The SAGE Handbook of
Interview Research

Second Edition

The SAGE Handbook of
Interview Research
The Complexity of the Craft

Second Edition

Edited by

Jaber F. Gubrium
University of Missouri

James A. Holstein
Marquette University

Amir B. Marvasti
Pennsylvania State University, Altoona

Karyn D. McKinney
Pennsylvania State University, Altoona

$SAGE

Los Angeles | London | New Delhi
Singapore | Washington DC

Los Angeles | London | New Delhi
Singapore | Washington DC

FOR INFORMATION:

SAGE Publications, Inc.
2455 Teller Road
Thousand Oaks, California 91320
E-mail: order@sagepub.com

SAGE Publications Ltd.
1 Oliver's Yard
55 City Road
London EC1Y 1SP
United Kingdom

SAGE Publications India Pvt. Ltd.
B 1/I 1 Mohan Cooperative Industrial Area
Mathura Road, New Delhi 110 044
India

SAGE Publications Asia-Pacific Pte. Ltd.
33 Pekin Street #02-01
Far East Square
Singapore 048763

Acquisitions Editor: Vicki Knight
Associate Editor: Lauren Habib
Editorial Assistant: Kalie Koscielak
Permissions Editor: Adele Hutchinson
Production Editor: Laureen Gleason
Copy Editor: QuADS Prepress (P) Ltd.
Typesetter: C&M Digitals (P) Ltd.
Proofreader: Scott Oney
Indexer: Molly Hall
Cover Designer: Candice Harman
Cover Image: Weber, Max. Tapestry. 1913. Max
    Weber. By Alfred Werner. New York: Harry Abrams
    Publishers, 1975. 89. Print.
Marketing Manager: Nicole Elliott

Printed in the United States of America

Library of Congress Cataloging-in-Publication Data

The SAGE handbook of interview research : the complexity of the craft / editors, Jaber F. Gubrium . . . [et al.]. — 2nd ed.

p. cm.
Rev. ed. of: Handbook of interview research : context & method / editors, Jaber F. Gubrium, James A. Holstein. c2002.
Includes bibliographical references and index.

ISBN 978-1-4129-8164-4 (cloth)

1. Interviewing—Handbooks, manuals, etc. I. Gubrium, Jaber F. II. Handbook of interview research.   III. Title: Handbook of interview research.

H61.28.H36 2012
158.3´9—dc23   2011034825

This book is printed on acid-free paper.

12 13 14 15 16 10 9 8 7 6 5 4 3 2 1

CONTENTS

PREFACE

As an approach to data collection, interviewing continues to expand, diversify, and evolve with the reflexive revision of long-standing assumptions. Core principles of the traditional model of the structured interview—such as the distinctive roles of the interviewer and the respondent—have been reformulated in a number of ways and across a wide range of disciplines. The first edition of the *Handbook of Interview Research* successfully delivered the latest developments in the enterprise. This revised edition both builds on and moves beyond the first edition by

- updating the book in terms of recent developments, especially in qualitative interviewing;

- shortening the volume so that it can be used as the main text for graduate seminars in qualitative research as well as a general reference book;

- featuring a how-to/instructional approach through empirically and theoretically informed discussions; and

- enhancing the multidisciplinary flavor of the first edition.

The contributing authors offer a survey of the field, with an emphasis on empirical diversity,

procedural options, and theoretical choices. In this edition, three new sections have been added:

- Logistics of Interviewing

- Self and Other in the Interview

- Ethics of the Interview

While there is ample coverage of more traditional interviewing approaches and concerns (see, e.g., the chapters on survey interviews and quantitative analysis), the new edition emphasizes the dynamic, interactional, and reflexive dimensions of the research interview. This is in keeping with newly emerging interests in the field and the editors' expertise in presenting the research interview in this way. The volume highlights the myriad dimensions of complexity that are emerging as researchers increasingly frame the interview as a communicative opportunity as much as a data-gathering format. Like the original volume, the second edition begins with the history and conceptual transformations of the interview. The subsequent chapters are organized around the following main components of interview practice:

- Part I: Interviewing in Context

- Part II: Methods of Interviewing

- Part III: Logistics of Interviewing

- Part IV: Self and Other in the Interview

- Part V: Analytic Strategies

- Part VI: Ethics of the Interview

- Part VII: Critical Reflections

As indicated by the subtitle of the new edition (*The Complexity of the Craft*), the research interview is being recast as a complex, multidimensional collection of assumptions and practices. Having shed the presumption that a particular model of interviewing is the "gold standard" of data collection, interviewing's persistent, ubiquitous presence in the social sciences is marked by an amazing diversity. Taken together, the contributions to the *Handbook* encourage readers simultaneously to learn the frameworks and technologies of interviewing and to

reflect on the epistemological foundations of the interview craft. We invite readers to view the chapter contents both as points of emphasis in a common enterprise and as reflexive reconsiderations that have taken an uncommonly imaginative direction.

It goes without saying that the *Handbook* would not have been possible without the superb work of the contributing authors. We deeply appreciate their scholarly insight, spirit of innovation, generosity, and consummate professionalism in working with us on this volume. We also thank the volume's editorial board and reviewers, who were called on for critical guidance and insight.

Last, but not the least, we are also extremely grateful to all the people in the editorial, production, and marketing departments at SAGE Publications who did so much to bring this project to fruition.

INTRODUCTION

The Complexity of the Craft

◆ Jaber F. Gubrium, James A. Holstein,
Amir B. Marvasti, and Karyn D. McKinney

n today's "interview society" (Silverman, 1997), we frequently learn about lives, feelings, and experiences by way of interviews. Interviewing flourishes as the stock-in-trade of journalism and contemporary news media. Its popularity as entertainment continues to grow. And the interview remains unquestionably a staple of social-scientific research. In the historical context of information about society, however, the interview is a relatively recent invention (see Benney & Hughes, 1956; Platt, 2002; Platt's chapter "The History of the Interview," this volume). But as straightforward a process as it may seem, interviewing and interview data posed complex challenges for those practicing the craft for research purposes.

◆ Early Challenges

Early on, the competence of potential interviewees was a major concern (see Holstein & Gubrium, 1995).

Henry Mayhew's four-volume study of *London Labour and the London Poor* (1861–1862) offers a revealing glimpse into the perceived ability of research subjects to convey useful information. In the preface to the first volume, Mayhew comments that he had initially believed the term *poverty* (or "poor people") signaled narrative incompetence. At the time, for purposes of information gathering, the poor were considered incapable of telling their own story; those considered more learned—their "social betters"—were viewed as more reliable and accurate when it came to describing the condition of the "humbler classes." To his credit, Mayhew broke with convention to discover that the poor, indeed, could speak authoritatively about their lives in "unvarnished language; and [social researchers could] portray the condition of their homes and their families by personal observation of the places, and direct communication with the individuals" (p. iii).

Mayhew used interviews and observations conducted among the London poor to document their living conditions from the point of view of the people themselves. The insights generated were extraordinary.

John Madge (1965) suggests that the idea of interviewing *anyone* about their lives, let alone the poor, was unprecedented at that time, even though the poor and poverty were topics of considerable public debate and social policy. He explains that the word *interview* does not even appear until about the time of Mayhew's study. Following Mayhew, the notion of interviewing as a means of gathering facts of experience in general, not to mention the experience of urban poverty, cut a new path for social research, establishing a broad spectrum of persons as potential sources of information. The emerging view was that people of all backgrounds were capable of giving credible voice to experience.

The nascent craft of interview research was grounded in the newly recognized principle that everyone possessed significant views and feelings about life, which were accessible by simply asking people about them. As William James (1892/1961) argued well over 100 years ago, this assumed that each and every individual had a sense of self that was owned and controlled by himself or herself, even if this self was interpersonally formulated. Everyone could meaningfully reflect on experience and enter into socially relevant dialogue about it. This became the new guiding principle: Interview practice since that time has assumed that "everyone" was capable of voicing their experience, even as the general practice might be circumscribed by cultural and political delimitations of what constituted research populations (Holstein & Gubrium, 1995).

◆ Technical Complexity

Interviewing traditionally has been viewed as a straightforward process in which interviewers solicit information from interviewees, who, in turn, respond to interviewers' inquiries. Ostensibly, those seeking information about others' thoughts, feelings, and actions merely have to ask the right questions, and the responses virtually pour out. Studs Terkel, the legendary journalistic and sociological interviewer, made this stance explicit, claiming at one point that he just turned on his tape recorder and asked people to talk unabashedly about their lives. Referring to the interviews done for his classic study *Working* (1972), Terkel indicated that his questions unlocked wellsprings of information that interviewees were all too ready to share. In Terkel's interviews, "the sluice gates of dammed up hurts and dreams were open" (p. xxv).

This straightforward approach to interviewing was fairly typical in the social sciences for much of the 20th century. If it was the imagined ideal, this is not to say that researchers were complacent about technical challenges. As Andrea Fontana and James Frey (2005) note, "Interviewing is not merely the neutral exchange of asking questions and getting answers. . . . Asking questions and getting answers is a much harder task than it may seem at first" (pp. 696–697). Social scientists had recognized this for decades and worked diligently to "get it right," as it were. Generations of sociologists, anthropologists, and other social researchers rigorously examined interview practices (see Platt, 2002), delving in great detail into the methods, forms, and functions of the interview (see Bradburn & Sudman, 1979; Hyman, Cobb, Feldman, Hart, & Stember, 1975; Richardson, Dohrenwend, & Klein, 1965); the strategies, techniques, and tactics of interviewing (see Cannell, Miller, & Oskenberg, 1981; Gorden, 1987; Kahn & Cannell, 1957; Sudman & Bradburn, 1983); and the variety of interactional problems that could derail the enterprise (see Suchman & Jordan, 1990).

Perhaps no other social science information-gathering technique has been subjected to such scrutiny. This was the first watershed of complexity for the craft. Because research on the interview process has been motivated by the perspective that the shortcomings of interviewing as a mode of information collection were technical problems, technical improvements could further open and clarify interviewing's window to the world.

Refinements grew at the technical forefront of survey research (see, e.g., Converse & Schuman, 1974). Much of this literature deals with the nuances of formulating questions and providing an atmosphere conducive to open and undistorted communication between the interviewer and the respondent. It specifies ways of asking questions that will not interfere with or contaminate information that resides with respondents, which is waiting to be set free (see Holstein & Gubrium, 1995). It offers myriad procedures for obtaining unadulterated facts and details, most of which implicate the interviewer and question neutrality. The underlying assumption is that if the interviewing process goes "by the book" and is unbiased, respondents will communicate the relevant facts of their lives. Contamination emanates from the interview setting, its participants, and their interaction, not from the interview subject, who is understood to provide authentic reports under the right conditions.

◆ *Epistemological Complexity*

Not all challenges to the craft have been technical. More recently, a second watershed of complexity emerged that has been equally concerned with epistemological issues. Qualitative researchers began to ask fundamental questions about the nature of interview communication and interview information. These questions challenged what previously have been primarily technical developments. The idealized view of the interview as a straightforward exercise in information extraction has given way to the perspective that interviewing, like communication in general, is as much collaboratively constructive of the meanings of experience as it is an efficient means of gathering information. Traditional technical concerns are now sharing the complexity terrain with concerns about the interview as a form of knowledge *production*.

The second edition of the *Handbook of Interview Research* features the interplay between the technical and epistemological challenges of the craft. It raises questions about what it means, in communicative practice, to be an interviewer or a respondent. How do time, place, culture, and sociohistorical circumstance affect interviews? And, as a result, how is interview material to be analyzed? The ideas that the interview can be conceptualized in relation to a universal standard, that particular rules of procedure guide good interviewing, and that outcomes are adequately understood in terms of the distribution of responses and the relationship between distributions still underpin much of interview research. But these views now sit alongside, rather than over and above, epistemological concerns. A key assumption of many of the *Handbook*'s chapters is that technical and epistemological issues are intertwined, that complexity presents itself most vividly and consequentially at their intersection.

◆ *The Contributions*

The chapters of Part I, "Interviewing in Context," lead the way in examining the multifaceted terrain of complexity. Jennifer Platt (Chapter 1) organizes her history around key texts, tracing the evolution of

validity, examining the shifting senses of the appropriate relationship between interviewer and respondent, and contrasting approaches to what constitutes useful data. Clearly, interviewing and how researchers conceptualize it have changed over time; what may have been standard at one time is not necessarily what was standard at another. Jaber Gubrium and James Holstein (Chapter 2) discuss the transformation in how researchers conceive of the subjectivity of interview participants. The chapter contrasts passive and active views of subjectivity, provides different conceptions of participants' roles, explains what to make of interview results, and offers a basis for considering the craft as narrative production. Michael Ian Borer and Andrea Fontana (Chapter 3) take us on the postmodern journey that has inspired some interview researchers. If there are postmodern sensibilities in evidence, there is no distinctive postmodern interview, according to the authors. Kathryn Roulston (Chapter 4) argues for the ultimate impossibility of designating the characteristics of a good interview, presenting a more modest way of evaluating the craft.

Part II, "Methods of Interviewing," features the complexity of existing interview procedures. The range of what is understood to be appropriate is striking, from the guiding principles of survey interviewing, discussed by Royce Singleton and Bruce Straits (Chapter 5), to the autoethnographic self-interview procedure described by Sara Crawley (Chapter 9). John Johnson and Timothy Rowlands (Chapter 6) consider in-depth interviewing as a social form whose procedural shape reflects a common mode of interpersonal communication. Robert Atkinson (Chapter 7) brings another social form into the mix; the life story interview is viewed as importing the mutually equitable and intimate format of how experience is shared through time. Carol Warren (Chapter 8) expands on the parallels between research procedure and daily living in a discussion of the interactive contours of qualitative interviewing. David Morgan (Chapter 10) considers the interactional dimensions of group interviews, and Nalita James and Hugh Busher (Chapter 11) feature interviewing that capitalizes on the Internet, a rapidly growing social form. Janice Morse (Chapter 12) combines qualitative and quantitative sensibilities—and social practices—into a discussion of mixed-method designs. It is evident throughout Part II that complexity derives as much from parallels with communicative formats in society as it does from a spectrum of procedural options.

The chapters of Part III, "Logistics of Interviewing," center on important practical challenges to interviewing of all kinds. Hanna Herzog (Chapter 13) is concerned with the effect of interview location on outcomes. Anne Grinyer and Carol Thomas (Chapter 14) address the question of trust and rapport in the context of interviewing on multiple occasions or longitudinally, figuring that the quality of data, not just interpersonal relations, is significantly affected. Jinjun Wang and Ying Yan (Chapter 15) take question selection beyond desired information to the issue of how power is exercised in the selection process. Here, complexity emerges in the contentious area of impartiality and neutrality, challenging researchers over and above technical concerns. Not leaving sample size to statistical considerations, Ben Beitin (Chapter 16) discusses the matter in terms of "who can provide information to present the most comprehensive picture possible." Shannon Carter and Christian Bolden (Chapter 17) reformulate what it means to figure culture in interview responses; the concept of "culture work" highlights how shared meaning is constructed within the interview, not just shaping responses from the outside. Christopher Faircloth (Chapter 18) discusses "what is left at the end" of the interview, dealing with the huge terrain of coding, analysis, and the representation of findings in terms of integral political considerations.

Part IV, "Self and Other in the Interview," deals with the personal side of interviewing, from how one manages the interviewer self (Annika Lillrank, Chapter 19) to how stigma (especially in relation to marginalized participants) can shape the data collected (Kay Cook, Chapter 23). John Talmage (Chapter 20) explains how practices of listening mediate the question–answer exchange, pointing to differences in the cultivated alertness of interviewers. Lara Foley (Chapter 21) outlines the many ways respondents are constructed in the interview, adding layers of subjectivity undervalued in information-centered approaches. Linda Finlay (Chapter 22) features the centrality of reflexivity in interviewing, offering a multifaceted perspective for increasing the richness and the integrity of understanding.

The chapters of Part V, "Analytic Strategies," take us out of the interviewing process and into the realm of data analysis. The distinction is somewhat artificial in qualitative inquiry, as analysis and data collection commonly transpire simultaneously. Kathy Charmaz and Linda Belgrave (Chapter 24) begin with a description of grounded theory analysis. Catherine Riessman

(Chapter 25) follows with a commentary on how to analyze personal narratives. Marjorie DeVault and Liza McCoy (Chapter 26) discuss the dynamics of interviewing in institutional ethnography, which is a form of analysis integral to the exploration of the "relations of ruling." Pirjo Nikander (Chapter 27) turns to the communicative details of the interview exchange, showing how analysis can extend to the ways in which interview information is solicited, constructed, and managed in the interview process. David Shemmings and Ingunn Ellingsen (Chapter 28) explain how to use Q methodology to unpack the everyday epistemological grounds of meaning making in the interview. And Clive Seale and Carol Rivas (Chapter 29) provide a handy discussion of the uses of qualitative analysis software, especially for examining video data.

Part VI, "Ethics of the Interview," turns to controversial moral and legal dimensions of the craft. Marco Marzano (Chapter 30) reviews the history of informed consent and its implementation in social research. Complexity emerges because the original domain of the consent issue—biomedicine—has decidedly different epistemological dimensions from its social science counterparts. Karen Kaiser (Chapter 31) examines the challenges of disseminating detailed data while simultaneously protecting the confidentiality of participants. Kristin Heggen and Marilys Guillemin (Chapter 32) offer a "situated ethics approach" to the protection of confidentiality. Anne Ryen (Chapter 33) reflects on the micropolitical dimensions of research ethics, which contrasts with debates that transpire as if ethical matters were not indigenous concerns of everyday life. Michelle Miller-Day (Chapter 34) offers an alternative perspective on the uneasy relationship between institutional review boards and qualitative researchers, proposing strategies for possible accord.

The chapters of Part VII, "Critical Reflections," pose a basic empirical question—What are interviews about?—which centers on the substantive bearings of the craft. To comprehend the interpretive frames of interviewing, Kirin Narayan and Kenneth George (Chapter 35) ask us to imagine that we, as interview researchers, are witnessing story formation, not just information gathering, as we talk with respondents about their lives. Laura Ellingson (Chapter 36) takes issue with the mind/body split that pervades social research, offering suggestions for consciously embodying the interview process to produce embodied results. Tim Rapley (Chapter 37) revisits the interaction-in-interviews issue, suggesting what can be learned from this research. Jonathan Potter and Alexa Hepburn (Chapter 38) close the volume with a discussion of eight challenges for interview researchers. Their chapter reflexively integrates epistemological and technical issues and offers suggestions for using noninterview data, especially records of natural interaction, more effectively in qualitative research.

◆ A Gentle Caution

The editors invite you to consider in detail the facets of complexity in interview research. The *Handbook* is an impressive array of contributions. From the technical to the analytic to the epistemological, complexity is clearly evident throughout. But we must be cautious not to let our fascination with complexity shortchange the interview's information-gathering potential. To recognize and elaborate the multifaceted shape of the interview should not mean that we pay less attention to its utility for learning about the world around us. Rather, it is just the opposite; we must think carefully about both technical and epistemological matters because they inventively construct our knowledge of the world we live in, as much as they serve to gather information about it. If the chapters of the *Handbook* stress complexity, they do so with an eye to improving the craft that interviewing creates.

◆ References

Benney, M., & Hughes, E. C. (1956). Of sociology and the interview. *American Journal of Sociology, 62,* 137–142.

Bradburn, N., & Sudman, S. (1979). *Improving interview method and questionnaire design.* San Francisco, CA: Jossey-Bass.

Cannell, C., Miller, P., & Oksenberg, L. (1981). Research on interview technique. In S. Leinhardt (Ed.), *Sociological methodology* (pp. 389–437). San Francisco, CA: Jossey-Bass.

Converse, J., & Schuman, H. (1974). *Conversations at random: Survey research as interviewers see it.* New York, NY: Wiley.

Fontana, A., & Frey, J. (2005). The interview: From neutral stance to political involvement. In N. Denzin & Y. Lincoln (Eds.), *The SAGE handbook of qualitative research* (3rd ed., pp. 695–727). Thousand Oaks, CA: Sage.

Gorden, R. (1987). *Interviewing: Strategy, techniques, and tactics.* Homewood, IL: Dorsey.

Holstein, J., & Gubrium, J. (1995). *The active interview.* Thousand Oaks, CA: Sage.

Hyman, H. H., Cobb, W. J., Feldman, J. J., Hart, C. W., & Stember, C. H. (1975). *Interviewing in social research.* Chicago, IL: University of Chicago Press.

James, W. (1961). *Psychology: The briefer course.* New York, NY: Harper. (Original work published 1892)

Kahn, R. L., & Cannell, C. F. (1957). *The dynamics of interviewing: Theory, technique, and cases.* New York, NY: Wiley.

Madge, J. (1965). *The tools of social science.* Garden City, NY: Anchor Books.

Mayhew, H. (1861–1862). *London labour and the London poor.* London, England: Griffin, Bohn.

Platt, J. (2002). The history of the interview. In J. Gubrium & J. Holstein (Eds.), *Handbook of interview research* (1st ed., pp. 33–54). Thousand Oaks, CA: Sage.

Richardson, S., Dohrenwend, B., & Klein, D. (1965). *Interviewing: Its forms and functions.* New York, NY: Basic Books.

Silverman, D. (1997). *Qualitative research: Theory, method, and practice.* London, England: Sage.

Suchman, L., & Jordan, B. (1990). Interactional troubles in face-to-face survey interviews. *Journal of the American Statistical Association, 85,* 232–241.

Sudman, S., & Bradburn, N. (1983). *Asking questions.* San Francisco, CA: Jossey-Bass.

Terkel, S. (1972). *Working.* New York, NY: Avon.

Part 1

INTERVIEWING IN CONTEXT

1

THE HISTORY OF THE INTERVIEW

◆ Jennifer Platt

The "interview" has existed, and changed over time, both as a practice and as a methodological term in current use. However, the practice has not always been theorized or distinguished from other modes of acquiring information. Interviewing has sometimes been treated as a distinct method, but more often it has been located within some broader methodological category, such as "survey," "case study," or "life story." It is not always easy to decide what should be treated as a part of interviewing as such; for instance, some discussion of interview questions is about the construction of schedules, without reference to how the questions are presented to the respondent. Here, the focus is on what happens while the interviewer is interacting with the respondent.

At each stage, the more fully institutionalized practices have been less likely to be written about in detail, except for the purpose of guiding trainees; therefore caution needs to be exercised in generalizing from the prescriptive literature to current practice. In principle, we aim here to look at both the theorization and the practice of the interview, without assuming that there has always

been a close correspondence between the two. But interview *practice* has been very unevenly described. Descriptions of it are more common when some aspect becomes salient because it is seen as novel, unconventional, or problematic. Even then, what is described is commonly a policy or strategy rather than the actual practice, which may not always conform to the policy. Thus, for our historical account, we have to draw largely on prescriptions for practice as it should be.

We concentrate on the book literature; the main points in the journals will have been taken up in books if they were practically influential, so this is adequate for a broad overview. It is with regret that the decision had also to be made, given the limitations of space, to focus almost entirely on the U.S. experience. For the prewar period, especially its earlier part, this can be quite misleading, as other national disciplines had some of their own distinct traditions and discussion. From about 1945 to 1960, U.S. social science and the survey became so hegemonic elsewhere that they can perhaps be treated as representing the whole; after the high period of U.S. hegemony, however, this approach becomes less reasonable. This chapter is written from a sociologist's perspective; the most likely bias is one toward work that sociologists have used and treated as important, whether or not the authors were sociologists. Those from other backgrounds are urged to supplement my examples with their own.

The U.S. book literature on interviewing falls into a number of categories, of which some illustrative examples are listed in Table 1.1. (Where possible these are chosen from works not extensively discussed below, to indicate more of the range of material.) There are relatively distinct intellectual and practical traditions here, despite overlaps and some strong influences across traditions, and this needs to be taken into account in placing the stances and concerns of single texts.

We concentrate on social-scientific interviewing, but that has not always been distinguished from the interviewing techniques of psychiatrists, social caseworkers, or personnel managers. When it has been so distinguished, work in such fields has still often been drawn on by social scientists. But the character of the literature has changed historically. The earliest relevant work was not specifically social scientific. As new practices such as polling and bodies such as survey organizations emerged, they generated writing that expressed their concerns and led to methodological research on issues they were interested in. Once an orthodoxy was established, there was room for critiques of it and declarations of independence from it. Those working on special groups developed special ways of dealing with them; then, with an understandable lag, theorists began to take an interest in the more philosophical aspects. Textbooks regularly strove to keep up with the main developments, while authors of empirical studies wrote about the experiences and needs specific to their particular topics. In later times, as the quantitative and qualitative worlds became increasingly separate, their discussions of interviewing diverged correspondingly. The quantitativists carried forward an established tradition with increasing sophistication, from time to time taking on technical innovations such as telephone interviewing, while qualitative workers blossomed out into focus groups, life histories, and own-brand novelties. However, an interesting link has recently been established in the use by surveyors of conversation-analytic techniques to analyze what is happening in their questions and answers.

Below, a broad outline of the trajectory of the field is sketched in via selected examples of such writings, starting with the prescriptive methodological literature and going on to empirical work that has been treated as methodologically important. We then review some key analytical themes. The literature of research on interviewing is looked at as much for

Table 1.1 Genres of Books Related to Interviewing

Genre	Examples
Practitioner textbooks	Garrett, *Interviewing: Its Principles and Methods*, 1942
Polling practice	Gallup, *A Guide to Public Opinion Polls*, 1944
Social science methods textbooks	Goode and Hatt, *Methods in Social Research*, 1952
Instructions to survey interviewers	University of Michigan, Survey Research Center, *Manual for Interviewers*, 1954
Critiques of method, general or particular	Christie and Jahoda, *Studies in the Scope and Method of "The Authoritarian Personality,"* 1954; Cicourel, *Method and Measurement in Sociology*, 1964
Empirical work discussing its methods	Kinsey, Pomeroy, and Martin, *Sexual Behavior in the Human Male*, 1948
Handbooks	Denzin and Lincoln, *Handbook of Qualitative Research*, 1994
Monographs on special groups, novel approaches	Dexter, *Elite and Specialized Interviewing*, 1970; Douglas, *Creative Interviewing*, 1985
Philosophical/theoretical discussion	Sjoberg and Nett, *A Methodology for Social Research*, 1968
Reports of methodological research	Hyman, *Interviewing in Social Research*, 1954

what the concerns reflected there show us about the researchers' focuses of interest as for what the findings have been, though research has surely influenced practice. The interlinked issues of changing interest in and thought about validity, conceptions of the appropriate social relations between interviewer and respondent, and the types of data sought by those working in different styles are briefly explored; some effort is made to draw out points of potential interest to researchers, whose concern is less with the history as such than it is with informing their own practice. Finally, the strands are drawn together to present a synthetic account of the ways in which interviewing and thinking about it have changed over time.

◆ *The Trajectory of Change in Methodological Writing*

To give a sense of the broad trajectory of change, a sequence of arguably representative accounts of interviewing, in particular its forms and purposes, is presented below in order of historical appearance. Key points of content and assumptions are outlined, and each is briefly placed in its context.

HOWARD W. ODUM AND KATHARINE JOCHER, AN INTRODUCTION TO SOCIAL RESEARCH, *1929*

This was one of the first general social science methods textbooks. In it, in addition to "interview," "schedule" (to be used by an enumerator) and "questionnaire" (to be answered unaided) are mentioned; for these, there is a discussion of questions and presentation but nothing on interviewing as such. (At this time, the conduct of structured interviews was not treated as being at all problematic and so was hardly discussed.) It is stated that

> an interview is made for the purpose of securing information . . . about the informant himself, or about other persons or undertakings that he knows or is interested in. The purpose may be to secure a life history, to corroborate evidence got from other sources, to secure . . . data which the informant possesses. [It] . . . may also be the means of enlisting the informant's cooperation . . . in the investigation. . . . If the student is not acquainted with the informant, some method of

introduction through a mutual acquaintance should be secured. (pp. 366–367)

Permission to take notes should be requested.

As here, in the 1920s and 1930s, an "interview" was often assumed to be of a key informant or gatekeeper rather than a respondent who is merely one member of a sample (cf. Bingham & Moore, 1931; Fry, 1934). The implicit model of the old, fact-finding survey in the Booth tradition is still in the background; Booth's data on the working-class family were provided by middle-class visitors (Bales, 1991). The interviewee may thus be an informant about the situation studied, as much as or more than being a part of it, and potentially of a status superior to the interviewer, another reason for allowing the respondent to structure the interaction. This does not mean that no questionnaires to mass samples were being used, though they were not common yet in academic social science, but that this was seen as a distinct method. It was often recommended that notes should not be taken during the interview, or only to a minimal extent, but that recording should be done as soon as possible afterward; questions might not be revealed or might be written on the back of an envelope to appear informal and spontaneous (see, e.g., Converse, 1987, p. 51). Clearly the role of respondent was not yet so institutionalized that no need to conceal the mechanics was felt.

PAULINE V. YOUNG, SCIENTIFIC SOCIAL SURVEYS AND RESEARCH, *1939*

This was a very successful general methods textbook. "Interview" is again distinguished from "schedule" and "questionnaire," which are dealt with separately. Young distinguishes respondents who are adequate sources on factual matters from those who are of interest as subjects, individually or in relation to the larger situation. A personal introduction to the respondent is still seen as desirable. "The interview proper does not begin until a considerable degree of rapport has been established. . . . The most important touchstone is probably the mutual discovery of common experiences" (p. 189). What does she see as the value of the interview?

> The personal interview is penetrating; it goes to the "living source." Through it the student . . . is able to go behind mere outward behavior and

phenomena. He can secure accounts of events and processes as they are reflected in personal experiences, in social attitudes. He can check inferences and external observations by a vital account of the persons who are being observed. . . . [T]he field worker . . . needs to know in a general way why he is interviewing this particular person or group and what he intends asking . . . [but] needs to be open to unforeseen developments. (pp. 175, 179)

As few questions as possible should be asked:

When people are least interrupted, when they can tell their stories in their own way, . . . they can react naturally and freely and express themselves fully. . . . [Interruptions and leading questions are likely to have the effect that] . . . the adventure into the unknown, into uncharted and hitherto undisclosed spheres, has been destroyed. (p. 190)

It is rarely advisable to complete an interview at one sitting (p. 195). It is better not to take notes, except maybe a few key words, and it is seen as controversial whether to record the interview in the first or the third person and whether a verbatim account is to be preferred to a summary by the interviewer (pp. 196, 200).

Young's department at the University of Southern California was oriented toward the training of practitioners; her *Interviewing in Social Work* (1935) was widely cited in sociology when there were few other such sources to draw on. Its perceived relevance owed something to the widespread use by sociologists, especially at the University of Chicago where she was trained, of case histories collected by social workers; this connects with the idea of the case study and of the significance of life history data, which are clearly the contexts she has in mind in the passages quoted above (Platt, 1996, p. 46). One may also perhaps detect formative traces of the participant observation she used in her doctoral work. George A. Lundberg's (1942) important—and intellectually far superior—textbook takes a similar approach, despite his strongly scientistic tastes, though with a slight twist in the direction of the more modern concern with personality and psychoanalytical interests.

By the 1949 edition of her text, Young had mentioned the modern survey, though she was far from treating it as the paradigm:

A specialized form of the interview is useful in the collection of personal data for quantitative purposes. This type of interview aims to accumulate a variety of uniform responses to a wide scope of predetermined specific questions. (Generally these questions appear on a printed form.) (p. 244)

This distanced account was in effect one of the last traces of an older conception.

CHARLES F. CANNELL AND ROBERT L. KAHN, "THE COLLECTION OF DATA BY INTERVIEWING," 1953

This is a chapter in what became a standard general methods text, written by a group from the University of Michigan's Institute for Social Research (ISR). Cannell and Kahn, the former a clinical and the latter a social psychologist, were members of the team that became the wartime Division of Program Surveys (DPS) and after the war transformed itself into the Institute for Social Research. In this chapter they attempt to go beyond current rules of thumb and to draw on work in counseling and communication theory to understand the psychology of the interview. (Their later book, *The Dynamics of Interviewing*, Kahn & Cannell, 1957, carries this forward, coming to the formulation of objectives and questions only after three chapters on the interviewing relationship.)

The following extract shows their relatively qualitative orientation, which nonetheless goes with a strong commitment to scientific procedure; one may detect some tensions between the two:

Even when the research objectives call for information which is beyond the individual's power to provide directly, the interview is often an effective means of obtaining the desired data. . . . Bias and lack of training make it impossible for an individual to provide such intimate information about himself, even if he is motivated to the utmost frankness. But only he can provide the data about his attitudes towards his parents, colleagues, and members of minority groups, from which some of his deeper-lying characteristics can be inferred. . . . [T]he interviewer cannot apply unvaryingly a specified set of techniques, because he is dealing with a varying situation. . . . [T]he best approximation to a standard stimulus is to word the question at a level which is understandable to all respondents and then to ask the question of each respondent in identical fashion. . . . [T]he interviewer's role with respect to the questionnaire is to treat it as a scientific instrument designed to administer a constant stimulus. (pp. 332, 358)

Cannell was a doctoral student of Carl Rogers, recruited to the DPS to draw on what he had learned with Rogers about nondirective styles of questioning. It is assumed in the book that a schedule is used, but this heritage was shown in the team's long-term commitment to more open-ended questions than those favored by other groups and explains some of the assumptions made here about interviewing. At an early stage, there was controversy between the proponents of closed and open questions, contrasted by one participant in the DPS as the "neat reliables" and the "sloppy valids." This was reflected in a classic article by Paul F. Lazarsfeld (1944), in which he aimed to resolve the conflict between wartime research outfits with divergent styles. Converse (1987, pp. 195–202) shows that the dispute was as much about the costs of more open-ended work, and whether the gains were worth it, as it was about validity. It became evident even to those committed in principle to the open style that it not only created coding problems but also was impossible to sustain with less educated interviewers scattered across the country, making training and supervision difficult.

SELLTIZ, JAHODA, DEUTSCH, AND COOK, RESEARCH METHODS IN SOCIAL RELATIONS, 1965

This classic textbook written by psychologists has passed through many editions. It still distinguishes between "interview" and "questionnaire," seeing the interview, which may be structured or unstructured, as practically advantageous because it does not require literacy and has a better response rate than postal questionnaires, is more flexible, and is "the more appropriate technique for revealing information about complex, emotionally laden subjects, or for probing the sentiments that may underlie an expressed opinion" (p. 242). However, much of the discussion is on question wording, without distinguishing interview from questionnaire, and clearly a standard survey interview, by now well

established, is what they have in mind. The interviewer should put the respondent at ease and create a friendly atmosphere but "must keep the direction of the interview in his own hands, discouraging irrelevant conversation and endeavoring to keep the respondent to the point" (p. 576) and must ask the questions exactly as worded and not give impromptu explanations. Complete verbatim recording is needed for free-answer questions—"aside from obvious irrelevancies and repetitions" (p. 580). Many of those involved in the early development of polling and market research using the survey were psychologists, and for them the experiment was usually the model, so they laid great emphasis, as here, on the importance of applying a uniform stimulus. This shows development well beyond the approach of the early Gallup (1944) conducting the simple political poll, designed for newspaper rather than academic publication. The interview there was unequivocally designed for quantification of the responses made to fixed questions by members of the general public, and the need for accuracy and precision was emphasized, but uniformity of stimulus was not given the importance that it later acquired; validity was seen primarily in terms of getting the public predictions right.

GIDEON SJOBERG AND ROGER NETT, A METHODOLOGY FOR SOCIAL RESEARCH, 1968

This is quite a new genre of work, reflecting wider movements in sociology. The authors were not closely involved with survey units and were not writing a conventional methods text but a textbook/monograph with a standpoint: "The scientist who employs . . . [structured interviews] is usually intent upon testing an existing set of hypotheses; he is less concerned with discovery per se. And, of course, standardization greatly enhances reliability"—as well as saving time and money. However, it has the drawback of imposing the investigator's categories on informants: "The unstructured type is most useful for studying the normative structure of organizations, for establishing classes, and for discovering the existence of possible social patterns (rather than the formal testing of propositions concerning the existence of given patterns)" (pp. 193–195).

Four types of unstructured interview are described: (1) the free-association method, (2) the focused interview, (3) the objectifying interview, and (4) the group interview. Of these, the objectifying interview is preferred:

> The researcher informs the interviewee from the start . . . concerning the kinds of information he is seeking and why. The informant is apprised of his role in the scientific process and is encouraged to develop his skills in observation (and even in interpretation). . . . Besides examining his own actions, the interviewee is encouraged to observe and interpret the behavior of his associates in his social group. Ideally, he becomes a peer with whom the scientist can objectively discuss the ongoing system, to the extent that he is encouraged to criticize the scientist's observations and interpretations. (p. 214)

Throughout the discussion, there is a stress on the social assumptions built into different choices of questions. Status effects in the interview situation, and the consequences of varying cultural backgrounds, especially for work in the Third World, are discussed.

The authors approached the matter from a theoretical and—in a turn characteristic of the period—a sociopolitical perspective; it was proposed to involve the respondent as an equal, not so much for instrumental reasons of technical efficacy as because a nonhierarchical, nonexploitive relationship is seen as intrinsically right. It is also noticeable that this is a sociologists' version; there is no orientation to psychologists' usual concerns. Although Galtung (1967) and Denzin (1970) wrote books more like conventional methods texts, those have key features in common with Sjoberg and Nett's book: the more theoretical and philosophical interests, the more distanced approach to surveys and their mundane practicalities, and a clearly sociological frame of reference. Interviewing of various kinds has now become a standard practice to which even those with theoretical interests relate their ideas.

STEVEN J. TAYLOR AND ROBERT BOGDAN, INTRODUCTION TO QUALITATIVE RESEARCH METHODS, 1984, SECOND EDITION

This is a specialized methods textbook, again with a strong standpoint:

In stark contrast to structured interviewing, qualitative interviewing is flexible and dynamic . . . [with] repeated face-to-face encounters between the researcher and informants directed toward understanding informants' perspectives on their lives, experiences, or situations as expressed in their own words. The in-depth interview is modeled after a conversation between equals, rather than a formal question-and-answer exchange. Far from being a robotlike data collector, the interviewer, not an interview schedule or protocol, is the research tool. The role entails not merely obtaining answers, but learning what questions to ask and how to ask them. (p. 77)

Without direct observation to give context to what people say in an interview, the responses may not be adequately understood, and there may be problems of deception and distortion; it is important, therefore, to interview in depth,

> getting to know people well enough to understand what they mean and creating an atmosphere in which they are likely to talk freely. . . . [I]t is only by designing the interview along the lines of natural interaction that the interviewer can tap into what is important to people. . . . [T]he interviewer has many parallels in everyday life: "the good listener," "the shoulder to cry on," "the confidante." . . . [T]here has to be some exchange in terms of what interviewers say about themselves. . . . The best advice is to be discreet in the interview, but to talk about yourself in other situations. You should be willing to relate to informants in terms other than interviewer/informant. Interviewers can serve as errand-runners, drivers, babysitters, advocates. (pp. 82–83, 93–94, 101)

This reaction against "robotlike" standard survey interviewing is part of the growth of a separate, "qualitative" stream, recommending many practices anathema to surveyors. The rhetoric is very distant from that of "science." These authors often refer to the Chicago School as a model, drawing on a widely current image of it—if one more useful for ideological than for historical purposes (Platt, 1996, pp. 265–269). The ideal is clearly participant observation or ethnography, and this type of interviewing again blurs the boundary with them. It could not be adapted to large representative samples without enormous costs, and makes implicit assumptions about likely research topics that, one somehow infers, exclude (for instance) the demographic or economic. Other representatives of this broad tendency are Douglas (1985), Holstein and Gubrium (1995), and Potter and Hepburn (2005). Potter and Hepburn set such high conversation-analytic standards and emphasize the significance of the interaction between interviewer and respondent so heavily that, after recognizing that the necessary quality would be bought at the expense of sample size, they suggest that it might be better anyway to use naturalistic records rather than interviews. (Perhaps their focus on interviewing for *psychology* may have led to a concern with fine detail less necessary for sociology or anthropology.)

Many feminists have practiced and argued in favor of similar styles on feminist grounds. Reinharz (1992) suggests that interviewing appeals to feminists because it

> offers researchers access to people's ideas, thoughts and memories in their own words rather than in the words of the researcher. This asset is particularly important for the study of women because [this] . . . is an antidote to centuries of ignoring women's ideas altogether or having men speak for women. (p. 19)

She points out, however, that having close relations with every subject is not practicable and that too much emphasis on rapport may unduly limit the range of topics covered. (It is noticeable that the work she cites in this chapter is almost all on topics such as rape and hysterectomies.) The emphasis here is on letting the respondent's perspective dominate rather than analyzing the interaction with the interviewer. Recent advocacy of "narrative interviewing" goes further in the attempt to elicit narration with minimal intervention by the interviewer: "It is assumed that [uninterrupted] narrations preserve particular perspectives in a more genuine form" (Jovchelovitch & Bauer, 2007, p. 1), though the final interpretive product fuses the informants' relevance structures with those of the researcher.

One might speculate how much of this qualitative tendency rests on the increased availability of good-quality portable tape recorders, which facilitate the detailed recording of free answers and their close textual analysis.[1] We may expect fresh creative developments facilitated by the digital revolution; there are already methodological and ethical discussions of the special features of online data collection.

◆ Empirical Work and Its Influence

Important contributions to discussion of interviewing have also been made by authors whose primary concern was their substantive topic; these do not necessarily relate directly to the professional methodological discussion and cannot be explained by their location within that. Below, we review some of them. It is probably not by chance that the empirical exemplars that come to mind, as well as much methodological research, are largely from work done in the period from 1935 to 1955. This was the time when the modern survey was emerging, and so the problems that its practice raised were live ones, confronted and argued over for the first time, while its high profile and popularity also encouraged those with criticisms, or alternatives suited to less usual topics, to write about them. None of the exemplars is a conventional survey because, where there is a structured schedule, the tradition has been to provide a copy of it without describing the interviewing process; what took place is implicitly assumed to be sufficiently described by the schedule.

Roethlisberger and Dickson (1939/1964) make an early contribution to unstructured interviewing technique, though the intellectual responsibility for this arguably lies more with Elton Mayo, who led the work—his ideas on method were influenced both by his interest in Jungian psychoanalysis and by his friendship with the anthropologist and fieldwork pioneer Malinowski. The interviewing program reported started to collect employees' views about their work (for use in improving supervisor training), but it was found that the workers often wanted to talk about "irrelevant" material, so in 1929 the decision was made to adopt an "indirect approach," following the workers' lead without changing the subject and asking only noncommittal questions. Interviews were recorded as far as possible verbatim,

---

[1]In an earlier version of this chapter, I said that research on the consequences for practice of changing recording techniques and technologies was strikingly absent; Lee (2004) has responded with a valuable step toward filling that gap.

rather than under target headings, and the data were seen as information not so much on real problems as on the meanings that the worker gave to the realities. "Rules of performance" were set up, such as "Listen in a patient, friendly but intelligently critical manner" and "Do not display any kind of authority," but these rules were to be treated as flexible: "If the interviewer understands what he is doing and is in active touch with the actual situation, he has extreme latitude in what he can do" (pp. 286–287). This program, not initially intended for social-scientific purposes, became used for social science.

Warner and Lunt (1941) said that in their work they used techniques suggested by Roethlisberger and Dickson (1939/1964), although their research, an intensive community study, was of a very different character; Warner was an anthropologist by training, and the anthropological fieldwork tradition seems more relevant to their research. Many of their "interviews" were done without the subject's awareness of being interviewed: "The activity of the investigator has been classed as observation when the emphasis fell on the observer's seeing behavior of an individual; as interviewing, when emphasis fell on listening to what was said" (Warner & Lunt, 1941, p. 46). Questionnaires were seen as liable to take items out of their social context and as useful only when one is already familiar with the general situation from interviews (Warner & Lunt, 1941, pp. 55–56). Although the authors called their main method "interviewing," it should probably be regarded primarily as part of the history of what we now call participant observation.

Our next example, Kinsey, Pomeroy, and Martin's *Sexual Behavior in the Human Male* (1948), is more idiosyncratic. Kinsey was a professor of zoology and devised techniques planned to suit his special topic. There was a list of items to be covered in the interview, but no fixed order or words for them, and additional items for subjects with uncommon ranges of experience. The questions placed the burden of denial of sexual practices on the subject and were asked very rapidly to increase the spontaneity of the answers (pp. 50–54). Interviewer neutrality was not valued:

> Something more than cold objectivity is needed in dealing with human subjects. . . . The interviewer who senses what these things can mean . . . is more effective, though he may not be altogether neutral. The sympathetic interviewer records his reactions in ways that may not involve spoken words but which are, nonetheless, readily comprehended by most people. . . . These are the things that . . . can never be done through a written questionnaire, or even through a directed interview in which the questions are formalized and the confines of the investigation strictly limited. (p. 42)

The aims of the interview were not at all concealed from respondents, and if they appeared not to be answering truthfully, the interview was broken off. Very long training was again seen as necessary for interviewers, who were also required, in the interests of confidentiality, to memorize a large number of codes for recording the answers. Any use of this method by others has not been identified in the mainstream sociological literature; Kinsey's reasoning suggests that it would only have been appropriate in areas posing the same problems as sexual behavior (Kinsey et al., 1948).

Radically different, almost equally famous, and more influential in social science method was Adorno, Frenkel-Brunswik, Levinson, and Sanford's *The Authoritarian Personality* (1950). Here again, there was a schedule, but interviewers were not expected to stick closely to its questions or order. The model followed was that of the psychotherapeutic encounter, and the instructions distinguished "underlying" from "manifest" questions. It was taken that "the subject's view of his own life . . . may be assumed to contain real information together with wishful—and fearful—distortions," and consequently, methods were needed

> to differentiate the more genuine, basic feelings, attitudes, and strivings from those of a more compensatory character behind which are hidden tendencies, frequently unknown to the subject himself, which are contrary to those manifested or verbalized on a surface level. (p. 293)

(Kinsey also distrusted overt statements of attitudes, but his solution was to ask only about behavior and—unless untruths were suspected—to accept what was offered at face value [Kinsey et al., 1948])

Perhaps surprisingly, given the lack of social-scientific precedent for Kinsey's approach (Kinsey et al., 1948), Adorno et al. (1950) were treated more harshly in published critiques. Where the former were criticized, it was concluded that empirical evidence for saying that their results were less valid than those of alternative approaches was not available (Cochran, Mosteller, & Tukey, 1954, pp. 78–79); Adorno et al. (1950) were, however, accused of inconsistency and speculative overinterpretation of data not appropriate for their use (Christie & Jahoda, 1954, pp. 97, 100).

What might be seen as a more social version of such an approach, used to generate large ideas about historical change in American society, is shown in other work from the same period, by David Riesman and colleagues. They carried out many interviews but certainly did not take them at face value:

> Everything conspired to lead to an emphasis not on the interview itself but on its interpretation. . . . [S]uch a method . . . requires repeated reading of the interview record . . . in search of those small verbal nuances and occasional Freudian slips that might be clues to character. (Riesman & Glazer, 1952, pp. 14–15).

Of course, character as a topic hardly lends itself to direct questions of a factual nature, but the extent of "interpretation" here goes strikingly beyond the literal data. It is interesting that there are two books from the project, the main interpretive one (Riesman, Glazer, & Denney, *The Lonely Crowd*, 1950), which contains almost no direct interview data, and *Faces in the Crowd* (Riesman & Glazer, 1952), consisting mainly of raw interview data without analysis; the issue of how securely the data support the interpretation is thus avoided.[2]

The genre of publication of raw interview data has a history—sometimes, like the work of Studs Terkel, a history not within academic social science, even if social scientists refer to it. However, material that looks raw may be at least lightly cooked. Terkel describes his own procedure thus:

> The most important part of the work, is the editing of the transcripts . . . the cutting and shaping of it into a readable result. The way I look at it is I suppose something like the way a sculptor looks at a block of stone: inside it there's a shape which he'll find. (Parker, 1997, p. 169)

Thus, to treat the published version as showing just what took place in the interview would be misleading. Whole "life stories" have been published in sociology, though sometimes written by their subjects rather than elicited by interviewing;[3] the genre was treated as of central importance in the interwar period, and much more recently, it has been revived. Some recent work on life stories (e.g., Atkinson, 1998) takes a similar approach—on the one hand, putting a very high value on the subject's own version of events while, on the other hand, permitting the interviewer a considerable editorial role. Note that this, interestingly, shifts the stage intended as active researcher intervention from data elicitation, as with a questionnaire or interview guide, to data presentation. The version presented is, though, nearer to raw data than are the figures and tables of the quantitative tradition.

Topics of research have their own traditions and intrinsic needs (Platt, 1996, pp. 129–130), and so some methodological ideas arise from the substance of the work being done: Kinsey's conceptions of interviewing technique followed directly from what they saw as the requirements of work on sexual behavior (Kinsey et al., 1948). One might expect the influence of such work to follow the same paths, though whether it has done so cannot be explored here. It is clear that the choices of method did not simply follow from the current state of methodological discussion, though the results fed into that, if only by evoking criticism. The level of attention paid to the methods of such work has depended on the extent to which it has departed from the survey paradigm as well as on the general interest in its substantive content.

◆ Some Analytical Themes

Discussions of empirical work have taken us a little nearer to what has happened in practice. Research on interviewing offers another window through which we may see something of the actual conduct of the interview, as distinct from the prescriptions for it. Practice has often been indeed distinct. Interviewers

---

[2]Later, however, in his chapter in *The Academic Mind* (Lazarsfeld & Thielens, 1958), Riesman (1958) contributed what is in effect—though he does not present it as such—an extended, research-based discussion of validity, based on respondent reports on the experience of being interviewed.

[3]James Bennett (1981) has suggested the circumstances under which some types of these appear appropriate.

are repeatedly shown to use their own ways of dealing with problems in eliciting the data wanted. Roth (1966) long ago documented a few cases where research employees had for their own reasons departed from the investigator's plan, in ways that damaged it. He argued that this was only to be expected when they were employed as "hired hands," without personal commitment to the research goal or control over the content and methods. Later authors have also identified interviewer cheating. Jean Peneff (1988) observed some of the most experienced and valued interviewers working for a French governmental survey organization, all highly motivated, and found that they regularly adapted their behavior and language to the social context: "They intuitively improvised a blend of survey norms and fieldwork practices" (p. 533). He queries whether departure from specifications should be regarded as cheating—though it tended to make what was intended as standard survey work more "qualitative." It sounds as though there was an implicit bargain between interviewers and their supervisors, in which good-quality work was exchanged for lack of close inquiry into the way in which the quality was achieved. (An under-researched and under-theorized area of interviewing is that of the social relations between employed interviewers and their supervisors, and their consequences.) We do not know how far patterns such as those found by Peneff have held more widely, but we

ought not to be surprised if sometimes they do. In a very different style, Brenner (1982) elicited a large number of recordings of routine survey interviews and found that departures from instructions were common; individual interviewers showed considerable differences in asking questions as required and in probing. He treats this as a problem of interviewer skills and training rather than either "cheating" or creative fieldwork; the emphasis is on uniformity of stimulus, and he shows how departure from instructions could often lead to the collection of inadequate information.

Roth's (1966) and Peneff's (1988) work is unusual; research on interviewing has come overwhelmingly from those active in specialist survey units. (A list of main book sources presenting research on interviewing is given in Table 1.2.) It is not surprising that it should be those with continuing professional concern with the matter who do such work, but it does mean that the research has been skewed toward their distinctive preoccupations. What was problematic about interviewing for them can be seen from the topics researched, and it is from that point of view that some of their themes are considered.

A major preoccupation over the years has been variation in the answers elicited by different interviewers. This is commonly taken as a measure of "error," implying that validity is defined as arriving at the correct overall figures rather than as fully

Table 1.2 Key Works Presenting Research and Analysis on Interviewing

1947	Hadley Cantril, *Gauging Public Opinion*
1954	Herbert H. Hyman, *Interviewing in Social Research*
1965	Stephen A. Richardson, B. S. Dohrenwend, and D. Klein, *Interviewing: Its Forms and Functions*
1969	Raymond L. Gorden, *Interviewing: Strategy, Techniques and Tactics*
1974	Jean M. Converse and Howard Schuman, *Conversations at Random*
1979	Norman M. Bradburn and Seymour Sudman, *Improving Interview Method and Questionnaire Design*
1981	Charles F. Cannell, P. V. Miller, and L. Oksenberg, "Research on Interviewing Techniques"
1982	W. Dijkstra and J. van der Zouwen, *Response Behaviour in the Survey-Interview*
1984	Charles Turner and Elizabeth Martin, *Surveying Subjective Phenomena*
1990	Lucy Suchman and Brigitte Jordan, "Interactional Troubles in Face-to-Face Survey Interviews"
1991	Paul P. Biemer, R. M. Groves, L. E. Lyberg, N. A. Mathiowetz, and S. Sudman, *Measurement Errors in Surveys*
2002	Douglas W. Maynard, H. Houtkoop-Steenstra, N. C. Schaeffer, and J. van der Zouwen, *Standardization and Tacit Knowledge: Interaction and Practice in the Survey Interview*

grasping individuals' meanings or correctly identifying their real opinions. Cantril (1947) suggested that the problem of interviewer biases could be dealt with by selecting interviewers with canceling biases. Other writers saw careful selection of interviewers for their personal characteristics, whether of race or of personality, as valuable—though the real labor market often made this difficult. Fowler (1991, p. 260) points out that the conventional definition of "error" that he uses makes standardization across interviewers tautologically necessary to reduce error; this approach inevitably ignores the possibility that some nonstandardized interviewers might be better than others. In the earlier work, there was a strong tendency to blame interviewers for problems and to see the answer as more control over them. An extreme of this definition of the situation is suggested by Bradburn and Sudman's (1979) chapter on interviewer variations in asking questions, where the nonprogrammed interviewer behavior studied by tape recordings included minutiae such as stuttering, coughing, false starts, and corrected substitutions.[4] Converse and Schuman (1974), in contrast, studied the interviewers' point of view, and were not concerned primarily with their errors and how to control their behavior—which may owe something to the fact that their interviewers were graduate students, members of "us" rather than "them." Consequently, they emphasize the tensions interviewers experience between conflicting roles and expectations.

Later work, however, more often recognizes respondents' contributions and takes the interview as interaction more seriously. For Cannell, Miller, and Oksenberg (1981), the aim was to decrease reporting error due to the respondent rather than the interviewer. Because the study used in the research was on topics appearing in medical records, which could, unlike attitudes, be checked, they were able to identify some clear factual errors made by respondents. It was found that interviewers were giving positive feedback for poor respondent performance, in the supposed interests of rapport, so that correction of this and clearer guidance to respondents on what was expected of them improved their performance.

More recent writing about "cognitive" interviewing has revived the issue of accuracy in ways that do deal with the issue of validity, if only in relation to "factual" questions. Suchman and Jordan (1990), anthropologists using a conversation-analytic perspective, stress the extent to which "the survey interview suppresses those interactional resources that routinely mediate uncertainties of relevance and interpretation" (p. 232), so that reliability is bought at the cost of validity. They recommend encouraging interviewers to play a more normal conversational role, so that respondents may correctly grasp the concepts used in the questions. This article raised considerable discussion; perhaps its ideas would not have seemed so novel to the readership of a more social-scientific journal. Schaeffer (1991) balances such considerations against the need for some uniformity if the answers are to be added to give a total. She points out that "artificiality" in the interview situation does not necessarily mean that the answers given are less valid, but that to elicit them as intended, the researcher needs to bear in mind the rules of interaction that the respondent brings to the situation. Schober and Conrad (1997) have shown that less standardized and more conversational interviewing can markedly increase the accuracy of the responses given—by, for instance, allowing the interviewer to help the respondents fit their relatively complicated circumstances into the categories of answer provided by the researcher. They illustrate the self-defeating extremes to which the pursuit of the uniform stimulus had gone, being used to forbid even the provision of guidance that would ensure that the meanings sought by the researcher were indeed conveyed in the answers chosen. It is noticeable that most of the examples used in these recent discussions are drawn from large-scale national surveys, often carried out for governmental purposes and with fact-finding as a key aim. This reflects the increasing tendency of academics doing quantitative work to use high-quality data not created for their own purposes; that has led discussion in the directions suitable to the character of such work, but not equally applicable to the whole range of surveys.

Schober and Conrad's (1997) study exemplifies a recurrent pattern in which research shows that

---

[4]Some kinds of error, such as mistakes in following the schedule's instructions on which question to put next, have been eliminated by the computer-assisted methods now commonly used in survey organizations. Lyberg and Kasprzyk (1991, p. 257) point out, though, that computer-assisted telephone interviewing (CATI)-specific errors may still arise.

commonly taught practices do not necessarily have the intended effects. That the limited benefits of "rapport" for data quality have repeatedly been (re)discovered suggests that, for whatever reasons, practice has not always followed research-based conclusions and that the folklore of the field has been powerful. Recommendations on the relations between interviewer and respondent have changed considerably, whether the aim is rapport or just access. One of the earliest statements on this subject is by Bingham and Moore (1931): "The interviewee is frank when he feels that his own point of view is appreciated and respected, that the interviewer has some right to the information, and that the questions are relevant and not impertinent" (p. 11). This is rationalistic, corresponding to the assumption that the respondent is of relatively high status and is being approached for factual information; this is not typical of later discussion with other assumptions. When the interview is seen as deep and richly qualitative, or as a large-scale survey interview with members of the general public, other approaches follow. The early survey literature typically suggested that rapport needed to be established to get access and cooperation but that the interviewer should also when questioning appear unshockable, have no detectable personal opinions, and behind the front of friendliness be objective and scientific.[5] Not every writer offered as business-like a conception of rapport as Goode and Hatt (1952), for whom rapport existed when the respondent "has accepted the research goals of the interviewer, and actively seeks to help him in obtaining the necessary information" (p. 190), but the ideal was clearly an instrumental relationship.

Before the modern survey was fully developed, it was often not seen as so important to keep the interviewer as a person out of the picture. Lundberg (1942) suggests as ways of getting an informant "started" some devices—"to refer to important friends of the informant as if one were quite well acquainted with them; to tell of one's own experiences or problems and ask the informant's advice or reactions to them" (pp. 365–366)—of just the kind that survey organizations train their interviewers to avoid. Kinsey's advocacy of a less impersonal and unbiased style was quoted above (Kinsey et al., 1948).

Elements of such an approach have now come round again in recent qualitative work, where there has often been a sociopolitical commitment to treat the respondent as an equal, which is taken to imply not playing a detached role while expecting the other party to reveal the self:

> We can no longer remain objective, faceless interviewers, but become human beings and must disclose ourselves, learning about ourselves as we try to learn about the other. . . . As long as . . . researchers continue to treat respondents as unimportant, faceless individuals whose only contribution is to fill one more boxed response, the answers we . . . get will be commensurable with the questions we ask and the way we ask them. (Fontana & Frey, 1994, p. 374)

This line can, however, be presented in a more manipulative way, as here in Douglas's (1985) unique style:

> Most Goddesses [beautiful women] feel the need for a significant amount of self-disclosure before they will . . . reveal their innermost selves in their most self-discrediting aspects. When they seem to be proceeding to the inner depths with reluctance, I normally try to lead the way with a significant bit of self-discrediting self-disclosure. (p. 122)

Research on their perceptions of each other has shown that respondents do not necessarily detect the interviewer's biases or manipulative strategies; to that extent, the impulse is moral or political rather than scientific. The barrier between the role and the self is broken down—or is it? Is this just another mode of instrumental presentation of self, as fellow-human rather than as detached professional?

Holstein and Gubrium (1995) do not stress the interviewer's revelation of self but treat the interviewer and the respondent as equal in another way, since both are creating meanings; both are also "active," rather than the respondent being seen as just the passive object of the interviewer's attempted control. For them, there is no such thing as the one correct answer to be found, but a range of possibilities depending on which of the respondent's resources and potential standpoints are brought to

---

[5]This is another area where CATI must have changed the issues, though it has been little written about from that point of view; perhaps the physical separation from the respondent has placed the focus on control of the interviewer rather than on understanding the respondent's reactions to the situation.

bear. The role of the interviewer is "to provide an environment conducive to the production of the range and complexity of meanings that address relevant issues and not be confined by predetermined agendas" (p. 17). The resultant conversation is not necessarily less authentic than "real," normal ones, though the use of interviewers may be justified by their capacity to raise for comment matters on which everyday conversation is rare. Coding, by both interviewer and respondent, is seen as "endogenous to the interview" (p. 66), implicit in the emergent categories that they develop together to describe experience. When the materials collected in this way are put together to make a broader picture,[6] it is certainly not done in quantitative terms, and this is clearly not an approach intended to be of use toward fact-finding or hypothesis-testing goals.

A method of data collection that cannot make plausible claims to validity is of no use, so it is surprising that a wide range of levels of concern for validity, and conceptions of it, have been shown in relation to interviews. It has commonly been agreed that less rigidly structured methods may score higher on validity, though this has to be traded off against the greater reliability of the more structured methods. Concern with the problem has come more from those who employ other people to do their interviews; those who carry out their own interviews have usually seemed to regard their validity as self-evident and not requiring checks. This sometimes reflects a hostility to "science" or "positivism" prevalent among qualitative researchers. However, in the literature of the standard survey too there has been surprisingly little concern shown about validity as such. The question of the substantive meaningfulness of the data, except on purely factual questions, somehow gets elided in the concern about interviewer error and questionnaire improvement.

It is, of course, in the survey, as in other contexts, difficult to demonstrate validity, though some authors have suggested ways of doing so. Maccoby and Maccoby (1954) proposed a traditional measure: "It remains to be seen whether unstandardized interviews have sufficiently greater validity so that ratings based upon them will predict criterion variables better than will ratings based on standardized interviews" (p. 454). Where there is a clear criterion to use as the standard of prediction, as in voting

results, it has been used, but for many topics there is none. There has been some discussion in terms of whether the respondent is telling the truth. Kinsey et al. (1948) take an inimitably robust stand on this:

> It has been asked how it is possible for an interviewer to know whether people are telling the truth. . . . As well ask a horse trader how he knows when to close a bargain! The experienced interviewer knows when he has established a sufficient rapport to obtain an honest record. (p. 43)

Even if one accepts the horse-trading approach as adequate, it could only be applied in relatively deep and unstructured types of interview, where the interviewer has time to establish a relationship. For the "depth" or psychoanalytical style, of course, the issue of validity has not arisen in the same sense, since the focus has been not on correct factuality but on the interpretations made by the analyst. Warner and Lunt (1941) take a different approach:

> The information gathered about social relations is always social fact if the informant believes it, and it is always fact of another kind if he tells it and does not believe it. If the informant does not believe it, the lie he tells is frequently more valuable as a lead to understanding his behavior or that of others than the truth. (p. 52)

They assume the researcher to have ways of *knowing* that the respondent is lying. In intensive, long-term studies of a community, such as Warner and Lunt's, that is a relatively plausible assumption; Vidich and Bensman (1954), conducting another such study, also report detecting much intentional misrepresentation. Plainly, however, in many other cases this assumption would not be met.

Galtung (1967) is one of the earliest representatives of what might be seen as a truly sociological position, even if it is not one that exactly solves the problem:

> The spoken word is a social act, the inner thought is not, and the sociologist has good reasons to be most interested and concerned with the former, the psychologist perhaps with the latter. But this only transforms the problem from correspondence

---

[6]A remarkable discussion of the choice of good respondents (as distinct from a quantitatively representative sample) that, despite its sophisticated style, is reminiscent of some of the much earlier literature on informants.

between words and thoughts to that of how representative the interview situation is as social intercourse. (p. 124)

Holstein and Gubrium (1995) take this one step further and, informed by ethnomethodological perspectives, stop worrying about such representativeness:

One cannot expect answers on one occasion to replicate those on another because they emerge from different circumstances of production. Similarly, the validity of answers derives not from their correspondence to meanings held within the respondent but from their ability to convey situated experiential realities in terms that are locally comprehensible. (p. 9)

This takes it that there is no stable underlying reality to identify, thus in a sense abolishing the problem. Mishler's (1986) emphasis on the interview response as a narrative in which the respondent makes sense of and gives meaning to experience has a similar stance. The issue has thus moved from the interview as an adequate measure of a reality external to it to the content of the interview as of interest in its own right. This is a long way from the concerns of some survey researchers to get correct reports of bathroom equipment or medical treatment received. Each of the extremes of the discussion may write about "the interview," but they have had in mind different paradigms and different research topics and have shown little interest in the problems relevant to the needs and concerns of the other.

◆ *The Historical Pattern*

Not all the work reviewed fits into a clear historical pattern, and empirical studies may be idiosyncratic in relation to the methodological literature, but nonetheless we sketch a broad trajectory that thinking has followed. The dates suggested are not meant as precise; different workers move at different speeds.

Up to the later 1930s, the "interview" was distinguished from the "questionnaire," which was generally thought of as for self-completion; if it was administered by an interviewer, her contribution was not seen as requiring serious attention. The "interview" was unstructured, if with an agenda, and wide-ranging; the interviewer was likely to be the researcher. Subjects were often used as informants with special knowledge to pass on, rather than as units to be quantified. This kind of interview was not strongly distinguished from interviews for job selection or journalism or, when interviewing down, for social casework. (Indeed, data from social work interviews in particular were widely used by social scientists, at a time when the idea of professors themselves going into the field was a new one.) Little concern with reliability or validity was shown. A few rules of thumb were suggested for success. It was assumed that subjects might not accept overt interviewing, so some concealment was necessary. In parallel to this, however, much work was done under rubrics such as "life history," "fieldwork," and "case study," which we might call "interviewing" even if the writers did not. For these, there was serious discussion of technical matters such as how to keep the respondent talking without affecting the direction of the conversation too much (see, e.g., Palmer, 1928, pp. 171–175).

Meanwhile, political polling and market research were developing. Here, interviews were conducted by forces of interviewers instructed and supervised from the center. The private research agency came into existence, alongside developments within government. The modern "survey" began to emerge and, hence, concern with the technique of interviewing with a relatively elaborate fixed schedule. The work done was often to be published in the newspapers or was of direct commercial interest to the client, which meant that predictions might be testable and numerical accuracy became important. There were also repeated studies of similar kinds carried out by the same agencies. Reliability began to be taken seriously as the data to evaluate it were available, and this led to concern with "interviewer effects" and the control of the interviewing force. The development of ideas about sampling was also important, because it was only when, in the late 1930s, it began to be seen as desirable to have nationally representative samples that the issue of how to control a large, scattered, and not very highly trained body of interviewers came to the fore. Whatever the intellectual preferences of the surveyors, the realities of dealing with such a labor force had weight. Less was left to the interviewer's initiative, and training became more detailed and serious. Much of the work was done by psychologists, so an experimental and stimulus–response model was influential, and attitudes rather than factual information became a focus of interest.

Then the hothouse atmosphere of wartime research brought different strands of work together, and the modern survey emerged fully. There were controversies between structured and unstructured approaches, or open and closed questions, and different teams developed different styles, but there was much cooperation and a consensus on many practical and technical issues. Nonexperimental aspects of psychology were prominent as inspiration; on the level of technique, Rogers's "nondirective" approach, and psychoanalytic approaches were popular in the more qualitative styles. For those in the lead on surveys, question construction, sampling, and scaling became of more interest than interviewing as such. Researchers not in the survey world developed their own detailed qualitative techniques, often planned to deal with their particular subject matter; some were heavily criticized by the methodologists from the perspectives that they had now developed.

After the war, new practices were incorporated into textbooks and training procedures (see, e.g., Sheatsley, 1951). Systematic research on interviewing started, and it showed that some of the folk wisdom was unfounded. Social scientists turned to the survey as a major method, and it became a standard practice. Those out of sympathy defended alternatives, often under the banner of "participant observation" (Becker & Geer, 1957), which was differentiated from the survey by laying stress more on direct observation than on questioning, though certainly much "conversation with a purpose" (a frequently cited definition of "interview") was part of the observation. Discussions of participant observation technique have, though, given attention to the social relations involved in such conversation rather than to the fine detail of what takes place in the encounter; obviously, repeated contacts with the same subjects raise different issues.

Soon surveys were widespread enough for nonmethodologists to take an interest in them—though often a skeptical one. From the later 1960s, the upheaval in the political and theoretical interests of the time was related to interviewing, and work was done on its implicit assumptions in areas such as epistemology. Much more interest was shown in its social relations; this was the heyday of reflexivity and autobiographical accounts of research. Specialist work on interviewing particular groups (children, elites) also started to be written as the general application of survey method brought to light the special problems involved.

By the 1970s, interviewing was taken for granted as an established practice in the survey world; specialists continued with increasingly sophisticated methodological research and refined details of method still further, often in relation to new technologies using telephones and/or computers. (Meanwhile, for members of the general public, the idea of polling with quantitative results, and of the role to be played by respondents, became established; Back & Cross, 1982,[7] and Igo, 2007, discuss what this meant.) The "qualitative" world became ideologically more separate and developed its own discussions, which showed little concern with the technical issues it might have in common with the survey world. Feminists often saw qualitative methods as particularly appropriate to women as subjects and developed ideas about their special requirements. The barrier between interviewer and respondent was attacked, and efforts were made to define ways of co-opting respondents rather than using them; whether these have been successful, and how it feels from the respondent's point of view, has hardly been investigated.

There is a sense in which interviewing has come full circle. Although in its early beginnings the typical stance toward mass respondents was that of the social worker rather than of the social equal, for some sociologists the interviewer again has a high degree of freedom and initiative and may make direct use of personal experience. In much of the survey world, however, the pattern has been different. From a starting point where the interviewer's behavior was not much programmed, it has gone through a phase of high programming with relatively unsophisticated techniques to one where the areas formerly left unexamined, such as probing, are themselves intended to be programmed. What really happens in the field might not live up to those hopes—but less was done "in

---

[7]"One can say that the interview proceeds best if the social situation of the interview has been solidified in the culture, if survey research is an accepted institution, and if people have definite expectations of the performance in the interview. If these social conditions are met, the interview can proceed smoothly, while the respondent can disregard the characteristics of the interviewer or the nature of the questions" (pp. 201–202).

the field." The telephone interviewing system opened up fresh possibilities of near-total surveillance and control of interviewer behavior. Thus, the flexibility needed for adaptation to the respondent's needs became no longer an area of initiative. Meanwhile, however, another strand of development, the cognitive approach, has reopened some of the earlier possibilities of unprogrammed conversational initiative by the survey interviewer, showing an interesting convergence between otherwise very separate areas of work.

Quantification can only be justified if it is in some sense instances of the same thing that are added up—but there is room for variation in how precisely uniform the stimuli need to be—and not all research has had goals to which quantification is appropriate. For exploratory or descriptive research, not aiming to test specific hypotheses, varying stimuli could be desirable if they help produce responses of more detail, precision, validity, and felt adequacy for the respondent—as long as those responses are not then fed into precodes. If the text of the answer is to be processed later, there are problems of recording and analysis, but many problems shift from the interviewing to the analysis stage. In the end, therefore, discussion cannot be confined to the interaction between interviewer and respondent.

Some of the changes over time in interviewing theory and practice have arisen internally, from methodological concerns, though which ones have been salient has depended on the topics studied and on the organizational and technological framework within which the studies have taken place. Other changes have responded to broader intellectual movements and to agendas defined in sociopolitical rather than methodological terms. Strong normative statements about method have often rested on assumptions appropriate to their original context but less relevant to other kinds of work. The interview remains an area of richly diverse practice about which few convincing generalizations can be made. We cannot tell which of the many current variants will appear to the later historian to have played a significant role or whether history will recognize all the distinctions made between them as meaningful.

◆ References

Adorno, T. W., Frenkel-Brunswik, E., Levinson, D. J., & Sanford, R. N. (1950). *The authoritarian personality*. New York, NY: Harper & Row.

Atkinson, R. (1998). *The life story interview*. Thousand Oaks, CA: Sage.

Back, K. W., & Cross, T. S. (1982). Response effects of role-restricted respondent characteristics. In W. Dijkstra & J. van der Zouwen (Eds.), *Response behaviour in the survey-interview* (pp. 189–207). London, England: Academic Press.

Bales, K. (1991). Charles Booth's survey of *Life and Labour of the People in London 1889–1903*. In M. Bulmer, K. Bales, & K. K. Sklar (Eds.), *The social survey in historical perspective 1880–1940* (pp. 66–110). Cambridge, England: Cambridge University Press.

Becker, H. S., & Geer, B. (1957). Participant observation and interviewing: A comparison. *Human Organization, 16*, 28–32.

Bennett, J. (1981). *Oral history and delinquency: The rhetoric of criminology*. Chicago, IL: University of Chicago Press.

Biemer, P. P., Groves, R. M., Lyberg, L. E., Mathiowetz, N. A., & Sudman, S. (Eds.). (1991). *Measurement errors in surveys*. New York, NY: Wiley.

Bingham, W. V. D., & Moore, B. V. (1931). *How to interview*. New York, NY: Harper.

Bradburn, N. M., & Sudman, S. (1979). *Improving interview method and questionnaire design*. San Francisco, CA: Jossey-Bass.

Brenner, M. (1982). Response effects of "role-restricted" characteristics of the interviewer. In W. Dijkstra & J. van der Zouwen (Eds.), *Response behaviour in the survey-interview* (pp. 131–165). London, England: Academic Press.

Cannell, C. F., & Kahn, R. L. (1953). The collection of data by interviewing. In L. Festinger & D. Katz (Eds.), *Research methods in the behavioral sciences* (pp. 327–380). New York, NY: Dryden Press.

Cannell, C. F., Miller, P. V., & Oksenberg, L. (1981). Research on interviewing techniques. In S. Lienhardt (Ed.), *Sociological methodology 1981* (pp. 389–437). San Francisco, CA: Jossey-Bass.

Cantril, H. (1947). *Gauging public opinion*. Princeton, NJ: Princeton University Press.

Christie, R., & Jahoda, M. (Eds.). (1954). *Studies in the scope and method of "The Authoritarian Personality."* Glencoe, IL: Free Press.

Cicourel, A. V. (1964). *Method and measurement in sociology*. New York, NY: Free Press.

Cochran, W. G., Mosteller, F., & Tukey, J. W. (1954). *Statistical problems of the Kinsey report*. Washington, DC: American Statistical Association.

Converse, J. M. (1987). *Survey research in the US: Roots and emergence, 1890–1960*. Berkeley: University of California Press.

Converse, J. M., & Schuman, H. (1974). *Conversations at random: Survey research as interviewers see it*. New York, NY: Wiley.

Denzin, N. K. (1970). *The research act in sociology*. Chicago, IL: Aldine.

Denzin, N. K., & Lincoln, Y. S. (1994). *Handbook of qualitative research*. Thousand Oaks, CA: Sage.

Dexter, L. A. (1970). *Elite and specialized interviewing*. Evanston, IL: Northwestern University Press.

Dijkstra, W., & van der Zouwen, J. (Eds.). (1982). *Response behaviour in the survey-interview*. London, England: Academic Press.

Douglas, J. D. (1985). *Creative interviewing*. Beverly Hills, CA: Sage.

Fontana, A., & Frey, J. H. (1994). Interviewing: The art of science. In N. K. Denzin & Y. S. Lincoln (Eds.), *Handbook of qualitative research* (pp. 361–376). Thousand Oaks, CA: Sage.

Fowler, F. J. (1991). Reducing interviewer-related error through interviewer training, supervision and other means. In P. B. Biemer, R. M. Groves, L. E. Lyberg, N. A. Mathiowetz, & S. Sudman (Eds.), *Measurement errors in surveys* (pp. 260–279). New York, NY: Wiley.

Fry, C. L. (1934). *The technique of social investigation*. New York, NY: Harper.

Gallup, G. (1944). *A guide to public opinion polls*. Princeton, NJ: Princeton University Press.

Galtung, J. (1967). *Theory and methods of social research*. London, England: Allen & Unwin.

Garrett, A. (1942). *Interviewing: Its principles and methods*. New York, NY: Family Service Association of America.

Goode, W. J., & Hatt, P. K. (1952). *Methods in social research*. New York, NY: McGraw-Hill.

Gorden, R. L. (1969). *Interviewing: Strategy, techniques and tactics*. Homewood, IL: Dorsey Press.

Holstein, J. A., & Gubrium, J. F. (1995). *The active interview*. Thousand Oaks, CA: Sage.

Hyman, H. H. (1954). *Interviewing in social research*. Chicago, IL: University of Chicago Press.

Igo, S. E. (2007). *The averaged American: Surveys, citizens and the making of a mass public*. Cambridge, MA: Harvard University Press.

Jovchelovitch, S., & Bauer, M. W. (2007). *Narrative interviewing*. London, England. Retrieved from http://eprints.lse.ac.uk/2633/1/Narrativeinterviewing.pdf

Kahn, R. L., & Cannell, C. F. (1957). *The dynamics of interviewing*. New York, NY: Wiley.

Kinsey, A. C., Pomeroy, W. B., & Martin, C. E. (1948). *Sexual behavior in the human male*. Philadelphia, PA: W. B. Saunders.

Lazarsfeld, P. F. (1944). The controversy over detailed interviews: An offer for negotiation. *Public Opinion Quarterly, 8*, 38–60.

Lazarsfeld, P. F., & Thielens, W., Jr. (Eds.). (1958). *The academic mind*. Glencoe, IL: Free Press.

Lee, R. M. (2004). Recording technologies and the interview in sociology, 1920–2000. *Sociology, 38*, 869–889.

Lundberg, G. A. (1942). *Social research*. New York, NY: Longmans, Green.

Lyberg, L., & Kasprzyk, D. (1991). Data collection methods and measurement error: An overview. In P. B. Biemer, R. M. Groves, L. E. Lyberg, N. A. Mathiowetz, & S. Sudman (Eds.), *Measurement errors in surveys* (pp. 237–257). New York, NY: Wiley.

Maccoby, E. E., & Maccoby, N. (1954). The interview: A tool of social science. In G. Lindzey (Ed.), *Handbook of social psychology* (Vol. 1, pp. 449–487). Reading, MA: Addison-Wesley.

Maynard, D. W., Houtkoop-Steenstra, H., Schaeffer, N. C., & van der Zouwen, J. (Eds.). (2002). *Standardization and tacit knowledge*. New York, NY: Wiley.

Mishler, E. G. (1986). *Research interviewing: Context and narrative*. Cambridge, MA: Harvard University Press.

Odum, H. W., & Jocher, K. (1929). *An introduction to social research*. New York, NY: Holt.

Palmer, V. (1928). *Field studies in sociology*. Chicago, IL: University of Chicago Press.

Parker, T. (1997). *Studs Terkel: A life in words*. London, England: HarperCollins.

Peneff, J. (1988). The observers observed: French survey researchers at work. *Social Problems, 35*, 520–535.

Platt, J. (1996). *A history of sociological research methods in America, 1920–1960*. Cambridge, England: Cambridge University Press.

Potter, J., & Hepburn, A. (2005). Qualitative interviews in psychology: Problems and possibilities. *Qualitative Research in Psychology, 2*, 281–307.

Reinharz, S. (1992). *Feminist methods in social research*. New York, NY: Oxford University Press.

Richardson, S. A., Dohrenwend, B. S., & Klein, D. (1965). *Interviewing: Its forms and functions*. New York, NY: Basic Books.

Riesman, D. (1958). Some observations on the interviewing in the Teacher Apprehension Study. In P. S. Lazarsfeld & W. Thielens Jr. (Eds.), *The academic mind* (pp. 266–370). Glencoe, IL: Free Press.

Riesman, D., & Glazer, N. (1952). *Faces in the crowd*. New Haven, CT: Yale University Press.

Riesman, D., Glazer, N., & Denney, R. (1950). *The lonely crowd*. New Haven, CT: Yale University Press.

Rocthlisberger, F. J., & Dickson, W. J. (1964). *Management and the worker*. New York, NY: Wiley. (Original work published 1939)

Roth, J. A. (1966). Hired hand research. *The American Sociologist, 1*, 190–196.

Schaeffer, N. C. (1991). Conversation with a purpose—or conversation? Interaction in the standardized interview. In P. B. Biemer, R. M. Groves, L. E. Lyberg, N. A. Mathiowetz, & S. Sudman (Eds.), *Measurement errors in surveys* (pp. 367–391). New York, NY: Wiley.

Schober, M. F., & Conrad, F. G. (1997). Does conversational interviewing reduce survey measurement error? *Public Opinion Quarterly, 61*, 576–602.

Selltiz, C., Jahoda, M., Deutsch, M., & Cook, S. W. (1965). *Research methods in social relations*. London, England: Methuen.

Sheatsley, P. B. (1951). The art of interviewing and a guide to interviewer selection and training. In M. Jahoda, M. Deutsch, & S. W. Cook (Eds.), *Research methods in social relations* (Pt. 2, pp. 463–492). New York, NY: Dryden Press.

Sjoberg, G., & Nett, R. (1968). *A methodology for social research*. New York, NY: Harper & Row.

Suchman, L., & Jordan, B. (1990). Interactional troubles in face-to-face survey interviews. *Journal of the American Statistical Association, 85,* 232–241.

Taylor, S. J., & Bogdan, R. (1984). *Introduction to qualitative research methods*. New York, NY: Wiley.

Turner, C., & Martin, E. (Eds.). (1984). *Surveying subjective phenomena*. New York, NY: Russell Sage Foundation.

University of Michigan. (1954). *Manual for interviewers*. Ann Arbor: University of Michigan, Survey Research Center.

Vidich, A., & Bensman, J. (1954). The validity of field data. *Human Organization, 13,* 20–27.

Warner, W. L., & Lunt, P. S. (1941). *The social life of a modern community*. New Haven, CT: Yale University Press.

Young, P. V. (1935). *Interviewing in social work*. New York, NY: McGraw-Hill.

Young, P. V. (1939). *Scientific social surveys and research*. New York, NY: Prentice Hall.

Young, P. V. (1949). *Scientific social surveys and research* (2nd ed.). New York, NY: Prentice Hall.

2

NARRATIVE PRACTICE AND THE TRANSFORMATION OF INTERVIEW SUBJECTIVITY

◆ Jaber F. Gubrium and James A. Holstein

The research interview was once viewed as a straightforward method of data collection. Respondents were contacted, interviews scheduled, a location determined, ground rules set, and the interviews begun. Questions were designed to elicit answers in an anticipatable form from respondents until interview protocols were complete. The respondent's job was to provide information pertinent to the research project. Knowing his or her role, the respondent waited until the questions were posed before answering. Duties did not extend to managing the encounter or raising queries of his or her own. This was the interviewer's responsibility. If the respondent asked questions, they were treated as requests for clarification.

This model of the interview informed social research for decades. Most people are now well acquainted with what it takes to play either role, recognize what it means to interview someone, and broadly know the aims of the interview process.

The requirements of interviewing are familiar, whether they take the form of demographic questionnaires, product use surveys, Internet polls, or health inventories. The roles and expectations cross the borders of scientific and professional interviewing.

Recently, researchers have begun to scrutinize the traditional model's epistemological bearings (see, e.g., Denzin & Lincoln, 2005, 2011). A more reflexive appreciation of knowledge production in general, not just interview knowledge, has prompted a reassessment of the procedures of empirical inquiry, including the interview. Given its centrality in a recent turn toward more sophisticated analyses of knowledge production (see Chase, 2011), the interview can no longer be viewed as a unilaterally guided means of excavating information. It is being reevaluated in terms of its structure, interactional dynamics, situational responsiveness, and discursive dimensions.

◆ 27

This chapter discusses the transformation of how researchers conceive of respondent and interview roles, the nature of interview information, and the relationship of the information to society. These themes are traced through critical commentary on models of interview subjectivity and their relation to narrative practice in the interview context. Reconceptualizing interview roles in terms of narrative practice presents a more active version of how interview participants actually operate. Their agency is recast as artful, collaborative, and suffused with discourse. If the responsive, yet relatively passive, respondent and the inquiring interviewer once characterized participant subjectivity, this is now considered deceptively simple. It has given way to a more interactionally sensitive and constructive perspective, featuring the active narrativity of the enterprise. The chapter explores the implications of this transformation for how interview data might be construed and analyzed.

◆ Public Opinion and Surveillance

Despite its familiarity, the interview is a relatively recent phenomenon and was once figured to be strange in the everyday scheme of things. As a systematic method for obtaining experiential knowledge, it is the product of a mere century of development (Platt, 2002). Undergirding the emergence of the interview was a new understanding that the individual person—each and every one of them—is an important source of knowledge. We can imagine, of course, that questioning and answering have been with us since the beginning of communication. As long as we have had parental authority, parents have questioned their children regarding their whereabouts and activities. Similarly, suspects and prisoners have been interrogated since suspicion and incarceration have been a part of human affairs. Healers, priests, employers, writers, and many others seeking knowledge about daily life for practical purposes have all engaged in interview-like inquiry.

Yet a century ago, it would have seemed peculiar for a complete stranger to approach us—any one of us, from the humblest to the most celebrated—and to ask for permission to discuss personal matters just for the sake of knowledge. Questioning and answering was more practical. Daily life was, in many ways, more intimate; everyday affairs were conducted on a face-to-face basis only between those well acquainted with each other. According to Mark Benney and Everett Hughes (1956), "The interview [as a behavioral format] is a relatively new kind of encounter in the history of human relations" (p. 193). It is not the asking and answering of questions that was new. Rather, the innovation was a preplanned conversation between strangers from all walks of life devoted to information gathering without an immediate purpose in view (Benney & Hughes, 1956).

Especially after World War II, with the emergence of standardized survey interviews, individuals became accustomed to offering their opinions for the sake of information gathering. "Public opinion" became a newfound and anonymous forum within which individuals could forthrightly express their most private thoughts and deepest feelings with the expectation that their published opinions were anonymous but important. No matter how insignificant their station in life, they were treated as equal elements of populations of interest. Each person had a voice, and it was imperative that each voice be heard. Seeking the gamut of thoughts and sentiments, the research interview democratized opinion.

THE MODERN TEMPER

Guided by the new "modern temper," the times progressively embraced routine conversational exchanges between strangers (Riesman & Benney, 1956). When they encountered an interview situation, people weren't immediately defensive about being asked for information about their lives, their associates, and even their heartfelt sentiments. They readily recognized and accepted two new roles associated with talking about oneself and one's life to strangers, (1) the role of interviewer and (2) the role of respondent, the centerpieces of the now familiar interview encounter.

Interviewing helped spread the understanding that all individuals have the wherewithal to offer a meaningful description of, or a set of opinions about, their lives. Experiential knowledge was no longer the principal responsibility of high-status commentators—of tribal chiefs, village headmen, or the educated classes—who in other times and places spoke for one and all. As Pertti Alasuutari (1998) explains, it wasn't so long ago that when one wanted to know something important about society or daily life, one asked those allegedly "in the know" (also see Platt, 2002). In contrast to what seems self-evident today—that is, questioning those individuals whose experiences are under consideration—the obvious and efficient choice was to ask informed citizens to provide answers to research questions. Those considered to be properly knowledgeable in the subject matter, Alasuutari notes, were viewed as informants. Not everyone's opinion counted, certainly not the opinions of the "humbler classes" (see Mayhew, 1851, pp. xv–xvi). But the modern interview changed this, giving rise to the importance of *all* opinion. (See, e.g., the proliferation of Internet interviews and surveys that derive entertainment value from the valorization of any and all publicly offered opinions.)

BIOPOLITICS

Along with the democratization of opinion came increasing life surveillance, what Michel Foucault (Dreyfus & Rabinow, 1982) calls "biopolitics." The survey interview became an efficient means of information gathering for populations of individuals. Foucault's (1973, 1975, 1977, 1978) seminal studies of the discursive organization of identity shed important light on the development of individualized subjectivity. Time and again, in institutional contexts ranging from the medical clinic and the mental asylum to the prison, Foucault showed how "technologies of the self" created and transformed sources of information about who and what we are (see Dreyfus & Rabinow, 1982; Foucault, 1988). The phrase refers to the concrete practices through which a sense of, and information about, individual identity is constructed. The notion that each and every one of us has an ordinary self, capable of reflecting on his or her experience, individually describing it, and communicating opinions about it and his or her surrounding world, created a new subjectivity worth communicating about.

The technologies Foucault especially had in view were the concrete, socially and historically located institutional practices, including individual interviews, through which the new democratic and individualized sense of who and what we are as human beings was being constructed. Prompted, this individualized subject would duly offer his or her outlook and sentiments within the self-scrutinizing regimens of what Foucault (1991) called "governmentality," the unwitting archipelago of surveillance

practices suffusing modern life. As James Miller (1993, p. 299) points out, governmentality extends well beyond the political and carceral, to include pedagogical, spiritual, and religious dimensions (also see Garland, 1997). If Bentham's original panopticon was an efficient form of prison surveillance, panopticism in the modern temper became the widespread self-scrutiny that "governs" all aspects of life in the very commonplace questions and answers we continually apply to ourselves both in our inner thoughts and in public inquiries. Now formalized in opinion surveys and increasingly in media interviews, these are inquiries about what we personally think and feel about every conceivable topic, including our most private actions.

The research interview was a constitutive part of this development. Indeed, this interview may be seen as one of the 20th century's most distinctive technologies of the self. It helped scientize the individualized self. As Nikolas Rose (1990, 1997) has shown in the context of the psychological sciences, the shaping of the private self, along with its descriptive data, was invented right along with the technologies we now associate with behavioral and attitude measurement. Scientific surveillance such as psychological testing, case assessments, and individual interviews of all kinds have created the experiencing and informing respondent we take for granted as the subject of our inquiries.

LEARNING FROM STRANGERS

The title of Robert Weiss's (1994) popular how-to book on interviewing, *Learning from Strangers*, affirms the importance of anonymous opinion seeking. Behind each bit of advice on how to interview effectively is the understanding that every stranger-respondent one encounters as an interviewer is someone worth listening to. The respondent is someone who can provide amazingly detailed descriptions of his or her thoughts, feelings, and activities—presumably better than anyone else—if one asks and listens carefully. The trick, in Weiss's judgment, is to present a concerned attitude, expressed within a well-planned and encouraging format. The aim is to derive as objectively as possible the respondent's *own* opinions on the subject matter, opinions that will readily be offered up and elaborated on by the respondent when circumstances are conducive to doing so and the proper solicitations extended.

The full range of individual experiences is accessible through interviewing, according to Weiss (1994), because the interview is a virtual window on experience. It is its own panopticon. In answering the question of why we interview, Weiss offers a compelling portrayal of the democratization of experiential knowledge:

> Interviewing gives us access to the observations of others. Through interviewing we can learn about places we have not been and could not go and about settings in which we have not lived. If we have the right informants, we can learn about the quality of neighborhoods or what happens in families or how organizations set their goals. Interviewing can inform us about the nature of social life. We can learn about the work of occupations and how people fashion careers, about cultures and the values they sponsor, and about the challenges people confront as they lead their lives.
>
> We can learn also, through interviewing, about people's interior experiences. We can learn what people perceived and how they interpreted their perceptions. We can learn how events affect their thoughts and feelings. We can learn the meanings to them of their relationships, their families, their work, and their selves. We can learn about all the experiences, from joy through grief, that together constitute the human condition. (p. 1)

◆ The Interview Society

Today, interviewing is ubiquitous. Think of how much is learned about people and their experiences by way of interviews, across a broad spectrum of venues and beyond the realm of social research. Interviews, for example, are an important source of celebrity, notoriety, and entertainment. News media interviewers introduce us to presidents and power brokers, who not only provide a mass audience with their thoughts, feelings, policies, and opinions but also cultivate fame in the process. The process implicates the deepest secrets and sentiments, not just the political, economic, or social savvy of high-profile figures. Interviewers like Barbara Walters or Oprah Winfrey plumb the emotional depths of luminaries and VIPs from across the political and entertainment gamut. To this, add television talk show hosts of all stripes, who daily invite ordinary men and women,

the emotionally tortured, and the behaviorally bizarre to "spill their guts" to millions. Questions and answers fly back and forth on the Internet, where blogs, chat rooms, Facebook, and Twitter are as inquisitive and intimate as back porches, bars, and bedrooms. The interview is a premier experiential conduit of the electronic age.

Interviews extend to professional realms as well. Countless institutions employ interviewing to generate useful and often crucial information. Physicians conduct medical interviews with their patients to formulate diagnoses and monitor progress in treatment (see Zoppi & Epstein, 2002). Employers interview job applicants, guided by consultants who formularize the process (see Latham & Millman, 2002). Psychotherapy always has been a largely interview-based human service, perhaps more diversified in its perspectives than any other professional interviewing (see Miller, de Shazer, & De Jong, 2002). Even forensic investigation has come a long way from the interview practices of the Inquisition, where giving the "third degree" was the last resort of interrogation (see McKenzie, 2002).

As interviewing became pervasive, an interviewing industry developed. Survey research, public opinion polling, and marketing research are in the vanguard. This crosses over as survey research is increasingly employed for commercial purposes. The interviewing industry now extends from individual product use inquiries to group-interviewing services, where focus groups are used to quickly establish everything from consumer product evaluations to voter preferences (see Morgan, 2002).

David Silverman (1993, 1997) argues that we live in an "interview society," in which interviews are central to making sense of life (see Gubrium & Holstein, 2002). The interview process and the interview society are reflexively related, the process giving discursive shape to the social form and the social form prompting us to present who and what we are writ large in its terms. Resonating with the modern temper and governmentality, Silverman (1997) identifies three requisite conditions for this development. First, the interview society requires a particular form of informing subjectivity, "the emergence of the self as a proper object of narration" (p. 248). Second, there is a need for the "technology of the confessional." The interview society requires a procedure for securing the narrative by-product of "confession," which, as Silverman points out, extends not only to "friend[ship] with the policeman, but with the priest, the teacher, and the 'psy' professional" (p. 248). Third, and perhaps most important, a mass technology must be widely available and easily accessible. The interviewing ethos and its technical realization must be recognizably in place throughout society, so that virtually everyone is familiar with the goals of interviewing as well as what it takes to participate in an interview.

Not only do communications media and human service professionals get their information from interviews, but it's been estimated that fully 90% of all social science investigations exploit interview data (Briggs, 1986). Internet surveys now provide instant questions and answers about every imaginable subject; we are asked for our inclinations and opinions regarding everything from political candidates to suggestions for which characters on TV serials should be retained or removed. The interview society is a contemporary fixture, flourishing as a leading milieu for addressing the subjective contours of daily living.

The prominence of the interview has served to promote the individualized subject (Atkinson & Silverman, 1997) as a key feature of the interview society. Ultimately, there is a fundamentally romantic impulse undergirding the interview enterprise. If we desire to really know the individual subject, then we must provide a means of hearing his or her authentic voice. "Really," "authentic," and "voice" are the bywords. Superficial inquiry and description are inadequate. Accordingly, interviewers are prompted to explore the deeper emotional grounds of the self by way of open-ended or in-depth interviewing. While, technically, these are merely alternative ways of structuring the interview process, Atkinson and Silverman (1997) argue that the words flag an epistemological understanding, namely, that the true voice of the subject is internal and comes through only when it is not externally screened or otherwise narratively fettered. The interview society, it seems, is the province of subjects harboring deep inner meanings, selves, and sentiments, whose stories retain the truths of the matters in question.

But Atkinson and Silverman (1997) caution that authenticity should not be taken as ultimate experiential truth. Authenticity itself is a methodically constructed product of communicative practice (see Gubrium & Holstein, 2009b). Authenticity has a constructive technology of its own, in other words. Recognizable signs of emotional expression and scenic practices such as direct eye contact and intimate gestures are widely taken to reveal deep truths about individual experience (also see Gubrium & Holstein, 1997, 2009a; Holstein & Gubrium, 2000). We "do" deep, authentic experiences as much as we "do" opinion offering in the course of the interview. It is not simply a matter of procedure or the richness of data that turns researchers, the interview society, and its truth-seeking audiences to in-depth and open-ended interviewing. Rather, discursive conventions make audible and visible the phenomenal depths of the individual subject.

◆ The Turn to Narrative Practice

If experience is increasingly generated and mediated by the interview, everyday reality is also becoming even more narratively formulated. As Charles Briggs (2007) puts it, interview narratives "produce subjects, texts, knowledge, and authority" (p. 552). As part of a recent narrative turn, social researchers aim to document and understand the discursive complexity of narratives of all sorts (see Chase 2005, 2011; Gubrium & Holstein, 2009a; Hyvärinen, 2008; Polkinghorne, 1988, 1995; Riessman, 2008). Texts and textual analysis have become de rigueur in the social sciences. Briggs and many others are especially interested in how interviews and their stories are assembled and communicated and how they circulate in various domains of society. The diversity is stunning, as particulars are worked up and presented in specific settings, performing different functions and having varied consequences.

Most researchers acknowledge the interactional bases of interviewing (see Conrad & Schober, 2008; Warren & Karner, 2005), but the technical literature typically stresses the need to keep conversational bias in check. Guides to interviewing—especially those oriented to standardized surveys—are primarily concerned with maximizing the flow of valid, reliable information while minimizing distortions of what the respondent knows (Fowler & Mangione, 1990; Gorden, 1987). But a heightened sensitivity to the constitutive properties of communication—characteristic of poststructuralist, postmodernist, constructionist, and ethnomethodological inquiry—has refocused attention on the in situ activeness of interviews (e.g., Hootkoop-Steenstra, 2000; Kvale, 1996). These perspectives view meaning as socially constituted; experience is the product of the actions undertaken to produce and understand it (see Cicourel, 1964, 1974; Garfinkel, 1967). Treating interviewing as a social encounter in which knowledge is actively formed and shaped implies that the interview is not so much a neutral conduit or source of distortion as an occasion for constructing accounts (Gubrium & Holstein, 1995; Holstein & Gubrium, 1995; see Warren & Karner, 2005).

Briggs (1986) explains that the social circumstances of interviews are more than obstacles to respondents' articulations. Interview situations fundamentally, not incidentally, shape the form and content of what is said. Interviews result in locally pertinent narratives—some longer than others—that represent versions of opinion, persons, events, and the world at large. The circumstances of narrative production are deeply and unavoidably implicated in creating the meanings that ostensibly reside within individual experience. Meaning is not merely directly elicited by skillful questioning, nor is it simply transported through truthful replies; it is strategically assembled in the interview process (Holstein & Gubrium, 1995). Interview participants are as much constructive practitioners of experiential information as they are repositories or excavators of experiential knowledge.

This view reconceptualizes interviews in terms of narrative practice. It suggests the need to concertedly attend to the meaning-making work and communicative conditions of interviewing (Gubrium & Holstein, 2009a). In this context, researchers pay explicit attention to both the constructive *hows* and the substantive *whats* of interviewing, taking care to give them equal status both in the research process and in reporting results (see Gubrium & Holstein, 1997, 2009a). Understanding *how* the narrative process constructively unfolds in the interview is as critical as appreciating *what* is selectively composed and preferred.

The new understanding, in turn, prompts a reimagining of the subjects behind interview participants. Regardless of the type of interview, there is always a model of the subject lurking behind those assigned the roles of interviewer and respondent (Holstein & Gubrium, 1995). Even the soberly rational and controlled survey interview has an implicit subjectivity. By virtue of the subjectivity we project—again regardless of the type of interview—we confer varying senses of agency on interviewers and respondents. Differential methodological sensibilities ensue.

PASSIVE SUBJECTIVITY

Recent developments in research interviewing have begun to transform interview subjectivity from fundamentally passive to concertedly and constructively active. In traditional interviewing, respondents are envisioned as being vessels of answers to whom interviewers direct their questions. Respondents are seen as repositories of facts, reflections, opinions, and other traces of experience. This extends to nonresearch interviews. Studs Terkel, journalistic interviewer *par excellence*, worked with the traditional image in place. He simply turned on his tape recorder and asked people to talk. Writing of the interviews he did for his book *Working*, Terkel (1972) explained,

> There were questions, of course. But they were casual in nature . . . the kind you would ask while having a drink with someone; the kind he would ask you. . . . In short, it was a conversation. In time, the sluice gates of dammed up hurts and dreams were open. (p. xxv)

Others have likened traditional interviewing to "prospecting" for the true facts and feelings residing within the respondent (cf. Kvale, 1996). The image of prospecting turns the interview into a search-and-discovery mission, with the interviewer intent on detecting what is already there within more or less cooperative respondents. The challenge lies in excavating information as efficiently as possible, without contaminating it. Highly refined interview techniques streamline, systematize, and sanitize the process. Occasionally, researchers acknowledge that it may be difficult to obtain accurate or honest information, but the information is still imagined, in principle, as embedded in the respondent's vessel of answers. The challenge is to formulate reliable questions and provide an atmosphere conducive to open communication between interviewer and respondent. The challenge is all up-front, in recalcitrant respondents and feckless interviewers, not in the vessel of answers.

In the vessel-of-answers approach, the image of the subject behind the respondent is passive, even while the subject's respondent may be actively reluctant or otherwise difficult to deal with (see Adler & Adler, 2002). The subjects themselves are not engaged in the production of knowledge. If the interviewing process goes "by the book" and is nondirective and unbiased, respondents will validly and reliably speak the unadulterated facts of experience. Contamination creeps in from the interview setting, its participants, and their interaction; the imagined subject, in contrast, is pristinely communicative, and under ideal conditions, his or her respondent serves up authentic reports when beckoned.

Much of the traditional methodological literature on interviewing deals with the nuances of aligning respondents with a passive subjectivity. Understandably, the vessel-of-answers view leads interviewers to be careful in how they ask questions, lest their method of inquiry bias what lies within the subject. This has prompted the development of myriad procedures for obtaining unadulterated information, most of which rely on interviewer and question neutrality. Successfully implementing neutral practices elicits truths held uncontaminated in this vessel of answers. "Good data" result from the successful application of these techniques.

This image evokes a complementary model of the subject behind the interviewer. Because the interviewer aims to extract information, he or she stands apart from the actual data; the interviewer merely unearths and collects what is already there. Interviewers are expected to avoid shaping the information they extract. This involves controlling one's opinions as an interviewer so as not to influence what the passive interview subject can communicate. Interviewers resist supplying particular frames of reference or personal information in the interview. Interviewers are expected to keep themselves and their preferences out of the interview conversation. Neutrality is the standard. Ideally, the interviewer uses his or her interpersonal skills to merely encourage the expression of, but not help construct, the attitudes, sentiments, and behaviors under consideration. The ideal interviewer is a facilitator, not a coproducer, of pertinent information. This stance relegates the interviewer's involvement in the interview to a preordained role, one that is constant from one interview to another. Should the interviewer introduce anything other than variations on prespecified questions, the generalizability of the interview is compromised. This is understandable given the subjectivity in place.

ACTIVE SUBJECTIVITY

Drawing on a contrasting image of active subjectivity, interview researchers are increasingly appreciating the narrative agency of the subjects behind the participants, of both respondents and interviewers. Interviews have been reconceptualized as formal occasions on which animated subjects collaboratively assemble accounts of experience (see Holstein & Gubrium, 1995). Conceiving the interview in this way casts participants as constructive practitioners of the enterprise, who work together to discern and designate the recognizable and orderly features of the experience under consideration (see Bamberg, 2006; Chase, 2011; Clandinin, 2007; Gubrium & Holstein, 2009a; Riessman, 2008).

This transforms the subject behind the respondent from a repository of information or wellspring of emotions into an animated, productive source of narrative knowledge (see Polkinghorne, 1988). The subject behind the respondent not only retains the details of his or her inner life and social world but, in the very process of offering them up to the interviewer, stories the information, assembling it into a coherent account (see Linde, 1993). The respondent can hardly spoil what is subjectively constructed in the first place. Indeed, the active subject pieces experience together before, during, and after occupying the respondent role. He or she is, in a phrase, "always already" a storyteller.

Active subjectivity also lurks behind the interviewer. His or her participation in the interview process is not ultimately a matter of standardization or constraint; neutrality is not the issue. One cannot very well taint the solicitation of knowledge if its response expectations do not exist in some pure form apart from the process of communication. Rather, the active subject behind the interviewer is a necessary counterpart, a working narrative partner, of the active subject behind the respondent. The subject behind the interviewer is fully engaged in the coproduction of accounts. From the time one identifies a research topic, to respondent selection, questioning and answering, and, finally, to the interpretation of responses, the interviewing enterprise is a narrative project.

◆ Contingencies of Narrative Practice

Active agency alters the quality of interview communication as well as its procedural sensibilities (see Gubrium & Holstein, 1997, 2009a)—the ways in which we think about and evaluate what is and is not permissible within the interview encounter. We can sort these matters in terms of the contingent *whats* and *hows* of the interview noted earlier. One family of contingencies centers on the *whats* of interviewing, dealing with the substantive demands and circumstances of the research project. They provide interpretive signposts and resources for developing interview narratives. The eventual narrative is to some degree always already told in the kind of story prompted by the research project through the interviewer. From there, it is constructively elaborated in terms that resonate with the salient circumstances involved in and evoked by the interview process. These circumstances constitute the interview's narrative environment. As interviewing practices are deployed, participants are encouraged to narratively link the topics of interest to biographical particulars, taking account of the circumstantial contingencies of the interview process, producing a subject who both responds to and is affected by the narrative environment. Analysis must take these environments into consideration so that results are not merely coded without regard for context but are also examined for circumstantial and cultural resonances.

Another family of contingencies centers on the constructive *hows* of the interview process. Interview narratives develop within ongoing interaction. The interaction is not merely incidental but is a constitutive part of the meanings and accounts that emerge. In this context, it is not in the nature of narratives to simply flow forth, but instead, they are formulated and shaped in collaboration between the respondent and the interviewer. Participants continually construct and reflexively modify their roles in the exchange of questions and answers as the interview unfolds. The *whats* of the interview have to be interactionally put into place, managed, and sustained. The interplay between these *hows* and *whats*—between narrative work and its narrative environments, respectively—constitutes narrative practice (see Gubrium & Holstein, 2009a).

NARRATIVE WORK

Eliot Mishler's (1986) discussion of empowering interview respondents has set a tone for the growing appreciation of narrative work in the interview context—the *hows* of the interview process.

Uncomfortable with the model of the interview as a controlled, asymmetric conversation dominated by the researcher (see Kahn & Cannell, 1957; Maccoby & Maccoby, 1954), Mishler examines the communicative assumptions and implications behind the standardized interview. His aim is to activate the interview by bringing the respondent more fully into the picture, to make the respondent an equal partner in the interview conversation.

Rather than modeling the interview as a form of stimulus and response, where the respondent is merely a repository of answers for the formalized questions asked by the interviewer, Mishler (1986) suggests that the interview encounter might more fruitfully be viewed as an interactional accomplishment. Noting that interview participants not only ask and answer questions in interviews but simultaneously engage in "speech activities," Mishler turns our attention to what participants do with words:

Defining interviews as speech events or speech activities, as I do, marks the fundamental contrast between the standard antilinguistic, stimulus-response model and an alternative approach to interviewing as discourse between speakers. Different definitions in and of themselves do not constitute different practices. Nonetheless, this new definition alerts us to the features of interviews that hitherto have been neglected. (pp. 35–36)

The key phrase "discourse between speakers" directs us to the integral and inexorable speech activities that even survey interview participants engage in as they ask and answer questions (see Schaeffer & Maynard, 2002), but that are treated as merely technical by survey researchers. Informed by conversation analytic sensibilities (see Sacks, 1992a, 1992b; Sacks, Schegloff, & Jefferson, 1974), Mishler (1986) turns the reader to the discursive machinery evident in interview transcripts, which provides evidence of the way the interviewer and the respondent mutually monitor speech exchanges. Focused on these *hows*, Mishler discusses the way in which participants collaboratively construct their senses of the developing interview agenda. Mishler notes, for example, that even token responses by the interviewer, such as "Hmmm . . . hmmm," can serve as a confirmatory marker that the respondent is on the right track for interview purposes, telling a pertinent story. The slightest or most mundane of speech acts is integral to an unfolding narrative. To eliminate them can, in effect, stop the conversation, hence the interview and the account. This observation points to the practical need for interview participants to be linguistically active and responsive, not just standardized and passive.

Mishler (1986) explains that each and every point in the series of speech exchanges that constitute an interview is subject to interactional work, activity aimed at producing interview data. This applies to both unstructured and standardized forms of interviewing. In contrast to the traditional asymmetric model of the interview, Mishler notes, in practice, that there is considerable communicative reciprocity and collaboration in interviewing:

> The discourse of the interview is jointly constructed by interviewer and respondent. . . . Both questions and responses are formulated in, developed through, and shaped by the discourse between interviewers and respondents. . . . An adequate understanding of interviews depends on recognizing how interviewers reformulate questions and how respondents frame answers in terms of their reciprocal understanding as meanings emerge during the course of an interview. (p. 52)

As an alternative, Mishler (1986) advocates more open-ended questions, minimal interruptions of accounts, and the use of respondents' own linguistic formulations to encourage elaborations of the experiences in view. He urges researchers to consider ways in which interviewing can be activated, designed so that the respondent's voice comes through in greater detail as a way of highlighting respondent relevancies (see Holstein & Gubrium, 2011).

This concern for voice privileges respondents' stories; experience, it is argued, takes meaningful shape as we narrate our lives (see, e.g., Chase, 2005; McAdams, 1993). We communicate experiences to each other in the form of stories. Encouraging elaboration, interviewers commonly use narrative devices such as "Go on," "Then what happened?" and so forth, prompting story-like formulations. In Mishler's (1986) view, it is difficult to imagine how an experience of any kind can be adequately conveyed except in such narrative terms.

Mishler (1986) recommends that we reconceptualize the research interview to "empower" respondents to tell their *own* stories. The word *own* is key

here and will be of critical concern as we consider the issue of narrative ownership. Empowerment can be gotten by lessening interviewer control in the interview. According to Mishler, the goal is to hear the respondents' own voices and, in turn, obtain their own story (see Gubrium & Holstein, 1997); empowerment, voice, and story are his leading concerns. But it is also important to explore the extent to which empowerment allows or provokes the respondent's *own* voice or the voicing of alternate subject positions to be expressed. In other words, when the respondent is actively encouraged to freely speak, whose voice do we hear? Does it assure us that we will hear the respondent's own story?

Conferring ownership, and by implication personal authenticity, on a particular narrative voice has major implications for what is taken to be the extent and purview of the narrative work involved. Mishler's (1986) sense of ownership locates authenticity within the narrator or storyteller, diminishing the role of the narrative-producing interaction and the broader narrative environment. This seems to contradict his call for "reciprocal understanding." If narrative analysis seeks the respondent's own voice and, as a result, his or her own story, as Mishler encourages, another form of passive image of the subject behind the respondent emerges, one that, in the final analysis, locates the true voice of the subject in the respondent's own vessel of answers. This effectively reappropriates passive subjectivity. The respondent is conceived as a subject who owns his or her story, who, on his or her own and under equalizing conditions, can and would narrate that story. The story is uniquely the respondent's in that only his or her own voice can articulate it authentically; any other voice or format detracts from this.

By resurrecting the subject as a vessel of answers, the respondent is reestablished as the ultimate repository of meaningful information, and the interviewer's job remains to extract that information. The process is now envisioned as interactively cooperative rather than interactionally controlled and directed. Nevertheless, as empowered or equalized as the interview conversation might be, the actual stories of respondents' lives are seen to emerge from a sort of internal repository.

While Mishler's (1986) strategy alters the shape of the discourse between speakers, it shortchanges the work that goes into producing authentic accounts. Narrative work does not stop with the extraction of the respondent's own stories but includes the integral production of authenticity, one common practical marker of which is equalized communication (see Gubrium & Holstein, 2009a). Paul Atkinson (1997) is aware of this problem and recommends critical attention to the cultural conventions used to produce authentically personal stories. Writing about narrative analysis generally, but with clear implications for analyzing interview narratives, Atkinson argues,

> The ubiquity of the narrative and its centrality . . . are not license simply to privilege those forms. It is the work of anthropologists and sociologists to examine those narratives and to subject them to the same analysis as any other forms. We need to pay due attention to their construction in use: how actors improvise their personal narratives. . . . We need to attend to how socially shared resources of rhetoric and narrative are deployed to generate recognizable, plausible, and culturally well-informed accounts. . . . What we cannot afford to do is to be seduced by the cultural conventions we seek to study. We should not endorse those cultural conventions that seek to privilege the account as a special kind of representation. (p. 341)

Atkinson (1997) is advocating a more fully interactional appreciation of interview accounts, especially those claimed to be personal narratives. Narrative work, from this perspective, includes any communicative activity involved in producing interview accounts: how interview participants work up adequate responses and what they attempt to accomplish in the process. Attention focuses on both how interview narratives are produced and the functions those narratives serve—in a word, what respondents *do* with the narratives (see Wittgenstein, 1953).

Ownership, and by implication personal authenticity, are established through the constructive voices of interacting narrative agents, which, as we'll illustrate shortly, also brings us to the *whats* of the matter. In practice, the idea of one's "own story"—which once was actually viewed as a methodological procedure and called the "own story method" (see Shaw, 1930/1966)—is not just a commendable research goal but is something participants themselves contend with as they move through the interview. They continuously and tentatively resolve the interactive

problems of ownership as a way of sorting the possible subjectivities of an account and collaboratively proceed on that basis for practical communicative purposes. When a respondent such as a young wife and mother responds to a question about her parenting style, she might note that "it depends" on whether she is thinking (and speaking) in terms of the parenting manuals she conscientiously consults or in terms of her own mother's caution about sparing the rod and spoiling the child. One's own voice, in other words, depends on one's footing and related perspective on the matter, on whose voice is empowered and asserted in responding to the question. This is as much the respondent's doing as it is a matter of interviewer guidance.

An illustration from one of the authors' doctoral supervision duties shows the complexities of the narrative work involved in shifting footings and establishing narrative ownership. It also underscores the way in which the *whats* of narrative practice are intertwined with the *hows* of narrative work. Gubrium was serving on the dissertation committee of a graduate student who was researching substance abuse among pharmacists. The student was committed to allowing the pharmacists being interviewed to convey in their own words their experiences involving illicitly using drugs, seeking help for their habits, and going through rehabilitation. The graduate student had put in place a version of Mishler's (1986) empowerment strategy. He hoped to understand how those who "should know better" would describe what they did and explain what happened to them afterward.

When the interviews were completed, the interview data were analyzed thematically and presented in the dissertation as individual accounts of experience. Interestingly, several of the themes identified in the pharmacists' stories closely paralleled the familiar recovery themes of self-help groups such as Alcoholics Anonymous and Narcotics Anonymous (NA). As it turned out, many, if not all, of the pharmacists had participated in such recovery groups and evidently had incorporated these groups' ways of narrating the substance abuse and recovery experience into their "own" stories. For example, respondents spoke of the experience of "hitting bottom" and organized the stepwise trajectory of the recovery process in familiar NA terms in this case. Noting this, Gubrium raised the issue of the extent to which the interview material could be analyzed as the pharmacists' own stories as opposed to the stories of their recovery programs. At a doctoral committee meeting, he asked, "Whose voice do we hear when these pharmacists tell their stories? Their own or NA's?" The question, in effect, asked whether the stories belonged to the individuals being interviewed or to the organizations that promulgated their discourse.

An equalized and unstructured interview environment does not so much guarantee narrative authenticity as help make its accomplishment and sources more visible. It opens to view the complex work and sources of subject positioning in storytelling (see Koven, in press). For example, in the best of interview circumstances, does a 50-year-old man offer the opinions of a professional at the height of his career, or might his voice be that of a husband and father reflecting on what he missed in family life along the way? Or will he speak as a church elder, a novice airplane pilot, or the "enabling" brother of an alcoholic at different points of the interview? All of these might be possible, given the range of subject positions that could underpin the accounts the man offers in response to interview questions. Each has multiple bases for authenticity. In practice, respondent subjectivity emerges out of the give-and-take of the interview process, even while the researcher might hope for a particular form of agency or footing to emerge out of an interview format designed to explore a specific research topic.

In contrast to the unwitting ways in which the preceding pharmacists' accounts drew on alternate subject positions, interview participants can also be openly strategic about this practice, which is the reason why both the *hows* and the *whats* of narrative practice must be examined. Consider a passing comment that might be made by a father being interviewed about parenting practices. Following a question asking him to place himself along a five-point continuum of parenting styles, from being an authority figure at one end to being a friend at the other, the man responds to another interview item:

> I figure that . . . what did you say? . . . I can be "friendly" [gestures quotation marks with his hands] when I have to and that usually works, unless they [his children] really get wound up, then another father comes out.

The inserted question "What did you say?" references a possible subject position articulated earlier *by the interviewer*, the implication being that, in the give-and-take of the interview, participants jointly figured the father's narrative positions and resulting interview data.

Verbal prefaces are frequently used to signal shifts in subjectivity, something often ignored in interview research. The phrases "to put myself in someone else's shoes" and "to put on a different hat" are speech acts that voice shifts in footing. For example, in an interview study of nurses' opinions on the qualities of good infant care, we probably wouldn't be surprised to hear a respondent say something like, "That's when I have my RN [registered nurse] cap on, but as a mother, I might tell you a different story." Some respondents are didactic in giving voice to alternative subject positions and their respective points of view, as when a respondent prefaces a response with "What I mean is . . . from the point of view of a . . ." or "Let me explain what I mean . . . it depends on whose shoes you're wearing, doesn't it?" Such phrases are not interview debris but skillfully do things with words, in this case conveying an important and persistent complication of interview subjectivity.

But things are seldom this straightforward. An interview, for example, might start with the presumption that a father or a mother is being interviewed, which the interview's introductions appear to confirm. But there is no guarantee that these subject positions will remain constant throughout. This isn't often evident in so many words or comments. Indeed, the possibility of an unforeseen change in subjectivity might not be broached, if broached at all, until the very end of the interview, when a respondent remarks, "Yeah, that's the way all of us who were raised down South do with our children," making it unclear who or what exactly has been providing responses to the interview's questions, this individual parent or her region of the country.

The work of establishing subject position and voice also implicates the interviewer. Who, after all, is the interviewer to the respondent? How will the interviewer role fit into the conversational matrix? For example, respondents in debriefings might comment that an interviewer sounded more like a company man than a human being or that one interviewer made the respondent feel that the interviewer was "just an ordinary person, like myself." This raises the possibility that the respondent's perceived subject position, and by implication the respondent's "own" story, is constructed out of the unfolding interpersonal sentiments of the interview participants.

If this isn't complicated enough, imagine what the acknowledgement of multiple subject positions does to the concept of sample size. To decompose the designated respondent into his or her subject positions raises the possibility that any sample unit or set of units can expand or contract in size in the course of the interview, increasing or decreasing the sample *n* in the process. Treating subject positions and their associated voices seriously, we might find that what we took to be a single interview, in practice, is an interview with several subjects, whose particular identities may only be partially, if at all, clear. To be satisfied that one has completed an empowered interview with a single respondent and to code it as such because it was conducted in a context of equalitarian exchange is to be rather cavalier about narrative practice.

All of this is reason enough for some researchers to approach the interview as a set of positions and accounts that are continuously accomplished. In standardized interviewing, one needs to conclusively settle on the matter of who the subject behind the respondent is, lest it be impossible to know to which population generalizations can be made—a dubious goal in the context of practice. A respondent who shifts the subjectivity to whom she is giving voice poses dramatic difficulties for the kind of generalization survey researchers aim for. Varied parts of a single completed interview, for example, would have to be coded as the responses of different subjects and be generalizable to different populations, which would be a conceptual, if not just a procedural, nightmare.

NARRATIVE ENVIRONMENTS

If they are not straightforwardly owned by individuals, where do interview narratives come from? This turns us to the *whats* of the matter and their complications, broached in our pharmacist illustration. It was evident in the previous discussion of the pharmacist drug abuse research that respondents made use of a very common notion of recovery in today's world, one that has percolated through the entire troubles treatment industry (Gubrium & Holstein, 2001). Does this industry, or other institutions dealing with human experiences, offer an answer to the question?

Erving Goffman's (1961) exploration of what he called "moral careers" provides a point of departure for addressing this. Goffman was especially concerned with the moral careers of stigmatized persons such as mental patients, but his approach is broadly suggestive. In his reckoning, each of us has many available identities and associated ways of accounting for our actions. Goffman described the prepatient, patient, and postpatient selves that individuals constructed, along with others, on their way into and out of mental hospitals. He referred to this trajectory of identities as a moral career because it had implications for the self-representation of those concerned, both the individual patients in question and those who interacted with them. The identities were moral because they related significantly to choices made about who one was, is now, and would be, implicating the appropriateness of the accounts conveyed in the process.

According to Goffman (1961), individuals obtain narrative footing as they move through the various moral environments that offer pertinent recipes for identity. A mental hospital, he noted, provides the individuals it serves with particular selves, which includes ways of storying who one is, one's past, and one's future. The moral environment of the mental hospital also provides others, such as staff members, acquaintances, and even strangers, with parallel footing, such as what to expect from and how to respond to patients as they move along the trajectory. As far as stories are concerned—both our own and those of others—moral environments are also narrative environments.

Goffman's (1961) analysis of moral careers focused on what he called "total institutions," environments whose narrative options are limited and engulf the self. What Everett Hughes (1942/1984) calls "going concerns" expand moral careers and their narrative options to the world at large, to the many and varied social locations, not just formal organizations, that specify pertinent identities and ways of accounting for ourselves. It was Hughes's way of emphasizing that institutions are not just formally mandated and, more important in practice, are not fixed establishments but that considerable narrative work keeps them going, to put it in our terms. How we story our lives is as varied as the narrative options available. Going concerns are a virtual landscape of narrative possibilities, stunningly complicating our moral careers and their accounts.

From the myriad formal organizations in which we work, study, play, and recover, to the countless informal associations and networks to which we otherwise attend, to our affiliations with racial, ethnic, and gendered groupings, we engage in a panoply of going concerns on a daily basis. Taken together, they set the conditions of possibility (Foucault, 1979) for narrative footing—for who and what we could possibly be. Many going concerns explicitly structure or reconfigure personal identity. Human service agencies, for example, readily delve into the deepest enclaves of the self to ameliorate personal ills, with the aim of re-storying our lives. Self-help organizations seem to crop up on every street corner, and self-help literature beckons us from the tabloid racks of most supermarkets and the shelves of every bookstore. "Psychobabble" on radio and TV talk shows constantly prompts us to formulate (or reformulate) our stories, aiming to give voice to the selves we do or should live by. Interviewing without these *whats* in view shortchanges the extensive communicative apparatus that prompts and supports accounts.

Narrative environments not only feed personal accounts but are also a source of socially relevant questions that interviewers pose to respondents. To the extent that those who conduct large-scale surveys are sponsored by the very agents who formulate applicable discourses such as recovery trajectories, the collaborative production of the respondent's own story is shaped, for better or worse, in agreements and markets well beyond the give-and-take of the interview conversation—such are the proprietary subjectivities of individual accounts in a world of going concerns (Gubrium & Holstein, 2000).

This observation returns us to the interview society. The research context is not the only place in which we are asked interview questions and are expected to respond in turn with opinions. Virtually all going concerns are in the interviewing business; they construct and marshal the subjects they need to do their work. Each provides a communicative context for narrative practice, for the collaborative production of the moral equivalents of respondents and interviewers. Medical clinics deploy interviews and, in the process, assemble doctors, patients, and their illnesses (see Zoppi & Epstein, 2002). Personnel officers interview job applicants and collect information that forms the basis for selection decisions (see Latham & Millman, 2002). Therapists of all stripes continue to interview as they have for decades and assemble narrative plots of illness experiences, which form the basis for further, rehabilitative interviewing (see Frank, 1995; Kleinman, 1988; Mattingly, 1998; Miller, de Shazer, & De Jong, 2002). The same is

true for schools, forensic investigation, and journalistic interviewing, among the broad range of concerns that enter our lives and help shape our stories (see Altheide, 2002; Gabriel, 2000; McKenzie, 2002; Tierney & Dilley, 2002).

As the interview society expands the institutional auspices of interviewing well beyond the research context, it would be a rather narrow perspective on the interview to limit ourselves to research environments. The research interview is only one of the many sites where subjectivities and the voicing of individual experience are storied. These going concerns can't be considered to be independent of each other. As our pharmacist illustration suggested, the narrative environments of therapy and recovery can be brought directly into the research interview, serving to commingle a spectrum of institutional voices.

Our understandings of subjectivity and voice are varied and deepened as new formats for interviewing are developed. These formats are themselves going concerns, providing distinctive narrative environments. The group interview, for example, can be a veritable swirl of subject positions and opinion construction, as participants share and make use of story material from a broader range of narrative resources than a single interview might muster on its own. Life story and oral history interviews extend biographical construction through time, which can be amazingly convoluted when compared with the often detemporalized information elicited in cross-sectional surveys (see Atkinson & Coffey, 2002; Cándida-Smith, 2002). The in-depth interview extends experience in emotional terms, affectively elaborating subjectivity by constructing it ever more deeply within experience (see Johnson, 2002).

◆ It's Like Jazz

To guard against overdetermining the role of either narrative environments or narrative work in the production of interview accounts, it is important to emphasize that the practice of interviewing refracts, but does not reproduce, the narratives proffered by going concerns. Interview participants themselves are biographically active in shaping how received subjectivities are put to use in the interview process. While institutional auspices provide resources for both asking questions and providing answers, prescribe possible roles for interview participants, and privilege or marginalize certain accounts, these resources and roles are not automatically adopted and reproduced in practice. If participants are accountable to particular circumstances, such as conducting social-scientific research, completing job interviews, or interrogating suspects in criminal procedures, they borrow from the variety of narrative resources available to them. They are more "artful" (Garfinkel, 1967) than mechanistic in managing their roles and giving voice to experience.

The pharmacist example is a case in point. While these were formal research interviews, it was evident that respondents were interpolating their stories in NA recovery terms. They drew from their experiences in recovery groups to convey to the interviewer what it felt like to be "taken over" by controlled substances. As noted earlier, several respondents used the familiar metaphors of "hitting bottom" and "12 steps" to convey a trajectory for the experience. But the respondents weren't simply mouthpieces for NA; they put individual spins on NA terminology. "Hitting bottom" could mean different things to the respondents, depending on biographical particulars. How hitting bottom narratively figured in one respondent's experience was no guarantee of how it figured in another's. Hitting bottom for the tenth time, for instance, could have different moral contours from hitting bottom for the first (or only) time.

As in producing jazz, themes and improvisation are the hallmarks of narrative practice. Interview narratives are artfully assembled, discursively informed, and circumstantially conditioned. Because the stories we live by refract a world of competing going concerns, they do not uniformly reproduce a collection of accounts. The interplay of narrative work and narrative environments—the constructive *hows* and substantive *whats* of the matter—provides interviews with a discernable range of possibilities for asking and responding to questions about what we are and what our worlds are like. In this scheme of things, the interview is far more than a technical way of extracting information. If the interview is now among our most commonplace and conventional means of gathering experiential information, the voices we hear within it represent a dispersed ownership, endless senses of who and what we could be, and variegated perspectives on our social worlds.

The relationship between this information and society is complex. In one sense, it derives from individualized accounts conveyed in diverse voices,

positioned in different locations in the empirical landscape. The democratization of opinion assures us that each and every one of us counts in the grander scheme of public opinion. But in a second sense, democratization is too simple a notion. It ignores the social forces and cultural frameworks that inform the *whats* and *hows* of individualized accounts. While the mechanism of data gathering in interviews and the analysis of responses draw from individualized testimony, we now realize that the modern temper that made this possible was always already up against the expanding discourses used to articulate what we think, how we feel, and how we expect to act. The increasing medicalization of experience, for example, has transformed much of this into accounts of illness and health, and lately of fitness. The once healthy, "chubby" baby is now subject to the gaze and resulting accounts of the medicalization of body weight, portending a future of illness or obesity for the person the child might become. In the 1980s, interview accounts of family members' experiences of caring for demented elderly loved ones gradually turned from accounts of caring for the normal confusion and senility of late life to the sickness of Alzheimer's disease and the hope for recovery (Gubrium, 1986). These changing *whats* of individual accounts drawn from interviews are immersed in new and emerging discourses of experience.

Complexity is asserted in a third sense because society is not merely a discursive template for individual articulation. While the shared themes of dominant and changing discourses provide narrative resources for asking interview questions and responding to them, the questions asked in interviews and the responses to them vary in their own right. They draw on biographical particulars in the context of specific research questions to collaboratively construct individualized articulations of shared understandings. The *hows* of the matter are, again like jazz, improvisational. Yes, there are discursive themes, but these are assembled and constructed in relationship to the narrative improvisations of biography, perspective, interests, and the immediate pertinences of the process.

The analogy to jazz encourages us to be ethnographically sensitive in conducting interview research (see Gubrium & Holstein, 2009a). The transformation of interview subjectivity has reached a point where the *whats* of interview questions and responses can no longer be left to the quantifying devices of traditional survey sensibilities. They must be extended to an understanding of the ways discourse and going concerns relate to individual accounts. The same sensibility encourages us to move beyond the turn-taking *hows* of interview practice. The *hows* can no longer be left to the everyday tool-identifying devices of conversation analysis. They must be extended to include the broader constructive *hows* of narration as it plays out in discursive practice (Gubrium & Holstein, 2009a; Holstein & Gubrium, 2000). Methods of analysis are accordingly informed by a model of narratively active subjectivity (see Cerwonka & Malkki, 2007).

◆ *References*

Adler, P. A., & Adler, P. (2002). The reluctant respondent. In J. F. Gubrium & J. A. Holstein (Eds.), *Handbook of interview research* (pp. 515–536). Thousand Oaks, CA: Sage.

Alasuutari, P. (1998). *An invitation to social research.* London, England: Sage.

Altheide, D. L. (2002). Journalistic interviewing. In J. F. Gubrium & J. A Holstein (Eds.), *Handbook of interview research* (pp. 411–430). Thousand Oaks, CA: Sage.

Atkinson, P. (1997). Narrative turn or blind alley? *Qualitative Health Research, 7,* 325–344.

Atkinson, P., & Coffey, A. (2002). Revisiting the relationship between participant observation and interviewing. In J. F. Gubrium & J. A. Holstein (Eds.), *Handbook of interview research* (pp. 801–814). Thousand Oaks, CA: Sage.

Atkinson, P., & Silverman, D. (1997). Kundera's *immortality*: The interview society and the invention of the self. *Qualitative Inquiry, 3,* 304–325.

Bamberg, M. (2006). Stories: Big or small, why do we care? *Narrative Inquiry, 16,* 139–147.

Benney, M., & Hughes, E. C. (1956). Of sociology and the interview. *American Journal of Sociology, 62,* 137–252.

Briggs, C. (1986). *Learning how to ask.* Cambridge, England: Cambridge University Press.

Briggs, C. L. (2007). Anthropology, interviewing, and communicability in contemporary society. *Current Anthropology, 48,* 551–580.

Cándida-Smith, R. (2002). Analytic strategies for oral history interviews. In J. F. Gubrium & J. A. Holstein (Eds.), *Handbook of interview research* (pp. 711–732). Thousand Oaks, CA: Sage.

Cerwonka, A., & Malkki, L. (2007). *Improvising theory: Process and temporality in ethnographic fieldwork.* Chicago, IL: University of Chicago Press.

Chase, S. (2005). Narrative inquiry: Multiple lenses, approaches, voices. In N. Denzin & Y. Lincoln (Eds.), *The SAGE handbook of qualitative research* (3rd ed., pp. 651–679). Thousand Oaks, CA: Sage.

Chase, S. (2011). Narrative inquiry: Still a field in the making. In N. Denzin & Y. Lincoln (Eds.), *The SAGE handbook of qualitative research* (4th ed.). Thousand Oaks, CA: Sage.

Cicourel, A. (1964). *Method and measurement in sociology.* New York, NY: Free Press.

Cicourel, A. V. (1974). *Theory and method in a study of Argentine fertility.* New York, NY: Wiley.

Clandinin, D. (Ed.). (2007). *Handbook of narrative inquiry.* Thousand Oaks, CA: Sage.

Conrad, F. G., & Schober, M. F. (2008). New frontiers in standardized survey interviewing. In S. N. Hesse-Biber & P. Leavey (Eds.), *Handbook of emergent methods* (pp. 173–188). New York, NY: Guilford Press.

Denzin, N. K., & Lincoln, Y. S. (Eds.). (2005). *The SAGE handbook of qualitative research* (3rd ed.). Thousand Oaks, CA: Sage.

Denzin, N. K., & Lincoln, Y. S. (Eds.). (2011). *The SAGE handbook of qualitative research* (4th ed.). Thousand Oaks, CA: Sage.

Dreyfus, H. L., & Rabinow, P. (1982). *Michel Foucault: Beyond structuralism and hermeneutics.* Chicago, IL: University of Chicago Press.

Foucault, M. (1973). *Madness and civilization.* New York, NY: Vintage Books.

Foucault, M. (1975). *Birth of the clinic.* New York, NY: Vintage Books.

Foucault, M. (1977). *Discipline and punish.* New York, NY: Vintage Books.

Foucault, M. (1978). *The history of sexuality: An introduction* (Vol. 1). New York, NY: Vintage Books.

Foucault, M. (1979). *Discipline and punish: The birth of the prison.* New York, NY: Vintage Books.

Foucault, M. (1988). *Technologies of the self* (L. H. Martin, H. Gutman, & P. H. Hutton, Eds.). Amherst: University of Massachusetts Press.

Foucault, M. (1991). Governmentality (R. Braidotti, Trans., & C. Gordon, Rev.). In G. Burchell, C. Gordon, & P. Miller (Eds.), *The Foucault effect: Studies in governmentality* (pp. 87–104). Chicago, IL: University of Chicago Press.

Fowler, F. J., & Mangione, T. W. (1990). *Standardized survey interviewing.* Newbury Park, CA: Sage.

Frank, A. (1995). *The wounded storyteller.* Chicago, IL: University of Chicago Press.

Gabriel, Y. (2000). *Storytelling in organizations: Facts, fictions, and fantasies.* Oxford, England: Oxford University Press.

Garfinkel, H. (1967). *Studies in ethnomethodology.* Englewood Cliffs, NJ: Prentice Hall.

Garland, D. (1997). "Governmentality" and the problem of crime. *Theoretical Criminology, 1,* 173–214.

Goffman, E. (1961). *Asylums.* New York, NY: Doubleday.

Gorden, R. L. (1987). *Interviewing: Strategy, techniques, and tactics.* Homewood, IL: Dorsey Press.

Gubrium, J. F. (1986). *Oldtimers and Alzheimer's: The descriptive organization of senility.* Greenwich, CT: JAI Press.

Gubrium, J. F., & Holstein, J. A. (1995). Qualitative inquiry and the deprivatization of experience. *Qualitative Inquiry, 1,* 204–222.

Gubrium, J. F., & Holstein, J. A. (1997). *The new language of qualitative method.* New York, NY: Oxford University Press.

Gubrium, J. F., & Holstein, J. A. (2000). The self in a world of going concerns. *Symbolic Interaction, 23,* 95–115.

Gubrium, J. F., & Holstein, J. A. (Eds.). (2001). *Institutional selves: Troubled identities in a postmodern world.* New York, NY: Oxford University Press.

Gubrium, J. F., & Holstein, J. A. (2002). From the individual to the interview society. In J. F. Gubrium & J. A. Holstein (Eds.), *Handbook of interview research* (pp. 3–32). Thousand Oaks, CA: Sage.

Gubrium, J. F., & Holstein, J. A. (2009a). *Analyzing narrative reality.* Thousand Oaks, CA: Sage.

Gubrium, J. F., & Holstein, J. A. (2009b). The everyday work and auspices of authenticity. In P. Vannini & J. P. Williams (Eds.), *Authenticity in culture, self, and society* (pp. 121–138). Surrey, England: Ashgate.

Holstein, J. A., & Gubrium, J. F. (1995). *The active interview.* Thousand Oaks, CA: Sage.

Holstein, J. A., & Gubrium, J. F. (2000). *The self we live by: Narrative identity in a postmodern world.* New York, NY: Oxford University Press.

Holstein, J. A., & Gubrium, J. F. (2011). Animating interview narratives. In D. Silverman (Ed.), *Qualitative research: Theory, method, and practice* (3rd ed., pp. 149–167). London, England: Sage.

Hootkoop-Steenstra, H. (2000). *Interaction and the standardized survey interview.* Cambridge, England: Cambridge University Press.

Hughes, E. C. (1984). *The sociological eye: Selected papers.* Chicago, IL: Aldine. (Original work published 1942)

Hyvärinen, M. (2008). Analyzing narratives and storytelling. In P. Alasuutari, L. Bickman, & J. Brannen (Eds.), *The SAGE handbook of social research methods* (pp. 447–460). London, England: Sage.

Johnson, J. M. (2002). In-depth interviewing. In *Handbook of interview research* (J. F. Gubrium & J. A. Holstein, Eds.). Thousand Oaks, CA: Sage.

Kahn, R. L., & Cannell, C. F. (1957). *The dynamics of interviewing: Theory, technique, and cases.* New York, NY: Wiley.

Kleinman, A. (1988). *The illness narratives.* New York, NY: Basic Books.

Koven, M. (in press). Speaker role analysis of personal narratives. In J. A. Holstein & J. F. Gubrium (Eds.), *Varieties of narrative analysis.* Thousand Oaks, CA: Sage.

Kvale, S. (1996). *InterViews: An introduction to qualitative research interviewing.* London, England: Sage.

Latham, G. P., & Millman, Z. (2002). Context and the employment interview. In J. F. Gubrium & J. A. Holstein (Eds.), *Handbook of interview research* (pp. 473–486). Thousand Oaks, CA: Sage.

Linde, C. (1993). *Life stories: The creation of coherence.* New York, NY: Oxford University Press.

Maccoby, E. E., & Maccoby, N. (1954). The interview: A tool of social science. In G. Lindzey (Ed.), *Handbook of social psychology* (Vol. 1, chap. 12). Cambridge, England: Addison-Wesley.

Mattingly, C. (1998). *Healing dramas and clinical plots: The narrative structure of experience.* New York, NY: Cambridge University Press.

Mayhew, H. (1851). *London labour and the London poor* (Vol. 1). New York, NY: Dover.

McAdams, D. (1993). *The stories we live by: Personal myths and the making of the self.* New York, NY: Guilford Press.

McKenzie, I. K. (2002). Forensic investigative interviewing. In J. F. Gubrium & J. A. Holstein (Eds.), *Handbook of interview research* (pp. 431–452). Thousand Oaks, CA: Sage.

Miller, G., de Shazer, S., & De Jong, P. (2002). Therapy interviewing. In J. F. Gubrium & J. A. Holstein (Eds.), *Handbook of interview research* (pp. 384–410). Thousand Oaks, CA: Sage.

Miller, J. (1993). *The passion of Michel Foucault.* New York, NY: Doubleday.

Mishler, E. (1986). *Research interviewing: Context and narrative.* Cambridge, England: Harvard University Press.

Morgan, D. L. (2002). Focus group interviewing. In J. F. Gubrium & J. A. Holstein (Eds.), *Handbook of interview research* (pp. 141–160). Thousand Oaks, CA: Sage.

Platt, J. (2002). The history of the interview. In J. F. Gubrium & J. A. Holstein (Eds.), *Handbook of interview research* (pp. 33–54). Thousand Oaks, CA: Sage.

Polkinghorne, D. E. (1988). *Narrative knowing and the human sciences.* Albany, NY: SUNY Press.

Polkinghorne, D. E. (1995). Narrative configuration in qualitative analysis. In J. A. Hatch & R. Wisniewski (Eds.), *Life history and narrative* (pp. 5–23). London, England: Falmer Press.

Riesman, D., & Benney, M. (1956). Asking and answering. *Journal of Business of the University of Chicago, 29,* 225–236.

Riessman, C. K. (2008). *Narrative methods for the human sciences.* Thousand Oaks, CA: Sage.

Rose, N. (1990). *Governing the soul: The shaping of the private self.* London, England: Routledge.

Rose, N. (1997). *Inventing ourselves: Psychology, power, and personhood.* Cambridge, England: Cambridge University Press.

Sacks, H. (1992a). *Lectures on conversation* (Vol. 1). Oxford, England: Wiley-Blackwell.

Sacks, H. (1992b). *Lectures on conversation* (Vol. 2). Oxford, England: Wiley-Blackwell.

Sacks, H., Schegloff, E. A., & Jefferson, G. (1974). A simplest systematics for the organization of turn taking for conversation. *Language, 40,* 696–735.

Schaeffer, N. C., & Maynard, D. W. (2002). Standardization and interaction in the survey interview. In J. F. Gubrium & J. A. Holstein (Eds.), *Handbook of interview research* (pp. 577–602). Thousand Oaks, CA: Sage.

Shaw, C. R. (1966). *The jack-roller: A delinquent boy's own story.* Chicago, IL: University of Chicago Press. (Original work published 1930)

Silverman, D. (1993). *Interpreting qualitative data.* London, England: Sage.

Silverman, D. (1997). *Qualitative research: Theory, method, and practice.* London, England: Sage.

Terkel, S. (1972). *Working.* New York, NY: Avon.

Tierney, W. G., & Dilley, P. (2002). Interviewing in education. In J. F. Gubrium & J. A. Holstein (Eds.), *Handbook of interview research* (pp. 453–472). Thousand Oaks, CA: Sage.

Warren, C. A. B., & Karner, T. (2005). *Discovering qualitative methods.* Los Angeles, CA: Roxbury.

Weiss, R. S. (1994). *Learning from strangers.* New York, NY: Free Press.

Wittgenstein, L. (1953). *Philosophical investigations.* New York, NY: Macmillan.

Zoppi, K. A., & Epstein, R. M. (2002). Interviewing in medical settings. In J. F. Gubrium & J. A. Holstein (Eds.), *Handbook of interview research* (pp. 355–384). Thousand Oaks, CA: Sage.

3

POSTMODERN TRENDS

Expanding the Horizons of Interviewing Practices and Epistemologies

◆ Michael Ian Borer and Andrea Fontana

Postmodernism is a dirty word in some academic circles and remains a subject of intense debate in many academic journals and at many academic conferences even as the term has lost some of its original luster (see Matthewman & Hoey, 2006). Regardless of one's position, it is undeniable that the influence of postmodernism has changed our society, the way in which we conceive it, and the way we see ourselves and relate to others. Whether we consider postmodernism as a radical break from modernism or merely the continuation of modernism, profound changes have occurred throughout the world and in the way we study it (see Best & Kellner, 1991; Dickens & Fontana, 1994; Lemert, 2005). We are no longer awed by metatheories about the nature of society and the self (Lyotard, 1984), theories that we now question and deconstruct. Today, we focus on smaller parcels of knowledge; we study society in its fragments, in its daily details (Silverman, 1997). Postmodernism has affected many fields, from architecture to literary criticism, from anthropology to sociology. It has provided few answers but raised more questions, rendering the "reality" of the social world extremely problematic. Postmodernism has also changed the very nature of experience. The everyday world and the world of media have been merged (Baudrillard, 1983), and as the boundaries between the two have collapsed, experience is mediated by the "hyperreality" of the likes of Disneyland, Real TV, and *The Jerry Springer Show*, where the imaginary becomes real and the real, imaginary (see Denzin, 2003). Many have lost the tools to distinguish between the multiple levels of social reality.

Influenced by postmodern epistemologies, interviewing also has changed; ours has become "the interview society" (Atkinson & Silverman, 1997; Gubrium & Holstein, 2003; Silverman, 1993). Interviewing is no longer reserved for social researchers or investigative reporters but has become the very stuff of life as members of society spend much of their time asking questions, being asked questions themselves, or watching TV shows about people being asked questions and answering them in turn. They all seem to have routine knowledge of the rules of interviewing, with no need for instruction. Both elites and common folk have "interview repertoires" filled with sound bites that often pass as legitimate opinions and acquired knowledge (Borer, 2009). Because interview repertoires are stocked with bits of informal knowledge that people can rely on and recall when asked questions about themselves or other issues, interviewee answers become problematic as truth claims. Prepackaged sound bites, however, should not impede the interviewer's task or craft. Instead the interviewer—as evidenced by those who have experimented with the content and form of interview practices—must move beyond the static nature of traditional interviewing techniques by recognizing the interview as a microsituation within a larger sociocultural context (e.g., "the interview society").

In this chapter, we show the impulses and consequences of the most discernible postmodern trends in interviewing. We begin by outlining some of the postmodern sensibilities that are relevant to interviewing. Although there is no such thing as postmodern interviewing per se, postmodern epistemologies have profoundly influenced our understanding of the interview as both a product and a process. Keeping in line with the postmodern blurring and fragmentation of theories and methods, we present only fragments of postmodern-informed interviewing rather than an overarching, modernistic formulation of the postmodern interview.[1] As such, we discuss some of the most cogent critiques of traditional interviewing and then present nuanced techniques that include phenomenological, feminist, virtual, theatrical, and sensuous practices.

◆ Postmodernism and Its Influence

Postmodernism, which is not a unified system of beliefs, has been presented and interpreted in diverse ways. It can be seen as a crisis of representation in a great variety of fields, from the arts to the sciences, and, more generally, in society at large (Dickens & Fontana, 1994). It has been conceptualized both as the continuation of modernism and as a break from it. In some views, postmodernism advocates abandoning overarching paradigms and theoretical and methodological metasystems (Lyotard, 1984). Postmodernism questions traditional assumptions and deconstructs them (Derrida, 1972); that is, it shows the ambiguity and contextuality of meaning. It proposes that, in the name of grand theorizing, we have suppressed this ambiguity in favor of a single interpretation, which is commonly touted as "the truth," rather than a choice among many possible truths. Postmodernism orients to theorizing and, indeed, to society itself, not as a monolithic structure but as a series of fragments in continuous flux. It persuades us to accept uncertainty and turn our attention to these fragments, to the minute events of everyday life, seeking to understand them in their own right rather than gloss over differences and patch them together into paradigmatic wholes (Silverman, 1997).

POSTMODERN SENSIBILITIES AND INTERVIEWING

Postmodern sensibilities have greatly affected the methodologies used by social scientists to uncover the dynamics of lives in our contemporary world(s). Researchers influenced by postmodernism have come to display a greatly heightened sensitivity to problems and concerns that previously had been glossed over or scantily addressed. These can be briefly described as follows:

- The boundaries between, and respective roles of, interviewer and interviewee have become blurred as the traditional relationship between

---

[1]Following Lee Harvey (1987), we see ethnography and in-depth interviewing as much more intertwined than most methodologists. Indeed, fieldwork relies on a combination of both methods. Harvey points out that many of the works of the Chicago school, which are commonly referred to as "ethnographic," actually rely on in-depth interviews. As early as Malinowski's fieldwork in New Guinea, the two methods have been combined. In fact, Malinowski did not actually live in the village with the natives but would go there only occasionally, with an interpreter, to interview them (Malinowski, 1989; see also Lofland, 1971).

the two is no longer seen as natural and is criticized for reproducing societal power dynamics.

- New forms of communication in interviewing are being used, as interviewer and respondent(s) collaborate together in constructing their narratives.

- Interviewers have become more concerned about issues of representation, seriously engaging questions such as "Whose story are we telling and for what purpose?"

- The authority of the researcher qua interviewer, but also qua writer, comes under scrutiny. Respondents are no longer seen as faceless numbers whose opinions we process completely on our own terms. Consequently, there is increasing concern with the respondent's own understanding as he or she frames and represents an "opinion."

- Traditional patriarchal relations in interviewing are being criticized, and ways to make formerly unarticulated voices audible are now center stage.

- The forms used to report findings have been hugely expanded. As the boundaries separating disciplines collapse, modes of expression from literature, poetry, and drama are being applied.

- The topic of inquiry—interviewing—has expanded to encompass the cinematic and the televisual. Electronic media are increasingly accepted as a resource in interviews as e-mail, Internet chat rooms, and other electronic modes of communication have become almost ubiquitous.

- Interviewers have become aware of the roles that the senses play in everyday life and in the interview exchange and have tried to capture and represent them in nuanced ways.

These sensibilities, some of which are now old and some new, provide a context for methodological exploration. Let us consider, initially, how these have informed and affected traditional interview roles. Note, especially, that some ostensibly postmodern trends have been close to the heart of qualitative inquiry for decades (see in this volume Johnson & Rowlands, "The Interpersonal Dynamics of In-Depth Interviewing"; Warren, "Interviewing as Social Interaction").

◆ From Traditional to Postmodern-Informed Interviewing

Traditional, structured interviewing establishes a priori categories and then asks preestablished questions aimed at capturing precise data that can be categorized, codified, and generalized (see Converse & Schuman, 1974; Singleton & Straits, "Survey Interviewing," this volume). The aim is to provide explanations about the social world. The method assumes that there is a set of discreet facts to be apprehended in the social world and that we can garner them through the use of rigorous techniques. The language of "natural" science permeates these techniques. The interviewer is not unlike a highly trained instrument and remains substantively detached from the situation and the respondent. Responses are quantifiable and allow generalizations about society. As such, respondents are viewed as "rational beings" in that they understand all the possible choices presented to them and answer as comprehensively and truthfully as possible. Fortunately, we no longer treat ourselves or our interviewees as robotic automatons, though positivistic traditions still remain at the core of mainstream social sciences.

CRITIQUES OF THE DETACHED INTERVIEWER

Some critics claim that the method of traditional interviewing is much more like science fiction than science, a perspective that has not been lost on qualitative researchers. Herbert Blumer (1969), for one, prefaces the introduction of his seminal book *Symbolic Interactionism* with an insightful critique of traditional methodologies. The work of Aaron Cicourel is also a milestone in unveiling the myth of "scientific" interviewing. Cicourel (1964) refers to the hidden complexity of the interview situation:

All social research includes an unknown number of implicit decisions which are not mirrored in the measurement procedures used. The abstraction process required to describe a set of properties, regardless of the measurement system, automatically imposes some amount of reification. (p. 80)

Discussing and quoting the work of Herbert Hyman and other survey researchers, Cicourel adds, "The authors are not aware that too much stress has been placed on asking questions and recording answers, and that the interviewer is overlooking . . . the many judgments he made in the process" (p. 91). Cicourel goes on to suggest that the interview is an interactional event based on reciprocal stocks of knowledge, a point we will explore again in our discussion of phenomenological influences on postmodern trends.

The response of interactionist sociologists to problems inherent in structured interviewing was to move interviewers center stage as constructive agents and acknowledge their influence on interview outcomes. They also recognized the importance of feelings on the part of both the interviewer and the respondent, as well as the possibility of deceit in the interview situation. Must we always believe what our respondents tell us, and what are the consequences of our disbelief? This is an important philosophy of social science question that interviewers must take into consideration.

In his book *Creative Interviewing*, Jack Douglas (1985) advocates lengthy, unstructured interviews in which the interviewer uses his or her personal skills by adapting to the changing interactional situation of the interview. For Douglas, the creativity is cultivated by the interviewer, who attempts inventively to reach a mutual understanding and intimacy of feelings with the interviewee. Still, it has been pointed out that the interviewee remains a rather passive participant even in this context. Jaber Gubrium and James Holstein (1997; Holstein & Gubrium, 1995) consider Douglas's interviewing techniques decidedly "romantic." As they explain, "Douglas imagines his subject, like the image implicit in survey research, to be a repository of answers, but in his case, the subject is a well guarded vessel of feelings, not simply a collection of attitudes and opinions" (Gubrium & Holstein, 1997, p. 65). As such, interviewers are pushed to view their interviewees not as treasure chests of knowledge that need to be cracked open but as co-constructers of the treasures themselves. In their comprehensive how-to and why-to text *InterViews*, Steinar Kvale and Svend Brinkmann (2009) successfully show the various types of knowledge—the varied treasures—that can arise from adopting postmodern interviewing techniques.

EMERGING VOICES OF INTERVIEWEES

In the 1980s, new trends appeared in qualitative sociology, in both ethnography and interviewing, as researchers attempted to secure the constructive voices of research subjects. Some were concerned with the authorial voice of the researcher speaking for his or her subjects (Geertz, 1988; Van Maanen, 1988); others took a broader epistemological approach (Marcus & Fischer, 1986).

George Marcus and Michael Fischer (1986) gave special attention to these issues, which was widely appreciated. They were concerned with the authority of traditional ethnographic texts, commonly derived through a combination of ethnographic work and in-depth interviews. They also addressed problems of representation and selectivity generated by the privileged position of the researcher both as a fieldworker and as an author. They felt that in "modernistic" interviewing, the researcher is in control of the narrative and highlights what best conveys, in his or her judgment, the social worlds of those being studied (see the discussion of "representational rights" in Bauman & Briggs, 2003).

Marcus and Fischer (1986) present postmodern alternatives in anthropology that allow diverse voices to come through. Some of these alternatives apply to interviewing as well as to ethnography. One is the need to take a "dialogic" approach that focuses "on the dialogue between anthropologist and informant as a way of exposing how ethnographic knowledge develops" (p. 69). An exemplar of this work is Kevin Dwyer's (1982) *Moroccan Dialogues*, in which the interviews are only minimally edited and show the problematic nature of interviewing for all participants. Another is the use of "polyphony," which is "the registering of different points of views in multiple voices" (p. 71). The aim here is to reduce the editorial authority of the researcher. Another alternative is found in Vincent Crapanzano's (1980) ethnography *Tuhami: Portrait of a Moroccan*, where the author presents transcripts from interviews and minimizes his interpretation of them, inviting the reader to help in the process of interpretation. This is rendered more difficult by the informant, Tuhami, who uses complex metaphors in his communication with the researcher, mixing real events with fantasy, both of which Crapanzano takes as valid data. Here, the concern turns from the *what* of the interview to the *how*. That is, ethnographers should pay attention to both what their interviewees say and how they say it. Indeed, this is somewhat akin to Erving Goffman's (1959) much earlier distinction between "expressions given" and "expressions given off." This approach is consistent with ethnomethodological concerns as well. This will be discussed later.

Sociological works have displayed a postmodern dialogic approach to interviewing, even reporting the mishaps, mistakes, and miscommunications between the researcher and the researched. Susan Krieger (1983) focuses on *polyphony* by presenting the various perspectives of respondents, highlighting discrepancies and problems rather than minimizing them. In a study of victimization, social process, and resistance that embraces notions of polyphony, Allen Shelton (1995) uses the machine and other powerful metaphors to convey his message. He mixes sociological data with stories from his past, using visual imagery from paintings to underscore his points. In another context, Shelton (1996) even goes back to the vespers to compellingly embellish his sociological findings.

Norman Denzin's work is a major impetus for applying postmodern sensibilities to research methodology. Denzin (1989) focuses on "the meanings persons give to themselves and their life projects" (pp. 14–15). Key elements of the approach are the essentially interpretive nature of fieldwork and interviewing and the attempt to let the members speak for themselves. In particular, Denzin borrows the concept of *epiphanies* from James Joyce and orients these as turning points that reshape people's lives, which, in turn, have significant implications for the selection of interview topics. By focusing on these existential moments, Denzin believes, we can gain access to the otherwise hidden feelings experienced by individuals and bring them to the fore for others, and the interviewees themselves, to appreciate and explore.

Denzin (1997) continues his dialogue with postmodernism in more recent work but becomes more distinctly partisan. Here, again, he begins with Joyce and the concern for meaning as perceived by the members of society. However, he is no longer happy with just trying to understand and make these meanings visible. He has become more politically involved with his research subjects. He rejects the traditional canons of researcher noninvolvement and objectivity and instead advocates "partnership" between researcher and subjects. He is especially partial to subjects' "underdog" status: "This model seeks to produce narratives that ennoble human experiences while facilitating civic transformation in the public (and private) spheres" (p. 277).

In summary, one change from traditional to postmodern-informed interviewing is that the so-called detached researcher and interviewer are recast as active agents in the interview process and attempts are made to de-privilege their agency. Another shift is that the interviewee's agency is privileged and in the name of the interviewee all manner of experimentation is undertaken to make evident his or her own sense of identity and representational practices. We turn now to the influences of various theoretical perspectives on this trend.

◆ Phenomenologically Informed Interviews

Phenomenological sociology first appeared in the 1960s, loosely based on the philosophy of Edmund Husserl and the writings of the social philosopher Alfred Schutz. Though Peter Berger and Thomas Luckmann (1966) are explicitly indebted to Schutz's phemonemology and lay some of the groundwork for postmodernism by way of social constructionsim, it is in Cicourel's (1964) work that we see the tie between phenomenology and interviewing most clearly, even as in Harold Garfinkel's (1967) own project there is an added phenomenological influence through ethnomethodology.

Cicourel argues forcefully early on that the interview, no matter how technically perfected its execution, is grounded in the world of commonsense thinking. In fact, according to Cicourel, it must be so, for without the participants' ability to share common or overlapping social worlds and their related communicative understanding, the interview would not be possible. Cicourel follows in Schutz's (1962, 1964, 1966) footsteps here. Schutz discusses the way in which members of a society share a common stock of knowledge that allows them to understand and reciprocate actions. This extends to markedly mundane and shared knowledge, such as speaking in the same language and knowing that the sun will set, that peanut butter will stick to the roof of your mouth, that the Chicago Cubs will never win the World Series, and that Pamela Anderson's beauty is surgically enhanced.

Following such postmodern trends, Irving Seidman (1991) resurrects Schutz's sentiments in his book *Interviewing as Qualitative Research*. Seidman explains that by establishing an "I–thou" relationship or reciprocity of perspectives, the interviewee (I) and the interviewer (thou) form a personal relationship. The result is that the interviewee is no longer objectified but becomes a co-member of a communicative partnership. In fact, in some instances, this may blossom into a full "we" relationship, according to Seidman (e.g., see Denzin's [1997] model of "collaboration").

Robert Dingwall (1997) recapitulates these sentiments as follows:

> If the interview is a social encounter, then, logically, it must be analyzed in the same way as any other social encounter. The products of an interview are the outcome of a socially situated activity where the responses are passed through the role-playing and impression management of both the interviewer and the respondent. (p. 56)

Dingwall adds elements of Goffman's dramaturgical view to the basic notions, which he attributes to both Mead and Schutz. Both within and outside the interview, action is mediated by others' responses and their co-contingent dramatic realizations. According to Dingwall, individuals in interviews provide organizing accounts; that is, they turn the helter-skelter, fragmented process of everyday life into coherent explanations, thus co-creating a situationally cohesive sense of reality.

Furthering the mission of co-creating knowledge, specifically about the meanings and experiences of places, Magarethe Kusenbach (2003) has created a phenomenologically informed method for interviewing that moves it beyond the unnatural stasis of sit-down conversations: "The physical constraints of most ethnographic interview encounters separate informants from their routine experiences and practices in 'natural' environments. These are serious disadvantages, especially if they obstruct themes that are the foci of the investigation" (p. 462). As a remedy to counter these disadvantages, Kusenbach proposes, uses, and encourages what she calls the "go-along." Participant observation and interviewing are systematically conflated. The researcher accompanies interviewees, either one by one or in groups, into their familiar environments to discuss, as in Kusenbach's work, their perceptions of their respective neighborhoods. As such, the go-along helps researchers take account of the ways in which "individuals connect and integrate the various regions of their daily lives and identities, which sociologists, including symbolic interactionists, too often treat as separate, autonomous entities" (p. 478). The go-along allows the informant to be an expert on his or her environs,

proving a useful way for co-constructing knowledge about personal and collective identities and perceptions.

ETHNOMETHODOLOGICAL IMPULSES

Ethnomethodologists put forward similar sentiments. They share a skeptical approach to standardized methodologies. Garfinkel (1967), for one, informs us that we cannot study social interaction except in relation to the interactive methods employed by the social actors themselves to create and maintain their sense of reality. As such, the impulse in interview research would be to attend as much to how participants assemble their respective communications as to what is asked and answered (Boden & Zimmerman, 1991; Maynard, Houtkoop-Steenstra, van der Zouwen, & Schaeffer, 2001).

Recently, Holstein and Gubrium (1995) have directly linked ethnomethodology with these distinctive questions in their discussion of the "active interview." They specifically apply to interviewing the perspective that the interview is a social production between interviewer and respondent. In other words, it entails collaborative construction between two active parties. Because the interview is situationally and contextually produced, it is itself a site for knowledge production rather than simply a neutral conduit for experiential knowledge, as traditionally believed.

Holstein and Gubrium are further inspired by the ethnomethodological distinction between topics (substantive elements of inquiry) and resources (procedures used to study the topics) (see Zimmerman & Pollner, 1970). They point out that, in interviews, researchers focus too much on the *whats*, or substantive foreground, and tend to gloss over the *hows*, which "refer to the interactional, narrative procedures of knowledge production, not merely to interview techniques" (p. 4). Indeed, given the irremediably collaborative and constructed nature of the interview, a postmodern sentiment would behoove us to pay more attention to the *hows*, that is, to try to understand the biographical, contextual, historical, and institutional elements that are brought to the interview and used by both parties. The interview should be understood in light of all these elements rather than as a discreet, neutral set of questions and ensuing responses, detached from both the interviewer's and the respondent's constructive and culturally informed agency.

Gubrium and Holstein (1998) continue this line of thinking in a discussion of personal narratives. Their point of departure is the argument that life comes to us in the form of stories, and personal narratives are approached as individualized constructions. In conveying life to us, respondents tell us stories about themselves, but they do not do so in a social vacuum (see Atkinson, "The Life Story Interview as a Mutually Equitable Relationship," this volume; Fontana, 1977). Rather, as Gubrium and Holstein explain, "Personal accounts are built up from experience and actively cast in the terms of preferred vocabularies" (p. 164; compare Garfinkel, 1967). A postmodern trend emphasizing social construction is evident in their goal: "We want to make visible the way narrative activities play out in everyday practice to both produce coherence and reveal difference" (p. 165).

Others share similar perspectives. The late Madan Sarup (1996), in analyzing the role of narrative in the construction of identity, distinguishes two parts to each narrative: "The story is the 'what' of the narrative, the discourse is the 'how'" (p. 170). And more, "When we talk about our identity and our life-story, we include some things and exclude others, we stress some things and subordinate others" (p. 16). Although Sarup's focus is identity, the message is much the same—the story (and its identities) is constructed in its communicative unfolding.

Dingwall (1997) takes this impulse further. Following Garfinkel, as well as Marvin Scott and Stanford Lyman (1968), he states that interviews are "an occasion for the elicitation of accounts" and that "accounting is how we build a stable order in social encounters and in society" (pp. 56, 57). Applying this to interviews, Dingwall concludes, "An interview is a point at which order is deliberately put under stress. It is a situation in which respondents are required to demonstrate their competence in the role in which the interview casts them" (p. 58). Once more, we are directed to the collaborative production of contextually based accounts.

◆ *Feminist Influences*

In analyzing the images of a nude man with his arm raised in greeting and a nude woman imprinted on the Pioneer spacecraft, Craig Owens (1983) states,

"For in this (Lacanian) image, chosen to represent the inhabitants of Earth for the extraterrestrial Other, it is the man who speaks, who represents mankind. The woman is only represented; she is (as always) already spoken for" (p. 61). It has been much the same in the methodological world of interviewing; women have always already been spoken for in the very structure of the traditional interview. This is exemplified in Earl Babbie's (1992) classic text on research, which has nothing to say about gender differences in interviewing. Indeed, as Carol Warren (1988) reports, female researchers in primitive patriarchal societies were, at times, temporarily "promoted" to the role of male in order to be allowed to witness events and ceremonies from which women were traditionally excluded (see Ryen, "Assessing the Risk of Being Interviewed," this volume).

Not any longer. One of the significant influences on the postmodern trends in interviewing comes from feminist quarters (see Hertz, 1997; Naples, 2003). An ongoing concern has been the elastic subject position of the respondent. A leading question here, for example, is "Do women always speak as women, or are other important subject positions part of their response repertoires?" While feminists have focused on gender differences, they have not ignored other important factors, such as race.[2] For instance, Kim Marie Vaz (1997) has edited an interdisciplinary book on African and African American women that "unearths" their experiences through telling personal portraits, focusing on how both their gender and their race have affected them. Patricia Hill Collins (1990) uses interviews as well as autobiographical accounts, songs, images, and fiction to bring out the viewpoints of black women. Her interviews are hardly "detached," as they are shaped to provide a sympathetic context for making visible the experiences of being both black and a woman.

Kath Weston (1998) explores another traditionally silenced subjectivity, sexual nonconformity. As she recounts, "Back in graduate school, when I first decided to study lesbians and gay men in the United States, the faculty members who mentored me pronounced the project 'academic suicide'" (p. 190). Weston persevered nevertheless, and in her book *Long Slow Burn* (1998), she rejects the idea that

[2]Shifting subject positions have traditionally been glossed over in interview research. Seidman (1991) recounts that in his study of community college faculty, he was treated either with deference because of his affiliation with what was perceived to be a higher-status institution (the university) or with suspicion because of his affiliation with the "ivory tower." The difference was important in how it mediated the organization of responses.

sexuality is merely a sociological specialization; rather, she considers sexuality as being at the often silent heart of the social sciences, deeply implicating the subject. We infer from this that the interview that realizes alternative sexualities can serve to reveal the sexual contours of all subject positions (see Plummer, 2003).

Contrary to the traditional belief that the relation between interviewer and interviewee is neutral and the results of the interview can be treated as independent of the interview process as long as the interviewer is methodologically skilled, gender consciousness changes the nature of interview results (Denzin, 1989). Seidman (1991) shares this view:

> All the problems that one can associate with sexist gender relationships can be played out in an interview. Males interviewing females can be overbearing. Women interviewing men can sometimes be reluctant to control the focus of the interview. Male participants can be too easily dismissive of female interviewers. (p. 78)

If we are to overcome these and other potential problems, the traditional relationship between interviewer and interviewee must change, according to many feminists. The two must become equal partners in a negotiated dialogue. The woman/interviewee should be allowed to express herself freely. Rather than saying or implying, "Answer my question, but don't tell me anything else," interviewers should indeed encourage all respondents to express their feelings, their fears, and their doubts. As Kathryn Anderson and Dana Jack (1991) explain, "If we want to know what women feel about their lives, then we have to allow them to talk about their feelings as well as their activities" (p. 15).

Hertz (1997) urges us to blur the distinction between the interviewer and the respondent. As the interviewer comes to realize that she is an active participant in the interview, she must become reflexive—acknowledge who she is in the interview, what she brings to it, and how the interview gets negotiated and constructed in the process. Doing so will alleviate an associated reification of methodological problems. But we need to go beyond methodology, as Hertz points out, to face the ethical problems associated with how much we are willing to become partners and disclose about ourselves (see also Behar, 1996). As we turn the interviewee

from a faceless member of a category to a person, how much should we divulge about her? How do we maintain her anonymity? Ruth Behar (1996) poses the matter succinctly: "Are there limits—of respect, piety, pathos—that should not be crossed, even to leave a record? But if you can't stop the horror, shouldn't you at least document it?" (p. 2).

A related ethical problem stems from researchers' traditional custom of using interviewees to gather material for their own purposes. As Daphne Patai (1987) explains, no matter how well-intentioned researchers are, if they use interview materials exclusively for their own purposes, they are exploiting the women they interview (Oakley, 1981; Reinharz, 1992; Smith, 1987). As a result, some interviewers take the notion of partnership one step further and become advocates for those they interview (Gluck, 1991). Others turn interview narratives into political acts as they uncover the injustices to which those studies are subjected (Cherot, 2009; Denzin, 1999a).

◆ Virtual Interviewing

For traditional interviewing, the transition to the Internet would seem flawless, moving from telephone questionnaires to the use of e-mail, chat rooms, and websites. In one way or another, all of these remain "distant" interviewing, with little or no face-to-face contact. While only about 50% of American households have personal computers and only about half of these have access to the Internet (Fontana & Frey, 2000) (though these numbers are both increasing and elusive), new software programs facilitate electronic interviewing and provide the ability to obtain returns of almost 100% from some specialized groups (Schaefer & Dillman, 1998). At the same time, new ethical problems are surfacing, because anonymity is not feasible in e-mail communication (Johns, Chen, & Hall, 2004; Markham & Baym, 2008). Even though the use of pseudonyms is possible in chat rooms, issues of deceit and misrepresentation need to be addressed (see Borer & Schafer, in press).

The move to electronic interviewing is perhaps most problematic for in-depth interviewing. Instead of the parties to the interview being face-to-face, interaction centers on "virtual" respondents and "virtual" interviewers, to which we might add the "virtual" researcher, all of whose empirical groundings are unclear. Indeed, the lack of clarity portends a version of Baudrillard's (1983) "hyperreality," the melding together of everyday and media realities, confounding the traditional boundaries of text, identity, and other.

To explore some of these issues online, Annette Markham (1998) created an Internet site where she interviewed and conversed with other online media users. In particular, Markham and the others were "trying to make sense of what it means to be there" (p. 18). The participants, including Markham, were experimenting with their sense of self online: "By logging onto my computer, I (or part of me) can seem to (or perhaps actually) exist separately from my body in 'places' formed by the exchange of messages" (p. 17). People exchanging messages online apply a text—online dialogue—to communicate with each other and create a sense of reality as well as a sense of online identity. According to Markham, despite the fact that communication takes place through fiber-optic cables, the interactants actually "feel a sense of presence" (p. 17) of the other: "We feel we meet in the flesh. . . . Everywhere we rub shoulders with each other" (Argyle, quoted in Markham, 1998, p. 17).

The identities that interactants create online may differ from their other identities, as the lack of visual communication and accountability allows one to create a practically new self if one so wishes. The interaction can also be very different from face-to-face communication, because the interactants, visually hidden as they are, can formulate "false nonverbals," claiming feelings and emotions that do not correspond to their demeanor. This type of interviewing takes away one of the traditional strengths of qualitative research, which is perennially based on the claim, "I saw it, I heard it, I was there." Internet interviewing and face-to-face interviews are, however, coming closer together with the rise of virtual worlds such as Second Life, which allow participants and researchers alike to interact using their virtually embodied "avatars" (Gottschalk, 2009; Malaby, 2009).

Researchers' increased reliance on computers has faced the criticism of social commentators for some time (see, among others, Dreyfus, 1979; Searle, 1984). These critics contend that computers are not mere aids that facilitate research; rather, they drastically change our lives and modes of communication. That modern-day "Luddite," Neal Postman (1993), states, "The fundamental metaphoric message of the computer, in short, is that we are machines—thinking machines, to be sure, but machines nonetheless" (p. 111). According to Postman, reliance on machines will increase human belief in scientism, with the result that we will try to scientize and cloak in the language of science the stories we tell. John Murphy (1999) echoes the sentiment. He sees qualitative researchers as being pressured by the ethos of the times and the demands of academia and granting agencies into using computers and software programs such as ETHNO, QualPro, and the Ethnograph (see Seale & Rivas, "Using Software to Analyze Qualitative Interviews," this volume). Murphy warns that computers will not merely help us sort out the data but will lead us to seek precise responses, removing ambiguity from the interview material. Rather than created, negotiated, face-to-face narratives, we will be left with artificially derived categories that will reify our results and have little to do with the world of everyday life.

◆ Making Sense of the Senses

One of the powerful and informative consequences of postmodernism is the move away from modernism's valorization, or perhaps even fetishization, of reason and rationality. This has opened paths for researchers to explore other elements of meaning making such as the imagination and less rigidly cognitive practices related to the senses. Expanding our focus on the senses can be viewed, then, as a postmodern attempt to move beyond the preconditioned repertoires that accompany citizens of interview societies.

Influenced by the work of Cornelius Castoriadis (1998), scholars have sought to uncover the ways in which both personal and collective imagination affect social behavior and perceptions of social life. For instance, Jacqueline Adams (2004) explored, through interviews, the ways in which cross-national couples—"couples whose partners grew up in different countries" (p. 277)—use their imagination when deciding where they will cohabit as well as how to cope with living in a foreign land. Michael Ian Borer (2010) used interviews to access the collective imagination of a neighborhood. Residents were asked about the present conditions of their neighborhood and whether they would like a recently defunct neighborhood firehouse to be reconstructed and redefined. While they were using their ideas about the past and the present as fodder, it was their imaginations that helped them envision potential futures for the firehouse and for their neighborhood. The neighborhood, City View, was for all intents and purposes forgotten during the redevelopment of the larger city it is embedded within. As such, many of the residents felt that "the stigmatized image of City View has reinforced the tradition of despair and culture of fear that is prevalent in the neighborhood" (p. 106). Borer prompted interviewees to wonder aloud about the way an adapted firehouse might change the image of City View. As one resident, a third-generation City Viewer, revealed,

> Turning that place [the firehouse] into something special would tell everyone that we haven't given up on our community, even though other people have. Some of us care . . . this place could show them that. . . . This is our community and we don't need to go somewhere else to feel good about ourselves. This place [the firehouse] could really help get us lookin' like other parts of Greenville, the nice parts. (p. 106)

From this quote, we can see how this respondent, with Borer, imagined ways in which the firehouse could change outsiders' imagined perceptions of the blighted neighborhood.

Even though both Adams and Borer used semistructured interviews, which are not inherently postmodern, their postmodern sensibilities made them aware of the use of their interviewees' imaginations. This was an unexpected finding from their respective studies because neither researcher entered the field with the intention to investigate the roles that imagination plays in the way people perceive their social worlds. By uncovering the importance of the imagination in everyday life, the postmodern distinction between "reality" and "fantasy" is further blurred, perhaps beyond repair, opening up new avenues for qualitative researchers to investigate such nonrational processes.

Researchers who have tried to capture the roles of the senses have done so in a variety of ways. The field of visual sociology, which is still in its adolescent phase (see Emmison & Smith, 2000), encompasses works that range from the positivistic (Collier & Collier, 1986) to the highly interpretive and postmodern (Moxey, 2008). Influenced by postmodern ethnography's disposition toward collaborative research with informants, Douglas Harper (2002) is a proponent of *photo elicitation*. One way of applying photo elicitation is to use photographs or other visual materials as objects for discussion between interviewer and interviewee. Harper purports that visuals afford both parties opportunities to produce knowledge beyond verbal interviewing. He contends that "images evoke deeper elements of human consciousness than do words. . . . [T]he photoelicitation interview seems like not simply an interview process that elicits more information but rather one that evokes a different kind of information" (p. 13). The kind of information, then, that is produced draws from participants' imaginations as well as other elements that exist beyond the realm of instrumental reason.

Influenced by the classic works of Merleau-Ponty and, more specifically, Paul Stoller's *Sensuous Scholarship* (1997), the *sensuous turn* in ethnographic interviewing has so far proven to be valuable. At the forefront of this turn are the works of Dennis Waskul and Phillip Vannini (2008) as well as Sarah Pink (2003, 2008). Relying on "research journals" provided by their informants, Waskul and Vannini (2008) have sought to connect the "habits of sensing" to larger, collective moral orders (p. 59). Focusing specifically on smells and odor, they contend that "through smell, meaning is reflexively bestowed unto odor in the context of negotiated somatic rules. . . . Clearly, odor is a subtle but significant component of the culturally normative and aesthetic rituals of expressive and impressive everyday life" (p. 68). The research journals became mediums for discussions—like the visuals in the photo elicitation method—about the roles that smell, as well as the other senses, play in their informants' everyday lives.

Pink, on the other hand, actively engages in the sensual and somatic order of her participants. In a representative article, Pink (2008) uses a guided walking tour of an urban neighborhood as her case study to "discuss how the sensory sociality of walking, eating, imagining, drinking, photographing, and audio- and video-recording, alongside and in collaboration with research participants, can be productive of place-as-ethnographic knowledge (pp. 176–177). Pink's technique is similar to Kusenbach's (2003) "go-along" method discussed earlier. Pink's goal, however, expands the notions of perception and meaning making to include all the senses. Moreover, by walking, talking, and eating with the tour guides and other participants, she was able to participate in and discuss the sensuous aspects of the places they were visiting as they were being guided through those places. Before being led on a tour of Mold, a town in Flintshire, Wales, Pink met with Fred, the town clerk, to discuss the influence of the "Slow City" movement—or Cittàslow as it is referred to locally—on Mold's social and built environment. Recognizing her role as a sensuous being in a purposely determined sensory environment, Pink (2008) writes,

> Although these talks are crucial in my research, in understanding the town and its locations that created its Cittàslow identity I was actually using all my senses. With Fred at the coffee morning I tasted the half-milk coffee, compared the warmth of the hall and the sunlight pouring through its windows with the December chill outdoors, and noticed how the floral table-cloths created a café space in a multi-use room. The coffee helped me to feel situated in this café context. Its biographical familiarity cut across the clear generational and occupational differences between middle-aged researcher and retired residents and enabled me to feel "in place." (p. 185)

Clearly, Pink uses her own senses to empathize with the sensations that the residents of Mold feel, from the weather outside to the indoor café to the "half-milk coffee" she ingests. The common sensations felt by Pink and her respondent Fred as they sipped their drinks also helped build mutual rapport and a sense of comfort.

◆ *Representational Practices*

One of the most controversial areas of postmodern-informed interview research centers on the question of how empirical material should be represented. Traditionally, the writing of social science has mimicked the sparse prose of the natural sciences (see Geertz, 1988). John Van Maanen (1988) has analyzed the more recent changes in reporting styles and found that they are moving toward the literary. In postmodern-informed reporting practices, writing

engages new, experimental, and highly controversial forms of representation. Mindful of the postmodern collapse of disciplinary barriers, social researchers are using literature, poetry, and even plays to represent interview narratives. Though scholars have tried to incorporate these new forms to display and share their findings, there still remains a considerable amount of reluctance toward following these emerging practices. New media outlets have helped provide opportunities for multimedia "reports," but they are yet to garner any significant status within the mainstream social-scientific fields.[3]

AUTOETHNOGRAPHY

Autoethnography offers a nuanced way of giving voice to personal experience while advancing sociological understanding. Carolyn Ellis (1995a, 2004) and others have been employing autoethnography to conflate the traditional distinction between the interviewer and the respondent. Ellis writes about her past experiences in what becomes a form of retrospective self-interview and narrative reconstruction of life events. The crucial difference between this work and traditional representation is that Ellis aims to recount her own feelings about interview topics that apply to her as a researcher and subject of the experience under consideration, thus combining the roles of interviewer and interviewee. As a result, we are witness to many personally conveyed epiphanic moments in her life, moments that could be our very own. For example, she has written about the agony of facing the death of her brother in an airplane crash (1993), her uneasy encounter with a friend dying of AIDS (1995b), and the slow spiral toward death of her beloved partner, who was stricken with a terminal illness (1995a). In the same vein, Laurel Richardson (1999) has written a personal narrative of her misadventures with paternalistic faculty colleagues after a car accident. Troy McGinnis's (1999) presentation "The Art of Leaving" is about his stumbling on his wife and a best friend in an intimate situation, and Norman Denzin (1999b, 1999c) has written stories about his hideout in Montana. These are just a few of the many recent autoethnographic (self-interviewing)

___
[3]Ben Agger (2002), who exists as somewhat of bridge between Frankfurt School–style Marxism and postmodernisms, argues for the necessity of a more literary sociology but, through stories of his own tenure process, warns budding sociologists of the dangers of embracing the controversial albeit significant "narrativity" of the postmodern turn.

representations of experience. Even though autoethnography has been criticized as self-indulgent and atheoretical (Wall, 2008), it offers explicit opportunities for self-reflection and use of the "ethnographic I" (Ellis, 2004).

POETRY

Laurel Richardson extends this trend to poetic representation. After lengthy interview sessions with a southern, middle-aged single mother, Richardson (1997) transformed the woman's sad and powerful tale into a poem, which she recites masterfully in a sorrowful southern drawl. A segment follows, which in Richardson's view comes fully to life only in its recitation.

So, the Doctor said, "You're pregnant."

I was 41. John and I

had had a happy kind of relationship,

not a serious one.

But beside himself with fear and anger,

awful, rageful, vengeful, horrid,

Jody May's father said,

"Get an Abortion."

I told him,

"I would never marry you.

I would never marry you.

I would never." (p. 133)

Others have followed Richardson's lead into the realm of sociological poetry. For example, Patricia Clough's (1999) angst-filled poetic presentation "A Child Is Being Killed" took the place of the keynote address at a symposium of the Society for the Study of Symbolic Interaction. Sociologically informed poetry—or poetically informed sociology—has been adopted by researchers exploring sensitive topics including those discussed above as well others such as homelessness (Clarke, Febbraro, Hatzipantelis, & Nelson, 2005) and Holocaust survivor testimonies (Rapport & Hartill, 2010).

STAGE PLAYS AND PERFORMANCES

Scripted performance has also been rallied to enhance the "scenic presence" (Holstein & Gubrium,

2000) of interview-based reports of experience. Richardson (1997), for example, not only constructs poetic accounts but uses plays to tell her stories, at times soliciting participation from her audience. Indeed, dramatic realization has become a broadly popular mode of expression. Jim Mienczakowski and Steve Morgan (1998) have dressed as police officers to act out their counseling interviews, which were completed in Queensland, Australia. Andrea Fontana donned black clothing and a white mask to portray Farinelli, the castrato, in reporting on a study of transsexuals (Fontana & Schmidt, 1998, 1999). Robert Schmidt and Fontana enlisted Jennifer O'Brien's help in producing a polyphonic play based on in-depth interviews with a lap dancer (Schmidt & Fontana, 1998).

At times, however, performances have moved from the sublime to the studiously ridiculous. For example, the sociologist Stephen Pfohl (1995) once stripped to black bikini bottoms at the culmination of his video-music play, and more recently, a graduate student smeared himself with bean dip to convey the ironies of the Latino identity. Postmodern trends have taken representation a long way from the guarded prose of research reports, yet stage plays and performances have the weakest following due, at least in part, to their inability to be reproduced outside and beyond the event. Perhaps a hypermediated Internet journal could provide videos of these performances. Until such a forum is established, the prestige level of this form of representation will likely continue to remain low.

◆ Conclusion

Clearly, postmodernism has influenced interviewing, loosening it from many of its traditional moorings. Perhaps it has accomplished its goal—imploding traditional interviewing to leave it in fragments, each crying out to be appreciated in its own way. Some see this fragmentation as a healthy sign, because we have many groups with different approaches and methods all presenting their wares (Adler & Adler, 1999). Others feel threatened by it and, in various ways, decry the ostensible chaos (Best, 1995; Dawson & Prus, 1993; Prus, 1996; Sanders, 1995; Shalin, 1993). Yet another response strikes a balance between the modern and the postmodern, staking a middle-ground approach to incorporate innovative postmodern ideas with more traditional precepts (Gubrium & Holstein, 1998; Holstein & Gubrium, 1995). And, finally, there are those who are oblivious to these trends, who continue to be guided by traditional rules of both qualitative and quantitative inquiry.

Shadowing the differences is the prospect that the interview can no longer be viewed as a discreet event, the straightforward result of asking questions and receiving answers. Indeed, even the traditional "conversation with a purpose," which until recently was a way of conceptualizing the survey interview, has increasingly given way to evidence of the systematic communicative work that produces interview data (see Maynard et al., 2001). Survey researchers themselves are systematically discovering something they have always suspected—that both the interviewer and the respondent negotiate and work together to accomplish the interview, the resulting "data" being as much a product of interview participants' collaborative efforts as of the experiences under consideration.

Postmodern trends in interviewing and qualitative research are seemingly coming full circle, back to where they began, though more reflexive and less positivistic. Increasingly, we are learning that what Paul Rabinow (1977) said about the informant and the researcher in ethnography also applies to the interviewer and the respondent: "The common understanding they construct is fragile and thin, but it is upon this shaky ground that anthropological inquiry proceeds" (p. 39). The shaky ground, the loose gravel, the cracked world of interviewing is much more of a blessing than a curse. These cracks open up the established protocol of interviews as dictated by postmodern "interview society." And through the cracks we see light and shadows that we never anticipated. This should provide all of us with enough motivation to continue to explore the world(s) around us.

◆ References

Adams, J. (2004). The imagination and social life. *Qualitative Sociology, 27,* 277–297.

Adler, P. A., & Adler, P. (1999). The ethnographer's ball: Revisited. *Journal of Contemporary Ethnography, 28,* 442–450.

Agger, B. (2002). Sociological writing in the wake of postmodernism. *Cultural Studies <=> Critical Methodologies, 2,* 427–459.

Anderson, K., & Jack, D. C. (1991). Learning to listen: Interview techniques and analyses. In S. B. Gluck & D. Patai (Eds.), *Women's words: The feminist practice of oral history* (pp. 11–26). New York, NY: Routledge.

Atkinson, P., & Silverman, D. (1997). Kundera's immortality: The interview society and the invention of self. *Qualitative Inquiry, 3,* 304–325.

Babbie, E. (1992). *The practice of social research* (6th ed.). Belmont, CA: Wadsworth.

Baudrillard, J. (1983). *Simulations* (P. Foss, P. Patton, & J. Johnston, Trans.). New York, NY: Semiotext(e).

Bauman, R., & Briggs, C. (2003). *Voices of modernity: Language ideologies and the politics of inequality.* Cambridge, England: Cambridge University Press.

Behar, R. (1996). *The vulnerable observer: Anthropology that breaks your heart.* Boston, MA: Beacon.

Berger, P. L., & Luckmann, T. (1966). *The social construction of reality: A treatise in the sociology of knowledge.* Garden City, NY: Anchor Books.

Best, J. (1995). Lost in the ozone again. In N. K. Denzin (Ed.), *Studies in symbolic interaction: A research annual* (Vol. 17, pp. 125–130). Greenwich, CT: JAI Press.

Best, S., & Kellner, D. (1991). *Postmodern theory: Critical interrogations.* New York, NY: Guilford Press.

Blumer, H. (1969). *Symbolic interactionism: Perspective and method.* Englewood Cliffs, NJ: Prentice Hall.

Boden, D., & Zimmerman, D. H. (Eds.). (1991). *Talk and social structure: Studies in ethnomethodology and conversation analysis.* Berkeley: University of California Press.

Borer, M. I. (2009, April). *The double-edged sword of sound bite culture.* Paper presented at the Pacific Sociological Association annual meeting, San Diego, CA.

Borer, M. I. (2010). From collective memory to collective imagination: Time, place, and urban redevelopment. *Symbolic Interaction, 33*(1), 96–114.

Borer, M. I., & Schafer, T. (in press). Culture war confessionals: Conflicting accounts of Christianity, violence, and mixed martial arts. *Journal of Media and Religion.*

Castoriadis, C. (1998). *The imaginary institution of society.* Cambridge, MA: The MIT Press.

Cherot, N. (2009). Storytelling and ethnographic intersections: Vietnamese adoptees and rescue narratives. *Qualitative Inquiry, 15,* 113–148.

Cicourel, A. V. (1964). *Method and measurement in sociology.* New York, NY: Free Press.

Clarke, J., Febbraro, A., Hatzipantelis, M., & Nelson, G. (2005). Poetry and prose: Telling the stories of formerly homeless mentally ill people. *Qualitative Inquiry, 11,* 913–932.

Clough, P. T. (1999, February). *A child is being killed: The unconscious of autoethnography.* Keynote address presented at the annual symposium of the Couch-Stone Society for the Study of Symbolic Interaction, Las Vegas, NV.

Collier, J., & Collier, M. (1986). *Visual anthropology: Photography as a research method*. Albuquerque, NM: University of New Mexico Press.

Collins, P. H. (1990). *Black feminist thought: Knowledge, consciousness, and the politics of empowerment*. New York, NY: Routledge.

Converse, J. M., & Schuman, H. (1974). *Conversations at random: Survey research as interviewers see it*. New York, NY: Wiley.

Crapanzano, V. (1980). *Tuhami: Portrait of a Moroccan*. Chicago, IL: University of Chicago Press.

Dawson, L., & Prus, R. (1993). Interactionist ethnography and postmodern discourse. In N. K. Denzin (Ed.), *Studies in symbolic interaction: A research annual* (Vol. 15, pp. 147–177). Greenwich, CT: JAI Press.

Denzin, N. K. (1989). *Interpretive interactionalism*. Newbury Park, CA: Sage.

Denzin, N. K. (1997). *Interpretive ethnography: Ethnographic practices for the 21st century*. Thousand Oaks, CA: Sage.

Denzin, N. K. (1999a). An interpretive ethnography for the next century. *Journal of Contemporary Ethnography, 28,* 510–519.

Denzin, N. K. (1999b). Performing Montana. In B. Glassner & R. Hertz (Eds.), *Qualitative sociology as everyday life* (pp. 147–158). Thousand Oaks, CA: Sage.

Denzin, N. K. (1999c, February). *Performing Montana, Part II*. Paper presented at the annual symposium of the Couch-Stone Society for the Study of Symbolic Interaction, Las Vegas, NV.

Denzin, N. K. (2003). *Performance ethnography: Critical pedagogy and the politics of culture*. Thousand Oaks, CA: Sage.

Derrida, J. (1972). Structure, sign and play in the discourse of the human sciences. In R. Macksey & E. Donato (Eds.), *The structuralist controversy* (pp. 247–272). Baltimore, MD: Johns Hopkins University Press.

Dickens, D. R., & Fontana, A. (Eds.). (1994). *Postmodernism and social inquiry*. New York, NY: Guilford Press.

Dingwall, R. (1997). Accounts, interviews and observations. In G. Miller & R. Dingwall (Eds.), *Context and method in qualitative research* (pp. 51–65). Thousand Oaks, CA: Sage.

Douglas, J. D. (1985). *Creative interviewing*. Beverly Hills, CA: Sage.

Dreyfus, H. (1979). *What computers can't do: The limits of artificial intelligence*. New York, NY: Harper & Row.

Dwyer, K. (1982). *Moroccan dialogues: Anthropology in question*. Baltimore, MD: Johns Hopkins University Press.

Ellis, C. (1993). "There are survivors": Telling a story of sudden death. *Sociological Quarterly, 34,* 711–730.

Ellis, C. (1995a). *Final negotiations: A story of love, loss, and chronic illness*. Philadelphia, PA: Temple University Press.

Ellis, C. (1995b). Speaking of dying: An ethnographic short story. *Symbolic Interaction, 18,* 73–81.

Ellis, C. (2004). *The ethnographic I: A methodological novel about autoethnography*. Walnut Creek, CA: AltaMira Press.

Emmison, M., & Smith, P. (2000). *Researching the visual*. London, England: Sage.

Fontana, A. (1977). *The last frontier: The social meaning of growing old*. Beverly Hills, CA: Sage.

Fontana, A., & Frey, J. H. (2000). The interview: From structured questions to negotiated text. In N. K. Denzin & Y. S. Lincoln (Eds.), *Handbook of qualitative research* (2nd ed., pp. 645–672). Thousand Oaks, CA: Sage.

Fontana, A., & Schmidt, R. (with O'Brien, J.). (1998, August). *The fluid self*. Paper presented at the annual meeting of the Society for the Study of Symbolic Interaction, San Francisco, CA.

Fontana, A., & Schmidt, R. (1999). Castrato: Predetermined to fluid self or a dialogue/performance script intended to inform Garfinkel about the possibilities of gendering. In N. K. Denzin (Ed.), *Studies in symbolic interaction: A research annual* (Vol. 23, pp. 83–91). Greenwich, CT: JAI Press.

Garfinkel, H. (1967). *Studies in ethnomethodology*. Englewood Cliffs, NJ: Prentice Hall.

Geertz, C. (1988). *Works and lives: The anthropologist as author*. Stanford, CA: Stanford University Press.

Gluck, S. B. (1991). Advocacy oral history: Palestinian women in resistance. In S. B. Gluck & D. Patai (Eds.), *Women's words: The feminist practice of oral history* (pp. 205–220). New York, NY: Routledge.

Goffman, E. (1959). *The presentation of self in everyday life*. New York, NY: Doubleday Anchor Books.

Gottschalk, S. (2009, August). *The virtual imagination: Second life, ethnography and the hypermodern self*. Paper presented at the meetings of the Society for the Study of Symbolic Interaction, San Francisco, CA.

Gubrium, J. F., & Holstein, J. A. (1997). *The new language of qualitative method*. New York, NY: Oxford University Press.

Gubrium, J. F., & Holstein, J. A. (1998). Narrative practice and the coherence of personal stories. *Sociological Quarterly, 39,* 163–187.

Gubrium, J. F., & Holstein, J. A. (2003). From the individual interview to the interview society. In J. Gubrium & J. Holstein (Eds.), *Postmodern interviewing* (pp. 21–49). Thousand Oaks, CA: Sage.

Harper, D. (2002). Talking about pictures: A case for photo-elicitation. *Visual Studies, 17*(1), 13–26.

Harvey, L. (1987). *Myths of the Chicago school of sociology*. Aldershot, England: Avebury.

Hertz, R. (Ed.). (1997). *Reflexivity and voice*. Thousand Oaks, CA: Sage.

Holstein, J. A., & Gubrium, J. F. (1995). *The active interview*. Thousand Oaks, CA: Sage.

Holstein, J. A., & Gubrium, J. F. (2000). *The self we live by: Narrative identity in a postmodern world*. New York, NY: Oxford University Press.

Johns, M. D., Chen, S., & Hall, G. J. (Eds.). (2004). *Online social research: Methods, issues, and ethics*. New York, NY: Peter Lang.

Krieger, S. (1983). *The mirror's dance: Identity in a women's community*. Philadelphia, PA: Temple University Press.

Kusenbach, M. (2003). Street phenomenology: The go-along as ethnographic research tool. *Ethnography*, 4(3), 455–485.

Kvale, S., & Brinkmann, S. (2009). *InterViews: Learning the craft of qualitative research interviewing* (2nd ed.). Thousand Oaks, CA: Sage.

Lemert, C. (2005). *Postmodernism is not what you think: Why globalization threatens modernity*. Boulder, CO: Paradigm.

Lofland, J. (1971). *Analyzing social settings*. Belmont, CA: Wadsworth.

Lyotard, J.-F. (1984). *The postmodern condition: A report on knowledge* (G. Bennington & B. Massumi, Trans.). Minneapolis: University of Minnesota Press.

Malaby, T. (2009). *Making virtual worlds: Linden Lab and Second Life*. Ithaca, NY: Cornell University Press.

Malinowski, B. (1989). *A diary in the strict sense of the term*. Stanford, CA: Stanford University Press.

Marcus, G. E., & Fischer, M. M. J. (1986). *Anthropology as cultural critique: An experimental moment in the human sciences*. Chicago, IL: University of Chicago Press.

Markham, A. N. (1998). *Life online: Researching real experience in virtual space*. Walnut Creek, CA: AltaMira.

Markham, A. N., & Baym, N. K. (Eds.). (2008). *Internet inquiry: Conversations about method*. Thousand Oaks, CA: Sage.

Matthewman, S., & Hoey, D. (2006). What happened to postmodernism? *Sociology*, 40(3), 526–547.

Maynard, D. W., Houtkoop-Steenstra, H., van der Zouwen, J., & Schaeffer, N. C. (2001). *Interaction and practice in the survey interview*. New York, NY: Wiley.

McGinnis, T. (1999, February). *The art of leaving*. Paper presented at the annual symposium of the Couch-Stone Society for the Study of Symbolic Interaction, Las Vegas, NV.

Mienczakowski, J., & Morgan, S. (1998, February). *Stop! In the name of love!* Paper presented at the annual symposium of the Couch-Stone Society for the Study of Symbolic Interaction, Houston, TX.

Moxey, K. (2008). Visual studies and the iconic turn. *Journal of Visual Culture*, 7, 131–146.

Murphy, J. (1999, February). *Computerized ethnography: Fad and disaster!* Paper presented at the annual symposium of the Couch-Stone Society for the Study of Symbolic Interaction, Las Vegas, NV.

Naples, N. A. (2003). *Feminism and method: Ethnography, discourse analysis, and activist research*. New York, NY: Routledge.

Oakley, A. (1981). Interviewing women: A contradiction in terms? In H. Roberts (Ed.), *Doing feminist research* (pp. 30–61). London, England: Routledge & Kegan Paul.

Owens, C. (1983). The discourse of others: Feminists and postmodernism. In H. Foster (Ed.), *The anti-aesthetic: Essays on postmodern culture* (pp. 57–82). Port Townsend, WA: Bay.

Patai, D. (1987). Ethical problems of personal narrative, or who should eat the last piece of cake? *International Journal of Oral History*, 8(1), 5–27.

Pfohl, S. (1995, May). *Venus in Microsoft*. Paper presented at the Gregory Stone Annual Symposium of the Society for the Study of Symbolic Interaction, Des Moines, IA.

Pink, S. (2003). Representing the sensuous home: Ethnographic experience and anthropological hypermedia. *Social Analysis*, 47(3), 46–63.

Pink, S. (2008). An urban tour: The sensory sociality of ethnographic place-making. *Ethnography*, 9(2), 175–196.

Plummer, K. (2003). Queers, bodies and postmodern sexualities: A note on revisiting the "sexual" in symbolic interactionism. *Qualitative Sociology*, 26(4), 515–530.

Postman, N. (1993). *Technopoly: The surrender of culture to technology*. New York, NY: Vintage Books.

Prus, R. (1996). *Symbolic interaction and ethnographic research*. Albany: State University of New York Press.

Rabinow, P. (1977). *Reflections on fieldwork in Morocco*. Berkeley: University of California Press.

Rapport, F., & Hartill, G. (2010). Poetics of memory: In defence of literary experimentation with Holocaust survivor testimony. *Anthropology and Humanism*, 35(1), 20–37.

Reinharz, S. (1992). *Feminist methods in social research*. New York, NY: Oxford University Press.

Richardson, L. (1997). *Fields of play: Constructing an academic life*. New Brunswick, NJ: Rutgers University Press.

Richardson, L. (1999, February). *Jeopardy*. Paper presented at the Forum Lecture Series, University of Nevada at Las Vegas, NV.

Sanders, C. (1995). *Stranger than fiction*. In N. K. Denzin (Ed.), *Studies in symbolic interaction: A research annual* (Vol. 17, pp. 89–104). Greenwich, CT: JAI Press.

Sarup, M. (1996). *Identity, culture and the postmodern world*. Athens: University of Georgia Press.

Schaefer, D. R., & Dillman, D. A. (1998). Development of a standard e-mail methodology. *Public Opinion Quarterly*, 62, 378–397.

Schmidt, R., & Fontana, A. (1998, February). *Deconstructing Peggy Sue*. Paper presented at the annual symposium of the Couch-Stone Society for the Study of Symbolic Interaction, Houston, TX.

Schutz, A. (1962). *Collected papers I: The problem of social reality*. The Hague, The Netherlands: Martinus Nijhoff.

Schutz, A. (1964). *Collected papers II: Studies in social theory*. The Hague, The Netherlands: Martinus Nijhoff.

Schutz, A. (1966). *Collected papers III: Studies in phenomenological philosophy*. The Hague, The Netherlands: Martinus Nijhoff.

Scott, M. B., & Lyman, S. (1968). Accounts. *American Sociological Review, 33*(1), 46–62.

Searle, J. (1984). *Minds, brains and science*. Cambridge, MA: Harvard University Press.

Seidman, I. (1991). *Interviewing as qualitative research: A guide for researchers in education and the social sciences*. New York, NY: Teachers College Press.

Shalin, D. (1993). Modernity, postmodernism and pragmatist inquiry. *Symbolic Interaction, 16*, 303–332.

Shelton, A. (1995). The man at the end of the machine. *Symbolic Interaction, 18*, 505–518.

Shelton, A. (1996, May). *Vespers*. Paper presented at the Gregory Stone Annual Symposium of the Society for the Study of Symbolic Interaction, Des Moines, IA.

Silverman, D. (1993). *Interpreting qualitative data: Methods for analysing talk, text and interaction*. London, England: Sage.

Silverman, D. (Ed.). (1997). *Qualitative research: Theory, method and practice*. London, England: Sage.

Smith, D. E. (1987). *The everyday world as problematic: A feminist sociology*. Boston, MA: Northeastern University Press.

Stoller, P. (1997). *Sensuous scholarship*. Philadelphia, PA: University of Pennsylvania Press.

Van Maanen, J. (1988). *Tales of the field: On writing ethnography*. Chicago, IL: University of Chicago Press.

Vaz, K. M. (Ed.). (1997). *Oral narrative research with black women*. Thousand Oaks, CA: Sage.

Wall, S. (2008). Easier said than done: Writing an autoethnography. *International Journal of Qualitative Methods, 7*(1), 38–53.

Warren, C. A. B. (1988). *Gender issues in field research*. Newbury Park, CA: Sage.

Waskul, D., & Vannini, P. (2008). Smell, odor, and somatic work: Sense-making and sensory management. *Social Psychology Quarterly, 71*(1), 53–71.

Weston, K. (1998). *Long slow burn: Sexuality and social science*. New York, NY: Routledge.

Zimmerman, D. H., & Pollner, M. (1970). The everyday world as a phenomenon. In J. D. Douglas (Ed.), *Understanding everyday life: Toward a reconstruction of social knowledge* (pp. 80–104). Chicago, IL: Aldine.

4

THE PEDAGOGY OF INTERVIEWING

◆ Kathryn Roulston

The proliferation and popularization of the interview in the opening decades of the 21st century has led to a point where interviewing has become a form of interaction that is frequently taken for granted. Thus, the mechanics underlying a "good" interview largely remain invisible. Projects such as the American Folklife Center's StoryCorps project, which has archived 16,000 interviews conducted by people of all ages exploring the experiences and lives of friends, colleagues, and family members from across the United States, support the idea that interviewing is a mundane skill—anyone might conduct interviews anytime, anywhere.

In this chapter, I focus specifically on providing resources for those in higher education who prepare researchers to conduct qualitative interviews for the purposes of doing social research. The ideas presented here are premised on the assumption that there are specific skills that might be learned about how to conduct research interviews and that these skills might be facilitated in professional learning contexts and higher education. I argue that what a "good" interview will look like will vary according to the epistemological and theoretical perspectives assumed by researchers in the design and conduct of research projects. Instruction in how to conduct interviewing must therefore (a) examine epistemological and theoretical assumptions concerning how interviews are used for research purposes, (b) encourage researchers to be reflective and consider reflexivity in the use of qualitative interviews, and (c) provide opportunities for researchers to critically observe their practice and analyze interaction methodologically. For this, I first provide historical insights into the use of interviewing for research purposes before reviewing research that focuses on interviewing and the teaching of the practical skills of interviewing as well as the reflective practices involved. I then review two common instructional approaches to teaching qualitative research interviewing. I end the chapter by discussing how I effectively combined these two approaches in one of my courses.

Author's Note: Thanks to Mike Healy and Karyn McKinney for comments on earlier drafts of this chapter.

◆ Methodological Considerations and the Preparation of Interviewers: Historical Insights

Numerous noted scholars have considered interview practices and the preparation of interviewers to conduct social science research. Jennifer Platt's (2002) historical review of research interviewing in the United States provides key research studies investigating methodological issues in interviewing—most of which focus on data from large-scale national surveys. One example of guidelines for interviewing drawn from actual practice that has influenced qualitative research practice is provided by the sociologist Robert Merton (1910–2003). Merton is well-known for the development of the "focused interview" as an approach to the generation of data at the Bureau of Applied Social Research at Columbia University, and he recollected in the introduction to the second edition of *The Focused Interview: A Manual of Problems and Procedures* (Merton, Fiske, & Kendall, 1956/1990) how he became involved in conducting interviews. He described his first encounter with research on listeners' responses to radio broadcasts conducted by Paul Lazarsfeld (1901–1976), the founding director of the Office of Radio Research:

> I begin passing notes to Paul about what I take to be great deficiencies in the interviewer's tactics and procedures. He was not focusing sufficiently on specifically indicated reactions, both individual and aggregated. He was inadvertently guiding responses; he was not eliciting spontaneous expressions of earlier responses when segments of the radio program were being played back to the group. And so on and on. (Merton et al., 1956/1990, p. xiv)

Merton went on to coauthor with Marjorie Fiske and Patricia Kendall a manual of procedures that codified how researchers might ask questions of listeners concerning their opinions and responses (Merton et al., 1956/1990). What Merton initially conceptualized as an approach to generating data from either individuals or groups has since morphed into what is known as focus group research—a method of generating data taken up in the field of marketing research and subsequently reappropriated for use in social science research (Morgan, 2002). An interesting corollary to Merton's critique of the interviewer's questioning practices cited above is reflected in a memo that he and Lazarsfeld cowrote that was circulated in 1950 at Columbia University. In the memo, Merton and Lazarsfeld (Lazarsfeld, 1972) argued that the preparation of social science researchers must include both academic knowledge and research skills, one component of which was the collection of qualitative field data.

A contemporary of Merton, the sociologist David Riesman (1909–2002), also demonstrated considerable interest in examining the research interview (see Lee, 2008, for a review), and he wrote a number of articles on the methodological aspects of interviewing. With Mark Benney, Riesman embarked on a study of interviewing as a research method in *The Interview Project* (Lee, 2008; Riesman & Benney, 1956). Riesman (1951) also argued for engaging ordinary citizens in research activities—what he called a "social science militia"—to complement the work of social science professionals. Riesman was not interested in "standardizing" the interview, as were many of his contemporaries involved in opinion polling, but saw the possibilities of exploring interview data for traces of the conscious and unconscious of speakers, claiming that

> there are no "bad" interviews; where rapport in the usual sense is poor, and answers are perfunctory, something else is gained: we at least know how the interviewee responded in *that* situation. Or to state the point more accurately, some interviews are of course more fruitful than others—they are richer in both opinions and in residues—but analysis can in large measure equate for these differences in degree. (Riesman & Glazer, 1948, p. 525)

Demonstrating his keen interest in the methodological issues that arose in interview practice, in *Faces in the Crowd*, and reiterating that there are "no bad interviews," Riesman (1952) commented that "inadequacies in communication could be as revealing as full and conspicuous rapport" (pp. 28–29), reflecting his interests in psychoanalytic theory (see Lee, 2008).

The two perspectives of interview practice expressed by Merton and Riesman in the 1940s and 1950s—first that poorly conducted interviews jeopardize the quality of data generated, and thus the outcomes of research studies, and second that there are no "bad" interviews—reflect disparate views still existent in a continuum of contemporary thought. From the former viewpoint, the preparation of researchers to conduct "quality" interviews is crucial to the enhancement of social science research. Merton et al.'s (1956/1990) one influential manual (see Platt, 2002, for others) exemplifies this approach by providing numerous recommendations to interviewers on how to ask questions and interact with research participants in the course of "focused interviews." Merton et al. comment that

> we do not suppose that interviewing procedures can be so completely routinized that individual differences in aptitude are eliminated. It is clear that fixed routine of mechanically applied procedures will not make for effective interviewing. Yet we do not conceive interviewing as a private incommunicable art. It is not necessary that the interviewer improvise anew, out of whole cloth, in each interview. Experience suggests a more tenable point of view than either of these two. (p. 17)

Following the path exemplified by Merton and his colleagues (1956/1990), along with other sociologists, contemporary methodologists have explicated an array of advice on how to design and conduct an array of interview formats.

◆ Methods Texts

This literature includes information on how to design and conduct research studies that use interviews and how to formulate and ask questions, and is informed by various epistemological and theoretical traditions. These include cognitive anthropology (Spradley, 1979), feminist epistemologies (DeVault, 1990; DeVault & Gross, 2007; Reinharz & Chase, 2002), grounded theory (Charmaz, 2002), hermeneutics (Dinkins, 2005; Freeman, 2006), phenomenology (deMarrais, 2004; Kvale & Brinkmann, 2009; Seidman, 2006), postmodernism (Denzin, 2001), and sociolinguistics (Briggs, 1986). Authors have also focused on specific interview methods such as biographic interviewing (Wengraf, 2001), focus groups (Barbour & Kitzinger, 1999; Morgan, 1997; Puchta & Potter, 2004; Stewart, Shamdasani, & Rook, 2007), narrative methods (Mishler, 1986),

oral history (Dunaway, 1996; Janesick, 2010; Ritchie, 2003; Yow, 2005), and photo elicitation (Frith & Harcourt, 2007). More recently, methodologists have explicated how online methods of communication may be used for the purposes of conducting qualitative interviews (James & Busher, 2009; Salmons, 2010). The literature cited here provides a cursory introduction to the broad array of perspectives on how qualitative research interviews may be designed and conducted. What is common across these texts, however, is that they demonstrate Merton's viewpoint that researchers may be prepared to conduct more effective interviews.

A second stream of literature takes up an idea highlighted in Riesman's view that methodological issues on how interview data are generated may be just as interesting to examine as the topics of talk. In a footnote, Riesman (1951) described his review of interviewers' reports received by the National Opinion Research Center that discussed the issues that had arisen during interviews as well as how questions worked in practice—commenting that these reports were often more interesting than the interview schedules. Riesman's work reveals an interest in the themes of this edition of the *Handbook of Interviewing*—the methodological issues and interactional dynamics involved in research interviews.

Some researchers take the view that since interviewers use the very same conversational skills that speakers use in ordinary conversation (Hester & Francis, 1994), interviewers simply need to be aware of how their conversational practices unfold in specific contexts with others and learn to listen to others respectfully. Rapley (2004) explains that "interviewers don't need massive amounts of detailed technical (and moral) instruction on how to conduct qualitative interviews" (p. 26). Rapley is careful to assert that this does not mean that "anything goes." On the contrary, he reminds researchers that although interviewing is "never just 'a conversation,' it may be conversation*al*" (p. 26). For researchers who view how interview data are co-constructed as just as interesting and informative as a study's findings, the methodological issues that arise in interview interaction (e.g., Holstein & Gubrium, 1995, 2004), whether problematic or not, become topics of examination (Roulston, 2011). Given the proliferation of writing on various forms of qualitative research interviews, what might be said about how qualitative interviewers might be prepared and taught?

◆ The Preparation of Qualitative Interviewers

Information for those involved in the preparation of qualitative interviewers may also be found in texts that more explicitly focus on teaching qualitative research methods. In this context, issues and approaches with respect to teaching qualitative research methods are discussed both generally and in reference to specific disciplines, including geography (Delyser, 2008), the health sciences (Rifkin & Hartley, 2001; Stark & Watson, 1999), management (Harlos, Mallon, Stablein, & Jones, 2003), marketing (Hopkinson & Hogg, 2004), and nursing (Cobb & Hoffart, 1999; McAllister & Rowe, 2003). (For a bibliography of interdisciplinary resources on teaching and learning qualitative research, see Chenail, 2010.) While many of these resources allude to the inclusion of interviewing as an experiential component of coursework on qualitative research, most provide few specific details concerning how this might be accomplished.[1] A cursory examination of qualitative research methods syllabi available online in 2010 suggests that interviewing is commonly presented as one component among other methods of qualitative data gathering (including document reviews and participant observation), with coursework entailing some form of practice.[1] This aligns with findings from a study conducted by Corinne Glesne and Rodman Webb (1993) in which they surveyed 73 professors teaching qualitative research methods in the United States. Of the 55 syllabi examined, 45 required some form of pilot research project or fieldwork exercises.

There is also no shortage of methodological articles that examine how qualitative interview interaction takes place in research contexts and discuss implications for practice (see, e.g., Mallozzi, 2009; Stephens, 2007). These kinds of articles focus on post hoc methodological analyses examining problems that have arisen. Likewise, there is an extensive body of research that has examined the practices of standardized interviewing—such as question formulation and sequencing—over many decades (e.g., Houtkoop-Steenstra, 2000; Schuman & Presser, 1981; see also Platt, 2002), particularly within the area of opinion polling and attitudinal surveys. In contrast, although there is a substantial body of literature that examines how clinical interviewing skills are taught, there are few studies that examine the teaching of qualitative research interviewing as a topic of analysis in its own right. More common are experiential accounts of teaching interviewing.

In the next section, I focus on how the teaching of qualitative interviewing has been approached in the methodological literature. I begin by reviewing how teachers of research methods have described ways to facilitate experiences that assist beginning researchers in developing their interview practice.

◆ Teaching Qualitative Interviewing

Apart from a focus on two aspects that emerge as critical in learning to interview effectively—*practice* and *reflection*—there are few commonalities to be found in the literature on teaching interviewing. Such texts largely comprise reflective accounts and recommendations drawn from authors' teaching practice. Writing from a variety of disciplinary backgrounds, authors describe different ways to incorporate interviewing into coursework with undergraduate and graduate students for a variety of purposes. The recommended strategies and areas of focus reported by teachers of qualitative interviewing vary considerably in scope, content, and area of emphasis. I begin by reviewing articles that address teaching interviewing by emphasizing the value of *practicing skills*.

◆ Interview Skills in Practice

Charmaz (1991) reports on how an intensive interviewing project incorporated into coursework in sociology benefits both graduate and undergraduate students. First, in teaching intensive interviewing, graduate students must go beyond technique to consider the philosophical, epistemological, and theoretical assumptions concerning interviews, how they unfold, and what interviewers do. Second, graduate students develop a repertoire of skills that involve both research and teaching that prepare them for careers in

---

[1]See the following websites for qualitative methods syllabi:

http://www.coe.uga.edu/syllabus/qual/index.html

http://www.nova.edu/ssss/QR/syllabi.html

higher education. Undergraduates, on the other hand, learn about how data are transformed into knowledge about the social world and are encouraged to "think sociologically" (p. 386). Students are actively involved in all aspects of the project, including topic selection and preparation of an interview protocol prior to conducting the interview. According to Charmaz, through designing and conducting an interview, undergraduates learn about others' definitions of events and behaviors, as well as working through the challenges involved in doing research. Pedagogical outcomes for students encompass learning how to ask questions, recruiting participants for research on sensitive topics, or even sorting out misunderstandings in interview interactions. Charmaz's article includes suggestions for how to plan for the interview assignment and how students might be assisted in the development of interview questions, and it also covers issues that instructors might address in teaching undergraduate students how to conduct interviews. Clearly, teaching interviewing, for Charmaz, incorporates much more than practicing interview skills. Through involvement in an intensive interviewing project, undergraduate or graduate students can gain practical expertise in asking questions and designing interview studies and expand their theoretical knowledge of their chosen discipline.

Similarly, Ronald Chenail (1997) recommends three exercises for teaching family therapists interviewing skills in a qualitative research methods course. First, instructors model a research interview "in the round" followed by a postinterview discussion and analysis. Chenail notes that the interview might be conducted as part of an authentic project carried out by the instructor in which a research participant agrees to be interviewed in front of a class, or a simulation in which a volunteer plays the role of interviewee. Chenail provides considerable detail concerning preparing students for the interview, what they might observe, and what topics might be discussed in a review of the session. Students are required to write up reflective observations for homework and may review the audiotape if necessary. Second, students participate in a "rotational interviewing" exercise in which they assume three alternating roles—the roles of interviewer, interviewee, and observer—in classroom practice taped interviews concerning topics of their choice. Via the rotational process, all students receive "180°" evaluations from others (interviewees and observers), which inform their own reflections on revisiting the recordings. Finally, students conduct

another interview in which they "self-supervise" and write a postinterview reflection. Chenail suggests that an alternative to this model may be drawn from family therapy, in which the interviewer takes "breaks" during the interview—consulting with a supervisor or team to discuss how the interview is going and plan for midcourse corrections if appropriate—and then resumes the interview.

Writing from a different disciplinary perspective, Chris Wellin (2007) provides a detailed description of how narrative interviewing might be included in undergraduate gerontology courses. Like Charmaz (1991), Wellin focuses on a particular form of interviewing—in this case, narrative interviews. He argues that narrative interviews are especially suited to exploring issues related to the life course in social gerontology. Learning objectives projected for students engaged in conducting a narrative interviewing project include (a) formulating research questions, (b) understanding how knowledge related to aging is created via interview encounters, (c) applying the concepts and theories from course readings in interpreting interview data, and (d) writing a final paper that students perceive to be a valuable record of participants' lives. Once students have defined a topical focus for their project and formulated interview questions, they conduct and transcribe a 45-minute interview. Students then code and analyze the transcript and develop a paper that relates the findings to concepts covered in the course. Issues reported to arise in this sort of project include (a) how students consider and deal with the trade-offs involved in interviewing close friends and family members as opposed to strangers, (b) whether interviewers select to explore potentially sensitive issues, and (c) how students navigate the process of connecting narrative data to conceptual issues in the relevant area of study.

In summary, these practice-oriented articles describe approaches to the incorporation of interview projects into undergraduate and graduate coursework in gerontology, sociology, and family therapy. The activities described by Chenail (1997) involve a stepwise gradation of difficulty. In this context, students participate in staged classroom interviews and interact with peers in a variety of roles (as observer, interviewer, and interviewee) before undertaking a full-fledged self-supervised interview. Similarly, the projects described by Charmaz (1991) and Wellin (2007) involve the supervision of students in the development of a research topic and interview protocol over the duration of a course. As a whole, these authors recommend that instructors and students incorporate epistemologies and theories from their respective fields into the development of the research project and the interpretation of interview data. In the next section, I discuss literature that emphasizes interviewer preparation in the form of reflective skills.

◆ Reflecting on Interview Practice

Lisbeth Uhrenfeldt, Barbara Paterson, and Elisabeth Hall (2007) draw on work in teaching clinical interviews in the health professions to outline how videotaping of practice interviews by novice researchers might be used as a tool for reflection to develop reflexivity. These authors argue that guided reflection with respect to video-recorded interviews provides students with insights that extend beyond those that may be offered by an instructor who only reviews transcripts. The guided-reflection framework offered by these authors seeks to involve students in examining elements of interviews that are usually omitted from transcriptions, specifically (a) paralinguistic communication (i.e., gestures, body language, vocal tone and pitch, speed of talk), (b) proxemics (i.e., use of space and eye gaze, distance), (c) timing (i.e., pauses, hesitations), and (d) the context of the interview (i.e., the context and conditions of the interview). The authors conclude by recommending empirical testing of the framework at different points in the development of an interviewer's practice to examine its effectiveness in developing researcher reflexivity.

Chenail (2009) recommends the use of a "prepilot study," in which the investigator is interviewed by another researcher using the protocol developed for his or her research study. This interview may be used by the researcher to investigate "potential biases" and revise interview protocols prior to submission of applications for research with human subjects to institutional review boards (IRBs) (p. 17). Through reflection on the interview process and findings, the researcher may be encouraged to (a) recognize personal feelings that occur during the interview, (b) develop an appreciation for the challenges inherent in answering questions about the research topic as well as the potential experience of "being and not being heard," (c) identify perspectives that may

potentially "bias" the study, (d) learn patience within the interview process, (e) appreciate the potential vulnerability that may be experienced by research participants, and (f) identify his or her a priori assumptions about participants (Chenail, 2009, p. 19).

Drawing on a graduate seminar on qualitative interviewing that she has taught over a number of years, Ping-Chun Hsiung (2008) focuses specifically on how to teach reflexivity in relation to interview practice. In this description, students begin by working with preexisting data to examine what "narrative-rich" or "narrative-thin" data might look like, as well as how the "conceptual baggage" of the interviewer manifests itself in interview interaction. Hsiung emphasizes the hands-on practice of interviewing in the classroom setting, in which students take turns as interviewer and interviewee. Students are expected to design, conduct, record, and transcribe a 40- to 50-minute interview and write a reflective essay that examines their experiences as both interviewer and interviewee. Hsiung argues that the interview practicum encourages students not only to reflect on the way they asked questions but also to deeply interrogate their own conceptual baggage. Although students are encouraged to reflect on their technical skills independently, Hsiung stresses the importance of facilitating their reflections.

In summary, these articles each represent different strategies designed to assist students to reflect on both their interview practice (i.e., how they ask questions and respond to research participants) as well as researchers' assumptions about knowledge construction and the use of interviews as a research method. Taken together, pedagogical literature emphasizing *interviewing in practice* or *reflecting on interview practice* encompasses a variety of strategies that might be included in coursework to prepare qualitative interviewers. These include the following:

1. *Course-related activities that may include self-initiated topics* (modeling of interviews; rotational interviews; peer interviews to experience the roles of interviewer, interviewee, and observer; and analysis of preexisting data)

2. *Interviews conducted prior to designing and conducting a self-initiated interview study* (e.g., interviewing the interviewer, reflection on and analysis of pilot interviews)

3. *Self-initiated interview projects* (including development of an interview protocol, recruitment of participants, and conducting, transcribing, and interpreting interview data)

In the third option, self-initiated projects are described as part of formal coursework, and as such, they are not deemed to be "research" in the sense that students might present and publish findings from their studies. Rather, findings are presented as class papers, and the projects themselves may or may not be subject to approval by IRBs, depending on the respective universities' policies.

◆ Studies of Student Experiences in Coursework on Interviewing

Ideally, the effectiveness of different instructional approaches to teaching interviewing skills should be determined through empirical research. To this end, my colleagues and I have examined students' experiences in learning how to interview in two studies. First, in Roulston, deMarrais, and Lewis (2003), we examined graduate students' experiences in a 15-day intensive-interviewing class. Our examination of data from the study (interview transcriptions, audiotapes and videotapes of student interviews, and reflective papers) showed that novice interviewers encountered a number of challenges in conducting interviews in the context of both in-class practice activities and interviews on self-initiated topics. These included (a) encountering unexpected participant behaviors (e.g., an interviewee arriving 30 minutes late and distractions from copresent children), (b) dealing with the consequences of their own actions and subjectivities during the interview process, (c) phrasing and asking questions, and (d) dealing with sensitive issues that arose in interviews. As a result of this study, we recommended that (a) students learn how to conduct interviews as a part of authentic projects, (b) instructors provide opportunities for students to engage in close, guided analysis of audiotaped interviews and transcripts, and (c) students participate in class discussions concerning research design and the researcher's assumptions.

Following from the first study, in Roulston et al. (2008), we examined students' involvement in an authentic research project that was incorporated within a course I myself taught. As a result of this

self-study, the students who took part in the study and I argue that this kind of project, as opposed to mock interviews, has several advantages. First, students tend to have little stake in mock or staged interviews. However, through working on a joint project, students are forced to focus on skill development and methodological issues rather than on a topic of personal interest. Although for some students this may be experienced as a constraint, for others, the guided practice in an authentic project provides more compelling learning experiences than participating in mock interviews. One participant in the study described above reflected, "Because we had an audience that was interested in our findings, I felt I was engaged in the 'community of practice' of research interviewing" (p. 238). Second, an actual research project compels students to go beyond their personal comfort zones and interview participants who are unknown to them—a practice that is less likely when students self-select interview topics and participants (see Wellin, 2007). Third, the group project provided students an opportunity to review and discuss one another's work in relation to a common topic. Finally, students collaborated to produce and present a report from the study for an external client as part of the applied project that was initiated by the instructor and approved by the IRB prior to the course.

Overall, Roulston et al. (2008) provides an overview of how a project of this type might be organized and conducted, in addition to students' reflections and perspectives of their involvement in an authentic project, including the technical issues and challenges that arose during their involvement, skill development, and critical self-reflection. In particular, we include analysis of the reflections-on-action generated during the course, as well as the critical reflections produced after the experience when students collaborated with me to describe their experiences of learning how to interview. In essence, this example serves as a bridge between the two instructional approaches discussed earlier: (1) the growth of students' interviewing skills in practice and (2) those articles that emphasize the development of reflective skills on interview practice.

As noted at the outset, the body of literature concerning teaching qualitative interviewing, while relatively small, shares two common features. First, students are *engaged in practicing their skills as interviewers*—either in class, in class interview assignments, or—less commonly—in authentic projects.

Second, students are called on to *reflect on their epistemological and theoretical assumptions as researchers and interviewers and on their interview practice*—that is, how they go about asking questions and interacting with participants. Reflective activities suggested in the literature include (a) interviewing the interviewer using the researcher's protocol; (b) examination of interview data generated from other research projects; (c) observing and being observed in practice interviews in which interviewers rotate among the roles of interviewer, interviewee, and observer; and (d) reviewing audiotapes and/or videotapes of one's practice interviews.

While considering the variety of options related to teaching qualitative interviewing, in Table 4.1, I draw on literature related to qualitative interviewing and qualitative research methods more broadly to summarize approaches and strategies that might be used by instructors working with researchers learning how to interview in the social sciences. In Column 1 of Table 4.1, possible activities that instructors might use to facilitate experiences that develop researchers' interview practices are represented. Also included are anticipated learning outcomes for interviewers (Column 2), along with further reading that might be discussed (Column 3).

Table 4.1 Strategies and Activities for Teaching Qualitative Interviewing

Activities and Descriptions	Pedagogical Purpose	References

Theorizing the researcher prior to and during a research study
 	
• Write subjectivity statements
• Interview the researcher
• Participate in "why-interview" (Maso, 2003)
   o What do you mean by each of the concepts embedded in the question?
   o Why is this question important to you?
• Participate in bracketing interview or "interview of the interviewer"
• Researcher journals
	Developing reflexivity
	
	• Investigate researcher's assumptions and perspectives about research topic/participants
	• Interrogate initial research topics and questions
	• Develop research proposal
	• Investigate researcher's presuppositions and perspectives about research topic/participants
	• Pilot interview questions and reflection on interview process/reflexivity
	• Examine subjectivities during research process
	• Record methodological issues arising during research process, analytic hunches, etc.
		Bradbury-Jones (2007), Chaudhry (1997), Cole and Knowles (2001), Goodall (2000), Krieger (1985), Peshkin (1988), Pillow (2003)
		
		Chenail (2009), Pollio, Henley, and Thompson (1997), Rolls and Relf (2006), Roulston (2010)

Examining other interviewers' practices
 	
• Observe model interviews
   o Review of interview practices in media (TV, radio, World Wide Web)
   o Modeling of interview by instructor (authentic or role play)
• Review interview transcriptions from other projects
	Developing critical observation and listening skills
	
	• Observe multiple examples of interview practice
	   o How do interviewers and interviewees ask and answer questions?
	   o How are data co-constructed by speakers?
	   o What are the outcomes for the generation of "data" for research purposes?
	   o What is the evidence in transcriptions of the interviewer's "conceptual baggage"?
		Chenail (1997)
		
		Hsiung (2008)

Activities and Descriptions	Pedagogical Purpose	References

Developing a reflective interview practice
 	
• Develop research questions and interview questions
• Conduct practice interviews (individual and/or focus group)
   o Participate and reflect on interviews conducted in interview triads (interviewer–interviewee–observer)
   o Reflect on audiotaped and/or videotaped pilot interviews
	Learning how to design research studies and conduct interviews
	
	• Consider epistemological and theoretical implications underlying assumptions about various forms of interviewing (e.g., ethnographic, phenomenological, feminist, oral and life history, focus group)
	• Develop interview questions that align with theoretical assumptions about interviewing
	• Use interview guide to ask questions
	• Formulate follow-up questions to elicit further details concerning participants' descriptions
	• Listen respectfully to participants
	• Critically observe how interviewers and interviewees orient to one another's utterances and actions
		See literature review on qualitative interviewing (p. 63 in the section Methods Texts)
		
		Chenail (1997), Puchta and Potter (2004), Uhrenfeldt, Paterson, and Hall (2007)

Developing a self-initiated interview project • Develop a research proposal that includes a statement of the problem and supporting literature, research questions, and interview protocol • Apply for human subjects review (subject to whether the project is approved as a course-based project or requires institutional review board approval)	Practicing designing a research study • Match epistemological and theoretical assumptions concerning social research with methods of data generation used • Match genre of interview selected with research questions posed (e.g., ethnographic, feminist, phenomenological, oral history interview, focus groups) • Develop interview questions that will elicit data to examine research questions posed • Understand institutional procedures required to conduct ethical research with human subjects	Mason (2002), Maxwell (2005), Roulston (2010)

Conducting an interview project
 	
• Recruit participant(s)
• Schedule interview(s)
• Conduct an interview in which the following occur:
   o Interview is recorded (audio/video)
   o Informed consent is explained
   o Respectful listening is demonstrated
   o Interview guide is followed to elicit descriptions
   o Follow-up questions are posed
	Learning how to generate interview data for the purposes of research
	
	• Understand work involved in recruitment of research participants (e.g., involvement of gatekeepers)
	• Locate appropriate venue for research interviews and schedule interviews
	• Demonstrate mastery of technical equipment involved in interviews (e.g., digital or analog equipment, external microphones)
	• Explain research purpose to participants
		Wanat (2008)
		
		Price (2002)
		
		Corbin and Morse (2003), deMarrais and Tisdale (2002)

(Continued)

Table 4.1 (Continued)

Activities and Descriptions	Pedagogical Purpose	References
	• Develop conversational skills to talk to friends/strangers • Develop follow-up questions to elicit further description • Demonstrate respect for participants • Consider ethical implications of studies (e.g., sensitive issues)	
Working with interview data • Transcribe interview	Learning how to interpret and analyze interview data • Match theoretical assumptions of ontological and epistemological properties of interview data with requirements of transcription (e.g., whether transcription conventions are appropriate) • Demonstrate mastery of technical equipment (e.g., transcription software, downloading and storage of digital files)	Davidson (2009), Ochs (1979), Oliver, Serovich, and Mason (2005), Poland (2002), Powers (2005)
Developing a reflective interview practice • Review interview transcriptions methodologically and topically (*how + what*) • Analyze and represent data	Developing reflexivity • Examine interview interaction for how interviewers and interviewees co-construct talk • Examine interview interaction for data that respond to research questions • Consider interview "problems" as prompts for thinking about the kinds of interview questions posed, and research design more broadly • Match theoretical assumptions of ontological and epistemological properties of interview data with assertions (evidence is used to warrant claims)	Holstein and Gubrium (1995, 2004), Nairn, Munro, and Smith (2005), Rapley (2004), Roulston (2010, 2011), Roulston, Baker, and Liljestrom (2001), Tanggaard (2007, 2008)

I present activities, outcomes, and readings as suggestions rather than as prescriptions for how to go about teaching interviewing. Since Table 4.1 includes a wide array of possibilities that might be used, instructors must choose judiciously from these options to plan for meaningful learning activities that meet the needs of particular learners.

Even experienced interviewers encounter challenges in practice, and most researchers will admit to interviews gone wrong for all kinds of reasons: exploding batteries; interviews that take much more time than planned; recording devices that run out of storage space; audio or video equipment that malfunctions; miscommunication with venues resulting in interviewers and interviewees missing one another; difficulties in recruiting participants; participants dissolving into tears, which leaves interviewers at a loss for what to say next; interruptions from family members, pets, and crying babies; and so forth. Of course, these are just a few of the issues that my colleagues and I have encountered. Undoubtedly, the list can be as lengthy and as complex as social life itself. Admittedly, it is impossible to instruct students on how to deal with an infinite list of scenarios. As the discussion in this chapter has shown, however, it is possible to prepare them.

◆ Conclusions

In this chapter, I have not provided a list of recommendations for "effective" and "good" qualitative open-ended questioning practices. There are many resources on this topic that suggest that asking open questions of interviewees is more effective in generating narrative-rich data than asking closed questions and that posing "leading" questions in which the interviewer's assumptions are inherent is poor practice. Although often this type of advice holds true, in closely examining transcriptions, I have found that there are also exceptions to these rules of thumb. Given the complexity of designing, organizing, and conducting interviews, rather than reiterate a list of "Dos and Don'ts" here, I focus on what I regard as three crucial components that researchers must accomplish to design and conduct interview studies of quality.

First, interviewers must understand both the epistemological and the theoretical implications of how they conceptualize interview data for the kinds of interviews they select to use, how questions are formulated, and how data are transcribed, analyzed, interpreted, and represented. For example, in some social contexts, researchers aiming to conduct decolonizing research (Smith, 1999) may well avoid the use of interviews because they are inappropriate (e.g., Iseke-Barnes, 2003). In other social contexts, researchers working from a decolonizing perspective may design and conduct an interview project in a way that aligns with the decolonizing aim of social justice for indigenous peoples (e.g., Iwasaki, Bartlett, Gottlieb, & Hall, 2009).

Second, interviewers must understand the social locations that they occupy as researchers—such as race, ethnicity, status, age, nationality, education, gender, language proficiency, and so forth—and how these may both limit and benefit the generation of interview data with research participants. Given that researchers come in all theoretical stripes, investigate all topics imaginable, and work with research participants all over the globe in unique social contexts, an understanding of what one brings to a study as a researcher and what the implications are for how participants view and interact with the researcher must be worked out on a case-by-case basis.

Third, interviewers must be able to rigorously analyze the transcriptions from their interviews for methodological purposes, with a view to learning how interview data are generated and what effective questions might look like in particular contexts. As the relevant chapters in this handbook indicate, numerous approaches have been used to analyze interview transcriptions. For example, Riessman (1987) uses narrative methods to reconsider an interview, Nairn et al. (2005) examine a "failed" interview from a poststructuralist perspective, and I have outlined how methods drawn from conversation analysis may be used to reexamine transcripts (Roulston, 2010).

In summary, I argue that instruction in interviewing must (a) examine epistemological and theoretical assumptions with respect to how interviews are used, (b) encourage researchers to be reflective and consider various theorizations and approaches to reflexivity in qualitative research, and (c) provide opportunities for researchers to critically observe their practice and analyze interaction methodologically. Such an approach to instruction will be open and flexible in allowing for diversity in epistemological and theoretical conceptualizations of knowledge production and interviewing as a research method, as well as in conversational and learning styles represented by students. There is no one-size-fits-all approach to preparing qualitative interviewers. By providing a variety of opportunities to meet the needs of learners who come to interviewing with different levels of expertise and a variety of research purposes, instructors can assist researchers in using interviews in theoretically consistent ways to design and conduct sophisticated studies of quality.

As a caveat, I recognize that some students may struggle with the ambiguity involved in an approach that emphasizes openness and flexibility rather than specification and recipes. Certainly, when learning a new task, some novices tend to gravitate toward applying rules in context-free ways. Yet newcomers to interviewing may also become overwhelmed and struggle when attempting to remember and apply too many rules. Instructors, therefore, need to be able to judge what is required for different learners and adapt their instructional methods accordingly.

◆ References

Barbour, R. S., & Kitzinger, J. (Eds.). (1999). *Developing focus group research: Politics, theory and practice* (pp. 140–161). London, England: Sage.

Bradbury-Jones, C. (2007). Enhancing rigour in qualitative health research: Exploring subjectivity through Peshkin's I's. *Journal of Advanced Nursing, 59*(3), 290–298.

Briggs, C. (1986). *Learning how to ask: A sociolinguistic appraisal of the role of the interview in social science research*. Cambridge, England: Cambridge University Press.

Charmaz, K. (1991). Translating graduate qualitative methods into undergraduate teaching: Intensive interviewing as a case example. *Teaching Sociology, 19*(3), 384–395.

Charmaz, K. (2002). Qualitative interviewing and grounded theory analysis. In J. F. Gubrium & J. A. Holstein (Eds.), *Handbook of interview research* (pp. 675–694). Thousand Oaks, CA: Sage.

Chaudhry, L. N. (1997). Researching "my people," researching myself: Fragments of a reflexive tale. *International Journal of Qualitative Studies in Education, 10*(4), 441–453.

Chenail, R. J. (1997). Interviewing exercises: Lessons from family therapy. *The Qualitative Report, 3*(2). Retrieved from http://www.nova.edu/ssss/QR/QR3-2/chenail.html

Chenail, R. J. (2009). Interviewing the investigator: Strategies for addressing instrumentation and researcher bias concerns in qualitative research. *The Weekly Qualitative Report, 2*(3), 14–21. Retrieved from http://www.nova.edu/ssss/QR/WQR/interviewing.pdf

Chenail, R. J. (2010). *Bibliography of resources for teaching and learning qualitative research and qualitative research design resources*. Retrieved from http://www.nova.edu/ssss/QR/teaching_042610.pdf

Cobb, A. K., & Hoffart, N. (1999). Teaching qualitative research through participatory coursework and mentorship. *Journal of Professional Nursing, 15*(6), 331–339.

Cole, A. L., & Knowles, J. G. (Eds.). (2001). *Lives in context: The art of life history research*. Walnut Creek, CA: AltaMira Press.

Corbin, J., & Morse, J. M. (2003). The unstructured interactive interview: Issues of reciprocity and risks with dealing with sensitive topics. *Qualitative Inquiry, 9*(3), 335–354.

Davidson, C. R. (2009). Transcription: Imperatives for qualitative research. *International Journal of Qualitative Methods, 8*(2), 35–52. Retrieved from http://ejournals.library.ualberta.ca/index.php/IJQM/article/view/4205/5401

Delyser, D. (2008). Teaching qualitative research. *Journal of Geography in Higher Education, 32*(2), 233–244.

deMarrais, K. (2004). Qualitative interview studies: Learning through experience. In K. deMarrais & S. D. Lapan (Eds.), *Foundations for research: Methods of inquiry in education and the social sciences* (pp. 51–68). Mahwah, NJ: Lawrence Erlbaum.

deMarrais, K., & Tisdale, K. (2002). What happens when researchers inquire into difficult emotions? Reflections on studying women's anger through qualitative interviews. *Educational Psychologist, 37*(2), 115–123.

Denzin, N. K. (2001). The reflexive interview and a performative social science. *Qualitative Research, 1*(1), 23–46.

DeVault, M. L. (1990). Talking and listening from women's standpoint: Feminist strategies for interviewing and analysis. *Social Problems, 37*(1), 96–116.

DeVault, M. L., & Gross, G. (2007). Feminist interviewing: Experience, talk, and knowledge. In S. N. Hesse-Biber (Ed.), *Handbook of feminist research: Theory and praxis* (pp. 143–154). Thousand Oaks, CA: Sage.

Dinkins, C. S. (2005). Shared inquiry: Socratic-hermeneutic interpre-viewing. In P. M. Ironside (Ed.), *Beyond method: Philosophical conversations in healthcare research and scholarship* (pp. 111–147). Madison: University of Wisconsin Press.

Dunaway, D. K. (1996). The interdisciplinarity of oral history. In D. K. Dunaway & W. K. Baum (Eds.), *Oral history: An interdisciplinary anthology* (2nd ed., pp. 7–22). Walnut Creek, CA: AltaMira Press.

Freeman, M. (2006). Nurturing dialogic hermeneutics and the deliberative capacities of communities in focus groups. *Qualitative Inquiry, 12*(1), 81–95.

Frith, H., & Harcourt, D. (2007). Using photographs to capture women's experiences of chemotherapy: Reflecting on the method. *Qualitative Health Research, 17*(10), 1340–1350.

Glesne, C., & Webb, R. (1993). Teaching qualitative research: Who does what? *International Journal of Qualitative Studies in Education, 6*(3), 253–266.

Goodall, H. L., Jr. (2000). *Writing the new ethnography*. Walnut Creek, CA: AltaMira Press.

Harlos, K. P., Mallon, M., Stablein, R., & Jones, C. (2003). Teaching qualitative methods in management classrooms. *Journal of Management Education, 27*(3), 304–322.

Hester, S., & Francis, D. (1994). Doing data: The local organization of a sociological interview. *British Journal of Sociology, 45*(4), 675–695.

Holstein, J. A., & Gubrium, J. F. (1995). *The active interview* (Vol. 37). Thousand Oaks, CA: Sage.

Holstein, J. A., & Gubrium, J. F. (2004). The active interview. In D. Silverman (Ed.), *Qualitative research: Theory, method and practice* (2nd ed., pp. 140–161). London, England: Sage.

Hopkinson, G. C., & Hogg, M. K. (2004). Teaching and learning about qualitative research in the social sciences: An experiential learning approach amongst marketing students. *Journal of Further and Higher Education, 28*(3), 307–320.

Houtkoop-Steenstra, H. (2000). *Interaction and the standardized survey interview: The living questions.* Cambridge, England: Cambridge University Press.

Hsiung, P.-C. (2008). Teaching reflexivity in qualitative interviewing. *Teaching Sociology, 36,* 211–226.

Iseke-Barnes, J. (2003). Living and writing indigenous spiritual resistance. *Journal of Intercultural Studies, 24*(3), 211–238.

Iwasaki, Y., Bartlett, J. J., Gottlieb, B., & Hall, D. (2009). Leisure-like pursuits as an expression of aboriginal cultural strengths and living actions. *Leisure Sciences, 31,* 158–173.

James, N., & Busher, H. (2009). *Online interviewing.* London, England: Sage.

Janesick, V. J. (2010). *Oral history for the qualitative researcher: Choreographing the story.* New York, NY: Guilford Press.

Krieger, S. (1985). Beyond "subjectivity": The use of the self in social science. *Qualitative Sociology, 8*(4), 309–324.

Kvale, S., & Brinkmann, S. (2009). *InterViews: Learning the craft of qualitative research interviewing* (2nd ed.). London, England: Sage.

Lazarsfeld, P. F. (1972). *Qualitative analysis: Historical and critical essays.* Boston, MA: Allyn & Bacon.

Lee, R. M. (2008). David Riesman and the sociology of the interview. *The Sociological Quarterly, 49,* 285–307.

Mallozzi, C. (2009). Voicing the interview: A researcher's exploration on a platform of empathy. *Qualitative Inquiry, 15*(6), 1042–1060.

Maso, I. (2003). Necessary subjectivity: Exploiting researchers' motives, passions and prejudices in pursuit of answering "true" questions. In L. Finlay & B. Gough (Eds.), *Reflexivity: A practical guide for researchers in health and social sciences* (pp. 39–51). Oxford, England: Blackwell Science.

Mason, J. (2002). *Qualitative researching* (2nd ed.). Thousand Oaks, CA: Sage.

Maxwell, J. A. (2005). *Qualitative research design: An interactive approach* (2nd ed.). Thousand Oaks, CA: Sage.

McAllister, M., & Rowe, J. (2003). Blackbirds singing in the dead of night? Advancing the craft of teaching qualitative research. *Journal of Nursing Education, 42*(7), 296–303.

Merton, R. K., Fiske, M., & Kendall, P. L. (1990). *The focused interview: A manual of problems and procedures* (2nd ed.). New York, NY: Free Press. (Original work published 1956)

Mishler, E. G. (1986). *Research interviewing: Context and narrative.* Cambridge, MA: Harvard University Press.

Morgan, D. L. (1997). *Focus groups as qualitative research* (2nd ed.). Thousand Oaks, CA: Sage.

Morgan, D. L. (2002). Focus group interviewing. In J. F. Gubrium & J. A. Holstein (Eds.), *Handbook of interview research: Context and method* (pp. 141–160). Thousand Oaks, CA: Sage.

Nairn, K., Munro, J., & Smith, A. B. (2005). A counter-narrative of a "failed" interview. *Qualitative Research, 5*(2), 221–244.

Ochs, E. (1979). Transcription as theory. In E. Ochs & B. Shieffelin (Eds.), *Developmental pragmatics* (pp. 43–72). New York, NY: Academic Press.

Oliver, D. G., Serovich, J. M., & Mason, T. L. (2005). Constraints and opportunities with interview transcription: Towards reflection in qualitative research. *Social Forces, 84*(2), 1273–1289.

Peshkin, A. (1988). In search of subjectivity: One's own. *Educational Researcher, 17*(7), 17–22.

Pillow, W. S. (2003). Confession, catharsis, or cure? Rethinking the uses of reflexivity as methodological power in qualitative research. *International Journal of Qualitative Studies in Education, 16*(2), 175–196.

Platt, J. (2002). The history of the interview. In J. F. Gubrium & J. A. Holstein (Eds.), *Handbook of interview research: Context and method* (pp. 33–54). Thousand Oaks, CA: Sage.

Poland, B. D. (2002). Transcription quality. In J. F. Gubrium & J. A. Holstein (Eds.), *Handbook of interview research: Context and method* (pp. 629–650). Thousand Oaks, CA: Sage.

Pollio, H. R., Henley, T. B., & Thompson, C. J. (1997). *The phenomenology of everyday life: Empirical investigations of human experience.* Cambridge, England: Cambridge University Press.

Powers, W. R. (2005). *Transcription techniques for the spoken word.* Lanham, MD: AltaMira Press.

Price, B. (2002). Laddered questions and qualitative data research interviews. *Journal of Advanced Nursing, 37*(3), 273–281.

Puchta, C., & Potter, J. (2004). *Focus group practice.* London, England: Sage.

Rapley, T. J. (2004). Interviews. In C. Seale, G. Gobo, J. Gubrium, & D. Silverman (Eds.), *Qualitative research practice* (pp. 15–33). London, England: Sage.

Reinharz, S., & Chase, S. E. (2002). Interviewing women. In J. F. Gubrium & J. A. Holstein (Eds.), *Handbook of interview research: Context and method* (pp. 221–238). Thousand Oaks, CA: Sage.

Riessman, C. K. (1987). When gender is not enough: Women interviewing women. *Gender & Society, 1*(2), 172–207.

Riesman, D. (1951). Some observations on social science research. *The Antioch Review, 11*(3), 259–278.

Riesman, D. (1952). *Faces in the crowd.* New Haven, CT: Yale University Press.

Riesman, D., & Benney, M. (1956). The sociology of the interview. *Midwestern Sociologist, 18,* 3–15.

Riesman, D., & Glazer, N. (1948). Social structure, character structure, and opinion. *International Journal of Opinion and Attitude Research, 2,* 512–527.

Rifkin, S. B., & Hartley, S. D. (2001). Learning by doing: Teaching qualitative methods to health care personnel. *Education for Health, 14,* 75–85.

Ritchie, D. A. (2003). *Doing oral history: A practical guide* (2nd ed.). Oxford, England: Oxford University Press.

Rolls, L., & Relf, M. (2006). Bracketing interviews: Addressing methodological challenges in qualitative interviewing in bereavement and palliative care. *Mortality, 11*(3), 286–305.

Roulston, K. (2010). *Reflective interviewing: A guide to theory and practice.* London, England: Sage.

Roulston, K. (2011). Interview "problems" as topics for analysis. *Applied Linguistics, 32*(1), 77–94.

Roulston, K., Baker, C. D., & Liljestrom, A. (2001). Analyzing the interviewer's work in the generation of research data: The case of complaints. *Qualitative Inquiry, 7*(6), 745–772.

Roulston, K., deMarrais, K., & Lewis, J. B. (2003). Learning to interview in the social sciences. *Qualitative Inquiry, 9*(4), 643–668.

Roulston, K., McClendon, V. J., Thomas, A., Tuff, R., Williams, G., & Healy, M. F. (2008). Developing reflective interviewers and reflexive researchers. *Reflective Practice, 9*(3), 231–243.

Salmons, J. (2010). *Online interviews in real time.* London, England: Sage.

Schuman, H., & Presser, S. (1981). *Questions and answers in attitude surveys: Experiments on question form, wording, and content.* New York, NY: Academic Press.

Seidman, I. (2006). *Interviewing as qualitative research: A guide for researchers in education and the social sciences* (3rd ed.). New York, NY: Teachers College.

Smith, L. T. (1999). *Decolonizing methodologies: Research and indigenous peoples.* London, England: Zed Books.

Spradley, J. P. (1979). *The ethnographic interview.* Fort Worth, TX: Harcourt Brace Jovanovich.

Stark, S., & Watson, K. (1999). Passionate pleas for "passion please": Teaching for qualitative research. *Qualitative Health Research, 9*(6), 719–730.

Stephens, N. (2007). Collecting data from elites and ultra elites: Telephone and face-to-face interviews with macroeconomists. *Qualitative Research, 7*(2), 203–216.

Stewart, D. W., Shamdasani, P. N., & Rook, D. W. (2007). *Focus groups: Theory and practice* (Vol. 20). Thousand Oaks, CA: Sage.

Tanggaard, L. (2007). The research interview as discourses crossing swords: The researcher and apprentice on crossing roads. *Qualitative Inquiry, 13*(1), 160–176.

Tanggaard, L. (2008). Objections in research interviewing. *International Journal of Qualitative Methods, 7*(3), 15–29. Retrieved from http://ejournals.library.ualberta.ca/index.php/IJQM/article/view/1827/3449

Uhrenfeldt, L., Paterson, B., & Hall, E. O. C. (2007). Using videorecording to enhance the development of novice researchers' interviewing skills. *International Journal of Qualitative Methods, 6*(1), 36–50. Retrieved from http://www.ualberta.ca/~iiqm/backissues/6_1/uhrenfeldt.pdf

Wanat, C. L. (2008). Getting past the gatekeepers: Differences between access and cooperation in public school research. *Field Methods, 20*(2), 191–208.

Wellin, C. (2007). Narrative interviewing: Process and benefits in teaching about aging and the life course. *Gerontology & Geriatrics Education, 28*(1), 79–99.

Wengraf, T. (2001). *Qualitative research interviewing: Biographic narrative and semi-structured methods.* London, England: Sage.

Yow, V. R. (2005). *Recording oral history: A guide for the humanities and social sciences* (2nd ed.). Walnut Creek, CA: AltaMira Press.

Part II

METHODS OF INTERVIEWING

5

SURVEY INTERVIEWING

◆ Royce A. Singleton Jr. and Bruce C. Straits

Until recently, surveys were carried out via telephone or face-to-face interviews or via mailed questionnaires. Developments in computer-assisted interviewing (CAI) and Internet-based surveys, however, have challenged the traditional distinction between an interview survey and a mail survey. Now, it is more appropriate to think of the various modes of data collection as falling along a continuum from the most to the least interactive. At one end of this continuum, involving all channels of communication, is the face-to-face interview; this is followed, in turn, by telephone interviews, Internet interviews, computer-assisted self-interviews, and self-administered questionnaires. Also, some surveys employ a mixture of data collection modes, such as a study incorporating a confidential self-administered form within face-to-face interviews as a means of collecting sensitive information about socially undesirable behaviors.

This chapter focuses on face-to-face and telephone interviews: surveys in which a researcher or, more commonly, an agent of the researcher interacts directly with a respondent. Face-to-face interviews were the dominant mode of survey data collection until the 1970s, when improved methods and an increasing proportion of households with telephones made telephone interviewing more viable and practical. Today, many polling agencies rely exclusively on telephone interviews, while many large-scale academic and government surveys are still conducted with face-to-face interviews.

In the past half-century, surveys have become ubiquitous data-gathering devices used by social scientists, federal government agencies, the media, and other commercial interests to test models of human behavior, estimate population trends, gauge public opinion, and assess consumer preferences. Regardless of purpose, the value of surveys ultimately rests on how accurately they measure population characteristics. Robert Groves's (1989) "total error perspective" identifies four types of errors that threaten the accuracy of survey results. *Sampling error*, the difference between a population value and a sample estimate of that value, occurs because only a sample rather than a complete census of the population is surveyed. Because sampling error is primarily a function of sampling design, sample size, and population heterogeneity, and not a function of the data collection process, our focus here is on the three other nonsampling errors: *coverage error*, resulting from the failure to give some members of the target population any chance of being included in the sample; *nonresponse error*, due to the failure to obtain data from all sampled persons; and *measurement error*, due to inaccuracies in what respondents report.

In describing interviewing, we review current knowledge regarding sources of interviewer-related error and common procedures for minimizing interviewer effects. Interviewer effects became an issue early in the history of survey research, when studies demonstrated the influence of interviewer ideology (Rice, 1929) and expectations (e.g., Hyman, 1954) on responses. By the 1950s, survey practitioners had developed widely accepted, standard survey interviewing practices designed to reduce interviewer error. These practices, still dominant in interviewer training, emphasized the highly structured role of the interviewer, who read questions as a neutral agent while the respondent passively answered them. As improved methods lessened concerns about interviewer effects, survey researchers gradually shifted the focus from the role of the interviewer to the role of the respondent and developed a more complex view of the interaction between interviewer and respondent (O'Muircheartaigh, 1997). This shift in perspective has renewed interest in interviewing techniques and stimulated considerable research.

Once the goals of the survey are established, the researcher initially must (a) develop a sampling plan, (b) devise appropriate questions, and (c) select the survey mode. Selection of the survey mode depends on several factors, including study goals, the nature of the questions, the target population, funds, and other available resources. The objective is to choose the survey mode that maximizes data quality (error reduction) within cost and resource constraints.

Face-to-face interviews, in comparison with telephone interviews, (a) offer more flexibility in terms of question content and target population, (b) tend to generate higher response rates, (c) are more appropriate for long interviews with complex questions, (d) permit visual aids in presenting questions and response options, and (e) enable unobtrusive interviewer observations of the respondents and their surroundings. By comparison, telephone interviews (a) are cheaper, (b) are easier to administer, (c) require a shorter data collection period, and (d) permit greater control over interviewer training, supervision, and data collection quality (Groves et al., 2009, pp. 160–175; Singleton & Straits, 2010, pp. 281–287).

Selecting a mode of data collection, developing a sampling design, and devising a preliminary survey instrument complete the planning phase of the survey. The fieldwork phase then begins. This phase starts with the recruitment of interviewers, continues with interviewer training and instrument pretesting, and concludes with interviewing and field supervision. Figure 5.1 depicts the steps in survey interviewing.

◆ Interviewer Recruitment and Selection

Interviewer selection may influence the quality of surveys insofar as interviewer attributes affect the interviewer's ability to perform the job or the manner in which respondents interpret and answer questions. Hence, survey researchers are concerned not only with hiring people who are competent to carry out interviewing tasks but also with identifying and controlling visible background traits that might affect responses. Although certain skills such as reading and writing are clearly necessary for interviewing, researchers have found no consistent correlates between interviewer characteristics, including formal education, and the quality of interviewing (Fowler, 1991). One meta-analysis of hundreds of studies (Sudman & Bradburn, 1974) showed only that interviewers under 25 (mainly college students) produced more errors than others;[1] however, this appeared to be an artifact stemming from the inexperience and lack of training of student interviewers (Bradburn, 1983).

With regard to the impact of interviewer demographic characteristics on how people respond, two

---

[1]Interviewer-related error has been measured in various ways. The most commonly used measure, the intraclass correlation, compares the variation in responses among different interviewers with the total variation in responses (see Groves, 1989). The more alike the responses obtained by one interviewer relative to those obtained by another, the higher the correlation. Researchers also have calculated the association between interviewer traits (e.g., race, gender) and answers to particular questions. Finally, in rare instances, researchers have directly measured response accuracy associated with different interviewers by comparing survey answers against records or other behavioral evidence (e.g., Anderson, Silver, & Abramson, 1988a).

Figure 5.1 Steps in Survey Interviewing

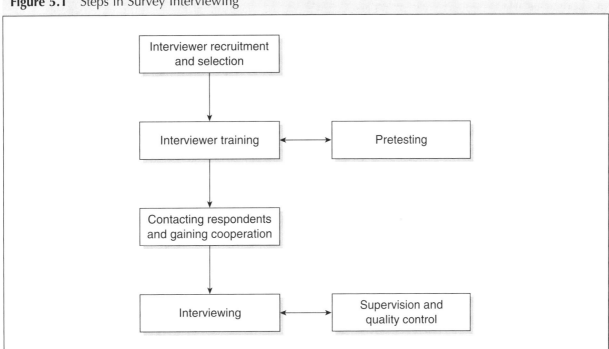

generalizations are consistent with research findings. First, despite abundant research, few studies have found any association; second, the few positive findings suggest that interviewer traits may have an effect when they stimulate respondents' apprehension about normatively appropriate responses (Fowler, 1991). Several studies (e.g., Anderson, Silver, & Abramson, 1988b; Davis, 1997; Finkel, Guterbock, & Borg, 1991; Hatchett & Schuman, 1976; Krysan & Couper, 2003; Schuman & Converse, 1971) have shown, for example, that the race of the interviewer affects racially relevant responses. In general, blacks express more antiblack and conservative sentiments to white interviewers than to black interviewers, and whites give more problack and liberal answers to black interviewers than to white interviewers. Less is known about whether other demographic variables such as age, gender, and class have the same effect as race, although this seems likely when a specific interviewer trait is particularly relevant. For instance, Emily Kane and Laura Macaulay (1993) found gender-of-interviewer effects on several items measuring gender role attitudes, with both male and female respondents tending to give more egalitarian responses to female interviewers than to male interviewers.[2]

What are the implications of these findings? Because interviewer attributes seldom have been found to affect responses, there is little basis for choosing one interviewer over another. The exception occurs when interviewer characteristics are particularly relevant to the question, which is most apparent in questions pertaining to race. When race is a major topic, researchers often attempt to control for race-of-interviewer effects by matching the race of the interviewer with the race of the respondent. The assumption is that an interviewer who resembles the respondent will obtain more valid data than one who does not. Even race matching may be of limited utility, however, as evidence suggests that the interviewer's race makes little difference on most survey questions (Schuman & Converse, 1971), and some research calls into question the assumption that race matching enhances validity (Anderson et al., 1988a).

[2]Both race- and gender-of-interviewer effects may be due to the general tendency to give socially desirable answers to controversial questions. Streb, Burrell, Frederick, and Genovese (2008) recently showed that "evidence of social desirability goes well beyond interviewer effects" (p. 79). Using an unobtrusive measure—the list experiment—they found considerably more discontent about the possibility of a "woman serving as president" than traditional public opinion polls indicate, suggesting a tendency to express opinions consistent with the norm of gender equality.

Rather than using race matching to control for race-of-interviewer effects, Robert Groves and associates (2009, p. 294) argue that the best approach may be to randomly assign interviewers to respondents, which makes it possible to measure interviewer-related error.

The process of recruiting interviewers is basically the same as hiring for any job. That is, positions are advertised; applicants are screened and selected. Beyond minimum reading and writing skills, availability and readiness to meet the job requirements are the principal selection criteria.[3] Other interviewer attributes are largely dependent on market forces. The majority of interviewers, according to data from a sample of interviewers at U.S. government statistical agencies, do not regard their job as a primary source of income or career, perhaps because of the intermittent nature of the work (Groves & Couper, 1998, p. 198). This work feature as well as the job requisites also may account for the composition of the interviewer workforce, which is predominantly female, young to middle-aged, and with above-average education. Since such attributes are largely beyond the control of the researcher, it is fortunate that they appear to be much less important in determining the quality of a survey than the interviewer's ability achieved through careful training and experience.

◆ *Interviewer Training*

Survey interviewers are required to do more than simply ask questions and record answers. In general, they must complete four tasks (Lessler, Eyerman, & Wang, 2008): (1) implement a procedure for locating or contacting respondents, (2) persuade respondents to participate, (3) collect information from respondents, and (4) edit and transmit the data. The first of these tasks is more complex in face-to-face interviews; the last is automatic in computer-assisted interviews. To carry out these tasks, interviewers receive training in general interviewing skills and techniques as well as in specific procedures required for a particular survey project. In practice, these two aspects of training

often are combined, with survey-specific materials (e.g., questionnaire or sampling procedures) used for practical application.

The typical training program combines home study with a series of classroom sessions. The first session might begin with a general introduction to the study, followed by a presentation and instruction in basic interviewing skills and responsibilities. In the second session, the researcher would thoroughly familiarize interviewers with the survey questionnaire, going over the entire instrument item by item, explaining the importance of each item, giving instructions for recording responses, and providing examples of problematic responses and ways to deal with them. Next, the researcher would conduct a demonstration interview and then divide interviewers into pairs for supervised practice interviewing. The third and subsequent sessions would involve further practice, possibly including field experience, and further evaluation. Experienced interviewers generally receive survey-specific training through home study of the project's special interviewing procedures and survey instrument followed by discussions or mock interviews with a field manager.

The length of the general training period varies, from less than 1 day in many surveys to 3 to 5 days in government and academic survey organizations (Fowler & Mangione, 1990). Telephone interviewing requires a shorter training period than in-person interviews. Studies that have examined the impact of training on interview skills suggest that less than 1 day is inadequate and 3 days may be optimal (Billiet & Loosveldt, 1988; Fowler & Mangione, 1990). For example, Floyd Fowler and Thomas Mangione (1990) found that interviewers with less than 1 day of training were significantly worse than those with 2 or more days of training on several skills, such as reading questions correctly and probing when respondents gave incomplete or ambiguous answers. Analyses further suggested that supervised practice made the critical difference in interviewer skills and that a protracted training period of 10 days was counterproductive, producing more interviewer-related error. Such findings imply that adequate training reduces measurement error associated with the interviewer's ability to follow instructions in

---

[3]Surveys of target populations with large percentages of non–English-speaking people may require the recruitment of bilingual interviewers. The need to conduct interviews in a foreign language raises numerous questions that are beyond the scope of the present chapter. Historically, most U.S. surveys, including virtually all of those reviewed here, have avoided such issues by limiting their target populations to those who speak English. Obviously, that solution may result in a large coverage error.

administering the survey instrument. On the other hand, Fowler and Mangione found no significant effects of training on response rates, a source of non-response error. More recently, training regimens have introduced special techniques for gaining a respondent's cooperation (e.g., O'Brien, Mayer, Groves, & O'Neill, 2002), which we discuss.

◆ Evaluating Survey Questions

The process of designing and evaluating survey questions and procedures may involve one or more phases or methods. Initially, experts may review drafts of survey questions, with persons knowledgeable in the survey topic assessing whether the questions meet the study objectives and survey methodologists assessing whether they are consistent with the principles of good questionnaire design (Groves et al., 2009). Also, at an early stage of the evaluation, skilled interviewers may conduct focused discussions with small groups of participants (usually five to eight). Having already identified key topics and developed preliminary questions, the researchers ask the focus groups to share their perceptions and reactions to these items. In this way, the participants can help evaluate the researchers' assumptions about reality and the appropriateness of the vocabulary (Fowler, 1995). In planning a survey of sexual practices among teenagers, for example, teen focus groups could provide insight into how teens cognitively organize, label, and retrieve sexual information.

PRETESTING THROUGH COGNITIVE INTERVIEWING

Once a draft of the survey instrument has been prepared, the next step is to pretest questions to determine if respondents clearly understand and are able to answer them. Traditionally, pretesting has been done solely "in the field"—that is, in the homes of respondents drawn from the target population. However, sparked by interest in the cognitive aspects of surveys (Sirken et al., 1999; Tanur, 1992; Willis, 2005), in the 1980s, researchers began to test questions in the laboratory. The goal of laboratory testing, or "cognitive interviewing," is to understand the thought processes involved when respondents answer survey questions and to use this information to identify problems and formulate better questions. The cognitive laboratories

established at the Census Bureau and other federal statistical agencies typically use paid subjects who are recruited to intensive sessions lasting 1 to 2 hours. The primary techniques are "think-aloud" interviews and probing (Beatty & Willis, 2007; Willis, 2005).

In think-aloud interviews, the respondents are asked to think out loud, reporting everything that comes to mind while arriving at answers to the questions. Either they verbalize their thought processes concurrently as they work out an answer to each question or retrospectively, after they answer each question or complete the survey. In a tobacco use survey, the think-aloud procedure uncovered ambiguities in the question "How many times during the past 12 months have you stopped smoking for 1 day or longer?" The question was intended to measure attempts to quit smoking; however,

> several respondents included instances when they had not smoked for at least one day because of illness, excessive drinking the previous day, or other extraneous circumstances. The revised version makes the intent clearer, asking specifically, "How many times during the past twelve months have you stopped smoking for one day or longer because you were trying to quit smoking?" (DeMaio & Rothgeb, 1996, pp. 182–183)

A more proactive approach involves asking follow-up questions that probe the basis of a respondent's answers. An interviewer can focus on particular aspects of cognitive processes by asking, for example, "What did you think I meant by 'stopping smoking'?" Probes may directly follow each question (when the information used to answer the question is freshest in memory) or come at the end of the survey (to avoid reactivity or bias associated with the probing). Probing also may vary in the extent to which it is standardized or can be used at the interviewer's discretion (Conrad & Blair, 2009). Here is an example of probes used to pretest a question intended for elderly people:

> Question: By yourself and without using special equipment, how much difficulty do you have bathing or showering, some, a lot, or are you unable to do it?
>
> Probes: "I said without using special equipment. What sort of things do you think would be special equipment?" "Do you use anything to help you bathe or shower?" (Jobe, Keller, & Smith, 1996, p. 201)

Think-aloud procedures are relatively standardized and can be administered by interviewers with limited training and knowledge of questionnaire design; however, respondents may have great difficulty describing their thought processes, and some research raises questions about whether thinking aloud literally reflects thought processes (Beatty & Willis, 2007). By comparison, probing is more artificial and subject to reactivity but focuses attention on pertinent issues and appears to interfere less with the actual process of responding. In practice, the two methods are complementary, with one or the other more optimal depending on the cognitive ability of respondents, the question topic, and the survey mode (Beatty & Willis, 2007). Both procedures generate useful information about respondents' thought processes, although research indicates that they are more effective in identifying question problems than in finding ways to resolve them (Forsyth, Rothgeb, & Willis, 2004).

FIELD PRETESTING

The information gained by these cognitive diagnostic procedures gives direction to revision efforts. Often, several pretests and revisions may be necessary to arrive at a good semifinal draft. Once the questionnaire is in this form, it routinely is tested in the field under more realistic interviewing conditions. This phase of pretesting may be carried out before or as part of interviewer training, either with experienced interviewers or with interviewers-in-training. Typically, field pretesting is based on 25 to 50 interviews with a convenience sample of persons having characteristics similar to those in the target population. Interviewers both administer the questionnaire and observe the process to identify practical problems in following procedures as well as questions that respondents have trouble answering. While they may take notes during the interviews and file reports afterward, their observations generally are conveyed in a group oral debriefing (Converse & Presser, 1986).

Field pretests provide the ultimate "dress rehearsal" of the instrument and procedures; however, they have several limitations (Fowler, 1995; Fowler & Cannell, 1996; Presser et al., 2004). Playing the role of interviewer may interfere with the task of observing the process; each interviewer's observations are based on a small number of interviews, which may not be adequate for reliably assessing question problems; the standards for evaluation may not be well articulated or may be applied inconsistently, resulting in a lack of agreement about problem questions; and the recognition of question comprehension problems is limited to items in which respondents ask for clarification or give inappropriate answers. Some of these problems may be addressed by cognitive laboratory interviewing. But recently, several strategies have been applied to make field pretesting more systematic and reliable. These include behavior coding, respondent debriefings, interviewing ratings, split-panel tests, and response analysis.

Behavior coding originally was developed to evaluate interviewer performance (e.g., Cannell, Miller, & Oksenberg, 1981). It consists of systematically coding the frequency of problematic respondent and interviewer behaviors with respect to each question in a live or taped interview. Such behaviors include (a) interviewers incorrectly reading or skipping questions, (b) respondents interrupting interviewers before the question is completely read, (c) respondents requesting that the question be repeated or clarified, and (d) interviewers probing to follow up on inadequate answers (Fowler, 1995, pp. 116–121).[4]

Whereas behavior coding may be conducted without respondents knowing the purpose of the inquiry, respondent debriefings enlist their cooperation. Like cognitive interviewing, this method uses probes to analyze respondents' interpretations of survey questions. Probes may test respondents' interpretations of terminology, question intent, or instructions; subjective reactions or thoughts during questioning; and missed or misreported information (Martin, 2004). As an example of the latter, to determine if a question on income is yielding accurate information, respondents could be asked if they reported net or gross income and if they included specific income sources (Martin, 2004, p. 167).

The pretest interviewers can provide another perspective on question-and-answer problems. Customarily, interviewer debriefings entailed informal group discussions with the interviewers, but

---

[4]This approach has been applied to electronically transcribed interviews (Bolton & Bronkhorst, 1996) and extended beyond the coding of individual behaviors to the sequence of interviewer–respondent interactions (van der Zouwen & Smit, 2004).

Fowler (1995, pp. 121–124) recommends that the interviewers fill out standardized ratings of each question prior to the debriefing session to collect more systematic information.

Finally, two other methods require somewhat larger pretest samples. Experimental manipulations of question ordering, wording, and formats, called split-panel or split-ballot tests, are a costly but effective way to check out suspected problems or weaknesses under field conditions. Split-panel tests require the random assignment of adequate-sized samples of pretest respondents to the version being tested. For example, the results of cognitive interviewing might suggest a serious problem of question-order effects. This suspicion could be experimentally tested by randomly assigning pretest respondents to two forms of the instrument in which the order of related questions differs and then comparing the responses on the two forms. In contrast to other pretesting methods, which are most useful in identifying question problems, experiments test whether question revisions solve the problem.

The responses of the pretest respondents also can be tabulated and examined for problems such as (a) a low response rate to sensitive questions, (b) the incidence of "don't know" responses, (c) items where nearly everyone makes the same response, and (d) the adequacy of responses to open-ended questions. The generalizability of a response analysis depends on the pretest sample size and the degree to which the pretest respondents resemble the target population.

Each of these pretesting techniques offers a slightly different window on the question-and-answer process: (a) behavior coding—interviewer–respondent interaction under actual field conditions, (b) respondent debriefings and other cognitive interviewing methods—problems from the respondent's perspective, (c) interviewer debriefings—problems from the interviewer's perspective, (d) response analysis—problems from the researcher's perspective, and (e) split-panel tests—differences among instrument versions. This suggests that some pretest methods are better than others at identifying particular types of question problems. To test this idea, Stanley Presser and Johnny Blair (1994) systematically compared four pretest methods: (1) conventional field pretesting with oral group debriefings, (2) behavior coding of live pretest interviews, (3) cognitive interviewing combining follow-up probes with concurrent and retrospective think-alouds, and (4) expert panels. Each method was applied to a single questionnaire in repeated trials. Results indicated that behavior coding was the most reliable and conventional pretesting the least reliable; expert panels identified the largest number of problems and were the least costly; expert panels and cognitive interviewing were the only means likely to spot problems affecting the data analysis; and conventional pretesting and behavior coding were the only effective methods for spotting problems involving the interviewer. Noting that the expert panel was the most cost-effective, Presser and Blair argued that questionnaire drafts should be routinely subjected to a peer review process. Their results also imply that questionnaires should be subjected to more than one form of pretesting. Indeed, the use of multiple techniques is critical to any comprehensive program of pretesting, as it capitalizes on the strengths of individual techniques while compensating for the unique weaknesses associated with each (Esposito & Rothgeb, 1997).

◆ Securing Respondents

Because only random samples provide unbiased estimates of population characteristics and the means of calculating the margin of sampling error, virtually all major surveys use some form of random or probability sampling. It is common in face-to-face surveys to randomly select individuals from randomly chosen households from randomly chosen blocks within sampled counties or metropolitan areas. Similarly, most telephone surveys use a technique called random digit dialing to choose telephone numbers randomly; in its simplest form, telephone prefixes (exchanges) within the target geographical area are sampled and then the last four digits of the telephone number are chosen randomly.

The interviewer's responsibility in the sampling process ordinarily consists of following specified rules to select an eligible respondent within each designated or telephone household. In most face-to-face interviews, prospective respondents first receive letters introducing them to the survey and notifying them that they will be contacted. Once someone answers the door, the interviewer introduces himself or herself, explains the purpose of the visit, presents credentials or other supporting documents (e.g., brochures, identification card), identifies the eligible household member, and asks for his or her cooperation. This scenario is similar in random digit dialing telephone surveys except that prior notification often is not possible and other means of legitimating the survey request are more limited.

To obtain responses, interviewers must contact or reach the sample person, and they must persuade him or her to cooperate by completing the survey. Statistical estimates from surveys are considered unbiased when all sampled persons are measured. Anything less may create nonresponse error or bias, which is a function of the proportion of noncontacts and refusals (nonresponse rate) and the difference between respondents and nonrespondents. Because the latter difference is almost always unknown, most surveys report the nonresponse rate as an indicator of sample quality. The implicit assumption is that "the higher the response rate, the lower the nonresponse bias" (Groves, 1989, p. 209). Although recent research calls into question the strength of this assumption (Groves, 2006), survey practice still emphasizes obtaining as large a proportion of the sample as possible to reduce error (see, e.g., Peytchev, Baxter, & Carley-Baxter, 2009).

Making contact with designated households is primarily a matter of persistence and overcoming barriers. To maximize the likelihood that respondents are at home at the time of the initial contact, some survey organizations limit the hours of contact to weekdays after 4 p.m. and weekends. If no one is available, interviewers make repeated callbacks, typically at least 6 for face-to-face surveys and 10 or more for telephone surveys (Fowler, 2009, p. 56). To increase the odds of contacting persons with different at-home patterns, they also vary the time of calls between daytime, evening, and weekends. Finally, interviewers may leave notes, ask neighbors or apartment managers when people are usually at home, and obtain telephone numbers to set up appointments.

Avoiding refusals is a more difficult problem with a more complex set of causes. Some of those causes lie in the social environment and in the demographic characteristics of nonrespondents. For example, some studies indicate that men, those living alone, and those living in urban areas are more likely to refuse than their counterparts (Groves & Couper, 1998; Groves et al., 2009). Other causes of refusals reside in the characteristics of the interviewer, the survey design and procedures, and interviewer–respondent interaction. Because survey design and interaction variables are under the control of the researcher or interviewer, they offer the most promising lines of inquiry for overcoming resistance to cooperation.

Many survey procedures that are intended to enhance the likelihood of gaining cooperation are based on a social exchange theory of human behavior (Dillman, Smyth, & Christian, 2009; Goyder, 1987). According to this view, the greater the perceived rewards relative to the perceived costs of complying with an interview request, the more likely it is that a householder will cooperate. Survey researchers may attempt to provide rewards by showing positive regard for respondents, expressing appreciation, and pointing out the social utility of the survey; they attempt to reduce costs by making the interview as short as possible or otherwise minimizing the burden of responding (Dillman et al., 2009, pp. 23–30). Research also supports the utility of promising or giving respondents cash or a token gift (e.g., a pen, a calendar) when they are contacted. Singer, Hoewyk, Gebler, Raghunathan, and McGonagle's (1999) meta-analysis of 39 experiments in telephone and face-to-face interview surveys showed that both monetary and nonmonetary incentives increased response rates even when the cash amount was relatively small (less than US$10) and the burden of the interview was low. Other research shows that respondents are more likely to comply when the survey topic is of high than of low salience to them (Goyder, 1987; Groves, Presser, & Dipko, 2004; Hox & de Leeuw, 1994), presumably because answering high-salience questions is more interesting and rewarding.

In survey interviews, it is the interviewer who ultimately mediates such design features. Indeed, the interaction between interviewer and respondent appears to play a large part in the decision to cooperate or refuse. According to Robert Groves and Mick Couper's (1996, 1998) theory of survey participation, in the initial moments of the survey encounter, the sample person is actively trying to comprehend the purpose of the interviewer's visit. He or she uses cues from the words, behavior, and physical appearance of the interviewer to arrive at an explanation (or identify a "script") and then evaluates the costs of continuing the conversation. Whether the person eventually agrees or refuses to participate depends on the interviewer's ability to quickly and accurately judge the particular script reflected in the householder's initial response and to react accordingly.

Consistent with the theory, experienced interviewers use two related strategies to convince respondents to participate. First, they tailor their approach to the sample unit, adjusting their dress, mannerisms, language, and arguments according to their observations of the neighborhood, the housing unit, and the immediate reactions of the householder. Second, they maintain interaction, which maximizes the possibility of identifying relevant cues for tailoring the conversation to present the most effective arguments.[5] Robert Groves and Katherine McGonagle (2001) demonstrated the merit of this theoretical framework in a telephone survey in which an interview training protocol was designed to impart skills in tailoring and to emphasize rapid interviewer response. In two experimental tests, interviewers who received the training had higher cooperation rates than those who did not. Eileen O'Brien and associates (2002) also demonstrated the effectiveness of a similar program, called refusal aversion training, in a national face-to-face interview survey; however, two other studies (McConaghy & Carey, 2004; Shuttles, Welch, Hoover, & Lavrakas, 2002) found no significant effect of refusal aversion training on cooperation rates.

The theory of survey participation applies mainly to face-to-face interviews. The cues for tailoring are much richer, and it is easier to prolong the conversation in face-to-face conversations than in telephone conversations. Fewer normative constraints for maintaining telephone conversations make telephone surveys easier to terminate; and refusals tend to occur in the first minute, before any argument for participating can be presented (Couper & Groves, 2002). In telephone surveys, there are also fewer means of legitimating the survey request, as there is no opportunity to present identification badges or brochures and no visual contact with the interviewer (de Leeuw & Hox, 2004). Given these more limited sources of influence, it is not surprising that refusal rates are higher and response rates consistently lower in telephone surveys than in face-to-face surveys (Hox & de Leeuw, 1994).[6] To increase response rates in telephone surveys, researchers increasingly have turned to prepaid incentives and advance letters, both of which have been shown to be effective

(Cantor, O'Hare, & O'Connor, 2008; de Leeuw, Callegro, Hox, Korendijk, & Lensvelt-Mulders, 2007; Link & Mokdad, 2005).

Other research suggests that in telephone surveys, the interviewer's vocalization, apart from the content of the communication, may affect compliance rates. Lois Oksenberg and Charles Cannell (1988; see also Oksenberg, Coleman, & Cannell, 1986) asked subjects to rate the tape-recorded voices of interviewers who were giving actual introductions to a telephone survey. Interviewers who obtained higher cooperation rates were perceived as speaking louder and more rapidly and as sounding more confident and competent. However, using a superior research design, Groves, O'Hare, Gould-Smith, Benki, and Maher (2008) recently failed to replicate the positive effects of fast speech and perceived confidence. They found that speech variation across contacts, for example, in pitch and speed, are important predictors of response rates and that the most successful interviewers were judged as less scripted, less breathy, and less masculine sounding. Moreover, unlike in prior research (Oksenberg & Cannell, 1988; Van der Vaart, Ongena, Hoogendoorn, & Dijkstra, 2005), acoustic measurements added predictive power. Although the practical value of these findings is not clear-cut, Groves et al. (2008) recommend training interviewers to guard against appearing to be scripted and speeding up their speech under stress.

Finally, survey practitioners use various methods to convert householders who are reluctant to cooperate when initially contacted. Often, they assign more experienced interviewers or supervisors to recontact those who refuse to participate, or they may employ highly effective interviewers known as "converters." Groves (1990) reports that a conversion rate of 20% to 40% is common in telephone surveys; and one academic-based, national face-to-face survey reports successful conversions of 35% to 45% (Davis & Smith, 1992).[7] Another common practice is to mail special persuasion letters that reiterate the importance

---

[5]Robert Groves, Eleanor Singer, and Amy Corning (2000) built on Groves and Couper's work in their formulation of leverage-saliency theory. They proposed that respondents are influenced to participate in a survey as a function of the importance (leverage) of various survey features and the degree to which each feature is emphasized (i.e., its salience) in requests to participate.

[6]Besides having lower rates of response than personal interviews, telephone interviews have shown a steady increase in nonresponse in recent decades due to massive changes in telephone technology and other social changes such as increased concern about privacy and the growth of telemarketing (Curtin, Presser, & Singer, 2005; de Leeuw & de Heer, 2002).

[7]As in research on the factors affecting initial cooperation in surveys, Kana Fuse and Doug Xie (2007) found that maintaining interaction with the respondent mattered most in converting a refused case.

of the survey and the respondent's participation in it. Some surveys may buttress these appeals by offering incentive fees to complete the survey, although such refusal conversion payments raise ethical issues regarding equity (Singer, Groves, & Corning, 1999). Also, in telephone and mail surveys, initially reluctant respondents may be contacted through a different, usually more expensive mode; thus, face-to-face contacts sometimes are made with initial refusals in telephone surveys, and telephone contacts may follow up nonreturns in mail surveys.

◆ Interviewing

Once the respondent has agreed to cooperate, the interviewer begins to ask questions and record answers. At this point, the researcher's concern shifts to measurement error, or inaccuracies in the responses to questions. The four principal sources of measurement error are (1) the interviewers, (2) the respondents, (3) the questions, and (4) the mode of data collection. With regard to survey mode, available evidence generally points to small differences between face-to-face and telephone interviews (see Groves et al., 2009, p. 175), suggesting that similar conclusions will be reached independent of the mode, provided that the surveys are competently implemented. A substantial literature exists on question design—the effects of question forms (e.g., open vs. closed), the type of questions (e.g., threatening vs. nonthreatening), question wording, and the order in which questions are asked (Schaeffer & Presser, 2003; Schuman & Presser, 1981). There also is an expansive literature on respondents' question comprehension, memory, motivation, and judgment (Schwarz & Sudman, 1994, 1996; Sudman, Bradburn, & Schwarz, 1996; Tourangeau, Rips, & Rasinski, 2000). Here, we examine the effects of the interviewer. One potential source of influence on respondents' answers, discussed earlier, is the interviewer's social background characteristics. Another is the interviewer's role demands and variations in role behavior.

INTERVIEWING PRACTICES

Survey interviewing is generally synonymous with standardized interviewing. The goal of standardization is to expose each respondent to the same interview experience, so that any differences in the recorded answers are due to differences among respondents "rather than differences in the process that produced the answer" (Fowler & Mangione, 1990, p. 14). To standardize the measurement process, researchers construct structured questionnaires consisting almost entirely of closed-ended questions that are presented in the same order for all respondents, and they carefully prescribe the procedures that interviewers must follow. Ideally, interviewers should be perfectly consistent, neutral intermediaries of the survey researcher. In short, "the goal [of standardized interviewing] is nothing less than the elimination of the interviewer as a source of measurement error" (Groves, 1989, p. 358).

Although specific practices vary from one survey organization to another (Viterna & Maynard, 2002), the following four rules of standardized interviewing, according to Floyd Fowler (1991, p. 264; see also Fowler & Mangione, 1990), are given almost universally to interviewers:

1. Read the questions exactly as written.

2. If a respondent does not answer a question fully, use nondirective follow-up probes to elicit a better answer. Standard probes include repeating the question, asking "Anything else?," "Tell me more," and "How do you mean that?"

3. Record answers to questions without interpretation or editing. When a question is open-ended, this means recording the answer verbatim.

4. Maintain a professional, neutral relationship with the respondent. Do not give personal information, express opinions about the subject matter of the interview, or give feedback that implies a judgment about the content of an answer.

Survey practitioners use several strategies to ensure standardization. Most important, they train interviewers to follow the above rules; as noted earlier, research has shown that interviewers with insufficient training are not adept at applying standardized protocols, especially nondirective probing. Second, field supervisors monitor and provide feedback on interviewers' performance (see discussion of supervision below).

Third, Fowler and Mangione (1990) argue that training respondents in how to participate in the question-and-answer process facilitates carrying out a standardized interview. If respondents better understand their role, they will feel more comfortable and interviewers will feel less awkward in following the rules of standardization. To train respondents, interviewers can read a brief statement before the interview starts that describes the nature of a standardized interview, and they can remind respondents of their role when they fail to perform it appropriately.

Fourth, in a similar vein, Cannell et al. (1981) contend that respondents also need to be *motivated* to perform their role, especially the reporting task. They recommended and tested three principal methods of promoting a good role performance: (1) adding instructional passages to the interview that explain the importance of producing complete and accurate information and how to answer questions adequately, (2) providing differential verbal feedback that positively reinforces good performance and negatively reinforces poor performance, and (3) asking respondents to make an overt agreement to answer questions conscientiously. To standardize the feedback process as much as possible, criteria for judging the respondent's performance and appropriate feedback statements are printed in the questionnaire, and interviewers are trained in their use. In experiments with both face-to-face and telephone interviews, Cannell and his associates (1981; Miller & Cannell, 1982) showed that the use of these techniques improved the quality of reporting. Despite their apparent value and relatively low cost, however, they are seldom used in surveys (Groves et al., 2009, p. 302).

A fifth way to ensure standardization is to reduce the need for interviewers to clarify the meaning of questions to respondents. Research shows that questions that produce the greatest variation among interviewers are those that require the use of follow-up probes to obtain an adequate answer (Mangione, Fowler, & Louis, 1992). And due to variable probing behavior, interviewer error also is correlated with the number of distinct answers to open-ended questions (Groves & Magilavy, 1986). Thus, interviewer error appears to be more likely to occur when questionnaire items are difficult to administer and to answer. One way of minimizing the impact of such questions is to specify more interviewer probes to certain

responses within the survey instrument. The best approach is to identify and correct poorly designed questions with cognitive laboratory and other pretesting techniques before the survey is undertaken.

Finally, for the past four decades, survey practitioners have attempted to increase standardization through the application of computer technology that automates various data collection tasks. CAI techniques replace paper-and-pencil forms with a laptop computer or computer terminal. Interviewers (or respondents) read the survey questions as presented on the computer screen and enter the answers via the keyboard. The application of this technology began in the 1970s with the development of computer-assisted telephone interviewing (CATI). CATI currently is used widely to manage the sampling process, control and monitor interviewer tasks, and expedite data processing. Specifically, CATI systems can automatically dial phone numbers, schedule callbacks, and even screen and select the person to be interviewed at each sampled phone number; prompt the interviewer by providing appropriate introductions, probes, and questions in the proper sequence, skipping irrelevant questions, and identifying responses inconsistent with the replies to earlier questions; alert the interviewer when an illegitimate code is entered and record responses into a computer data file; and maintain records of interviewer productivity that are accessible to survey supervisors and reproduce an interviewer's screen at a supervisor's terminal to allow for audio monitoring (Nicholls, 1988).

With the advent of microcomputers in the 1980s, CAI was extended to face-to-face surveys. In computer-assisted personal interviewing (CAPI), interviewers carry out the survey through a laptop computer, which they bring to the respondent's home; in computer-assisted self-administered interviewing (CASI), the respondent records his or her own answers on a computer provided by an interviewer or researcher.[8] By the late 1990s, Mick Couper and William Nicholls (1998) reported an inexorable movement toward computer-assisted methods, with leading government and private sector survey organizations in Europe and North America already using or in the process of converting to this technology. A decade later, a new technology trend is toward self-administration, as CASI increasingly is used either as an adjunct to CAPI or as a stand-alone

---

[8]In addition to CAPI and CASI, new data collection technologies include audio computer-assisted self-administered interviewing and audio computer-assisted telephone surveys that use voice recording or Touch Tone data entry.

method (Couper, 2008). This may be due in large part to a parallel trend to collect increasingly sensitive information in surveys (Tourangeau & Yan, 2007); abundant evidence shows that respondents give more honest answers on sensitive topics (e.g., illegal or embarrassing activities such as illicit drug use, alcohol consumption, and sexual activity) in self-administered surveys, which create a sense of privacy (Aquilino, 1994; Jobe, Pratt, Tourangeau, Baldwin, & Rasinski, 1997; Tourangeau & Smith, 1996).

CAI methods offer several advantages apart from automating interviewer tasks. They can reduce the costs of data collection, speed up data delivery, and improve data quality by reducing item omissions and data inconsistencies (Baker, Bradburn, & Johnson, 1995; Nicholls, Baker, & Martin, 1997; Weeks, 1992); they also make it easier to randomize question sequences and question wording for experimental tests. Based on their comprehensive review of studies comparing CAI surveys with paper-and-pencil interview surveys, Nicholls et al. (1997) concluded that both respondents and interviewers accept, often enthusiastically, the use of a computer during interviewing and that CATI enhances supervisory quality control. Some research also shows that interviewers may make fewer recording errors in CAI surveys (Lepkowski, Sadosky, & Weiss, 1998).

In the end, Nicholls et al. (1997, p. 242) deduced that comparisons of CAI and paper-and-pencil interview methods may become irrelevant "as CAI becomes the new standard for survey data collection." As this occurs, they argue, research on CAI methodology "should be refocused to inform choices of collection mode, questionnaire design, and field work procedures." Instrument design or layout is particularly important in CAI surveys because the computer exerts greater control over the flow of the interview and the interviewer becomes more dependent on the work of the designer (Couper & Hansen, 2002; Edwards, Schneider, & Brick, 2008).

EVALUATIVE STUDIES

Considerable empirical evidence and sound theoretical arguments justify standardization principles (Fowler, 1991; Fowler & Mangione, 1990). For example, if questions are not asked as worded, one cannot know what question was posed; and numerous experiments have shown that small changes in the wording of questions can alter the distribution of answers (Schuman & Presser, 1981). Also, experiments have demonstrated that suggestive questioning (presenting only a subset of answer alternatives that are presumed to be relevant) and suggestive probing can affect response distributions and relationships with other variables (Smit, Dijkstra, & van der Zouwen, 1997).

Indirect evidence of the effectiveness of standardization derives from studies of interviewer error in well-conducted surveys. When interviewer error is measured in terms of interviewer variation, or the extent to which answers to a question are correlated with the interviewer, the estimates tend to be relatively small (Groves, 1989; de Leeuw & Collins, 1997).[9] There is little direct evidence, however, on the relationship between prescribed interviewer behavior and data quality. On the one hand, observational studies applying behavior coding indicate that even well-trained interviewers often depart from standardized protocols. Fowler (1991) reported studies that showed a range of 5% to 60% of questions at least slightly reworded and a range of 20% to 40% of interviewers using directive or leading probes (see, e.g., Bradburn, Sudman, & Blair, 1979; Cannell & Oksenberg, 1988; Fowler & Mangione, 1990). On the other hand, few studies have related such behavior to interviewer-related error, and even fewer have found a significant correlation. For example, Groves and Magilavy (1986) found no relationship between errors in question reading and interviewer variability. One study (Dykema, Lepkowski, & Blixt, 1997), reportedly the first to test the effect of nonstandardized interviewer behavior on the *accuracy* of responses, analyzed audiotaped in-home interviews in a survey of health and health care utilization. When the researchers compared responses with hospital records, they found no consistent relationship between interviewers' departures from the exact reading of questions and response accuracy. The only exception was one item in which changes in question wording produced *more* accurate reporting.

---

[9]Edith de Leeuw and Martin Collins (1997) report that the intraclass correlation averages around .02 in well-conducted face-to-face surveys and .01 in centrally controlled telephone surveys; however, the total error that is interviewer related is a function of both the intraclass correlation and the number of interviews conducted per interviewer.

More information clearly is needed on what interviewer behaviors contribute most to interviewer-related error. Still, there is little doubt that standardization reduces the interviewer's contribution to measurement error. A more serious, long-standing concern, which resurfaced in the 1990s, is that presenting a standard stimulus in and of itself can produce measurement error. According to this view, standardized interviewing stifles interviewer–respondent communication in two ways: (1) it inhibits the ability to establish rapport, which motivates respondents to cooperate and give complete and accurate answers, and (2) it ignores the detection and correction of communication problems (Beatty, 1995).

The issue of rapport received the most attention during the early development of standardization. By the mid-1970s, a smattering of evidence that personalizing interviews was counterproductive led survey researchers to discredit the value of rapport (Beatty, 1995). Interest in the interviewer–respondent relationship survives today in research on different styles of interviewing. Wil Dijkstra (1987; see also van der Zouwen, Dijkstra, & Smit, 1991) investigated the consequences of a personal versus formal style of interviewing with interviewers who maintained the general rules of standardization. Interviewers trained in the "personal" style were instructed to express a sympathetic attitude toward respondents by making statements such as "I understand what moving to this house meant for you" and "How nice for you!" Those trained in a "formal" style were instructed to be polite but neutral. Results indicated that respondents interviewed in a personal style gave more accurate answers on a map-drawing task, more socially undesirable answers, and fewer "Don't know" responses than those interviewed in a formal style did. But interviewers trained in the personal style also were more likely than interviewers trained in a formal style to use leading probes and accept incomplete answers. Thus, respondent performance may be better with the personal style, but additional training and close supervision may be necessary to offset its undesirable effects.

The second controversy—that standardization sidesteps communication problems—has received a great deal of attention. In a widely cited article, Lucy Suchman and Brigitte Jordan (1990) argued that standardization suppresses elements of ordinary conversation that are crucial for establishing the relevance and meaning of questions. Interviewers who are trained to read questions as written and to discourage elaboration are not prepared to listen carefully for misunderstandings and correct them. From videotapes of standardized interviews, Suchman and Jordan gave several examples of miscommunication, such as an interviewer failing to correct a respondent who interpreted "alcoholic beverages" to include hard liquor but exclude wine, which led to invalid responses. Such problems could be resolved, they claimed, if interviewers were granted the freedom and responsibility to negotiate the intended meaning of questions through ordinary conversational conventions.

While acknowledging the communication problems identified by Suchman and Jordan (1990), advocates of standardized interviewing tend to disagree with them about causes and remedies. Some advocates contend that problems arise chiefly because of poorly worded questions, and whether respondents interpret questions consistently and accurately depends on adequate question pretesting (Kovar & Royston, 1990). Detractors of standardization maintain that efforts to improve question wording are rarely, if ever, sufficient. Researchers need interviewers to help ensure consistent interpretations, but this is unlikely unless interviewers are given a freer hand in communicating with respondents than standardization allows.

Paul Beatty (1995) notes that advocates on both sides of this debate tend to take extreme positions that seem incompatible. He argues, following Nora Cate Schaeffer (1991), that while the problems of standardization should not be overlooked, it is also foolish to ignore its merits. The real issue for him is "How can researchers solve communication problems while harnessing the full benefits of standardization?" One means is the development of better questions; another may involve adapting the role of the interviewer. Both Beatty and Schaeffer (see also Maynard & Schaeffer, 2002) call for empirical research on interaction within the interview to investigate breakdowns in establishing mutual understanding.

At the least, the debate over standardization will continue to raise questions about restrictions on interviewer behavior. Michael Schober and Frederick Conrad's (1997) line of research suggests, for example, that it may be beneficial to give interviewers more leeway in clarifying terms or concepts in survey questions. According to the most stringent view of standardization, interviewers should not attempt to define terms for the respondent, even if scripted definitions are available, because this would make the stimulus inconsistent (Fowler & Mangione, 1990). Initially, Schober and Conrad (1997) conducted a laboratory experiment comparing this form of standardized interviewing with a more flexible method that encouraged interviewers to paraphrase questions, provide definitions in their own words, and ask questions or intervene if they thought the respondent misunderstood the question. In ongoing government surveys, experienced interviewers trained in one of these two interviewing techniques were given fictional scenarios on which to base their answers; in half the scenarios, the circumstances corresponded straightforwardly to government definitions of the terms in the question, and in the other half, they did not. When the mapping between the scenario and question was straightforward, both interviewing methods produced nearly perfect accuracy. But when the mapping was complicated, response accuracy was much higher for the flexible than for the standardized interviewers. This increased accuracy came at a cost, however, as flexible interviewers took nearly three times as long to complete the interview.

In subsequent studies, Schober and Conrad replicated this basic finding—that is, greater response accuracy but more lengthy interviews with flexible interviewing—when they measured natural interviewer deviations from standardization (Schober & Conrad, 1999), when respondents in a household telephone survey were reinterviewed and accuracy was inferred from measures of response change and explanations for answers (Conrad & Schober, 2000), and when interviewers could clarify concepts either with scripted definitions or in their own words and the clarification was either solicited or unsolicited (Schober, Conrad, & Fricker, 2004). Although promising, this research is limited, and the potential of flexible interviewing to improve data quality has not been demonstrated across multiple questions in lengthy, complex surveys (Groves et al., 2009). Groves et al. (2009, p. 314) caution that writing good questions and providing adequate training "are less controversial paths to successful standardized interviews" than allowing interviewers autonomy in helping respondents to understand survey questions. Still, the controversy already may have had an impact on survey practice as evidence shows that many survey centers now allow considerable interviewer autonomy, especially in probing inadequate answers (Viterna & Maynard, 2002).

THE INTERVIEW AS A SOCIAL OCCASION

Schober and Conrad's research draws on theoretical analyses of the process of understanding in ordinary conversations. A key proposition of this theory is that addressees make sense of questions by relying on speakers to help interpret the question—that is, to make sure that the question was understood as intended (Schober, 1999). From this perspective, the problem with strictly standardized interviewing is that interviewers are not supposed to help the respondent interpret the questions, which leaves respondents to arrive at their own, sometimes erroneous, interpretations.

Schober and Conrad's theoretical focus is on the interview as an interactive process. Many other survey methodologists concentrate on the role of the respondent; in so doing, they have drawn heavily on theories of conversational processes as well as from cognitive and social psychology (for detailed discussions, see Schwarz & Sudman, 1996; Sirken et al., 1999; Sudman et al., 1996). While scientifically the survey interview is an occasion to obtain valid responses to a series of questions, it also is a social occasion subject to the influences of the social world. Being interviewed is an uncommon, sometimes apprehensive, experience for many respondents. Unfamiliar with the canons of structured interviewing, they turn to the social and linguistic rules governing everyday conversation for guidance on how they should behave as a respondent. In answering each question, they also attend to a sequence of cognitive tasks with a certain level of ability and motivation. What can each of these perspectives tell us about survey interviewing?

Survey interviews are social encounters between highly trained interviewers and respondents who, at best, receive limited "on-the-job" training. In deciphering their proper role in answering questions, respondents may be unintentionally influenced by subtle aspects of the survey instrument and administration, such as prior questions, response formats, and other cues irrelevant to the intended purpose of the current question. From the perspective of conversational analysis, respondents may rely on the tacit assumptions underlying ordinary conversations, as described by the philosopher of language H. Paul Grice (1989, pp. 22–40), to make sense of survey interviews. According to Grice, conversations generally run smoothly because speakers and listeners follow four maxims:

1. Speakers should not say things that they believe to be false. (Truthfulness)

2. Speakers should make comments that are relevant to the purposes of the conversation. (Relevance)

3. Speakers should make their contributions as informative as possible and not repeat themselves. (Nonredundancy)

4. Speakers should express themselves as clearly as possible. (Clarity)

The principle of relevance, for example, implies that respondents will see everything about the survey as relevant to a given question, including seemingly irrelevant design features such as the numeric values on a rating scale. Schwarz, Knauper, Hippler, Noelle-Neumann, and Clark (1991) demonstrated this by asking respondents to answer the question "How successful would you say you have been in life?" on an 11-point scale, with the end points labeled *not at all successful* and *extremely successful*. The answers, as it turned out, depended on the numeric values assigned to these end points. When the end points ranged from 0 (*not at all successful*) to 10 (*extremely successful*), 34% endorsed a value from 0 to 5, whereas when the end points ranged from −5 (*not at all successful*) to +5 (*extremely successful*), only 13% endorsed a formally equivalent value of −5 to 0. Follow-up questions revealed that the numeric values affected how respondents interpreted the end points. When accompanied by a value of 0, they interpreted "not at all successful" to mean the absence of success, but when accompanied by a value of −5, they interpreted this to mean explicit failure.

These principles imply that interviewers will ask only clear questions that respondents are capable of answering promptly. That is, asking the question presupposes that it can and should be answered. Since respondents will perceive vague, ambiguous, and difficult questions as being relevant, they will feel pressure to respond immediately, even if their reply is a haphazard guess or a hasty estimate. Unless an explicit "Don't know" option is part of an attitudinal question, people without opinions may feel obligated to provide one.

From the perspective of cognitive processing, answering survey questions requires that respondents (a) comprehend the question, (b) retrieve the information requested from memory, (c) formulate a response in accord with the question and the information retrieved, and (d) communicate a response deemed appropriate (Sudman et al., 1996, pp. 58–75; see also Tourangeau et al., 2000). Each of these steps involves mental tasks that can give rise to response errors. For example, to comprehend a question according to what the researcher had in mind, the respondent must understand both its literal and its intended meaning. Therefore, the question–answer task breaks down not only when the question wording is vague but also when the purpose of the question is misunderstood.

Consider the question "What have you done today?" While the literal meaning of the words may be clear, it may not be sufficient to answer the question as the respondent still needs to know what sort of activities are of interest to the researcher. Would this include, for example, mundane activities such as brushing one's teeth and taking a shower? (Schwarz, Groves, & Schuman, 1998). Analyses of the other cognitive steps in the response process indicate that response errors are likely to occur when there is insufficient time to access relevant information from memory, when the accessed information does not fit the response options provided in the question, and when the respondent modifies the information to project a favorable image to the interviewer.

Another theoretical perspective, rational choice theory, focuses on how respondents' *motivation* to provide acceptable answers to survey questions can affect their responses (Alwin, 1991; Krosnick, 1991, 1999). Answering survey questions requires a great deal of mental effort. Some questions, such as those that require memory recall or thoughtful opinions on controversial issues, require more work than others; and lengthy interviews require more effort than shorter ones. When respondents exert the maximum effort to generate a complete and unbiased answer, they are said to be "optimizing"; when they do not expend the necessary effort but take shortcuts, such as not searching their memories thoroughly, they are said to be "satisficing."

Theoretically, the likelihood of satisficing behavior increases with question difficulty and decreases with the respondent's motivation and ability to answer the question. One study (Holbrook, Green, & Krosnick, 2003) compared evidence of satisficing responses in telephone versus personal interview surveys. As evidence of their lesser motivation to provide optimal answers, telephone respondents were judged to be less cooperative and engaged in the interview and expressed more dissatisfaction with the length of the interview. Consistent with the theory, they also evidenced more satisficing behavior. For example, they were more likely to give "No opinion" answers on several attitudinal items and more likely to express agreement on Yes/No and Agree/Disagree questions.

Efforts to apply communication and cognitive theories to the survey process began in the 1980s. With a few notable exceptions, for instance, Groves and Couper's (1996, 1998) theory of survey participation, most applications have been to questionnaire design, including the development of diagnostic procedures for pretesting, described earlier. The time now appears to be ripe for the integration of this work into a broader theory of survey interviewing that fully integrates the interviewer, the respondent, and the task.

◆ Supervision and Quality Control

Once the interviewing phase of the survey begins, the researcher or an interviewer supervisor oversees all aspects of data collection. The supervisor's role involves three interrelated sets of activities: (1) managing the work of interviewers, (2) monitoring their performance, and (3) administering quality control procedures. In their management role, supervisors provide materials, collect completed questionnaires, pay for work done, make themselves available to answer questions and provide help, identify and resolve problems, hold regular meetings with interviewers, and review and give feedback on the interviewers' work.

To detect problems and review interviewers' progress, supervisors monitor their performance. In virtually all surveys, part of performance monitoring involves careful record keeping and evaluation of completed interviews. Records kept on the number of hours worked, amount paid, number of eligible contacts, and number of refusals provide critical information on interviewer productivity, survey costs

(e.g., time and dollars per interview), and survey quality (response and refusal rates). By reviewing completed questionnaires, supervisors also can clarify uncodable responses and check to see if interviewers are following instructions and recording answers appropriately. As Fowler and Mangione (1990, p. 122) point out, however, none of this information assesses the quality of measurement, because it does not reveal what actually occurs during the question-and-answer process. To tell if interviewers ask questions exactly as written, use neutral probes, and record answers correctly, many survey organizations also monitor or observe the interview process.

In face-to-face interview surveys, supervisors may observe interviewers by either accompanying them on interviews or making recordings of all or a sample of their interviews. Direct field observation is much more costly and possibly more intrusive, although it provides the most information, including what occurs from the initial contact to the beginning of the interview and nonverbal communication during the interview. More commonly, interviewers make audiotape recordings of selected interviews; however, this practice may soon be replaced by digital recordings of interview segments, now possible with CAPI software (Biemer, Herget, Morton, & Willis, 2000).

Monitoring as well as all other supervisory activities are much simpler in telephone surveys than in face-to-face surveys. When a telephone survey is conducted from a central facility, special monitoring phones allow supervisors to listen to ongoing interviews unobtrusively. This allows for prompt feedback and retraining, if necessary, which helps minimize interviewer error.

For both in-person and telephone monitoring, Fowler and Mangione (1990) recommend that supervisors monitor 1 in 10 interviews using standard forms to provide a systematic evaluation of interviewer performance. Although evaluation criteria vary across survey organizations, interviewer monitoring forms typically include the following behaviors: (a) voice characteristics such as enunciation and rate of speech, (b) reading questions as worded, (c) nondirective probing, (d) gaining respondent cooperation and countering reluctance to participate, and (e) data entry errors (Steve, Burks, Lavrakas, Brown, & Hoover, 2008). Fowler and Mangione (1990) found that interviewers who received feedback on face-to-face interviews rated being a standardized interviewer as more important than interviewers who received feedback only on productivity indicators such as cost, the number of hours worked, and response rates. Otherwise, there is a dearth of systematic evidence on the impact of monitoring interviewer performance on data quality (Groves et al., 2009, p. 318).

Reviewing completed questionnaires and observing interviews are two mechanisms of controlling the quality of interviewers' work and thereby determining the quality of the data. Two other processes are retrieving missing data and validating interviews. When data are missing, particularly for factual items that are critical to the survey, respondents may be recontacted to retrieve the information. Also, all well-conducted surveys employ procedures to detect and guard against interview falsification. The most blatant form of falsification is fabricating an entire interview; more subtle forms include fabricating answers to some questions but not others, purposely skipping some questions, and deliberately interviewing a nonsampled person. The few, dated estimates of falsification vary from less than 1% of interviewers in ongoing surveys to as high as 6.5% in a one-time survey (Biemer & Stokes, 1989; Schreiner, Pennie, & Newbrough, 1988). But it seems likely that the prevalence of falsification currently is much lower given the increased awareness of the problem and the newly established guidelines for its solution (see American Association for Public Opinion Research, 2009).

Validation may be carried out through observation, recontact, and data analysis (Ann Arbor Summit on Interviewer Falsification, 2004). The most effective method for detecting and deterring falsification is observation: listening to interviews in progress or tape recorded, as in monitoring interview performance. This is common practice in telephone surveys. In face-to-face surveys, the usual procedure is recontact, in which a staff member reinterviews or asks a subset of questions of a sample of respondents for each interviewer. To reduce costs, reinterviews most often are carried out by telephone. For recurring surveys, they may be used not only to detect cheating but also to evaluate and provide feedback on interviewers' performance (Forsman & Schreiner, 1991). The third method of detecting falsification, data analysis, involves examining completed data records for outliers such as very short interviews, an abnormally

high percentage of interviews obtained on first contact, and unusual patterns of response.

The supervision of interviewers is an extension of another form of quality control: interviewer training; it cannot replace training, but it can reinforce the need for honesty, precision, and accuracy and ensure that interviewers are using the skills that they have learned.

◆ Conclusions

Survey interviews are both a type of survey and a type of interview. In this chapter, we have emphasized the former, drawing attention to how interviewing operates to accomplish survey aims. It also is important, however, to consider survey interviews as a special case of conversations between individuals. Although the survey interview has a definite structure and rules of its own that differ from those of other conversations (Bradburn, 1992), it shares many elements of ordinary conversations, as we saw in our discussion of the interview as a social encounter. By focusing on these common elements, in particular the cognitive, communicative, and social processes involved in answering questions, survey methodologists have gained important insights into interviewing practice as it relates to the quality of survey data.

This theoretical focus represents one of two major changes in survey interviewing over the past quarter-century. First, theorizing about cognitive and communicative processes has resulted in a fundamental shift in methodological research on surveys (Tourangeau, 2003). Whereas the previous paradigm focused on statistical models of survey estimates based on sampling error, the new paradigm emphasizes "theories about how people decide whether to take part in surveys [a source of nonresponse error] and theories about how they come up with answers to the questions [a source of measurement error]" (Tourangeau, 2003, p. 4). This work led to the development of new training procedures for interviewers to avert refusals and to the growth of cognitive interviewing methods for evaluating survey questionnaires. It will continue to have an impact on survey practice.

Second, beginning with CATI, new communication technology has altered the way data are collected in survey interviews. The primary modes of data collection now consist of CATI and CAPI, but survey researchers are exploring many other new modes that blur the lines between interviewer- and self-administered surveys (Schober & Conrad, 2008). These include interactive voice response surveys, in which respondents listen on their telephones to a prerecorded voice reading the questions and answer by speaking or pressing numbers on the telephone keypad, and audio- and video-CASI surveys, where respondents listen to a prerecorded voice or watch a full-screen video stimulus on a computer while typing answers or clicking a selection with the mouse. The use of computerized voices and images raises many measurement issues that will challenge survey researchers for years to come.

◆ References

Alwin, D. F. (1991). Research on survey quality. *Sociological Methods & Research, 20,* 3–29.

American Association for Public Opinion Research. (2009). *Interviewer falsification: Practices and policies.* Deerfield, IL: Author. Retrieved from http://www .aapor.org/Content/NavigationMenu/AboutAAPOR/ StandardsampEthics/InterviewerFalsificationPractices andPolicies/default.htm

Anderson, B. A., Silver, B. D., & Abramson, P. R. (1988a). The effects of race of interviewer on measures of electoral participation by blacks in SRC national election studies. *Public Opinion Quarterly, 52,* 53–83.

Anderson, B. A., Silver, B. D., & Abramson, P. R. (1988b). The effects of race of the interviewer on race-related attitudes of black respondents in SRC/CPS national election studies. *Public Opinion Quarterly, 52,* 289–324.

Ann Arbor Summit on Interviewer Falsification. (2004). Interviewer falsification in survey research: Current best methods for prevention, detection, and repair of its effects. *Survey Research, 35*(1), 1–5.

Aquilino, W. S. (1994). Interview mode effects in surveys of drug and alcohol use. *Public Opinion Quarterly, 58,* 210–240.

Baker, R. P., Bradburn, N. M., & Johnson, R. A. (1995). Computer-assisted personal interviewing: An experimental evaluation of data quality and cost. *Journal of Official Statistics, 11,* 413–431.

Beatty, P. (1995). Understanding the standardized/nonstandardized interviewing controversy. *Journal of Official Statistics, 11,* 147–160.

Beatty, P. C., & Willis, G. B. (2007). Research synthesis: The practice of cognitive interviewing. *Public Opinion Quarterly, 71,* 287–311.

Biemer, P., Herget, D., Morton, J., & Willis, G. (2000). The feasibility of monitoring field interview performance using computer audio recorded interviewing (CARI). In *Proceedings of the Survey Research Methods Section of the American Statistical Association* (pp. 1068–1073). Washington, DC: American Statistical Association.

Biemer, P. P., & Stokes, S. L. (1989). The optimal design of quality control samples to detect interviewer cheating. *Journal of Official Statistics, 5,* 23–39.

Billiet, J., & Loosveldt, G. (1988). Improvement of the quality of responses to factual survey questions by interviewer training. *Public Opinion Quarterly, 52*(2), 190–211.

Bolton, R. N., & Bronkhorst, T. M. (1996). Questionnaire pretesting: Computer-assisted coding of concurrent protocols. In N. Schwarz & S. Sudman (Eds.), *Answering questions: Methodology for determining cognitive and communicative processes in survey research* (pp. 37–64). San Francisco, CA: Jossey-Bass.

Bradburn, N. M. (1983). Response effects. In P. H. Rossi, J. D. Wright, & A. B. Anderson (Eds.), *Handbook of survey research* (pp. 289–328). New York, NY: Academic Press.

Bradburn, N. M. (1992). What have we learned? In N. Schwarz & S. Sudman (Eds.), *Context effects in social and psychological research* (pp. 315–323). New York, NY: Springer-Verlag.

Bradburn, N. M., Sudman, S., & Blair, E. (1979). *Improving interview method and questionnaire design: Response effects to threatening questions in survey research.* San Francisco, CA: Jossey-Bass.

Cannell, C. F., Miller, P. V., & Oksenberg, L. (1981). Research on interviewing techniques. In S. Leinhardt (Ed.), *Sociological methodology 1981* (pp. 389–437). San Francisco, CA: Jossey-Bass.

Cannell, C., & Oksenberg, L. (1988). Observation of behavior in telephone interviews. In R. M. Groves, P. P. Biemer, L. E. Lyberg, J. T. Massey, W. L. Nicholls II, & J. Waksberg (Eds.), *Telephone survey methodology* (pp. 475–495). New York, NY: John Wiley.

Cantor, D., O'Hare, B. C., & O'Connor, K. S. (2008). The use of monetary incentives to reduce nonresponse in random digit dial telephone surveys. In J. M. Lepkowski, C. Tucker, J. M. Brick, E. de Leeuw, L. Japec, P. J. Lavrakas, M. W. Link, & R. L. Sangster (Eds.), *Advances in telephone survey methodology* (pp. 471–498). Hoboken, NJ: John Wiley.

Conrad, F. G., & Blair, J. (2009). Sources of error in cognitive interviewing. *Public Opinion Quarterly, 73,* 32–55.

Conrad, F. G., & Schober, M. F. (2000). Clarifying question meaning in a household telephone survey. *Public Opinion Quarterly, 64,* 1–28.

Converse, J. M., & Presser, S. (1986). *Survey questions: Handcrafting the standardized questionnaire.* Beverly Hills, CA: Sage.

Couper, M. P. (2008). Technology and the survey interview questionnaire. In F. G. Conrad & M. F. Schober (Eds.), *Envisioning the survey interview of the future* (pp. 58–76). Hoboken, NJ: John Wiley.

Couper, M. P., & Groves, R. M. (2002). Introductory interactions in telephone surveys and nonresponse. In D. W. Maynard, H. Houtkoop-Steenstra, N. C. Schaeffer, & J. van der Zouwen (Eds.), *Standardization and tacit knowledge: Interaction and practice in the survey interview* (pp. 161–178). New York, NY: John Wiley.

Couper, M. P., & Hansen, S. E. (2002). Computer-assisted interviews. In J. F. Gubrium & J. A. Holstein (Eds.), *Handbook of interview research: Context and method* (pp. 557–575). Thousand Oaks, CA: Sage.

Couper, M. P., & Nicholls, W. L., II. (1998). The history and development of computer assisted survey information collection methods. In M. P. Couper, R. P. Baker, J. Bethlehem, C. Z. F. Clark, J. Martin, W. L. Nicholls II, & J. M. O'Reilly (Eds.), *Computer assisted survey information collection* (pp. 1–22). New York, NY: John Wiley.

Curtin, R., Presser, S., & Singer, E. (2005). Changes in telephone survey nonresponse over the past quarter century. *Public Opinion Quarterly, 69,* 87–98.

Davis, D. W. (1997). The direction of race of interviewer effects among African Americans: Donning the black mask. *American Journal of Political Science, 41,* 309–322.

Davis, J. A., & Smith, T. W. (1992). *The NORC general social survey: A user's guide.* Newbury Park, CA: Sage.

de Leeuw, E., Callegro, M., Hox, J., Korendijk, E., & Lensvelt-Mulders, G. (2007). The influence of advance letters on response in telephone surveys: A meta-analysis. *Public Opinion Quarterly, 71,* 413–443.

de Leeuw, E., & Collins, M. (1997). Data collection methods and survey quality: An overview. In L. Lyberg, P. Biemer, M. Collins, E. de Leeuw, C. Dippo, N. Schwarz, & D. Trewin (Eds.), *Survey measurement and process quality* (pp. 199–220). New York, NY: John Wiley.

de Leeuw, E., & de Heer, W. (2002). Trends in household survey nonresponse: A longitudinal and international comparison. In R. M. Groves, D. A. Dillman, J. L. Eltinge, & R. J. A. Little (Eds.), *Survey nonresponse* (pp. 41–54). New York, NY: John Wiley.

de Leeuw, E. D., & Hox, J. J. (2004). I am not selling anything: 29 experiments in telephone introductions. *International Journal of Public Opinion Research, 16,* 464–473.

DeMaio, T. J., & Rothgeb, J. M. (1996). Cognitive interviewing techniques: In the lab and in the field. In N. Schwarz & S. Sudman (Eds.), *Answering questions: Methodology for determining cognitive and communicative processes in survey research* (pp. 177–195). San Francisco, CA: Jossey-Bass.

Dijkstra, W. (1987). Interviewing style and respondent behavior: An experimental study of the survey-interview. *Sociological Methods & Research, 16,* 309–334.

Dillman, D. A., Smyth, J. D., & Christian, L. M. (2009). *Internet, mail, and mixed-mode surveys: The tailored design method* (3rd ed.). Hoboken, NJ: John Wiley.

Dykema, J., Lepkowski, J. M., & Blixt, S. (1997). The effect of interviewer and respondent behavior on data quality: Analysis of interaction coding in a validation study. In L. Lyberg, P. Biemer, M. Collins, E. de Leeuw, C. Dippo, N. Schwarz, & D. Trewin (Eds.), *Survey measurement and process quality* (pp. 287–310). New York, NY: John Wiley.

Edwards, B., Schneider, S., & Brick, P. D. (2008). Visual elements of questionnaire design: Experiments with a CATI establishment survey. In J. M. Lepkowski, C. Tucker, J. M. Brick, E. de Leeuw, L. Japec, P. J. Lavrakas, . . . R. L. Sangster (Eds.), *Advances in telephone survey methodology* (pp. 276–296). Hoboken, NJ: John Wiley.

Esposito, J. L., & Rothgeb, J. M. (1997). Evaluating survey data: Making the transition from pretesting to quality assessment. In L. Lyberg, P. Biemer, M. Collins, E. de Leeuw, C. Dippo, N. Schwarz, & D. Trewin (Eds.), *Survey measurement and process quality* (pp. 541–571). New York, NY: John Wiley.

Finkel, S. E., Guterbock, T. M., & Borg, M. J. (1991). Race-of-interviewer effects in a pre-election poll: Virginia 1989. *Public Opinion Quarterly, 55,* 313–330.

Forsman, G., & Schreiner, I. (1991). The design and analysis of reinterview: An overview. In P. P. Biemer, R. M. Groves, L. E. Lyberg, N. A. Mathiowetz, & S. Sudman (Eds.), *Measurement errors in surveys* (pp. 279–301). New York, NY: John Wiley.

Forsyth, B., Rothgeb, J. M., & Willis, G. B. (2004). Does pretesting make a difference? An experimental test. In S. Presser, M. P. Couper, J. T. Lessler, E. Martin, J. Martin, J. M. Rothgeb, & E. Singer (Eds.), *Methods for testing and evaluating survey questionnaires* (pp. 525–546). Hoboken, NJ: John Wiley.

Fowler, F. J., Jr. (1991). Reducing interviewer-related error through interviewer training, supervision, and other means. In P. P. Biemer, R. M. Groves, L. E. Lyberg, N. A. Mathiowetz, & S. Sudman (Eds.), *Measurement errors in surveys* (pp. 259–278). New York, NY: John Wiley.

Fowler, F. J., Jr. (1995). *Improving survey questions: Design and evaluation.* Thousand Oaks, CA: Sage.

Fowler, F. J., Jr. (2009). *Survey research methods* (4th ed.). Thousand Oaks, CA: Sage.

Fowler, F. J., Jr., & Cannell, C. F. (1996). Using behavioral coding to identify cognitive problems with survey questions. In N. Schwarz & S. Sudman (Eds.), *Answering questions: Methodology for determining cognitive and communicative processes in survey research* (pp. 15–36). San Francisco, CA: Jossey-Bass.

Fowler, F. J., Jr., & Mangione, T. W. (1990). *Standardized survey interviewing: Minimizing interviewer-related error*. Newbury Park, CA: Sage.

Fuse, K., & Xie, D. (2007). A successful conversion or double refusal: A study of the process of refusal conversion in telephone survey research. *Social Science Journal, 44*, 434–446.

Goyder, J. (1987). *The silent minority: Nonrespondents and sample surveys*. Boulder, CO: Westview.

Grice, H. P. (1989). *Studies in the way of words*. Cambridge, MA: Harvard University Press.

Groves, R. M. (1989). *Survey errors and survey costs*. New York, NY: John Wiley.

Groves, R. M. (1990). Theories and methods of telephone surveys. *Annual Review of Sociology, 16*, 221–240.

Groves, R. M. (2006). Nonresponse rates and nonresponse bias in household surveys. *Public Opinion Quarterly, 70*, 646–675.

Groves, R. M., & Couper, M. P. (1996). Contact-level influences on cooperation in face-to-face surveys. *Journal of Official Statistics, 12*, 63–83.

Groves, R. M., & Couper, M. P. (1998). *Nonresponse in household interview surveys*. New York, NY: John Wiley.

Groves, R. M., Fowler, F. J., Jr., Couper, M. P., Lepkowski, J. M., Singer, F., & Tourangeau, R. (2009). *Survey methodology* (2nd ed.). Hoboken, NJ: John Wiley.

Groves, R. M., & Magilavy, L. J. (1986). Measuring and explaining interviewer effects in centralized telephone surveys. *Public Opinion Quarterly, 50*, 251–266.

Groves, R. M., & McGonagle, K. A. (2001). A theory-guided interviewer training protocol regarding survey participation. *Journal of Official Statistics, 17*, 249–265.

Groves, R. M., O'Hare, B. C., Gould-Smith, D., Benki, J., & Maher, P. (2008). Telephone interviewer voice characteristics and the survey participation decision. In J. M. Lepkowski, C. Tucker, J. M. Brick, E. de Leeuw, L. Japec, P. J. Lavrakas, . . . R. L. Sangster (Eds.), *Advances in telephone survey methodology* (pp. 385–400). Hoboken, NJ: John Wiley.

Groves, R. M., Presser, S., & Dipko, S. (2004). The role of topic interest in survey participation decisions. *Public Opinion Quarterly, 68*, 2–31.

Groves, R. M., Singer, E., & Corning, A. (2000). Leverage-saliency theory of survey participation: Description and illustration. *Public Opinion Quarterly, 64*, 299–308.

Hatchett, S., & Schuman, H. (1976). White respondents and race of interviewer effects. *Public Opinion Quarterly, 39*, 523–528.

Holbrook, A. L., Green, M. C., & Krosnick, J. A. (2003). Telephone versus face-to-face interviewing of national probability samples with long questionnaires: Comparisons of respondent satisficing and social desirability response bias. *Public Opinion Quarterly, 67*, 79–125.

Hox, J. J., & de Leeuw, E. D. (1994). A comparison of nonresponse in mail, telephone, and face-to-face surveys. *Quality & Quantity, 28*, 329–344.

Hyman, H. H. (1954). *Interviewing in social research*. Chicago, IL: University of Chicago.

Jobe, J. B., Keller, D. M., & Smith, A. F. (1996). Cognitive techniques in interviewing older people. In N. Schwarz & S. Sudman (Eds.), *Answering questions: Methodology for determining cognitive and communicative processes in survey research* (pp. 197–219). San Francisco, CA: Jossey-Bass.

Jobe, J. B., Pratt, W. F., Tourangeau, R., Baldwin, A. K., & Rasinski, K. A. (1997). Effects of interview mode on sensitive questions in a fertility survey. In L. Lyberg, P. Biemer, M. Collins, E. de Leeuw, C. Dippo, N. Schwarz, & D. Trewin (Eds.), *Survey measurement and process quality* (pp. 311–329). New York, NY: John Wiley.

Kane, E. W., & Macaulay, L. J. (1993). Interviewer gender and gender attitudes. *Public Opinion Quarterly, 57*, 1–28.

Kovar, M. G., & Royston, P. (1990). Comment. *Journal of the American Statistical Association, 85*, 246–247.

Krosnick, J. A. (1991). Response strategies for coping with the cognitive demands of attitude measures in surveys. *Applied Cognitive Psychology, 5*, 213–236.

Krosnick, J. A. (1999). Survey research. *Annual Review of Psychology, 50*, 537–567.

Krysan, M., & Couper, M. P. (2003). Race in the live and the virtual interview: Racial deference, social desirability, and activation effects in attitude surveys. *Social Psychology Quarterly, 66*, 364–383.

Lepkowski, J. M., Sadosky, S. A., & Weiss, P. S. (1998). Mode, behavior, and data recording error. In M. P. Couper, R. P. Baker, J. Bethlehem, C. Z. F. Clark, J. Martin, W. L. Nicholls II, & J. M. O'Reilly (Eds.), *Computer assisted survey information collection* (pp. 367–388). New York, NY: John Wiley.

Lessler, J. T., Eyerman, J., & Wang, K. (2008). Interviewer training. In E. D. de Leeuw, J. J. Hox, & D. A. Dillman (Eds.), *International handbook of survey methodology* (pp. 442–460). New York, NY: Lawrence Erlbaum.

Link, M. W., & Mokdad, A. (2005). Advance letters as a means of improving respondent cooperation in random digit dial studies: a multistate experiment. *Public Opinion Quarterly, 69*, 572–587.

Mangione, T. W., Fowler, F. J., Jr., & Louis, T. A. (1992). Question characteristics and interviewer effects. *Journal of Official Statistics, 8*, 293–307.

Martin, E. (2004). Vignettes and respondent debriefing for questionnaire design and evaluation. In S. Presser, M. P. Couper, J. T. Lessler, E. Martin, J. Martin, J. M. Rothgeb, & E. Singer (Eds.), *Methods for testing and evaluating survey questionnaires* (pp. 149–171). Hoboken, NJ: John Wiley.

Maynard, D. W., & Schaeffer, N. C. (2002). Standardization and its discontents. In D. W. Maynard, H. Houtkoop-Steenstra, N. C. Schaeffer, & J. van der Zouwen (Eds.), *Standardization and tacit knowledge: Interaction and practice in the survey interview* (pp. 3–45). New York, NY: John Wiley.

McConaghy, M. W., & Carey, S. (2004, May). *The ART of persuasion: A controlled experiment to evaluate the impact of avoidance refusal training (ART) in Britain.* Paper presented at the 2004 Annual Meeting of the American Association for Public Opinion Research, Phoenix, AZ.

Miller, P. V., & Cannell, C. F. (1982). A study of experimental techniques for telephone interviewing. *Public Opinion Quarterly, 46,* 250–269.

Nicholls, W. L., II. (1988). Computer-assisted telephone interviewing: A general introduction. In R. M. Groves, P. P. Biemer, L. E. Lyberg, J. T. Massey, W. L. Nicholls II, & J. Waksberg (Eds.), *Telephone survey methodology* (pp. 377–385). New York, NY: John Wiley.

Nicholls, W. L., II, Baker, R. P., & Martin, J. (1997). The effect of new data collection technologies on survey data quality. In L. Lyberg, P. Biemer, M. Collins, E. de Leeuw, C. Dippo, N. Schwarz, & D. Trewin (Eds.), *Survey measurement and process quality* (pp. 221–248). New York, NY: John Wiley.

O'Brien, E. M., Mayer, T. S., Groves, R. M., & O'Neill, G. E. (2002). Interviewer training to increase survey participation. In *Proceedings of the Annual Meeting of the American Statistical Association* (pp. 2502–2507). Arlington, VA: American Statistical Association.

Oksenberg, L., & Cannell, C. (1988). Effects of interviewer vocal characteristics on nonresponse. In R. M. Groves, P. P. Biemer, L. E. Lyberg, J. T. Massey, W. L. Nicholls II, & J. Waksber (Eds.), *Telephone survey methodology* (pp. 257–269). New York, NY: John Wiley.

Oksenberg, L., Coleman, L., & Cannell, C. F. (1986). Interviewers' voices and refusal rates in telephone surveys. *Public Opinion Quarterly, 50,* 97–111.

O'Muircheartaigh, C. (1997). Measurement error in surveys: A historical perspective. In L. Lyberg, P. Biemer, M. Collins, E. de Leeuw, C. Dippo, N. Schwarz, & D. Trewin (Eds.), *Survey measurement and process quality* (pp. 2–25). New York, NY: John Wiley.

Peytchev, A., Baxter, R. K., & Carley-Baxter, L. R. (2009). Not all survey effort is equal: Reduction in nonresponse bias and nonresponse error. *Public Opinion Quarterly, 73,* 785–806.

Presser, S., & Blair, J. (1994). Survey pretesting: Do different methods produce different results? In P. Marsden (Ed.), *Sociological methodology 1994* (pp. 73–104). San Francisco, CA: Jossey-Bass.

Presser, S., Couper, M. P., Lessler, J. T., Martin, E., Martin, J., Rothgeb, J. M., & Singer, E. (2004). Methods for testing and evaluating survey questions. *Public Opinion Quarterly, 68,* 109–130.

Rice, S. A. (1929). Contagious bias in the interview: A methodological note. *American Journal of Sociology, 35,* 420–423.

Schaeffer, N. C. (1991). Conversation with a purpose—or conversation? Interaction in the standardized interview. In P. P. Biemer, R. M. Groves, L. E. Lyberg, N. A. Mathiowetz, & S. Sudman (Eds.), *Measurement errors in surveys* (pp. 367–391). New York, NY: John Wiley.

Schaeffer, N. C., & Presser, S. (2003). The science of asking questions. *Annual Review of Sociology, 29,* 65–88.

Schober, M. F. (1999). Making sense of questions: An interactional approach. In M. G. Sirken, D. Herrmann, S. Schechter, N. Schwarz, J. M. Tanur, & R. Tourangeau (Eds.), *Cognition and survey research* (pp. 77–93). New York, NY: John Wiley.

Schober, M. F., & Conrad, F. G. (1997). Does conversational interviewing reduce survey measurement error? *Public Opinion Quarterly, 61,* 576–602.

Schober, M. F., & Conrad, F. G. (1999). Response accuracy when interviewers stray from standardization. In *Proceedings of the American Statistical Association, Section of Survey Research Methods, 1998* (pp. 940–945). Alexandria, VA: American Statistical Association.

Schober, M. F., & Conrad, F. G. (2008). Survey interviews and new communication technologies. In F. G. Conrad & M. F. Schober (Eds.), *Envisioning the survey interview of the future* (pp. 1–30). Hoboken, NJ: John Wiley.

Schober, M. F., Conrad, F. G., & Fricker, S. S. (2004). Misunderstanding standardized language in research interviews. *Applied Cognitive Psychology, 18,* 169–188.

Schreiner, I., Pennie, K., & Newbrough, J. (1988). Interviewer falsification in census bureau surveys. In *Proceedings of the Survey Research Methods Section of the American Statistical Association* (pp. 491–496). Washington, DC: American Statistical Association.

Schuman, H., & Converse, J. (1971). Effects of black and white interviewers on black responses in 1968. *Public Opinion Quarterly, 35,* 44–68.

Schuman, H., & Presser, S. (1981). *Questions and answers in attitude surveys: Experiments on question form, wording, and context.* San Diego, CA: Academic Press.

Schwarz, N., Groves, R. M., & Schuman, H. (1998). Survey methods. In D. T. Gilbert, S. T. Fiske, & G. Lindzey (Eds.), *The handbook of social psychology* (Vol. 1, 4th ed., pp. 143–179). Boston, MA: McGraw-Hill.

Schwarz, N., Knauper, B., Hippler, H.-J., Noelle-Neumann, E., & Clark, L. (1991). Rating scales: Numeric values may change the meaning of scale labels. *Public Opinion Quarterly, 55*, 570–582.

Schwarz, N., & Sudman, S. (Eds.). (1994). *Autobiographical memory and the validity of retrospective reports.* New York, NY: Springer-Verlag.

Schwarz, N., & Sudman, S. (Eds.). (1996). *Answering questions: Methodology for determining cognitive and communicative processes in survey research.* San Francisco, CA: Jossey-Bass.

Shuttles, C. D., Welch, J. S., Hoover, J. B., & Lavrakas, P. (2002, May). *The development and experimental testing of an innovative approach to training telephone interviewers to avoid refusals.* Paper presented at the 2002 Annual Meeting of the American Association for Public Opinion Research, St. Petersburg, FL.

Singer, E., Groves, R. M., & Corning, A. D. (1999). Differential incentives: Beliefs about practices, perceptions of equity, and effects on survey participation. *Public Opinion Quarterly, 63*, 251–260.

Singer, E., Hoewyk, J. V., Gebler, N., Raghunathan, T., & McGonagle, K. (1999). The effect of incentives on response rates in interviewer-mediated surveys. *Journal of Official Statistics, 15*, 217–230.

Singleton, R. A., Jr., & Straits, B. C. (2010). *Approaches to social research* (5th ed.). New York, NY: Oxford University Press.

Sirken, M. G., Herrmann, D. J., Schechter, S., Schwarz, N., Tanur, J. M., & Tourangeau, R. (Eds.). (1999). *Cognition and survey research.* New York, NY: John Wiley.

Smit, J. H., Dijkstra, W., & van der Zouwen, J. (1997). Suggestive interviewer behaviour in surveys: An experimental study. *Journal of Official Statistics, 13*, 19–28.

Steve, K. W., Burks, A. T., Lavrakas, P. J., Brown, K. D., & Hoover, J. B. (2008). Monitoring telephone interview performance. In J. M. Lepkowski, C. Tucker, J. M. Brick, E. de Leeuw, L. Japec, P. J. Lavrakas, . . . R. L. Sangster (Eds.), *Advances in telephone survey methodology* (pp. 401–422). Hoboken, NJ: John Wiley.

Streb, M. J., Burrell, B., Frederick, B., & Genovese, M. A. (2008). Social desirability effects and support for a female American president. *Public Opinion Quarterly, 72*, 76–89.

Suchman, L., & Jordan, B. (1990). Interactional troubles in face-to-face survey interviews. *Journal of the American Statistical Association, 85*, 232–241.

Sudman, S., & Bradburn, N. M. (1974). *Response effects in surveys: A review and synthesis.* Chicago, IL: Aldine.

Sudman, S., Bradburn, N. M., & Schwarz, N. (1996). *Thinking about answers: The application of cognitive processes to survey methodology.* San Francisco, CA: Jossey-Bass.

Tanur, J. M. (Ed.). (1992). *Questions about questions: Inquiries into the cognitive bases of surveys.* New York, NY: Russell Sage.

Tourangeau, R. (2003). Cognitive aspects of survey measurement and mismeasurement. *International Journal of Public Opinion Research, 15*, 3–7.

Tourangeau, R., Rips, L. J., & Rasinski, K. (2000). *The psychology of survey response.* Cambridge, England: Cambridge University Press.

Tourangeau, R., & Smith, T. W. (1996). Asking sensitive questions: Impact of data collection mode, question format, and question context. *Public Opinion Quarterly, 60*, 275–304.

Tourangeau, R., & Yan, T. (2007). Sensitive questions in surveys. *Psychological Bulletin, 133*, 859–883.

Van der Vaart, W., Ongena, Y., Hoogendoorn, A., & Dijkstra, W. (2005). Do interviewers' voice characteristics influence cooperation rates in telephone surveys? *International Journal of Public Opinion Research, 18*, 488–499.

van der Zouwen, J., Dijkstra, W., & Smit, J. H. (1991). Studying respondent–interviewer interaction: The relationship between interviewer style, interviewer behavior, and response behavior. In P. P. Biemer, R. M. Groves, L. E. Lyberg, N. A. Mathiowetz, & S. Sudman (Eds.), *Measurement errors in surveys* (pp. 419–437). New York, NY: John Wiley.

van der Zouwen, J., & Smit, J. H. (2004). Evaluating survey questions by analyzing patterns of behavior codes and question–answer sequences. In S. Presser, M. P. Couper, J. T. Lessler, E. Martin, J. Martin, J. M. Rothgeb, & E. Singer (Eds.), *Methods for testing and evaluating survey questionnaires* (pp. 109–130). Hoboken, NJ: John Wiley.

Viterna, J. S., & Maynard, D. W. (2002). How uniform is standardization? Variation within and across survey research centers regarding protocols for interviewing. In D. W. Maynard, H. Houtkoop-Steenstra, N. C. Schaeffer, & J. van der Zouwen (Eds.), *Standardization and tacit knowledge: Interaction and practice in the survey interview* (pp. 365–397). New York, NY: John Wiley.

Weeks, M. F. (1992). Computer-assisted survey methods information collection: A review of CASIC methods and their implications for survey operations. *Journal of Official Statistics, 8*, 445–465.

Willis, G. B. (2005). *Cognitive interviewing: A tool for improving questionnaire design.* Thousand Oaks, CA: Sage.

6

THE INTERPERSONAL DYNAMICS OF IN-DEPTH INTERVIEWING

◆ John M. Johnson and Timothy Rowlands

The contributors to this volume describe many different types of interviewing. Each type has its distinct style, methods, advantages, and limitations. Each uses and builds on our commonsense knowledge about talking to others. Each type of interviewing uses our common cultural wisdom about people, places, manner, and contexts. Each is no better than the person using it. This chapter examines in-depth interviewing. In-depth interviews tend to be of relatively long duration. They commonly involve one-on-one, face-to-face interaction between an interviewer and an informant and seek to build the kind of intimacy that is common for mutual self-disclosure. They tend to involve a greater expression of the interviewer's self than do some other types of interviews, as well as a personal commitment on the part of participants that spans several or many interview segments. In-depth interviewing offers great advantages, but it also entails some risks and dangers as well as some distinct ethical considerations.

In this chapter, we first describe in-depth interviewing as a social form and explain how this form is commonly used along with other methods of collecting data. We then discuss the goals and purposes of in-depth interviewing, emphasizing the importance of clarifying the research question to maximize the utility of this method, and describe some methods for locating informants. Next, we discuss the role of emergence in the dynamics of conducting such interviews. This is followed by an examination of the life cycle of an in-depth interviewing project. The chapter concludes with a discussion of some common ethical issues associated with in-depth interviewing.

◆ In-Depth Interviewing as a Social Form

In-depth interviewing involves a certain style of social and interpersonal interaction. As a social form, it differs from the kind of interactions one usually finds in sales pitches, public lectures, job interviews, counseling sessions, sexual pickups, board meetings, monologues, or marital conflicts. To be effective and useful, in-depth interviews develop and build on intimacy; in this respect, they resemble the forms of talking one finds among close friends. They resemble friendship, and they may even lead to long-term friendship. But in-depth interviews are also very different from the kind of talking one finds between friends, mainly because the interviewer seeks to use the information obtained in the interaction for some other purpose.

A researcher who uses in-depth interviewing commonly seeks "deep" information and knowledge—usually deeper information and knowledge than is sought in surveys, informal interviewing, or focus groups, for example. This information usually concerns very personal matters, such as an individual's self, lived experience, values and decisions, occupational ideology, cultural knowledge, or perspective. When two close or "best" friends talk, there is no pragmatic purpose that transcends the friendship itself. That kind of talk is an end in itself. But when an in-depth interviewer talks to an informant, the goal is to collect data. Some specific ethical issues arise because of this difference.

In-depth interviews rarely constitute the sole source of data in research. More commonly, they are used in conjunction with data gathered through avenues such as the lived experience of the interviewer as a member of or participant in what is being studied, naturalistic or direct observation, informal interviewing, documentary records, and team field research. In many cases, researchers use in-depth interviewing as a way to check out theories that they have formulated through naturalistic observation, to verify independently (or triangulate) knowledge that they have gained through participation as members of particular cultural settings, or to explore multiple meanings of or perspectives on some actions, events, or settings.

This was true of the famous case of the anthropologist Margaret Mead's (1928/1960) *Coming of Age in Samoa*. Mead supplemented her field experience, direct or naturalistic observations, and other interviews with in-depth interviews with informants. Years later, however, in his reexamination of Mead's research in *Margaret Mead and Samoa*, Derek Freeman (1983) raised serious questions about these interviews. Freeman argues that Mead was misled by her female adolescent informants, even though she had lived in the Samoan villages for many months,

because of the Samoan suspicion of outsiders and other contextual features of their recent contacts with Westerners. When Freeman later interviewed some of the same women who had been Mead's adolescent informants, they told him that they had told Mead what they thought she wanted to hear.

Another well-known case is represented by the studies of the Mexican village of Tepoztlan done over several decades by two different researchers, Robert Redfield (1930, 1941, 1960) and Oscar Lewis (1951). Redfield and Lewis made different inferences from their observations and interviews and drew diverse conclusions from their lengthy experiences of living in this small, remote village. Each justified and legitimated what he reported by referring to his heroic fieldwork and interviews. The two men's findings were different, however, in large part because of certain basic assumptions each made about the nature of "conflict" and "shared meanings" (or consensus) in everyday life, assumptions that predated their research observations and experiences.

Another heated debate arose recently concerning what is arguably the most famous sociological ethnography of all time, William Foote Whyte's (1943, 1955, 1981, 1993) *Street Corner Society*, the classic study of an Italian American community in north Boston. Whyte also used in-depth interviewing in his study to supplement and complement other forms of data collection. Years later, W. A. Marianne Boelen (1992) returned to north Boston and reinterviewed virtually all of the people Whyte had interviewed; she then contested the truth of what he had reported (see Denzin, 1992; Vidich, 1992; Whyte, 1992).

All of the studies noted above involved multiple research methodologies in addition to in-depth interviews. They illustrate that each research project involves the observer or interviewer as an active sense maker and interpreter of what is seen or heard in the research context. Each inevitably depends on the researcher's own standpoint and place in the community as well as his or her own self-understandings, reflection, sincerity, authenticity, honesty, and integrity.

Whether in-depth interviewing should be used in research depends on the nature of the research question. Achieving clarity in the formulation and articulation of the research question commonly enhances the clarity of the methodological goals and objectives. If one is interested in an area of study in which the information sought is relatively limited, such as the marketing choices of individuals, then there is every reason to think that the use of focus groups or fixed-choice questionnaires might be appropriate. If one is interested in understanding forms of urban sociation, then direct observation would seem to be a reasonable approach for gathering data. But if one is interested in questions of greater depth, where the knowledge sought is often taken for granted and not readily articulated by most members, where the research question involves highly conflicted emotions, and where different individuals or groups involved in the same line of activity have complicated, multiple perspectives on some phenomenon, then in-depth interviewing is likely the best approach despite its known imperfections. In-depth interviewing is often a very appropriate method to use in qualitative research, life story research, the gathering of personal narratives and oral histories, and the use of grounded theory methodology to analyze the accounts of members of some social setting.

The important point is this: The nature of the research question determines whether or not the use of in-depth interviewing is advisable. Largely associated with an inductive mode of research, in-depth interviewing is best suited to research questions of the descriptive or exploratory type (i.e., questions that focus on *what* and *how* rather than *why* social processes are enacted in everyday life). Given the emphasis on how individuals and groups make their experiences meaningful and the typical lack of quantification during analysis, in-depth interviews are not well suited for producing generalizable results. As such, they are not typically used in explanatory studies that aim to produce causal explanations according to the deductive criteria of the association, logical time order, and nonspuriousness of predetermined independent and dependent variables. They can, however, help researchers interested in causality explore the context and mechanism of a causal explanation in ways surveys, experiments, or even direct observation often cannot.

◆ The Goals and Purposes of In-Depth Interviewing

Many talented researchers have analyzed in-depth interviewing as a method or technique of collecting data (see Atkinson, 1998; Cicourel, 1964; Denzin, 1989a, 1989b; Douglas, 1985; Fontana & Frey, 1994; Fontana & Prokos, 2007; Geertz, 1988; Holstein & Gubrium, 1995; Kvale & Brinkmann, 2008; Lofland & Lofland, 1984, 1995; Merton, Fiske, & Kendall, 1956;

Rubin & Rubin, 1995; Spradley, 1979; Wax, 1971). Many authors have taken up the issue of "how to do" qualitative or in-depth interviewing, and most additionally affirm the importance of the researcher's goals and purposes, the researcher's moral commitment to seek out what is true, and the researcher's ethical imperative to examine his or her own personal ideas, occupational ideologies, assumptions, common sense, and emotions as crucial resources for what he or she "sees" or "hears" in a particular research interview or project.

Many reflective parents have had to learn this important lesson from their children, often painfully: Children do not hear what their parents tell them but what they are prepared and ready to hear. The same holds good for in-depth interviewers: They don't necessarily "hear" what their informants tell them but only what their own intellectual and ethical development has prepared them to hear. The Mead/Freeman, Lewis/Redfield, and Whyte/Boelen conflicts emphatically underscore this point. In each of the complicated community settings that these researchers study, it is not the case that there is just "one truth" that the observer or interviewer either does or does not "see" or "hear." Rather, each researcher implicitly draws on his or her common-sense cultural knowledge—or "stock of knowledge," as Alfred Schutz (1967) terms it—and creates or constructs a truth or interpretation—meaning—that will work for all practical (intellectual) purposes.

As the name implies, in-depth interviewing seeks "deep" information and understanding. The word *deep* has several meanings in this context. First, deep understandings are held by the real-life members of or participants in some everyday activity, event, or place. The interviewer seeks to achieve the same deep level of knowledge and understanding as the members or participants. If the interviewer is not a current or former member or participant in what is being investigated, he or she might use in-depth interviewing as a way to learn the meanings of participants' actions. In the words of the famous ethnographer and student of daily life Erving Goffman (1989), the goal here is one of

> subjecting yourself . . . and your own social situation, to the set of contingencies that play upon a set of individuals, so that you can physically and ecologically penetrate their circle of response to their social situation, their work situation, or their ethnic situation. (p. 125)

In this respect, the informant would be a kind of teacher and the interviewer a student, one interested in learning the ropes or gaining member knowledge from a veteran informant. If the interviewer happens to be a current or former member of or participant in this activity, he or she may use in-depth interviews to explore or check his or her understandings and to see if they are shared by other members or participants. Former or returning members can fruitfully use in-depth interviews to check, stimulate, or inspire their own self-reflections and to see if their understandings are the same as those shared by others who are also members or participants.

Second, deep understandings go beyond commonsense explanations for and other understandings of some cultural form, activity, event, place, or artifact. In-depth interviewing is an irremediably commonsensical (or intersubjective) enterprise. It begins with commonsense perceptions, explanations, and understandings of some lived cultural experience (which include scientific explanations) and aims to explore the contextual boundaries of that experience, or perception, to uncover what is usually hidden from ordinary view or reflection or to penetrate to more reflective understandings about the nature of that experience. For example, in previous research, Johnson (2002) used in-depth interviewing to explore the complicated phenomenon of "stalking"; he sought to learn how those who stalk others actually see or interpret their actions as well as to explore the nature of the (often conflicted) emotions that lie underneath these actions.

Third, deep understandings can reveal how our commonsense assumptions, practices, and ways of talking partly constitute our interest and how we understand them. In his self-revealing book *Creative Interviewing*, for example, Jack Douglas (1985) tells how his own deeply hidden and conflicted emotions about his mother's prostitution influenced what he was able to "hear" in the in-depth interviews he conducted on the nature of love and intimacy (Douglas, 1985, 1988).

Fourth, deep understandings allow us to grasp and articulate the multiple views of, perspectives on, and meanings of some activity, event, place, or cultural object. To illustrate with an example from Johnson's research with Beth McLin, we are currently seeking to understand the multiple perspectives on the death penalty. At a commonsense level, one might think this would include studying the

views of those who advocate the death penalty and those who oppose it. Although this is a useful distinction for some limited purposes, it fails to grasp the variety among the many groups involved in this issue: death penalty abolitionists and protesters, executioners, death row prisoners' wives and other family members, victims' family members, prison guards, legislators, clerics, pro–death penalty demonstrators, wardens, prosecutors, defense lawyers, and death row prisoners. Knowing whether an individual is "for" or "against" the death penalty tells us little about the complicated, multifaceted perspectives on and meanings of capital execution. Jaber Gubrium (1975, 1988; Buckholdt & Gubrium, 1985) is a longtime qualitative researcher who has successfully combined observations with in-depth interviewing in several settings to gain explicit understanding of the multiple interpretations of and perspectives on the activities and settings he investigated.

To gain clarity on the goals for conducting in-depth interviews, the research must achieve clarity on the research questions. An important issue is the researcher's relationship with member knowledge and lived experience. Is the researcher completely ignorant of and inexperienced in the issues to be addressed in the interviews? If so, the interviews will take on the nature of instruction, with the more experienced members teaching the novice interviewer. Such interviews are commonly very uneven in quality, with the early ones usually telling more about the novice's ignorance than about the phenomenon being studied. John Lofland and Lyn Lofland (1995) have observed that virtually all of such interviews will prove as worthless as empirical data. They may play an important role in the education and learning curve of the neophyte interviewer, but it usually takes a long time for a novice to begin to "hear" what a veteran is saying about the important matters of lived experience. This aspect of interviewing is of such importance that the authors of a book on the topic elevate it to the very subtitle of their work: *Qualitative Interviewing: The Art of Hearing Data* (Rubin & Rubin, 1995).

In prior decades, social researchers who possessed experiential knowledge of some activity or scene that they were studying commonly chose to hide that fact to avoid a professional disrepute or even some more severe stigma. The many legendary examples (including quantitative researchers as well) provide fodder for the informal gossip one finds at professional meetings. These tales are commonly transmitted orally, and one begins to achieve "inside" or "member" status as a social science professional by learning these sad and joyous tales of heroism, cowardice, and perseverance in the face of adversity. In earlier times, the professional ideal was that of "detachment" and "objectivity," which was taken to mean that actual lived experience or actual membership status could "taint" the research or its findings. John Irwin's (1970) perception that he had to conceal his 9-year prison sentence as an important experiential resource in the research that went into the writing of *The Felon* is a good example from this era. H. Laud Humphreys's (1970) concealment of his gay identity in his award-winning *Tearoom Trade* is another.

Lived experience and member status are no longer stigmatized among social scientists, and some even extol their relative merits (Denzin, 1997; Ellis & Flaherty, 1992). Today, there are many researchers who use their investigations and interviews to explore phenomena about which they have prior or current member-based knowledge. Jeffrey Reiman (1979), who terms this *opportunistic research*, provides many examples of individuals who have conducted such research (see also Higgins & Johnson, 1988). Lofland and Lofland (1995) advocate the advantages of "starting where you are," by which they meant that potential researchers should seriously consider studying those social phenomena to which they have ready or advantaged access. Even our own first research experiences and in-depth interviews fit this pattern. Making use of his knowledge and membership as a former U.S. Navy officer, Johnson (1972, 1980a, 1980b) conducted in-depth interviews to explore others' perceptions and knowledge of routine bureaucratic record-keeping activities and "gundecking" (fudging) of official reports. Later, active participation in the battered women's shelter movement as a founder and as a worker in a shelter provided Johnson with a foundation from which to conduct in-depth interviews with battered women about their experiences with domestic violence (Adhikari, Reinhard, & Johnson, 1993; Ferraro & Johnson, 1983; Johnson, 1981, 1985, 1992; Johnson & Ferraro, 1984; Johnson, Luna, & Stein, 2003). And even today, Johnson's years of activist participation as a death penalty abolitionist serve to inform his works as he conducts in-depth interviews with respondents who hold multiple perspectives on these actions.

When charting a research project that includes in-depth interviewing, is it better to be an experienced veteran or a relatively ignorant novice? Each status has its strengths and advantages, and each has its pitfalls and dangers. Novices are less inclined to possess hardened assumptions about what they are studying, but they often have more difficulty seeing the nuances or layered meanings of participating members. When undertaking a research project through in-depth interviews, they are likely to have a longer learning curve. Veterans with actual lived experience may already possess member knowledge, but they may also take that knowledge for granted. Additionally, their current or former status as members may constitute a barrier when they interview others. It is important that researchers recognize these nuances in advance, so that they can undertake the planning of in-depth interviewing in a manner that will help them assess these influences on the accounts and reflections collected during the interviewing process. Whether the researcher is a neophyte or a returning veteran, in-depth interviewing involves an interactive process in which both the interviewer and the informant draw on and use their commonsense knowledge to create some intelligible sense of the questions posed and the ensuing discussions about them.

◆ *Locating Informants*

Planning and preparation are essential for successful in-depth interviews, but few researchers do everything they think they should before beginning them. Hardly anyone reads everything he or she feels should be read or achieves the kind of clarity he or she really wants on the protocol of questions. In their work on interviewing, Herbert Rubin and Irene Rubin (1995, p. 42) liken the planning for an interviewing session to planning for a vacation—that is, making plans sufficient to meet practical and emotional expectations while at the same time providing for the possibility of "hanging loose," or altering the course of the interview to go where the informant wants to lead. At some point, the research must make a leap of faith and just dive into the process.

The research process is a learning process. Interviewers make mistakes; they make gaffes and alienate informants. They learn that their race, age, gender, social class, appearance, and even achieved statuses make one kind of difference with some informants and another kind of difference with other informants. The point is that researchers can learn from all this—learn what makes a difference for their specific projects, learn their strengths and how to play them, and learn how to cover or compensate for their weaknesses.

Individuals have performed the basic forms of not only asking questions but also answering them countless times before they ever come to their first formal, in-depth interviews. The role of informant is part of the cultural stock of commonsense knowledge for the vast majority of children and adults. As friends, we talk in an informal manner and engage in cooperative, mutual self-disclosure. Those who elect to conduct research in a more formal fashion draw and build on these cultural forms and commonsense practices. When a researcher begins an in-depth interview, he or she behaves in a friendly and interested manner so as to help build trust and good rapport.

An in-depth interviewer begins slowly with small talk (chitchat), explains the purpose of the research, and commonly begins with simple planned questions (often referred to as icebreakers) that are intended to "get the ball rolling" but not to move so quickly into the issues of the key interview questions as to jeopardize intimate self-disclosure (or trust). Good rapport is signaled by emotions that feel harmonious and cooperative, and trust can commonly be discerned through eye contact, facial expression, and bodily idiom.

In-depth interviewing differs from other forms because it involves a great involvement of the interviewer's self. To progressively and incrementally build a mutual sense of cooperative self-disclosure and trust, the interviewer must offer some form of strict or complementary reciprocity. Strict reciprocity is possible only if the interviewer is a former or current member of the group under study and would take the form of the interviewer's sharing with the informant his or her own views, feelings, or reflections on the topics being discussed.

It is more common for an interviewer to bring some form of complementary reciprocity to the informant—not a strict exchange of perceptions, feelings, or reflections but rather some form of assistance or other form of information. When Johnson interviewed the women who came to the battered women's shelter that he helped establish in the late 1970s, for example, he could hardly offer them strict

reciprocity for their views on battering (given that he was not a battered woman!). Rather, he could share with them what many other women had told him they felt in similar circumstances, and after a while, he could even offer well-grounded advice on what they might do next (Ferraro & Johnson, 1983; Johnson & Ferraro, 1984). Johnson did the same in two subsequent interview studies on the effectiveness of domestic violence protection orders (Adhikari et al., 1993; Johnson et al., 2003). In later interviews with male stalkers, Johnson found that he could not offer his informants the solace of strict reciprocity, given that he had never stalked anyone himself. He could, however, share the wisdom he had culled from working in the field of domestic violence for 30 years, including almost two decades of work and counseling with violent men.

To conduct in-depth interviews, then, researchers must undertake considerable self-reflection to get to know themselves; they must also make a self-conscious effort to observe themselves in interaction with others. The development and cultivation of trust with informants is slow, incremental, and emotional, in most cases, and the relationship can change quickly (Johnson, 1975). The ideal goal is that the informant becomes a collaborative partner with the researcher in the intellectual endeavor at hand.

Gender is inevitably important in interviewing, but it is difficult to generalize about the precise nature of its importance. The nature of the research question is commonly the main issue. Some research questions may elicit responses or perspectives for which gender has great relevance, whereas others may not. Feminist scholars such as Carol Gilligan (1982) assert that many researchers interpret women's responses according to hegemonically masculine standards (hierarchy, individualization, rationality) while neglecting women's relatively greater uses of relational categories and perspectives. Dorothy Smith (1987, 1990) notes that the prevailing institutional priorities and agendas often devalue women's lived experiences in the world and that the very formulation of the questions that animate a research project often implicitly contains hidden gender evaluations or perspectives. She proposes that researchers place the issue of women's daily lived experiences at the center of the research process itself. All researchers would be wise to develop a special sensitivity to the explicit or deeply obscured meanings of gender in any particular research topic.

The process of locating informants is simplified if members of the group of interest are usually or regularly located at the same place or scene; it is more complicated if potential informants do not regularly congregate at one locale. However, not everyone who is a member of some scene or community or who participates in some activity is equally valuable as an informant. Informants differ greatly in their intelligence, knowledge, and ability to reflect. Informants also differ in their motivations to assist in or cooperate with an in-depth interview or series of interviews. Informants differ widely in their responses to specific individuals, whether because of racial, class, gender, age, or other characteristics or perhaps just because of timing. It is realistic for the researcher to anticipate that this will happen. Because those who do in-depth interviews for research purposes have no interest in "counting" them or "adding them up" through an analytic strategy of quantitative coding, this reality of noncomparable interviews poses no problem.

Many research projects have been "made" by the researcher finding that rare, reflective inside informant who seems to know just about everything that seems to be important and has thought about it and reflected on it for some considerable period of time before he or she even meets the ethnographer or does an in-depth interview. Legendary examples include "Doc" (Dean Pecci), William Foote Whyte's key informant in his research for *Street Corner Society* (1943, 1955, 1981, 1993); "Tally," Elliot Liebow's (1967) key informant for *Tally's Corner*; and "Vincent Swaggi," Carl Klockars's (1974) key informant for *The Professional Fence*. The kinds or types of individuals who are likely to become key informants like these can be found in many settings. They are often marginal to the setting or scene being studied and are often seen by others in the setting as "lay intellectuals," thinkers, eggheads, or know-it-alls. Sometimes they are politically ambitious individuals in the setting, those who have strenuously studied the setting and its personnel for the purposes of occupational or material gain or advancement. Sometimes they are the "outsiders" of the setting, stigmatized for some quality that is depreciated or deprecated.

Ethnographers and interviewers should always develop an awareness of such individuals and be ready to cultivate their trust and friendship for the purpose of gaining member knowledge. Marginal membership status in the setting or activity seems to

provide many with an invitation to reflection and usually a certain sense of intellectual detachment from the "official line" among the membership. Finding such individuals and making them collaborators in the research process can yield wonderful results. Researchers should take care, however, to check out the observations and reflections of such individuals by getting independent verification through other interviews if and when possible. Researchers who fail to do such checking can jeopardize the integrity of their research findings and possibly their own reputations.

Some informants are better than others. Not all members of a setting or community are equally valuable for the purpose of in-depth interviews. Not all of those who participate in some activity have a sufficient motive or interest to be interviewed about it. The best informants are those who have been thoroughly enculturated in the setting or community, have recent membership participation, have some provisional interest in assisting the interviewer, and have adequate time and resources to take part in the interviews. The best informants are those who can describe a scene or setting or activity, those who can provide "thick description," as Clifford Geertz (1973, 1988) terms it, but not necessarily those who analyze or theorize. In some settings or situations, such individuals may "click" with the interviewer, or they may not—this is inevitable.

The issue of "sampling," or how researchers decide which informants to include and which to exclude, is one that is rarely addressed in research reports and publications. Nevertheless, it is important for researchers to provide accounts or explanations of how this selection was done in specific projects, so that readers may assess the researchers' findings (Altheide & Johnson, 1994, pp. 494–495). That said, typically, in-depth interviewers employ purposive or theoretical sampling methods that aim to identify specific interviewees because of their perceived ability to answer specific questions of substantial or theoretical importance to the research.

◆ *Conducting In-Depth Interviews*

The act of conducting the first in-depth interviews on a new study is often tinged with not only anxiety but also great anticipation and excitement. The first interviews usually yield great leaps forward in learning.

The learning curve is steep at this point. It is best for the interviewer to begin with an actual protocol of questions: usually two or three introductory icebreakers to get the ball rolling; several transition questions, which may again explain the purpose of the interviewing project, secure informed consent, or elicit permission from the respondent to use a tape recorder; and then perhaps five to eight main or key questions that address the heart or essence of the research question(s). An in-depth interview commonly concludes with the interviewer summarizing some of the main points he or she has understood or giving the informant some information about what others have said about the issues discussed. Although interviewers might anticipate following such a nice, neat, rational plan before they begin interviewing, they inevitably find that the path, tone, and trajectory of actual interviews rarely follow this sequence.

USING THE AUDIO RECORDER TO LEARN INTERVIEWING SKILLS

We now know with some certainty that a human being's individual memory does not remember what the person sees or hears but rather organizes it into some intelligible coherence based on the individual's past experience. Thus, it is essential that interviewers audio record in-depth interviews to obtain verbatim records of those interviews. Handwritten field notes are important for any research project, and there exists considerable wisdom about how to make such notes (Emerson, Fretz, & Shaw, 1995; Lofland & Lofland, 1995; Strauss & Corbin, 1990), but field notes are far inferior to audio recording for in-depth interviews.

One of the main goals of qualitative research has always been to capture the words and perceptions of informants, or, as Bronislaw Malinowski (1922) puts it, "to grasp the native's point of view, his relation to life, to realize his visions of his world" (p. 25). So obtaining a verbatim record is the ideal, if the subsequent analysis is to be valid and meaningful. Whether or not the researcher records an interview, it is imperative that he or she take process notes regarding the interview itself, to gain an understanding of the interview as a social occasion and how the questions and answers mutually constitute the sense of what is said. The questions asked guide and influence the answers given, and so it is important for the interviewer to grasp why the informant proffers one segment of talk as an answer rather than another.

Researchers can develop and cultivate the skills needed for in-depth interviewing with practice. Although in-depth interviewing is perhaps the form of interviewing closest to the kind of talking done between friends, the individual who conducts an in-depth interview exercises greater control over the flow and tone of the conversation than does the respondent. The beginning of the interview is different from the beginning of a conversation between friends in that the interviewer commonly explains the purposes of the research and, these days, perhaps gets the informant's signature on an informed consent statement. The turn taking is also different from that in a conversation between friends, with the interviewer deferring to the informant.

The asking and answering of questions is asymmetrical, with the interviewer having previously prepared a protocol of questions and the necessity to keep the informant on track, attending to the business at hand. The interviewer is more passive in the role of listener, and if the interviewer is successful, the informant is more active as a speaker. During interviews, the rules for pausing are usually different from those in talks between friends, as are the rules for physical proximity. The interviewer's aim is to develop progressively with the informant the kind of mutual and cooperative self-disclosure that is associated with the building of intimacy and trust, but it takes great skill to accomplish this when one is working with asymmetrical communication norms very dissimilar to those one usually associates with building intimacy and trust, as in actual friendship. The interviewer's goal is to solicit the informant as a collaborative partner in the sense making and interpretations that flow from the interviewing process. Reflecting on one's own performance during interviews by reviewing audio recordings can thus provide essential feedback and an invaluable learning tool.

USING INTERVIEWS TO EXPLORE VERSUS USING INTERVIEWS TO VERIFY

In the early stages of a research project, the in-depth interviewer may feel relatively ignorant about what he or she is studying. After several interviews, however, the interviewer begins to build a stock of knowledge about the research questions and, in most cases, feeds some of this information back to the informants in subsequent interviews, after those same questions have been covered. This information exchange becomes part of the complementary reciprocity so necessary to the continued building of intimacy, and it also begins the process of verification in the research process. Data collection and verification become inextricably intertwined in most in-depth interviewing projects. As the research develops, the interviewer should keep and review his or her own jottings and notes (see Emerson et al., 1995; Lofland & Lofland, 1995) and review prior interviews when possible, or when transcripts become available, and should begin progressively to focus on the nature of the questioning and probing in later interviews. The later interviews of an in-depth interviewing project are usually more focused on specific probes and verification of what has been learned in the earlier interviews.

In more traditional or standardized interviewing, interviewers are commonly told to stick to the questions on the research protocol, to ask the questions precisely as they are given, to probe for clarifications only in ways that will not influence the respondents' answers, and to record only what the respondents say. Furthermore, traditional interviewers are trained to be impersonal; that is, they are trained to avoid offering any kind of personal information or revelations about any of their own values, beliefs, or opinions that might influence respondents in any way (see, e.g., Fowler & Mangione, 1990). This is not a realistic ideal for in-depth interviewing, because the nature of the research question itself usually entails a deeper process of mutual self-disclosure and trust building.

◆ The Dynamics of In-Depth Interviewing

As an interview progresses, it often takes unexpected turns or digressions that follow the informant's interests or knowledge. Such digressions or diversions are likely to be very productive, so the interviewer should be prepared to depart from his or her prepared plan and "go with the flow"—that is, consider following for a while where the informant wants to lead. It is essential that the interviewer be assertive enough to return the interview to its anticipated course when necessary, but not so rigid as to preclude his or her obtaining some unexpected information. Go with the flow, be playful, and adopt

an experimental attitude—these are all good pieces of advice for a novice in-depth interviewer in the early stages of the project.

With experience, skilled in-depth interviewers may often deviate from the research protocol, to go where the informant seems to want to go or perhaps to follow what appear to be more interesting leads. The interviewer should record these moves in his or her process notes, so that he or she can see later how one set of interviewing actions influenced and thereby constituted what the informant said. The interviewer can use subsequent interviews with the same informant or other interviews with additional informants to check the interpretive validity of this strategy.

◆ The Life Cycle of In-Depth Interviewing

Excitement runs high when an interviewer is in the springtime of a research project. Genuine students are usually enthusiastic about gaining new knowledge from informants and learning what they have to teach. Eventually, however, the excitement begins to wane. The doldrums of the summer monsoons appear. The animating enthusiasm begins to lessen, and researchers find themselves using all sorts of excuses, rationalizations, and self-deceptions to alter their involvement with the research interviews. In some cases, boredom appears. This happens because the learning curve has peaked and it is less satisfying to do all the pragmatic work required to set up interviews when one learns progressively less from them. Barney Glaser and Anselm Strauss (1967, pp. 120–145) refer to this as the "saturation point" of a research project. It is commonly in this context that the researcher begins to ask, How many interviews are needed? How many interviews are enough?

Interestingly, the academic literature on interviewing includes various answers to the question of how many interviews are needed. James Spradley (1979, p. 51), an anthropologist usually interested in using interviews to understand cultural forms and members' perspectives, has noted, for example, that for him, one in-depth interview commonly involves six or seven 1-hour sessions, and a given research project might include between 25 and 30 of these. Grant McCracken (1988, p. 37), a researcher with a business background who uses in-depth interviews (which he terms *long interviews*) to gain knowledge about marketing and business questions, says eight such interviews are usually enough. The progenitors of grounded theory methodology in qualitative research, Glaser and Strauss (1967), do not recommend a specific number of interviews or observations but say that the researcher should continue until a state of *theoretical* saturation is achieved; the identification of this point, however, is left ambiguous in their writings on this issue. Many others have shared their opinions on this question, but as the researchers cited above illustrate, there is no specific, set answer.

The number of interviews needed to explore a given research question depends on the nature of that question and the kind or type of knowledge the interviewer seeks. To those students who have asked him how many interviews they need, Johnson has often responded, "Enough." By this, he means that enough interviews must be conducted so that the interviewer feels that he or she has learned all there is to be learned from the interviews and has checked out those understandings by reinterviewing the most trusted and most knowledgeable informants.

It has been a common ideal in in-depth interviewing for the interviewer to check out his or her understanding with one or more key informants since this practice was first articulated and reported by William Foote Whyte (1943, pp. 279–358); this is usually called the "member's test of validity." In research that uses interviewing as a basic form of data collection, whether the researcher is a neophyte or a returning member, early interviews will embody much more "grand tour" questioning (Lofland & Lofland, 1995, pp. 78–86; Spradley, 1979, pp. 86–92) than later interviews, which tend to be more focused on checking out and verifying research observations, analyses, and presumptive findings.

In a very important sense, all research is "team research" in that it occurs in social, interactional, and community contexts. Even in the case of the heroic "lone ranger," the individual who is for the most part working on his or her own out in the field, there is usually a social support system of family members and friends and a small coterie of professional colleagues who provide intellectual and social support for the project. Researchers usually acknowledge such ties in the introductions, prefaces, or notes of the reports they publish on their studies. In other cases, interviewers may work in teams on projects with other researchers and share the interviewing duties. The interpersonal dynamics among research team members can be a source of problems, from the beginning of negotiations concerning the "research bargain" (the division of labor and reward) to the eventual analysis and report. Members of an interviewing team may feel violated or "ripped off" just as informants may feel violated or "ripped off" if their confidentiality is breached or if promises are not kept (Adler, Adler, & Rochford, 1986; Douglas, 1976). In one of the extensive team research projects on which Johnson worked, proprietary rights to the interviewing records were specified in a divorce agreement.

In addition to the social relationships implicated in, and by, a particular research project, research reports claim membership in some kind of interpretive community. They do this through the idiom, language, and issues that they embody. Qualitative research is a diverse and multifaceted field. The editors of the *Handbook of Qualitative Research*, Norman Denzin and Yvonna Lincoln (2000a), identify "seven moments" of qualitative research; in their work, Jaber Gubrium and James Holstein (1997) identify four major "idioms" of qualitative method. However one classifies qualitative research communities, each implicates its own standards of acceptable and reportable truth. Researchers would be wise to make their connection to particular research communities explicit and to incorporate these into their research processes and reporting, so that competent readers may assess how standards were created and embodied in actual research situations.

◆ Ethical Issues Raised by In-Depth Interviewing

In-depth interviewing commonly elicits highly personal information about specific individuals, perhaps even about the interviewer. This information may include participants' personal feelings and reflection as well as their perceptions of others. It may include details about deviant or illegal activities that, if made known, would have deleterious consequences for lives and reputations. It may include expressions of private knowledge about some setting or occupation that goes against that setting or occupation's public front or public presentation. Collecting this kind of information raises some specific ethical issues.

HOW DEEP?

One ethical issue concerns how far an interviewer should go in probing informants' answers. As noted previously, in-depth interviewers should be prepared to follow where informants might lead, because this often leads to fruitful territory for those informants who wish to use the interviewing situation as an occasion for self-reflection and their own increased understanding. It is sometimes difficult, if not impossible, however, for a researcher to anticipate fully the consequences of such probing. In the case of one in-depth interview conducted by Rubin and Rubin (1995, p. 98), an informant's suicide followed a revealing interview by a matter of weeks; the timing of this informant's death led the researchers to wonder if there was any connection between their interview and the suicide.

Given this uncertainty, in-depth interviewers have an ethical obligation to anticipate and prepare for worst-case scenarios regardless of how rarely they might occur in practice. One strategy adopted by many researchers is the provision of resources to all informants as part of the informed consent and ice-breaking process. By making available the numbers of relevant toll-free hotlines and/or the hours and locations of local crisis counseling centers, an in-depth interviewer is not only providing options should the interview stir up painful or traumatic memories; he or she is also making an open and explicit commitment to the psychological, emotional, physical, and social well-being of the informants.

PROTECTING SUBJECTS

Professional social science organizations have traditionally addressed potentially difficult issues in their published codes of ethics (see Neuman, 1994). One traditional ethical principle has been that the researcher must do whatever is necessary "to protect research subjects." There are several different ways in which such a principle can be interpreted, however, and so there exists some ambiguity about what is required of the researcher. One interpretation of this ethical principle is that the researcher should do what is necessary *to protect the specific individuals who have assisted him or her in the research, as individuals.* This means that a researcher or interviewer would feel obligated to take whatever steps are necessary to protect the individuals who have cooperated in the research from any misuse of the information they have shared.

In one well-known case, a researcher coded all his interview records and kept them in a safe deposit box in a bank located in a state different from the one where the research was conducted (Humphreys, 1970). In another famous case, a researcher went to jail rather than yield research and interview materials to court officials (Brajuha & Hallowell, 1986; Hallowell, 1985). In this case, Mario Brajuha was a graduate student who was studying a restaurant that was "torched" (burned down), and when police investigators suspected mob arson, they went to the courts in an effort to obtain Brajuha's research records. In another case, a sociology graduate student spent 5 months in jail to study his subjects in a sociological field project on ecoterrorism; his incarceration produced further reflections on this ethical dilemma (Scarce, 1994, 1995, 1999). Knowing about such potential complexities in advance should stimulate researchers to give prior consideration to their ethical commitments and the lengths to which they will go to protect research informants.

At universities today, research proposals are submitted to the local institutional review board (IRB). While most student research for courses is exempt, research done for theses and dissertations must pass through this bureaucratic screening, which is mandated for the purpose of protecting the rights and interests of human subjects who participate in research and is often oriented to the legal protection of the institution as well. One of the guiding ethical rules is that human subjects must give their "informed consent" to the conditions and consequences of the research, but today we have a large literature that explores the flaws of this relatively narrow standard and the way it is implemented (American Historical Association, 2008; Christians, 2005; Denzin, 2009; Lincoln, 2009; Lincoln & Canella, 2004; Speigelman & Spear, 2009). Scholars from many disciplines have been critical of how narrow this standard is or how narrowly it is implemented. Scholars who do research in oral history have been especially critical of the IRB standards, and since 2000 the Oral History Association (2000) has developed its own ethical perspective and guidelines, now followed by many other professional associations. (For a summary, see Denzin, 2010, p. 76; see also Howard, 2006.) The Belmont Report of the Office for Human Research Protection (2009) advocates for a broader ethical perspective for research, a view that is more inclusive and scrupulous than most IRB applications, an ethic guided by three fundamental principles: (1) respect for all persons, (2) beneficence, and (3) social justice.

PROTECTING COMMUNITIES

Another issue concerning the protection of research informants is whether researchers should feel any obligation to avoid causing harm to the reputation, social standing, or social prestige of their informants' professions, occupations, communities, or groups *as collectives*. Predicting future consequences of this kind is highly problematic, so it is exceedingly difficult to assess the risk of such harm with any certainty.

Another issue concerning the protection of informants is whether a research report will play some role in "deprivatizing" their lived experience (Gubrium & Holstein, 1995). The risk of this is also very difficult to assess, and so it is reasonable to anticipate that different individuals will reach different ethical judgments, even individuals within the same support community or research team. This seems like one reasonable reading of what occurred when Carolyn Ellis (1986, 2009), an ethnographer, published an award-winning book about two fishing villages near Chesapeake Bay. Ellis studied the villages over a period of 19 years, but when she returned in the early 1990s, she discovered that her published accounts had offended some of the community members, leading her to express some reservations about the standards she had used in the research publication (Ellis, 1995). It seems clear that Ellis did not use the criteria for privacy that existed in the communities she studied but instead used a much broader standard familiar to most cosmopolitans who live and work in and around universities today. The problematic nature of such ethical judgments does not reduce the need for interviewers to face and address them as best they can.

TELLING THE TRUTH

The most important ethical imperative is to tell the truth. This issue has become especially important during the current period, which Denzin and Lincoln (2000b, p. 3) call "the postmodern moment." This moment is defined by two crises: (1) the crisis of

presentation and (2) the crisis of legitimation (for qualitative research). One response to these crises is the advocacy of "standpoint epistemologies" (Denzin, 1997, pp. 53–89), where the research interviewer not only *self-consciously empathizes* with the informants as individuals but also *self-consciously sympathizes* with the political or community goals of those informants *as a category or collective*.

John Lofland (1995), a strong advocate of analytic ethnography, heartily disagrees with this position, saying that it amounts to a promotion of "fettered research." Most of the complex settings or situations that the vast majority of social scientists are likely to study are highly variegated, pluralistic, and filled with multiple perspectives and interpretations, so the adoption of a standpoint epistemology does not address certain important ethical questions (Altheide & Johnson, 1994, in press).

In a situation with multiple perspectives or interpretations, whose standards or criteria of truth are to prevail in the final report? This is the critical ethical question for in-depth interviewing. In several publications, Denzin discusses a short story written by Raymond Carver (1989) about a writer who returns to his hometown to find out that everyone there is angry with him because of what he has written about them. Denzin (1997, pp. 285–287) interprets the import of this story to be that "a writer is always selling someone out," meaning that, in virtually all complex settings in today's world, all interpretations and voices are subject to conflict and dispute. To resolve this problematic dilemma, Denzin suggests "upping the ante" on the guilt and other professional consequences for not telling a defensible truth in one's writings.

Robert Emerson and Melvin Pollner (1992) advocate another way to address this issue: Take the final ethnographic report back to the informants and other members of the setting that was studied, not so much to verify the findings independently (as in Whyte's "member's test of validity") as to gain their impressions and feedback on what has been written about them. The goal is not necessarily to seek a consensus but to open a dialogue on what is written in the final report. E. Burke Rochford (1992) is one researcher who has actually followed this path. His experiences indicate that this practice may be very problematic, however; it can lead to conflict among members who later dispute even what they accept as a true interpretation, because of subsequent considerations about the consequences of publication.

Carl Klockars (1977) offers the opinion that "the true test of ethics of research with human beings is whether or not it forces the researcher to suffer with his subjects" (p. 225). This is an ambiguous standard, to be sure. And Jeffrey Reiman (1979, p. 57) would add to this the consideration of whether the publication of the research results enhances the author's career or the informant's freedom. Denzin (2010) argues that qualitative research is embedded in complex historical and cultural contexts. He identifies eight distinct historical moments and concludes that our present moment is or should be defined by explicit conversations or dialogues about how our research is located in larger ethical concerns with human rights and justice. The successive waves of epistemological theorizing have blurred all existing paradigms or genres and call for qualitative scholars to transcend narrow disciplinary and methodological boundaries to see how our small contributions fit in with the large picture of justice.

◆ References

Adhikari, R. P., Reinhard, D., & Johnson, J. M. (1993). The myth of protection orders. In N. K. Denzin (Ed.), *Studies in symbolic interaction: A research annual* (Vol. 14, pp. 294–311). Greenwich, CT: JAI Press.

Adler, P. A., Adler, P., & Rochford, E. B. (1986). The politics of participation in field research. *Urban Life, 14,* 363–376.

Altheide, D. L., & Johnson, J. M. (1994). Criteria for assessing interpretive validity in qualitative research. In N. K. Denzin & Y. S. Lincoln (Eds.), *Handbook of qualitative research* (pp. 485–499). Thousand Oaks, CA: Sage.

Altheide, D. L., & Johnson, J. M. (in press). Criteria for assessing interpretive validity in qualitative research. In N. K. Denzin & Y. S. Lincoln (Eds.), *Handbook of qualitative research* (4th ed.). Thousand Oaks, CA: Sage.

American Historical Association. (2008, February). *AHA statement on IRBs and oral history research, perspectives and history.* Washington, DC: Author.

Atkinson, R. (1998). *The life story interview.* Thousand Oaks, CA: Sage.

Boelen, W. A. M. (1992). Street Corner Society: Cornerville revisited. *Journal of Contemporary Ethnography, 21,* 11–51.

Brajuha, M., & Hallowell, L. (1986). Legal intrusion and the politics of fieldwork: The impact of the Brajuha case. *Urban Life, 14,* 454–478.

Buckholdt, D. R., & Gubrium, J. F. (1985). *Caretakers.* Beverly Hills, CA: Sage.

Carver, R. (1989). Intimacy. In R. Carver (Ed.), *Where I'm calling from* (pp. 444–453). New York, NY: Vintage Books.

Christians, C. G. (2005). Ethics and politics in qualitative research. In N. K. Denzin & Y. S. Lincoln (Eds.), *Handbook of qualitative research* (3rd ed., pp. 139–164). Thousand Oaks, CA: Sage.

Cicourel, A. V. (1964). *Method and measurement in sociology.* New York, NY: Free Press.

Denzin, N. K. (1989a). *Interpretive interactionism.* Newbury Park, CA: Sage.

Denzin, N. K. (1989b). *The research act: A theoretical introduction to sociological methods* (3rd ed.). Englewood Cliffs, NJ: Prentice Hall.

Denzin, N. K. (1992). Whose Cornerville is it, anyway? *Journal of Contemporary Ethnography, 21,* 120–132.

Denzin, N. K. (1997). *Interpretive ethnography: Ethnographic practices for the 21st century.* Thousand Oaks, CA: Sage.

Denzin, N. K. (2009). *Qualitative inquiry under fire: Toward a new paradigm dialogue.* Walnut Creek, CA: Left Coast Press.

Denzin, N. K. (2010). *The qualitative mandate.* Walnut Creek, CA: Left Coast Press.

Denzin, N. K., & Lincoln, Y. S. (Eds.). (2000a). *Handbook of qualitative research* (2nd ed.) Thousand Oaks, CA: Sage.

Denzin, N. K., & Lincoln, Y. S. (Eds.). (2000b). Introduction: The discipline and practice of qualitative research. In N. K. Denzin & Y. S. Lincoln (Eds.), *Handbook of qualitative research* (2nd ed., pp. 1–28). Thousand Oaks, CA: Sage.

Douglas, J. D. (1976). *Investigative social research.* Beverly Hills, CA: Sage.

Douglas, J. D. (1985). *Creative interviewing.* Beverly Hills, CA: Sage.

Douglas, J. D. (1988). *Love, intimacy, and sex.* Newbury Park, CA: Sage.

Ellis, C. (1986). *Fisher folk: Two communities on Chesapeake Bay.* Lexington: University Press of Kentucky.

Ellis, C. (1995). Emotional and ethical quagmires in returning to the field. *Journal of Contemporary Ethnography, 24,* 711–713.

Ellis, C. (2009). *Revision: Autoethnographic reflections on life and work.* Walnut Creek, CA: Left Coast Press.

Ellis, C., & Flaherty, M. G. (Eds.). (1992). *Investigating subjectivity: Research on lived experience.* Newbury Park, CA: Sage.

Emerson, R. M., Fretz, R. I., & Shaw, L. L. (1995). *Writing ethnographic fieldnotes.* Chicago, IL: University of Chicago Press.

Emerson, R. M., & Pollner, M. (1992). Difference and dialogue: Members' readings of ethnographic texts. In G. Miller & J. A. Holstein (Eds.), *Perspectives on social problems* (Vol. 3, pp. 79–98). Greenwich, CT: JAI Press.

Ferraro, K. J., & Johnson, J. M. (1983). How women experience battering. *Social Problems, 30,* 325–339.

Fontana, A., & Frey, J. H. (1994). Interviewing: The art of science. In N. K. Denzin & Y. S. Lincoln (Eds.), *Handbook of qualitative research* (pp. 361–376). Thousand Oaks, CA: Sage.

Fontana, A., & Prokos, A. H. (2007). *The interview: From formal to postmodern.* Walnut Creek, CA: Left Coast Press.

Fowler, F. J., Jr., & Mangione, T. W. (1990). *Standardized survey interviewing: Minimizing interviewer-related error.* Newbury Park, CA: Sage.

Freeman, D. (1983). *Margaret Mead and Samoa: The making and unmaking of an anthropological myth.* Cambridge, MA: Harvard University Press.

Geertz, C. (1973). Thick description: Toward an interpretive theory of culture. In C. Geertz (Ed.), *The interpretation of cultures: Selected essays* (pp. 3–30). New York, NY: Basic Books.

Geertz, C. (1988). *Works and lives: The anthropologist as author.* Palo Alto, CA: Stanford University Press.

Gilligan, C. (1982). *In a different voice: Psychological theory and women's development.* Cambridge, MA: Harvard University Press.

Glaser, B. G., & Strauss, A. L. (1967). *The discovery of grounded theory: Strategies for qualitative research.* Chicago, IL: Aldine Press.

Goffman, E. (1989). On fieldwork. *Journal of Contemporary Ethnography, 18,* 123–132.

Gubrium, J. F. (1975). *Living and dying at Murray Manor.* New York, NY: St. Martin's Press.

Gubrium, J. F. (1988). Rationality and practical reasoning in human service organizations. In P. C. Higgins & J. M. Johnson (Eds.), *Personal sociology* (pp. 103–117). New York, NY: Praeger.

Gubrium, J. F., & Holstein, J. A. (1995). Qualitative inquiry and the deprivatization of experience. *Qualitative Inquiry, 1,* 204–222.

Gubrium, J. F., & Holstein, J. A. (1997). *The new language of qualitative method.* New York, NY: Oxford University Press.

Hallowell, L. (1985). The outcome of the Brajuha case: Legal implications for sociologists. *Footnotes, American Sociological Association, 13*(1), 13.

Higgins, P. C., & Johnson, J. M. (Eds.). (1988). *Personal sociology.* New York, NY: Praeger.

Holstein, J. A., & Gubrium, J. F. (1995). *The active interview.* Thousand Oaks, CA: Sage.

Howard, J. (2006). Oral history under review. *Chronicle of Higher Education, 53*(12), 14.

Humphreys, H. L. (1970). *Tearoom trade: Impersonal sex in public places.* Chicago, IL: Aldine Press.

Irwin, J. (1970). *The felon.* Englewood Cliffs, NJ: Prentice Hall.

Johnson, J. M. (1972). The practical use of rules. In R. A. Scott & J. D. Douglas (Eds.), *Theoretical perspectives on deviance* (pp. 145–162). New York, NY: Basic Books.

Johnson, J. M. (1975). *Doing field research.* New York, NY: Free Press.

Johnson, J. M. (1980a). Battle efficiency reports as propaganda. In D. L. Altheide & J. M. Johnson (Eds.), *Bureaucratic propaganda* (pp. 205–228). Boston, MA: Allyn & Bacon.

Johnson, J. M. (1980b). Military preparedness as propaganda. In D. L. Altheide & J. M. Johnson (Eds.), *Bureaucratic propaganda* (pp. 179–204). Boston, MA: Allyn & Bacon.

Johnson, J. M. (1981). Program enterprise and the official co-optation of the battered women's shelter movement. *American Behavioral Scientist, 24,* 837–842.

Johnson, J. M. (1985). The changing meanings of child abuse. In J. Peden (Ed.), *The American family and the state* (pp. 123–140). San Francisco, CA: Pacific Institute.

Johnson, J. M. (1992). The church response to domestic violence. In N. K. Denzin (Ed.), *Studies in symbolic interaction: A research annual* (Vol. 13, pp. 245–259). Greenwich, CT: JAI Press.

Johnson, J. M. (2002). The stalking process. In J. A. Kotarba & J. M. Johnson (Eds.), *Postmodern existential sociology* (pp. 189–206). Boulder, CO: Blackwell.

Johnson, J. M., & Ferraro, K. J. (1984). The victimized self: The case of battered women. In J. A. Kotarba & A. Fontana (Eds.), *The existential self in society* (pp. 119–130). Chicago, IL: University of Chicago Press.

Johnson, J. M., Luna, Y., & Stein, J. (2003). Victim protection orders and the stake in conformity thesis. *Journal of Family Violence, 18*(9), 317–323.

Klockars, C. B. (1974). *The professional fence.* New York, NY: Free Press.

Klockars, C. B. (1977). Field ethics for the life history. In R. S. Weppner (Ed.), *Street ethnography: Selected studies of crime and drug use in natural settings* (pp. 210–226). Beverly Hills, CA: Sage.

Kvale, S., & Brinkmann, S. (2008). *Interviews: Learning the craft of qualitative research interviewing.* Thousand Oaks, CA: Sage.

Lewis, O. (1951). *Life in a Mexican village: Tepoztlan restudied.* Urbana: University of Illinois Press.

Liebow, E. (1967). *Tally's corner: A study of Negro street corner men.* Boston, MA: Little, Brown.

Lincoln, Y. S. (2009). Ethical practices in qualitative research. In D. M. Mertens & P. E. Ginsberg (Eds.), *The handbook of social research ethics* (pp. 150–170). Thousand Oaks, CA: Sage.

Lincoln, Y. S., & Canella, G. S. (2004). Dangerous discourses: Methodological conservatism and governmental regimes of truth. *Qualitative Inquiry, 10,* 5–14.

Lofland, J. (1995). Analytic ethnography. *Journal of Contemporary Ethnography, 24*, 30–67.

Lofland, J., & Lofland, L. H. (1984). *Analyzing social settings* (2nd ed.). Belmont, CA: Wadsworth.

Lofland, J., & Lofland, L. H. (1995). *Analyzing social settings* (3rd ed.). Belmont, CA: Wadsworth.

Malinowski, B. (1922). *Argonauts of the Western Pacific: An account of native enterprise and adventure in the Archipelagoes of Melanesian New Guinea.* London, England: Routledge & Kegan Paul.

McCracken, G. (1988). *The long interview.* Newbury Park, CA: Sage.

Mead, M. (1960). *Coming of age in Samoa: A psychological study of primitive youth for Western civilization.* New York, NY: Mentor. (Original work published 1928)

Merton, R. K., Fiske, M., & Kendall, P. L. (1956). *The focused interview: A manual of problems and procedures.* Glencoe, IL: Free Press.

Neuman, W. L. (1994). *Social research methods: Qualitative and quantitative approaches* (2nd ed.). Boston, MA: Allyn & Bacon.

Office for Human Research Protection. (2009). *Belmont report.* Washington, DC: Author.

Oral History Association. (2000). *Oral history evaluation guidelines* (Pamphlet No. 3, adopted 1989, revised September 2000). Lexington, KY: Author. Retrieved from http://www.oralhistory.org

Redfield, R. (1930). *Tepoztlan—a Mexican village: A study in folk life.* Chicago, IL: University of Chicago Press.

Redfield, R. (1941). *The folk culture of Yucatan.* Chicago, IL: University of Chicago Press.

Redfield, R. (1960). *The little community and peasant society and culture.* Chicago, IL: University of Chicago Press.

Reiman, J. H. (1979). Research subjects, political subjects, and human subjects. In G. Miller & J. A. Holstein (Eds.), *Deviance and decency: The ethics of research with human subjects* (pp. 33–57). Greenwich, CT: JAI Press.

Rochford, E. B. (1992). The politics of member validation: Taking findings back to Hare Krishna. In G. Miller & J. Holstein (Eds.), *Perspectives on social problems* (Vol. 3, pp. 99–116). Greenwich, CT: JAI Press.

Rubin, H. J., & Rubin, I. S. (1995). *Qualitative interviewing: The art of hearing data.* Thousand Oaks, CA: Sage.

Scarce, R. (1994). (No) trial (but) tribulation: When courts and ethnography conflict. *Journal of Contemporary Ethnography, 23*, 123–149.

Scarce, R. (1995). Scholarly ethics and courtroom antics: Where researchers stand in the eyes of the law. *American Sociologist, 26*, 87–112.

Scarce, R. (1999). Good faith, bad ethics: When scholars go the distance and scholarly associations do not. *Law and Social Inquiry, 24*(4), 977–986.

Schutz, A. (1967). *The phenomenology of the social world* (G. Walsh & F. Lehnert, Trans.). Evanston, IL: Northwestern University Press.

Smith, D. E. (1987). *The everyday world as problematic: A feminist sociology.* Boston, MA: Northeastern University Press.

Smith, D. E. (1990). *Texts, facts and femininity: Exploring the relations of ruling.* London, England: Routledge.

Speigelman, R., & Spear, P. (2009). The roles of institutional review boards: Ethics now you see them, now you don't. In D. M. Mertens & P. E. Ginsberg (Eds.), *The handbook of social research ethics* (pp. 121–134). Thousand Oaks, CA: Sage.

Spradley, J. P. (1979). *The ethnographic interview.* New York, NY: Holt, Rinehart & Winston.

Strauss, A. L., & Corbin, J. (1990). *Basics of qualitative research: Grounded theory procedures and techniques.* Newbury Park, CA: Sage.

Vidich, A. J. (1992). The historical context of *Street Corner Society. Journal of Contemporary Ethnography, 21*, 99–119.

Wax, R. H. (1971). *Doing fieldwork: Warning and advice.* Chicago, IL: University of Chicago Press.

Whyte, W. F. (1943). *Street corner society: The social structure of an Italian slum.* Chicago, IL: University of Chicago Press.

Whyte, W. F. (1955). *Street corner society: The social structure of an Italian slum* (2nd ed.). Chicago, IL: University of Chicago Press.

Whyte, W. F. (1981). *Street corner society: The social structure of an Italian slum* (3rd ed.). Chicago, IL: University of Chicago Press.

Whyte, W. F. (1992). In defense of *Street Corner Society:* Response to Boelen. *Journal of Contemporary Ethnography, 21*, 52–68.

Whyte, W. F. (1993). *Street corner society: The social structure of an Italian slum* (4th ed.). Chicago, IL: University of Chicago Press.

7

THE LIFE STORY INTERVIEW AS A MUTUALLY EQUITABLE RELATIONSHIP

◆ Robert Atkinson

We are the storytelling species. Storytelling is in our blood. Telling the stories of our lives is so basic to our nature that we are largely unaware of its profound implications. The stories we tell of our own lives bring us into deep relationship with one another; they connect us on many levels, as few other things could. Hidden within our life stories are myriad themes, all expressions of timeless and universal motifs and archetypes, reminding us every day that we are in relationship, linked with each other through the stories we share.

We think in story form, speak in story form, and bring meaning to our lives through story. Stories connect us to our roots. In traditional communities of the past, stories played a central role in the lives of the people. Stories told from generation to generation carried enduring values as well as lessons about life lived deeply. Traditional stories followed a timeless and universal pattern that can be represented as separation, transition, incorporation (Van Gennep, 1960); birth, death,

rebirth (Eliade, 1954); or departure, initiation, return (Campbell, 1968). This pattern is like a blueprint, or an original form, within which the story communicates a balance between opposing forces. The pattern actually forms the basis for the plot of a story and aids the storyteller in remembering the story's key elements while keeping it on the course it was meant to follow.

The stories we tell of our own lives today are still guided by the same pattern and enduring elements. Our life stories connect us to our roots, give us direction, validate our own experience, and restore value to our lives. Life stories can fulfill important functions for us, and as we recognize now more than ever, everyone has a story to tell about his or her life, and they are indeed important stories (Atkinson, 1995, 1998; Gubrium & Holstein, 1998; Kenyon & Randall, 1997; Randall, 1995).

The life story interview is designed to help the storyteller and the listener, as well as readers and scholars, to understand better how life stories serve to facilitate meaning making. The life story interview provides a practical and holistic methodological approach for the sensitive collection of personal narratives that reveal how a specific human life is constructed and reconstructed in representing that life as a story.

The life story interview, first and foremost, brings forth the voice and spirit of the storyteller within a life-as-a-whole context. This approach is fundamentally built on the deepest respect for individual storytellers, the highest regard for the subjective meaning carried within their stories, and the goal of achieving the most equitable interpersonal exchange possible. The life story offers a way, perhaps more than any other, for another to step inside the personal world of the storyteller and discover larger worlds.

Primarily, there is a very important mutuality to the life story interview. There may well be an undeniable research agenda for the interviewer, but there is just as much a high level of sensitivity required because of the inherent interactional nature of the interview. When it comes to telling and sharing a life story, no other kind of interview could be more personal, more intimate, for the person doing the sharing. Interviewees receive great benefit in being listened to and guided through the telling of their life story, even though they may not be aware of it until they've had time to reflect on the experience. The interviewer's primary job is to be a sensitive, respectful listener in guiding the life storyteller's narration.

◆ The Life Story in Historical and Disciplinary Context

The life story interview is a qualitative, ethnographic, and field research method for gathering information on the subjective essence of one person's entire life experience. As a method of looking at life as a whole and of carrying out an in-depth study of individual lives, the life story interview stands alone. It has become the central element of the burgeoning subfield of the narrative study of lives (Cohler, 1988; Josselson & Lieblich, 1993) for understanding single lives in detail and how the individual plays various roles in society (Cohler, 1993; Gergen & Gergen, 1993).

The life story interview produces a first-person text, in the words of the storyteller, that can stand on its own, as any other text, or that can be examined through the lens of any theory or research question

applied to it. This methodology has broad applications across disciplines: A researcher from any discipline can choose to apply this methodology to get at the particular research or disciplinary questions in hand, within the context of a life story, or a researcher from any field can turn to an existing life story text to examine it for the questions at hand. The life story approach has come into being through varied applications in a variety of disciplines.

Having evolved from many disciplinary and theoretical perspectives, what has become the life story interview can be traced back across time and disciplines through terms such as *life narratives*, *the narrative study of lives*, *personal documents*, *personal history*, *life history*, and *oral history*, though each term, or categorization, is not synonymous with *life story* and has its own unique approach, perspective, and uses.

◆ The Research Uses of Life Stories

PSYCHOLOGY

The ideographic use of life narratives for serious academic study is considered to have begun in psychology with Sigmund Freud's (1910/1957, 1911/1958) psychoanalytic interpretation of individual case studies although these were based on secondary documents. Henry Murray (1938, 1955) was one of the first to study individual lives using life narratives primarily to understand personality development. Gordon Allport (1942) used personal documents to study personality development in individuals, focusing on primary documents, including narratives, while also considering the problems of reliability and validity of interpretation using such materials. Distinguishing between the ideographic and the nomothetic approaches, he raised the important question of "why not ask the person first if that is who you want to know something about."

The use of personal documents reached its maturation in Erik Erikson's studies of Luther (Erikson, 1958) and Gandhi (Erikson, 1969). Erikson (1975) also used the life history to explore how the historical moment influenced lives. This approach further led to the pursuit of psychobiography (biography informed by psychological theory), a method used to understand the inner workings of the minds of individuals of historical significance (Runyan, 1982).

Another related approach is that of Robert Coles (1989), who, after having learned the value of stories from his parents, who read to him as a child, listened to the stories of his patients, his students, and others and continued to learn yet more important lessons about life. For him, it was as much about the relationship involved in the telling and the listening—or as he put it, "We owe it to each other to respect our stories and learn from them."

Theodore Sarbin (1986) uses narrative as the *root metaphor* and places it at the core of self-formation, for understanding human experience, while Jerome Bruner (1986) uses narrative as an important means for discovering how we *construct* our lives.

Dan McAdams (1985, 1993) uses the life story approach to understand better the formation of identity and the role of generativity in individual lives, two of Erikson's (1963) key developmental constructs. The narrative study of lives series furthers the theoretical understanding of individual life narratives through in-depth studies, methodological examinations, and theoretical explorations (Josselson, 1996; Josselson & Lieblich, 1993, 1995, 2000; Josselson, Lieblich, & McAdams, 2003; Lieblich & Josselson, 1994, 1997; Lieblich, McAdams, & Josselson, 2004; McAdams, Josselson, & Lieblich, 2002, 2006).

First-person narratives are an effective means of gaining an understanding of how the self evolves over time. Through the self-narrative process, researchers can secure useful information and come to the desired understanding of the self as a meaning maker with a place in society, culture, and history (Freeman, 1992).

GERONTOLOGY

It is commonly recognized in gerontology that the primary developmental task for the elder is the review of one's life (Butler, 1963). This is the process of remembering and expressing the experiences, struggles, lessons, and wisdom of a lifetime. Long before Butler described the "life review" process and referred to it as the "elder function," it was the traditional role of elders to pass on their values and wisdom through their stories. This is a time of life for remembering, clarifying, and even writing down one's "ultimate concerns" (Erikson, 1964; Tillich, 1957) before it is too late. "Narrative gerontology" is an emerging subfield focusing on the possibilities of the life story as a metaphor in the field of aging

and the ways narrative approaches, such as "guided autobiography" and life review, can be incorporated into practice to bring many benefits to the participants, including clarity, a deeper understanding of one's life themes, connection with others, and a new perspective on and meaning in one's life (Birren & Cochran, 2001; Birren, Kenyon, Ruth, Schroots, & Svensson, 1996; Kenyon, Clark, & de Vries, 2001).

SOCIOLOGY

The nomothetic approach to life stories can be linked to the early narrative turn in sociology or to the Chicago School of Sociology, represented by Thomas and Thomas (1928) and Shaw (1929). These groundbreaking works were followed up in sociology by Blumer (1969) and Becker (1976) and later by other sociologists using life histories to understand a social reality existing outside the story but described by the story, to define relationships and roles in a community, to explain an individual's understanding of social events, or to simply invite stories rather than reports during interviews (Bertaux, 1981; Chase, 1995; Linde, 1993; Mkhonza, 1995; Rosenthal, 1993).

ANTHROPOLOGY

The life history has long been a methodology of anthropological fieldwork. L. L. Langness (1965) sees the life history as primarily biographical, not autobiographical, because of the way it is used to learn more about culture than about the individuals in it. He further defines the real nature of the life history as "seldom the product of the informant's clearly articulated, expressive, chronological account of his life" (p. 48).

James Spradley (1979) points out that some life histories are heavily edited by the ethnographer (often only 60% of the description is actually in the insider's own words or language), while others may be presented in the same form in which the recording occurred.

FOLKLORE

The term *life story* has more of a home in folklore (Ives, 1986; Titon, 1980), defined simply as a person's story of his or her life or of what he or she thinks is a significant part of that life. Titon (1980) takes the distinction between terms an important step further, making it clearer how to distinguish *life story* from *biography* (the history of a life), *oral history*, and *personal history* or *life history*. He notes that history is ultimately *found out* in the sense of discovery of knowledge, while a story, charged with the power of lived experience, is *made* not as in fiction or a lie but in the creative or imaginative sense. The life *history* typically removes, at least in part, the voice of the storyteller, putting the narrative more in the voice of the researcher, while a life story more often retains the voice of the storyteller, often in its entirety.

HISTORY

The oral history approach has long been used as an important source for enhancing local history (Allen & Montell, 1981). Memory and narrative are intricately linked in the *incomprehensibility* of the events of the Holocaust and the many testimonies resulting from this and other needs to remember on the part of survivors (Funkenstein, 1993; Langer, 1991).

EDUCATION

The pioneering work of John Dewey (1938) focused on *experience* as identified in both the personal and the social levels along with the importance of the continuity of experience within both realms. Recently, other educators have used life stories and personal narratives as new ways of knowing in teaching and learning (Connelly & Clandinin, 1999; Elbaz-Luwisch, 2007; Lyons, 2007; Witherell & Noddings, 1991).

LITERATURE

Literary scholars use autobiography as texts through which to theoretically and critically explore questions such as design, style, content, literary themes, and personal truth (Olney, 1980). Autobiographies also hold much potential for other research endeavors, such as reconstructing ways of knowing in women's lives (Helle, 1991) or charting cultural memory (Freeman, 2002).

RELIGION

Religious autobiographies, as well as life stories, can portray religion and spirituality as a lived experience. Researchers can ask specific questions of the story. What beliefs, or worldviews, are expressed in the story? Is the transcendent expressed? Did a spiritual community play a role in the life lived deeply (Comstock, 1995)?

PHILOSOPHY

Personal stories can be examined to see how subjective accounts of one's life often contain a personal worldview, a personal philosophy, a personal value system, a personal ideology, and a view of what is morally, if not politically, correct; in other words, how life is to be lived and how people make sense of the world we now live in could lead to important insights (Brockelman, 1985). Hermeneutic perspectives on personal narratives have been taken to explore the relation between life and story—life as a process of narrative interpretation and stories as interpretations of life (Widdershoven, 1993).

INTERDISCIPLINARY ISSUES

Beyond disciplinary boundaries, some researchers conceive of life narratives as a circumstantially mediated, constructive collaboration between the interviewer and interviewee. This approach stresses the situated emergence of the story told as opposed to the subjectively faithful, experientially oriented account. In this constructionist perspective, stories are evaluated not so much for how well they accord with the life experiences in question but more for how the accounts of lives are used by others for various descriptive purposes (Holstein & Gubrium, 2000a, 2000b).

Life narratives are needed especially of individuals from groups underrepresented in research studies to at least balance out the databases that have been relied on for so long in generating theory. More narratives in the voice of women would help eventually achieve a synthesis of knowledge that would benefit both genders (Gergen & Gergen, 1993). A wide range of uses and applications of narrative knowing in relation to gender issues already exist (Abu-Lughod, 1993; Helle, 1991; Lieblich &

Josselson, 1994). For similar reasons, since how we tell our stories is mediated by our culture (Josselson & Lieblich, 1995), we need to hear the stories of individuals from culturally unheard from groups. Life stories of gay men and lesbians would also contribute to a more complete understanding of the issues related to change in people's lives (Ben-Ari, 1995; Boxer & Cohler, 1989).

In any field, the life story itself could serve as the centerpiece for published research, or segments could be used as data to illustrate any number of research needs. The life story interview allows for more data than you may actually use, which is good practice and also provides a broad foundation of information to draw on.

◆ Defining a Life Story

With so many disciplinary applications and other narrative approaches providing many definitions to consider, I will offer the definition of a life story I have previously used:

> A life story is the story a person chooses to tell about the life he or she has lived, told as completely and honestly as possible, what is remembered of it, and what the teller wants others to know of it, usually as a result of a guided interview by another. . . . A life story is a fairly complete narrating of one's entire experience of life as a whole, highlighting the most important aspects. (Atkinson, 1998, p. 8)

To this can be added Dilthey's succinct framework: putting one's life as a whole, one's entire lived experience, into story form (Rickman, 1979).

A person's life story, the one he or she chooses to tell others, is what is most real, most important to him or her and is what gives us, the casual reader as well as the researcher, the clearest sense of the person's subjective understanding of his or her lived experience, his or her life as a whole. The key to the life story is keeping the story in the words and voice of the one telling it. The life story narrative that results from the life story interview, after it is transcribed, with the interviewer's questions left out and the storyteller's words put into sentence and paragraph form, becomes the essence of what has happened to a person. It presents an insider's perspective on, and understanding of, a life lived.

A recorded life story can take a factual form, a metaphorical form, a poetic form, or any other creatively expressive form. What is important is that the life story be told in the form, shape, and style most comfortable to the person telling the story. It can cover the time from birth to the present, or before and beyond. It includes the important events, experiences, and feelings of a lifetime and is a way of understanding better the past and the present and a way of leaving a personal legacy for the future. The point of the life story interview is to give people the opportunity to tell their story the way they choose to tell it, so we can learn from their voice, their words, and their subjective meaning of their experience of life.

An important distinction between the life story and an oral history is made by Titon (1980):

> In oral history the balance of power between the informants and historian is in the historian's favor, for he asks the questions, sorts through the accounts for the relevant information, and edits his way toward a coherent whole. . . . But in the life story the balance tips the other way, to the storyteller, while the listener is sympathetic and his responses are encouraging and nondirective. If the conversation is printed, it should ideally be printed verbatim. (p. 283)

It is this sense of encouragement in guiding the telling, the sympathetic listening for the subjective meaning of one's life story, or the subjective interpretation of one's lived experience as told to others (usually at least implicit in the story itself), along with the mutually equitable approach and outcome, that is most characteristic of the life story.

◆ Benefits of the Life Story Interview

It is impossible to anticipate what a life story interview will be like, not so much for how to do it but for the power of the experience itself. I find this to be the case over and over with students who report how meaningful it was for them to have done the interview, especially when it was with someone they were already close to, like a parent or spouse. Just witnessing—really hearing, understanding, and accepting without judgment—another's life story can be transforming (Birren & Birren, 1996).

There may be no equal to the life story interview for revealing more about the inner life of a person. Historical reconstruction may not be the primary concern in a life story; what is important is how people see themselves at this point in their lives and want others to see them. A life story offers sometimes a hidden glimpse of the human qualities and characteristics that make us all so fascinating *and* fun to listen to.

I have found that the vast majority of people really want to share their life story. All that most people usually need is someone to listen or someone to show a sincere interest in their story, and they will welcome the interview. For those who may be reluctant for reasons of being intimidated, feeling embarrassed or shamed, or simply being unsure about it or uncomfortable with it, here are a few of the many valuable benefits that can come with sharing a life story for those who are willing and able to reflect on the process and the content of their story:

1. A clearer perspective on personal experiences and feelings is gained, which brings greater meaning to one's life.

2. Greater self-knowledge, a stronger self-image, and self-esteem are gained.

3. Cherished experiences *and* insights are shared with others.

4. Joy, satisfaction, and inner peace are gained in sharing one's story with others.

5. Sharing one's story is a way of purging, or releasing, certain burdens and validating personal experience—it is in fact central to the recovery process.

6. Sharing one's story helps create community and may show that we have more in common with others than we thought.

7. Life stories can help other people see their lives more clearly or differently and perhaps be an inspiration to help them change something in their life.

8. Others will get to know and understand us better, in a way that they hadn't before.

9. A better sense of how we want our story to end, or how we could give it the "good" ending

we want, might be gained. By understanding our past and present, we also gain a clearer perspective of our goals for the future.

Not everyone will experience the life story interview in the same way. Some may look back on certain parts of their lives with regret, and for some, it could even be a painful process. But even this kind of reaction to the interview could have its eventual positive outcomes.

♦ The Life Story Interview as Process

Doing a life story interview is both an art and a science. Although a fairly uniform research methodology can be used to gain a large quantity of important data, there is also much left to individual variation in the depth of reflection and reporting involved in telling one's life story. The life story interview is essentially a template that will be applied differently in different situations, circumstances, or settings.

For example, there are more than 200 questions suggested in *The Life Story Interview* (Atkinson, 1998) that can be asked to obtain a life story. These are suggested questions only, with only the most appropriate few to be used for each person interviewed. There are times when a handful of the questions might actually be used and other times when two or three dozen might be used, and in each case, very likely a different set of questions are chosen. The key to getting the best interview is being flexible and being able to adapt to specific circumstances.

In my view, the life story interview can be *approached* scientifically, but it is best *carried out* as an art. Though there may be a structure (a set of questions) that can be used, just as there are good and better artists, there are good and better interviewers. The execution of the interview, whether structured or not, will vary from one interviewer to another.

A life story interview involves the following three steps: (1) *planning* (pre-interview)—preparing for the interview, including understanding why a life story can be beneficial; (2) *doing the interview itself* (interviewing)—guiding a person through the telling of his or her life story while recording it on either audiotape or videotape; and (3) finally, *transcribing the interview* (postinterview)—leaving questions and comments by the interviewer, and other repetitions, out (only the words of the persons telling their story remain, so that it then becomes a flowing, connected narrative in their own words). One might then give the transcribed life story to the person to review and check over for any changes he or she might want to make in it. Once the final draft of the life story has been read and approved by the storyteller, then the interviewer or researcher can respond to the life story in the form of a personal reaction, substantive interpretation, or theoretical analysis.

The length of a life story interview can vary considerably. Ideally, it is best to let the interview take its course naturally to cover all that the life storyteller wants to cover of his or her life. What may be typical is anything from a 1-hour interview to two or three interviews of 1 hour each with the person to record his or her entire life story. In some cases, this may be considered a brief life story interview, but much can be learned about a person's life in a two- or three-part interview that extends over 3 hours.

Some life story interviews could even go on for 2 or 3 dozen hours. This length of interview would be more like a full-length assisted autobiography. I have done a life story interview of more than 40 hours that was later published as the autobiography of Babatunde Olatunji, the African drummer (Olatunji & Atkinson, 2005). The interviews took place as we were able to fit them into our respective schedules, and with time needed for transcriptions, editing, and the publication process, the entire project took 12 years to complete.

◆ The Life Story Interview as Product

What we will end up with is a flowing life story narrative in the words of the person telling the story, essentially a verbatim transcription, leaving out only repetitions, other completely extraneous information that has nothing to do with the life story itself, and the interviewer's questions. Some reordering of content to make it chronological may or may not be necessary to add to the clarity or readability of the story.

A great advantage of the life story approach in arriving at a reliable and valid research product is that the life storyteller is always consulted in resolving any questions or concerns that may come up

after the transcription. They are the ones who have the final say in what their life story will look like in its final form. They are the authors of the first as well as the final draft of their life story. The person telling his or her life story should always have the last word in how his or her story is presented in written or published form.

◆ A Question of Theory

The life story interview, as used here, avoids debates on theoretical approaches because it is first and foremost concerned with getting the entire subjective story of the life lived in the words of the person who has lived it rather than with addressing a particular research agenda. The need for specific research questions is expected, but this is not an essential, inherent part of the methodology.

The life story itself, as told to an interviewer, is atheoretical in that people do not tell their own story based on a preconceived theory. As individuals, we experience the world not as scientists, through a theoretical lens, but as persons who are trying to give meaning to our own unique or universal lived experiences. We do not approach understanding our own lives with the rigor of a scientific experiment or research project, but we do, however, bring our own subjective understanding or interpretation to our lived experience based on an inner sense of what our experience means to us. Individual lives do carry at least personal meaning of their own, and it is the purpose of the life story interview to help bring forth this meaning. The life story interview is therefore not typically guided by specific theoretical or research questions, other than the questions that would be used to help elicit the story itself.

The subjective, first-person, atheoretical life story text can also, therefore, be seen as pretheoretical—a narrative gathered initially as much for the service provided to the storyteller in guiding his or her process as for its potential research use in a variety of ways. A researcher can, however, add, apply, or assign his or her theoretical stance or understanding to it, just as a literary scholar could add a theoretical perspective to an autobiography. It is also possible, under any methodological circumstances, for a researcher to undertake a life story interview with specific research questions embedded into the interview itself along with those designed to elicit the entire life story. What the life story interview approach shows is that people do not tell their story based on a theoretical framework, yet there can be much meaning expressed in the story, and any theory that fits can be applied to it.

◆ The Life Story Interview as a Deep Relational Exchange

My own evolution toward the life story interview, its ideographic approach, and wanting to view a life as a whole began when, as an undergraduate philosophy major, I was introduced to the work of Wilhelm Dilthey by my professor, William Kluback (1956), one of his translators. In the 19th century, Dilthey's work in the scientific study of the whole person, or the human sciences (*geisteswissenshaften*), laid a foundation for an appreciation of the actual *lived experience* of individual persons and recognized that describing lived experience is fundamentally an act of narrative interpretation. Dilthey's concept of *life* (*das Leben*) referred to life as we experience it in our daily lives (Schwandt, 2001, p. 273). This represents a classical grounding for both narrative and interpretive approaches that look at human beings as whole persons. Dilthey understood that the individual's experience of life is something not to be discounted by the desire to achieve scientific knowledge since each individual life experience is simultaneously in some ways like no one else's (unique), in some ways like some others', and in some ways like everyone else's (universal). The life story interview builds on each of these perspectives of lived experience and brings them into clearer focus through (a) the relationship that is established by the interactional exchange and (b) the respect for the person that is generated in the process.

For a master's degree thesis project in American folk culture, I undertook my first life story interview, sitting with Harry Siemsen, a Catskill mountain farmer-singer, at his kitchen table, recording his life and songs for many wonderful weekends. I was profoundly moved by his willingness to share his complete life story with someone he hadn't known before and even more aware of learning how a new and lasting connection can be forged between people through this unique and powerful personal exchange. It was during this time that I began to look at the bigger picture of stories in their role of strengthening traditional communities and carrying enduring values and lessons about life lived deeply that were key tools for communicating and recognizing our common humanity.

During my second master's degree, in counseling, I began to see the power not only in telling but in retelling, or composing and recomposing, recasting and reframing, one's story and especially in getting to one's deeper or inner story. My doctoral work, focusing on cross-cultural human development, further explored how life story interviews could shed light on the cultural values of elder tradition bearers while creating the quickest and most direct means to experience an in-depth relationship with another, even without any previous experience with the person. In my postdoctoral research work, I further explored how Henry Murray's (1938) study of the lives approach connected with Bert Cohler's (1982) life history interests and Dilthey's human studies (Rickman, 1979).

All along, I have felt that it is important, in trying to understand people's experience in life or their relation to others, to let their voice be heard, to let them speak for and about themselves first, and to look for the wholeness in their life. If we want to know the unique perspective of an individual, there is no better way to see it, and how the parts fit together, than in the person's voice in his or her life story. What is new about *the new ethnography* that Holstein and Gubrium (1995) describe is first allowing the storytellers' construction of their own reality and then, as researchers, learning what we can from it about who they are.

All of this is but a brief outline to express the process I experienced in coming to the strong realization that the real significance, beyond any research agenda or even findings, of the life story interview is most often the relationship that emerges from the experience itself.

Since I created the Life Story Center at the University of Southern Maine in 1988, many of my graduate students, after having done a life story interview for a class project, have said in one way or another how powerful the experience was, especially in bringing them so much closer to the person they interviewed than they were before the interview.

Just one example of this deeper relationship that is the unintended but completely natural outcome of the life story interview is from a woman in her late 30s who interviewed her father:

Sitting with my father for three hours listening to his life story was a wonderful experience for both of us. Our relationship has not been one of sharing feelings and innermost thoughts. I've always felt that he loves me, although he has seldom shown his love through words or behavior. What started out to be a slightly uncomfortable experience for both of us ended up being a very special time. It was like we had both been lifted out of our worlds and placed in this room together. . . . He shared more with me that day than he had in my entire lifetime. At the end of our three hours together we hugged each other. I told him that I loved him, and was glad he was my father. He told me that he loved me, and was glad that I was his daughter. Our eyes both filled up and then this special time ended, although the effects of this time together will stay with us. That door within him that was slammed shut when he was thirteen years old opened up a crack, and I was allowed to peek in and see my father from the inside out— and I am thankful for this.

What individuals reveal about themselves in a life story interview is not only the essence of who they are but also what most makes them human and therefore what most connects us, as listeners, to them.

◆ *Developing a Sensitivity to the Relational Dynamics of the Interview*

The movement toward life stories, where we tell our own story in our own words, is a movement toward acknowledging the importance of personal truth from the subjective point of view. This movement is championed by Jerome Bruner (1986, 1987, 1990, 1991), who has illustrated that personal meaning (and reality) is actually constructed during the making and telling of one's narrative, that our own experiences take the form of the narratives we use to tell about them, and that stories are our way of organizing, interpreting, and creating meaning from our experiences while maintaining a sense of continuity through it all. Robert Coles (1989) also honors the primacy of narrative authority and the relational responsibility in assisting anyone in the telling of their life story. In referring to these life storytellers, he says, "We have to remember that what we hear is *their* story."

The meaning-making nature of telling the stories of our lives carries both the teller and the listener into a personally sacred realm. This is a realm where everything that is exchanged is felt as having a power beyond the temporal, beyond the fleeting changes of day-to-day life. Here, the life story exchange suddenly becomes an interaction charged with a purpose greater than the content of the story itself. The interaction goes beyond the personal, taking all involved to a collective realm of being, where all human beings can readily recognize all that they have in common.

This creates a clear and strong sense of coming to know something new and valuable through the relationship created by the interview itself. How else can we come to know the living, dynamic, interactional nature of a lived experience that the personal narrative expresses but through a relational exchange? Indeed, relationships form the nexus of narrative knowing. It is this learning through an awareness of the deepening relationship that results in a richer and meaningful experience, beyond anything that a research agenda anticipates (Craig & Huber, 2007).

Furthermore, the life story interview approach sees the relationship naturally created through the highly personal exchange as collaborative research in its purest sense. The interviewer/guide takes on the responsibility, then, of becoming a true and equal collaborator—or better yet, a partner—with the life storyteller in keeping the life story presented to others true to the story told, or the story the teller wants to tell, since, as Clandinin and Connelly (1988) have aptly pointed out, "collaborative research constitutes a relationship."

Thus, the primary values that a life story interview approach upholds in carrying out this highly personal exchange are as follows:

1. *The power in telling the life story rests with the teller*, not the interviewer; it is the teller's story being told in the way he or she wants to tell it, and the interviewer's job is to ensure this.

2. *The interviewer*, while being an encouraging and nondirective guide in the process, *is sympathetic to the way the life story is told*, *to achieve a mutually equitable and beneficial outcome.*

3. *The interviewer/guide assists in* the process of shaping and telling the life story, while also *helping to bring forth the unique voice and spirit of the storyteller.*

4. *A life story approach seeks to build a respectful relationship with the storyteller and to hold the highest regard for the subjective meaning shared from his or her life.*

5. *The guide is providing a service to the storyteller*, as much as fulfilling a research interest.

6. *A life story approach reveals* the essence of who a person is, what makes him or her most human, and, therefore, *what most connects us all, despite our differences.*

7. *A life story approach can potentially be a transformative experience*, from the power of the exchange itself, from the depth of the bond that is created, and from the meaning that is shared.

◆ The Ethics of Relational Interviews

Because we are asking real people to tell us their personal stories, and potentially taking their story to a larger audience, we, therefore, have to ask ourselves and be able to answer satisfactorily several questions, starting with these: What is ethically prudent of us to make this exchange mutually beneficial to our interviewee and to our research agenda? How do we make sure that we maintain a consistency between our original intention and the final product and that this is clear all the way through? These are important questions, especially if we ask people for their stories and then write only *about* them, not using their own words to tell their story (Josselson, 1996).

Ultimately, the ethics of an interactional relationship involving a highly personal exchange make the life story interview a value-laden encounter. What may be most intriguing to consider about the inherent values that a life story interview approach upholds (highlighted at the end of the last section) is that these place this particular methodology in a somewhat unique position in relation to other methodologies. This approach consists of a very fluid form of research, one that the interviewer might have to adapt or change while the interview is in progress, depending on each response; it is therefore not designed for the "research precision" demanded by the human subject agreements enforced by universities (Clandinin & Connelly, 2000, p. xxii; Craig & Huber, 2007). Yet, at the same time, it is the very

values themselves that a life story interview approach is founded on that, if genuinely followed, will do more to ensure the equitable and ethical outcome that the human subject agreements are meant to protect than any attempt at "research precision" could.

Clearly, the life story interview approach is, and all interview research for that matter should be as well, deeply grounded in ethical beliefs about the relationship it creates and depends on, as Noddings (1986) has noted. All release forms, or informed consents, should include at least a statement acknowledging the ethical understanding of the interviewer and interviewee, as well as something on the values inherent in the mutually beneficial exchange.

When such relational values are the foundation of a life story interview, the result could be even more positive than expected. Beyond the relationship that is built, the interview itself could become a healing conversation, as it is understood and approached in narrative therapy (White & Epston, 1990) or in other clinical practices where this is the outcome in what is referred to as healing narratives or healing dramas (Mattingly, 2007).

This also can affect considerably the way this highly personal encounter shapes whatever findings might be required as part of the outcome. What has really been entered into in a life story interview is an "implicit contract" based on the trust and rapport the interviewer is able to build with the interviewee. The greater the degree of trust, the greater is the degree of self-disclosure and, with this, the greater the degree of respect and compassion that the interviewer will put into the life story presentation itself as well as into any findings (Josselson, 2007). Underlying all of this is a relational process built on an ethics of care rather than rights (Gilligan, 1982).

The practice of becoming a respectful, honoring, active, empathic listener/guide is not only the goal and approach of the life story interview; it is a highly ethical way of carrying out any research or narrative inquiry work.

◆ Conclusion

Beyond the interpersonal relationship that frames and defines the life story interview, it would also be prudent to consider the current movement in social, cultural, and economic realms toward recognizing the interrelatedness between the parts and the whole on all levels. We might want to ask, if the world we live in is being seen as more and more interconnected, how this might shine a new light on the interviewer–interviewee relationship. Will this change in any way the relationship between a person being interviewed and the one doing the interviewing? If a greater connection between human beings conducting research and generating data were felt, could this mean a greater openness to really explore various research questions, a greater desire to want to learn more or maybe even different kinds of things, both objectively and subjectively, about each other? Could it ultimately lead to an even deeper understanding of how, why, and in what ways we, as human beings, are connected?

As we have seen, this possibility is already somewhat built into the life story interview methodology. The life story interview is more than a methodology. It is a way of being in relationship with another that is rarely found in today's harried world. The opportunity for a deep connection between the teller and the listener in a life story interview is unparalleled.

From my own experience, when I had the honor of listening to and recording Baba Olatunji's entire life story for his autobiography, from his traditional Yoruba upbringing to his becoming a cultural ambassador for Africa to his role in the civil rights movement to his vision for Voices of Africa, I was literally hearing a story that no one else in this world today could tell (Olatunji & Atkinson, 2005). This experience brought me closer to not only Baba the person but to his culture and his world. Yet this is as it could be for any life story interviewer. The experience becomes a rare and unique opportunity to fully enter another's life, culture, and world. This then becomes part of one's own life, culture, and world. The life story interview—and other interview research methodologies—could play a role in the greater realization of our understanding of the world as a network of multiple and diverse, yet interrelated, relationships.

If the notion of interviewer as separate from the interviewee shifted with the trends of our time to a notion of interconnectedness, we might also come closer to what Erikson (1987) spoke of as a "wider identity," which he described as "a future all-human, all-inclusive identity" (p. 497), one that would acknowledge what we already are—one species. He says identity is an issue reaching much deeper than

the conscious choice of roles; moving toward a wider identity, our narrower identities loosen, and we gradually identify with mankind. If identity in the future becomes as bound up with others as it now is with one's self, how might the research relationship change, and how would this affect interview research methods?

These possible changes would not necessarily threaten research as an endeavor but could enhance and enrich our efforts. An individual consciousness usually comes with clear boundaries that separate us from others and our environment. A consciousness of the whole and of our identities as interpenetrating each other, however, would overcome boundaries and could enable us to be as eager and committed to learn as much as possible about others as we ever were. Such a shift could also affect the existing power differentiation between researcher and interviewee.

Finally, a life story is not a history that is discovered; it is a story that arises from lived experience. Life stories serve as an excellent means for understanding how people see their own lives and their interactions with others. They allow us to learn more than almost any other methodology about individual lives and society from one person's perspective. Life stories make connections, shed light on the possible paths through life, and lead us to our deepest feelings, the values we live by, and the commonalities of life. More life stories need to be brought forth that respect and honor the personal meanings the life storytellers give to their stories. The more we share our own stories, the closer we all become.

◆ References

Abu-Lughod, L. (1993). *Writing women's worlds: Bedouin stories*. Berkeley: University of California Press.

Allen, B., & Montell, L. (1981). *From memory to history: Using oral sources in local historical research*. Nashville, TN: American Association for State and Local History.

Allport, G. (1942). *The use of personal documents in psychological science*. New York, NY: Social Science Research Council.

Atkinson, R. (1995). *The gift of stories: Practical and spiritual applications of autobiography, life stories, and personal mythmaking*. Westport, CT: Bergin & Garvey.

Atkinson, R. (1998). *The life story interview* (Qualitative Research Methods, No. 44). Thousand Oaks, CA: Sage.

Becker, H. (1976). The career of the Chicago public school teacher. In M. Hammersley & P. Woods (Eds.), *The process of schooling: A sociological reader* (pp. 75–80). London, England: Routledge & Kegan/Open University Press.

Ben-Ari, A. (1995). It's the telling that makes the difference. In R. Josselson & A. Lieblich (Eds.), *The narrative study of lives: Interpreting experience* (Vol. 3, pp. 153–172). Thousand Oaks, CA: Sage.

Bertaux, D. (1981). *Biography and society.* Beverly Hills, CA: Sage.

Birren, J. E., & Birren, B. A. (1996). Autobiography: Exploring the self and encouraging development. In J. E. Birren, G. M. Kenyon, J. E. Ruth, J. J. F. Schroots, & T. Svensson (Eds.), *Aging and biography: Explorations in adult development* (pp. 283–299). New York, NY: Springer.

Birren, J. E., & Cochran, K. N. (2001). *Telling the stories of life through guided autobiography groups.* Baltimore, MD: Johns Hopkins University Press.

Birren, J. E., Kenyon, G. M., Ruth, J. E., Schroots, J. J. F., & Svensson, T. (Eds.). (1996). *Aging and biography: Explorations in adult development.* New York, NY: Springer.

Blumer, H. (1969). *Symbolic interactionism: Perspective and method.* Englewood Cliffs, NJ: Prentice Hall.

Boxer, A. M., & Cohler, B. (1989). The life course of gay and lesbian youth: An immodest proposal for the study of lives. *Journal of Homosexuality, 17,* 315–355.

Brockelman, P. (1985). *Time and self.* New York, NY: Crossroads.

Bruner, J. (1986). *Actual minds, possible worlds.* Cambridge, MA: Harvard University.

Bruner, J. (1987). Life as narrative. *Social Research, 54*(1), 11–32.

Bruner, J. (1990). *Acts of meaning.* Cambridge, MA: Harvard University Press.

Bruner, J. (1991). The narrative construction of reality. *Critical Inquiry, 18,* 1–21.

Butler, R. (1963). The life review: An interpretation of reminiscence in the aged. *Psychiatry, 26,* 65–67.

Campbell, J. (1968). *The hero with a thousand faces.* New York, NY: Meridian Books.

Chase, S. E. (1995). *Ambiguous empowerment: The work narratives of women school superintendents.* Amherst: University of Massachusetts Press.

Clandinin, D. J., & Connelly, F. M. (1988). Studying teachers' knowledge of classrooms: Collaborative research, ethics, and the negotiation of narrative. *Journal of Educational Thought, 22*(2A), 269–282.

Clandinin, D. J., & Connelly, F. M. (2000). *Narrative inquiry: Experience and story in qualitative research.* San Francisco, CA: Jossey-Bass.

Cohler, B. (1982). Personal narrative and the life course. In P. B. Baltes & O. G. Brim (Eds.), *Life span development and behavior* (Vol. 4). New York, NY: Academic Press.

Cohler, B. (1988). The human studies and life history. *Social Service Review, 62*(4), 552–575.

Cohler, B. (1993). Aging, morale, and meaning: The nexus of narrative. In T. R. Cole, W. A. Achenbaum, P. L. Jakobi, & R. Kastenbaum (Eds.), *Voices and visions of aging* (pp. 107–133). New York, NY: Springer.

Coles, R. (1989). *The call of stories: Teaching and the moral imagination.* Boston, MA: Houghton Mifflin.

Comstock, G. L. (1995). *Religious autobiographies.* Belmont, CA: Wadsworth.

Connelly, R. M., & Clandinin, D. J. (1999). *Shaping a professional identity: Stories of educational practice.* New York, NY: Teachers College Press.

Craig, C. J., & Huber, J. (2007). Relational reverberations: Shaping and reshaping narrative inquiries in the midst of storied lives and contexts. In D. J. Clandinin (Ed.), *Handbook of narrative inquiry* (pp. 251–279). Thousand Oaks, CA: Sage.

Dewey, J. (1938). *Experience and education.* New York, NY: Collier.

Elbaz-Luwisch, F. (2007). Studying teachers' lives and experience. In D. J. Clandinin (Ed.), *Handbook of narrative inquiry* (pp. 357–382). Thousand Oaks, CA: Sage.

Eliade, M. (1954). *The myth of the eternal return.* Princeton, NJ: Princeton University Press.

Erikson, E. (1958). *Young man Luther: A study in psychoanalysis and history.* New York, NY: W. W. Norton.

Erikson, E. (1963). *Childhood and society.* New York, NY: W. W. Norton.

Erikson, E. (1964). *Insight and responsibility.* New York, NY: W. W. Norton.

Erikson, E. (1969). *Gandhi's truth: On the origins of militant nonviolence.* New York, NY: W. W. Norton.

Erikson, E. (1975). *Life history and the historical moment.* New York, NY: W. W. Norton.

Erikson, E. (1987). *A way of looking at things: Selected papers.* New York, NY: W. W. Norton.

Freeman, M. (1992). Self as narrative: The place of life history in studying the life span. In T. M. Brinthaupt & R. P. Lipka (Eds.), *The self: Definitional and methodological issues* (pp. 236–290). Albany: State University of New York Press.

Freeman, M. (2002). Charting the narrative unconscious: Cultural memory and the challenge of autobiography. *Narrative Inquiry, 12,* 193–211.

Freud, S. (1957). Leonardo da Vinci and a memory of his childhood. In J. Strachey (Ed. & Trans.), *The standard edition of the complete psychological works of Sigmund Freud* (Vol. 11, pp. 59–137). London, England: Hogarth. (Original work published 1910)

Freud, S. (1958). Psycho-analytic notes on an autobiographical account of a case of paranoia. In J. Strachey (Ed. & Trans.), *The standard edition of the complete psychological works of Sigmund Freud* (Vol. 12, pp. 3–82). London, England: Hogarth. (Original work published 1911)

Funkenstein, A. (1993). The incomprehensible catastrophe: Memory and narrative. In R. Josselson & A. Lieblich (Eds.), *The narrative study of lives* (pp. 21–29). Newbury Park, CA: Sage.

Gergen, M. M., & Gergen, K. J. (1993). Narratives of the gendered body in popular autobiography. In R. Josselson & A. Lieblich (Eds.), *The narrative study of lives* (Vol. 1, pp. 191–218). Newbury Park, CA: Sage.

Gilligan, C. (1982). *In a different voice*. Cambridge, MA: Harvard University Press.

Gubrium, J. F., & Holstein, J. A. (1998). Narrative practice and the coherence of personal stories. *Sociological Quarterly, 39*, 163–187.

Helle, A. P. (1991). Reading women's autobiographies: A map of reconstructed knowing. In C. Witherell & N. Noddings (Eds.), *Stories lives tell: Narrative and dialogue in education* (pp. 48–66). New York, NY: Teachers College Press.

Holstein, J. A., & Gubrium, J. F. (1995). The active interview. In *Qualitative research methods series* (Vol. 37). Thousand Oaks, CA: Sage.

Holstein, J. A., & Gubrium, J. F. (2000a). *Constructing the life course* (2nd ed.). Dix Hills, NY: General Hall.

Holstein, J. A., & Gubrium, J. F. (2000b). *The self we live by: Narrative identity in a postmodern world*. New York, NY: Oxford University Press.

Ives, E. (Ed.). (1986). Symposium on the life story. *Folklife Annual*, 154–176.

Josselson, R. (Ed.). (1996). *The narrative study of lives: Ethics and process in the study of lives* (Vol. 4). Thousand Oaks, CA: Sage.

Josselson, R. (2007). The ethical attitude in narrative research. In D. J. Clandinin (Ed.), *Handbook of narrative inquiry* (pp. 537–566). Thousand Oaks, CA: Sage.

Josselson, R., & Lieblich, A. (Eds.). (1993). *The narrative study of lives* (Vol. 1). Newbury Park, CA: Sage.

Josselson, R., & Lieblich, A. (Eds.). (1995). *Interpreting experience: The narrative study of lives* (Vol. 3). Thousand Oaks, CA: Sage.

Josselson, R., & Lieblich, A. (Eds.). (2000). *Making meaning of narratives in the narrative study of lives* (Vol. 6). Thousand Oaks, CA: Sage.

Josselson, R., Lieblich, A., & McAdams, D. (2003). *Up close and personal: The teaching and learning of narrative research*. Washington, DC: American Psychological Association.

Kenyon, G., Clark, P., & de Vries, B. (Eds.). (2001). *Narrative gerontology: Theory, research, and practice*. New York, NY: Springer.

Kenyon, G., & Randall, W. (1997). *Restorying our lives: Personal growth through autobiographical reflection*. Westport, CT: Praeger.

Kluback, W. (1956). *Wilhelm Dilthey's philosophy of history*. New York, NY: Columbia University Press.

Langer, L. L. (1991). *Holocaust testimonies: The ruins of memory*. New Haven, CT: Yale.

Langness, L. L. (1965). *The life history in anthropological science*. New York, NY: Holt, Rinehart, & Winston.

Lieblich, A., & Josselson, R. (Eds.). (1994). *Exploring identity and gender: The narrative study of lives* (Vol. 2). Thousand Oaks, CA: Sage.

Lieblich, A., & Josselson, R. (Eds.). (1997). *The narrative study of lives* (Vol. 5). Thousand Oaks, CA: Sage.

Lieblich, A., McAdams, D., & Josselson, R. (2004). *Healing plots: The narrative basis of psychotherapy*. Washington, DC: American Psychological Association.

Linde, C. (1993). *Life stories: The creation of coherence*. New York, NY: Oxford University Press.

Lyons, N. (2007). Narrative inquiry: What possible future influence on policy or practice? In D. J. Clandinin (Ed.), *Handbook of narrative inquiry* (pp. 600–631). Thousand Oaks, CA: Sage.

Mattingly, C. F. (2007). Acted narratives: From storytelling to emergent dramas. In D. J. Clandinin (Ed.), *Handbook of narrative inquiry* (pp. 405–426). Thousand Oaks, CA: Sage.

McAdams, D. (1985). *Power, intimacy and the life story: Personological inquiries into identity*. New York, NY: Guilford Press.

McAdams, D. (1993). *Stories we live by: Personal myths and the making of the self*. New York, NY: William Morrow.

McAdams, D., Josselson, R., & Lieblich, A. (2002). *Turns in the road: Narrative studies of lives in transition*. Washington, DC: American Psychological Association.

McAdams, D., Josselson, R., & Lieblich, A. (2006). *Identity and story: Creating self in narrative*. Washington, DC: American Psychological Association.

Mkhonza, S. (1995). Life histories as social texts of personal experiences in sociolinguistic studies: A look at the lives of domestic workers in Swaziland. In R. Josselson & A. Lieblich (Eds.), *Interpreting experience: The narrative study of lives* (Vol. 3, pp. 173–204). Thousand Oaks, CA: Sage.

Murray, H. A. (1938). *Explorations in personality*. New York, NY: Oxford University Press.

Murray, H. A. (1955). American Icarus. In A. Burton & R. E. Harris (Eds.), *Clinical studies in personality* (Vol. 3, pp. 615–641). New York, NY: Harper & Row.

Noddings, N. (1986). Fidelity in teaching, teacher education, and research for teaching. *Harvard Educational Review, 56*(4), 496–510.

Olatunji, B., & Atkinson, R. (2005). *The beat of my drum: An autobiography*. Philadelphia, PA: Temple University Press.

Olney, J. (Ed.). (1980). *Autobiography: Essays theoretical and critical*. Princeton, NJ: Princeton University Press.

Randall, W. (1995). *The stories we are*. Toronto, Ontario, Canada: University of Toronto Press.

Rickman, H. P. (1979). *Wilhelm Dilthey: Pioneer of the human studies*. London, England: Paul Elek.

Rosenthal, G. (1993). Reconstruction of life stories: Principles of selection in generating stories for narrative biographical interviews. In R. Josselson & A. Lieblich (Eds.), *The narrative study of lives* (Vol. 1, pp. 59–91). Newbury Park, CA: Sage.

Runyan, W. M. (1982). *Life histories and psychobiography: Explorations in theory and method*. New York, NY: Oxford University Press.

Sarbin, T. R. (1986). The narrative as root metaphor for psychology. In T. R. Sarbin (Ed.), *Narrative psychology: The storied nature of human conduct* (pp. 3–21). New York, NY: Praeger.

Schwandt, T. A. (2001). *Dictionary of qualitative inquiry* (2nd ed.). Thousand Oaks, CA: Sage.

Shaw, C. (1929). *Delinquency areas*. Chicago, IL: University of Chicago Press.

Spradley, J. (1979). *The ethnographic interview*. New York, NY: Holt, Rinehart, & Winston.

Thomas, W. I., & Thomas, D. S. (1928). *The child in America: Behavioral problems and programs*. New York, NY: Knopf.

Tillich, P. (1957). *Dynamics of faith*. New York, NY: Harper & Row.

Titon, J. (1980). The life story. *Journal of American Folklore*, 93(369), 276–292.

Van Gennep, A. (1960). *The rites of passage*. Chicago, IL: University of Chicago Press.

White, M., & Epston, D. (1990). *Narrative means to therapeutic ends*. New York, NY: W. W. Norton.

Widdershoven, G. A. M. (1993). The story of life: Hermeneutic perspectives on the relationship between narrative and life history. In R. Josselson & A. Lieblich (Eds.), *The narrative study of lives* (Vol. 1, pp. 1–20). Newbury Park, CA: Sage.

Witherell, C., & Noddings, N. (1991). *Stories lives tell: Narrative and dialogue in education*. New York, NY: Teachers College Press.

INTERVIEWING AS
SOCIAL INTERACTION

◆ Carol A. B. Warren

An interview transcript sits in front of me, on top of a pile. I did the interview, tape-recorded it, and transcribed it. The topic is older women married to younger men; this interview is with a 50-year-old woman married to a 30-year-old man. At the time I did this project, I was married to a man 12 (or 13, depending on when the years were counted) years older than me. My respondents knew that my interest in this topic stemmed from my own situation.

Another interview transcript sits in front of me on another pile. I am a hired hand; the principal investigator who hired me did the interview and tape-recorded it, and her assistants transcribed it. I am to analyze it. The topic is satisfaction versus depression in assisted living (AL). It is not my interest but that of the principal investigator that led up to this interview. I am grimly aware, though, that at nearly 70 years I am being forced to take an interest in this topic. But I am not there yet. I can read the words of this interview, but I cannot feel (echoes of) the feelings, as I did when

I interviewed the 50-year-old woman. These interview transcripts are records of social encounters and can be analyzed as such, although the first one gives an access far beyond the printed word. What do I do with these interviews, as documents of social interaction and/or vessels of topics?

An ethnomethodologist would approach each of these interview transcripts, and the others on the pile, as a slice of everyday life: an interaction between "ethnics," illustrating "methods" of interaction, and not much else. Briggs (1986) and Mischler (1986) would look at it as a speech event, focusing on the ways in which questions are structured and answers shaped by those questions. A conversation analyst, combining these two traditions, might spend 3 hours of seminar time discussing a particular "um" in the transcript.

Not being an ethnomethodologist, however—just a plain old (literally) qualitative sociologist—I see the transcript before me as a document not only of social interaction but of the topic. To play on Gubrium and Holstein's (2002) metaphor of

◆ 129

the respondent as a vessel of answers, I see interview transcripts not only as speech events or social interactions but as vessels of topics. I wrote this methodological chapter, and many other methodological chapters, based on my own and others' interview research, including on AL (Warren & Williams, 2008). I have written vessel-of-topics articles on older women and younger men (Warren, 1996) and on AL (Warren & Williams, 2008; Williams & Warren, 2009).

The focus of this chapter is on the interview as interaction, but its conclusions pertain not only to interaction. The point is to try to grasp the relationship between the interview as social interaction and as vessel of topics. In this chapter, I explore what has been written about the social interaction of the interview, then bring the topic of the interview as interaction back—albeit briefly—into the context of the interview as vessel of topics. None of this is a novel endeavor. Jennifer Platt (2002) and others have explored the history of the interview as one aspect of social science research. There are also numerous anecdotal accounts of interviewing issues that arise while conducting ethnographic and other interviews.

In sociology, the analysis of the interview as social interaction can be traced to the work of Harold Garfinkel (1967) and Aaron Cicourel (1964), who pointed out that social science methods are encounters that can be analyzed as such. Analysis of the interview as social interaction began in the 1980s, with its philosophical debates on the relationship between reality and representation. Empirically based 1980s articles on the interview as social interaction included Grace DeSantis's (1980) article on interviewing doctors. The French sociologist Jean Peneff (1988) followed census takers around as they did their jobs, noting the qualitative context of what was supposed to be a simple quantitative matter of obtaining numerical accounts of household residents. From the 1990s onward, analyses of the interview as social encounter—including feminist interviews—appeared regularly in the literature.

◆ Interviews, Interviewers, and the Missing Respondent

Interviews—from the planning stages to after the interview—have participants, contexts, times, and places. In this chapter, I explore the various "stages"

of face-to-face social science research interviews as social interaction. Interviews that do not involve face-to-face contact, such as those using the telephone or Internet, are considered in other chapters. I am also, in this chapter, limiting the discussion to dyadic rather than triadic or focus group interviews. Although interviews have numerous purposes other than research—such as job, media, or psychiatric interviews—this chapter considers those that have social science research purposes, in particular sociology (since this is my field of familiarity). My focus is on the broad tent of "qualitative" interviewing (including terms such as *naturalistic*, *in-depth*, *oral history*, and *ethnographic*) but with some examples from quantitative interviewing and a few from celebrity journalism.

The content of interviews can be recorded in a number of ways, ranging from notes taken by the interviewer to videotaping. The examples given in this chapter mostly involve an interviewer using an audiotape rather than a videotape. Discussions of the social interaction of the interview, in such cases, rest on examining transcripts of it (e.g., my AL transcript) or experiencing the interview as an interviewer and transcriber as well as through the transcript (e.g., my age-discrepant marriage transcript).

People may be interviewed only once or more than once over a given period of time. Although most examples of interviewing as social interaction are gleaned from one-shot interviewing experiences, repeated interviews can bring different perspectives. Jack Douglas (1985), in *Creative Interviewing*, recommended using multiple interviews to prompt respondent self-revelation. In this chapter, I use the longitudinal "Bay Area" study of the late 1950s and early 1960s to illustrate the changes that occur when the same dozen or so people are interviewed repeatedly for upward of 2 years during different stages of their life (Warren, 1987).

The expectation of what an interview could, would, or should be is culturally variable. Other chapters in this text explore issues of cross-national interviewing. In this chapter, I focus on interviewing in what Gubrium and Holstein (2002) have referred to as the "interview culture" of contemporary Western society. Interviews are virtually inescapable in the mass media. It is the rare respondent who would not have a mental picture of an interview: two people (usually) seated, with the one asking the questions, mainly, and the other answering them; the interaction is bounded in time and place.

The language of dyadic interviewing is worth noting as a background to exploring its interactional facets. The interviewer is just that: the one who interviews, who turns the audio recorder on and off, and who asks all or most of the questions. The one who is interviewed may be referred to as the interviewee, the respondent, or the subject. "Interviewee" is the obverse of "interviewer," and arguably the most egalitarian of these terms. "Subject," evoking psychological experimentation, is arguably the least. The "respondent" is one who responds, as opposed to the one who queries.

And the respondent is missing from most of the discourse on the interview as social interaction. The analysis of interaction in the interview is almost entirely based on the interviewer's experience of it. Although we sometimes think that we know what different categories of people—by gender, class, nationality, or race—might think of being interviewed, we don't know much, if anything, about what individual respondents make of it. Occasionally, subjects' responses in journalistic interviews are recorded. In a telephone interview with Lily Tomlin (Wood, 2010, p. 10), for example, the comedian reflected on her interview interactions: "I don't mind interviews because I rant and meander. Today I'll hang up and say, 'What did I say to that woman?' Hopefully, my meandering during interviews keeps it fresh."

Social science research respondents' perspectives on the interview interaction can sometimes be found in social scientists' interviews of other social scientists. As an example, in an interview by the anthropology student Eric Haanstad (EH; 2001) with the anthropologist Philippe Bourgeois (PB), this exchange occurred following a very long answer on Professor Bourgeois's part:

PB: Now I'm talking too long.

EH: No, you're actually answering most of my questions as we go along.

The tact with which EH responds to PB is perhaps reflective of their relative status positions within anthropology. In an interview with Gary Alan Fine (GAF) conducted by Roberta Sassatelli (RS; 2010) of the University of Milan, Roberta displays her knowledge of what she is interviewing him about; Gary, in turn, guides the interview into his own channels:

RS: I appreciate that fieldwork did not come all of a sudden, that it was part of a broader intellectual development.

GAF: Yes. Let us go back a little bit about my intellectual history, my biography. To talk about that there are a number of places where I could begin. After high school I attended the University of Pennsylvania. (p. 82)

I wish I could say that this chapter would reintroduce the missing respondent to the discourse on the interview as social interaction, but there are not enough bits and pieces of information to make this claim. Social scientists propose numerous generalizations concerning how various types of respondent—by gender, age, nationality, or class—might or should respond to interview questions, but we know little about how individual respondents feel or think about the interview encounter. My discussion of the social interaction of the interview, therefore, is based on the point of view of the interviewer—as she mirrors herself and her respondent—inscribed within the transcript of the interview.

◆ The Interview as Social Interaction

To understand the interview as social interaction, it is useful to understand its preparatory stages—its participants and their contexts—as well as the conduct of the interview itself. Prior to the actual interview—and shaping its interaction to some degree—there are the multiple and changing contexts within which the interaction takes place. The interview encounter is framed by the circumstances that got the interviewer and the respondent to the moment of it. For the interviewer, these circumstances include prior interest in the topic, training in the method, and negotiations such as those between graduate students and mentors, granting agencies and principal investigators, and researchers and human subjects committees. For the respondents, they include the biographical and current features of their lives. And all of these contexts are historically variable.

For both interviewer and respondent, the situation of the interview—its time and place—is of relevance, as well as the selves mirrored within it. As Dingwall (1997) puts it,

If the interview is a social encounter . . . it must be analysed in the same way as any other social encounter. The products of an interview are the outcome of a socially situated activity where the responses are passed through the role-playing and impression management of both the interviewer and the respondent. (p. 56)

The social science interview, with its "role-playing and impression management," is presumed to involve strangers. In some studies, however, acquaintances, friends, or family are interviewed, either by design (Richardson, 1985) or as an accident of sampling (Harkess & Warren, 1993). Interviewing nonstrangers may pose special interactional problems, beginning with the interviewer asking questions to which he already knows the answer. In an interview with a colleague and friend, I hemmed and hawed, half trying to be formally interviewer-ish, half attempting jocularity. The social situation of interviews involving strangers is different from that of interviews involving acquaintances to friends, or family.

RESEARCHERS AND THEIR QUESTIONS

The prior relationship, or lack of it, between interviewer and respondent is one of the myriad contexts that precede and shape the interview encounter. For researchers, interviews are embedded in social science research purposes, which can range from a large-scale census or survey to a dissertation project with 20 respondents. The social interaction of the interview is framed by planned questions and audio or video technologies. Interviewers are selected and trained according to interactional as well as technical concerns. Even the lone-wolf dissertation research interviewer may read up on how to present herself in the best light when attempting to locate, pin down, and actually interview the respondent.

Plans for interviewing involve questions as well as participants. An interviewer such as myself—retired, unpaid, and unconnected with any organization—can approach anyone and ask any questions that come to mind. For researchers in colleges and universities, paid by grants, there are a plethora of human subject committee and governmental constraints on the topics and the framings of the interview, as well as on the cadre of respondents (don't even think about discussing sex with children or anything at all with prisoners). Quantitative researchers' questions are carefully scrutinized for "biasing" possibilities, while qualitative researchers' have to be stripped of the emotionally upsetting.

Interviewers' characteristics and qualifications have been the subject of much debate throughout the history of the interview. For Alfred Kinsey in the first part of the 20th century, males were the only viable interviewers. As O'Connell and Layder (1994) note,

Kinsey "refused to employ women, black people, or people with Jewish names because he believed that only WASPS [white Anglo-Saxon Protestants] could interview everybody" (p. 130). Kinsey considered "matching" interviewers with respondents by race, class, and occupational ranking but concluded that "the qualities of the interviewer, not his sex, race, or personal history, were the important variables" (p. 130)—within his WASP world, of course.

Later in the century, the "matching" theory of interviewing was followed, in which the best interviewer was framed as of the same gender as the respondent, and perhaps of the same race or ethnicity, if not the same age and social class. But not everything was matched. Interviewers were advised to dress in a manner than honored but did not mimic the respondent's style and to observe an unthreatening, calm, and interested demeanor. They were advised to maintain this demeanor throughout the interview; respondents might become ruffled, emotional, or angry but not the interviewer.

Later in the century, too, there arose a literature on "feminist interviewing": interviewing of women by feminist academics not only to obtain information but also to empower respondents in some presumptively unempowered sector(s) of their lives (e.g., Oakley, 1981). In feminist interviewing, interviewers might be permitted to become ruffled or emotional (probably not angry) and also to answer respondents' questions and share personal stories. By the 1990s, some feminist interviewers had come to question the idea of a presumptive bond between interviewer and respondent on the basis of gender.

In addition to the issue of *what* questions to ask, there is also the *how*—how to ask questions and follow up with probes and prompts. I have dispensed some of this advice myself (Warren & Karner, 2010). The Berkeley Oral History Office (Regional Oral History Office [ROHO]; see http://bancroft.berkeley.edu/ROHO), for example, provides the following guidelines for questioning respondents:

An interview is not a dialogue. The whole point of the interview is to get the narrator to tell her story. . . . Ask questions that require more of an answer than "Yes" or "No." Ask questions one at a time. . . . Start with questions that are not controversial. . . . Ask brief questions.

Interviewers and their questions set the background for the social interaction of the interview, as do the specific times and spaces within which the interview takes place. The respondent brings to the table his own interests, agenda, and biography.

RESPONDENTS AND THEIR LIVES

Respondents come to the interview willingly (presumably), interested enough in the topic—and whatever lures are thrown out—to show up. But their agendas and understandings of what the interview is for, and how it unfolds, depend on the biographical and situated context of their lives—which, in turn, is also historically situated. A busy housewife in Napa, California, may not be as inclined to agree to, or prolong, an interview as a bored mental patient. A Napa housewife might be more willing to be interviewed in her home in 2010 than in 1959, being concerned less about "what the neighbors would say."

In the Bay Area study of "schizophrenic" Napa housewives and their husbands in the late 1950s and early 1960s (Warren, 1987), the interviewers interviewed the respondents both during and after their mental hospitalization—multiple interviews, not one-shot interviews, a research design difference that brings up interactional differences. From the interviewers' point of view, the respondents were the same people at both those times. From the respondents' points of view, they might not be—they might be a new, well self, changed completely from the old schizophrenic one. The consequences for the post-hospital interviews of these changes in the respondents' selves in time were manifold.

Interview interaction—indubitably a speech event—is also a temporal and spatial one. It takes place in a location often selected by the respondent, at a time convenient to the respondent. The historical and local context of the interview can shape these choices. In the 1950s and 1960s, gender roles being what they were, several of the women did not want male interviewers coming to their homes, in case the neighbors talked. In his ethnographic and interview research on American Nazis, Pete Simi attempted to limit his interview interactions to times and places where there were more than a couple of people around, in order to limit his chances of being beaten up or possibly killed (Simi & Futrell, 2010). In Hanna Herzog's (2005) study of Palestinian female residents of Israel, she claims that the interviewee's choice of location—at home, at the workplace, or in a neutral location—was political:

> The participants used their choice of location to redefine themselves and their role as interviewees—but no less so, of their place in the gender and national order. The decision of where to hold the interview allowed the participants to demand that the interviewers, particularly the Jewish ones, traverse both geographic and social boundaries. (p. 44)

In studies of elderly persons in AL (Warren & Williams, 2008; Williams & Warren, 2009), interview questions about satisfaction with the AL facility and personal depression were interpreted within the contexts of home and a home. No home could match, for most of these women, their own homes, in which they had reigned as wife, mother, and cook. But on the other hand, they "could not complain," because they perceived the context of the AL facility as one in which complaining could lead to trouble—specifically, being moved on to the next, worse stage of old age: the nursing home. We refer to this interview context as that of "fear."

The institutional context of fear promoted vague answers or nonanswers from the elderly residents of AL. The institutional context of loneliness, however, moved them in the other direction, toward elaborating and extending communication with the interviewer. The residents were lonely, often because they were without spouses, family, or friends in everyday life, and they did not necessarily get along with the other residents. So the middle-aged female nurse practitioner interviewer—not demented, not blind or deaf, and interested in them—was a welcome visitor. As one AL resident said of the interviewer, "I'm glad you helped fill in the morning" (Warren & Williams, 2008, p. 409).

In the Bay Area study, the participants were repeatedly reinterviewed, which meant engaging and reengaging the interviewee from the patient to the ex-patient stages of her moral career. Initially, the social science interviewers seemed to the woman like just another medical stranger encountered on her road to patienthood, and she responded as she was "supposed" to, by answering questions. After a few months or years, after discharge, however, the researchers' interview beginnings shifted in a number of ways, including role reversal and changing the definition of the situation from "scientific" to "sociable."

Several of the respondents attempted to reverse roles, attempting to analyze the interviewer clinically:

[Referring to the interviewer] Jack Oren said, "I think you are a kid that missed happiness somewhere along the line." He then started speculating about my past life and thought that something had happened to me . . . to make me feel like that. Mr. Oren first was critical about my interviewing technique, then started to question me about my life, and so on. (Warren, 1987, p. 62)

In addition to role reversal, Mr. Oren attempted to redefine the interview situation as a sociable one: "Mr. Oren asked me if I wanted to join them for dinner, and was rather insistent about this despite my repeated declining" (Warren, 1987, p. 261). Similarly, June Mark asked if the interviews could be redirected into more sociable, everyday, or what she called "normal" channels. In response to the interviewer's introductory "How are you?" the ex-patient answered, "How are *you*?" in a pointed attempt at role reversal (Warren, 1987, p. 261). Ann Rand

repeated that she would only see [me] again if I would have her over to my house. While the interviewer was evasive, Ann said, "Then I suppose you still see me as a patient. To me you are either a friend or some kind of authority, now which is it? The way I see it, you either see me as a friend or a patient." (Warren, 1987, p. 261)

To the ex-patients, the point of attempting role reversal and sociability was the erasure of the old, patient self. The interview reminded them that they had been mental patients. June Mark, for example, said that

she cannot fully participate in the research simply because the research in itself signifies the stigma of deviance which she is struggling to avoid. . . . "You keep asking a lot of questions . . . things I want to forget about. . . . It's not normal, my talking to you. . . . It's just that I am reminded I'm a patient. If you're a patient, you're always a patient."

The interviewer can be or become a dangerous listener in the social interaction of the interview, depending on the context of the respondents' lives.

The interviewer becomes dangerous by the simple act of listening: when the speaker has put on the

mantle of a new self seeking to bury the old in an unmarked grave, yet must confront the presence of an interviewer who has knowledge of the past self. The listener is also dangerous as a participant in the retelling of the past by a respondent who feels unable to escape from that past and the self constituted by it. (Karner & Warren, 1995, p. 81)

◆ The Social Interaction of the Interview

Within its chosen time and place, the interview has a beginning, an end, and in the middle an expectation of questioning and answering. This process is built on the assumption of an interviewer and a respondent, strangers to each other, sitting down somewhere private, close but not too close together, with the interviewer in charge of a well-tested and functioning tape recorder. Indeed, many interviews follow this model; others, however, may involve other interactional frames. The Bay Area study began with the first interview following this model, but as the years went by, the interviewer and the respondent were no longer strangers.

As researchers who have had their interviews interrupted have observed, the unintended presence of other people in an interview (as opposed to, say, a purposely dyadic or focus group interview) can affect the social interaction. Ferraro (2008) describes one such situation, saying,

It is important to be aware of the social situation in which the interview takes place. . . . What effect does the presence of other people have on the answers given? . . . Early in the initial stage of the research a single adult male, who was being interviewed in the presence of his single male friend, mentioned that he spent the night with his girlfriend. When the two friends were interviewed the next day, they mentioned that they too had spent the night with their girlfriends. (p. 101)

Later, we will see what Ferraro (2008) did about this sequence of storytelling.

BEGINNING THE INTERVIEW

Koltnow (2010) gives an interesting description of a celebrity interview with the then 18-year-old Lindsay Lohan. The interview began at 6:30 p.m., 3 hours late. "When I entered her hotel suite, she rose from a sofa and extended her hand. 'I'm sorry for being late,' she said. . . . 'No, you're not,' I snapped back." The interview was supposed to—and did—take place in the bedroom, where "I sat down across from her and asked her about her injuries. She lifted her leg up and laid it across my lap to show me her bruises. I asked her to remove her leg from my lap" (p. E2). Such an approach to the beginning of an interview is not for the faint of heart—or the social scientist.

For the qualitative interviewer, it is up to the interviewer to make the introductions, set the tone, and ask the questions—politely. Although there are debates in academic circles over whether or not interviewers should self-disclose, the matter is, again, up to the interviewer (not the respondent, who may or may not want the interlocutor to self-disclose) (Viruru & Cannella, 2006). Interviewers are trained or told to greet the respondent with the proper polite formalities, then to proceed to the beginning of the interview as rapidly as courtesy permits. The beginning of the interview is signaled often by the participants sitting down and arranging themselves and the interviewer taking out pen and paper (perhaps as props), setting up the tape recorder, and bringing out the consent form to sign. There are anecdotal, but not so many published, accounts of respondents balking at precisely this point, asking not to be tape-recorded, or even walking away from the interview altogether.

Walking away from the interview may be precipitated by second thoughts or fears, by the intrusion of the respondent's own agendas, or by the specter of the consent form. As a student of mine was attempting to interview mental patients for an **electroconvulsive therapy** (ECT) study, I was attempting to interview mental health lawyers and psychiatrists. Several of her patients—poor and lower class, with time on their hands—walked away from the beginning of the interview, as did several of mine—upper class, pressed for time, and called urgently away.

I have found that for some respondents the signing of the consent form is the sticking point. In a 1980s (aborted) study of lesbians, I discussed the research with one respondent, turned on the tape recorder, and presented her with the consent form to sign. She said, "What is this—you tell me you are going to protect my identity AND NOW YOU WANT MY SIGNATURE ON THIS FORM?" This respondent had recognized the tension between informed consent and protection from (stigma) harm, and needless to say, she walked away from the study.

Some cross-cultural research has encountered similar (but, of course, contextually different) opposition to the signing of consent forms. In her study of being "poor and pregnant in New Delhi, India," Helen Vallianatos (2006) describes the beginning of her interviews with pregnant women:

My assistants and I visited the women in their homes, explained the study, and if the women were interested, obtained their consent. . . . I did not ask the women to sign a consent form, because I had been advised . . . that because these women were illiterate, they would not readily sign their names to a document they could not read. Stories circulated in the community about people foolishly signing a paper without being able to read the document, and, by doing so, they had given up their land or other valuables. (p. 41)

Helen Vallianatos (2006) was lucky: "I approached a total of 156 women. Only one woman refused to participate, and another turned out not to be pregnant and was dropped from the study" (p. 4).

These various preambles to the beginning of question asking in the interview may be dispensed with in interviews with fellow social scientists. In the Italian sociologist Roberta Sassatelli's (2010) interview with the sociologist Gary Alan Fine, she went straight to the heart of the matter:

RS: I want to start this interview with your intellectual trajectory from social psychology to sociology and ethnography, which was not an obvious path. I mean, you could have taken a different direction . . .

GAF: Absolutely . . . (p. 81)

Following Gary Alan Fine's "Absolutely," there are 11 inscribed lines of commentary by Sassatelli, indicating that she does not take to heart the qualitative researcher's dictum to allow the respondent to do most of the talking.

Another approach to beginning an interview with a fellow social scientist is illustrated by Nadine Wilmot's (NW) 2005 interview with University of California, Berkeley, Professor Emeritus Harry Edwards (HE):

NW: October 18, Professor Harry Edwards. Interview 1 with the Regional Oral History Office, this is Nadine Wilmot. So, good morning.

HE: Thank you for having me here to do this.

NW: We're very glad to. I guess the way we usu-
        ally start these things is by saying when and
        where you were born, and could you tell us
        a little bit about your family background?

In this exchange, Nadine Wilmot proffers the
usual beginning-of-the-interview courtesies, but then
she frames them as mutual, taken-for-granted, background knowledge: "the way we usually start these
things." Topically, this oral history literally begins at
the beginning, with the birth of the respondent.

In the Bay Area study, with its repeated interviews
and thus repeated beginnings, some of the women
some of the time dreaded the arrival of the researcher,
while others looked forward to it. Those who looked
forward to the interviews found them to be therapeutic; in one case, the start of an interview (on April 3,
1959) had a calming effect on the patient, Joyce
Noon. The interviewer, Sheldon Messinger, said,

I had the feeling that Irene James was desperately
trying to gain some control over her feelings and
thoughts by talking about them to me . . . Irene
says that when I arrive for my interview that seems
reassuring.

Just as the interview as a whole is framed by its
contexts as well as its times and spaces, so is each of
its parts. Frankland (2007), in describing his ethnographic and interview research in Kampala, Uganda,
gives this description of the ritualized greetings/
questions/answers provided by researcher and
respondent at the beginning of research encounters:

In response to the standard greeting of "how's
life?" a regular answer from the young men would
be either "surviving" or "fifty-fifty." The follow-up
would move further along the same lines: "life is
tough, there is no money around"; "my pockets
are empty"; "you know how it is . . . no money,
no life." (p. 44)

Once the interview has set its course, the next
stage is (presented as) engaging the respondent in
some way to keep the interview going.

ENGAGING THE RESPONDENT

There is a social history to the sort of interactions
seen as likely in or appropriate to the interview.

In the early 20th century (Palmer, 1928), models of
the research interview resembled models of the welfare interview, in which a subordinate (in social class
and income) was reviewed by a superordinate for
worthiness and truthfulness. The stance of the interviewer was to be in charge, cool and collected. In the
1920s, Vivienne Palmer (1928) suggested that the
interviewer maintain a "detached attitude" to guard
against "distorting the story of the personal interview . . . causing him to express himself in terms of
the interviewer" (p. 175).

During the next few decades, rapport rather than
coolness became the truth-eliciting strategy. Alfred
Kinsley adopted a presumptively rapport-building
folksy style with respondents such as this "older
Negro male":

Kinsey enquired if he had ever "lived common
law." The man admitted he had, and that it had
first happened when he was fourteen. "How old
was the woman?" Kinsey asked. "Thirty-five," he
admitted, smiling. Kinsey showed no surprise. "She
was a hustler, wasn't she?" At this, the subject's
eyes opened wide, he smiled in a friendly way, and
said, "Well, sir, since you appear to know something about these things, I'll tell you straight."
(quoted in O'Connell & Layder, 1994, p. 131)

O'Connell & Layder (1994), critics of Kinsey's
interview interactions, question the "rapport" interpretation of this exchange:

Why did [Kinsey] not consider the possibility that
the man was exaggerating the age difference, or
that the smile and wide-eyed "Well, sir," could
have been a straightforward mockery of Kinsey's
rather transparent line of thought? (p. 131)

By the late 20th century, the trajectory of the typical interview was presumed to unfold in stages, from
socially correct to more nuanced answers, or from
cool formalities to ardent truth telling (see Douglas,
1985). The topic of rapport between interviewer and
interviewee, and its relationship to truth, has been
the subject of considerable debate, as has been the
purported "natural history" of the successful interview from courtesies to rapport to truth revelation.

Even the seemingly ill-fated interview of Lindsay
Lohan by the journalist Barry Koltnow (2010) seems
to have been successful in its middle stage. Taking
a hard line, Koltnow says that once Lindsey Lohan

understood that I was not going to be easily charmed or manipulated, she settled down and turned into a perfect interview subject. She was never defensive, and answered every question fully. She complained about becoming a tabloid obsession, which did not sound like complaining but rather a statement of fact. (p. E2)

A similar "natural history" of the celebrity interview is described by Eric Wilson (2010) as he interviewed Courtney Love. Wilson met Love at 7 p.m. in the lobby of her hotel, where she said she wanted to finish her cocktail, and asked him to go up to her room. She showed up 2 hours later naked, with a man (p. D1). During the interview, however, "she came across as calm, funny, and well read. . . . I was tempted to agree with the writer Dennis Cooper, who defended Ms. Love as misunderstood" (p. D12).

Within the "stage" model of the interview there has often been the assumption that what comes later is more truthful than what comes first. The respondent may indeed say one thing toward the beginning of the interview and another toward the end, and the parameters of this difference need to be explored. In a 1970s ethnographic and interview study of Weight Watchers (Laslett & Warren, 1975), I had noticed that much of the group meeting time was devoted to the subject of food. When I asked my first interview respondent if she thought that the meetings focused on food, she said, "Oh no." About an hour and a half later—much of which time was spent discussing food—she said, "That earlier question of yours—well it does seem we spend a lot of time discussing food, doesn't it!"

Given that this was an ethnographic interview, the "truth" of these interview comments can or could be located ethnographically—yes, there is a focus on food in Weight Watchers (at least there was in the early 1970s). Without the ethnographic component to the study, the researcher would not, from these interview contradictions, be able to make any comment about whether or not Weight Watchers focused on food.

But what is happening here interactionally? I have the sense, and have had a similar sense in other interview contexts, that the unfolding of the interview—as long or short as the respondent wished—permitted the student to reflect on the parameters of her experience in the Weight Watchers meeting as the questions and answers of the interview proceeded. The shaping of interview interaction by topic is part of its unique power.

The topic of an interview is obviously one of interest to the interviewer (with the possible exception of research with hired hands, where it might not be). Interviewers hope that it will be of interest to the respondents also, but at times, it is perhaps of too much interest or of too little. The classic interviewing problem of stubby "Yes" and "No" answers to questions when thick description is wanted can be traced to several sources: respondents who aren't very verbal or have little interest in the topic, respondents who are fearful of discussing the topic, and respondents who use silence loudly.

Napolitano (2009) describes 5 interviews with homeless young people in a shelter—out of 28—as "unsuccessful." Although she refers to the interaction of the "successful" interview as "ritual," its components equally reflect earlier concerns with rapport: a mutual focus of attention, synchronization of body microrhythms and emotions, turn taking, and nonverbal cues such as sitting forward in one's chair and head nodding (p. 6). In the absence of such rapport, the interaction proceeded thus: "OK, do you think it's easy to go to school and raise your daughter?" Respondent: "No."

There are even shorter answers than "No" in interviews. Viruru and Cannella (2006) speak of the power of silence on the part of research subjects:

The link between language and power is not as simple and natural as dichotomous ways of thinking have led us to believe. Silence can be used as a "strategic defense against the powerful." . . . Silence . . . becomes the opposite of passivity. . . . Qualitative interviews . . . have yet to transcend the boundaries that would allow discourses such as silence to be an integral part of research. (p. 187)

ROHO advises similarly—although from a less wordy epistemology—"Don't let periods of silence fluster you." I remain unconvinced, flustered by periods of silence during interviews.

Then, there is the issue of too much interest on the part of the respondent in the researcher or the topic of the interviewer—or both. Students of the interview worry about the problem of overrapport between interviewer and respondent, perhaps resulting in the respondent trying to please the interviewer by saying what seems to be expected. Overinvestment in the topic on the part of respondents can lead to moments of interview drama. For example, a student studying the identities of biracial people had to terminate one interview when the respondent became distraught talking about the experience of being biracial. This is the sort of nightmare that human subjects committee members dream about.

Between the engaging of the respondent and the ending of the interview is the end of the interview—the last questions asked and comments made. It is commonplace to advise the interviewer to introduce controversial or difficult questions later in the interview, after trust and rapport have been established; this may mean that the last stage of the interview is more fraught than the earlier stages. Others suggest that the interviewer should be prepared with "ending questions" that are upbeat rather than fraught, to terminate the interview on a positive note (Platzer, 2006, p. 76).

ENDING THE INTERVIEW

Not many social scientists are likely to—or would admit to—ending interviews abruptly or impolitely. Angry at being kept waiting for 3 hours for his celebrity interview with Lindsay Lohan, the journalist Barry Koltnow (2010) questioned her for 45 minutes. Then,

> realizing . . . that the interview might go on forever . . . [I] turned off my tape recorder. I looked up at the actress and said, "That's about all I can take of you." . . . I have to admit she won me over during the interview. (p. E2)

We social scientists are taught to be more careful of the feelings of our respondents than Koltnow (2010) seems to be. As generations of interviewers know, the kind of focused attention required by the method is tiring, if not exhausting, and it may also be tiring to the respondent. Although some interviews take more and others less time, between 1 hour and a maximum of 1½ hours is generally enough for this form of intensive social interaction. As Berkeley's ROHO website advises, "End the interview at a reasonable time. An hour and a half is probably the maximum. First, you must protect your narrator against over-fatigue; second, you will be tired even if she isn't."

Ending the interview can be a simple or complicated process depending on whether or not the respondent goes along with the interviewer's wish to terminate it. Many factors come into play here.

Among the factors that prompt the respondent to prolong the interaction are the search for therapy from the interview interactions, a desire to help, and loneliness (Warren & Williams, 2008; Williams & Warren, 2009). Among the factors that prompt respondents to want to terminate the interview—wishing, perhaps, that they had never acceded to it at all—are being at work or busy with many other tasks or, for the elderly in particular, a fear of consequences (Williams & Warren, 2009) or simply tiredness.

The social researchers in the Bay Area study were warned repeatedly not to confuse or infuse their interviews with therapeutic interventions. Some of the respondents, however, did not see the matter in this light: They wanted to prolong the interviews, and the set of interviews, because they experienced the interview interactions as therapeutic and thus did not want to terminate them:

> I had originally anticipated that I would stop the interview after about one tape, but since Joyce [Noon] seemed to be getting some benefit from talking to me and expressing her feelings, I went on for another tape to give her further opportunity to do so.

In many biomedical and social science research studies the respondent is asked to participate not only for his own sake but also for the sake of others who might be suffering from or experiencing what the interviewee has gone through. Prolonging the interview may be prompted by a desire to help as well as by the other agendas discussed. When the AL interviewer apologized for taking 30 minutes longer for the interview than originally promised, the resident said, "I'm here to help you" (Warren & Williams, 2008, p. 409).

For many of the women in our AL studies, institutional loneliness fought with the institutional fear of negative consequences in their response to being interviewed. One consequence was that when areas such as staff competence or satisfaction with the facility were touched on, they were vague with their replies. But some of them wanted to prolong the interview because it was a social interaction and helped alleviate their loneliness.

Interviews may be tiring not only for the interviewer but also for the respondent, especially if that respondent is elderly. In an interview with 90-year-old Deborah Cavendish, Duchess of Devonshire—the last of the Mitford sisters—by the journalist

Sarah Lyall (2010), at one point, the elderly respondent interjects, "'Haven't we had enough?' . . . making it somehow seem gracious" (p. A6). The journalist terminated the interview. Not many interviewers—journalists or sociologists—would "carry on regardless" after such a demonstration of a respondent's wishes.

AFTER THE INTERVIEW AND INTERVIEW AFTERMATHS

Even after the interview has "officially" ended, the interaction may be prolonged—especially if turning off the tape recorder frees the respondent from the fear of being "on the record." While the interviewer may perceive the interview as over—switching off the tape recorder and rising from a sitting position—respondents may not share that perception. There seem to be two circumstances under which the end of the interview and the end of the interaction may not correspond: (1) the respondent is willing to talk "off the record" or (2) the respondent has her own agenda.

"Off the record" remarks are made by people who do not want certain topics to be covered in the "on the record" taped interview. In my experience and those of my graduate students, these are often respondents with some relationship to the law, whether this is the kind of relationship typified by a criminal or the kind of legal liability personified in a doctor or lawyer. As I turned off the tape recorder in a 1980 interview with a hospital psychiatrist concerning ECT, he said, "Now that we can talk off the record, I will tell you about billing." In Geoff Harkness's videotaped interviews at pawnshops, the pawnbrokers spoke about the stigma of being a pawnbroker. After the video camera was shut down, the pawnbrokers spoke to Geoff (a young white man) in stigmatizing terms about the ethnic, racial, and class characteristics of their customers (Warren et al., 2003, p. 101).

Some respondents have agendas that differ from those reflected in the interviewer's questions; in such cases, they may wait until the interview is over to bring their concerns to the fore. After an interview with a Bay Area husband, Sheldon Messinger was asked his opinion of what ECT is for: "As I packed up the tape recorder, Mr. W asked me what ECT does for people. I muttered something about 'I wish I knew.' He responded with, 'Well, what's it supposed to do?'"

In a study of women quilters, one respondent talked during the interview about competition from foreign, machine quilters. After the tape recorder was turned off, the interviewer, Tori Barnes-Brus, reports that the respondent "talked for nearly 5 minutes about these imported quilts . . . and said, 'WOW! I really feel strongly about that, I didn't realize'" (Warren et al., 2003, pp. 101–102).

Other agendas revolve around wanting company or comfort, the same situations that prompt respondents to agree to and continue the interview in the first place (Warren & Williams, 2008; Williams & Warren, 2009). In *Tearoom Trade*, Laud Humphreys (1970) describes an interview with "a jobless Negro" who said, "I really wish you'd stay awhile . . . I haven't talked to anyone about myself in a hell of a long time!" (p. 117). In Napolitano's (2009) study of homeless youth in a shelter, one young man said after the interview, "We had fun and we spent a brief amount of time after the interview chatting" (p. 14). In a graduate student interview project on elder caregiving, most of the respondents continued to talk after the interview:

> The caregivers . . . talked about their experience caring for their parents. Some of them remembered something else they wanted to add, while others continued to express their feelings. About a third of the women . . . seemed to find the interviews therapeutic: "They expressed pleasure in being able to talk with someone about this, they didn't really ever get the chance to talk about it much, or if the caregiving stint was over, they could explore it with a new perspective." (Warren et al., 2003, p. 104)

Eventually, the interaction of the interview and after comes to an end, with the parting of ways of interviewer and respondent. This moment has not been much described; it might be a verbal closure, a handshake, or a physical gesture. Meghan McCain, daughter of once presidential candidate John McCain, gives us a rare glimpse into this moment from the point of view of the respondent. Ms. McCain has said that she distrusts journalists because they "do not care about the person being interviewed. . . . If they seem to, it is an act. So whatever happens, don't hug them goodbye" (Shillinger, 2010, p. 12). At the end of an interview with the journalist Liesl Shillinger (2010), "she hugged me goodbye." We can perhaps discern the effect this hug might have had on the tone of Ms. Shillinger's article; she refers to it as "the reflex of a woman who can't separate inclusiveness from effusiveness, and perhaps doesn't need to" (p. 12).

Beyond the ending of the interview and the after-the-interview strip of interaction, the interviewer, the respondent, or both may have echoes of the interview in their lives or thoughts—interview aftermaths. Eric Wilson (2010), despite his conclusion that Courtney Love might be misunderstood, realized that "there is no way I could forgive her for making me wait for three hours" (p. D12). And Love did not forget Wilson either. In this communicative era, interview aftermaths can take electronic form:

Courtney Love sent me a series of lengthy text messages. . . . She apologized for what happened the night before and she said she felt embarrassed. . . . I'm so humiliated . . . I trust you understand that our hearts can take us all to dark and ill timed places. Warmly, Courtney. xx (p. D12)

◆ The Interview as Interaction and as Vessel of Topics

Interviews can be analyzed as social interaction and as sources of data on topics outside the interview: as vessels of topics. Analyzing interviews as social interaction, as I have done here, implies that this interaction is a distinct social form. Contemporary Western interviews involve a strip of interaction that can be analyzed as five stages: (1) introductions and setting up, (2) the beginning of the interview, (3) the middle part of the interview, (4) the end of the interview, and (5) any interactions that occur after the interview's formalities (usually the turning off of the tape recorder) have wound down.

Using interview transcripts as vessels of topics means that we background their interactional frames and mine them for insights on, say, electroshock therapy, pawnbrokers, or pregnant Indian women. The question for the interview researcher is whether or not the socially interactive nature of the interview makes it unsuitable for use as a vessel of topics. This is what ethnomethodologists and linguists might claim. Ferraro (2008), who was quoted at the beginning of this chapter, seems to agree. This is what he concluded about the three interviews he conducted with young men who said that they had

spent the night with their girlfriends: "It seemed fairly transparent that the two friends, in order to preserve their reputations as sexually active bachelors, had at least the motivation to fabricate that part of their . . . history" (p 101). The study's author, given his "situated fabrication" interpretation, "threw out" all three interviews. Although the Ferraro book was published in a 2008 edition, the antique nature of this discussion makes it likely that the interviews took place many years, if not many decades, ago. Young men spending the night with girlfriends would not merit a raised eyebrow in 2008, let alone the throwing out of three interviews.

When we analyze interviews, we acknowledge that "the veridical is intertwined with the rhetorical" (Platzer, 2006, p. 74). But unlike Ferraro (2008), most of us don't throw out our interviews, even when there might be some "fabrication." In one of our AL analyses (Warren & Williams, 2008), for example, we suspected that some of the residents some of the time suddenly became afflicted with confusion, deafness, or memory loss when asked, in the context of institutional fear, questions they did not want to answer. In one of many examples, the researcher, KW, asked two residents, whom we will call GP and NB, if they had "trouble understanding" the mostly African staff; these residents' answering strategies were different, and interesting:

GP: Maybe a little, but not, you know, not too much.

NB: I didn't understand what you said. (Warren & Williams, 2008, p. 417)

Sociologists are famous for pointing things out that they then ignore; the interactionally contingent aspects of the interview are among those things. We write methodological articles about these contingent aspects, and then we go on to analyze the data as if this were not so. That is why we have a fair number of titles and themes in our published methodological literature like this one: "Theorizing From the Neck Down: Why Social Research Must Understand Bodies Acting in Real Space and Time (and Why It's So Hard to Spell Out What We Learn From This)" (Eliasoph, 2005, p. 159).

In our AL research, we concluded the following:

Mostly . . . residents have to suck up and get by, do for themselves as much as possible, comply with staff directives, socialize and participate in activities, and refrain from criticizing the facility or its staff. Given this institutional fear factor . . . recorded interviews may be somewhat threatening—the interviewer could be a spy for the facility, or report back to the facility, no matter what [the reassurances]. On the other hand, many of these residents are lonely, and the interview has a more positive meaning—filling time, someone listening to them. (Warren & Williams, 2008, p. 415)

This analysis was based on interviews analyzed both as social interaction and as vessels of topic—and, not incidentally, with a background of ethnographic work. AL residents attempt, at all times, to project a self competent enough not to be forwarded to the nursing home; thus, they know to comply, socialize, participate, and not be critical—their words are vessels of the topic "The AL Experience." Their interaction with the interviewer is shaped both by loneliness and by fear in the context of this particular environment. Despite their infirmities, these old people "suck it up . . . get by . . . and do for themselves" both in the AL facility and in the interview. Let one of them—an 87-year-old former college teacher, DW—have the last word. The interviewer is attempting to administer Likert-type health and satisfaction scales and asks, "Would you say your health has been good in general?":

DW: Well I tell people I am good considering the shape I am in.

KW: Uh huh, well that's . . .

DW: Is that what you mean?

KW: Yeah, I think it's a good attitude.

DW: Should I say very good because of course I have hearing and vision problems? Or should I just say very good to allow for those?

KW: Well it's just kinda how you think. There's no right or wrong answers.

DW: That's why I don't like this kind of a question.

KW: I know. It's kinda hard to know what they mean. So if you think you're doing good.

DW: I think I'll put very good. Now do I mark it or do you?

We—the interviewer and the respondent—both mark it, don't we?

◆ References

Briggs, C. L. (1986). *Learning how to ask*. Cambridge, England: Cambridge University Press.

Cicourel, A. (1964). *Method and measurement in sociology*. New York, NY: Free Press.

DeSantis, G. (1980). Interviewing as social interaction. *Qualitative Sociology, 2*, 72–78.

Dingwall, R. (1997). Accounts, interviews, and observations. In G. Miller & R. Dingwall (Eds.), *Context and method in qualitative research* (pp. 51–65). London, England: Sage.

Douglas, J. D. (1985). *Creative interviewing*. Beverly Hills, CA: Sage.

Eliasoph, N. (2005). Theorizing from the neck down: Why social research must understand bodies acting in real space and time (and why it's so hard to spell out what we learn from this). *Qualitative Sociology, 28*(2), 159–169.

Ferraro, G. (2008). *Cultural anthropology: An applied perspective* (7th ed.). Belmont, CA: Thomson Wadsworth.

Frankland, S. (2007). No money, no life: Surviving on the streets of Kampala. In J. Staples (Ed.), *Livelihoods at the margins: Surviving the city* (pp. 31–51). Walnut Creek, CA: Left Coast Press.

Garfinkel, H. (1967). *Studies in ethnomethodology*. Englewood Cliffs, NJ: Prentice Hall.

Gubrium, J. F., & Holstein, J. A. (2002). From the individual to the interview society. In J. F. Gubrium & J. A. Holstein (Eds.), *Handbook of interview research: Context and method* (pp. 3–32). Thousand Oaks, CA: Sage.

Haanstad, E. (2001). Being a public anthropologist: An interview with Philippe Bourgois [*sic*]. Retrieved from www.publicanthropology.org/Journals/Gradj/Wisconsin/Bourgint.htm

Harkess, S., & Warren, C. A. B. (1993). The social relations of intensive interviewing: Constellations of strangeness and science. *Sociological Methods and Research, 21*, 317–339.

Herzog, H. (2005). On home turf: Interview location and its social meaning. *Qualitative Sociology, 28*, 25–47.

Humphreys, L. (1970). *Tearoom trade: Impersonal sex in public places*. Chicago, IL: Aldine Press.

Karner, T. X., & Warren, C. A. B. (1995). The dangerous listener: Unforeseen perils in intensive interviewing. *Clinical Sociology Review, 13*, 80–105.

Koltnow, B. (2010, July 16). Jailed Lohan earned her public disapproval. *San Diego Union-Tribune*, p. E2.

Laslett, B., & Warren, C. A. B. (1975). Losing weight: The organizational production of behavior change. *Social Problems, 23*, 69–80.

Lyall, S. (2010, November 6). A duchess with a common touch. *The New York Times*, p. A6.

Mischler, E. G. (1986). *Research interviewing: Context and narrative*. Cambridge, MA: Harvard University Press.

Napolitano, L. (2009, August). *The qualitative interview as interaction ritual*. Paper presented at the annual meetings of the American Sociological Association, San Francisco, CA.

Oakley, A. (1981). Interviewing women: A contradiction in terms? In H. Roberts (Ed.), *Doing feminist research* (pp. 30–61). London, England: Routledge & Kegan Paul.

O'Connell, J. D., & Layder, D. (1994). *Methods, sex and madness*. London, England: Routledge.

Palmer, V. (1928). *Field studies in sociology: A student's manual*. Chicago, IL: University of Chicago Press.

Peneff, J. (1988). The observers observed: French census takers at work. *Social Problems, 35,* 520–535.

Platt, J. (2002). The history of the interview. In J. F. Gubrium & J. A. Holstein (Eds.), *Handbook of interview research: Context and method* (pp. 33–54). Thousand Oaks, CA: Sage.

Platzer, H. K. (2006). *Positioning identities: Lesbians' and gays' experiences with mental health care*. Alberta, British Columbia, Canada: Qual Institute Press.

Richardson, L. (1985). *The new other woman: Contemporary single women in affairs with married men*. London, England: Collier Macmillan.

Sassatelli, R. (2010). A serial ethnographer: An interview with Gary Alan Fine. *Qualitative Sociology, 33,* 79–96.

Shillinger, L. (2010, September 12). The rebel. *The New York Times,* pp. 1–12.

Simi, P., & Futrell, R. (2010). *American swastika: Inside the white power movement's hidden spaces of hate*. Lanham, MD: Rowman & Littlefield.

Vallianatos, H. (2006). *Poor and pregnant in New Delhi, India*. Walnut Creek, CA: Left Coast Press.

Viruru, R., & Cannella, G. S. (2006). A postcolonial critique of the ethnographic interview. In N. K. Denzin & M. D. Giardina (Eds.), *Qualitative inquiry and the conservative challenge* (pp. 175–191). Walnut Creek, CA: Left Coast Press.

Warren, C. A. B. (1987). *Madwives: Schizophrenic women in the 1950s*. Chapel Hill, NC: Rutgers University Press.

Warren, C. A. B. (1996). Older women, younger men: Self and stigma in age-discrepant relationships. *Clinical Sociology Review, 14,* 62–86.

Warren, C. A. B., Barnes-Brus, T., Burgess, H., Wiebold-Lippisch, L., Kennedy, V., Dingwall, R., . . . Shuy, R. (2003). After the interview. *Qualitative Sociology, 26,* 93–110.

Warren, C. A. B., & Karner, T. X. (2010). *Doing qualitative research: Interviewing, ethnography and analysis*. New York, NY: Oxford University Press.

Warren, C. A. B., & Williams, K. N. (2008). Interviewing elderly residents in assisted living. *Qualitative Sociology, 30,* 407–424.

Williams, K. N., & Warren, C. A. B. (2009). Communication in assisted living. *Journal of Aging Studies, 23,* 24–36.

Wilson, E. (2010, November 7). I'd like to be trusted again. *The New York Times,* pp. D1, D12.

Wood, B. (2010, January 20). Just a "regular" gal. *San Diego Union-Tribune Night and Day,* p. 10.

9

AUTOETHNOGRAPHY AS FEMINIST SELF-INTERVIEW

◆ Sara L. Crawley

As I read a glossy national lesbian magazine, I marvel at the tough, leather-
jacketed (female-to-male) transgender
men who seem the new fascination of the hip,
urban queer media. As I sit in my suburban,
mid-20th-century, ranch-style block house in
Florida, these images, as gorgeous as they may be,
do not ring so familiar to my lesbian experience
or my identity. How do trans men differ from
butch lesbians? Why are cutting-edge queers
always represented as residing in urban hotspots
such as New York or San Francisco? Are they
more progressive than me? How did transgender
become the hottest new identity? If an identity is
a deeply felt, interior self, how can an identity be
trendy? Why do I often feel that my suburban life
is somehow less queer than that of urban dykes? I
am a social theorist. I should be able to answer
these questions. Yet as a social theorist, the lens is

very rarely turned on me, as if somehow that
would constitute clinical counseling, not sociological reflection. If I am truly committed to a
constructionist explanation of identities and sexualities, shouldn't I be able to theorize my own
identity? How did I come to identify as butch, not
trans? And so the self-interview begins.

Bingo! It hits me. I didn't have a leather jacket
when I was growing up and coming out in subtropical, suburban South Florida—50 miles directly
west of Grand Bahama. It is hard to be transgendered in hot places, where the body is almost of
necessity exposed to visible surveillance. As a result,
I feel my body differently than if I had lived in a
northerly climate. Perhaps this is why I have always
envisioned myself as butch but not trans. Maybe
identity (including mine) is more about geography
and place than I had previously considered.
Mentally, I comb through my past, asking myself

Author's Note: This book chapter is dedicated to my scholarly mentors, Kendal Broad, Spencer Cahill, Carolyn Ellis, Kim Emery, Joe Feagin, Jay Gubrium, and Doni Loseke, whose work and teachings have so profoundly affected my own. Thank you for always encouraging me to work and play at the edges of discipline.

◆ 143

about the times and places of my coming out. How does it feel to embody butchness as I understand it? I have to actively reflect. How do I understand butch or trans? The finished work is published in the *Journal of Lesbian Studies* as an autoethnography called "The Clothes Make the Trans" (Crawley, 2008a). It reads like a cross between theory and memoir, and I produced it through a process of vigorous self-reflection, not so different from a self-interview.

Is autoethnography social science? What does autoethnography have in common with interviewing? How does one write autoethnography? Having published this style of work (Crawley, 2002, 2008a, 2009; Crawley & Broad, 2004; and selections in Crawley, Foley, & Shehan, 2008), I hear these questions often. The debates in which these questions are situated are compelling and contentiously unresolved (which I describe below). In this chapter, I situate autoethnography as a kind of self-interview, which is not a defined method with specific parameters but rather a balancing act between modernist empirical science, postmodernist deconstructions of science and subjectivity, and the activist pursuit of recording marginalized ideas and voices. Its usefulness lies in an interdisciplinary place between humanities and social science—like most critical theory, especially that of bodily experience—evoking and theorizing simultaneously but refusing to be boxed into categorical notions of method and the ruling relations of knowledge production. Like the iridescence inside a clam shell, it appears to change color as you turn its angle to the sun. For a tenure review committee, it is sociological theory making few claims to empiricism, only speculating as to new directions for future research. Lesbian readers may read it as expressing the truth of an identity—that butchness *is* ableness (Crawley, 2002). Or perhaps they read it as treasonous: How could geography affect identity (Crawley, 2008a)? To my family and friends, it is a loving memoir to our past that is now recorded with a Library of Congress number—not bad for a working-class kid. For me, it is postmodern catharsis in recording how I understand events that are deeply personal to me yet are clearly the purview of my social location in the world, edging ever closer to the elusive original theoretical breakthrough.

In this chapter, my goal is to define the methodological and epistemological bases of autoethnography as based in active interviewing and feminist standpoint theory, respectively. I begin by opening with some methodological debates between modernism and postmodernism. I then outline a brief history of autoethnography as method; offer a brief literature review of styles of autoethnography, including some rather contentious debates; argue for an epistemological shift from these debates toward feminist standpoint theory as a basis for writing autoethnography; and conclude with my view of the limitations and cautions of writing this kind of work.

◆ Between Modernist Interviews and Postmodernist Deconstruction

Postmodernism troubles the premise of modernist interview methods (Fontana, 2002; Kong, Mahoney, & Plummer, 2002). A poststructuralist historian, Joan Scott (1991/1993), argues that any interview project, presumably pursuing truth claims that turn on the "evidence of experience," would fail to fully theorize a broader, historicized understanding of discursive subjectivity, knowledge construction, and power over time and space. Does Scott's argument invalidate phenomenological interviewing? From a critical theory stance, is there no value to giving voice to everyday actors? Henry Rubin (2003) encountered this problem in his wonderful book on female-to-male transsexuals, *Self-Made Men*. Rubin opens the book with a deeply historicized, postmodernist, Foucauldian genealogy of transsexuality. He then proceeds to the empirical chapters wherein his respondents offer the exact opposite view. Following a phenomenological approach, Rubin respectfully interviews his respondents, who assure him that gender and sexuality are strictly essentialist—a truth of the body. They would know, they argue; it is their experience of the body in this world. The crux of Rubin's conundrum emanates from the methodological premise of the interview method—to confirm with members in the social world how their worlds work. Rubin handles this conundrum with analytic grace, turning the focus on the problem of methods while taking his respondents seriously. Though many chapters in this *Handbook* problematize traditional, positivist interviewing methods, few would disagree that the most basic premise of engaging in interview work is to collect empirical data about people's lives. The example of Rubin's work offers some important methodological questions.

How do we regard phenomenological accounts that fully disagree with widely accepted, historicized postmodern theory? Are members simply underinformed, lacking a privileged exposure to dense theory to better narrate their own experiences (an elitist position suggesting that academic theorists somehow always already know the "truth" of social relations)? Conversely, are academic theorists too deeply focused on the world of received theoretical knowledge to give a fair account of lived experience (a position that seems to greatly undervalue the potential of rational thought, my chosen profession)? It seems that we are at a methodological standoff. Perhaps the issue revolves around the differing stocks of knowledge available to each. Everyday actors tend to be immersed in a world of politics and pragmatics filled with media pundits of all stripes hollering at electoral audiences about commonsense moralities. Meanwhile social scientists are commonly trained to focus on rational explanation and clinical evidence devoid of experiential feeling (Simmonds, 1999). Indeed, given this divide, how can we come to understand experiences of the body? In this chapter, I suggest that feminist standpoint theory, including *black feminist thought* and critical race theory, which honors multivocality, can help us moderate these intractable positions such that autoethnography written by academics about their experiences as everyday members of social life can provide interesting insights into experiences, especially of the body, perhaps otherwise impeded by epistemological and methodological hard-lining. In other words, what might be learned if members describing their own lived experience were also critical, poststructuralist theoreticians? There is epistemic gain from being able to utilize both everyday and academic stocks of knowledge. What I argue here is both methodological and epistemological—first, that autoethnography at the margins of modernist interviewing and postmodernist theorizing can offer valuable insights into bodily experience in social interaction and, second, that feminist standpoint theory has always supported this kind of methodological hybridity. The first issue addresses the Schutzian problem of consciousness (Schutz, 1970), while the second addresses the epistemological issue of whose knowledge matters the most in social research. I address these issues in turn.

Interview projects contend with the Schutzian problem of consciousness (Schutz, 1970)—that is, can humans share consciousness? Can we know if what is spoken by one person is understood by any

listener? For philosophers, this may be an unanswerable question. For empiricists, it implies a methodological hiccup in the process of the telling, which is attended to variously according to epistemology. How shall we regard interview data (Gubrium & Holstein, 1997)? Positivist interviewers search for valid and reliable answers from a respondent, wary that politics, rationalizations, stigma, Goffmanian personal fronts, and other murkiness get in the way of attaining truths from the respondent. They worry whether respondents are telling tales and, even if not, whether they themselves have "gotten it right"—ever unsure of the accuracy of the data. Phenomenologists will be seeking authenticity from respondents such that "truths" take a backseat to the realities that respondents narrate for themselves, leaving strict methodologists little room to generalize data to explanatory theory or make claims comparing responses across time or communities. Postmodernists, as I noted above, often avoid interviewing altogether, turning the critique on the process of science itself. Autoethnography from academics who are also members sheds new methodological light on this problem of consciousness. I am not suggesting that politics, rationalizations, stigma, and fronts disappear as issues when interviewers use introspection into their own self as method, but at least analysts who have had theoretical training can argue with the member in their own head about the central experiential and ethical issues to be presented in a text. As such, autoethnography offers one view of the embodiment of social locations that other methods lack—a direct line from the analyst to the member, unobstructed by the Schutzian problem of conveying language *out loud*. In a Meadian sense, the Me and I in one's own internal conversation can offer points and counterpoints, reflecting on members' realities, taking evocation into account, reflecting on methodology and epistemology, and engaging theories of historicity without worrying about a hiccup of consciousness in the telling. This is not without methodological difficulty. Holding one's multiple selves accountable to honesty and rigor continues to be an issue. Nonetheless, angst-ridden struggles of consciousness over whether the interviewer understood the respondent diminish in favor of the struggle over conveying the results on paper (an ever-present issue).

Epistemologically, feminist standpoint theory is a logical premise for this method on at least three bases. First, feminist standpoint theory alters the standard interview project as it argues that members and academics offer equally important components of the knowledge project. Implicitly questioning the relationships between the knower and the known and the researcher and those researched, *black feminist thought*, in particular, works to reduce the hierarchy between academic knowledge and everyday lived experience, finding both potentially mutually informing (Collins, 1990; McClaurin, 2001a, 2001b; Simmonds, 1999). Academics and members offer different stocks of knowledge, if you will, for articulating social relationships, but both positions must work together to formulate a theory that works for people (Smith, 2005), not just for the academic elite. Second, for standpoint theory, social life requires theorizing. A standpoint is an earned, formulated theoretical position that is deeply informed by personal experience and body knowledge. It is not simple essentialism (as in, you have to be one to get it). As W. E. B. DuBois (1903/1989) expresses with his notion of "double consciousness," structural inequality is much more apparent for marginalized people than for those in the mainstream. Double consciousness is understood as a holistic experience of the world through the body, not an innate understanding of fixed races. Still, following the example of DuBois's life, it is not enough to simply experience marginality (i.e., not all black people can articulate a theory of racism like DuBois himself); the experience of double consciousness must be theorized—a work in concert between lived experience and analytic theory. Third, the embodiment of this lived experience involves emotion and analytics. It recognizes the usefulness of rage, sadness, and frustration in articulating experiences of the social world. As such, standpoint theory does not split the actor into rational minds and emotional bodies, instead fusing both into the analysis. I outline these relationships in further detail below.

I do not offer autoethnography as a purer or more accurate form of investigation. Rather, autoethnography becomes one of the tools in the tool kit of methods, but one that can be particularly timely and powerful. My goal is to outline an epistemological basis for autoethnography as I have understood and practiced it—one that honors methodological hybridity, troubles the perceived divide between modernism and postmodernism, and focuses squarely on theorizing social phenomena, rather than curtailing projects according to the rules of received methods. As such, I hope to use autoethnography to preempt the possibility that rules of method operate as "relations of ruling" (Smith, 1988, 2005) in our own knowledge production projects.

◆ A Brief History and Literature Review of Autoethnography

What is autoethnography, where did it begin, and who writes it? The term *autoethnography* has been used by several scholars, sometimes with discordant methodological perspectives. Working to breach the positivist edict of objective distance from the data, the method involves using the researcher's own life experiences as data for theoretical analysis. If researchers interview members for empirical science and researchers can be members of the groups they research, why not engage in the kind of introspection that resembles a self-interview? Among autoethnographers, the issue of bridging the distance between researcher and member seems mostly uncontested. What autoethnographers tend to disagree on are the goals of writing. What should one be attempting to convey with autoethnography? Here, I give a very brief history of this method, review three forms of autoethnography that I believe characterize the current landscape of the literature, and discuss some ongoing debates.

Emerging from the ethnographic tradition in anthropology, autoethnography is not necessarily new. Heider introduced the term *autoethnography* in 1975 to mean allowing *respondents* to speak in their own words with little intervention by the interviewer (Chang, 2007; Reed-Danahay, 1997). In a postcolonialist move, "colonized" subjects were intended to attain some control over an anthropological text by self-representing, reducing the power researchers of the Metropole have with regard to the "Other" whom they study (Pratt, 1994). However, today this pursuit sounds more like interview research than the more current form of autoethnography, in which researchers write about their own life experiences. Some current authors continue to use this definition and method (Besio & Butz, 2004; Butz & Besio, 2004; Reed-Danahay, 1997); but more commonly today, the notion of "auto" refers to the self of the researcher rather than the researched. In 1979, Hayano defined autoethnography as a method of "how anthropologists conduct and write ethnographies of their 'own people'" (p. 99), in which the insider status of the "native-as-ethnographer" is seen as central to the method. He explains that he first heard the term in a graduate seminar in 1966, during which his professor recounted the story of an ethnography of the Kikuyu people done by a Kikuyu researcher in 1938. Apparently when the native Kikuyu ethnographer presented the data, a white African disagreed with some point being made, but none of the observers were able to follow the line of argument because the two broke into a heated argument in Kikuyu. Hayano writes, "Their argument pointedly raised the question of judging the validity of anthropological data by assessing the characteristics, interests, and origin of the person who did the fieldwork" (p. 100). This example demonstrates the centrality of perspective of the "native-as-ethnographer," rather than the ethnographer-gone-native, even where the ethnographer learns to speak the language. It raises the following methodological question: Could a white African ethnographer come to know the Kikuyu people better than a native Kikuyu ethnographer? Both have become ethnographers. It is hard to imagine that the native experience of the one who grew up Kikuyu does not trump that of a nonnative if only on the basis of time spent "in the field."

Focusing on sociological beginnings, both Anderson (2006a) and Plummer (2001) trace back the history of autoethnography and life story writing (which I only briefly summarize here) to the symbolic interactionist ethnographic traditions of the Chicago School, linking the method to classic sociological works such as Thomas and Znaniecki's *The Polish Peasant in Europe and America* (1920), Anderson's *The Hobo* (1923), Liebow's *Tally's Corner* (1967), Whyte's *Street Corner Society* (1969), and Sudnow's *Ways of the Hand* (1978). Although never taken as a distinct part of the analysis, the biography of the ethnographer/students and their seat-of-the-pants experiences in the field were always bound up in the type of ethnography that Robert Park, the school's ostensible patriarch, encouraged (Anderson, 2006a). Anderson argues that Park "encouraged many of his students to pursue sociological involvement in settings close to their personal lives, arenas with which they had a significant degree of self-identification" (p. 375). This type of ethnography often narrowed the distance between the ethnographer and those researched by living among them and trying to experience their lives firsthand. As I will argue shortly, none of the works above fit the criteria of autoethnography as I define it, yet the Chicago School's ethic of being deeply involved predicts the next step offered by the so-called postmodern turn.

The prolific writings of Laurel Richardson (1991, 1994, 1997, 2000, 2002) champion the postmodern cause of narrowing the divide between teller and knower, science and literature, author and audience, and begin to ask the following question: Why shouldn't researchers write about their own member experiences in the theoretical pursuit of understanding various life experiences? Writing the self as data grows out of the postmodern turn and its related critique of the truth claims of positivist social science (see also Clough, 1997; Collins, 1992; Denzin, 1994). Similar to the methodological innovations regarding the auspices of interviewing offered throughout this *Handbook*, scholars with postmodernist interests recognize that knowledge is jointly produced between researchers and respondents, but postmodernists add to this a concern for historically situating subjectivity in time and geography, especially as it relates to power and the sociology of knowledge. As such, the self of the researcher and that of members are placed in a broader historical and political context beyond the specific site of data collection.

There are at least three common forms of autoethnography in publication: (1) evocative autoethnography, (2) analytic autoethnography, and (3) performance autoethnography. I outline each below.

EVOCATIVE AUTOETHNOGRAPHY

Perhaps the most widely written form has been variously termed *emotional sociology* (Ellis, 1991a), *evocative autoethnography* (Anderson, 2006a; Ellis, 1997), or *heartful autoethnography* (Ellis, 1999). Carolyn Ellis has been the most widely cited proponent of this form (1991a, 1991b, 1993, 1995, 1996, 1997, 1998, 1999, 2004, 2009; Ellis & Berger, 2002; Ellis & Bochner, 1996, 2000; Ellis & Flaherty, 1992; see also Bochner & Ellis, 2002; Ellingson & Ellis, 2008), and she offers perhaps the most exhaustive list of this style of work in her article with Arthur Bochner (2000). Ellis's stated goal "is to extend ethnography to include the heart, the autobiographical, and the artistic text" (p. 669)—by way of including "researchers' vulnerable selves, emotions, bodies and spirits," considering "moral, ethical and political consequences" of ethnography, "featur[ing] multiple voices" in dialogue that "repositions readers and 'subjects' as co-participants," and "seek[ing] a fusion between social science and literature." The work seeks to evoke the feeling of lived emotional experience from the reader, and *evocative* is clearly the best term to describe this form of writing. Writing in the first person with vivid recounts of conversations, interactions, and memories, Ellis has given several heartrending examples of this work from her life experiences on topics such as the sudden death of a sibling from an airplane crash (1993), the death of an intimate partner from long-term illness (1995), agonizing with a partner over the decision to abort a fetus (1992), physical care of an ailing parent (1996), and "minor bodily stigmas," such as having a lisp (1998). Other examples of this form of work include the publications of Ellis's students on experiences such as exotic dancing (Rambo Ronai, 1992), having a mentally handicapped parent (Rambo Ronai, 1996), and child sexual and physical abuse (Rambo Ronai, 1995, 1996), among others. The experience of reading such work takes readers to their own dark, painful places—or perhaps opens a view to them if they have yet to have such experiences. These autoethnographers want the reader to *feel* their writing. I have often had to pause during or after reading such work, literally to catch my breath or to wipe away tears. The style is effective at evoking emotion.

Traditional empiricists are often not receptive to the evocative purposes of this kind of autoethnography. Quoting in detail from actual review notes received from reviewers of their own autoethnographic attempts, both Holt (2003) and Sparkes (2000) write of the difficulties of publishing in this genre because of confusion or discord over the method. Their reviewers offer critiques over the "inappropriate criteria" of using only one case as data, crossing the ethical boundary of using self as data, and lack of "rigor." Others have critiqued evocative ethnography as insufficiently analytic, with the potential to be interpreted as self-absorbed (Anderson, 2006a). As a result, both Holt and Sparkes as well as Clough (1997) attempt to offer helpful hints for authors or alternative reviewing criteria for reviewers of this genre. Perhaps the most damning critique of evocative autoethnography comes from Gingrich-Philbrook (2005), when he worries about it

being read as a bad "burlesque" of literary artistry and self-congratulatory elitism from the academy. Ouch! I confess that I have similarly been concerned, albeit with much less vehemence than Gingrich-Philbrook, about the potential usurpation by a purportedly new methodological genre of a literary tradition hundreds of years in the making. Writing in a style that feels more akin to writing fiction than social science, I have questioned my own skills: How will I know if my attempts at evocation are any good? My own hope is that if evocative autoethnographers avoid making sweeping claims about the quality of their artistry in favor of a more theoretical (whether evocative or analytic) intent, literary critics will not see their work as competing for artistry. Furthermore, perhaps recognition that the events discussed are a rendering of actual life events of the author will allow readers to focus on the interpretation of life experience and grant some latitude to authors for their (our?) aesthetics.

ANALYTIC AUTOETHNOGRAPHY

Intending to shift gears, Anderson (2006a) argues for a second form with more traditionally sociological goals in his call for "analytic autoethnography." Specifically addressing the popularity of evocative work but wishing to differentiate his own interest in writing autoethnography as oriented toward the analytic, realist goals of his Chicago School sympathies, Anderson calls for authors to consider theoretical explanation also as a valid focus of this form of writing. Similarly pursuing a realist approach in her attempt to recuperate a distinctly anthropological approach to autoethnography, Chang (2007) argues that autoethnography moves beyond autobiographical field notes in the interpretive, analytical stages of writing. She writes, "Autoethnographers need to keep in mind that what makes autoethnography ethnographical is its ethnographic intent of gaining a cultural understanding of self that is intimately connected to others in the society" (p. 212). Grinenko-Baker (2001) articulates this ethnographic interest as follows: "I became convinced that in order to hold carefully the stories of adolescent females—stories about death, race, gender, bodies, God—I had to tell carefully some of the stories of my own experience" (p. 406).

Many examples of this work include investigations of gender, identity, and the body (Ettorre, 2005; Munt, 1998; Taber, 2005), including my own work (Crawley, 2002, 2008a; Crawley & Broad, 2004; Crawley et al., 2008, pp. 37–38, 49). Nancy Taber (2005) cites and develops sociological gender theory in her article on learning and unlearning "how to be a woman" from her experiences in the military and later in academia. Elizabeth Ettorre (2005) engages medical sociology and Foucault's "technologies of the self" with her analysis of her own experience with illness. Furthermore, there is a sort of unstated tradition among lesbian, gay, bisexual, and transgendered authors of many disciplines to tell their life stories by way of theorizing a life not widely published or publicly encouraged (Gamson, 2000; Plummer, 1995). (Of course, in feminist circles, this is the stated tradition of consciousness-raising, which I will discuss in the next section.) In telling a life story, explicit theorizing of bodies, identities, sexualities, performativities, and subjectivities is the analytic goal. The example of Joan Nestle's (1988, 1992) activist, not specifically academic, collections of everyday life stories about butch and femme is taken up by Sally R. Munt (1998) in her book anthologizing 26 academic writers who explicitly write autoethnographies theorizing butch and/or femme experiences.

My own work is influenced by and participates in this genre, and my intention as I composed it was expressly an analytic one: What can my lived experiences add to social theories of gender, identity, and the body? I have written on the relationship of butch identity to the cultural perception of the female body as not fully abled (Crawley, 2002), on the interplay of geography with butch and transgender identity development (Crawley, 2008a), on Schutzian typification and the experience of announcing one's sexual identity to anonymous audiences in college classrooms (Crawley & Broad, 2004), and as part of a larger theoretical project connecting interactionism, gender performance theories, and the production of gender on bodies (Crawley et al., 2008, pp. 37–38, 49). Betsy Lucal (1999) has written similarly on misrecognition of gender and sociological gender theory.

PERFORMANCE AUTOETHNOGRAPHY

A final form of autoethnography comes from performance theory and has explicit political goals—statedly to change the world toward progressive, democratic goals (Adams & Holman Jones, 2008; Clough, 2000; Denzin, 1997, 2000a, 2003; Holman

Jones, 2005; Spry, 2001). Originating in cultural studies and performance studies, performance autoethnography describes "particularly involved and dramatized oral narrative" (Langellier, 1999, p. 127) in which "the phenomenon being described is created through the act of representation. . . . A good performance text must be more than cathartic; it must be political, moving people to action and reflection" (Denzin, 2000b, p. 905).

Norman Denzin has been one of the more prolific purveyors of performance autoethnography, sponsoring an annual conference on qualitative inquiry as well as having edited several editions of the *Handbook of Qualitative Research* and several peer-reviewed journals that publish autoethnography. In his post–9/11 treatise on the political importance of this work, Denzin (2003) defines the work as such:

> At stake is an "insurgent cultural politics" that challenges neo-fascist state apparatuses. . . . Performance ethnography is more than a tool of liberation. It is a way of being moral and political in the world. Performance ethnography is moral discourse. (p. 258)

He grounds this work in the aesthetics of critical race theory, black feminist thought, and the use of performance, art, and other experimental forms to pursue progressive politics. Both evocative and political, it is intended to change minds.

Holman Jones (2005) similarly argues for making narrative more bodily focused and bodily produced by linking the notions that identities and daily practices are "performance choices" (p. 770). With the title "Autoethnography: Making the Personal Political," Holman Jones claims feminism but does not fully explicate the link of performance to feminism. In her 2008 article with Tony Adams, they also argue for autoethnography as aligned with queer theory—encouraging indeterminacy and elasticity over clarity and concreteness. In an interesting move, they assert Garfinkel's ethnomethodology—penned a full 20 years prior to the emergence of queer theory—as queer in that identities are a relational achievement and actors are held accountable to categories such that identities are characterized by requiring constant attention.

There are far too many examples of performance autoethnography to list here, as the conference organized by Denzin and the journals he edits have been quite prolific. Still, a couple of examples are Magnet's (2006) investigation into whiteness and privilege and Taylor's (2000) discussion of being "an exemplary lesbian" and the impossibility of being a role model.

ALIGNMENTS AND DEBATES

Describing autoethnography as method in three distinct forms as though they are clearly separable is itself a questionable task. There is much overlap, such that most work that I aligned as an analytic form is also statedly feminist with clear political commitments. Carol Rambo (2007) clearly attempts to engage analytic and evocative ends. My article (2002), which I situate above as analytic, cites Ellis's work, was published by Norman Denzin, and is clearly political. Furthermore, I could not locate Elizabeth Ettorre's (2010) article on the entirety of her life story as a former nun turned lesbian feminist turned sociologist to a specific form in my own rubric, as she cites C. Wright Mills, separatist feminist philosophy, and Ellis and Bochner. So to overstate the differences between the forms is to indulge in hairsplitting. Nonetheless, it is worth noting that debates over the purposes of the method are not uncommon and sometimes are quite contentious.

As one might expect, in defense of "the postmodern turn," autoethnographers have had to instruct and persuade the traditional realists about the intellectual merits of autoethnography (Denzin, 1991, 1997, 2000b; Reed-Danahay, 2002; and nearly all the works of Ellis and Bochner). For example, in a 2006 issue of *Journal of Contemporary Ethnography* (*JCE*) dedicated to the discussion, Anderson (2006a) introduces analytic autoethnography, which he bases in realist-style ethnography from the Chicago School of symbolic interactionism to counter a trend toward the popularity of evocation. In their rebuttal in the same issue of the journal, Ellis and Bochner (2006) take up the cause for evocation by calling for a (premature?) "autopsy" of analytic autoethnography. They call Anderson's work "aloof autoethnography" and essentially dismiss the validity of realist epistemologies. Interestingly, an early collection edited by Carolyn Ellis and Michael Flaherty (1992) contains an article by John H. Gagnon that similarly links "investigating subjectivity" to G. H. Mead, whose theories of the self are later linked to the Chicago School.

Denzin's (2006) response to Anderson's analytic autoethnography in the same *JCE* issue overtly calls for the demise of not only analytic autoethnography but the entire Chicago School. Anderson (2006b) rebuts the rebuttals by reclaiming what he refers to as a more constructionist history of the Chicago School (with which I agree) as realist but sensitized to the production of reality in people's worlds, as opposed to grand generalized theory, as stated by Ellis and Bochner. Clearly the debate is contentious, but we should not be surprised. Anderson is a sociologist. Ellis and Denzin, although both trained as sociologists, currently work in communication departments, as does Bochner. Hence, the disciplinary leanings of each seem to emerge in their debates.

My own interest leans toward finding common ground and pursuing interdisciplinary approaches. In my view, the underrecognized potential of autoethnography in this debate is offered by Burnier's article in the *JCE* special issue (2006), in which she describes coming to autoethnography as a feminist response to the limitations of positivism inherent in her discipline. Burnier suggests that autoethnography allows her to both value her work as a political scientist *and* stretch her discipline by introducing self-reflexive writing. Here, she makes a distinctly feminist move (inspired by Patricia Hill Collins) by offering a "both/and" (p. 414) solution that supports the legitimacy of both methods. Both Rambo (2007) and Gingrich-Philbrook (2005) also agree with the premise that the analytic/epistemic versus evocative/aesthetic standoff can be avoided. If we shift the epistemological premise away from disciplinary debates toward feminist standpoint theory, we can find productive, perhaps interdisciplinary, ways to engage *both evocative and analytic* purposes with autoethnography.

◆ Feminist Standpoint Theory, the Body, and the Necessity of the Personal

Autoethnography as situated on an epistemological basis of feminist standpoint theory can accommodate both realism and evocation. Similar to C. Wright Mills's (1959) call for a sociological imagination, autoethnography calls for reflection on the social organization (public issues) and structuring one's own life (personal troubles) (Collins, 1990; Denzin, 2003; Ettorre, 2010). It is striking how feminist this call by Mills is and yet how divergent the histories of sociology and feminist epistemologies have generally been

(Acker, 2006; Lorber, 2006; Ray, 2006; Rupp, 2006; Stacey, 2006; Stacey & Thorne, 1985; Thorne, 2006; Williams, 2006).

I came to autoethnography in graduate school by way of finding the work of Carolyn Ellis. Writing my first autoethnography felt like (self)consciousness-raising in the old-school feminist tradition—simultaneously deeply personal, politically engaged, and theoretically aware of social organizations and power structures. It was painful, analytic, and freeing. From this experience, I understand Ellis's interest in the value of emotional autoethnography, but I also find it exciting to articulate something so personally experienced as a broader theory of the social order.

Feminist standpoint theory can take both analysis and evocation as its goal, refusing to see a narrative/theoretical split in scholarship. When I attend public events sponsored by our university's Africana Studies Department, I find that they have a curious practice of opening an academic talk by having someone sing a song, signaling a lack of necessary split between the humanities and social science. This practice demonstrates an important epistemological premise: The substantive issue—a focus on African and African diaspora experiences—is more important than methodological skirmishes over who studies it best. Outlining a *Black Feminist Anthropology*, McClaurin (2001b) seems similarly ambivalent to methodological skirmishes; she writes,

> I found myself drawn to the idea that self (auto), collective/nation (ethno), and writing (graphy) offered possibilities for scholars such as myself in that I am always in search of a theory, a concept, an innovation, that will allow me to describe and interpret the kind of anthropology I do. (p. 65)

Feminist theory is most recognized for reclaiming women from exclusion in history and the academy (i.e., the idea that women's studies is about women). This is a vital pursuit but, in my opinion, not the most important contribution of feminism. Feminism's greatest contribution is an epistemological shift away from androcentric, boundary-specific methods that enforce traditional binaries—rational over emotional, authoritative voices over voices of the oppressed, public over private, transcendental truths over everyday experiences—toward refusing binaries—thought as rational and emotional, multiple views and truths, everyday private and public worlds (Collins, 1990;

Fonow & Cook, 1991). A standard premise of feminist work is that the researcher cannot be separated from the research. Research is never objective in the sense of being devoid of power relations. When we pretend as though it can be, we are employing what Donna Haraway (1989) calls the "God trick"—implying that knowledge simply exists, as though handed down by God. Haraway argues cogently that this perspective hides power relations rather than making them transparent and that feminist researchers must always be open about their affiliations and attentive to their own place in reproducing power in the research process.

Feminist epistemologies have altered traditional methods such as ethnography and interviewing (Abu-Lughod, 1991; Burnier, 2006; Candida Smith, 2002; Chapman Sanger, 2003; Ellis & Bochner, 2000; Fontana, 2002; Oakley, 1981; Narayan & George, 2002; Plummer, 2001; Richardson, 1991; Warren, 2002). Indeed, volumes have been written on feminist revisions to methods (Hesse-Biber, 2007; Reinharz, 1992). More recent queer epistemologies also push methods to examine the researcher's self and its rootedness in the body and sexual subjectivity (Gamson, 2000; Kong, Mahoney, & Plummer, 2002). Furthermore, feminist and queer epistemologies have much crossover with interactionist traditions. Plummer (2001) argues that any writing of life stories "cross[es] the embodied and emotional 'brute being' with the rational and irrational 'knowing self'" (p. 395).

The body and lived experience is the very ground of feminist standpoint epistemologies. Dorothy Smith (1992) intends to write "a method of inquiry beginning from the site of being" (p. 88). She explains, "I emphasize this embodied ground of our experiencing as women. . . . The Cartesian subject escapes the body, hence escaping the limitations of the local historical particularities of time, place, and relationship" (p. 89). Smith's institutional ethnography starts from the perspective of someone going through the institution and works to understand how institutions and texts—which she terms *the relations of ruling*—mediate what a person can be and how an experience can be lived. "For this sociology, there is no outside, no Archimedean point from which a positionless account can be written" (Smith, 1999, p. 8). Smith's entire career, then, has been a kind of methodological consciousness-raising for social theory. She writes, "Taking up women's standpoint as a place to begin locates the knower in her body, in a lived world in which both theory and practice go on, in which theory is itself a practice" (p. 7).

Writing a "sociology for people" (Smith, 2005), Smith (1992) is clear that institutional ethnography should not be married to any epistemological boundary or particular method. The goal is to use various methods as necessary to uncover the substance of the issue—the relations of ruling in social organization. Furthermore, while Smith's project is poststructurally aware of the constructedness of knowledge, she is also clear to frame her work in Marxist materialism. Unlike psychoanalytic materialists, who frame the subject via unconscious desires, Smith's materialism focuses on a much more sociological project— the ways in which the Enlightenment project brought to social interaction a public world of mediating texts that structure relations between people (Denzin, 1997, pp. 59–60; Smith, 1988, 1990, 1999, 2005). Smith (1999) writes, "Text in its material as well as symbolic aspect [is] the bridge between the everyday/everynight local actualities of our living and the ruling relations" (p. 7). For Smith, then, the actor is neither transcendental nor postructurally discursive. Experience is located, situated, and material, if often undertheorized by members because the textual relations of ruling are transparent in the everyday world. Of course, missing from Smith's work is a similar critique of race.

Both academic and nonacademic feminists of color followed a similar trajectory of writing themselves into knowledge by writing their experiences, as is evidenced by the wildly popular anthology *This Bridge Called My Back* (Moraga & Anzaldua, 1984). Irma McClaurin (2001a) traces this genealogy through feminism and critical race theory to include "the writings and speeches of Sojourner Truth, Frederick Douglass, W. E. B. DuBois, Ida B. Wells, Anna Cooper, [and] Zora Neale Hurston" (p. 5) to bell hooks (feminist cultural critic), Patricia Hill Collins (sociologist), Elizabeth Fox-Genovese (historian), Nancy Hartsock (feminist standpoint theorist), and Nikki Giovanni (poet). Grounded in W. E. B. DuBois's (1903/1989) notion of "double consciousness"—that people who experience oppression develop a consciousness of the mainstream society as well as a consciousness of the experience of oppression— McClaurin (2001a, 2001b) argues that black women have had to develop a consciousness of "multiplicity" as well as to write against tradition in order to write black feminism.

Patricia Hill Collins is widely recognized as having written a definitive work in her book *Black Feminist Thought* (1990). Like Smith, Collins grounds her work in life experience and bases it in feminist theory, Marxist social theory, sociology of knowledge, and postmodernism. But Collins also includes critical race theory and Afrocentric philosophy, which highlights multiple voices, not a dominating intellectual voice, uses a "both/and" conceptual stance to "reconcile subjectivity and objectivity in producing scholarship" (p. xiv), and theorizes the "outsider-within" positionality that is shared by black domestic workers (Rollins, 1985) as well as by Collins herself as a black woman in a traditionally white academy with androcentric, Eurocentric knowledge structures. Clearly Marxist in her sociology of knowledge project, Collins articulates a power structure of knowledge and a justifiable fear that too much value placed on constructionism will diminish the harsh realities of living inequality.

Both Smith and Collins ground their epistemologies in the experiences of structural inequalities that have governed Western history for several centuries, including the entire history of the United States. Hence, the feminist standpoint is grounded in bodily experience and in a sociology of knowledge that must situate knowledge in history. Still true to feminist standpoint theory, both Smith and Collins are careful not to engage in essentialism. Collins (1990) writes,

A definition of Black feminist thought is needed that avoids the materialist position that being Black and/or female generates certain experiences that automatically determine variants of a Black and/or feminist consciousness. . . . But a definition of Black feminist thought must also avoid the idealist position that ideas can be evaluated in isolation from the groups that create them. . . . I suggest that Black feminist thought consists of specialized knowledge created by African-American women which clarifies a standpoint of and for Black women. In other words, Black feminist thought encompasses theoretical interpretations of Black women's reality by those who live it. (pp. 21–22)

Hence, this position recognizes the construction of gender and racial classification systems present in historical power structures but also notes that living in such an oppressed social location gives one a particular angle of vision for theorizing the social. As such, consciousness is earned, not innate, and must be cultivated, as in Smith's notion of uncovering the relations of ruling.

Norman Denzin (1997) has offered a full explication of feminist standpoint theory, including the work of Smith and Collins, but ultimately calls the project too utopian to create political change. Rejecting a realist approach, he calls for what he believes to be a more activist and engaging project using performance texts. I believe that neither Collins nor Smith would agree with Denzin's (2006) call for an end to realism, as both their positions are centrally grounded in empiricism—the everyday lives of people. Furthermore, his recent work (2003) envisions the "ethnographer as public intellectual who produces and engages in meaningful cultural criticism" (p. 259). To me, his recent turn to pure, unadulterated politics seems to take up an unfortunate return to ethnographer as spokesperson for the masses. I imagine Collins asking, "Who gets to be a public intellectual?" The understanding of pragmatic lived experiences requires multiple voices, not just public intellectuals.

Following the "both/and" approach of black feminist thought, it is imminently clear that identities are based in narrative and discourse, profoundly grounded in constructions of history, time, and context, and it is equally true, at least to members, that their lived experiences of identities, places, communities, and especially inequalities feel real in a Marxist sense of consciousness. These realities coexist at the level of lived experience. We can measure a theory by what it makes clear that was previously cloudy—considering multivocality a positive character of the work while not letting go of the realist project of describing a world that exists if only in the way that some experience it. In that way, both analytic and evocative ends are valid and useful, informative and enlightening—both/and, not either/or. Not coincidentally, this vision of sociology would not shy away from Henry Rubin's (2003) problem: that we can both take seriously the experiences of our members and offer intellectual critiques of knowledge, even when these positions diverge.

◆ *Producing Autoethnography as Self-Interview*

Authoethnography, as I envision it, is also an extension of the active interview approach set out by Holstein and Gubrium (1995) and pursued via this

Handbook on at least three bases. First, in the opening article of the first edition of this anthology, they write, "No method of research can stand outside the cultural and material world" (p. 11). As researchers, we are embodied in the material world and always have been. There is no objectivity, even for analyses of social locations of which we are not members (e.g., a white person writing about African American communities). Second, following Holstein and Gubrium's notion of the active interview, "The interview is being reconceptualized as an occasion for purposefully animated participants to *construct* versions of reality interactionally rather than merely purvey data" (p. 14). If the interview is seen as a site of "joint action" (Plummer, 2001, p. 399) between a "respondent" and an interviewer (especially the native-as-interviewer), why pretend to ignore or obfuscate that relationship of the researcher to the site, content, and lived experience of the issues being investigated? Third, "interview formats are themselves going concerns" (Gubrium & Holstein, 2002). Researchers mull over the events of an interview, an instance of fieldwork, and/or a focus group interactively in the Meadian mind—speaking to and about the members in their mind—while attempting to get the analysis on paper. Why not extend the ground of this interview format to self-interrogation? Indeed, researchers probably always have, whether they explicitly acknowledged the practice or not.

How, then, is autoethnography written? As described earlier, there is no single way of defining and practicing autoethnography. Nonetheless, I offer some practices or orientations across the diverse landscape of autoethnography. To outline a few suggestions, I generally agree with four of the five sensitizing key characteristics of Anderson's (2006a) analytic autoethnography: (1) analytic reflexivity, (2) a visible and active researcher, (3) dialogue with informants beyond the self, and (4) commitment to a theoretical agenda of understanding lived experience (which, unlike Anderson, I believe can have epistemic or aesthetic goals). I do not agree with Anderson's view of membership, which I will take up in the next section.

Autoethnography, as I have practiced it, works best as part of a larger project of interviews or fieldwork, or perhaps even a life's work, but not as a quick reflection on a short project. Consistent with analytic reflexivity, Anderson (2006a) writes, "It entails self-conscious introspection guided by a desire to better understand both self and others through examining one's actions and perceptions in reference to and dialogue with those of others" (p. 382). As such, reflections on one's own life might be more fertile while simultaneously focusing on the lives of others in social context. Furthermore, Anderson suggests that autoethnography shows a commitment to an analytic agenda, which he defines as "a broad set of data-transcending practices that are directed toward theoretical development, refinement, and extension" (p. 387). Similarly for me, the issue is rigor, in the conceptual sense, not the realist sense of "getting it right." The strongest measure of any project, for me, is whether it has rigorously attended to the relevant literatures, the stated methodology, the contents under review (data? art? narrative?), and their place in the larger, theoretical academic conversation. If one has a fleeting experience and decides to just sit down and bang out reflections about it, one is likely to miss a strong connection to existing academic and nonacademic literatures as well as clear attention to the local, social context. Consistent, then, with the active interview model, a fleeting idea about a single social experience does not meet the standard of rigor that I think characterizes strong scholarly work.

Similarly, autoethnography does not assume a transcendental subject free-floating around its own bootstraps. As a result, authoring situatedness in time, place, and context relative to the relations of ruling is key to this method. As I have written elsewhere (2002), I see autoethnography as the inverse of autobiography. Autobiography logs the intricacies of a famous person's life because a readership wants to know the gory details of a specific life. I write autoethnography because I am commonplace; my lived experience is interesting because my social location is likely shared by many others and informative to a broader project of understanding power in everyday lives. Focusing on the mundane trappings of daily events orchestrated by texts, interactions, and social structure—such as having to wear bridesmaid dresses (Crawley, 2002) or having been a nun (Ettorre, 2010)—illuminates the relations of ruling in our lives. In organizing these connections into an argument, I have tended to focus on the concepts of my argument, rather than on a chronology of my experiences, so as to make an argument of my interpretations, not just a log of my life.

Engaging both evocation and analysis, my favorite kind of format for autoethnography engages "scenes" from one's reflected life experiences followed by theoretical analysis. The "scenes" from one's life put the reader in the emotional place of experiencing a world while the analytic self *simultaneously* organizes that life experience into one's own theory of social location. The recurrent memories that pop up regularly over the course of everyday life continue to surface because people regularly try to theorize a self if only to themselves (Crawley, 2008b). These memories are not random. Thousands of events take place over the course of a life. If certain memories recur, they must be relevant to some unexplained part of self that the member-turned-ethnographer grapples with, academically or not. Chang (2007) succinctly encapsulates the practice I envision as such: "When autoethnographers recall past experiences, they do not randomly harvest bits of fragmented memories. Rather, they select some according to their research focus and data-collection criteria" (p. 212). In other words, the act of focusing analytically or aesthetically on a particular subject matter predisposes one for certain memories to surface: "It's like that time when . . . "

With only these few hints for structure (as well as the long list of examples cited here), the author attempting an autoethnographic work for the first time may still be unclear as to how to write one well. In addition to the steps or focal points outlined above based on Anderson's article, there are numerous other sources on what authoethnography is and how it is to be done. For example, a special symposium of *Qualitative Inquiry* in 2000 was dedicated to considering criteria for evaluating "alternative modes of qualitative and ethnographic research." In the issue, Ellis, Bochner, Richardson, Denzin, and Clough all began with the postmodern unwillingness to impose standards, but ultimately, each offered up criteria that they use for reviews in peer-reviewed journals and that provide great ideas to authors (which I need not replicate here).

◆ Embodiment Matters: Some Cautions and Limits to Autoethnography

Autoethnography is too free a form to come with prescriptions, but it may come with proscriptions. There are some cautions that I would like to offer first, briefly, on the ethics of talking about people in your life and then on membership.

Authors of autoethnographic accounts should consider the people about whom they are simultaneously telling tales as they write their life experiences. There are some people whose identities cannot be hidden—such as your mother—or whose identities will be presumed—such as siblings or ex-lovers—even if you are speaking about one and not the other, and some people will not be pleased to see their names in print, even in trivial ways. Can you mask identities where prudent? Do you have permission to use real names, even if only first names? Apart from institutional review board (IRB) issues, consider whether this will cause you to lose a friend and, if so, whether the intent can be accomplished in alternative ways. I strive to focus on the scholarly intent over juicy content. If a topic does not enhance the argument or story, it need not take shape in print. Even if it might enhance an argument or story, some issues or relationships are prudently left out of academic writing. This does not mean that some topics are unapproachable. For example, I am currently working on an autoethnography of butch sexuality. To accomplish this, I focus on writing my thoughts, feelings, and experiences about *my body* during sex and purposefully disclaim any specific time or relationship. Autoethnography is about my experience; telling tales on others is inconsistent with the intent and may be unethical. My goal is to hold myself to a higher personal standard than the litigious concerns of the IRB.

A last caution concerns the premise of feminist standpoint theory and the issue of membership: About what can I write *as a member*? Anderson (2006a) references Adler and Adler's (1987) concept of "opportunitistic" and "convert" CMR (complete member researcher status), in which "opportunistic" CMRs are born into or already live in a setting whereas "convert" CMRs go into fieldwork and become so enamored that the field becomes a lifelong pursuit. Anderson endorses both. I do not. To me, "convert" CMRs are not doing autoethnography based on feminist standpoint theory. Feminist standpoint theory has an important axiom that anyone can learn about the life experiences of others, as standpoint is acquired. Indeed, no one is excused from the conversation about social inequalities. But to write about social location (gender, race, class, sexuality) as *auto*ethnography and not simply as ethnography, the experience of a particular social location must be your own—in your own body—otherwise

you risk colonizing the voices of the marginalized. You also run the risk of overstating your claims—to come to understand another's experience is not the same as to have *become* that experience, primarily because *the researcher can still elect to leave the field.* For me, a central tenet of the method of autoethnography is that if researchers can ever "leave the field," they are writing ethnography (which is a perfectly honest and valuable contribution, in my opinion), not autoethnography. Because my own interest in autoethnography, as well as the central focus of feminist theory, is to understand major structural social inequalities (which are usually written on the visible body, e.g., sex or race categorization or cultural capitals that accompany class stratification), it is imperative for the experiences to be long term and thoroughly experienced, such that being able to leave the field does not constitute the "lived experience" of entrenched social inequalities. The evocation of such experiences is exactly the realization that one cannot leave the racialized body or the sexed body, to which one experiences ever-present accountability (Crawley et al., 2008). The rage of that recognition is so deeply felt that one cannot approach it by "trying it on" in ethnography, although hopefully such rage can be expressed in the descriptive project of autoethnography. What characterizes autoethnography as a project of bodily experience is that the experiences described as autoethnography must have occurred naturalistically in one's own civilian life, if you will, not as a project that began as fieldwork.

As an example, Wacquant's (2003) excellent ethnography of boxing gyms among poor, inner-city, primarily black, men has many self-reflexive moments, but it is a mistake to call it autoethnography (which I do not believe Wacquant claims) because Wacquant, as a researcher, can come and go into or from the field as he prefers. While Wacquant's embeddedness in the field is an exemplar for fieldwork, it would overdrive any methodological claims to suggest that Wacquant has become a full member (an inner-city black man?). If Wacquant were to write an autoethnography from those experiences, it would have to be as a white, French-native man from the privilege of the academy, encountering his own whiteness and privilege while in the field (which is closer to what Wacquant intends in the book). Erich Goode (2002) provides an exemplar of what autoethnography is not when he writes of an unpublished, "failed" fieldwork project wherein he (inadvertently?) has sex with self-identified "fat women." He calls this autoethnography, but I disagree. Reflection pieces about how to avoid unwanted circumstances in future research can be helpful, but entering the field to do fieldwork cannot later constitute membership from a feminist standpoint.

Resonant with feminist standpoint theories, my focus for autoethnography is on lifelong experiences of inequalities and their impact on the body and the production of self (see Crawley, 2008a; Crawley et al., 2008). Like the argument about butch identity and subtropical climate with which I opened this chapter, sexuality and gender identity are long-term productions of identity that are written on and felt through the body (as are experiences of race, ethnicity, and class, which is not to say that they are not inflexible), not fleeting dalliances to be tried out by a researcher on entering "the field." Convert CMRs may work for analytic autoethnographies of pastimes—such as Anderson's skydiving—and they may change the lives of the researchers doing this work, but they cannot substitute for issues of social location among entrenched social inequalities. For autoethnography on structural inequalities from a feminist standpoint, to be a member you must first be there in your life. That is, white people can talk about experiences of whiteness, but moving into a black community to see "what it is like to be Black" is not autoethnography. It is fieldwork—however well or ill conceived, however deep or surface level the investigation—and all knowledge claims from such a project must carefully navigate tricky waters to avoid colonizing the voice of the Other. I do not mean to set the methods of ethnography or autoethnography up in hierarchal relation to each other. There is much to be learned from each method, and neither should be understood as providing a truer or more real result. Yet, for me, one *begins a project* to do ethnography, whereas one writes autoethnography from reflections of what one has already experienced—from a life that one cannot step outside.

◆ Concluding Thoughts

Autoethnography from the position of feminist standpoint theory takes up a serious, rigorous, respectful analysis and/or evocation from the lived experience of the researcher as member. It intends to illuminate politics, knowledge construction, subjectivity, and methodology and offers exciting potential that is unavailable with many other methods. Yet it remains only one of the tools in the methodological tool kit, one that must be treated with ethical and claims-making care. Autoethnography cannot claim to resolve a theoretical issue, as if to speak for the essentialized masses. In its best usage, it can shine a light on the relations of ruling and connect members' voice to theory, but we must remain ever careful to guard against the assumption that any method can represent "the people" or constitute the final ruling on best practices. Scholarship, even autoethnography, is best understood as part of the group conversation we call knowledge construction.

◆ References

Abu-Lughod, L. (1991). Writing against culture. In R. G. Fox (Ed.), *Recapturing anthropology: Working in the present* (pp. 137–162). Santa Fe, NM: School of American Research Press.

Acker, J. (2006). Introduction: "The Missing Feminist Revolution" symposium. *Social Problems, 53,* 444–447.

Adams, T. E., & Holman Jones, S. (2008). Autoethnography is queer. In N. Denzin, Y. Lincoln, & L. T. Smith (Eds.), *Handbook of critical and indigenous methodologies* (pp. 373–390). Thousand Oaks, CA: Sage.

Adler, P. A., & Adler, P. (1987). *Membership roles in field research.* Newbury Park, CA: Sage.

Anderson, L. (2006a). Analytic autoethnography. *Journal of Contemporary Ethnography, 35,* 373–395.

Anderson, L. (2006b). On apples, oranges, and autopsies: A response to commentators. *Journal of Contemporary Ethnography, 35,* 450–465.

Besio, K., & Butz, D. (2004). Commentary: Autoethnography: A limited endorsement. *The Professional Geographer, 56*(3), 432–438.

Bochner, A. P. (2000). Criteria against ourselves. *Qualitative Inquiry, 6*(2), 266–272.

Bochner, A. P., & Ellis, C. (Eds.). (2002). *Ethnographically speaking: Autoethnography, literature, and aesthetics.* Walnut Creek, CA: AltaMira Press.

Burnier, D. (2006). Encounters with the self in social science research: A political scientist looks at autoethnography. *Journal of Contemporary Ethnography, 35,* 410–418.

Butz, D., & Besio, K. (2004). The value of autoethnography for field research in transcultural settings. *The Professional Geographer, 56,* 350–360.

Candida Smith, R. (2002). Analytic strategies for oral history interviews. In J. Gubrium & J. Holstein (Eds.), *Handbook of interview research* (1st ed., pp. 711–732). Thousand Oaks, CA: Sage.

Chang, H. (2007). Autoethnography: Raising cultural consciousness of self and others. In G. Walford (Ed.), *Methodological developments in ethnography: Studies in educational ethnography* (Vol. 12, pp. 207–221). Amsterdam, The Netherlands: Elsevier.

Chapman Sanger, P. (2003). Living and writing feminist ethnographies. In R. P. Clair (Ed.), *Expressions of ethnography: Novel approaches to qualitative methods* (pp. 29–44). Albany: State University of New York Press.

Clough, P. T. (1997). Autotelecommunication and autoethnography: A reading of Carolyn Ellis's *Final Negotiations*. *The Sociological Quarterly, 38,* 95–110.

Clough, P. T. (2000). Comments on setting criteria for experimental writing. *Qualitative Inquiry, 6,* 278–291.

Collins, P. H. (1990). *Black feminist thought: Knowledge, consciousness, and the politics of empowerment.* New York, NY: Routledge.

Collins, P. H. (1992). Transforming the inner circle: Dorothy Smith's challenge to sociological theory. *Sociological Theory, 10,* 73–80.

Crawley, S. L. (2002). "They still don't understand why I hate wearing dresses": An autoethnographic rant on dresses, boats and butchness. *Cultural Studies ⇔ Critical Methodologies, 2,* 69–92.

Crawley, S. L. (2008a). The clothes make the trans: Region and geography in experiences of the body. *Journal of Lesbian Studies, 12*(4), 365–379.

Crawley, S. L. (2008b). Full-contact pedagogy: Lecturing with questions and student-centered assignments as methods for inciting self-reflexivity for faculty and students. *Feminist Teacher, 19*(1), 13–30.

Crawley, S. L. (2009). When coming out is redundant: On the difficulties of remaining queer and a theorist after coming out in the classroom. *Feminism and Psychology, 19*(2), 210–215.

Crawley, S. L., & Broad, K. L. (2004). "Be your [real lesbian] self": Mobilizing sexual formula stories through personal (and political) storytelling. *Journal of Contemporary Ethnography, 33,* 39–71.

Crawley, S. L., Foley, L. J., & Shehan, C. L. (2008). *Gendering bodies.* Lanham, MD: Rowman & Littlefield Press.

Denzin, N. K. (1991). Representing lived experiences in ethnographic texts. *Studies in Symbolic Interaction, 12,* 59–70.

Denzin, N. K. (1994). The art and politics of interpretation. In N. K. Denzin & Y. S. Lincoln (Eds.), *Handbook of qualitative research* (pp. 500–515). Thousand Oaks, CA: Sage.

Denzin, N. K. (1997). *Interpretive ethnography: Ethnographic practices for the 21st century.* Thousand Oaks, CA: Sage.

Denzin, N. K. (2000a). Aesthetics and the practices of qualitative inquiry. *Qualitative Inquiry, 6,* 256–265.

Denzin, N. K. (2000b). The practices and politics of interpretation. In N. K. Denzin & Y. S. Lincoln (Eds.), *Handbook of qualitative research* (2nd ed., pp. 897–922). Thousand Oaks, CA: Sage.

Denzin, N. K. (2003). Performing [auto] ethnography politically. *The Review of Education, Pedagogy, and Cultural Studies, 25,* 257–278.

Denzin, N. K. (2006). Analytic autoethnography, or déjà vu all over again. *Journal of Contemporary Ethnography, 35,* 419–428.

DuBois, W. E. B. (1989). *The souls of black folk.* New York, NY: Penguin Books. (Original work published 1903)

Ellingson, L. L., & Ellis, C. (2008). Autoethnography as constructionist project. In J. Holstein & J. Gubrium (Eds.), *Handbook of constructionist research* (1st ed., pp. 445–466). Thousand Oaks, CA: Sage.

Ellis, C. (1991a). Emotional sociology. *Studies in Symbolic Interaction, 12,* 123–145.

Ellis, C. (1991b). Sociological introspection and emotional experience. *Symbolic Interaction, 14,* 23–50.

Ellis, C. (1993). "There are survivors": Tell a story of sudden death. *The Sociological Quarterly, 34,* 711–730.

Ellis, C. (1995). *Final negotiations: A story of love, loss, and chronic illness.* Philadelphia, PA: Temple University Press.

Ellis, C. (1996). Maternal connections. In C. Ellis & A. P. Bochner (Eds.), *Composing ethnography: Alternative forms of qualitative writing* (pp. 240–243). Walnut Creek, CA: AltaMira Press.

Ellis, C. (1997). Evocative ethnography: Writing emotionally about our lives. In W. G. Tierney & Y. S. Lincoln (Eds.), *Representation and the text: Reframing the narrative voice* (pp. 115–139). New York: State University of New York Press.

Ellis, C. (1998). "I hate my voice": Coming to terms with minor bodily stigmas. *The Sociological Quarterly, 39,* 517–537.

Ellis, C. (1999). Heartful autoethnography. *Qualitative Health Research, 9,* 669–683.

Ellis, C. (2004). *The ethnographic I: A methodological novel about autoethnography.* Walnut Creek, CA: AltaMira Press.

Ellis, C. (2009). *Revision: Autoethnographic reflections on life and work.* Walnut Creek, CA: Left Coast Press.

Ellis, C., & Berger, L. (2002). Their story/my story/our story. In J. Gubrium & J. Holstein (Eds.), *Handbook of interview research* (1st ed., pp. 849–875). Thousand Oaks, CA: Sage.

Ellis, C., & Bochner, A. P. (1992). Telling and performing personal stories: The constraints of choice in abortion. In C. Ellis & M. G. Flaherty (Eds.), *Investigating subjectivity* (pp. 79–101). Newbury Park, CA: Sage.

Ellis, C., & Bochner, A. P. (Eds.). (1996). *Composing ethnography: Alternative forms of qualitative writing*. Walnut Creek, CA: AltaMira Press.

Ellis, C., & Bochner, A. P. (2000). Autoethnography, personal narrative, reflexivity: Researcher as subject. In N. K. Denzin & Y. S. Lincoln (Eds.), *Handbook of qualitative research* (2nd ed., pp. 733–768). Thousand Oaks, CA: Sage.

Ellis, C., & Bochner, A. P. (2006). Analyzing analytic autoethnography: An autopsy. *Journal of Contemporary Ethnography, 35,* 429–448.

Ellis, C., & Flaherty, M. G. (Eds.). (1992). *Investigating subjectivity: Research on lived experience*. Newbury Park, CA: Sage.

Ettorre, E. (2005). Gender, older female bodies and autoethnography: Finding my feminist voice by telling my illness story. *Women's Studies International Forum, 28,* 535–546.

Ettorre, E. (2010). Nuns, dykes, drugs and gendered bodies: An autoethnography of a lesbian feminist's journey through "good time" sociology. *Sexualities, 13*(3), 295–315.

Fonow, M. M., & Cook, J. A. (1991). *Beyond methodology: Feminist scholarship as lived research*. Bloomington: Indiana University Press.

Fontana, A. (2002). Postmodern trends in interviewing. In J. Gubrium & J. Holstein (Eds.), *Handbook of interview research* (1st ed., pp. 161–175). Thousand Oaks, CA: Sage.

Gagnon, J. H. (1992). The self, its voices, and their discord. In C. Ellis & M. G. Flaherty (Eds.), *Investigating subjectivity* (pp. 221–243). Newbury Park, CA: Sage.

Gamson, J. (2000). Sexualities, queer theory, and qualitative research. In N. K. Denzin & Y. S. Lincoln (Eds.), *Handbook of qualitative research* (2nd ed., pp. 347–365). Thousand Oaks, CA: Sage.

Gingrich-Philbrook, C. (2005). Autoethnography's family values: Easy access to compulsory experiences. *Text and Performance Quarterly, 25,* 297–314.

Goode, E. (2002). Sexual involvement and social research in a fat civil rights organization. *Qualitative Sociology, 25*(4), 501–534.

Grinenko-Baker, D. (2001). Future homemakers and feminist awakenings: Autoethnography as a method in theological education and research. *Religious Education, 96,* 395–407.

Gubrium, J. F., & Holstein, J. A. (1997). *The new language of qualitative method*. New York, NY: Oxford University Press.

Gubrium, J. F., & Holstein, J. A. (2002). From the individual interview to the interview society. In J. Gubrium & J. Holstein (Eds.), *Handbook of interview research* (1st ed., pp. 3–32). Thousand Oaks, CA: Sage.

Haraway, D. (1989). *Primate visions: Gender, race, and nature in the world of modern science*. New York, NY: Routledge.

Hayano, D. M. (1979). Auto-ethnography: Paradigms, problems, and prospects. *Human Organization, 38,* 99–104.

Hesse-Biber, S. N. (Ed.). (2007). *Handbook of feminist research: Theory and praxis*. Thousand Oaks, CA: Sage.

Holman Jones, S. (2005). Autoethnography: Making the personal political. In N. Denzin & Y. Lincoln (Eds.), *Handbook of qualitative research* (pp. 763–791). Thousand Oaks, CA: Sage.

Holstein, J. A., & Gubrium, J. F. (1995). *The active interview*. Thousand Oaks, CA: Sage.

Holt, N. L. (2003). Representation, legitimation, and autoethnography: An autoethnographic writing story. *International Journal of Qualitative Methods, 2,* 18–28.

Kong, T. S. K., Mahoney, D., & Plummer, K. (2002). Queering the interview. In J. Gubrium & J. Holstein (Eds.), *Handbook of interview research* (1st ed., pp. 239–258). Thousand Oaks, CA: Sage.

Langellier, K. M. (1999). Personal narrative, performance, performativity: Two of three things I know for sure. *Text and Performance Quarterly, 19,* 125–144.

Lorber, J. (2006). Shifting paradigms and challenging categories. *Social Problems, 53,* 448–453.

Lucal, B. (1999). What it means to be gendered me: Life on the boundaries of a dichotomous gender system. *Gender and Society, 13,* 781–797.

Magnet, S. (2006). Protesting privilege: An autoethnographic look at whiteness. *Qualitative Inquiry, 12,* 736–749.

McClaurin, I. (2001a). Introduction: Forging a theory, politics, praxis, and poetics of black feminist anthropology. In I. McClaurin (Ed.), *Black feminist anthropology: Theory, politics, praxis, and poetics* (pp. 1–23). New Brunswick, NJ: Rutgers University Press.

McClaurin, I. (2001b). Theorizing a black feminist self in anthropology: Toward an autoethnographic approach. In I. McClaurin (Ed.), *Black feminist anthropology: Theory, politics, praxis, and poetics* (pp. 49–76). New Brunswick, NJ: Rutgers University Press.

Mills, C. Wright. (1959). *The sociological imagination*. London, England: Oxford University Press.

Moraga, C., & Anzaldua, G. (1984). *This bridge called my back: Writings by radical women of color*. New York, NY: Kitchen Table, Women of Color Press.

Munt, S. R. (1998). *Butch/femme: Inside lesbian gender*. London, England: Cassell.

Narayan, K., & George, K. M. (2002). Personal and folk narratives in cultural representation. In J. Gubrium & J. Holstein (Eds.), *Handbook of interview research* (1st ed., pp. 815–832). Thousand Oaks, CA: Sage.

Nestle, J. (1988). *A restricted country*. Ann Arbor, MI: Firebrand Books.

Nestle, J. (1992). *The persistent desire: A femme-butch reader*. Boston, MA: Alyson.

Oakley, A. (1981). Interviewing women: A contradiction in terms. In H. Roberts (Ed.), *Doing feminist research* (pp. 30–61). London, England: Routledge & Kegan Paul.

Plummer, K. (1995). *Telling sexual stories*. London, England: Routledge.

Plummer, K. (2001). The call of life stories in ethnographic research. In P. Atkinson, A. Coffey, S. Delamont, J. Lofland, & L. Lofland (Eds.), *Handbook of ethnography* (pp. 395–406). Thousand Oaks, CA: Sage.

Pratt, M. L. (1994). Transculturation and autoethnography: Peru 1615/1980. In F. Barker, P. Hulme, & M. Iversen (Eds.), *Colonial discourse/postcolonial theory* (pp. 24–46). Manchester, UK: Manchester University Press.

Rambo, C. (2007). Sketching as practice. *Symbolic Interaction, 30,* 531–542.

Rambo Ronai, C. (1992). The reflexive self through narrative: A night in the life of an erotic dancer/researcher. In C. Ellis & M. G. Flaherty (Eds.), *Investigating subjectivity* (pp. 102–124). Newbury Park, CA: Sage.

Rambo Ronai, C. (1995). Multiple reflections on child sex abuse: An argument for a layered account. *Journal of Contemporary Ethnography, 23,* 395–426.

Rambo Ronai, C. (1996). My mother is mentally retarded. In C. Ellis & A. P. Bochner (Eds.), *Composing ethnography: Alternative forms of qualitative writing* (pp. 109–131). Walnut Creek, CA: AltaMira Press.

Ray, R. (2006). Is the revolution missing or are we looking in the wrong places? *Social Problems, 53,* 459–465.

Reed-Danahay, D. (1997). *Auto/ethnography*. New York, NY: Berg.

Reed-Danahay, D. (2002). Turning points and textual strategies in ethnographic writing. *Qualitative Studies in Education, 15*(4), 421–425.

Reinharz, S. (1992). *Feminist methods in social research*. New York, NY: Oxford University Press.

Richardson, L. (1991). Speakers whose voices matter: Toward a feminist postmodernist sociological praxis. *Studies in Symbolic Interaction, 12,* 29–38.

Richardson, L. (1994). Writing: A method of inquiry. In N. K. Denzin & Y. S. Lincoln (Eds.), *Handbook of qualitative research* (pp. 516–529). Thousand Oaks, CA: Sage.

Richardson, L. (1997). *Fields of play*. New Brunswick, NJ: Rutgers University Press.

Richardson, L. (2000). Evaluating ethnography. *Qualitative Inquiry, 6,* 253–255.

Richardson, L. (2002). Poetic representations of interviews. In J. Gubrium & J. Holstein (Eds.), *Handbook of interview research* (1st ed., pp. 877–891). Thousand Oaks, CA: Sage.

Rollins, J. (1985). *Between women: Domestics and their employers*. Philadelphia, PA: Temple University Press.

Rubin, H. (2003). *Self-made men: Identity and embodiment among transsexual men*. Nashville, TN: Vanderbilt University Press.

Rupp, L. J. (2006). Is the feminist revolution still missing? Reflections from women's history. *Social Problems, 53,* 466–472.

Schutz, A. (1970). *On phenomenology and social relations* (H. R. Wagner, Ed.). Chicago, IL: University of Chicago Press.

Scott, J. W. (1991/1993). The evidence of experience. In H. Abelove, M. A. Barale, & D. M. Halperin (Eds.), *The lesbian and gay studies reader* (pp. 397–415). New York, NY: Routledge.

Simmonds, F. N. (1999). My body, myself: How does a black woman do sociology? In J. Price & M. Shildrick (Eds.), *Feminist theory and the body: A reader* (pp. 50–63). New York, NY: Routledge.

Smith, D. E. (1988). *The everyday world as problematic: A feminist sociology*. Toronto, Ontario, Canada: University of Toronto Press.

Smith, D. E. (1990). *Texts, facts, and femininity: Exploring the relations of ruling*. New York, NY: Routledge.

Smith, D. E. (1992). Sociology from women's experience: A reaffirmation. *Sociological Theory, 10,* 88–98.

Smith, D. E. (1999). *Writing the social: Critique, theory, and investigations*. Toronto, Ontario, Canada: University of Toronto Press.

Smith, D. E. (2005). *Institutional ethnography: A sociology for people*. Lanham, MD: AltaMira Press.

Sparkes, A. C. (2000). Autoethnography and narratives of self: Reflections on criteria in action. *Sociology of Sport Journal, 17,* 21–43.

Spry, T. (2001). Performing autoethnography: An embodied methodological praxis. *Qualitative Inquiry, 7,* 706–732.

Stacey, J. (2006). Feminism and sociology in 2005: What are we missing? *Social Problems, 53,* 479–482.

Stacey, J., & Thorne, B. (1985). The missing feminist revolution in sociology. *Social Problems, 32,* 301–316.

Taber, N. (2005). Learning how to be a woman in the Canadian forces/unlearning it through feminism: An autoethnography of my learning journey. *Studies in Continuing Education, 27,* 289–301.

Taylor, J. (2000). On being an exemplary lesbian: My life as a role model. *Text and Performance Quarterly, 20,* 58–73.

Thorne, B. (2006). How can feminist sociology sustain its critical edge? *Social Problems, 53,* 473–478.

Wacquant, L. (2003). *Body and soul: Notebooks of an apprentice boxer*. New York, NY: Oxford University Press.

Warren, C. A. B. (2002). Qualitative interviewing. In J. Gubrium & J. Holstein (Eds.), *Handbook of interview research* (1st ed., pp. 83–102). Thousand Oaks, CA: Sage.

Williams, C. (2006). Still missing? Comments on the twentieth anniversary of "The Missing Feminist Revolution in Sociology." *Social Problems, 53*(4), 454–458.

10

FOCUS GROUPS AND SOCIAL INTERACTION

◆ David L. Morgan

The primary topic of this chapter is a practical approach to interaction in focus groups. This approach is practical in two ways. First, it examines how the process of interaction is related to the *substantive information* that the group participants generate. Second, it describes how a project's *research design* can affect the nature of the interaction in the participants. My methodological orientation derives from the version of pragmatism associated with John Dewey and George Herbert Mead, while my general orientation to the understanding of interaction in focus groups comes from symbolic interaction—which also originated from Mead's work.

Based on the symbolic interactionist tradition (Mead, 1934), I treat interaction as based on shared meanings that are created and negotiated by the participants in the course of their interaction. Following the classic framework of interactionism, all the participants in a focus group simultaneously conceive of both their own role and the roles that others play. This close connection between identity and interaction can be traced back to Cooley's (1909) concept of the "looking-glass self," where individuals find the meanings of their own actions in the reactions of others. It is also important to recognize that Mead (1934) considered most aspects of thought to be a form of interaction that occurs within "the little theater of the mind." In addition, Mead treated interaction as inseparable from the broader social context that extended beyond the boundaries of face-to-face contact, to include the host of other identities that participants possess. Thus, the interaction that occurs in focus groups involves all the elements of *Mind, Self, and Society* (Mead, 1934).

The pragmatic orientation in this chapter is devoted to the connections between research design and group interaction. Although it is up to the participants themselves to initiate and sustain their own discussion, the decisions that we make as researchers can have a major influence on the nature of that discussion. As a philosophy, pragmatism has a central emphasis on action and experience (e.g., Dewey, 1933), with a process of deliberation and decision making standing between past experience and future action. Making decisions about research design is a process of anticipating what difference it would make to conduct focus groups in one way rather than another, and this deliberation on our possible actions and their likely outcomes is at the core of pragmatism. From a research point of view, we need to decide on research designs that are likely to create the desired forms of interaction within our focus groups. Specifically, as we think about decisions that can affect the nature of interaction in focus groups, we need to consider the differences that arise from choices such as setting up the group composition, writing the interview questions, and selecting the style of moderating.

Taken together, this joint emphasis on symbolic interactionism and pragmatism converges on the topic of shared meanings. On the one hand, my interactionist outlook shapes my thoughts about how participants create shared meanings through their interactions. On the other hand, my pragmatic orientation shapes my thoughts about how my own actions, as a researcher, also have an impact on the participants' interactions, and thus on the meanings that they share in their conversations. It needs to be clear, however, that creating "shared meanings" is not the same as having participants agree with each other, and this chapter will pay attention to a variety of forms of interaction. Ultimately, what matters most is not the form a focus group takes but what the participants actually say to each other and to us.

This chapter is divided into three basic sections. The first section lays out the current approach to interaction in focus groups, which concentrates on the "co-construction of meaning." This approach falls between the two most common approaches to designing and analyzing focus groups, which emphasize either the meaning of the content in the discussion or the conversational dynamics that occur within that discussion. The second section proposes a process of "sharing and comparing" as a basic element in participants' co-construction of meaning in focus groups. The participants use this process to share similar ideas and compare different ideas with regard to the research topic, and this interaction helps them develop a shared perspective on that

topic. The third major section proposes "organizing and conceptualizing" as a higher-level process in the co-construction of meaning. Once the early interaction in the groups gives participants a shared sense of the various aspects of the topic, this creates the opportunity for the participants to organize these basic elements into a more abstract set of concepts, which helps them express why they feel the way they do about the topic.

Each of the two sections on the co-construction of meaning will include practical advice on how to design focus groups that will promote sharing and comparing as well as organizing and conceptualizing. On the one hand, there is more information about the process of sharing and comparing. The advice in that section will be on specific techniques for designing focus groups that generate sharing and comparing as a desired form of interaction. On the other hand, there is less specific information about how to achieve organizing and conceptualizing in focus groups; the advice in that section will concentrate on techniques that can produce a better understanding of this more abstract process. Overall, the emphasis on the co-construction of meaning matches the chapter's symbolic interactionist orientation, while the emphasis on design decisions that encourage the co-construction of meaning matches the chapter's pragmatic orientation.

◆ Studying Interaction in Focus Groups

CONTENT-ORIENTED AND CONVERSATION-ORIENTED RESEARCH

Although focus groups are indeed a form of interviewing, the source of the data is the interaction among the participants in these interviews. Surprisingly, the study of interaction continues to receive relatively little attention, although a number of articles have criticized this lack of attention (e.g., Kitzinger, 1994; Wilkinson, 1998b). Duggleby (2005) provides a useful review of two of the most common targets for this critique: (1) the analysis of data from focus groups and (2) the reporting of the results from that analysis. It is impossible to deny the importance of interaction in focus groups, but even so, I have argued (Morgan, 2010) that this does imply that interaction is the central concern for every project that uses focus groups. In particular, saying that the interaction in focus groups produces the data is not the same as saying that the interaction itself is the data. . . . [C]hoices about the analysis and reporting of interaction in focus groups must be made within the context of the needs and goals of the overall project. (p. 718)

Along with making a strong argument for paying more attention to interaction in focus groups, Duggleby (2005) also agrees with the fundamental pragmatist point that the goal of the research must determine the use of the methods (see Macnaghten & Myers, 2004, for a similar argument).

In describing the different goals that focus groups can serve, I have distinguished between purposes that are oriented to substantive content and those that relate to the conversational dynamics (Morgan, 2010). Content-oriented studies are by far the most common of the two, largely because they include almost all the work devoted to applied goals and practical uses for focus groups. For this purpose, the microdynamics of the conversation are largely irrelevant. In contrast, the less common studies that use either conversation analysis (Schegloff, 2007) or discourse analysis (Puchta & Potter, 2004) represent the most explicit attention to the actual conversations in focus groups. In this case, the conversations in focus group discussions are almost always used as a convenient site for studying interaction in general, so the specific subject of the discussion is largely irrelevant.

The difference between content-oriented and conversation-oriented research is exemplified by the long-term coauthorship team of Phil Macnaghten and Greg Myers, who have used their mutual experience to compare these two approaches (Macnaghten & Myers, 2004). Thus, content-oriented researchers such as Macnaghten typically use a more directive style of moderating to elicit useful content on their topic of interest, while conversation-oriented researchers such as Myers typically use a less structured style that lets them hear how the participants set their own agenda. For analysis, the difference is between using a well-defined goal to locate the most important themes in the discussion and searching for patterns in the way participants talk to each other and to the moderator. For interpretation of data, the difference is between finding statements that are relevant to the final report of the data and treating focus groups as a particular example of conversation

that makes it possible to hear ongoing interaction. For reporting the research, content-oriented researchers apply their results to debates and decisions related to a specific topic, while conversation-oriented researchers contribute to the academic debate within their field of interest.

Macnaghten and Myers (2004, p. 74) provide a useful summary of these distinctions by comparing the approaches to focus groups. Whereas Phil Macnaghten represents researchers who are interested in the substantive content of focus groups and concentrate on "*what* was said," Greg Myers represents researchers in conversation analysis, who concentrate on "*how* it was said." By coincidence, I used the same language (Morgan, 2010) to argue for "the inherent connection between the substantive content of 'what' participants say and the interactive dynamics of 'how' participants say those things" (p. 718). Acknowledging this connection between the content of interaction and the processes that produce that content only takes us so far, however. The real problem is getting back and forth between these two forms of analysis. In my opinion, the most reasonable way to bridge this gap is by introducing a middle level, where the substance of the current conversation is linked to both the content of the ongoing discussion and the dynamics of the associated interaction. This intermediate course of action avoids asking either substantive-oriented researchers or conversation analysts to expand their domains in ways that are radically disconnected from their traditional interests. To do this, I propose an emphasis on what has been called the *co-construction of meaning* in focus groups.

THE CO-CONSTRUCTION OF MEANING

The idea of the co-construction of meaning in focus groups comes from the work of Sue Wilkinson (1998a):

Focus group data offer considerable potential for exploring the co-construction of meaning through an analysis of interactive processes. Sensitively analysed, such data can offer insights into the relational aspects of self, the processes by which meanings and knowledges are constructed through interactions with others, and the ways in which social inequalities are produced and perpetuated through talk. (p. 123)

In addition, Wilkinson (1998b) discusses five "specific mechanisms through which focus groups elicit participants' own meanings" (p. 334):

1. By enhancing disclosure

2. By providing access to participants' own language and concepts

3. By enabling participants to follow their own agendas

4. By encouraging the production of elaborated accounts

5. By providing an opportunity to observe the co-construction of meaning in action

Once again, however, these processes give an excellent summary of *what* researchers can learn by observing the participants' interaction, but they provide less insight into *how* the participants accomplish these activities. Thus, from a middle-range point of view, this approach reproduces the earlier distinction between the content of the interaction and the conversational processes that produce that content. Closing this gap requires *actively moving back and forth between the interactive dynamics of focus groups and the content of that interaction.* The next two sections each develop an example of connecting conversational dynamics and substantive content. The first part describes "sharing and comparing" as a process that focus group participants typically use in the early stages of their co-construction of meaning, as a way to develop the basic content of their ongoing conversation. The next part looks at "organizing a conceptualizing" as a higher level of the co-construction of meaning, where the participants create and use more abstract versions of the content in their conversations.

◆ Basic Forms of Interaction in Focus Groups, Part 1: Sharing and Comparing

My earlier works contain several explicit mentions of "sharing and comparing" as a fundamental aspect of interaction in focus groups. For example, at a procedural level, my chapter in the first edition of this volume described how my own moderating style encourages sharing and comparing as a form of interaction among participants (Morgan, 2002). At the level of purposes, the "Introduction to the Focus Group Kit" highlighted the process of sharing and comparing as one of the strengths that focus groups as a specific method added to the general strengths of qualitative methods as a whole (Morgan, 1998, p. 12).

The entry for "focus groups" in the *Sage Dictionary of Social Research Methods* provides a more explicit description of this process (Morgan, 2006):

When the participants are mutually interested in the discussion, their conversation often takes the form of sharing and comparing thoughts about the topic. That is, they share their experiences and thoughts, while also comparing their own contributions to what others have said. This process of sharing and comparing is especially useful for hearing and understanding a range of responses on a research topic. The best focus groups thus not only provide data on *what* the participants think but also explicit insights into *why* they think the way they do. (p. 123)

A similar statement in the second edition of *Focus Groups as Qualitative Research* (Morgan, 1997) pays more attention to the interactive exchanges that are central to symbolic interactionism:

From the researcher's point of view, this process of sharing and comparing provides the rare opportunity to collect direct evidence on how the participants themselves understand their similarities and differences. This actual observation of consensus and diversity is something that can happen quite powerfully through group interaction. (p. 20)

These statements about sharing and comparing are, however, quite general. In contrast, the current treatment will offer a great deal more detail. To provide some perspective, my emphasis on sharing and comparing comes from my observations of interactions in focus groups, followed by examining the transcriptions to check on my interpretation. Thus, my assertions about the importance of sharing and comparing emerge from the same essentially "inductive" process that guides qualitative research in general.

Following a pragmatic orientation, both this section and the next include coverage of both broad purposes and specific procedures. For this section, the first question is this: What are the *purposes* of sharing and comparing that make this process an essential form of interaction in a focus group? In particular, what purposes does it serve for the participants as they create and maintain their discussion? The next question is this: How can researchers design a set of *procedures* that will produce both the levels of and the types of sharing and comparing that are most appropriate for a given project? This is followed by another question: What are the *procedures* that will affect the process of sharing and comparing among the participants? In particular, which procedures should researchers use to encourage the kind of interaction that is most appropriate for a given project? The last questions provide the core content of this section.

PURPOSES FOR SHARING AND COMPARING FROM THE PARTICIPANTS' PERSPECTIVE

Imagine that the moderator has just asked the first question in a focus group. In addition, assume that it is a well-chosen question, so that each of the participants is interested in the question, has something to say about it, and is interested in hearing what others have to say. Like virtually all conversations, this discussion will involve a process of "turn taking," where every statement follows the one before it and is in turn followed by the next statement. From the participants' point of view, this need to maintain an orderly conversation means that each of their statements should have an obvious connection to what has already been said and should give particular importance to the remark immediately before their own contribution.

This summary of the mechanics of turning taking in conversations is both intuitively obvious and well established by decades of research. What has received considerably less attention, however, is the way participants link the *content* of what they say with the content of what was just said. This is the most basic element in the co-construction of meaning, and I am proposing sharing and comparing as a basic interactive process that establishes this ongoing connection in focus group interaction. Sharing consists of statements that connect to the previous remark by adding similar content to that remark. Participants thus use sharing to *join* existing elements of the topic. Alternatively, comparing consists

of noting a difference between the content of the current statement and the previous remark. Participants thus use comparing to *differentiate* elements of the topic that separate from each other.

Sharing and comparing are clearly distinct processes, but they serve related purposes for the participants' discussion of the topic. In particular, they each make it possible for participants to *expand* on the content of the ongoing conversation. If this conversation were a continuous piece of speech, sharing and comparing would serve as the "conjunctions" that mark the connection between different segments of the overall content. Like conjunctions as parts of speech, sharing and comparing connect the substantive content of the conversation in focus groups, rather than simply linking the end of one speaker's turn to the beginning of the next. From the participants' point of view, beginning a statement with a form of sharing or comparing signals the relationship between what they are about to say and the content of the previous remark. Thus, a statement that indicates sharing joins similar elements within the topic as a whole, and a statement that indicates comparing points to different aspects of the topic.

For the English language, the analogy of conjunctions to sharing and comparing would match "and" with sharing, while "but" would correspond to comparing. Just as "and" adds to the previous content in a sentence, sharing joins the content in a remark to the previous conversation. Alternatively, just as "but" separates the content in the two halves of a sentence, comparing differentiates the current content from the previous remarks. When participants want to add to and extend the previous remark, they will often begin what they have to say with either the literal word "and" or its equivalent. When they want to differentiate or separate their statement from the previous remark, they will often begin their statement with "but" or its equivalent. Together, sharing and comparing serve as conversation-level "conjunctions" that allow participants to expand on the prior topics in the conversation.

Of course, the English language has a third conjunction, "or," which is a means of offering an alternative. In some instances, "or" signals an alternative that is similar to the content that preceded it, much as "and" does (e.g., "Or another thing that's like that is . . ."). In other instances, it signals a different alternative, much as "but" does (e.g., "Or a different way of looking at that . . ."). Thus, "or" as a third English conjunction essentially serves as a way for focus group participants to express one of the other two forms of conjunction, with the specific usage being clear in the context.

Here are some illustrations of "and" and "but" from actual focus groups:

Forms of "And"

And along with that . . .

And you've got the same thing when . . .

That's a great idea, and another piece of it is . . .

Forms of "But"

But I was thinking of it more as . . .

One of the big differences is . . .

In my family, we do almost the exact opposite of that . . .

Here are two additional, more detailed examples from a study of "Dual Earners in the Sandwiched Generation" (Neal & Hammer, 2006), in which both the partners of a couple were working and the couple had both child care and parent care responsibilities. In this example of sharing, a discussion of issues related to combining work and family duties leads one participant to introduce the topic of the characteristics of a good supervisor, and the next participant adds to the set of experiences that help a supervisor "understand," followed by validation from the first participant.

#1: I've found that where I work, usually the supervisors that are the best are the ones that came up through the ranks, they were workers like you at one time. They seem to understand . . .

#2: Or if they've "been there." If they have a family then they understand a lot more.

#1: Oh yeah, that makes a difference.

For comparing, the following example involves the topic of sharing your house with an older parent. When the first participant notes that she would be more likely to share her home than her sisters would, the next person differentiates the overall issue of parents living with siblings according to how well it works out for the older parent.

#1: We've thought about it. . . . [There is an] extra bedroom, and we have teased my mom about it, you know, "If and when you ever need to stay somewhere . . ." She would probably live with us, but it would not be easy at all. So I don't know. Neither one of my sisters would come through.

#2: But see, then that's where you have got to think, too, "How would I feel if I pushed it on to a sister and then my mom died?" I would feel like I didn't do my part or, I didn't try hard enough or, you know what I mean?

Sharing and comparing are obviously not the only way that participants can create substantive links between what they are about to say and what has already been said, and the two most obvious alternatives are agreement and disagreement (e.g., Kitzinger, 1994). Conversation analysis, in particular, pays a considerable amount of attention to agreement and disagreement in the context of turn taking (Schegloff, 2007), where they are known as a "preferred" or "dispreferred" response to the prior remark (for a different treatment of this topic, see Hollander & Gordon, 2004, who examine turns as support, challenge, and nonresponse). Although it is tempting to pair sharing with agreement and comparing with disagreement, their function as ways to expand the content of the conversation typically makes them less "charged" than outright agreement or disagreement. Because disagreement is more problematic than agreement, it has received notably more attention (see Myers, 1998, for an application to focus groups). The importance of disagreement makes it worth considering "but" as a conjunction that can indicate a literal form of disagreement. Within the context of sharing and comparing, however, "but" is seldom interpreted as a potential source of conflict; instead, it is far more likely to be treated as a useful contribution to the development of the discussion.

Consider the following example from Macnaghten and Myers (2004), where Myers as a conversation analyst interprets a section of interaction from one of Macnaghten's focus groups on the substantive topic of genetic engineering in animals:

Phil: Can I just say, so in what ways do you think these animals are natural?

M: Well, they won't be natural will they?

Paul: They're not natural, they're man made aren't they.

M: They're engineered.

Iris: But we do that now through interbreeding don't we?

M: But even more so now . . .

Phil: But that's a point, how is it different from conventional selective breeding? (pp. 74–75)

Myers points out that the last two remarks by participants "both begin [with] 'but,' implying a kind of agree/disagree structure." Yet even though there is a little element of disagreement here, I would argue that it is more useful to interpret this exchange (starting with M's statement, "They're engineered") as an example of comparing, where the idea of interbreeding is differentiated from genetic engineering. Interestingly, this clearly seems to be how Macnaghten, as a moderator, interprets this exchange.

It is also worth noting that agreement and disagreement, in their milder forms, are not necessarily mutually exclusive options for responding to a previous remark. The most common way to convey this kind of mixed message is a kind of "hybrid" conjunction, which often takes the form of "Yes, but . . ." (e.g., "I agree, but another thing from my perspective is . . ."). Rather than conveying a mixed message, conjunctions such as "Yes, but . . ." are more likely to *both* acknowledge the relevance of what was just said and point out different aspects of the topic that would be more relevant in a different context. Using expressions such as "Yes, but . . ." as a way to signal a *context-dependent form of differentiation* allows participants to describe how shifts in circumstances expand on the topic. Here is a more detailed example of a "Yes, but . . ." construction from the "Dual Earners in the Sandwiched Generation" study. In this case, the first participant describes her negative experience of living too far from an older parent, while the second participant begins by agreeing about the value of living closer and then shifts over to the alternative advantages of living farther away.

#1:   I would say that we need to live in a central location for our jobs and our families. We tried moving out to [a small town], we bought a house out there. It was a disaster. I thought I could handle it and I couldn't. It was too far.

#2:   I live close to my parents, too. About a block and half away. And so it is helpful to be close by sometimes. But, on the other hand, being farther away, you aren't called on as often to be there.

Up to this point, my presentation of sharing and comparing has concentrated on the purposes these processes serve in connecting the content in two statements. But they also play an important part in the larger process of co-constructing meaning. More broadly, sharing and comparing are an ongoing process that elicits and shapes the substantive content of the discussion, by establishing connections across the separate contributions from individual participants. Treating sharing and comparing as an ongoing process tells us how participants implicitly define the research topic by what they include within the boundaries of their discussion. From this perspective, participants co-construct their definition of the topic through their interpretation of what is most meaningful with regard to the topic.

Overall, the joint process of sharing and comparing defines the core content of the topic, and this content serves as a continuing context for further development of the discussion. Thus, the co-construction of meaning requires both a continuing series of connections with the earlier content of the conversation and a substantive expansion of that earlier material. In focus groups, the discussion emerges from participants' efforts to connect and expand on the separate statements in their conversation. But the discussion in focus groups is also a function of the research design that guides the participants, and that is the subject of the next section.

PROCEDURES THAT PROMOTE SHARING AND COMPARING: THE RESEARCHER'S PERSPECTIVE

This section examines four basic issues that affect the nature of interaction in focus groups. Each of these issues amounts to a decision about the design of a focus group project:

• Who will the participants be?

• How will the group discussion be introduced to the participants?

• What questions will the participants be asked?

• How will the moderator interact with the group during the discussion?

Following the pragmatic emphasis in this chapter, these decisions will be addressed through explicit attention to the overall goals of the research project and the procedures that can address those goals.

The Role of Group Composition in Shaping the Discussion

The first and most important influence on sharing and comparing occurs during the design process, when the research team decides who the participants will be. In terms of how the group composition affects group interaction, the core question is "How will these participants relate to each other in terms of this topic?" The minimum requirement for a good group discussion is that these participants need to be comfortable with talking to the other participants about this topic. Beyond that minimum, sharing and comparing is most likely to occur when the participants are genuinely interested in what each of them has to say about the research topic.

The classic solution to the problem of choosing a group composition that will facilitate interaction is to choose a set of homogeneous participants. The more the participants share similarities before they even start the discussion, the less they will have to explain themselves to each other and the easier it will be to react appropriately to what others say. It is important to note, however, that this kind of homogeneity is *based on similarity with regard to the topic*. Despite the repeated emphasis on this point in most textbooks about focus groups, too many researchers still think of homogeneity in terms of background characteristics and demographics; even these factors typically do little to encourage meaningful interaction.

In symbolic interactionist terms, the shared experiences that go with homogeneity make it more straightforward for participants to "take the role of the other." For interactionists, everything that participants say during the discussion is shaped by their sense of how the other participants will react to what they might say. Once the conversation is well under way, direct experience will drive the process of role taking, but the beginning of the group inherently poses more challenges for estimating the likely reactions of the other people around the table. Homogeneity reduces this uncertainty by providing realistic assumptions about how the rest of the group is likely to react.

The Role of the Introduction in Shaping the Discussion

To help participants become engaged in their discussion, the research team has to portray the nature of that discussion, and this matches another key concept from symbolic interactionism: *the definition of the situation*. One basic design dimension that needs to be introduced is the desired degree of structure in the discussion, ranging from less structured groups, where the participants can explore the topic, to more structured groups, where the researcher's predetermined agenda seeks depth and detail about the topic. Once there is a decision about the level of structure that is most appropriate for a given set of research goals, the research team needs to "define the situation" for the participants by describing the nature of the focus group in ways that promote the desired level of structure. From an interactionist perspective, this means helping the participants understand their role as "participants in a group discussion."

In less structured groups, encouraging a process of sharing and comparing involves using the introduction and "ground rules" to create a climate that encourages the expression of a diverse range of opinions. Too often, moderators address issues of diversity in opinions by saying little more than "Remember, there are no right and wrong answers." This is not only a trite expression that participants have heard too many times in too many situations, but it also fails to provide any practical advice on how to handle differences in experiences and viewpoints. In my own instructions, I encourage the expression of diverse viewpoints by extending that all-too-common phrase with something like the following: "For all the questions you'll be discussing, you are free to talk about your different experiences and opinions. So, if you think 'that's not how I feel,' then you should speak up."

This definition of the situation helps participants understand our genuine interest in hearing different opinions and experiences, while also indicating when they should be sharing their differences, and providing a model for how to state their differences.

In contrast, defining the situation by a moderator means giving the moderator more control over the discussion. Here is an example of instructions that are designed to encourage a more structured discussion: "I'll be asking the questions I want you to discuss. So, I want to hear lots of different experiences and opinions—as much as you can tell me about my questions."

This definition of the situation allows moderators to pursue their own agenda by simply saying something like, "Remember how I said that I might have to apologize and break into the discussion? So, in the interest of time, I'd like to hear what you have to say about . . ."

Once the instructions help define the situation for the participants, the next step is to follow through on these expectations *during the group itself*. Ultimately, it is the questions that have the most powerful effect on the definition of the situation for any form of interviewing, and that is the topic for the next section.

The Role of the Interview Questions in Shaping the Discussion

The first question in the focus group can have a crucial impact on the discussion as a whole. It is also important to note that the first question occurs immediately after the instructions—which means that it should follow through on those instructions. For example, when the instructions call for a less structured discussion that asks for different points of view, then the first question should encourage a diverse range of contributions to the discussion. Moving forward from the groundwork laid during the instructions, the first question should serve as a "discussion starter" that matches the goals laid out in the introduction. An example would be something like "Let's start by having you make as long a list as you can of everything that is involved, one way or another, with [topic]" (see Krueger, 1998, for other examples).

There are several basic principles for starter questions that successfully promote interaction in the discussion. A starter question should be

- Something that is easy for each of the participants to answer

- Something that makes participants want to hear what the other participants have to say

- Something that creates the opportunity to express a diverse range of views

In terms of sharing and comparing, starting with a question that is easy to answer supplies each participant with a reasonably substantial number of potential

contributions to the conversation, at the same time that it also creates a comfort level that increases the likelihood of making those contributions. The idea of asking a question where the participants will be interested in what the others have to say corresponds to the earlier advice about selecting a group composition that meets this same standard. Finally, asking questions that create space for multiple points of view means that each participant has a continuing set of options for connecting to the conversation. Taken together, these elements of a successful first question provide the participants with resources that help them discover their similarities and differences through a mutually informative process of sharing and comparing.

One of the key elements of all discussion starter questions is that they need to pay careful attention to participants' needs for generating a discussion. The research team thus needs to balance both their own need for information from the discussion and the participants' need for comfortable interaction. Ultimately, getting high-quality data from the discussion depends on the interaction among the participants. To achieve this goal, the members of the research team have to engage in different forms of role taking: They take the roles of the participants as they are writing the questions. In other words, they need to think as if they were not only participants who are going to respond to these questions as individuals but also ones who can create and maintain an active group discussion around each question.

This first question sets the discussion in motion, but that obviously needs to be followed up by further questions that build on the directions the first question establishes. This means that the sequence of questions in a focus group should flow smoothly with regard to both the substantive topic and the developing group dynamic. Interview guides that produce this level of coherence make all of the other aspects of conducting focus groups much less problematic. In particular, when the situation is well-defined by the instructions and questions, this greatly reduces the potential challenges involved in moderating focus groups.

The Role of the Moderator in Shaping the Discussion

There is a common, but often mistaken, assumption that the moderator is responsible for creating the conversation in focus groups. What I am claiming, however, is that it is possible to produce the preferred types of group interaction through careful decisions about research design. All of these design decisions help frame the discussion before the moderator takes any action other than delivering the instructions and asking the first question. When these decisions successfully channel the discussion in the desired direction, the moderator's primary job is to assist with the ongoing group dynamics rather than taking responsibility for creating those dynamics.

Consider the moderator's role after a discussion starter question has created a process of sharing and comparing about topics that match the research team's interests. Then the main thing that the moderator needs to do is to listen to the discussion and learn from it. Sooner or later, the moderator will want to probe the group in ways that match the goals for their discussion. For example, in a less structured group with instructions that encourage sharing a wide range of questions, the probes should follow through on that message, with comments such as "Who has something that we haven't heard yet?" If, however, the participants are already meeting the discussion goals on their own, then even this minimal degree of probing may not be necessary.

This final piece of procedural advice reinforces the larger point that appropriate decisions about the group composition, the instructions for the participants, the interview questions, and the role of the moderator have a major influence on the degree of sharing and comparing that occurs in focus groups. Note, however, that this section consistently points out the research team's need to take the participants' perspectives into account. For example, what kind of homogeneity would be most likely to encourage comfortable exchanges about the research topic? Or what kind of discussion starter question would lead to a dynamic where these participants were interested in what the others had to say about the topic? Thus, at every step, researchers need to consider the participant's perspective in order to produce the sharing and comparing that will meet their own research goals.

◆ Basic Forms of Interaction in Focus Groups, Part 2: Organizing and Conceptualizing

Compared with sharing and comparing, the processes of organizing and conceptualizing typically occur during the later part of focus groups. Once the participants have co-constructed a set of topics that define the topic, they can engage in more interpretive forms of interaction. In particular, the sharing and comparing that happen earlier provide the subject matter that participants organize into broader categories and convert into more abstract concepts. Hence, the co-construction of meaning that results from organizing and conceptualizing is at a "higher level" than the more concrete topics that participants consider in sharing and comparing.

Like the previous section, this one is also divided between the purposes that organizing and conceptualizing can serve for the participants and the procedures that the research team can use to promote these processes. As noted in the introduction, however, the state of knowledge about organizing and conceptualizing is still at a basic level. Thus, the section on the purposes will be more speculative, as opposed to the inductively grounded basis for the description of sharing and comparing. Similarly, the coverage of procedure designs related to organizing and conceptualizing will be more about potential options rather than specific advice. Overall, the goal of this section is to emphasize the importance of organizing and conceptualizing and to encourage more attention to both participants' and researchers' perspectives on these two processes.

PURPOSES OF ORGANIZING AND CONCEPTUALIZING FROM THE PARTICIPANTS' PERSPECTIVE

From a symbolic interactionist perspective, organizing and conceptualizing topical material in focus group discussions can be treated as creating and using *social objects*. Callero (1986) summarizes Mead's thinking on this point: "Social objects are said to emerge in the course of interaction and exist only in relation to others" (p. 346). The participants will bring many of these shared social objects with them, based on their shared culture, but they will construct more specific social objects through their immediate conversation. This emphasis on shared social objects is similar to the idea that focus group participants use their interaction to locate a "common ground." Hyden and Bulow (2003) introduced this term to capture the extent to which participants used prior identities or roles to act as a group rather than as a collection of individuals. Later work (Lehoux, Poland, & Daudelin, 2006; Moen, Antonov, Nilson, & Ring, 2010) followed this tradition by treating common ground as a preexisting characteristic that helps participants act in a coherent, grouplike fashion. In contrast, a co-construction of meaning approach concentrates on creating a common ground through the focus group interaction itself. In this case, participants begin with only their shared relationship to the topic, and while this may include similar characteristics, that shared background is neither necessary nor sufficient for achieving a common ground.

The idea that groups can "go beyond" sharing and comparing to "reach the level" of organizing and conceptualizing points to a typical difference between the co-construction of social objects during the earlier and later portions of focus group discussions. After the participants *expand* on the research topic by using sharing and comparing to uncover a broad range of material related to that topic, they can *consolidate* their discussion through the more abstract processes of organizing and conceptualizing. Of course, actual focus groups are quite likely to blend these two processes, but it is still quite reasonable to expect a broad progression from expanding a topic through sharing and comparing toward consolidating that topical material through organizing and conceptualizing.

This two-step process bears a resemblance to a three-part theoretical system from one of my first articles on focus groups, where Margaret Spanish and I examined the interaction in discussions about who has heart attacks and why (Morgan & Spanish, 1985). Our analysis was based on cognitive theories of learning, which pointed to the sequential development of three forms of knowledge. First, the participants generated "episodic knowledge" by telling stories about people they knew who had heart attacks. Second, they compared these stories to produce "categorical knowledge" that almost always used risk factors to discuss who has heart attacks and why. Finally, at least a few groups in this study created "abstract knowledge" about what causes and what prevents heart attacks, through theories that systematically related various risk factors.

The two end points of the previous system correspond to the current description of processes for the co-construction of meaning. On the one hand, episodic knowledge corresponds to the topical content of the conversation that participants develop and expand through sharing and comparing. On the other hand, abstract knowledge matches the products of organizing and conceptualizing. From this perspective, the intermediate level of producing categories can be considered as one component in the more general process of organizing either topical materials into categories or categorical materials into concepts. Thus, in our study on heart attacks, the participants could categorize stories according to the risk factors in each case, or they could categorize risk factors according to how they fit into more abstract conceptual frameworks. Consider this simple example:

#1: Who did you write about?

#2: A friend of my parents. He had the usual life with a lot of work and a lot of food, a lot of smoking.

#3: How old was this fellow?

#2: Seventy, something like that. But my guess is that lifestyle is very important . . . (Morgan & Spanish, 1985, p. 409)

In this example, the second speaker uses the emerging system of risk factors to present a "story" that is already more conceptual than the ones that preceded it. Then, when the third speaker inquires about age, the reply emphasizes "lifestyle" as a package of risk factors. This illustrates the common process of organizing concrete categories into more abstract concepts, which can in turn be organized into more complex conceptual frameworks. This architectural metaphor of creating a "conceptual framework" reflects a progressive co-construction of meaning.

Many qualitative researchers will recognize these processes as having much in common with the analysis of qualitative data. In particular, qualitative data analysis often creates categories from topical codes and then converts this category system into a set of themes. These themes organize a number of related ideas into a "conceptual tool" for interpreting the content in a topic area. Interestingly, focus group participants can also label related ideas to produce concepts that are very similar to themes. These self-labeled themes serve an important additional purpose in the ongoing interaction by giving the participants a compact way to refer to a larger package of related material. For example, in one of the heart attack groups, the participants developed the mechanical metaphor of the heart as a pump, leading to a description of one person's stress as so destructive that it was "eating his pump out."

Perhaps it should not be surprising to find this parallel between qualitative analysis and the interaction among focus group participants, because there is a distinct sense in which they share the same purpose: constructing meaning from the content of the focus group discussion. This also makes perfect sense from a pragmatic point of view, because it points to the fundamental equivalence of research and everyday life. Thus, for pragmatists, the quest for understanding is always a matter of what Dewey (1933) called inquiry, and Dewey also emphasized that the only difference between "lay" and "scientific" inquiry was the degree of care and self-awareness in the latter. Hence, the more solitary construction of meaning that goes into qualitative analysis corresponds to the more active *co*-construction of meaning that occurs during focus groups.

In comparison with researchers, however, participants do not have the liberty to go over the content of the discussion at their leisure. Instead, they have to do their "coding, categorizing, and conceptualizing" during the ongoing flow of the conversation itself. As the conversation proceeds, the meanings that participants construct at earlier points become social objects that they can use in their later discussions. In some cases, these earlier constructions will serve as the basis for further processes of organization and conceptualization. In other cases, the earlier material may be either explicitly examined and found wanting or implicitly ignored as less relevant to the emerging direction of the discussion.

One key point underlying this whole section is the idea that *the ongoing conversation serves as the context for the participants' co-construction of meaning*. Thus, the expansion of the topic through sharing and comparing provides material for consolidation through organizing and conceptualizing. Similarly, some of those "social objects" become themes, and some of those themes provide the basis for conceptual frameworks. All of this assumes a process that moves from lower to higher levels of organization and from more concrete topics to more abstract conceptualizations. Thus, researchers who want to observe phenomena that depend on organizing and conceptualizing will need procedures that can promote this form of interaction.

PROCEDURES THAT PROMOTE ORGANIZING AND CONCEPTUALIZING: THE RESEARCHER'S PERSPECTIVE

This section will examine three possible techniques for encouraging the process of organizing and conceptualizing. The first involves variations in interviewing techniques, while the second relies on concept mapping, and the third uses repeated interviews. Each of these procedures fits the general pragmatic model of examining possible solutions to a problematic situation—that is, the desire to create research designs that promote organizing and conceptualizing.

Among the various strategies for influencing interaction described in the previous section, the content of the interview questions is most relevant to encouraging conceptualization. In particular, if this set of strategies establishes a comfortable process of sharing and comparing in the earlier parts of the discussion, then the later questions could build on that as a way to move the conversation in more conceptual directions. More specifically, a deeper understanding of both the similarities and the differences among the participants makes it more likely that they will find a common ground for developing shared concepts and themes. Thus, the strategy is to create appropriate interview questions that can help them create both a common ground and a set of shared concepts and goals.

Interestingly, one of the currently most common forms of organizing interview guides may actually be holding back the kind of interaction that encourages conceptualization. "Funnel-style" interviews, as shown in Figure 10.1, move from broader, more participant-oriented questions to more specific, researcher-oriented questions. This format is especially useful

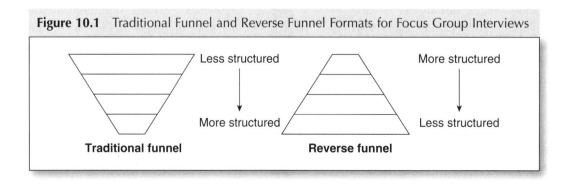

Figure 10.1 Traditional Funnel and Reverse Funnel Formats for Focus Group Interviews

in applied research, where the goal is to learn "what" the participants have to say. If, however, the goal is to learn about the more conceptual aspects of participants' thinking, then the funnel format is less useful, because it moves progressively toward narrower, externally defined questions. In contrast, each of the two other question formats in Figure 10.1 is not only relatively more familiar in current practice but also more likely to lead the discussion in a conceptual direction.

The reverse (or inverted) funnel moves from more specific to more general aspects of the topic, so this is a natural match to encouraging more conceptualization. One widely used implementation of this format begins by asking the participants to think of specific examples that are related to the topic (e.g., "I want you each to tell the rest of the group about someone you know who. . ."). Following this path, the next question might ask the participants to think about "all the stories you" told and "all the things that mattered with regard to [topic]," and that might be followed by hearing how they would group together the various ideas that are generated, to talk about "how all these things relate to [topic]." This reverse funnel matches the format for the interviews on "who has heart attacks and why" (Morgan & Spanish, 1985). In that case, the broad topic provided the basis for requesting specific stories about people who had heart attacks, followed by using those stories to consider "what makes some people more likely to have heart attacks and other people less likely," with a final question that asked, "What causes and what prevents heart attacks?" To understand the value of this design in this situation, consider what would have happened if we began with the last question. The participants could undoubtedly have discussed that question, but their answers would almost certainly have consisted of highly general statements about various risk factors. That starting point would have created not only little opportunity for sharing and comparing but also equally little incentive to construct personally meaningful conceptual systems.

Beyond the opportunities offered by alternative formats for interview guides, there are a number of other strategies that are oriented toward either smaller or larger aspects of research designs for focus groups. Other techniques that can be used to encourage conceptualization can be found in a book chapter I coauthored with two of my students (Morgan, Fellows, & Guevara, 2008). The most specific strategy from that chapter relies on concept maps as a

form of "stimulus material" that requests participants to organize the content from their prior discussion. It should be obvious how this direct request to organize and conceptualize the discussion material can encourage the more abstract thinking that is the goal in this section. This approach typically relies on a two-part question, where the participants begin by either generating a list of concepts or using a predetermined list, with the goal of creating a "map" (actually a structured diagram) that shows the relationships among the concepts. The second part of the question asks the participants to step back from their map and talk about how they chose to create it the way they did—that is, why they organized the concepts into this set of relationships. For example, in the heart attacks study, we could have replaced the last question about "what causes and what prevents" with a request to list and map all the various things that either cause or prevent heart attacks. Follow-up discussions of those maps would have been likely to produce more explicit organizational and conceptual material than we found through our rather generic question.

Another technique from Morgan et al. (2008) involves repeated focus groups, where the first round of groups provides participants who return for further discussions. The easiest way to set up repeated focus groups is to draw the participants for the second round of groups from the "pool" of participants who were in the first round. Because these participants have already engaged in a great deal of topic development during their earlier rounds, they will be in a favorable position for taking that material to the next level. A useful tactic for bringing out that prior topic development is to take advantage of the fact that the "pooled" participants will have been in different groups and therefore to ask them to "compare notes on the different things you discussed in each of your groups." In the Morgan and Spanish study (as reported in Morgan, 1997), we used the first round of participants as a pool for creating a repeated group, to build on their earlier discussions about what causes and what prevents heart attacks.

A more difficult technique for conducting repeated focus groups is to bring the same set of participants together twice. Although this strategy requires very careful attention to recruitment, it can have very notable benefits with regard to observing interaction. For example, McGregor (2004, 2005) worked with members of environmental organizations. What is especially interesting from the current perspective is that the second round of interviews constructed a degree of consensus that also required a certain amount of "silencing" of alternative views. As I argued at the beginning of this section, outcomes such as consensus seldom evolve in some passive manner; instead, they require active interaction devoted to organizing and conceptualizing, both emphasizing some standpoints and de-emphasizing others.

In considering these procedures for promoting organizing and conceptualizing, it is important to recognize that many focus groups do not need to reach this level of abstraction. Returning to the pragmatic principle that purposes should drive procedures, it is clear that the processes of organizing and conceptualizing are more relevant for some kinds of focus groups than for others. In particular, the classic reason for using a funnel form is to begin by letting the participants expand on the topic, so that the researchers themselves can consolidate the discussion around their own specific interests. Hence, there is nothing inherently valuable in groups that move beyond sharing and comparing to organize their ideas at a higher conceptual level; instead, as always, it depends on the purposes of the research.

◆ Conclusions

Every conversation is about something, and that "something" is the core of focus groups. When we design our data collection, we want to hear what the participants have to say about our research topic. When we analyze the data, we want to understand what the participants have said. At every step, our goal is to listen to and learn from participants' conversations about the topics that interest us.

The first of the four core sections in this chapter dealt with participants' use of sharing and comparing as a type of conversation that develops their understanding of the research topic. Although it is quite literally the interaction in focus groups that produces these conversations, it is participants' interests that move the conversation in one direction or another, as well as favoring one process over another as a way to advance the conversation. From the standpoint of symbolic interaction, this process of sharing and comparing amounts to using sets of social objects that make interaction possible. Whatever meanings the individual participants associate with the topic prior to the focus group, sharing and comparing

these meanings allow participants to co-construct shared meanings. While individual segments of sharing and comparing are a way to sort out the meanings of specific aspects of the research topic, the overall outcome of this process serves as a way to expand the topic as a whole. This points to the importance of the conversation as an ongoing context, where the earlier parts of the discussion have a continuing influence on what is said later. It is also worth noting that this immediate and local "context" is a major addition to the broader forms of context that surround any given focus group (Hollander, 2004). Overall, the process of sharing and comparing often plays a crucial, early role by developing the topic in ways that sustain the remainder of the discussion.

The section on research procedures for encouraging sharing and comparing showed that there are already a considerable number of techniques available in this area. This does not, however, eliminate the need for innovation. One limitation of the current literature on focus groups is an overreliance on well-accepted procedures, as opposed to experimentation with new and better ways to do focus groups. Hence, there are undoubtedly a large number of procedures related to sharing and comparing that are yet to be discovered, and one goal of this chapter is to raise the awareness of sharing and comparing, to stimulate more research on this fundamental aspect of interaction in focus groups. In particular, if this form of interaction serves as a way of expanding on the research topic, then processes that increase sharing and comparing should produce a richer range of materials. Overall, our procedures for sharing and comparing have been successful, but largely implicit, so more direct attention to these procedures has the potential to make a substantial contribution.

Turning to organizing and conceptualizing, the interactive purposes that these processes serve for participants can be captured with the idea that the conversation is an ongoing context for the co-construction of meaning. In particular, it helps explain how the earlier development of more concrete material is a necessary precursor for the more abstract work that occurs during organizing and conceptualizing. From the perspective of the overall conversation, the process of sharing and comparing has the advantage of expanding the topic, but this occurs at the "expense" of managing that increasing volume of material. When the participants do continue their discussion through organizing and conceptualizing, it is hardly surprising that this type of interaction is more self-conscious and, thus, more self-evident. Overall, the process of consolidation that arises for organizing and conceptualizing inherently occurs within that context of a developmental trajectory that is unique to each focus group.

In contrast to sharing and comparing, procedures for organizing and conceptualizing constitute an area that explicitly needs more development, and this section of the chapter presented three ideas along this line. The first suggestion recommended the use of the inverted funnel as a format for asking questions in a focus group, but we need more ideas about the specific types of questions and lines of questioning that will move participants into a higher level of abstraction. The second suggestion was to use concept mapping as a form of "stimulus material" creating connections between the separate aspects of the research topic, but there are undoubtedly many other forms of stimulus material that accomplish similar goals. The final suggestion was to use repeated focus groups to boost familiarity with the topic, but there are undoubtedly easier ways to do this, such as bringing together participants who are already acquainted with each other—especially when the research topic is a reason for their relationships. Overall, however, it is important not to lose track of the point of these procedures, which is to pursue purposes that engage participants in more complex and abstract aspects of the co-construction of meaning.

As a concluding message, I would interpret this chapter as a relatively rare attempt at systematically addressing interaction in focus groups, in terms of both the value of this interaction for participants and the procedures that researchers can use to encourage the desired forms of interaction. I believe that the best way to move forward with this agenda is to follow the current use of Wilkinson's concept of the co-construction of meaning. The co-construction of meaning is the ultimate source of the data from focus groups, so our own goals and purposes provide a direct justification for investigating how our procedures influence this essential process. Ultimately, we need to think of the co-construction of meaning not only as the way in which participants pursue their discussions but also as the key to pursuing our own research goals.

◆ References

Callero, P. L. (1986). Toward a median conceptualization of role. *Sociological Quarterly, 49,* 343–358.

Cooley, C. H. (1909). *Social organization: A study of the larger mind.* New York, NY: Scribner's.

Dewey, J. (1933). *How we think, a restatement of the relation of reflective thinking to the educative process.* Boston, MA: D. C. Heath.

Duggleby, W. (2005). What about focus group interaction data? *Qualitative Health Research, 15,* 832–840.

Hollander, J. (2004). The social contexts of focus groups. *Journal of Contemporary Ethnography, 33,* 602–637.

Hollander, J., & Gordon, H. (2004). The processes of social construction in talk. *Symbolic Interaction, 29,* 183–212.

Hyden, L. C., & Bulow, P. H. (2003). Who's talking: Drawing conclusions from focus groups. *International Journal of Social Research Methodology, 6,* 305–321.

Kitzinger, J. (1994). The methodology of focus groups: The importance of interaction between research participants. *Sociology of Health and Illness, 82,* 103–121.

Krueger, R. A. (1998). *Developing questions for focus groups.* Thousand Oaks, CA: Sage.

Lehoux, P., Poland, B., & Daudelin, G. (2006). Focus group research and "the patient's view." *Social Science and Medicine, 63,* 2091–2104.

Macnaghten, P., & Myers, G. (2004). Focus groups: The moderator's view and the analyst's view. In G. Gobo, J. Gubrium, C. Seale, & D. Silverman (Eds.), *Qualitative research practice* (pp. 65–79). Thousand Oaks, CA: Sage.

McGregor, A. (2004). Sustainable development and "warm fuzzy feelings": Discourse and nature within Australian environmental imaginaries. *Geoforum, 35,* 593–606.

McGregor, A. (2005). Negotiating nature: Exploring discourse through small group research. *Area, 37*(4), 423–432.

Mead, G. H. (1934). *Mind, self, and society.* Chicago, IL: University of Chicago Press.

Moen, J., Antonov, K., Nilson, L., & Ring, L. (2010). Interaction between participants in focus groups with older patients and general practitioners. *Qualitative Health Research, 20,* 607–617.

Morgan, D. L. (1997). *Focus groups as qualitative research* (2nd ed.). Thousand Oaks, CA: Sage.

Morgan, D. L. (1998). *The focus groups guidebook.* Thousand Oaks, CA: Sage.

Morgan, D. L. (2002). Focus group interviewing. In J. Gubrium & J. Holstein (Eds.), *Handbook of interview research* (pp. 141–160). Thousand Oaks, CA: Sage.

Morgan, D. L. (2006). Focus group. In V. Jupp (Ed.), *The Sage dictionary of social research methods* (pp. 121–123). Thousand Oaks, CA: Sage.

Morgan, D. L. (2010). Reconsidering the role of interaction in analyzing and reporting focus groups. *Qualitative Health Research, 20,* 718–722.

Morgan, D. L., Fellows, C. E., & Guevara, H. (2008). Emergent approaches to focus groups research. In S. N. Hesse-Biber & P. Leavy (Eds.), *Handbook of emergent methods* (pp. 189–206). New York, NY: Guilford Press.

Morgan, D. L., & Spanish, M. (1985). Social interaction and the cognitive organisation of health-relevant knowledge. *Sociology of Health and Illness, 73,* 401–422.

Myers, G. (1998). Displaying opinions: Topics and disagreement in focus groups. *Language in Society, 27,* 85–111.

Neal, M. B., & Hammer, L. B. (2006). *Working couples caring for children and aging parents: Effects on work and well-being.* Hillsdale, NJ: Lawrence Erlbaum.

Puchta, C., & Potter, J. (2004). *Focus group practice.* Thousand Oaks, CA: Sage.

Schegloff, E. A. (2007). *A primer in conversation analysis.* Cambridge, England: Cambridge University Press.

Wilkinson, S. (1998a). Focus groups in feminist research: Power, interaction and the co-construction of meaning. *Women's Studies International Forum, 21,* 111–125.

Wilkinson, S. (1998b). Focus groups in health research: Exploring the meanings of health and illness. *Journal of Health Psychology, 33,* 329–348.

11

INTERNET INTERVIEWING

◆ Nalita James and Hugh Busher

◆ Introduction—The Developing Cyber Context of Research Interviews

In the past 10 years, there has been a global spread of the Internet. In 2007, there were 1.24 billion Internet users (Burkeman, 2008). This has had a significant impact on the conditions of social interaction, providing opportunities for individuals to construct the reality of their everyday lives online and off-line and for these two to interact. It is no longer a special place that people visit occasionally. It has reconfigured the way in which individuals communicate and connect with each other. The "trajectory of acquaintanceship development" (Zhao, 2006, p. 471) has become such that individuals can now get to know each other first online through chat rooms before using other media such as e-mail, telephone, and face-to-face contact. There has been a rapid increase in websites such as YouTube, MySpace, Facebook, and blogs (online diaries or journals) of many

descriptions. Websites such as these not only offer opportunities for "social networking" but are reshaping the way in which news and views are gathered and disseminated (Goodfellow, 2007). They allow people to present themselves, create presentations of themselves, present their views, and invite the views of others.

As the Internet has expanded globally, it has come to be used as a research medium in social research, opening up innovative ways for researchers to examine human interactions and experiences, as individuals and communities. It provides a virtual social arena where practices, meanings, and identities can intermingle between researchers and participants in ways that may not be possible in the real world (Dominguez et al., 2007). It has altered the nature of the context in which research can take place and how knowledge is constructed by offering a different space and dimension in which conventional research designs and methods can be used and adapted to allow individuals to write about who they are and what they know. "Electronic virtuality is now embedded within actuality in a more dispersed and active way than ever before" (Hammersley, 2006, p. 8).

The context of research is now more febrile. Along with the embedding of the virtual world in everyday life has come concerns about how it might undermine the stability of societies, giving rise to cultures of surveillance in many countries, especially since the terrorist attack on the World Trade Center and the Pentagon in the United States on September 11, 2001. In Western countries, it has given rise to governments, quasi-governmental organizations, and employers justifying monitoring citizens'/employees' e-mail and Internet connections to find out if they are linked with potential terrorist activity (Coleman, 2006). For example, the Australian government requires Internet Service Providers to implement a mandatory Internet filtering/blocking system, which limits the availability of content to people. The U.S. central government can read and track e-mails sent by people to anywhere in the world (Hessler et al., 2003). In some non-Western countries, such as the Gulf States and China, surveillance of Internet activities is routinely carried out by governments. This is to prevent citizens from having access to websites or news that might carry information or views against the government. Consequently, online researchers cannot assume that participants have the freedom to speak freely on the Internet. Nor can they assume that there may be any widely supported norms in many countries about how people's communications on the Internet might be used by third parties. Both these factors undermine the trustworthiness of online research in many countries (Madge, 2007).

Such intercepting of Internet activity or suspicion of it by government or quasi-governmental agencies helps make people cautious about engaging in online communication, whether or not for research purposes, for fear of having their privacy invaded or their economic or personal safety compromised. Despite being a violation of the International Bill of Rights (comprising the Universal Declaration of Human Rights, the International Covenant on Civil and Political Rights, and the International Covenant on Economic, Social and Cultural Rights), promulgated by the United Nations and supported by 151 of the 189 member states in 2003 (Coleman, 2006, p. 21), monitoring of Internet activity is common.

For example, "lurking" on newsgroups and online communities is an illegitimate use of power to survey people's activities through technological means without first gaining their permission, even if the action is for utilitarian and potentially socially beneficial purposes, such as to explore the viability of a site for research (Bakardjieva & Feenberg, 2000).

Furthermore, the Internet is not equally accessible to all people. Despite the global reach of the Internet, different people in different societies have different levels of access to it because they lack computer equipment, software, or literacy skills (Janelle & Hodges, 2000). People who are without access to online communications often are disadvantaged economically and not sure how to secure access to them (Evans, 2004). This makes online research more difficult in some parts of the world and with certain social groups since in every society some social groups are "less connected" than others. It raises uncomfortable questions for online researchers about the construction of representative samples and the extent to which certain voices in society are further marginalized by having insufficient access to Internet technologies.

Research on and through the Internet has been marked "as a distinct topic worthy of specific note by the introduction of new epithets to familiar methods" (Hine, 2005, p. 5). It has offered researchers exciting possibilities to explore and understand human experience by taking conventional research designs and methods and adapting them for the virtual environment. This has led to the emergence of virtual focus groups, online ethnography, and cyber research to distinguish old familiar methods from their new counterparts.

One such method that this chapter will focus on is that of Internet or online interviewing and the methodological and ethical potential, versatility, and challenges that the medium offers for social researchers. Their use has led to a broad range of discussions about how they are designed and used as methods of data collection and where they are located epistemologically and methodologically. In examining the nature of synchronous and asynchronous interviews that have been used in the online environment, the chapter will also explore how online researchers engage in online interactions and communications as part of their commitment to develop the research relationship and, in turn, facilitate the online interview. Finally, the chapter will also consider how online researchers are confronted by a range of ethical issues in the conduct of their online interviews and how these issues can be addressed.

◆ Synchronous and Asynchronous Interviews: Establishing Research Relationships Online

Interviews as social arenas provide both vehicles and sites through which people construct and contest explications for their views and actions (Foucault, 1977). They can take the form of group interviews to explore the generation of social representations and social knowledge of the viewpoints of a small number of participants (Schneider, Kerwin, Frechtling, & Vivari, 2002), as well as one-to-one semistructured and unstructured interviews that include ethnographic, life history, and narrative approaches. Both group and individual interviews can produce a wealth of data about people's experiences, thoughts, and feelings from their perspectives and can become a series of representations, as conversations, text, or notes. These methods then can become the site for the construction, interpretation, understanding, and representation of experience. The commitment to and reliance on the interview to produce narrative experience led Atkinson and Silverman (1997) to argue that this has created an interview society.

Online or Internet interviews have become popular tools for data collection. To date, researchers have taken face-to-face approaches to interviewing and adapted them for the online environment. Over the past decade, there has been a wealth of academic research, particularly in the social sciences, that has used a range of approaches to online interviewing. These approaches have included virtual discussion/focus groups (Gatson & Zweerink, 2004; Stewart & Williams, 2005) and one-to-one interviews via e-mail (Bampton & Cowton, 2002; Hinton-Smith, 2006) to gather textual data in naturalistic settings online. Online interviews can be broadly divided into two main categories: synchronous and asynchronous. Synchronous interviews mirror a traditional interview in that they take place in real time but in an online environment. Asynchronous online interviews are non–real time. This means they are carried out in a time-lapsed manner that makes it possible for researchers to work easily with participants living in different time zones or working different time shifts

from their own. As discussed later in the chapter, which of these two modes is chosen will affect the construction of participant–researcher relationships during online interviews.

SYNCHRONOUS INTERVIEWS

Synchronous interviews can be complicated to set up as the researcher needs access to the appropriate software, such as chat room facilities. Furthermore, the researcher has to accommodate time zone differences at the time of scheduling and throughout the interview (Kazmer & Xie, 2008). However, they do offer opportunities for real-time responses from participants as well as a high level of participant involvement. To this extent, they mirror the traditional face-to-face interview, providing greater spontaneity than asynchronous interviews and thus allowing individuals to answer right away (Chen & Hinton, 1999). Furthermore, in the concealing contexts of online discussions, where people's social and personal characteristics are not immediately visible, participants who are reticent or shy in face-to-face contexts may find that they have more confidence to "speak" freely and make extensive contributions to conversations (Rheingold, 1994, pp. 23–24).

In synchronous interviews, the interaction and sharing of experiences is framed by researchers' and participants' online presence. The real-time nature of online interviews, as in face-to-face interviews, if managed appropriately by the researcher, can encourage spontaneous interactions between participants and researcher, whether involved in one-on-one or group interviews of various sorts. The immediate and dynamic form of dialogue can elevate participants' awareness of each other and narrow the psychological distance between them, as well as enhancing the feeling of joint involvement (Bowker & Tuffin, 2004).

One of the disadvantages of this mode of interviewing is that only people with access to the Internet and/or who have keyboard skills and experience of online communication facilities will be able to participate in fast-paced, synchronous, text-based interviews. Literacy in dealing with computers and online communication facilities is therefore essential, as taking part in a synchronous interview using either a chat room or conferencing software can be complex for participants who have basic technological expertise. Furthermore, the fast-paced nature of synchronous interviews means that participants can fall behind. The distinction between responding and sending can also become blurred as conversational turn taking develops into overlapping conversations. This can lead to brief responses from the participants and less opportunity for researchers to reciprocate or clarify questions (Bowker & Tuffin, 2004). However, new forms of online synchronous interviews are beginning to emerge that allow researchers to make use of VoIP (Voice over Internet Protocols) to construct audio interviews, even if researcher and participants are invisible to each other on the Internet, reducing the need for researcher and participants to be dependent on text-based communications. This form of synchronous Internet interview is similar to telephonic interviews in its process.

ASYNCHRONOUS INTERVIEWS

Interviews that are conducted in non–real time, or asynchronously, are mainly facilitated via e-mail and, in terms of technological requirements, are far easier to set up than synchronous interviews. With this mode of interview, participants can answer at a time suitable to their personal or work-based schedules. As there are no time restrictions on the relationships and interactions between researcher and participants in this mode of interviewing, this type of interview is particularly useful for research projects that need the researcher to work with participants who are located in different time zones or work in different time patterns, such as shift work, or who may be difficult to reach or interview face-to-face or by telephone. The absence of a temporal dimension also allows participants and researchers to take as much time as they wish to consider the questions and potential responses, rereading and reflecting on what they have previously written before actually responding or sending a prompt or request, thus enriching the interview text (James & Busher, 2006). Such an approach may help provide more open and honest exchanges than socially desirable responses.

This type of interview can be simpler to administer when conducted through e-mail. Researchers can send interview questions to participants one at a time or a set of questions as an e-mail attachment and then just wait for a response. This can take several

days or even weeks as participants do not necessarily reply to questions in the time frame set by the researcher (James & Busher, 2009). Furthermore, there is a greater risk of nonresponse from participants than with synchronous interviews as participants can be distracted by other demands on their time and not feel pressed to respond. Participants' everyday lives, let alone exceptional circumstances, such as surges in workloads or family crises, of which a researcher may be unaware, can inhibit participation in a research project, interrupting the flow of the online interview. In the worst circumstances, this can lead to a participant's temporary disengagement from the project or withdrawal from it (James, 2007). Kazmer and Xie (2008) argue that this may affect participant attrition for a number of reasons. First, people may stop using e-mail at specific times, such as during summer. Second, e-mail can be used inconsistently, and third, people may disconnect from their service provider. Researchers may have to work hard to maintain rapport with participants who engage spasmodically with a research project. Probes or prompts to main questions can get lost in participants' e-mail traffic. Furthermore, it is relatively easy for participants to delete or ignore e-mails with requests for further information if they are too busy or lose interest in the research project, especially if they do not wish to open up (Kivits, 2005).

However, the long-term nature of e-mail interviews does allow for the collection of in-depth data through repeated interactions and a closer reflection of the interview issues. While some researchers see this as the sole advantage of e-mail (James & Busher, 2006), this approach can also create more socially desirable responses rather than a spontaneous response generated through a synchronous interview. Participants may also digress to subjects outside the research project, making it difficult to maintain the flow of the dialogue (Sanders, 2005). Yet in their e-mail study of pregnancy loss, McCoyd and Kerson (2006, p. 397) found that many participants wrote their responses "in a stream-of-consciousness manner" that included both prior and immediate emotional responses. This seemed to empower the participants to present themselves in the ways they chose. In terms of the data analysis, this helped reduce the effects of interpretation error, which can occur when analyzing qualitative interview data. Nonetheless, the researchers also recognized the need to ensure the credibility and truth worth of the interviews by going back to the participants to clarify the meaning of their texts and obtaining further feedback where necessary. As Burns notes (2010), "It is important, nonetheless, even amid the pleasure of how easy producing this immediately analysable text, to continue to reflect what other changes this email interviews format produces in the production and consumption of research data."

As with synchronous interviews, there is no need for transcription in asynchronous interviews, as there is a continuous and visible text-based record of each interview constructed during its course on e-mail or on some other form of online communication. This can reduce participants' apprehension about speaking and being recorded since the records of the interviews are more likely to be accurate and, particularly in e-mail interviews, can easily be checked by participants during the course of an interview as they can scroll back and forth through the text. Misrepresentation of what has been said during an interview, which sometimes occurs during transcription, does not happen here, and participants do not have to wait for some time after the end of a research interview to have an opportunity to validate their record of it.

ESTABLISHING RESEARCH RELATIONSHIPS ONLINE

Whichever type of online interview researchers choose, they need to consider as part of their research practice how they are going to develop the research relationship online. This includes the nature of the online interactions and communications with participants and the impacts of these on those being researched. Unless researchers are using web cameras, such issues become more complicated as online participants and researchers are hidden from each other by the "veil" of the Internet. This affords them visual anonymity and pseudonymity if they wish. In a face-to-face interview, the presentation of self is based not only on what we choose to show, for example, through gesture or tone of voice, but also how that is perceived by others in the space of social interaction (Matthews, 2006). Online interviews are devoid of the normal social frameworks of face-to-face encounters between researchers and participants, in which both interpret the social characteristics of the other, either verbally or nonverbally through gesture, tone

of voice, and facial expressions (James & Busher, 2007). When the face-to-face contact is absent, "we cannot ignore the potential obstacles that anonymity and disembodiment pose in attempting to arrive at a relationship of trust with other people online" (Orgad, 2005, p. 55).

This visual anonymity can reduce researcher/participant effects as the physical characteristics of the other are absent. As the social frameworks of face-to-face encounters are missing online, this may make it easier to discuss more sensitive topics or state unpopular views. On the other hand, it makes it easier for people to distort and disguise their views and perspectives (Jacobson, 1999) and their identities. The written texts generated during the online interchanges of a research project can lead to the creation of personae that bear little relationship to participants' "'interactional self' in everyday 'non-screen life'" (Denzin, 1999, p. 114). In such circumstances, researchers need to test what is authentic against regular patterns of interaction in participants' online communications (Mann & Stewart, 2000).

Even if e-mail is not as full a mode of contact, the personalization of an e-mail interview exchange is largely lost when there is any perception of mass mailing (as happens in e-mail surveys). While the labor of transcription might be addressed by e-mail interviewing, especially en masse, any reduction in the emotional or personal labor of a one-to-one correspondence is likely to significantly affect the quality of information offered. The personalization of an e-mail exchange can be strengthened by prior individual or telephone conversations to establish the willingness of the potential participant to receive and participate in the e-mail interview (Burns, 2010). This reemphasizes the importance of maintaining trust through continuing e-mail contact to ensure the credibility of the e-mail interview data (Mann & Stewart, 2000).

E-mail interviews are more naturally communications with one person, a series of exchanges forming an interview (setting aside for the present discussion longitudinal research). Though this e-mail interview exchange might be a one-off, a sequence, or a period of interaction, within this framework is the potential for multiple rounds of question and response—two, three, or many more, depending on the arrangements or how the exchange develops in the lived circumstances of e-mail query and response. At the very minimum, an e-mail acknowledgment by the researcher of participant views and comments (question–response–acknowledgment/thanks) takes the process further than surveys (question–response).

Some researchers have argued that online interactions are deeply embedded in, and shaped by, off-line situations and relationships (Xie, 2007). Off-line discussions can add depth to a researcher's interpretations of participants' identities, reinforcing how the construction and understanding of online texts can be shaped by the nature of interactions that transcend both online and off-line boundaries (James & Busher, 2006). Busher (2001) and James (2003) conclude that a successful way to check the authenticity of research project participants' online texts is to see how closely participants' stories align with their selves and identities, especially through off-line contact with them.

Off-line discussions can add depth to a researcher's interpretations of participants' identities. In her online study of academic identities, James (2007) found that when she met her participants face-to-face, she was able to follow up some of the issues that had emerged in her e-mail interviews. In part, this was because some participants' responses were superficial and playful and it was evident that they did not always want "to participate in substantive discussion" (Gaiser, 1997, p. 142). Other researchers argue that online discourses and identities are valid in themselves and do not need to be verified off-line (Hine, 2000), accepting the socially constructed nature of the online environment that contains shared understandings and information. Individuals do not leave the body and all its material inequalities behind when they enter cyberspace (O'Connor & Madge, 2003). It is the embodied participant who interacts online, and they can never escape from their lived experiences (Jones, 1999). Indeed, perhaps the most convincing way of establishing the authenticity of online research conversations may be through considering the extent to which researchers and participants construct credible and consistent stories in the course of their text-based exchanges (Lee, 2006). Gatson and Zweerink (2004) found in their synchronous interviews that the identities portrayed by their participants emphasized the importance of discourse and experience in shaping both the real and the virtual worlds. This intertextual construction of self can be facilitated by online researchers trying to generate an open and honest dialogue with their participants.

Identities are inextricably linked with who we are, our commitments and values, and are "integral and continuous" (Kendall, 1999, p. 61). It is not possible to physically isolate our social faces as we all inhabit the same space and are identified as one person by those around us (Kolko & Reid, 1998). Cavanagh (2007) uses the example of a blog, an online diary to which other "bloggers" can post comments in a public forum, to highlight how "one's identity emerges from whom one knows and one's associations and connections" (Turkle, 1995, p. 258). An important implication of this is that identity formation can be as much a product of membership in online/"virtual" communities as it can be about belonging to "actual" face-to-face communities. Individuals have to be part of a context in which they can identify with others and be identified (Waskul & Douglass, 1997). This suggests that when participants take part in a virtual group interview, their identity formation is mediated by membership in that group. Online, the interview context can provide a space in which participants can identify with others and be identified, an issue that is discussed in more detail later in the chapter.

If the development of online interviews is exclusively reliant on textual communication, researchers must more quickly and with greater explicit clarity "establish their bona fide status and the boundaries of the online interview . . . than they might in a face-to-face situation" (Sanders, 2005, p. 78). The written word in online interviews becomes an important means of building rapport and trust as the absence of visual and social gestures and cues in online interviews means that conversational elements of simple gestures (nodding, agreeing, eye contact) have to be translated into text. Consequently, within the research context, the evidence for the existence, attitudes, and values of participants and researchers is text based (Markham, 2004). This can represent a significant challenge for the online researcher. Orgad (2005) has argued that "there is a real challenge in building rapport online. Trust, a fragile commodity . . . seems ever more fragile in a disembodied, anonymous and textual setting" (p. 55).

Researchers then must be proactive in establishing a permissive and friendly atmosphere (Mann & Stewart, 2000). In e-mail interviews, this can be achieved by providing prompt replies to their participants' messages, thus demonstrating a commitment to their written texts (Orgad, 2005), "as part of the live connection that is more instantly sustained in a face-to-face situation: recognizing both content and manner; honouring the process, not simply the substantive focus of the interview" (Burns, 2010). Where research has involved sensitive topics, others have used the technique of self-disclosure, or providing personal information about themselves such as family life and work, to maintain a certain level of rapport (Kivits, 2005). Such approaches can also be enhanced through repeated interaction and mutual disclosure, which creates a context of trust and a good level of rapport (Mann & Stewart, 2000). This highlights the importance of online researchers constructing a nonthreatening environment, which minimizes the risk to participants' privacy and anonymity, to ensure a creative, collaborative relationship with other people online.

In e-mail interviews, this can include sending participants a welcome letter about the aims and content of the research study and who the researchers are. However, even when researchers try to do this, potential participants in a research project may still be suspicious of the ethical framework within which the research is being carried out and the protection it will afford them. Despite sending potential participants in their research projects a framework setting out how e-mail interviews would be carried out, James and Busher (2006) found that some participants were still worried about the protection of their privacy and anonymity online, especially as they were revealing personal (and sometimes sensitive) information about their professional lives and identities. While not questioning the researchers' integrity, some participants expressed concerns that a technical aspect of e-mail communication posed a risk to their privacy. Views expressed through e-mail to one person can be transmitted easily to third parties deliberately as well as inadvertently, for example, when online communications are backed up on researchers' and participants' institutional servers.

When conducting synchronous group interviews, a welcome page, where participants wait between logging in and starting the discussion, can offer space for researchers to identify the purpose and expected conduct of the group and encourage active participation (Fox, Morris, & Rumsey, 2007). This approach can act as a starting point for building good rapport with participants. O'Connor and Madge (2001) took this a step further by replicating the kind of rapport they believe occurs in a face-to-face interview. In their online interviews with new parents, the

researchers attempted to build rapport by using both textual exchanges and visual posting that included pictures. Their participants were directed to a project website, which included information on the project as well as photographs of the researchers, to find out more about the research. This meant that once the participants commenced the interview, they had an idea of what the researchers looked like in real life. For them, the use of visual personal information via e-mails also helped create and facilitate rapport.

Participants may feel better able to discuss sensitive topics in an online environment than in a face-to-face interview. However, this may not always be the case. As Illingworth (2001) found in her study of infertility, many of her participants did not want the interviews to be facilitated in a chat room. This was because the open format of a chat room environment was viewed as an inappropriate space for the discussion of private and sensitive matters. Consequently, the study used e-mail interviews instead. When engaging in online interviews, the choice of interview medium is clearly significant.

◆ Addressing Ethical Issues in Online Interviews

Participating in any research involves ethical risks to the individuals concerned (Chadwick, 2001). Consequently, online research projects are no different from face-to-face ones in seeking to protect their participants from harm. Researchers have to consider the "moral consequences" of their actions in terms of research conduct and responsibility (to themselves and to other participants in the research) (Knoebel, 2005). This includes acknowledging "the direct and indirect contributions of colleagues, collaborators and others" (Economic and Social Research Council [ESRC], 2005, p. 32). Just as researchers need to protect research participants by ensuring that society's benefit from the research is not at the expense of individual participants' engagement with it, they also need to ensure that the research is "conducted so as to ensure the professional integrity of its design, the generation and analysis of data [that can be trusted], and the publication of results" (ESRC, 2005, p. 23). Constructing ethical research is not merely a matter of applying ethical codes of practice (Usher, 2000). It is an imminent and emergent ethical practice that researchers have to follow throughout the life cycle of a research project and the publication of its findings. Researchers have to balance the needs of participants, society, and themselves by using a variety of technologies: ethical frameworks, ontological and epistemological perspectives, and research methods and techniques.

How these ethical risks can be successfully managed and minimized in the online environment is different from but related to how they might be managed in off-line research. Some researchers argue that online research interviews entail greater ethical risk to individual privacy and confidentiality than face-to-face interviews and greater challenges to a researcher in terms of gaining informed consent and deciding what is a public versus a private interview, and they are more difficult in terms of ensuring and ascertaining trustworthiness and data authenticity (Ess & Association of Internet Researchers [AoIR], 2002). Such issues are discussed in detail below.

THE NATURE OF INFORMED CONSENT

As do researchers in face-to-face interviews, online researchers need to gain participants' informed consent to take part in research right from the time they join the project and before the online interviews are begun. However, gaining informed consent online can be more problematic as it can be easier for participants to deceive the researcher. Researchers too have to be cautious when accepting participants into research projects, and participants need to be cautious in agreeing to join online projects.

To gain informed consent, as discussed earlier, researchers will need to identify themselves and their purposes to potential participants. The absence of the physical presence of a researcher can make identity verification difficult, as discussed earlier. Identities can be negotiated and reproduced and indexed in a variety of ways (Wilson & Peterson, 2002). Individuals too can express themselves in ways that are different from everyday life, allowing improvisation and word play to flourish (Danet, 1998). While it is more difficult for the researcher to authenticate the identity of his or her participants in e-mail and synchronous interviews, this does not make the research less valid. Researchers also need to be aware of the impact that participants' anonymity can have on the research and should explain this clearly to their putative participants as well as reassure them that their privacy is not being infringed. It is important therefore for researchers to explain

the medium that they are going to use for interviews, whether they are going to conduct the interviews on a private website or a public bulletin board or by e-mail, and how they intend to protect the privacy and anonymity of participants. Researchers will also need to explain and construct a means through which members can check and confirm the meaning of their text/speech acts and any accompanying photographic or video material before these are used outside the conversations of the research or online/off-line communities for which they were originally intended.

An important element of the informed consent that participants give to researchers when joining a project is the voluntary nature of their participation in it, which allows them to withdraw from it at any time. The technology of the Internet facilitates this. In online interviews, the absence of the physical and temporal presence of a researcher makes it possible for participants to write their responses as and when it suits them irrespective of any reminders the researcher might send asking them to respond to an interview question (James & Busher, 2006). "Silence" or the absence of any obvious signal from participants during the course of an online research interview might also be an indication that they are, even if only temporarily, withdrawing from the project. In online interviewing, the reasons for participants dropping out of the research may not be transparent or amenable to investigation (Hodgson, 2004). This in turn raises ethical questions about what a researcher should do when participants terminate the process of replying to questions and reminders. This becomes a significant risk for long-term interviews. In particular, asynchronous e-mail communication means that the research becomes dependent on, and is vulnerable to, the commitment of participants, who can easily disappear from the study (Kivits, 2005). In James's (2003) research, some participants dropped out after several e-mail exchanges. While some clearly justified their reasons for not being able to continue with the interview, others simply "disappeared." Such disappearances can leave the researcher with the dilemma of how strongly to pursue the disappearing participants. James (2003) contacted her participants two or three times, as she was aware that to continually pester them would not facilitate good rapport if the participants finally responded. She was also prepared to move the interview off-line if necessary. She also had to decide whether to include the unfinished interview data as part of the final data analysis. Researchers therefore must be aware of these potential points of "participant loss" so that they can work to retain the participants during the research process and make decisions about how to handle incomplete interview data (Meho, 2006). Such issues also reiterate the provisional nature of the informed consent that participants give to a researcher. It is not merely garnered at the start of a project for its lifetime but must be sustained throughout the study by researcher practices. These include, ironically, empowering participants to feel free to withdraw consent whenever they wish (Hewson, 2003).

CONSTITUTING PUBLIC AND PRIVATE SPACES

As the Internet "blurs the traditional boundaries between interpersonal and mass communications, ethical concepts like privacy and dignity of participants become more difficult to determine" (Delorme, Zinkhan, & French, 2001, p. 272). One argument suggests that what constitutes private and public conversations on the Internet is ambiguous because of the open-access designation of so many Internet sites. "The taken-for-granted boundaries of the public/private dichotomy [are being dissolved]" (Bowker & Tuffin, 2004, p. 231). Waskul and Douglass (1997) argue that online texts are both publicly private and privately public. For example, chat rooms and virtual communities can be viewed as public spaces, whatever conversations are taking place in them and to whatever degree participants consider their conversations "private." Anyone with access to the Internet may connect to them either as a registered member or as a temporary visitor, and usually, there are no restrictions on membership. Other researchers think that it depends on how the members of the online group/community perceive their communications with each other (Robson & Robson, 2002). Participants in online discussion groups may consider their communications private, even if that privacy extends to the whole group (Gatson & Zweerink, 2004), although their discussions might be accessible to the public through the Internet. Furthermore, they may not want the information that is shared with other group members to go beyond their own community (Elgesem, 2002). Where online interviews are conducted in open spaces such as e-mail, and researchers use their institutional e-mail addresses to conduct their online interviews, it can become relatively easy for participants to identify them and their geographical locations, at least at work.

Such issues can potentially undermine the ethical basis of a research project (Orgad, 2005). This is because the open nature of much of the Internet makes it problematic for participants in online conversations to know the extent to which the information they have divulged is likely to be visible publically and potentially able to be broadcast in an even more public domain. Participants have to take it seriously that during their conversations with other members of an online community, whether or not for research, strangers may be "lurking" on it and possibly harvesting information from it without their consent. Researchers must also take seriously the level of perceived privacy that group members attach to their communications and not lurk on a site or harvest information from it in any way, when constructing research projects, without the overt consent of site members, however justifiable the reasons for lurking (King, 1996). Lurking on discussion forums is akin to eavesdropping on conversations without first gaining permission from the other participants to do so (Bakardjieva & Feenberg, 2000; Coleman, 2006). The National Committee for Research Ethics in the Social Sciences and the Humanities (2003) considers lurking unethical and insists that Internet researchers should declare their presence and purpose when entering an online group. Researchers therefore need to consider the extent to which they share personal information with participants and ask them to do the same in an attempt to develop respectful, trusting, and collaborative online relationships with participants. They also need to respect the definitions of "private" being used by participants in an online discussion, whether constructed as part of a research project conversation or discovered fortuitously by a researcher, and only publish those elements of a discussion for which they are given overt permission by the participants to publish.

It is for these reasons that Ess and the AoIR (2002) argue that researchers are more likely to persuade participants to disclose personal information if they establish a secure online interview environment that minimizes the risk to participants' privacy and carefully defines what is meant by "private spaces" in a research project. This might include a project-dedicated website or chat room to collect, curate, and disseminate interview data, instead of an open environment such as e-mail, where identity verification is possible. Irrespective of the type of online interview, every research project has to negotiate its own agreed norms between researchers and participants to establish an ethical framework of process. This nego-tiation is central to persuading participants that they are protected from intentional or unintentional harm and so are free to (re)present themselves truthfully. Such a framework from the outset should include an "ethics of care" that at the very least involves a respect for the interests and values of those who participate in online research (Capurro & Pingel, 2002, p. 194). It must also make clear whether or not the environment in which the discussions are conducted is secure so that participants are aware of the risks.

USING LANGUAGE AND NETIQUETTE

Another aspect of creating an ethical framework for online conversations is researchers and partici-pants agreeing on the nature and style of their online communications that will be considered appropriate, polite, and respectful. Thurlow, Lengel, and Tomic (2004) suggest that much face-to-face etiquette is unnecessary in Internet communications, in part because of the lack of visual cues available to par-ticipants. Netiquette (communication etiquette on the Internet) is an important help in clarifying this to prevent aggressive and insulting behavior (Madge, 2007). Based on their research with newsgroups, Hall, Frederick, and Johns (2004) have identified a number of netiquette considerations:

- The subject header used in any posting to a newsgroup must not misinform the participant or create misunderstandings between the researcher and participants.

- Self-identification and self-presentation of the researcher are critical, as receivers of the research will form their evaluations about the credibility of the research and the researcher.

- To ensure respect for those being researched, the researcher must be familiar with the common language used by the participants/communities, including jargon, abbreviations, acronyms, emo-ticons, and common grammatical rules.

- Researchers should always ask appropriate questions, and to do this, they must acquaint themselves with the subject matter before ask-ing for help.

- Prior understanding of the specific culture of the group/community should be attained either by observing the group for a period of time or through a review of online FAQs and archives prior to "jumping in."

- The researcher has an obligation to inform the participants about the purpose, nature, proce-dures, and risks of the research.

Where online research interviews have been con-ducted, the communication has tended to be carried out in English. This has been viewed as a form of linguistic colonialism that limits the power of peo-ple who do not speak English as a first language to express their views (Madge, 2007). This challenge to participants is compounded because "most research on the Internet is centered in Anglo-American cultural contexts" (Jankowski & Van Selm, 2005, p. 203). In online research interviews, then, nonnative speakers of English can feel particu-larly threatened. They have to become adept at expressing themselves on sensitive personal topics and feelings in a language that is not their own. The lack of visual and nonverbal cues in online commu-nication further limits their power to express them-selves. Understandably, such circumstances may lead to participants withdrawing from research projects or reverting to text discussions in their native lan-guage. Writing rather than speaking in a second language may, however, help empower some nonna-tive speakers (Mann & Stewart, 2000). The ano-nymity of online research denies people the potential embarrassment (loss of social status/"face," loss of power) of trying to express themselves orally in ways they consider less than sufficiently fluent. In a study of East Asian participants, online communica-tion enabled more direct communication and greater self-disclosure (Ma, 1996). Participants had less fear of rejection or disagreement in the virtual environ-ment. Being unable to discriminate subtly, the social situation and the anticipated perspectives of the researcher may help participants develop highly personal and intimate replies to the interview ques-tions (James, 2003).

ENSURING ANONYMITY AND CONFIDENTIALITY

Researchers have the responsibility to ensure the anonymity and confidentiality of participants and data at all stages of the research interview, during all interactions with participants, when data are trans-mitted between participants and researchers, and when they are stored and published. Confidentiality is of particular concern when personal or sensitive information is collected or when conducting research with vulnerable participants, as defined by the *Research Ethics Framework* (ESRC, 2005).

In setting up the online interview, researchers need to think about the nature of the virtual environment and whether it is well suited to the needs of the participants to ensure that the research is not compromised both legally and ethically. Researchers need to ensure that arrangements for interviewing online are such that participants feel safe during the research and are not victimized. Where possible, threats to the confidentiality and anonymity of research data generated by online interviews should be anticipated by researchers. Participants may wish to contact the researchers directly about the project, yet directly e-mailing the researchers can compromise anonymity in several ways. The identities of those participating in any type of online interview should be kept invisible whether or not an explicit pledge has been given. Yet e-mail addresses often contain identifiers such as name, organization, and geographical location, as noted earlier. Even if carefully processed, this can make participants' views instantly visible, because their e-mail addresses, especially their domain names, contain part or all of their real names or their locations, making it possible in public sites to retrieve their messages (Eysenbach & Till, 2001). So the apparent privacy of individuals is instantly breached by some of the characteristics of online communications. Researchers then need to think carefully about the implications of using their e-mail address to conduct the online interviews and the extent to which they share personal information in an attempt to develop an online relationship that also respects the confidentiality and anonymity of their participants. Such issues are potential risks to anonymity (Orgad, 2005) but can be essential in arriving at a relationship of trust with other people online. The issue of ensuring confidentiality while interacting with research participants can arise at all stages throughout the research process.

When storing or publishing online data, researchers need to assure participants about the confidentiality of the information. This might include the use of pseudonyms and hiding user names, domain names, and other personal identifiers. Yet such data will be retained on the server of the transmitting and sending account. Even if e-mail messages can be encrypted only by the intended recipient, this is still reliant on both participants and researcher sharing the same software (Meho, 2006).

Confidentiality is also a concern where personal information is collected, when conducting research interviews with participants who may be vulnerable, or if the topic is sensitive. If members of a research project team know the private e-mail addresses of their participants and these participants have given their written consent to take part in a project, which has to include their real name whatever aliases they use online, it is relatively easy for anybody to find out who the participants are and where they live and to link their data to them (Fox, Murray, & Warm, 2003). One way to reduce this risk is to store research data not on institutional servers but on project-dedicated laptops and hard drives. Another is not to store together in the same folder or filing cabinet personal information about participants and their interview data. A third is to give participants a dedicated and different e-mail address than that of the research project or the research project website for them to contact researchers if they have any queries about the research process that do not form part of the research interview. A fourth is to construct a dedicated project website that has restricted access segments on it, on which participants and researchers can converse or exchange views without this being visible on the project website's public spaces.

Of course, an advantage of online interviews is that participants do not have to divulge any personal information. This is useful for sensitive research topics and where participants do not want to be identifiable. Online interviews, especially those conducted in chat rooms, can be conducted on an anonymous basis. It allows online researchers to read messages and observe without participating, even if with the permission of participants, the natural conversations and linguistic behavior of their participants engaged in real-time chat. Participants engaged in the "chat" can also observe the ongoing actions of others, especially if they do not have the confidence to fully participate and share their values (James & Busher, 2009).

◆ Conclusions: Living Through Interviews Formally, Informally, and Collectively

The Internet offers researchers exciting possibilities for exploring and understanding human experiences. Through it, they can investigate the social realities of everyday life in its online and off-line phases and the interaction between the two. It has also offered researchers the opportunity to take a range of conventional research methods, such as interviewing, and adapt them for the virtual environment. We would argue that the Internet has presented opportunities for the evolution of traditional methods, but the extent of the evolution still largely amounts to researchers constructing online interviews by adapting traditional face-to-face research practices for use in text-based communications.

Online research practice requires an epistemology and ontology of research that stresses "the hybrid and unfinished character of cyberspace" (Teli, Francesco, & Hakken, 2007). The rapid developments in Internet technology in the 21st century mean that face-to-face interviews can now take place in the online environment. Researchers no longer have to physically meet face-to-face to supplement and verify data collected through online interviews. There is a greater capacity to conduct online interviews that are not simply restricted to text-based communications. It is now possible to talk, chat, or make video calls using Skype, a software application that allows users to make voice calls over the Internet. Such technology also means that it is possible to conduct online interviews face-to-face using web cameras, video links, and voice chat software between computers. Social networking sites such as Facebook are now being explored as an avenue where "live" interviews can take place rather than sending questions via e-mail. Blogs, or web logs, shared online journals where people can post diary entries about their personal experiences, can also offer scope for synchronous chat. These virtual sites can allow more than one voice to speak, and the text can now include discourse, character, voice, tone, and visual imagery, adding a richness of possibilities to how and where qualitative researchers conduct their interviews and engage with participants' online interactions, visibility, and discourses. Yet they also continue to blur the way in which participants' experiences are interconnected and shaped by cultural and social elements that are both real and virtual, public and private, online and off-line, and in turn, they make the ethicality of using such methods more difficult to determine. To capture this interconnectedness needs methods and methodologies that can research the spaces of the online and off-line worlds, the contexts and actions of the research participants in the multiple sites of their lived realities. To do so, researchers need to keep abreast of technological innovations in interviewing and the myriad ways in which they can be used to enhance the research process.

In particular, researchers too need to establish their online research practice rather than just adapting face-to-face research methods for the virtual world linked to the cautious epistemology of qualitative research. This includes developing a coherent ethical framework for online research that protects participants from harm. If the Internet is "a unique medium that necessitates its own conventions" (Best & Krueger, 2004, p. 1) because of the virtual (disembodied) and often anonymous nature of its social interactions, then applying recognized codes of ethical conduct for onsite research in online situations can no longer be an option. Yet there is still no consensus among online researchers about how to deal with the ambiguities around informed consent, public/private spaces, language and netiquette, ensuring confidentiality, authenticity, and data security. The complexity of such issues is further compounded by the rapid developments in Internet technology, so that researchers now have to ensure that the ethical conventions adopted in online interviews take into consideration not only online texts but visual imagery and discourse as well.

The use of online interviews in social research should not be seen as an easy option, although such instruments do provide a range of methods that complement face-to-face interactions. Researchers who use such methods need to demonstrate the viability of the method used, by making explicit what benefits it can bring to their research projects. The effectiveness of online research interviews of all sorts depends on who is being researched, what is being researched, and why.

◆ References

Atkinson, P., & Silverman, D. (1997). Kundera's immortality: The interview society and the invention of self. *Qualitative Inquiry, 3,* 304–325.

Bakardjieva, M., & Feenberg, A. (2000). Involving the virtual subject. *Ethics and Information Technology, 2,* 233–240.

Bampton, R., & Cowton, C. J. (2002). The E-interview. *Forum: Qualitative Social Research, 3.* Retrieved from http://www.qualitative-research.net/fqs/

Best, S. J., & Krueger, B. S. (2004). *Internet data collection.* London, England: Sage.

Bowker, N., & Tuffin, K. (2004). Using the online medium for discursive research about people with disabilities. *Social Science Computer Review, 22,* 228–241.

Burkeman, O. (2008, January 2). The Internet. *The Guardian,* p. 19.

Burns, E. (2010). Developing email interview practices in qualitative research. *Sociological Research Online, 15*(8). Retrieved from http://www.socresonline.org.uk/15/4/8.html

Busher, H. (2001, March). *Being and becoming a doctoral student: Culture, literacies and self-identity.* Paper presented at the TESOL Arabia Conference, Dubai, UAE.

Capurro, R., & Pingel, C. (2002). Ethical issues of online communication research. *Ethics and Information Technology, 4,* 189–194.

Cavanagh, A. (2007). *Sociology in the age of the Internet.* Maidenhead, England: Open University/McGraw-Hill.

Chadwick, R. (2001). Ethical assessment and the human genome issues. In P. Shipley & D. Moir (Eds.), *Ethics in practice in the 21st century.* Proceedings of the Interdiscplinary Conference of the Society for the Furtherance of Critical Philosophy. Oxfordshire, England: Society for the Furtherance of Critical Philosophy.

Chen, P., & Hinton, S. M. (1999). Realtime interviewing using the World Wide Web. *Sociological Research Online, 4.* Retrieved from http://www.socresonline.org.uk/socresonline/4/3/chen/html

Coleman, S. (2006). Email, terrorism, and the right to privacy. *Ethics and Information Technology, 8,* 17–27.

Danet, B. (1998). Text as mask: Gender, play and performance on the Internet. *Cybersociety 2.0: Revisiting computer-mediated communication and community.* Thousand Oaks, CA: Sage.

Delorme, D. E., Zinkhan, G. E., & French, W. (2001). Ethics and the Internet: Issues associated with qualitative research. *Journal of Business Ethics, 33,* 271–286.

Denzin, N. (1999). Cybertalk and the method of instances. In S. Jones (Ed.), *Critical issues and methods for examining the net, doing Internet research* (pp. 107–125). London, England: Sage.

Dominguez, D., Beaulieu, A., Estalella, S., Gomez, E., Schnettler, B., & Read, R. (2007). Virtual ethnography. *Forum: Qualitative Social Research, 8.* Retrieved from http://www.qualitative-research.net/fqs-texte/3-07/07-3-E1-e.htm

Economic and Social Research Council. (2005). *Research ethics framework.* Swindon, England: Author.

Elgesem, D. (2002). What is special about the ethical issues in online research? *Ethics and Information Technology, 4,* 195–203.

Ess, C., & Association of Internet Researchers. (2002). *Ethical decision-making and Internet research.* Retrieved from www.aoir.org/reports/ethics.pdf

Evans, K. F. (2004). *Maintaining community in the information age: The importance of trust, place and situated knowledge.* Melbourne, Victoria, Australia: Palgrave Macmillan.

Eysenbach, G., & Till, J. E. (2001). Ethical issues in qualitative research on Internet communities. *British Medical Journal, 323,* 1103–1105.

Foucault, M. (1977). *Discipline and punish: The birth of the prison* (A. Sheridan, Ed. & Trans.). Harmondsworth, England: Penguin.

Fox, E. F., Morris, M., & Rumsey, N. (2007). Doing synchronous online focus groups with young people: Methodological reflections. *Qualitative Health Research, 17,* 539–547.

Fox, J., Murray, C., & Warm, A. (2003). Conducting research using web-based questionnaires: Practical, methodological and ethical considerations. *International Journal of Social Research Methodology, 6,* 167–180.

Gaiser, T. (1997). Conducting on-line focus groups: A methodological discussion. *Social Science Computer Review, 15,* 135–144.

Gatson, S. N., & Zweerink, A. (2004). Ethnography online: "Natives" practicing and inscribing community. *Qualitative Research, 4,* 179–200.

Goodfellow, R. (2007, January). *The impact of emerging web2.0 Internet practices on future developments in teaching and learning.* Paper presented at the *Learning Futures Conference,* University of Leicester, England.

Hall, G. J., Frederick, D., & Johns, M. D. (2004). "NEED HELP ASAP!!!": A feminist communitarian approach to online research ethics. In M. D. Johns, S. L. S. Chen, & G. J. Hall (Eds.), *Online social research: Methods, issues and ethics* (pp. 239–252). Oxford, England: Peter Lang.

Hammersley, M. (2006). Ethnography: Problems and prospects. *Ethnography and Education, 1,* 3–14.

Hessler, R. M., Downing, J., Beltz, C., Pellicio, A., Powell, M., & Vale, W. (2003). Qualitative research on adolescent risk using email: A methodological assessment. *Qualitative Sociology, 26,* 111–124.

Hewson, C. (2003). Conducting research on the Internet. *The Psychologist, 16,* 290–293.

Hine, C. (2000). *Virtual ethnography.* London, England: Sage.

Hine, C. (2005). *Virtual methods: Issues in social research on the Internet.* Oxford, England: Berg.

Hinton-Smith, T. (2006, December). *Lone parents as higher education students: A qualitative email study.* Paper presented at the ESREA Access, Learning Careers and Identities Network Conference, Louvain-la-Neuve, Belgium.

Hodgson, S. (2004). Cutting through the silence: A sociological construction of self-injury. *Sociological Inquiry, 74,* 162–179.

Illingworth, N. (2001). The Internet matters: Exploring the use of the Internet as a research tool. *Sociological Research Online, 6.* Retrieved from http://www.socresonline.org.uk/6/2/illingworth.html

Jacobson, D. (1999). Doing research in cyberspace. *Field Methods, 11,* 127–145.

James, N. (2003). *Teacher professionalism, teacher identity: How do I see myself?* (Unpublished doctoral dissertation). University of Leicester, England.

James, N. (2007). The use of email interviewing as a qualitative method of inquiry in educational research. *British Educational Research Journal, 33,* 963–976.

James, N., & Busher, H. (2006). Credibility, authenticity and voice: Dilemmas in web-based interviewing. *Qualitative Research Journal, 6,* 403–420.

James, N., & Busher, H. (2007). Ethical issues in online educational research: Protecting privacy, establishing authenticity in email interviewing. *International Journal of Research & Method in Education, 30,* 101–113.

James, N., & Busher, H. (2009). *Online interviewing.* London, England: Sage.

Janelle, D. G., & Hodges, D. C. (2000). *Information, place and cyberspace.* New York, NY: Springer.

Jankowski, N. W., & Van Selm, M. (2005). Epilogue: Methodological concerns and innovations in Internet research. In C. Hine (Ed.), *Virtual methods: Issues in social research on the Internet* (pp. 199–207). Oxford, England: Berg.

Jones, S. (1999). *Doing Internet research.* Thousand Oaks, CA: Sage.

Kazmer, M., & Xie, B. (2008). Qualitative interviewing in Internet studies: Playing with the media, playing with the method. *Information, Communication & Society, 11,* 257–278.

Kendall, L. (1999). Recontextualising cyperspace: Methodological considerations for online research. In S. Jones (Ed.), *Doing Internet research* (pp. 57–75). Thousand Oaks, CA: Sage.

King, S. A. (1996). Researching Internet communities: Proposed ethical guidelines for reporting results. *The Information Society, 12,* 119–127.

Kivits, J. (2005). Online interviewing and the research relationship. In C. Hine (Ed.), *Virtual methods: Issues in social research on the Internet* (pp. 35–50). Oxford, England: Berg.

Knoebel, M. (2005). Rants, ratings and representation: Ethical issues in researching online social practices. In K. Sheehy, M. Nind, J. Rix, & K. Simmons (Eds.), *Ethics and research in inclusive education: Values into practice* (pp. 150–167). London, England: Routledge-Falmer/The Open University.

Kolko, B., & Reid, E. (1998). Dissolution and fragmentation: Problems in online communities. In S. Jones (Ed.), *Cybersociety 2.0: Revisiting computer-mediated communication and community* (pp. 212–229). Thousand Oaks, CA: Sage.

Lee, H. (2006). Privacy, publicity and accountability of self-presentation in an online discussion group. *Sociological Inquiry, 76,* 1–22.

Ma, R. (1996). Computer-mediated conversations as a new dimension of intercultural communication between East Asian and North American college students. In S. Herring (Ed.), *Computer-mediated communication: Linguistic, social and cross-cultural perspectives* (pp. 173–189). Amsterdam, The Netherlands: John Benjamins.

Madge, C. (2007). Developing a geographers' agenda for online research ethics. *Progress in Human Geography, 31,* 654–674.

Mann, C., & Stewart, F. (2000). *Internet communication and qualitative research: A handbook for research online.* London, England: Sage.

Markham, A. N. (2004). Representation in online ethnography. In M. D. Johns, S. L. S. Chen, & G. J. Hall (Eds.), *Online social research: Methods, issues and ethics* (pp. 141–157). Oxford, England: Peter Lang.

Matthews, S. (2006). On-line professionals. *Ethics and Information Technology, 8,* 61–71.

McCoyd, J., & Kerson, T. (2006). Conducting intensive interviews using email: A serendipitous comparative opportunity. *Qualitative Social Work, 5,* 389–406.

Meho, L. (2006). E-mail interviewing in qualitative research: A methodological discussion. *Journal of the American Society for Information Science and Technology, 57,* 1284–1295.

National Committee for Research Ethics in the Social Sciences and the Humanities. (2003). *Research ethics guidelines for Internet research* (L. G. Lundh & C. Ess, Trans.). Oslo, Norway: Author.

O'Connor, H., & Madge, C. (2001). Cybermothers: Online synchronous interviewing using conferencing software. *Sociological Research Online, 5.* Retrieved from http://www.socresonline.org.uk/9/2/hine.html

O'Connor, H., & Madge, C. (2003). Focus groups in cyberspace: Using the Internet for qualitative research. *Qualitative Market Research: An International Journal, 6,* 133–143.

Orgad, S. (2005). From online to offline and back: Moving from online to offline relationships with research participants. In C. Hine (Ed.), *Virtual methods: Issues in social research on the Internet* (pp. 51–66). Oxford, England: Berg.

Rheingold, H. (1994). *The virtual community: Finding connection in a computerised world.* London, England: Secker & Warburg.

Robson, K., & Robson, M. (2002). Your place or mine? Ethics, the researcher and the Internet. In T. Welland & L. Pigsley (Eds.), *Ethical dilemmas in qualitative research* (pp. 94–107). London, England: Ashgate.

Sanders, T. (2005). Researching the online sex work community. In C. Hine (Ed.), *Virtual methods: Issues in social research on the Internet* (pp. 67–80). Oxford, England: Berg.

Schneider, S. J., Kerwin, J., Frechtling, J., & Vivari, B. J. (2002). Characteristics of the discussion in online and face-to-face focus groups. *Social Science Computer Review, 20,* 31–42.

Stewart, K., & Williams, M. (2005). Researching online populations: The use of online focus groups for social research. *Qualitative Research, 5,* 395–416.

Teli, M., Francesco, P., & Hakken, D. (2007). The Internet as a library-of-people: For cyberethnography of online groups. *Forum: Qualitative Social Research, 8.* Retrieved from http://www.qualitative-research.net/index.php/fqs/article/view/283/622

Thurlow, C., Lengel, L., & Tomic, A. (2004). *Computer mediated communication: Social interaction and the Internet.* London, England: Sage.

Turkle, S. (1995). *Life on the screen, identity in the age of the Internet.* London, England: Phoenix/Orion.

Usher, R. (2000). Deconstructive happening, ethical moment. In H. Simons & R. Usher (Eds.), *Situated ethics in educational research* (pp. 162–185). London, England: RoutledgeFalmer.

Waskul, D., & Douglass, M. (1997). Cyberself: The emergence of self in on-line chat. *Information Society, 13,* 375–398.

Wilson, S. M., & Peterson, L. C. (2002). The anthropology of online communities. *Annual Review of Anthropology, 31,* 449–467.

Xie, B. (2007). Using the Internet for offline relationship formation. *Social Science Computer Review, 25,* 396–404.

Zhao, S. (2006). The Internet and the transformation of the reality of everyday life: Towards a new analytic stance in sociology. *Sociological Inquiry, 76,* 458–474.

12

THE IMPLICATIONS OF INTERVIEW TYPE AND STRUCTURE IN MIXED-METHOD DESIGNS

◆ Janice M. Morse

The difficulty in mixed-method design has often been described as the problem of combining textual and numerical data, and this "mixing of paradigms" remains the major challenge (Greene, 2007; Hesse-Biber, 2010; Lieber & Weisner, 2010). Obviously, textual interview data cannot be merged into a quantitative data set for analysis unless the text is coded and transformed into numerical data. If such transformation is to occur, it may be conducted only when particular conditions in the qualitative data set are met (these will be described later). Similarly, the use of numerical data obtained from a qualitative data set introduces problems of meaning, sampling, and boundaries. Numerical data may be relatively meaningless in a textual data set unless again special conditions have been met that are not usually possible or desirable in a qualitative research design.

Nevertheless, despite the recognition of the problems in combining these two types of interview data, the general principles of design for selecting the type of interviews and analytic procedures in qualitatively driven mixed-method design (QUAL-*quan*) or in quantitatively driven mixed-method design (QUAN-*qual*) have been poorly addressed in the literature. Therefore, in this chapter, I will describe the structure (or form) of the major types of interviews and how that structure relates to the types of analyses that may be used in QUAL-*quan* and in QUAN-*qual*. Of course, in mixed-method design, the qualitative data may not necessarily be interview data (e.g., they may be observational data), but in this

◆ 193

chapter I will primarily restrict this discussion to textual interview data.

◆ Clarifying Terms

Herein, *mixed methods* refers to one method (called the *core component*), which is complete in itself and might be published alone, and the *supplementary component(s),* which use uses additional data and an analytic strategy from another method. The supplementary component is not a complete method, and while this component adds additional understanding to the project as a whole, it must be interpreted within the context of the core component and is too "thin" to be published alone (Morse & Niehaus, 2009). In multiple-method designs where each method is complete, the dilemmas of inappropriate sampling and analysis are not an issue, and both studies may have been published separately and are integrated in the results narrative of a publication that combines both complementary studies (Morse & Niehaus, 2009).

The difficulty in conducting mixed-method research occurs in two positions in the research process: (1) in sampling and (2) when combining data during or following an analysis. In this chapter, I will focus on the latter—how the types of textual data produced from various interview techniques and analyses fit with the quantitative data, when the textual interview data form either the core or the supplementary component. The *point of interface* (Morse & Niehaus, 2009) is the position in the mixed-method research design in which the two data components meet—either for a combined analysis (i.e., in the *analytic point of interface*) or in the description of the results (the *results narrative point of interface*).

◆ The Form of Interview Data

Qualitative interviews and quantitative structured interviews have differing characteristics that require each type to obtain data in a particular form, for a particular method of analysis. The characteristics of these major types of interviews are summarized in Table 12.1. In this table, for the sake of completeness, I have included details of the interview type according to the researcher's knowledge of the phenomena, the inductive versus deductive approach, the derivation of the questions and responses, the sample and sample size, and the pacing of the analysis.

STRUCTURED INTERVIEWS

In quantitative analysis, the form of the numerical data is crucial for determining the type of analysis. Quantitative questionnaires are *structured*, with all subjects asked the same questions, in the same order, and with subjects responding from a "forced choice" by selecting one option from an assigned set of choices. Numerical values represent each choice. Should a subject decide not to answer, leaving a response blank, the "missing data" may be left as missing or, if too many subjects have not answered a particular question, the researcher may decide to omit that item from the analysis. The data set is always in the form of a matrix, with subjects' responses listed line by line in rows listing each item value and the variables forming columns. Data are analyzed statistically at one point in time following the completion of data collection.

UNSTRUCTURED INTERVIEWS

In qualitative interviews, *unstructured* refers to a type of interview in which the researcher asks minimal questions—often just a "grand tour" question (Spradley, 1979) that presents the general topic to focus the participant—and then primarily assumes a listening stance to elicit the participant's "story." The researcher's goal is to obtain the participant's perspective without "leading" the participant (which is one of the major threats to the validity of the unstructured interview). Unstructured interviews (Kvale, 1996; Roulston, 2010; Rubin & Rubin, 1995) are also referred to as "long" (McCracken, 1988), nonstandard (Kvale, 1996), narrative (Kvale, 2007), or "open-ended" (Johnson & Weller, 2002) interviews. A major subset of these interviews are *guided interviews* or *guided conversations* (Rubin & Rubin, 1995), in which the researcher may prepare 6 to 10 questions providing a general order to guide the course of the interview. Both of these approaches, unstructured and guided, give the participants the freedom to "tell their story" in their own way with minimal interruption from the researcher, hence the label *unstructured*. These interviews are considered optimally *emic* (from the participant's perspective), which, with the lack of interference or interjection from the researcher, increases validity.

Analysis. Importantly, analysis of the unstructured interview may be conducted in one of two styles.

Table 12.1 Characteristics and Use of Interview Types With Mixed-Method Design

Characteristics	Type of Interviews				
	Unstructured (Narrative) Interviews	Guided Interviews	Focus Group Interviews	Semistructured Interviews	Quantitative Questionnaires (Closed-Ended)
Domain	Not known	Partially known	Partially known	Known	Known
Direction of inquiry	Inductive	Inductive	Usually inductive	Deductive or inductive	Deductive
Approach	Investigator learns about phenomena during the course of the inquiry Investigator assumes listening mode	Investigator guides the order and direction of the interview but not the specific content	Interviewer develops questions designed to stimulate conversation among participants, thereby eliciting the necessary data	Investigator knows the questions that need to be asked but not all the possible responses	Investigator knows that questions and responses are necessary
Questions	Not planned in advance but developed during the course of the inquiry	Broad questions (6–10) developed to guide the course (but not the content) of the interview	Questions and prompts planned in advance	Question stems (and sometimes prompts) planned in advance	Questions and response choices planned in advance
Responses	"Long responses" conducted with minimal interruption Interviews not equivalent	Interviewer guides participants' "long responses" Interviews only partly equivalent	Discussion among participants with facilitator prompts to elicit various perspectives Group interviews only partly equivalent	Unscripted (free) responses to set open-ended questions All respondents are asked the same questions	All respondents are asked the same questions in the same order Participant selects responses
Sample	Sample changes according to the informational needs of the emerging analysis	Sample characteristics identified	Sample characteristics identified	Sample characteristics identified	Sample randomly selected from the selected population
Sample size	Depends on the scope and complexity of the phenomena	Depends on the scope and complexity of the phenomena	Number of groups and number of participants and purpose of study must be considered	If data are to be numerically transposed, at least 30 participants are required.	Large: size determined by number of questions
Analysis	Concurrent with collection	Concurrent with collection	Concurrent or at end of data collection	Analysis at end of data collection	Analysis at end of data collection
Point of interface for QUAL	QUAL-*qual*, results narrative point of interface	QUAL-*qual*, results narrative point of interface	QUAL-*qual*, results narrative point of interface	QUAL-*qual*, results narrative point of interface	QUAL-*quan*, results narrative point of interface
Point of interface for QUAN	QUAN-*qual*, results narrative point of interface	QUAN-*qual*, results narrative point of interface	QUAN-*qual*, results narrative point of interface	QUAN-*quan*, results; if textual data are transformed, analytic point of interface	QUAN-*quan*, results

Note: QUAL-*quan* = qualitatively driven mixed-method design; QUAN-*qual* = quantitatively driven mixed-method design.

In the first style, *synthesized interviews*, all participants have a similar story to report arising from similar circumstances in the interview topic and the research question, so that the content from all interviews is reasonably consistent and approximately follows a similar course (see Figure 12.1). For instance, the researcher may be asking the participants to relate their experience of caring for a spouse with Alzheimer's disease. In such cases, the interviews from all participants will consist of stories that follow a rather similar course, from when the symptoms first appeared, learning the diagnosis, seeking treatment, managing day-to-day activities, and so forth. These interviews may then be combined or synthesized into a *general story* of what happens overall during the process of caring for a spouse with Alzheimer's disease (or whatever the topic is). The results are presented in narrative form, describing the phenomenon or experience. Theoretical development of these results varies from thick description, to interpretation, to concept or theory development.

The second style, which I call *progressive comprehension* (see Figure 12.2), is one in which the researcher is learning about the phenomena as the interviews accrue and as the analysis progresses. In this case, to gain an overall (but superficial) understanding, the initial interviews are general and broad in scope, with the researcher asking an overall "grand tour" question (Spradley, 1979). Later, the researcher may ask more specific questions, and the content of these interviews will become more direct and targeted toward various aspects of whatever needs to be known, or more saturated. Data may be used to verify the earlier findings or will be directed, using the emerging theory, to the selection of participants, and interview questions will be derived from the emerging theoretical needs of the analysis (Glaser, 1978).

Figure 12.1 Interviews Cover Approximately the Same Material; the "Main Story" Becomes Evident With That Consistency, and Individual Variation Is Shown Outside the Overlap

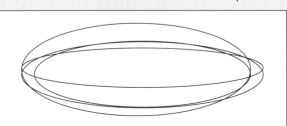

Figure 12.2 Progressive Interviews: The Main Theoretical Scheme Is Derived From the Grand Tour Questions; Subsequent Interviews Target Missing or Thin Data, Support the Emerging Theory, or Verify Data by Supplementing Previous Interviews With Greater Depth

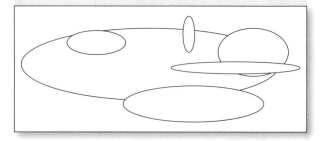

Analysis. With progressive interviews, information that is obtained from the interviews is pieced together to create an understanding of the whole, rather than a general common experience described, as in synthesized analysis. Because later interviews have different content from those conducted earlier, as the study progresses, the process of analysis pieces together the descriptions. Note that this analytic process differs from that used with synthesized interviews, where the interviews are combined to produce a general story for all participants. Again, these results are presented in narrative form, as description, interpretation, concept, and theory development.

Focus Group Interviews

Focus group interviews consist of a series of questions (usually 10–20) intended to facilitate discussion and elicit opinions among, and from, a small group of people. While the same questions are asked in all focus groups within a single study, the intent of the facilitator is to stimulate discussion about the questions. Each participant in the group does not necessarily answer every question, and the approach to analysis cannot, for instance, include counts of agreement or disagreement. Rather, data are much less precise than if a quantitative survey had been conducted and less in-depth than if an unstructured or guided interview had been used. However, focus groups do provide valuable information about, and the rationale for, beliefs and attitudes.

Analysis. The analysis of focus group data may be content analysis by question, although occasionally thematic analysis is conducted. The responses from each group are synthesized question by question. Counting by participant is not valid as each participant may not have had the opportunity to be asked every question, but the overall consensus of each group may be noted, and if an adequate number of focus groups have been held, statistical analysis by groups may be conducted.

SEMISTRUCTURED INTERVIEWS

The third category of interviews, usually considered qualitative, is the semistructured interview (McIntosh & Morse, 2012; Merton, Fiske, & Kendall, 1990; Richards & Morse, 2007). These interviews consist of a question stem, to which the participant may respond freely. Probing questions, planned or arising from the participant's response, may be asked.

Semistructured interviews are used when the researcher knows enough about the topic or phenomenon to identify the domain (i.e., knows the limits of the topic and what is and is not pertinent to the research question) but does not know and cannot anticipate all of the answers. Questions are asked of all participants in the same order. These interviews may be conducted face-to-face, in written format, or by Internet survey. Because the questions cannot be changed once the data collection begins, pretesting of the questions is important. This ensures that the questions are adequately covering the topic and that the expected responses are being obtained. Data are analyzed all at once at the end of data collection, using content analysis (Morse & Field, 1995; Richards & Morse, 2007).

THE MODE OF ANALYSIS OF QUALITATIVE INTERVIEWS

Content Analysis Versus Thematic Analysis

For qualitative interviews, there are two standard approaches to analysis, developing themes and content analysis, and these are sometimes confused (Morse, 2008).

Content Analysis. Processes of content analysis separate data from the interview context for analysis and place them in a separate file, forming a category for conceptualization and further analysis. There are no rules about how much or how little content is needed

before the data are placed in the category, how many coded pieces may be placed in the category, or how many may be taken from a single interview; nor is it necessary that every interview contribute to a particular category.

Thematic Analysis. Themes, on the other hand, may be evident or hidden (i.e., behind the text) and are found using interpretative techniques such as the analysis of metaphors or studying what is implied. When conducting thematic analysis, there is no requirement that all themes appear in all interviews. There may be more than one theme in a single interview, depending on the scope of the research question and the specificity of the interview.

When are thematic analyses or content analyses used? Themes or content analysis may be used with unstructured and guided interviews, depending on the method used and the analytic goal of the investigator. Content analysis should be used with focus group and semistructured interviews and analysis conducted item by item once the data collection has been completed (McIntosh & Morse, 2012). In part, researchers' use of themes or content analysis is dictated by the method used. For instance, in grounded theory, the identification of stages is by content analysis, and the core variable (Strauss, 1987) or basic social process (Glaser, 1978) is a theme that runs through the data; in phenomenology, themes are used, and generally in ethnography, content analysis.

What is the difference between a theme or content analysis? Basically, a theme moves throughout the interview. Sometimes the theme is foregrounded, sometimes it is backgrounded, and sometimes it is present only by inference and revealed through indicators, signs, metaphors, or other means of interpretation. If the theme is also present in other participants' interviews, the theme may be synthesized across interviews. Because of their inferential and fluid nature, themes are best used for interpretative qualitative inquiry, such as phenomenology (see Van Manen, 1990).

On the other hand, when conducting content analyses, the researcher identifies pieces of text with similar content. These paragraphs are then separated from the interview by copying them into a category, along with similar text/paragraphs from other interviews. Once the category contains an adequate number of segments or examples, the characteristics of the category itself are analyzed. Common characteristics are identified, the category is labeled and defined, and, finally, its relationship to other categories is identified. Content analysis should be used with semistructured interviews, and in this case, analysis is conducted item by item once the data collection has been completed (McIntosh & Morse, 2012). Themes or content analysis may be used with unstructured and guided interviews, depending on the method used and the analytic goal of the investigator. In summary, content analysis is therefore a concrete and descriptive technique best used for descriptive analysis, while themes are more interpretative and used for interpretative description.

◆ The Problem of Counting With Unstructured Interview Research

Counting is generally considered inappropriate with unstructured interviews unless certain conditions are met. Further concerns must be considered and, if necessary, countered:

1. If the researcher is certain that all participants have been asked the same questions and that only one instance from each interview is counted, then counting may be used. More appropriately, in qualitative inquiry, approximate quantities (most, some, many, few, etc.) may be used as textual descriptors replacing the actual numerical values.

2. The second concern is that the purposeful sample "stacks the deck": The sample is not representative of the general population, and for that reason, the sample (and therefore the data) may be considered biased. Of course, the sample is also "biased," selected to facilitate inquiry to elicit meaning—which is the goal of purposeful sampling—so that the bias here has two meanings, one negative and one positive in its contribution to qualitative inquiry.

3. The third problem is that researchers tend to count without considering the meaning of what it is they are counting. The golden rule is that whatever is counted "must make sense." Some researchers count words, sentences (and even sentence length), the number of pages of the interview, and so forth, without justifying the meaning or usefulness of quantifying such indicators.

I will discuss these issues in greater depth later in the chapter. The bottom line is that counting *may* be used with unstructured, guided, or focus group interviews, but with much care and caution.

◆ Appropriate Modes of Quantifying Qualitative Interviews

CLASSIFYING THE INTERVIEWS BY IDENTIFYING TWO (OR MORE) CHARACTERISTICS IN EACH INTERVIEW

If a general question has been asked in every interview (including in unstructured, guided, and focus group interviews), one type of quantitative analysis is to use the broad response from each participant (or focus group) and code these responses. Depending on the question asked, they may be coded as present/yes/agree (1) or absent/no/disagree (0). Provided that the minimal number of interviews (or participants) meet the minimal nonparametric requirements of two or more variables and the sample size is adequate, a statistic such as chi-square may be used to determine significance.

Sandelowski, Voils, and Knafl (2009) are less rigid in their criteria for judging "similarities and differences as bases for counting" (p. 214). They recognize that the researcher's judgment of the *presence* of whatever is being counted in the interview depends on whether it "a) spontaneously came up in the discussion [interview], b) was directed to come up in the discussion, c) was seen by the analyst between the lines, [or] d) truly was a dimension of the experience" (p. 217).

They continue that the absence of what is being counted may mean that it

a) did not come up; b) was not seen by the analyst; c) was forgotten as a factor by the participant; d) was thought by the participant to be so understood as to not require bringing it up; e) was a factor, but the participant did not want to bring "it" up; f) was not brought up because the conversation veered away from "it"; [or] g) truly was not a dimension of the experience. (p. 217)

The unstructured nature of qualitative interviews therefore leaves the text wide open to false positive or false negative ratings that subsequently contribute to the invalidity of the study. The use of interpretative techniques to "read between the lines" for data that may be rated is particularly troublesome, and it is recommended that if participants have not been asked specifically for the necessary data, they be contacted a second time.

QUALITATIVE INTERVIEWS THAT MEET THE MATRIX REQUIREMENTS FOR COUNTING

Semistructured Interviews

Semistructured interviews are a qualitative method of interviewing that is used when the researcher knows a reasonable amount about the topic—enough to identify the domain and the questions to be asked—but does not know enough to anticipate the participant's responses. Therefore, the semistructured questionnaire adds form to the interview: All participants are asked the same questions in the same order but have the option of responding to the question as they choose (called an unstructured, open-ended response) (Bernard & Ryan, 2010; Morse & Field, 1995). Because in semistructured interviews all questions have been asked of all participants, data are in the form of a matrix, similar to quantitative data. Provided the sample is large enough (generally $n \geq 30$), researchers may tabulate data and use nonparametric statistics in analysis (Morse & Field, 1995).

Because the interview schedule does not change over the course of the study, all responses are analyzed at the end of the study. Data may be analyzed qualitatively, using content analysis by item (or similar groups of items), and/or quantitatively, using techniques of data transformation to transform textual to numerical data (described later). Therefore, given the fit between the form of qualitative semistructured data sets and quantitative data sets, it is not surprising that in his survey of mixed-method research, Bryman (2006) found that semistructured interviews were the most common type of qualitative interviews used in mixed-method design.

◆ Modes of Analysis in Mixed-Method Designs

The difficulties in mixed-method qualitative and quantitative designs extend from the characteristics of each method that violate the principles of the other design. These are summarized in Table 12.2, and the features listed are the most important for "compatibility" when combining qualitative and quantitative analysis:

1. All participants must be asked the same questions. That is, data must be available for all cases. In qualitative unstructured interviews (including guided interviews and individuals in focus groups), this does not occur.

2. Data must be structured in a matrix for statistical analysis. Again, unstructured interviews, guided interviews, and focus groups are not in this form.

3. The sample must be representative of the phenomenon. This is difficult in quantitative sampling; the "average" experiences that would be obtained from a random sample dilute the data usually obtained in qualitative purposeful sampling. Such "less strong" data make the analysis more difficult and slow, requiring a larger sample.

4. The sample must be representative of the population. This is a criterion that must be carefully considered, for the necessity for purposeful sampling in qualitative inquiry negates the use of random sampling. The process of randomization leads to a situation of oversampling near the mean (which is expensive for qualitative research) and the danger that the oversampling will make the scarce data at the ends of the distributions more difficult to see. Rather, good qualitative inquiry has an even distribution, with approximately the same amount of data required at the tails of the distribution as at the center.

The most important consideration for the use of interviews with mixed-method design is whether or not the data needed are available for each and every participant or subject. By definition, this occurs with quantitative and semistructured interviews (all participants or subjects are asked the same question) and may or may not occur if two or more questions (variables) are included in all of the unstructured interviews. However, if the researcher's approach in a qualitative study is to learn about the phenomena as the study progresses (as in ethnography), the purpose and the content of the interviews change as the

Table 12.2 The Fit of Strategies Used in Different Types of Interviews and Mixed-Method Design

Aspect	Unstructured (Narrative) Interviews	Guided Interviews	Focus Group Interviews	Semistructured Interviews	Quantitative Questionnaires (Closed-Ended)
Themed	Y	Y	y	y	N/A
Category formation	Y	Y	Y	Y	N/A
Saturated	Y	Y	n	Y	N/A
Count	N	N	N	Y	Y
Same questions asked of all participants	N	N	N	Y	Y
Structured matrix (columns and rows)	N	N	N	Y	Y
Sample representative					
of phenomenon	Y	Y	y	y	y
of population	N	N	N	n	Y
Conditions for textual–numerical transposition	N	N	N	Y	N/A

Note: The uppercase Y (Yes) and N (No) represent a clear fit; the lowercase y (yes) and n (no) represent cases in which there are exemptions.

study progresses. The initial interviews are comprehensive overviews; the later interviews are targeted for specific information or are confirmatory. In this "learning as you go along" model, all interviews do not contain the same information and therefore are not suitable for transforming into numerical data: The investigator will find that he or she has too much missing data.

◆ *Integration of Interview Styles in Quantitatively Driven Mixed-Method Designs*

Next, I will discuss the possibility of quantifying semistructured interviews so that qualitative data may be incorporated into a quantitative data set.

DATA TRANSFORMATION

As noted above, quantitative interview data are usually in the form of a forced-choice questionnaire, such as a survey or a Likert scale. The format is a fixed matrix, and the scale is analyzed statistically. However, with QUAN-*qual*, a qualitative strategy is added to increase the scope of the quantitative component, to make data accessible that would not be so otherwise, or to obtain data that would not be possible to acquire quantitatively. Hence, the qualitative strategy increases the validity of the quantitative component, provided the two components, the qualitative and the quantitative, can be brought together in a complementary manner without violating the assumptions of either method.

Techniques of Data Transformation

The procedures for transformation of qualitative data to quantitative are well described (Morse & Niehaus, 2009; Srnka & Koeszegi, 2007): The qualitative items are coded, and definitions are developed for each code and a codebook developed. Two or more raters then code the qualitative text, and interrater reliability is established. Once an adequate level of interrater reliability is attained, the remaining qualitative text is coded and imported into the quantitative data set as new variables (see Figure 12.3).

Example of QUAN-qual
With Data Transformation

The unstructured nature of qualitative inquiry made the institutional review boards (IRBs) uneasy: Qualitative researchers studied vulnerable populations, their unstructured methods made their research difficult for IRBs to evaluate risk, and qualitative researchers tended to select sensitive topics for research. If qualitative researchers insisted that the risk of their research was no greater than in everyday life, the IRBs often insisted on a full review; if qualitative researchers insisted that there was minimal harm in their research, the IRBs insisted on counseling and other interventions. Yet a survey of qualitative researchers to determine the incidence of acute distress in their participants or investigation of their participants to determine if indeed they were distressed during qualitative data collection had not been conducted.

A quantitative online survey was developed for qualitative researchers to report the perceived harm in their studies. However, in some areas where not enough information was available to write closed-ended questions, a few questions in the survey had to be written as semistructured questions—with the question stem listed and space for respondents to write an unstructured qualitative response. These questions were included in the closed-ended questionnaire.

The semistructured questions were then analyzed in two ways. If they contained data suited for qualitative analysis, they were content analyzed, and these

Figure 12.3 Management of Interview Data for Quantitatively Driven Simultaneous Designs (a) at the Analytic Point of Interface and (b) at the Results Narrative Point of Interface

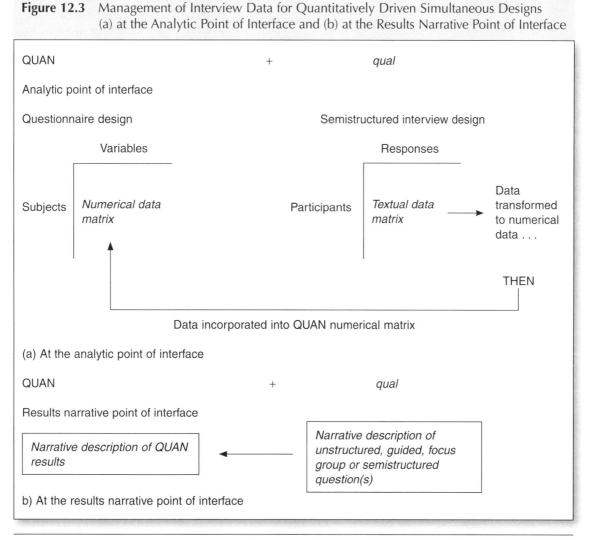

Note: QUAN-*qual* = quantitatively driven mixed-method design.

results were incorporated into the *results narrative point of interface* (Figure 12.3b). These descriptive results expanded on the quantitative findings. If the responses were "patterned," they were transformed into quantitative variables using standardized techniques (described previously). They were then imported into the quantitative data set as variables at the *analytic point of interface* and included in the statistical analysis (see Figure 12.3a). Note that the qualitative semistructured interviews may possibly contribute to the analysis textually and numerically.

◆ Merging Supplemental Qualitative Interview Data Without Data Transformation

If the supplemental *qual* component consists of unstructured or semistructured interview questions and the core QUAN component is a fixed-choice questionnaire, can the textual, supplemental data be used in a mixed-method design? The qualitative questions may be given simultaneously to the same sample as those who respond to the QUAN questionnaire. There are advantages in using the same sample: The *n* is the same, and all are asked the same questions, so that if the researcher decides to quantify the responses (as previously described), that option is possible.

However, if the questions have not been asked of the entire sample, a separate sample is usually drawn for the qualitative components. Certainly, this is the case if sequential mixed methods are used. In this case, the results of the questions are analyzed separately using content analysis, and the results are incorporated into the results narrative point of interface. The qualitative description is then used to expand the narrative describing the qualitative results.

We must consider two additional and important questions regarding QUAN-*qual*:

1. Can the researcher *count* features of the unstructured interview with the small nonequivalent sample? Bazeley (2004) argues that counting is always more appropriate than using textual descriptors (some, few, most, etc.). However, as the sample has not been randomly selected and is small (usually less than 30; Bazeley, 2004, uses 20 as her cut point), counting may be meaningless or, worse, misleading.

2. How much interview data is needed in the supplemental sample to support the quantitative core component? Elsewhere (Morse & Niehaus, 2009), we have suggested that the sampling should continue until the researcher is *certain of the answer*. Such certainty suggests a certain amount of stability in the responses, but saturation may not have been reached. Because the questions are targeted, the supplemental responses are of use only in the context of the major QUAN component and may not be separately publishable (Morse & Niehaus, 2009).

MISSING DATA

When preparing to transpose data in, for instance, a quantitative questionnaire that contains several open-ended questions and has been administered to a large sample, it is smart to review the qualitative answers before commencing the transposition to make certain that there is a reasonable response rate. If many participants have left the qualitative questions blank, do not waste your time transposing, for the mean or average value cannot be substituted for missing data in the qualitative items as they can in the quantitative. Rather, if there are adequate interesting responses, keeping these data textual and conducting content analysis may be possible.

◆ Quantitative (Same Paradigm) Research: QUAN-quan

While most researchers define mixed-method research as a qualitative–quantitative methods mix, I suggest that the principles of mixed-method design may also apply to two methods from the same paradigm, either both qualitative or both quantitative, when the form of the data are of a different type or different level of measurement (e.g., micro/macro).

In this light, QUAN-*quan* may be considered a mixed-method design when, for instance, the QUAN component is a survey or fixed-choice questionnaire and the supplemental component is a quantitative physiological measure that is administered to the entire QUAN sample. If the supplemental sample is nonequivalent or a different sample, those data have to be analyzed separately, perhaps interpreted using external norms, and the results incorporated into the results narrative point of interface.

◆ Integration of Interview Styles in Qualitatively Driven Mixed-Method Designs

In QUAL-*quan*, the qualitative study is complete and serves as the core project, and the supplemental *quan* component may be structured interview questions (even forced-choice demographic questions or a formal test, e.g., an IQ test or an anxiety questionnaire).

If the researcher is using case study design, then the results of each participant's *quan* test are analyzed with the data from the QUAL component, participant by participant. If the researcher is using a pooled design, participants' results from the *quan* component may be analyzed as a group, but because the sample is probably small, it should be compared with external norms (available with standardized tests) and incorporated into the core component at the results narrative point of interface (see Figure 12.4).

◆ Qualitative (Same Paradigm) Research: QUAL-qual

As with QUAN-*quan*, some methodologists may not consider QUAL-*qual* to be a mixed method. However, as with QUAN-*quan*, I again argue that it is appropriate when the data are of different types. Even two

interview types, such as the core consisting of grounded theory and the supplemental components of conversational analysis, are appropriately used with a mixed-method design. Again, the supplemental component is analyzed separately, and those results are incorporated into the results narrative point of interface.

◆ Writing at the Results Narrative Point of Interface

When writing the results, is it important to keep the two types of information, that from the core and that from the supplemental project, separate? The answer is that it depends on the nature of the information, the topic, and the style of writing. Even when two components are integrated in the same paragraph, it is probably easy to "tag" or label the supplemental data (e.g., "From the conversational analysis component, we found that . . ."). This integrates the data sources and, at the same time, identifies the data source for those auditing and critiquing your study. Writing the results in separate paragraphs is not integrating the studies and should be avoided if possible.

◆ Conclusion

In this chapter, I described the necessary structure (or form) of interviews for QUAL-*quan* and QUAN-*qual* mixed-method design. Unstructured and guided interviews do not have the matrix form necessary for

Figure 12.4   Management of Interview Data for Qualitatively Driven Simultaneous Designs at the Results Narrative Point of Interface

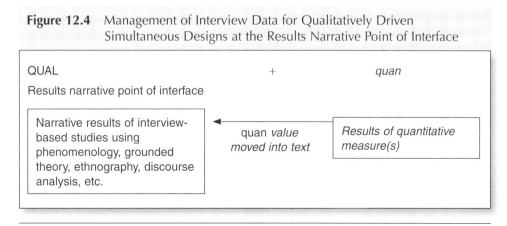

Note: QUAL-quan = qualitatively driven mixed-method design.

analysis with qualitative interviews, and in QUAN-*qual*, they must link at the results narrative point of interface. When these unstructured interviews form the core method, as in QUAL-quan, the quantitative supplemental component also links at the results point of interface.

The interview structure that best fits the QUAN mixed-method design is the semistructured interview. This type of interview has the matrix configuration and the data that, following transformation of the textual data, permit their transference into the quantitative data set. The implications extending from the type of interview are important and must be considered at the design stage.

◆ References

Bazeley, P. (2004). Issues in mixing qualitative and quantitative approaches to research. In R. Buber, J. Gadner, & L. Richards (Eds.), *Applying qualitative methods to marketing management research* (pp. 141–156). Basingstoke, UK: Palgrave Macmillan.

Bernard, H. R., & Ryan, G. W. (2010). *Analyzing qualitative data: Systematic approaches*. Newbury Park, CA: Sage.

Bryman, A. (2006). Integrating qualitative and quantitative research: How is it done? *Qualitative Research, 6*(1), 97–113.

Glaser, B. G. (1978). *Theoretical sensitivity*. Mill Valley, CA: Sociology Press.

Greene, J. C. (2007). *Mixed methods in social inquiry*. San Francisco, CA: Wiley.

Hesse-Biber, S. N. (2010). *Mixed methods research: Merging theory with practice*. New York, NY: Guilford Press.

Johnson, J. C., & Weller, S. C. (2002). Elicitation techniques for interviewing. In J. F. Gubrium & J. A. Holstein (Eds.), *Handbook of interview research* (pp. 491–514). Thousand Oaks, CA: Sage.

Kvale, S. (1996). *InterViews: An introduction to qualitative research interviewing*. London, England: Sage.

Kvale, S. (2007). *Doing interviews*. London, England: Sage.

Lieber, E., & Weisner, T. S. (2010). Meeting the practical challenges of mixed methods research. In A. Tashakkori & C. Teddlie (Eds.), *Sage handbook in mixed methods in social and behavioral research* (pp. 559–580). Thousand Oaks, CA: Sage.

McCracken, G. (1988). *The long interview* (Qualitative Research Methods Series 13). Newbury Park, CA: Sage.

McIntosh, M. J., & Morse, J. M. (2012). *The diversification, utilization and construction of the semi-structured interview*. Manuscript submitted for publication.

Merton, R. K., Fiske, M., & Kendall, P. L. (1990). *The focused interview: A manual of problems and procedures* (2nd ed.). New York, NY: Free Press.

Morse, J. M. (2008). Confusing categories and themes [Editorial]. *Qualitative Health Research, 18*(7), 727–728. doi: 10.1177/1049732308314930

Morse, J. M., & Field, P. A. (1995). *Qualitative methods for health professionals*. Thousand Oaks, CA: Sage.

Morse, J. M., & Niehaus, L. (2009). *Mixed-method design: Principles and procedures*. Walnut Creek, CA: Left Coast Press.

Richards, L., & Morse, J. M. (2007). *A user's guide to qualitative methods* (2nd ed.). Thousand Oaks, CA: Sage.

Roulston, K. (2010). *Reflective interviewing: A guide to theory and practice*. Thousand Oaks, CA: Sage.

Rubin, H. J., & Rubin, I. S. (1995). *Qualitative interviewing: The art of hearing data*. Thousand Oaks, CA: Sage.

Sandelowski, M., Voils, C. I., & Knafl, G. (2009). On quantitizing. *Journal of Mixed Methods Research, 3*(3), 208–222.

Spradley, J. P. (1979). *The ethnographic interview*. New York, NY: Holt, Rinehart & Winston.

Srnka, K. J., & Koeszegi, S. T. (2007). From words to numbers: How to transform qualitative data into meaningful quantitative results. *Schmalenbach Business Review, 59*, 29–57.

Strauss, A. L. (1987). *Qualitative analysis for social scientists*. Cambridge, UK: Cambridge University Press.

Van Manen, M. (1990). *Researching the lived experience: Human science for an action sensitive pedagogy*. London, Ontario, Canada: University of Western Ontario, Althouse Press.

Part III

LOGISTICS OF INTERVIEWING

13

INTERVIEW LOCATION AND ITS SOCIAL MEANING

◆ Hanna Herzog

Of the various components of the interview process, relatively little attention has been paid to the question of where the interview takes place and who selects the interview location, how, and why. This chapter fills this deficiency by critical and reflexive review of the various strategies scholars have used for setting interview locations and the rationales they have suggested for their decisions. The chapter argues that the interview location plays a role in constructing reality, serving simultaneously as both cultural product and producer. Thus, the choice of interview location (who chooses and what place is chosen) is not just a technical matter of convenience and comfort. It should be examined within the social context of the study being conducted and analyzed as an integral part of the interpretation of the findings.

Specifically, I begin by locating the issue of selecting the interview location in the wider paradigm of qualitative research. I then continue with a critique of the traditional understanding of how and why interview locations are selected. This critique is followed by my suggestion to rethink the interview location as an element of the broader sociopolitical context and as a site of crossing boundaries. While my case study on Palestinian women citizens of Israel serves as an example, the chapter concludes with general assertions. First, the meaning of location is never immanent but is produced and reproduced within contested social relations. Second, the interview location as negotiated site becomes an integral part not only of the findings and their analysis but also of the construction of the reality under study and the consolidation of cultural knowledge.

◆ Locating the Interview Location Within the Qualitative Research Paradigm

Is the issue of where the interview takes place and who selects the interview location a procedural, technical one, or should it be discussed and understood in the wider context of the logic of qualitative methods in general and in-depth interviews in particular? Qualitative research has recently become an established field of knowledge. What form does the establishment of this field of knowledge take? First and foremost, there are an increasing number of studies that define themselves as belonging to this field. Second, it is recognized that this is a separate field, and there are publications devoted exclusively to it, such as entire journals, special issues in journals, books, and more. Third comes the teaching of courses at universities. Fourth, conferences are held, and professional organizations or sessions at general conferences are devoted to this topic. And, finally, there are consumers of the accumulated knowledge of this field. Here we do not mean only students but also professionals and advisors who need this knowledge as part of a process of planning and decision making. There is no doubt that qualitative research methods fit these criteria and are not just step-children of various quantitative methodologies. In the expanding space of disciplines and professions, even in the case of scientific disciplines that have given precedence to quantitative research, such as psychology, medicine, management, political science, and public policy, there has been an increase in the use of qualitative research that facilitates uncovering of new levels of knowledge and of human experience. This process of institutionalization of the field paves the way for the generation of instructional literature on how to plan and conduct a qualitative study, including detailed manuals for interviews. At the same time, there is a growing critical literature discussing these instruction manuals.

The critical, reflexive examination of various aspects of the use of interviews has enhanced this research tool and led to a broadening of its role and significance in research and certainly in research findings. Alongside handbooks for qualitative interviews (e.g., Rubin & Rubin, 1995; Seidman, 1991), there are a growing number of published compilations filled with empirical, theoretical, and epistemological discussions (e.g., Berg, 2001; Denzin & Giardina, 2006; Denzin & Lincoln, 2000; Gillham, 2000, 2005; Gubrium & Holstein, 2002; Hesse-Biber & Leavy, 2004; Mishler, 1986; Schostak & Schostak, 2008; Silverman, 1997; Warren & Karner, 2005). The common thread in all these works is the argument that the interview is not

merely a technique for gathering data; rather, it should be examined as part of the structuring of an "interview society," to use David Silverman's (1997, p. 248) term. Interviews of various types have become part of our everyday routine, from physicians' interviews with patients to determine the best course of treatment to job interviews, media interviews, opinion polls and consumer surveys, state censuses, and—last but not least—interviews for research purposes (Gubrium & Holstein, 2002). For many users, the interview is an instrument to collect relevant data in order to fulfill their needs and achieve their aims. However, one of the major insights that emerges, especially from open, in-depth interviews, is that the data considered "relevant" are changed and redefined through the interview itself and/or through its analysis. Interviews broaden and deepen the concept of knowledge and its sources, incorporating the subjects' experiential truths into the process of the creation of knowledge (Atkinson & Silverman, 1997). According to Kvale (1996), the human interaction of the interview itself produces scientific knowledge. As such, interviews constitute an integral part of our society and culture (Holstein & Gubrium, 1995).

Interviews are social processes in themselves. They are an integral part of constructing individual subjectivity. Numerous researchers specializing in qualitative interviewing stress that the interview is, as its name suggests, an "inter-view," that is, an interchanging of views on a common subject between people—people who travel together on a conversational journey (Kvale, 1996). It is a social event, or "speech event," according to Mishler (1986); an "act of communication" (Herzog, 1995); a "narrative practice" (Abu-Lughod, 1993; Behar & Gordon, 1995; Josselson & Lieblich, 1995; Josselson, Lieblich, & McAdams, 2007); and a conversation between partners, according to Rubin and Rubin (1995).

Participants in the interview—the interviewer and the interviewee—become practitioners of everyday life (Gubrium & Holstein, 2002, p. 15), and the interview is part of the practices of constructing a reality anchored in the social, structural, historical, cultural, and circumstantial contexts in which it exists (DeVault, 1990; Warren, 2002, p. 91). According to Schostak (2006), the interview is both an ethical and a political space articulated by acts of witnessing, judging, and deciding. The very fact of the interview, along with what takes place around and during it, or is generated by it, plays a role in the analysis of the findings and in the construction of the reality being studied. As Gubrium and Holstein (2002) suggest, interviews are "the procedural scaffolding of a broad, culturally productive enterprise. . . . The interview's ubiquity serves to produce communicatively and ramify the very culture it ostensibly only inquires about" (p. 30).

This theoretical position compels us to inquire into the significance of various selections made by the interviewer and the interviewee during the course of embarking on and conducting the interview. Such selections might be the location of the interview, the language in which the interview will be conducted in a multicultural or immigrant society, who the interviewer will be, and so forth. These are all not merely technical considerations but analytical moves aimed at understanding the dialogic space of the interview and the world of knowledge produced by it.

◆ *Who Determines the Interview Location: Literature Survey*

Among the most neglected components of the interview process is the *choice* of location. In the interview society in which we live, the person who usually dictates the location of the interview is the interviewer: the doctor, the psychologist, the employer, the police, the judge, the journalist, and so on. They are also the ones who dictate to the interviewee how and, to a great extent, when the interview will take place. Most interviews are conducted under the aegis of institutionalized relationships that are usually hierarchical. Even studies based on telephone surveys and interviews are based on the same logic. But what do we know about the selection of location in the context of face-to-face research interviews? In what follows, I shall attempt to examine whether, and how, this question has been addressed in research studies.

Many studies do make a reference to the setting in which the interview was conducted but only as a footnote or a parenthetical comment, with no further explanation of why it was chosen and the relevance of the interview location, if any, to the research findings. Similarly, most of the classic handbooks do not problematize the issue of interview location. For example, in Rubin and Rubin's (1995) classic study,

which constituted one of the pillars of qualitative research, and which suggested integrating interpretive principles and the feminist approach, the authors assert that anything can affect the interview, but they do not address the issue of the interview location. This disregard is also evident in later works dealing with interviews, such as the 11th edition of Babbie's (2007) book. Similarly, Denzin and Lincoln (2003) emphasize that in planning the interview we must take into account the interviewee as social agent, his or her voice, the relationship between the interviewer and interviewee, and the significance of the interviewer's gender, as well as the role of race, socioeconomic status, and age. This is particularly important in relation to a structured interview: "It is hoped that in a structured interview, nothing is left to chance" (p. 125). Nevertheless, they do not explicitly discuss the location of the interview, although a very minor reference to this issue appears in their discussion of the group interview:

Fieldwork settings provide both formal and informal occasions for group interviews. The field researcher can bring respondents into a formal setting in the field context and ask directed questions. Or, a natural field setting, such as a street corner or a neighborhood tavern, can be conducive to casual but purposive inquiries. (p. 127)

In the handbooks for conducting an interview, however, the issue of location, if dealt with at all, generally comes under the heading of logistics. While logistical considerations are indeed analytically important and central to the interview process, the standard pedagogical texts seem to relegate them to matters of rapport or creating a comfortable atmosphere that is sensitive to the needs of the participants (Adler & Adler, 2002, p. 528; Berg, 2001, pp. 99–100). Seidman (1991), for example, states,

The place of the interview should be convenient to the participant, private, yet if at all possible, familiar to him or her. It should be one in which the participant feels comfortable and secure. A public place such as a cafeteria or a coffee shop may seem convenient, but the noise, lack of privacy, and the likelihood of the interview's becoming an event for others to comment upon undermine the effectiveness of such a place for interviews. (p. 40)

Gillham (2000), presenting a similar position regarding the common assumption that people talk more freely "on their own ground," cautions us that familiar places can also be distracting due to the presence of other people and the constraints of daily surroundings. He thus suggests giving interviewees the *choice* but with an explanation of the pros and cons of each location to enable them to make the best judgment for themselves. If practical problems arise with meeting on *their* territory and recording is impossible because of sound quality, background noise, or other difficulties, the interviewer will "have to adapt" (p. 8). According to the above citations, the guiding principle in determining the location, date, and time of an interview should be equity. The interviewer is the "taker," and the participant is the "giver"; hence, the interviewer must be flexible and willing to adapt him- or herself to the preferences of the participant.

However, some claim that the aims and constraints of the interviewer must also be taken into account. Adler and Adler (2002, p. 528) argue that the subject of the interview should be the determining factor in terms of location. Interviews dealing with highly emotional, sensitive, or private issues are best conducted in the home of the participant, since such a setting offers a sense of intimacy and friendliness. For other topics, it is preferable to hold the interview in the workplace, particularly when it involves subjects that the interviewee does not wish to talk about in the presence of family members. In these cases, Adler and Adler prefer to leave the selection of interview location in the hands of the interviewer.

Underlying these discussions is the notion that researchers cannot resolve all the problems of inequity that creep into the research process; however, they must be aware of them and strive to create the most congenial conditions to facilitate the flow of the interview process. In the following, I argue that the location of an interview is not just a logistical tool but rather constitutes an integral part of the interview.

◆ Rethinking the Interview Location

In contrast to the approach that seeks to refine and enhance the interview as a research tool and to overcome its technical limitations, I argue that "logistical issues" should be regarded as constructive practices in their own right, mediating the interview as a social event involving two parties—the interviewer and the participant—in an "I–Thou relationship" (Schulz, 1967, p. 164). In Goffman's (1959/1990) terms, the parties negotiate the social definition of the interview situation through the "logistical" choices they make or impose on each other. Warren (2002) hints at such negotiations when she notes that the accepted approach is to allow the participants to set the time and place best suited to them. But in her experience, it is not always easy for the participant to decide where to hold the interview. The interview location is not the result of a "well-defined methods procedure" but is affected by temporary circumstances as well as the fact that the participant who consents to being interviewed is raced, gendered, and classed. "In retrospect," she writes, "it is evident that the negotiation of perspectives on this matter filtered many of these preliminary issues, just as many seasoned qualitative researchers have noted that such negotiations indeed reverberate throughout the interview process itself" (p. 90).

My suggestion is to relate to every interview as a socially constructed, negotiated event. While the interviewer's primary aim is to grasp and interpret the interviewee's social world, the interviewer and his or her behavior are also interpreted by the participant (Rubin & Rubin, 1995, p. 39). Consequently, the determination of the interview location should not be viewed solely as a minor technical matter. Rather, one should examine what takes place *around* the logistics of the interview and include this as part of the study as important "findings" about the social structuring of reality. This argument conforms to the approaches that perceive the interview as an active process and a locus for the creation of knowledge of and about society (Holstein & Gubrium, 1995). As part of this process, "democratization" is interactionally achieved as both interviewer and participant become partners in arranging the event and, consequently, in consolidating the knowledge.

Indeed, the concept of an interview society incorporates assumptions about democratization and the granting of space to different voices. But one must also take into account critiques, such as those of Briggs (2002), that seek to expose the discursive and sociopolitical mechanisms of control underpinning the illusion of equality in the interview society.

Influenced by Foucault and Bourdieu, Briggs argues that interviews of all types are aspects of political technology and symbolic capital that reproduce the power relations of modern society

> by producing representations of social life that are deeply and invisibly informed by class relations, and by providing modes of screening individuals, through employment, counseling, social services, and other interviews, for the forms of competence that will position them in relation to institutions. Dominated communities are common targets for interview projects, providing both the models of difference and objects of surveillance and regulation. (p. 914)

Briggs (2002) proposes that interviews not be seen as monolithic political technologies but as "politically situated and interested practices for producing and re-contextualizing discourse" (p. 919)—that is, as a framework for the creation of discourse. By adopting this approach, we can be more sensitive to the ways in which participants attempt to demonstrate resistance to the dominant discourse, and be more attentive to new forms of framing and interpreting social experiences.

In the remainder of this chapter, I will illustrate this more analytically sensitive approach to choosing an interview site using examples from my own research. I first examine how the selection of a location is part of a larger sociopolitical context. I then demonstrate how the interview serves as a means for crossing social boundaries.

◆ *Interview Location as a Broader Sociopolitical Context*

Studies based on surveys frequently make note of the proportion of respondents (or alternatively of the proportion of those who refused) to indicate that the sample is not biased. Following Briggs's (2002) logic, the question that must be asked is not so much how many refuse to participate in the study but, more importantly, *how* they refuse and *what* the meaning of this refusal is. He suggests that we question what is meant by the term *uncooperative* with reference to interviewees and find out which strategies are used to cope with the codes dictated by the interview narrative.

This position leads us to rethink when the interview event begins and what data should be included in the analysis. Refusal to be interviewed, even when it can be justified by the respondents in various ways, might be an indication of unwillingness to cooperate with the researcher's research agenda. This unwillingness is a form of resistance, a resistance that can also be manifested during the interview itself when respondents are evasive or refuse to answer a question or answer it in a way that the interviewer does not consider to be an answer to the question. As Carol Warren notes (see her chapter, "Interviewing as Social Interaction," this volume), everything that transpires between the interviewer and the interviewee before, during, and after the recording is an integral part of the interview. This is part of the journey—to use Kvale's (1996) metaphor. The researcher "wanders along with the local inhabitants, asks questions that lead the subjects to tell their own stories of their lived world, and converses with them in the original Latin meaning of conversation as 'wandering together with'" (p. 4). In other words, a qualitative interview is about the ability to traverse social boundaries and to acknowledge that as part of this process. It is about our understanding that the interview, almost by definition, recontextualizes social relations. The physical location in which the interview is conducted is one of the most concrete expressions of this process of boundary crossing (a topic that I shall discuss later on in the chapter).

The refusal to be interviewed, negotiations over the conditions of participating in the interview, and the selection of and agreement on the interview location are all part of the "wandering" in unknown worlds as well as in those that we seem to be familiar with. This is a way to meet people and through conversation with them to locate the interview in social and political contexts, to uncover and chart meanings (Holstein & Gubrium, 1995). So all these are not merely technical issues but rather lie at the heart of the qualitative analysis.

Rubin and Rubin (1995, p. 103) note that, in the American context, there is a tendency to agree to take part in a study simply because people are pleased that someone is taking an interest in them. Whether one consents to being interviewed or fears it is often related to the role attributed to the interviewer—a perception frequently influenced by the cultural context of the group being studied. For example, residents of slum neighborhoods tend to perceive the interviewer as a social worker, an undercover policeman, a landlord, or some other official agent (p. 115). Adler and Adler (2002) argue that studies that touch on "delicate or sensitive" issues will meet with a higher rate of refusal; this rate is greatest among groups at either extreme of the hierarchy of power, prestige, and socioeconomic class. In my studies, I learned that in the case of Palestinian citizens of Israel (also known as Israeli Arabs), their consent to being interviewed must be examined against the historical backdrop of Jewish–Arab relations in Israel (Herzog, 2002, 2004, 2005), for no interview takes place in a situation of total neutrality. Any interview voyage should begin with understanding of and sensitivity to the culture of the "interview society" under study.

When it comes to Israeli Arabs, one should remember that until 1966 they were under a military regime that oversaw their movements and monitored their activities. The watchful eye of the security services became part of everyday life. From the perspective of the Israeli administration, there was always the fear that the Arabs could become a hostile element or collaborate with such elements from the Arab states or the Communist bloc. Even after the termination of the military regime, Arab citizens were still watched—although less closely and less overtly. Individuals suspected of political activity or nationalist involvement were regularly summoned before the General Security Service (commonly known as the "Shin Bet") for interrogation. Many lost their jobs due to the suspicion that they had collaborated, or were connected in some way, with hostile elements. For many Israeli Arabs, life under constant surveillance created a permanent sense of mistrust, directed against their own people as well, since many were suspected of being informants or otherwise collaborating with the Israeli government. Finding themselves cast in the role of "suspects," they constantly had the fear that anything they said might be used to incriminate them. To this day, any attempt to interview Palestinian Arab citizens of Israel, whether by the media or by researchers, is met with great apprehension on their part. While the civil status of Israeli Arabs has changed greatly over the past several decades, this suspicion, rightly or wrongly, is still entrenched among them.

Moreover, in the Israeli interview society, Arabs are frequently the interviewees (being questioned rather than questioning others) since the inherent inequality of Jewish–Arab relations in Israel creates a situation in which the vast majority of professionals, employers, pollsters, media people, and academic researchers are Jews. While the geographic segregation that defines the internal map of Israel creates separate, presumably semi-autonomous, local communities of Palestinian Arabs (Yiftachel, 1997), in many cases, the local "interviewers" (in most fields of inquiry) depend on the government of Israel, even if they do not directly represent it. It is noteworthy that for many years academic social research altogether avoided addressing Arab society in Israel (Smooha, 1978, 1984). Public opinion polls also excluded Palestinian Arabs, and it was only in the 1990s that they began to be included in representative samples of the country's population. For years, the study of Arabs in Israel was the province of the professional "Orientalists," of whom the vast majority were connected in various ways with military intelligence and assorted government bodies (Eyal, 2006).

Thus, the inclusion of the Palestinian Arab citizens of Israel in research studies and surveys is surely an expression of the process of democratization and expansion of the collective boundaries of Israeli society (Herzog, 2000; Kimmerling, 1993). Indeed, there are a growing number of Arab scholars who initiate and conduct their own studies, and this has been accompanied by the emergence of independent Palestinian Arab research institutes. However, as a result of the prolonged Arab–Israeli conflict, Arabs are still labeled as "others" within the Jewish nation-state (Peled, 1992). Regular, everyday encounters between Jews and Arabs are not typical of Israeli society.

Consequently, the request for an interview signifies a recontextualization, to use Briggs's terminology, of the unequal Jewish–Arab relations. The negotiations surrounding the consent to participate in a research interview should be interpreted in light of this sociopolitical background. In this sense, the refusal to be interviewed reflects a genuine fear, but it is also a gesture of resistance. Even the eventual consent to be interviewed constitutes a social statement. In analyzing the interviews, one cannot help but notice that the consent, as well as the place where the interview itself takes place, is socially situated in the embedded meaning of the term *interview*. The contribution of the in-depth interview lies in revealing the various strategies people use to confront, or adapt to, the cultures of the interviews.

◆ Interview Location as Crossing Boundaries

In keeping with Briggs's argument, I propose a cautiously critical discussion of the meaning of the participant's selection of the interview location. This also includes a reflexive understanding of the term *choice* and the presumption of a *free* place to talk. More and more researchers are allowing the interviewee to decide where the interview will take place. As mentioned earlier, the justification for this position is usually the desire to make things easier for the interviewee and to offer him or her the maximum degree of comfort and convenience. Giving interviewees the option of choosing in this sense is taken to be a practical strategy for conducting the research. But we must give some analytical consideration to whether in giving interviewees this presumed "right" without considering its significance for them, the researcher is subordinating the interview to a dominant frame of thinking in the discourse of choice. To put it another way, we should ask whether the logistic approach to selecting a location glosses over important analytical insights about the meaning that research participants attach to the interview.

The gradual incorporation of the discourse of choice into research is not new. Choice is a concept that has made inroads into various branches of the social sciences with the development of rational choice theories. The concept of choice is rooted in liberal thinking and has been bolstered by the neoliberal knowledge regime. It has been applied to everything, from parents' choice of a school for their child to the choice of health services, to reproductive technologies, to sexual identity, to the decision to engage in prostitution, and, in recent writings, to research procedures such as the choice of interview place. This thinking presupposes, in the spirit of Kant, autonomous and rational individuals, free to choose their actions. This is combined with an assumption about the existence of free markets in the spirit of the capitalist market. In this sense, choice is a value that places the individual at the center and sees him or her as a human agent shaping his or her own life. The expansion of critical discourses such as the feminist, postcolonial, and queer theories has strengthened the discussion of choice by casting minority groups not as passive victims but as active agents opposing or undermining mainstream cultural norms. This perception in turn establishes and legitimizes the notion of "social diversity" within and among social groups (Bhabha, 1994; Butler, 2004; Friedan, 1974; Narayan, 2001). In particular, giving the interviewee the option to choose the interview location is greatly influenced by feminist discourse, which emphasizes the importance of creating as equitable a relationship as possible between interviewer and participant. This stems from the viewpoint that the interview is inherently inequitable and from the feminist goal of reducing power differences even if they cannot be avoided completely (Reinharz, 1992).

Critics of this approach argue that, more than genuine choice itself, there exists an ideology of choice that masks social inequality and disregards the social, economic, and political constraints that delimit choice or do not allow its existence in the first place. Many choices contain an illusion of choice as opposed to true, autonomous, and/or rational choice. Often, choices depend on information disseminated by assorted social agents, experts of various types whose authority and/or control of the flow of information dictate what people know or don't know when choosing. The end result is that choices based on information actually increase the measure of power and control (Bakera, 2007; Lowenberg, 1995; Sherwin & Parish, 2001; Solinger, 2001). In academic studies, granting the interviewee the option to choose the location of the interview might also involve reproduction of power relations. For example, poor people very often are not able or are reluctant to host the interviewer in their home. Conversely, choice by elite groups very often reaffirms their privileged status when they cordially invite the interviewee to their office, their home, or even to a fine coffee shop.[1]

The contrast between choice as an empowering and liberating personal resource and choice as a silencing, subjugating mechanism presents a picture of "either/or." It ignores the context in which choice, as a discursive mechanism, exists and is used. A discussion based on social contexts will reveal a complex

---

[1]On interviewing various groups, see Gubrium and Holstein (2002, chap. 15).

reality of contemporaneousness. Choice may serve as an empowering and challenging discursive practice for some and, at the same time, as a social force that silences and subjugates for others (Herzog, 2009). Therefore, the question of which interview location is chosen, by whom, and in what social circumstance is an important component in understanding the lived world qualitative analysis aims to reveal. This leads us to question the meaning of a "neutral" place, such as a coffeehouse, hotel lobby, park, or university hall, as well as more "familiar" places, such as the home and workplace. There is no universal meaning of "a place."

Gieryn (2000), in his review of the rich literature of place sensitiveness in sociology, indicates that the sociological understanding of place combines three major elements: first, the demarcation of boundaries to define the physical location; second, material form, that is, a compilation of things or objects at some particular spot in the universe with unique local characteristics; and finally, the meaning and value people confer on a place. The three elements are mutually dependent. Places are made by human practices and interpretation and simultaneously shape human practices. Places are interpreted, perceived, understood, experienced, narrated, negotiated, and imagined (Soja, 1996). A sense of place is continuously produced and reproduced by ordinary people (De Certeau, 1984; Herzog & Kemp, 2010). The meaning of a chosen place is part of the interview voyage. The significance of the place is not fixed but fluctuates according to the context as inferred by the interviewee and in accordance with the message that the interviewee wishes to transmit to the interviewer.

My experience with interviewing Palestinian Arab women revealed that, in general, they preferred places that were more convenient for them. But in addition to the dimension of convenience, the interviewees made use of their power of choice to articulate their sociopolitical views to both groups of interviewers—"insiders" (e.g., Palestinians) and "outsiders" (e.g., Jews) alike (Herzog, 2005). The study of Palestinian women citizens of Israel was conducted in two rounds. The first was with women who were active in peace organizations (most of whom have higher education), and the second was with university-educated women. I found that women used the selection of the interview location as a means of expressing a social and political

position rooted in the inequality between Jews and Arabs in Israel and between men and women in general and in Palestinian society in particular. Inviting an interviewer from the outside (i.e., the Jewish interviewer) into one's home means inviting the person to *cross boundaries*—geographical, certainly, but social as well—and moving from the public to the private sphere. Peace activists invited Jewish interviewers to their homes more often than Palestinian interviewers. They required the Jewish partner to "demonstrate" her willingness to cross boundaries and place herself in an equal position. And the women who were politically aware demanded this of their interviewers to a greater extent than those who were less involved politically. In any event, it is worth noting that even when the location chosen was the workplace, the Jewish interviewer was still being asked to traverse a certain boundary and enter the Arab Palestinian living space, since in most cases the place of work was in an Arab locality or in the Arab section of a mixed city of Jews and Arabs, such as Haifa, Acre, or Nazareth. In my case, the interviewer and the interviewees were women, but certainly the choices could be different if the interviewees and the interviewer were of different genders. Here, different gender codes come into play within and between cultures.

The participants' attempts to balance the unequal relations between themselves and the interviewers and to create a situation in which they enjoy a broader control base are also related to the objectives of the study and to the messages that the women wished to convey by the very locations they chose. The Palestinian women used their choices as vehicles to negotiate directly or symbolically with societal norms and to express their re/positioning in Israeli society and in their own community. Thus, for example, there were different uses of the choice of the home as the location of the interview. Approach roads leading into the Arab villages are in poor condition. In many places, only the main roads inside the villages are paved, and homes can be reached only via dirt roads. An invitation to the participant's home is an invitation to the interviewer to witness firsthand the extent of governmental neglect and discrimination.

An interview in the home of the participant places her in the context of her family, her community, and her locality and introduces the interviewer to the home environment of the interviewee. Both of these factors become an integral part of the interview as "event." The invitation to the participant's home enables the interviewer to make use of the event as a way of defining the interviewee's status in her home and community. In many cases, the interview incorporates a restatement of cultural norms; in others, it points to the ability to combine home and career. Through such dialogic relations, the women in my study structured their individual subjectivity.

Only 1 of the 108 participants in my study asked to meet at the interviewer's home, and this request was made of a Jewish interviewer. This interviewee was an exception to the rule in many ways. Her mother is from Jordan and her father, from a village near Shechem (Nablus). She was born and raised in Shechem, married an Israeli citizen, and moved to Israel. Her siblings are scattered around the world (Italy, the United States, Bahrain, and Jordan), and her older sons also live abroad. She described herself as rebelling against convention, a woman critical of both the gender division within her community and the discriminatory political-national order in Israel. In her words, "I am always the odd [wo]man out . . . I am not an anomaly politically but personally, socially," as reflected in the fact that she is a partner in running the business owned by her and her husband, is active in peace organizations, is continuing her studies, and is very involved in the education of her children. Challenging many aspects of social life, she asked to *cross boundaries* to enter the Jewish interviewer's home. At the end of the interview, the participant expressed a great deal of interest in the study, asking to read it when it was completed. She also invited the interviewer to come to her home and meet her daughters "so that we can have a less business-like and friendlier conversation." It was important to her to receive the telephone number of the interviewer's parents as well, so as to ensure that she and the interviewer could remain in touch.

♦ Conclusion

As these examples show, it is not the setting or even the research topic per se that determines the significance of the interview location but rather the interaction between the two and the verbal or symbolic dialogue that takes place between interviewer and participant around the meaning of the location. All of these are situated within the broader contexts of culture, politics, and society.[2]

The interviewer and the participants, as "practitioners of everyday life" (Holstein & Gubrium, 1995), took part in a study that addressed the complex relationship between the Jewish and Palestinian citizens of Israel, Jewish and Palestinian women, and Palestinian women in and among themselves and as they relate to men in an ethno-nationalist, gendered society. A range of meanings was attributed to the practical matter of interview location. Some of the interviews perpetuated an asymmetrical relationship, while in other instances, interview location served as a subversive strategy against social inequality in a number of spheres. Frequently, the participants used their choice of location to propose a redefinition not only of themselves and of their role as interviewees but no less so of their place in the gender and national order. The decision about where to hold the interview allowed the participants to demand that the interviewers, particularly the Jewish ones, traverse both geographic and social boundaries.

As such, the interview not only structured the individual subjectivity of the interviewer and the participants but also broadened and deepened the concept of knowledge and its sources and incorporated the subjects' experiential truths. In doing so, the interview became simultaneously a part of the knowledge and of the process by which that knowledge emerged from the issues addressed in this study. These, in turn, became an integral part not only of the findings and their analysis but also of the construction of the reality under study and the consolidation of cultural knowledge.

It is apparent that the Israeli case applies to highly politicized situations in which space is strongly contested. Nevertheless, the accumulating studies on the meaning of space indicate that the Israeli case might be an extreme and explicit example but is not an exception. Place is the spatial form that anchors people to a social world, providing them the basis for a stable identity (Zukin, 1991, p. 223), but at the same time, place is a constructed, negotiated social arena (Keith & Pile, 1993; Pile & Keith, 1997) within an ongoing landscape of powers. The meaning of location is never immanent but is produced and reproduced within

---

[2]For similar problematizing of the language used in interviews, see Lomsky-Feder and Rapoport (2004).

contested social relations. Leaving the social and political meaning of such recontextualizing outside the research analysis might create an illusion of openness and equality. Using terms such as *comfortable atmosphere*, *convenience*, *intimacy*, or *friendliness* as explanations for the choice of interview location depoliticizes the research practice. It ignores the power relations that are produced, reproduced, and challenged continuously within the interview process. Locations, their boundaries, and their social meaning are negotiated, contested, and constituted in the interview process as in other social arenas. At the same time, these socially constructed locations are part of our knowledge production and, therefore, must be part of our research.

◆ References

Abu-Lughod, L. (1993). *Writing women's worlds: Bedouin stories*. Berkeley: University of California Press.

Adler, P. A., & Adler, P. (2002). The reluctant respondent. In J. A. Holstein & J. F. Gubrium (Eds.), *Handbook of interview research: Context and method* (pp. 515–535). Thousand Oaks, CA: Sage.

Atkinson, P., & Silverman, D. (1997). Kundera's immortality: The interview society and the invention of self. *Qualitative Inquiry, 3*, 304–325.

Babbie, E. R. (2007). *The practice of social research*. Belmont, CA: Thomson Wadsworth.

Bakera, J. (2007). The ideology of choice: Overstating progress and hiding injustice in the lives of young women: Findings from a study in North Queensland, Australia. *Women's Studies International Forum, 31*, 53–64.

Behar, R., & Gordon, D. A. (Eds.). (1995). *Women writing culture*. Berkeley: University of California Press.

Berg, B. (2001). *Qualitative research methods for the social sciences*. Boston, MA: Allyn & Bacon.

Bhabha, H. K. (1994). *The location of culture*. London, England: Routledge.

Briggs, C. L. (2002). Interviewing, power/knowledge, and social inequality. In J. A. Holstein & J. F. Gubrium (Eds.), *Handbook of interview research: Context and method* (pp. 911–922). Thousand Oaks, CA: Sage.

Butler, J. (2004). *Undoing gender*. New York, NY: Routledge.

De Certeau, M. (1984). *The practice of everyday life*. Berkeley: University of California Press.

Denzin, N. K., & Giardina, M. D. (2006). *Qualitative inquiry and the conservative challenge: Confronting methodological fundamentalism*. Walnut Creek, CA: Left Coast Press.

Denzin, N. K., & Lincoln, Y. S. (2000). *Handbook of qualitative research*. Thousand Oaks, CA: Sage.

Denzin, N. K., & Lincoln, Y. S. (2003). *The landscape of qualitative research: Theories and issues*. Thousand Oaks, CA: Sage.

DeVault, M. (1990). Talking and listening from women's standpoint: Feminist strategies for interviewing and analysis. *Social Problems, 37*, 96–117.

Eyal, G. (2006). *The disenchantment of the orient: Expertise in Arab affairs and the Israeli state*. Palo Alto, CA: Stanford University Press.

Friedan, B. (1974). *The feminine mystique*. Ithaca, NY: Dell.

Gieryn, T. F. (2000). A space for place in sociology. *Annual Review of Sociology, 26*, 463–496.

Gillham, B. (2000). *The research interview*. London, England: Continuum.

Gillham, B. (2005). *Research interviewing: The range of techniques*. Maidenhead, England: Open University Press.

Goffman, E. (1990). *The presentation of self in everyday life*. London, England: Penguin Books. (Original work published 1959)

Gubrium, J. F., & Holstein, J. A. (Eds.). (2002). *Handbook of interview research: Context and method*. Thousand Oaks, CA: Sage.

Herzog, H. (1995). Research as a communication act: A study on Israeli women in local politics. In R. Hertz & J. B. Imber (Eds.), *Studying elites using qualitative methods* (pp. 171–186). Thousand Oaks, CA: Sage.

Herzog, H. (2000). Sociology and identity: Trends in the development of sociology in Israel. *Soziologie, 2*, 5–17.

Herzog, H. (2002). Redefining political spaces: A gender perspective on the Yishuv historiography. *Journal of Israeli History, 21*, 1–25.

Herzog, H. (2004). Both an Arab and a woman: Gendered racialized experiences of female Palestinian citizens of Israel. *Social Identities, 10*, 53–82.

Herzog, H. (2005). On home turf: Interview location and its social meaning. *Qualitative Sociology, 28*, 25–47.

Herzog, H. (2009). Choice as everyday politics: Female Palestinian citizens of Israel in mixed cities. *International Journal of Politics, Culture, and Society, 22*, 5–21.

Herzog, H., & Kemp, A. (2010). Do we have a home? The "sense of home" in the narratives of Jewish women survivors of Ravensbrück. In I. Dublon-Knebel (Ed.), *A Holocaust crossroads: Jewish women in Ravensbruck* (pp. 176–204). Portland, OR: Vallentine Mitchell.

Hesse-Biber, S. N., & Leavy, P. (2004). *Approaches to qualitative research: A reader on theory and practice*. New York, NY: Oxford University Press.

Holstein, J. A., & Gubrium, J. F. (1995). *The active interview*. Thousand Oaks, CA: Sage.

Josselson, R., & Lieblich, A. (Eds.). (1995). *Interpreting experience: The narrative study of lives*. Thousand Oaks, CA: Sage.

Josselson, R., Lieblich A., & McAdams, D. P. (2007). *The meaning of others: Narrative studies of relationships.* Washington, DC: American Psychological Association.

Keith, M., & Pile, S. (Eds.). (1993). *Place and the politics of identity.* London, England: Routledge.

Kimmerling, B. (1993). State building, state autonomy and the identity of society: The case of the Israeli state. *Journal of Historical Sociology, 6,* 396–429.

Kvale, S. (1996). *Interviews: An introduction to qualitative research interviewing.* Thousand Oaks, CA: Sage.

Lomsky-Feder, E., & Rapoport, T. (2004). Speaking their language? Identity, home and power relations in interviews with immigrants. In M. H. M. B. Abrahao (Ed.), *The autobiographic adventure: Theory and practice* (pp. 329–353). Porto Alegre, Brazil: EDIPUCRS.

Lowenberg, J. S. (1995). Health promotion and the "ideology of choice." *Public Health Nursing, 12,* 319–323.

Mishler, E. G. (1986). *Research interviewing: Context and narrative.* Cambridge, MA: Harvard University Press.

Narayan, U. (2001). Minds of their own: Choices, autonomy, cultural practices and other women. In L. M. Antony (Ed.), *A mind of one's own* (pp. 418–433). Boulder, CO: Westview Press.

Peled, Y. (1992). Ethnic democracy and the legal construction of citizenship: Arab citizens of the Jewish state. *American Political Science Review, 86,* 432–443.

Pile, S., & Keith, M. (Eds.). (1997). *Geographies of resistance.* London, England: Routledge.

Reinharz, S. (1992). *Feminist methods in social research.* New York, NY: Oxford University Press.

Rubin, H. J., & Rubin, I. S. (1995). *Qualitative interviewing: The art of hearing data.* Thousand Oaks, CA: Sage.

Schostak, J. F. (2006). *Interviewing and representation in qualitative research.* Maidenhead, England: Open University Press.

Schostak, J. F., & Schostak, J. (2008). *Radical research: Designing, developing and writing research to make a difference.* London, England: Routledge.

Schulz, A. (1967). *The phenomenology of the social world.* Chicago, IL: North Western University.

Seidman, I. E. (1991). *Interviewing as qualitative research.* New York, NY: Teachers College Press.

Sherwin, S., & Parish, B. (2001). *Women, medicine, ethics and the law.* Burlington, VT: Ashgate.

Silverman, D. (1997). *Qualitative research: Theory, methods and practice.* London, England: Sage.

Smooha, S. (1978). *Social research on Arabs in Israel, 1948-1977: Trends and an annotated bibliography.* Ramat Gan, Israel: Turtledove.

Smooha, S. (1984). *Social research on Arabs in Israel, 1977–1982: A bibliography.* Haifa, Israel: University of Haifa Jewish-Arab Center, Institute of Middle Eastern Studies.

Soja, E. W. (1996). *Thirdspace: Journeys to Los Angeles and other real-and-imagined places.* Cambridge, MA: Blackwell.

Solinger, R. (2001). *Beggars and choosers: How the politics of choice shapes adoption, abortion, and welfare in the United States.* New York, NY: Hill & Wang.

Warren, C. A. B. (2002). Qualitative interviewing. In J. F. Gubrium & J. A. Holstein (Eds.), *Handbook of interview research: Context and method* (pp. 83–101). Thousand Oaks, CA: Sage.

Warren, C. A. B., & Karner, T. X. (2005). *Discovering qualitative methods: Field research, interviews, and analysis.* Los Angeles, CA: Roxbury.

Yiftachel, O. (1997). Israeli society and Jewish-Palestinian reconciliation: "Ethnocracy" and its territorial contradictions. *Middle East Journal, 51,* 505–519.

Zukin, S. (1991). *Landscapes of power: From Detroit to Disney World.* Berkeley: University of California Press.

THE VALUE OF INTERVIEWING ON MULTIPLE OCCASIONS OR LONGITUDINALLY

◆ Anne Grinyer and Carol Thomas

◆ *Introduction*

This chapter addresses issues relating to multiple interviews and interviewing across a period of time during the course of a lengthy program of research. This poses questions about researchers' relationships with both the research participants and the data they provide, especially about matters of trust and rapport in long-term engagements in the field. The focus is on qualitative research designs organized around the longitudinal collection of interview data from cohort samples. Anne Grinyer's research program about cancer in teenagers and young adults provides the case study used here; it illuminates the pragmatic and theoretical issues for interview research relating to studies with a longitudinal dimension. Grinyer's program is one example

of a recent trend to mount qualitative longitudinal studies, a much larger example in the United Kingdom being the *Timescapes* program (2007–2012), funded by the Economic and Social Research Council. This multicenter study explores how personal relationships and identities unfold through the life course and involves core projects that follow the lives of 400 people—using in-depth interviews together with other qualitative research methods:

We are using the method of "walking alongside" people to document their growing up, relationships, having children, living in families and growing older. We are interested in how these experiences impact on people's well-being and life chances. We also want to explore what this means for the long term resourcing of families.[1]

[1]http://www.timescapes.leeds.ac.uk/

Whatever the scale and topic of interviewing on multiple occasions or across a lengthy period of time, the purpose is to obtain interviewees' interpretations of their own experiences and understanding of the world in which they live—as these move forward.

◆ Advantages and Disadvantages of the Longitudinal Approach

When 20th-century social scientists were relatively new to interviewing techniques, the coupling of "interviews and longitudinal study" seemed to represent a contradiction in terms. Going back to Black and Champion (1976, p. 355), the interview was defined as "a fleeting, momentary experience" based on a one-off encounter, and it thus involved a transitory relationship between interviewer and interviewee. Longitudinal research projects were commonly associated with quantitative studies using statistically representative samples and cohort panels in large *repeat* surveys deploying either "tick the box" *self-completion* questionnaires or structured interview questionnaires *administered* and analyzed by research staff. Repeat questionnaire engagements with members of samples or panels were designed to capture temporal changes in lives and social contexts. However, methodological developments in favor of *mixed methods* showed that longitudinal research could "build a bridge" between quantitative and qualitative methods by employing both extensive and intensive approaches in a staged design (Robson, 1993; Ruspini, 2000, p. 3).

Longitudinal research, whether quantitative or qualitative, can pose particular challenges. For example, studies based on returning to the same participants face the problem of sample attrition: Some participants cannot be traced because they have moved location, may have become unable to commit to long-term participation for lifestyle reasons, may have become too ill to see another interview through, or may have died. In addition, there is the risk that some participants may regret becoming involved and decide to limit or purposively distort their responses in subsequent interviews; and another limitation may simply be recall bias (Ruspini, 2000). Such studies are also demanding of the time and resources of the researchers and are subject to the changed priorities of funders (Robson, 1993, p. 50).

Despite such drawbacks, there are a number of advantages to be gained by using the longitudinal approach to data collection in qualitative research, apart from the production of a greater volume of data. Earthy and Cronin (2008) list the following advantages of interviewing a research participant on more than one occasion:

- It may assist the development of trust and rapport between the researcher and interviewee.

- It may be less exhausting for both parties, particularly in comparison with a single attempt to capture a person's life story.

- For interviewees who are unwell or who find aspects of the conversation distressing, the possibility of ending the interview knowing that the conversation can continue on another day may be particularly helpful.

- The gap between interviews provides an opportunity for both the interviewee and the researcher to reflect.

- Aspects discussed in one interview can be clarified and explored in greater depth in a subsequent conversation. (Earthy & Cronin, 2008, p. 431)

Indeed, some researchers recommend two, three, or more interviews with the same participant, convinced that this multiple and staged approach can uncover greater detail, depth, and complexity of meaning of the interviewee's experiences (Hollway & Jefferson, 2000). For example, Hollway and Jefferson undertook two interviews with each of their study participants, a week apart, in their research on the fear of crime in a British city. In the intervening week, the researchers engaged in the first phase of data analysis—listening analytically to the recorded interview—so that questions could be formulated with precision for the second interview, thus building up familiarity and trust between the interlocutors. An oft-cited example of undertaking multiple interviews with participants is Kathy Charmaz's (1991) study of living with chronic illness. Because the interviews were designed to unlock very sensitive experiences and narratives of *suffering*, multiple interviews were thought to offer the best approach; indeed, these laid the foundation for Chamaz's influential conceptualization of *loss of self*. Moreover, building in degrees of temporality and multi-occasion interviewing in an interview study design seems fitting when the research is focused on the psychosocial impacts of long-lasting but changing experiential phenomena.

Another well-known study using repeat interviews is Jocelyn Cornwell's (1984) research on health and illness in East London. Cornwell's approach led her to draw a distinction between "public" and "private" accounts. The public accounts were those that participants offered in the first interview when rapport was minimal—accounts that interviewees thought the interviewer wanted or expected to hear. Private accounts were those that participants offered when trust and familiarity with the researcher had been established in a second or subsequent interview; later interviews could lead to the disclosure of more closely guarded and "difficult" health matters. The feminist researcher Beverly Skeggs (1994) makes a related observation: that researchers who build up personal relationships with study participants on the ground cannot claim to practice or theorize in "an ivory tower or a vacuum" (p. 88). Clearly, researchers need to be skilled both in the design of research studies and in interviewing techniques in order to carry multi-occasion interviewing through successfully.

TRUST AND RAPPORT

That multiple interviews help build researcher–interviewee relationships that generate trust and rapport, resulting in data of high quality, is central to the claims in many of the studies cited above. But these qualities are not necessarily established in an easy or straightforward fashion. For example, in his classic book *Creative Interviewing*, Jack Douglas (1985) highlights a number of challenges involved in achieving multiple interviews. With regard to one female interviewee, Douglas tells us that "*some of the most important facts of her life did not come out in a first interview and the depth remained heavily shrouded, as happens on all first interviews except the most miraculously creative*" (italics added; p. 99). In fact, this interviewee had questioned the point of another interview and put Douglas on the defensive. He had to explain and justify the second interview and even disclose personal details concerning his own feelings. Fortunately, this reciprocity succeeded

in engaging the interviewee emotionally in a way that allowed the interview to reach unexpected depths. As Holstein and Gubrium (1995, p. 12) observe, Douglas established a climate for mutual and deep disclosure that allowed the "emotional wellsprings" of his participants to be accessed.

Douglas emphasizes the need for the shared emotions to be genuine and says that fabricating them will not serve the researcher well. However, he acknowledges that warmth is not his own "trump card" (Douglas, 1985, p. 106) and that achieving intimacy has always been a challenge; nevertheless, he learned warmth in part from his interactions with study participants—reaching what he hopes is an 8 on a scale of 1 to 10.

Darlington and Scott (2002) support these reflections on the necessity of emotional bonding when they point out that participation in research about personal and perhaps traumatic experiences requires a great deal of ongoing trust. Without some sense of connection with the interviewer, participants are unlikely to be either relaxed or trusting enough to share their innermost feelings. That is, trust needs to be nurtured and, as with rapport, cannot be taken for granted as a "once and for all":

> Rapport is often included in research texts as an entity that is established at the beginning of the research, and once this is done the researcher can get on with the business of researching. But rapport is not a finite commodity that can be turned on and off by the researcher. It is relational. . . . Like all relationships, the researcher-participant relationship is subject to continuing negotiation and reworking; this extends to the participant's trust in the researcher's behaviour at every stage of the research. (p. 54)

Once again, we can see that implicit in the idea of meaningful trust between the researcher and the participant is the notion of positive relational continuity across a period of time—a period during which the individual or the community come to understand the researchers and their purpose and are willing to disclose private and personal feelings and contextual information.

However, it must be noted that shared emotions may not be sufficient to build trust and rapport in an interview. That is, *shared experience* may be a necessary addition. In *Gender Issues in Field Research*,

Carol Warren (1988) explains that being a female ethnographer was not enough to gain trust and secure access to women participants in the field. Rather than shared gender being the key, there was also a necessity to share experiences of marital and maternal status. Yet as Warren and Hackney (2000) maintain, the nature of relationships changes when researchers are in the field for any length of time. They suggest that a fluid, dynamic process of interaction and negotiation is set in train; desired outcomes are not, therefore, guaranteed.

TAKING TRUST AND RAPPORT INTO "PRIVATE" OR DANGEROUS TERRITORY

Some longitudinal research may make exceptional personal demands on the researcher or may venture into the challenging topics and territory associated with illicit or deviant behaviors. On each occasion that both interviewer and participant meet, they can take nothing for granted because each encounter will yield unique interactional outcomes (Holstein & Gubrium, 1995). Indeed, there are cases where one might argue that the researcher *steps over the line*.

One way of looking at this is to explore how trust is established, over a lengthy period, in situations where the researched social activity is illegal. One illustration is Patricia Adler's (1993) study of drug dealing and smuggling with a group whose occupation made them secretive and mistrustful. This meant that she needed to gain trust slowly by adopting a "peripheral membership role" (p. 11). Over a period of 6 years of daily participant observation, she reports offering favors to participants such as lending her phone or car and, eventually, the use of her home to establish trust, but she acknowledges that "real" trust was established with only some members of the drug-dealing group. This suggests that personal familiarity and "giving" may be key components in establishing trust in some longitudinal research settings. In another study, Patricia Adler and Peter Adler (2004) discuss their research with hotel workers, which involved extended visits and sometimes sharing accommodation with their participants. Their continuing and repeated, but not constant, presence appears to have been central to their success in gaining the confidence of the interviewees: "We thus settled into a regular lifestyle, travelling to Hawaii twice a year for two weeks in March and six weeks in the summer. . . . [S]pending eight weeks there a year gave us a consistent presence" (p. 31).

Despite these extended and repeated stays in the resort, Adler and Adler (2004) say that "it never felt like enough." Nevertheless, they were able to use their March visit to reconnect and set up interviews in the summer, thereby never losing touch. These authors describe themselves as "recurring, permanent fixtures but not people who were completely there" (p. 35).

However, as Miller and Glassner (2004) argue, identifying too closely with participants may actually distort or restrict the stories they choose to share. These observations suggest that overfamiliarity can undermine the research endeavor and that any attempt at objectivity is sacrificed in the effort to establish what might even be interpreted as "inappropriate" relationships with research participants. Warren (1988) cites examples of situations where extended relationships in the field result in levels of intimacy that complicate the research process:

> We are told for example that Carolyn Fleuhr-Lobban, as a married woman, was treated to oil massages, and we are told that for Dona Davis rapport was enhanced by taking a lover. The implication—sometimes the explicit indication—is that the events described in these anecdotes resulted in greater rapport, which in turn resulted in access to more (and presumably more truthful) information. (p. 41)

Thus, it is possible to envisage scenarios in which the complications of being intimate with participants might result in relationships becoming strained and disclosures, as a result, being more guarded. Adler and Adler (1987) also acknowledge the danger of overinvolvement, citing a study where a researcher had to wait 7 years after it was completed before she felt able to write about it; her loyalties left her in fear that her writing would offend the participants, who would feel that their trust had been betrayed.

Of course, the practice of immersion in the field and gaining long-term membership of the study community is a rich Chicago School tradition exemplified by, for example, Whyte's *Street Corner Society: The Social Structure of an Italian Slum* (1981). However, it must be noted that many of the early studies gained the trust of participants because the research purpose remained *covert*. Current academic thinking tends to frown on such practices, and the ethical approvals process for research will normally demand full and frank disclosure of the purpose of the research to participants to get their *informed consent*—a basic doctrine of ethical behavior (Bulmer, 2008).

MEANINGS, DATA QUALITY, AND "TRUTH"

Goudy and Potter (1975) argue that while rapport is frequently mentioned as important in interviewing, the concept is ill defined and is used in different and ambiguous ways. For example, rapport might be understood as respondent motivation, the generation of free and frank answers, harmonious or friendly relations, or respondents accepting the goals of the research and assisting in their achievement. The measures of rapport may be eye contact, frequency of smiles and nods, the level of embarrassment when sensitive questions are asked, the liking of each party for the other, and willingness of the participant to be reinterviewed. Given these variations, is it possible to claim "rapport" for one's study without clarifying the meanings one employs?

Moreover, Goudy and Potter (1975) warn against "overrapport" and suggest that there is an optimum level of rapport that should be aimed at—rather than maximal rapport. These authors cite studies that suggest that there may be a tendency for validity to be low when rapport is high: That is, the higher the rapport, the greater is the bias in the interview. Goudy and Potter cite what Gordon calls the "rather haunting specter" of the "neophyte" researcher coming away from an interview feeling that it has gone particularly well because the "rapport was perfect" only to discover, when undertaking the analysis, that the data were "incomplete, superficial and ambiguous" (p. 541). That is, the two parties had established such a pleasing relationship that the purpose of the interview became obscured. Thus, Goudy and Potter argue that the purpose of the interview is not simply to establish rapport in and of itself but to use rapport as a means to generate data of high quality.

While Darlington and Scott (2002) emphasize the importance of rapport, they too warn that researchers may assume shared researcher–interviewee understandings in multiple interviews that are misleading. Moreover, if we accept that each encounter with a participant carries with it a unique interactional outcome that is "not predefined but is instead constructed in relation to the ongoing communicative contingencies of the interview process" (Holstein &

Gubrium, 1995, p. 14), what are we to take as the "truth" in what is said? In repeat interviews, do we expect participants to try to recall what they said in previous encounters and deepen their account, or do we want them to feel free to move on, to divulge new, perhaps contradictory, information? Which interview gets nearer the truth, and how do we manage the interaction when we spot discrepancies? This clearly has implications for validity and reliability in research and suggests that multi-occasion interviews may not necessarily result in "accumulative" or "better" data. Indeed, the resulting contradictions may simply serve to confuse our research.

One way of verifying the truth, or at least clarifying what our participants meant at any one time, is to return to the field with our data (usually the printed transcripts) for confirmation. This practice is recommended by some researchers and viewed as essential by others. That is, to return to the field with the output is to make some form of "payment" and a recognition of the fact that without the participants' goodwill and cooperation there would be no data at all (Emerson & Pollner, 2002). However, Emerson and Pollner (1988) point out that these "going back for validation" occasions are actually new social encounters that should be analyzed in their own right.

"Going back to participants with the data" or, at least, with the research results, is viewed by some researchers as ethically and/or politically necessary—giving back to those who gave and avoiding simply relegating findings to dusty journals on academics' shelves. Adler and Adler (1987) suggest that it is appropriate to take research results "back to the field" either by presenting them personally or by publishing them in members' journals. However, too often researchers have to get on with planning the next research project, applying for the next grant, or even finding their next job, so any kind of extended contact with the research field might be limited to the data collection period. While this may not threaten the research in question, it may damage the field—giving research and researchers a bad name and making it more difficult to secure trust in future research encounters. However, it would also be wrong to assume that the "take the data back" practice is always welcomed by the participant—or all participants—especially if repeat requests are made to participants to read their interview transcripts and feedback comments.

Of course, not all projects have the capacity for repeat interviews or for returns to the field to debrief participants. This may be for reasons of cost, scale, or other practicalities. Nevertheless, any study that requires an understanding of *prospective change across time* will necessitate a longitudinal study design. However, on occasion, the dynamics are reversed. That is, it is the relationship established with participants or with the interview data they generate that propels a study in a longitudinal direction and demands repeat interviews or generates further research questions. This is true for the case study that follows, drawing on Grinyer's research on cancer in teenagers and young adults over a 10-year period.

◆ *Case Study*

The selected case study lays out the natural history of a 10-year qualitative research program that developed incrementally and recruited participants, at least in part, as a result of the trust and rapport built up with individuals in a wider community. The case study illuminates some of the issues, challenges, and contradictions raised above in a particular set of circumstances.

It began in 2000, when Anne Grinyer and Carol Thomas embarked on a small-scale and very modestly funded study on the experiences of parents of young adults with cancer. The research was initiated and funded by a couple, Helen and Geoff, known to Anne for 25 years as close family friends. After their 23-year-old son, George, died of cancer, his parents set up a small charity to fund research and approached the university department in which Anne and Carol were employed. Anne was asked to take on the research, but because Anne's own children had grown up alongside George, she felt too personally involved to pursue the research alone—and Carol agreed to join in. Thus, it was crucial at the outset that an academic with no personal involvement in the scenario become a coresearcher; although Carol's involvement lasted only a year, it was of fundamental importance in the early stages.

From these small beginnings, a cancer research program of 10 years' duration evolved, with some repeat interviewing of both the "cancer respondents" and the health professionals. Directed by Anne, this program involved ongoing relationships with participants and continues at the time of writing. The program developed incrementally into five

phases, each using mixed qualitative research methods. As this case study illustrates, researchers may set off with a time-limited study in mind, one designed to involve single data collection encounters with participants, only to find themselves involved in research that has a lasting momentum and emergent qualities because the social actors involved propel the researcher into an extended engagement that builds on the advantages of repeat interviews and long-term relationships.

PHASE 1

From our current vantage point, we can report that Phase 1 in this case study did not start with interviews (with one exception) but with the *narrative correspondence method* used by Carol in her earlier research with disabled women (Thomas, 1998, 1999a, 1999b). This method involved receiving 28 written accounts about lived experiences from parents (mostly mothers) whose sons or daughters had been diagnosed with cancer when they were young adults; all but 7 of these young adults had died. These written narratives were responses to an appeal letter written by George's mother, Helen, and distributed via cancer networks in diverse publications—both local and national. The charitable trust, set up in memory of George by his parents, provided the funding for the project.

The rationale for the use of the narrative correspondence method was largely pragmatic in that such parents were a hard-to-reach and geographically dispersed group; indeed, two of the correspondents lived in Germany and Australia. There was also an important ethical consideration: Using this method gave privacy and control to the participants because they could pick up and put down their accounts as and when they felt able to do so and were under no obligation to submit their written narratives. The storied material that was supplied in response to the appeal letter was immensely moving and informative: Parents poured out their thoughts and feelings about what had occurred—often with an insightful edge that had the potential to inform and assist both other parents in the same situation and health professionals in the cancer field.

However, while the majority of participants in this phase wrote narrative accounts of their experience, there was a notable exception: Helen, the mother who set the research in motion. So, at the start of each chapter in the resulting book (Grinyer, 2002), Anne includes an extract of interviews with Helen—giving her account of how she, her family, and George experienced a particular issue. The seven interviews with Helen took place over a period of weeks because the recollection of the events was emotionally demanding. In this case, in contrast to the other data collection throughout the whole subsequent program, Anne was interviewing a personal friend whom she had known for years and whose charitable trust was funding the research. This close, preexisting personal relationship could have resulted in some of the challenges documented above that emerge in research encounters. However, while the interviews were successful, they did feel like rather "artificial" encounters because of the familiarity of each with the other; here were two women used to having conversations across the kitchen table without a recording device in between them. Roles certainly had to be negotiated—and subsequently renegotiated to return to their former status. However, this did not appear to overcomplicate the process, and the discussion and sharing of the intimate details surrounding Helen's son's death may even have required the friendship context. The quality of the data generated was rich and meaningful and captured the essence of Helen's experience. Interestingly, for one particularly sensitive issue, Helen preferred to write her own account. The resulting text had a different quality from the interview data, and Anne and Helen decided that they would try an interview instead. This was achieved, and the resulting book extract is more "in keeping" with the other extracts from her interviews. The difference in the tone of the two versions—one written and one spoken—was subtle but significant.

Anne undertook a cross-sectional thematic analysis of all the narrative accounts and interviews and was able to publish full details of the study in book form (Grinyer, 2002). A copy of the book was sent to all the participants after verification that they would welcome a copy.

PHASE 2

Following the publication of this book, the assumption had been that the data accrued would constitute the sum total of the project and that further engagement with the participants would be limited to "Thank you" messages. However, this was

not the case because social relationships with temporal qualities were set in motion. Despite the participants not having had any personal, face-to-face, or even telephone contact with the researchers during the data collection process, the participants clearly felt a strong connection and personal commitment to the project. It seems likely that this was in part because the initial appeal letter had been written by Helen, a mother in the same emotionally fraught and difficult position; this raises the question of whether an appeal from a university researcher would have sparked the same interest and commitment.

The effort invested by parents in their written accounts transformed the study, and follow-up events ensued. The first of these was the setting up of a meeting to launch the book based on the parental accounts: *Cancer in Young Adults: Through Parents' Eyes* (Grinyer, 2002). This meeting was attended by at least half of the parents and involved Anne and Helen in face-to-face meetings with their narrative correspondents. This was also the first time that the parents met with one another. The preparatory spoken and written communication that took place between the research team and the parents prior to the launch had suggested that it should be linked to a series of workshops and events on the following day, because the emotionally charged nature of the launch demanded further opportunities for talk and mutual support. These linked events were not treated as focus groups or any other type of research forum, but they certainly generated ideas for further research and facilitated the growth of personal bonds and friendships among *all* the participants, Anne and Helen included. Moreover, several participants spoke of the cathartic and therapeutic effects of their involvement in the research.

Even at this stage, it was not obvious that the research would progress any further over the subsequent months, but a new momentum and ethical imperative was now in play. Anne felt compelled to return to the participants in order to undertake a follow-up study on the impact of their involvement in the Phase 1 project. There is a paradox here in that returning to them to find out if they had been caused any discomfort by their first engagement risked further intrusion; however, nearly half agreed to participate (Grinyer, 2004). In the ensuing months, Anne returned to the data to undertake further thematic analysis and realized that there were unanswered questions that should be followed up—but this time via semistructured interviews. For example, implicit within the narratives, written mainly by the mothers, was the suggestion that their own health and well-being had been affected. So Anne returned to the participants again to ask if an interview could be arranged (see Grinyer, 2004). Although these were not repeat interviews in the conventional sense, the interviews had many of the beneficial qualities outlined above because the previous encounters with the participants, on paper and in person, had established trust and mutual respect. For example, the relationship that had been generated with the participants in Phase 1 and Phase 2 created a partnership that resulted in them becoming familiar with and committed to the research to the extent that they became in some sense "core-searchers." Such a development would seem to accord with Skeggs's (1994) notion of not working in an ivory tower or vacuum but instead engaging in meaningful ways with research participants. Indeed, it was this engagement that led to the next phase of the research on the young peoples' experience of treatment and care as suggested by the participants.

After the interviews, all involvement with the participants might have drawn to a natural conclusion but for two factors: the first was that the participants had become very involved in the project, wanting updates on its progress and information about publications and presentations, and a few had become frequent correspondents with Helen. Put another way, the research program had become *participative*—and lay people were influencing the research agenda. At the time of writing, it is more than 10 years since the first phase of the project, yet Christmas letters and cards are still sent to Helen with family updates, and all pass on their best wishes to Anne and inquire about current research activities. These communications may not be "data" per se, but they do tell us something about the significance of a continuing connection with a project when it has touched the lives of participants in a meaningful way.

PHASE 3

As had been suggested by the parents at the book launch events, and as a consequence of other influences, the research moved into Phase 3: the experiences of young adults in treatment for cancer, with an emphasis on the effects of the care setting. Anne's cancer research program was thus expanding and gathering renewed momentum, though conducting semistructured interviews with young adults in treatment for cancer was not an easy venture (see Grinyer, 2007).

An important relationship was established at this stage with the Teenage Cancer Trust (TCT). The TCT had been approached at the outset, but they were clearly unsure of the credentials of these newcomers to the field. However, as the program delivered tangible outcomes in terms of publications, conference presentations, and international recognition, the TCT became more interested in the research and began to use the outcomes for training purposes. They also became crucial "research partners" in terms of their support in gaining access to settings of care in Phase 3 and introducing Anne to long-term survivors in Phase 4 and to bereaved families in Phase 5. To gain the respect and support of such an organization is again something that takes time, cannot be expedited, and is inextricably linked to the temporal nature of the process as a whole. Additionally, over time, key personnel from the TCT also agreed to be interviewed. As with Phase 1, a book based on the interview data was published, and once more a copy of the book was sent to all participants after verification that they would welcome it.

PHASE 4

During the course of data collection in Phase 3, the health professionals interviewed suggested that it would be helpful for them to understand more about long-term survivorship as they tended to lose touch with their young adult patients after discharge. Participants for this phase of the program were identified in a range of ways, and some of the health professionals interviewed in Phase 3 helped Anne to recruit interviewees for Phase 4 (i.e., semistructured interviews with "survivors"—see Grinyer, 2009b). Another group of young adults to be approached were the surviving daughters and sons of the participants in Phase 1. Of these, one young woman agreed to be interviewed (Grinyer, 2009b). As well as recruiting via long-term follow-up clinics and appealing for participants in relevant cancer-related publications, other young people were contacted via a network that had grown around the program over the years. For example, the TCT approached survivors to ask if they would agree to Anne being put in touch with them. The implicit trust placed by the TCT in the program was related directly to the length of time it had taken to establish the research as valuable, ethical, and committed to furthering the understanding of cancer in teenagers and young adults (see especially Grinyer, 2002, 2007, 2009b). The program was by definition not in the "smash and grab" line of research, where the researcher moves on to the next topic when the money runs out. As with the previous phases, a book based on the interview data was published, and again a copy of the book was sent to all participants after verification that they would welcome one.

PHASE 5

As a consequence of many of the relationships built up with people in Phases 1 to 4, the research program is currently in its fifth phase, on "palliative and end-of-life care and place of death" (see also Grinyer & Thomas, 2004). This took Anne back, once again, to the data supplied by the parents in Phase 1—but this time only to data about sons and daughters who had died. Thus, some of the original participants again contributed to the program more than 10 years after their first involvement. One interview was with a bereaved mother from Phase 1 who also arranged for Anne to make a research visit to the hospice where she now worked; this led to Anne undertaking a series of interviews with the participant's hospice colleagues. Furthermore, in this participant's capacity as a hospice librarian, Anne had been kept informed throughout about publications that might be relevant to the research program; in this way, the participant became a type of coresearcher.

This fifth phase of the research is ongoing at the time of writing and has thus far recruited 40 interview participants for semistructured interviews. Some of these are health professionals, and others, such as staff from the TCT, have participated in the previous phases. There is no doubt that willingness and commitment to support the program have gradually and almost imperceptibly developed as a result of its longevity. This not only has offered the opportunity to return to participants who have been previous interviewees but has, within the field, generated the type of trust and respect that is inevitably missing in some programs of shorter duration. This is not to say that this program is more deserving of such trust, simply that many projects do not have the prolonged existence necessary to generate it.*

◆ Further Observations

This case study presents a possibly unique set of conditions and unusual circumstances, yet it does have relevance for research design and conduct in other fields and tells us much about the significance of longitudinal relationships with research participants as well as about researchers' relationship with the data generated and the wider research field.

For Anne, relationships with participants developed slowly, based on accumulating trust. As Douglas (1985) emphasized, mutual self-disclosure is of great importance in establishing trust and rapport and, thus, in gaining meaningful insights into participants' lives. A significant number of participants asked Anne why she was doing the research. She explained that her motivation was her lifelong friendship with George's family and, having known George since his birth, her personal commitment to realize the family's wish to make the research "successful." This explanation seemed to satisfy the participants; they valued the fact that there was a personal dimension to the commitment—even if Anne did not share their experience directly.

As noted, each participant in all phases of the research was offered a copy of Anne's resulting book. This commitment has cost the trust a great deal financially but has more than paid off in terms of validating the participants' decision to contribute. And when sons and daughters have been lost to cancer, a book featuring the participants' personal stories (Phase 1) or extracts from their interviews (Phase 2) acts as a lasting memorial. The significance of this relatively simple commitment to show appreciation for participation echoes Emerson and Pollner's (2002) observations that failure to return to the field with research findings is unethical because it exacerbates the imbalance between researcher and participant. In some cases, the recipients of Anne's books became participants in later phases of the research program, but even when this did not happen, the reputation of the research was enhanced, and this has, in turn, laid the foundations for establishing trust and credibility with future participants.

Since the participants have seen how their data have been used, and as they have been kept informed as well as consulted and included, they have shown

---

*At the time this handbook went to press, a book based on Phase 5 was in the process of publication (Grinyer, 2012). All participants in the research have been contacted about the book's publication, and all have said that they wish to receive a copy.

trust in Anne by introducing her to other family members and research participants. Moreover, they have suggested ideas for further research. Unlike much longitudinal research, which does not deliver an outcome until the end of the process, the phased relationship with participants has, in this case, seen the delivery of outcomes at regular intervals. This meant that the participants' immersion in the field and ongoing awareness of how their data are treated have strengthened their interaction with the researcher. It has allowed them to exercise their agency and influence the development of the research program.

The case study also illustrates how researchers are motivated to maximize the impact of the data supplied. That is, because the interviews have been so demanding on the participants in terms of recalling illness, loss, or bereavement—and on the interviewer in listening to these accounts—there is an imperative to maximize the weight, quality, and dissemination of research findings and outputs. However, to keep returning to the participants—particularly when the subject matter is sensitive—carries with it ethical implications. As noted above, in the case study, there was a potential clash between the researcher's wish to understand the long-term impact of participation and the right of the participants to remain undisturbed or cease further involvement (Grinyer, 2004). There is also the matter of the researcher's long-term relationship with the data per se. This too has ethical implications. Carrying out a project in distinct phases, each of which involves the analysis of a further data set, might lead researchers to make connections and comparisons that are greater than the sum of the parts. This can only occur in research that is spread across time, and it carries with it theoretical and ethical challenges. For example, is it legitimate to compare and contrast the findings from different phases in the research, especially phases that have used different data collection methods? What are the theoretical implications involved in contrasting a data set using interview methods with one that has used observational or narrative techniques? Such a departure from the "recipes" often described and recommended in methods texts can prove challenging during the peer review process and requires justification of the kind discussed in Grinyer (2009a). There is also the matter of having to obtain renewed "consent" in order to return to interview data for further analysis (Grinyer, 2009a). While research participants may wish to remain connected, they do not necessarily want to be asked for renewed consent each time researchers wish to return to the

data for different analytical purposes, but this is the common expectation of research ethics committees.

In this chapter, the interview method has been largely unquestioned due to its ubiquitous nature. However, Nunkoosing (2005) reminds us that its popularity should not mean that we take it for granted, and he proceeds to problematize the interview on a number of levels. For example, he suggests that *power* is always present in the interview situation and questions whether it is ever possible to establish nonhierarchical relationships; even reciprocity rarely involves equality. Issues of *truth* and authenticity are also questioned by Nunkoosing; he suggests that accounts from participants may offer a selective or preferred self-image—such as the man who claims to go to the gym every day but whose account is doubted by the interviewer. *Consent* is also problematized; Nunkoosing points out that we seek consent prior to the interview at a moment when neither the interviewer nor the participant can predict the details of what will be discussed or the effect that the interview will have.

However, "power," "truth," and "consent" might all be addressed by research designs that build in longitudinal elements, including multi-occasion interviewing. The case study has shown, first, that the inevitable power relationship between the interviewee and interviewer can be gradually made more equitable over time. When both parties became more familiar with each other, and were more relaxed and at ease, the relationship became more trustful and evenly balanced. Indeed, the participant became an active coproducer of data rather than a passive provider, and the rapport was genuine rather than an artifact of the *interviewer as technician* (Nunkoosing, 2005, p. 701). Second, in relation to truth, the growth of familiarity between the researcher and the participants over time meant that any "deception" would have been harder to sustain. The defensiveness that may have been felt at first by some participants surely faded away as they formed a relationship with Anne and Helen. And the accounts were authenticated when Anne was able to return to the participants to sensitively probe their narratives. At no point did Anne feel that her research participants presented themselves in an exaggerated or favored light. Her understanding deepened as ongoing relationships with participants opened up aspects of their very private lives, thoughts, and fears. Third, with regard to "informed" consent, Phase 1 involved a research method that ceded control of disclosure to the participants. The participants agreed to being interviewed at a later date, and by then they had acquired a sophisticated knowledge of the consequences of consenting. Thus, their consent was informed in a more meaningful way than it might have been in a one-off research encounter. Some of Anne's long-term participants have acknowledged that it is their belief in the project, based on evidence of its beneficial outcomes and impact on policy and practice, that has bound them to the research and resulted in their ongoing willingness to participate.

While we argue that the longevity of Anne's research program is one of its strengths, it would be a mistake to assume that the early narrative data (Phase 1) were in any sense less rich and informative than what followed. Rather, it was the high quality of the original data that led to high-quality outputs and encouraged the further development of the research. Johnson (2002) suggests that exhaustion can set in, and enthusiasm wane, as a project progresses; that is, researchers can experience "interview fatigue" as interviews lead to more of the same type of data and a saturation point is reached (Glaser & Strauss, 1967). However, in this case study, while theoretical saturation of the data was achieved in each phase, freshness was retained by the new questions posed at each turn. Despite the extraordinary length of the research program, and Anne's lone-scholar status in the field (Johnson, 2002), ongoing originality has been its hallmark, with intellectual and social support along the way being provided by the charitable trust and academic colleagues. In addition, the embeddedness and longevity of the program acted as a way to establish the research within what Johnson calls an interpretive community—in this case of families and professionals.

The trust that was built up during the course of the research program was based for the most part not on extended interaction with participants, as might be the case with an anthropological or ethnographic study, but rather by the reputation of the study's previous outputs. Thus, while Douglas (1985) and others argue that only by extended interactions with a participant can *deep disclosure* be achieved, this has not been Anne's experience. Rather, rapport was achieved by disclosure of a personal connection and commitment, and trust was established through the reputation of the project and the endorsement of its credentials by trusted health and social care professionals.

Central to both the longevity of the research and the achievement of trust, rapport, and credibility was

Helen; her own son's death was the starting point of the research program and its lasting rationale. Helen did not act as a "gatekeeper"; rather she acted as a "gateway." She was an enabling actor whose constant presence and endorsement helped establish trust and rapport, which might have been more difficult to achieve had a true member of the community not been the conduit for much of the recruitment of and continuing connection with the participants. It is perhaps relevant that Christmas cards are sent to Helen rather than to Anne, though Anne's well-being and progress with the project are always inquired about.

With regard to claims about the "truth" of the interview data in the case study, it has to be acknowledged that there were some interviews in which it was possible to discern differences between participants' accounts. In the main, these discrepancies were manifested in differences in interpretation between the patients' and families' accounts and the professionals' versions of the same events and issues. This does not mean that either cohort was "untruthful"; rather, as Johnson (2002) acknowledges, all interpretations are subject to conflict and dispute and depend on whose criteria of "truth" prevails. It was best to treat any discrepancies as findings in themselves, and it was often found that these tended to indicate a failure of communication between professionals and patients and their families. Nevertheless, to publish such conflicting data and maintain the respect of the entire "interpretive community" required diplomacy and skill in the presentation of the material.

This raises issues about the analysis of interview data. As noted, Anne undertook cross-sectional thematic analyses of her interview data, but narrative analysis was also an option available to her given the semistructured nature of the interviews and the quantity of data captured in each interview. Whether interviews with individuals are singular or multiple, both methods of data analysis are suitable, as long as attention is paid to the type of data to be generated. However, in sociology, the analysis of *illness narratives* has generated a great deal of disagreement and debate—recently reviewed by Carol (Thomas, 2010). The implications of the debate extend to research using narrative methods on *any* topic. Clearly, in planning research designs and in decision making about whether to undertake repeat interviews, researchers need to give careful consideration to methods of analysis as well as to the methods of data collection. But that is another story . . .

◆ References

Adler, P. A. (1993). *Wheeling and dealing: And ethnography of an upper-level drug dealing and smuggling community.* New York, NY: Columbia University Press.

Adler, P. A., & Adler, P. (1987). *Membership roles in field research* (Qualitative Research Methods Series, No. 6). Newbury Park, CA: Sage.

Adler, P. A., & Adler, P. (2004). *Paradise laborers: Hotel work in the global economy.* Ithaca, NY: Cornell University Press.

Black, J. A., & Champion, D. J. (1976). *Methods and issues in social research.* New York, NY: Wiley.

Bulmer, M. (2008). The ethics of social research. In N. Gilbert (Ed.), *Researching social life* (3rd ed., pp. 145–161). London, England: Sage.

Charmaz, K. (1991). *Good days, bad days: The self in chronic illness and time.* New Brunswick, NJ: Rutgers University Press.

Cornwell, J. (1984). *Hard-earned lives: Accounts of health and illness from East London.* London, England: Tavistock.

Darlington, Y., & Scott, D. (2002) *Qualitative research in practice: Stories from the field.* Buckingham, England: Open University Press.

Douglas, J. (1985). *Creative interviewing.* Beverley Hills, CA: Sage.

Earthy, S., & Cronin, A. (2008). Narrative analysis. In N. Gilbert (Ed.), *Researching social life* (3rd ed., pp. 420–439). London, England: Sage.

Emerson, R. M., & Pollner, M. (1988). On the uses of members' responses to researchers' accounts. *Human Organization, 47*(3), 189–198.

Emerson, R. M., & Pollner, M. (2002). Difference and dialogue: Members' readings of ethnographic texts. In D. Weinberg (Ed.), *Qualitative research methods* (pp. 154–170). Oxford, England: Wiley-Blackwell.

Glaser, B. G., & Strauss, A. L. (1967). *The discovery of grounded theory.* Chicago, IL: Aldine Press.

Goudy, W. J., & Potter, H. R. (1975). Interview rapport: Demise of a concept. *Public Opinion Quarterly, 39,* 529–543. Retrieved from http://poq.oxfordjournals.org/cgi/reprint/39/4/529

Grinyer, A. (2002). *Cancer in young adults: Through parents' eyes.* Buckingham, England: Open University Press.

Grinyer, A. (2004). The narrative correspondence method: What a follow up study can tell us about the longer-term effect on participants in emotionally demanding research. *Qualitative Health Research, 14*(10), 1326–1341.

Grinyer, A. (2007). *Young people living with cancer: Implications for policy and practice.* Buckingham, England: Open University Press.

Grinyer, A. (2009a). Contrasting parental perspectives with those of teenagers and young adults with cancer: Comparing the findings from two qualitative studies. *European Journal of Oncology Nursing, 13,* 192–198.

Grinyer, A. (2009b). *Life after cancer in adolescence and young adulthood: Late effects and long term survivorship.* Oxford, England: Routledge.

Grinyer, A. (2012). *Palliative and end of life care for children and young people: Home, hospice, hospital.* Oxford, England: Wiley-Blackwell.

Grinyer, A., & Thomas, C. (2004). The importance of place of death in young adults with terminal cancer. *Mortality, 9*(2), 114–131.

Hollway, W., & Jefferson, T. (2000). *Doing qualitative research differently: Free association, narrative and the interview method.* London: Sage.

Holstein, J. A., & Gubrium, J. F. (1995). *The active interview* (Qualitative Research Methods Series, No. 37). Thousand Oaks, CA: Sage.

Johnson, J. M. (2002). In-depth interviewing. In J. F. Gubrium & J. A. Holstein (Eds.), *Handbook of interview research* (1st ed., pp. 103–120). Thousand Oaks, CA: Sage.

Miller, J., & Glassner, B. (2004). The "inside" and the "outside": Finding realities in interviews. In D. Silverman (Ed.), *Qualitative research: Theory, method and practice* (2nd ed., pp. 125–139). Thousand Oaks, CA: Sage.

Nunkoosing, K. (2005). The problems with interviews. *Qualitative Health Research, 15*(5), 698–706.

Robson, C. (1993). *Real world research.* Oxford, England: Blackwell.

Ruspini, E. (2000). Longitudinal research in the social sciences. *Social Research Update, 20.* Retrieved from http://sru.soc.surrey.ac.uk/SRU28.html

Skeggs, B. (1994). Situating the production of a feminist methodology. In M. Maynard & J. Purvis (Eds.), *Researching women's lives from a feminist perspective* (pp. 72–92). New York, NY: Taylor & Francis.

Thomas, C. (1998). Parents and family: Disabled women's stories about their childhood experiences. In C. Robertson & K. Stalker (Eds.), *Growing up with disability* (pp. 85–96). London, England: Jessica Kingsley.

Thomas, C. (1999a). *Female forms: Experiencing and understanding disability.* Buckingham, England: Open University Press.

Thomas, C. (1999b). Narrative identity and the disabled self. In M. Corker & S. French (Eds.), *Disability discourse* (pp. 47–55). Buckingham, England: Open University Press.

Thomas, C. (2010). Negotiating the contested terrain of narrative methods in illness contexts. *Sociology of Health & Illness, 32*(4), 647–660.

Warren, C. A. B. (1988). *Gender issues in field research* (Qualitative Research Methods Series, No. 9). Newbury Park, CA: Sage.

Warren, C. A. B., & Hackney, J. K. (2000). *Gender issues in ethnography* (Qualitative Research Methods Series, No. 9). Thousand Oaks, CA: Sage.

Whyte, W. F. (1981). *Street corner society: The social structure of an Italian slum* (3rd ed.). Chicago, IL: University of Chicago Press.

15

THE INTERVIEW QUESTION

♦ Jinjun Wang and Ying Yan

♦ About the Interview

According to the *Oxford English Dictionary*, the term *interview* originates from the French word *entre voir* (meaning "to be in sight of"), which refers to a face-to-face meeting. By the end of the 19th century and the rise of modern journalism, the term *interview* came to have a different and more current meaning. *Webster's Revised Unabridged Dictionary* in 1913 defined an interview as "a conversation, or questioning, for the purpose of eliciting information for publication" and of "recent use, originating in American newspapers, but apparently becoming general" (p. 781). Later on, many dictionaries, such as the *Macmillan English Dictionary for Advanced Learners* and the *Oxford Advanced Learner's English–Chinese Dictionary*, followed Webster's definition that "interview is a meeting in which someone asks another person, especially a famous person, questions about themselves, their work, or their ideas, in order to publish or broadcast the information" (*Macmillan English Dictionary for Advanced Learners*, 2003, p. 753). More specifically, Wikipedia (n.d.)

defines an interview as "a conversation between two or more people (the interviewer and the interviewee) where questions are asked by the interviewer to obtain information from the interviewee." According to their functions and methods, interviews can be classified as job interviews, case interviews, news interviews, telephone interviews, mall-intercept personal interviews, and so on.

From the above definitions, one can discern these common features of interviews:

1. An interview is a goal- or task-oriented talk to gather information, in which the interviewer and the interviewee have their respective roles to play.

2. The interviewer acts in the role of questioning and the interviewee in the role of answering.

3. The question–answer sequence is the predominant sequential structure in an interview.

4. The interviewer is empowered to ask questions, and the interviewee is confined to responding.

♦ 231

These features of the interview conform to the description of institutional dialogue by many scholars, such as Drew and Heritage (1992), who hold that institutional dialogue is goal oriented, involving constraints of different degrees and associated with an inferential framework under special institutional contexts. Similarly, Thornborrow (2002) identifies institutional dialogue as "talk which sets up positions for people to talk from and restricts some speakers' access to certain kinds of discursive actions" and also "a form of interaction in which the relationship between a participant's current institutional role and their current discursive role emerges as a local phenomenon which shapes the organization and trajectory of the talk" (pp. 4–5).

Institutional talk can be described as characteristically asymmetrical (Drew & Heritage, 1992). In fact, such asymmetry depends on unequal turn allocation between participants and unequal distribution of social power and status (Habermas, 1984). Therefore, institutional asymmetry implies both the asymmetry of the overall structural organization and the asymmetry of right and obligation or power and status. According to Wang (2006), "The institutional asymmetry of the overall structural organization often concerns the sequence organization and the turn-taking system. The most distinctive and dominant sequence in institutional dialogue is the questions/answer sequence when an interaction proceeds" (p. 540).

As questions constitute a crucial speech act in an interview, the definition and the classification of questions will be introduced in the following section.

◆ The Definition and Classification of the Question in English

For a long time, the concept of question or questioning has been of interest to many linguists and scholars. "Question" has been defined generally from syntactic, semantic, and structural-functional perspectives. The traditional syntactic research on questions focuses on the formal classification of questions. Jespersen (1933) divides questions into two categories in terms of word order: One is x-questions, and the other is nexus questions, which have a special interrogative word and intonation. For example, (1) Did Mary see it? is a nexus question that connects an object with a particular subject, and (2) What did

Mary see? is an x-question that inquires about the status of an unknown object. For Jespersen, nexus questions refer to Yes/No questions, and x-questions refer to "Wh-" questions (what, where, who, why, etc.). Most grammarians (see, e.g., Dixon, 1991; Morenberg, 1991) have adopted the dual division of questions by Jespersen (1933). However, some grammarians, such as Quirk, Greenbaum, Leech, and Svartvik (1985) and Biber, Johansson, Leech, Conrad, and Finegan (2000), insist on the three-type division of questions: Yes/No questions, Wh- questions, and alternative questions. Following their description, alternative questions are regarded as questions that present two or more possible answers and presuppose that only one is true, such as (3) Shall we go by bus or by train?

The structural-functional approach to understanding questions focuses on discourse structure and further explores the functions of questions in everyday talk and in institutional settings. For example, in Sinclair and Coulthard's (1975) model, the grammatical forms and functions of questions are considered in the context of classroom discourse. Questions are considered as eliciting a discourse act and at the same time are in possession of discourse functions. Accordingly, elicitation as an act that is expressed by questions can represent an initiating move in an exchange.

According to their analysis of a classroom encounter, the highest unit of classroom discourse, consisting of one or more than one transaction, is called a lesson. Transactions are made up of different exchanges, which are realized by moves and acts. A typical exchange in the classroom consists of an initiation by a teacher, followed by a response from a student, and then followed by feedback from the teacher. Moves and acts in discourse are similar to words and morphemes in grammar. Sinclair and Coulthard (1975) assume that there are three major acts—elicitation, informative, and directive—that occur in all forms of spoken discourse. Usually, there are three grammatical categories (interrogative, declarative, and imperative) and three situational categories (question, statement, and command) corresponding to the three major acts, as shown in Table 15.1.

Sinclair and Coulthard (1975) define elicitation as "an act, the function of which is to request a linguistic response—linguistic, although the response may be a non-verbal surrogate such as a nod or raised hand" (p. 28). Elicitation, as a discourse act to

Table 15.1 Grammatical Categories, Situational Categories, and Discourse Categories

Grammatical Categories	Situational Categories	Discourse Categories
Declarative	Statement	Informative
Interrogative	Question	Elicitation
Imperative	Command	Directive

Source: *Towards an Analysis of Discourse: The English Used by Teachers and Pupils* by J. McHardy Sinclair, M. Coulthard (1975), p. 29, Table. By permission of Oxford University Press.

describe any utterance, can be realized by a question, a situational category, which in turn is realized by its grammatical category—an interrogative. Thus, an interrogative as a grammatical category can realize the situational function of a question and the discourse function of initiation.

As this brief review indicates, a range of theoretical models have considered the linguistic structure and function of questions. For the purpose of this chapter, however, we will primarily rely on the two classifications of questions provided by grammarians: Yes/No questions and Wh- questions.

◆ Defining Power

Power has been investigated in a variety of disciplines, such as physics, technology, religion, politics, philosophy, linguistics, cultural studies, and so on. In this chapter, power is confined to the field of discourse. As Althusser (1971) argues, power operates through discourse by constructing particular subject positions for people to occupy. Similarly, Foucault (1980) regards the concept of power as a complex and continuously evolving web of social and discursive relations. Fairclough (1989) argues that "power in discourse is to do with powerful participants controlling and constraining the contributions of nonpowerful participants" (p. 46). Van Dijk (2001) holds that power accrues in verbal interaction and is determined by participants' institutional roles and their socioeconomic status, gender, or ethnic identity. For Watts (1991), the possession of power suggests that "s/he has the freedom of action to achieve the goals s/he has set her/himself, regardless of

whether or not this involves the potential to impose A's will on others to carry out actions that are in A's interests" (p. 60). Therefore, power can be characterized as the ability to control and constrain others, as the capacity to achieve one's aim, as the freedom to achieve one's goals, and as the competence to impose one's will on others.

The exercise of power, according to Lukes (1974), means that one affects or coerces another person in a manner contrary to that person's interest, and affecting or coercing another person may be done covertly or overtly. In institutional settings (e.g., courtroom cross-examination, news interviewing, a medical encounter, or classroom encounters), as there exists an asymmetrical conversational organization—namely, participants' unequal turn allocation, topic control, and asymmetrical distribution of social power and status—power can be easily detected, and the exercise of power tends to be overt. By contrast, it is more difficult to discern the differentiation of power between family members, intimate friends, and so on, as the exercise of power in these settings is covert, because in less formal settings power is always negotiable and is indeed frequently negotiated by the participants. For example, whereas a judge in a courtroom might explicitly remind the defendant of his or her authority, such overt claims of power would be regarded as unreasonable or downright taboo in intimate relations (e.g., in a marital relationship).

The research interview, a form of interviewing, has notably the features of institutional dialogue. As an increasingly popular type of interview, the research interview is used by governments in Western countries to describe and analyze peoples' actions and attitudes, and it is often conducted in person or by telephone. Among the different types of research interview, the survey interview is the most widely used and "is designed for gathering data with which to measure the intentions, actions, and attitudes of large numbers of people, usually representative samples of the populations being studied" (Hanneke, 2000, p. 1). In the context of survey interviews, the overt or covert exercise of power would thus depend on the degree to which social roles or interactional responsibilities are formalized and differentiated. For example, a traditional survey with closed-ended questions is founded on a very clear allocation of conversational authority, with the interviewer exclusively in charge of the questions and the respondents confined to a set of fixed answers. By contrast, in an in-depth interview the power dynamics are more subtle since the give-and-take, as it were, is less structured by the design.

In fact, although power is more easily scrutinized in institutional dialogue, there also exists a power struggle, as Fairclough (1989) points out: "Power relations are always relations of *struggle*. Social struggle occurs between groupings of various sorts—women and men, black and white, young and old, dominating and dominated groupings in social institutions, and so on" (p. 34). Discourse is the site of power struggle (Fairclough, 1989), and undoubtedly the power struggle is a universal phenomenon in all forms of verbal communication, including institutional dialogue and casual conversation.

◆ *Interview Questions and the Exercise of Power*

Questioning is the main linguistic device for an interviewer to control an interviewee's contribution to the conversation, which confines the interviewee to answering. Consequently, there is a great difference in the use of questions between interviewer and interviewee. According to Wang (2006), in an interview encounter, 96.1% of the questions are posed by the interviewer, compared with only 3.0% by the interviewee.

An interviewer has the right to ask questions to initiate an interview and has the privilege of terminating it. Through the interviewer's choice of questions, she or he selects the topic of the interview; the interviewer even has the prerogative to ask questions so deliberately designed that no new information is introduced (as in closed-ended surveys). An interviewee only has the right to ask questions with the interviewer's explicit permission. In the process of interviewing, interviewers essentially function as catalysts whose task is to provide a context in which interviewees can communicate information and opinion, and on occasion, depending on the research design, interviewers challenge or press interviewees to clarify their answers. Additionally, by limiting the interviewee's response or shifting the topic, interviewers exercise authority regarding the relevance or appropriateness of the matter under discussion.

In the remainder of the chapter, we illustrate these various features of questions and questioning using empirical examples.

INTERVIEW QUESTIONS CONTROLLING THE TURN-TAKING SYSTEM

Interview questions are unequally distributed as interviewers are endowed with the power to ask questions but interviewees are confined to doing so only if invited. Therefore, interview questions noticeably control the turn-taking system.

Harris (1951) defines "turn" as "a stretch of talk, by one person, before and after which there is silence on the part of that person" (p. 14). Goodwin (1981) defines turn as "a static unit with fixed boundaries and a time-bound process" (p. 41). Edmondson (1981) holds that "turn" refers to a chance for an interlocutor to talk during the conversation and the stretch of talk uttered by the interlocutor. Despite the subtle variations, these definitions seem to converge on a common point of interest; that is, a turn is the stretch of talk uttered by a speaker at one period of time during a conversation. In terms of the description by Schegloff and Sacks (1974), participants in a conversation always follow a turn-taking system. When a turn is transferred from one participant to another, there are two possibilities. The first is that the current speaker can select the next speaker by way of using vocatives, gaze, or posture or by asking the listener questions. The second possibility is that the next speaker may self-select. Within a turn-taking system, only one person speaks at a time, and the pattern of speaker change recurs.

However, this turn-taking model overlooks power and inequality in communicative contexts. In casual conversation, power and inequality are covert and not easy to scrutinize, while in institutional dialogue, power is more or less overt and is easier to scrutinize owing to the highly conventionalized structures and roles. In traditional research interviews (surveys, in particular), the interviewer dominates the position of asking questions, while the interviewee or respondent has to answer the questions or has very limited opportunity to ask questions. When the interviewer asks a question, she or he will acquire an opportunity to take a turn and, at the same time, she or he will assign a turn to the interviewee. When the interviewer asks successive questions or a number of questions, she or he will continuously control the turn-taking mechanism. Therefore, the interviewer will dominate the role of initiating and force the interviewee to act in the role of responding. Additionally, the interviewer not only initiates turns and controls the question–answer sequence but also restricts the other participants' opportunity to initiate. The interviewer's position as the initiator implies a higher status, whereas the interviewee's limited obligation to answer assigns him or her to a lower, subordinate status. To illustrate this point, let us consider the following excerpt from Bill O'Reilly's interview with the newly elected U.S. president Barack Obama:

O'Reilly: But I was worried there for awhile. It's been nine months since we last met in New Hampshire.

Obama: It took a little while. I've had a few things to do in between, but I appreciate you having me on the show.

O'Reilly: OK. Let's start with national security. Do you believe we're in the middle of a War on Terror?

Obama: Absolutely.

O'Reilly: Who's the enemy?

Obama: Al Qaeda, the Taliban, a whole host of networks that are bent on attacking America, who have a distorted ideology, who have perverted the faith of Islam, and so we have to go after them.

O'Reilly: Is Iran part of that component?

Obama: Iran is a major threat. Now, I don't think that there is a—the same—they are not part of the same network. You've got Shia, and you've got Sunni. We've got to have the ability to distinguish between these groups, because, for example, the war in Iraq is a good example, where I believe the administration lumped together Saddam Hussein, a terrible guy, with Al Qaeda, which had nothing to do with Saddam Hussein. (Fox News, 2008)

In this excerpt, the interviewer, O'Reilly, takes four turns, and three of them are questions. With the three questions, O'Reilly controls the turn-taking mechanism by initiating a turn and distributing a responding turn to President Obama. As O'Reilly dominates the role of asking questions, he not only holds the initiative but also forces President Obama to play the role of an interviewee. Although President Obama has a much higher social status than O'Reilly, President Obama is cast in the role of an interviewee in the institutional framework of journalistic interviewing.

Similarly, in a survey interview, an interviewer and an interviewee or a respondent have to play their fixed roles; that is, the interviewer asks a question, and sometimes presents the answering categories by reading from the questionnaire, and the respondent has to take the turn of answering. Finally, the interviewer acknowledges that the answer has been received and accepted. In the hierarchical relationship between the interviewer and the respondent, questions are predetermined by the interviewer before they are asked of the respondent. This question–answer–acceptance sequence is very typical of survey interviews. By way of asking questions, the interviewer controls the turn-taking mechanism; in particular, the interviewer's turn of accepting answers further strengthens his or her control over the respondent. Look at the following excerpt from a survey interview ("I" stands for the interviewer and "R" for the respondent):

1 I: how many people ((pause)) live in this house?

2 R: three.

3 I: three

4: Okay, ((continues)). (Schober & Conrad, 1997, p. 592)

The interviewer controls the conversation by asking a Wh- question, and the respondent has to take the turn of answering the question. What's more, the interviewer continues to dominate the conversation by repeating or confirming the respondent's answer, "Three." The interviewer's "Okay" can be regarded as the signal to end the present survey or start another round of questioning.

INTERVIEW QUESTIONS MANIPULATING TOPIC SHIFT

"Topic" is often considered as an intuitive notion. Presumably, participants in a conversation tend to have a "feel" for whether a speaker talks topically (Brown & Yule, 2000). Renkema (2004) holds the same idea, that "topic is usually defined as the 'aboutness' of a unit of a discourse." That is to say, "a topic is what a discourse, a discourse fragment or a sentence is about. It is the shortest summary of a discourse, the main proposition of a paragraph or what is commented on in a sentence" (p. 90).

What a speaker is talking about is inevitably based on how she or he structures what she or he is saying. When an interviewer asks a question, she or he restricts the topic of discussion to the extent that the addressee has to respond according to the question. The question–answer sequence sets up a horizon of meaning aimed at keeping the verbal exchange topically focused (Gubrium, 1993). Questions not only topicalize matters to which the interviewees should respond; the change in questions also manipulates the shift of topics.

As institutionalized dialogue, an interview can be seen as a goal-oriented practice whereby an interviewer asks a question to set up a sequence of talk with local relevance. According to Gubrium and Holstein (1998), interviewing produces narratives, which combine diverse human activities and happenings together. Moreover, narratives provide links, connections, coherence, and meaning. A typical way of maintaining narrative coherence is through the question–answer sequence. Usually, the interviewer's questions help the respondent talk topically. As the interviewer's questions set up a topical framework, the interviewee's contributions have to be confined to the existing topic framework under normal conditions. Therefore, the interviewer's questions and the interviewee's answers lead to conversational relevance and topical unity. In other words, the interviewer's questions and the ensuing sequential topics produce narrative coherence (Gubrium & Holstein) in a conversation and will ultimately constitute a conversational topic as a whole.

Topics in research interviewing, in particular, center on eliciting information for publication purposes. In this context, an interviewer's questions control both the whole structure of a dialogue and the relevance of local and global topics to be discussed. Through asking questions, the interviewer also controls the trajectory and the development of the topic of concern, introducing new subtopics or redirecting the old ones if necessary.

Therefore, a series of topics introduced by questions collectively constitute the larger global heading of the interview and help serve its larger institutional objectives. The following is an extract from the famous host Chris Wallace's interview of the former U.S. president Bill Clinton on September 24, 2006, on the television program *Fox News Sunday*.

Wallace: How do you rate, compare the powers of being in office as president and what you can do out of office as a former president?

Clinton: Well, when you are president, you can operate on a much broader scope. So, for example, you can simultaneously be trying to stop a genocide in Kosovo and, you know, make peace in the Middle East, pass a budget that gives millions of kids a chance to have after school programs and has a huge increase in college aid at home. In other words, you've got a lot of different moving parts, and you can move them all at once. But you're also more at the mercy of events. That is, President Bush did not run for president to deal with 9/11, but once it happened it wasn't as if he had an option. . . .

Wallace: So what is it that you can do as a former president?

Clinton: So what you can do as a former president is—you don't have the wide range of power, so you have to concentrate on fewer things. But you are less at the mercy of unfolding events. So if I say, look, we're going to work on the economic empowerment of poor people, on fighting AIDS and other diseases, on trying to bridge the religious and political differences between people, and on trying to, you know, avoid the worst calamities of climate change and help to revitalize the economy in the process, I can actually do that. I mean, because tomorrow when I get up, if there's a bad headline in the paper, it's President Bush's responsibility, not mine. That's the joy of being a former president. . . .

Wallace: When we announced that you were going to be on "Fox News Sunday," I got a lot of e-mail from viewers. And I've got to say, I was surprised. Most of them wanted me to ask you this question: Why didn't you do more to put bin Laden and Al Qaeda out of business when you were president? . . .

Clinton: OK, let's just go through that.

Wallace: Let me—let me—may I just finish the question, sir? And after the attack, the book says that bin Laden separated his leaders, spread them around, because he expected an attack, and there was no response. I understand that hindsight is always 20/20. . . .

Clinton: No, let's talk about it.

Wallace: . . . but the question is, why didn't you do more, connect the dots and put them out of business?

Clinton: OK, let's talk about it. Now, I will answer all those things on the merits, but first I want to talk about the context in which this arises. (Fox News, 2006)

The interviewer, Chris Wallace, takes five turns, and all the turns are realized by five questions. By way of questioning, Wallace firmly controls the turn taking, and he also sets up a specific topical domain and then controls the local and global topics. Wallace's first two questions are concerned with Clinton's present situation as a former president. However, his third question is much more challenging; it takes Clinton by surprise, and he replies, "OK, let's just go through that." However, Wallace continues with his topical interest by interjecting, "Let me—let me—" and then insisting, "May I just finish the question, sir?" In his fifth turn, Wallace still insists on his question: "Why didn't you do more, connect the dots and put them out of business?" Clinton has no other way out but to make a concession saying, "Let's talk about it."

This example illustrates the interviewer's control over the interviewee and the topic of discussion. It clearly demonstrates how an interviewer can manipulate topics and force interviewees to follow topics of his choosing.

What's worth mentioning is that it is hard to find such examples in empirical research interviews. Unlike the live televised or live news interview, in a research interview, the interviewer does not badger the respondent like Wallace did. Normally, the research interview follows the sequence of question–answer–acceptance. The third turn of the exchange is often the interviewer repeating or accepting the respondent's answers. The survey interview is, to some degree, pre-organized by the questionnaire. All interviewers have to ascertain whether or not the respondent's talk is an appropriate response to the question, and its appropriateness is dictated by

the response categories in the questionnaire. The interviewer's repetition of the respondent's answer gives the interview analyst the opportunity to learn what may be recorded as the answer. Interviewers sometimes transform a respondent's answer into an answer that better matches the precoded response options. Usually, interviewers rephrase questions, change the order of the questions, and probe in a leading manner, but they seldom badger the respondent or become aggressive toward the respondent. Look at the following survey on adult education:

1. I: how did you know about that course?
2. how did you learn about it?
3. R: u:h from a u:h so:cial uh worker with us.
4. I: social work.
5. R: yes.
6. I: so-ci-al wo:rk ((at dictation speed)). (Hanneke, 2000, p. 26)

In the extract of the survey interview, the interviewer asks the question twice. After the interviewer asks the first question, "How did you know about that course?" she asks the second question, "How did you learn about it?" for the sake of further explanation and the respondent's better understanding. Under such a topic framework, the respondent provides a nearly acceptable answer, "U:h from a u:h so:cial uh worker with us." Later, the interviewer makes a minor improvement, "Social work," which is further acknowledged by the respondent and then accepted and repeated by the interviewer. Consequently, the interviewer's questions help the respondent speak topically and relevantly and produce the narrative coherence.

As a matter of fact, as research interview manuscripts tend to be heavily edited before they are published, we really do not know to what extent such practices are carried across from the world of journalism to social research, but we can speculate that the basic rules of turn taking and control of topic apply.

INTERVIEW QUESTIONS LIMITING THE INTERVIEWEE'S RESPONSE

Yes/No questions and Wh- questions have their own ways of exercising power in interviewing. Yes/No questions, common in survey interviews, require affirmative or negative answers. They are often used to seek confirmation or denial from the respondent or addressee. In general, Yes/No questions are more constraining on an interviewee as they cannot be used to extend the scope of a conversation. The questioner, in using them, restricts the information that is introduced. In comparison, Wh- questions can set the parameters of response more broadly. A Wh-question expects a reply from an open range of replies. In other words, Wh- questions require the addressee to introduce new factual material in response to questions beginning with interrogative pronouns such as *which, where, who, when, why, how,* and so on. Accordingly, Wh- questions are also called information-seeking questions. In particular, *what, why,* and *how* questions are more open and can require more exposition than questions starting with the interrogatives *who, when,* and *where.*

In light of Wang's (2006) statistics, Yes/No questions constituted 56.1% and Wh- questions 43.9% of all news media questions from a sample of 42 news interviews collected in 13 volumes of *Newsweek,* of which 6 volumes are from May 1 to June 19, 2000, and 7 volumes from October 23 to December 18, 2000. Thus, it appears that in the world of news, Yes/No questions are more frequently used by interviewers than Wh- questions. (Given the prevalence of closed-ended surveys, one can assume that the same pattern holds in social science research.) This type of questioning is more prevalent in part because it affords the interviewer greater control over the content and flow of the topic. That is to say, interviewers tend to use Yes/No questions more frequently because they allow them to constrain interviewees' replies to a greater degree than Wh- questions.

The ability of an interviewer to control the content and the turn-taking system of a conversation through Yes/No questions is well illustrated by the following two examples:

Jeremy Paxman:	And you believe American intelligence?
Tony Blair:	Well I do actually believe this intelligence . . . (BBC News, 2003)
O'Reilly:	And he never said inflammatory stuff?
Obama:	He didn't say stuff like that, all right, so . . .

O'Reilly:	Did he say white people were bad?
Obama:	No. (Fox News, 2008)

In the exchange between Jeremy Paxman and the former British prime minister Tony Blair, Jeremy Paxman asks a question that presents a declarative ending with a question mark and a rising tone. Tony Blair responds with a very short, affirmative answer, "Well I do actually believe this intelligence." In the second exchange between O'Reilly and U.S. president Obama, O'Reilly asks two Yes/No questions, and President Obama provides two brief, negative answers. As seen in these examples, the rigid structure of Yes/No questions does not allow interviewees to contextualize or elaborate on their answer, but the brief answers nevertheless appear to be a verification of factual details. Similar to a police interrogation or courtroom testimony, the linguistic space for providing context-specific answers is all but eliminated through Yes/No questions.

By comparison, Wh- questions allow greater freedom for interviewees to elaborate on their replies. Particularly, it is much easier for interviewees to extend their answers when asked Wh- questions that start with *what, how,* and *why.* Consider the following extract, for example:

Wallace:	So what is the B.S.?
Clinton:	Well, every even-numbered year, right before an election, they come up with some security issue. In 2002, our party supported them in undertaking weapons inspections in Iraq and was 100 percent for what happened in Afghanistan, and they didn't have any way to make us look like we didn't care about terror. And so, they decided they would be for the homeland security bill that they had opposed. And they put a poison pill in it that we wouldn't pass, like taking the job rights away from 170,000 people, and then say that we were weak on terror if we weren't for it. They just ran that out. (Fox News, 2006)

Wallace asks a 5-word Wh- question starting with *what,* and Clinton takes the responding turn and provides a very detailed answer of 108 words. Note that Wh- questions essentially elevate the authority and voice of the respondent. They signal that the interviewee has specific expertise and knowledge on the topic and provide the conversational space for its expression.

Likewise, in survey interviews, open questions and closed-ended questions have their own roles to play. Open questions do not limit the response alternatives. Respondents are free to formulate their own answers. The interviewers have to repeat the answers. Comparatively, closed-ended questions, such as Yes/ No questions, constrain respondents' replies, permitting only "Yes" or "No" answers. Closed-ended survey questions present two or more response options from which the respondent is supposed to choose.

INTERVIEW QUESTIONS EMBODYING PRESUPPOSITIONS ABOUT THE MATTER UNDER DISCUSSION

According to Yule (2000) and Levinson (1983), presupposition is any kind of background assumption against which an expression or utterance makes sense or is rational. Presuppositions refer to the conditions that must be met for the intended meaning of a sentence to be regarded as acceptable. In other words, it is "something the speaker assumes to be the case prior to making an utterance" (Yule, 2000, p. 25).

Words or phrases can often be regarded as presupposition triggers as they can presuppose the truth of the information that is discussed. In addition, some sentence structures can also be considered as resources to generate presuppositions. These sentence structures are called structural presupposition triggers, as Yule (2000) holds that "certain sentence structures have been analyzed as conventionally and regularly presupposing that part of the structure is already assumed to be true" (p. 28). For example, the Wh- question construction in English is conventionally interpreted by presupposing the information that is embedded in the question and already known to be true: for example,

When did the dog bark at the window?

This Wh- question presupposes that the dog barked at the window, which helps listeners believe that the information provided is true instead of being given just for the sake of asking a question. See the following question:

Where have you met Lucy?

In this case, it is much easier for a listener to accept the presupposition that the person has already met Lucy as the question focuses on the location of the meeting rather than on whether the meeting has taken place. Therefore, the presupposition interpreted from the Wh- question is assumed to be true.

When an interviewer asks Wh- questions, she or he presupposes, or takes for granted, at least some aspects of the matter under discussion. Additionally, Wh- questions implicitly indicate the interviewer's attitudes, challenge the interviewee, or altogether express hostility toward the interviewee. To illustrate this point, let us return to our example of the Wallace interview with the former U.S. president Clinton:

Wallace: When we announced that you were going to be on "Fox News Sunday," I got a lot of e-mail from viewers. And I've got to say, I was surprised. Most of them wanted me to ask you this question: Why didn't you do more to put bin Laden and Al Qaeda out of business when you were president?

Wallace: . . . but the question is, why didn't you do more, connect the dots and put them out of business? (Fox News, 2006)

Wallace uses two consecutive *why* questions to express his attitude toward Clinton—namely, that "[Clinton] didn't do more to put bin Laden and Al Qaeda out of business when [he was] president." The two Wh- questions convey Wallace's dissatisfaction and criticize Clinton's previous (lack of) action against bin Laden and Al Qaeda.

Additionally, some rhetorical questions asked by interviewers have obvious presuppositions, and moreover, they often have "hostile question content" (Heritage, 2002, p. 1427) or can be "used as challenges" (Koshik, 2003, p. 51). According to Heritage (2002), negative interrogatives with frames such as "isn't," "don't," and "shouldn't" can produce assertions as these questions do not ask for information but express a position or point of view.

O'Reilly: So you're going to have to confront Putin.

Obama: That's exactly right.

O'Reilly: Maybe not militarily. Maybe you can do it other ways. But Europe is weak, and Europe is cowardly.

Obama: Right.

O'Reilly: You know, what are they going to have, another meeting? Yes, Putin's quaking, aren't they? Isn't Putin quaking about . . .

Obama: Well, you know, here's the one thing I've said.

O'Reilly: I know you're going to rally them all. They're going to be terror warriors, right . . . (Fox News, 2008)

In this extract, O'Reilly asked Obama a grammatically negative Yes/No question beginning with *isn't*. His question makes a noticeable presupposition to express his attitude clearly that Putin is "quaking."

In fact, Wh- questions or some rhetorical questions in interviews always contain discernible presuppositions and embody the noticeable attitudes and points of view of interviewers, even an interviewer's hostility toward the interviewee.

◆ Interview Questions and Power Dynamics

As expounded in the previous sections, interview questions are a major means for the interviewer to exercise power over the interviewee and control the turn-taking mechanism and topic shifts. Different types of interview questions exercise power over interviewees to different degrees.

Undoubtedly, questioning as a fixed formulation has been a powerful resource for interviewers. Thus, the asymmetry of social power and status is overt or noticeable in interviews; that is, interviewers are more powerful than interviewees or have control over interviewees.

However, it should be pointed out that power relations are dynamic rather than fixed. As Fairclough (1989) argues,

> Power is not a permanent and undisputed attribute of any one person or social grouping. On the contrary, those who hold power at a particular moment have to constantly reassert their power, and those who do not hold power are always liable to make a bid for power. (p. 68)

In other words, a power conflict does exist between the layperson and the professional and between the powerful and the less powerful. More specifically, in interviewing there is a power struggle between interviewer and interviewee.

Every participant in a verbal interaction has his or her own comparatively fixed social role. Hasan (1977) holds that social roles are often influenced by three dimensions of tenor, that is, status, contact, and affect. The transformation of status, contact, and affect will result in change in social relations. As status is concerned with education, wealth, information, age, sex, specific mental or physical abilities, and so on, in a social relationship people with a higher status always have a better opportunity to possess more power. When the transformation of the social status of the interviewer and the interviewee does occur, the degree of transformation will differ depending on the different factors that determine social status, and the power relation between interviewer and interviewee will change subtly. A veteran interviewer is more likely to exercise control over an interviewee than a new interviewer. Likewise, an interviewee with a higher status or social power is more likely to resist the interviewer's agenda and to hold the floor.

In empirical interviews, interviewees always adopt different ways to resist question formulation, such as avoiding a direct response to the question, hedging, confronting or challenging the interviewer, and even asking the interviewer questions.

Look at the following survey interview:

1. I: what is your civil status?

2. R: what do you mean?

3. I: are you single, or marr↑ied or living togeth↑er

4. R: oh.

5. R: no single. (Hanneke, 2000, p. 26)

The interviewer asks the first question concerning the civil status of the respondent. However, the interviewer does not get the expected answer. Instead, the interviewer is encountered by the interviewee's question, "What do you mean?" In the third turn, the interviewer makes a further explanation by posing an alternative question with three options. The interviewee does not choose any of the three alternatives but gives an indefinite response: "No single." This is an example of confrontation between the interviewer and the interviewee.

When an interviewee has a higher status, he or she is more likely to question the interviewing procedure. The following extract taken from BBC Radio 4's *Start the Week* is from an interview of the former

U.S. secretary of state Henry Kissinger by the veteran interviewer Jeremy Paxman:

Interviewer:	can we t'ba-turn to indo-China for which you (.) t-received the Nobel peace prize in 1973 that (.) deal did not bring peace to Indo-China m. hhh (.) was there any part of you felt a fraud in accepting it ↑
Kissinger:	(ye-) felt a what ↑
Interviewer:	a fraud in accepting the Nobel peace prize
Kissinger:	I wonder what you do when you do a uh (.) a hostile interview=
Interviewer:	= uh hu ((slight laugh)) I was merely trying to explore ↓
Kissinger:	em [yeah
Interviewer:	[this is Mr. Paxman being very kind↓]. (Thornborrow, 2002, p. 103)

At the initiating turn, Paxman asked Kissinger two rather hostile and embarrassing questions concerning whether Kissinger deserved the Nobel Peace Prize. However, Kissinger confronted Paxman with an affirmative sentence ending with a question mark: "Felt a what?" Not only did this question imply his resentment, but he also tried to exercise his power and authority as former U.S. Secretary of State. Shortly after getting the response from the interviewer, Kissinger challenged the interviewer with a sarcastic, embedded question: "I wonder what you do when you do a uh (.) a hostile interview=," which embarrassed the interviewer, and a with slight, ashamed laugh, he explained that "[he] was merely trying to explore."

These two examples indicate that when the interviewer exercises power over the interviewee, the interviewee has his or her own resources to challenge or resist the interviewer's agenda. Hence, there is a power struggle between the two parties. It can be safely concluded that power dynamics is a constant theme in all verbal communication.

◆ Conclusion

As a form of institutional dialogue, the interview highlights the conversational sequence of questions and answers between interviewers and interviewees. By asking questions of different types, the interviewer

not only controls the turn-taking mechanism and topic shifts but also exercises conversational power over what information is relevant and what attitudes or points of view are to be expressed. In a sense, the interview is an interesting stereotype of the power differences encoded in discourse, "a specialized, institutionally validated, variety of the interactions revolving around power differences which go on all the time in our society" (Kress & Fowler, 1979, p. 80).

Another interesting phenomenon is that interviewees with higher social status or political power (e.g., Clinton and Obama) are not immune from the struggle for power inherent in interview exchanges. Of course, cultural norms and variations also mediate the more micro-interactional dynamics of the interview. For example, many world dictators are rarely challenged, accused, or put on the defense, as it were, when giving interviews to their own domestic media outlets. By comparison, a sort of "gotcha" ("I got you!") style of media interviewing seems to characterize U.S. news interviews (perhaps this is best exemplified by the news program *60 Minutes* and its former hosts). Interestingly, in the field of research interviews, university research ethics committees have made a concerted effort to minimize any "abuses of power" by researchers, through the use of informed consent and preapproved interview scripts. Future research should examine to what extent these institutionalized ethical safeguards help resolve the power inequalities inherent in interview encounters.

◆ References

Althusser, L. (1971). Ideology and ideological state apparatus. In *Lenin and philosophy and other essays* (B. Brewster, Trans.). London, England: New Left Books.

BBC News. (2003, February). *Transcript of Blair's Iraq interview*. Retrieved from http://news.bbc.co.uk/2/hi/programmes/newsnight/2732979.stm

Biber, D., Johansson, S., Leech, G., Conrad, S., & Finegan, E. (2000). *Longman grammar of spoken and written English*. Beijing, People's Republic of China: Foreign Language Teaching and Research Press.

Brown, G., & Yule, G. (2000). *Discourse analysis*. Beijing, People's Republic of China: Foreign Language Teaching and Research Press.

Dixon, R. (1991). *A new approach to English grammar on semantic principles*. Oxford, England: Clarendon Press.

Drew, P., & Heritage, J. (Eds.). (1992). *Talk at work: Interaction in institutional setting*. Cambridge, England: Cambridge University Press.

Edmondson, W. (1981). *Spoken discourse: A model for analysis.* London, England: Longman.

Fairclough, N. (1989). *Language and power.* London, England: Longman.

Foucault, M. (1980). *Power/knowledge: Selected interviews and other writings 1972–1977* (C. Gordon, Trans.). Brighton, England: Harvester Press.

Fox News. (2006, September). *Transcript: William Jefferson Clinton on "Fox News Sunday."* Retrieved from http://www.foxnews.com/story/0,2933,215397,00.html

Fox News. (2008, September). *Part 1: Obama talks War on Terror, Iran and Pakistan in first-ever interview with O'Reilly.* Retrieved from http://www.foxnews.com/story/0,2933,417563,00.html?loomia_ow=t0:s0:a16:g12:r3:c0.816279:b25434102:z0

Goodwin, C. (1981). *Conversational organization: Interaction between speakers and hearers.* New York, NY: Academic Press.

Gubrium, J. (1993). *Speaking of life: Horizons of meaning for nursing home residents.* New Brunswick, NJ: Aldine Transaction.

Gubrium, J. F., & Holstein, J. A. (1998). Narrative practice and the coherence of personal stories. *Sociological Quarterly, 39*(1), 163–187.

Habermas, J. (1984). *Theory of communicative action: Vol. 1. Reason and the rationalization of society* (T. McCarthy, Trans.). London, England: Heinemann.

Hanneke, H.-S. (2000). *Interaction & the standardized survey interview: The living questionnaire.* Cambridge, England: Cambridge University Press.

Harris, Z. S. (1951). *Methods in structural linguistics.* Chicago, IL: University of Chicago Press.

Hasan, R. (1977). Text in the systemic-functional model. In W. Dressler (Ed.), *Current trends in text linguistics* (pp. 226–246). Berlin, Germany: Walter de Gruyter.

Heritage, J. (2002). The limits of questions: Negative interrogatives and hostile question content. *Journal of Pragmatics, 34,* 1427–1446.

Jespersen, O. (1933). *Essentials of English grammar.* London, England: Allen & Unwin.

Koshik, I. (2003). Wh-questions used as challenges. *Discourse & Society, 5*(1), 51–77.

Kress, G., & Fowler, R. (1979). Interviews. In R. Fowler, B. Hodge, G. Kress, & T. Trew (Eds.), *Language and control* (pp. 63–80). London, England: Routledge & Kegan Paul.

Levinson, S. C. (1983). *Pragmatics.* Cambridge, England: Cambridge University Press.

Lukes, S. (1974). *Power: A radical view.* London, England: Macmillan.

Macmillan English Dictionary for Advanced Learners. (2003). Interview (p. 753). Oxford, England: Macmillan Education.

Morenberg, M. (1991). *Doing grammar.* Oxford, England: Oxford University Press.

Quirk, R., Greenbaum, S., Leech, G., & Svartvik, J. (1985). *A comprehensive grammar of the English language.* London, England: Longman.

Renkema, J. (2004). *Introduction to discourse studies.* Amsterdam, The Netherlands: John Benjamins.

Schegloff, E. A., & Sacks, H. (1974). Opening up closings. In R. Turner (Ed.), *Ethnomethodology* (pp. 233–234). London, England: Penguin.

Schober, M. F., & Conrad, F. G. (1997). Does conversational interviewing reduce measurement error? *Public Opinion Quarterly, 61,* 576–602.

Sinclair, J. M., & Coulthard, M. (1975). *Towards an analysis of discourse.* Oxford, England: Oxford University Press.

Sinclair, J. M., & Coulthard, M. (1992). Towards an analysis of discourse. In M. Coulthard (Ed.), *Advances in spoken discourse analysis* (pp. 1–34). London, England: Routledge.

Thornborrow, J. (2002). *Power talk.* London, England: Pearson Education.

Van Dijk, T. A. (2001). Critical discourse analysis. In S. Deborah, D. Tannen, & H. E. Hamilton (Eds.), *The handbook of discourse analysis* (pp. 352–371). Oxford, England: Blackwell.

Wang, J. (2006). Questions and the exercise of power. *Discourse & Society, 17*(4), 529–548.

Watts, R. J. (1991). *Power in family discourse.* Berlin, Germany: Mouton de Gruyter.

Webster's Revised Unabridged Dictionary. (1913). Interview (p. 781). Springfield, MA: G. & C. Merriam.

Wikipedia. (n.d.). *Interview.* Retrieved from http://en.wikipedia.org/wiki/Interview

Yule, G. (2000). *Pragmatics.* Oxford, England: Oxford University Press.

16

INTERVIEW AND SAMPLING

How Many and Whom

◆ Ben K. Beitin

Sample size and composition in qualitative interviews have been discussed in the literature at great length, with assorted recommendations on the size and makeup of sample participants. Researchers have shifted from a clearly defined, predetermined number of participants to a focus on the research process as informing the ultimate number of participants. Focus on process is understanding sample size as fluid and emerging throughout a research design, from research questions to data analysis. This shift is not accepted by all qualitative researchers as there continues to be an identification of predetermined numbers of necessary participants (Guest, Bunce, & Johnson, 2006).

The makeup of participants in interviews has also been changing. Research originally focused on homogeneous samples of people who experienced a particular area of interest. Samples were generally white college students and soldiers in the post–World War II era (Taylor, 1998). This broadened to more diverse samples and recently to multiple perspectives as discussion began about the representativeness of college students and soldiers to general populations (Highhouse & Gillespie, 2009). This chapter will review the literature on sample size and multiple perspectives as well as who should be considered to participate in an interview.

◆ Sample Size

The early development of qualitative research followed quantitative research in that there were attempts to establish numerical requirements for the selection of participants. There were two challenges in this approach. The first was that qualitative theorists could not agree on an optimal sample size. Researchers have discussed a range of numbers for samples in phenomenological studies. Thomas and Pollio (2002) suggest that an appropriate sample size for phenomenological research can range from 6 to 12 participants—provided there is thematic redundancy after hearing the narratives of 6 participants. Creswell (1998) recommended between 5 and 25 participants, with another researcher (Boyd, 2001) prescribing a more flexible range of 2 to 10. These differences extend to other common qualitative approaches, such as grounded theory, and make it difficult for qualitative researchers to predetermine a sample size.

Theoretical saturation is becoming the most common approach to sample size. Guest et al. (2006) write, "Saturation has, in fact, become the gold standard by which purposive sample sizes are determined in health science research" (p. 60). The authors go on to point out that theoretical saturation is not without its own deficiencies. The main flaw is the lack of a common description of how saturation is reached. This shortcoming especially affects the advancement of qualitative methodology. Particularly, researchers with little qualitative experience and funding applicants who need to establish and justify their budgets are more likely to follow the quantifiable approach and identify sample sizes in their proposals (Cheek, 2000). Since grant funders continue to favor quantitative designs over qualitative designs (Morse, 2003), qualitative researchers are pressured to identify a preestablished sample size to navigate the politics of grant funding. With vague guidelines on the use of saturation, a priori sample sizes will remain a part of qualitative research and reinforce the mind-set that the quality and validity of qualitative research should be measured with quantitative criteria.

◆ *Sample Composition*

There are many possible configurations of people who can participate in research interviews, including individuals, couples, families, and groups. In addition, interviews can be conducted with people individually or in groups. Groups may be composed of people with different relationships to the topic of interest. It is also possible for researchers to conduct interviews with different configurations of people (Arksey, 1996). For example, a couple may be interviewed together and then individually or participants may be interviewed individually and then as part of a focus group. As discussed later in this section, each configuration carries certain

issues and challenges that must be addressed as part of the research process.

INDIVIDUAL INTERVIEWS

One choice is to interview individuals who have knowledge about the area of focus and can provide a perspective on it. Individual interviews are the most commonly used data collection strategy in qualitative research (Nunkoosing, 2005; Sandelowski, 2002). Although individual interviews contribute in-depth data, they must be considered in light of their benefits and limitations. As is the case with all interview formats, individual interviews must be connected to the purpose and research questions.

This approach is less susceptible to members holding back or altering information in the presence of another member for fear the information would negatively affect the relationship. On the other hand, individual interviews are more susceptible to participants withholding certain descriptions or alternatively embellishing them if the truth is inconsistent with their preferred self-image or if they wish to impress the interviewer (Fielding, 1994). Logistically, interviews with more than one person, such as with a couple or family, can be harder to arrange than interviews with an individual. Also, a family member may use the word *we* and attempt to speak for the family (Valentine, 1999). This may also happen with a dominant family member. An interviewer must be aware of this dynamic and determine whether to engage other members or focus on the vocal member. This decision is influenced by design and sample characteristics, such as research questions and culture. If research questions are focused on violence or an area that might pose a safety risk to participants, then the interviewer should not push other members to participate and should be more observant of the nonverbal interactional dynamics. Also, if a culture has clear rules about who speaks for a family and this member is dominating the interview, then the interviewer should respect this and continue with the dominant member while allowing for other members to contribute as they feel comfortable.

There are instances when a researcher is studying a topic in which he or she wishes to compare potentially conflicting accounts, such as work productivity. This could justify interviewing staff and administration separately. Safety and comfort of participants is an important factor in the decision to interview individuals. For example, in their study of couples with a history of violence, Jory, Anderson, and Greer (1997) discuss the need to interview partners separately in the interest of safety.

MULTIPLE-PERSON INTERVIEWS

Another option for researchers is to interview many individuals at once if the research questions are focused on relationships and interaction between people. This allows for people to interact around a question and create meaning or supplement each other's answers. This is particularly relevant when a researcher is interested in interactions between couples, families, or groups of people connected through relationships, such as at work or in neighborhoods. Interviews with people who share a relationship also reveal patterns of social interaction otherwise unseen in individual interviews (Allan, 1980).

However, it seems that many studies involving interviews with multiple participants fail to systematically and empirically analyze interactions between participants. For example, Allen, Armstrong, Riemenschneider, and Reid (2006) interviewed women in information technology positions in the same company and their supervisors to discuss barriers and turnover of women in the information technology field. Yet the authors did not report any of the interactions between the employees and supervisors in the groups. The results section was limited to quotes from individual employees.

Morgan (2010) has noted that discussion of interaction in interviews has been missing and "assertions about the importance of interaction in the analysis of focus groups have ignored the fundamental principle that the research goals should determine the analysis methods" (p. 719). The key idea is that research goals and questions should inform whom to involve in an interview and whether to focus more on the content or the process (Beitin, 2008).

Additionally, there is some debate in the field about participants altering their answers in the presence of others. In their interviews of adult children of alcoholics and their spouses, Bennett, Wolin, and McAvity (1988) found that couples were more forthcoming when interviewed together rather than separately. Yet Pahl and Pahl (1971) interviewed middle-class couples living in major cities in Britain about their experience of marriage and reported that they could sense their answers were influenced by the spouse's presence. Indeed, after one interview, a male respondent reported that his wife's presence helped shape the way he replied to questions. This could also occur in interviews of workers and those in authority over them, such as Allen et al.'s (2006) interviews of employees and their supervisors or of teachers and their principals.

Different ideas have emerged in the literature about how to handle data in which participants report disagreement on a topic. From a positivist viewpoint, one could analyze and report only the points of agreement, or if there is only one set of participants (e.g., one set of family members in a sample of 10 families) who disagree, they could be treated as an exception. A researcher can explore whether the format was responsible for producing different results or whether changes need to be made in the research design to accommodate the divergences in responses (Erzberger & Prein, 1997). For example, a researcher could interview family members in separate interviews to seek out the "truth."

From a postpositivist or constructivist framework, disagreement provides a rich source of information (Perlesz & Lindsay, 2003). Disagreement is examined in the context of participants, the worldview of the interviewer, and the relationships between family members and between the interviewer and the family. Beitin and Allen (2005) studied Arab American couples' experiences after September 11, 2001. One couple disagreed about the term *backlash*, which was being used by the researchers. The wife agreed that there was a backlash, but the husband did not. The disagreement was meaningful on many levels. The researchers had incorporated the word *backlash* into the study. After examining this disagreement, the researchers discovered the influence of the media on their view of the topic, since leading up to the study, *backlash* was a term used frequently in the media. The couple's context was also influential since the husband was interacting regularly in his community, which was predominantly European American, and as a result would be risking relationships if he alienated anyone. Also, in Arab culture, men are predominantly responsible for family stability, and acknowledging a backlash could heighten tension in his family. Since the wife was wearing a hijab, she was less able to "pass" off as part of her local community and reported more instances of discrimination than her husband. Together, there were multiple layers within the interviewer and the couple as well as in their relationships.

There are also issues of one member speaking disproportionately more than the others. Hertz (1995) warns of the dangers of a simplified account of experience resulting if one member is more talkative and dominates the conversation. This could also be evidence of a cover-up for other behaviors that the couple or family wishes to keep out of the interview. Finally, couple, family, and group interviews can be challenging in that there is more time required, generally, for responses since multiple people are participating.

INDIVIDUAL AND MULTIPLE-PERSON INTERVIEWS

A third format is the use of both individual and couple/family/group interviews. In this format, participants may be interviewed individually and then together with other members of their group, or in reverse order. This allows for each person to elaborate on his or her experiences in a more private setting with more time to expand on his or her answers. Then, the researcher can look at some preliminary themes and bring the group together to investigate these themes further or ask the group to process questions as a unit to see if new meaning arises through interaction.

Lambert and Loiselle (2008) explored the information-seeking behavior patterns of individuals diagnosed with breast, prostate, or colorectal cancer by interviewing participants individually and in groups. They found that

> the analysis of individual data showed how participants might have proceeded through the decision-making process (procedural description) and how this was related to cancer information-seeking. Focus group discussions did not emphasize the actual process of decision-making, but rather broad contextual factors that might have been involved (e.g., physicians' preferences for patient involvement). (p. 232)

This study demonstrates how individual and group interviews can complement each other and provide multiple levels of information through the interviewees' answers to the research questions. The group interaction also showed the value of multiple perspectives interacting. The following is one of the statements from a participant discussing his decision-making process:

> There are a lot of people giving you advice as well and people trying to compare themselves to you. And saying why are you getting chemo . . . how long is your radiation treatment is it 30 seconds, is it 45, and I thought, I don't know how long is my treatment nobody told me how long it was. I only know that I'm going through it, like I'm not you know that precise. I assume the doctor knows what they are doing. (Lambert & Loiselle, 2008, p. 233)

This statement in isolation might make a reader believe that cancer patients have a lot of trust in the process and the doctors. Here is a second participant responding to the previous member's view:

Second Participant:	That's quite interesting because I asked how long the [radiation treatment takes; everybody laughing] and I know that I got 43 seconds from one angle and 44 seconds from another. I don't know if its . . .
First Participant (Interrupting):	What's the difference?
Second Participant:	I wanted to know. It's a total of one minute and a half. It's just different coping strategies. (Lambert & Loiselle, 2008, p. 233)

With this added interaction, a reader is able to see the difference between decision making and coping. Also, participants are able to react to different points of view.

Additionally, individual interviews can be a valuable way to follow up on the responses given in group interviews, particularly when the follow-up information is potentially damaging or just too embarrassing to air in the presence of others. Jones and Bugge's (2006) study of patient participation in the health care process illustrates the importance of this observation. In the following excerpt, a nurse describes her approach to doing intakes involving sensitive topics (e.g., sexually transmitted diseases):

> Just say a girl came and she has lower abdominal pain and breakthrough bleeding. Well, I'm

think[ing] Chlamydia—but this is like a new partner or something she's with. Normally I would say, if she was on her own, have you had unprotected sex with several partners and they would normally go "Yes," you know, "I've had ten." But you don't really want to ask that kind of question when the new boyfriend or the husband's sitting in there because that's confidential between us. (p. 614)

The researchers then record the following interview between this nurse (N) and a patient (P):

N: I don't know if you have ever heard of implanan

P: (silence)

N: it's a

P: Mmm. Oh yes

N: A rod

P: I have. Yeah.

N: Yes and you

P: (Silence)

N: It's got zero percent failure rate at the moment. Nobody has become pregnant using this and lots of the

P: Uh huh

N: Students are finding it quite useful.

P: (Silence) Okay (Silence)

N: Em, so its an option. (Jones & Bugge, 2006, p. 614)

Relying on a conversation analysis framework, Jones and Bugge (2006) speculated that the long silences in the above excerpt indicated reluctance or disagreement. To test this assumption, the authors used individual interviewing to better understand the patient's own perception of the interview and silence. The patient reported the following:

She [the nurse] was telling me about that rods that they put in the arm and she told me there was so far a 0% failure rate. Well, one of my pals is now pregnant with it and I didn't want to tell her that [because] I just felt that it wasn't my place to go around telling—that's my friend's choice. . . . And I just feel that it's her decision and how she wants

to tackle it, because so far they've had a 0% failure chance but now they've not. (p. 615)

Collectively, the three interviews present a more complete picture of patients' participation in their health care than each interview alone. The nurse has a viewpoint of patients as difficult to elicit information from. The interaction suggests as much, but on interviewing the patient, it is evident that the patient has information that could challenge the authority.

Lambert and Loiselle (2008) conducted a literature review of all studies that combined individual interviews with group interviews. They found that researchers conducted interviews with multiple groupings, but it was not always for enhancing the data. Many times it was for logistical reasons or for comparing responses and was not often used to build a more coherent narrative.

◆ Interaction Among Participants

Researchers generally recognize interviews as social interaction (Holstein & Gubrium, 1995). Interviews allow people to give meaning to constructs and phenomena through language and interaction. Postmodern theorists see knowledge as socially constructed between people through language (McNamee & Gergen, 1992). Social constructionists argue that as soon as we attempt to describe an individual, we automatically enter into discourse and social interchange (Gergen, 1994). Therefore, individuals may give different meaning to objects, events, or situations that occur between themselves and their outside world. The experience of the nurse mentioned earlier was that gathering information from patients is difficult. The perspective is valuable but could be limited if we did not also know the perspective of the patient and the interaction between the two. Interviews with a whole family or multiple members allow researchers to analyze the interactional processes through which meanings and perspectives emerge.

There are situations that are better addressed by individual interviews, such as when a researcher believes that the research questions focus on individual experiences, when there are safety issues, or when there are time and budget limitations. Safety issues can arise in interviews focused on topics that could bring harm to one or many participants, such as violence or discussion of workplace administrators (Jory et al., 1997). When the research purpose and questions become more strongly influenced by multiple viewpoints or when the topic under analysis is intrinsically based on interaction, interviews with multiple people allow for intricate and rich description.

For example, interviewing couples, families, or groups allows for an understanding of how relationships develop or change. Many relational processes are formed over time through interaction and communication. For example, a group of company employees may have developed a break or lunch routine that helps reduce stress. The routine by itself is telling, but the story of how the workers developed the ritual and how it can be used to protect them against future uncertainties (e.g., layoffs) also is meaningful for interviewers.

In this context, one should also consider the role of the researcher in the process of interviewing multiple respondents (Echevarria-Doan & Tubbs, 2005). Each interview is different and in some ways reflects the personalities of both the interviewer and the interviewees (Seidman, 1998). The meaning derived from interviews can differ depending on one's epistemological framework (e.g., a critical/feminist standpoint is more likely to consider the researcher's values and perspectives in the research than a positivistic paradigm of science). Researcher values and bias are also evident in leading participants with particular questions and prompts. Rennie (2000) cites the example of a colleague who discards interview transcripts if he judges them to be too actively shaped by the researcher's questions and prompts.

The interview also can be affected by the structure and process of the group. An enmeshed family may need more guidance on turn taking in the interview process, whereas a more rigid family may have clearly delineated roles for who talks when. An interviewer may have to block an interruption so that a member can finish his or her thoughts. There may also be times when quiet members may have to be drawn out or members may start talking about their own perceptions of a topic or issue and the researcher has to decide how long this is going to be productive for the research and when it is overly focused on the individual respondent's experience. For example, in a group interview with employees about their experiences of mourning while at work the death of a coworker, if a member begins discussing how he or she dealt with the grief outside the workplace, the

interviewer would have to decide if this is relevant or is simply taking time away from the group response.

The researcher also influences the process through his or her choice of questions and the related decisions inherent in the interview, such as asking a question of one member rather than another. Also, trust or rapport, considered an important factor in all interviews, becomes especially crucial in interviews with multiple people. For example, Eggenberger and Nelms (2007) suggest becoming part of the environment from where families will be recruited rather than using flyers or other less personal methods to recruit respondents. For example, face-to-face contact is more engaging than flyers, so a researcher may choose to spend time at the recruiting location introducing himself or herself and explaining the study. A researcher may recruit more participants if he or she spends time at the location learning about the location and the area around it before introducing the study. Astedt-Kurki, Hopia, and Vuori (1999) interviewed family units twice in an effort to build rapport and found that in their second round of interviews, the families were more likely to confide in the interviewer.

◆ Multiple Perspectives

Quantitative and qualitative researchers seek representativeness yet have different understandings of how many and who constitute representativeness. Quantitative researchers are in search of large, random samples that are representative of a larger population and can be generalized. Qualitative researchers are more interested in a small number of participants who represent the phenomena of interest. Participants or informants are purposively selected to represent rich knowledge about the research questions.

Among qualitative researchers, triangulation is frequently used to strengthen research through the combining of multiple methods, measures, researchers, theories, and perspectives. Denzin (1978) identified four types of triangulation: (1) data triangulation, the use of a variety of data sources; (2) investigator triangulation, the use of multiple researchers; (3) theory triangulation, using multiple perspectives to interpret a data set; and (4) methodological triangulation, using multiple research methods to study one problem. This section will focus on data triangulation through the use of multiple perspectives on the phenomenon of interest.

Most discussions of interviews in qualitative research have focused on how many participants are enough and when saturation has been reached. Recently, researchers have considered the question "How can a sample include as many perspectives as possible on a topic?" The most common way to address this question is by relying on multiple roles. Asking who can provide a different perspective on a topic by nature of their role can be just as important as asking how many people are needed to answer the question.

Mishna (2004) investigated children's experiences of victimization by bullying, comparing the children's perspectives with those of their parents and educators and exploring the child–adult interactions related to peer victimization. She interviewed five children, five of their parents, three teachers, one vice principal, and one principal. The use of multiple people who were involved with the bullying helped researchers provide a nuanced understanding of the problem. If the children had been interviewed alone, the likely outcome would have been a clear definition of bullying as behaviors that range from nonphysical acts such as teasing to physical ones such as assault. But with the inclusion of parents, teachers, and administrators, the question of bullying became more complex as many of these adults did not consider certain nonphysical incidents as bullying whereas the children did. This was further complicated when the bully was a child's friend. Child respondents were less likely to view behavior as bullying if it was inflicted by a friend. Likewise, parents were not always clear on how to view or handle bullying behavior from their child's friend.

Examples of multiple-perspective interviewing can be gleaned from a wide range of disciplines. Lawrence, Murray, Ffytche, and Banerjee (2009) were interested in the experiences and needs of older adults with dementia and visual impairment. They interviewed adults struggling with these medical issues as well as their caregivers and various health care professionals involved in their care, such as nurses, activity coordinators, and occupational therapists. In the same way, Hiatt, Stelle, Muslow, and Scott (2007) used qualitative interviews with multiple stakeholders to conduct a program evaluation of hospice care. They interviewed patients, their family members, bereaved family members, volunteers at the hospice, staff, and community members such as funeral directors and pastors.

However, variations in social roles do not necessarily correspond with variations in perspective. It is, for example, possible that the diverse members of a social setting share a common perspective, discourse, or narrative. For example, teachers, students, parents, and so on might voice in their interviews a common institutional culture about formal education being a stepping stone to a better future. Similarly, people from different cultural or ethnic groups might share a common vision of a social problem (e.g., fear of crime). Variations in social roles do offer the opportunity for a diverse range of meaning. In their social roles, each person can bring a different relationship to the topic, and through the interaction of a group interview, the participants can build a broad narrative that consists of similarities as well as differences in their relationship to the topic.

◆ Multiple Selves

In addition to multiple people, there are also multiple selves within each person. Holstein and Gubrium (1995) refer to a person's various identities as footings, or the multiple roles and perspectives people act out in their life that can influence their responses in interviews. A participant can tell his or her story from one footing or shift between footings. The answers given depend on the roles accessed by participants. For example, a person might take on the role of a parent, romantic partner, employee, and son or daughter. If asked about the impact of a traumatic event on one's self, one may answer from any or all of these roles depending on what is salient at the moment. It is likely that all of a person's roles were affected, and to ask for the perspective of just one is narrowing their experience. Shifts in perspective are encouraged by an interviewer because of the recognition that roles are boundary-less and cannot be isolated from one another.

It is not always the case that people present narrative perspectives that are coherent with their internal selves. Furthermore, a person may not present the same perspective in two different contexts. A person chooses a perspective to present based on who is listening and the culture around them. The influence of the people around a person implies that narratives are relational and interactional. Perspective can be influenced by the relationship with the interviewer as well as if the interview is with one's spouse or supervisor.

An interviewer can influence footings based on how and what questions are asked. If a question is left open-ended, the interviewee is left to decide which footing to take on in his or her answer. The interviewer can also ask a person to answer from the perspective of a certain footing. For example, Sands and Roer-Strier (2006) interviewed mothers and daughters coping with a daughter's religious intensification. The interviewer asked a specific question suggesting that the daughter take on the perspective of a daughter:

Interviewer: Can you just tell me about the role your mother played at the time of the birth of your children?

Daughter: The devoted grandmother. No, she was there to help. We were all, you see, basically it wasn't only, only my mother. It was my sisters as well. We were all . . . there to help. (p. 245)

In either case, a respondent needs flexibility to answer from the footings that help him or her develop a narrative.

A respondent will also use narrative linkages as a way of building coherence and context for stories (Holstein & Gubrium, 1995). Linkage is connecting a story to past and future experiences as a way of providing a perspective for experiences. Interviewers encourage linking to understand how people make meaning of their narratives. This is the "how" of the interview process—discovering how participants construct meaning.

This quote from a Palestinian woman illustrates both footing and linkage. She discusses her experience of September 11, 2001:

This is very tough for me. I felt like I was dreaming that day. I worried about the fact my children were far away. What if we never saw them again? I was away from my husband. I worried what if something happened to him and I wouldn't be there to say goodbye. I was traveling (on September 11th) and I wanted to be home. Obviously I wasn't that productive that day. The very next day I wanted to find a way home. No planes were flying and no cars were for rent. It took me 76 hours to get home on a train. I think what happened to me at that time and I don't know if it was denial but somehow it was far away from me. I remembered wars before.

I started remembering the '67 war in the Middle East, when I was in elementary school and I was the only non Jew. I remember I was on my cell phone on the bus to get the train and my husband said to me be careful what you are saying because people may be listening. (Beitin, 2003, p. 50)

Her footing shifted as she spoke as a mother and then a wife. The effects of the trauma of September 11, 2001, affected her footings as a mother and a wife. Her experience of September 11, 2001, was linked to living through the 1967 war between Israel and Egypt, Jordan, and Syria. She experienced September 11, 2001, with a similar feeling of panic to get to her family.

◆ Analysis Issues

When interviewing multiple people, there are certain analysis issues that must be considered. Above all else, one's theoretical framework must guide the analysis and decisions, whether it is grounded theory, phenomenology, ethnography, or another approach. Statements must be evaluated in terms of not only the research questions and framework but also whether they are capturing the experience of the whole or focusing on one member's experience. Also, does a member's experience contribute to the understanding of the whole or mainly of that individual?

A major issue commonly faced in coding is dissonant data between members. Members may disagree in group interviews or may give responses in individual interviews that contradict their group responses or another member's responses. This is particularly relevant in couple interviews. Mansfield and Collard (1988) wrote about their experience of dissonance when interviewing spouses:

The identical issue may be described by each spouse so differently that it can appear to the interviewer that each is referring to a completely different issue. This highlights the paradox we so often found that it can appear as if there are two different relationships cohabiting in the one marriage. (p. 39)

When responses are similar between members, a coherent narrative is easier to build. Responses can be fit together to create rich themes that are supported by multiple views of a phenomenon. Convergent data can indicate either a shared social reality or an environment where members feel social pressure to present a facade of conformity.

Challenges arise when responses diverge. McCarthy, Holland, and Gillies (2003) discuss the many possible options for dealing with dissonant data. The decision is informed by the researcher's worldview. A realist, objective worldview will lead one to seek ways to determine which viewpoint is more likely or true. This may be done by examining the responses and making a judgment about the response that is the most likely to be true. A researcher may go with the numerically higher response as representing the norm or the "valid" response. Another possibility is to look at the dissonant data in the context of other answers and choose the response that seems to fit the other data. A researcher with an interpretationist, postmodern worldview would be less interested in a single truth and more interested in multiple versions of reality, with no single view valued more than the others.

Alternatively, when faced with contradictory accounts, a researcher may choose to look at the context rather than the content per se. For example, a company employee may be seen as hard to work with by his employer, while the employee may see his boss as restrictive and limiting his productivity. An objectivist may examine the work output of the employee as well as others in his or her position as an added factor to see whose truth is more accurate. An interpretationist may look at the work context and discover that the employer strongly believes in strict mentorship while the employee wants more independence, and this conflict in perspectives is the source of the lower productivity.

◆ Recommendations

Research questions and previous literature can be a starting point in determining whom to interview. A researcher must consider the interactional nature of the questions, recommendations of previous studies, and who can provide a perspective on the topic. The area of focus may be more individually oriented or can be viewed as interactional. Settings for interaction can be subdivided into large units, such as corporations, or smaller units, such as couples.

A researcher must also consider the time and resources needed to conduct interviews with both individual members and the couple/family/group together. It requires considerable coordination and motivation to schedule interviews with large groups. There are also space and privacy issues. Risk must be assessed for each member of a group and whether a member of a connected group will answer openly in front of other members.

In particular, the decision of whom to interview should be guided by the aims of the study. If the purpose of the study is to examine social realities that are constructed through the interaction, the researcher is encouraged to consider a mixture of individual and couple, family, or group interviews or group interviews alone. Of course, such an approach requires that researchers attend to who is speaking in the interview or whose voice is being articulated (see Holstein & Gubrium's [1995] *Active Interview*). For example, if family members are interviewed individually, the interviewer might have to discern if a participant is speaking from the position of "we" or "I." Depending on the theoretical paradigm adopted by the interviewer, he or she might wish to distinguish one perspective from another, attributing its ownership to one respondent versus another. For example, the perspective of a wife might be treated as being separate from that of other family members.

Conducting a mixture of individual and couple/family/group interviews may offer the best of both worlds for researchers as it allows for the comparison of individual perspectives with jointly constructed meanings and accounts. Of course, this approach represents its own challenges. For example, a researcher has to make sense of possible discrepancies between the two sets of interviews. More important, should such inconsistencies be treated as "contradictions" or meaningful responses that differ because of their grounding in each person's context?

Interview questions should help guide an interviewer but not so rigidly that an interviewee is not able to shift footings and perspectives. Interviewers should encourage participants to discuss how they constructed their narrative.

Ultimately, it remains important that researchers be transparent and vigorous during every step of the research design and reporting as they look at the implications of the decisions in sampling. Researchers should publish their decisions and rationale for how their sample and sample configuration could give the most comprehensive data to answer the research questions. If multiple people were interviewed, a researcher can ask himself or herself if the chosen quotes capture the interaction that carries much of the meaning or whether more voices can be included in a quote. Transparency is necessary in how disagreement, narrative footing, and narrative linking are handled. Finally, researchers further enrich the data by describing their own influence on the interactions as well as their observations of nonverbal interactions.

◆ *References*

Allan, G. (1980). A note on interviewing spouses together. *Journal of Marriage and the Family, 42*, 205–210.

Allen, M. W., Armstrong, D. J., Riemenschneider, C. K., & Reid, M. F. (2006). Making sense of the barriers women face in the information technology work force: Standpoint theory, self-disclosure, and causal maps. *Sex Roles, 54*, 831–844.

Arksey, H. (1996). Collecting data through joint interviews. *Social Research Update, 15*, 1–4.

Astedt-Kurki, P., Hopia, H., & Vuori, A. (1999). Family health in everyday life: A qualitative study on well-being in families with children. *Journal of Advanced Nursing, 29*, 704–711.

Beitin, B. K. (2003). *Resilience in Arab American couples in the wake of the terrorist attacks on New York City: A family systems perspective* (Unpublished doctoral dissertation). Virginia Polytechnic Institute and State University, Blacksburg, VA.

Beitin, B. K. (2008). Qualitative research in marriage and family therapy: Who is in the interview? *Contemporary Family Therapy, 30*, 48–58.

Beitin, B. K., & Allen, K. (2005). Resilience in Arab–American couples after September 11, 2001: A systems perspective. *Journal of Marital & Family Therapy, 31*, 251–268.

Bennett, L. A., Wolin, S. J., & McAvity, K. J. (1988). Family identity, ritual, and myth: A cultural perspective on life cycle transition. In C. J. Falicov (Ed.), *Family transitions: Continuity and change over the life cycle* (pp. 211–234). New York, NY: Guilford Press.

Boyd, C. O. (2001). Philosophical foundations of qualitative research. In P. L. Munhall (Ed.), *Nursing research: A qualitative perspective* (3rd ed., pp. 65–89). Sudbury, MA: Jones & Bartlett.

Cheek, J. (2000). An untold story? Doing funded qualitative research. In N. K. Denzin & Y. S. Lincoln (Eds.), *Handbook of qualitative research* (2nd ed., pp. 401–420). Thousand Oaks, CA: Sage.

Creswell, J. W. (1998). *Qualitative inquiry and research design: Choosing among five traditions.* Thousand Oaks, CA: Sage.

Denzin, N. K. (1978). *The research act: A theoretical introduction to sociological methods.* New York, NY: McGraw-Hill.

Echevarria-Doan, S., & Tubbs, C. Y. (2005). Let's get grounded: Family therapy research and grounded theory. In D. H. Sprenkle & F. P. Piercy (Eds.), *Research methods in family therapy* (2nd ed., pp. 41–62). New York, NY: Guilford Press.

Eggenberger, S. K., & Nelms, T. P. (2007). Family interviews as a method for family research. *Journal of Advanced Nursing, 58*, 282–292.

Erzberger, C., & Prein, G. (1997). Triangulation: Validity and empirically-based hypothesis construction. *Quality & Quantity, 31*, 141–154.

Fielding, N. (1994). Varieties of research interviews. *Nurse Researcher, 1*, 4–13.

Gergen, K. J. (1994). Exploring the postmodern: Perils or potentials? *American Psychologist, 49*, 412–416.

Guest, G., Bunce, A., & Johnson, L. (2006). How many interviews are enough? An experiment with data saturation. *Field Methods, 18*, 58–82.

Hertz, R. (1995). Separate but simultaneous interviewing of husbands and wives: Making sense of their stories. *Qualitative Inquiry, 14*, 429–451.

Hiatt, K., Stelle, C., Mulsow, M., & Scott, J. P. (2007). The importance of perspective: Evaluation of hospice care from multiple stakeholders. *American Journal of Hospice & Palliative Medicine, 24*, 376–382.

Highhouse, S., & Gillespie, J. Z. (2009). Do samples really matter that much? In C. E. Lance & R. J. Vandenberg (Eds.), *Statistical and methodological myths and urban legends: Doctrine, verity and fable in the organizational and social sciences* (pp. 249–268). New York, NY: Routledge.

Holstein, J. A., & Gubrium, J. F. (1995). *The active interview.* Thousand Oaks, CA: Sage.

Jones, A., & Bugge, C. (2006). Improving understanding and rigour through triangulation: An exemplar based on patient participation in interaction. *Journal of Advanced Nursing, 55*, 612–621.

Jory, B., Anderson, D., & Greer, C. (1997). Intimate justice: Confronting issues of accountability, respect, and freedom in therapy for abuse and violence. *Journal of Marital & Family Therapy, 23*, 399–420.

Lambert, S. D., & Loiselle, C. G. (2008). Combining individual interviews and focus groups to enhance data richness. *Journal of Advanced Nursing, 62*, 228–237.

Lawrence, V., Murray, J., Ffytche, D., & Banerjee, S. (2009). Out of sight, out of mind: A qualitative study of visual impairment and dementia from three perspectives. *International Psychogeriatrics, 21*, 511–518.

Mansfield, P., & Collard, J. (1988). *The beginning of the rest of your life: A portrait of newly-wed marriage.* London, England: Macmillan.

McCarthy, J. R., Holland, J., & Gillies, V. (2003). Multiple perspectives on the family lives of young people: Methodological and theoretical issues in case study research. *International Journal of Social Research Methodology: Theory and Practice, 6,* 1–23.

McNamee, S., & Gergen, K. J. (Eds.). (1992). *Therapy as social construction.* London, England: Sage.

Mishna, F. (2004). A qualitative study of bullying from multiple perspectives. *Children & Schools, 26,* 234–247.

Morgan, D. L. (2010). Reconsidering the role of interaction in analyzing and reporting focus groups. *Qualitative Health Research, 20,* 718–722.

Morse, J. M. (2003). The adjudication of qualitative proposals. *Qualitative Health Research, 13,* 739–742.

Nunkoosing, K. (2005). The problems with interviews. *Qualitative Health Research, 15,* 698–706.

Pahl, J. M., & Pahl, R. E. (1971). *Managers and their wives.* London, England: Allen Lane.

Perlesz, A., & Lindsay, J. (2003). Methodological triangulation in researching families: Making sense of dissonant data. *International Journal of Social Research Methodology, 6,* 25–40.

Rennie, D. L. (2000). Grounded theory methodology as methodological hermeneutics. *Theory & Psychology, 10,* 481–502.

Sandelowski, M. (2002). Reembodying qualitative inquiry. *Qualitative Health Research, 12,* 104–115.

Sands, R. G., & Roer-Strier, D. (2006). Using data triangulation of mother and daughter interviews to enhance research about families. *Qualitative Social Work: Research and Practice, 5,* 237–260.

Seidman, I. (1998). *Interviewing as qualitative research: A guide for researchers in education and the social sciences.* New York, NY: Teachers College Press.

Taylor, S. E. (1998). The social being in social psychology. In D. Gilbert, S. T. Fiske, & G. Lindzey (Eds.), *The handbook of social psychology* (3rd ed., pp. 58–95). Boston, MA: McGraw-Hill.

Thomas, S. P., & Pollio, H. R. (2002). *Listening to patients: A phenomenological approach to nursing research and practice.* New York, NY: Springer.

Valentine, G. (1999). Doing household research: Interviewing couples together and apart. *Area, 31,* 67–74.

17

CULTURE WORK IN THE RESEARCH INTERVIEW

◆ Shannon K. Carter and Christian L. Bolden

As Christian began searching for self-identified gang members to interview, he announced the study in his college courses and stated his need for research participants. After class, a student approached and declared himself a gang member who would participate in the study. By identifying himself as a potential participant for the study, this student activated a cultural identity. By doing so, contextual boundaries and status positions shifted from student and professor to participant and researcher. The participant, who could have been interviewed as a "student," came into the interview understanding that he was being interviewed as a "gang member." Christian sat down with the participant as a researcher to conduct a semistructured interview, guided by a set of questions prepared for "gang members," which the individual who sat down with him now had become.

Cultural identities are created and negotiated within the context of social interaction. To the other professors, this student was simply another student in one of their classes. But because of Christian's interest in "gang members" and this student's identification of himself as a member of that category, the two sat down to create a narrative of gang membership. Even before this exchange took place, Christian had defined "gang members" as a collective worthy of sociological inquiry. Through Christian's identification of this population as a topic of study and his student's identification of himself as a member of that population, the two have sustained a definition of "gangs" as a socially significant group that exists in contemporary society.

The emergence of culture that takes place in the dyadic dialogue and situational contexts of an interview setting is the focal point of our analysis. In particular, we analyze *culture work*, or the interactional labor involved in creating, defining, and negotiating perceptions of culture and the relationships between these perceptions and individuals' socially constructed identities. Because of its multiplicity, culture work is a complex matter. First, culture work involves identifying and articulating what culture *is*. This task alone is difficult because culture is often invisible, hidden in the taken-for-granted knowledge and mundane activities of everyday life (Frankenberg, 1993; Pattillo-McCoy, 1998). In addition, culture is not a static and finite entity but a fluid and changing one. Second, culture is often part and parcel of individuals' identities. Culture work involves explicating the role of culture—in its fluid and changing forms—for individuals' identities, which are also fluid and changing (Holstein & Gubrium, 2000). Third, culture work takes place in a *cultural context*. That is, the interactive labor to define culture is situated within a particular social, historical, and cultural moment. Indeed, the research interview is itself a cultural phenomenon, produced and popularized in a specific time and place (Gubrium & Holstein, 2002; Silverman, 1997).

The goal of this chapter is to theorize what culture means for the research interview and provide some recommendations for effectively activating culture in an interview setting—what we call *culture work*. We would like to emphasize that simply interviewing an individual whom the researcher perceives as belonging to a particular culture or subculture does not constitute what we mean by culture work. Instead, as the phrase suggests, culture work requires that both researcher and participant actively engage in labor to articulate and analyze culture during the interview. First, we begin by examining some previous definitions of culture to help us create a working definition that guides our discussion. Second, we analyze existing understandings of culture in more depth through a comparison of essentialist and constructionist perspectives and the implications of each for the research interview. Finally, we describe specific strategies researchers can use to facilitate culture work in the interview setting. We draw on examples from Christian's research on gang members (Bolden, 2010a, 2010b), Shannon's research on recent mothers (Carter, 2009a, 2009b, 2010; Houvouras, 2004, 2006), and other published works to illustrate these strategies.

◆ Toward a Working Definition of Culture

In the social sciences, culture has been defined in many ways. For example, anthropologists tend to define culture as a shared way of life (Grillo, 2003),

or "the total way of life of a people" (Geertz, 1973, p. 4). Culture is also commonly viewed as something everyone has (e.g., language) or that can be specified as *a* culture, which is a collective of individuals who can be identified as carriers of a particular culture (Grillo, 2003). Culture can also be understood as the imprint of social groups on the individual, often manifested in language, symbols, beliefs, values, norms, rituals, and material objects (Geertz, 1973; Tsekeris, 2008). In this sense, culture is referred to more generally as the knowledge people use to activate collective behavior and relay social meaning (McCarthy, 1995; Spradley, 1972). In the following sections, we expand on these rudimentary definitions to establish a theoretical foundation for culture as "work" or "interpretive practice." In particular, after reviewing and critiquing the essentialist approach to culture, we outline a constructionist understanding of the topic that informs our analysis of culture work in the research interview.

ESSENTIALIST VIEWS OF CULTURE

An essentialist perspective views culture as something that has a concrete existence. It is viewed as a stable and unchanging external force that shapes people's lives and produces particular kinds of people. As a consequence of belonging to a particular culture, individuals obtain certain kinds of selves that are deterministic of who they are inside. Fuchs's (2001) concept of essentialism "holds that things are what they are because that is their nature, essence, or definition" (p. 3). Thus, cultural essentialism views groups of individuals as fundamentally different from one another based on their cultural membership. Culture is viewed as a "bounded" system (Wikan, 1999), with clear distinctions between members and nonmembers, who are assumed to be influenced by it uniformly.

An essentialist view of culture uses a naturalistic approach to interview research. Naturalism requires researchers to physically locate themselves in "natural settings" where everyday life takes place and become accepted features of participants' daily lives (Douglas, 2003). The naturalistic researcher focuses on the subjective "member's meanings" individuals attribute to their everyday lives (Douglas, 2003). The goal of naturalistic inquiry is to tell "their story" from their point of view (Gubrium & Holstein, 1997), which requires the ability to "put oneself in the place of the other" (Liebow, 1993, p. xv). Hammersly and Atkinson (1983) state, "As participant observers we can learn the culture or subculture of the people we are studying. We can come to interpret the world in the same way as they do" (p. 7).

A naturalistic approach could also view the product of an interview not as an individual's personal narrative but as a representation of a historical time and place. In this view, "interviews are windows into collective thought processes; incidents and characters, even if presented in individualized performative style, are conventionalized and shaped by a long history of responses to previous tellings" (Smith, 2002, p. 713). Using this strategy, the individual narrative is considered a reflection of the culture in which it is produced.

Critiques of Essentialism

Critics argue that essentialists inaccurately presume that a stable and unchanging cultural subject resides within the participant. Holstein and Gubrium (1995) argue that this approach views the participant as a passive vessel of feelings, emotions, and experiences that, with good rapport and the right line of questioning, can be extracted by the interviewer. The assumption here is that individuals and their identities are concrete and unchanging rather than fluid and negotiated. Such a position also assumes that narratives produced in the research interview are direct reflections of individuals' experiences. Riessman (1993) argues that the product of an interview is not the participant's lived experience but rather a narrative, or a story of experience, imbued with meanings, interpretations, additions, and deletions. Furthermore, narratives are told through the medium of language, which also shapes and constrains the story in significant ways (Foucault, 1977; Gubrium & Holstein, 1997). Essentialism also relies on the notion that there is a singular culture, an entity that has an objective reality available for the researcher to extract.

Additionally, essentialism is critiqued as a driving force of social inequality. Critics posit that essentialism ignores the roles of language and discourse in creating categories of people (Foucault, 1977, 1978) who, once assigned to a category, are presumed to be substantively different from nonmembers. Categories are often constructed in dichotomous terms, such as "Western" and "non-Western" cultures (Narayan, 1998), and then characterized as polar opposites, which exaggerates the differences and ignores the similarities between groups (Bem, 1993). Since powerful groups have the privilege of defining both themselves and "others," they define themselves as inherently superior and use these socially created definitions to justify further exploitation, often framed as bringing civilization to otherwise "uncivilized" groups (Ani, 1994; Narayan, 1998; Said, 1978, 1993). Said (1978) traces the creation of "the Orient" in "Western" popular and academic literature, arguing that such images project an "Oriental" other, characterized as exotic, primitive, barbaric, and feminine, and the "Occident" as rational, civilized, democratic, and masculine. These definitions of the Western self were created during a historical moment when those same societies practiced slavery, colonization, and exploitation (Narayan, 1998).

Critiques of Anti-essentialism

Some scholars suggest that the rigid understanding of culture we have described as "essentialist" does not adequately represent the views of those charged with being "essentialists," particularly in academia. Sahlins (1999) argues, "Ethnography has always known that cultures were never as bounded, self-contained and self-sustaining as postmodernism pretends that modernism pretends" (p. 411). Others argue that anti-essentialism can have negative consequences for subordinate groups, as efforts to avoid essentialism have resulted in the dissolution of attention to categories that remain politically significant, such as race, and the creation of apolitical and individualized understandings of identity (Mohanty, 2003). Gilroy (1991) advocates an "anti anti-essentialist view," whereby individuals are not viewed as sharing some common internal essence yet are acknowledged as a potentially political group based on socially constructed perceptions of similarity that have resulted in common social and material conditions. Spivak (1990) suggests that marginalized groups can engage in a "strategic use of essentialism," whereby essentialist notions are drawn on as a political tool to advocate for emancipation.[1] She states, "Since it is not possible

---

[1] In a subsequent interview (Danius, Jonsson, & Spivak, 1993), Spivak stated that she no longer wanted to use this idea because it was commonly misunderstood and used as a way to justify "essentialism" without really considering what she meant by "strategic."

not to be an essentialist, one can self-consciously use this irreducible moment of essentialism as part of one's strategy" (p. 109).

Studies also show individuals often rely on essentialist understandings of culture when constructing their own identities in everyday life. In a study of youth who identify with the "straightedge" subculture, Williams (2006) found that many claimed to *be* straightedge before they knew what straightedge was. Essentialization of culture was one of the tools the straightedgers used to claim authenticity in their subcultural identification and to distinguish themselves from those they perceived as having inauthentic identities. Constructions of essentialist cultural identities have also been identified among jazz musicians (Becker, 1997), Filipina mail-order brides (Mahalingam & Leu, 2005), and rappers (McLeod, 1999). Others contend that essentialist definitions have been evoked by subordinate groups to negate negative images of themselves and advocate for certain rights and privileges (Grillo, 2003; Mahalingam & Leu, 2005).

CONSTRUCTIONIST VIEWS OF CULTURE

An alternative and more contemporary viewpoint is that culture is not something that has a concrete, objective reality but is an active process that is continuously constructed and negotiated through social interaction. A social constructionist perspective views culture as an ongoing production that unfolds as social life is carried out by active agents who engage in actions and interactions in everyday life. From this point of view, culture is not a concrete and stable entity that can be identified once and for all. Nor does it have an objective reality that is separate from social interaction and everyday life. It is not something that exists *out there* but instead is *right here*, being constructed and reconstructed through ongoing social interaction. As a product of social interaction, we view culture as a practice, a subject position, and a narrative resource.

Culture as Practice

Frankenberg (1993) uses the phrase "cultural practice" to emphasize the active component of culture. She argues that culture is not some separate sphere, existing apart from the concrete world of social interaction, but conceptualizes culture as *practice*, as

something people engage in. As something that is practiced, we can think of culture as a social accomplishment. West and Zimmerman (1987) argue for an understanding of gender as an interactional accomplishment, a set of actions engaged in by individuals within particular situational and institutional contexts that are subsequently interpreted by others as "gendered action." Through ongoing interactions, "masculinity" and "femininity" are created, interpreted, and negotiated. Just as West and Fenstermaker (1995) argue that this approach can be expanded beyond gender and applied to race and class, we suggest that it can also be applied to culture. As individuals engage in the activities of everyday life based on their interpretations of social situations, their practices create and reproduce what is considered "culture." In this sense, culture is not something that has a fixed, predetermined existence, but it is *emergent* in the ongoing interactions that take place in everyday life. Furthermore, it is not a feature of individuals but is an emergent component of social situations. West and Zimmerman (1987) state, "When we view gender as an accomplishment, an achieved property of situated conduct, our attention shifts from matters internal to the individual and focuses on the interactional and, ultimately, institutional arenas" (p. 126).

One way culture is interactionally accomplished is through the research interview. In this sense, culture becomes a topic of inquiry, something to be articulated and theorized by participants. The goal of the interview in this context is for the participant to construct and negotiate social meanings associated with culture. Topics include definitions of culture, its key components, perceptions of cultural membership (or the lack of it), and cultural identities. Articulating culture might be difficult for participants, as "cultural" practices are often not recognized, but may consist of a set of routines that are practiced every day. Pattillo-McCoy (1998) states, "The commonsense character of culture makes specifying cultural practices extremely difficult but painfully elementary" (p. 769). Nevertheless, the interview setting can be used as a situation in which participants can work to articulate the "mundane" and theorize its significance.

Culture as Subject Position

As something that is practiced, either deliberately or not, culture is often a component of individuals' identities. We view culture as part of one's identity, as a *subject position*, or a social position from which an individual can speak, act, and interact. In an interview, culture is a *voice* (Gubrium & Holstein, 2002) from which individuals can answer questions or narrate their experiences. Culture is not something individuals automatically *are*, but it is a social position one can assume in everyday life. Consequently, we view culture as a *fluid subject position*, or one subject position among many, that may or may not be activated during an interview. For example, an individual might speak from the subject position of a woman, a mother, a daughter, or a physician, or she might speak as a member of a certain culture.

Individuals also inhabit different subject positions within a culture based on their various social relationships. In an interview setting, a participant might speak as a woman in American culture, as a mother in American culture, and so on. In analyzing culture, we must take into consideration the other subject positions of the individuals who articulate culture in our interviews. Individuals who identify as different genders, races, social classes, and sexual orientations may create different perspectives of the same culture. At the same time, we have to be careful not to make generalizations based on the patterns we might think we see in the data, such as gender differences in perceptions of culture. Such a conclusion risks essentializing gender, as the assumption would be that men and women have different cultural experiences, which may or may not be true. Rather than making such assumptions, researchers can ask participants to theorize whether or not individuals who hold different social positions experience culture differently. In such an interview context, participants will negotiate multiple definitions of culture. Some individuals might also affiliate with more than one culture or with one culture and an array of subcultures. A single participant might speak from any, all, or none of their cultural subject positions throughout the course of an interview.

In an interview setting, participants articulate a sense of reality in relation to an interviewer, who also holds a particular subject position in the participant's imagination. It is not only the researcher who activates the cultural position of the participant but also the participant who contextually constructs who the researcher is. Marcuse (1965) argued that culture is the process of humanization, with the distinct requirement that there are "others" or "aliens" who do not belong. Whether the participant perceives the researcher as an insider or outsider will affect the kind of narrative that is produced in the interview setting. Subject positions may not be static throughout the interview, but cultural boundaries and perceptions of inclusion and exclusion can be created and negotiated throughout the interview processes (Gubrium & Koro-Ljungberg, 2005). How these subject positions are negotiated will affect the kind of story that unfolds throughout the interview.

Culture as a Narrative Resource and Narrative Constraint

A social constructionist perspective also views culture as a *narrative resource* (Gubrium & Holstein, 1997), or a tool that is available for use in the narration of identities, practices, and experiences. As a narrative resource, culture is a conceptual apparatus participants can draw on as they actively and artfully construct their realities through social interaction. It is an available resource participants can mold and reshape in creative ways as they craft narratives of identity and experience. At the same time, culture also serves as a *narrative constraint*, setting limits to the kind of selves, experiences, and realities participants can construct in social life, including in the interview setting. Gubrium and Holstein (1997) argue that individuals exert agency in everyday life as they work to produce social reality; however, the view of the individual as a free agent must be balanced by an understanding that agency and activity take place in *social contexts*. That is, individuals do not exist alone, creating a unique sense of reality that is unsituated and uncontextualized, but instead, reality construction takes place through interactions with others. The social and historical contexts of situated action necessarily limit the kinds of realities that can be created as these realities must be produced, conveyed, and interpreted through interactions with other human beings. Because of the interactional nature of reality production, individuals are limited by the kinds of resources that are available to them. Culture is one of these limitations.

Gubrium and Holstein (1997) advocate a view of culture within the Foucauldian framework (Foucault, 1975) of "conditions of possibility." In this view, culture provides a "toolkit" (Pattillo-McCoy, 1998) that not only allows individuals to create their own realities but also limits the kinds of realities that can be created. According to Foucault (1978), language and discourse are powerful forces that limit and constrain perceptions of reality. In particular, Foucault analyzes the role of discourse in the formation of objects. Once an object is created through discourse, it is available to be thought about, talked about, and negotiated through social interaction. However, not all possible objects are created in a given language. Because much of social interaction takes place through language—including individuals' "internal conversations" with themselves in their heads (Mead, 1934)—language limits the objects that are available in a society. As an integral component of cultures and subcultures, language and discourse serve as narrative constraints that limit the kinds of realities that can be produced.

◆ Doing Culture Work in the Research Interview

Doing *culture work* in the research interview means activating culture as a topic to be constructed, theorized, and negotiated in the context of the interview setting. The methods used to activate culture will depend on the particular goals of the research project and the dynamic interactions that unfold between researcher and participant in the interview setting. We provide recommendations for doing culture work, including methods of activating culture as a topic of analysis, activating and negotiating cultural subject positions, and analyzing culture as a narrative resource and narrative constraint.

ACTIVATING CULTURE AS A TOPIC OF ANALYSIS

One way to activate culture work in an interview is to place culture at the center of the discussion, to be analyzed by participants. This can be accomplished by asking participants specific questions about a particular culture, such as how they define it, what they see as its key elements, what it means to them, and how it relates to their identities. Activating culture in this way opens culture up as a topic for the participant to navigate and explore. Using probes to keep conversations active will encourage participants to expand their narrative constructions of culture.

Because cultural practice is often invisible, broad questions such as "tell me about your culture" may not suffice in activating talk about culture. Alternatively, researchers can ask questions about mundane, everyday life activities and routines. In his interviews with current and former gang members, Christian Bolden (CB) asked participants about "typical activities" that were "engaged in day to day" to activate discussions of cultural practice.

CB: What were the typical activities that the group engaged in day to day?

Giggles: Hanging out, chilling, smoke weed and drink and basically talk shit to anybody who would get near us or come by us. . . . So a lot of times, the girls would just sit around on the porch the whole day, just kind of kicking it, chilling, just whatever, and would watch the comings and goings of neighbors of people, and they would break into garages later and take stuff.

By asking participants about mundane, everyday life, Christian elicits a construction of the everyday, ordinary routines of the group.

Another method of activating culture as a topic of discussion is to ask participants more specific questions about their group. In this way, the participant is asked to theorize components of cultures or subcultures that are typically deemed significant, such as group structure, membership, rituals, and so on. This provides an opportunity for participants to construct and negotiate the significance of these components for their cultural group. For example, Christian asked some of his participants if their gang had a particular system. In asking such a question, the researcher is requesting that the participants theorize the nature and structure of the group.

CB: Speaking of that, I don't know a whole lot about Jamaican gangs. Can you explain to me how they work, like what is the, do they have a system?

Machete: System, well, as long as you join, you can't get out of gang scene. . . . You have to become brave, you have to, you cannot be scared, you have to be, you have to learn to take a life if you want to be in a gang. Joining a gang, it is not really a gang, we call it a family. They look after each other in that gang.

Here, Christian's question about a Jamaican "gang system" activates narrative about the group as the participant constructs member personalities and rituals.

A traditional approach to placing culture at the center of an interview would recommend the broad, open-ended questions we have discussed so far that avoid leading participants in a particular direction. We agree that these kinds of questions are useful for encouraging participants to engage in culture work. However, we part from traditional approaches in that we also recommend asking leading questions to see how participants respond. Researchers can state a certain opinion to see how participants grapple with it or even play "devil's advocate" to encourage participants to explore and articulate their ideas about culture more fully.

For example, in online interview/discussion groups with "straightedge" youth, Williams (2006) posted a leading question on a discussion board:

> Does punk rock, hardcore, or whatever it is called nowadays still have a role in the straightedge movement? I guess what I'm asking is, can you separate the music from the scene or are they intertwined? I think the music and the "punk rock" culture is what makes straightedge unique so the two cannot and should not be separated. (p. 183)

Here, Williams (2006) poses a question and states a particular opinion to see how participants respond. His question incites a debate between what he identifies as *music-straightedgers* and *net-straightedgers*, in which participants construct and negotiate the definitions and boundaries of straightedge subculture. They argue over who is and is not a member and what kinds of activities constitute membership. They engage in cultural identity work, as each participant defines himself or herself as a part of the subculture and works to authenticate his or her own identity.

A conventional approach would contend that researchers should not suggest a particular opinion, as such a suggestion might "contaminate" participants' responses. The conventional logic is that participants may not have thought of the topic in that particular way until the researcher suggested it. A constructionist approach views all interview data as a collaborative product of interactions between the researcher and the participant. Indeed, a participant may not have thought about a topic at all until the researcher brought it up. By simply asking a question,

the researcher constructs a topic as something worthy of discussion. Rather than deny or try to escape this unavoidable impact the researcher has on the narrative produced in the interview, constructionists believe that researchers should embrace this impact and work with it rather than against it (Holstein & Gubrium, 1995).

Of course, the researcher should not do *all* the reality constructing in the interview process, since the interview, after all, is expected to reveal something about the participant's perspective. Researchers can work to find the right balance by (a) carefully considering the order of interview questions and (b) developing and refining questions throughout the data collection process. In considering the order of questions, we recommend beginning with broad, nonleading questions, such as "Tell me about your culture." These questions allow participants to choose the direction of their answers and avoid steering them a particular way. After these open questions, researchers can ask more direct, leading questions that ask participants to respond to a particular opinion or engage in a debate. These questions might be developed as part of the research questions derived from the literature review that drive the research project or that developed during data collection. Drawing from the logic of grounded theory (Charmaz, 2002; Glaser & Strauss, 1967), researchers can begin analyzing data as soon as the first interview is under way. As themes emerge from the interviews, subsequent participants can be asked what they think about the other participants' constructions of reality. In particular, contrasting views can be framed in a debate to ask participants what they think about what earlier participants have said. This gives participants an opportunity to grapple with some of the conflicting views that emerge and provides researchers an opportunity to elicit rich data on the topic.

ACTIVATING PARTICIPANTS' CULTURAL SUBJECT POSITIONS

Both interviewer and interviewee have the capacity to activate culture during an interview. Holstein and Gubrium (1995) point out that interview participants "not only offer substantive thoughts and feelings pertinent to the topic under consideration but simultaneously and continuously monitor who they are in relation to the person questioning them" (p. 15). One way participants accomplish this is by shifting the voice—or subject position—from which they speak (Gubrium & Holstein, 2002). As simultaneous members of various social groups, cultures, and/or subcultures, interviewees can activate different cultural identities throughout an interview. In the process, a single participant may speak as a member of several different cultures or subcultures and from different subject positions within a single culture or subculture.

In many cases, a particular cultural subjectivity will be activated simply by an individual agreeing to participate in a study. When a project is advertised to solicit participants, either through formal advertisements or by word of mouth, there is typically some sort of specification of the "type" of person solicited for the study. For an individual to agree to participate, she or he must identify herself or himself as a member of the group being solicited. This mutual understanding between researcher and participant about the focus of the study might be enough to activate a particular subjectivity in the research participant. In Christian's interviews with self-identified current and former gang members, both he and the participants came to the interview with the mutual understanding that "gang membership" was the topic of interaction. This mutual understanding was typically enough to activate gang member subjectivities among the participants. When Christian asked his opening question, "Which group are/were you a part of?" most responded with the name of the gang they were affiliated with, often introducing the term *gang* into the interviews themselves.

However, agreement to participate did not always suffice for activating a gang member subjectivity. For example, Twista continuously resisted a gang member identity, choosing instead to identify himself with the music industry.

Twista: I'm not in no gang, I created my own stuff. But it's just an organization of a lot of dudes that's just about making money and helping each other out.

CB: Does your group ever have conflicts with other groups?

Twista: Yeah, I done had some conflicts, but I'm about doing music, trying to be an artist or producer, you know what I'm saying.

Although Twista volunteered to participate in an interview with gang members, he resists defining himself as a gang member and his "organization" as a gang. When asked to further describe the group, Twista begins by drawing on discourse typically associated with gang activity but then again shifts toward a discussion of music.

Twista: I'd say, what's the word, organized crime. We're not really organized crime but you know what I'm saying. Out of anybody in the group, if ya'll gonna go out and do something, everybody needs to know because it affects all of us and it makes us look bad. Like, if I go to try to get a show and I'm talking to a promoter, they be like "naw, I don't think I wanna pay ya'll to perform, because we heard about ya'll." And stuff like that.

CB: You referenced the group as organized crime. Why did you reference the group that way?

Twista: Basically, we don't go out and start any trouble. It's basically self-defense. Like, if somebody say something to us, we'll try to keep it down, but somebody walks out behind me and hits me in the back of the head with a bottle, it's gonna be a problem.

Here, Twista identifies organized crime as a characteristic commonly associated with gangs but dissociates his group from the concept in his effort to reject defining the group as a gang. Although he resists the subject position of gang member, he is still engaging in culture work as he works to define himself as a non–gang member and construct his identity in relation to the concept of a gang. The significance of this excerpt is the *interactional techniques* the participant uses to identify himself as a non–gang member while voluntarily participating in an interview with "gang members." Specifically, Twista engages in *typification* (Schutz, 1970) as he describes the ordinary or typical gang, and he then performs *distancing* (Snow & Anderson, 2003) as he constructs his group as different from the "typical" gang. He uses *particularization* (Potter & Wetherell, 2003) as he speaks about himself in individual terms, insisting that he is "all about the music." Rather than identify him as a non–gang member or a recalcitrant subject, we view his interview as a rich source of data on gang identity and methods of identity construction.

Depending on the focus of the project, researchers may want to facilitate *cultural deactivation*, whereby a participant minimizes his or her cultural subject position in favor of a different subject position. Cultural deactivation involves the occurrence of a narrative shift (Gubrium & Holstein, 1997) in which participants change the voice from which they speak. Many of Christian's participants who identified themselves as former gang members engaged in cultural deactivation when asked why they had left the gang.

CB: You told me something off the record, so I'll ask it again. If there was any one thing that caused you to get away from it or decide to leave, what would that be?

Apostle: My girlfriend at the time getting pregnant. And my dad was involved in gangs, you know? And I already saw myself slowly becoming who I hated the most. So, once I had a kid, it was like, well, here's my chance to stop the cycle, it doesn't have to go in a circle. . . . Once I had the kid it was like it was something greater than me in life that I could love. I just chose to pursue that instead of fight.

CB: You said your dad was involved in gangs?

Apostle: Yeah, in New York. . . . My father was a real violent man, you know what I mean? . . . This was a man that was just used to violence every day and it was normal to him and I just don't want to be like that. To me, once the option was put in front of me, it was an easy choice, just because I didn't want to be what I hated.

By asking why he left the gang, Christian encourages Apostle to deactivate his subject position of gang member and speak instead as a father. Apostle's narrative shifts from a focus on "gang" themes to fathering themes, in which he talks about his love for his child and the kind of parent he wants to be.

If research questions do not spontaneously produce cultural deactivation, researchers can encourage a narrative shift by asking participants to speak in a different voice (Gubrium & Holstein, 2002). Interviewers can ask participants to discuss a topic

from the perspective of one of their other subject positions or to theorize what the topic might look like from another person's subject position. In interviews with nursing home residents, Gubrium and Holstein (2002) note that a participant indicated a shift in voice by stating, "Speaking as a woman" (p. 16), before proceeding with her narrative. A shift in voice can also be activated by interviewers through questions such as "Tell me about it from a woman's perspective" or "from a mother's perspective" and so on. Such questions may deactivate cultural subject positions and activate other subject positions. Alternatively, they may activate *situated cultural subject positions*, such as a woman or a mother in a particular culture. Engaging in culture work requires the researcher to activate these different subject positions and attend to shifts in voice throughout the analysis.

◆ Negotiating Cultural Subject Positions

Participants' narratives are not created in a vacuum but are told *to* interviewers who also hold subject positions. From a constructionist perspective, the research interview is always a situational conversation in which two people are constructing and negotiating identities and boundaries. When interviewer and participant meet, they often engage in impression management (Goffman, 1959) by portraying a certain identity to influence the image of themselves in the other's imagination. Researchers may work to create separation between participants and themselves, purposefully maintaining "outsider" status, or they may try to portray themselves as more of an "insider." Either selection is a conscious choice in impression management with consequences that may not always be clear. Particularly in cross-cultural interviewing, researchers may be unsure of how their behavior is received by participants (Kenney & Akita, 2008). From a constructionist perspective, a participant's view of the researcher as an insider or outsider will not automatically affect the quality or utility of the interview but may shape the kind of narrative that unfolds.

Hall (2004) discusses the physical and linguistic creation of boundaries in interviews with women she classified as South Asian immigrants, whereby the participants constructed her as an "outsider." In some cases, the participants viewed her as more powerful or important because she was white and assumed that she could help with immigration application efforts, or else she was constructed as harmless or neutral due to her lack of ties to the immigrant community. In one interview, the participant reduced Hall's status position by speaking in another language and using disparaging and derogatory words in reference to the researcher. Hall did understand what was said but pretended to be unaware of it. Notably, she could have made the participant aware of her understanding, which would likely have resulted in a shift in boundaries in the interview.

In several of Christian's interviews, he was viewed initially as an oblivious and judgmental outsider (i.e., a white man from a university setting). Challenging this construction often involved demonstrating knowledge about gangs and, particularly, using "insider" language. For example, a participant appeared tense and suspicious until a certain point in the interview when Christian demonstrated gang knowledge through his use of language. The participant subsequently relaxed and became more forthcoming.

CB: Start with the Dragons. Were they People or Folks?

Stripe: People

CB: People?

Stripe: You know a little bit about your gangs (laughs). They were People. They became Folks.

After he had demonstrated gang knowledge by using the relevant terminology, the boundaries between interviewer and participant were renegotiated, and the participant began to view Christian as more of an insider. Responses to the remaining questions became highly detailed rather than short and succinct, which was important for narrative production in this scenario.

The physical setting of the interview can also affect participants' perceptions of the researcher and influence the kind of data generated through the interaction. In Christian's interviews, subject positions were heavily influenced by the interview location. Interviews held in a classroom or in Christian's office reinforced perceptions of him as an authority figure. Participants took on demeanors that were sometimes meek and almost supplicating, often explaining that they were "trying to do better." On the other hand, at public

places, usually fast-food joints or parks, the interview began with researcher and participant on an equal yet unsure footing, followed by a process of feeling each other out and working to establish boundaries of inclusion and exclusion. Participants' homes offered participants a potential position of power and seemed to provide the highest comfort level. On several occasions, participants pulled out a marijuana joint or bong and began smoking during the interview, which may be an indication that a certain level of trust and comfort had been established that did not appear to be present in the interviews that took place on the university campus.

The significance of the researcher obtaining "insider" or "outsider" status varies depending on the topic of discussion and participants' perceptions of the researcher. Due to the sensitive, often illegal nature of Christian's research topic, establishing rapport and facilitating at least partial insider status was important for obtaining detailed information from participants. On the other hand, purposeful antagonism may be more effective for activating narrative production. While studying the sex trade in Sri Lanka, Miller's (2010) field interviewer, described as a feminist and modernist with outspoken views about legitimizing prostitution, interviewed a series of police officers. The officers typically began with standardized legal answers to each question, until the interviewer intentionally antagonized them with oppositional viewpoints. This resulted in the participants shifting their subject positions from police officers to ordinary citizens, in which they constructed more conservative viewpoints. Negotiating participants' perceptions of the researcher's subject position can be an important tool for activating culture work in the research interview.

◆ Audience Shifts and Imaginary Audiences

In addition to negotiating subject positions, interview participants can create an *audience shift* in which they change the interviewer's preestablished subject position or role from that of a "researcher" to a presumed cultural "insider" or "outsider." An audience shift can change the subject position of the interviewer only temporarily or for the remainder of the interview. For example, in Shannon's interview with Aimee regarding her pregnancy and childbirth experience, Aimee narrated her pregnancy to Shannon as the two spoke woman to woman, mother to mother, as subjects with a shared cultural experience both of being pregnant and of giving birth in U.S. society. As Aimee proceeded into her birth story, she introduced an audience shift by verifying that Shannon had given birth without anesthesia. After confirming Shannon's birth methods, Aimee's narrative changed to accommodate the new subject positions she created. She articulated more clearly the physical sensations associated with epidural anesthesia, as the audience of her story was one who had not shared the experience. In this scenario, the audience shift from insider to outsider resulted in a richer and more detailed description as a result of the participant's perception of dissimilarity between herself and the interviewer.

Interviewers can also create an audience shift by activating different subject positions for themselves. Such a shift can be created by simply asking the participant to speak to the interviewer as a different subject. In the example with Aimee, Shannon could have said something like this: "I gave birth in a birth center with a midwife. What was it like giving birth in a hospital?" To create similar subject positions but to position them in a cultural context, the same question could be asked in the following way: "I gave birth in the midwifery home birth/birth center subculture. What was it like giving birth in the dominant U.S. cultural model?" Such a question highlights that the audience of the narrative is not someone with a similar experience, which will require the participant to adjust her narrative to this new audience. It also puts culture at the center of the analysis for the participant to work out in her story. It is likely that the participant has not analyzed the birth experience within the framework of culture, but by asking her to speak as one who gave birth in a "cultural" way to one who gave birth in a "subcultural" way, the participant is incited to grapple with the notion of culture in her narrative.

Another way to create an audience shift is to introduce an *imaginary audience*. In Shannon's interviews on childbearing it became clear early on that the participants went into less depth in their explanations of experiences they believed were shared between researcher and participant. Participants said things such as "You remember what it was like . . ." or "I'm sure you experienced that too" when narrating a part of their pregnancy or labor they thought

was similar to Shannon's experience. Concomitantly, they went into greater depth in those parts of their stories they believed were different from hers. To encourage further elaboration, Shannon evoked an imaginary audience by asking participants questions such as "How would you describe being pregnant to someone who has never been pregnant before?" This question shifted the audience from the infinite roles attributed to or held by Shannon in her research to an imaginary audience who has never been pregnant. She asked questions of this nature after a series of more general questions, such as "Tell me about your pregnancy?" "What was it like being pregnant?" and "How did you feel while you were pregnant?" The imaginary audience provides a fresh narrative context for the participants to retell their story, now to a second audience. In the retelling of the story, a new set of themes are likely to emerge.

Evoking an imaginary audience is another way culture can be activated in an interview. Imaginary audiences may be particularly useful in interviews that involve culture because they can allow the researcher to take on a cultural subjectivity that may not otherwise be possible. For example, in Christian's interviews, participants perceived him as a non–gang member. Following discussions of their decisions to join a gang and their day-to-day activities, Christian could have asked his participants how they would describe gang activity to other gang members, potential gang members, dating partners, or police. Such questions would activate an imaginary audience that the researcher is unable to physically present to his or her participants, for both logistic and ethical reasons.

◆ *Analyzing Culture as a Narrative Resource and Narrative Constraint*

Analyzing culture as a *narrative resource* and *narrative constraint* involves focusing on the methods individuals use to actively construct their realities and the ways in which these constructions are limited by the concepts available in language and discourse. In particular, it entails careful examination of participants' active and artful engagement in reality production, the limitations of their agency, and how they negotiate the balance between the two—what Gubrium and Holstein (1997; Holstein & Gubrium, 2000) refer to as *interpretive practice*. Interpretive practice combines *discursive practice*, or the ethno-methodological view of individuals as active agents engaging in reality production, with *discourses-in-practice*, or the constraining impact of language and discourse. Our view of culture as a narrative resource and a narrative constraint is consistent with interpretive practice, whereby culture is used as a narrative resource in discursive practice yet serves as a narrative constraint in discourses-in-practice. The analytic task of the researcher is to identify the ways in which individuals use agency to craft cultural narratives and the ways their stories are constrained by the cultural concepts available to them.

In some sense, participants may become more active and artful in moments of greater cultural constraint. In particular, when the common ways or "clichés" for understanding and articulating the self or social experience are deemed inadequate, participants are likely to draw on more artful techniques to convey their experiences. They become more artful in such scenarios out of necessity, as the common concepts and ways of thinking embedded in cultural discourses inhibit explication of their identities, experiences, or worldviews. For example, in Gubrium's (2003) research on caregivers of individuals with Alzheimer's, he observed close friends and family experiencing difficulty in describing their feelings in a caregiver support group. Participant after participant explained how difficult it was to articulate what was happening, until one participant read an original poem about the experience. Gubrium noted that the words in the poem were the same as the words that had been expressed throughout the group discussion, but the participants agreed that the poem captured what they were unable to articulate through ordinary talk.

In Shannon's research on women's childbearing experiences, she examined participants' constructions and negotiations of the concepts of body, mind, emotions, and self throughout their narratives (Houvouras, 2004). The participants drew on these concepts in creative ways, often crafting relationships between them, such as the body influencing the mind, and so on. However, Shannon noted that in a few cases, particularly as labor contractions grew in intensity, the participants became more creative in their articulation of their experiences. For example, some participants talked really fast, as they described what they were feeling physically, emotionally, and cognitively all at the same time. They used the speed of their speech, facial expressions, and hand gestures to convey the intensity of their experience. Since our cultural mode of thinking primarily conceptualizes body, mind, emotions, and self as distinct, separable entities, the participants seemed to experience more difficulty describing experiences in which these various components may have worked together as a whole. They, therefore, used alternative, creative techniques to convey these experiences.

In another analysis (Carter, 2009a), Shannon noted that many participants stated that they were unable to explain what pregnancy and childbirth were like because there was an element of childbearing that could only be known through experience. The depiction of their experience as "indescribable" suggests that the existing cultural resources for communicating the childbirth experience were deemed insufficient by the women in Shannon's research interviews. For these women, rather than being a narrative resource, the common stock of knowledge about childbirth (e.g., the discourse of physical pain) failed to fully capture, and in a sense restrained, the experiential quality of their stories.

◆ Conclusion

In this chapter, we presented a view of culture (or subculture) as a socially constructed concept that is not intrinsically meaningful but is given meaning through the interactions among people. In our view, culture is a fluid, ongoing creation that is formed, interpreted, practiced, contested, negotiated, and transformed through social interactions. It is also a category of meaning used in the formation of groups and attribution of characteristics that are socially and historically situated. In everyday life, culture serves as a narrative resource, something that is available for use in the construction of identities, the explanations of beliefs and practices, and the production of stories of experiences. At the same time, culture sets parameters for the kind of reality construction that can take place in a given situation. In other words, individuals are not able to construct whatever realities they choose through social interaction but must work within the "conditions of possibility" (Foucault, 1977) that are available in the sociohistorical, cultural contexts in which those realities are produced. In this sense, culture provides a "toolkit" (Pattillo-McCoy, 1998) or set of "received, yet unfolding maps, recipes, and templates" (Gubrium & Holstein, 1997, p. 169) for the production of selves, social groups, and realities.

The research interview provides an avenue for both the articulation and the analysis of culture. As we have noted throughout this chapter, culture itself is not necessarily something drawn from the "vessels of responses" (i.e., the research participants). Instead, culture is "work"; it is a product of active researcher–participant interactions in the context of a social occasion classified as an "interview." Specifically, "culture" is constructed, and *used*, in the research interview as a topical focus, subject position, narrative resource, or imagined audience.

More broadly, culture is relevant to all research on human subjects. Just like all humans are presumed to have, in some sense, a gender and a race—and therefore all research has something to do with gender and race—all humans are presumed to belong to some culture, at least marginally. This is not to suggest that gender, race, or culture are static categories that determine individuals' identities, experiences, or worldviews but rather that they are potential resources that can be used to construct identities, interpret experiences, and create worldviews.

◆ References

Ani, M. (1994). *Yurugu: An African-centered critique of European cultural thought and behavior.* Trenton, NJ: Africa World Press.

Becker, H. (1997). The culture of a deviant group: The "jazz" musician. In K. Gelder & S. Thornton (Eds.), *The subcultures reader* (pp. 55–65). New York, NY: Routledge.

Bem, S. L. (1993). *The lenses of gender: Transforming the debate on sexual inequality.* New Haven, CT: Yale University Press.

Bolden, C. L. (2010a). Charismatic role theory: Towards a theory of gang dissipation. *Journal of Gang Research, 17*(4), 39–70.

Bolden, C. L. (2010b). *Evolution of the folk devil: A social network perspective of the hybrid gang label* (Unpublished doctoral dissertation). University of Central Florida, Orlando, FL.

Carter, S. K. (2009a). Gender and childbearing experiences: Revisiting O'Brien's dialectics of reproduction. *NWSA Journal, 21*(2), 121–143.

Carter, S. K. (2009b). Gender performances during labor and birth in the midwives model of care. *Gender Issues, 26*(3/4), 205–223.

Carter, S. K. (2010). Beyond control: Body and self in women's childbearing narratives. *Sociology of Health & Illness, 32*(7), 993–1009.

Charmaz, K. (2002). Qualitative interviewing and grounded theory analysis. In J. F. Gubrium & J. A. Holstein (Eds.), *Handbook of interview research: Context and method* (pp. 675–694). Thousand Oaks, CA: Sage.

Danius, S., Jonsson, S., & Spivak, G. C. (1993). An interview with Gayatri Chakravorty Spivak. *Boundary 2, 20*(2), 24–50.

Douglas, J. D. (2003). The sociology of everyday life. In J. A. Holstein & J. F. Gubrium (Eds.), *Inner lives and social worlds: Readings in social psychology* (pp. 30–35). New York, NY: Oxford University Press.

Foucault, M. (1975). *The birth of the clinic.* New York, NY: Vintage Books.

Foucault, M. (1977). *Discipline & punish: The birth of the prison.* New York, NY: Vintage Books.

Foucault, M. (1978). *The history of sexuality: Vol. 1. An introduction.* New York, NY: Vintage Books.

Frankenberg, R. (1993). *White women, race matters: The social construction of whiteness.* Minneapolis: University of Minnesota Press.

Fuchs, S. (2001). *Against essentialism: A theory of culture and society.* Cambridge, MA: Harvard University Press.

Geertz, C. (1973). *The interpretation of cultures.* New York, NY: Basic Books.

Gilroy, P. (1991). *There ain't no black in the Union Jack: The cultural politics of race and nation.* Chicago, IL: University of Chicago Press.

Glaser, B. G., & Strauss, A. L. (1967). *The discovery of grounded theory: Strategies for qualitative research.* Chicago, IL: Aldine Press.

Goffman, E. (1959). *The presentation of self in everyday life.* Garden City, NY: Doubleday.

Grillo, R. D. (2003). Cultural essentialism and cultural anxiety. *Anthropological Theory, 3*(2), 157–173.

Gubrium, E., & Koro-Ljungberg, M. (2005). Contending with border making in the social constructionist interview. *Qualitative Inquiry, 11*(5), 689–715.

Gubrium, J. F. (2003). The social preservation of mind: The Alzheimer's disease experience. In J. A. Holstein & J. F. Gubrium (Eds.), *Inner lives and social worlds: Readings in social psychology* (pp. 180–190). New York, NY: Oxford University Press.

Gubrium, J. F., & Holstein, J. A. (1997). *The new language of qualitative method.* New York, NY: Oxford University Press.

Gubrium, J. F., & Holstein, J. A. (2002). From the individual interview to the interview society. In J. F. Gubrium & J. A. Holstein (Eds.), *Handbook of interview research: Context and method* (pp. 3–32). Thousand Oaks, CA: Sage.

Hall, R. R. (2004). Inside out: Some notes on carrying out feminist research in cross cultural interviews with South Asian women immigrant applicants. *International Journal of Social Research Methodology, 7*(2), 127–141.

Hammersly, M., & Atkinson, P. (1983). *Ethnography: Principles and practice*. London, England: Routledge.

Holstein, J. A., & Gubrium, J. F. (1995). *The active interview*. Thousand Oaks, CA: Sage.

Holstein, J. A., & Gubrium, J. F. (2000). *The self we live by: Narrative identity in a postmodern world*. New York, NY: Oxford University Press.

Houvouras, S. K. (2004). Negotiated concepts: Body, mind, emotions and self in women's childbearing narratives. *Dissertation Abstracts International, 65*(6), 2378A.

Houvouras, S. K. (2006). Negotiated boundaries: Conceptual locations of pregnancy and childbirth. *The Qualitative Report, 11*(4), 665–686.

Kenney, R., & Akita, K. (2008). When West writes East: In search of an ethic for cross-cultural interviewing. *Journal of Mass Media Ethics, 23*, 280–295.

Liebow, E. (1993). *Tell them who I am: The lives of homeless women*. New York, NY: Penguin Books.

Mahalingam, R., & Leu, J. (2005). Culture, essentialism, immigration and representations of gender. *Theory & Psychology, 15*(6), 839–860.

Marcuse, H. (1965). Remarks on a redefinition of culture. *Daedalus, 94*(1), 190–207.

McCarthy, E. D. (1995). *Knowledge as culture: The new sociology of knowledge*. New York, NY: Routledge.

McLeod, K. (1999). Authenticity within hip-hop and other cultures threatened with assimilation. *Journal of Communication, 49*(4), 134–150.

Mead, G. H. (1934). *Mind, self, and society: From the standpoint of a social behaviorist*. Chicago, IL: University of Chicago Press.

Miller, J. (2010). The impact of gender when interviewing offenders on offending. In W. Bernasco (Ed.), *Offenders on offending: Learning about crime from criminals* (pp. 161–183). Cullompton, UK: Willan.

Mohanty, C. T. (2003). *Feminism without borders: Decolonizing theory, practicing solidarity*. Durham, NC: Duke University Press.

Narayan, U. (1998). Essence of culture and a sense of history: A feminist critique of cultural essentialism. *Hypatia, 13*(2), 86–106.

Pattillo-McCoy, M. (1998). Church culture as a strategy of action in the black community. *American Sociological Review, 63*(6), 767–784.

Potter, J., & Wetherell, M. (2003). Categories in discourse. In J. A. Holstein & J. F. Gubrium (Eds.), *Inner lives and social worlds: Readings in social psychology* (pp. 62–78). New York, NY: Oxford University Press.

Riessman, C. K. (1993). *Narrative analysis*. Newbury Park, CA: Sage.

Sahlins, M. (1999). Two or three things that I know about culture. *Journal of the Royal Anthropological Institute, 5*(4), 399–422.

Said, E. W. (1978). *Orientalism*. New York, NY: Vintage Books.

Said, E. W. (1993). *Culture and imperialism*. New York, NY: Alfred A. Knopf.

Schutz, A. (1970). *On phenomenology and social relations*. Chicago, IL: University of Chicago Press.

Silverman, D. (1997). *Qualitative research: Theory, method and practice*. London, England: Sage.

Smith, R. C. (2002). Analytic strategies for oral history interviews. In J. F. Gubrium & J. A. Holstein (Eds.), *Handbook of interview research: Context and method* (pp. 711–732). Thousand Oaks, CA: Sage.

Snow, D. A., & Anderson, L. (2003). Salvaging the self. In J. A. Holstein & J. F. Gubrium (Eds.), *Inner lives and social worlds: Readings in social psychology* (pp. 139–160). New York, NY: Oxford University Press.

Spivak, G. C. (1990). *The post-colonial critic: Interviews, strategies, dialogues*. New York, NY: Routledge.

Spradley, J. (1972). Foundations of cultural knowledge. In J. Spradley (Ed.), *Culture and cognition* (pp. 3–38). San Francisco, CA: Chandler.

Tsekeris, C. (2008). Sociological issues in culture and critical theorizing. *Humanity & Social Sciences Journal, 3*(1), 18–25.

West, C., & Fenstermaker, S. (1995). Doing difference. *Gender & Society, 9*(1), 8–37.

West, C., & Zimmerman, D. H. (1987). Doing gender. *Gender & Society, 1*(2), 125–151.

Wikan, U. (1999). Culture: A new concept of race. *Social Anthropology, 7*(1), 57–64.

Williams, J. P. (2006). Authentic identities: Straightedge subculture, music, and the Internet. *Journal of Contemporary Ethnography, 35*, 173–200.

18

AFTER THE INTERVIEW

What Is Left at the End

◆ Christopher A. Faircloth

The interview has certainly come a long way in, well, a long time. While the analytic quandary of the interview as a situational encounter has now been bandied around by methodologists and theorists, and those who consider themselves both, seemingly without an end in sight, something else is strangely lacking, and it is a part of the interview process that any methodologist will tell you is a vital part of the process—what happens after the actual interview is completed (see Warren et al., 2003, for an exception). It is this part of the interview process that I wish to discuss here. It is important to note, however, that I refer to this as part of the ongoing process. The "after" is part and parcel of the interview, from beginning to end: from how the interviewer conceptualizes the interview, to the proceedings of the interview itself, to the coding of the data, and to how the data are to be represented. The "after" exists very much in the "before" and in the "during."

To begin, it is important that we revisit the interview as a theoretical project to establish the arguments to follow. From there, I will discuss the "after-interview process" in four sections: (1) sensitizing concepts and coding, (2) narrative analysis, (3) shift in representation, and (4) its politicization.

◆ The Interview as Situational Encounter: A Brief History of the Theorized Interview

As Gubrium and Holstein (2001) note, when first viewing the interview, it seems like a rather "simple and self-evident" event. The interviewer organizes a session with a respondent, schedules the interview and its geographical location, establishes the rules and procedures of the interview, initiates the question-and-answer period of the interview, and then ends the session. As such, the interview is a remarkably functional data-mining method for the social sciences and other fields such as journalism.

However, underlying all this is a very important theoretical assumption—the respondent as a passive vessel of answers. This has been the long-standing assumption within the "interview world," if you will, and has important implications. In this model, it is up to the interviewer to simply ask the right questions, to probe the respondent correctly, and the subject's "real world" will be revealed for all to see (Gubrium & Holstein, 2001). In this model, the interview respondent simply conveys what the passive subject already possesses as knowledge. It is unmediated by the social contours of the interview as an interactive encounter or the social factors of the world outside the interview. The data, important to the arguments presented later, are uncontaminated. In fact, it is only possible for the data to be contaminated through the mistakes made by the interviewer. Importantly, this removes the respondent as an agent in the interview process and, if we turn the tables, so to speak, also removes the interviewer as an agentic subject in the process. The different interview protocols employed produce different notions of agency in terms of the interview encounter itself. For example, in the survey interview, it is the speaker who has to be regulated or controlled. By comparison, the agent in the open-ended interview is liberated to speak freely. In short, different interview protocols produce different subjects or subjectivities.

However, as theorizing methodologists began to investigate the interview, this view was called into question. Were the interview respondents actually so passive, playing out roles already laid out for them in the many interviews that preceded them before? Or were they active, animate, and working to interactively construct an ongoing reality (Holstein & Gubrium, 1995)? The implications are significant and represent an enormous and momentous shift in how we see the interview today.

If the interview subject is seen as active, not passive, then choice must enter into the equation of the interview. That is to say, the active respondent, as subject, holds a vast repository of available information, of life experiences, and in providing answers to questions, he or she actively constructs the information provided in the interview session. The interview, especially the data, is a *constructed* thing. Again, this has important implications for "after the interview,"

for, as Gubrium and Holstein (2001) so adroitly point out, "When researchers take this active subject into account, what is otherwise a contradictory and inconclusive data set is transformed into the meaningful, intentionally crafted responses of quite active respondents" (p. 15).

In this case, the truth, or validity, of a respondent's answers cannot be judged as they were when the subject was seen as passive. Instead, the value, or use of their answers, lies in their meanings and in the manner in which these meanings were constructed. Gubrium and Holstein (1997) orient us to this by referring to it as the *whats* and *hows* of meaning-making action in the interview. In this view, the interview is inherently "active," fueled by the contribution and interaction of all participants and the various subject positions they hold as the question-and-answer banter unfolds. Again, this has important implications for data, because it implicates what researchers actually analytically choose to highlight as data and how they choose to represent it.

The switch to the active subject has had important implications. One of these is the urge, if you choose this word, to empower respondents in the interview process, on both a practical and a political level. One of the most important methodologists behind the arguments to empower respondents on a purely practical level has been Eliot Mishler. Notably, Mishler (1986) has provided means to do this, specifically with regard to medical practice and a more patient-centered medicine (Mishler, 1984).

For example, drawing on the discourse of the active subject, Mishler (1986) wishes to bring the respondent into the interview interaction as a more equal partner. Mishler argues, similar to the discussion above, that the interview should be seen as an interactional accomplishment, not simply one of call-and-response. To do this, he turns his attention to the "discourse between speakers" engaged in the interview event. By focusing on the discursive machinery of the interview, he focuses analytic attention on the ongoing speech acts and exchanges that mutually constitute the interview and by extension the subject in the interview. By viewing it as a mutually constitutive process, Mishler points out the, "considerable communicative equality and interdependence in the speech activities of all interviewing" (Gubrium & Holstein, 2001, p. 16).

For Mishler, and central to his project, communicative interdependence has enormous practical implications. Dating back to the publication of his work *The Discourse of Medicine: Dialectics of Medical Interviews*, Mishler (1984) had displayed a long-standing interest in patient-centered medicine—in this particular instance, the all-important medical encounter between doctor and patient. In an interactional example of power/knowledge at work, the doctor–patient encounter in today's medical world provides a setting for a certain type of medical interview in which the patient is systematically and discursively reduced to a mere "illness factory" as the doctor searches for the patient's medical history in a tightly scripted format. The voice at play is that of medicine, not of the patient and lay interpretations of illness.

To remedy this and empower the patient, Mishler (1984) advocates a more minimalistic interview, allowing extended narratives and illness stories by patients, a vast departure from the medical encounter as we know it. This is part and parcel of Mishler's (1986) project of empowering respondents, as he focuses his attention on, as he phrases it, "respondents' modes of understanding themselves and the world, on the possibility of their acting in terms of their own interests" (pp. 117–118). This is empowerment—acting in one's *own* interest through speaking in one's *own* voice. While there are analytic quandaries to Mishler's arguments (see Gubrium & Holstein, 2001), his romantic journey toward providing a greater voice for the patient in medicine provides us with a practical application of the goal to empower respondents within the active subject framework.

The discourse of empowerment is not merely a "practical" matter; it also has distinct political overtones. This is not to say that political empowerment is not practical; it most certainly is, but not in the sense of Mishler's (1984, 1986) arguments regarding the medical encounter and patient-centered medicine.

It is not so easy to dismiss Mishler from this story, however. His arguments concerning *participants* and *participation* in the interview process are central to the politicization of the interview and its representation. Mishler, drawing from his initial interest in the medical encounter, advocates an overtly collaborative model of the research interviewing. This collaborative goal is part of his overall project to "redistribute power" in the interview process and, in turn, to redistribute power/knowledge in discourse.

This issue of empowerment in the interview process, as noted above, takes us clearly into the political realm, most notably identity politics as a going concern (Hughes, 1942/1984). Obviously, an inherent concern here is voice. Gender, race, ethnicity, and sexuality, among other voices, all emerge as going concerns in the interview process when the power structures of the interview process are themselves taken into play. What voice is used, as an active subject, to give rise to experience is an important part of the power rubric of the interview process.

This leads us to power and representation, certainly an important concern when considering the empowerment of respondents, as well as what happens "after the interview." Indeed, we have entered what some term a *crisis in representation*. Different forms of data representation, or, as Laurel Richardson (2001) phrases it, "alternative textual choices," provide different voices, or at least ways of hearing these voices. Richardson begins by suggesting that interviews, at least in the academic context, are most often (if not always) conducted for research audiences. This has important implications. In short, the questions and, in turn, the "expected" answers and their portrayal are developed with the "analytic interests" of researchers in the forefront.

However, interview respondents might not think in these terms. While a sociologist of health and illness might be studying breast cancer and its intersection with race and class in a study on health disparities, respondents might not think that their opinions or answers are best understood or comprehended in this manner, or with this blueprint. Vital to our understanding of what happens after the interview, Richardson (2001) further alerts us to how coding itself works to take power away from respondents by changing and altering their narratives into *our* terms, away from *their* sense-making mechanisms. She suggests radically different forms of representation, such as poetry instead of prose, to more capably reproduce a respondent's conveyed narrative meanings. Others, such as Carolyn Ellis and Arthur Bochner (1996), have taken up this calling, using different forms of representational texts to convey respondents' experience and empower their voices.

In this section, I have focused attention on a historical analysis of the interview—that is to say, a theoretical analysis of the interview as a research methodology primarily employed in the social sciences. My focus here has been on the interview as a situational encounter, particularly the question of agency as it is implied in the interview encounter to the respondent, according to specific interview practices. Extending this, I have investigated the ramifications of the questions of agency in the interview in terms of respondent empowerment and political overtures. However, inclusive to all of this is an overarching focus on what happens "after the interview." That is, we must see the interview as a holistic process both involving the encounter itself and extended into interview work postinterview.

◆ After the Interview as Process

As we turn our attention further toward the holistic nature of the interview as process, in this section, we will focus on the actual means and methods of the postinterview process as discussed in the introduction. Each of these provides important indicators of how interviews, from beginning to end, and the interviewing methods, from conceptual apparatus to methodological techniques, work to construct the actual data presented. In short, each method, or approach, constructs, from its initiation to its completion, postinterview, the actual representation of interview data for reporting and writing.

SENSITIZING CONCEPTS AND CODING

The term *sensitizing concept* originated with Herbert Blumer (1954), founder of the Symbolic Interactionist School, who contrasted definitive concepts with sensitizing concepts. Blumer explained that

> a definitive concept refers precisely to what is common to a class of objects, by the aid of a clear definition in terms of attributes or fixed benchmarks. . . . A sensitizing concept lacks such specification of attributes or benchmarks and consequently it does not enable the user to move directly to the instance and its relevant content. Instead, it gives the user a general sense of reference and guidance in approaching empirical instances. Whereas definitive concepts provide prescriptions of what to see, sensitizing concepts merely suggest directions along which to look. (p. 7)

Importantly, qualitative researchers view sensitizing concepts as interpretive devices and as a starting point for a qualitative study and, for our purposes, interview research (Bowen, 2006; Glaser, 1978; Padgett, 2004). Sensitizing concepts point analytic attention to important features of social interaction and provide guidelines for interpretation of research. Key to the arguments made in this chapter, according to Gilgun (2002, as cited in Bowen, 2006), "Research usually begins with such concepts, whether researchers state this or not and whether they are aware of them or not" (p. 4). In short, sensitizing concepts inform the actual initiation of the interview project, the coding, and the interpretation of data. While seemingly perhaps just affecting the coding process, they instead affect the whole interview as process, from beginning to end.

Charmaz (2001) points us farther along in this direction, alerting us to sensitizing concepts as an overriding juggernaut, to borrow a concept from Anthony Giddens, in the interview process. She points out that in her own research, symbolic interactionist concepts such as "identity" and "self-concept" have provided ongoing themes for her research, most notably identity, "alerting [her] to look for its implicit meanings in the lives of participants" (p. 683). As a noted researcher on chronic illness (see Charmaz, 1987), she has connected identity with a variety of respondents' going concerns, including identity goals and identity hierarchy, as these were tied with physical condition and social circumstance.

As a constructivist grounded theorist, Charmaz (2006) acknowledges the *reflexivity* inherent in researchers' work, which further explains the interplay between interview questions, preconceptions, assumptions, and interpretations of their data. The coding process of grounded theory requires, in fact demands, this. There is an open acknowledgment of the preconceptions of data and the use of sensitizing concepts, such as identity or self, though also a reflexivity between these concepts and data, something positivistic that researchers do not theoretically acknowledge. Charmaz (2001) openly notes this when she states, "Constructivist grounded theorists acknowledge that they *define* what is happening in their data" (p. 684).

Grounded theory (Glaser & Strauss, 1967), whether constructionist in nature or not, is heavily valued and used by many in interview research, especially researchers in health-related fields. As such, it is an important arena to investigate in terms of "after the interview." Comments by Charmaz and others alert us to the implications that the use of sensitizing concepts have for the interview process, from beginning to end, and the importance of reflexivity in determining the construction of data and its interpretation. "After the interview" is shown to be a process that exists before the interview, during the interview, and after the interview, working back and forth at all points in between.

NARRATIVE ANALYSIS

We are in the midst of the "narrative turn" (Riessman, 2001). Beyond sociology (Chase, 1995; Frank, 1995; Holstein & Gubrium, 2000), the analysis of narratives has been extensively used in disciplines as diverse as history (Carr, 1986; Cronon, 1992), anthropology (Mattingly & Garro, 2000), psychology (Bruner, 1986; Mishler, 2000; Sarbin, 1986), nursing (Sandelowski, 1991), and occupational therapy (Mattingly, 1998), among others. Narrative analysis takes as its data, its object of interest, storytelling, or the act of "storying." What is important to us here is how narrative is defined in research, how it is analyzed, and how it is represented.

As Riessman (2001) so adroitly points out, "There is considerable variation in how investigators employ the concept of personal narrative and, relatedly, in the methodological assumptions" (p. 697). This has enormous methodological implications. For example, Barbara Myerhoff (1978) used narrative to study elderly Eastern European Jews living in Venice, California. Her choice of narrative representation has important implications for "data representation." In using the narratives of her respondents, she builds portraits of them by inserting herself into the text, building her story inside theirs. According to Riessman (2001), this allows her to "speak her truth without 'erasing the others' viewpoint and social language'" (p. 697; Kaminsky, 1992, pp. 17–18). While this point can certainly be argued, it does alert us to one representational technique, among many, and the way in which narrative data can be represented by the researcher. Representation is data.

To reach this point, however, an important step must be taken. The researcher has to define what exactly narrative is for the purpose at hand. Is all talk in interviews narrative? Are we to treat questions,

answers, utterances, pauses, and entrances and exits of talk in social interaction as narratives? Stories are rarely clearly bounded with an entrance and exit and are often negotiated in the interview as social encounter between respondent and interviewer, or teller and listener (though these positions are not so clearly defined at all moments). Defining and establishing boundaries as to what is and what is not narrative, then, is clearly an interpretive task of the researcher with methodological consequences.

Riessman (2001) provides us with an empirical example of this complex problem as she reflects on her own narrative study of stigma and infertility, primarily conducted in South India. She focuses on the singular narrative of a woman she calls "Gita" and begins her discussion at a point where teller and listener discuss the topic of infertility. Gita provides a fascinating story of terminated pregnancies, political demonstration and resistance, and her own spouse's anger. Then, her narrative shifts to a story of her in-laws and her husband's own refusal to be tested for possible infertility. Gita's story spanned many years and extended across various social settings, encounters, and dimensions. Perhaps surprisingly, she alludes to no emotional distress or sadness over the story being told.

But what are the boundaries of Gita's narrative? How do we interpret it? How do we represent it as data? Initially, Riessman decided to conclude the narrative with this statement by Gita: "But afterwards I never became—[pregnant]." Her rationale was that this ended Gita's discussion of pregnancy. However, on further reflection, she decided to include what she refers to as the "next scene," Gita's narrative about her husband and the extended family. Why? Because Riessman's own theoretical markers, her sensitizing concept, as discussed in the previous subsection, were altered with regard to identity construction to resistance to stigma. Therefore, what was to be included in the narrative, what *had* to be represented as data, was subsequently altered.

Riessman (2001) ends her discussion by summarizing that this "discernment" of a particular narrative text for analysis and representation, as with all narrative analysis and representation, is affected by researchers' evolving (or reflexive) understandings, their own disciplines, and beginning and developing research questions. As she points out, at all levels, the researcher, both teller and listener, I suggest, "infiltrates" the text. This alludes to my ongoing point that "after the interview" cannot be separated as a temporal moment distinct from the rest of the interview but, rather, can only be seen as part and parcel of the interview as process.

THE SHIFT IN REPRESENTATION

Postmodernism, as an epistemological shift, has had an enormous and profound impact on our understanding of the interview as process (Fontana, 2001). Strangely, this has occurred at the same time as a romantic shift in representation, making for, if you wish, rather strange analytic bedfellows (Gubrium & Holstein, 2001; Marvasti & Faircloth, 2002). Nevertheless, the two discourses, whether seen as competing or mutually coproductive, have led to an important shift in representation of the interview subject and data.

Rather than enter into a long discussion of postmodernism, I wish to only briefly discuss its impact on the interview. As Fontana (2001) points out, those interview researchers alert to postmodernism are inherently theoretically aware of the boundary blurring between the traditional roles of interviewer and interviewee. This, in turn, leads to the production of new forms of representation concerned with the ownership of story and the possession of "voice" in data. From this, new forms of representation have exploded on the scene—poetry, literature, drama, and a comingling of narratives. Last, the "cinematic society" (Denzin, 1991) is on us with its own implications for the interview as process and representation. Indeed, we are at a crisis point.

As noted earlier in the chapter, it is Richardson who perhaps most forthrightly urges us toward these representational and alternative textual choices. Acknowledging that research interviews are conducted for specific audiences (as Goffman would certainly allude to), these audiences are not, however, the audiences that respondents are speaking to. These are the audiences that the researchers are speaking to, usually, when representing their data in conventional forms. However, in doing so, they "disenfranchise" the research subjects, remove them from their own folk sensibilities, and turn their narratives into foreign objects. Richardson (2001) argues that a shift in textual form is needed to convey the authentic experience of subjects in the interview format. In her case, it is the use of poetry as a representational form that most authentically reproduces the interview subject's true meanings and feelings. Prose as a textual form is seen to be inadequate. It cannot convey what poetry can as text. So in this postmodern moment, poetry takes precedence as data over narrative or other forms of representation.

Richardson (2001) even offers advice on how to achieve better representation through poetry in the interview process. She suggests taking classes in poetry writing, joining a poetry circle, and attending poetry readings. As she states, "The more you immerse yourself in it, the better you can communicate with it" (p. 881). If you, as a researcher and a reporter of the knowledge claims of respondents, are going to write poetry, then you need to learn to do it "right"! She goes on to provide further tips such as "Revise, revise, revise," suggesting that the researcher write various poems to represent the interview material.

Focusing on poetry as a representational tool has implications on the interview from the very beginning of the process, not simply at the end. As Richardson (2001) comments, the researcher should construct his or her interview schedule in such a way "as to elicit images and similes" (p. 882). This has implications for the very type of questions to be asked by the interviewer, leading to questions that probe for metaphors and images from the subject—simply put, data that are more conducive for inclusion into poetry as a representational form. Richardson (2001) concludes by speaking to the inherent reflexivity of this project, suggesting that the researcher start with one goal in mind, but as the project unfolds, another goal might emerge. Seeing representation as a creative activity, as Richardson does, this is in no way surprising. As she puts it, "It is as if the writing has a mind of its own, strange as that may sound" (p. 883).

Ellis and Berger (2001) tell us another tale of the shift in representation, though one that is remarkably similar. Long involved in new forms of interviewing and representation, Carolyn Ellis, along with Arthur Bochner (see Bochner & Ellis, 1996; Ellis & Bochner, 1996), provides a valuable resource for this discussion. A useful example for this discussion is "interactive interviews," which takes us from the beginning of the interview process to the end, from the interview as setting to the interview as data representation, and all through its many pathways and byways.

According to Ellis and Berger (2001), in this form of interviewing, the interviewer self-consciously inserts himself or herself into a collaborative, group interview setting (Ellis, Kiesinger, & Tillman-Healy, 1997). The goal is for *all* participating in the interview to see and act as *both* researchers and research subjects. Like Richardson, Ellis and Berger provide a blueprint when they suggest that this format works best when all participants are trained as interviewers/ researchers. However, there is a primary researcher. The emotions, insights, comments, narratives, and stories of the primary researcher are as important and as vital as those of the other participants; they are all equally valuable interview subjects. The meanings and shared understandings that emerge through the interview interactions are developed together, interactively. While all bring their own stories to the interview, a collaborative story is developed through the interactive process of the interview.

This is brought to life in Ellis et al. (1997), which describes a research project on bulimia. The researcher has no experience with the condition, but all others in the group interview have. However, all the participants share common concerns with food and women's bodies as culturally constructed commodities, as well as an interest in the particular research methodology. Out of the interview sessions, a paper emerged that consisted of four stories, drawn from different occasions, the last from a dinner at a local restaurant, alerting us to the nongeographical boundaries of the interview setting. Each story adds another "layer," another texture, to the data. Ellis inserts herself into the text as an "outsider" at various points, discussing methodological difficulties, quandaries, and various problems she faces, as well as her own emotions and developing understanding in performing this research. We are left with a fascinating representation of story, or stories, as data, emerging from the very initiation of the interactive interview as an interview methodology to its chosen form of representation after the interview is concluded.

THE POLITICIZATION OF THE INTERVIEW

In recent decades, we have seen an increasing concern with identity politics in interview research (Gubrium & Holstein, 2001). Obviously, this is part of an overarching increased awareness of identity, and its shifting political nature, within the social sciences on the whole. But it is important to note that the interview has not been immune to this. Interview subjects are now seen as historically, culturally, and politically constructed, embedded in a matrix of identities—gender, race, ethnicity, sexuality, class, age groups, and others. This has important implications for how the interview is seen as a methodological tool, how the subject is constructed for data-gathering purposes, and how data are to be represented. In short, it has enormous implications throughout the interview process.

While the politicization of the interview process and its implication for "after the interview" can be explored from various angles and identities, for the sake of argument, in this chapter, I wish to look at what Kong, Mahoney, and Plummer (2001) term *queering the interview*—in other words, the interviewing of LGBT (lesbian, gay, bisexual, transexual) subjects, the inherent political nature of this act, and its methodological implications. Apart from the interviewing of "homosexuals," the queering of the interview process, with its postmodern and poststructuralist theoretical underpinnings, opened up a new world of methodological considerations with regard to the interviewing of the "gay subject," voice, subject positioning, and textual representation of data.

As Kong et al. (2001) note, it was the shift to reflexivity in feminist research in the 1980s that led to an understanding of the research process as something that is inherently "moral and political." Furthering this was the onset of HIV/AIDS, which led to more community-based approaches to research, directly involving participants in data interpretation and representation and incorporating findings into a "public social science." There was now an increase of gay interviewers and interviewees who shared meanings, going concerns, and "ways of knowing" (Kong et al., 2001). The interview had been "gayed."

From here, it was but a short step to the "queering" of the interview. Drawing from the theoretical movements of poststructuralism and postmodernism, queer theory pushed its way into the world of the interview. The implications for the construction of the subject were immediate. No longer was there simply the "gay subject" but now a decentered, unstructured subject, multiple and fragmented, constructed by discourses of sexuality, race, gender, and class. All of these subject positions, then, entered the interview world, and all had moral and political dimensions.

This queering of the interview and the concept of multiple subject positions led to new concerns with representation as a political problem. What do "interview stories" of gays or lesbians really represent? Whose story is it anyway? In a very poststructuralist question, who is the author of the story, or narrative? The research subject? The researcher? To deal with these questions, as we discussed in the previous section, new forms of representation, new strategies of narrative or performance, must be found, embraced, and used. Politics, morality, and representation of data, of writing the interview, are expressly linked (Plummer, 1995). New interview sites such as Internet chat rooms and virtual worlds are opened up as methodological tools for queering the interview itself, and representational forms centering on queering the voice and the subject become paramount concerns and goals in data interpretation and presentation.

◆ Conclusion

In this chapter, I have "taken on" a subject matter that has been vastly undertheorized. This is quite unusual given the seemingly endless amount of theorizing we have had in recent years concerning the interview as methodology. However, what happens "after the interview" has been almost completely left alone, as if self-evident for all to see. After all, everyone knows what you do when an interview is completed, right? Well, not if you look a little deeper. What one does after the interview is implicated and complicated by the choices made before the interview and throughout the "interview as process" due to the reflexive nature of the method. In fact, I suggest that there is no separate moment such as "after the interview." It is only an extended moment of the interview as process, beyond the specific situational encounter itself.

To explore this, I have investigated the interview as process through four specific areas: (1) sensitizing concepts and coding, (2) narrative analysis, (3) the shift in representation, and (4) the politicization of the interview. Each of these areas illuminates different aspects of the interview as process and its implications on the emergent final product. Taken together, these four areas shed light on the process nature of the interview as a research methodology—for example, how sensitizing concepts, at the initiation of a project, influence how the researcher will "see" the data and, in turn, develop coding schemes. The section on different forms of representation displays the importance of the choices made in terms of how data and findings are presented to the audience. While this might seem to many as a choice to be made at the end, it is influenced by theoretical and epistemological stances of the researcher that exist from before the interview and reflexively constitute themselves throughout the interview as process.

All in all, the interview, as a whole, is a fascinating process fraught with theoretical and methodological questions and quandaries, as the many other chapters in this *Handbook* indicate. It is hoped that this chapter will provide an impetus to future discussion on what happens after the interview. As mentioned previously, it is an immensely undertheorized area of the interview as a datagathering technique increasingly employed in the "interview society" we live in today.

◆ References

Blumer, H. (1954). What is wrong with social theory. *American Sociological Review, 18,* 3–10.

Bochner, A. P., & Ellis, C. (Eds.). (1996). Talking over ethnography. In C. Ellis & A. P. Bochner (Eds.), *Composing ethnography: Alternative forms of qualitative writing* (pp. 13–45). Walnut Creek, CA: AltaMira Press.

Bowen, G. (2006). Grounded theory and sensitizing concepts. *International Journal of Qualitative Methods, 5,* 1–9.

Bruner, J. (1986). *Actual minds, possible worlds.* Cambridge, MA: Harvard University Press.

Carr, D. (1986). *Time, narrative, and history.* Bloomington: University of Indiana Press.

Charmaz, K. (1987). Struggling for self: Identity levels of the chronically ill. In J. A. Roth & P. Conrad (Eds.), *Research in the sociology of health care: The experience and management of chronic illness* (Vol. 6, pp. 283–321). Greenwich, CT: JAI Press.

Charmaz, K. (2001). Qualitative interviewing and grounded theory analysis. In J. Gubrium & J. Holstein (Eds.), *Handbook of interview research* (1st ed., pp. 675–694). Thousand Oaks, CA: Sage.

Charmaz, K. (2006). *Constructing grounded theory: A practical guide through qualitative analysis.* Thousand Oaks, CA: Sage.

Chase, S. (1995). *Ambiguous empowerment: The work narratives of women school superintendents.* Amherst: University of Massachusetts Press.

Cronon, W. (1992). A place for stories: Nature, history, and narrative. *Journal of American History, 78,* 1347–1376.

Denzin, N. (1991). *Images of postmodern society: Social theory and contemporary cinema.* London, England: Sage.

Ellis, C., & Berger, L. (2001). Their story/my story: Including the researcher's experience in interview research. In J. Gubrium & J. Holstein (Eds.), *Handbook of interview research* (1st ed., pp. 849–876). Thousand Oaks, CA: Sage.

Ellis, C., & Bochner, A. P. (Eds.). (1996). *Composing ethnography: Alternative forms of qualitative writing.* Walnut Creek, CA: AltaMira Press.

Ellis, C., Kiesinger, C. E., & Tillman-Healy, L. M. (1997). Interactive interviewing: Talking about emotional experience. In R. Hertz (Ed.), *Reflexivity and voice* (pp. 119–149). Thousand Oaks, CA: Sage.

Fontana, A. (2001). Postmodern trends in interviewing. In J. Gubrium & J. Holstein (Eds.), *Handbook of interview research* (1st ed., pp. 161–175). Thousand Oaks, CA: Sage.

Frank, A. (1995). *The wounded storyteller.* Chicago, IL: University of Chicago Press.

Glaser, B. (1978). *Theoretical sensitivity: Advances in the methodology of grounded theory.* Mill Valley, CA: Sociology Press.

Glaser, B., & Strauss, A. (1967). *The discovery of grounded theory: Strategies for qualitative research.* Chicago, IL: Aldine Press.

Gubrium, J., & Holstein, J. (Eds.). (1997). *The new language of qualitative method.* New York, NY: Oxford University Press.

Gubrium, J., & Holstein, J. (Eds.). (2001). *Handbook of interview research* (1st ed.). Thousand Oaks, CA: Sage.

Gubrium, J., & Holstein, J. (Eds.). (2001). *Institutional selves: Troubled identities in a postmodern world.* New York, NY: Oxford University Press.

Holstein, J., & Gubrium, J. (1995). *The active interview.* Thousand Oaks, CA: Sage.

Holstein, J., & Gubrium, J. (2000). *The self we live by: Narrative identity in a postmodern world.* New York, NY: Oxford University Press.

Hughes, E. C. (1984). *The sociological eye: Selected papers.* Chicago, IL: Aldine Press. (Original work published 1942)

Kaminsky, M. (1992). Introduction. In B. Myerhoff (Ed.), *Remembered lives: The work of ritual, storytelling, and growing older* (pp. 1–98). Ann Arbor: University of Michigan Press.

Kong, T. S., Mahoney, D., & Plummer, K. (2001). Queering the interview. In J. Gubrium & J. Holstein (Eds.), *Handbook of interview research* (1st ed., pp. 239–258). Thousand Oaks, CA: Sage.

Marvasti, A., & Faircloth, C. (2002). Writing the exotic, the authentic, and the moral: Romanticism as discursive resource for ethnographic text. *Qualitative Inquiry, 8,* 760–784.

Mattingly, C. (1998). *Healing dramas and clinical plots: The narrative structure of experience.* Berkeley: University of California Press.

Mattingly, C., & Garro, L. C. (Eds.). (2000). *Narrative and cultural construction of illness and healing.* Berkeley: University of California Press.

Mishler, E. (1984). *The discourse of medicine: Dialectics of medical interviews.* Norwood, NJ: Ablex.

Mishler, E. (1986). *Research interviewing: Context and narrative.* Cambridge, MA: Harvard University Press.

Mishler, E. (2000). *Storylines: Craftartists' narratives of identity.* Cambridge, MA: Harvard University Press.

Myerhoff, B. (1978). *Number our days.* New York, NY: Simon & Schuster.

Padgett, D. K. (2004). Coming of age: Theoretical thinking, social responsibility, and a global perspective in qualitative research. In D. K. Padgett (Ed.), *The qualitative research experience* (pp. 297–315). Belmont, CA: Wadsworth/Thomson Learning.

Plummer, K. (1995). *Telling sexual stories: Power, change, and social worlds.* London, England: Routledge.

Richardson, L. (2001). Poetic representation of interviews. In J. Gubrium & J. Holstein (Eds.), *Handbook of interview research* (1st ed., pp. 877–892). Thousand Oaks, CA: Sage.

Riessman, C. K. (2001). Analysis of personal narratives. In J. Gubrium & J. Holstein (Eds.), *Handbook of interview research* (1st ed., pp. 695–710). Thousand Oaks, CA: Sage.

Sandelowski, M. (1991). Telling stories: Narrative approaches in qualitative research. *Image: Journal of Nursing Scholarship, 23*(3), 161–166.

Sarbin, T. R. (Ed.). (1986). *Narrative psychology.* New York, NY: Praeger.

Warren, C., Barnes-Brus, T., Burgess, H., Wiebold-Lippisch, L., Hackney, J., Harkness, G., . . . Ryen, A. (2003). After the interview. *Qualitative Sociology, 26*(1), 93–110.

Part IV

SELF AND OTHER IN THE INTERVIEW

19

MANAGING THE INTERVIEWER SELF

◆ Annika Lillrank

◆ Introduction

A reflexive turn in the social sciences and qualitative research has acknowledged the interviewer as an inevitable part of the interview process and empirical evidence claims in the research results. This means that the interaction between the interviewer and interviewees needs to be included in the analytic work as the context in which interviewees' responses are articulated. To focus only on respondents' answers without taking the entire dialogue into account is not enough (Holstein & Gubrium, 2003; Hydén, 2008b, p. 97; McIlveen, 2008; Mishler, 1986). To *"activate narrative production,"* an active interviewer facilitates the interview interaction to "direct and harness the respondent's constructive storytelling to the research task at hand" (Holstein & Gubrium, 1995, p. 39). Respondents' answers could be seen as part of an ongoing process where the interviewer continuously tries to make sense of the unfolding interaction (Holstein & Gubrium, 2003; Hydén, 2008a, p. 124; Riessman, 2000).

This way of looking at interviewing also directs our attention to the complexity of emotional labor in researcher–respondent interactions and the various ways in which it is incorporated into the research process and writing (Andrews, 2007; Arendell, 1997; Hoffman, 2007; Holstein & Gubrium, 2003; Hydén, 2008b). This sensitivity to the interactional dynamics of the interview is founded on the proposition that "knowledge cannot be separated from the knower" (Steedman, 1991, as cited in Alvesson & Sköldberg, 2005, p. 1). Instead, knowledge is assumed to be embodied in subjective lived experiences and the management of identity in social interaction. In this context, researchers must attend to both the thematic and the dynamic dimensions of the interview: "thematically with regard to producing knowledge, and dynamically with regard to the interpersonal relationship in the interview" (Kvale, 2007, p. 57).

How interviewers reflexively elaborate the thematic and dynamic aspects of interview interactions has a long history. It has ranged from early anthropological "realist tales" to personal "confessional tales" and toward more transparent descriptions of intersubjective understandings of the research process. Today, its countless forms are "the defining features of qualitative research" (Finlay, 2002, pp. 210–211; Holstein & Gubrium, 2003). However, the apparent consensus on the importance of interaction in interview data collection has not resulted in uniform or unified practices. Indeed, the related body of research and pedagogy is "full of muddy ambiguity and multiple trails" (Finlay, 2002, p. 212).

In this chapter, I specifically focus on the range of interviewer self-presentation and identity management practices. For my purpose, the core area of the interviewer's self-management is about self-presentation and listening. Thus, I suggest rethinking and theorizing about the vital dimensions of the interview as relational work. Compared with standardized interview practice, where an interviewer simply coordinates interviews, designed to result in certain responses (Holstein & Gubrium, 2003), I propose that the interviewer needs to first engage in active listening—meaning, suspending one's own perspective to focus on what the interviewee has to say. In this way, listening becomes interactive, relational work that theoretically means more than just hearing things correctly. It means reflective work, or trying to understand the responses or an emerging story from the interviewee's point of view, and to theorize flexibly about what comes next regarding related follow-up questions.

Second, an interviewer needs to attend to multifaceted power shifts during the interview interaction. I suggest that the standardized interview practice with an active interviewer and a passive interviewee merely offering information of personal experiences (Holstein & Gubrium, 2003) be reworked to a joint construction of an explicit give-and-take interaction. Since power is always relational and based on resources, such as values or specific knowledge, the interviewer's dominant position may become subordinate when asking for something valuable, for example, interviewees' experiences (Hydén, 2008a, pp. 126–127; Mishler, 1986).

Third, and perhaps most important, the interviewer needs to manage emotions during the interview to *facilitate interviewer–interviewee* knowledge production. Compared with the positivist thinking in standard interview practice, which emphasizes objectivity and neutrality in the pursuit of truth (Holstein

& Gubrium, 2003), I suggest that managing emotions during the interview is an essential skill for an interviewer's self-management. For example, an interviewer benefits from developing strategies to support and empower interviewees—and not challenge them—to ensure a reciprocal interaction resulting in rich data gathering (Hydén, 2008a, pp. 133–134; Mishler, 1986). By highlighting these three areas of the active interviewing model, I would like to expand it in these new directions.

Accordingly, the chapter is divided into two main parts. The first part consists of reflections on listening and focuses on interviewers managing the self in interviewing practices. Using excerpts from Margareta Hydén's (2000, 2008b) study with abused women, several examples are provided to highlight the management of an interviewer self as an active listener and as a "helping voice." This section explores how "conversational collaboration" (Gubrium & Holstein, 2009, p. 94) facilitates and lends support to a teller-focused interview interaction. The second part examines emotions and emotional work as dynamic aspects of an interviewer's self-management. Concepts such as autoethnography, "vulnerable observer," and "defended subjects" highlight the different ways of managing the interviewer self and are discussed using various examples. I conclude the chapter by reemphasizing the complexity of emotional management, particularly for the interviewer self, and considering the trajectory of this topic, particularly in relation to qualitative research.

◆ Reflections on Listening

Since research questions often originate from personal interests and commitments that researchers care deeply about, the involvement is usually both personal and professional. It is common knowledge these days that most researchers are personally invested in their research topics. As Molly Andrews (2007) points out, "Sometimes we might even feel that our questions choose us" (p. 27). This has inevitable consequences for the interview practices that challenge conventional, standard interviewing as an asymmetrical encounter, where an interviewer actively asks for information from interviewees, who are seen as passive "vessels of answers" (Holstein & Gubrium, 2003, p. 12).

Because the active interview indicates a reciprocal personal interaction about mutually shared interests, neither interviewers nor interviewees are necessarily expected to omit their subjective selves or keep their emotional reactions outside the interview process. Indeed, the interview, in some cases, could become "interpersonal drama" with a range of emotional reactions, power negotiations, and other mundane interpersonal questions that help generate knowledge and construct meaning (Holstein & Gubrium, 1995). Certainly, if we were to view the interview from an "active" standpoint, there is no reason why the interviewee and the interviewers should not be encouraged to speak in their personal ways.

THE INTERVIEWER AS AN ACTIVE LISTENER

Margareta Hydén (2000, 2008b) and Molly Andrews (2007) emphasize the importance of *active listening* as a critical but underanalyzed dimension of interview research. As far as the pedagogy of interviewing is concerned, listening is both about the microdynamics of the interview and about a larger, thematic research agenda.

The ability to listen actively requires more than being quiet. Telling and listening are like twin sisters in a complementary relationship. Listening is hard work since it involves risking one's self to an unexpected framework of meanings. It takes time to develop confidence. And it is mentally demanding, since it requires openness to the unknown and that the listener be both intellectually and emotionally engaged and attentive (Andrews, 2007, pp. 15–16; Hydén, 2008b, p. 89). A good listener creates a mental space for the other. It means that the listener is able to leave his or her own perspective and concentrate on what the narrator has and wants to say. It also means to take care, interpret, and respond to a story and to avoid taking for granted one's own hypothetical framework of the subject matter. In addition, a good listener recognizes shifts, contradictions, or gaps in a story (Andrews, 2007; Gubrium & Holstein, 2009; Hydén, 2008b, pp. 89–96).

How is it practically possible to create a mental space that oscillates between closeness and distance? One possibility is to continually encourage the interviewee to expand the telling, using statements such as these: "Please go on telling me what happened."

"Did this remind you of something you have experienced before?" "Can you give me an example?" "Could you possibly relate this story to a picture, a color, a fragrance that could help express what you are talking about?" (Hydén, 2008b, p. 96). This way of interviewing allows for several possibilities to explore an experience. At the same time, it facilitates management of the interviewer self. Last, but not the least, it underlines respect for the interviewees; it suggests that their experiences are valuable and worth listening to from multiple angles (Andrews, 2007; Hydén, 2008b, pp. 95–96; Mishler, 1986; Riessman, 2000, 2003).

In encouraging respondents to elaborate on their stories, researchers must keep in mind that individual narratives take forms that are specific to the culture that they construct and are constructed by. The stories interviewees tell, and the stories interviewers hear, are immersed in the cultural norms of a community. Individuals are socialized to think of their lives in a particular way, and they usually construct stories about their own lives in relation to culturally expected tales. That is why the "tell-ability" of individuals' experiences is influenced by the level of intimacy between speaker and listener and especially by the larger cultural context in which the narrative is told (Andrews, 2007, p. 33).

In the next section, I present a teller-focused interview method, developed by Margareta Hydén (2000, 2008b). She demonstrates how an interviewee can be helped to articulate better when the interviewer acts as a supporting "helping voice." The battered women, whom she interviewed, have never talked about their experiences; instead, they have been actively suppressed and encouraged to silence their experiences.

THE INTERVIEWER ACTING AS A "HELPING VOICE"

The concept of a "helping voice" means something like "a voice that makes itself available to help an interviewee articulate her- or himself more clearly," especially if somebody speaks with a weak or evasive voice. In such situations, an interviewer "lends her own voice" to encourage interviewees to try out different ways of talking until they find a comfortable mode of self-expression (Hydén, 2000, p. 143; Mishler, 1986).

An interviewee who talks with an evasive voice usually gives indefinite answers such as "I do not know" or "Maybe." In the beginning of an interview, such responses should not be automatically regarded as obstacles to real data collection. Instead, such maneuvers might be "natural" when two strangers begin talking to each other, especially about a sensitive topic. If in interviews with battered women—and others who have lived in traumatic circumstances—the interviewee speaks in an evasive manner, one way of understanding this behavior is to see it as an expression of the interviewee's uncertainty about the demands of the social setting (i.e., the interview itself). Also, such verbal strategies might be reflections of earlier, futile dialogues between her and an abusive partner. In such relations, an abused woman has a lot to gain by being vague. For example, a woman may trigger a violent reaction if she makes clear statements and articulates her own opinions. From this point of view, speaking with an evasive voice is very appropriate. However, this may turn against herself or the telling of her experience in a meaningful way, especially in a research interview (Hydén, 2000, p. 144). To illustrate this point, let us consider the following excerpt from an actual interview with a battered woman leaving an abusive husband.

Fredrika, a 21-year-old Swedish woman, has been seriously battered and sexually harassed. This interview took place 4 weeks after she arrived at a women's shelter in Stockholm. Fredrika had agreed to participate in Margareta Hydén's (2000) study but was uncertain if she had anything valuable to contribute to the study. The following dialogue developed between Fredrika (F) and Margareta (M):

M: So I am somewhat curious about how you are now . . . are you happy with yourself nowadays?

F: Yes, it could be said . . . yes . . . both this and that . . .

M: Mm . . .

F: About that?

M: Mm

F: It is clear that today I feel . . . I feel happier with myself than I was a year ago . . . only to look back one year . . . (pp. 144–146)

In her analysis of this case, Margareta Hydén (2000) explains,

My comments were limited to a few supporting "mmm's." I articulated a more positive support in these "mmm's" than what can be read from the transcriptions. I was hoping Fredrika should continue telling without much interference from me. I felt that she was very uncertain and was afraid that she should become quiet or uncritically agree to what I was saying. But I did not get much reaction to my minimal utterances. All I learned initially was that both "this and that" could be told about being happy with oneself and that she was happier with herself now than a year ago. Then Fredrika became quiet. In an attempt to continue our dialogue, I took hold of her last sentence:

M: Why did you feel so unhappy about a year ago?

F: Yes oh . . . afraid and uncertain and I felt that I would never be able to get out of that box that I am in . . .

M: Mm

F: It felt like I was trapped . . .

M: Did it have something to do with Janno [the husband] or was it in general . . . ?

F: I thought more about that with Janno . . . I think . . .

M: You told about the years before Janno, you moved out of your parents' home early . . . it gave an impression that you did not really know what you were up to . . . (p. 145)

In this short part of the interview, two topics became obvious: "being trapped" and "uncertainty." The sense of being trapped is spoken out, while uncertainty is framed more indirectly by statements such as "I think" and pauses between words and sentences. Hydén had a possibility and a demand to choose from. So she chose to continue the interview by focusing on the "uncertainty" expressed in Fredrika's last reply: "I think." As the interviewer, she continued by connecting it to the uncertainty Fredrika had talked about earlier in the interview— her traveling when she was a very young woman moving from her childhood home. Hydén hoped, by focusing on a negative topic such as "uncertainty," to make it meaningful in the interview, thus acknowledging that no topics were too trivial or unclear for a discussion. However, her initial attempts failed. To explore openly seemed to make Fredrika even more uncertain. The interviewee's *uncertainty* made the interviewer *uncertain*—Hydén (2000, p. 145) could not shield herself from this feeling.

Hydén (2000) concludes,

My attempt to explore the theme of "uncertainty" seemed to be doomed to end in—uncertainty itself [italics added]. However, as the interview process continued, Fredrika became more articulated in her talk and was able to introduce rather articulated issues for discussions. This way of interviewing required a research design that included several interviews with each interviewee. Regardless of repeated or one-interview sessions, the interviewer's emotional and cognitive empathic statements were important. By empathy *I mean ability to see the things from the interviewees' point of view* [italics added]. Cognitive empathy means ability to follow an interviewee's thoughts and ways of thinking. This could mean verifying what an interviewee has said by asking her to continue a line of thoughts. (pp. 145–146)

The interviewer's ability to function as a helping voice for interviewees who talk with an evasive voice is founded on the idea that when an interviewee tells about herself, it also invites increased self-reflection and awareness. This became evident in the study of battered women's process of leaving abusive husbands. Only on rare occasions had these women talked with someone else about the issues that were covered in the interviews. Women who talk with an evasive voice are not able to easily develop an articulated story. It is the interviewer's task to develop an interaction practice that enables interviewees to create a more clearly articulated story (Gubrium & Holstein, 2009, p. 37; Holstein & Gubrium, 2003; Hydén, 2000, p. 146). As evident from this discussion, active listening involves attending to both the talk about the substantive area or theme of the interview and the emotional labor of the talk itself. These two dimensions of active listening are interdependent. In the next section, I will discuss the emotional management of the interviewer self from different angles.

◆ Reflecting on Emotional Labor

Emotions are defined by Hochschild (2003) as "bodily cooperation with idea, thought, or attitude and the label attached to that awareness" (p. 75). By "feelings," she means simply milder emotions (p. 75). An active interviewing strategy acknowledges that to be able to listen to and understand an interviewee means to enter into an emotional relationship. Reflecting on emotional atmosphere becomes an important part of interviewing (Ezzy, 2010, pp. 168–169). The focus on emotions as an inevitable part of research interviews has developed within the past decades (Arendell, 1997; Blee, 1998, p. 395; Ellis, 1999; Hoffman, 2007; Kleinman & Copp, 1993). An increasing amount of research has focused on managing the interviewer self when it comes to emotions since "emotional labor is central to the trade. But we might be made somewhat more comfortable . . . if more of our efforts were directed to the understanding, expression, and reporting of [our emotions]" (Kleinman & Copp, 1993, p. viii). This has revealed emotions as an inevitable part of interviewing skills (Hochschild, 2003; Hoffman, 2007; Hydén, 2008a; Kleinman & Copp, 1993; Riessman, 2002).

Hochschild (1983) defined emotional labor as "the management of feeling to create a publicly observable facial and bodily display" (p. 7). Emotional interactions in research encounters, while not exempt from the more general "feeling rules" in everyday life, require systematic attention in the course of data collection and analysis, especially since "emotional dynamics in fieldwork often require continual negotiations and renegotiations" (Blee, 1998, p. 383).

Skillful interviewers try to anticipate what is likely to develop into an emotionally painful topic or area of questions. What is a sensitive matter for one individual might not be so for another, and thus it becomes difficult to anticipate in advance how an individual interview interaction might develop. Or a seemingly neutral topic might suddenly run into an interviewee's personally sensitive area. Thus, it is important to make a distinction between an event that involves emotionally sensitive experiences and a sensitive topic. A topic is something that appears in a discussion, while an event is individually experienced and has the potential to become a sensitive topic (Hydén, 2008a, p. 123). Hydén (2008a, pp. 123–124) suggests that what is an emotionally sensitive topic, or what is not, depends on *relational circumstances* rather than personal ones, as Renzetti and Lee (1993) have suggested.

Renzetti and Lee (1993) define a sensitive topic as "one that potentially poses for those involved a substantial threat, the emergence of which renders problematic for the researcher and/or researched the collection, holding, and/or dissemination of research data" (p. 5). They emphasize that almost all topics could become sensitive, while they especially list such areas

(a) where research intrudes into the private sphere or delves into some deeply personal experience, (b) where the study is concerned with deviance and social control, (c) where it impinges on the vested interests of powerful persons or the exercise of coercion or domination, and (d) where it deals with things sacred to those being studied that they do not wish profaned. (p. 6)

Hydén (2008a, pp. 124–125) proposes an alternative understanding of a sensitive topic that emphasizes *relational* circumstances. It means the relationship between the listener and the teller, in addition to the personal and cultural circumstances of this relationship (p. 135). When conducting interviews that allow both the interviewee and the interviewer to *actively shape* the interviews as a joint process, the "questions" and "answers" will be part of an ongoing process where the interviewer tries to continually understand what the discussion is all about. If Hydén had conducted her interviews on domestic violence according to standard (stimulus–response) interviewing practice, she would probably have encountered several difficulties (pp. 124–125). First, since domestic violence meets many of the criteria Renzetti and Lee (1993, p. 6) have said characterize a sensitive topic and, second, since interviewees talked with "evasive voices" when they had difficulties articulating their experiences, these kinds of stories may never have been told if the interviewer had practiced a stimulus–response model of interviewing.

Hydén (2008a) emphasizes the role of the researcher as that of an *active interviewer*, who together with the interviewee actively shapes the form of the interview in a joint process. In the relational interview interaction, the joint discussion of "untold stories" invites interviewees to increase self-reflection and relate previously unknown experiences

to a subjectively known experience. Thus, "without having experienced the cognitive process of 'having been through' an experience and rendering it some meaning so you 'know about it,' it is difficult to discuss the experience" (p. 125).

EXAMPLES OF EMOTIONAL LABOR

Emotionally laden interactions often move in unanticipated directions and require continuous management (Blee, 1998, p. 398). In her study of workplace grievances, Elisabeth Hoffman (2007, p. 323) underlines the challenges of emotional labor by focusing on the multiple, often conflicting roles that a researcher must assume in the course of an interview. Her large project on workplace dispute resolution investigated workers' strategies for resolving workplace problems and how social power and status mediated the outcome of dispute resolution (p. 326). Hoffman worried that her emotional response—in any way—could have a poor impact on the interviewee. Thus, for example, when respondents spoke with much despair about the limitations of their professional roles, she tried to "blink with compassion." In her words,

I tried to look very engaged in what they were saying so that they would know that I was listening carefully to them. I did not want to open up further than the most minimal response. This was because, beneath my intense, somewhat neutral emotional display, my deeper layer of emotion was much more volatile and passionate. To control my own emotions, I did not want to allow myself to speak and express more than I believed I should. (p. 340)

Hoffman (2007) managed her interviewer self by not showing or sharing her own emotional reactions. The emotional labor in this case involved the suppression of emotional expression itself. Hoffman suggests that the management of emotions for the interviewer varies from situation to situation. In some cases, *not* sharing emotions would have a clearly negative impact on the interview interaction. For example, in the case of home care workers who cared for elderly clients, their work relationship often developed into friendship. In interviews, home care workers discussed their sadness when a client passed away. When discussing such relationships in the context of a research interview, health care providers expressed particularly strong emotions, especially when they arrived at a client's home and found a lifeless body. In such circumstances, for an interviewer "to not display some emotion—such as compassionate expressions, gestures of comfort, or emphatic tears—would seem either disconcertingly obtuse or cold-heartedly indifferent" (p. 341). Such shifts in interviewers and interviewees' emotional relationship require skillful management. Hoffman emphasizes that the emotional reactions exhibited in the interview by both the interviewee and the interviewer are as important as data "as any other product of the interview" (p. 342).

Hoffman's (2007, pp. 339–343) examples highlight the interviewer's complex management of emotions during interview interactions. Such emotion work involves being in charge of one's emotions and managing the outward displays of emotions according to the situation. Let us now consider some of the more nuanced challenges involved in managing emotions in the context of research interviews.

CHALLENGES OF EMOTIONAL LABOR

Emotionally demanding topics affect all who are involved in the social encounter, and the interviewer is not exempt from this basic rule (Dickson-Swift, James, Kippen, & Liamputtong, 2009, pp. 62–63; Wray, Markovic, & Manderson, 2007). For example, when interviewing traumatized individuals, researchers may become a target to vicarious traumatization. Consequently, individual and research-related emotions become so mixed together that it may take years to sort them out before they can be used as relevant research data (Lillrank, 1999, pp. 101–103). The complex character of emotional labor has been acknowledged in interview interactions mostly as a procedural matter to enhance data collection, but the personal impact of emotional labor on researchers is not fully understood or analyzed in the literature. It may be that the mantra of scientific objectivity contributes to this neglect. More important, it seems that emotional labor has not yet established itself to the level where the emotional data become as important as the more analytical, empirical observations (Dickson-Swift et al., 2009, p. 63; Kleinman & Copp, 1993; Lillrank, 1999; Riessman, 2002; Wray et al., 2007).

Nonetheless, emotional labor is never far removed from the conduct and analysis of interviews. For example, in their study of public health care researchers, Dickson-Swift et al. (2009, pp. 66–68) show how they had to manage their conflicting emotions in their interviews. In the course of their research, the management of emotion sometimes involved the interviewers giving a bodily display that conflicted with their personal feelings at the time: "I nodded to let her know that I was listening but all the while I was feeling ill, in my head I was telling her to stop, wanting her to stop talking, but I kept on smiling and nodding" (p. 68). This may indicate that interviewers' emotional reactions are mediated by how they personally relate to the interview topic or the emerging data. According to Dickson-Swift et al., many interviewers reflect on their area of research as closely related to their own life experiences and the related emotional background (p. 72).

Many researchers report using informal networks of colleagues, trusted friends, and family members for support. Coping strategies and practices for dealing with the emotional challenges of research interviews seem to vary across disciplines. For example, Wray et al. (2007) in their study of gynecological cancer used both the university counselor for debriefing after distressing interviews and a fee-for-service psychotherapist to assist in dealing with distress. A discussion of how interviewers could care for themselves emotionally and include this work in the research design would be important. For example, James and Platzer (1999) suggest, "Self-care is crucial, but where there is considerable emotional labor involved in research interviews we suggest that there is a requirement for formal supervision, not only of the academic but also of the therapeutic kind" (p. 76).

Such knowledge of demanding emotional labor in research interviews was taken seriously by the social policy research unit at the University of York in the United Kingdom. It was funded to use group psychotherapy to support researchers who interviewed parents following a child's death—to help them deal with the emotionally demanding work (Corden, Sainsbury, Sloper, & Ward, 2005). Training and supervision were considered beneficial for interviewers with emotionally demanding topics (Johnson & Clarke, 2003; Wray et al., 2007). They could facilitate the use of empathy as a tool in the interviewer–interviewee relationship and to reflect on research-related emotional labor. Other solutions for managing the interviewer self have been developed within the autoethnographic literature, which is discussed briefly below.

THE AUTOETHNOGRAPHIC TURN

Autoethnography is a method for reflecting on researchers' emotions—and selves (Ellis, 1999, p. 669). In the social sciences, autoethnography, or introspective self-awareness, is being recognized as a valuable research tool:

Auto-ethnography is an autobiographical genre of writing and research . . . focusing outward on social and cultural aspects of . . . personal experience . . . (and) inward, exposing a vulnerable self that I moved by and may move through, refract, and resist cultural interpretations. (Ellis & Bochner, 2000, p. 736)

Using empathic observation, the researcher becomes a full insider and tries to understand the interviewee's experience by connecting it to similarities in his or her own life and writing about it in the first person (Ellis & Bochner, 2000).

According to Manning (2005, p. 150), the term *autoethnography* comes from the research of Hayano (1982), who studied the world of professional gamblers. It describes situations where researchers become so involved in the social worlds they study that it is no longer possible, or necessary, "to distinguish them from their informants. In a literal sense, they become one of their own informants" (Manning, 2005, p. 150). Hayano (1982) described his study of poker players as something that "is completely interwoven with my personal involvement and analysis as an inside member" (as cited in Manning, 2005, pp. 150–151). In short, autoethnography emphasizes a reflective attitude aimed at bringing the interviewer self into the data collection process and thus opening up new understandings of both the interviewee and the interviewer self and their relationship (Jones, 2006; McIlveen, 2010, p. 6). Another way of managing the interviewer self is the use of a secondary analysis in qualitative research, which is discussed next.

"DOING JUSTICE" IN MANAGING THE INTERVIEWER SELF

Active interviewing as a joint construction requires that the research interactions' unexpected turns between the interviewer and interviewees need to be included in the analytic work in order to do justice to the interviewees' responses (Behar, 1996; Hydén,

2008b, p. 97; Riessman, 2002). To some degree, this means that researchers must locate themselves in their own text, without turning the entire enterprise into personal confessions and self-aggrandizement. In other words, the process requires "deeper connections between one's personal experience and the subject under study," which requires a keen-eyed understanding of what areas of the self are the most significant filters through which an interviewer perceives the studied topic (Behar, 1996, p. 13). Self-closure needs to be purposeful and should focus on the self as an observer who has enabled gathering information. Without deliberate researcher self-reflection, this type of knowledge would have otherwise been unavailable (Behar, 1996, pp. 13–14; Finlay, 2002; Riessman, 2002, pp. 208–209).

The anthropologist Ruth Behar (1996), who coined the concept "the vulnerable observer," emphasizes that there is "no easy route [with] which to confront the self who observes" (p. 6), especially when struggling with very demanding emotional labor following fieldwork encounters. She continues, "Writing vulnerably takes as much skill, nuance, and willingness to follow through on all the ramifications of complicated ideas as does writing invulnerably and distantly" (p. 13).

Cathy Riessman (2002, pp. 193–195) positioned herself as a vulnerable observer when she reinterpreted a previous interview interaction. She explores the complexity of subjectivity and witnessing one interview that addressed a brutal marriage. Riessman notes that interviewers essentially translate the lives of others, and as such, they bear a heavy responsibility. Such a responsibility highlights the complexity of the researcher's self-management; when witnessing "provoking emotions nearly impossible to bear, doing justice means that we cannot look away" (p. 194). Behar (1996, p. 2) explains how vulnerability is both the clue and a serious dilemma of such witnessing. Accordingly, Riessman (2002) asks, "If one decides to document the horror, where is the witness to take her emotions?" (p. 194). To comprehend how she as an interviewer was able to manage herself, she quoted Nancy Chodorow (1999), who argues, "What Freud discovered in the analytic encounter goes well beyond the specialized analytic relationship. The capacity for transference (in this sense subsuming counter-transference) is thus one of the great abilities and defining capacities of the human mind" (p. 21). Riessman (2002) suggests that by examining transference processes we can connect the emotions developed in our own interpersonal encounters and not run from them: "We can look back, as I do here, and describe dilemmas of past witnessing that configured interpretations. We can reinterpret narratives from current positioning and give new meanings to them" (p. 195; see also Gadd, 2004).

To do justice to an interviewee's experiences, Riessman (1990) reexamined her analysis of a divorcing woman's narrative that was published in *Divorce Talk*. She chose to look back and describe the dilemmas of past interview experiences that shaped her interpretation according to the academic practices at that time. She reflectively analyzes her previous interpretations and explains why in the past she developed them as she did. To do justice both to the interviewee and to herself, Riessman reinterpreted the text in a different way from what she had written 20 years before. By doing so, she gives new meanings and interprets parts of the interview she was unable to include in the previous publication. Thus, Riessman (2002) has moved the management of the interviewer self into new possibilities, to revisit the interviewer's "representations in their past work, to reveal the historical situatedness of interpretation—the professional, theoretical, political, disciplinary, and yes, autobiographical imperatives that draw us to certain interpretations and not to others" (p. 210).

Overall, this means that research knowledge (its construction, representation, and dissemination) is embedded in history and the interviewer's own life experiences. How we make sense of what we hear is heavily influenced by the changing frameworks of understandings; and the meaning of our text itself is not fixed and certain, even after it has been published (Andrews, 2008, p. 86). Rather, the most convincing interpretation of human interactions is one that displays as closely as possible all of the unexpected paths of what it means to be human—a meaning that is always partial (Andrews, 2008, pp. 92–93; Ellis, 1999; Holstein & Gubrium, 2003).

In the final section, I present a case study from my own study (Lillrank, 1998a, 1998b, 1999, 2002) of how parents managed their experiences of their children's struggle with cancer. In particular, this study serves as an example of how an interviewer in a joint construction with interviewees manages herself or himself by becoming a "defended subject."

MANAGING THE INTERVIEWER SELF IN ILLNESS NARRATIVES

At the time of the interviews, I had much experience as a clinical social worker for families with disabled children. In my clinical work, I practiced therapeutic interviewing (Kvale, 1999). However, as a novice social scientist interviewer, I was trained to be an objective and emotionally neutral interviewer. Although I hadn't planned for them to do so, my research interviews became a mixture of these two interview traditions. As illustrated here through my interview with a respondent named Maire, I felt that my respondents had gone through something so emotionally painful that I personally found it impossible to deal with. The interviewees seemed able to cope by reverting to a social discourse of childhood cancer as a manageable illness experience while avoiding talking about their feelings and fears. Thus, both the interviewer and the interviewee became engaged as anxious "defended subjects" in an unconscious intersubjectivity of acknowledging but being unable to talk more explicitly about "how it really is" to have a child diagnosed with cancer (Lillrank, 1998a; 2002, p. 112). Accordingly, both interviewer and interviewees are seen as anxious, defended subjects, "whose mental boundaries are porous where unconscious material is concerned" (Hollway & Jefferson, 2000, p. 45). It means that both interviewer and interviewees will be subject to projections and introjections of feelings and thoughts appearing in the interview interaction.

THE INTERVIEW AS JOINT CONSTRUCTION

Maire was a married secretary in her early 40s and the mother of two children. My interview with her lasted for 1½ hours. At the time of our interview, about 3 years had passed since her son was diagnosed with cancer. I suggested that she should feel free to say what she thought and decide how much she would like to elaborate on my questions. When the interview moved to emotionally difficult illness experiences, Maire became more reserved in her talk, limiting verbal expressions of her feelings and related thoughts about the tragedy. In particular, Maire avoided talking about her feelings and fears of the illness's life-threatening character, the prolonged uncertainty of the prognosis, its unknown medical cause, and how much it had changed their family life. However, I did not want to challenge her unwillingness to talk about it. Even when Maire's talk was rational and well organized, intuitively I felt that she was extremely afraid of her complex emotions and that she was not aware of them and consequently was unable to talk about them (Lillrank, 1998a, p. 67; 2002, p. 116).

After general discussions concerning her family life prior to the diagnosis of cancer, I (Annika Lillrank [A]) asked Maire to describe the first symptoms and how the cancer was eventually discovered. This question moved the interview to her emotionally vulnerable illness experience:

Maire: On Monday my work was scheduled to begin. What actually happened was that on Sunday Ari (her five year old son) fell off the swing and hurt his teeth, so that he was bleeding from the mouth. On Monday I went to work as planned, but I had organized Ari's day so he was taken care of. In the morning I did not look very carefully, but he had been bleeding during the night. I worked the whole day and when I came home in the evening Ari was very tired and had a fever. When he lay down beside me, his gums started to bleed again. I suspected that he had an infection in his teeth, which caused the fever and bleeding. That is how I explained it to myself. Next morning we went to the dentist, but they did not discover anything. It was strange, but when he was standing he wasn't bleeding at all; it was maybe because his heart didn't beat so strongly. After the visit to the dentist, Ari was taken to the HCC (Health Care Center). There they noticed some changes. From HCC we were sent to the University clinic, and that is how everything started . . . so actually this was the story. The illness was discovered because of a lucky accident.

A: Was it within a week or was it . . . ?

Maire: Within a day, a day, that on Tuesday we were already in the hospital when he fell off the swing on Sunday . . .

A: Well, how much were you then able to be in the hospital with Ari? (Lillrank, 2002, p. 117)

For me, the emotionally demanding part of Maire's story was not her factual and coherently told story. Instead, a nonverbally transferred exhaustive emotional pain overwhelmed me like an opaque cloud. Her nonverbally communicated emotional pain took me by surprise, and I felt an overwhelming sense of anxiety, despair, and helplessness. Maire did not have words for her emotional pain, something I repeatedly observed in my respondents (Lillrank, 1998a, p. 66). In a similar way, Arthur Frank (1995) has characterized "the chaos story" as incommunicable. It is told in silence because the storyteller has no words for it. Thus, "it is what is always *lacking* in speech" (p. 101). Frank explains how in chaos stories individuals have lost control of their own experiences because nothing redeems their suffering as an ordinary occurrence; instead, it feels arbitrary (p. 104). Such a serious life crisis forced Maire to rationally acknowledge the life-threatening illness of her beloved child. Consequently, she cut off all the related emotional (bad) experiences from herself and projected them onto me, probably because that was the easiest way of dealing with such anxiety in the interview interaction.

For me as an interviewer, it became a challenge to hear the rest of her story because I felt emotionally threatened. So I myself became a defended subject, trying to defend myself against emotional pain. That is why I was unable to comment on her story. Instead, I changed the subject and asked her how she had practically managed the hospital care (Lillrank, 2002, p. 118).

MANAGING THE INTERVIEWER SELF DURING MY INTERVIEW WITH MAIRE

I used a narrative interview strategy based on semistructured questions. They were divided into three major categories: (1) the prediagnostic social world, (2) the diagnosis, and (3) the postdiagnostic life. I managed to complete the interview(s) by relying on my loosely constructed interview guide. It helped to give structure, continue, and complete the interview(s). However, to be able to continue, it became necessary to reformulate the questions in order to defend myself from too much anxiety. For example, I was unable to ask directly, "How did you experience the situation when the diagnosis was delivered?" Instead, I asked if the child was present and how she or he reacted. I assumed that the interviewees would have liked to discuss my original question, "How did you experience the situation when the diagnosis was delivered?" However, as a defended subject I would have been unable to listen to their experiences. The interviewees went on at length answering my reformulated question, "If the child was present, how did the child react when the diagnosis was delivered" (Lillrank, 1999, p. 101).

During the interview interactions, my "coping strategies" were to continue to be emotionally and intellectually available for the interviewees. I verbally encouraged the interviewees to feel free to decide what they wanted to discuss and share with me about their difficult illness experiences. Since the interviewees were unable to verbalize their emotions, it was not possible to verbally share with them my own emotional pain. Indeed, it may have been entirely inappropriate to load them with my feelings. I was careful not to break down myself, relying on and following my training as a social worker. So I concentrated on my role as a professional interviewer and made efforts to communicate trust and understanding through supporting nods and gestures (Lillrank, 1999).

I could not always predict which questions or topics would spark emotionally intense reactions. For example, several interviewees began crying when talking of painful memories. In such situations, I comforted them by handing them a paper handkerchief and suggesting that they should feel free to cry as long as they needed to. At the same time, I stopped the tape recorder and said that we would continue the interview when they felt comfortable doing so. Only one interviewee became so upset that she could not calm down, and when I asked if she would prefer to terminate the interview, she was happy to do so. At the end of the interview, several interviewees thanked me for the opportunity to talk about their illness experience—they seemed to have experienced and benefitted from the interview as a therapeutic encounter (Lillrank, 1998a, pp. 66–69).

INTERACTING AS DEFENDED SUBJECTS

Despite how Maire and I interacted as defended subjects, my ability to recognize her emotional pain and allow the dialogue to continue without demands kept the interview going. In a sense, I functioned as a "holding environment," which refers to a concept developed by Donald Winnicott (1971). It describes the intersubjectivity between mother and baby,

where a sensitive and "good enough mother" functions as a container and coordinator of the baby's chaotic emotions. In a similar way, I managed to function as a "good enough interviewer." To continue the interview on less vulnerable issues, I asked how Maire and her family acknowledged the illness to other people:

A: So who told this to your relatives, friends and neighbors and how did they respond to you?

Maire: I probably told them, I cannot really remember. Yes, besides when somebody was told it spread very quickly to others. So I did not need to tell everybody. But there was a lady; she and I had taken our children to music school, which ended in the beginning of May. One month has passed and then Ari was already hospitalized. She [the lady] was not a close friend of mine; we just knew each other because of our children. Once I met her in the shop and she greeted me very happily and asked how we were doing. At that moment I of course said that we are not doing well and told her about Ari. So the situation became upside down because she started to cry and I had to comfort her "please don't, . . . we are doing fine," and told her in greater detail about it. So that it is how sensitive people react. I did not think that I should need to take care of her feelings. If I can endure it, others have to endure it too.

A: [1] In telling others were these kinds of situations, in your opinion, the most difficult ones?

Maire: No, I don't know. I am not unemotional, but in my opinion, this needs to be managed with pure reason. [2] *I do not know where I have my emotions and perhaps they ooze up somehow in form of rash and that sort of thing* [italics added]. I have had this before [she showed me her arms] but now it is quite bad. Maybe this is possibly psychological.

A: Well, when you had such a special situation, you had recently begun working and then Ari was seriously ill, so who took care of the practical management of everyday life? (Lillrank, 2002, p. 120)

When I attempted to interpret a friend's reaction as emotionally demanding, Maire became defensive and emphasized her rational way of dealing with the illness. However, the interview interaction was probably safe enough because Maire continued talking about her rash as a sign of suppressed emotions. When she gave me a clue [2] for a possible discussion of her suppressed emotions, I was not ready to take it. Instead, I changed the subject by asking about the practical illness management at home. Maire responded to my emotional indifference by giving very short answers to my following questions. And the tone of her voice revealed that she felt offended.

These interview excerpts show how both the interviewer and the interviewee behaved as defended subjects in a joint construction of avoiding anxiety. Analyzing this joint construction of such emotional logic was crucial to understanding the depth of the illness experience that otherwise would have remained incomprehensible. Of course, this is mainly "my story" and thus a partial and tentative interpretation of the interview encounter (Lillrank, 2002, pp. 120–124).

◆ Conclusions

Using various examples, this chapter has underlined how qualitative research interviewers manage the self during interview interactions. This chapter presents multiple practices regarding the intertwined knowledge production and emotional management involved in research interviews. The analytical focus on knowledge production goes hand in hand with repeated practice and the ability to keep a "conversational collaboration" focused on specific topics and procedural data collection methodology. Furthermore, to convince readers of the importance of the interviewer's self-management strategies, all the relevant interactions need to be documented and made transparent (Gubrium & Holstein, 2009, pp. 94–95). Margareta Hydén (2008a, 2008b) and Molly Andrews (2007) discussed the demands of active listening and how it requires one to continually open up to the unknown. This may be particularly difficult for interviewers who have been trained to focus on a research agenda.

The many examples I have discussed here focus on the interviewer's management of emotions and his or her emotional labor during the interview in the context of the behavioral and interactional demands of the situation. As Hochschild (2003, p. 92) points out, this approach is closely linked with Erving Goffman's conceptualization of identity management in everyday life. However, Goffman seems to be concerned mostly with overt performances, or empirically observable behavioral manifestations. Thus, he may have underestimated the "power of social forces on our inner grip of ourselves" (p. 92). When applied to social sciences and to qualitative research in particular, this bias toward the overt has left the interviewer's internal (emotional) self unacknowledged.

Concepts such as a "vulnerable observer," "defended subject," and "autoethnography" highlight the often unexpected complexities of interviewers' participation in the painful experiences of the respondents. Of course, this attention to the internal can considerably slow down analysis and raises questions about what interviewers should feel or express during an interview and their analysis of postinterview interactions (Gadd, 2004, p. 387; Riessman, 2002). According to Hochschild (2003, p. 75), this debate mirrors partly the division between thinking and emotions in Western culture, where rational thinking is considered superior to feelings and emotions. On the other hand, Hochschild is aware of this theoretical weakness in sociology, especially in Goffman's "black-box psychology" (p. 92). She presents the strengths and weakness of Goffman's account in the following way:

> In Goffman's theory the capacity to act on feeling derives only from the occasion, not from the individual. The self may actively choose to *display* feelings in order to give outward impressions to others. But it is passive to the point of invisibility when it comes to the private act of managing emotion. The "I" is there, of course, in the many stories from the *San Francisco Chronicle,* in the passages from novels, in hangmen's accounts, in Ionesco plays, in Lillian Gish's autobiography. But the private "I" is simply not there in theory. Feelings are contributions to interactions via the passive medium of a bodily self. We act behaviorally, not affectively. The system affects our behavior, not our feelings. (Hochschild, 1983, p. 218; also quoted in Manning, 2005, p. 135)

Merging these two positions is part of Hochschild's pathbreaking suggestion to establish a theory of emotions (Manning, 2005, p. 135). She fuses these two ways of defining the self (the cognitive self and the emotional self) and proposes a third image—"that of the *sentient self, a self that is capable of feeling and aware of being so*" (Hochschild, 2003, p. 77). If we choose to see a self as capable of feeling, a sentient self, it becomes possible to discover an individual's *own* definition of his or her personal emotions and feelings (Hochschild, 2003, p. 78). This broadened conceptualization of the self could be applied in the social sciences and the methodology of qualitative research and can make visible interviewers' complex management of their own feelings and emotions, a central part of the interviewer self.

◆ References

Alvesson, M., & Sköldberg, K. (2005). *Reflexive methodology: New vistas for qualitative research*. London, England: Sage.

Andrews, M. (2007). *Shaping history: Narratives of political change*. Cambridge, England: Cambridge University Press.

Andrews, M. (2008). Never the last word: Revisiting data. In M. Andrews, C. Squire, & M. Tamboukou (Eds.), *Doing narrative research* (pp. 86–101). Thousand Oaks, CA: Sage.

Arendell, T. (1997). Reflections on the researcher-researched relationship: A woman interviewing men. *Qualitative Sociology, 20*(3), 341–366.

Behar, R. (1996). *The vulnerable observer: Anthropology that breaks your heart*. Boston, MA: Beacon Press.

Blee, K. M. (1998). White-knuckle research: Emotional dynamics in fieldwork with racist activists. *Qualitative Sociology, 21*(4), 381–399.

Chodorow, N. J. (1999). *The power of feelings: Personal meanings in psychoanalysis, gender and culture*. New Haven, CT: Yale University Press.

Corden, A., Sainsbury, R., Sloper, P., & Ward, B. (2005). Using a model of group psychotherapy to support social research on sensitive topics. *International Journal of Social Research Methodology, 8*(2), 151–160.

Dickson-Swift, V., James, E. L., Kippen, S., & Liamputtong, P. (2009). Researching sensitive topics: Qualitative research as emotion work. *Qualitative Research, 9*(1), 61–79. Retrieved from http://qrj.sagepub.com/cgi/content/abstract/9/1/61

Ellis, C. (1999). Heartful autoethnography. *Qualitative Health Research, 9*(5), 669–683. Retrieved from http://qhr.sagepub.com/cgi/content/abstract/9/5/669

Ellis, C., & Bochner, A. P. (2000). Autoethnography, personal narrative, reflexivity. In N. K. Denzin & Y. S. Lincoln (Eds.), *Handbook of qualitative research* (pp. 733–786). Thousand Oaks, CA: Sage.

Ezzy, D. (2010). Qualitative interviewing as an embodied emotional performance. *Qualitative Inquiry, 16*(3), 163–170. Retrieved from http://qix.sagepub.com/cgi/content/abstract/16/3/163

Finlay, L. (2002). Negotiating the swamp: The opportunity and challenge of reflexivity in research practice. *Qualitative Research, 2*(2), 209–230. Retrieved from http://qrj.sagepub.com/cgi/content/abstract/2/2/209

Frank, A. W. (1995). *The wounded storyteller*. Chicago, IL: University of Chicago Press.

Gadd, D. (2004). Making sense of interviewee–interviewer dynamics in narratives about violence in intimate relationship. *International Journal of Social Research Methodology, 7*(5), 383–401.

Gubrium, J. F., & Holstein, J. A. (2009). *Analyzing narrative reality*. Thousand Oaks, CA: Sage.

Hayano, D. (1982). *Poker faces: The life and work of professional card players*. Berkeley: University of California Press.

Hochschild, A. R. (1983). *The managed heart: Commercialization of human feeling*. Berkeley: University of California Press.

Hochschild, A. R. (2003). *The commercialization of intimate life*. Berkeley: University of California Press.

Hoffman, E. A. (2007). Open-ended interviews, power, and emotional labor. *Journal of Contemporary Ethnography, 36*(3), 318–346. Retrieved from http://jce.sagepub.com/cgi/content/abstract/36/3/318

Hollway, W., & Jefferson, T. (2000). *Doing qualitative research differently: Free association, narrative and the interview method*. London, England: Sage.

Holstein, J. A., & Gubrium, J. F. (1995). *The active interviewer* (Qualitative Research Methods Series, No. 37). Thousand Oaks, CA: Sage.

Holstein, J. A., & Gubrium, J. F. (2003). Inside interviewing: New lenses, new concerns. In J. A. Holstein & J. F. Gubrium (Eds.), *Inside interviewing: New lenses, new concerns* (pp. 3–32). Thousand Oaks, CA: Sage.

Hydén, M. (2000). Den berättarfokuserade intervjun [The teller-centered interview]. *Socialvetenskaplig tidskrift, 1*(2), 137–158.

Hydén, M. (2008a). Narrating sensitive topics. In M. Andrews, C. Squire, & M. Tamboukou (Eds.), *Doing narrative research* (pp. 121–136). Thousand Oaks, CA: Sage.

Hydén, M. (2008b). Om den svåra konsten att lyssna till berättelser [About the difficult task of listening to narratives]. In S. Larsson, Y. Sjöblom, & J. Lilja (Eds.), *Narrativa metoder i socialt arbete* [Narrative methods in social work] (pp. 85–110). Studenttlitteratur, Hungary: Reaszisztema Dabas.

James, T., & Platzer, H. (1999). Ethical considerations in qualitative research with vulnerable groups: Exploring lesbians' and gay men's expressions of health care—a personal perspective. *Nursing Ethics, 6*(1), 73–81.

Johnson, B., & Clarke, J. M. (2003). Collecting sensitive data: The impact on researchers. *Qualitative Health Research, 13*(3), 421–434. Retrieved from http://qhr .sagepub.com/cgi/content/abstract/13/3/421

Jones, R. (2006). Dilemmas, maintaining "face," and paranoia: An average coaching life. *Qualitative Inquiry, 12*(5), 1012–1021. Retrieved from http://qix.sagepub .com/cgi/content/abstract/12/5/1012

Kleinman, S., & Copp, M. A. (1993). *Emotions and field-work.* Newbury Park, CA: Sage.

Kvale, S. (1999). The psychoanalytic interview as qualitative research. *Qualitative Inquiry, 5*(1), 87–113. Retrieved from http://qix.sagepub.com/cgi/content/ abstract/5/1/87

Kvale, S. (2007). *Doing interviews.* London, England: Sage.

Lillrank, A. (1998a). *Living one day at a time: Parental dilemmas of managing the experience and the care of childhood cancer* (Stakes Research Report No. 89). Jyväskylä, Finland: Gummerus.

Lillrank, A. (1998b). Päivä kerrallaan: Vanhempien selviytymisstrategiat lapsen sairastuttua syöpään [Living one day at a time: Parental dilemmas of managing the experience and the care of childhood cancer]. *Yhteiskuntapolitiikka, 63*(4), 317–326.

Lillrank, A. (1999). Samspelet mellan verbal och icke-verbal interaction i forskningsintervjuer [The interplay between verbal and non-verbal interaction in research interviews]. *Sosiologia, 2,* 95–108.

Lillrank, A. (2002). The tension between overt talk and covert emotions in illness narratives: Transition from clinician to researcher. *Culture, Medicine and Psychiatry, 26,* 111–127.

Manning, P. (2005). *Freud and American sociology.* Cambridge, England: Polity Press.

McIlveen, P. (2008). Autoethnography as a method for reflexive research and practice in vocational psychology. *Australian Journal of Career Development, 17*(2), 13–20.

McIlveen, P. (2010). *Autoethnography as a method for reflexive research and practice in vocational psychology.* Retrieved from USQ ePrints, http://eprints.usq.edu .au/4253/1/McIlveen_2008_AJCD_Autoethnography .pdf (Author's postprint version)

Mishler, E. G. (1986). *Research interviewing: Context and narrative.* Cambridge, England: Harvard University Press.

Renzetti, C. M., & Lee, R. M. (Eds.). (1993). *Researching sensitive topics.* Newbury Park, CA: Sage.

Riessman, C. K. (1990). *Divorce talk: Women and men make sense of personal relationships.* New Brunswick, NJ: Rutgers University Press.

Riessman, C. K. (2000). Even if we don't have children [we] can live: Stigma and infertility in South India. In C. Mattingly & L. C. Garro (Eds.), *Narrative and the cultural construction of illness and healing* (pp. 128–152). Berkeley: University of California Press.

Riessman, C. K. (2002). Doing justice: Positioning the interpreter in narrative work. In W. Paterson (Ed.), *Strategic narratives: New perspectives on the power of personal and cultural stories* (pp. 193–214). Boston, MA: Lexington Books.

Riessman, C. K. (2003). Analysis of personal narratives. In J. A. Holstein & J. F. Gubrium (Eds.), *Inside interviewing: New lenses, new concerns* (pp. 331–346). Thousand Oaks, CA: Sage.

Winnicott, D. W. (1971). *Playing and reality.* London, England: Tavistock.

Wray, N., Markovic, M., & Manderson, L. (2007). Researcher saturation: The impact of data triangulation and intensive-research practices on the researcher and qualitative research process. *Qualitative Health Research, 17*(10), 1392–1402. Retrieved from http:// qhr.sagepub.com/cgi/content/abstract/17/10/1392

LISTENING TO, AND FOR, THE RESEARCH INTERVIEW

◆ John B. Talmage

◆ *Introduction*

In the context of the social science research interview, discussions of listening as a foundational practice are rare. While considerable attention is given to asking the "right" question and following it up with the "right" probe, there is little discussion of how listening mediates the question–answer exchange. In this chapter, I examine listening as a constructive/interpretive practice that shapes the content of the research interview, particularly in the context of in-depth and narrative interviews. For the purpose of this chapter, I distinguish hearing (the registration or sensing of sound waves) from listening (the interpretation of those sounds and words as meaningful talk) (Wolvin & Coakley, 1988). Hearing requires virtually no interpretation, while listening involves making sense of sounds and words. McCracken (1988) states it succinctly when he notes, "Hearing is the capacity to be aware of and to receive sounds. Listening involves not only receiving sounds, but, as much as possible, understanding their meaning" (p. 51).

In the context of research interviews, "understanding meaning" is, however, more than a passive task of deciphering what a respondent has in mind. It involves determining the central theme of the respondent's talk, relating the talk of the respondent to the research topic and to the questions and prompting of the interviewer, and determining the biographical linkages and other horizons of meaning that the respondent references. As Holstein and Gubrium (1995) have suggested, meaning making in the research interview involves active collaboration between the interviewer and the respondent. By extension, the research interview involves "active listening" (see also Annika Lillrank's "Managing the Interviewer Self," this volume), or active collaboration between the interviewer and respondent so that the respondents' utterances are appropriately directed and framed for the research interview.

The listening interviewer clarifies what the respondent has said, suggests alternative interpretations that seem to be consistent with the narrative construction of the respondent, and facilitates significant linkages between the evolving narrative of the respondent and the different meanings and events that the respondent has previously articulated. The role of the interviewer in the interview is that of active listener and collaborating participant. In this sense, all interviews (whether qualitative or quantitative) are to some degree actively constructed through interviewer–respondent collaboration.

In the traditional face-to-face survey interview, the goal is noninvolvement by the interviewer in the interview, other than asking the questions and either mentally or mechanically recording the answers that the interviewer only hears. Of course this kind of neutrality is impossible to achieve. Even the most disengaged researcher is likely to reveal agreement or disagreement, shock, amusement, or confusion. Body language, failure to attend to the respondent, or other, more subtle means of verbal or nonverbal communication all implicate the interviewer in the joint activity of meaning making. Survey researchers contend that with the proper training objective interviewers can minimize such reactions and transform themselves into a neutral data collection instrument, or the logical parallel to their view of the respondent as a "vessel of knowledge" (Holstein & Gubrium, 1995).

The active interview model assumes that the interviewer, rather than being a nonfeeling, nonresponsive neutral sponge that is merely there to absorb information, is involved in the meaning-making enterprise. We might go further and say that the partnership in meaning making between researcher and respondent is the primary task of the interview. Consequently, active interviewing, particularly in the context of qualitative research, assumes a more flexible approach to the interview, with fewer formulaic restrictions on how the interviewer presents herself or himself in the interview. Rather than following a rigid interview schedule, the active interviewer is thought to be engaged in a conversation around a topic. As John Johnson (2002) notes,

> In more traditional standardized interviewing, interviewers are commonly told to stick to the questions on the research protocol, to ask the questions precisely as they are given, [and] to probe for clarification only in ways that will not influence the respondents' answers. . . . This is not a realistic ideal for in-depth interviewing, because the nature of the research question usually entails a deeper process of mutual self-disclosure and trust building. (pp. 112–113)

In a sense, this takes the starch out of the research interview. From an active-interview standpoint, the interviewer is involved in shaping the interview by suggesting alternative voices, pointing out conflicts, raising relevant alternative points of view, or facilitating coherence in the narrative construction (Holstein & Gubrium, 1995).

Similarly, active listening entails not only accurately comprehending the speaker's communications but also demonstrating in some manner that the respondent has been understood. The researcher is actively listening for those potential points of engagement at which he or she will find ways to shape the narrative construction of the respondent (Holstein & Gubrium, 1995). In the remainder of this chapter, I will outline critical elements of active listening in terms of its context and filtering mechanisms.

◆ Context and Listening

When considering the task of listening, the question of context emerges as a primary concern. While "context" is related to many topics (e.g., geographical, cultural, institutional, or discursive contexts), here I use the term to refer to (a) the physical setting of the interview event and (b) the social frames of reference that the research participants draw from for the utterances and interpretations.

PHYSICAL CONTEXT

In the interview, the setting enables the respondent to organize and articulate his or her story and/or perspective. As such, it is a key component in facilitating the ability of the interviewer to listen closely to what the respondent is saying without the need for redundancy, clarification, or other methods used to clarify meaning. When an interview is scheduled, the time and place of the interview are established. The location may be the researcher's office or another place that is quasi-official or that is linked to the group or organization that the researcher is investigating. The physical characteristics of the setting inform the type of listening that is to take place in the interview, with more formal settings providing for fewer unwanted interruptions. In a more formal environment, such as the office of the researcher, the researcher has control over the setting. Some of the factors that need to be controlled are the use of a tape recorder, noise levels, whether or not to offer coffee or another beverage, seating arrangements, distracting decor, lighting, access to note pads, time management, access to restrooms, and other things that create a comfortable and, in many cases, effective context for the interview.

The use of an audio recorder, in particular, presents unique challenges for the active listener. For example, in my training as a counselor, we were required to prepare verbatim records of our therapy sessions for analysis and discussion in our training group. The possibility of using an audio recorder became a topic of conversation and was quickly vetoed by the psychiatrist in charge of the group. His rationale was that people would tend to be more guarded in what they said if they knew that they were being recorded. Since then, I have found that some people are more guarded and others are not.

It is always appropriate to ask a respondent if he or she is comfortable with the use of a recorder. If not, I assure them that I could work just as well by taking notes. The use of an audio recorder is helpful in listening but does not eliminate the need for notes, as eye contact, voice inflections, or other nonverbal cues are not accessible. In either case, it is helpful to make notations regarding the above nonverbal elements, keeping the note taking discreet as it may be distracting.

In a more informal setting, it is frequently more difficult to control many of these things as some informal settings are not the native work setting of the interviewer. One example of the difficulties involved in agreeing to a location that allows significant respondent input is illustrated from an experience I had when studying race relations in a southern city. I had requested an interview with a man who was an unofficial leader in a civil rights racial demonstration. He agreed to the interview but felt that it needed to take place in his community for him to maintain contact with different participants. With my agreement, we met at a barbeque stand. The best time for him was in the late afternoon, and the barbeque stand was packed. The noise of the customers and the music playing on the juke box made conversation all but impossible. In addition, with my being

a white male, we attracted attention as we were forced to shout back and forth and the eyes of the clientele of the barbeque stand were focused on us. After attempting to talk for a reasonable amount of time, I suggested to him that we go outside and talk for just a minute. In that conversation, I pointed out that while I understood his need for remaining in that setting, it was not a good locale for an interview. We agreed to meet late that night at another restaurant in another part of the town that was quieter, and then we went back inside. He introduced me to several people and explained what I was doing there. I spent the next hour as a participant observer, made notes, and used many of these as background for the interview that was conducted later.

One cannot, however, automatically assume that a formal setting necessarily provides for "better" listening. Indeed, a formal setting (e.g., an office) may be threatening for people whose work or lifestyle does not include such environments. An example from the world of business illustrates this. A man responsible for human resources (HR) in a relatively large manufacturing plant told me the story of the problems he had with employees who came to his office to talk about some of their problems with supervisors or other problems affecting their work. As he spoke with several of them, he sensed that he was not hearing what was at the heart of the employees' concern and that the employees were not being candid with him about their problems. He asked one of them, "Why the discomfort?" The employee responded that the office was "too uptown" and that he felt like he didn't belong there. From that point on, the HR director met employees with these types of problems in a small restaurant about three blocks from the plant at off-hours. This would afford the quiet and the anonymity needed for these more personal conversations. As this translates into the research interview, it is important for the researcher to conduct interviews in places that allow the respondents to feel comfortable and do not inadvertently make them feel subservient or otherwise ill at ease.

SOCIAL CONTEXT

In the context of active listening, "context" also refers to biographical details, social roles, and cultural expectations embedded and invoked in the research interview. In an informal conversation between friends or acquaintances, context is typically part of the taken-for-granted knowledge of everyday life. For example, in a conversation between friends, the context is understood to be that of two people with shared experiences, common interests, and a general liking for each other. If the context is not understood and defined by mutual understanding, conversation or speaking/listening becomes, in essence, unintelligible (Schlesinger, 1994, p. 32).

In the research interview, social context is equally important as an aid to making sense of the occasion and facilitating listening. However, whereas in everyday life many contexts are familiar and taken for granted, the context from which the researcher comes and his or her expectations from the exchange may be less clearly understood by the respondents. To a large extent, the research interview context and its norms are universally understood in Western societies (see, e.g., Gubrium & Holstein's [2002] discussion of "interview society"). Nonetheless, in most cases, respondents need to be provided with some degree of background about the research and its purposes prior to the interview. Institutional review boards (IRBs) try to ensure this, for example, by requiring that respondents be provided with informed consent agreements. By contrast, or perhaps as a complement to the IRB protocol, ethnographic researchers emphasize the importance of prior contact and relationships with respondents. Thus, whether from the point of view of contractual obligations or the desire for better data, it is safe to say that without at least a modicum of rapport, the respondent has little investment in developing his or her perspective or articulating it to the interviewer. But rapport also enables the researcher to attend to and engage the respondent, or actively listen.

Two dimensions of rapport that this understanding of context includes are (1) mutual interest and (2) interpersonal comfort. In the legal interview, the therapeutic interview, the medical interview, or other professional interviews this is typically not relevant as the client or patient has a taken-for-granted investment in the interview. In comparison, in the typical research interview, the respondents have no intrinsic or vested interest in the exchange. The primary interest in initiating the interview is that of the researcher. The interviewer will need to listen for the level of interest in the respondent, and if the interest is not there, or if there is insufficient investment, then the interviewer will have to devise responses to generate interest or investment in the topic. Rapport-building

practices are well documented in the how-to literature (see, e.g., John Johnson and Timothy Rowlands's "The Interpersonal Dynamics of In-Depth Interviewing," this volume; Berger, 2001; Reinharz, 1992; Yow, 2005). In my own research with the homeless, I routinely disclosed biographical details of my own life, hoping that the respondent would be able to relate and use this material to illustrate the ways she or he relates to the topic (Jourard, 1964; Seidman, 2006, p. 73; Simon, 1988; Weiner, 1978). In addition, I presented my respondents with my academic or hearsay knowledge of the topic under analysis and asked them to comment on the validity of this information.

To illustrate these techniques of generating mutual interest, consider this example from my interview with a homeless man, Larry (fictional name), in a park. I asked Larry how he saw himself with no place to call home. Larry replied that this was not something that he thought about and that the only reason he had been asked that question was because I was "just trying to write a book or something like that." I explained to him that I might possibly write a book but that I chose to explore the lives of homeless people because I had a concern for them and hoped that whatever I wrote would eventually be of help to homeless people. I then told Larry that I had heard him state earlier that people never really looked at him and that he felt invisible. The question, then, was how this related to his experience as a homeless man.

Larry: Yeah, I did say that, didn't I?

John: (smiling) Yes, you did. Now what do you think made you feel invisible?

Larry: You think that's got something to do with me not having a home?

John: You tell me.

Larry: Yeah, I guess it do. You see, folks can tell by looking at me, and all of us out here, that we're homeless. They can tell because our clothes is ragged, we just settin' around doin' nothin' while other folks is working, and so they know I'm homeless and they don't want to look at me.

From this point on, Larry talked almost nonstop for the next 40 minutes. Toward the end of the conversation, Larry told me that maybe we did have something in common after all and that he didn't feel invisible while he had been talking to me. As this example shows, one way to initiate an interview and active listening is by simply indicating one's willingness, interest, or desire to listen. In this case, once I indicated to Larry that I genuinely was interested in what he had to say, both as a researcher and as a man interested in the plight of others, Larry became personally involved in the conversation and related a rich narrative of his life as a homeless man that both resulted in a successful interview and appeared to be personally rewarding to Larry.

The interview with Larry is closely related to another dimension of rapport and active listening, which is interpersonal comfort. Larry found that he and the researcher had a genuine mutual interest in the conditions of homelessness. This resulted in his sense that what he had to say was important and that he had human value to the researcher and was not just a source of data or information. This sense of personal value and ensuing openness further encouraged his personal comfort with the research interview. Key to this was the ability of the researcher to listen before the interview had even begun. At the start of our interaction, Larry essentially indicated to me that he feared I wanted to use him to "write a book" and that his story did not have an intrinsic value to me. I actively listened to his concerns and was subsequently able to frame the interview in a social context that made sense to him (i.e., I want to help homeless people).

◆ Filtering

We do not listen to everything equally, but we pick and choose what we attend to. Active listening in this case is a process of filtering what we hear. There are a number of things that serve as filters in our listening. Some of these include filtering out parts of the discourse, while others serve to select information to be "admitted" or "listened to" in the interview. Among the significant filters are (a) the self that we bring to the interview; (b) the ideology that we hold (which may be a part of the self); (c) what we perceive as shared experience and what the respondent means by what he or she is saying; (d) junk filters, or the process of tuning out bits of interview talk; and (e) filtering for topics of relevant concern in the research project.

SELF AS FILTER

Perhaps the most important among these filters is the self that we bring to the interview (see Annika Lillrank's "Managing the Interviewer Self," this volume; Lillrank, 2002). Admittedly, the nature and very reality of a "core sense of self" is a matter of some debate in the social sciences, and it is not my purpose here to rehash this argument. Rather, I simply use the idea of self here as a person with a perspective or point of view, whatever its "true" or ontological nature might be, that mediates the act of listening in the research interview.

Regardless of the theoretical underpinnings that underlie the interview, the purposes of the interview, or the techniques employed in the interview, the interview is inevitably shaped to some degree by the self that is doing the interviewing (Brooks, 1978; Brownell, 2006; Wolvin & Coakley, 1988). This has implications for the entire research process, including selection of the research topic, the interview component, and the listening that is involved within it. Just as it is the sense of self that determines the research interest, it is also the self that shapes the research plan, shapes the interview, and listens to the discourse of the respondent. Moustakas (1994) argues that "the self of the researcher is present throughout the process and, while understanding the phenomenon with increasing depth, the researcher also experiences growing self-awareness and self knowledge. Heuristic processes incorporate creative self-processes and self-discoveries" (p. 17).

In his discussion of listening in anticipation of the interpretive process, Schlesinger (1994) says that

> it matters a great deal what goes on in the analyst's mind prior to the beginning of an interpretive process, and it also matters a great deal what the analyst selects to say first to the patient from among the possibilities that may come to mind. (p. 31)

He then goes on to argue for listening through the filters of our previous experience as "that experience is translated, more or less accurately, into an appreciation of our current context" (p. 31).

These arguments run counter to the understanding that the interviewer is but an instrument whose purpose is to absorb information from the respondent, who is but a vessel of that information. An extension of this thinking goes further, as was illustrated in a collaborative research project in which I was involved. One point of contention among the researchers was that it was inevitable that any collaboration between researcher and respondent would add additional voices and perspectives to the interview that would affect the objectivity of the research. They believed that this would influence the respondents' perspectives and their consequent answers. In this way, they argued, active listening would have an undue influence on the respondent and thus influence what he or she said or how he or she thought about fair housing in the city that was being studied, and thus it would bias the study. This seems to mirror McCracken's (1988) argument for the investigator as instrument (pp. 19–20). More specifically, he goes on to argue that "active listening strategies must not be used by the qualitative researcher. They are obtrusive in precisely the manner that this research wishes to avoid, and they are likely to be almost completely destructive of good data" (p. 21).

Thus, the researcher's self is implicated in the conduct and interpretation of the interview. This has implications for what the interviewer hears or doesn't hear, the significance that he or she attaches to the "data," the frame in which the interview is interpreted as the interviewer listens to the respondent, and the ongoing theorizing that the interviewer does as he or she listens. It is the self that listens, and as such, it is the self that is a filter for what we hear, and consequently for our listening.

The sense of self is the umbrella under which many other filters fall. First, as real, live human beings, we are concerned to some degree about our psychological well-being. As the respondent speaks, we may be on guard for the integrity of our own self and our standing as a person in the interview. Consider the researcher who becomes the object of passive hostility for a respondent. The respondent may project onto the researcher a belief that the researcher is viewing the respondent with an air of condescension, that the researcher considers himself or herself as superior because of education, position, or myriad other reasons. If the respondent becomes openly challenging and suggests to the interviewer that he or she is really not in a position to evaluate what the respondent is saying, it may become a source of psychic threat to the interviewer. If the interviewer is secure, that is, comfortable in his or her own skin, this may well be a time for overcoming the respondent's hostility and building an appropriate relationship. But if the researcher is insecure, he

or she may then discount other things that the respondent may say and thus "tune out" or "filter out" much of what the respondent is saying.

Closely related to this is the desire to see the interview progressing in a way that makes the interviewer look or feel good. This is particularly true when the interviewer is invested in a particular point of view and the respondent makes statements that challenge that perspective. This might result in the interviewer having a sense of being intimidated. The secure interviewer will, however, inquire about the origins, linkages, or meanings of that perspective and enrich the interview process. The interviewer who is less secure may well focus on defending his or her perspective and miss the significance of what the respondent is saying.

Finally, the interviewer may have what is called in the vernacular "too large an ego." My own experience with my own interviewing, and in discussions with others who interview, is that this may result in an inability to focus on listening to the respondent because of an inappropriate focus on the self. Another result of this is that the interviewer becomes engrossed in his or her own ego and simply talks too much, thus precluding respondents from fully articulating their point of view or confusing the respondents so that they are dealing with the point of view of the interviewer rather than their own.

In the world of research interviews, appropriate awareness of the self is critical for how we listen. All of these concerns regarding the self require at a minimum some self-reflection. The point is that it is the respondent who is at the center of the interview and not the interviewer. One way of confronting this is for the researcher to discuss his or her interviews, including both the techniques and the findings, with colleagues. There is, however, another remedy that is even more significant. In graduate school curricula, there is a distinct need for training in listening as a part of training in interviewing techniques (Wolvin & Coakley, 1988). In my own department, we have included a required course in interviewing. This includes methods of interviewing, but more to the point here, there is an emphasis on the self who listens, speaks, and is actively engaged in the interview.

IDEOLOGICAL FILTERS

In the process of lifelong socialization, the interviewer has internalized beliefs and values that are linked to his or her role in the social world, that is, the culture. In the course of their career, researchers will interview people with different beliefs and values. This applies both to people who live in different ethnic or cultural contexts and people who live within different contexts of beliefs and values within one's own culture. In speaking of beliefs and values, I am including political agendas, social values, religious orientation, and racial and gender perspectives. These may be learned from childhood, or they may be beliefs and agendas that have been adopted later on in life. They are, however, cultural artifacts that shape our perspective on the social world and, as such, affect our listening.

It is not unusual to consider different cultures, or cultural perspectives, as either inferior to or at least different from one's own. This difference frequently influences the perspective one has of "the other." This difference in turn has the potential to influence what the interviewer hears as he or she listens to the respondent, as we constantly interpret and reinterpret what we hear in light of our own experience (Schlesinger, 1994).

All of this suggests that if respondents represent different ideologies that diverge from that of the interviewer, it is wise for the interviewer to probe and ask questions about his or her own linkages, generalizations, and perceptions. The research interview is not the time for arguing or attempting to "win an ideological argument." The researcher's investment is to be in the quality of the interview, with the primary goal of facilitating the cultural narrative of the respondent.

PRESUMED SHARED EXPERIENCE AS A FILTER

The assumption of shared experience presents additional filtering problems for listening in the context of the research interview. By assuming shared experience, researchers run the risk of glossing over the meaning of the experience and related biographical or narrative linkages. The meanings of the experience of the respondent are replaced by the meanings of the interviewer. To undo the listening filter of presumed shared experiences, researchers can "bracket" (Garfinkel, 1984) their respondents' comments. Listening from the position of an outsider, if done successfully (without alienating the respondent by being offensively obtuse or dense), can facilitate a richer and deeper understanding of the biographical details of both the researcher and the respondent.

Different types of probes can be particularly effective in the listening process, aimed at removing taken-for-granted filters. Such probes fall into two categories. The first is probes based on the researcher's own autobiography. In this case, the interviewer may briefly relate a story from her or his own background and then ask if it is similar to the experience that the respondent has related. I will say a few words of caution from my own experience. With this type of potentially lengthy probe, it is wise for researchers to be careful not to disrupt the respondent's concentration or narrative construction to the point that the researcher's story replaces the construction and/or meaning of the respondent's account.

The second category probes for confirmation of the respondent's perspective and meaning. This is accomplished by either restating what the respondent has said in a clear and unambiguous way and asking if that is what the respondent meant or by asking the respondent to state what he or she has said in a different way. Probes in this general category are intended to confirm that the researcher is both hearing and understanding what the respondent is saying rather than hearing the researcher's own thoughts that he or she has projected onto the respondent. This is particularly important when the respondent uses a large number of pronouns, which may be confusing, or when the respondent is attempting to relate a coherent narrative with which he or she is struggling. The other consequence of this is that the respondent is assured that the researcher is listening and is taking what is being said seriously.

JUNK FILTERS

An important dimension of filtered listening is designating certain material as irrelevant. Many words and phrases that we hear in an interview are filtered out as extraneous material or "junk." For example, I often ignore editorial comments by the respondent that are said in passing. An example is a white woman talking about racial attitudes, who briefly said, "You know how they are [referring to racial minorities]!" While this was offensive, this was not the time or place to argue with her or correct her. I ignored the comment, and she resumed telling her story. The challenge is to prevent junk filters from indirectly constructing the respondent's story for research and analysis purposes and to avoid listening to an interview with so many junk filters that one no longer attends to what the respondent is saying.

The obvious question here is "For what are we listening?" One answer to this question might be that we are genuinely curious and want to learn more about the respondent and his or her perspective(s): We are listening to, and for, the respondent. This is to be distinguished from either listening to our own sense of self or validation of our own existing view of the world. When we take the respondent seriously and listen to him or her, we express an understanding of the respondent that becomes noticeable to the respondent. In his discussion of active listening in the counseling context, Nelson-Jones (1988) recommends that therapists understand the internal frame of reference of the client. This, he argues, confirms to the client that we are taking seriously who he or she is and what he or she means. This is directly translatable into the interview situation. Consider the African American respondent whom I interviewed about housing. He stated, "You don't have any idea what it's like to be black." If this goes unanswered, or answered superficially or dishonestly, the respondent is likely to believe and feel that what he says will not be taken seriously (i.e., his comment was "junked"). This was a real interview situation in which I found myself. In an earlier time, I might well have said something like this: "I'm not sure what difference that makes, but I'm sure that it is difficult for you to find suitable housing." Instead, my response was

> Of course I don't have any idea of what it means to be black, but if you can tell me about your experience as a black man, I can have a better idea. So can you tell me what it's like to be a black man who is looking for housing, and how it seems to be different from being a white man?

The respondent then openly discussed his experience as an African American struggling to find suitable housing, and from that point on, he referenced the difference between white and black in a number of situations. This gave me the dual perspective of the black experience and the respondent's perception of the white experience.

RELEVANCE/THEME FILTERS

Research interviewers are particularly trained to listen for themes: congruence or contradictions in the narrative, layers of meaning attached to different experiences, and the overall sense of self that the respondent conveys in the interview. As these are noted, it is frequently helpful for the interviewer to respond by restating what has been heard. This will indicate to the respondent that he has been heard and taken seriously. Additional note should be made of the respondent's own interpretation of what has been said. Essentially, this amounts to applying "respondent validation," or "feedback" (Kadushin & Kadushin, 1997), to the ongoing act of the interview, as opposed to something that is done in postinterview analysis. Again, from my own experience, it is better to ask if our understanding of these elements is accurate. If the respondent says that our understanding is not accurate, it makes possible the respondent's clarification and thus enhances the joint construction of the narrative.

In my experience, if asked, respondents frequently provide their own theories or interpretations of their world. To illustrate this point, consider the following example. A colleague related an incident in which the respondent indicated that people could not be trusted. He asked the respondent to articulate the source of this distrust. The respondent explained that he and another man had conducted their own social experiment on honesty by placing a dollar bill on the floor of a store and observing people's reactions. The two men, playing amateur social scientists, observed one person ignore the bill and then saw a second one look around and cautiously pick it up and put it in his pocket. They then placed another dollar bill on the floor, and the first person who noticed it likewise put it in his pocket after first mentioning that he must have dropped it. This was repeated for the third time, and again, the first customer who noticed it picked it up and put it in his pocket without comment. Thus, if listened to, far from being "cultural dopes" (Garfinkel, 1984, pp. 68–75), interview respondents are quite capable of theorizing their own experiences by linking biographical experiences to theoretical or abstract formulations.

In the research interview, we are listening in a focused manner as we listen for themes and connect the dots as we listen to our interviewees. However, focused listening is by definition partial and can in fact get in the way of listening to the whole narrative (Schlesinger, 1994). Therefore, it may be appropriate to borrow from the counseling field by presenting what has been heard to the respondent and then asking if what the researcher has noted is at all significant to the respondent and, if it is, what it means.

◆ Silent Listening and Listening to Silences

There are listening responses that are time honored and that are helpful in responding to the listener. The first of these is the artful use of silence (Knapp, 1978; Yow, 2005). This does not mean to simply be quiet. It does mean to respond with attention in viewing the respondent, making notes that may be referred to in the future and that will also indicate to the respondent that he or she has been heard. Respondents themselves, however, may fall silent. When this occurs, there is frequently the impulse on the part of interviewers to fill the silent spaces with their own words and thus relieve their anxiety. This, however, may be counterproductive as several things may be occurring. The respondent may be collecting his or her thoughts before continuing with the narrative. The respondent may not know what to say but if left to silence may find ways to fill the silent vacuum. Finally, silence may be used to evaluate or reevaluate what has occurred in the interview thus far. The astute interviewer will listen both to what the respondent is saying and to what is not being said. There may be reasons for silence on the part of the respondent. It is the task of the interviewer to listen to the silence in the context of the interview and determine appropriate responses, if any.

Closely related to allowing silence within the interview is sensitivity to appropriate turn taking (i.e., when it is one's turn to "shut up"). In an ideal world, a conversation is an exercise in turn taking. One speaks and the other listens; then the roles are reversed. In the meantime, while one is speaking, the other is silent, absorbing and interpreting what is being said.

In interview situations such as the social work interview or therapeutic interview, the protocol dictates who speaks and who listens. In a counseling situation, the focus of the interview is the client and the issues that are central to his or her problem. In this instance, the therapist or counselor is listening to the client's troubles to devise appropriate interventions or therapeutic techniques. When the counselors believe that some verbal intervention would be either helpful or necessary, they speak. Otherwise they are silent. In research interview situations, while the respondent is talking, it is almost never helpful to interrupt but to wait for an appropriate time to interject a thought, question, or observation (i.e., to probe). Of course, the pitfall here is that the researcher may only be listening for the opportune moment to inject his or her ideas into the conversation as a way of changing the topic of the conversation.

◆ Conclusion

My experiences as researcher, counselor, and business executive form the basis of my thoughts on listening as I have considered both the fact of listening and the components of listening and have embedded techniques within these thoughts. Throughout this chapter, I have drawn attention to different techniques of listening in the context of conversations labeled as "research interviews." In more informal conversations, there may be lapses in attention, brief periods of boredom, or some tolerance of irrelevance in the conversation at hand; all that is really expected in a "polite" informal conversation is sufficient attention to maintain the continuity of the conversation. However, the research interview is based on a different agenda and is geared toward a different type of listening. Additionally, it should be noted that different methods of research require different types of listening. For example, in a survey interview, the listening is more likely to be directed toward factual details and "when," "where," or "why" questions. In comparison, an in-depth interview might focus on the quality of the experience and "how" follow-up questions. Accordingly, what the interviewer listens for varies considerably depending on the style of interview.

Active listening, as described in this chapter, is essentially about being self-reflexively aware of interview interactions. It is unnerving, to say the least, to lecture to a class or speak to a friend and have no sign of recognition that one has been heard. Responding to the speaker is not to agree with the speaker but to affirm that what he or she has said has been taken seriously. The same is true of listening in an interview. The collaboration between interviewer and listener in an interview situation mandates that the interviewer give evidence that the speaker has been heard and that what he or she has said has been appreciated as authentic, serious, and reflective of his or her narrative.

However, the importance and relevance of self-awareness in the interview process is not necessarily shared by all researchers, even the practitioners of qualitative research methods. In the course of writing this chapter, I spoke with a colleague with some experience in qualitative research and interviewing and asked him to describe how he dealt with self-awareness in the interview process. His immediate response was telling as he said, "What do you mean?" I clarified what I meant as follows:

John: It makes sense to me for anyone in the interview business to psychologically monitor the process of the interview and himself within that process. Through this monitoring, he is able to remain finely attuned both to what the other is saying and to observe what seems to be occurring between him and the respondent so that he can listen. . . .

Respondent: Hell, I just listen. Don't you just listen? It really doesn't make any difference what I feel or think, or what the respondent feels or thinks. That's all psychological stuff. All I want is the answers to my questions.

This was not the answer I expected, but it does represent the attitude of many who view the researcher as nothing more than a human tape recorder. This is not to say that the research interview process is best served by the interviewer playing counselor or therapist. It is to suggest, however, that the researcher needs to spend time understanding his or her participation in the interview and how and why others are responding to him or her in the interview situation in specific ways.

◆ References

Berger, L. (2001). Inside out: Narrative autoethnography as a path toward rapport. *Qualitative Inquiry, 7*(4), 504–518.

Brooks, W. D. (1978). *Speech communication* (3rd ed.). Dubuque, IA: Wm. C. Brown.

Brownell, J. (2006). *Listening: Attitudes, principles, and skills.* Boston, MA: Pearson.

Garfinkel, H. (1984). *Studies in ethnomethodology.* Cambridge, MA: Polity Press.

Gubrium, J., & Holstein, J. (2002). From the individual interview to interview society. In J. Gubrium & J. Holstein (Eds.), *Handbook of interview research: Context and method* (pp. 3–32). Thousand Oaks, CA: Sage.

Holstein, J. A., & Gubrium, J. F. (1995). *The active interview.* Thousand Oaks, CA: Sage.

Johnson, J. (2002). In-depth interviewing. In J. Gubrium & J. Holstein (Eds.), *Handbook of interview research: Context and method* (pp. 103–119). Thousand Oaks, CA: Sage.

Jourard, S. (1964). *The transparent self.* Princeton, NJ: D. Van Nostrand.

Kadushin, A., & Kadushin, G. (1997). *The social work interview* (4th ed.). New York, NY: Columbia University Press.

Knapp, M. L. (1978). *Non-verbal communication in human interaction.* New York, NY: Holt, Rinehart, & Winston.

Lillrank, A. (2002). The tension between overt talk and covert emotions in illness narratives: Transition from clinician to researcher. *Culture, Medicine and Psychiatry, 26,* 111–127.

McCracken, G. (1988). *The long interview.* Thousand Oaks, CA: Sage.

Moustakas, C. (1994). *Phenomenological research methods.* Thousand Oaks, CA: Sage.

Nelson-Jones, R. (1988). *Practical counseling and helping skills* (2nd ed.). New York, NY: Holt, Rinehart, & Winston.

Reinharz, S. (1992). *Feminist methods in social research.* New York, NY: Oxford University Press.

Schlesinger, H. J. (1994). How the analyst listens: The presages of interpretation. *International Journal of Psychoanalysis, 75,* 31–37.

Seidman, E. (2006). *Interviewing as qualitative research* (3rd ed.). New York, NY: Teachers College Press.

Simon, J. (1988). Criteria for therapist self-disclosure. *American Journal of Psychotherapy, 42*(3), 404–415.

Weiner, M. F. (1978). *The use of self in psychotherapy.* Boston, MA: Butterworth.

Wolvin, A., & Coakley, C. G. (1988). *Listening* (3rd ed.). Dubuque, IA: Wm. C. Brown.

Yow, V. R. (2005). *Recording oral history* (2nd ed.). Walnut Creek, CA: AltaMira Press.

21

CONSTRUCTING THE RESPONDENT

◆ Lara J. Foley

n recent decades, the literature on interviewing has considered the interview as a social interaction in which the interviewer and the respondent jointly construct meanings (Chase, 2005; DeVault, 1999; Dingwall, 1997; Holstein & Gubrium, 1995; Rapley, 2004; Silverman, 1993). The pedagogy and theory of interviewing, however, still seem very interviewer centered (Emerson, 1983; Miller & Dingwall, 1997; Rubin & Rubin, 1995; see Presser, 2004, and Riach, 2009, for interesting exceptions). We recognize that the respondent plays a role, but there is little systematic examination of the diversity of this role.

In this chapter, I examine different constructions of interview respondents in relation to different methods of interviewing. I explore the ways respondents are constructed in relation to ethical concerns. Next, I demonstrate how researchers work to construct the respondent through the selection of participants, in the course of the interview, through the analysis of the transcripts, and in the production of manuscripts. Finally, I discuss interview respondents as engaged in their own project of constructing self and interviewer.

◆ Constructing Respondents in Relation to Methods

To conduct particular kinds of research, researchers must imagine a certain type of respondent. Therefore, the method of data collection usually dictates the way a researcher expects a respondent to act, behave, talk, and produce useful data. In this section, I will address the construction of respondents in relation to survey interviews, in-depth interviews, and ethnographic interviews. Researchers using these methods construct respondents as reporters, teachers, and members, respectively.

SURVEY INTERVIEWS: RESPONDENT AS REPORTER

Some approaches to interviewing assume a concrete reality that can be accessed through the respondent. The respondent is seen as a relatively passive reporter of information. Following these assumptions, interviewers see the need to standardize interviews and typically do so through

◆ 305

survey interviews or structured interviews (Fontana & Frey, 2005; Singleton & Straits, 2002). These types of interviews rely on preestablished questions, usually with a limited set of responses. Each respondent receives the same questions, in the same order, and interviewers are trained to present themselves in the same, neutral way for each interview. If these conditions are not met, then the data resulting from the interviews are presumed to be contaminated or biased. Selection of respondents in these cases is ideally based on either a random sample or at least a sample that is representative of the study population. The material (data) that is produced from this approach is then thought to be generalizable to a larger population (Converse & Schuman, 1974). Using this model of data collection, the researcher maintains a great deal of control over the interaction (Corbin & Morse, 2003).

The idea that there is a truth to be told shapes the construction of the respondent as a reporter of truth. As long as a researcher can ask a question in the right way and respondents can be conditioned to remember, cooperate, and be honest, the data collected will reveal that truth.

In this context, respondents can be viewed as honest and helpful; lying, uncooperative, or forgetful; or unable to comprehend the questions. This way of viewing the respondent can be seen in the language used to describe problems in this approach to interviewing—response inconsistency, item omission, and response error. There is also the frequent concern that respondents will succumb to social desirability by trying to make a favorable impression on the interviewer rather than answering truthfully (Singleton & Straits, 2002).

In the model of the survey interview, researchers are trained to be neutral, to ask questions in a very structured manner, and to attempt to elicit the truth from respondents. Not only are interviewers trained, but respondents are "trained" as well (Singleton & Straits, 2002). The survey researcher may read brief statements to the respondent, describe to the respondent the nature of standardized interviews, instruct the respondent that it is important to give complete and accurate information, or ask the respondent to agree to answer conscientiously. Although this model relies on a relatively passive respondent who retrieves and relays information about her- or himself, the training of the respondent hints at the recognition of a more active respondent, one who

could venture off script if not trained properly. In this model, however, a respondent who is too active is cast as undesirable.

IN-DEPTH INTERVIEWING: RESPONDENT AS TEACHER

Another approach to interviewing, in-depth interviewing, sees the interview as a social interaction that takes place within a particular social context created by the interaction of the interviewer and the respondent (Johnson, 2002). The interviewer initially creates the interview context, or defines the situation, but the interviewee may either comply with or resist that definition of the situation. In other words, the interviewee is an active participant and a source of knowledge. In this approach to interviewing, standardized interview schedules are often rejected in favor of unstructured or open-ended interviews, which permit respondents to raise and explore issues that they find to be relevant and allow their *voices* to be heard. In this model, the respondent has much more control over the pacing of the interview, the topics that will be discussed, and what she or he will disclose.

In addition to the assumptions and practices mentioned above, interviewers using this approach recognize that the interviewer cannot be neutral. Instead of aiming for objective neutrality on the part of the interviewer, this approach calls for mutual understanding and intersubjective depth between interviewer and respondent. Many researchers taking this approach to interviewing would insist that to reach deep understanding, interviewers must build rapport and trust with the interviewee, and some suggest that self-disclosure on the part of the interviewer helps build this trust (Carpenter, 2005; Douglas, 1985; Johnson, 2002; Schilt, 2006; Webb, 1984). For example, in her study of transgendered people's work experiences, Schilt (2006) was concerned about how she, as a nontransgendered person, would be received in her research setting and chose to take an approach of openness and self-disclosure. She writes,

> I went into the study being extremely open about my research agenda and my political affiliations with feminist and transgender politics. I carried my openness about my intentions into my interviews, making clear at the beginning that I was

happy to answer questions about my research intentions, the ultimate goal of my research, and personal questions about myself. Through this openness, and the acknowledgement that I was there to learn rather than to be an academic "expert," I feel that I gained a rapport with my respondents that bridged the "outsider/insider" divide [Merton, 1972]. (p. 469)

Like Schilt, researchers using this model often present themselves as learners, asking the respondent to play the role of the "expert" or teacher. In-depth interviewers typically recognize the existence of multiple truths and see the interview as a collaboration between researcher and respondent (Johnson, 2002). This approach, however, has an analytical focus on the substance of what is being said rather than on the process of interaction or collaboration between researcher and respondent. Researchers encourage respondents to dig deep into their stocks of knowledge to provide more and richer data.

In this context, the respondent's distinct characteristics become especially relevant as lenses that color her or his view of reality. Researchers in this vein are often interested in the *voices* of members of distinct groups—children, men, women, older people, elites, the ill, and people of varying sexual identities and varying races and ethnicities. While it is important to recognize that members of each distinct group are likely to have a different set of experiences than members of other distinct groups, researchers must be careful not to construct respondents as a "set of distinctions" (e.g., "the black respondents" or "the gay respondents"), but rather, they should recognize the more complex nature of respondent identities.

ETHNOGRAPHIC INTERVIEWING: RESPONDENT AS MEMBER AND INFORMANT

Ethnographic interviews can take the form of in-depth interviews or the form of "spontaneous 'conversations'" (Atkinson & Pugsley, 2005). They are very different from the structured interview of survey interviewing. And what sets them apart from in-depth interviewing is the context in which they take place. Ethnographic interviews are typically set in a fieldwork or participant observation setting. The level of immersion in the setting can vary widely for researchers. Some researchers may live, work, and socialize within a particular community for long stretches of time, while others might keep moving in and out of the community. For example, in my work, I often attend the training classes, staff meetings, and court appearances of the nurses I study. I primarily get to know the respondents only in a professional context. Although in my writing, my primary source of data is in-depth interviews, I consider those interviews to be ethnographically informed because of my participation in the work settings of the nurses.

In the context of ethnographic interviewing, respondents are often chosen for their special knowledge of a setting. The special respondent is typically referred to as an informant and may be a longtime member of the community or organization. The informant may be in a position within the organization or community to give the researcher access to other members. It is important that the informant not only have significant knowledge about the group but also that she or he demonstrate communicative competence (Warren, 2002). This means that the informant must be able to effectively teach the researcher about the community. While I discussed the respondent as teacher in the section on in-depth interviewing, the role of teacher is expanded with ethnographic respondents. Beyond teaching about a specific kind of life experience, the ethnographic informant may teach the researcher how to be a member of the community. For example, in his study of a halfway house for paroled ex–drug addicts, Lawrence Wieder (1983) describes how after asking a question about the use of drugs in the house, his informant, Sanchez, tells him he can't ask that question and proceeds to instruct Wieder in very specific ways:

He [Sanchez] suggested that I should publicly argue with the staff about their treatment of the residents, that I should not spend time with the staff, and that I should take guys out for beer and the like. . . . He suggested that if I followed his instructions, then perhaps after several weeks I might find out something. (p. 80)

Like many ethnographers, Wieder found that he had to earn the trust of the residents and build rapport with them before they would take his presence or questions seriously.

Unlike in the survey model, respondents in the ethnographic model are not thought of as potential liars but as possibly being "reluctant," as Adler and Adler (2002) might put it. For example, Marvasti and

McKinney (2004) found Middle Easterners living in the United States to be initially reluctant to speak to researchers following the events of September 11, 2001. Given the discourses prominent during that time relating to war and terror, potential respondents were reasonably concerned about researchers having hidden agendas or being sponsored by the government. It required a great deal of time and effort on the part of the researchers to build the trust and rapport necessary for respondents to be willing to talk and share their experiences. When researchers find themselves coming up against reluctant respondents, they engage in various strategies to secure trust and rapport. These strategies can fall anywhere on the continuum from extreme measures such as engaging in the same illegal activities as their respondents (Adler & Adler, 2002) to simpler tactics, such as asking a different sort of question. For example, Seimsen (2004) initially found the women defense attorneys she interviewed to be reluctant until she changed the way she asked her questions. She writes,

> After the interview was over I asked [the respondent], "What kinds of questions were you expecting me to ask?" Her response was, "well, I guess I didn't realize it was going to be quite so feminist slanted, how-do-you-represent-those-rapists kind of thing." . . . I found the women in future interviews more responsive if I asked, "how do you respond to people who question your work by asking, 'how can you defend that guy'?" (p. 6)

Although ethnographic interviews can be distinguished to some degree from in-depth interviews, in both approaches, there is the sense that with enough trust and rapport and asking the right kinds of probing questions, the researcher will eventually uncover truer or richer data.

In the approaches to interviewing above, we have seen a move from highly structured to unstructured, from a relatively passive to an active respondent, and from no acknowledgment to recognition of the constructed nature of the interview context. In-depth and ethnographic approaches to interviewing recognize the interactive nature of the interview, that there can be multiple truths, and that respondents speak from multiple subject positions. Even in these approaches, however, the analytic focus typically remains on *what* is being said (Holstein & Gubrium, 1995). Later, I will talk about the importance of turning analytic attention to *how* stories are told and how respondent and researcher work together to create the interview data.

◆ Constructing Respondents in Relation to Ethical Concerns

Not only are respondents constructed in relation to research methods, but they are also constructed in response to certain ethical concerns. This is often done in an effort to avoid exploitation of respondents and to reduce the possibilities for misunderstanding them, although occasionally different motives come into play. In this section, I will outline the ways in which respondents are variously constructed as learners, vulnerable, and same/other.

LEARNERS

Earlier in this chapter, I discussed the respondent as teacher. At times, respondents are also constructed as learners. We have already seen how respondents in the survey interview model are often trained to be "good" respondents—for example, by being instructed to give accurate answers. Another way in which respondents are painted as learners is when scholars describe them as learning about themselves (Reinharz & Chase, 2002; Saylor, 2010). For example, in a discussion on interviewing women, Reinharz and Chase (2002) write that sometimes the interview context is an opportunity for the respondent to "discover her thoughts, learn who she is, find her voice" (p. 225). One more way that respondents are cast as learners is by researchers who feel a moral and ethical obligation to offer counterarguments to respondents who hold inaccurate information or negative views about a group of people (McKinney, 2005). Writing about studying whiteness and white privilege, McKinney (2005) cites other authors who engage in this practice and adds that

> I too sometimes offer counterevidence to respondents' statements. I discuss how certain beliefs they espouse about being white are "fictions" that, left unchallenged, help to sustain societal racism. I believe that I as the researcher can take this position while still maintaining the respect for my respondents that my ethics require. (p. xviii)

McKinney and others who take this approach cast the respondent as someone who can potentially learn or benefit from participation in the interview.

VULNERABLE

Respondents may also be painted as vulnerable. For example, respondents who have experienced violence or trauma or who have been stigmatized for one reason or another could experience anxiety (or worse) when being interviewed about their experience. Some authors recommend that the interviewer be prepared to offer referrals for counseling in these cases (Brzuzy, Ault, & Segal, 1997; Reinharz & Chase, 2002). While it is certainly important to protect respondents from harm, researchers should be careful not to assume that violence and trauma have the same meaning for all respondents (Corbin & Morse, 2003). In my work looking at forensic exams of sexual assault patients, it has been clear that not everyone experiences assault in the same way. One forensic nurse working in an urban hospital said it best when she described to me that

> for some of our clients, being raped is not the worst thing that ever happened to them, nor is it the worst thing that happened that day. I mean it could be, "I need my drugs, I'm homeless, I have no place to eat, I'm afraid for my life and by the way I was raped." (Unpublished interview transcript)

As a researcher, I need to be careful not to make too many assumptions about what makes a respondent vulnerable. It may turn out that what I think makes the respondent vulnerable could really differ from what the respondent thinks makes him or her vulnerable. In a study with sexual minority young adults, Saylor (2010) found that some of her respondents seemed perplexed by her preemptive presentation of referrals:

> I preemptively provided the young adult participants in this study a list of helpful organizations should our interview leave them upset and in need of someone to talk to, reasoning that I might not appropriately gauge someone's emotional state and therefore leave an upset participant without resources. Some of the participants found the resources I provided puzzling, perhaps even offensive. (p. 22)

Sometimes interviewers can position the participants as at-risk even when the researchers and/or the respondents themselves do not think they are vulnerable (Saylor, 2010). This may be done out of necessity for a particular audience—a funding agency or an institutional review board (IRB), for example. For example, to obtain permission to waive parental consent for LGBTQ (lesbian, gay, bisexual, transgender, queer) minors, some researchers have portrayed these young people as a vulnerable group to IRBs, even though "young sexual minorities may object to and resent the implication that their status as LGBTQ somehow marks them as more vulnerable than their heterosexual peers" (Saylor, 2010, p. 20). There are certainly times when groups of people are in vulnerable situations and as research participants should absolutely be protected. I have used this strategy myself with IRB applications, asking to waive written consent when working with undocumented immigrants and transgender individuals, some (but not all) of whom may have been vulnerable to law enforcement or employer sanctions.

In another example of constructing respondents as vulnerable who may not define themselves as such, McCracken (1988) reports that a funding agency was concerned when he wanted to conduct long interviews with people who were between the ages of 65 and 75 years. There was concern that these interviews would be too exhausting for the respondents. But, as the researcher discovered, this fear turned out to be unfounded, and instead, he claims, "almost without exception, respondents proved more durable and energetic than the interviewer" (p. 27).

SAME/OTHER

A final ethical concern relates to the long-standing insider/outsider problem in qualitative research. Typically, this concern is addressed from the perspective of the researcher—is she or he part of the community being studied or not? This question is not typically addressed from the point of view of the respondent. What does this mean for how respondents are constructed? If a researcher is an insider, that suggests that the respondent and researcher are the same; if the researcher is an outsider, then the respondent would be constructed as other.

Despite the dichotomized way this debate continues to be presented, many scholars have provided evidence that it is not so clear-cut (Bhopal, 2010; Dunbar, Rodriguez, & Parker, 2002; Furman, 1997; Kusow, 2003; Litt, 2000; Naples, 1996; Riessman, 1987). Often researchers recognize that they are "insiders" in one sense and "outsiders" in another. For example, in a study of older Jewish women and beauty shop culture, Furman (1997) recognized that she shared ethnicity, gender, and class status with her respondents but was separated from them by nationality, age, and education level.

The insider/outsider discussion often revolves around access to, rapport with, and the ability to gain truer or richer data from respondents. But it seems that authors can make arguments for how their insider/outsider status served them well regardless of where they fall on the insider/outsider spectrum. For example, two different studies of drag queens have authors making different arguments regarding the insider/outsider issue. Taylor and Rupp (2005) suggest that as lesbians, they were able to facilitate access and rapport with the drag queens they studied because of shared identities as sexual minorities. Berkowitz and Belgrave (2010) make a distinctly different claim. They claim that access and rapport were facilitated by their status as heterosexual women, citing "crude wisecracks about lesbians" (p. 164) as part of the rapport work. The authors of both of these studies recognize that identities, access, and rapport are all much more complicated than a simple insider/outsider dichotomy would have us believe. For example, Taylor and Rupp (2005) recognized that while in some ways their gender and sexual identities facilitated access, in other ways it complicated it. They also came to learn during their fieldwork that other statuses, such as education and socioeconomic status (which differed from their respondents), played out in complicated ways.

There are many researchers, and a vast and growing body of literature, that recognize respondents as active subjects with multiple and complex standpoints (Chase, 2005; Choo & Ferree, 2010; Collins, 1991; DeVault, 1999; Holstein & Gubrium, 1995). In other words, during an interview, a respondent may speak at one moment as a parent, at another moment as an African American man, and at yet another moment as a professional. What has been less often addressed is the interaction of the multiple subject positions of the researcher and the respondent.

◆ The Work of Constructing Respondents

The various constructions of respondents discussed above are not mutually exclusive. Respondents can be all of these things: teachers and learners, active and passive, empowered and vulnerable. Ultimately, interviewers work with respondents. This is done in the practice of the interview, in the analysis of the interview data, and in the representation of the interview in print.

INTERVIEW PRACTICE

Interviewers engage in the work of constructing respondents in several different ways. I will discuss this work in relation to analytic categories, rapport work, and the talk of the interview. Researchers work to construct respondents as analytic categories. This likely takes place before the interview even begins, in the selection of respondents. If I want to study yoga enthusiasts, I will probably go to a yoga studio instead of a ski lodge (although I'm sure I could find some yoga enthusiasts at a ski lodge). Once I start meeting people who like to do yoga, I might discover that I should interview people who practice Bikram yoga (or hot yoga) and people who practice Iyengar yoga. Next, I might discover that in the particular geographic community I'm studying, some people engage in yoga as a spiritual practice and others only to stay in shape. Not only are researchers constantly engaged in the work of finding respondents who fit these analytic categories; they also may be charged with seeking out variations or cases that do not fit the constructed analytic categories (Corbin & Strauss, 1990). In my own work with midwives, everyone I interviewed claimed to practice and believe in the philosophy of holistic health care. Without exception, both direct-entry midwives and nurse midwives constructed themselves against a "medical model" of birth. In doing this, though, they frequently referred to "baby docs" or "really medical model types" of midwives that I should interview. They even gave me names. I tracked down these so-called medical model midwives, only to discover that they defined themselves as holistic as opposed to medical and suggested that I talk to so-and-so, who really follows a medical model. The defining of analytic categories as well as seeking out people to fill them takes a great deal of work on the part of the researcher.

Second, after the respondents are selected, researchers typically try to build a sense of trust and rapport with them. This takes work (Rapley, 2004). One way to do rapport work is through self-disclosure. In her study of virginity loss, Carpenter (2005) shows how her own self-disclosure helped a respondent open up a bit. She writes,

> Although [the respondent] answered me when I asked how old she'd been when she lost her virginity, she really opened up after I answered her question about how old I was—and it turned out we'd been the same age. (p. 211)

But Carpenter (2005), like some other researchers (Klatch, 1987; McCracken, 1988; Reinharz & Chase, 2002), recognizes that self-disclosure does not always lead to more or better information from respondents. In fact, it can be counterproductive. Carpenter (2005) says,

> When it came to sharing my own *opinions* with women and men whose beliefs appeared to differ substantially from mine, I confess that I was less forthcoming—without lying outright—for fear that being entirely open would "poison" the interview and destroy my rapport with the respondent. (p. 211)

So we see that rapport work can take the form of self-disclosing or opting not to self-disclose, whichever approach works best for the task at hand.

Finally, once respondents are found and trust and rapport are built, researchers must turn to the interview itself. Chase (2005) suggests that researchers *invite* respondents to be narrators. From there, researchers introduce a topic, listen to the answers, ask follow-up questions, perhaps interject personal experiences or opinions, and provide the embodied performances of nodding, smiling, and frowning to make the respondent feel heard (Rapley, 2004). If a respondent gets "off topic," researchers will work in different ways depending on their approach to interviewing. Survey researchers may try to bring the respondent back on track, while in-depth and ethnographic interviewers might try to find out more about this new direction.

INTERVIEW ANALYSIS

After the interviews are over, the researcher continues to construct the respondent through the analysis of the interview. Riessman (1993) suggests

that when "investigators interact with subjects, analytic ideas change" (p. 57). Here, she is actually referring to interacting with the narratives of the respondents after the interview, through interview transcripts. Returning to the example of studying yoga enthusiasts, a researcher might initially interview a respondent because he or she practices Bikram yoga as a spiritual practice, but later, during the analysis of the interview transcript, the interviewer may realize that the respondent also subtly interweaves a physical fitness narrative in and through the narratives of spiritual practice. In my research with midwives, I expected to outline some differences between nurse midwives and direct-entry midwives. There were some differences between the two groups. As the analysis of interview data proceeded, however, I discovered that in the narratives that I chose to focus on, the differences did not fall along the lines of type of training.

INTERVIEW REPRESENTATION

Even after the analysis of interviews is completed, researchers continue to work to construct respondents. At this stage, the results of the research, ultimately the respondents' answers or stories, are crafted to appear a certain way in the research manuscripts. Perhaps the most common example here is that while respondents are usually interviewed as individuals, they are sometimes presented in manuscripts as a broader collection of voices (Rapley, 2004). Researchers can make choices about how they represent respondents. For example, prisoners could be presented as dangerous or as victims of childhood traumas. Gay men could be presented as pathological or as sympathetic resisters of gender and sexuality norms (Kong, Mahoney, & Plummer, 2002). Chase (2005) argues that researchers have the ability to demonstrate the way larger cultural discourses affect the lives of respondents. She writes, "When researchers' interpretive strategies reveal the stranglehold of oppressive metanarratives, they help to open up possibilities for social change" (p. 668).

Regardless of the efforts researchers may make to be neutral during the interview and during analysis, their concerns shape the kinds of questions that are asked, how they code and quote field notes or interview data, and how they represent the data in manuscript form (Harris, 2001). At each stage, researchers work to construct the interview respondent they need to do the work they are trying to do. This last comment has not been a popular one. Several reviewers have expressed concern with the sentiment, suggesting that it sounds cynical. However, just as scholars of the sociology of work and occupations demonstrate that service providers often construct the clients they need to do the work that they do (see Martin, 2005, for a great example), I do not mean to be cynical when I suggest that interviewers are engaged in the same sort of practice.

◆ The Active Respondent

Many of the constructions discussed in this chapter recognize an active respondent (even if it is viewed as undesirable). Some go further to see the respondent as interactive or as a co-collaborator (Ellis, Kiesinger, & Tillman-Healy, 1997; Holstein & Gubrium, 1995; Johnson, 2002). Less often do we turn our attention to the respondent's work of self-construction, and even less often to how the respondent views or constructs the researcher and the research. In both of these instances, the respondent is actively helping define the situation of the interview. Respondents engage in this project not only through talk but also through embodied performance.

EMBODIED PERFORMANCE

In recent decades, sociology has paid a great deal of attention to bodies and embodiment (Crawley, Foley, & Shehan, 2008; Faircloth, 2003; Featherstone, 1982; Turner, 1984). Qualitative researchers have asked people about their bodies (Carter, 2010; Dumas, Laberge, & Straka, 2005; Furman, 1997; Vannini & McCright, 2004), they have observed the bodily practices of themselves and respondents in a fieldwork setting (Desmond, 2007; Paap, 2006), and some have even touched on the topic of the embodied researcher (Ellingson, 2006). What about the body of the respondent in the context of the interview? How do respondents use their embodied performances to shape interaction during the interview? In my interviews with midwives, I had a respondent breast-feed her 4-year-old child during the interview, another show me tattoos, and yet another remove items of clothing that seemed to be "constraining." As a well-trained ethnographer, I did not let on to any awkwardness I might have felt—actually, I had

been in the field for so long that I wasn't surprised by any of these performances. But I never took the time to think about how these body practices were influencing the interview itself and the resulting data. The examples that I've given are some of the more unusual body presentations that I've encountered during interviews, but in every interview setting, what respondents wear, how they sit, and how closely they pay attention are all part of the presentation of self being enacted (Goffman, 1959).

Rapley (2004) argues that respondents actively work to present themselves as an "adequate interviewee" or as a "specific type of person in relation to this topic" (p. 16). I can't be sure if my midwife respondent was breast-feeding because her child happened to be hungry at that moment or if she was actively presenting herself as someone committed to the philosophy and practice of breast-feeding, or both.

REFLEXIVE, INTERACTIVE CO-COLLABORATORS

Not only do respondents contribute to the construction of the interview context through embodied performances, but they do so in many other ways as well. McCracken (1988) asks the question, "Who does the respondent think the interviewer is?" (p. 25). He argues that respondents make assumptions and judgments about the researcher's institutional affiliation and appearance as well as about the project itself. This issue has presented itself numerous times in my research. For example, in a study of domestic violence shelter directors that I was involved in during graduate school, one of the directors, a white, middle-class woman, referring to the low-income, African American clients of the shelter, said to my coresearcher during a phone interview, "The majority of the ones [referring to black women] that we get through here are lower socioeconomic, not folks like you and me who can afford a hotel room" (Donnelly, Cook, Van Ausdale, & Foley, 2005, p. 25). Here, the respondent makes an assumption that she and the researcher share a social class identity (and maybe a racial identity). The researcher is a white, middle-class woman, but the respondent's assumptions about her reveal interpretive work, particularly since this was a phone interview and thus visible cues were not available.

Another example from my work appears in my interviews with nurse midwives and direct-entry midwives. Nurse midwives typically have a 4-year degree in nursing plus a master's degree in midwifery. Direct-entry midwives in Florida, the state where I conducted my research, typically have 3 years of training outside a university context. This difference in training influenced how respondents approached me and the research project. Without exception, every single nurse midwife whom I interviewed asked me "What's your hypothesis?" Not a single direct-entry midwife asked me that question, although some expressed interest in the project, asking other sorts of questions such as "Why are you interested in midwifery?" The nurse midwives had clearly been trained in the scientific method and had an expectation that research should be conducted in a certain way. My inductive, open-ended approach did not mirror the deductive, structured model they had learned during their training. Because I approached research in a different way from what they were accustomed to, it may have influenced the stories they told (Foley, 2004).

While I have not given a great deal of analytic attention (yet) to the performance work of my respondents, their assumptions about me, and the effect they have on the data, other researchers have (Dunbar et al., 2002; Hawkins, 2010; Presser, 2004; Riach, 2009). Dunbar et al. (2002) point out that respondents are often quite savvy to the "subtleties and complexities" influencing the "kinds of subjects/ respondents they will be if they choose to be interviewed" (p. 281). In the context of interviewing poor African American children, the authors show how as a result of being frequently interviewed and tested and questioned, these kids develop a "keen ear for what is being asked *implicitly*" (p. 294). In the following example from Dunbar's research, we can see how the respondent's response could change the direction of the interview—influencing the data that are collected. The researcher asks a question about whether "there was anyone at home to help him do his homework" (p. 294), and the young respondent replies in the form of a question, asking if the researcher thinks that there is something wrong with his family. Using an active interview model, this response is not a misunderstanding of the question or a refusal to answer the question; rather, it is part of an interactively constructed narrative.

Riach (2009) shows how her respondents like the respondent described above, actively work to shape the interview. She points out that while there is much attention paid to researcher reflexivity, very little attention has been devoted to the reflexivity of

the participant or respondent. She goes on to discuss how the questions that respondents asked her about her age may have simply been about expectations that a researcher be a person older than she but that given the context of her research—age discrimination—there may be more going on. These questions did not only arise on meeting the researcher, but comments about the researcher's age continued during the interviews. For example, one 60-year-old respondent said,

It would be hard for you to understand . . . what it feels like when you're working hard, making sure your skills are up to date and then you don't get the promotion because of a high flyer—I don't know, maybe your colleagues feel the same about you (laughs)! (p. 362)

In this case, the respondent used the young interviewer as a resource around which to construct her narrative (Holstein & Gubrium, 1995).

The respondents in Presser's (2004) study of violent offenders also refer to the researcher in their responses to her questions. Presser examines how the respondents constructed and presented themselves and their identities in relation to the researcher. They often did so by constructing her opinion of them. While she did not necessarily offer an assessment of the respondents, they worked to construct it, as in the following example:

Respondent: Now, I don't know—based on me having this interview, or—How do you feel? Do you feel comfortable? Do you feel like you in here with some nut (chuckle)?

Interviewer: (Shake head).

Respondent: Huh, okay (laughing). You know wah' I mean. I'm—people have a sense of understandin' and feelin' comfortable with people. You know wha'm sayin'? They know when a person is—sincere or they know when a person is real or they know when they around somebody that just ain't got all they scruples. (p. 94)

Here, the respondent works hard to try to get the interviewer to help him construct the person he wants to be for the purposes of the interview.

◆ Conclusion

As I've demonstrated throughout this chapter, interview respondents can be constructed differently based on the data collection methods of the researcher and based on ethical concerns. None of this, however, simply happens. Rather, researchers *work* to construct respondents during the interview and in the analysis and representation of data. Respondents also are engaged in a practice of self-construction and constructing the researcher and the research project. Scholars should explore the notion of the *active respondent* in greater depth. In addition, it would be valuable for scholars to engage in further theorizing about the complex interaction of the multiple subject positions of the interviewer and the respondent.

◆ References

Adler, P., & Adler, P. (2002). The reluctant respondent. In J. F. Gubrium & J. A. Holstein (Eds.), *Handbook of interview research: Context and method* (pp. 515–535). Thousand Oaks, CA: Sage.

Atkinson, P., & Pugsley, L. (2005). Making sense of ethnography and medical education. *Medical Education, 39,* 228–234.

Berkowitz, D., & Belgrave, L. L. (2010). "She works hard for the money": Drag queens and the management of their contradictory status of celebrity and marginality. *Journal of Contemporary Ethnography, 39*(2), 159–186.

Bhopal, K. (2010). Gender, identity and experience: Researching marginalised groups. *Women's Studies International Forum, 33,* 188–195.

Brzuzy, S., Ault, A., & Segal, E. A. (1997). Conducting qualitative interviews with women survivors of trauma. *Affilia, 12*(1), 76–83.

Carpenter, L. M. (2005). *Virginity lost: An intimate portrait of first sexual experiences.* New York, NY: New York University Press.

Carter, S. K. (2010). Beyond control: Body and self in women's childbearing narratives. *Sociology of Health and Illness, 32,* 993–1009.

Chase, S. E. (2005). Narrative inquiry: Multiple lenses, approaches, voices. In N. K. Denzin & Y. S. Lincoln (Eds.), *The SAGE handbook of qualitative research* (3rd ed., pp. 651–679). Thousand Oaks, CA: Sage.

Choo, H. Y., & Ferree, M. M. (2010). Practicing intersectionality in sociological research: A critical analysis of inclusions, interactions, and institutions in the study of inequalities. *Sociological Theory, 28*(2), 129–149.

Collins, P. H. (1991). *Black feminist thought.* New York, NY: Routledge.

Converse, J. M., & Schuman, H. (1974). *Conversations at random: Survey research as interviewers see it.* New York, NY: Wiley.

Corbin, J., & Morse, J. M. (2003). The unstructured interactive interview: Issues of reciprocity and risks when dealing with sensitive topics. *Qualitative Inquiry, 9,* 335–354.

Corbin, J., & Strauss, A. (1990). Grounded theory research: Procedures, canons and evaluative criteria. *Qualitative Sociology, 13*(1), 3–21.

Crawley, S., Foley, L., & Shehan, C. (2008). *Gendering bodies.* Lanham, MD: Rowman & Littlefield.

Desmond, M. (2007). *On the fireline: Living and dying with wildland firefighters.* Chicago, IL: University of Chicago Press.

DeVault, M. L. (1999). *Liberating method: Feminism and social research.* Philadelphia, PA: Temple University Press.

Dingwall, R. (1997). Accounts, interviews, and observations. In G. Miller & R. Dingwall (Eds.), *Context and method in qualitative research* (pp. 51–65). Thousand Oaks, CA: Sage.

Donnelly, D. A., Cook, K. J., Van Ausdale, D., & Foley, L. (2005). White privilege, color blindness, and services to battered women. *Violence Against Women, 11*(1), 6–37.

Douglas, J. (1985). *Creative interviewing.* Beverly Hills, CA: Sage.

Dumas, A., Laberge, S., & Straka, S. M. (2005). Older women's relations to bodily appearance: The embodiment of social and biological conditions of existence. *Ageing & Society, 25,* 883–902.

Dunbar, C., Rodriguez, D., & Parker, L. (2002). Race, subjectivity, and the interview process. In J. F. Gubrium & J. A. Holstein (Eds.), *Handbook of interview research: Context and method* (pp. 279–298). Thousand Oaks, CA: Sage.

Ellingson, L. L. (2006). Embodied knowledge: Writing researchers' bodies into qualitative health research. *Qualitative Health Research, 16,* 298–310.

Ellis, C., Kiesinger, C. E., & Tillman-Healy, L. M. (1997). Interactive interviewing: Talking about emotional experience. In R. Hertz (Ed.), *Reflexivity and voice* (pp. 119–149). Thousand Oaks, CA: Sage.

Emerson, R. M. (Ed.). (1983). *Contemporary field research: A collection of readings.* Prospect Heights, IL: Waveland Press.

Faircloth, C. A. (Ed.). (2003). *Aging bodies: Images and everyday experience.* Walnut Creek, CA: Rowman & Littlefield.

Featherstone, M. (1982). The body in consumer culture. *Theory, Culture, and Society, 1,* 18–33.

Foley, L. (2004). How I became a midwife: Identity, biographical work, and legitimation in midwives' work narratives. In M. T. Segal & V. Demos (with J. J. Kronenfeld) (Eds.), *Gender perspectives on reproduction and sexuality: Advances in gender research*

(Vol. 8, pp. 87–128). Amsterdam, The Netherlands: Elsevier/JAI Press.

Fontana, A., & Frey, J. H. (2005). The interview: From neutral stance to political involvement. In N. K. Denzin & Y. S. Lincoln (Eds.), *The SAGE handbook of qualitative research* (3rd ed., pp. 695–727). Thousand Oaks, CA: Sage.

Furman, F. K. (1997). *Facing the mirror: The older woman and beauty shop culture.* New York, NY: Routledge.

Goffman, E. (1959). *The presentation of self in everyday life.* New York, NY: Doubleday.

Harris, S. (2001). What can interactionism contribute to the study of inequality? The case of marriage and beyond. *Symbolic Interaction, 24*(4), 455–480.

Hawkins, R. (2010). Outsider in: Race, attraction, and research in New Orleans. *Qualitative Inquiry, 16,* 249–261.

Holstein, J. A., & Gubrium, J. F. (1995). *The active interview.* Thousand Oaks, CA: Sage.

Johnson, J. M. (2002). In-depth interviewing. In J. F. Gubrium & J. A. Holstein (Eds.), *Handbook of interview research: Context and method* (pp. 103–119). Thousand Oaks, CA: Sage.

Klatch, R. (1987). *Women of the new right.* Philadelphia, PA: Temple University Press.

Kong, T., Mahoney, D., & Plummer, K. (2002). Queering the interview. In J. F. Gubrium & J. A. Holstein (Eds.), *Handbook of interview research: Context and method* (pp. 239–258). Thousand Oaks, CA: Sage.

Kusow, A. M. (2003). Beyond indigenous authenticity: Reflections on the insider/outsider debate in immigration research. *Symbolic Interaction, 26*(4), 591–599.

Litt, J. S. (2000). *Medicalized motherhood: Perspectives from the lives of African-American and Jewish women.* New Brunswick, NJ: Rutgers University Press.

Martin, P. Y. (2005). *Rape work: Victims, gender and emotions in organization and community context.* New York, NY: Routledge.

Marvasti, A., & McKinney, K. D. (2004). *Middle Eastern lives in America.* Lanham, MD: Rowman & Littlefield.

McCracken, G. (1988). *The long interview.* Newbury Park, CA: Sage.

McKinney, K. D. (2005). *Being white: Stories of race and racism.* New York, NY: Routledge.

Merton, R. (1972). Insiders and outsiders: A chapter in the sociology of knowledge. *American Journal of Sociology, 78*(1), 9–47.

Miller, G., & Dingwall, R. (Eds.). (1997). *Context and method in qualitative research.* London, England: Sage.

Naples, N. (1996). A feminist revisiting of the insider/outsider debate: The "outsider phenomenon" in rural Iowa. *Qualitative Sociology, 19*(1), 83–106.

Paap, K. (2006). *Working construction: Why white working-class men put themselves and the labor movement in harm's way.* Ithaca, NY: Cornell University Press.

Presser, L. (2004). Violent offenders, moral selves: Constructing identities and accounts in the research interview. *Social Problems, 51*(1), 82–101.

Rapley, T. (2004). Interviews. In C. Seale, G. Gobo, J. F. Gubrium, & D. Silverman (Eds.), *Qualitative research practice* (pp. 15–33). London, England: Sage.

Reinharz, S., & Chase, S. (2002). Interviewing women. In J. F. Gubrium & J. A. Holstein (Eds.), *Handbook of interview research: Context and method* (pp. 221–238). Thousand Oaks, CA: Sage.

Riach, K. (2009). Exploring participant-centered reflexivity in the research interview. *Sociology, 43,* 356–370.

Riessman, C. K. (1987). When gender is not enough: Women interviewing women. *Gender & Society, 1*(2), 172–207.

Riessman, C. K. (1993). *Narrative analysis.* Newbury Park, CA: Sage.

Rubin, H. J., & Rubin, I. S. (1995). *Qualitative interviewing: The art of hearing data.* Thousand Oaks, CA: Sage.

Saylor, T. (2010). *Stumbling over ethics: Considering autonomy, beneficence and justice in research with queer adolescent participants* (Invited Panel: Division D Exemplary Work From Promising Researchers). Paper presented at the annual meeting of the American Educational Research Association (AERA), Denver, CO.

Schilt, K. (2006). Just one of the guys: How transmen make gender visible at work. *Gender & Society, 20*(4), 465–490.

Seimsen, C. (2004). *Emotional trials: The moral dilemmas of women criminal defense attorneys.* Boston, MA: Northeastern University Press.

Silverman, D. (1993). *Interpreting qualitative data: Methods for analysing talk, text, and interaction.* London, England: Sage.

Singleton, R. A., Jr., & Straits, B. C. (2002). Survey interviewing. In J. F. Gubrium & J. A. Holstein (Eds.), *Handbook of interview research: Context and method* (pp. 59–82). Thousand Oaks, CA: Sage.

Taylor, V., & Rupp, L. (2005). When the girls are men: Negotiating gender and sexual dynamics in a study of drag queens. *Signs: Journal of Women in Culture and Society, 30*(4), 2115–2139.

Turner, B. (1984). *The body and society.* Oxford, England: Blackwell.

Vannini, P., & McCright, A. M. (2004). To die for: The semiotic seductive power of the tanned body. *Symbolic Interaction, 27*(3), 309–332.

Warren, C. A. B. (2002). Qualitative interviewing. In J. F. Gubrium & J. A. Holstein (Eds.), *Handbook of interview research: Context and method* (pp. 83–101). Thousand Oaks, CA: Sage.

Webb, C. (1984). Feminist methodology in nursing research. *Journal of Advanced Nursing, 9,* 249–256.

Wieder, L. D. (1983). Telling the convict code. In R. M. Emerson (Ed.), *Contemporary field research: A collection of readings* (pp. 78–90). Prospect Heights, IL: Waveland Press.

22

FIVE LENSES FOR
THE REFLEXIVE INTERVIEWER

◆ Linda Finlay

Reflexivity has been defined as "disciplined self-reflection" (Wilkinson, 1988, p. 493).[1] It is employed in various guises in clinical and research practice as explicit, self-aware reflection and analysis toward increasing richness and integrity of understanding.

This chapter focuses specifically on research applications, although the ideas can be imported into all practice. Mason (1996) explains that reflexive research requires researchers to take "stock of their actions and their role in the research process" and subject these to the "same critical scrutiny as the rest of their 'data'" (p. 6). More than being a tool to improve the quality, rigor, and validity of research, reflexivity can be used to expose relational and ethical dilemmas that permeate the entire research process.

The reflexive interviewer looks through a critical lens at the process, context, and outcomes of research and interrogates the construction of knowledge. Aided by tools such as field notes, reflective diaries, and supervision, the interviewer is a "thoughtful and ever-present subject who throughout has an impact on the what, why and how of the research" (King & Horrocks, 2010, p. 140). Key questions asked include the following: What am I trying to do? Why am I carrying out the interview this way? How is my approach affecting the research?

Beyond offering a way to reflect on the interviewer's role and the research process, reflexive analysis can also form part of the data to be analyzed. In phenomenologically oriented interviews, for example, an interviewer may use his or her

---

[1]The terms *reflection* and *reflexivity* are often confused. Reflection can be defined as "thinking about" something after the event. Reflexivity, in contrast, involves an ongoing *self*-awareness (Finlay & Gough, 2003).

own understandings along with bodily/emotional intuitions to shed light on the interviewee's experience. In discursively focused interview research, the "rhetorical strategies," "discursive repertoires," and culturally situated understandings of both interviewer and interviewee can be scrutinized.

In this chapter, I propose five "lenses" through which researchers can reflexively evaluate interviews at several levels: (1) *strategic reflexivity* looks through a lens focused on methodological/epistemological aspects; (2) *contextual-discursive reflexivity* examines situational and sociocultural elements; (3) *embodied reflexivity* focuses on the researcher's embodied felt sense and the gestural duet between interviewer and interviewee; (4) *relational reflexivity* examines the intersubjective, interpersonal realm; and (5) *ethical reflexivity* monitors processual aspects and power dynamics, enabling the possible ethical implications to be revealed.

Each of these lenses will be theoretically explored and research examples provided to demonstrate the concepts in practice. Extracts from my own interview dialogues, research diaries, and published reflections will be used as illustrations. I interject a further reflexive voice (RV) related to writing this chapter to make my own choices explicit and thereby acknowledge the constructed nature of this chapter (Steier, 1991).

> RV: I agree with Bonner (2001) when he says that "reflexivity raises the most fundamental issue that can be raised for modern social enquiry" (p. 267). I have an investment in raising its profile in the research world, and I want to raise the quality of how reflexivity is engaged in practice. Too often, I see researchers paying lip service to reflexivity, assuming that the job is done when the interviewer's interests or subjectivity has been declared. For me, the value of reflexivity is the critical analysis that takes place when examining how the researcher (or research relationship/context) influences the research. Reflexivity is a tool to understand better. I hope that my different examples from practice will demonstrate some of the layers of critically reflective activity involved.

◆ Different Versions of Reflexivity in Research

A number of typologies exist identifying different ways of doing reflexivity in research. For instance, Wilkinson (1988) offers her feminist distinction between personal (subjective), functional (as related to one's researcher role), and disciplinary (looking at the place and function of the research) reflexivity. Marcus (1994) pinpoints four styles of reflexivity: (1) self-critique and personal quest, (2) objective reflexivity as a methodological tool, (3) reflexivity as the "politics of location," and (4) feminist experiential reflexivity as the practice of epistemological "positioning." Lynch (2000) offers an inventory of "reflexivities": (a) mechanical, (b) substantive, (c) methodological, (d) metatheoretical, (e) interpretative, and (f) ethnomethodological. Willig (2001) identifies two kinds of reflexivity: (1) epistemological reflexivity (reflecting on theory and how assumptions about the world infuse the research) and (2) personal reflexivity.

In previous articles, I have defined reflexivity as being thoughtfully and critically self-aware of personal/relational dynamics in the research and how these affect the research (Finlay, 2002a, 2002b, 2003b). How this reflexivity is applied, however, varies in practice. The chosen variant of reflexivity needs to take into account the specific epistemological values and assumptions underpinning the particular methodologies. I have suggested that the *social critique* and *ironic deconstruction* variants of reflexivity are favored by postmodernists, sociologists, and social constructionists; the *introspective* versions are embraced by phenomenologists and psychodynamic researchers; *intersubjective reflection* can be descriptive (phenomenological) or explanatory (when psychodynamic interpretations come into play); and *mutual collaboration* can be employed by a broad range of methodologies, from humanistic, relationally orientated research to more discursive, feminist and/or sociological approaches.

In a similar vein, Gough (2003) notes the broad distinction between *realist* uses of reflexivity, where researcher "confessions" are deployed to persuade readers of the validity and authenticity of the research, and postmodern *relativist* versions of reflexivity, which aim to deconstruct and disrupt claims of narrative coherence. Lynch (2000) says, "What reflexivity does, what it threatens to expose, what it reveals and who it empowers depends upon who does it and how they go about it" (p. 36).

> RV: I feel an internal struggle about what I am doing in this chapter. I want to make sure that I have sufficiently acknowledged that there is no *one* way of doing reflexivity but also that there are wrong ways to do it (such as using a variant of reflexivity that contradicts the epistemological assumptions of the research). But I wonder if, by mapping different possibilities, I am simply creating yet another typology, in a sense reinventing the wheel. As I brace myself to drop this strategy and find another way of constructing this chapter, I think about my students and other novice researchers who are hungry for a heuristic tool to help them know what they are supposed to reflect on. My new typology specifically considers the interview context and offers several ways into reflexivity. Because it does not require sophisticated knowledge of methodology, it can readily be put into action. Perhaps it can work. I'll be happier once I ground myself in applied practical examples.

◆ Strategic Reflexivity

Strategic decisions need to be taken at every point of carrying out and analyzing research interviews. Ideally, the researcher will be explicitly self-aware and relatively in control of (or at least explicitly monitoring) this process. Often researchers will choose to write reflexive field notes[2] to plot their progress and ongoing reflections.

Strategic reflexivity involves researchers reflecting critically about research aims, methods, and how to set up and approach research. For instance, before interviewing a participant, researchers need to think through issues about their own role, presentation, dress, behavior, and planned approach. During the interview, the researcher will monitor the participant's responses and shape questions accordingly. After the interview, the researcher works strategically to consider how to analyze, re-present, and disseminate findings. All these processes need to be accounted for and, ideally, need to be sufficiently transparent to enable external audit and support validity claims:

> Transactions and the ideas that emerge from [the research process] . . . should be documented. The construction of analytic or methodological memoranda and working papers, and the consequent explication of working hypotheses, are of vital importance. It is important that the processes of exploration and abduction be documented and retrievable. (Coffey & Atkinson, 1996, p. 191)

As the quote above suggests, strategic reflexivity involves a kind of *methodological self-consciousness*. How this is enacted varies according to the methodology used; in a grounded theory study, reflexivity will be used to demonstrate transparency toward making validity claims, while in discursive approaches, reflexivity offers a critical tool to deconstruct discourse. It also varies according to the historical context, as shown by the way ethnographers and other qualitative researchers have over recent decades reworked the nature of their field notes. In early-20th-century "realist tales," anthropologists conscientiously recorded observations in an effort to prove their scientific credentials. These forms gradually gave way to more personal accounts where researchers explicated the dilemmas and decisions arising during their fieldwork. The ethnographic critique, led by writers such as Clifford and Marcus (1986), nudged qualitative researchers into a "new paradigm, placing discovery of reflexivity at the centre of methodological thinking" (Seale, 1999, p. 160). Now, highly subjectivist accounts of fieldwork can be seen as qualitative researchers unravel their own biographies and explore how these might intersect with interpretations of field experiences (see, e.g., Anderson, 2006; Reed-Danahay, 1997).

In my own case, I made use of strategic reflexivity during an existential-phenomenological case study on the lived experience of multiple sclerosis (Finlay, 2003a). In this study, I interviewed my friend

---

[2]The form these take will vary according to the research: One researcher may make straightforward diary entries; another might choose to write poetry. I have even supervised a researcher who engaged a "two-chair dialogue," talking in turn from each position to reflect her different takes on her interviews as she came at them as a woman and as a researcher.

Ann, who had been first diagnosed with this condition the year before. Ann and I embarked on the research collaboratively with an eye to disseminating "insider" findings to therapists (she was a physiotherapist, and I was an occupational therapist). Our aim was to attempt to "bring to life" Ann's immediate lived experience.

As therapists, we had both believed that we knew about multiple sclerosis. We were familiar with its signs and symptoms, and we understood how awful and devastating it could be as the person headed toward life in a wheelchair. But Ann's experience had shown her the flawed and inadequate nature of that "understanding," and it was this that she wanted to share more widely.

I went to stay with Ann one weekend. It was a social occasion, but we managed to include two relatively formal interviews held in Ann's kitchen: one to explore her lived experience, the next to discuss some provisional themes that I had sensed. We agreed that while Ann's symptoms were still relatively minor, her life, relationships with others, hopes, projects, and dreams had all been derailed by a sense of global uncertainty that permeated her being. Her response to her condition was to throw herself into being a good mother and to compartmentalize her existence while seeking the oasis of "hyper"-normality.

Our friendship contributed a more personal tone to the interview, yet by mutual unspoken consent, we avoided dwelling on more personal details, such as how her marital relationship had been affected. We also agreed that while we were collaboratively engaged with co-creating the interview findings, I would retain authorial control of my analysis and writing. I would ultimately choose where, when, how, and what to publish. For her part, she was prepared to rein in any of my excesses and overly fanciful interpretations. This she did in our second interview, as I describe in the following reflexive passage:

> She affirmed certain themes, suggesting I had captured her experience "nicely." At other points she suggested that my analysis needed to be toned down as she didn't feel they represented her ordinary, everyday experience. One notable example here was my initial use of an analogy: that of Ann's situation being akin to "living with an alien monster." I rather liked this metaphor, regarding it as both punchy and poetic, and was reluctant to let it go. However, it was not something Ann could

relate to. I therefore deleted all references to the monster while retaining (I acknowledge ruefully) some sense of the notion of alien infiltration.

> In retrospect, I can see that it was useful to get Ann's feedback. For one thing, it helped me to better appreciate how Ann had, in fact, managed to reconnect with her "disconnected" arm. . . . I stop short of claiming that Ann has "validated" this study in any way. I do not seek a "truth" that can be validated in this way. Instead, I tend towards a more relativist position, one recognising that my findings have emerged in a specific context, that my telling of Ann's story is specific to the time, place and individuals concerned. Another researcher working with Ann would have unfolded a different story. So most likely would I, had I undertaken the research at a different point in time or in different circumstances. (Finlay, 2006b, pp. 195–196)

As this passage shows, I used strategic reflexivity to examine my epistemological commitments and critically interrogate my methodology with regard to both the legitimacy of my interpretations and participant validation. These concerns overlap with those of contextual-discursive reflexivity discussed in the next section.

RV: The book editors have asked that I use examples from research practice to situate, explain, and justify. Have I been persuasive with my exemplar? Is my strategy of mixing quotations from published pieces with reflections from both past projects and the here and now unduly complicated and confusing? I am starting to doubt my strategy of providing examples from my own interviews rather than offering those of other people. At the same time, these examples are the ones at hand, and they do allow me to offer a richer, insider account.

◆ Contextual-Discursive Reflexivity

A different way of critically interrogating the research process can be found in the use of what I call contextual-discursive reflexivity. This more sociological, poststructuralist version considers the social context and world of shared meanings, in terms of both the proximal research *situation* and the broader *structural* (sociocultural) domain. This genre of reflexivity is most commonly found in ethnographic and ethnomethodological studies and in those using discourse or conversation analysis (e.g., Potter & Wetherell, 1995).

While interview data (e.g., participants' narratives) may be presented as reflecting something of an individual's reality, reflexivity would acknowledge the co-constructed, collaborative nature of that data. Actual stories told by participants are invariably more "chaotic" than when they appear as "findings" (Frank, 1998). The story heard, interpreted, and analyzed by one researcher is likely to be different therefore from that of another. Researchers need to distinguish reflexively between a life story that is *lived* and one that is *told* and then *retold* by a researcher (Clandinin & Connelly, 1994). Narratives drawing extensively on participants' verbatim quotes from interviews can be persuasive, but published versions usually remain the researcher's construction.

The fragility of the results rests on the fact that participants present what they want to be known about themselves in interviews and that the resulting narratives arise from a cocreated dialogue between participant and researcher. The whole is then repackaged and re-versioned as "research findings" (Finlay & Evans, 2009). A reflexive account of these *situational* variables can be invaluable. Pels (2000) argues that it is both "feasible and important to talk about something and simultaneously talk (at least a little) about the talking itself" (p. 3).

In my PhD research (Finlay, 1998) on the life-world of occupational therapists, I interviewed 11 therapists about their work experience. Beneath their apparently straightforward stories lurked other stories. In particular, there was the story of the complex, and entirely hidden, negotiation that took place between my participants and myself as "listener." I invited them to share the story of their experiences. They chose what story to tell, but they did so in the context of my responses and the questions I was asking. The stories told were, at least in part, created through our dialogue and set within a broader professional/disciplinary context. Our relationship had an impact on the way the therapists spoke to me, particularly in terms of what they felt I would understand and what they felt safe to reveal.

It is significant that I was a therapist interviewing other therapists. I had insider knowledge: I understood their pressures, their work contexts, their professional humor, and I had shared similar experiences. At the same time, I needed to caution myself not to assume shared experience. As I noted in my diary, "My research participants and I are all white, middle-class therapists, concerned about people, engaged in a project of being 'nice.' . . . We share the same language and jargon, even the same jokes. But I can't assume commonality" (Finlay, 1998, p. 226).

That my participants also knew me as an academic was also relevant. I had taught several of them as students, and they knew me as something of an "expert" as I had written articles and books about occupational therapy practice. It would not be surprising if, at some level at least, some of my participants were trying to "perform" for me, showing off their competence while minimizing their insecurities. When one therapist repeatedly engaged in abstract, theoretical concepts, I suspected she might have been trying to impress me with her knowledge. For my part, I felt frustrated that she did not seem to be telling me about her actual experience of her work world. I wondered if she was hiding her practice from me, consciously or unconsciously, to preempt any criticism from me. As Riessman (2003) says, "Individuals negotiate how they want to be known in the stories they develop collaboratively with their audiences. . . . Social actors shape their lives retrospectively for particular audiences" (p. 8).

Here, Riessman is drawing on Goffman's (1959) drama metaphor: the idea that people "perform" desirable selves to preserve "face" in difficult situations. If the world is like a stage, our narratives are part of the show (Finlay, 2004).

In terms of the macro-sociopolitical forces shaping the narratives emerging from interviews, researchers need to recognize how the social world (consisting of the community and cultures around us and in which we are embedded) is ever present. *Structural* dimensions such as our class, gender, ethnicity, age, race, sexuality, religion, language, nationality, and discourse all influence who we are and how we interact with the other in the interview situation. "Self-reflexivity unmasks complex political/ideological agendas hidden in our writing," says Richardson (1994, p. 523). Our research interview can benefit from scrutinizing the complex political/ideological agendas that exist around our participants and within the broader research context.

These structural dimensions came to the fore in my narrative interview case study research on the experience of having mental health problems (Finlay, 2004). Here, "Kenny" shared his story of surviving and overcoming anxiety and depression. In the narrative we co-constructed, Kenny described himself as moving from being a "gibbering idiot" to getting better and becoming an "iceman," with emotions firmly in check. This shift of self-identity coincided with the move from being long-term unemployed to having a job. My challenge as researcher was to recognize our divergent social locations: The values and beliefs of Kenny, a working-class man, needed to be understood from his perspective rather from than mine. When he called himself an "iceman" he saw this as a good thing, while my therapist self metaphorically shuddered.

> Kenny's performance can . . . be understood as a way of "doing" masculinity (Edley, 2002). His struggle to respect himself through finding a work role needs to be seen in the context of the stigma attached by his working class community to an unemployed man who is not fulfilling his family breadwinner role. Through his narrative performance focused on returning to work and becoming an "iceman," he reasserts his preferred masculine identity. As Bourdieu and others have noted, "narratives about the most 'personal' . . . articulate the deepest structures of the social world." (Bourdieu et al., 1993, cited in Riessman, 2003, p. 24)
>
> At a different level, Kenny's performance can be understood as an attempt to teach me what it was like to experience mental illness. He wanted to persuade me (as someone who had not experienced mental illness) just how bad it could be. He also wanted to give hope to other sufferers and show how it was possible to claw your way back to health. So, he wove his tale of trials towards a "happy" ending and I was encouraged to "spread the word." (Finlay, 2004, p. 479)

These examples alert us to the view favored by social constructionists, that narrators—participant or interviewer—are strategic in their choices about positioning themselves, their characters, and the audience. At the same time, the broader talk/text of the discursive context plays a part in actively shaping the world we are attempting to represent.

> RV: Harper (2003) notes that there is a "danger when researchers lose their reflexivity and see themselves as lying outside the arena of discourse" (p. 85). So, I have tried to acknowledge my own positioning. Yet I'm all too aware that my version of contextual reflexivity falls short of a full-blooded discursive critique. I am a phenomenologist, not a social constructionist, more comfortable explicating lived experience than deconstructing context. Then, I wonder if, in noting this, I am just making a fresh rhetorical move, stating my failings in an effort to excuse and justify myself. Am I inoculating myself against likely criticism that I am "watering down" contextual reflexivity? Am I now displaying sufficient discursive credentials?

◆ Embodied Reflexivity

While spoken language is central to contextual-discursive reflexivity, the language of the body is the focus for embodied reflexivity. This lens puts under the microscope the wisdom of our embodied felt sense (Gendlin, 1996) and the gestural duet of nonverbal communication that occurs between interviewer and interviewee. The focus is on the potentially significant implicit meanings arising beneath participants' words in a "more than verbal" way. "What one feels is not 'stuff inside' but the sentience of what is happening in one's living in the outside" (Gendlin, 1997, p. 41). With this genre of reflexivity, we as interviewers can use the technique of Focusing[3] to read our body's response to—and relationship with—the bodies of our participants during research encounters.

Elsewhere, I have written about *reflexive embodied empathy* (Finlay, 2005). This concept highlights

---

[3]"Focusing" is a therapeutic technique elaborated by Gendlin (1996) that amounts to a form of bodily self-reflection where mind and body are in dialogue. Focusing involves learning to let a deeper bodily felt sense come into awareness in relation to a problem or situation. The body has its own wisdom and often "knows" when something feels uncomfortable or just "right."

the way in which an interviewer's empathy is not just about emotional knowing but a *felt*, embodied experience that helps us understand our participants: Our corporeal commonality enables the possibility of empathy. In phenomenological terms, our embodied intersubjective horizon of experience gives us access to others' experience (Wertz, 2005). I suggest that it can be fruitful to engage reflexively with our participant's lived body, our own body, and our embodied intersubjective relationship with the participant.

A good example of the practice of reflexive embodied empathy emerged in my interview research with Kenny exploring his experience of mental health problems (Finlay, 2004). During our interview, I became aware of our mutual bodily responses. I wondered if I was mirroring the bodily posture he had adopted on re-membering the trauma of his emotions. (I deliberately hyphenate the word *re-member* to emphasize the fact that the process is not just a cognitive function; we re-member and reiterate responses in the body.) In the following extract, I show my dawning awareness of bodily responses and how I checked out my emerging hypothesis about what his posture might mean to him. Our embodied communication thus became a part of the interview and the reflexive data I later analyzed.

I remember noticing how my arms were folded tightly across my stomach. I was protecting myself, but also "holding my self in" and somehow "holding myself together." I then saw that Kenny had adopted the same posture as he recalled his trauma (had I mirrored his posture or had he followed mine?) . . .

With us both holding ourselves, it seemed an important moment, one that called for me to tune into what we were both doing. I was a little surprised at the sensations and my reactions. Usually, I would interpret this non-verbal gesture as representing a symbolic wish to protect oneself from others or a way of giving oneself some nurturing/ comforting. But here in this situation I was somehow sensing an additional, even different, interpretation. I checked it out with Kenny:

Linda: As you're speaking and remembering, Kenny, I can see you're holding yourself tightly. And I'm doing the same as I'm listening to you [shared laughter]. It's like you're trying to hold yourself together. Is it like, kinda to stop yourself falling apart. Is that what it was like for you?

Kenny: Yeah, I would go off to bed and just hold myself like that. Sometimes it seemed like for hours. One minute I was alright and the next I could just go into a rage about the simplest thing. And again, it could be a trivial thing and I'd lose it completely. Again I sought the sanctuary of the bedroom. I knew there I wouldn't hurt people. The worse thing was because I was feeling guilty I was getting more angry about it.

I felt his confusion: his rage against himself and this crazy "alien" it seemed he had become. I felt his fear of losing himself, of losing it in general, and his concern that he might hurt others in his anger and craziness. I felt his guilt about this anger and understood why he might want to lock himself away. It was the only place he could be safe. Perhaps it was the only place he could recover himself to reassure himself that he was still there. (Finlay, 2006a, pp. 2–3)

Replaying this dialogue (including my reflexive notes) over and over helped me focus on what Kenny might be experiencing. Again, I found myself adopting that holding posture and "re-membered" the (my? his?) emotions and felt this powerful intuitive sense of "holding together" that which was falling apart. It felt as if "I" was containing the rage and craziness and if "I" let go, the rage/craziness might break out and destroy others (Finlay, 2006a).

Not every researcher will want to pursue my version of reflexive embodied empathy that has evolved through my practice of integrative psychotherapy. However, awareness of the bodily communication between participant and researcher is invariably fruitful. At the very least, interviewers will want to attend reflexively to their communication skills and how participants have been engaged nonverbally in dialogue. This attention should also lead to a deeper awareness of relational components—the topic of the next section.

> RV: What is my feeling and felt sense as I write this now? My felt sense is in my belly; it is "stuffy struggling." I am probably trying too hard to make my point. As I acknowledge this, I feel an "easing shift." But then I become aware of an underlying tension and
>
> *(Continued)*

(Continued)

discomfort in my ribs, "a tight self-consciousness." Alert to the possibility that you, the reader, will want to distance yourself from my "fanciful" practice of using my body as a way of understanding others, my writing comes to a halt.

A shadow of shame lurks. I have a choice: Should I regularize my embodied approach with references to established literature or excuse myself for my idiosyncratic approach by explaining that I am a "therapist"? Or might I offer a more radical provocation? Taking a deep breath, I opt for the latter . . .

Merleau-Ponty (1964/1968) writes of the intersubjective interconnecting of the human way of being, the "intertwining of my life with the lives of others, of my body with the visible things, the intersection of my perceptual field with that of others" (p. 49). Here, Merleau-Ponty (1964/1968) calls our attention to the way human beings are caught up in a dynamic of doubling and mirroring. "The mirror's ghost lies outside my body . . . man is the mirror for man" (1961, as cited in Churchill, 2000–2001, pp. 29–30).

Now I imagine your impulse to distance yourself has been confirmed. Once more I nudge my shame aside as I want to show the provenance of my idea of embodied reflexive empathy and how reflexivity can be theoretically informed as well as personal. More than this, I want to share my love of phenomenological philosophy. I resolve to keep this contentious (and personally revealing) insert in.

◆ Relational Reflexivity

The interview examples of Ann and Kenny, above, highlight the point that participants are involved (explicitly or implicitly) in co-constructing findings and that there is a research relationship involved. The processes involved in interviewing, says Nicolson (2003), can never be "neutral, objective and unbiased acts: interviewer and respondent are engaging (or failing to engage) with each other" (p. 144). Even if the interviewer attempts to be objective and nondirective, this very effort will have an impact, resulting in particular kinds of answers. The dynamics between researcher and participant need attention, and this is the domain of relational reflexivity.

This version of reflexivity is of particular interest to researchers engaged in feminist, phenomenological, psychoanalytic, and ethnographic research. Here, the lens of relational reflexivity allows us to put the intersubjective and relational dimensions between interviewer and interviewee under the microscope. Researchers have the possibility of focusing on the *overt* relational dimension between researcher and participant as well as the tacit, *implicit* intersubjective realm, where less conscious dynamics flourish.

The (inevitably) emergent, situated, and negotiated nature of the interviewer–participant relationship demands reflexive attention, whatever the focal point. An interviewer approaching an informant will want to consider how his or her own relational style is affecting the informant, and vice versa. Reflexivity begins the process of separating what belongs to the researcher from what pertains to the researched (Finlay & Evans, 2009).

The relationship under scrutiny is not simply that between two people in straightforward dialogue. There are multiple interacting "selves" or subjectivities involved. DeYoung (2003) describes the therapy relationship as a "thickly populated" encounter, a concept that applies equally to the research interview. Reinharz (1997), in her study of an Israeli kibbutz, acknowledged some 20 different researcher selves, which she categorized as *researcher-based* selves, *brought selves*, and *situationally created* selves. King and Horrocks (2010) elaborate on this:

> When we interview we bring our understandings of how people exist in the world (social constructionist, critical realist selves), we bring our political agendas (feminist, ecologist, socialist selves), our caring roles (father, daughter selves), our professional selves (nurse, academic, social worker, teacher selves). We also situationally *create* different selves in the field—being a member of a group, being a friend, being sympathetic. (p. 135)

The idea of multiple interacting subjectivities came to the fore in my interview with "Kath" concerning her experience of the phenomenon of mistrust: This was a collaborative project undertaken by a group of phenomenologists interested in explicating the commonalities and divergences of our various approaches to analysis (King et al., 2008). We were, in effect, engaging in "reflexivity as a team," where we negotiated and debated subtle disciplinary, methodological, and epistemological differences (Barry, 2003).

I was responsible for interviewing Kath. She described her lived experience of mistrust as being "attacked" and becoming reduced to a "ghost" of herself. Feeling forced, in an unsafe environment, to pull in her normally big presence and personality, she had lost her previously vivacious embodied way of being. Using my approach of embodied reflexive empathy, I sensed that Kath, having lost her customary way of being, felt vulnerable and "lost." At the same time, paradoxically, "losing herself" was a protective *strategy*. I checked this interpretation out with Kath, who responded with the comment "That sums it up."

Other researchers in our group, who had also analyzed the interview transcript, challenged my interpretation. They suggested that in the dialogue between Kath and myself, my interventions carried a therapeutic whiff that had fostered an explicit concern with emotionality. My style of reflecting back (developed in my training as a therapist) may, they thought, have nudged Kath's narrative from having a neutral tone to one of being a "brave and battling victim." This encouraged me to do some further reflecting:

I may have introduced into the mix something from my own history as a "caring therapist." This, in turn, may have triggered something in Kath, encouraging her to edge towards the stance of "victim." However, this process is probably even more complicated. While I had several roles which I was inevitably juggling (chief among them in this instance, the roles of therapist and researcher), questions can also be raised about my habitual interactional roles and pattern of operating. . . . If I reflexively probe my motivations, I understand that I have an emotional need to give care to others, perhaps as a result of significant gaps in the care I received as a child. I know that I tend to thrive on the empathy I once longed to receive; my providing of care can be seen as an effective way to deny my own need to be cared for. My child self can be seen as entwined with my adult therapist and researcher selves. . . . What selves were activated in Kath? (Finlay, 2009a, p. 10)

In my practice of interviewing using a relational-centered research approach (Finlay & Evans, 2009), I draw on my skills, values, and interests as a relational psychotherapist. I am familiar with the need to explore relational processes, including the possibilities of transferences/countertransferences and parallel process. But to what extent should these be foregrounded?

Relationally oriented researchers assume that both researcher and participant "bring to the encounter the sum total of who they are in all their complexity and with their own individual histories and ways of organizing their experience [and] their unconscious processes" (Evans & Gilbert, 2005, pp. 74–75). As these complexities of the research relationship are brought to the fore, so too are ethical considerations. As Ellis (2007) notes, "relational ethics requires researchers to act from our hearts and minds, to acknowledge our interpersonal bonds to others, and initiate and maintain conversations" (p. 4).

RV: Relational reflexivity, more than any other lens, excites and inspires me. It would be too easy for me to wallow self-indulgently in complex relational dynamics where multiple selves are mirrored and reflected back. There is a risk of getting trapped in a mire of infinite regress.

I am reminded of McCleary's phrase "a mirror of moving shadows" (as cited in Merleau-Ponty, 1945/1962, p. xviii). We should not mistake our "reflections" for reality and, like Narcissus, become seduced by our own image. Relational reflexivity works best as a way of seeing and understanding the other. It is not a backdoor opportunity for self-analysis. The lens needs to stay focused on the relational world beyond ourselves. Have I been clear enough about this?

◆ Ethical Reflexivity

When we present—and *re*-present—our interview findings, we lay claim to professional guidelines for the ethical conduct of social research (e.g., that we will respect and protect participants). Through these guidelines, we assert the ethical integrity of our work. In practice, however, every interview brings up context-specific ethical challenges. They raise numerous *relational* ethical challenges that go far beyond procedural ones (Christians, 2000; Ellis, 2007; Guillemin & Gillam, 2004). Situations arise in the field that make our heads spin and hearts ache (Ellis, 2007). Negotiating an ethical path can be tricky, and compromises are invariably made. Is Wise (1987, p. 56) right to claim that professional guidelines have "little bearing on actual research practice"? How often do we explicitly and reflexively acknowledge and work through the uncertainty and muddiness of our research?

As part of revealing my "muddy boots" (Fielding, 1982), I would like to offer an extended discussion of my experience of feeling taxed by the ethical demands placed on me during some collaborative interview research. The example below shows how reflexivity is enacted throughout the research process, including the writing-up phase.

The research involved collaborating with Pat to explore her lived experience of receiving a cochlear implant (Finlay & Molano-Fisher, 2008). Our collaboration involved not only interviews but also some participant observation and an extended e-mail dialogue over the course of several months.

In what follows, I hope to demonstrate how ethical reflexivity monitors the ethical implications of particular processual aspects and power dynamics. I discuss how Pat and I negotiated consent, engaged in barter within our relationship, handled emotional intensity, and wrote up our research with an ethical eye.

NEGOTIATING CONSENT

Throughout the research, Pat and I were committed to "honoring" her story by embracing an egalitarian, dialogical, and reflexive approach. Despite this, gaps appeared between our ideals and our practice, between the rhetoric of collaborative research and the reality (Finlay, 2009b). For my part, I was exercised over the power issues that arose, the emotional intensity stirred by our research, and our division of labor and the way in which we represented our voices as "coresearchers."

Pat was able to give consent that was particularly well-informed: She had herself carried out a phenomenological study for her master's dissertation. But we

adhered to Grafanaki's (1996) suggestion of engaging in *process consent*. Rather than just seeking consent at the start of the study, the emergent nature of our project demanded that we continually check out with each other that we were both content to proceed.

By mutual agreement, we included only the material that seemed directly to concern Pat's hearing experience and put out of play particularly sensitive and personal material. When initially drafting and co-constructing her narrative, for example, we removed any material that might have had a negative impact on her family or professional relationships. This involved something of a balancing act: We sought to facilitate disclosure while at the same time taking steps to protect Pat from too much exposure. We acknowledged the oppositions involved as we moved between expression and protection, disclosure and restraint (Bochner, 1984; Ellis, 2007).

BARTERING THE RELATIONSHIP

In practice, the process of negotiating our project was more unpredictable, complex, and dynamic than we anticipated:

In our early discussions it became clear that Pat hadn't been entirely comfortable with our earlier supervisor-student relationship. She wanted the opportunity to collaborate on a "more equal" footing. For my part, I was interested in researching her experience and I intended to write up the research and present it at conferences. As I shared this, Pat put some brakes on saying that in looking for "academic glory," she did not want to feel I was exploiting or "using" her. This challenge unsettled me. While realising Pat had particular sensitivities about potential inequalities which I needed to respect, I needed to carefully and critically scrutinise my motives: to what extent did Pat's research represent a necessary expedient for my own professional project? How was I to act in a non-exploitative way while being mindful of my researcher responsibilities (Guillemin and Gillam, 2004)? I shared my perspective with Pat via my diary writings. . . .

Over time through our mutually respectful dialogue, Pat became more trusting and accepting of my role as "researcher." We realised the need to put effort into keeping the communication channels open and the value of reflexivity to acknowledge emotional and political tensions arising from our different social positions and to deconstruct the "researcher's authority" (Finlay and Gough, 2003; Hertz, 1997). We sought to use reflexivity to "mute the distance and alienation" which comes from objectifying those being studied (Wasserfall, 1997, p. 152). (Finlay, 2009b, p. 31)

Part of our reflexive discussion involved recognizing that power was not simply being exerted in one direction. Power is complex and can be enacted in multilayered ways. Pat, too, had power. If process consent was to be taken seriously, she had the power to control the course of the research, and it was in her power to call a halt to the research and/or any subsequent publication. The challenge is to accept that power as well as to reflexively grapple with the ethical dilemmas arising from it. As Wolf (1996) notes, "The most central dilemma for contemporary feminists in fieldwork is power and the unequal hierarchies or levels of control that are often maintained, perpetuated, created and re-created during and after the field research" (p. 2).

HANDLING EMOTIONAL INTENSITY

During the interview itself, ethical issues concerning emotional intensity came to the fore. The story that Pat shared with me was as much about deafness and disability as it was about new hearing and well-being. Profoundly deaf for much of her life, Pat found herself, after her implant, in a surreal, alien world filled with hyper-noise. Her life was turned upside down. Although she was connecting with others at a hearing/physical level, at a psychological-social level, a part of her felt more disconnected than before (Finlay & Molano-Fisher, 2008).

As Pat learned to map an expanding range of sounds, she also had to confront the fact that her relationships with people were changing. People somehow *felt* different, but Pat recognized that she was in fact the one who was changing. It was all something of a struggle, both physically and emotionally. Pat said, "Everything has been affected, my body, my thinking." She was seeing and feeling the world in a radically different way.

Given all this, and her battered confidence, Pat found herself wanting to withdraw from social contact, to hide from the gaze of others. She craved solace from the tensions of her deafness, which continued to be revealed to her in her disrupted interactions. While struggling to accept herself, she also wanted to hide from herself:

I don't like deafness as other people see it. . . . I don't like . . . that I cannot follow things like others do even with the implant. It scares me that I really like my silence and I miss it and I found it hard to cope with the noise even if it helps and makes me *more part of things.* . . . What is the hard thing is trying to be part of the hearing, have the expectations of the hearing . . . and having to struggle all the time to do what your body is not able to do effortlessly. (Finlay & Molano-Fisher, 2008, p. 261)

Loss of confidence, anger, shame, alienation, and isolation were some of the emotional themes that surfaced repeatedly. For example, in the following extract, Pat shares her shame about her disability:

Pat: My sense of confidence is battered. . . . How many mistakes have I made in my [past] work and interactions? . . . I cringe when I think about it. . . . (Finlay & Molano-Fisher, 2008, p. 263)

The fact that the research tapped sensitive emotions made me worry whether our project to explore her lived world was making Pat experience her pain more than she would have otherwise. Was the retelling of her story actually retraumatizing her? As I reflected on these questions, I realized that I had entered into the research somewhat naively, vaguely expecting some sort of "celebration of new hearing." I had not expected such emotional intensity, and neither of us had predicted that her postimplant experience would be so much about disability. I was reminded that "trauma" (be it physical, emotional, or spiritual) is something that is lived and needs to be defined from the inside.

At one stage, I wondered if Pat was actually angry with me for highlighting her vulnerability, and I had to ask myself if the research was worth continuing, given the possible threats to our relationship (Ellis, 2007). I became more sensitive to the point made by Guillemin and Gillam (2004) that "the potential harms to participants in qualitative social research are often quite subtle and stem from the nature of the interaction between researcher and participant" (p. 272).

We both had to weigh the potential harm of our focus on Pat's emotional world against the potential benefit of telling her story. Our decision was to carry on. Pat felt she wanted to share her experience as there were lessons to be learned by professionals as well as those deaf individuals considering the possibility of implants. As Cutcliffe and Ramcharan (2002) and others acknowledge, emotionally charged research may be distressing for some, but it can also often be therapeutic and validating.

WRITING UP WITH AN ETHICAL EYE

The writing process, like the research, is replete with ethical challenges. There is the discomfort researchers may feel when "reducing" people's stories to a few pages of an academic article. As Josselson (1996) puts it, "Language can never contain a whole person, so every act of writing a person's life is inevitably a violation" (p. 62).

From the beginning, I had concerns about not being able to do justice to Pat's experience. I felt this more acutely than I normally do when I write up research, as I felt that Pat had given me the responsibility to "tell her story" and that she had a greater investment in the outcome than I did.

There are no easy ways to evade or preclude such feelings of discomfort. However, being reflexively aware both of the nature of our project and of our ethical responsibilities is a good place to start. Just as in life, in research too we have to make choices in difficult, uncertain circumstances and cope with competing demands and responsibilities. It is these choices that ethical reflexivity brings to our attention.

> RV: Even now, some 3 years after completing our research, I feel a sense of discomfort about treating Pat and our research as *objects* to "talk about" rather than "talking with" her. Put in Levinas's (1969) terms, the power we can misuse is a function of the way we objectify others in relation; we should choose to act to reduce such dominance. I am experiencing a slight guilt that comes in part from knowing that while I am no longer in close collaboration with Pat, I have continued to

> "work" our research. While Pat has encouraged me to continue sharing and discussing our research, I wonder if I betray her even now with this instrumental, if not exploitative, rehashing of our work for this chapter.

◆ Discussion and Reflection

In this chapter, I have suggested a typology of five lenses of reflexivity: strategic, situational-discursive, embodied, relational, and ethical. I have sought to show how the application of these lenses opens up the *content* and the *process* of research interviews—prior to, during, and after the encounter.

As with any typology, some categories overlap and are less than clear-cut in practice. And the lenses should not be seen as mutually exclusive: Researchers may well find themselves applying both the contextual and the relational, the relational and the ethical, and so forth.

The choice of which reflexive lens to use will vary depending on the interviewer's own predilections and methodological commitments. Phenomenological, autoethnographic, and feminist researchers are likely to be drawn toward embodied and relational lenses, while interviewers using ethnomethodology, discourse, or conversation analysis will probably favor contextual-discursive reflexivity as part of their quest to deconstruct and unsettle.

In practice, the way reflexivity is enacted varies considerably. Some interviewers may choose to use reflexivity in a thoughtful, systematic fashion, as a methodological audit to ensure trustworthiness. Others might prefer more spontaneous, creative approaches, employing more artful evocations. Some may keep a log of their methodological journey (i.e., focusing on the process) separate from their actual research. Others (like myself) inject reflexivity into every corner of the project, using reflexivity to color and permeate all aspects of both presentation and production (Georgaca, 2003).

However, there are limits to what can be offered for publication. Given the constraining word counts for journal articles, there may be neither opportunity nor need to give a reflexive account. It is hoped that there will be space in other forums (e.g., specifically focused pieces and conference presentations) to demonstrate reflexivity.

As researchers, we always face the inherent problem of providing "packaged" accounts of reflexivity. The process is invariably more "confusing, complex, multilayered, situated, enactive, emergent, precarious and messy than we could ever express." The challenge, as ever, is to retain sufficient critical awareness to guard against "getting sucked into a vortex of narcissism, pretentiousness or infinite regress" (Finlay & Gough, 2003, p. xi). Ultimately, the reflexive focus on the researcher/ process should be used to advance understanding and should not distract from the participants and/or the topic being studied.

In this chapter I have laid out my typology; I've also laid myself open. Have I achieved the balance of critical analysis and transparency without undue self-preoccupation? By using examples from my own interview research, I hope to have shown my commitment to being reflexive throughout every stage of the process.

I wonder which lens you, the reader, are drawn to. Which lens seems the most useful, significant, or irresistible? As for me, as I go about my research, I'm going to keep wearing my richly colored, endlessly intriguing varifocal spectacles.

◆ References

Anderson, L. (2006). Analytic autoethnography. *Journal of Contemporary Ethnography, 35*, 373–395.

Barry, C. A. (2003). Holding up the mirror to widen the view: Multiple subjectivities in the reflexive team. In L. Finlay & B. Gough (Eds.), *Reflexivity: A practical guide for researchers in health and social sciences* (pp. 214–228). Oxford, England: Blackwell.

Bochner, A. P. (1984). The functions of communication in interpersonal bonding. In C. Arnold & J. Bowers (Eds.), *The handbook of rhetoric and communication* (pp. 544–621). Beverly Hills, CA: Sage.

Bonner, K. M. (2001). Reflexivity and interpretive sociology: The case of analysis and the problem of nihilism. *Human Studies, 24*, 267–292.

Christians, C. G. (2000). Ethics and politics in qualitative research. In N. Denzin & Y. Lincoln (Eds.), *Handbook of qualitative research* (2nd ed., pp. 133–155). Thousand Oaks, CA: Sage.

Churchill, S. D. (2000–2001). Intercorporeality, gestural communication, and the voices of silence: Towards a phenomenological ethology (Part 1). *Somatics, 13*, 28–32.

Clandinin, D. J., & Connelly, F. M. (1994). Personal experience methods. In N. K. Denzin & Y. S. Lincoln (Eds.), *Handbook of qualitative research* (pp. 413–427). Thousand Oaks, CA: Sage.

Clifford, J., & Marcus, G. E. (Eds.). (1986). *Writing culture: The poetics and politics of ethnography.* Berkeley: University of California Press.

Coffey, A., & Atkinson, P. (1996). *Making sense of qualitative data analysis: Complementary strategies.* Thousand Oaks, CA: Sage.

Cutcliffe, J. R., & Ramcharan, P. (2002). Leveling the playing field? Exploring the merits of the ethics-as-process approach for judging qualitative research proposals. *Qualitative Health Research, 12*(7), 1000–1010.

DeYoung, P. (2003). *Relational psychotherapy: A primer.* New York, NY: Brunner-Routledge.

Edley, N. (2002). The loner, the walk, and the beast within: Narrative fragments in the construction of masculinity. In W. Patterson (Ed.), *Strategic narrative: New perspectives on the power of personal and cultural stories* (pp. 127–145). Lanham, MD: Lexington Books.

Ellis, C. (2007). Telling secrets, revealing lives: Relational ethics in research with intimate others. *Qualitative Inquiry, 13*(1), 3–29.

Evans, K. R., & Gilbert, M. (2005). *An introduction to integrative psychotherapy.* Basingstoke, England: Palgrave Macmillan.

Fielding, N. (1982). Observational research on the national front. In M. Bulmer (Ed.), *Social research ethics* (pp. 80–104). London, England: Macmillan.

Finlay, L. (1998). *The lifeworld of the occupational therapist: Meaning and motive in an uncertain world* (Unpublished doctoral dissertation). The Open University, Milton Keynes, England.

Finlay, L. (2002a). Negotiating the swamp: The opportunity and challenge of reflexivity in research practice. *Qualitative Research, 2*(2), 209–230.

Finlay, L. (2002b). "Outing" the researcher: The provenance, principles and practice of reflexivity. *Qualitative Health Research, 12*(3), 531–545.

Finlay, L. (2003a). The intertwining of body, self, and world: A phenomenological study of living with recently diagnosed multiple sclerosis. *Journal of Phenomenological Psychology, 34*(6), 157–178.

Finlay, L. (2003b). The reflexive journey: Mapping multiple routes. In L. Finlay & B. Gough (Eds.), *Reflexivity: A practical guide for researchers in health and social science* (pp. 3–20). Oxford, England: Blackwell.

Finlay, L. (2004). From "Gibbering idiot" to "Iceman," Kenny's story: A critical analysis of an occupational narrative. *British Journal of Occupational Therapy, 67*(11), 474–480.

Finlay, L. (2005). Reflexive embodied empathy: A phenomenology of participant-researcher intersubjectivity. *The Humanistic Psychologist, 33*(4), 271–292.

Finlay, L. (2006a). Dancing between embodied empathy and phenomenological reflection. *Indo-Pacific Journal of Phenomenology, 6,* 1–11.

Finlay, L. (2006b). An embodied experience of multiple sclerosis: An existential-phenomenological analysis. In L. Finlay & C. Ballinger (Eds.), *Qualitative research for allied health professionals: Challenging choices* (pp. 185–199). Chichester, England: Wiley.

Finlay, L. (2009a). Ambiguous encounters: A relational approach to phenomenological research. *Indo-Pacific Journal of Phenomenology, 9,* 1–17.

Finlay, L. (2009b). Reflexively probing relational ethical challenges. *Qualitative Methods in Psychology Newsletter, 7,* 30–34.

Finlay, L., & Evans, K. (2009). *Relational centred research for psychotherapists: Exploring meanings and experience.* Chichester, England: Wiley-Blackwell.

Finlay, L., & Gough, B. (Eds.). (2003). *Reflexivity: A practical guide for researchers in health and social sciences.* Oxford, England: Blackwell.

Finlay, L., & Molano-Fisher, P. (2008). "Transforming" self and world: A phenomenological study of a changing lifeworld following a cochlear implant. *Medicine, Health Care and Philosophy, 11*(2), 255–267.

Frank, A. W. (1998). Just listening: Narrative and deep illness. *Families, Systems & Health, 16*(3), 197–212.

Gendlin, E. T. (1996). *Focusing-oriented psychotherapy.* New York, NY: Guilford Press.

Gendlin, E. T. (1997). How philosophy cannot appeal to reason and how it can. In D. M. Levin (Ed.), *Language beyond postmodernism: Saying and thinking in Gendlin's philosophy* (pp. 3–41). Evanston, IL: Northwestern University Press.

Georgaca, E. (2003). Analysing the interviewer: The joint construction of accounts of psychotic experience. In L. Finlay & B. Gough (Eds.), *Reflexivity: A practical guide for researchers in health and social sciences* (pp. 120–132). Oxford, England: Blackwell.

Goffman, E. (1959). *The presentation of self in everyday life.* New York, NY: Penguin.

Gough, B. (2003). Deconstructing reflexivity. In L. Finlay & B. Gough (Eds.), *Reflexivity: A practical guide for researchers in health and social sciences* (pp. 21–36). Oxford, England: Blackwell.

Grafanaki, S. (1996). How research can change the researcher: The need for sensitivity, flexibility and ethical boundaries in conducting qualitative research in counselling/psychotherapy. *British Journal of Guidance & Counselling, 13.*

Guillemin, M., & Gillam, L. (2004). Ethics, reflexivity and "ethically important moments" in research. *Qualitative Inquiry, 10*(2), 261–280.

Harper, D. (2003). Developing a critically reflexive position using discourse analysis. In L. Finlay & B. Gough (Eds.), *Reflexivity: A practical guide for researchers in health and social sciences* (pp. 78–92). Oxford, England: Blackwell.

Hertz, R. (Ed.). (1997). *Reflexivity and voice.* Thousand Oaks, CA: Sage.

Josselson, R. (1996). On writing other people's lives: Reflections of a narrative researcher. In R. Josselson (Ed.), *Ethics and process in the narrative study of lives* (Vol. 4, pp. 60–71). London, England: Sage.

King, N., Finlay, L., Ashworth, P., Smith, J. A., Langdridge, D., & Butt, T. (2008). Can't really trust that, so what can I trust? A polyvocal, qualitative analysis of the psychology of mistrust. *Qualitative Research in Psychology, 5*(2), 80–102.

King, N., & Horrocks, C. (2010). *Interviews in qualitative research.* Thousand Oaks, CA: Sage.

Levinas, E. (1969). *Totality and infinity: An essay on exteriority.* Pittsburgh, PA: Duquesne University Press.

Lynch, M. (2000). Against reflexivity as an academic virtue and source of privileged knowledge. *Theory, Culture & Society, 17*(3), 26–54.

Marcus, G. E. (1994). What comes (just) after "post"? The case of ethnography. In N. K. Denzin & Y. S. Lincoln (Eds.), *Handbook of qualitative research* (pp. 563–574). Thousand Oaks, CA: Sage.

Mason, J. (1996). *Qualitative researching.* Thousand Oaks, CA: Sage.

Merleau-Ponty, M. (1962). *Phenomenology of perception* (C. Smith, Trans.). London, England: Routledge & Kegan Paul. (Original work published 1945)

Merleau-Ponty, M. (1968). *The visible and the invisible* (A. Lingis, Trans.). Evanston, IL: Northwestern University Press. (Original work published in 1964)

Nicolson, P. (2003). Reflexivity, "bias" and the in-depth interview: Developing shared meanings. In L. Finlay & B. Gough (Eds.), *Reflexivity: A practical guide for researchers in health and social sciences* (pp. 133–145). Oxford, England: Blackwell.

Pels, D. (2000). Reflexivity: One step up. *Theory, Culture & Society, 17*(3), 1–25.

Potter, J., & Wetherell, M. (1995). Discourse analysis. In J. A. Smith, R. Harre, & L. Van Langenhove (Eds.), *Rethinking methods in psychology* (pp. 80–92). London, England: Sage.

Reed-Danahay, D. (1997). *Auto/ethnography: Rewriting the self and the social.* Oxford, England: Berg.

Reinharz, S. (1997). Who am I? The need for a variety of selves in the field. In R. Hertz (Ed.), *Reflexivity and voice* (pp. 3–20). Thousand Oaks, CA: Sage.

Richardson, L. (1994). Writing: A method of inquiry. In N. K. Denzin & Y. S. Lincoln (Eds.), *Handbook of qualitative research* (pp. 516–529). Thousand Oaks, CA: Sage.

Riessman, C. K. (2003). Performing identities in illness narrative: Masculinity and multiple sclerosis. *Qualitative Research, 3*(1), 5–33.

Seale, C. (1999). *The quality of qualitative research*. London, England: Sage.

Steier, F. (Ed.). (1991). *Research and reflexivity*. London, England: Sage.

Wasserfall, R. R. (1997). Reflexivity, feminism, and difference. In R. Hertz (Ed.), *Reflexivity and voice* (pp. 150–168). Thousand Oaks, CA: Sage.

Wertz, F. (2005). Phenomenological research methods for counseling psychology. *Journal of Counseling Psychology, 52*(2), 167–177.

Wilkinson, S. (1988). The role of reflexivity in feminist psychology. *Women's Studies International Forum, 11*, 493–502.

Willig, C. (2001). *Introducing qualitative research in psychology*. Buckingham, England: Open University Press.

Wise, S. (1987). A framework for discussing ethical issues in feminist research: A review of the literature. In V. Griffiths, M. Hum, J. Batsleer, F. Poland, & S. Wise (Eds.), *Writing feminist biography: Issue 2. Using life histories* (Studies in Sexual Politics, No. 19). Manchester, England: University of Manchester.

Wolf, D. (Ed.). (1996). *Feminist dilemmas in fieldwork*. Boulder, CO: Westview Press.

STIGMA AND THE
INTERVIEW ENCOUNTER

◆ Kay E. Cook

The issue of stigma in the research interview is an interesting and complex one. Thinking about the stigmatizing effects of in-depth interviews on marginalized participants focuses attention on the purpose of our research, our relative power with respect to the interviewee, and how the formalized nature of contemporary research shapes the ways in which our intentions may be interpreted by the participant. In this chapter, I seek to explore some of this terrain as it relates to the conduct of qualitative research interviews. The purpose of this chapter is not to revisit theories of interview interaction, which are well documented elsewhere in this *Handbook*; rather, I aim to examine the nature of stigma as it applies to the interview encounter. By conducting this exploration, I am not suggesting that stigma is the dominant force that shapes the nature of all interaction between interviewees and interviewers. Rather, I suggest that in certain circumstances, particularly when working with marginalized participants, relations of stigma can shape the nature

of the data collected, and as such, this is an issue to which the researcher must be attuned. As such, this chapter seeks to examine the interactional approaches of impression management that are inherent in the processes of interview data collection and analysis.

To begin this investigation into stigma in the interview encounter, I first examine studies where stigma was either the focus of the investigation or emerged as an analytical category. These studies shed light on the definition of stigma and the nature of its enactment; however, they offer little critique of the interview encounter itself. I then turn to focus on a small body of work where researchers have reflected on the potentially stigmatizing nature of their interviews with people from marginalized groups. In this section, the socially constructed nature of stigma in the interview encounter will be examined first in light of the definitions and processes of stigma, followed by an examination of the implications of specific research processes that may shape this power-laden interaction. Attention will now be turned, however, to defining the nature of stigma, so as to begin this process with a common understanding of the issue at hand.

◆ Stigma

In the social sciences, definitions of stigma are typically derived from the work of Erving Goffman (1963), who defined stigma as an "attribute that is deeply discrediting, but it should be seen that a language of relationships, not attributes, is really needed" (p. 3). In such social relations, inferior attributes are associated with those who violate socially constructed norms, and the person is reduced "from a whole and usual person to a tainted, discounted one" (p. 3). As a result of such stigma, "shame becomes a central possibility, arising from the individual's perception of one of his own attributes as being a defiling thing to possess" (p. 7).

Goffman's work has informed countless studies and position papers on stigma, including those put out by the World Psychiatric Association (Sartorius, 2006), which positions stigma as a self-confirming process whereby stigmatizing markers become loaded with the negative connotations that produce stigma and subsequent discrimination. Through such a process, stigmatizing markers are amplified, and the person is more likely to be identified and stigmatized in the future (Link & Phelan, 2001; Tindal, Cook, & Foster, 2010).

Goffman (1963) identified three "types" of stigma or facets by which a person could be stigmatized: (1) bodily (physical deformities), (2) moral (deficits in character), and (3) tribal (lineal inadequacies) attributes. Each of these stigmas produce marks of social disgrace that leave a person either discredited, where their stigma is evident, or discreditable, where the stigma is yet to be exposed. Strategies for dealing with evident stigma include "hiding the discredited status (secrecy), avoiding social interaction (withdrawal), and education (preventative telling)" (Winnick & Bodkin, 2008, p. 300), whereas strategies for concealing an as yet unexposed stigma are what Goffman (1963) terms as "passing," which "because of the great rewards of being considered normal, almost all persons who are in a position to pass will do so on some occasion by intent" (p. 74). Each of these has implications for the interview encounter.

To examine the role of stigma in the interview encounter, it is necessary to first examine the processes through which stigmas are enacted and the implications for both those who typically bear them (the interviewee) and those who typically inquire about them in the interview setting (the interviewer). The socially constructed nature of Goffman's (1963) conception of stigma thus leads to an examination of the social processes underlying both stigma and the interview encounter. My discussion of these processes focuses on the work of Link and Phelan (2001), who draw on Goffman's original conception to describe stigma as occurring when the following interrelated components converge:

1. Human differences are noted and labeled.

2. Human differences are associated with negative stereotypes.

3. Social labels connote a separation of "us" and "them."

4. Labeled persons experience status loss and discrimination.

The mechanism that Link and Phelan (2001) proposed through which these four interrelated components converge is the exercise of power, where either power is obvious or it is overlooked, taken for granted, or seen as unproblematic. As stigma research focuses typically on the "perceptions of individuals and the consequences of such perceptions for micro-level interactions" (p. 366), the research interview can be seen as a microcosm of the larger social processes of stigma.

◆ Stigma in the Research Interview

The following discussion of stigmas constructed during the interview encounter, therefore, draws on the work of Kvale (2005, 2006), who describes the asymmetrical power relations of the interview, and Watson (2009), who describes the "shockwaves" experienced by interview researchers when interviewees did things such as violating social taboos, akin to engaging in discrediting behavior, or changing the footing of the interview to save face and maintain dignity (Cook & Nunkoosing, 2008).

The research interview represents a site where the four interrelated components of stigma described by Link and Phelan (2001) converge in overt and/or covert ways. Stigma necessarily involves power differentials and the exercise of social superiority over another, and such power differentials are inherently involved in the research interview (Briggs, 2001). While differences between the researcher (not to be confused with a peer interviewer) and the participant are essential to the research process, it is the result of this process that also makes the research interview relevant to the processes of stigmatization. As Briggs (2001) notes, "Interviews are saturated by images of the social dynamics of the interview itself, projections of the social context in which it takes place, the roles and power dynamics of the interviewer and respondent, and their respective agendas" (p. 914). Even within cocreated accounts, relations of power and social hierarchies exist. As theorists such as Gramsci (1971) and Foucault (1980), however, contend, "Those with less power are not simply trapped within the totalization of an asymmetrical power relation: the less powerful find innumerable, creative, even powerful ways to resist inequity" (Scheurich, 1997, p. 71).

With respect to the research interview, I posit that all interview participants, particularly those occupying socially marginalized positions, have the potential to be discredited, and as such, identity management is of both theoretical and practical significance to all qualitative researchers. In the following analysis, I draw on empirical examples to examine these social dynamics and the roles of both interviewee and interviewer. While some authors correctly note that research with marginalized groups can be used to give voice to and empower those who are disaffected (Liamputtong, 2007), I, like Briggs (2001), argue that research interviews are typically predicated on institutional and social conventions that are heavily weighted toward the wishes of the more powerful party. As such, while it can be argued that power in the interview context is discursively constructed through each participant's attempts to steer the interview as it is simultaneously steered by the other party (Enosh, Ben-Ari, & Buchbinder, 2008), in sensitive research, the interview may often become threatening or discrediting for the interviewee, who is left to accept or resist, but rarely so for the interviewer. As such, the interviewer is essentially an agent of power who can divest as little or as much as he or she feels is required to effect the best possible data. This is a fact not lost on the interview participant, who must then decide what (if any) vulnerabilities to expose. The participant may invoke face-saving methods to minimize the threats posed during the interview,

which manifest themselves in the data collected. This relationship, however, does not cast the participant as passive to the dominance of the researcher. Far from it. While the researcher has initial power over the intent and conduct of the interview, the participant then assumes an equally powerful role in deciding how much access to grant—from complete acceptance of the overtones of the researcher to complete resistance, or something in between.

To return to the discussion of stigma, it is possible to divide the empirical qualitative interview research reviewed here into two broad categories, reflecting Goffman's (1963) distinction between those who are already discredited and those who are at that moment discreditable. While this represents a simple dichotomy for illustrative purposes, I intend these poles to examine the extreme paradigms of interview research where the interview is either an occasion for gauging, exploring, or unearthing an existent stigma or a descriptive resource or context where the interviewer and the discredited can coconstruct stigma or provide an opportunity for stigma management. This is not to suggest, however, that there is nothing in between. Rather, the discredited and discreditable domains of stigma research presented here are not regarded by Goffman to be mutually exclusive, as at any time one can be both discredited and discreditable. Similarly, both formulations can also occur within the one interview encounter. As Goffman notes with respect to social interaction, which can be applied equally to the interview encounter,

> The stigmatized and the normal are part of each other; if one can prove vulnerable, it must be expected that the other can, too. For in imputing identities to individuals, discreditable or not, the wider social setting and its inhabitants have in a way compromised themselves; they have set themselves up to be proven the fool. (p. 135)

The following sections of this chapter, however, break away from the dynamic and interactive nature of stigma, as described by Goffman (1963), to discuss these domains separately. This is not to suggest that these can be discretely divided but, rather, to provide a mechanism through which existing interview research can be discussed with respect to the divergent ways through which researchers have arrived at the topic of stigma. One could think of this work as occurring along a continuum (Figure 23.1).

Figure 23.1   A Continuum of Stigma in the Interview Encounter

The Discredited   The Discreditable

Self-evident   Constructed

| Researchers aim to explore, describe, and examine how the discredited participants experience their stigmas outside the interview encounter. | Stigma is constructed during the interview encounter by the nature of the research question and the interview dynamics OR Researchers aim to investigate the experiences of the discredited but acknowledge that interview practices need to be carefully managed in order to avoid further stigmatizing participants and affecting data quality. | Researchers acknowledge that the interview itself is a site where participants may experience stigma and manage their identities to avoid being (further) discredited. These strategies have implications for both the identity of the interviewee and the nature of the data collected. |

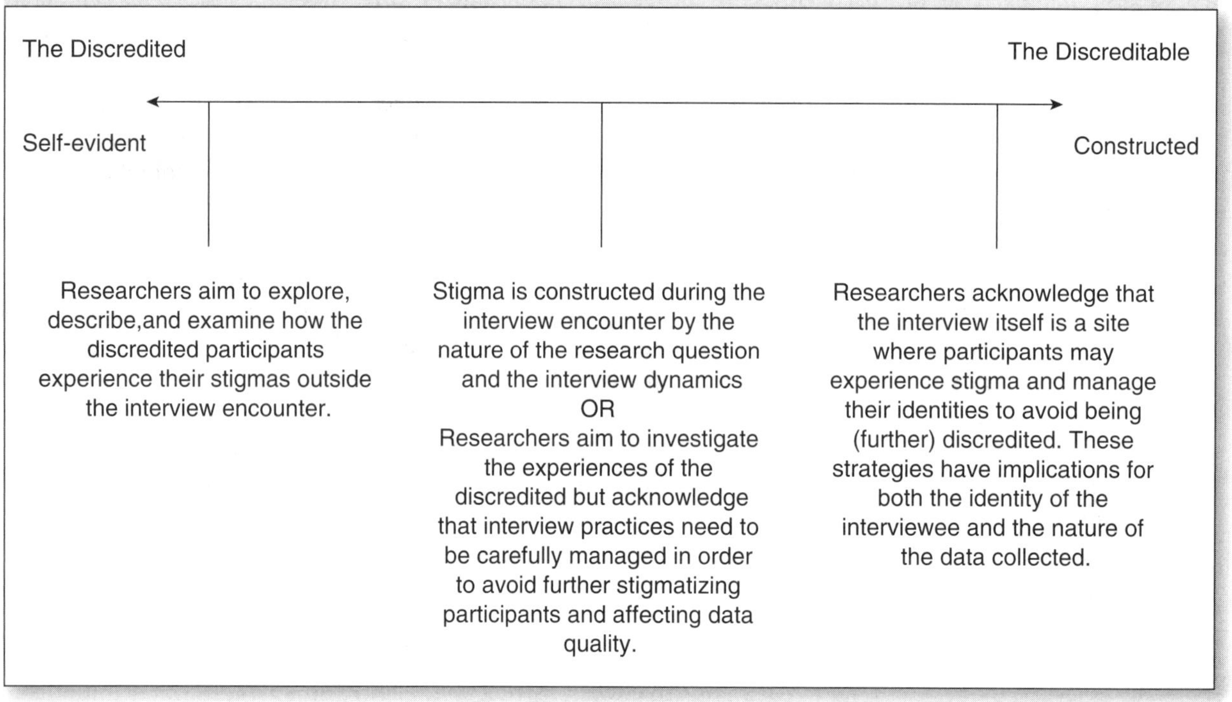

At one end of the continuum are researchers examining the apparently self-evident stigma of the discredited. At the other end are those exploring how the interview itself poses the requirement for impression management by discreditable participants and how discreditable or discredited participants shape the nature of the interview. Finally, the middle of the continuum is occupied by researchers who inadvertently construct stigma during the interview encounter due to the nature of the research question and the dynamics of the interview encounter. Here, we may also find researchers who investigate the experiences of the discredited and/or discreditable yet who are reflexive about their interview practices insofar as they may affect the quality of data collected, but not to the extent to which they view the interview as a site for active identity management and resistance that needs to be accounted for in the analysis and reporting of results.

The following sections then describe the three points on the continuum, in the same order: beginning with the poles and using research examples to illustrate the key issues associated with interview practice and the associated discussions that relate to ethical practice and the quality of data collected. As such, the central question being asked here, and to be asked anew for each research project, is to what extent marginality is itself internal or external to the interview interaction.

◆ *Exploring the Stigmas of the Discredited*

The literature is replete with examples of research studies that have employed qualitative interviews to elicit data on the experiences of stigmatized participants and subsequently report on the nature and implications of this stigma. These studies typically focus on the discredited—those participants who are explicitly acknowledged to be stigmatized at the outset of the study. Recent examples of such research span disciplines and include research on poverty (Cook, 2009; Kusenbach, 2009; Reutter et al., 2009); disability and chronic illness (Green, 2009; Karim, Chowdhury, Islam, & Weiss, 2007), including hepatitis C and HIV/AIDS (Buseh & Stevens, 2007; Ware, Wyatt, & Tugenberg, 2006); mental illness (Phelan & Basow, 2007); white supremacy (Simi & Futrell, 2009); and sexuality and "deviant" sexual identities or behavior (Balfe et al., 2010; Bradley, 2007; Scambler, 2007), to name but a mere few. These studies, which examine and report on the experience of stigmatization, can be further categorized into two groups: (1) those studies that set out to examine the nature and imposition of stigma from the outset and (2) those studies in which stigma emerged as an analytical category through in-depth unstructured or semistructured interviews with participants typically constructed as "marginalized." In these cases, the stigmatized experiences of participants provided the impetus for a publication beyond the originally intended auspice of the project. In all cases, the stigmas explored or unearthed during the interviews were regarded as distinct from the interview encounter itself. For example, in their study of physically disabled female college students, Taub, McLorg, and Fanflik (2004) note as follows:

> Respondents indicate being very aware that their educational experiences occur in a social environment primarily consisting of able-bodied professors, staff, and students. From the interview data, it became apparent that during their collegiate experiences, these women used interactional approaches to deal with the imposition of stigma by others. (p. 172)

In this and other research with the discredited, however, these interactional approaches of impression management are not considered relevant to the processes of data collection and analysis.

To turn Goffman's (1963) discussion of the interaction between stigmatized persons and normals around to focus on the interview process, he states that in such interactions, it is the evident nature of the stigma that shapes the interaction. For those whose stigma is immediately apparent, "the cooperation of a stigmatized person with normals in acting as if his known differentness were irrelevant and not attended to is one main possibility for life of such a person" (pp. 41–42). In the interview encounter, however, the stigma of the person is often the very subject of the interview. Their experiences of living in poverty, with a disability, or with an illness make their difference from the researcher impossible to avoid. To draw again on Goffman's parlance, being discredited thus requires the management of tensions that might arise in interactions with others, including researchers.

While often focusing on social processes, these studies occupy an ontological and epistemological space where stigma is regarded as something that exists separately from the interview encounter. Here, the stigmatizing experiences of the participant are acknowledged, discussed, and reported as if the stigma being discussed is not influenced by the interview itself. While typically acknowledging the interpersonal stigmatizing processes similar to those put forward by Goffman (1963) and Link and Phelan (2001), the studies reviewed here make no reference to the interaction between the researcher and the participant in terms of the construction or operation of this stigma, or how the participant's reporting of a stigma shapes the social construction and management of further stigmas. For example, Reutter and colleagues' (2009) examination of the perceptions and responses to poverty stigma focused on "the microlevel processes that are used to manage stigma interpersonally" (p. 298). Yet this study focused only on those processes that occurred outside the interview context.

Arguably, there is nothing inherently wrong with this approach to stigma research; indeed, my own work is included in the articles examined here. There is certainly a need to describe the experience of those people who are marginalized; however, this work does ignore the social processes of the interview encounter, the same social processes that help produce the meanings of the stigmas under investigation. In fact, these studies grow out of Goffman's (1963) original conceptualization of stigma, which is located in a similar epistemological paradigm where the interactions between researcher, participants, and data are not considered relevant to his emerging theory. In this respect, researchers working with the discredited seem to operate on the basis of an arbitrary analytical division between the social interactions they describe as shaping participants' experiences and the social interactions of the interview encounter itself.

To turn now to the other end of the continuum, we find researchers primarily concerned with the impression management strategies staged during the interview. In these studies, the stigmatizing relations created in the interview encounter are the focus of the research.

◆ Interviewing the Discreditable

In contrast to studies that view the research interview as a neutral setting where the meaning of stigma and stigma management can be accessed and described, the studies outlined in this section examine the research interview as a site where stigmatization occurs in the context of the power hierarchies inherent in the research interview, including the dialogical dominance of interviewers over interviewees (Kvale, 2005, 2006). While not directly concerned with stigma, regard for the asymmetrical nature of modern research interviews has been prevalent among researchers. To locate these power-laden interviews within Goffman's (1981) domain, one can think of research interviews as encounters that provide the research participant with a forum where face-saving performances of the desirable self can be staged. These performances, however, carry with them social risks, such as the risk of becoming discredited or being disregarded as a moral agent (Goffman, 1959, 1961, 1963).

In comparison with the abundance of articles employing qualitative interviews (typically conducted by privileged, white, middle-class researchers) to probe discredited people's stigma, there are relatively few articles that take up a close examination of such interviews as a microcosm of normative society, where these very stigmas are reproduced. Moreover, those articles that do take stock of the potentially stigmatizing nature of the research interview often do so as a result of unanticipated events occurring within the interview encounter (see, e.g., Cook & Nunkoosing, 2008; Hagan, 1986; Tanggaard, 2007; Watson, 2009). These articles describe how power dynamics in the setup and conduct of the interview unintentionally discredited the interviewee or created sites where face-saving performances were required. These instances have implications for data collection, analysis, and reporting. For example, I, along with my colleague Karl Nunkoosing, came to explore such issues in our unanticipated examination of paid-for participation. Here, atypical and resistant interview interactions led us to examine how third-party recruitment methods and the payment of $20 for each interview led to the stigmatization of impoverished participants (Cook & Nunkoosing, 2008). To regain agency over the interview process, interviewees employed tactics that limited their disclosure, while they maintained enough semblance of the conversational genre required to warrant the $20 payment. Hagan (1986), in her article titled "Interviewing the Downtrodden," reported a similar situation:

> Some of those in my sample who agreed to be interviewed were distinctly uncooperative throughout, either poking fun at the whole exercise as not

something to be taken seriously, or chose to take on a disinterested enactment of the part whilst making sure nothing of any real consequence was said. (p. 341)

In situations such as these, silence becomes a powerful tool through which interview participants can subvert an intrusive and controlling research process and save face (Huby, 1997; Taket, Foster, & Cook, 2009).

To overcome respondent reluctance and resistance, researchers such as Adler and Adler (2002) have put forward various strategies from which researchers can choose their preferred path. These include decisions on whether to conduct single interviews with each participant, which provide "an ironic security in detachment" (Adler & Adler, 2002, p. 523), or develop trust over time through multiple interviews; whether to pay or not; reducing perceived asymmetry by employing researchers more similar to the respondent population; and being attentive to conduct during the interview. While some of these strategies are discussed in more detail below, regardless of the strategies assumed to reduce asymmetrical power dynamics and the unintentional enactment of stigma, I agree with both Briggs (2001) and Nunkoosing (2005) that "power is always present in the transactions of the interview" (p. 699) and that interviewers cannot pretend that their "status, race, culture, gender and their interviewee's status, race, culture and gender do not influence what can be said, how it can be said, and what can be written about" (p. 704).

With the power-laden dynamics of the interview in mind, the following section describes the strategies put forward to manage the explicit stigma to be discussed in the interview or arrange the interview interaction in such a way as to avoid stigmatizing relations, representing the midpoint on the continuum presented earlier. These techniques have been put forward to protect vulnerable participants from processes such as the stigmatizing nature of the interview and/or improve data quality; however, they illustrate the inescapable nature of the power dynamics inherent in the interview encounter.

◆ Power Dynamics in the Interview Encounter

The following section outlines the practical issues that shape the stigmatizing nature of the interview encounter. The issues presented below critique several typical qualitative researcher practices. The discussion of these practices, however, does not suggest that researchers apply these mechanisms carte blanche, as researchers working with the discredited and discreditable necessarily engage in serious reflection about the nature of their practice (see, e.g., Liamputtong, 2007; Mkandawire-Valhmu, Rice, & Bathum, 2009). Rather, this section is designed to provide an overview of some of the issues debated by researchers working with the discredited and discreditable in order to illuminate the thinking that takes place before conducting research with discredited or discreditable participants.

THE CONTRACTUAL NATURE OF RESEARCH

With respect to the contractual nature of contemporary qualitative research, Kvale and Brinkmann (2009) and Miller-Day (Chapter 34 in this handbook) have outlined some of the issues with institutional review boards as they apply to interview-based research in general. Their main point is that the procedural and static approach to ethics, as found in most Western countries, is often too rigid to be relevant and can potentially be stifling to the fluid and inductive nature of qualitative research. However, when reflecting on stigma in light of the contractual nature of contemporary Western interview research, the work of Carter, Jordens, McGrath, and Little (2008) provides an interesting insight. Drawing on the work of Guillemin and Gillman (2004), they distinguish between the procedural ethics required by institutional review boards, such as the distribution of participant information sheets and the signing of consent forms, and the micro-ethics of practice that arise during the interview encounter.

While Carter and colleagues (2008) argue that participant information sheets do little to prepare participants for the likely experience of participating, I take their argument on a different track, as I contend that these information sheets do indeed prepare participants for participation in their role as subordinate to the expert, authorized researcher in the formalized, contractual interview that is about to take place (Cook & Nunkoosing, 2008). Even the title of the project, which is typically required to be printed on top of the information sheet, may contain words that draw attention to the participants' marks of social disgrace. These information sheets

may contain symbols of participants' discredited status—such as by acknowledging and thus drawing attention to their HIV/AIDS status, their poverty, their single parenthood, their disability, or whatever attribute makes them of interest to the researcher. The formalized nature of the interview thus places moral demands on the speaker to discuss those characteristics outlined in the information sheet that made the participant a subject of interest to the researcher. The interviewees are discredited from the outset. Their options thus include the identity management strategies described by Goffman (1981) and others that I have outlined above, which may effectively label them as a difficult or reluctant participant.

THE UNNATURAL NATURE OF THE RESEARCH INTERVIEW

There has been a long succession of researchers describing problems with the research interview in terms of the detachment of this artificial question-and-answer format from the discourses of everyday life (see, e.g., Cicourel, 1982; Lazarsfeld, 1935; Mishler, 1986; Nunkoosing, 2005; Riesman & Benney, 1956). The problem for researchers employing qualitative research interviews is that formalized interviews attempt to construct a "natural" and "comfortable" setting for a conversational interview yet operate in a context and adopt a pattern of interaction that is far from natural. Despite the best intentions of researchers employing tactics to minimize the discomfort faced by participants (see, e.g., Liamputtong, 2007), unlike social conversation, research interviews involve two (or more) agents with differing degrees of control and perhaps vastly different agendas. Such asymmetrical conversations are rare in normal social life, and when they are encountered (e.g., in a police interrogation, doctor–patient consultation, or social service caseworker/client interview), the more powerful party is largely unconcerned with the social comfort of the interviewee and the illusion of replicating everyday conversation. The addition of stigma to these already awkward and forced social interactions propels the research interview into uncharted territory:

When normals and stigmatized do in fact enter on another's immediate presence, especially when they there attempt to sustain a joint conversational encounter, there occurs one of the primal scenes for sociology; for, in many cases, these moments will be the ones when the causes and effects of stigma must be directly confronted by both sides. The stigmatized individual may find that he feels unsure of how we normals will identify him and receive him. (Goffman, 1963, p. 13)

The interview represents one such instance where participants and researchers openly discuss a discrediting mark. Here, the tactics of the interviewer shape how the participants perceive that they are identified and received. In particular, two vastly different sets of tactics are worth noting here: (1) employing empathy and (2) positioning the interview as a battle.

On the use of empathy, researchers working with vulnerable populations have often cited the need to self-disclose to participants in order to let them "know that they really did understand what the participant was going through, sometimes having had the same or similar experiences themselves" (Dickson-Swift, James, Kippen, & Liamputtong, 2006, p. 857). While disclosures on the part of the researcher may lessen the power differentials inherent in the interview process, such disclosures are predicated on the assumption that both researcher and participant share a common experience. As such, empathetic disclosures crystallize the nature of the stigma by making it evident, albeit shared. Similar to the dynamics of a counseling session, here, the researcher attempts to normalize the stigmatizing attribute so as to make a "safe place" for the participants to reveal more of their "true selves." While this tactic is often successful, and widely employed, the danger is that the researcher's disclosure may not be regarded as similar to that of the participant or as deeply discrediting. As a result, the researcher's disclosure may further stigmatize the participant by trivializing his or her experience.

Watson (2009) has further criticized the use of empathy as an analytic tool in qualitative inquiry, drawing on Shields's (1996) analysis of *Verstehen*, claiming, like Dickson-Swift and colleagues (2006) above, that empathy seeks to unite the experiences of the researcher and the participant. Watson (2009) and Shields (1996) claim that this "logic of unity" creates a monological interpretation of the experience that ultimately silences the participant. As such, while empathy may lessen the stigma felt by the participant in the interview encounter, at the other extreme, "if interviewers assume commonalities in

identification in the context of such differentness, they are liable to reproduce structures of oppression and exploit research respondents" (Bondi, 2003, p. 66). This issue may be resolved through the use of a peer interviewer, but in most research, it is often not practical for academic researchers to divulge an experience that disqualifies them from being a "normal" and places them in the camp of the "stigmatized." Furthermore, to draw again on Goffman's (1963) discussion of the self and its others in a conversational setting,

there is the much less gentle art of "putting the other on," whereby militant members of disadvantaged groups, during sociable occasions, build up a story, about themselves and their feelings, to normals who clumsily profess sympathy, the story reaching a point where it becomes patent that the story was designed to reveal itself to be a fabrication. (p. 136)

As such, the lived reality of the participant is silenced, which may be what McKeganey (2001) and others (Adler & Adler, 2002; Cook & Nunkoosing, 2008) speak of when they refer to the "truthfulness" of data obtained from a reluctant respondent, as discussed below. The dangerous territory of performing empathy with research participants has led some researchers to suggest openly acknowledging the sites of difference, leading to my second extreme—the research interview as a battle.

With respect to the proposed recognition of qualitative interviews as combative in nature, Lene Tanggaard (2007) provides a recent discussion. She is wary of strategies that aim to achieve symmetry with participants, noting that such attempts "make it difficult to reflect on critical aspects of power and ethics in qualitative research" (p. 163). The alternative she provides is to take "an agnostic conception of conversation as fighting," where meanings are contested and negotiated and each party asks questions and answers with a critical attitude. Such interview processes provide the participant with more control to refute or resist stigmatizing constructions, using tactics such as those of deflection, normalization, or disidentification, described previously. As such, "each interview becomes an arena where interviewer and interviewee negotiate the implicit question of 'What are the moral and identity implications of what is being said here *for me*?'" (Enosh et al., 2008, p. 463).

A focus on differentness and active knowledge construction, which Tanggaard (2007) has conceived as the "battle" of the interview, provides a challenge to interview-based stigma research that seeks to describe the experiences of the discredited. Combining the critical gazes of stigma management "out there" in the social world with management "in here" in the interview context allows both a description of the everyday social relations experienced by the participant and greater analytical insight into the processes of dignity preservation and identity management that are fundamentally linked to the relational concept of stigma the researcher seeks to describe.

PAID-FOR PARTICIPATION

The third and final issue that I will explore regards the decision whether to pay research participants or not. Conventions regarding payment vary between disciplines and research contexts (for a brief review, see Fry et al., 2005). Internationally, ethical review bodies have scrutinized such relationships with respect to the effect payments have on free and informed consent. The nature and extent of undue inducement has been the primary area of concern (Ackerman, 1989; Brody, 2005; Emanual, 2005; Macklin, 1989), particularly within the health and medical sciences, where the payment of injecting drug users has highlighted the contentious nature of the issue (Fry et al., 2005; Ritter, Fry, & Swan, 2003). Within the clinical paradigm, this debate has focused largely on whether payments are a fair reimbursement for participation contribution, effort, and expenses incurred and whether payments represent an undue influence on the choice to participate or not (Fry et al., 2005). These issues, however, focus on the legal contract of the interview rather than examining the ethical implications paid-for participation has on the micropractices of the interview encounter, especially with respect to socially vulnerable groups.

In this space, several researchers have identified issues of particular relevance to qualitative interviews. McKeganey (2001) states,

It is comforting to think that the only reason why an individual should involve himself or herself in our research is because they wish to tell their story. If we introduce money into the equation we start to worry that the individual may be less motivated to tell the truth and may instead start to tell us what he or she feels we want to know in order to earn whatever money we have deemed should be paid to them. (p. 1237)

While I am not particularly concerned here with the "truth" of the narrative produced, as I agree with Polkinghorne (2007) that the "truths" sought in research interviews are narrative rather than historical, the commodification of the narrative is an issue of particular importance when working with discredited or discreditable participants. As I have noted elsewhere (Cook & Nunkoosing, 2008), stigmatizing conditions such as "poverty makes it possible for a stranger to invite the participant to talk about sensitive aspects of her life. The participant is being asked to commodify the personal" (Polkinghorne, 2007). To draw on Stones and McMillan's (2010) development of Titmuss's (1970) discussion of the gift relationship involved in human blood donation, payment for research participation redistributes both knowledge and money between academics and the poor (or other socially marginalized groups who find themselves the object of inquiry). The net worth of each commodity, however, is often not equal. In protecting vulnerable participants from undue inducements, ethics review boards have placed a value on narrative that may inadvertently define it and its creator as of limited social value. In my research with impoverished elders, a $20 payment for each interview commodified the transaction as if the participant's life story had been purchased. Impoverished participants who were discredited by the exchange subverted the interview process to reclaim their dignity.

To counter feelings of domination and subordination produced through coerced [i.e., paid-for] participation, we suggest that the acts of resistance and subversive tactics are strategies through which participants might retain control over their narratives and identity, despite relinquishing this control by selling their commodified narrative. (Cook & Nunkoosing, 2008, p. 422)

Such occurrences mirror the empirical investigation of Flicker (2004) and the theoretical work of Bolle and Otto (2010), again building on Titmuss's classic investigation, who claim that intrinsic motivation (such as is assumed to motivate interview participation) is not acknowledged if payment is offered. Following the experimental work of Gneezy and Rustichini (2000) in their article titled "Pay Enough or Don't Pay at All," Bolle and Otto (2010) claim that "paying a low amount leads to worse results than paying nothing, and paying a high amount leads to better results than paying a low amount" (p. 10). Similarly, VanderWalde (2005) claims that paying too little can be as unethical as paying too much, particularly if the payment takes advantage of participants' relative poverty by getting them to accept a price that is lower than what is a fair reimbursement, for example, for their life story. Such worse results in the context of interview participation may well include the resistance and subversive tactics outlined above.

Rather than ignoring instances of reluctance and resistance by removing such "unsuccessful" interviews from data analysis, I suggest that these micro-interactional sites of resistance and subversion offer crucial insight into the processes of stigmatization experienced by participants. At such points, the rich point analytic techniques of Michael Agar (1999) or the analysis of meaning horizons offered by Phil Carspecken (1996) may be useful mechanisms through which the larger normative social processes that operate to create and sustain these stigmas can be drawn out.

The issues presented above illustrate some of the considerations that must be made when working with vulnerable and marginalized groups, as they highlight the inescapable nature of the power dynamics within the interview encounter. As in all qualitative research, however, while the issues outlined above offer insight into some of the processes at play, careful consideration is required by researchers to distill the nature of their research, their role in the process of data generation, and the characteristics of both the participant and the interviewer with respect to stigma management.

◆ Conclusions

In this chapter, I have sought to examine the nature of stigma as it applies to the interview encounter. In doing so, I have explored the interactions between researchers and participants, drawing on the work of previous researchers to illustrate key points at which the discreditable status of participants may become known through the interview process.

While there is a considerable amount of interview-based research conducted with vulnerable participants that has sought to illustrate the nature of participants' stigma, far less work has been done that focuses the critical gaze on the research process itself to understand the stigmatizing processes inherent in contemporary qualitative research. This chapter has sought to begin this discussion, although it in no way offers a "solution" to these deeply institutional and socially entrenched practices. Work is continually needed to throw light on the often problematic nature of taken-for-granted research practices such as the qualitative interview, as has been undertaken in this *Handbook*. This work is required to inform more sensitive and reflexive ethical review processes at an institutional level and provide a richer account of qualitative interview research in research training.

◆ References

Ackerman, T. F. (1989). An ethical framework for the practice of paying research subjects. *IRB: Ethics & Human Research, 11*(4), 1–4.

Adler, P., & Adler, P. (2002). The reluctant respondent. In J. F. Gubrium & J. A. Holstein (Eds.), *Handbook of interview research* (pp. 515–535). Thousand Oaks, CA: Sage.

Agar, M. (1999). How to ask for a study in qualitatisch. *Qualitative Health Research, 9*(5), 684–698.

Balfe, M., Brugha, R., O'Connell, E., McGee, H., O'Donovan, D., & Vaughan, D. (2010). Why don't young women go for Chlamydia testing? A qualitative study employing Goffman's stigma framework. *Health, Risk & Society, 12*(2), 131–148.

Bolle, F., & Otto, P. E. (2010). A price is a signal: On intrinsic motivation, crowding-out, and crowding-in. *Kyklos, 63*(1), 9–22.

Bondi, L. (2003). Empathy and identification: Conceptual resources for feminist fieldwork. *ACME: An International E-Journal for Critical Geographies, 2*(1), 64–76.

Bradley, M. S. (2007). Girlfriends, wives, and strippers: Managing stigma in exotic dancer romantic relationships. *Deviant Behavior, 28*(4), 379–406.

Briggs, C. L. (2001). Interviewing, power/knowledge and social inequality. In J. F. Gubrium & J. A. Holstein (Eds.), *Interviewing, power/knowledge, and social inequality* (pp. 911–922). Thousand Oaks, CA: Sage.

Brody, H. (2005). The welcome reassessment of research ethics: Is "undue inducement" suspect? *American Journal of Bioethics, 5*(5), 15–16.

Buseh, A. G., & Stevens, P. E. (2007). Constrained but not determined by stigma: Resistance by African American women living with HIV. *Women & Health, 44*(3), 1–18.

Carspecken, P. F. (1996). *Critical ethnography in educational research.* New York, NY: Routledge.

Carter, S. M., Jordens, C. F. C., McGrath, C., & Little, M. (2008). You have to make something of all that rubbish, do you? An empirical investigation of the social process of qualitative research. *Qualitative Health Research, 18*(9), 1264–1276.

Cicourel, A. V. (1982). Interviews, surveys, and the problem of ecological validity. *The American Sociologist, 17*(1), 11–20.

Cook, K. (2009). Not measuring up: Low-income women on welfare. In A. Taket, B. R. Crisp, A. Nevill, G. Lamaro, M. Graham, & S. Barter-Godfrey (Eds.), *Theorising social exclusion* (pp. 55–67). Oxfordshire, England: Routledge.

Cook, K., & Nunkoosing, K. (2008). Maintaining dignity and managing stigma in the interview encounter: The challenge of paid-for participation. *Qualitative Health Research, 18*(3), 418–427.

Dickson-Swift, V., James, E. L., Kippen, S., & Liamputtong, P. (2006). Blurring boundaries in qualitative health research on sensitive topics. *Qualitative Health Research, 16*(6), 853–871.

Emanual, E. J. (2005). Undue inducement: Nonsense on stilts? *American Journal of Bioethics, 5*(5), 9–13.

Enosh, G., Ben-Ari, A., & Buchbinder, E. (2008). Sense of differentness in the construction of knowledge. *Qualitative Inquiry, 14*(3), 450–465.

Flicker, S. (2004). "Ask me no secrets, I'll tell you no lies": What happens when a respondent's story makes no sense. *Qualitative Report, 5*(3), 528–537.

Foucault, M. (1980). Two lectures (C. Gordon, Trans.). In C. Gordon (Ed.), *Power/knowledge: Selected interviews and other writings 1972–1977* (pp. 78–108). Brighton, England: Harvester.

Fry, C. L., Ritter, A., Baldwin, S., Bowen, K. J., Gardiner, P., Holt, T., . . . Johnston, J. (2005). Paying research participants: A study of current practices in Australia. *Journal of Medical Ethics, 31*(9), 542–547.

Gneezy, U., & Rustichini, A. (2000). Pay enough or don't pay at all. *Quarterly Journal of Economics, 115*, 791–810.

Goffman, E. (1959). *The presentation of self in everyday life.* London, England: Allen Lane.

Goffman, E. (1961). *Encounters: Ten studies in the sociology of interaction.* Indianapolis, IN: Bobbs-Merrill.

Goffman, E. (1963). *Stigma: Notes on the management of spoiled identity.* Middlesex, UK: Penguin Books.

Goffman, E. (1981). *Forms of talk.* Oxford, UK: Basil Blackwell.

Gramsci, A. (1971). *Selections from the prison notebooks* (Q. Hoare & G. Nowell-Smith, Trans. & Eds.). London, England: Lawrence & Wishart.

Green, G. (2009). *The end of stigma? Changes in the social experience of long-term illness.* Oxfordshire, England: Routledge.

Guillemin, M., & Gillam, L. (2004). Ethics, reflexivity, and "ethically important moments" in research. *Qualitative Inquiry, 10*(2), 261–280.

Hagan, T. (1986). Interviewing the downtrodden. In P. D. Ashworth, A. Giorgi, & A. J. J. de Koning (Eds.), *Qualitative research in psychology* (pp. 332–360). Pittsburgh, PA: Duquesne University Press.

Huby, G. (1997). Interpreting silence, documenting experience: An anthropological approach to the study of health service users' experince with HIV/AIDS care in Lothian, Scotland. *Social Science & Medicine, 44*(8), 1149–1160.

Karim, F., Chowdhury, A. M. R., Islam, A., & Weiss, M. G. (2007). Stigma, gender, and their impact on patients with tuberculosis in rural Bangladesh. *Anthropology & Medicine, 14*(2), 139–151.

Kusenbach, M. (2009). Salvaging decency: Mobile home residents' strategies of managing the stigma of "trailer" living. *Qualitative Sociology, 32*(4), 399–428.

Kvale, S. (2005). The dominance of dialogical interview research. *Implus, 1,* 5–13.

Kvale, S. (2006). The dominance through interviews and dialogues. *Qualitative Inquiry, 12*(2), 480–500.

Kvale, S., & Brinkmann, S. (2009). *Interviews: Learning the craft of qualitative research interviewing* (2nd ed.). Los Angeles, CA: Sage.

Lazarsfeld, P. (1935). The art of asking why: Three principles underlying the formulation of questionnaires. *National Marketing Review, 1*(1), 26–38.

Liamputtong, P. (2007). *Researching the vulnerable: A guide to sensitive research methods.* Thousand Oaks, CA: Sage.

Link, B. G., & Phelan, J. C. (2001). Conceptualizing stigma. *Annual Review of Sociology, 27,* 363–385.

Macklin, R. (1989). The paradoxical case of payment as benefit to research subjects. *IRB: Ethics & Human Research, 11*(6), 1–3.

McKeganey, N. (2001). To pay or not to pay: Respondents' motivation for participating in research. *Addiction, 96*(9), 1237–1238.

Mishler, E. G. (1986). *Research interviewing: Context and narrative.* Cambridge, MA: Harvard University Press.

Mkandawire-Valhmu, L., Rice, E., & Bathum, M. E. (2009). Promoting an egalitarian approach to research with vulnerable populations of women. *Journal of Advanced Nursing, 65*(8), 1725–1734.

Nunkoosing, K. (2005). The problems with interviews. *Qualitative Health Research, 15*(5), 698–706.

Phelan, J. E., & Basow, S. A. (2007). College students' attitudes toward mental illness: An examination of the stigma process. *Journal of Applied Social Psychology, 37*(12), 2877–2902.

Polkinghorne, D. E. (2007). Validity issues in narrative research. *Qualitative Inquiry, 13*(4), 471–486.

Reutter, L. I., Stewart, M. J., Veenstra, G., Love, R., Raphael, D., & Makwarimba, E. (2009). "Who do they think we are, anyway?" Perceptions of and responses to poverty stigma. *Qualitative Health Research, 19*(3), 297–311.

Riesman, D., & Benney, M. (1956). The sociology of the interview. *The Midwest Sociologist, 18*(1), 3–15.

Ritter, A. J., Fry, C. L., & Swan, A. (2003). The ethics of reimbursing injecting drug users for public health research interviews: What price are we prepared to pay? *International Journal of Drug Policy, 14*(1), 1–3.

Sartorius, N. (2006). Lessons from a 10-year global programme against stigma and discrimination because of an illness. *Psychology Health and Medicine, 11*(3), 383–388.

Scambler, G. (2007). Sex work stigma: Opportunist migrants in London. *Sociology, 41*(6), 1079–1096.

Scheurich, J. J. (1997). A postmodernist critique of research interviewing. In J. J. Scheurich (Ed.), *Research method in the postmodern* (pp. 61–79). London, England: Falmer Press.

Shields, R. (1996). Meeting or mis-meeting? The dialogical challenges to Verstehen. *British Journal of Sociology, 47*(2), 275–294.

Simi, P., & Futrell, R. (2009). Negotiating white power activist stigma. *Social Problems, 56*(1), 89–110.

Stones, M., & McMillan, J. (2010). Payment for participation in research: A pursuit for the poor? *Journal of Medical Ethics, 36*(1), 34–36.

Taket, A., Foster, N., & Cook, K. (2009). Understanding processes of social exclusion: Silence, silencing and shame. In A. Taket, B. R. Crisp, A. Nevill, G. Lamaro, M. Graham, & S. Barter-Godfrey (Eds.), *Theorising social exclusion* (pp. 173–183). Oxfordshire, England: Routledge.

Tanggaard, L. (2007). The research interview as discourses crossing swords: The researcher and apprentice on crossing roads. *Qualitative Inquiry, 13*(1), 160–176.

Taub, D. E., McLorg, P. A., & Fanflik, P. L. (2004). Stigma management strategies among women with physical disabilities: Contrasting approaches of downplaying or claiming a disability status. *Deviant Behavior, 25*(2), 169–190.

Tindal, C., Cook, K., & Foster, N. (2010). Applying a model of stigma to injecting drug users in Australia. *Australian Journal of Primary Health, 16*(2), 119–125.

Titmuss, R. (1970). *The gift relationship: From human blood to social policy*. London, England: Allen & Unwin.

VanderWalde, A. (2005). Undue inducement: The only objection to payment? *American Journal of Bioethics, 5*(5), 25–27.

Ware, N. C., Wyatt, M. A., & Tugenberg, T. (2006). Social relationships, stigma and adherence to antiretroviral therapy for HIV/AIDS. *AIDS Care: Psychological and Socio-medical Aspects of AIDS/HIV, 18*(8), 904–910.

Watson, C. (2009). The "impossible vanity": Uses and abuses of empathy in qualitative inquiry. *Qualitative Research, 9*(1), 105–117.

Winnick, T. A., & Bodkin, M. (2008). Anticipated stigma and stigma management among those to be labeled "ex-con." *Deviant Behavior, 29*(4), 295–333.

Part V

ANALYTIC STRATEGIES

24

QUALITATIVE INTERVIEWING AND GROUNDED THEORY ANALYSIS

◆ Kathy Charmaz and Linda Liska Belgrave

Researchers across disciplines and professions adopt grounded theory more frequently than any other method of analyzing qualitative data (Bryant & Charmaz, 2007b; Morse, 2009; Yamazaki et al., 2009), and consistent with other forms of qualitative inquiry, they use interviewing more frequently to collect data than any other form of data collection. Interviewing for a grounded theory study both resembles and differs from interviewing for thematic qualitative inquiry. We will point out the main points of divergence. Grounded theory is primarily a method of data analysis, with profound implications for collecting data that have largely remained unaddressed (but see Charmaz, 2009b; Charmaz & Bryant, 2011). In this chapter, we show how grounded theory methods shape qualitative interviewing and how they guide the analysis of interview data.

What is grounded theory? The term *grounded theory* refers to a systematic method for constructing a theoretical analysis from data, with explicit analytic strategies and implicit guidelines for data collection. In addition, the term refers to the *products* of the method, the completed theoretical analysis. We emphasize the flexible strategies that constitute this method and aid the researcher to (a) study social and social psychological processes, (b) direct data collection, (c) manage data analysis, and (d) develop and test an abstract theoretical framework that explains the studied process. These methods are guides for grappling with constructing this abstract analysis rather than an inflexible series of procedures. As Janice Morse (2009) argues, grounded theory cannot be standardized.

Grounded theory is an inductive, comparative, iterative, and interactive method (Charmaz, 2006). Researchers subject their inductive data to rigorous comparative analysis that successively moves from studying concrete realities to rendering a conceptual understanding from these data. Successive data collection and analysis each inform and focus the other as the iterative process proceeds.

The logic of grounded theory and enactment of its strategies keep researchers interacting with their data and nascent analyses.

The founders of grounded theory, Barney G. Glaser and Anselm L. Strauss (1967), aimed to develop middle-range theories through successive analysis of qualitative data that generated abstract theoretical categories, demonstrated relations among these categories, and specified the conditions under which theoretical categories and relationships emerge, change, or are maintained. Glaser and Strauss constructed a method for studying fluid, emergent processes. Since 1967, grounded theory has become both a general method (Charmaz, 2005, 2010; Corbin & Strauss, 2008; Strauss & Corbin, 1994) and a generalized method (Charmaz, 2009c, 2010). It is a general method because versions of its strategies have become part of the common lexicon of qualitative inquiry and stretch across disciplines and professions. It is a generalized method because qualitative researchers have adopted its strategies, but in diluted ways. What strategies do grounded theorists use? The strategy of simultaneous data collection and analysis has been a hallmark of grounded theory that has permeated qualitative inquiry. Ironically, numerous researchers who claim to use grounded theory state that they conduct their interviews first and analyze them later. This strategy weakens the analysis because it curtails the iterative, comparative process that fundamentally defines grounded theory.

Grounded theorists cannot identify the most significant processes beforehand, so we start with an area of interest and form preliminary interviewing questions to explore it. We learn about research participants' concerns and experiences and then successively develop our interview guides from the data and our emerging analysis of these data. Grounded theory methods can keep us close to our gathered data and compel us to question our assumptions and set aside our presuppositions to see past them. These methods give us expeditious tools for obtaining additional focused data that inform, extend, and refine our emerging analytic categories. We may go back and forth between data collection and analysis several times during a research project. Thus, our successively focused interviews strengthen the fit between data and analysis. The power of grounded theory lies in its integration of data collection and increasingly more abstract levels of analysis.

In-depth qualitative interviewing fits grounded theory methods particularly well. In-depth interviewing provides an open-ended, detailed exploration of an aspect of life in which the interviewee has substantial experience and, often, considerable insight. Both in-depth interviewing and grounded theory are emergent methods (Charmaz, 2008b) that combine flexibility and control. An interviewer assumes more direct control over the construction of data than do practitioners of most other methods such as ethnography or textual analysis. The interviewer engages the interviewee in a "directed conversation" (Lofland & Lofland, 1995), although the interviewee's concerns and comments shape this direction. As Witz (2006) advocates, many researchers can bring interviewees explicitly into the project as allies. Grounded theory methods require that researchers take control of their data collection and analysis, and in turn these methods give researchers more analytic control over their material.

Throughout the chapter, we draw on earlier explications of the method and grounded theory studies, including our own. In the past, most discussions of grounded theory have taken data collection practices for granted, giving them scant attention. Yet obtaining rich interview data is crucial for developing robust theories. Thus, we outline the logic of grounded theory and show how to obtain and use rich data with which to construct viable grounded theories. We also discuss the potential of focus group interviews in grounded theory studies and introduce ways of integrating grounded theory work in mixed-methods research.

◆ Variations of Grounded Theory

Since 1967, originators and students of grounded theory have developed different variants of the method but share some basic strategies. All variants include (a) conducting simultaneous data collection and analysis; (b) engaging in early data analysis of emergent ideas; (c) using comparative methods throughout the inquiry; (d) analyzing basic social processes within the data; (e) constructing tentative inductive abstract categories that explain and synthesize these processes; (f) sampling to expand, refine, and check these tentative categories; and (g) integrating robust categories into a theoretical framework that specifies relationships between categories and explicates the conditions under which the categories develop, their properties, and their consequences as well as those of the studied process(es) of which these categories are a part (see Charmaz, 1990, 1995, 2006, 2010; Glaser, 1978, 1992; Glaser & Strauss, 1967; Strauss, 1987, 1995).

The variants take three main forms: (1) constructivist, (2) objectivist, and (3) postpositivist grounded theory (Charmaz, 2000, 2009c). The constructivist approach places priority on the studied phenomenon and sees both data and analysis as created from shared experiences and relationships with participants (see Bryant, 2002, 2003; Bryant & Charmaz, 2007a, 2007b; Charmaz, 1990, 2000, 2006, 2007, 2009c; Clarke, 2003, 2005, 2006, 2009; Clarke & Friese, 2007; Mills, Bonner, & Francis, 2006; Witz, 2006). In this view, any method is always a means rather than an end in itself. Methods do not ensure knowing; they may only provide more or less useful tools for learning. Constructivists study how participants construct meanings and actions from as close to the inside of the experience as possible. In this perspective, we view data analyses as constructions that not only locate our data in time, place, culture, and context but also reflect our social, epistemological, and research locations. Thus, our standpoints, starting points, and end points influence our data analyses. Meanings of our data do not inhere entirely within or solely emerge from the data.

Objectivist grounded theory, in contrast, assumes the construction of data and the relationship of the viewer to the viewed as unproblematic. In this approach, grounded theorists are neutral analysts of a knowable external world.[1] Here, researchers aim to approach the data uncontaminated by preconceived notions and theories. Meaning inheres in the data, and the grounded theorist discovers it (see, e.g., Glaser, 1978; Glaser & Strauss, 1967; Strauss & Corbin, 1990).

Postpositivist approaches see the purpose of research as conceptualizing empirical findings. These grounded theorists aim to use qualitative data for theory construction as the means of generating new knowledge. They assume that employing analytic methods and procedures aids this quest. Postpositivist approaches rely on scientific method and aim for scientific credibility but acknowledge that research

participants may have varied ways of defining their situations. Like most researchers, Corbin (2008) had earlier viewed her previous contributions to grounded theory as consistent with earlier statements (Glaser, 1978; Glaser & Strauss, 1967; Strauss, 1987) of this method and with trends in qualitative inquiry. The postmodern critique, however, challenged her assumptions and subsequently altered the methodological stance she took in the third edition of *Basics of Qualitative Research* (Corbin & Strauss, 2008).

Nonetheless, the influence of Strauss and Corbin's (1990, 1998) editions extended their postpositivist approach across fields and continues to influence diverse researchers. In these books, Strauss and Corbin (1990, 1998) made objectivist assumptions about inquiry, emphasized description, offered new procedures to apply to the data rather than making methodological decisions indicated by the emergent analysis, and appeared rigid and rule bound (see also Atkinson, Coffey, & Delamont, 2003). As such, their version of grounded theory bore faint resemblance to Glaser's (1978; Glaser & Strauss, 1967) earlier statements or with the emergent, open-ended interpretive inquiry inherent in Strauss's early studies (Charmaz, 2007, 2009a; Strauss, 1961, 1959/1969). Corbin (2008, 2009) provides excellent discussions of the epistemological and practical tensions involved in conducting research in the 1980s and 1990s and of how she has rethought her position, which we see as closer to constructivist grounded theory.

Our approach to grounded theory builds on a symbolic interactionist theoretical perspective with constructivist methods (Charmaz, 1990, 2000, 2006, 2007, 2008a, 2008b). We make the following assumptions: (a) multiple realities exist, (b) data reflect researchers' and research participants' mutual constructions, and (c) the researcher enters, however incompletely, the participant's world and is affected by it. This approach explicitly provides an *interpretive* portrayal of the studied world, not an exact picture of it (Charmaz, 2000, 2007, 2009c). The interviewer aims to learn participants' implicit meanings of their experience to build a conceptual analysis of them. A constructivist approach takes implicit meanings, experiential views, and grounded theory analyses as constructions of reality. Constructivist

---

[1]For a more complete statement of contrasts distinguishing the variants of grounded theory, see Charmaz (2000, 2006, 2007, 2009c).

grounded theory complements symbolic interactionism because both emphasize studying how action and meaning are constructed.

◆ Grounded Theory Interviewing

FORMING GROUNDED THEORY INTERVIEW QUESTIONS

Interview data are useful for grounded theory studies that address organizations, social worlds, discourses, communications, and policy questions as well as individual experience. Individual and, increasingly, focus group interviewing are major sources of useful data for researchers who study people who experience disrupted lives, grief, illness, marital dissolution, or financial crises but do not have sustained contact with other people who face similar troubles; thus, in-depth interviewing is a particularly useful form of generating data (Charmaz, 1991, 2007).

Grounded theory objectives of studying processes and of developing theoretical analyses raise potential interviewing problems. One hazard is to define the collective analytic story at the expense of the participant's story. Dey (1999) has criticized Glaser and Strauss for advocating a "smash and grab" (p. 119) data collection strategy that exploits research participants. Sharing the interview "space," especially ceding control of an interview to a participant, can be difficult. Both interviewers and participants come to the interview with agendas and work together but with differential power (Gubrium & Koro-Ljungberg, 2005). Grounded theorists need to balance hearing the participant's story in its fullness with probing for the analytic properties and implications of major processes, particularly if they combine narrative methods and grounded theory strategies. Elisabeth Scheibelhofer (2008), for example, aimed to learn about migrants' constructions of their experiences from Austrians who had moved to New York City. She realized early in her data collection that viewing her interviewees as migrants was her presupposition, not theirs. Subsequently, Scheibelhofer changed her interviewing strategy and began her interviews with statements such as the following:

Could you please tell me everything that is involved in your coming to New York and how your life went on since then? I will listen and make some notes and I will not interrupt you until you have finished. Please take as much time as you feel necessary and tell me all the details you remember that, in your opinion, are connected to your living in New York. (p. 407)

After hearing their stories, Scheibelhofer (2008) asked open-ended questions about topics that these interviewees had brought up but had not detailed. She found that they often offered substantial accounts in response. Maines (2001) makes a similar point when comparing autobiographical accounts with interviews of the same people: The interviews contained richer and more detailed stories. An interested interviewer can engage interviewees in conversations that reveal their narrative constructions rather than gloss over them.

Grounded theory interviewers start with the participant's story and fill it out by attempting to locate it within a basic social process, which may be implicit. This fundamental question drives a grounded theory study: "What is happening here?" (Glaser, 1978). Thus, the "happening" is the experience or central problem addressed in the research. Constructivist grounded theorists attend to the construction of the interview, the construction of the research participant's story, and silences, as well as the explicit content of the interview (Charmaz, 2009d).

Interviewing has come under sharp criticism for generating contrived data rather than representing observed data in natural settings (see, e.g., Silverman, 2007; Potter & Hepburn's chapter "Eight Challenges for Interview Researchers," this volume). In-depth interviews are, of course, performed retrospective accounts in response to open-ended questions. Through constructing a performance, interviewees present themselves to their respective interviewers and, however silently, make and negotiate identity claims. Social scientists sometimes forget that their interviewees may also be silently monitoring the "directed conversation" and redirecting it to suit their own purposes (Charmaz, 2009b; Charmaz & Bryant, 2011). Interviewees' accounts explain and justify their behavior as well as report past events from the vantage point of the present, as George Herbert Mead (1932) would point out. Yet interviews can also give research participants a space and time to reflect on these events anew and to clarify meanings and actions—while providing rich data that spark analytic insights (Charmaz, 2011).

Chapter 24. Qualitative Interviewing and Grounded Theory Analysis ◆ 351

Like any interviewer, grounded theorists try to elicit their interviewees' stories, to the extent that they are willing to share them. We strive to gather as complete accounts as possible and to represent our data and research participants fairly. Nonetheless, grounded theorists attend more to whether their participants' accounts are *theoretically plausible* than whether they have constructed them with unassailable accuracy. From a grounded theory perspective, collecting a substantial amount and depth of data offsets the negative effects of several misleading accounts and thus reduces the likelihood of the researcher making misleading claims or writing a superficial analysis. The iterative process of grounded theory provides one check on limited, misleading, or fabricated accounts; other researchers' further study of the generated theoretical categories provides another. Another major benefit accrues from gathering data that have breadth and depth: The researcher can better define the range and types of variation occurring in his or her data.

Framing questions takes skill and practice.[2] Questions must explore the interviewer's topic and fit the participant's experience. In the following excerpt, Kristine N. Williams (Warren & Williams, 2008) asks an elderly resident a question that breaks two rules of interviewing: (1) do not ask loaded questions that slant the interviewee's response and (2) do not ask for more than one potential response in a question. Nevertheless, the multiple, loaded question may fit residents' experience in this facility. Warren and Williams (2008) state,

Margaret Smith was one of several residents who told the interviewer that they were routinely reprimanded by the Arden Director of Nursing for "dwelling on the past":

KW: During the past four weeks, have you been bothered by emotional problems or feeling anxious, depressed, irritable, or down-hearted and blue?

MS: Well, you can always feel that way when you have to give up your old home and everything else.

KW: Uh huh.

MS: That's normal for me, to wish I still had it.

KW: Yeah, that's true.

MS: That's what I think. [Director of Nursing] doesn't like that very well, but it's normal. You just like things that you had before. (p. 412)

Charmaz provides sample questions below to illustrate how constructivist grounded theorists frame questions to study processes in individual experiences, thoughts, feelings, and actions. Sometimes we study event-centered processes, but other times we pursue more subtle or mundane phenomena that involve less visible processes. A detailed interview guide is not always necessary. The first question may suffice for the whole interview if stories tumble out.

Grounded theory interview questions need to be sufficiently general to cover a wide range of experiences and narrow enough to elicit and explore the participant's specific experience. Probes and follow-up questions concerning participants' responses open up interviews. We devise these probes and follow-ups as we proceed. Charmaz's questions reflect a symbolic interactionist emphasis on learning the participant's subjective meanings and on stressing his or her actions. For a project concerning organizational or social processes, she directs questions to collective practices first and later attends to the individual's participation in and views of those practices.

The questions below are merely examples to consider. Charmaz has never asked all of them and often does not get beyond the initial set of questions in one session. She seldom takes an interview guide with her to the interview, as she prefers to keep the interview informal and conversational. Belgrave, in contrast, does bring one for jotting brief notes and keeping track of what she has and has not covered.

Interviewees may tell stories during the interview that they never dreamt of revealing. Their comfort level should have higher priority than obtaining juicy data. Thus, ending questions should elicit positive responses to bring the interview to closure at a normal conversational level. No interview should end abruptly after the researcher has asked the most searching questions or while the participant appears distressed. The following abbreviated examples of interview questions about a significant life change

---

[2]For analyses of the interview, see Foster-Fishman, Nowell, Deacon, Nievar, and McCann (2005), Gubrium and Koro-Ljungberg (2005), Gudmundsdottir (1996), Raz (2005), and Tanggaard (2009); for wording questions, see Ezzy (2010).

illustrate the above points. An actual interview guide would have far more intermediate questions and, depending on the topic, more initial or ending questions.[3]

EXAMPLES OF GROUNDED THEORY INTERVIEW QUESTIONS

Initial Open-Ended Questions

1. Tell me about what happened [or how you came to _____].

2. When, if at all, did you first experience _____ [or notice _____]?

3. [If so,] what was it like? What did you think then? How did you happen to _____? Who, if anyone, influenced your actions? Could you tell me about how he/she or they influenced you?

4. If you recall, could you describe what was going on in your life then? How would you describe how you viewed _____ before _____ happened? How, if at all, has your view of _____ changed?

5. How would you describe the person you were then?

Intermediate Questions

1. Could you tell me about your thoughts and feelings when you learned about _____. Who, if anyone, was involved? In which ways were they involved?

2. How, if at all, have your thoughts and feelings about _____ changed since _____?

3. Tell me about how you learned to handle _____.

4. Could you describe a typical day for you when you are _____? (Probe for different times.) Now tell me about a typical day when you are _____.

5. Would you tell me how you would describe the person you are now? What do you think most contributed to this change [or continuity]?

Ending Questions

1. Could you describe the most important lessons you learned about _____ through experiencing _____?

2. Tell me about how your views [and/or actions depending on topic and preceding responses] may have changed since you have _____.

3. How have you grown as a person since _____? Tell me about your strengths that you discovered or developed through _____. [If appropriate] What do you most value about yourself now? What do others most value in you?

4. After reflecting on your experiences with _____ is there something else you would like to add?

5. Is there anything you would like to ask me?

These questions overlap to allow the interviewer to return to an earlier thread in order to gain more information, or to winnow unnecessary or potentially uncomfortable questions. Note that Question 4 in the "Ending Questions" asks about "something" rather than the more common "anything." Conversational analysts have learned that making this minor change elicits more details rather than closing the conversation.[4] Taking notes on key points during the interview helps as long as it does not distract either interviewer or participant. Notes remind the interviewer to return to earlier points and suggest how he or she might frame follow-up questions.

Grounded theory researchers must guard against forcing the data into preconceived categories (Glaser, 1978). Interviewing, more than most other forms of qualitative data collection, challenges researchers to ask significant questions without forcing responses. We must pay attention to language, meaning, and participants' lives; otherwise, we can easily allow our notions to overshadow those of our participants (Gubrium & Koro-Ljungberg, 2005). Constructivist grounded theorists attempt to be alert to their participants' language and to ask questions about it. In the following initial interview, Charmaz uses intonation, slows her pacing, repeats

---

[3]For a more complete list, see the first edition of this handbook (Charmaz, 2002).

[4]Personal communication, David Silverman, June 28, 2008.

key points, and gently turns the interviewee's words into open-ended questions.

K: You told me that you're 68 now.

J: I'm 68 now. I was an extremely healthy person up until the day I guess, the night when I was 60 years old.

K: You were 60.

J: It happened very dramatically.

K: Dramatically?

J: Almost overnight, looking back at it with hindsight which is always . . . , looking back on it, given the fact that I most likely have Lyme disease and that is another subject, and since I've been bitten by ticks all my, you know, for the last 20 years, because of where we live in rural areas, it's not known if I had contracted the illness but [it] had stayed silent until all of a sudden, bang—it does happen with Lyme disease and probably a lot of other things because everybody carries a lot of bacteria but not everybody gets sick.

Like other skilled interviewers, grounded theorists must remain active in the interview and must remain alert for interesting leads (for suggestions, see Holstein & Gubrium, 1995; Kvale & Brinkmann, 2009; Rubin & Rubin, 2005; Seidman, 2006; Witz, 2006). Sound interview strategies help the researcher go beyond commonsense tales and subsequent obvious categories that add nothing new.

When we ask people to go beneath the surface and reveal impolite or unacceptable views or actions, we should make it easy for them to do so. In Belgrave's ongoing study of elders' views of well-being, she wanted to get beyond the "expected" values about topics such as family and health and tap more mundane, day-to-day values. She approached these values by interspersing pointed questions throughout the interview (see below), using Rubin and Rubin's (2005) advice to use long, wordy questions to get long answers. Reasoning that people express values in what they do as well as what they claim to value, she began her interviews by asking participants to tell how they spend their time; moved on to the pleasures and pains of life in an intermediate question, asking for both "big" and "little" things; and only came to values explicitly in her ending questions (below).

Included in Intermediate Questions

Life typically has some good and some bad, some things that bring us pleasure, or even joy, and some things we don't like or make us miserable. Some of these are big things, while some are more ordinary, day to day kinds of things. We're interested in both.

a. First, let's talk about the good things.

b. What about the bad things?

What are some of the things that are important to you?

Probe here for: family, health, money, friendship, religion, and commitment/obligation.

Included in Ending Questions

What makes a "good" old age good?

In response to the intermediate question above, one participant, Abby Smith, talked of furniture shopping, a prospect directly tied to resisting and accepting her mortality. Here is an excerpt.

Oh, God, I think, "If I buy this, maybe it'll be the last ones I'll ever buy." I don't think I like that idea. [So you're talking about replacing them, but you're not doing it?] I'm not doing it. And I ought to be doing it, because at one time I would have done it. Happily! You know, scoured every sofa in Miami-Dade. But I don't think I'm being, ah, pessimistic about the future. It's just, "Why? What do I need another sofa for? Mine are clean."

Carmen Fernandez also spoke to accepting mortality, but in a more philosophical, less personal fashion, in response to the ending question above (and probes):

Well, the "good" in good aging is when you have an interior life that is rich in understanding . . . You accept your old age. [And what are some of those internal things that a person should have to be able to accept old age?] Well, firstly, conformity. You have to know that everything is born and then dies, because sometimes old people do not accept that they are old and are afraid of death. And I think that death is nothing but a transition in one's life.

The interviewer went on to probe what "conformity" meant to Carmen. Thus, we use multiple questions to circle and home in on relevant issues; various questions resonate with different participants.

Grounded theorists adopt this basic rule: *Study your data*. However, to do it well, grounded theory interviewers must invoke another rule first: *Study your interview questions!* In other words, grounded theorists combine data analysis with data collection by simultaneously attending to the questions they ask and the answers they receive. In this sense, grounded theory has much in common with ethnographic methods, in which researchers adapt their data collection techniques to the nuances of the emerging observation. For example, in his ethnographic studies of children's reasoning about moral rules and bystander behavior, Robert Thornberg (2010b) developed a grounded theory of the moral frames that schoolchildren invoke. Thornberg's acquaintance with the children permitted his direct questions. As shown in the following excerpt, he routinely constructed his questions in the field in direct relation to his emerging observations and analytic categories:

> After observing a bystander situation in which a student was lying on the classroom floor with a flushed face expressing pain and crying very quietly, I talked to some of his classmates who had observed him:
>
> RT: How come everyone just passed him by and went to their places?
>
> Sandra Because that's what we usually do. We go to our places, and it's Margot [the teacher] who goes over to him and asks what has happened. (p. 593)

FOCUS GROUP INTERVIEWING IN GROUNDED THEORY

Researchers increasingly use focus group interviews as a tool for grounded theory in fields ranging from the social sciences to health care disciplines, informatics, and more, sometimes in stand-alone work and sometimes in combination with individual interviews (e.g., Belgrave & Smith, 1995; Lambert & Loiselle, 2008; Moore, 2006) and/or participant observation (Belgrave, Allen-Kelsey, Smith, & Flores, 2004). Focus group interviews provide an efficient means for data collection, an important feature when researchers face limited resources for qualitative work (Morgan, 2002). This very efficiency, however, might be an impediment to their use for grounded theory.

When researchers use focus group interviews as the sole method for data collection for grounded theory studies, they often relegate grounded theory methods only to data analysis. For instance, Ahmad, Hudak, Bercovitz, Hollenberg, and Levinson (2006) conducted six focus group interviews with family practitioners and used grounded theory analysis techniques to examine physicians' perceptions of patients who come to them with Internet-based health information. Although they outline their analytic choices, Ahmad et al. do not indicate that they engaged in successive analysis that influenced their subsequent interviewing. In an innovative approach, Fox, Rumsey, and Morris (2007) used online focus groups with young people to tap their experiences of chronic skin conditions. Their approach might be especially useful for other vulnerable populations because, as Madriz (1998) and Morgan (2002) demonstrate, focus groups are valuable for collecting data from minority group members or other groups, especially when a significant gap in social status exists between researchers and participants. For some, it is easier to open up in a group interview with peers than one-on-one with a person of higher status, which can be intimidating.

The practice of combining focus group interviews with grounded theory analysis, without integrating the interviewing and analytic processes, is well illustrated in large studies that are conducted across multiple research sites. For example, Beard, Fetterman, Wu, and Bryant (2009) conducted 14 focus groups to interview 85 persons (Alzheimer's disease sufferers and their caregivers) across four sites, using a single interview guide for all focus groups. The authors explain that they used "the constant comparative method and coding paradigm of grounded theory" (p. S42). Specifically, they describe how they began with more than 450 pages of transcribed interviews. They developed a master codebook at one center, while each site collected themes into condensed codebooks. They used this procedure as preparatory to line-by-line, open coding of all data by a single author. Beard et al. consolidated their codes into "core variables," which they found in more than 60% of the interviews. Next, investigators at all sites reviewed these variables to ensure consensus. They used ATLAS.ti to "validate the reliability of those themes identified manually" (i.e., before moving to the computer-assisted phase of analysis; p. S42). Like many researchers, Beard et al. adopted some grounded theory strategies, although the extent to which they followed the analysis techniques in their cited sources, Glaser and Strauss (1967) and Strauss and Corbin (1990), remains unclear. Beard et al.'s findings increase our understanding of aging, although they might have generated further ideas had they used an iterative, emergent approach.

Combinations of individual and focus group interviews have also proven to be fertile ground for developing grounded theories. For example, Moore (2006) integrated individual interviews and focus groups with biographical questionnaires to examine the career trajectories of African American men who entered the field of engineering, and he discovered themes that shaped these men's career trajectories. Similarly, Furness, Garrud, Faulder, and Swift (2006) used focus groups and interviews with 29 facial surgery survivors to develop a grounded theory model of adaptation to the functional and disfigurement challenges that such surgery poses. Taking a somewhat different tack, Lambert and Loiselle (2008) conducted individual and focus group interviews as a form of triangulation in their grounded theory study of cancer information seeking. They concluded that their dual methodological approach yielded an iterative process in which their initial model influenced further data collection and led to a richer conceptualization. They add that the convergence of findings across the two methods generated more confidence in their validity.

Thus, focus groups are valuable for grounded theory if we use them strategically. When researchers rely on focus groups to produce large quantities of data in little time, they might lose sight of the conceptual strength of grounded theory. Moreover, standardized focus group interviews with strictly defined analytic techniques and a concern for documenting evidence may reflect the encroachment of the evidence-based research movement (Denzin, 2009). Such uses are fine for many purposes but not for the development of grounded theory.

◆ Grounded Theory Guidelines for Analyzing Data

CODING DATA

Coding is the pivotal first analytic step that moves the researcher from description toward conceptualizing that description. Coding requires close attention to the data. Nonetheless, the codes reflect the

researcher's interests and perspectives as well as information in the data. Grounded theorists' disciplinary knowledge provides "sensitizing concepts" (Blumer, 1969; van den Hoonaard, 1997) for beginning to code and to develop more refined and precise concepts. In particular, symbolic interactionism provides a rich array of sensitizing concepts such as "identity," "self-concept," "negotiation," and "definition of the situation," although grounded theorists may draw on such concepts implicitly.

Proponents of objectivist grounded theory avoid being influenced by existing theoretical assumptions and thus direct researchers not to study the extant theoretical and research literatures on their topics. Constructivist grounded theorists, in contrast, assume that researchers already possess theoretical and research knowledge concerning their substantive field. Therefore, constructivist grounded theory encourages researchers to be reflexive about the constructions—including preconceptions and assumptions—that inform their inquiry. Objectivist grounded theorists view attending to prior theory as preconceiving and thus shaping the researcher's analysis (see Glaser, 1992, 1998, 2001). Ryan and Bernard (2003) observe that dismissing prior theory risks ignoring the links between data and important research questions. If researchers make their sensitizing concepts more explicit, they can then examine whether and to what extent these concepts cloud or crystallize their interpretations of data. We write down these concepts as we become aware of them—before beginning and throughout a project—to remember that they came before the data. Researchers can use sensitizing concepts if they spark ideas for coding and take the nascent analysis further, or they can drop them if they do not further the analysis. Questions to ask about sensitizing concepts include the following: (a) What, if anything, does the concept illuminate about these data? (b) How, if at all, does the concept specifically apply here? (c) Where does the concept take the analysis? As researchers answer such questions, they make decisions about the boundaries and usefulness of the sensitizing concept. Grounded theorists believe that extant concepts should earn their way into their analyses (Glaser, 1978).

From a broader grounded theory perspective, the first question to ask is "What is happening in the data?" (Glaser, 1978). Constructivist grounded theorists acknowledge that they *define* what is happening in the data. Objectivist grounded theorists assume that they *discover* what is happening in the data. The second question is "What is this data a study of?" (Glaser, 1978, p. 47). This question prompts the researcher to think of both the substantive problem and the theoretical direction of inquiry, either of which may have been anticipated.

On a more fundamental level, coding involves constructing short labels that describe, dissect, and distill the data while preserving their essential properties. Grounded theory coding is at least a two-step coding process: (1) initial or open coding forces the researcher to make beginning analytic decisions about the data and (2) selective or focused coding uses the most

frequent and/or significant initial codes to sort, synthesize, and conceptualize large amounts of data.

The line-by-line coding in Figure 24.1 generated several categories, "suffering as a moral status," "making a moral claim," and "having a devalued moral status" (Charmaz, 1999). Line-by-line coding with gerunds[5] prompts us to (a) study our interviews, (b) preserve processes and discern sequences, (c) illuminate participants' implied and explicit meanings and actions, and (d) make comparisons between data.

Action codes show what is happening and what people are doing. These codes move us away from topics, and if they address structure, they reveal how

Figure 24.1 Initial Coding

Christine Danforth, a 43-year-old receptionist, had returned to work after eight recent hospitalizations and a lengthy convalescence from a flare-up of lupus erythematosus and Sjogren's syndrome (see Charmaz, 1999).

Initial Coding	Interview Statement
Recounting the events
Going against medical advice

Being informed of changed rules
Suffering as a moral status
Accounting for legitimate rest time
Distinguishing between "free" and work time
Receiving an arbitrary order
Making a moral claim
Finding resistance; tacit view of worth
Having a devalued moral status because of physical suffering
Taking action
Learning the facts

Making a case for legitimate rights

Trying to establish entitlement

Meeting resistance

Comparing prerogatives of self and other

Seeing injustice

Making claims for moral rights of personhood | And so I went back to work on March 1st, even though I wasn't supposed to. And then when I got there, they had a long meeting and they said I could no longer rest during the day. The only time I rested was at lunchtime, which was my time, we were closed. And she said, my supervisor, said I couldn't do that anymore, and I said, "It's my time, you can't tell me I can't lay down." And they said, "Well you're not laying down on the couch that's in there, it bothers the rest of the staff." So I went around and I talked to the rest of the staff, and they all said, "No, we didn't say that, it was never even brought up." So I went back and I said, "You know, I just was talking to the rest of the staff, and it seems that nobody has a problem with it but you," and I said, "You aren't even here at lunchtime." And they still put it down that I couldn't do that any longer. And then a couple of months later one of the other staff started laying down at lunch time, and I said, you know, "This isn't fair. She doesn't even have a disability and she's laying down," so I just started doing it. |

Source: Charmaz (2002).

[5]A gerund is the noun form of a verb.

it is constructed through action. Charmaz tried to make action in the data visible by looking at the data as action. Hence, she uses terms such as *going, making, having,* and *seeing.* Using action codes helps us remain specific and not take theoretical leaps of fancy. In addition, action codes help grounded theorists compare data from different people about similar processes, data from the same individuals at different times during the course or trajectory of the studied experience, new data with a provisional category, and a category with other categories (Charmaz, 2006; Glaser, 1978, 1992; Strauss, 1987).

Selective or focused coding means adopting frequently reappearing initial codes to sort and synthesize large amounts of data. Focused codes are more abstract, general, and simultaneously analytically incisive than many initial codes that they subsume (Charmaz, 1983, 1995; Glaser, 1978). The reciprocal relation between coding data and creating analytic categories now becomes apparent: Grounded theorists develop categories from their focused codes. Subsequently, entire analytic frameworks are constructed through developing and integrating the categories. Focused codes cut across multiple interviews and, thus, represent recurrent themes. When deciding which focused codes to adopt, we check the fit between emerging theoretical frameworks and their respective empirical realities. For example, of the initial codes listed above, "suffering as a moral status" received greater analytical attention, as illustrated in the next section. Comparisons of different interviews netted similar statements about learning what it meant to have an impaired and unpredictable body. In contrast to Charmaz, Belgrave codes longer passages, often putting multiple codes on a single passage. Computer packages for qualitative data analysis make it easy to multicode and later pull out all passages marked with a single code, or view all the codes for a single passage simultaneously. Seeing these simultaneous codes helps Belgrave make connections in later stages of analysis.

Although major software programs were designed for grounded theory analysis, none of them can actually "do" grounded theory analysis in the way that quantitative analysis software can "run" a regression or factor analysis (Seale, 2002). Software can relieve much of the tedium of our work but not the hours devoted to reading, coding, rereading, pondering, writing memos, coding again, and more rereading. Whether we use software simply to code and retrieve (Seale, 2002) or use different features at different points in analysis (Bringer, Johnston, & Brackenridge, 2006; Peters & Wester, 2007), we will benefit from considering the meanings, as well as processes, involved in our grounded theory work. Konopásek (2007) argues that we should view our analyses less as mysterious achievements of the mind and more as "material praxis," seeing our results flowing from "practical manipulations with bodies of text" (p. 281). Essentially, her analysis shows that how we manipulate our data in the "virtual environment" of software matters. The software cannot think for us, but it can help us see what we've been thinking. In short, while theory cannot be generated by formula, new technologies have more to offer than we sometimes recognize.

MEMO WRITING

Memo writing links coding to writing the first draft of the analysis; it is the crucial intermediate step that moves the analysis forward. As grounded theorists, we use memos to elaborate the processes defined in our focused codes. Hence, memo writing prompts us to raise our codes to tentative conceptual categories. Through memo writing, grounded theorists take these categories apart analytically and, therefore, "fracture" the data. We define the properties of each category; specify the conditions when the category develops, is maintained, and changes; as well as delineate its consequences and relationships with other categories. As we analyze categories, we ground them in the illustrative interview excerpts included in our memos. Memos may range from loosely constructed "freewrites" about the codes to tightly reasoned analytic statements. They may also include the researcher's experiential struggles in making sense of data (Wengraf, 2001). Memos join data with the researcher's original interpretations of them, and the researcher thus avoids forcing the data into extant theories. Charmaz (2006, 2008a) recommends reworking memos to make them increasingly analytic. With each reworking, the researcher brings the empirical evidence forward as well as analyses of relevant new data and comparative material.

By analyzing data and codes in memos early in the research process, we avoid becoming overwhelmed by stacks of undigested data and remain involved in our research and writing. Memos provide the foundation for building whole sections of papers and chapters. The excerpt below is the first section of an early memo (see Charmaz, 1999, for the published version). Charmaz wrote this memo quickly after comparing data from a series of interviews.

Example of a Grounded Theory Memo: "Suffering as a Moral Status"

Suffering is a profoundly moral status as well as a physical experience. Stories of suffering reflect and redefine that moral status. With suffering comes moral rights and entitlements as well as moral definitions—when suffering is deemed legitimate. Thus, the person can make certain moral claims **and** have certain moral judgments conferred upon him or her.

> Deserving
>
> Dependent
>
> In Need

Suffering can bring a person an elevated moral status. Here, suffering takes on a sacred status. This is a person who has been in sacred places, who has seen and known what ordinary people have not. . . .

Although suffering may first confer an elevated moral status, views change. The moral claims from suffering typically narrow in scope and in power. The circles of significance shrink. Stories of self within these moral claims may entrance and entertain for a while, but grow thin over time—unless someone has considerable influence or power. The circles narrow to most significant others.

The moral claims of suffering may only supersede those of the healthy and whole in crisis and its immediate aftermath. Otherwise, the person is less. WORTH LESS. Two words—now separate may change as illness and aging take their toll. They may end up as "worthless." Christine's statement reflects her struggles at work to maintain her value and voice.

> They had a long meeting and they said I could no longer rest during the day. The only time I rested was at lunch time, which was my time, we were closed. And she said, my supervisor, said I couldn't do that anymore, and I said, "It's my time, you can't tell me I can't lay

down." And they said, "Well you're not laying down on the couch that's in there, it bothers the rest of the staff." . . . And then a couple of months later one of the other staff started laying down at lunch time, and I said, you know, "This isn't fair. She doesn't even have a disability and she's laying down," so I just started doing it.

Christine makes moral claims, not only befitting those of suffering, but of PERSONHOOD. She is a person who has a right to be heard, a right to just and fair treatment in both the medical arena and the workplace.

In the memo above, Charmaz addressed the following concerns: (a) establishing suffering as a moral status, (b) explicating the tacit moral discourse that occurs in suffering, and (c) sketching a moral hierarchy. She had long realized that the term *stigma* did not capture all that she saw in key interviews. Subsequently, she recoded earlier interviews, talked further with select participants about these topics, and then formed questions to ask other participants. In this way, she may tap participants' unstated assumptions that shape her categories. Ultimately, however, categories represent researchers' ways of asking and seeing as well as participants' ways of experiencing and telling.

The memo above differs slightly from the published version (Charmaz, 1999), which includes more empirical examples and discusses a range of social conditions that affect moral status in suffering. It helps to include interview excerpts in the memo in order to compare them with other data and to preserve quotes for later drafts. After exhausting the analytic potential of categories in the memo, researchers can make analytic connections and comparisons between their memos and relevant literatures.

THEORETICAL SAMPLING

Theoretical sampling, that is, sampling to develop the researcher's theory, not to represent a population, endows grounded theory studies with analytic power. Grounded theorists use theoretical sampling primarily for filling out the properties of a tentative category. They may return to the field or seek new cases to develop their theoretical categories. Thus, theoretical sampling builds a pivotal self-correcting step into the analytic process. An incomplete category or one without sufficient evidence shows clear gaps. Obtaining further data to fill these gaps makes the categories more precise, explanatory, and predictive. Charmaz sought further data on an "elevated moral status" to flesh out this category. When a category is incomplete, grounded theorists then interview select participants about specific key ideas to extend, refine, or check their categories. Thus, Charmaz returned to earlier participants to learn more about suffering and, later, sought new interviewees and read personal accounts to illuminate the categories. Specifically, theoretical sampling helps grounded theorists (a) gain rich data, (b) further develop theoretical categories, and (c) discover variations and gaps within or across their categories.

Through theoretical sampling, researchers define the properties of a category, the conditions under which it is operative, how and when it is connected with other categories, and its range of variation. For example, Charmaz explored "making moral claims" with a number of participants to discern to what extent the category was evident and when and how it fit into her emerging analytic framework and their experience.

Theoretical sampling involves asking more focused, even pointed questions in interviews than researchers ordinarily ask in early interviews. Obtaining answers at all may depend on the strength of the relationship between the interviewee and the interviewer. Note how Robert Thornberg (2010a) poses direct questions in the excerpts below and makes explicit links between his interview data and the respective category.

Bullying as a Reaction to Deviance

The most prevalent social representation on bullying causes among the children in this study is to view *bullying as a reaction to deviance*. . . . This social representation means that the victim is interpreted as deviant, different, or odd, which in turn provokes others to bully him or her.

Interviewer:	What do you think caused the bullying?
Child:	Being different.
Interviewer:	Different? What do you mean?
Child:	Well, different clothes, and talking differently, looking different.

Interviewer:	Can you tell a bit more about this? Looking different?
Child:	Tall, short, fat, different styles of clothes and such things. (Interview with a 13-year-old boy) (p. 315)

Bullying as a Revengeful Activity

A fourth social representation on bullying causes is about explaining bullying in terms of revenge, payback, or punishment. . . . For example, he or she said something mean, was teasing, started a fight, was nasty to the bully's little brother, spread negative rumors, snitched and told teachers, and so on.

Child:	He [the victim] does something bad, and then he gets shit back.
Interviewer:	What could he have done?
Child:	Well, it could be that he asks if he can join in a game, and they say no to him, and then he goes in and tells a teacher so you get a lot of telling-off. And then, the others usually think, "well, that wasn't so smart [of him]." And then a lot of things happen during the lessons and we can't go outdoors and have breaks because of that.
Interviewer:	So it's like a bit of punishment then?
Child:	Yeah, and then the whole class gets it.
Interviewer:	Well, okay, but how come that the bullying occurs?
Child:	Well, because he [the victim] has done something or has started something, that he has said something. (Interview with a 10-year-old boy) (p. 317)

Presumably, grounded theorists will keep seeking data until a category is "saturated," that is, until they find no new information about the properties of this category (Bowen, 2008; Charmaz, 2006). In practice, saturation is an elastic category that researchers use to suit their definitions (see also Morse, 1995; Robrecht, 1995). Guest, Bunce, and Johnson (2006) correctly point out that saturation originally referred to saturating theoretical concepts and was vaguely defined. Their interest in saturation, however, derives from a practical concern of identifying how many interviews to plan. As a result, they dropped the notion of theoretical saturation and instead advocate that researchers treat saturation as referring to the point "when new information produces little or no change to the codebook" and look for themes in the data (p. 65). Guest et al.'s approach is not consistent with grounded theory practice. Grounded theorists use emergent coding rather than structured codebooks and aim for explication of emergent categories rather than identification of themes. Thus, these authors further obfuscate saturation, a term with origins and applicability in grounded theory, and thus perpetuate the error of other researchers who claim to conduct grounded theory studies but do not use theoretical sampling for developing categories. Through an experiment, Guest et al. determined that data were saturated in 12 interviews, but that would hardly demonstrate the range of variation of a category or process, much less establish its properties. Saturating data is insufficient and misleading and renews questions about how many interviews researchers "should" have for a grounded theory study (Crouch & McKenzie, 2006).

After deciding which categories best explain what is happening in the study, grounded theorists treat them as concepts, to understand many incidents or issues in the data (Strauss & Corbin, 1990). Strauss (1987) advocates theoretical sampling early in the research. Charmaz recommends conducting it later, so that relevant data and analytic directions emerge without being forced. Otherwise, early theoretical sampling may bring premature closure to the analysis.

INTEGRATING THE ANALYSIS

Memos provide the substance of a paper or chapter. Typically, grounded theorists select some memos with analytic power for understanding a specific process or phenomenon and set aside others for later projects. Each memo can be used as a section or subsection of the draft. Some memos fit together so well that ordering them seems obvious. Integrating the memos may simply reflect the theoretical direction of the analysis, or stages of a process. But for many topics, researchers must create the order and make connections for their readers. The first draft of a paper often represents the first attempt to integrate a set of memos into some kind of coherent order. How does one go about integrating memos? What makes the most sense? Here are some suggestions:

- Sort memos by title of category.

- Map several ways to order memos and outline the draft.

- Choose an order that works for the analysis and the prospective audience.

- Create clear links between categories.

When ordering memos, a grounded theorist may think about how a particular order reflects the logic of participants' experience and whether it will fit the reader's experience. The grounded theorist will attempt to create a balance between them. That may mean collapsing categories for clarity and readability. Grounded theory methods serve as powerful tools for honing an analysis. One inherent danger in using them is to create a scientistic report overloaded with jargon. Like other social scientists, grounded theorists may become enamored of their concepts, especially when they provide a fresh perspective on the data.

◆ Grounded Theory in Mixed-Methods Research

Proponents and analysts of mixed-methods research (e.g., Alise & Teddlie, 2010; Bergman, 2008a, 2008b; Creswell, 2009b; Creswell & Tashakkori, 2007; Johnson, Onwuegbuzie, & Turner, 2007) do not advocate including grounded theory methods, per se, in the mix or often cite grounded theory works. Nonetheless, grounded theory is becoming increasingly used in mixed-methods research because of the priorities of funding agencies (Hesse-Biber, 2010a) and the growing popularity and familiarity of grounded theory.

Qualitative research often serves as the "handmaiden" of quantitative work, simply for instrument development and/or for fleshing out quantitative findings. We can, however, do much more when coming at mixed methods from a qualitative perspective (Hesse-Biber, 2010b). For instance, Ginsburg et al. (2009) conducted 10 focus groups of providers and convened an expert panel to develop a patient safety event learning response before testing it in a cross-sectional survey. Although grounded theory served instrumentation goals, Ginsburg et al. grounded the measure both theoretically and practically for practice settings.

Other researchers used grounded theory in a primary role with quantitative methods. Thornberg (2010b) grounded his theory of students' representations of school bullying in individual qualitative interviews and connected these representations to moral disengagement. Subsequently, he buttressed his findings with descriptive statistics and frequencies. Ferreira, Antunes, Chadwick, and Correia (2010) began their sequential mixed-methods work on access control policies for electronic medical records with focus groups, analyzed via grounded theory methods. They followed up their analysis with structured questionnaires, an explicitly secondary piece of the study. Their goal was to integrate their final results in these professionals' workflows. Teti et al. (2010) used grounded theory to analyze semistructured interviews with a small subsample to flesh out the impact of an intervention they tested. Although grounded theory played a secondary role, they found it valuable for understanding how and why the intervention that they tested had the effect it did.

These examples demonstrate some of the ways researchers use grounded theory in mixed-methods research, as they approach problems from a variety of perspectives (see Creswell, 2009a; Creswell & Tashakkori, 2007). (See Morse's "The Implications of Interview Type and Structure in Mixed-Method Designs," this volume, for combining the qualitative and quantitative components of mixed-methods work in analysis.) In well-integrated work, the grounded theory aspect of studies ensures that the overall result will be meaningful for its intended audience or will illuminate the processes underlying quantitative results. Morse (2008) urges investigators to give equal space and attention to both qualitative and quantitative aspects of their work, using a team approach for expertise if needed.

Too often, mixed-methods studies take a "methods-centric approach" or are dominated by a positivist assumption of objectivity (Hesse-Biber, 2010b). Creswell (2009b) finds a pragmatist paradigm useful for mixed-methods work, while Bergman (2008b) argues that the apparent paradigm dichotomy between quantitative and qualitative methods is false. Fielding

(2008) would have us put aside uncritical combinations of methods in favor of deeper analyses to reach analytic density. In keeping with Denzin (2009) and Denzin and Giardina (2009), we think it is important to attend to paradigms, because of their ontological, epistemological, and methodological implications.

◆ Conclusion

A grounded theory interview can be viewed as an unfolding story. It is emergent, although studied and shaped; open-ended, however framed and focused; intense in content yet informal in execution; and conversational in style but not casual in meaning. The relationship of the research participant to the studied phenomena as well as to the interviewer and the interview process also shapes the type, extent, and relative depth of the subsequent story. This unfolding story arises as interviewer and participant together explore the topic and imprint a human face on it. The story may develop in bits and pieces from liminal, inchoate experience. It may tumble out when participants hold views on their experience but are not granted voices to express them or audiences to hear them.

Focus group interviews are a viable, growing part of grounded theory studies. We use them effectively when we recognize their unique dynamics and, more important, do not allow this innovative (for us) data collection technique to short-circuit the iterative process at the heart of grounded theory.

New issues arise as we see grounded theory increasingly used in mixed-methods research. Is grounded theory a handmaiden to larger, quantitative, positivist, and currently evidence-based goals, or is it a well-integrated, core piece of the overall project for explicating relevant processes or contributing to analytic density? Fundamentally, researchers must effectively acknowledge, analyze, and manage the underlying epistemological tensions to use multiple methods to their best advantage.

Grounded theory interviews, whether individual or focus group, are used to tell a collective story, not an individual tale given in a single interview. The power of grounded theory lies in piecing together a theoretical narrative that has interpretive power. Inherent tensions are apparent between the emphasis on the subjective story in the interview and the collective analytic story in grounded theory studies. Grounded theorists place decided priority on developing a conceptual analysis of the material rather than on presenting participants' stories in their entirety.

Are these inherent tensions irresolvable? No. Not if the researcher intends to follow grounded theory strategies and stays on the analytic path. Not if the researcher outlines the place of interview stories in the final report and the research participant agrees. Not if the researcher believes that reciprocities are possible between interviewer and participant during the interview process itself. Priorities may legitimately differ during data collection and analysis. So, too, may the roles of researcher and participant. Although roles are always emergent and may take a novel turn, clarity about reciprocities and ethics can mitigate later dilemmas. Interviewers can minimize hierarchical relationships through their active involvement (see also Fontana & Frey, 2005). Interviewers can give full attention to what their participants want to tell—even when it seems extraneous or requires additional visits. And an interviewer can pace the interview to fit the participant's needs first. During data collection, then, participants take precedence. When analyzing data and presenting findings, the researcher's emerging theoretical categories take precedence. If grounded theorists critically assess their actions during all phases of inquiry, they may learn how their grounded theory discoveries are constructed.

◆ References

Ahmad, F., Hudak, P. L., Bercovitz, K., Hollenberg, E., & Levinson, W. (2006). Are physicians ready for patients with Internet-based health information? *Journal of Medical Internet Research, 8*(3), e22.

Alise, M. A., & Teddlie, C. (2010). A continuation of the paradigm wars? Prevalence rates of methodological approaches across the social/behavioral sciences. *Journal of Mixed Methods Research, 4,* 103–126.

Atkinson, P., Coffey, A., & Delamont, S. (2003). *Key themes in qualitative research: Continuities and changes.* New York, NY: Rowan & Littlefield.

Beard, R. L., Fetterman, D. J., Wu, B., & Bryant, L. (2009). The two voices of Alzheimer's: Attitudes toward brain health by diagnosed individuals and support persons. *The Gerontologist, 49,* S40–S49.

Belgrave, L. L., Allen-Kelsey, G. J., Smith, K. J., & Flores, M. C. (2004). Living with dementia: Lay definitions of Alzheimer's disease among African American caregivers and sufferers. *Symbolic Interaction, 27,* 199–222.

Belgrave, L. L., & Smith, K. J. (1995). Negotiated validity in collaborative research. *Qualitative Inquiry, 1,* 69–86.

Bergman, M. M. (2008a). *Advances in mixed methods research: Theories and applications.* Thousand Oaks, CA: Sage.

Bergman, M. M. (2008b). The straw men of the qualitative–quantitative divide and their influence on mixed methods research. In M. M. Bergman (Ed.), *Advances in mixed methods research: Theories and applications* (pp. 11–21). Thousand Oaks, CA: Sage.

Blumer, H. (1969). *Symbolic interactionism.* Englewood Cliffs, NJ: Prentice Hall.

Bowen, G. A. (2008). Naturalistic inquiry and the saturation concept: A research note. *Qualitative Research, 8,* 137–152.

Bringer, J. D., Johnston, L. H., & Brackenridge, C. H. (2006). Using computer-assisted qualitative data analysis to develop grounded theory project. *Field Methods, 18,* 245–256.

Bryant, A. (2002). Re-grounding grounded theory. *Journal of Information Technology Theory and Application, 4,* 25–42.

Bryant, A. (2003). A constructive/ist response to Glaser. *Forum Qualitative Sozialforschung/Forum: Qualitative Social Research, 4.* Retrieved from http://www .qualitative-research.net/index.php/fqs/article/view Article/757/1642

Bryant, A., & Charmaz, K. (2007a). Grounded theory in historical perspective: An epistemological account. In A. Bryant & K. Charmaz (Eds.), *The SAGE handbook of grounded theory* (pp. 31–57). London, England: Sage.

Bryant, A., & Charmaz, K. (2007b). Introduction. In A. Bryant & K. Charmaz (Eds.), *The SAGE handbook of grounded theory* (pp. 1–28). London, England: Sage.

Charmaz, K. (1983). The grounded theory method: An explication and interpretation. In M. R. Emerson (Ed.), *Contemporary field research* (pp. 109–126). Boston, MA: Little-Brown.

Charmaz, K. (1990). Discovering chronic illness: Using grounded theory. *Social Science and Medicine, 30,* 1161–1172.

Charmaz, K. (1991). Translating graduate qualitative methods into undergraduate teaching: Intensive interviewing as a case example. *Teaching Sociology, 19,* 384–395.

Charmaz, K. (1995). Body, identity, and self: Adapting to impairment. *The Sociological Quarterly, 36,* 657–680.

Charmaz, K. (1999). Stories of suffering: Subjects' stories and research narratives. *Qualitative Health Research, 9,* 362–382.

Charmaz, K. (2000). Constructivist and objectivist grounded theory. In N. K. Denzin & Y. Lincoln (Eds.), *Handbook of qualitative research* (2nd ed., pp. 509–535). Thousand Oaks, CA: Sage.

Charmaz, K. (2002). Qualitative interviewing and grounded theory analysis. In J. F. Gubrium & J. A. Holstein (Eds.), *Handbook of interview research: Context and method* (pp. 675–694). Thousand Oaks, CA: Sage.

Charmaz, K. (2005). Grounded theory in the 21st century: Applications for advancing social justice studies. In N. K. Denzin & Y. E. Lincoln (Eds.), *Handbook of qualitative research* (3rd ed., pp. 507–535). Thousand Oaks, CA: Sage.

Charmaz, K. (2006). *Constructing grounded theory: A practical guide through qualitative analysis.* London, England: Sage.

Charmaz, K. (2007). Constructionism and grounded theory. In J. A. Holstein & J. F. Gubrium (Eds.), *Handbook of constructionist research* (pp. 35–53). New York, NY: Guilford Press.

Charmaz, K. (2008a). Grounded theory. In J. A. Smith (Ed.), *Qualitative psychology: A practical guide to research methods* (2nd ed., pp. 81–110). London, England: Sage.

Charmaz, K. (2008b). Grounded theory as an emergent method. In S. N. Hesse-Biber & P. Leavy (Eds.), *The handbook of emergent methods* (pp. 155–170). New York, NY: Guilford Press.

Charmaz, K. (2009a). The legacy of Anselm Strauss for constructivist grounded theory. In N. K. Denzin (Ed.), *Studies in symbolic interaction* (Vol. 32, pp. 127–141). Bingley, England: Emerald.

Charmaz, K. (2009b). Recollecting good and bad days. In A. Puddephatt, W. Shaffir, & S. Kleinknecht (Eds.), *Ethnographies revisited: Constructing theory in the field* (pp. 48–62). London, England: Routledge.

Charmaz, K. (2009c). Shifting the grounds: Constructivist grounded theory methods for the twenty-first century. In J. Morse, P. Stern, J. Corbin, B. Bowers, K. Charmaz, & A. Clarke, *Developing grounded theory: The second generation* (pp. 127–154). Walnut Creek, CA: Left Coast Press.

Charmaz, K. (2009d). Stories, silences, and self: Dilemmas in disclosing chronic illness (Expanded version). In D. E. Brashers & D. J. Goldstein (Eds.), *Communicating to manage health and illness* (pp. 240–270). New York, NY: Routledge.

Charmaz, K. (2010). Studying the experience of chronic illness through grounded theory. In G. Scambler & S. Scambler (Eds.), *New directions in the sociology of chronic and disabling condition: Assaults on the lifeworld* (pp. 8–36). London, England: Palgrave MacMillan.

Charmaz, K. (2011). A constructivist grounded theory analysis of losing and regaining a valued self. In F. J. Wertz, K. Charmaz, L. J. McMullen, R. Josselson, R. Anderson, & E. McSpadden, *Five ways of doing grounded theory, discourse analysis, narrative research, and intuitive inquiry.* New York, NY: Guilford Press.

Charmaz, K., & Bryant, A. (2011). Grounded theory and credibility. In D. Silverman (Ed.), *Qualitative research: Issues of theory, method and practice* (3rd ed., pp. 291–309). London, England: Sage.

Clarke, A. E. (2003). Situational analysis: Grounded theory mapping after the postmodern turn. *Symbolic Interaction, 26,* 553–576.

Clarke, A. E. (2005). *Situational analysis: Grounded theory after the postmodern turn.* Thousand Oaks, CA: Sage.

Clarke, A. E. (2006). Feminisms, grounded theory, and situational analysis. In S. Hesse-Biber & D. Leckenby (Eds.), *Handbook of feminist research methods* (pp. 345–370). Thousand Oaks, CA: Sage.

Clarke, A. E. (2009). From grounded theory to situational analysis. In J. Morse, P. Stern, J. Corbin, B. Bowers, K. Charmaz, & A. Clarke, *Developing grounded theory: The second generation* (pp. 194–233). Walnut Creek, CA: Left Coast Press.

Clarke, A. E., & Friese, C. (2007). Situational analysis: Going beyond traditional grounded theory. In A. Bryant & K. Charmaz (Eds.), *The handbook of grounded theory* (pp. 694–743). London, England: Sage.

Corbin, J. (2008). Preface. In J. Corbin & A. Strauss (Eds.), *Basics of qualitative research* (3rd ed., pp. vii–xiii). Thousand Oaks, CA: Sage.

Corbin, J. (2009). Taking an analytic journey. In J. M. Morse, P. N. Stern, J. Corbin, B. Bowers, K. Charmaz, & A. E. Clarke (Eds.), *Developing grounded theory: The second generation* (pp. 35–53). Walnut Creek, CA: Left Coast Press.

Corbin, J., & Strauss, A. (2008). *Basics of qualitative research* (3rd ed.). Thousand Oaks, CA: Sage.

Creswell, J. W. (2009a). Editorial: Mapping the field of mixed methods research. *Journal of Mixed Methods Research, 3,* 95–108.

Creswell, J. W. (2009b). *Research design: Qualitative, quantitative, and mixed methods approaches.* Thousand Oaks, CA: Sage.

Creswell, J. W., & Tashakkori, A. (2007). Editorial: Differing perspectives on mixed methods research. *Journal of Mixed Methods Research, 1,* 303–308.

Crouch, M., & McKenzie, H. (2006). The logic of small samples in interview-based qualitative research. *Social Science Information, 45*(4), 483–499.

Denzin, N. K. (2009). The elephant in the living room: Or extending the conversation about the politics of evidence. *Qualitative Research, 9,* 139–160.

Denzin, N. K., & Giardina, M. D. (2009). *Qualitative inquiry and social justice: Toward a politics of hope.* Walnut Creek, CA: Left Coast Press.

Dey, I. (1999). *Grounding grounded theory.* San Diego, CA: Academic Press.

Ezzy, D. (2010). Qualitative interviewing as an embodied emotional performance. *Qualitative Inquiry, 16,* 163–170.

Ferreira, A., Antunes, L., Chadwick, D., & Correia, R. (2010). Grounding information security in healthcare. *International Journal of Medical Informatics, 79,* 268–283.

Fielding, N. (2008). Analytic density, postmodernism, and applied multiple method research. In M. M. Bergman (Ed.), *Advances in mixed methods research: Theories and applications* (pp. 37–52). Thousand Oaks, CA: Sage.

Fontana, A., & Frey, J. H. (2005). The interview: From neutral stance to political involvement. In N. K. Denzin & Y. S. Lincoln (Eds.), *Handbook of qualitative research* (3rd ed., pp. 695–727). Thousand Oaks, CA: Sage.

Foster-Fishman, P., Nowell, B., Deacon, Z., Nievar, M. A., & McCann, P. (2005). Using methods that matter: The impact of reflection, dialogue, and voice. *American Journal of Community Psychology, 36*(3/4), 275–291.

Fox, F. E., Rumsey, N., & Morris, M. (2007). "Ur skin is the thing that everyone sees and you cant change it!" Exploring the appearance-related concerns of young people with psoriasis. *Developmental Neurorehabilitation, 10,* 133–141.

Furness, P., Garrud, P., Faulder, A., & Swift, J. (2006). Coming to terms: A grounded theory study of adaptation to facial surgery in adulthood. *Journal of Health Psychology, 11,* 453–466.

Ginsburg, L. R., Chuang, Y.-T., Norton, P. G., Berta, W., Treguhng, D., Ng, P., & Richardson, J. (2009). Development of a measure of patient safety event learning responses. *Health Services Research, 44,* 2123–2147.

Glaser, B. G. (1978). *Theoretical sensitivity.* Mill Valley, CA: Sociology Press.

Glaser, B. G. (1992). *Basics of grounded theory analysis.* Mill Valley, CA: Sociology Press.

Glaser, B. G. (1998). *Doing grounded theory: Issues and discussions.* Mill Valley, CA: The Sociology Press.

Glaser, B. G. (2001). *The grounded theory perspective: Conceptualization contrasted with description.* Mill Valley, CA: The Sociology Press.

Glaser, B. G., & Strauss, A. L. (1967). *The discovery of grounded theory.* Chicago, IL: Aldine.

Gubrium, E., & Koro-Ljungberg, M. (2005). Contending with border making in the social constructionist interview. *Qualitative Inquiry, 11,* 689–715.

Gudmundsdottir, S. (1996). The teller, the tale, and the one being told: The narrative nature of the research interview. *Curriculum Inquiry, 26*(3), 293–306.

Guest, G., Bunce, A., & Johnson, L. (2006). How many interviews are enough? An experiment with data saturation and variability. *Field Methods, 18,* 59–82.

Hesse-Biber, S. (2010a). Emerging methodologies and methods practices in the field of mixed methods research. *Qualitative Inquiry, 16,* 415–418.

Hesse-Biber, S. (2010b). Qualitative approaches to mixed methods research. *Qualitative Inquiry, 16,* 455–468.

Holstein, J. A., & Gubrium, J. F. (1995). *The active interview.* Thousand Oaks, CA: Sage.

Johnson, R. B., Onwuegbuzie, A. J., & Turner, L. A. (2007). Toward a definition of mixed methods research. *Journal of Mixed Methods, 1,* 112–133.

Konopásek, Z. (2007). Making thinking visible with ATLAS.ti: Computer assisted qualitative analysis as textual practices. *Historical Social Research* (Suppl. 19), 276–298.

Kvale, S., & Brinkmann, S. (2009). *InterViews: Learning the craft of qualitative research interviewing.* Thousand Oaks, CA: Sage.

Lambert, S. D., & Loiselle, C. G. (2008). Combining individual interviews and focus groups to enhance data richness. *Journal of Advanced Nursing, 62,* 228–237.

Lofland, J., & Lofland, L. H. (1995). *Analyzing social settings* (3rd ed.). Belmont, CA: Wadsworth.

Madriz, E. I. (1998). Using focus groups with lower socioeconomic status Latina women. *Qualitative Inquiry, 4,* 114–128.

Maines, D. R. (2001). Writing the self vs. writing the other: Comparing autobiographical and life history data. *Symbolic Interaction, 24*(1), 105–111.

Mead, G. H. (1932). *Philosophy of the present.* LaSalle, IL: Open Court Press.

Mills, J., Bonner, A., & Francis, K. (2006). The development of constructivist grounded theory. *International Journal of Qualitative Methods, 5*(1), 1–10.

Moore, J. L. (2006). A qualitative investigator of African American males' career trajectory in engineering: Implications for teachers, school counselors, and parents. *Teachers College Record, 108,* 246–266.

Morgan, D. L. (2002). Focus group interviewing. In J. F. Gubrium & J. A. Holstein (Eds.), *Handbook of interview research: Context and method* (pp. 141–159). Thousand Oaks, CA: Sage.

Morse, J. M. (1995). The significance of saturation. *Qualitative Health Research, 5,* 147–149.

Morse, J. M. (2008). Serving two masters: The qualitatively-driven, mixed-method approach. *Qualitative Health Research, 18,* 1607–1608.

Morse, J. M. (2009). Tussles, tensions, and resolutions. In J. M. Morse, P. N. Stern, J. Corbin, B. Bowers, K. Charmaz, & A. E. Clark (Eds.), *Developing grounded theory: The second generation* (pp. 13–22). Walnut Creek, CA: Left Coast Press.

Peters, V., & Wester, F. (2007). How qualitative data analysis software may support the qualitative analysis process. *Quality & Quantity, 41,* 635–659.

Raz, A. (2005). A note on inter-viewing: Using symbolic interactionism for interview analysis. *Studies in Symbolic Interactionism, 28,* 323–339.

Robrecht, L. C. (1995). Grounded theory: Evolving methods. *Qualitative Health Research, 5,* 169–177.

Rubin, H. J., & Rubin, I. S. (2005). *Qualitative interviewing: The art of hearing* (2nd ed.). Thousand Oaks, CA: Sage.

Ryan, G. W., & Bernard, H. R. (2003). Techniques to identify themes. *Field Methods, 15*(1), 85–109.

Scheibelhofer, E. (2008). Combining narration-based interviews with topical interviews: Methodological reflections on research practices. *International Journal of Social Research Methodology, 11*(5), 403–416.

Seale, C. (2002). Computer-assisted analysis of qualitative interview data. In J. F. Gubrium & J. A. Holstein (Eds.), *Handbook of interview research: Context and method* (pp. 651–670). Thousand Oaks, CA: Sage.

Seidman, I. (2006). *Interviewing as qualitative research: A guide for researchers in education and the social sciences* (3rd ed.). New York, NY: Teacher's College Press.

Silverman, D. (2007). *A very short, fairly interesting and reasonably cheap book about qualitative research.* London, England: Sage.

Strauss, A. L. (1961). *Images of the American city.* Chicago, IL: University of Chicago Press.

Strauss, A. L. (1969). *Mirrors and masks: The search for identity.* Mill Valley, CA: Sociology Press. (Original work published 1959)

Strauss, A. L. (1987). *Qualitative analysis for social scientists.* New York, NY: Cambridge University Press.

Strauss, A. L. (1995). Notes on the nature and development of general theories. *Qualitative Inquiry, 1,* 7–18.

Strauss, A., & Corbin, J. (1990). *Basics of qualitative research: Grounded theory procedures and techniques.* Newbury Park, CA: Sage.

Strauss, A., & Corbin, J. (1994). Grounded theory methodology: An overview. In N. K. Denzin & Y. S. Lincoln (Eds.), *Handbook of qualitative research* (pp. 273–285). Thousand Oaks, CA: Sage.

Strauss, A., & Corbin, J. (1998). *Basics of qualitative research: Grounded theory procedures and techniques* (2nd ed.). Thousand Oaks, CA: Sage.

Tanggaard, L. (2009). The research interview as a dialogical context for the production of social life and personal narratives. *Qualitative Inquiry, 15*(9), 1498–1515.

Teti, M., Bowleg, L., Cole, R., Lloyd, L., Rubinstein, S., Spencer, S., et al. (2010). A mixed methods evaluation of the effect of the protect and respect intervention on the condom use and disclosure practices of women living with HIV/AIDS. *AIDS Behavior, 14,* 567–579.

Thornberg, R. (2010a). School children's social representations on bullying causes. *Psychology in the Schools, 47,* 311–327.

Thornberg, R. (2010b). A student in distress: Moral frames and bystander behavior in school. *The Elementary School Journal, 110*(4), 585–608.

van den Hoonaard, W. C. (1997). *Working with sensitizing concepts: Analytical field research.* Thousand Oaks, CA: Sage.

Warren, C. A. B., & Williams, K. N. (2008). Interviewing elderly residents in assisted living. *Qualitative Sociology, 31*(4), 407–424.

Wengraf, T. (2001). *Qualitative research interviewing.* London, England: Sage.

Witz, K. G. (2006). The participant as ally and essentialist portraiture. *Qualitative Inquiry, 12,* 246–268.

Yamazaki, H., Slingsby, B. T., Takahashi, M., Hayashi, Y., Sugimori, H., & Nakayama, T. (2009). Characteristics of qualitative studies in influential journals of general medicine: A critical review. *BioScience Trends, 3,* 202–209.

25

ANALYSIS OF PERSONAL NARRATIVES

♦ Catherine Kohler Riessman

t is a common experience for investigators to carefully craft discrete interview questions, only to have participants respond with lengthy accounts—long responses that appear, on the surface, to have little to do with the question. Survey interviews discourage such "digressions," and participants typically learn to limit their responses to the categories provided (Mishler, 1986). Interviewing practice need not reduce participants to passive containers of information. Although dehumanizing practices persist, feminist investigators and qualitative researchers generally advocate less dominating and more relational modes of interviewing that reflect and respect participants' ways of organizing meaning (DeVault, 1999). We have made efforts to give up communicative power and follow participants down their trails. But what happens if the response to a question has little to do with our research topic? We hope that it gets recorded and transcribed, but what then?

I will argue that certain "digressions" can be extremely productive for the analytic process.

They provide contextual and associative cues and sometimes force us to confront the very assumptions of our research topics. They can also expose fissures in the interviewing relationship. These possibilities are especially likely when participants develop long narrative accounts in response to discrete factual questions that we might ask in qualitative interviews. I illustrate the process with a woman's personal narrative that emerged unexpectedly in an interview I conducted in South India. But first some necessary background on narrative methods in social research that I draw on to interpret the interview segments.

♦ Narrative Inquiry

Narrative applications have mushroomed in the past 20 years, now spanning many topical areas and incorporating widely different methodologies. Virtually every discipline and profession has a stream of narrative work, including history, anthropology

Author's Note: My thanks to Amir Marvasti, Marj DeVault, and Wendy Luttrell for their suggestions on an earlier draft.

and folklore, psychology, sociolinguistics, sociology, and the fields of law, medicine, nursing, education, occupational therapy, and social work. Going beyond the tendency merely to celebrate lengthy autobiographical accounts (Atkinson & Delamont, 2006), narrative inquiry takes as its object of investigation the story itself. I limit discussion here to analysis of spoken discourse—talk—from face-to-face encounters, including interviews, putting aside other kinds of narratives (e.g., those about the self of the investigator, accounts of extended fieldwork, media representations of events, Internet accounts of lives, or narratives that develop in everyday conversational settings). My interview research has focused on disruptive life events—personal accounts of experiences that fundamentally alter expected biographies. I have studied personal accounts of divorce, chronic illness, and infertility and draw on several of these examples in this chapter.

Narrative analysis, however, is not only relevant for the study of disruptive life events; the methods are equally appropriate for studies of social movements, political change, and macrolevel phenomena. Storytelling has fostered the development of constituencies—communities of action (Polletta, 2006). Plummer (1995) puts it vividly thus: "Stories gather people around them" (p. 174), dialectically connecting people and social movements. The identity stories of members of historically "defiled" groups (rape victims, gays and lesbians) reveal shifts in language over time, which shaped (and were shaped by) the mobilization of these actors in collective movements, such as "Take Back the Night" and gay rights groups. "For narratives to flourish there must be a community to hear; . . . for communities to hear, there must be stories which weave together their history, their identity, their politics" (p. 87).

Storytelling is a relational activity that gathers others to listen and empathize. It is a collaborative practice that requires attentive listening and questioning. If investigators believe that they can have unmediated access to someone's "story," they will not attend to the interactional and institutional contexts that shaped the particular version of it. In contrast to this naive position, many of us in narrative studies attend to the research relationship, the unfolding interview conversation, and the positioning of a story in it. We interrogate the influence of the setting, the historical context, and other dimensions that shape any speech act. The extent to which an investigator represents these dimensions will vary,

of course, with the purpose of a project, but to neglect to notice them strips context from research; conscious decisions are needed regarding the degree of detail of a transcript (Riessman, 2008).

Interviewers are active participants in interview narratives, subtly prodding the interviewee to "say more" about a topic or pausing at key points in the expectation that "more" could be said. By this receptive stance, narrative interviewing invites expanded accounts of lives. Attention to the actions of all participants in producing particular accounts brings the interview conversation into view—an essential aspect of the local context that is illustrated in the example below. Excluding the actions of the questioner/listener and other aspects of the production of a narrative reflects a rationalist and monologic philosophy of language, and it can encourage essentialist thinking: The properties of an "experience" as conveyed in a narrator's speech exist independent of context—that is, when, how, and to whom it is described.

Narrative analysts assume that tellers and listeners/questioners interact in particular cultural milieus—historical contexts essential to interpretation. Narrative inquiry opens up forms of telling about experience, not simply the content to which language refers. We can ask the following questions: Why was the story told *that* way? How did the local context and research relationship shape *this* account? What broader social discourses are taken for granted by the participants (Riessman, 1993, 2008).

Narrative inquiry, like oral history and autobiographical studies, is a form of case-centered research (Mishler, 1996). The "case" could be an individual, family, community, group, organization, or other unit of social life (for examples that focus on groups and organizations, see Boje, 2001; Cain, 1991). Building on the tradition of sociology articulated most vividly by C. W. Mills (1959), case studies of individuals can illuminate the intersection of biography, history, and society. The "personal troubles" that participants represent in their narratives of divorce, for example, tell us a great deal about social and historical processes—contemporary beliefs about gender relations and marriage at a particular juncture in American history (Riessman, 1990). Coming-out stories, similarly, where narrators proclaim their gayness to themselves and others, reveal a shift in genre over time: The linear, "causal" modernist tales of the 1960s and 1970s give way in contemporary stories to identities that blur and change (Plummer, 1995). Historical shifts in the understanding of women's health issues and their growing politicization occur over time in the stories of women with cancer whose mothers were exposed to diethylstilbestrol during pregnancy (Bell, 2009). As Mills (1959) said long ago, what we call "personal troubles" are located in particular times and places, and individuals' narratives about their troubles are works of history as much as they are about individuals, the social spaces they inhabit, and the societies they live in. In a word, *personal* narratives are deeply social.

Narrative analysis opens up a "methodological repertoire" (Quinn, 2005, p. 6), rather than a canon, that investigators can draw on and expand to suit the demands of a particular project. In this spirit of methodological diversity, I have developed elsewhere a typology and illustrative exemplars of four general approaches to interpreting narrative: (1) thematic, (2) structural, (3) dialogic/performative, and (4) visual analysis (Riessman, 2008; for other perspectives and inquiry methods, see Andrews, Squire, & Tamboukou, 2008; Cortazzi, 2001; Emerson & Frosh, 2009; Gubrium & Holstein, 2009; Mishler, 1995). In different ways, these analytic approaches resist automatic readings of a text—that is, the focus merely on the information communicated by a research participant. We can question the omniscient narrator and examine instead how an account was generated, its effects, the positioning of self and characters in the story, and other aspects of narrative construction. Language use can come into view—an angle of vision missing from many qualitative studies. In interview studies, the analyst can ask what the specific words participants select carry on their backs from prior uses. We can attend to meaningful silences—what *isn't* spoken—and offer possible readings of a personal narrative that go beyond what the narrator may have intended. Finally, we can interrogate our positions as researchers and interviewers, including the assumptions embedded in our questions. I illustrate below how theoretically productive such a stance can be, using the example of a "digression" in an interview. Because the concept of "narrative" has ambiguous uses, I begin the next section with a brief introduction to definitional issues.

◆ *Defining Narrative for Analysis*

Given the explosion of a literary vocabulary into everyday life, some boundaries around the concept are useful. Take the term *narrative*, which originated

of course in literary studies but in the contemporary period has taken on commonsense meanings. Journalists now use the word to refer to what in the past would have been called an ideological position or argument. Many qualitative researchers are appropriating a narrative vocabulary to refer to interview segments of any kind. If investigators plan to use narrative concepts analytically, terminology needs to be taken seriously. Determining the boundaries—that is, the beginnings and endings of narrative segments—becomes a complex analytic task.

Sociolinguists generally make a sharp distinction between *narrative* and *story*: The former refers to the broad class of discourse types that have certain properties in common (identified below). A story is one prototypic form of narrative that recounts a discrete set of events with "sequential and temporal ordering" (De Fina, 2003, p. 13). I would add spatial ordering—*where* a sequence of events unfolded. Following Aristotle, De Fina (2003) reserves the term *story* for oral discourses "that include some kind of rupture or disturbance in the normal course of events . . . an action that provokes a reaction and/or adjustment" (p. 13). All scholars, particularly those working with the subtype "story," owe a debt to the canonical work of Labov (1972, 1982) and the prior work of Labov and Waletzky (1967), even if they didn't always make a distinction between *narrative* and *story*, and the field has moved beyond their theory of narrative. As narrative studies have developed, our language and conceptual apparatus have grown more precise.

In social research in the recent decades, considerable variation exists in how investigators employ the concept of personal narrative and, relatedly, in their methodological assumptions and strategies of analysis (i.e., how they solicit and make sense of narrative data). These, in turn, are usually tied to a disciplinary background. In one tradition of work (typical of social history and anthropology), narrative refers to the entire life story, an amalgam of autobiographical materials. Barbara Myerhoff's (1978) work offers an early example of the life story approach and well illustrates its potentials and problems. She constructs compelling portraits of elderly Eastern European Jews living their remaining lives in Venice, California, from the many incidents informants shared with her during extended fieldwork. She artfully "infiltrates" her informants, "depositing her authorial word inside others' speech" to speak her truth without "erasing the others' viewpoint and social language" (Kaminsky, 1992, pp. 17–18). In this genre, the stories informants recount merge with the analyst's interpretation of them, sometimes to the point of becoming indistinguishable from them.

In a very different tradition of work, the concept of personal narrative is quite restrictive, used to refer to brief, topically specific stories organized around characters, setting, and plot. These are discrete stories told in response to single questions; they recapitulate specific events the narrator witnessed or experienced. Labov (1982) analyzes the common structures underlying a series of bounded stories of inner-city violence told in response to a single question. Narrators recapitulate sequences of action that erupt and bring the danger of death. This approach has been modified by others, who include more extended accounts (Bamberg, 1997, 2004; Bell, 2009; Rich & Grey, 2005; Riessman, 1990).

In a third tradition, personal narrative refers to large sections of talk and interview exchanges—extended accounts of lives that develop in conversation over the course of interviews and other fieldwork interactions. The discrete story as the unit of analysis of the second tradition gives way in the third one to an evolving series of stories that are framed in and through interaction (for examples, see Bell, 2009; Brown, 1998; Luttrell, 2003). In a classic study, Mishler (1999) analyzed the trajectories of identity development among a group of artist-craftspersons that emerged from his extended interviews with them. His approach, which I have adapted, is distinguished by the following features:

1. Presentation of and reliance on detailed transcripts of interview excerpts

2. Attention to language use and other structural features of discourse

3. Analysis of the coproduction of narrative (including "digressions") through the dialogic exchange between interviewer and participant

4. A comparative approach to interpreting the similarities and differences among participants

In sum, there is considerable diversity in the operational definition of personal narrative in social research and, consequently, large methodological variation. Despite the differences, most investigators share some basic understandings. Accepting that oral narrative refers to a broad class of discourse types (of which the "story" is only one), what are the defining features that distinguish narrative from other kinds of interview discourse, such as brief question-and-answer exchanges, expository statements of beliefs, chronicles, listings, and other speech acts? Bell builds on Hinchman and Hinchman (1997) to define narrative as

> a sequence of ordered events that are connected in a meaningful way for a particular audience in order to make sense of the world or people's experience in it. . . . This definition assumes one action is consequential for the next, that a narrative sequence is held together with a "plot," and that the "plot" is organized temporally and spatially. . . . More than a list or chronicle, a narrative adds up to "something." (Bell, 2009, p. 8)

Determining that "something," of course, is a central task for the listener and subsequently for the analyst as they interpret meaning, or the "point" the speaker wishes to make, and it is not always an easy task. A long story about a particular moment must be worth telling to take up so much space in a conversation.

Narrators create plots from disordered experience,[1] giving reality "a unity that neither nature nor the past possesses so clearly" (Cronon, 1992, p. 1349). Relatedly, narrators structure their tales temporally and spatially; "they look back on and recount lives that are located in particular times and places" (Laslett, 1999, p. 392). Temporal ordering of a plot is most familiar (and corresponds to the characteristic Western listener's preoccupation with forward-marching time—"What happened next?"), but narratives can also be organized thematically and episodically (Gee, 1991; Michaels, 1981; Riessman, 1987). Narrators use particular linguistic devices to hold their accounts together and communicate their meanings to listeners. Human agency and imagination are vividly expressed:

> With narrative, people strive to configure space and time, deploy cohesive devices, reveal identity of actors and relatedness of actions across scenes.

---

[1]There is a lively philosophical debate about whether primary experience is "disordered"—that is, whether narrators create order out of chaos. See Hinchman and Hinchman (1997, pp. xix–xx).

They create themes, plots, and drama. In so doing, narrators make sense of themselves, social situations, and history. (Bamberg & McCabe, 1998, p. iii)

In a particular study, how does an investigator identify narratives and put some boundaries around them? Sometimes the decision is clear: Informants signal that a story is coming and indicate when it is over with entrance and exit talk (Jefferson, 1979). In my divorce interviews, for example, responding to a question about the "main causes" of separation, one man provided a listing and then said, "I'll clarify this with an example," an utterance that introduced a lengthy story about judging a dog show—an avocation his wife did not share. He exited from the story many minutes later with "That is a classic example of the whole relationship . . . she chose *not* to be with *me*" (Riessman, 1990, pp. 102–108).

Stories in research interviews are rarely so clearly bounded, and often there is negotiation between teller and listener about placement and relevance, a process that can be analyzed with transcriptions that include paralinguistic utterances, false starts, interruptions, and other subtle features of interaction. Deciding the beginnings and endings of narrative segments can be a complex interpretive task, especially when they emerge in bits and pieces over the course of the interview—trauma narratives and the accounts of children and youth provide vivid examples here. I confronted the problem in a study of stigma and infertility as I began to analyze a woman's narrative account. The research was conducted in Kerala, South India, and elsewhere (Riessman, 2000a, 2000b, 2005). I describe the fieldwork in detail. Here, I present a portion of an interview with a woman I call Gita: 55 years old, married and childless, Hindu, and from a lower caste. Because of progressive social policies and related opportunities in her South Indian state, Gita is educated, has risen in status, and works as a lawyer-advocate in a small municipality. When asked, she enthusiastically agreed to be interviewed for a study of infertility, preferring to talk to me in English. The particular interaction represented in the extract took place after she and I had talked for nearly an hour in her home about a variety of topics, most of which she introduced—her schooling, how her marriage was arranged, and her political work in the "liberation struggle of Kerala." We enter the interview as I reintroduce the topic of infertility, which was the purpose of my visit. My transcription conventions are adapted from Gee (1991): Lines about a single topic are grouped into stanzas, which I then group into scenes. Unlike earlier versions of the transcript (Riessman, 2002a), here I represent my participation to a much greater degree, specifically with interruptions and clarifying comments that reveal the interactional dimension of the narrative.

Transcript 1

Cathy: Now I am going to go back and ask some specific questions.
         Were you ever pregnant?

Gita: Pregnant means—You see it was 3 years [after the marriage]   Scene 1
         then I approached [name of doctor]
         then she said it is not a viable—[pregnancy].
         ==
         So she asked me to undergo this operation, this D&C
         and she wanted to examine him [husband] also.

         Then the second time in 1974—in 1975,   Scene 2
         next time—4 months.
         Then she wanted [me] to take bed rest
         advised me to take bed rest.

(Continued)

(Continued)

Because I already told you	Scene 3

Because I already told you
it was during that period that [name] the socialist leader
led the gigantic procession against Mrs. Indira Gandhi,
the Prime Minister of India, in Delhi.

And I was a political leader [names place and party]
I had to participate in that.

So I went by train to Delhi
but returned by plane.
After the return I was in [name] Nursing Home
for 16 days bleeding.

And so he [husband] was very angry   Scene 4
he said "Do not go for any social work
do not be active" this and that.
But afterwards I never became—[pregnant]
==

Then, my in-laws, they are in [city]   Scene 5
they thought I had some defect, really speaking.
So they brought me to a gynecologist,
one [name], one specialist.

She took 3 hours to examine me
and she said "You are perfectly—[normal], no defect at all"
even though I was 40 or 41 then.
"So I have to examine your husband."

Then I told her [doctor] "You just ask his sister."
She was—his sister was with me in [city].
So I asked her to ask her to bring him in.
He will not come.
Then we went to the house
so then I said "Dr. [name] wants to see you."
Then he [husband] said "No, no, I will not go to a lady doctor."
Then she [sister-in-law] said she would not examine him
they had to examine the—what is it?—the sperm in the laboratory.
But he did not allow that.

Although Gita could have answered my discrete question ("Were you ever pregnant?") directly (with a "Yes"), she chose instead to digress with a complex narrative that describes two miscarriages, going to a political demonstration, and coming home to her husband's anger, whereupon the scene shifts to the actions of in-laws and her husband's refusal to have his sperm examined. This account was unlike others

I had collected: Although temporally organized, Gita's plot spans many years and social settings, and there is little reference to sadness, disappointment, or other emotions common to narratives of miscarriage and infertility.

In an effort to interpret the account, I struggled to define some boundaries, initially deciding to end my representation of the personal narrative with what seems like a coda at the end of Scene 4: "But afterwards I never became—[pregnant]." The utterance ends the sequence about pregnancy—the topic of my initial question. Later, I decided to include the next scene, which communicates various family members' actions and the reported speech of Gita's husband ("No, no, I will not go to a lady doctor"). The change in decision coincided with a theoretical shift as I began to focus on the construction of positive identities. The few older women in my sample seemed to perform narratives that defied stigma (Riessman, 2002b). It was crucial, then, to include the episode about Gita's in-laws, the interaction with the gynecologists, and the husband's response to the request that his sperm be tested. Selection of segments for closer analysis—the textual representation of a spoken narrative we create and the boundaries chosen—is strongly influenced by the researcher's evolving theory, disciplinary leanings, and research questions. In these ways, the investigator variously "infiltrates" a transcript (see Riessman, 2008, chap. 2).

◆ *Analyzing Narrative as Performance*

In earlier interpretations of the personal narrative (Riessman, 2002a), I interpreted the above narrative as an identity performance by Gita. Obviously, personal narratives can serve many purposes in conversations—to remember, argue, convince, engage, or entertain their audience (Bamberg & McCabe, 1998). Consequently, investigators have many points of entry: Personal narratives can be interpreted thematically (Williams, 1984), structurally (Gee, 1991; Labov, 1982), conversationally (Ochs & Capps, 2001; Polanyi, 1989), culturally (Mattingly & Garro, 2000; Rosaldo, 1989), psychologically (Josselson, Lieblich, & McAdams, 2007; Linde, 1993), politically/historically (Mumby, 1993; White, 1981), and performatively (Langellier, 2001; Langellier & Peterson, 2004). My thinking about the interview transcript has evolved over time, and here, I extend my earlier performative focus by examining the interactional aspects of the performance. Going beyond my previous interpretation, I now see my role in the evolving conversational dance more critically.

Using a dramaturgical metaphor, Goffman (1963, 1969, 1981) extended symbolic interaction theory toward the performative, thus transforming studies of identity. We are forever composing impressions of ourselves, projecting a definition of who we are, and making claims about ourselves and the world that we test out and negotiate with others. In situations of difficulty and potential stigma, social actors stage performances of a desirable self to preserve "face." To do this, they develop accounts to "explain unanticipated or untoward behavior—whether that behavior is his or her own or that of others, and whether the approximate cause of the statement arises from the actor himself or someone else" (Lyman & Scott, 1989, p. 112). A personal narrative is a major site for developing accounts that try to repair identities that have been spoiled by biographical disruptions such as infertility and divorce (Riessman, 1990). As Goffman (1974) elegantly put it, "What talkers undertake to do is not to provide information to a recipient but to present dramas to an audience. Indeed, it seems that we spend more of our time not engaged in giving information but in giving shows" (pp. 508–509). To emphasize the performative element is not to suggest that identities are inauthentic, only that they are situated and accomplished in social interaction.

Applying these insights to interviews, informants negotiate how they want to be known by the stories they perform for the immediate audience—a particular listener/questioner. Informants do not "reveal" an essential self as much as they perform a preferred self, selected from the multiplicity of selves or personae that individuals switch between as they go about their lives. Approaching identity as a "performative struggle over the meanings of experience" (Langellier, 2001, p. 173) brings the audience in and opens up analytic possibilities that are missed with static conceptions of identity and essentializing theories that assume the unity of an "inner" self. Audience reception to an identity performance is a factor in its success.

Personal narratives contain many performative features that try to pull the audience into the narrator's experience and point of view. Tellers intensify words and phrases; they enhance segments with narrative detail, direct speech, repetition, asides to the audience, gestures, and even sound effects (Bauman, 1986; Wolfson, 1982). Analysts can ask questions of a performance: In what kind of a story does the narrator place herself? How does she position herself with respect to the audience, and vice versa? How does she position characters in relation to one another and in relation to herself? How does she position herself to herself—that is, make identity claims (Bamberg, 2004)? Social positioning in stories—how narrators choose to position the audience, characters, and themselves—is a useful point of entry because "fluid positioning, not fixed roles, are used by people to cope with the situations they find themselves in" (Harre & Van Langenhove, 1999, p. 17). Narrators can position themselves, for example, as victims of one circumstance or another in their tales, giving over to other characters, and not themselves, the power to initiate action. Alternatively, narrators can position themselves as agentic beings that assume control over events and actions: They purposefully initiate and cause action. They can shift among positions, giving themselves agentic roles in certain scenes and passive roles in others. To create these fluid semantic spaces for themselves, narrators use particular grammatical resources to construct who they are—verbs, for example, that frame actions as voluntary rather than compulsory or grammatical forms that intensify vulnerability (Capps & Ochs, 1995). Subject positions assigned in personal narratives are key features of an identity performance. How the audience reacts, by either entering into or resisting the presentation of self, is an indicator of performative success (i.e., one way the narrative is "infiltrated" by the audience).

I illustrate this reciprocity by returning to the conversation with Gita (see Transcript 1). In the larger research project of which this interview is a part, I theorize how the cultural discourse of gender defines women by their marital and childbearing status. In India and many parts of the world, married women are stigmatized when they cannot reproduce (Riessman, 2000a, 2000b). Gita deviated from the general pattern in my sample. She was beyond childbearing age. The absence of motherhood did not seem to be a particularly salient topic for her. (I was always the one to introduce it in the conversation, and she expressed little sadness and negative self-evaluation, as the younger women did.) Gita had built a life around principles other than marriage and motherhood. Close examination of the narrative reveals precisely how she constructs this preferred (positive) identity, not falling victim to stigma and subordination as a childless woman. She defies the dominant cultural narrative about gender identity in her performance. But her audience on this occasion is a reluctant partner in the improvisational dance: I repeatedly try to lead her toward my topic—pregnancy rather than politics.

During the hour-long conversation before the segment in Transcript 1, Gita had introduced and talked at length about various aspects of her biography: her caste origins and schooling opportunities in Kerala, her developing career as a lawyer-advocate, the state's socialist politics and her activism in the movement, and her mother's insistence on arranging a marriage when Gita was 35 ("I will not be here, I am old . . . very old. I cannot safeguard you all the time . . . So get married."). After a year, Gita finally agreed: "I am ready . . . you fix the marriage." It was a big affair, and Gita brought out a photograph album to educate me about the Hindu ritual and especially a brother's central role, in the place of her deceased father ("The girl is given as a gift to her husband"). She pointed out and named in the photographs the many wedding guests (judges, "all the lady lawyers . . . all in good positions").

In an effort to regain control of a research interview that had gotten away from the topic of infertility, I introduce a question ("Now I'm going to go back and ask some specific questions"; see Transcript 1). Gita obliges by developing a performance that I have represented in five "scenes." Each offers a snapshot of action, located in a different time and setting. Attention to how the scenes are sequenced and organized is my point of entry. The first two scenes are prompted by a request ("Were you ever pregnant?")—my attempt after an hour's conversation that digressed from the topic we had agreed to talk about. She reluctantly moves into the role of pregnant woman in these brief scenes, quickly chronicling two pregnancies several years apart—the outcomes of which I have to clarify by interrupting her several times ("==" in Transcript 1). She does not provide narrative detail or elaborate meanings; the audience must fill in. Gita constructs the first two scenes, which contain only one character apart from her, a doctor. She "approached" the doctor, who "asked" her to have a D&C. A quick aside states that the doctor wanted to examine the husband, but we infer that this did not happen. (With this utterance, Gita prefigures her husband's responsibility, anticipating the final scene and the point of the narrative.)

She casts the doctor as the active agent again in Scene 2: She "wanted" and "advised" Gita to take bed rest. Through her choice of verbs and positioning of characters, Gita constructs scenes in which she plays a relatively minor role. The lack of narrative detail in the plot up to this point suggests that the events are not particularly salient for her.

The narrator's position and the salience of events radically change in the third scene. Gita shifts topics, from pregnancy "to what I already told you," which is the primacy of her political life. Gita constructs Scene 3, where she is the central character: A "political leader" in her Kerala community who "had to" participate in a demonstration in Delhi against Mrs. Indira Gandhi, who was seeking reelection. A well-known component of her policy was forced sterilization. Ironically, this public discourse intersects the personal narrative about a miscarriage. Gita locates her private fertility story in the public story of "Mother India" and its socialist movement—the audience should not wonder which is most important (although I didn't see it at the time). Verbs frame the narrator's intentional actions,[2] situated in the political exigencies of the time, and here there is considerable narrative elaboration, in sharp contrast to the spare, "passive" grammar of the previous scenes, where Gita was the object of the doctor's actions.[3] Ignoring her doctor's advice "to take bed rest" during her second pregnancy, she travels to Delhi to participate in a mass demonstration, which probably involved a 3-day train trip in 1975. Despite her return by plane and a 16-day nursing home stay for "bleeding," she suggests that she lost the pregnancy, a fact I interrupt to confirm a few lines later (see Transcript 1). She constructs a narrative around oppositional worlds—family life, on the one hand, and the socialist movement of India, on the other. The personal and the political occupy separate spheres of action and, as such, do not infringe on each other.

In the next two scenes, Gita shifts the plot to the family world. In Scene 4, she again introduces her husband as a character and reports that he was "very angry" at her "social work," meaning her activism. She communicates a one-way conversation, not giving herself a speaking role. She positions herself as the object of her husband's angry speech. We do not know what she said to him, if anything. Her passive position in this scene is in sharp contrast to her activity in the previous one. Is she displaying here a typical practice in South Indian families, in which wives are expected to defer to the husband's authority (Riessman, 2000b)? If so, her choice of language is intriguing: He said "this and that." Could she be belittling his anger and directives? She concludes Scene 4 with a factual utterance ("But afterwards I never became—[pregnant]"). Her break-off here is significant perhaps. In an effort to finally get an answer to some basic questions about her reproductive history, I summarize, "So you had two miscarriages, two abortions,[4] right?"

After a quick "Yes," Gita picks up the plot right where she left off ("Then, my in-laws, they are in [city] . . ." In this fifth and final, lengthy scene, Gita introduces new characters—her parents-in-law, an infertility specialist, a sister-in-law—and an intricate plot, before the narrative moves toward its point, which is that Gita is not to blame for the situation. The final scene has the most elaboration, suggesting importance, and the performance of identity is most vivid here. Gita begins by constructing a passive position for herself: Her in-laws "brought" her for treatment to a gynecologist in the major South Indian city where the parents live, because "they thought I had some defect." As in earlier scenes involving pregnancy, others suggest or initiate action. She intensifies meaning and thematic importance with repetition ("defect") in the next stanza; the gynecologist determined after a lengthy examination that Gita has "no defect at all." She is "perfectly" normal. Blame for infertility, Gita intimates, resides elsewhere. In reported speech, she performs several conversations on the topic of getting her husband tested. Everyone is enlisted in the effort—gynecologist, sister-in-law—but he refuses: "No, no, I will not go to a lady doctor." Nor is he willing to have his sperm

[2]The verb construction "had to" is ambiguous. It might refer to others' expectations that Gita participate in the political demonstration as a leader in the community, or it might refer to a personal desire to participate, arising out of her own political convictions and priorities. The narrative context supports the latter interpretation.

[3]Other interpretations are possible here. Perhaps the passive voice in the first two scenes reflects medicine's dominant role in medical discourse during the historical period in question.

[4]In South India, the term *abortion* refers to miscarriage.

tested in a laboratory. (Gita returned several other times in our conversation to his refusal to be tested.) The narrator has crafted a performance, not unlike a legal argument that reviews the evidence and hints at a causal claim: She is not to blame. Gita doesn't have to say directly that her husband is the one with the "defect."

Years after the interview, I still find myself resisting the message of the identity performance. The attributions can certainly be questioned: Gita ignored her physician's advice to "take bed rest" during her second pregnancy, choosing to travel instead to Delhi. She gave primacy to political commitments, valuing work in the socialist movement over her gendered position in the home. She was also "40 or 41" years old when she was finally examined by a specialist. Age may have been a factor. Gita had conceived twice but could not sustain the pregnancies, implying a possible "defect." Gita's performance, however, suggests how she wants to be known: as a "perfectly" normal woman "with no defect at all." The way she organizes scenes within the performance, the choices she makes about positioning of characters and audience, and the grammatical resources she employs put forth the preferred identity of a committed political activist, not a disappointed would-be mother. In case I missed this point, she repeats it a little later when I attempt again to return to my topic: "Because I am not having [children], I have no disappointments because mine is a big family." She goes on to list her sister who has 10 children ("seven boys and three girls, all married except one") and other siblings who have children. She mentions her four brothers—"all of them married, all have children," two of whom "come here in the evening to take their meals," except on days when there is "some festival or something." I finally understand and say, "So you have many children in your life." Gita answers, "Yes," and she adds, "That is why I have no disappointment." Had I been the defective subject with naive, bipolar notions of parental status—either you have children or you don't? Although it took me a while to get it, analysis of the narrative shows how hard Gita worked to resist my research interest—infertility—and my related positioning of her. She had an agenda for the conversation, an identity she wanted to perform and stories she wanted to tell. Her preferred identity required many long "digressions" to accomplish, especially given her reluctant audience. She secured

a wider descriptive space than the plan for the interview had allowed.

Looking beyond the immediate context, the gender identity Gita performs challenged India's master cultural narrative—biological motherhood is the central axis of identity for married women. Ironically, this prevalent cultural belief had provided the rationale for my project: Infertility disrupts the expected biography, as divorce does. I began the infertility project wanting to understand what happens when South Indian married women can't become mothers, and over the course of the research, I heard many stories of stigma and blame and even of violence against women when they did not conceive. As a "deviant case," Gita forced me to take a look at the very assumptions of my project. Subsequently, I searched for and found in later interviews other fissures in the master narrative—women who were resisting the pull of the cultural mandate. Intentionally childless women were rare in South India in 1993 to 1994, but subtler forms of resistance did become visible to me (Riessman, 2000b, 2002b).

In sum, a "digression" and the interactional context that produced it turned out to be extremely productive, changing the course of a research project. In the years since I completed the research, opportunities for women besides marriage and childbearing have only increased. Although debate continues about women's "proper" place in modern India, the fast-developing nation is developing new spaces (besides home and field) for women to labor.

◆ Concluding Thoughts

Personal narratives can emerge at unexpected moments in research interviews, even in response to fixed-response questions. What may appear at the time to be an unrelated response can become important analytically, telling us a great deal about our interviewing practices and participants' preferred topics. Obviously, digressions can mean many things, but at a minimum, they momentarily shift power in the conversational dance, from the investigator's lead to control by the participant. The excerpt above from my long interview with Gita vivifies this process. In analyzing the excerpt here, I chose to emphasize the interactional dimensions of an identity performance, extending a previous analysis that had emphasized the narrator primarily.

We get drawn into compelling stories and the power of narrative to persuade and justify a particular course of action—this is how it "really" happened. An effective storyteller in a conversation sets up a situation where there's no way to "read" the text in another way. To maintain a critical stance toward our research materials, I've suggested that we resist instant interpretation and examine how a narrative is composed collaboratively and its consequent effects—what it accomplishes in the conversation for the identity-building project of the narrator. With the example from my interview with Gita, and analysis of it later, I tried to show how the narrative *functioned* in the conversational context to construct a *version* of events and a *subject position* that made a good life possible for Gita, given India's master narrative of compulsory motherhood. A participant's identity performance is contained (and constituted) in narrative accounts, but the literature in the social sciences has not paid sufficient attention to the audience side of interview performances, in particular, the way interviewers manage "digressions" in the research materials.

The personal narrative constituted in my interaction with Gita is obviously open to many interpretations. No analysis of discourse can be expected to do a multiplicity of tasks. Perhaps Gita didn't want to talk about infertility the way I expected because the events happened long ago and were painful to recollect. What remained unsaid and the gaps in her account might be explored. Investigators interested in psychological processes could analyze Gita's account for its closed, sealed-off features; she displays a set of understandings that seem to defy redefinition, and she is reluctant to talk about emotions. Investigators might speculate about a defensive process: Is she working to counter the implicit charge that she is not a "true woman?" Alternatively, the personal narrative could be analyzed with a primary focus on cultural context, for example, the prominent role of the wife's in-laws in defining and managing a childless woman in India. The personal narrative is social in this and other ways, connected to larger cultural and historical discourses about gender and politics in India. Certainly, my cultural location is relevant: Gita had to educate me repeatedly about facets of her life story that she thought a North American woman wouldn't understand (e.g., Hindu marriage rituals). I don't think my cultural otherness was the only (or even the primary)

reason for the conversational "trouble," but it was probably relevant to some degree. When interviewing across cultural divides, missteps are to be expected; participants usually have to teach us even if we fail to hear them the first time (Riessman, 1987). More important, cross-cultural interviews present a greater risk of the listener dismissing meaningful narrative linkages or footings (Gubrium & Holstein, 2009) as pointless "digressions" that have to be minimized.

Looking back on data collected and interpreted in the past is useful theoretically and practically, and it is one way to remediate such cultural misframings of interview data. Taking the opportunity to listen again to a tape recording and/or reexamine a transcript from a completed project opens up issues that may have been missed. Just as participants' accounts of their lives are situated in particular times and cultural contexts, so, too, our interpretations are situated in perspectives and histories that can shift over time. Looking back on past interviews from the present context reveals the contingency of all our observations.

◆ References

Andrews, M., Squire, C., & Tamboukou, M. (2008). *Doing narrative research*. London, England: Sage.

Atkinson, P., & Delamont, P. (2006). Rescuing narrative from qualitative research. *Narrative Inquiry, 16,* 164–172.

Bamberg, M. G. W. (Ed.). (1997). Oral versions of personal experience: Three decades of narrative analysis [Special issue]. *Journal of Narrative and Life History.*

Bamberg, M. (2004). Form and functions of "slut-bashing" in male identity constructions of 15-year-olds. *Human Development, 47,* 331–353.

Bamberg, M. G. W., & McCabe, A. (1998). Editorial. *Narrative Inquiry, 8,* iii–v.

Bauman, R. (1986). *Story, performance, and event: Contextual studies of oral narrative*. Cambridge, England: Cambridge University Press.

Bell, S. E. (2009). *DES daughters: Embodied knowledge and the transformation of women's health politics*. Philadelphia, PA: Temple University Press.

Boje, D. M. (2001). *Narrative methods for organizational and communication research*. London, England: Sage.

Brown, L. M. (1998). *Raising their voices: The politics of girls' anger*. Cambridge, MA: Harvard University Press.

Cain, C. (1991). Personal stories: Identity acquisition and self-understanding in alcoholics anonymous. *Ethos, 19,* 210–253.

Capps, L., & Ochs, E. (1995). *Constructing panic: The discourse of agoraphobia*. Cambridge, MA: Harvard University Press.

Cortazzi, M. (2001). Narrative analysis in ethnography. In P. Atkinson, A. Coffey, S. Delamont, J. Lofland, & L. Lofland (Eds.), *Handbook of ethnography* (pp. 384–394). Thousand Oaks, CA: Sage.

Cronon, W. (1992). A place for stories: Nature, history, and narrative. *Journal of American History, 78*, 1347–1376.

De Fina, A. (2003). *Identity in narrative: A study of immigrant discourse*. Amsterdam, The Netherlands: John Benjamins.

DeVault, M. L. (1999). *Liberating method: Feminism and social research*. Philadelphia, PA: Temple University Press.

Emerson, P., & Frosh, S. (2009). *Critical narrative analysis in psychology: A guide to practice*. London, England: Palgrave Macmillan.

Gee, J. P. (1991). A linguistic approach to narrative. *Journal of Narrative and Life History/Narrative Inquiry, 1*, 15–39.

Goffman, E. (1963). *Stigma: Notes on the management of spoiled identity*. Englewood Cliffs, NJ: Prentice Hall.

Goffman, E. (1969). *The presentation of self in everyday life*. New York, NY: Penguin.

Goffman, E. (1974). *Frame analysis: An essay on the organization of experience*. Cambridge, MA: Harvard University Press.

Goffman, E. (1981). *Forms of talk*. Oxford, England: Blackwell.

Gubrium, J. F., & Holstein, J. A. (2009). *Analyzing narrative reality*. Thousand Oaks, CA: Sage.

Harre, R., & Van Langenhove, L. (Eds.). (1999). *Positioning theory*. Malden, MA: Blackwell.

Hinchman, L. P., & Hinchman, S. K. (Eds.). (1997). *Memory, identity, community: The idea of narrative in the human sciences*. Albany: State University of New York Press.

Jefferson, G. (1979). Sequential aspects of storytelling in conversation. In J. Schenkein (Ed.), *Studies in the organization of conversational interaction* (219–248). New York, NY: Academic Press.

Josselson, R., Lieblich, A., & McAdams, D. P. (Eds.). (2007). *The meaning of others: Narrative studies of relationships*. Washington, DC: American Psychological Association.

Kaminsky, M. (1992). Introduction. In B. Myerhoff (Ed.), *Remembered lives: The work of ritual, storytelling, and growing older* (pp. 1–97). Ann Arbor: University of Michigan Press.

Labov, W. (1972). *Language in the inner city: Studies in the black English vernacular*. Philadelphia: University of Pennsylvania Press.

Labov, W. (1982). Speech actions and reactions in personal narrative. In D. Tannen (Ed.), *Analyzing discourse: Text and talk* (pp. 219–247). Washington, DC: Georgetown University Press.

Labov, W., & Waletzky, J. (1967). Narrative analysis: Oral versions of personal experience. In J. Helm (Ed.), *Essays on the verbal and visual arts* (pp. 12–44). Seattle: American Ethnological Society/University of Washington Press.

Langellier, K. (2001). "You're marked": Breast cancer, tattoo and the narrative performance of identity. In J. Brockmeier & D. Carbaugh (Eds.), *Narrative identity: Studies in autobiography, self, and culture* (pp. 145–184). Amsterdam, The Netherlands: John Benjamins.

Langellier, K. M., & Peterson, E. E. (2004). *Storytelling matters: Performing narrative in daily life*. Philadelphia, PA: Temple University Press.

Laslett, B. (1999). Personal narrative as sociology. *Contemporary Sociology, 28*, 391–401.

Linde, C. (1993). *Life stories: The creation of coherence*. New York, NY: Oxford University Press.

Luttrell, W. (2003). *Pregnant bodies, fertile minds: Gender, race and the schooling of pregnant teens*. New York, NY: Routledge.

Lyman, S. M., & Scott, M. B. (1989). *A sociology of the absurd*. Dix Hills, NY: General Hall.

Mattingly, C., & Garro, L. C. (Eds.). (2000). *Narrative and the cultural construction of illness and healing*. Berkeley: University of California Press.

Michaels, S. (1981). "Sharing time": Children's narrative styles and differential access to literacy. *Language in Society, 10*, 423–442.

Mills, C. W. (1959). *The sociological imagination*. New York, NY: Oxford University Press.

Mishler, E. G. (1986). *Research interviewing: Context and narrative*. Cambridge, MA: Harvard University Press.

Mishler, E. G. (1995). Models of narrative analysis: A typology. *Journal of Narrative and Life History, 5*, 87–123.

Mishler, E. G. (1996). Missing persons: Recovering developmental stories/histories. In R. Jessor, A. Colby, & R. A. Shweder (Eds.), *Ethnography and human development: Context and meaning in social inquiry* (pp. 74–99). Chicago, IL: University of Chicago.

Mishler, E. G. (1999). *Storylines: Craftartists' narratives of identity*. Cambridge, MA: Harvard University Press.

Mumby, D. K. (1993). *Narrative and social control: Critical perspectives*. Newbury Park, CA: Sage.

Myerhoff, B. (1978). *Number our days*. New York, NY: Simon & Schuster.

Ochs, E., & Capps, L. (2001). *Living narrative: Creating lives in everyday storytelling*. Cambridge, MA: Harvard University Press.

Plummer, K. (1995). *Telling sexual stories: Power, change, and social worlds*. London, England: Routledge.

Polanyi, L. (1989). *Telling the American story: A structural and cultural analysis of conversational storytelling.* Cambridge, MA: MIT Press.

Polletta, F. (2006). *It was like a fever: Storytelling in protest and politics.* Chicago, IL: University of Chicago.

Quinn, N. (2005). *Finding culture in talk: A collection of methods.* New York, NY: Palgrave Macmillan.

Rich, J. A., & Grey, C. M. (2005). Pathways to recurrent trauma among young black men: Traumatic stress, substance use, and the "code of the street." *American Journal of Public Health, 95,* 816–824.

Riessman, C. K. (1987). When gender is not enough: Women interviewing women. *Gender & Society, 1,* 172–207.

Riessman, C. K. (1990). *Divorce talk: Women and men make sense of personal relationships.* New Brunswick, NJ: Rutgers University Press.

Riessman, C. K. (1993). *Narrative analysis.* Newbury Park, CA: Sage.

Riessman, C. K. (2000a). "Even if we don't have children [we] can live": Stigma and infertility in South India. In C. C. Mattingly & L. C. Garro (Eds.), *Narrative and cultural construction of illness and healing* (pp. 128–152). Berkeley: University of California Press.

Riessman, C. K. (2000b). Stigma and everyday resistance practices: Childless women in South India. *Gender & Society, 14,* 111–135.

Riessman, C. K. (2002a). Analysis of personal narratives. In J. A. Gubrium & J. F. Holstein (Eds.), *Handbook of interview research* (pp. 695–710). Thousand Oaks, CA: Sage.

Riessman, C. K. (2002b). Positioning gender identity in narratives of infertility: South Indian women's lives in context. In M. C. Inhorn & F. van Balen (Eds.), *Infertility around the globe: New thinking on childlessness, gender, and reproductive technologies* (pp. 152–170). Berkeley: University of California Press.

Riessman, C. K. (2005). Exporting ethics: A narrative about narrative research in South India. *Health: An Interdisciplinary Journal for the Social Study of Health, Illness and Medicine, 9,* 473–490.

Riessman, C. K. (2008). *Narrative methods for the human sciences.* Thousand Oaks, CA: Sage.

Rosaldo, R. (1989). *Culture and truth: Remaking of social analysis.* Boston, MA: Beacon Press.

White, H. (1981). The value of narrativity in the representation of reality. In W. J. T. Mitchell (Ed.), *On narrative* (pp. 1–23). Chicago, IL: University of Chicago Press.

Williams, G. (1984). The genesis of chronic illness: Narrative re-construction. *Sociology of Health & Illness, 6,* 175–200.

Wolfson, N. (1982). *The conversational historical present in American English narrative.* Dordrecht, The Netherlands: Foris.

26

INVESTIGATING RULING RELATIONS

Dynamics of Interviewing in Institutional Ethnography

◆ Marjorie L. DeVault and Liza McCoy

Social researchers usually think of interviews as sources for learning about individual experience. In this chapter, however, we discuss interviewing as part of an alternative to conventional forms of interview research, in which investigators use informants' accounts to examine the "relations of ruling" that shape local experiences (Smith, 1996). The researcher and interviewee are conceived as exploring together the social relations in which both are situated, and the interview is conducted to produce something like a map (Smith, 2005) of institutional processes.

We use the term *institutional ethnography*, following the Canadian sociologist Dorothy E. Smith, to refer to investigation of the empirical linkages among local settings of everyday life, organizations, and translocal processes of administration and governance. These linkages constitute a complex field of coordination and control

that Smith (1999) identifies as "the ruling relations"; these increasingly textual forms of coordination are "the forms in which power is generated and held in contemporary societies" (p. 79). Those who have followed Smith in developing institutional ethnography have investigated many different social processes and regimes of power, including the regulation of sexuality (Kinsman, 1996); the organization of health care (Rankin & Campbell, 2006), education (André-Bechely, 2005), and social work practice (De Montigny, 1995); the development of policies toward violence against women (Walker, 1990); employment and job training (Ng, 1996); welfare and workfare (Ridzi, 2009); international development regimes (Campbell & Teghtsoonian, 2010); relations of funding in the nonprofit sector (Nichols, 2008); environmental policy (Eastwood, 2005); and the organization of home and community life (Luken & Vaughan, 2005, 2006).

Over the past three decades, a loosely organized network of institutional ethnographers has emerged in North America and internationally.[1] This chapter draws from the work of that network. In preparing the discussion that follows, we have examined published examples of institutional ethnographic research, interviewed practitioners (individually and in small groups), and collected accounts of research practices and reflections via e-mail. We understand institutional ethnography as an emergent mode of inquiry, always subject to revision and the improvisation required by new applications. Thus, we wish to emphasize that we do not intend any prescriptive orthodoxy. Rather, we hope to introduce this approach, provide practical information about it that is often unarticulated in published work, and highlight the distinctive practices associated with institutional ethnographic interviews.

In the following section, we provide an introduction to the various uses of interviewing in institutional ethnography projects. Next, we discuss the conduct and dynamics of interviews. The subsequent section foregrounds the key role of texts and institutional discourses in institutional ethnography, showing how interviews can be oriented toward these aspects of social organization and how that orientation may affect the interview process. Finally, we turn briefly to analysis and writing. For more detailed and extended discussions of institutional ethnography as a project of inquiry, with a focus on methods of research and analysis, see Smith (2005, 2006), Campbell and Gregor (2002), McCoy (2006, 2008), and Campbell (2010). For a longer version of this chapter, see Smith (2006).

◆ Institutional Ethnography as a Mode of Inquiry

Dorothy Smith describes institutional ethnography as an alternative, feminist "sociology for people" (2005) grounded in "the ongoing activities of actual individuals" (Smith, 1999, p. 232, Note 5). Analytically fundamental to this approach is an ontology that views the social as the concerting of people's activities. This is an ontology shared by phenomenologists, symbolic interactionists, and ethnomethodologists.

Smith expands this shared ontology through the concept of social relations, which, as in Marx, refers to the coordinating of people's activities on a large scale, as this occurs in and across multiple sites, involving the activities of people who are not known to each other and who do not meet face-to-face.

In contemporary global capitalist society, our everyday worlds are organized in powerful ways by translocal social relations that pass through local settings and shape them according to a logic of transformation that begins and gathers speed somewhere else (e.g., if the local hospital closes, the explanation will not be wholly local). D. E. Smith (1990) refers to these translocal social relations that carry and accomplish coordination and control as "relations of ruling":

> They are those forms that we know as bureaucracy, administration, management, professional organization, and the media. They include also the complex of discourses, scientific, technical, and cultural, that intersect, interpenetrate, and coordinate the multiple sites of ruling. (p. 6)

Practices of rule or governance in contemporary society rely extensively on text-based discourses and forms of knowledge, and these are central in institutional ethnography (a topic we will return to later).

Building on this conception of ruling, Smith's (1987, 2005) notion of institution points to clusters of text-mediated relations organized around specific ruling functions, such as education or health care. "Institution," in this usage, informs a project of empirical inquiry, directing the researcher's attention to coordinated and intersecting work processes taking place in multiple sites. Institutional ethnographers reject the conventional, nominal view of institutions as discrete entities and instead adopt a view that is always focused on people's coordinated doings and the relations that connect them. The researcher looks for some entry point to these activities, always recognizing that researcher and informants are "part of the action," in some sense. Strategies for interviewing are shaped not only by institutional contexts (which goes without saying) but also—and in this approach, more important—by how the researcher locates himself or herself within those contexts and by the standpoint from which the

[1]The Institutional Ethnography Division within the U.S.-based Society for the Study of Social Problems has provided a space where practitioners gather annually to share ideas and work. See http://www.sssp1.org/index.cfm/pageid/1236.

research proceeds. The aim of the institutional ethnographer is to explore particular corners or strands within a specific institutional complex, in ways that make visible their points of connection with other sites and courses of action and always with a focus on how they are produced through the coordinated activities of people and the consequences they carry.

Institutional ethnography takes for its entry point the experiences of specific individuals whose everyday activities are in some way hooked into, shaped by, and constituent of the institutional relations under exploration. The term *ethnography* highlights the importance of research methods that can discover and explore these everyday activities and their positioning within extended sequences of action. When interviews are used in this approach, they are used not to reveal subjective states but to locate and trace the points of connection among individuals working in different parts of institutional complexes of activity. The interviewer's goal is to elicit talk that will not only illuminate a particular circumstance but also point toward next steps in an ongoing, cumulative inquiry into translocal processes. As Peter Grahame (1999) explains, "The field continuously opens up as the researcher explores the institutional nexus that shapes the local" (p. 7; see also P. R. Grahame, 1998).

The researcher's purpose in an institutional ethnography is not to generalize about the group of people interviewed but to find and describe social processes that have generalized effects. Thus, interviewees located somewhat differently are understood to be subject, in various ways, to the discursive and organizational processes that shape their activities. These institutional processes may produce similarities of experience, or they may organize various settings to sustain broader inequalities (as explored in DeVault, 1999, chap. 5); in either case, these generalizing consequences show the lineaments of ruling relations. Locating and specifying the ways in which people are hooked into social relations—and whether in similar or different ways—is part of the project of inquiry and the analytic work it entails. For example, George W. Smith (1998) treated the gay young men he interviewed not as a population of subjects but as informants knowledgeable about school life for gay youth. He explains,

The interviews opened various windows on different aspects of the organization of this regime. Each informant provides a partial view; the work

of institutional ethnography is to put together an integrated view based on these otherwise truncated accounts of schools. (p. 310)

The general relevance of the inquiry comes, then, not from a claim that local settings are similar but from the capacity of the research to disclose features of ruling that operate across many local settings. It is in this way that institutional ethnography works as a "sociology for people": It "investigate[s] the social forms of knowledge, coordination, and control that shape our and others' lives and in which we participate"; the research is meant to "extend rather than replace our everyday knowledge of the world" (McCoy, 2008, p. 702).

POSSIBLE SHAPES OF INSTITUTIONAL ETHNOGRAPHIC PROJECTS

There is no "one way" to conduct an institutional ethnographic investigation; rather, there is an analytic project that can be realized in diverse ways. Institutional ethnographies are rarely planned out fully in advance. Instead, the process of inquiry is rather like grabbing a ball of string, finding a thread, and then pulling it out. Institutional ethnographers know what they want to explain, but they can discover only step by step whom they need to interview or what texts and discourses they need to examine. In the discussion that follows, we describe some common "shapes" or trajectories of institutional ethnographic research.

A common—even a "classic"—approach to institutional ethnography begins with an experience or area of everyday practice whose determinants are to be explored. The researcher seeks to "take the standpoint" of the people whose experience provides the starting point of investigation. The researcher can employ a range of data collection techniques to explore the experiences and actualities that provide the starting place. Most common among these techniques are interviews and focus groups, participant observation, and the researcher's reflection on her or his own experience, all of which serve to generate descriptions of what people do in their everyday lives. The analytic enterprise is paramount, however, and ways of realizing it are diverse. Many institutional ethnographers use individual and group interviews. For example, Khayatt (1995) conducted interviews with young lesbians in secondary school.

Weigt (2006) interviewed mothers about their work of balancing the care of their children with the demands of low-wage employment. Mykhalovskiy and McCoy (2002) conducted focus groups with men and women living with HIV/AIDS about their work of looking after their health. Through informants' stories and descriptions, the researcher begins to identify some of the translocal relations, discourses, and institutional work processes that are shaping the informants' everyday work. Of particular interest to institutional ethnographers are the points of disjuncture or trouble that arise for people at the interface between their everyday lives and translocal relations of knowledge and coordination.

Some institutional ethnographers spend considerable time at this point of entry (for it can take time to understand the complexity of people's experiences and sites of everyday practice, and data from this exploration can provide material with much analytic potential). Eventually, however, the researcher will usually need to shift the investigation to begin examining those institutional processes that he or she has discovered to be shaping the experience and generating the trouble but that are not wholly known or visible to the original informants. Thus, a second stage of research commonly follows that usually involves a shift in research site, although not in standpoint. Often, this shift carries the investigation into organizational and professional work sites. At this stage, other forms of research and analysis may come to be used. The researcher may employ observation and the analysis of naturally occurring language to examine institutional work processes, for example. Or the researcher may use text and discourse analysis to examine the textual forms and practices of knowledge that organize those work processes. But interviews continue to play an important role here as well, whether as the primary form of investigation or as a way of filling in the gaps of what the researcher can learn through observation and document analysis. For example, Li-Fang Liang's (2010) study of migrant careworkers in Taiwan began with the workers themselves, but as she pursued the analysis she also interviewed labor brokers, employers and care recipients, and the physicians whose assessments of care needs determined whether Taiwanese employers would be allowed to hire migrant workers.

A common aspect of institutional ethnographic research at this second stage involves the researcher investigating institutional work processes by following a chain of action typically organized around and

through a set of documents, because it is texts that coordinate people's activity across time and place within institutional relations. For example, Turner (2001) traced the trajectory of a developer's planning proposal as it passed through a review process involving the city planning office, the local conservation authority, the railroad company, and a meeting of the city council.

In some institutional ethnographic research, the point of entry is in organizational work processes and the activities of the people who perform them. Rather than arriving at these processes through an exploration of the experience of people who are the objects of that work or who are in some way affected by it, here the researcher jumps right into the examination of organizational work sites. The researcher already knows about a set of administrative or professional practices and sets about studying how they are carried out, how they are discursively shaped, and how they organize other settings. For example, Elizabeth Townsend (1998) studied the work of professionals in the mental health system and the contradictions between their professional goal of empowering people and the system processes organized to control deviance, starting from the practice of occupational therapy. Lauren Eastwood (2005) investigated UN processes of forest policy making to illuminate the challenges facing activist NGOs attempting to intervene in policy decisions. This type of institutional ethnography emphasizes the detailed examination of administrative and professional work processes. It still begins, however, with a focus on the activities and work knowledges of actual people in actual settings, and it relies on their ability to speak from their own experience about how things are done. It also involves tracing institutional relations of power, coordination, and control beyond the everyday knowledge of the people at work in the starting place.

CONCEPTUALIZATION AND PLACE OF INTERVIEWING

Interviewing is present in some form in just about all institutional ethnographic studies. But "interviewing" in institutional ethnography is perhaps better described as "talking with people," and institutional ethnographic uses of interviewing should be understood in this wide sense, as stretching across a range of approaches to talk with informants. At one end of the continuum are planned interviews and focus groups occurring at appointed times. Then, there is the kind of "talking with people" that occurs during field observation, when the researcher is watching someone do her or his work. For example, Janet Rankin is exploring what nurses can know about their patients within the current organization of acute care, how that knowledge is made available to them through the information systems of the hospital, and how that shapes the way the nurses are able to do their work. She job-shadows nurses who have volunteered for her project and periodically asks them to explain what they are doing; she records these moments of interview using a digital recorder, which she also uses to record (with permission) relevant work conversations between the nurse and other nursing or medical staff. Rankin reports that the times when she asks the nurses to explain how they are reading and getting information about their patients from the computerized information system provide some of her richest data (interview, May 2010). On-the-spot interviews such as these can be combined with later, planned interviews to which the researcher brings a set of questions or topics based on the earlier observation-and-talk.

An institutional ethnographer conducts interviews to piece together a larger picture; that project of inquiry is radically open-ended, so that interviewing is typically less structured and more collaborative than in other kinds of interview projects. Often, interviewees are surprised—but also engaged—by the interest of institutional ethnographers in mundane organizational processes; they are engaged because the interview focuses on the details of their daily work. Institutional ethnographic interviews may also go beyond the usual research format of asking questions and listening to answers. Eric Mykhalovskiy comments,

> Describing interviews as a set of questions doesn't get at the actual work involved. For me, analytic thinking begins in the interview. It's like an analytic rehearsal. I'm checking my understanding as it develops; I offer it up to the informant for confirmation or correction. (Interview, September 1999)

◆ Conducting Institutional Ethnographic Interviews

Institutional ethnographic interviewing is open-ended inquiry, and institutional ethnographic interviewers are always oriented to sequences of interconnected activities. Thus, in many investigations, informants are chosen as the research progresses, as the researcher learns more about the social relations involved and begins to see avenues that need exploration. Liang's (2010) study of migrant careworkers in Taiwan provides an example: She was aware of the role of labor brokers and sought them out early in her research, but only later did she learn that physicians had a role in the implementation of Taiwan's migrant labor policy. Given that the purpose of interviewing is to build up an understanding of the coordination of activity in multiple sites, the interviews need not be standardized. Rather, each interview provides an opportunity for the researcher to learn about a particular piece of the extended relational chain, to check the developing picture of the coordinative process, and to become aware of additional questions that need attention.

Dorothy Smith reports that when she conducted interviews jointly with George Smith in their study of job training (Smith & Smith, 1990), they thought of the interviews as a way to build "piece by piece" a view of an extended organizational process. Rather than using standard questions, they based each interview on what they had learned from previous ones. She explains, "You have a sense of what you're after, although you sometimes don't know what you're after until you hear people telling you things. . . . Discovering what you don't know—and don't know you don't know—is an important aspect of the process" (interview, September 1999). As in any qualitative interviewing, there is a balance between directing the interview and encouraging informants to talk in ways that reflect their activity. The distinctiveness of institutional ethnographic interviews is produced by the researcher's developing knowledge of institutional processes, which allows a kind of listening and probing oriented toward institutional connections. Again, Smith explains, "The important thing is to think organizationally, recognizing you won't know at the beginning which threads to follow, knowing you won't follow all possible threads, but noting them along the way."

INTERVIEW STRATEGIES

Institutional ethnographic interviewing is typically organized around the idea of work, defined broadly or "generously" (Smith, 1987), and the "work knowledge" associated with it (Smith, 2005). Whether the paid work of an organizational position, the activist work of challenging a regime, or some everyday life work such as caring for children or managing an illness, the point of interest is the informant's activity, as it reveals and points toward the interconnected activities of others. The idea of work provides a conceptual frame and guides interview talk; the point is not to insist on the categorical status of any activity but to hold in place a conception of the social as residing in the coordination of people's actual activities.

The generous understanding of work deployed by institutional ethnographers is related to early feminist insights about women's unpaid and often invisible work—the recognition that although various kinds of work sustain social life, some are uncompensated, unacknowledged, or mystified as aspects of personality (e.g., women's "caring" work, as explored in DeVault, 1991). An institutional ethnographic study aims at a picture that displays all the activity sustaining a particular institutional nexus or arena, and this analytic goal gives rise to several distinctive strategies for the conduct of interviews. In the following subsections, we identify several kinds of work and discuss the strategies associated with each.

No matter which strategy is adopted, institutional ethnographic interviews engage both researcher and participant in a project of inquiry. Both are at work in the moment of the interview, participating in, as well as reporting and reflecting on, social relations. The researcher's goals—arising from the standpoint adopted in the research—shape the initial choices made, about whom to interview and what to ask about, but they also continue to shape the interview conversation, as both participants (or all, in the case of focus groups) develop shared understandings and thus know better how to talk about the relations of interest in the study. Quite often, interviews begin with a focus on work practices of everyday life, and those interviews suggest additional avenues of inquiry—so that the strategies we discuss below should not be seen as distinctly associated with particular types of research but as offering an array of choices that will most often be made as the research proceeds.

Work Practices of Everyday Life

Some researchers conduct institutional ethnographic interviews with a view to understanding the everyday/everynight experiences of people living particular lives—single mothers, people with AIDS or disabilities, older women, or recent immigrants,

for example. In these interviews, researchers seek detailed accounts of activities: What do mothers do when their children have trouble at school? How do individuals work at managing their health? What work do older women do to maintain their housing? How do new immigrants seek employment, education, or training? For example, Nancy Naples (1998) studied the implementation of an Iowa jobs program that allowed recipients to work toward a college degree. Her interviews produced accounts of women participants' everyday routines, which she used to uncover the tensions between their lives as mothers and college students and the demands of the program—thus bringing an "everyday life" dimension to policy analysis.

Informants may or may not think of what they do as a form of "work"; there is no need to insist on agreement about the status of the activity. The point is to learn about what the informant actually does. In a study of a public school choice program, Lois André-Bechely (2005) interviewed parents using the program. She notes, "Not all of them saw their involvement as work—it was just what they did—while others did actually use words like, 'it's my job,' etc." (e-mail communication, September 1999). On the other hand, Debra Brown (2006), who conducted group interviews with mothers involved in the child protection system, found that the women eagerly took up the notion of work as they collectively described the skills and effort that went into meeting the expectations of their caseworkers. When Griffith and Smith (2005) interviewed mothers, they found that it "worked well to take them through the school day, to ask them what they did at each point, such as what is involved in getting the kids ready for school, getting them there on time" (interview, September 1999).

Interviews about everyday life work may also be used to point toward the work practices of others. For example, George Smith (1998) uses the stories of young gay men as windows onto the work processes that affect them—both the "everyday work" of students upholding a heterosexist regime through surveillance and gossip and the paid work of teachers and administrators, which was not organized to interrupt that regime and sometimes reinforced it. Similarly, Mykhalovskiy and McCoy (2002) worked with AIDS activists on a research project that explored the everyday experience of people living with HIV/AIDS. Interviews and focus groups explored people's efforts to find health care providers, negotiate with them about treatment options, and manage the demands of complex medication regimens. Those interviews provided windows onto the organization of health care and treatment information and the obstacles that some people living with HIV/AIDS face as they pursue treatment.

Frontline Organizational Work

Frontline professionals such as teachers, nurses, trainers, social workers, and community agency personnel often become informants in institutional ethnographic research. Individuals in such positions are especially important because they make the linkages between clients and ruling discourses, "working up" the messiness of an everyday circumstance so that it fits the categories and protocols of a professional regime. Frank Ridzi (2009), for example, focused on intake workers implementing U.S. welfare-to-work policy; he used both formal and informal interviews to analyze how the workers come to "buy in" to a new policy discourse. Yoko Ueda (1995) interviewed human resource professionals to learn about policies that shaped the family work of Japanese expatriate wives in Toronto. In other studies, researchers may be more directly focused on the work situations of these frontline workers and concerned with the organization and control of such work. For example, Janet Rankin and Marie Campbell's (2006) studies of nursing work focus on managerial strategies that limit nurses' autonomy at work; Henry Parada and his associates examine similar issues for social workers (Parada, Barnoff, & Coleman, 2007). Ann Manicom's (1995) examination of health work undertaken by teachers in low-income schools explores how these teachers are drawn into work that goes beyond official accounts of their jobs.

Here again, institutional ethnographers seek detailed accounts of work processes, but interviewing frontline workers presents distinctive challenges. These workers have been trained to use the very concepts and categories that institutional ethnographers wish to unpack, and they are accustomed to speaking from within a ruling discourse. Thus, the interviewer must find ways of moving the talk beyond institutional language to "what actually happens" in the setting. Marie Campbell teaches such interviewing strategies in part by offering the following advice: "Listen to the person tell her story. Pay attention to the sequencing. Then ask yourself, can you tell exactly how she gets from one point to another? If not, ask questions, clarify so that you can" (interview, January 2000).

Such strategies require practice, because "we're all very good at filling in the blanks." But the organizational orientation of institutional ethnographers leads them, with practice, to see both gaps in these accounts and the filling in that is needed. The challenge of moving beyond institutional language is so central to institutional ethnographic interviewing that we will return to it in the following section.

In some studies, interviews might include discussion of possible modifications of frontline work. For example, Pence's (2001) study of safety for battered women involved interviews with advocates, hospital staff, and criminal justice workers. As she gained an understanding of the interlocking activities of these workers, she could see that women's safety was only one of the concerns that shaped their work and, in fact, was often subordinated to organizational imperatives. She and her team began to ask workers not only how the system operated but also how it might be organized differently. She explains,

> We ask, "Is there something you don't have in your job, that if you did have, would help prevent that woman getting beat up?" "If you were going to build victim safety into this process, how would you do it?" It's an eye-opener. People in an institution rarely get asked, do you want to change something as basic as a form you fill out every day? How would you change it? And when you ask them, "Why is this on the form?" they can be quite insightful [about how the form works in the system], even though they might never have thought about it that way before. (Focus group, August 1999)

This dual emphasis on analysis and change is important for those researchers who work in partnership with activists or policymakers.

"Ruling" Work

Institutional ethnographers are always interested in moving beyond the interchanges of frontline settings to track the macroinstitutional policies and practices that organize those local settings. Thus, interviews are often conducted with managers and administrators who work at the level of translocal policy making and implementation, and these interviews also require a distinctive orientation and strategy. Kamini Maraj Grahame (1998), who studied federally funded job training for immigrant women in the United States, emphasizes the complexity of this kind of institutional process and the amount of "legwork and conversation" required, even to have a sense of where in the structure one might need to conduct interviews. She learned about the institutional complex of job training while working in and with community organizations, and she eventually conducted interviews not only within those organizations but also with managers in the local, state, and federal agencies that funded and oversaw their programs. With each interviewee, she focused on that worker's role in the overall job training system. She would ask, "What do you do?" Recognizing that she was interviewing each at a particular point in time, and therefore at a particular point in what she came to call "the training cycle," she would ask what the interviewee was doing that day or week, and then she would ask, "Why are you doing this now?" Whenever someone mentioned a document, she would ask to see a copy of it and then ask what the worker did with that document. In these ways, she built an accumulating understanding of how work processes were textually linked across sites and levels of administration.

Often, interviews with managers and administrators are conducted in the later phases of institutional ethnographic studies, so that researchers can use the information gained from clients and frontline workers to direct the interviewing. For example, Lois André-Bechely reports,

As I got farther up the chain of command, I had already done preliminary analysis of parent interviews and policy documents and my questions were focused on trying to uncover the social and textual organization of school choice practices that parents encounter and participate in. (E-mail communication, September 1999)

André-Bechely also used her knowledge as a former teacher to organize questions for administrators, but the talk still proceeded in the searching and open manner characteristic of institutional ethnography.

Processing Interchanges

Institutional ethnographers are especially alert to the intersections of work processes, points that Pence (2001) has labeled "processing interchanges":

Processing interchanges are organizational occasions of action in which one practitioner receives from another a document pertaining to a case

(e.g., a 911 incident report, a warrant request, or a motion for a continuance), and then makes something of the document, does something to it, and forwards it on to the next organizational occasion for action. It is the construction of these processing interchanges coupled with a highly specialized division of labor that accomplishes much of the ideological work of the institution. Workers' tasks are shaped by certain prevailing features of the system, features so common to workers that they begin to see them as natural, as the way things are done and—in some odd way—as the only way they could be done, rather than as planned procedures and rules developed by individuals ensuring certain ideological ways of interpreting and acting on a case. (p. 204)

In her study of the processing of domestic violence cases, Pence (1997, 2001) attends to the spaces and tools that organize the tasks of workers—how dispatchers use computers, the police use dictaphones, and so on—and to the forms required at each point of connection. As Pence (1997) points out, it is not "the woman who was beaten who moves from one point to the next in the stages of case processing"; rather, the "file stands in for the woman who was assaulted" (p. 67). In studying how this extremely important file is produced, Pence watched workers in these processing interchanges and also asked them about their work, querying police officers, for instance, on "how they decide when to write a report, how they decide what to record in their narratives, and how much leeway they have in making these decisions" (p. 71). At each processing interchange, she explains, "An institutional investigation helps to determine how such an objective (i.e. accounting for victim safety) could be incorporated into the design at each of these occasions" (p. 89). Working with practitioners in the system, Pence has developed an "audit" procedure—basically, an institutional ethnographic investigation to be used collaboratively to provide "a place for advocates and practitioners to work together" (p. 187).

Campbell, Copeland, and Tate (1998) used a similar approach in participatory research on home support for people with disabilities. Campbell's team used interviews to identify processing interchanges they wished to examine in detail and then arranged to conduct observations of these moments in the management of home support. Watching a scheduler at a computer screen, for example, they asked questions to help her make explicit the choices she was making. "People think the computer does it," Campbell notes, "but that glosses the judgment involved in her work" (interview, January 2000). The researchers found that continuity in scheduling home support workers was important for people with disabilities and a goal shared by workers in the system. As they observed the scheduler, however, and asked about her work, they could see how organizational priorities disrupted a focus on continuity.

SELECTING INFORMANTS

Institutional ethnographers are not oriented toward descriptive reporting on a population, and they do not think of informants as a "sample." Still, when exploring everyday experience, some seek informants who can report on varied circumstances and situations. For institutional ethnographers, these efforts allow them to explore how the people living in different circumstances are drawn into common organizational processes. Some report that attention to differences among informants can easily pull them toward the kinds of categorical analyses embedded in ruling activities, as when Smith and Griffith (1990) found themselves thinking much like school administrators about the class composition of student groups. One solution is to conceive of this kind of selection in terms of diversity of experience. For example, when interviewing people living with HIV/AIDS about their health work, Mykhalovskiy and McCoy (2002) thought about diversity in their informants' circumstances, reasoning that they needed to include women caring for children, people living in prison, and people on welfare, for example, to understand how these social and institutional positionings shape the work people can do around their health.

As discussed above, institutional ethnographers typically use such interviews as pointers toward informants working elsewhere. Those interviewees might be chosen in more varied ways. Some researchers follow "chains of action" (e.g., K. M. Grahame, 1998; McCoy, 1998). Some choose informants in and around sites of confrontation: George Smith (1990), for example, located the field of the AIDS bureaucracy through work with other activists attempting to gain access to treatments. And in some studies, it seems useful for researchers to select "good thinkers" as interviewees. When Pence interviewed police personnel, for example, she sought those who wrote especially complete or useful reports:

> If you read 50 police reports, you can say, "I want to talk to the cop who wrote these four." But I also try to interview one dud, so I can see how much is the institutional process and how much is the person. (Focus group, August 1999)

Often, as George Smith (1990) explains, researchers rely on the informants they encounter as their investigations proceed, using each conversation to expand understanding of the terrain.

While the selection of informants is open-ended, the process is not haphazard. Rather, fieldwork and interviewing are driven by faithfulness to the actual work processes that connect individuals and activities within an institutional complex. Rigor comes not from technique—in sampling or analysis—but from the corrigibility of the developing map of social relations. When George Smith (1990) was learning about placebo-controlled trials of experimental AIDS treatments, for example, he did not need to identify recurring themes in the accounts of multiple physician informants. Rather, he sought their help in filling in his knowledge of how such trials work, continuing to check the account he was building as he proceeded with the investigation and returning to physician (and other) informants as needed when questions or inconsistencies arose.

◆ Interviewing About Textual Practices

Text-based forms of knowledge and discursive practices are central to large-scale organization and relations of ruling in contemporary society. They function like a central nervous system running through and coordinating different sites. To find out how particular translocal relations work, a researcher needs to find the texts and text-based knowledge forms in operation. Thus, institutional ethnographic investigation often involves close attention to textual practices, and interviewing is important in this regard.

When institutional ethnographers talk about texts, they mean some kind of document or semiotic material that has a relatively fixed and replicable character, for it is that aspect of texts—that they can be stored, transferred, copied, produced in bulk, and distributed widely, allowing them to be activated by users at different times and in different places—that allows them to play a standardizing and mediating role. In this view, a text can be any kind of document, on paper or on computer screens; it can also be a drawing, a photograph, a printed instrument reading, or a video or sound recording. It can involve words, numbers, images, or any other shared symbolic system.

Much institutional ethnographic research has focused on standardized texts used in professional and bureaucratic settings, such as care pathway forms in hospitals (Mykhalovskiy, 2001), intake forms and applications at an employment agency (Ng, 1996), patients' charts (Diamond, 1992), patient satisfaction surveys (Rankin & Campbell, 2006), and course information sheets used in competency-based education reform (Jackson, 1995). Other bureaucratic texts studied have included job descriptions (Reimer, 1995) and developers' maps used in land-use planning (Turner, 1995). Griffith (1992, 2001) and Ng (1995) have examined legislative texts, and Eastwood (2005, 2006) has analyzed the conceptual frameworks of international environmental policy. Sometimes institutional ethnographers look at the creation or generation of texts, such as the work of producing a newsletter for doctors (Mykhalovskiy, 2003), creating materials for job skills training (Smith & Smith, 1990), or taking wedding photographs (McCoy, 1995).

Institutional ethnographers are also interested in the text-mediated discourses that frame issues, establish terms and concepts, and in various ways serve as resources that people draw into their everyday work processes, for example, health services research and evidence-based medicine (Mykhalovskiy, 2001, 2003), the literature on child development (Griffith, 1995), the literature on "deviant" sexuality as an aspect of the policing of gay men (Kinsman, 1996), the terms of an international development regime (Campbell & Teghtsoonian, 2010; Mueller, 1995), and popular cultural discourses of femininity (D. E. Smith, 1990, chap. 6) or housing (Luken & Vaughan, 2006). Whatever the text or textual process, in institutional ethnography, it is examined for the ways it mediates relations of ruling and organizes what can be said and done.

ASKING ABOUT TEXTS

Whenever texts come to be identified as central to the relations under study—whether through exploratory interviews, through preparatory work, or through the researcher's prior knowledge—the research at some stage may involve interviews with people who can talk in detail about a text or those aspects of a textual process they know. One effective way for an interviewer to structure such an interview is to sit down with the informant and the text in question and talk very concretely about what is in the text and how the informant works with it.

If the document in question is a standardized form, some researchers like to do the interview around a form that has been completed, rather than a blank one, as that will result in more concrete description. For example, when Dorothy Smith was interviewing a probation officer about a presentencing investigation form, she worked from an actual, completed form to ask about the sources of information (predominantly textual) and the practices of judgment that went into filling it out (interview, September 1999). Of course, this strategy requires institutional access to what is often confidential information about clients, students, or patients, and ethics board approval of that access. Since what the institutional ethnographer is interested in are practices of knowledge and decision making, it often works well to obtain copies of completed forms and case notes with the personal information (e.g., names and addresses) removed by agency staff before being given to the researcher. What remains is the language through which the client's needs or actions are depicted in institutionally relevant terms as a warrant for institutionally accountable forms of action.

In other cases, the text in question is not one the informant creates or completes but one he or she activates in some way, such as a report or a memo. Here, the interviewer might focus on practices of reading to learn how the text is taken up within an accountable work process. For example, in his research on health services research and its use in health care restructuring, Eric Mykhalovskiy (2001) interviewed a hospital administrator about her use of reports that show comparative data on different hospitals' average length of stay. He learned how her administrative work oriented to the forms of visibility created by the reports as she worked to improve her hospital's standing in the comparative tables.

What the researcher wants to learn about a text and the practices of making or using it will vary, depending on the nature of the text and the focus of the investigation, but in general institutional ethnographers are after the following:

- How the text comes to this informant and where it goes after the informant is done with it

- What the informant needs to know in order to use the text (create it, respond to it, fill it out, etc.)

- What the informant does with, for, and on account of the text

- How the text intersects with and depends on other texts and textual processes as sources of information, generators of conceptual frames, authorizing texts, and so on

- The conceptual framework that organizes the text and its competent reading

THE PROBLEM AND RESOURCE OF INSTITUTIONAL LANGUAGE

Institutional work processes are organized by conceptual schemes and distinctive categories. These are the terms in which the accountability of the work is produced, and procedures of accountability provide one of the main ways in which various local settings are pulled into translocal relations. Institutional ethnography therefore pays strong attention to institutional categories and the interpretive schemata that connect them.

In interviews, it is common—and understandable—that people in an institutional setting describe their work using the language of the institution. This is especially the case with people who have been taught a professional discourse as part of their training or people whose work requires them to provide regular accounts of institutional processes. "Some people do jobs where public relations is part of their job, so they are doing that work while talking to me" (K. M. Grahame, focus group, August 1999). The challenge for the institutional ethnographer is to recognize when the informant is using institutional language. Not to do so is to risk conducting interviews that contain little usable data beyond the expression of institutional ideology in action, because institutional language conceals the very practices institutional ethnography aims to discover and describe. Dorothy Smith elaborates as follows:

These terms are extraordinarily empty. They rely on your being able to fill out what they could be talking about. During the interview, you do that

filling in while you listen, but when you look at the transcript afterward, the description isn't there. (Interview, September 1999)

As an example, Ann Manicom reports as follows:

One challenge I've faced in interviewing professionals is . . . to get them beyond saying something like, "Well, I have a lot of ADHD kids" to getting them to actually describe day-to-day work processes. The discourses are of course also interesting and an important piece of the analysis, but shifting them out of the discourse is important for actual descriptions of the work process. (E-mail communication, September 1999)

An informant's comment that she has "a lot of ADHD kids" would not be treated by an institutional ethnographer as a straightforward description of her work, although it does show the teacher using institutional concepts to make sense of and talk about her day-to-day actuality. Within the institution of schooling, it is certainly a competent description; other teachers would nod and feel that they knew exactly what the teacher was talking about. A school administrator would understand something about that classroom relevant to her work of allocating resources. This is because the term references a discourse and practice of knowledge operative within the institution. An interviewer who knows something about teaching and professional discourses might also find, as Smith suggests above, that he or she too knows what the teacher is talking about. An alert institutional ethnographer, however, would try to get the teacher to describe, for example, what her work with "ADHD kids" involves. This might be done by asking the teacher to describe particular classroom events, thereby shifting the teacher's talk to the concrete practices and lived experiences of her work. The researcher would also try to learn how the teacher uses the ADHD concept to organize her work with the children and her conferences with their parents. Furthermore, the researcher might try to learn how ADHD as a category operates in the administration of schooling: For example, in some school districts, classroom assistants and other resources are allocated through a procedure that takes into account the number of students in a class who are entered in school records as having "special needs," such as ADHD. An institutional ethnographer encountering institutional language has thus a twofold objective: (1) to obtain a description of the actuality that is assumed by, but not revealed in, the institutional terms and, at the same time, (2) to learn how such terms and the discourses they carry operate in the institutional setting.

◆ *Analysis and Presentation*

Institutional ethnography is fundamentally an analytic project, so in this section we briefly address the work that comes after the interview. The studies we have cited throughout the chapter provide models for analysis; our comments here are meant to extend the preceding discussion of this distinctive type of interview by considering its use in the analytic project at hand.

In general, institutional ethnographers look at interview data as raising questions; analysis involves moving back and forth between collected speech and the contexts that produce it—not only the context of the interview but also the immediate and broader contexts of the participant's work. According to Khayatt, the key is to ask, "How is it that these people are saying what they're saying?" (focus group, October 1999). Griffith says of analysis, "It's never instances, it's always processes and coordination. It's all these little hooks. To make sense of it, you have to understand not just the speech of the moment, but what it's hooked into" (focus group, October 1999). Ng (1996, 1999), whose research explores the work experiences of immigrant women, believes that conventional analyses of immigrants' lives often "produce ethnicity" by linking informants' comments back to their "home cultures." Her goal, instead, is to find clues to "how things happen" for the people identified as immigrants in Canadian institutions (focus group, October 1999).

John McKendy (1999, 2006), who interviewed men incarcerated for violent crimes, focuses his analysis on the interview itself as a conversation, to make visible the juxtaposition of primary narratives and ideological, institutionally oriented accounts: "In doing the analysis . . . I am on the lookout for segments of the interviews where 'fault lines' can be detected, as the two modes of telling—the narrative and the ideological—rub up against each other" (McKendy, 1999).

Institutional ethnographers try to maintain a focus on institutional relations in their writing practices as well. George Smith (1998) uses the notion of the "exhibit" to specify a distinctive use of interview excerpts:

> As exhibits, the excerpts create windows within the text, bringing into view the social organization of my informants' lives for myself and for my readers to examine. Though what is brought into view emerges out of the dialogic relations of the interview, excerpts must not be read as extensions of my description. As exhibits, they make available the social organization of the everyday school lives of the individuals I interviewed. Dialogically they enter the actual social organization of schools into the text of the analysis. (p. 312)

Many institutional ethnographers find that they collect considerably more information than they use in a single analysis, because the analysis eventually follows some more specific thread of social organization. Dorothy Smith explains, "You don't have to use the whole interview. You can be quite selective, because you're not interested in all aspects of the institutional process" (interview, September 1999). As in most aspects of institutional ethnography, there is no fixed analytic technique or writing format to which all practitioners adhere; instead, writers have the goal of keeping the institution in view and different ways of realizing that goal.

◆ *Conclusion*

In one view, our brief discussion here risks misrepresenting institutional ethnography because of the artificiality of separating out the "interview" parts of the approach. For practitioners, institutional ethnography always combines theory and method, and these are understood not as dichotomized "ingredients" for an analysis but as constituting a coherent approach to "writing the social" (Smith, 1999). We have also been concerned with the danger of reifying the approach as technique. These risks seem worth taking, however, because we believe that institutional ethnography approaches offer distinctive advantages for researchers seeking to unmask the relations of ruling that shape everyday life.

Institutional ethnography is one of the new modes of inquiry that have grown from the cracks in monolithic notions of "objective" social science, as women of all backgrounds, people of color, and others previously excluded from knowledge production have found the space and "voice" to explore their experiences and pose questions relevant to their lives. In this context, the distinctiveness of institutional ethnography lies in its commitment to going beyond the goal of simply "giving voice." While participants' accounts are key to institutional ethnographies, these studies aim to build on those accounts in order to disclose the power of social relations that are organized and coordinated outside of people's intentions and interpretations. Much of the work we have discussed here has occurred among professionals concerned with their relations to clients and the forces shaping their work or among activists working to understand the institutions they confront and seek to change. In addition, many institutional ethnographers have found that the approach provides a powerful teaching tool, because it can provide anyone with a strategy for investigating the lineaments of ruling (Naples, 2002).

Institutional ethnographies explicate ruling processes that are pervasive, consequential, and not easily understood from the perspective of any local experience. But the approach suggests that an understanding grounded in such a vantage point is possible—and necessary if we are to build on excluded perspectives the kind of "map" of institutional processes that might be used in making changes to benefit those subject to ruling regimes. The institutional ethnographic interview can be understood as an interaction designed for collaborative inquiry; it brings together interviewee and researcher as co-inquirers, extending their knowledge of the forces shaping their experiences.

◆ References

André-Bechely, L. N. (2005). *Could it be otherwise? Parents and the inequities of public school choice.* New York, NY: Routledge.

Brown, D. (2006). Working the system: Re-thinking the role of mothers and the reduction of "risk" in child protection work. *Social Problems, 53,* 352–370.

Campbell, M. (2010). Institutional ethnography. In I. Bourgeault, R. Dingwall, & R. Devries (Eds.), *The SAGE handbook of qualitative methods in health research* (pp. 497–512). London, England: Sage.

Campbell, M., Copeland, B., & Tate, B. (1998). Taking the standpoint of people with disabilities: Experiences with participation. *Canadian Journal of Rehabilitation, 12,* 95–104.

Campbell, M., & Gregor, F. (2002). *Mapping social relations: A primer in doing institutional ethnography.* Aurora, Ontario, Canada: Garamond.

Campbell, M., & Teghtsoonian, K. (2010). Aid effectiveness and women's empowerment: Practices of governance in the funding of international development. *Signs: Journal of Women in Culture and Society, 36*(1), 177–202.

De Montigny, G. (1995). *Social working: An ethnography of front-line practice.* Toronto, Ontario, Canada: University of Toronto Press.

DeVault, M. L. (1991). *Feeding the family: The social organization of caring as gendered work.* Chicago, IL: University of Chicago Press.

DeVault, M. L. (1999). *Liberating method: Feminism and social research.* Philadelphia, PA: Temple University Press.

Diamond, T. (1992). *Making gray gold: Narratives of nursing home care.* Chicago, IL: University of Chicago Press.

Eastwood, L. E. (2005). *The social organization of policy: An institutional ethnography of UN forest deliberations.* New York, NY: Routledge.

Eastwood, L. E. (2006). Making the institution ethnographically accessible: U.N. document production and the transformation of experience. In D. E. Smith (Ed.), *Institutional ethnography as practice* (pp. 181–197). Lanham, MD: Rowman & Littlefield.

Grahame, K. M. (1998). Asian women, job training, and the social organization of immigrant labor markets. *Qualitative Sociology, 21,* 75–90.

Grahame, P. R. (1998). Ethnography, institutions, and the social organization of knowledge. *Human Studies, 21,* 347–360.

Grahame, P. R. (1999). Doing qualitative research: Three problematics. *Discourse of Sociological Practice, 2*(1), 4–10.

Griffith, A. I. (1992). Educational policy as text and action. *Educational Policy, 6,* 415–428.

Griffith, A. I. (1995). Mothering, schooling, and children's development. In M. Campbell & A. Manicom (Eds.), *Knowledge, experience, and ruling relations* (pp. 108–121). Toronto, Ontario, Canada: University of Toronto Press.

Griffith, A. I. (2001). Texts, tyranny, and transformation: Educational restructuring in Ontario. In J. Portelli & P. Solomon (Eds.), *The erosion of democracy in education* (pp. 83–98). Calgary, Alberta, Canada: Detselig.

Griffith, A. I., & Smith, D. E. (2005). *Mothering for schooling.* New York, NY: RoutledgeFalmer.

Jackson, N. (1995). "These things just happen": Talk, text, and curriculum reform. In M. Campbell & A. Manicom (Eds.), *Knowledge, experience, and ruling relations* (pp. 164–180). Toronto, Ontario, Canada: University of Toronto Press.

Khayatt, D. (1995). Compulsory heterosexuality: Schools and lesbian students. In M. Campbell & A. Manicom (Eds.), *Knowledge, experience, and ruling relations* (pp. 149–163). Toronto, Ontario, Canada: University of Toronto Press.

Kinsman, G. (1996). *The regulation of desire: Homo and hetero sexualities*. Montreal, Quebec, Canada: Black Rose.

Liang, L.-F. (2010). *Constructing migrant care labor: A study of institutional process and the discourse of migration and work* (Doctoral dissertation, Sociology: Dissertations and Theses, Paper 63). Syracuse University, Syracuse, NY.

Luken, P. C., & Vaughan, S. (2005). "Be a genuine homemaker in your own home": Gender and familial relations in state housing practices, 1917–1922. *Social Forces, 83*, 1603–1626.

Luken, P. C., & Vaughan, S. (2006). Standardizing childrearing through housing. *Social Problems, 53*, 299–331.

Manicom, A. (1995). "What's health got to do with it"? Class, gender, and teachers' work. In M. Campbell & A. Manicom (Eds.), *Knowledge, experience, and ruling relations* (pp. 135–148). Toronto, Ontario, Canada: University of Toronto Press.

McCoy, L. (1995). Activating the photographic text. In M. Campbell & A. Manicom (Eds.), *Knowledge, experience, and ruling relations* (pp. 181–192). Toronto, Ontario, Canada: University of Toronto Press.

McCoy, L. (1998). Producing "what the deans know": Cost accounting and the restructuring of postsecondary education. *Human Studies, 21*, 395–418.

McCoy, L. (2006). Keeping the institution in view: Working with interview accounts of everyday experience. In D. E. Smith (Ed.), *Institutional ethnography as practice* (pp. 109–125). Lanham, MD: Rowman & Littlefield.

McCoy, L. (2008). Institutional ethnography and constructionism. In J. A. Holstein & J. F. Gubrium (Eds.), *Handbook of constructionist research* (pp. 701–714). New York, NY: Guilford Press.

McKendy, J. P. (1999). *Bringing stories back in: Agency and responsibility of men incarcerated for violent offences*. Unpublished manuscript.

McKendy, J. P. (2006). "I'm very careful about that": Narrative and agency of men in prison. *Discourse & Society, 17*, 473–502.

Mueller, A. (1995). Beginning in the standpoint of women: An investigation of the gap between *Cholas* and "women of Peru." In M. Campbell & A. Manicom (Eds.), *Knowledge, experience, and ruling relations* (pp. 96–107). Toronto, Ontario, Canada: University of Toronto Press.

Mykhalovskiy, E. (2001). Troubled hearts, care pathways and hospital restructuring: Exploring health services research as active knowledge. *Studies in Cultures, Organizations, and Societies, 7*, 269–298.

Mykhalovskiy, E. (2003). Evidence-based medicine: Ambivalent reading and clinical recontextualization of science. *Health, 7*, 331–352.

Mykhalovskiy, E., & McCoy, L. (2002). Troubling ruling discourses of health: Using institutional ethnography in community-based research. *Critical Public Health, 12*, 17–37.

Naples, N. (1998). Bringing everyday life to policy analysis: The case of white rural women negotiating college and welfare. *Journal of Poverty, 2*, 23–53.

Naples, N. (2002). Negotiating the politics of experiential learning in women's studies: Lessons from the community action project. In R. Wiegman (Ed.), *Women's studies on its own* (pp. 383–415). Durham, NC: Duke University Press.

Ng, R. (1995). Multiculturalism as ideology: A textual analysis. In M. Campbell & A. Manicom (Eds.), *Knowledge, experience, and ruling relations* (pp. 35–48). Toronto, Ontario, Canada: University of Toronto Press.

Ng, R. (1996). *The politics of community services: Immigrant women, class and state*. Halifax, Nova Scotia, Canada: Fernwood.

Ng, R. (1999). Homeworking: Dream realized or freedom constrained? The globalized reality of immigrant garment workers. *Canadian Woman Studies, 19*(3), 110–114.

Nichols, N. (2008). Understanding the funding game: The textual coordination of civil sector work. *Canadian Journal of Sociology, 33*, 61–87.

Parada, H., Barnoff, L., & Coleman, B. (2007). Negotiating "professional agency": Social work and decision-making within the Ontario child welfare system. *Journal of Sociology and Social Welfare, 34*, 35–56.

Pence, E. (1997). *Safety for battered women in a textually mediated legal system* (Doctoral dissertation). University of Toronto, Ontario, Canada.

Pence, E. (2001). Safety for battered women in a textually mediated legal system. *Studies in Cultures, Organizations, and Societies, 7*, 199–229.

Rankin, J. M., & Campbell, M. L. (2006). *Managing to nurse: Inside Canada's health care reform*. Toronto, Ontario, Canada: University of Toronto Press.

Reimer, M. (1995). Downgrading clerical work in a textually mediated labour process. In M. Campbell & A. Manicom (Eds.), *Knowledge, experience, and ruling relations* (pp. 193–208). Toronto, Ontario, Canada: University of Toronto Press.

Ridzi, F. (2009). *Selling welfare reform: Work-first and the new common sense of employment*. New York, NY: New York University Press.

Smith, D. E. (1987). *The everyday world as problematic: A feminist sociology*. Boston, MA: Northeastern University Press.

Smith, D. E. (1990). *Texts, facts and femininity: Exploring the relations of ruling*. New York, NY: Routledge.

Smith, D. E. (1996). The relations of ruling: A feminist inquiry. *Studies in Cultures, Organizations and Societies, 2,* 171–190.

Smith, D. E. (1999). *Writing the social: Theory, critique, investigations.* Toronto, Ontario, Canada: University of Toronto Press.

Smith, D. E. (2005). *Institutional ethnography: A sociology for people.* Lanham, MD: AltaMira Press.

Smith, D. E. (Ed.). (2006). *Institutional ethnography as practice.* Lanham, MD: Rowman & Littlefield.

Smith, D. E., & Griffith, A. I. (1990). Coordinating the uncoordinated: Mothering, schooling, and social class. In G. Miller & J. A. Holstein (Eds.), *Perspectives on social problems: A research annual* (pp. 25–44). Greenwich, CT: JAI Press.

Smith, D. E., & Smith, G. (1990). Re-organizing the jobs skills training relation: From "human capital" to "human resources." In J. Muller (Ed.), *Education for work, education as work: Canada's changing community colleges* (pp. 171–196). Toronto, Ontario, Canada: Garamond.

Smith, G. W. (1990). Political activist as ethnographer. *Social Problems, 37,* 629–648.

Smith, G. W. (1998). The ideology of "fag": The school experience of gay students. *Sociological Quarterly, 39,* 309–355.

Townsend, E. A. (1998). *Good intentions overruled: A critique of empowerment in the routine organization of mental health services.* Toronto, Ontario, Canada: University of Toronto Press.

Turner, S. M. (1995). Rendering the site developable: Texts and local government decision making in land use planning. In M. Campbell & A. Manicom (Eds.), *Knowledge, experience, and ruling relations* (pp. 234–248). Toronto, Ontario, Canada: University of Toronto Press.

Turner, S. M. (2001). Texts and the institutions of municipal government: The power of texts in the public process of land development. *Studies in Cultures, Organizations and Societies, 7,* 297–325.

Ueda, Y. (1995). Corporate wives: Gendered education of their children. In M. Campbell & A. Manicom (Eds.), *Knowledge, experience and ruling relations* (pp. 122–134). Toronto, Ontario, Canada: University of Toronto Press.

Walker, G. A. (1990). *Family violence and the women's movement: The conceptual politics of struggle.* Toronto, Ontario, Canada: University of Toronto Press.

Weigt, J. (2006). Compromises to carework: The social organization of mothers' experiences in the low-wage labor market after welfare reform. *Social Problems, 53,* 332–351.

◆ *Interviews*

Campbell, M. Telephone interview with M. L. DeVault, January 2000.

Grahame, K. M. Focus group conducted by L. McCoy, Duluth, MN, August 1999.

Griffith, A. I. Focus group conducted by L. McCoy, Toronto, Ontario, Canada, October 1999.

Khayatt, D. Focus group conducted by L. McCoy, Toronto, Ontario, Canada, October 1999.

Mykhalovskiy, E. Interview conducted by L. McCoy, Toronto, Ontario, Canada, September 1999.

Ng, R. Focus group conducted by L. McCoy, Toronto, Ontario, Canada, October 1999.

Pence, E. Focus group conducted by L. McCoy, Duluth, MN, August 1999.

Rankin, J. Interview conducted by L. McCoy, Calgary, Alberta, Canada, May 2010.

Smith, D. E. Interview conducted by M. L. DeVault and L. McCoy, Toronto, Ontario, Canada, September 1999.

27

INTERVIEWS AS DISCOURSE DATA

◆ Pirjo Nikander

The term *discourse analysis* (DA) has a wide reference and is often characterized as an umbrella designator for a growing range of different theoretical approaches, analytic emphasis, and typical or preferred data types (e.g., Phillips & Hardy, 2002; Wetherell, Taylor, & Yates, 2001a, 2001b; Wodak & Meyer, 2009). Despite the range of approaches and disciplinary locations of DA, the common ground for variants within the DA enterprise consists of social constructionist epistemology; an interest in the dynamics of interaction, talk, and texts; and systematic analysis on recurrent elements of discursive, cultural meaning making (e.g., Koro-Ljungberg, 2008; Nikander, 2008). Research materials in DA, in the broadest sense of the term, consist of all forms of talk transcribed into a written format from audio or video recordings, and a wide variety of written and visual documents. These may vary from dyadic or multiparty interaction in everyday and institutional settings to (group) interviews and focus groups; the analysis of documents, records, phone and online conversations, diaries and newspaper items, media products, political gatherings,

speeches, TV interviews or talk on radio; and, increasingly, the analysis of visual materials and the semiotics of place.

In recent years, however, the status of qualitative interviews as a means of data generation has been a topic of live debate, and the discursive social-scientific field is of two minds when it comes to using research interviews and their relative advantages and disadvantages. The key question in this debate, raised particularly within discursive psychology, is this: Does rendering a topic analyzable necessarily require interview data, or should researchers increasingly or perhaps solely turn to naturally occurring data? This chapter takes stock of this live debate concerning the epistemological status of interview data. It provides an overview of some of the key points of the so-called natural versus contrived debate (e.g., Speer, 2002a, 2002b, 2008) and discusses the analytic mileage and the problems and possibilities of interviews as qualitative and discourse data (see Gubrium and Holstein's "Narrative Practice and the Transformation of Interview Subjectivity," Potter and Hepburn's "Eight Challenges for Interview Researchers," and

Tim Rapley's "The (Extra)Ordinary Practices of Qualitative Interviewing," this volume, for parallel discussions). The treatment of the topic and the perspective adopted here is marked by my own background in discursive psychology and by the fact that my empirical work draws on both interview and naturally occurring or naturalistic data (Nikander, 2000, 2002, 2003, 2007, 2009a).

The chapter is divided into three sections. The first discusses the debate concerning natural versus contrived data and the key arguments typically voiced for and against the use of interviews (Griffin, 2007a, 2007b; Have, 2002; Henwood, 2007; Holstein & Gubrium, 1995, 1997; Nikander, 2007, 2008; Rapley, 2001; Silverman, 1993, 1998, 2006; Speer, 2002a, 2002b, 2008). The second section, devoted to classic and more recent discourse studies, illustrates how the analysis of interviews as *pieces of interaction in their own right* does away with notions of bias and contamination and provides ample examples of the analytic force and richness of findings that originate from these data. The empirical examples show that when analyzing interviews from the point of view of discourse, notions of contrived or researcher-provoked data have and can be turned into an asset, a tool, and a starting point for analysis and that this has resulted in perhaps some of the most influential analysis to date. In the final section of the chapter, I revisit the natural versus contrived debate and discuss the *hows* and the *whats* of interviews as well as the cross-fertilization between different analytic traditions, data sets, and potential future developments of DA.

◆ *"Natural" Versus "Contrived" Data*

As chapters in this book and in its predecessor (Gubrium & Holstein, 2002) show, interviews as the commonplace means of data generation throughout the history of social sciences have, to date, generated numerous debates, deconstructions, and discussions. As a result, the ideals, objectives, proper procedures, and notions of mutual roles and ideal rapport between participants, as well as the analytic status of interview data, have continuously shifted. In the course of this history, new forms, ideals, and technical means of interviewing have been introduced, and various interview types and elicitation techniques both implicitly and explicitly are pitted against each other, producing better, less biased, more in-depth, and "authentic" knowledge of participants. For some

time, however, social scientists have started to make increasing reference to the distinction between "naturally occurring," "natural," or "naturalistic" data as opposed to "contrived" or "nonnaturally occurring" data. The former have been characterized as perhaps preferable and as gaining precedence, while interviews and other researcher-provoked materials are viewed as artificial and lacking. *The question in the natural versus contrived debate is no longer what genre of interviewing or analysis one should choose or how the status of these data should be conceived but, rather, whether one should choose to use interviews at all.* The debate is partly an outcome of the exponential growth in the scope of empirical discourse-analytic research, the range of potential data sets available for analyses, and particularly the increasing cross-fertilization between discourse and conversation analysis; for it is clearly in conversation analysis that one finds the strongest and most quintessential preference for working with "tapes and transcripts of naturally occurring interactions" (Schegloff & Sacks, 1973, p. 291; see also Have, 1999, 2004). Within the broad field of DA, some researchers whose earlier work routinely devoted time to interview data now acknowledge (e.g., Rapley, 2001; Speer, 2008) and advocate the relative advantages of naturally occurring materials (e.g., Potter, 2003; Potter & Hepburn, 2005; Potter & Mulkay, 1985).

The debate has been heated at times as proponents on both sides of the fence seek to understand and come to grips with each other's agendas (e.g., Griffin, 2007a, 2007b; Henwood, 2007; Potter, 2002; Potter & Hepburn, 2005, 2007; Speer, 2002a, 2002b, 2008). The debate trades in adversarial images and notions of "natural" versus "unnatural" data—not unlike "regular" versus "in-depth interviews"—which typically means that mentioning one out of necessity leaves the other somehow lacking, "shallow," or "unsatisfactory." Advocacy for "naturally occurring data" has been interpreted as academic arrogance that builds unnecessary data hierarchies and is deemed hypercritical (Henwood, 2007). In a similar vein, proponents of a variety of discourse data view the strict ideals concerning transcription and research procedures originating from conversation analysis as brought in to function as a more general yardstick and touchstone for *all* qualitative inquiry (Griffin, 2007a). According to proponents of naturally occurring data, however, it is rather the *pull* from such materials as "an extraordinarily rich topic of study rather than the *push* of problems with interviews that has sustained the research" (Potter & Hepburn, 2007, p. 278). Other voices in the debate warn against treating "any data as untouched by human hands" and advise social scientists to "treat any appeals to nature with considerable caution" (Silverman, 2006, p. 159). Taking such obvious problems of terminology into account, the term *naturalistic* is increasingly being used instead of *natural* (Potter, 2002, p. 540), and conversation analysts themselves see the natural/contrived distinction as somewhat crude (Have, 1999, 2004; Speer, 2008).

The discussion concerning the naturalistic and contrived nature of interview materials is of course part of the broader critical discussion on interview practice and conceptions (see, e.g., Fontana & Frey, 2000; Jennifer Platt's chapter, "The History of the Interview," this volume). Nonnatural data have been "got up" or produced by the researcher by using an interview schedule, an experiment, a survey questionnaire, or some other social research technology (Potter, 1997, p. 149) and "would not exist apart from the researcher's intervention" (Silverman, 2006, p. 201). Data that are affected by the presence of the interviewer and the recording equipment, in other words, do not pass the so-called dead scientist's test (Potter, 1997, 2002). Such a conceptual test is passed only by data that occur entirely irrespective of the researcher's activities and intervention, even if the scientist had never been born or had got run down by a car on the way to the university (Potter, 1997, 2003; Speer, 2002a). Everyday conversations over dinner, on the phone, in courtrooms, or in meetings are examples of data that pass such a test. The immediate, often voiced counterargument to

this distinction is that *no data are completely pure or removed from any researcher involvement*. Ethics and consent procedures concerning recordings are also normally an inseparable part of research when working with naturally occurring materials, and spontaneous everyday interaction is still staged and interactionally managed but by persons *other* than the interviewer (Holstein & Gubrium, 1997).

Furthermore, arguments against using interview data concern the unavoidable asymmetry and lack of reciprocity resulting from the question–answer format, the deletion of the interviewer's activities in the makeup of the interview, the flooding of the interview with social science agendas and categories, and the difficulty of extrapolating analytic research findings and observations to other interactional settings (for further points of challenge, see Potter & Hepburn, 2005; Potter and Hepburn's "Eight Challenges for Interview Researchers," this volume). To consider and weigh these particular points of criticism, let us start by looking at an extract drawn from my own study that concerned interactional constructions of ageing in one-on-one open-ended interviews and age as a discursive membership category. The participants in the study represented the so-called baby-boom generation and were also approached using this colloquial category. During the interviews, the topic of conversation, ageing and, particularly, "turning 50," were among those introduced as the agenda for discussion (Nikander, 2002; also see 2000, 2008, 2009a). The data extract (see Extract 27.1) is presented in a two-column format that preserves the original Finnish alongside the translation into English (for further details on data translation, validity, and transparency, see Nikander, 2009b).

Extract 27.1 PN (Pirjo Nikander): W (woman) 2: Anita (A)

1.	PN:	Well (0.2) so if we talk	No (0.2) tota jos puhutaan
2.		about the like about (.)	tosta niinkun (.)
3.		ageing or the passing	ikääntymisestä tai ajan
4.		of time then what	kulumisesta niin mitä
5.		do you like (.)	niinku (.)
6.		<u>what</u> sorts of things do	<u>mitä</u> kaikkee sää aattelet
7.		you think when you think	ku sää aattelet niinku
8.		about the passing of time	ylipäänsä ajan kulumista

(Continued)

Extract 27.1 (Continued)

9.		in general we've	tässön nyt
10.		[alrea]dy talked about	tullu [jo]
11.		like=	semmoset niinku=
12.	A:	[mm]	[mm]
13.	PN:	= like becoming more	=tämmöset niinku
14.		independent	itsenäistymistä
15.	A:	mm	mm
→ 16.	PN:	but like what <u>else</u> does	mut et mitä <u>muuta</u> niinku
17.		like time passing mean	ajan kuluminen sulle
18.		(0.2) to you	(0.2) merkitsee
19.		(1.0)	(1.0)
20.	A:	You mean time passing <u>in</u>	Siis <u>yleensä</u> ajan
21.		<u>general</u>	kuluminen
22.	PN:	↑ Right	↑ Niin
23.	A:	Well the thing that (.)	No se että (.)
24.		well I've got no fear of	no <u>kuolemanpelkoo</u> mullei oo
25.		<u>dying</u> et cetera	sun muuta

Working with interviews, a discourse researcher takes the collaborative production of talk into account and approaches the interview as a specific type of space for interaction (Nikander, 2008; Rapley, 2001). Interviews remain an economic and efficient means of eliciting "talk on topic," and open-ended interviews can topicalize past, current, and future perspectives on virtually any issue. Participants produce talk from their own perspective: They describe events experienced and witnessed, account for their personal actions and opinions, express past and current feelings, and do so within a limited time-space. These, of course, are key reasons for the continued popularity of interviewing. In addition to being efficient and economic, interviews also enable the interviewer to control the "information stream" of participants, through questions and reactions, and to keep the speakers' talk "on topic." The pre-allocation of roles, turns, and the relative power of the interviewer as the agenda setter are also key points raised against the interview.

Looking at Extract 27.1, it is obvious that the asymmetrical distribution of interactional roles and control clearly structures the unfolding of the interaction (Nikander, 2002, p. 63). The interviewer (PN), in other words, typically produces utterances that can be heard as questions even when their format is not always strictly questionlike. The interviewer also has the right to choose to respond, comment on, or evaluate whatever the other party produces before moving the interaction along. Given the pre-allocated roles and the sequential structure of interviews, the job of the interviewee is to produce something hearable as a related "answer" to questions posed. Questions, as "forward-looking conversational objects" (Have, 2004, p. 66), then "project frames into which the answers have to be fitted, while the questioner can come back after the question to evaluate that fit" (Have, 2004, p. 58). In Extract 27.1, the interviewer's turn is clearly a follow-up question on the issues discussed earlier in the interview and an elicitation for further talk on the same topic. Markedly, the positive aspects of ageing are mentioned as already covered (Lines 9–14: "we've already talked about like . . . like becoming more independent"), and the interviewer moves on to pursue the theme and to elicit further description on the same topic. The fact that the interviewee's account so far is treated as insufficient or nonexhaustive is marked by the use of *but* (Line 16: "but like what <u>else</u> does"). After a second's pause and having echoed the interviewer's initial question, the respondent comes up with a very specific claim: "well I've got no fear of <u>dying</u> et cetera" (Lines 24–25).

The answer that surprised me somewhat during the interview and while working with the transcripts is, in the end, directly explainable by the setup of the interview situation. The interviewee can be heard as anticipating or second-guessing the kinds of preferred answers expected from her, and given that noticeably positive aspects of ageing have already been covered, she produces fear of dying as a suitable negative candidate. Note that death, in this context, is offered as a specific, par excellence example from a larger culturally available group of negative mentionables. Although no list is produced, the *et cetera* (Line 25) can, in other words, be heard as marking the sentence as relevantly incomplete and as pointing to the existence of a wider culturally shared group of such listable items.[1]

So focusing on the interviewer's turns alongside those of the respondents and analyzing interviews as interactions in their own right, discursive analysis shows how both parties follow situational interactional cues, how interviewees produce talk on and off topic, and how "being a competent interviewee/interviewer" is achieved and oriented to. To fulfill the characteristics of an interview, the researcher needs to set the agenda for the talk, but respondents are not total captives to such agenda setting to the degree suggested by critics of interview data. *Discursive research on interviews clearly demonstrates that both parties are equally implicated in meaning making and participate jointly as active agents and agenda setters.* This can be illustrated by looking at how the interaction in Extract 27.1 continues (see Extract 27.2).

Extract 27.2 PN: W2: A (cont.)

26.	A:	Well the thing that (.)	No se että (.)
27.		well I've got no fear of	no <u>kuoleman</u>pelkoo mullei oo
28.		<u>dying</u> et cetera	sun muuta
29.	PN:	mm-m	mm-m
30.		(0.2)	(0.2)
31.	A:	and sometimes I like think	ja joskus mä niinku aattelen et
32.		like what's it	et mitähän sit et ku täyttää
33.		gonna be like when you	viiskymmentä ja
34.		turn fifty or fifty-five	viiskytviis
35.		Like are you then like my	Et onks sitä sit niinku
36.		gran was way back or those	mun mummo oli joskus tai ne
37.		Then I think like wow	Sit mä mietin et jukra
38.		my mother is seventy-two	mun äiti on seitkytkaks
39.		and she's this quite	sehän on ihan
40.		perky person	pirtee ihminen
41.		So at the end of the day	Ni loppujen lopuks
42.		now at forty so	nyt kun on neljäkymmentä ni
43.		that fifty doesn't feel so	se viiskymppinen ei tunnu enää
44.		like terribly old at all	et se ois kauhee vanha mitenkä
45.	PN:	Yep	Joo
46.	A:	And then again I know	Sit se et mä taas tunnen
47.		this woman (.) she's	yhen sellasen naisen (.) se
48.		going to be sixty soon	täyttää kohta kuuskymmentä
49.		and she's really like	Se on hirveen tämmönen
50.		energetic well-groomed	energinen hyvin hoidettu
51.		Outgoing	menevä
52.		((continues the account))	((jatkaa kuvausta))

[1]See Jefferson (1990, p. 68) and also Hutchby and Wooffitt (1998, pp. 235–237) for a more detailed discussion on list constructions, followed by a generalized completer.

Without going into all the details of the account in Extract 27.2, we can simply note how having first conformed to the in situ interpreted expectations of the interviewer and following the interviewer's continuer, or minimal feedback token on Line 29, the respondent immediately pursues a more positive line of argumentation. The interviewer's agenda and elicitation to produce "something else" are, in other words, quickly acknowledged (Lines 26–28) but subsequently brushed to one side, followed by the reintroduction of more positive examples of ageing and a list of discursive characters (*my gran, my mother, this woman soon to be sixty*). The interviewer's agenda is thus acknowledged, but the interviewee still persistently follows her own chosen line of narration.

Ways of distinguishing between interviewer and interviewee agendas in discursive analysis have also been discussed by Griffin (2007a, 2007b). Her discussion of a study that concerned the meanings of consumption for young people directly challenges the notions that interviews inevitably and primarily produce material that is simply "got up" by the researcher, and that these are produced solely and primarily for the consumption of the interviewer. Griffin (2007a) also challenges the idea that interview data are "so ridden with methodological difficulties and pitfalls that it is of questionable value to the purposes of meaningful discourse analysis" (pp. 249–250). Using episodes from her focus group data, she (2007a) seeks to show that any research agenda or set of questions does not determine but rather forms but a part of the interview context and that the agendas of the interviewer and of the interviewees overlap to the point that one might define interview talk as "researcher-inspired interaction" (2007a, p. 261). Similar points can be drawn from recent research focusing on the ethical perspectives of studying various topics, including sensitive ones, and the experiences and accounts of people who had recently participated in social-scientific interview studies. Interviews based on experiences of being interviewed (perhaps a doubly dubious source to base claims on) show that participants make well-judged and situational decisions on how much and on what level they engage with the topic, exert their own power, and bring in their own agendas and interpretations to bear on the interview situation (Graham, Grewal, & Lewis, 2007).

Here, we come back to one of the key questions of the natural versus contrived debate: Can one claim that all interviewing is flooded with "etic" social science agendas and categories to the point that they are rendered unsatisfactory and unusable? Or rather, do respondents act like skillful politicians, taking the categories and the speaking identity implicitly or explicitly offered by the researcher only to then run away with them, countering and redetermining what the question is to smuggle in alternative agendas, categories, and conceptualizations when necessary? This being the case, one of the fascinating tasks in the discursive analysis of interviews is to follow how the cultural categories brought in by the active interviewer are recycled in and through the interaction and how their meanings shift and become challenged, redefined, and refuted. According to critics, however, the research interview easily ends up "chasing its own tail, offering up its own agendas and categories and getting those same agendas and categories back in a refined or filtered or inverted form" (Potter & Hepburn, 2005, p. 51). The critique also claims that the interview format in itself encourages general formulations and that the talk produced is self-monitored to a greater degree than is "naturally occurring." As a result, interview talk has features of a public performance to it. Interview data gathered by the researcher is seen as unhelpful because it "*generates* categories instead of looking at how categories are ordinarily deployed" (Silverman, 1998, p. 60).

Obvious counterarguments, also touched on by Potter and Hepburn (2005, p. 50), concern the image of both participants' and the interviewer's relative agency in the interview situation as well as notions of social science categories as the conversational currency readily available to both parties. From a discursive perspective, interviewees can hardly be conceptualized as captives of the interview agenda or as complete strangers to scientific categories and theorizing, but rather, these are an inseparable part of the everyday vernacular, and both parties already trade in concepts that originate from scientific theorization and debate. In addition, as Holstein and Gubrium (1997) remind us, the continuous development of the interview society and the deprivatization of personal experience mean that public mundane theorizing "for the record" and "opening up" to an interviewer are more commonplace, to the point that the interview is almost a "naturally occurring" occasion for narrating one's personal experience (p. 126).

◆ Embracing Interviews as Interaction

From the discussion so far, it is already clear that discursive work on interview materials acknowledges, celebrates, and actively investigates the active roles of all parties involved and treats *interviews as discursive spaces and as interactions in their own right* (e.g., Potter & Wetherell, 1987; Wetherell, 2003; Wetherell & Potter, 1992). This discursive reframing of interviews entails the methodological understanding that questions are not seen as a medium into the inner world or opinions of respondents or as linguistic precision tools carefully designed and tested to reach and tap into the same target area of true or authentic thought, beliefs, and attitudes in each interviewee. Rather, the questions posed and the interviewer's active involvement are a central part of the data and as such are not to be hidden away from the reader (Nikander, 2002, 2008; Rapley, 2001; Speer, 2002a, 2002b). Edwards (2003) raises another key point when reminding us that DA does not "try to apply a litmus test" (p. 32) to see whether accounts, opinions, or attitudes are 100% true reports on some "inner reality" of the interviewee but, rather, celebrates the variability, contradictions, and inconsistencies to look at what it achieves in interaction, rhetorically, on each occasion.

Notions concerning the active co-construction of interview data by both the interviewer and the interviewee(s) have been well rehearsed, and a consensus has been reached over the fact that "any technical attempts to strip interviews of their interactional elements will be futile" (Holstein & Gubrium, 1997, p. 114). DA is one seminal part of this wider constructionist criticism against interviews as a standardized or standardizable instrument for harvesting knowledge (Koro-Ljungberg, 2008). To use the distinction made by Pertti Alasuutari (1995, p. 63) between *factist* and *specimen* perspectives on social-scientific qualitative data, the discursive take on interviews seeks not to excavate the underlying truth items behind accounts or to treat them as direct reflections of inner or outside reality but rather as a cultural specimen of the reality and topic area being studied. A number of writers have made a parallel distinction by stating that

interview materials can be approached as either a *resource* or a *topic* (e.g., Rapley, 2001; Seale, 1998; Silverman, 1973, 2006). In the former, one uses interviews as a means of gaining information about events, or about the respondent, whereas in the latter case, interest is on the processes of interaction and on the realities jointly constructed therein. Research communities representing either side of the factist/specimen debate or interviews as resource versus topic have largely remained two distinct research cultures with little communication between them.

◆ Empirical Discourse Analysis Examples

Despite recent criticism, DA has never been inimical to using interviews as relevant data, but rather, some of the most often cited and influential pieces originate from such studies. Discourse analysts have worked with naturalistic interviews that take place outside research settings—say between social workers and clients, nurses and patients, or job seekers and employers—as well as interviews conducted by researchers themselves. For the benefit of this chapter, I will focus only on the latter. In what follows, I first discuss two specific areas of research that have proven to be particularly pertinent within the field of DA: first, the analysis of *identities and cultural categories in talk* and, second, the analysis of interview accounting as the interactional site for *constructing factuality, morality, and authenticity in talk*. Third, I will discuss DA research that makes local organizational features and the sequential makeup of the interview its primary concern and studies the *interactional and sequential architecture of interviews as an interview*. All the three traditions inevitably overlap in their interests and analytic foci, as it is impossible to look for the detailed ways of self- and other categorization or detailed constructions of accounts and identities in talk, for instance, without looking at morality or the joint local activities of all parties. However, for no other reason than clarity, I discuss the three in turn.

CATEGORIES AND IDENTITIES IN TALK

Interviewees are typically approached as representatives of a particular group of people: as mothers, immigrants, Swedes, grandparents, ageing ballet dancers, bankers, gay men, white middle-class persons, members of the baby-boom generation, firefighters, farmers, or sex workers. They can be chosen to represent a typical sample in terms of demographic categories such as gender or because they belong to a specific, limited category (Taylor, 2001, p. 24). When studying race talk, class and ethnicity may work as selection and recruitment criteria (Wetherell, 2003); on the other hand, when studying the changing cultural meanings of ageing and men's body image, interviews with men who have recently gone through cosmetic surgery may prove more useful. Those practicing DA do not see participants as directly representative of various demographic categories in the same sense as statistical researchers do. The task is to collect a corpus large enough to allow for discursive repetition and recurrent patterns of argumentation to emerge and then proceed to form data collections on particular discursive phenomena of interest for further analysis (for a discussion, see Nikander, 2008; Taylor, 2001). In this sense, the data represent a *specimen* (Alasuutari, 1995) of routine, repetitive, and highly consensual cultural resources that participants draw on in making sense of their own experiences. This means that discourse-analytic work on identities in talk focuses on the ways in which people make sense of themselves and of each other—that is, how they negotiate various cultural meanings, categories, and identities of "us and them" or "me and others" to build versions and social order into their worlds in collaboration with the interviewer.

Accounting and narrating versions of one's place and identity in the social world, participants draw on their wider cultural knowledge and organize and describe various social categories and their varied and contradictory meanings. *The fine-grained detail of this accounting work, the cultural and analytic resources and logic at work, is then taken as the core for the discursive analysis of such data.* Instead of treating any identity label or categorization as an unproblematic starting point for analysis, discursive analysis of identities in interaction looks at how participants themselves *orient to, mobilize, (re)define, contest, and manage various meanings and how they use identity as a discursive resource* (see Antaki & Widdicombe, 1998; Benwell & Stokoe, 2006; Nikander, 2002; Shotter & Gergen, 1989).

In one variant of DA research drawing on ethnomethodological analyses of interviews (Baker, 1984, 1997, 2002), the focus is on participants' ways of doing membership and nonmembership in social categories and on how members draw on interactional and interpretive resources, build versions of their social reality, and create and sustain social order (Baker, 2002). In practice, this means that instead of treating demographic categories such as gender, age, or nationality as a priori given, the constructionist epistemology guides us toward the analysis of how membership and identity in various groups are produced, accounted for, organized, legitimized, and justified (Antaki & Widdicombe, 1998; Nikander, 2009a). The discursive starting point for the analysis of identity, defined by Benwell and Stokoe (2006) as "who we are to each other, then is accomplished, disputed, ascribed, resisted, managed and negotiated in discourse" (p. 4), can perhaps be clarified through another data example. In Extract 27.3, a male participant from my baby-boom interview corpus has just been describing his 50th birthday party and the various points of view on age and ageing voiced during the party. The extract opens with the interviewer's (PN) question (see Nikander, 2002, p. 142).

Extract 27.3		PN: M (man) 2: Timo (T)	
1.	PN:	Which view did y'represent then	Kumpaa kantaa sä sit ite edustit
2.	T:	Well no I mean (.) I've said	No ei kun mää (.) oon sanonu
3.		that I live my life and	että mää elän elämääni ja
4.		accept that I'm (0.2)	hyväksyn sen että mää oon (0.2)
5.		<u>fifty</u> years old	<u>viiskyt</u>vuotias
6.		and (.) that I'm just as old as	ja (.) ett mä oon juuri niin vanha
7		I (.) happen to be at a time	kuin mää (.) kulloinkin olen
8.		and I don't (.) imagine being	enkä mää (.) kuvittele olevani
9.		(0.4) younger or older	(0.4) nuorempi taikka vanhempi

	10.		but like I don't (.)	mutta että en mää (.)
	11.		nonetheless	siitä huolimatta silti
→	12.		<u>behave</u> the way in	<u>käy</u>ttäydy sillai niin kun
	13.		a fifty-year-old	viiskytvuotiaana
	14.		<u>should</u> (.) behave like	<u>pitäis</u> (.) käyttäytyä että
→	15.		I don't go to symphony concerts	en minä käy sinfoniakonserteissa
	16.	PN:	heh heh	heh heh

From this short data sample, we can already start to see how, in the case of the interviews on turning 50, speakers enter a discursive or argumentative space with shared cultural resources for defining and intelligibly talking about age. Rhetoric, justification, and dialogic arguments and counterarguments—a variety of discursive practices of maneuvering within the theme at hand—are, in other words, an inescapable part of the situated rhetorical business of doing membership and identity. In the example above, we can see various alternative models, "musts," and cultural scripts of being 50 and the age-bound activities, preferences, and characteristics that interlock with those scripts and models. We can also hear the speaker doing both membership and nonmembership. Accepting one's ageing process without delusions of being any younger gets mentioned, but the speaker makes clear that such an acceptance does not mean blindly conforming to, or living, the stereotype. Membership in the *category* is acknowledged, whereas certain culturally available *category-bound activities* are not, and the speaker sharply and very economically distances himself from any middle-of-the-road cultural image of being 50. This is done by making reference to a specific *place category*: the symphony concert (Line15).[2] This achieves important discursive work in immediately mobilizing a host of images and categories of people, their tastes and attributes, which are rendered opposite to those of the speaker and also somewhat ridiculous. Interview talk, descriptions, and categorizations of who we are, like in any other situated interaction, thus build on and endlessly reshuffle culturally available images and meanings, this time of ageing.

Discursive accomplishment of identity in discourse has produced a wealth of empirical research through the years (for overviews, see Antaki & Widdicombe, 1998; Benwell & Stokoe, 2006).

Examples of discursive work on identity construction in interview talk, in particular, include work on youth subculture (Widdicombe & Wooffitt, 1995), age (Baker, 1984; Nikander, 2000, 2002), gender (e.g., Edley & Wetherell, 1997; Gill, 1993), occupation (Marshall & Wetherell, 1989), ethnicity (Day, 1998), social class (Holt & Griffin, 2005), and homosexual identity (Watson & Weinberg, 1982). The common denominator in discursive studies in the identity-in-interaction tradition is the joint interest in both the substantive *cultural conceptions mobilized* when talking about gender, class, age, occupation, or nationality and the *procedural knowledge*, the everyday commonsense methodology and discursive resources, put to use by members to communicate these to an interviewer (Watson & Weinberg, 1982, p. 59).

Some of the early DA studies on identities in interaction explicitly challenged traditional (social-) psychological theorizing concerning identity. This meant treating the variability and inconsistency in speakers' accounts as the analytic starting point, looking at the action orientation of language use, and analyzing how speakers managed and actively moved between various versions and meanings of their lived reality to achieve different interactional goals. This is the case, for instance, in studies focusing on gender and occupational identities, where different interpretative repertoires were identified in interview talk concerning one's gender and one's career, for example, as a lawyer (Marshall & Wetherell, 1989), or when identifying "broad types of accounts" when talking about gender and occupation (Gill, 1993). Variations in self and other representation in these and numerous other studies were seen not only as discursive action but also as consequential in terms of their ideological, gendered implications. In Gill's study (1993), for instance, the

---

[2]For further analysis of place categories in interaction, see Schegloff (1972).

interviews with broadcasters, DJs, and program controllers of radio stations on the lack of female DJs on air revealed a whole range of ways of accounting for possible reasons. While discussing interview accounts and how speakers selectively use various accounts and simultaneously preserve and protect their own identity as nonsexist, Gill also shows how ideology is not "a fixed subset of all discourse . . . but rather a way of accounting," and therefore "what is ideological is an analytical question" (p. 91). In a similar vein, Wetherell and Potter's already classic piece titled *Mapping the Language of Racism* (1992) focuses on how speakers construct interview accounts concerning racial relationships and how they move between, manage, and use different interpretative repertoires. While doing this, Wetherell and Potter simultaneously attend to some serious identity implications of the accounts produced.

Widdicombe and Wooffitt's (1995; see also Widdicombe, 1998) study on interviewees' negotiation of subcultural identities, such as being punk, hippy, gothic, and so on, provides another excellent example of analyzing identities in interview talk. Drawing on membership categorization analysis, Widdicombe and Wooffitt (1995) thoroughly challenge the claims put across by social identity theories and instead approach identity as made relevant for, and realized through, the fine grain of verbal interaction. The writers do not see social identity as a property of a person that in some way is conceived of as existing independently of language use and merely reflected in their language. Rather, identity is approached as "produced through, and embedded in, everyday forms of language use" (p. 66). Widdicombe and Wooffitt's treatment of youth identities in talk shows notions of category membership and social identity to be fundamentally linked; that social identities cannot be taken for granted; and that categorization, as an inference-rich means of doing identity, carries across not simple social labels but, rather, conventionally associated typical activities, predicates, and other hearable characteristics of the people being categorized.

A final, more recent example of the richness of analysis based on researcher-provoked data concerns the ways in which social class and "othering" on the basis of class status are accomplished as part of group interview accounts. In their refreshingly resourceful and rare study, Holt and Griffin (2005) set out to analyze the ways in which social class is constituted and mobilized in accounts of leisure and consumption. To do this, they conducted what could be described as a semi-experimental group interview study, where 42 middle-class students from Birmingham, England, were first taken on "nights out" to bars and pubs and then subsequently interviewed to generate group accounts of the places and people encountered. Analyzing the minute detail and specific categorizations in focus group discussions, the authors show how producing class boundaries, or "othering," is not a straightforward discursive process. Their study also shows the mundane features and dynamics through which the class system is sustained and reinforced in talk, how discourses of territoriality function as part of the positioning of the working-class other, and how, while describing social places and spaces and their organization and regulation, participants also created spaces and identities for themselves. In sum, the empirical examples briefly described above, and numerous others left unmentioned, show the insightful nature and the clear empirical and theoretical input analyses of "nonnatural" interview data can have within the broader discursive field.

FACTUALITY, AUTHENTICITY, AND MORALITY IN INTERVIEW INTERACTION

The second empirical theme I wish to discuss concerns the analysis of interviews as the interactional site for *constructing factuality, morality, and authenticity in talk*. Again, the focus is on the relative advantages of using interview materials. Embracing the "researcher-provoked talk-for-the-record" features of interview material, discursive analysis has turned participants' tendency to monitor the factual or moral adequacy of their accounts into a topic of analysis in itself. An early, already classic, example of interview talk as accounting is Dorothy Smith's (1978, 1990) study on fact construction: "K Is Mentally Ill." Smith's (1978) study concerned how an interviewee's story of a girl's gradual descent into mental illness was constructed in ways that turned the story into a factual description of things that happened in the world, untouched by any special interest, stake, or motivation of the person reporting it (see Wooffitt, 1992, for more detailed discussion). Smith (1978) shows, among other things, how carefully signposting that the teller of the tale is K's friend, listing several independent eyewitnesses to the gradual change in K, and including other minute details in the discursive anatomy of the story generate a consensus that the story is a factual case of mental illness, as opposed to something else. According to Smith, "To describe something as a fact or to treat something as a fact implies that the events themselves—what happened—entitle to authorize the teller of the tale to treat that categorization as ineluctable" (p. 35). The tale of K's mental illness and Smith's elegant analysis of the means by which it becomes established as a factual account, independent of the perception of any motivated interpretation by those witnessing it, is an impressive example of DA studies on constructions of "mental illness" and "deviance."

Another empirical example of describing events as factual comes from Robin Wooffitt (1992). His interview study concerned people's encounters with paranormal phenomena—a topic often greeted with a degree of skepticism—and therefore provides a showcase for the construction of factuality in interaction. Wooffitt identified several discursive patterns and devices that interviewees across the data corpus resorted to, to help manage their identity as a normal person while telling their "tales of the unexpected" to the interviewer. Stories on the paranormal were repeatedly in the following format: "I was just doing X when Y happened" or alternatively "At first I thought X, but then I realized Y" (Wooffitt, 1991). The former constructs the speaker as having been engaged in "normal" everyday actions (X), for example, washing dishes, watching TV, when the paranormal incident (Y) took place. The second device was used to underline that the interviewee's first reaction or line of interpretation of the phenomenon originated from a "normal source," for example, the first thought of the speaker was that it must be the light from the highway (X), only to be followed by the realization that no normal cause could explain the phenomenon, and so the speaker had to resort to an abnormal explanation (Y). Collected in a specific interview context, many of the empirical findings by Wooffitt (1992) have subsequently fed into and continue to inspire discursive analysis on orientations to factuality in other surroundings.

A further aspect of the accounts produced in interviews and other interactional sites concerns their status as authentic reports of events, one's identity, and so on. One pertinent example of this comes from the youth subculture study already discussed briefly above. In Widdicombe and Wooffitt's

study (1995), the young people who were approached were judged by their outward appearance to be members of a particular subculture: gothic, punk, hippy, and so on. One of the key questions posed concerned the process of becoming a member of a youth subculture. The authors point out that the interviewees' accounts were constructed against various academic and lay assumptions about the potential or likely reasons for and the typical processes of such youth affiliations. These include, among others, numerous reasons to do with peer pressure, ideas of passing through a normal phase, or notions of rebelling against parental influence. This meant that speakers typically also oriented to how their accounts were being heard and interpreted and engaged in carefully constructing their own authenticity as members of a subculture. Extract 27.4 is an example of this (p. 144; MR = Interviewee, I = Interviewer).

Extract 27.4

1.	MR:	it's like I was always int'rested-
2.		I know it sounds a cliché looking like this- but
3.		I was always interested in the:: (.) things like
4.		horror horror stories (.) and horror and I was always
5.		writing horror stories in school ever since I can
6.		remember (.)
7.	I:	ahha
8.	MR:	and it's like (.) it was just a (.) an escape from
9.		everything else and I was interested in things like
10.		the supernat'ral (.) and I I jus
11.		((a few lines omitted re. the supernatural))
12.		and that's why: it started to show with clothes, and hair,
13.		and make up n everything as ↓well

Analyzing this and several other data extracts like it, Widdicombe and Wooffitt (1995) point out how portraying a deep-rooted commitment to certain activities and using extreme case formulations (e.g., "always") together build the speaker's status as a member of a subculture as a simple expression of an intrinsic and authentic self-identity. The speaker in Extract 27.4 makes reference to the enduring characteristics and preferences that precede any subcultural affiliation and thus form the authentic and natural impulse for affiliation rather than the result of it. Similar discursive use of longer-term prototypical personal characteristics or aspects of the inner world of the speaker has been identified in other interview data.

Interview talk always places moral demands on its participants and the accounts produced (Silverman, 1993). Despite the somewhat slippery character of the term *morality* (Nikander, 2002), DA of interviews has focused on how moral adequacy is achieved and focused specifically on the moral aspects of people's stories and accounting practices. Two studies can be mentioned here. First, Geoffrey Baruch (1981), while studying stories told by parents of severely ill children, identified some of the discursive means by which interviewees, when talking about their encounters with health professionals, simultaneously attended to and established the rationality of their own actions and their moral and reasonable character. The interviews and the stories told by the parents all concerned situations where something had gone wrong with their child, and the parents were accounting for allowing something so drastic and potentially life

threatening to happen to their child. Baruch's analyses show how parents account for their own moral adequacy, how they mitigate their own potential responsibility or failure to identify problems and act accordingly, and how the discursive demarcation between the lay, everyday world of parents and the world of health professionals protects the moral character of the storyteller. Baruch also makes clear how the analysis of stories produced as part of research interviews can have important policy implications for professional encounters, this time between parents and pediatricians.

The factual, hierarchical, and positioned nature of stage-of-life categories makes the discursive take on age identity another interesting showcase for examining morality in interaction. Life course categories carry normative expectations for particular types of actions. Particularly, notions of maturity and immaturity have been identified as devices that can be "mapped onto the stage of life" (Hester, 1998, p. 140). The analysis of the baby-boom interview corpus thus also meant analyzing how the age-appropriateness of actions and issues of maturity were monitored by participants and how moral notions concerning age surfaced in interaction. Extract 27.5 presents but one example of how *discursive moral buffering* was achieved in the data more widely.

Extract 27.5   PN: W1: Laura (L)

	1.	L:	Somehow one is (1.2)	Että jotenkin sitä on (1.2) mää oon
	2.		I've often (.) like thought	monta kertaa (.) niinkun aatellukin
	3.		that have I ever	sitä et oonks mä ikinä
	4.		like in a way I've got	et mulla on niinkun tavallaan
→	5.		this feeling that inside (.)	semmoinen tunne et sisällä (.)
	6.		that in a way inside one is	et tavallaan sisimmältään on
	7.		this (0.2) somehow a little	semmoinen(0.2) jotenkin
	8.		girl still=	tyttö vielä=
	9.	PN:	mm	Mm
	10.	L:	=that one hasn't	=ettei oo niinkun
	11.		necessarily quite grown	ihan kasvanu
→	12.		to be a mature woman yet	välttämättä aikuiseksi naisekskaan
	13.		that (1.4) like one (0.4)	et (1.4) et sitä (0.4)
	14.		wants to sometimes like (.)	haluu tietyissä asiois niinkun (.)
	15.		play the fool and	heittäytyy silleen hullutella ja
	16.		somehow even (.) act quite	jotenkin (.) olla aika
→	17.		childishly and (2.4) and then	lapsellinenkin ja (2.4) ja sit
→	18.		you notice that your friends	huomaa et ystävät

19.		are doing exactly the <u>same</u>	tekee ihan <u>samaa</u>
20.		Like I think it's terribly	Et just must sekin on kauheen
21.		typical to y'know to	tyypillistä että et sitä niinku
22.		say that we're going there	puhutaan et mennään
23.		and here with the girls and	tyttöjen kanssa sinne ja tänne
24.		but it may well be that	mut voi olla ett niin tekee
25.		<u>seventy</u>-year-olds do	<u>seit</u>semänkytvuotiaatkin
26.		say the [same]=	sanoo [niin]=
27.	PN:	[mm]	[mm]
→ 28.	L:	=that <u>no one</u> says that I'm	=niin et ei <u>kukaan</u> sano et
29.		going with my (.) auntie	menen nyt noitten (.) tätiystävieni
30.		friends some(h)whe(h)re	kanssa jo(h)nne(h)kin

In this short section of talk, Laura describes a discrepancy between her age, the "way she feels inside," and particular activities she sometimes engages in. The hedges and pauses combined with the tentative features of the delivery and the repeated use of modifiers ("sometimes," "somehow," "in a way," "not quite") clearly mark some difficulty in conveying the message. It would seem then that Laura is working toward something that *she herself takes to be an incongruent description.* Claiming the category of "a little girl" is first done via descriptions based on the speaker's inner reality, which immediately makes the claim robust and difficult to refute (Nikander, 2000, 2002). As discourse analysts, we need not be interested in what possibly motivated the speaker to give an answer or to design her account in one specific way or another, nor do we need to look for any other possible explanation or truth value "behind" it. Instead, the focus should be on the specifics of descriptions: on the means through which certain elements in interviews are formulated in discreet or careful ways (cf. Bergmann, 1992; Silverman, 1993) and on how the moral aspects of age are negotiated in and for the interaction at hand.

Laura mobilizes notions of childlike behavior (Line 17), only to then mark her account as incongruent with some other available images concerning "being 50." Note how, after the "2.4" pause, she bridges the incongruence by explicitly naming further categories of people and their practices. Her list grows gradually more generalized—"friends," "70-year-olds," "no one,"—and brings together either groups of people engaging in similar, potentially inappropriate and immature behavior or people who, like Laura, defy the use of age-specific terms.

The potential problem with Laura's self-categorization as "a little girl" is finally played down by an extreme generalization (Line 28: "no one says"). She thus portrays a predictable, logical sequence that produces a general and consensual sense for the account. The gradual discursive disarming of a description in Extract 27.5 is but one example of the diverse means by which participants in collaboration with the interviewer achieve moral insulation and construct moral buffers for their accounts (Nikander, 2000, 2002). The interactional business—that is, being interviewed—is perhaps in part consequential for the design and shape of the things people say and how issues such as age and ageing are addressed. One can equally claim, however, that talk originating from the interview and other surroundings tells something about, and provides a specimen of, cultural notions and the moral landscape of age and ageing at a particular time and place in history.

STUDYING THE INTERACTIONAL ARCHITECTURE OF INTERVIEWS

Following Cicourel (1964) and others, a sizable tradition in DA and conversation-analytic literature now predominantly focuses solely on the architecture of interviews and the features of interview talk as locally and jointly produced. This increasing body of research topicalizes the research interview, studies what goes on in it, and studies the specific activities that are a part of the methodological instrument itself. Research within this tradition includes work on survey interviews and standardization (Houtkoop-Steenstra, 2000; Suchman & Jordan, 1990), interviewing as practical action (Hester & Francis, 1994; Potter & Mulkay, 1985; Silverman, 1973; Widdicombe & Wooffitt, 1995), different question formats (Have, 2004; Mazeland & Have, 1996), the mechanics of questionnaires (Houtkoop-Steenstra & Antaki, 1997; Rapley & Antaki, 1998), the interviewer's role (Rapley, 2001), the elicitation of "topic talk" with prompts (Speer, 2008), and the organization of focus group (marketing) research (Myers, 1998; Puchta & Potter, 1999), to name but a few.

Studies in this tradition have helped us understand the various, formerly unnoticed, logics behind interviewing as a research act, raised reflexivity in terms of the tools in use, and opened interview dynamics for detailed scrutiny. Discursive and interactional analysis of the architecture of interview interaction does not, however, aim to identify new methodological ideals or standards for interview practice. Nor does it wish to create new guidelines concerning more efficient means of elicitation of views, prompting, or obtaining feedback. The research does show, however, that whatever we choose in terms of the form of interviewing or as our style of analyzing the data, we are still left with talk locally and collaboratively produced. The interview remains an active and dynamic meaning-making occasion (Holstein & Gubrium, 1997, p. 117), and research into the fine detail of interview interaction sensitizes us to see the role of the interviewer as well as the fine detail that goes into joint collaboration, and it perhaps guides us toward more informed and reflective use of such data.

◆ Hows *and* Whats *and the Debate Revisited*

This chapter focuses on the analytic mileage and the theoretical and practical reasons for continuing to use interviews as data in discourse-analytic research. The chapter was built on three key premises for the discursive analysis of interview data:

1. DA treats interview talk as *accounting* rather than *reporting*.

2. Interviews are a specific discursive space, and the interview questions as well as the interviewer's participation are a crucial part of the data.

3. Interview data are analyzed both for their local organization as interviews and as a specimen of cultural knowledge, logic, and meaning making.

Given these points, a final theme key of the "natural" versus "contrived" debate concerns the *hows* and the *whats* (Holstein & Gubrium, 1997), or the "inside" and the "outside," of interviews (Miller & Glassner, 1997). Discourse researchers differ on how they view the different discursive patterns and observations drawn from a corpus of interview data. Critics of interview data claim that any findings can be viewed primarily as a local-situational accomplishment that recycles the social scientist's categories, agendas, and formulations in a noninteresting fashion. Other voices in the debate wish to strike a balance between the *hows* and the *whats*, the process and the meanings, and to sustain a dual interest so as not to "obviate interview material by deconstructing it" (Holstein & Gubrium, 1997, p. 115). Many texts, this chapter included, thus advocate methodologically a somewhat broader view and underline interview accounts not just as self-contained but also as empirical windows onto a cultural universe and the interpretative resources at hand to make sense of the world and social reality. In addition, examples of the reanalyses of research interview data show a rich variety of analytic and theoretical perspectives on both the *how* and the *what* of this discourse genre (e.g., Van den Berg, Wetherell, & Houtkoop-Steenstra, 2003).

Discussing questions of extrapolating research findings from interviews to other, for example, "natural," settings, scholars often adopt somewhat different stands. Writers like Rapley (2001, p. 308) claim that particular discursive patterns identified in interviews *may* travel into everyday interaction, while other presentations of self *are equally possible*. Margaret Wetherell (2003), on the other hand, adopts a broader perspective. She acknowledges the distal context and sees interview talk as generalizable beyond its immediate occasioned activities and situated discourse. According to this view, wider collective practices are not "outside" but rather infuse and are continuously rehearsed in the individual voices of the interview. Despite being a discursive genre for cultural meaning making, interview accounts still build on cultural categories, and speakers do "not invent these resources each time" (Wetherell, 2003, p. 25; see also Miller & Glassner, 1997).

So are interviews essential? Are there good practical reasons for the continued use of interviews as a data set alongside others? The discussion in this chapter shows that distinguishing "natural or naturalistic" data from various other social science data is not a straightforward task. Characterizations such as "natural" or "ordinary" language are problematic, the edges of "ordinary" are blurred and hard to define, and we can easily "become smug about the status of naturally-occurring data" (Silverman, 1993, p. 208). Rendering a topic analyzable does not require generation of interview talk. The examples in this chapter aimed to show, however, that the informed and reflective use of interview materials as discourse data has clear benefits and continues to provide insight into a range of topics and their characteristics in specific social and cultural contexts. The growing understanding of the *hows* of interviews as interaction need not mean condemning the use of interviews as qualitative-discourse data, but instead may result in a more informed scholarly understanding and use of them and thereby in better-quality research. In the end, methodological debates such as the natural versus contrived one should not obscure the reasons and processes of our analyses or result in academic arrogance and data hierarchies but, rather, should lead to a fruitful cross-fertilization between different data types and discussion across competing camps. Given this, the debate is worthwhile.

◆ References

Alasuutari, P. (1995). *Researching culture: Qualitative method and cultural studies*. London, England: Sage.

Antaki, C., & Widdicombe, S. (Eds.). (1998). *Identities in talk*. London, England: Sage.

Baker, C. D. (1984). The search for adultness: Membership work in adolescent-adult talk. *Human Studies, 7*, 301–323.

Baker, C. D. (1997). Membership categorization and interview accounts. In D. Silverman (Ed.), *Qualitative research: Theory, method and practice* (pp. 130–143). London, England: Sage.

Baker, C. D. (2002). Ethnomethodological analysis of interviews. In J. F. Gubrium & J. A. Holstein (Eds.), *Handbook of interview research: Context and method* (pp. 777–785). Thousand Oaks, CA: Sage.

Baruch, G. (1981). Moral tales: Parents' stories of encounters with the health professions. *Sociology of Health & Illness, 3*(3), 275–295.

Benwell, B., & Stokoe, E. (2006). *Discourse and identity*. Edinburgh, Scotland: Edinburgh University Press.

Bergmann, J. R. (1992). Veiled morality: Notes on discretion in psychiatry. In P. Drew & J. Heritage (Eds.), *Talk at work: Interaction in institutional settings* (pp. 137–162). Cambridge, England: Cambridge University Press.

Cicourel, A. V. (1964). *Method and measurement in sociology*. New York, NY: Free Press.

Day, D. (1998). Being ascribed, and resisting membership of an ethnic group. In C. Antaki & S. Widdicombe (Eds.), *Identities in talk* (pp. 151–170). London, England: Sage.

Edley, N., & Wetherell, M. (1997). Jockeying for a position: The construction of masculine identities. *Discourse & Society, 8*(2), 203–217.

Edwards, D. (2003). Analyzing racial discourse: The discursive psychology of mind-world relationships. In H. Van den Berg, M. Wetherell, & H. Houtkoop-Steenstra (Eds.), *Analyzing race talk: Multidisciplinary approaches to the interview* (pp. 31–48). Cambridge, England: Cambridge University Press.

Fontana, A., & Frey, J. H. (2000). The interview: From structured questions to negotiated text. In N. K. Denzin & Y. S. Lincoln (Eds.), *Handbook of qualitative research* (2nd ed., pp. 645–672). Thousand Oaks, CA: Sage.

Gill, R. (1993). Justifying injustice: Broadcasters' accounts of inequality in radio. In E. Burman & I. Parker (Eds.), *Discourse analytic research: Repertoires and readings of texts in action* (pp. 75–93). London, England: Routledge.

Graham, J., Grewal, I., & Lewis, J. (2007). *Ethics in social research: The views of research participants*. London, England: National Centre for Social Research, Government Social Research Unit. Retrieved from http://www.civilservice.gov.uk/Assets/ethics_participants_tech_tcm6-5784.pdf

Griffin, C. (2007a). Being dead and being there: Research interviews, sharing hand cream and the preference for analysing "naturally occurring data." *Discourse Studies, 9*(2), 246–269.

Griffin, C. (2007b). Different visions: A rejoinder to Henwood, Potter and Hepburn. *Discourse Studies, 9*(2), 283–287.

Gubrium, J. F., & Holstein, J. A., (Eds.). (2002). *Handbook of interview research: Context and method*. Thousand Oaks, CA: Sage.

Have, P. ten. (1999). *Doing conversation analysis: A practical guide*. London, England: Sage.

Have, P. ten. (2002). Ontology or methodology? Comments on Speer's "natural" and "contrived" data: A sustainable distinction. *Discourse Studies, 4*(4), 527–530.

Have, P. ten. (2004). *Understanding qualitative research and ethnomethodology*. London, England: Sage.

Henwood, K. (2007). Beyond hypercriticality: Taking forward methodological inquiry and debate in discursive and qualitative social psychology. *Discourse Studies, 9*(2), 270–275.

Hester, S. (1998). Describing "deviance" in school: Recognisably educational psychological problems. In C. Antaki & S. Widdicombe (Eds.), *Identities in talk* (pp. 133–150). London, England: Sage.

Hester, S., & Francis, D. (1994). Doing data: The local organization of a sociological interview. *British Journal of Sociology, 45*(4), 675–695.

Holstein, J. A., & Gubrium, J. F. (1995). *The active interview*. Thousand Oaks, CA: Sage.

Holstein, J. A., & Gubrium, J. F. (1997). Active interviewing. In D. Silverman (Ed.), *Qualitative research: Theory, method and practice* (pp. 113–129). London, England: Sage.

Holt, M., & Griffin, C. (2005). Students versus locals: Young adults' constructions of the working-class other. *British Journal of Social Psychology, 44*, 241–267.

Houtkoop-Steenstra, H. (2000). *Interaction and the standardized interview: The living questionnaire*. Cambridge, England: Cambridge University Press.

Houtkoop-Steenstra, H., & Antaki, C. (1997). Creating happy people by asking yes-no questions. *Research on Language and Social Interaction, 30*(4), 285–313.

Hutchby, I., & Wooffitt, R. (1998). *Conversation analysis: Principles, practices and applications*. Cambridge, England: Polity Press.

Jefferson, G. (1990). List construction as a task and resource. In G. Psathas (Ed.), *Interaction competence* (pp. 63–92). Lanham, MD: University Press of America.

Koro-Ljungberg, M. (2008). A social constructionist framing of a research interview. In J. A. Holstein & J. F. Gubrium (Eds.), *Handbook of constructionist research* (pp. 429–444). New York, NY: Guilford Press.

Marshall, H., & Wetherell, M. (1989). Talking about career and gender identities: A discourse analysis perspective. In S. Skevington & D. Baker (Eds.), *The social identity of women* (pp. 106–129). London, England: Sage.

Mazeland, H., & Have, P. ten. (1996). Essential tensions in (semi)open interviews. In I. Maso & F. Wester (Eds.), *The deliberate dialogue: Qualitative perspectives on the interview* (pp. 87–113). Brussels: VUB University Press.

Miller, J., & Glassner, B. (1997). The "inside" and the "outside": Finding realities in interviews. In D. Silverman (Ed.), *Qualitative research: Theory, method and practice* (pp. 99–112). London, England: Sage.

Myers, G. (1998). Displaying opinions: Topics and disagreement in focus groups. *Language in Society, 27*, 85–111.

Nikander, P. (2000). "Old" vs. "little girl": A discursive approach to age categorization and morality. *Journal of Aging Studies, 14*(4), 335–358.

Nikander, P. (2002). *Age in action: Membership work and stage of life categories in talk*. Helsinki, Finland: Finnish Academy of Science and Letters.

Nikander, P. (2003). The absent client: Case description and decision-making in interprofessional meetings. In C. Hall, K. Juhila, N. Parton, & T. Pösö (Eds.), *Constructing clienthood in social work and human services: Identities, interactions and practices* (pp. 112–128). London, England: Jessica Kingsley.

Nikander, P. (2007). Emotions in meeting talk. In A. Hepburn and S. Wiggins (Eds.), *Discursive research in practice: New approaches to psychology and interaction* (pp. 50–69). Cambridge, England: Cambridge University Press.

Nikander, P. (2008). Constructionism and discourse analysis. In J. A. Holstein & J. F. Gubrium (Eds.), *Handbook of constructionist research* (pp. 413–428). New York, NY: Guilford Press.

Nikander, P. (2009a). Doing change and continuity: Age identity and the micro-macro divide. *Ageing & Society, 29*(6), 863–881.

Nikander, P. (2009b). Working with transcriptions and translated data. *Qualitative Research in Psychology, 5*(3), 225–231.

Phillips, N., & Hardy, C. (2002). *Discourse analysis: Investigating processes of social construction* (Qualitative Research Methods Series No. 50). Thousand Oaks, CA: Sage.

Potter, J. (1997). Discourse analysis as a way of analysing naturally occurring talk. In D. Silverman (Ed.), *Qualitative research: Theory, method and practice* (pp. 144–160). London, England: Sage.

Potter, J. (2002). Two kinds of natural. *Discourse Studies, 4*(4), 539–542.

Potter, J. (2003). Discourse analysis. In M. Hardy & A. Bryman (Eds.), *Handbook of data analysis* (pp. 607–624). London, England: Sage.

Potter, J., & Hepburn, A. (2005). Qualitative interviews in psychology: Problems and prospects. *Qualitative Research in Psychology, 2*, 38–55.

Potter, J., & Hepburn, A. (2007). Life is out there: A comment on Griffin. *Discourse Studies, 9*(2), 276–282.

Potter, J., & Mulkay, M. (1985). "Scientists" interview talk: Interviews as a technique for revealing participants' interpretative practices. In M. Brenner, J. Brown, & D. Canter (Eds.), *The research interview: Uses and approaches* (pp. 247–271). London, England: Academic Press.

Potter, J., & Wetherell, M. (1987). *Discourse and social psychology: Beyond attitudes and opinions*. London, England: Sage.

Puchta, C., & Potter, J. (1999). Asking elaborate questions: Focus groups and the management of spontaneity. *Journal of Sociolinguistics, 3*(3), 315–335.

Rapley, M., & Antaki, C. (1998). "What do you think about . . . ?" Generating views in an interview. *Text, 18*(4), 587–608.

Rapley, T. J. (2001). The art(fullness) of open-ended interviewing: Some considerations on analyzing interviews. *Qualitative Research, 1*(3), 303–323.

Schegloff, E. (1972). Notes on a conversational practice: Formulating place. In D. Sudnow (Ed.), *Studies in social interaction* (pp. 75–119). New York, NY: Free Press.

Schegloff, E., & Sacks, H. (1973). Opening up closings. *Semiotica, 8,* 289–327.

Seale, C. (1998). Qualitative interviewing. In C. Seale (Ed.), *Researching society and culture* (pp. 202–216). London, England: Sage.

Shotter, J., & Gergen, K. J. (Eds.). (1989). *Texts of identity.* London, England: Sage.

Silverman, D. (1973). Interview talk: Bringing off a research instrument. *Sociology, 7*(1), 31–48.

Silverman, D. (1993). *Interpreting qualitative data: Methods for analysing talk, text and interaction.* London, England: Sage.

Silverman, D. (1998). *Harvey Sacks: Social science and conversation analysis.* Cambridge, England: Polity Press.

Silverman, D. (2006). *Interpreting qualitative data: Methods for analysing talk, text and interaction* (3rd ed.). London, England: Sage.

Smith, D. (1978). K is mentally ill: The anatomy of a factual account. *Sociology, 12,* 23–53.

Smith, D. (1990). *Texts, facts, and femininity: Exploring the relations of ruling.* London, England: Routledge.

Speer, S. A. (2002a). "Natural" and "contrived" data: A sustainable distinction? *Discourse Studies, 4*(4), 511–525.

Speer, S. A. (2002b). Transcending the "natural"/"contrived" distinction: A rejoinder to ten Have, Lynch and Potter. *Discourse Studies, 4*(4), 543–548.

Speer, S. A. (2008). Natural and contrived data. In P. Alasuutari, L. Bickman, & J. Brannen (Eds.), *The SAGE handbook of social research methods* (pp. 290–312). London, England: Sage.

Suchman, L., & Jordan, B. (1990). Interactional troubles in face-to-face survey interviews. *Journal of the American Statistical Association, 85,* 232–241.

Taylor, S. (2001). Locating and conducting discourse analytic research. In M. Wetherell, S. Taylor, & S. J. Yates (Eds.), *Discourse as data: A guide for analysis* (pp. 5–48). London, England: Sage and Open University.

Van den Berg, H., Wetherell, M., & Houtkoop-Steenstra, H. (Eds.). (2003). *Analyzing race talk: Multidisciplinary approaches to the interview.* Cambridge, England: Cambridge University Press.

Watson, R. D., & Weinberg, T. S. (1982). Interviews and the interactional construction of accounts of homosexual identity. *Social Analysis, 11,* 56–78.

Wetherell, M. (2003). Racism and the analysis of cultural resources in interviews. In H. Van den Berg, M. Wetherell, & H. Houtkoop-Steenstra (Eds.), *Analyzing race talk: Multidisciplinary approaches to the interview* (pp. 11–30). Cambridge, England: Cambridge University Press.

Wetherell, M., & Potter, J. (1992). *Mapping the language of racism.* London, England: Harvester Wheatsheaf.

Wetherell, M., Taylor, S., & Yates, S. J. (Eds.). (2001a). *Discourse as data: A guide for analysis.* London, England: Sage and Open University.

Wetherell, M., Taylor, S., & Yates, S. J. (Eds.). (2001b). *Discourse theory and practice: A reader.* London, England: Sage.

Widdicombe, S. (1998). "But you don't class yourself": The interactional management of category membership and non-membership. In C. Antaki & S. Widdicombe (Eds.), *Identities in talk* (pp. 52–70). London, England: Sage.

Widdicombe, S., & Wooffitt, R. (1995). *The language of youth subcultures: Social identity in action.* Hemel Hempstead, England: Harvester Wheatsheaf.

Wodak, R., & Meyer, M. (Eds.). (2009). *Methods of critical discourse analysis* (2nd Rev. ed.). London, England: Sage.

Wooffitt, R. (1991). "I was just doing X . . . when Y": Some inferential properties of a device in accounts of paranormal experiences. *Text, 11*(2), 267–288.

Wooffitt, R. (1992). *Telling tales of the unexpected: The organization of factual discourse.* London, England: Harvester Wheatsheaf.

28

USING Q METHODOLOGY IN QUALITATIVE INTERVIEWS

◆ David Shemmings and Ingunn T. Ellingsen

◆ Introduction: What Is Q Methodology?

Q methodology (QM) is an empirical research method to explore and investigate patterns of shared viewpoints, attitudes, beliefs, opinions, and other subjective aspects of social life. QM offers an innovative and complementary approach to qualitative analysis by developing conceptual categorization through the quantification of "patterned subjectivity."

In a Q study, the respondents participate by sorting different "subjective" statements in accordance with how they relate themselves to the statements (often referred to as a Q sorting procedure). The Q analysis[1] reveals how participants are grouped together with respect to their shared views. In most Q studies, the sorting procedure can be treated as an interview because respondents are encouraged to comment and elaborate on their positioning of the statements. Interviews are also the most common way of generating the statements, and when sorting the statements, the participants often make comments and elaborate on the different statements. Consequently, it is useful to consider QM as an interview method; it is particularly helpful when the researcher's plan includes participants who find it difficult to participate when more traditional interview methods are used.

The "Q" in QM denotes something different from "R," the convention used to denote correlation coefficients (McKeown & Thomas, 1988). Despite the quantitative techniques used in the analysis of QM, at heart it employs a qualitative approach to both data collection and analysis; it

[1]Q analysis makes use of correlation and factor analysis (by person and not traits); however, researchers using QM really do not need detailed knowledge on factor analysis or how to perform statistical analysis to perform a Q study.

also offers the richness and depth that typify qualitative research (Ellingsen, Størksen, & Stephens, 2010; Shemmings, 2006; Stenner, Watts, & Worrell, 2008). The dichotomy of qualitative and quantitative research is often used to describe and classify research. In its simplest terms, the distinction between qualitative and quantitative research is that the former is concerned with questions that focus on *what* and *how*, whereas the latter is interested in finding out *why*, *how much* (i.e., costs and efficiency), and *how good* (i.e., effectiveness). But this bifurcation into polar opposites is regularly questioned. Julia Brannen (2005), for example, advocates the "mixing of methods." She sees it as more than just a rapprochement between two epistemologically "opposing" traditions, partly because she questions these distinctions because

> claims that qualitative research uses words while quantitative research uses numbers is overly simplistic. A further claim that qualitative studies focus on meanings while quantitative research is concerned with behaviour is not supported since both may be concerned with people's views and actions. The association of qualitative research with an inductive logic of enquiry and quantitative research with hypothetic-deduction can often be reversed in practice; both types of research may employ both forms of logic. That qualitative research lacks quantitative research's power to generalise is moreover only true if generalisability is taken to refer only to statistical inference, that is, when the findings of a research sample are generalised to the parent population. Qualitative findings may be generalised in a different sense; they may be generalised to other settings or contexts or they may involve theoretical generalisation, where findings are extrapolated in relation to their theoretical application. (p. 175)

The uniqueness of QM is that it does not link the approaches sequentially; instead, qualitative and quantitative methods are joined concurrently. QM does not intend to measure anything (Stenner & Stainton-Rogers, 2004). Rather, aims and objectives are by and large qualitative (exploring points of view, perspectives, attitudes), and the research process makes use of qualitative (interviews, sorting procedure, and the interaction between the researcher and the participant) and quantitative (statements as "items," correlation, and by-person factor analysis) techniques. Mixed methods are often associated with triangulation; however, in QM, qualitative and quantitative aspects are intermingled throughout the research process. To use a metaphor, QM is like a bicycle, with one wheel being qualitative and the other quantitative. To get the cycle running, both wheels have to be in motion. Hence, qualitative and quantitative research methods are combined into *one* approach (Good & Brown, 2008).

Recently, an increasing number of researchers have become aware of the advantages of QM, and the method has been applied in many fields, such as social policy (Brown, 1980; Dryzek & Berejikian, 1993), health science (Stainton-Rogers, 1991; Valenta & Wigger, 1997), social work (Daniel, 2000; Ellingsen et al., 2010), psychology (Goldstein & Goldstein, 2005; Shemmings, 2006), and pedagogy (Thorsen, 2009).

Social research often has to deal with challenges when the research topic is of a contentious nature or when the participants' cognitive skills (e.g., verbal and reading skills) preclude the use of more conventional interview methods. Equally, when the research question touches on sensitive topics, it can be difficult even for respondents with good verbal skills to respond and express their views and experiences. QM's inclusive, participatory (Donner, 2001; Van Exel & de Graaf, 2005) and empowering (Brown, 2006) approach can overcome or reduce such barriers. Thus, the method makes it possible to include participants who are often excluded from taking part in research (Ellingsen et al., 2010).

In this chapter, we give an introduction to QM. We provide an overview of the research process and some practical examples from our own research using QM in a study of the meaning of "family" for foster children. In this particular study, the Q analysis revealed three distinct perspectives among the participants. In the following, we will portray examples from this research to illustrate how QM can be a good method for exploring perspectives and views. First, we will pay some attention to the epistemological aspects of QM, in particular subjectivity, self-reference, and concourse, which form an epistemological ground for the research process. Then we will look briefly into how to conduct a Q study, before we discuss how QM can complement conventional qualitative interview methods.

◆ Subjectivity and Self-Reference

QM deals with subjectivity. Perspectives on objective versus subjective research reflect the two different research traditions of "positivism" and "constructivism." These two perspectives are often, unhelpfully in our view, portrayed as binary opposites and result in the now familiar paradigm wars between positivists and social constructionists. More recently, there has been a rapprochement between these two "opposing" perspectives; QM offers a unique method reconciling them in such a way that "either/or" becomes "both/and."

Social life is subjectively influenced by how we reflect on, feel, and experience the world surrounding us. For example, when we hear a weather forecaster state that "it will be 2 °C tomorrow, but with the wind chill factor, it will feel more like –4 °C," the temperature is still 2 °C (try observing the temperature gauge on a car—it remains the same whether you are stationary or traveling at speed!). Nonetheless, it does *seem* colder. In other words, the subjective experience and objective realities coexist in a "both/and" configuration. Research preoccupied with subjectivity is not unique to QM. Qualitative research is, in general, concerned with subjectivity to explore different contours of social life. However, the research procedure and the unique way of comparing different points of view distinguish QM from other methods.

In QM, a subjective viewpoint or perspective is a person's "self-reference" on a topic, and the method seeks to preserve such self-reference (McKeown & Thomas, 1988). Statements based on self-reference are

> statements a person makes about himself, with reference to his personality and interaction with others, as in a diary, journal, or autobiography or in the course of talks, interviews, and the like. All have reference to himself as a self in action, reflection, retrospection, or the like, as more or less conscious matters; or they are statements he makes about others which might be projections of such self-notions and are therefore to be regarded as non-conscious notions. . . . It is with such statements, gathered in natural settings as far as possible (or in careful retrospections or the like), that Q-technique begins its study of the self. (Stephenson, 1953, p. 247)

William Stephenson, who first introduced the method in the United Kingdom in the 1950s, was particularly interested in "subjective communication" and "patterns of subjectivity." He provided an example to illustrate the important distinction between factual statements and subjective communication:

> "It is raining," as a statement of fact, is singular; the information can be tested by observing the rain outside. Subjectively, however, it may involve innumerable possibilities of thought and feeling—that one hates the rain, that it will spoil the picnic, that it will break the drought, and so on "ad infinitum." (1978, p. 23)

That said, a statement such as "It is raining" also shows some of the problems that we encounter when trying to divide the world into objective and subjective terms, as drawing attention to the fact that it is raining is itself an act of subjectivity. Such subjective statements are essential in QM, and the statements used in a Q study derive from a universe of such subjective statements relevant to the research topic. This universe of statements is referred to as the "concourse." However, while QM is concerned with exploring subjectivity, this is not to say that the statements *themselves* reveal subjectivity. Rather, *it is in the way the respondents relate to the statements and the way they sort the statements that participant subjectivity is revealed.*

◆ Concourse Theory of Communication

A *concourse* can be described as "the flow of communicability surrounding any topic" (Brown, 1991–1992, p. 3). It refers to communication about any topic that derives from self-reference rooted in a person's point of view, attitudes, feelings, and experience. The concourse can be expressed verbally or through pictures, arts, objects, and other possible manifestations of meaning, feelings, or ideas (Brown, 1991–1992; Smith, 2001; Stephenson, 1978). In QM, the concourse is eventually reflected in a series of statements or pictures about the topic of interest, which participants are asked to arrange into a grid against polarized "conditions of instructions" (e.g., "True for me"/"Untrue for me" or "Most like my view"/"Most unlike my view"). Identifying the concourse is the first of five steps in a QM study, and we now outline briefly how this is undertaken.

◆ *Conducting a Q Study: The Five Steps in the Research Process*

The research process of QM is often presented as steps or phases (Brown, 1991–1992; Ellingsen et al., 2010; Van Exel & de Graaf, 2005), as follows:

1. Identifying the concourse of the research topic

2. Developing the Q sample representing the concourse

3. Defining the P set, or sample of participants

4. Administering the Q sort

5. Q factor analysis and interpretation

STEP 1: IDENTIFYING THE CONCOURSE

As already stated, the concourse is a variety of subjective communication about a topic of interest, and the research question in a Q study is concerned with such subjective opinions and viewpoints; it is about identifying a variety of viewpoints on the research issue, often by conducting in-depth interviews, typically with individuals or in focus groups but also through the analysis of daily conversations. Secondary sources such as newspapers and political or public debates can also be included as part of the concourse (Brown, 1991–1992; Corr, 2006).

Donner (2001) suggests asking "umbrella questions that allow multiple possible answers" (p. 26) as the aim is to generate the great variety of subjective communication that exists about the research topic. Examples of such umbrella questions in our study exploring the meaning of "family" for children in foster care are as follows:

- When you think of the word *family* what do you think then?

- What "makes" a family?

- In what way do you think foster children reflect on family compared with other children living with their birth family?

We interviewed three children in foster care (individual interviews) and conducted focus group interviews with foster parents and birth parents to identify the concourse on the research topic (Ellingsen, 2011; Ellingsen, Shemmings, & Størksen, 2011).

When interviewing for the purpose of identifying the concourse, the researcher often ends up with a large number of statements, even if only a few people were interviewed. In the study of the meaning of "family" in foster care, we identified more than 240 *different* statements concerning "family" for children in foster care. A few examples follow:

- "I am sometimes afraid that my foster parents will let go of me."

- "If I get my own children some day, I think that both my foster parents and birth parents will be grandparents to my kids."

- "It's difficult to show my birth parents that I care about them."

- "It is actually quite good to have foster siblings."

- "My birth mother will always be an important part of me, but still, it is my foster family that is my family."

- "I used to think that I just lived here and not that they were my family, but now I think that they—my foster family—are my family."

It would be too much to hold in mind if we had included all the statements about family that we identified in the interviews; therefore, they needed to be reduced to a manageable number for a Q sort (39 statements constituted the Q sample of our study). This is the next step of the research process.

STEP 2: DEVELOPING THE Q SAMPLE REPRESENTING THE CONCOURSE

According to Stephenson (1978), the researcher must reduce the concourse to a realistic number of statements. It is, however, important that the statements be selected carefully to maintain the representativeness of the concourse. Defining the Q sample is considered the most crucial and challenging part of the method (Brown, 1991–1992). Developing the Q sample is not about selecting statements to represent the majority viewpoint; rather, it is the *variety* of viewpoints held by different people that the process seeks to capture. The Q sort grid (or matrix) is usually a quasi-normal distribution scale,[2] with one side (the positive side) to place statements that are agreeable or like the respondents' viewpoints and the other side (the negative side) for statements that are not agreeable or that are unlike the respondents' viewpoints[3] (Table 28.1).

This is also why the Q sample needs variety to make it possible to fill in statements both in the positive and in the negative side of the grid. In our study, we divided all the statements into subcategories such as "identity and attachment," "feelings and emotions," "conflicts," and so on. This gave us a better overview of the content of the concourse and was helpful in getting a Q sample representing the identified concourse.[4] The final Q sample normally consists of between 20 and 50 statements. However, the number and complexity of the statements will be adjusted depending on the respondents. Some groups may be able to relate to more ambiguous and more numerous

statements than others. As stated earlier, the Q sample may comprise pictures or illustrations. Illustrations have, for example, been used as "statements" in children's studies (see, e.g., Størksen, Thorsen, Øverland, & Brown, 2011; Taylor, Delprato, & Knapp, 1994). We will return later in this chapter to the way images have been used in a study involving young children.

A Q study sorting procedure is one based firmly on "self-reference." Hence, it is important that the statements possess a "scalability" that allows such self-reference; this is in contrast to factual statements, which tend to reduce self-reflectivity. For example, "I am a boy" is a factual statement that is (in the main) either true or false; scaling the statement into a Q sort grid, based on self-reference, would be meaningless. However, perspectives, feelings, and/or beliefs a person has about "boys"—and certainly deeper, more complex notions around "gender"—make self-reference possible (e.g., "Boys are less empathic than girls").

STEP 3: DEFINING THE P SET, OR SAMPLE OF PARTICIPANTS

In a Q study, the number of participants included does not need to be large; in fact, they rarely exceed 50 (Brown, 1991–1992). Also, single case studies can sometimes become the focus of interest in QM (McKeown & Thomas, 1988; Størksen, Thorsen, & Berner, 2008). It is important to note that the participants in a Q study do not "represent" a population, because the aim of QM is not quantitative generalizability; rather, it seeks to explore whether and how subjectivity is clustered among the participants. The selection of participants is usually based on a structured sample of specific interest to the research topic; it is also possible to include people of specific, theoretical interest in the P set (McKeown & Thomas, 1988; Van Exel & de Graaf, 2005). Such "theoretical sampling" can be useful if the researcher wishes to compare two or more distinctive groups of respondents (e.g., teachers in private

Table 28.1 Example of a Q Sort Grid Consisting of 39 Spaces Ranging From +4 (Most Like My Situation) to −4 (Most Unlike My Situation) With a Center (0) for Statements That Are Neutral or "Undecidable"

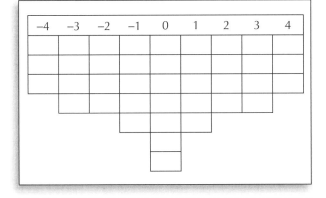

Note: The size of the grid varies depending on the number of statements and the controversy of the topic. Some issues are expected to be more controversial, and the researcher may therefore want to have more spaces on the extremes (and perhaps a more flat shape for the grid).

---

[2]A quasi-normal distribution means the number of spaces on one side correspond with the number of spaces on the other side.

[3]The size of the grid varies depending on the number of statements and the controversy of the topic. Some issues are expected to be more controversial, and the researcher therefore may want to have more spaces on the extremes (and perhaps a more flat shape of the grid).

[4]Stephenson developed a tool to help the researcher in the process of selecting statements for the Q sample, called Fisherian Block Balance Design (see Brown, 1991–1992; Stephenson, 1953).

schools, teachers in public schools, or the teacher's vs. the head teacher's perspectives).

STEP 4: ADMINISTERING THE Q SORT

When participants perform a Q sort, statements (selected to represent the concourse) are presented on separate cards, randomly numbered. Respondents sort the cards against binary anchors, referred to as the *conditions of instruction*. For example, participants might be asked to "sort the cards in accordance with what is 'most like' or 'most unlike' your situation" or "sort the cards in accordance with what is 'most true' or 'most untrue' for you." It can sometimes be of interest to suggest that respondents do several Q sorts, with different conditions of instructions (e.g., against a "past," "present," and "future" perspective). Alternatively, they can be specified to reveal perceptions of different viewpoints (e.g., "Please sort the cards in accordance with how you think your mother sees the situation . . . your teacher . . . etc."), or an "ideal" compared with a "real" situation might be considered. When QM is used in single case studies, such multiple instructions are often given.[5] It is important to make it clear to the respondents that there is no "right" or "wrong" answer when sorting statements. Figure 28.1 illustrates a Q sorting process with an adolescent placing statements into a Q sort grid.

Figure 28.1 Illustration of an Adolescent Doing a Q Sort

It is during the sorting process that the researcher can ask participants if they would mind being recorded—ideally filmed as this reveals more nonverbal communication than can be achieved by audiotaping alone. (Naturally, the usual provisos regarding anonymity, confidentiality, and tape ownership and eventual destruction must be adhered to openly and rigorously.) When completing the Q sort, participants often add comments to the statements as well as about their particular way of sorting the statements. This gives valuable insights into how the participants reflect on the statements. Such comments are especially valuable during the interpretation of the results in a Q study. It is therefore advisable to treat the sorting procedure as an interview and to write down or record comments in detail soon afterward.

The sorting procedure itself sometimes generates thoughts and reflections that the participant has not necessarily been aware of before. For example, in our study of "family" in the minds of children in foster care, one statement asked them to consider who they thought would be the grandparents if they ever had children of their own (i.e., the birth parents or foster carers). One of the participants (a 15-year-old) commented,

I don't know . . . I think maybe my mum in (name of place). I don't really know why, but I guess it's because . . . she is going to care—about the baby . . . I don't know. Well, I guess the others (the foster parents) would care as well, but maybe differently . . . I don't know.

Such comments are useful when interpreting the results, as they add a richness and provide insights on how to understand the value given to the statement (by the way the statement is placed into the Q sort grid).

Participants sometimes find it difficult to talk to a researcher about their situation, but relating to statements can be easier. For some of the children in our study, finding "the right words" to express how they felt was difficult, but they were more comfortable relating to different statements (irrespective of whether those statements were "most like" or "most unlike" their own situation). Putting feelings into words is a challenge for many, but when participating in research by doing a Q sort, an individual does not necessarily

---

[5]"Presorting" the statements into three piles will usually make it easier for the participants to sort the cards into the Q sort matrix (Brown, 1991–1992), for example, one pile with the cards "most like," a second comprising the cards "most unlike," and the remaining cards constituting an "undecided," third pile.

have to express or elaborate on the different statements: It is the sorting process itself that provides insight into how the participant relates to the research topic. Consequently, the sorting procedure may very well function as a substitute for an interview question.

STEP 5: Q FACTOR ANALYSIS AND INTERPRETATION

Many qualitative researchers are unfamiliar with the use of quantitative techniques and with factor analysis. Despite the qualitative aspects of QM, correlation and factor analysis are used to reveal a cluster of viewpoints. These quantitative techniques are used differently than in traditional factor analysis, by using a "by-person" factor analysis. This means that it is each participant's Q sort, containing all the statements in the Q sample (representing that person's view), that are factor analyzed. Participants who have sorted the statements in similar ways, and therefore have similar views with other participants on the research topic, are most likely to end on the same factor. Consequently, Q factor analysis reveals how the participants are grouped by the way they share the views and perspectives of other participants (McKeown & Thomas, 1988). The Q factor analysis does not simply reveal how individuals group themselves by shared beliefs, viewpoints, or attitudes; it also uncovers the divergences *within* groups. QM is therefore useful to compare and investigate commonalities and differences.

Although Step 5 uses complex statistical procedures, the researcher does not need to have detailed knowledge of either statistics or factor analysis in order to do a Q study (Brown, 1991–1992)—nevertheless, some understanding of the principles of factor analysis helps. A software program[6] carries out the statistical procedures after all the Q sorts have been entered into the "PQ program." Each of the statements is randomly numbered, and when adding a Q sort into the program, it is actually the number of each statement and its value given by the participants that are entered into the program.[7] The manual provided with the PQMethod program provides an easy, step-by-step guide on running the analysis.

In our study on what "family" means for children in long-term foster care, three factors emerged, suggesting three different perspectives on family among the foster children who took part in our study. The first factor indicated a pattern of adjustment in the placement, with bonding to both the foster family and the birth family. The second and third factors suggest a strong and weak bonding, respectively, to the birth family as opposed to the foster family.[8] When interpreting Q factors, factor loadings as well as the normalized factor scores are of specific interest (Shemmings, 2006). The normalized factor scores show the typical way of sorting the statements for each of the three emerging perspectives (factors). The factor loadings show to what extent the children are associated or correlated with each factor. When interpreting the factor, the researcher often makes an inspection of the following:

- "Distinguishing statements"—statements with scores that are statistically unique for a specific factor

- "Characteristic statements"—statements that are typically rated positively ("most like") or negatively ("most unlike") for each of the factors

- "Consensus statements"—statements that do not differ statistically between factors

- "Overall configuration" of the statements on each of the factors

- Comments given by the respondents on their Q sort

Insights and comments obtained by interviewing participants during the Q sorting procedure help understand, define, and elucidate each factor. In most cases, such comments complement and amplify the Q sort in rich ways, typical of qualitative research. But sometimes the researcher gets unexpected results. This occurs typically when follow-up interviews (e.g., participants with the highest loading on the factor) are conducted as they help the researcher explore the patterns revealed by the factors. Persons strongly associated with the factor help clarify its structure.

---

[6]"PQmethod," written by Peter Schmolck (2002), can be downloaded as freeware from http://www.lrz-muenchen .de/~schmolck/qmethod/#PQMethod.

[7]For newcomers to QM, it is advisable to do a trial run using principal component analysis (with varimax rotation), which will facilitate insight into how the participants share perspectives.

[8]See Ellingsen, Shemmings, and Størksen (2011) for an overall presentation and discussion of the results.

◆ How QM Can Complement "Traditional" Qualitative Interview Methods

TREATING THE Q SORT AS AN INTERVIEW

As we have shown through the research process, interviews are a central part of QM, and audio- or videotaping the sorting procedure can usefully be treated as an interview. While doing the Q sort, participants are encouraged to think deeply about the interrelationships *between* the statements; crucially, they are given time to do this without having to respond immediately to the researcher, as in a "traditional" interview situation. Indeed, in some crucial respects they are not being "interviewed"; rather, their ruminations are being witnessed and occasionally lubricated through the use of probing questions (e.g., "I see you've placed this statement under +4 ('most like'); could you say something more about that?"). Participants comment on the statements while sorting the cards or afterward (or both).

In our study, we also addressed some specific questions after the participants had completed their Q sort. All participants were asked if they wanted to comment on statements they had placed on the "most like" side of the scale, and many of them elaborated these statements and what they meant to them. The same was the case on the "most unlike" side of the scale. The statements placed in the center of the grid may represent statements that are neutral to the respondents, but they also may include statements about which they feel some degree of ambivalence (Brown, 1991–1992). It is important to understand such mixed feelings more fully. Another way of exploring ambivalence is to ask the participants if they found any statements particularly difficult to relate to or to place into the grid. For example, one of the participants (a 15-year-old boy) in our study about the meaning of "family" for children in foster care commented on this question:

> I feel that I have to consider my birth parents . . . I don't want them to get hurt. I guess foster children feel different about this, but for me it is like this . . . It was difficult placing the statements about loyalty because I don't want to hurt them; if I were to choose one of them (the foster parents or the birth parents) I would hurt the other. . . . When I am here, little by little I change . . . pretty much actually—that is difficult to admit to my mum and dad, really, and I am afraid I'll hurt them.

These reflections about ambivalent feelings of loyalty toward one's birth parents illustrate the potential richness interviews can bring to a Q study, partly because they refer not only to a specific statement but also to a cluster of several statements, in combination. Seen in connection with other comments from participants loading on the same factor, the ideas expressed were congruent with the overall configuration of the statements, revealing that "loyalty" was a central feature embedded within one of the Q factors.

QM PROMOTES AND STRENGTHENS INCLUSION AND PARTICIPATION

QM offers several possibilities to researchers seeking to include groups normally excluded from participating in research. For example, much contemporary research has viewed children's perspectives from the adult's standpoint (Greene & Hill, 2005; O'Kane, 2008). But even relatively young children can participate actively in a Q study. Images, pictures, and single phrases can be used as "statements" to help the children express their viewpoint when reading and comprehension skills are not developed fully (Corr, 2006; Størksen, 2010; Taylor et al., 1994; Thorsen & Størksen, 2010).

The visual images shown in Figures 28.2 to 28.4 were included in a study of 5-year-old children of divorced families (Størksen et al., 2011; Thorsen & Størksen, 2010).

The illustrations are very expressive and easy for children to "read" and "inject" meaning. The study offers a good example of how images used in a Q study helped very young children "tell their story" and how such tools can increase and deepen communication in research. (The children were asked to select the picture of a child whose expression was "most/least" like their own feelings.)

Using images can also be helpful for other groups by making it easier to "frame a narrative" and express experiences less amenable exclusively to verbalization. For example, professionals and volunteers who work with people with learning disabilities will be familiar with the use of pictograms (e.g., "smiley faces") to assist communication in daily life.

Although QM can be used to *assist* in communication, it is also a tool for communication in itself. As already stated, respondents do not necessarily need to elaborate on the statements. As we have seen, the unique way in which participants sort statements

Figure 28.2 Example of a Visual Statement Expressing Feelings of Anxiety (Størksen et al., 2011)

Source: Illustrations are by Ole Andre Hauge and belong to the Center for Behavioral Research at the University of Stavanger, Norway.

Figure 28.3 Example of a Visual Statement Expressing Good Friendship (Størksen et al., 2011)

Source: Illustrations are by Ole Andre Hauge and belong to the Center for Behavioral Research at the University of Stavanger, Norway.

Figure 28.4 Example of a Complete Q Sort With Visual Statements (Størksen et al., 2011)

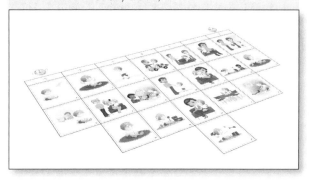

Source: Illustrations are by Ole Andre Hauge and belong to the Center for Behavioral Research at the University of Stavanger, Norway.

conveys a considerable amount of information about how the participant relates to the different statements, but the overall configuration of the statements reveals a more in-depth narrative than is possible by examining the statements in isolation.

We have sometimes heard participants in traditional interviews express the view afterward that they have revealed or unearthed "too much," which can leave some participants with uncomfortable feelings of vulnerability or even regret for having participated in the research. The Q sorting procedure may lessen or ease such feelings by giving more control to a participant over the pace and degree of self-disclosure. For example, one young person (an 18-year-old boy) in our study of foster children's perspective on "family" was interviewed as part of the first stage of the research process. He also participated later by completing a Q sort, and so he had experienced two quite different ways of engaging in the research. He put it this way: "This way might give a better feeling about what you have 'given' away of information about yourself compared to when you sit and talk more freely."

When using QM in a more narrative sense, it is useful to let participants complete several Q sorts, with different "conditions of instruction." When we talk about ourselves, we focus on different things—in a past, present, or future perspective—how we feel, how we would like others to see us, and so on. All of these perspectives are narratives of ourselves but may appear very different. One cannot say that one perspective is truer than the other. These stories coexist and are all patterns of narratives that we hold. In a Q study, respondents can relate to the same sample of statements, but from different angles—which makes it easier to reveal such "patterned" narratives compared with more conventional interview methods. Størksen et al. (2008) conducted a single case study using QM to reveal a richly contoured picture of how one adult participant experienced divorce as a child, which was explored from different angles and perspectives to reveal different "family" narratives.

◆ What Q Sorts Reveal and, Conversely, What Is Left Out

To what extent do the participants feel that participating in a Q study provides an accurate picture of their situation? The answer to this question depends on three features of the research process.

First, it depends on the extent to which the Q sample represents the different viewpoints that exist within the concourse. As we have seen, this step is actually the most crucial point in a Q study, and it is important that the researcher work thoroughly on Q statement selection. Some participants may feel that key aspects of the topic are missing from the set of statements; as the concourse usually consists of a large number of statements, consequently some statements must be left out. This is where interviewing is especially fruitful, as it reduces the danger of ignoring or overlooking pivotal features within the area of study. The eventual analysis of the Q sort and the interpretation of emerging factors depend on the representativeness of the statements selected in the Q sample. That said, it is possible to include comments on what the participants feel are missing in the Q sample, as well as other points related to the research topic. Encouraging respondents to comment on their Q sort when arranging it, as an in vivo research activity in its own right, not only provides the researcher with valuable information for the interpretation of the results but also offers respondents the opportunity to "fill out" the picture.

Second, as a consequence of the "acquiescence effect" (answering questions in a way that predicts what the respondent thinks the researcher wants), some individuals may be afraid of completing the Q sort "incorrectly." It is important that the researcher explain the Q sorting procedure to clarify and emphasize to participants that there is no right or wrong way to sort the statements into the Q matrix; rather, it is the way they read, understand, and relate to the statements that should determine how each participant arranges the statements.

Third, an advantage of QM is that it is the participants who "paint the picture," because the sketches, lines, contours, and colors are arranged by the research subjects doing the Q sort, not the researcher. This leaves the researcher free and open to address what is most important to *participants*. In much research, the researcher categorizes the data to search for patterns and important perspectives in the data. This is quite a challenge when the information is gathered from large, complex data sets. When the participants in a Q study sort the statements, none of the statements are left out when running the analysis, and the researcher has minimal influence on the results. The researcher will not know in advance the structure of the factors or how many clusters of views will eventually be distilled (Brown, 1991–1992). The researcher's "influence" on the data is centered mainly on the first three stages of the research process: identifying the concourse, selecting the Q sample (statements to represent the concourse), and selecting the P set (participants). By interviewing the participants at each step, not only are they actively and demonstrably involved, but also the researcher can stay more "grounded."

We asked the children who participated in our study whether they thought that their Q sort gave an accurate picture of how they felt or thought about "family." Checking out how the respondents feel about the accuracy of their "picture" is also a way to let them validate their Q sort. Respondent validation is referred to in the literature as respondents' feedback on the tentative results and analysis (Kvale, 1997; Silverman, 2000). In this study, the respondents did not give their feedback on the resulting factors. However, this is also possible, for example, by interviewing the people with the highest loading on each of the emerging factors (the persons most associated with the perspective) about the perspective revealed by the factor. On the one hand, this can be seen as respondent validation, but more than that, it actually adds new data to the research. In our study, all of the children's responses indicated agreement to a greater or lesser extent: No one disagreed. A few pointed to certain aspects they felt were missing, but based on the statements in the Q set, they felt that the Q sort gave a correct picture:

> Absolutely, I feel this gives a good picture of how I feel and how I think. It is not like . . . some cards could be read differently by different people, but really, this is how I feel—at least the way I read them.

Another participant said that she had not thought of all the aspects in the statements before, but still, she felt that it gave a picture of how she felt: "I think it does give a correct picture of how I think about family. Yeah, I guess it does. We are just a family. I haven't really thought that much about family—some things just are, you know."

The participant who also participated in the interviews to identify the concourse expressed it clearly: "Yes, this was a really clever way of doing it."

◆ Final Reflections

QM is, after a little practice, easy to use and offers researchers a way of making sense of participants' views, impressions, and perspectives on the topic of interest. It can complement and sometimes even replace other analytic methods (such as grounded theory) that involve detailed and painstaking analysis of lengthy transcripts. In many ways, it extracts the strengths of both qualitative and quantitative research traditions, by the way patterns of subjectivity are revealed systematically with little interference from the researcher's preconceptions, and at the same time, it preserves the richness typically associated with qualitative research. Mixed methods have a rather short history, and QM can therefore be viewed as a pioneer to contemporary research approaches acknowledging the strengths of qualitative and quantitative research. That said, the growing interests of QM in many fields and disciplines is perhaps the result of a greater acceptance of mixed-methodology research (Newman & Ramlo, 2010).

The potential of QM is truly realized when participants are interviewed during the completion of the Q sorts; it is enhanced even further when they help derive the statements for sorting and are involved in the final analysis. QM is thus ideally suited to maximize the full involvement of participants at each stage of the research process. Table 28.2 gives an overview of key concepts (vocabulary) in Q methodology.

Table 28.2 Vocabulary

	Q Vocabulary
Concourse	The variety of viewpoints, meanings, beliefs, etc., existing on a topic
P set	Persons participating in the Q study
Q sample/Q set	The sample of statements used in a Q study performed by the participants
Q sort	The sorting of statements into a matrix or grid
Q sort matrix/Q sort grid	A matrix or grid, often quasi-normal in shape, with spaces corresponding with the number of statements used in the Q sorting procedure
Q analysis	Correlation of participants' Q sort and by-person factor analysis
Q factor	The results are presented as a Q factor, revealing how participants are clustered with others sharing their view or perspective
Abduction	A way of understanding the Q factor by finding the most plausible explanation for the clusters of shared views (Q factors)

◆ References

Brannen, J. (2005). Mixing methods: The entry of qualitative and quantitative approaches into the research process. *International Journal of Social Research Methodology, 8*(3), 173–184.

Brown, S. (1980). *Political subjectivity: Applications of Q methodology in political science.* New Haven, CT: Yale University Press.

Brown, S. (1991–1992). *A Q methodological tutorial.* Retrieved from http://facstaff.uww.edu/cottlec/QArchive/Primer1.html

Brown, S. (2006). A match made in heaven: A marginalized methodology for studying the marginalized. *Quality & Quantity, 40,* 361–382.

Corr, S. (2006). Exploring perceptions about services using Q methodology. In G. Kielhofner (Ed.), *Research in occupational therapy: Methods of inquiry for enhancing practice* (pp. 389–400). Philadelphia, PA: E. A. Davis.

Daniel, B. (2000). Judgements about parenting: What do social workers think they are doing? *Child Abuse Review, 9*(2), 91–107.

Donner, J. C. (2001). Using Q-sorts in participatory processes: An introduction to the methodology. In R. A. Krueger,

M. A. Casey, J. Donner, S. Kirsch, & J. N. Maack (Eds.), *Social analysis: Selected tools and techniques* (Paper No. 36, pp. 23–49). Washington, DC: Social Development Department, The World Bank.

Dryzek, J. S., & Berejikian, J. (1993). Reconstructive democratic therapy. *American Political Science Review, 87*(1), 48–60.

Ellingsen, I. T. (2011). Designing a Q sample for a study with adolescent foster children. *The International Journal of Q Methodology, 13*(5), 395–409.

Ellingsen, I. T., Shemmings, D., & Størksen, I. (2011). The concept of "family" among Norwegian adolescents in long-term foster care. *Child & Adolescent Social Work Journal, 28*, 301–318.

Ellingsen, I. T., Størksen, I., & Stephens, P. (2010). Q methodology in social work research. *International Journal of Social Research Methodology, 13*(5), 395–409. doi:0.1080/13645570903368286

Goldstein, D. M., & Goldstein, S. E. (2005). Q methodology study of a person in individual therapy. *Clinical Case Studies, 4*, 40–56.

Good, J. M. M., & Brown, S. (2008, October). *The relationship of Q methodology to quantitative, qualitative, and mixed methods.* Paper presented at the meeting of the International Society for the Scientific Study of Subjectivity, Hamilton, Ontario, Canada.

Greene, S., & Hill, M. (2005). Researching children's experience: Methods and methodological issues. In S. Greene & D. Hogan (Eds.), *Researching children's experiences: Approaches and methods* (pp. 1–21). London, England: Sage.

Kvale, S. (1997). *Det Kvalitative Forskningsintervju* [Qualitative research interview]. Oslo, Norway: Ad Notam.

McKeown, B. F., & Thomas, D. B. (1988). *Q methodology* (Quantitative Applications in the Social Sciences series, Vol. 66). Newbury Park, CA: Sage.

Newman, I., & Ramlo, S. (2010). Using Q methodology and Q factor analysis in mixed method research. In A. Tashakkori & C. Teedlie (Eds.), *Handbook of mixed methods in social and behavioural research* (2nd ed., pp. 505–530). Thousand Oaks, CA: Sage.

O'Kane, C. (2008). The development of participatory techniques. In P. Christensen & A. James (Eds.), *Research with children: Perspectives and practices* (pp. 123–155). London, England: Taylor & Francis.

Schmolck, P. (2002). PQMethod Download Mirror [Computer software]. Retrieved from http://www.lrz-muenchen.de/~schmolck/qmethod/downpqx.htm

Shemmings, D. (2006). Quantifying qualitative data: An illustrative example of the use of Q methodology in psychological research. *Qualitative Research in Psychology, 3*, 147–165.

Silverman, D. (2000). *Doing qualitative research: A practical handbook.* London, England: Sage.

Smith, N. W. (2001). *Current systems in psychology: History, theory, research, and applications.* Belmont, CA: Wadsworth/Thomson Learning.

Stainton-Rogers, W. (1991). *Explaining health and illness: An exploration of diversity.* New York, NY: Harvester Wheatsheaf.

Stenner, P., & Stainton-Rogers, R. (2004). Q methodology and qualiquantology: The example of discriminating between emotions. In Z. Todd, B. Nerlich, S. McKeown, & D. D. Clarke (Eds.), *Mixing methods in psychology: The integration of qualitative and quantitative methods in theory and practice* (pp. 103–117). New York, NY: Psychology Press.

Stenner, P., Watts, S., & Worrell, M. (2008). Q methodology. In C. Willig and W. Stainton-Rogers (Eds.), *The SAGE handbook of qualitative research in psychology* (pp. 215–239). London, England: Sage.

Stephenson, W. (1953). *The study of behavior: Q technique and its methodology.* Chicago, IL: University of Chicago Press.

Stephenson, W. (1978). Concourse theory of communication. *Communication, 3*, 21–40.

Størksen, I. (2010). Bruk av Q-metode i Bambi-prosjektet [The use of Q-method in Bambi-project]. *Psykologisk tidsskrift, 1*, 16–21.

Størksen, I., Thorsen, A., & Berner, K. L. (2008). Family narratives through the eyes of an adult child of divorce. *Journal of Human Subjectivity, 6*(2), 27–47.

Størksen, I., Thorsen, A. A., Øverland, K., & Brown, S. R. (2011). Experiences of daycare children of divorce. *Early Child Development and Care.* Advance online publication. doi:10.1080/03004430.3011.585238

Taylor, P., Delprato, D. J., & Knapp, J. R. (1994). Q-methodology in the study of child phenomenology. *Psychological Record, 44*(2), 171–184.

Thorsen, A. A. (2009). *Teachers' priorities and beliefs: A venture into beliefs, methodologies and insights* (Doctoral thesis, University of Stavanger, Stavanger, Norway). Retrieved from http://idtjeneste.nb.no/URN:NBN:no-bibsys_brage_12466. (UiS No. 63)

Thorsen, A. A., & Størksen, I. (2010). Ethical, methodological, and practical reflections when using Q methodology in research with young children. *Operant Subjectivity, 33*, 3–25.

Valenta, A., & Wigger, U. (1997). Q-methodology: Definition and application in health care informatics. *Journal of American Medical Informatics Association, 4*(6), 501–510.

Van Exel, J., & de Graaf, G. (2005). *Q methodology: A sneak preview.* Retrieved from http://www.qmethodology.net/index.php?page=1&year=2005

29

USING SOFTWARE TO ANALYZE QUALITATIVE INTERVIEWS

◆ Clive Seale and Carol Rivas

S ocial researchers have long appreciated the usefulness of computers for data analysis. Statistical software (such as SPSS[1] [an IBM company] or SAS) used on increasingly powerful personal computers has automated mathematical calculations on large data sets to the extent that quantitative analysis can be increasingly interactive. Analysts can run procedures and get instant feedback on the results, freeing up time for the creative interplay of ideas and research data. In the humanities, the development of word list and concordance software (e.g., WordSmith Tools) has made possible the subdiscipline of "corpus linguistics" (McEnery, Xiao, & Tono, 2006), and as we shall see in this chapter, this is now beginning to attract the interest of social scientists, particularly discourse analysts (Baker, 2006).

These developments began in the 1960s and 1970s with software written for mainframe computers but have become increasingly sophisticated and interactive as personal computing has proliferated. Generalist qualitative data analysis software (QDA software) for social research data, on the other hand, only began to be written once personal computers had become easily available, ETHNOGRAPH being the first software to be used on a widespread basis from 1984 onward. Since then, a number of programs building on the basic "code and retrieve" architecture of ETHNOGRAPH have been developed, the most well-known being NVIVO, MaxQDA, and ATLAS.ti. Specialized software for the analysis of video data (such as ELAN and Transana) has also been developed, in association with an increasing preference among social researchers to work with video data over audio recording, made possible by the availability of cheap, handheld digital video cameras.

Developers of generalist QDA software have sought to add components to their products that offer some of the capabilities of more specialized

---

[1]SPSS was acquired by IBM in October 2009.

software. For example, ATLAS.ti and MaxQDA offer a "word frequency" feature that mirrors the word lists produced by WordSmith Tools; these programs and NVIVO now offer the capacity to import and code video data, similar to the more specialized ELAN or Transana; many QDA programs now offer the capacity to export counts of codes and other features of data in spreadsheet format, suitable for statistical analysis by programs such as Microsoft Excel or SPSS. The major issue in software choice for researchers, then, will be whether to choose one of the generalist QDA software packages that allow them to do a lot of different things, each to a limited degree, or specialized software that enables one type of data or a particular analytic approach to be thoroughly exploited.

In this chapter, we first review something of the history of QDA software in social research and summarize some of the core procedures it supports. The finer details of individual programs are not given as these change from one release to the next. Suffice it to say that programs vary, and if particular features are unavailable on one, then they are available on another. (Some useful resources for those who wish to explore particular packages are given at the end of this chapter.) We then consider the uses of specialized word list and concordance software for analyzing transcripts of social research interviews. Finally, we turn to the use of specialized software for helping in the analysis of video data.

◆ Generalist QDA Software

The chief contribution of QDA software is automation of the retrieval of text segments (e.g., within an interview) that have been categorized as examples of some analytic concept. Such categorization of data is usually called *coding*. To appreciate the difference computers make in code-and-retrieve operations, it is instructive to consider what preceded the development of QDA software.

HISTORY

As Nigel Fielding and Ray Lee (1998) point out, market researchers had been coding responses to open questions in surveys some time before qualitative researchers discovered the attractions of coding unstructured qualitative data. In the 1940s, some market researchers had even begun to code less structured interview material. Fielding and Lee observe that the first sustained sociological discussion of coding unstructured data is found in publications associated with Howard Becker, Geer, Hughes, and Strauss's *Boys in White* (1961). It is, however, clear that basic indexing operations were in use before this. For example, William Foote Whyte, in his appendix to the third edition of *Street Corner Society* (1943/1981), describes his initial difficulty in deciding whether to organize his field notes "topically, with folders for rackets, the church, the family, and so on" (p. 308) or according to the different social groups he was observing. Eventually, as the volume of material "grew beyond the point where my memory would allow me to locate any given item rapidly" (p. 308), Whyte devised what he calls "a rudimentary indexing system" (p. 308), which served both to reduce his data and to remind him what was in the folders. Other researchers have used card indexes, different-colored pens, scissors and tape, and a host of other manual devices to organize masses of otherwise unwieldy material.

Becker (1970), however, is rightly identified as expounding a more systematic approach to coding and retrieval, which coincided with his concern to address with methodological rigor the problems of inference and proof from fieldwork data. Becker wanted researchers to be able to avoid anecdotalism, identify negative instances, produce quasi statistics, and thereby represent without analytic bias the full range of phenomena in a data set. To this end, he recommended that coding should be done inclusively, so that all instances of a relevant phenomenon would be made available for inspection and perhaps further analysis.

At around the same time, Barney Glaser and Anselm Strauss (1967) were developing their approach to grounded theorizing (see Kathy Charmaz and Linda Belgrave's chapter, "Qualitative Interviewing and Grounded Theory Analysis," this volume). Like Becker, they built on earlier attempts at imposing analytic rigor on qualitative data (e.g., analytic induction) and on an appreciation of developments in quantitative data analysis that involved a creative interaction between theoretical ideas and data (e.g., Lazarsfeld & Rosenberg, 1955). The rigor and system made available by procedures such as the constant comparison of properties and their categories to generate theory, all of which were based on a fundamental code-and-retrieve logic, had a wide appeal that continues to this day. Apart from the real analytic gains, a generation of qualitative researchers learned the strategic advantages of citing grounded theory on grant application forms. Early QDA software programs (such as ETHNOGRAPH and NUD*IST) were designed in large part to relate to the analytic logic of grounded theorizing, so that the basic procedures they make available reflect this tradition in sociological ethnography. This influence is still seen in the structuring of today's QDA software.

The advantages of automated code and retrieval, compared with manual versions of the same thing, can be illustrated with an example involving the use of ETHNOGRAPH by Clive Seale in the early 1990s on data derived from interviews with people recalling the last year of life of deceased relatives or friends. This was an unusually large data set for this early version of ETHNOGRAPH. Only 80 interviews could be processed at any one time (there were a total of 639), so it was necessary to repeat many operations several times. Nevertheless, computerized retrieval saved a lot of clerical work that would have been necessary with manual methods. Using the "filter" operation, which enables the user to select interviews according to the values of "face sheet" variables (e.g., the age or gender of the interviewee), it was possible to make selective retrievals of coded segments. Thus, people who had died in hospitals were compared with people who had died in private homes, by selecting the segments where interviewees described learning of the deaths. Respondents whose deceased relatives or friends had lived alone at home and had died there often described finding the person dead; in hospitals, on the other hand, people were never "found dead" in this way, as hospital personnel ensured that relatives and friends "learned" of the deaths before they witnessed the bodies (Seale, 1995a).

In this and other publications, the software enabled the reporting of counts of the numbers of times particular respondents said particular kinds of things, regardless of where the sentiments were expressed in the interviews (e.g., Seale, 1995b, 1996). Further comparisons of groups of interviewees were made (e.g., reports for people who had cancer were different in various respects from reports for people who had other kinds of illnesses) and negative instances identified, where particular examples ran counter to the majority picture. In this respect, the software's requirement that the analyst code systematically and the tireless capacity of the

computer to confront the researcher with all the coded instances enforced a rigor that might otherwise have been daunting to achieve.

FEATURES

Generalist QDA software programs are capable of performing a variety of procedures, several of which can be described here. Data entry in most of the earlier programs was quite restrictive, often requiring text files only, shaped in a particular way and subject to a line limit, with additional restrictions as to the number of data files processed and unalterable once imported. Then, it became possible to import text files in any format (e.g., downloaded from the Internet, with graphics and colors in place), to alter them at any point, and, more recently, to import, code, and search audio, pdf, video, and scanned images. With the most recent developments, data do not even need to be imported; hyperlinks can be made to data held virtually in situ, for example, on a webpage. This has enabled the geodata application, in which hyperlinked codes may be placed within Google Earth itself. In the future, we may see more use of hyperlinking technology in the "hypermedia" format for disseminating findings. Results may be presented through multiple pathways that involve the reader negotiating, interpreting, and creating his or her own way through the data, or findings may be presented as a series of video clips or pictures instead of text narratives (see, e.g., Gibson, Callery, Campbell, Hall, & Richards, 2005).

Coding data by attaching code labels to segments of data, such as a section of a transcript or a part of an image, is a basic facility of code-and-retrieve QDA software. In addition, most programs allow users to categorize whole data files. For example, a series of interviews may have been carried out, and a researcher may want to attach information about the gender, age, race, or educational level of the interviewee to relevant transcripts or audio files. In addition, most software supports the attachment of analytic memos relating to parts of the data files, in which the researcher jots down his or her own observations and reflections.

The ability to search for coded segments of data according to variables attached to whole data files is a basic feature of a code-and-retrieve program. For example, a researcher may wish to compare men and women on how they discuss a particular topic in an interview. Generalist QDA programs may allow both expanded and restricted views of search results: At times, the researcher may need to see the text that occurs on either side of a coded segment in order to see its context (an expanded view). Beyond this, programs can feature a variety of Boolean search combinations. For example, in the project described above, involving interviews with bereaved people, the researcher might have asked the software to show segments in which respondents discussed the quality of health care and the topic of pain simultaneously, in order to investigate respondents' judgments about the adequacy with which pain was attended to by health care providers. This would have involved a simple overlap between two codes, perhaps called "Pain" and "Hcarequal." Other kinds of Boolean searches involve manipulation of "and," "or," and "not in" commands to specify the conditions under which segments should be retrieved. Alternatively, there may be support for proximity searches—that is, searches for differently coded segments that occur within specified distances of each other. Such searches can help an analyst test hypotheses; for example, a researcher may ask whether Event A always precedes Event B or whether this sequence occurs only under certain conditions of C.

Some of the analytic operations developed in the humanities' computing tradition for linguistic analysis are supported by generalist QDA programs for social research data. The capacity to do automatic searches for strings of letters (and therefore words) is fundamental to these operations. Some QDA users remain suspicious of such "autocoding," as it raises the specter of automatic thinking. The capacity to stop at each "hit" of a string in order to indicate whether a code should be applied in each case helps avoid this problem. This means that "I had a pain here" can be coded differently from "The doctor was a pain in the ass." But this does not solve the problem that arises when an individual talks about pain without using the actual word *pain*, which can only be dealt with by conventional coding procedures that involve reading the text before deciding how to code it. Other features of string searches that are useful include the use of "wildcard" letters (so that "coug*" returns "cough," "coughing," "coughed," etc.) and pattern searching, whereby a particular pattern of characters is identified (e.g., all words ending with "ing" and no more than 10 characters long). These latter features, however, are more likely to be found in specialist software for linguistic content analysis, such as WordSmith Tools, which is discussed in some depth later in this chapter.

Statistical output is another way to view the results of searches, and the ability to create data matrices amenable to statistical analysis by other software is now a common feature of QDA software. For example, Shepherd and Seale (2010) compared the coverage of eating disorders in U.S. and U.K. newspapers. Articles were imported into NVIVO, and segments where profiles of people with eating disorders occurred were coded. Within this, information about whether the person profiled was male or female, recovered or not, a celebrity or not was attached to each profile. In addition, codes for different causes and treatments for eating disorders were developed and applied to the text. This information was exported from the software program into Excel and then SPSS to generate tables in which different groups were compared. U.S. newspapers were much more likely to depict people who had recovered from their eating disorder. Qualitative analysis of depiction of recovery supplemented this broad statistical finding.

Increasingly, QDA software is designed to enable researchers working as a team to share their work. Of course, it was always possible for one researcher to work on a project, save his or her work, and send the project file to another researcher to work on. But this "serial" method of sharing work meant that only one person could work on a project at a time, and there was always a danger that coordination would break down, resulting in two or more versions of the same project. The capacity to merge different versions of a project solves this problem, enabling simultaneous work by different members of a team. This has developed in some programs into "virtual" sharing. For example, the specialist video analysis program Transana (described later in this chapter in more detail) has a multiuser version that allows "real-time" synchronized collaboration, with the video and all its analysis stored remotely on a secure server and accessible by password.

A further feature of QDA software is the capacity to draw conceptual maps that assist the development of theoretical models. Concepts can be linked with connecting lines to indicate different kinds of relationships (e.g., A causes B, A is a strategy for doing B, A loves B), with the added advantage that elements of the model are linked to data files. An early example of the use of this, supported by ATLAS.ti, is in Susanne Friese's (1999) account of her interviews with shoppers exhibiting different degrees of addiction to compulsive buying. She interviewed 55 shoppers about their behavior. Figure 29.1 reproduces her conceptual map summarizing the links made by addicted buyers that they

Figure 29.1 Reasons for Impulse Buying

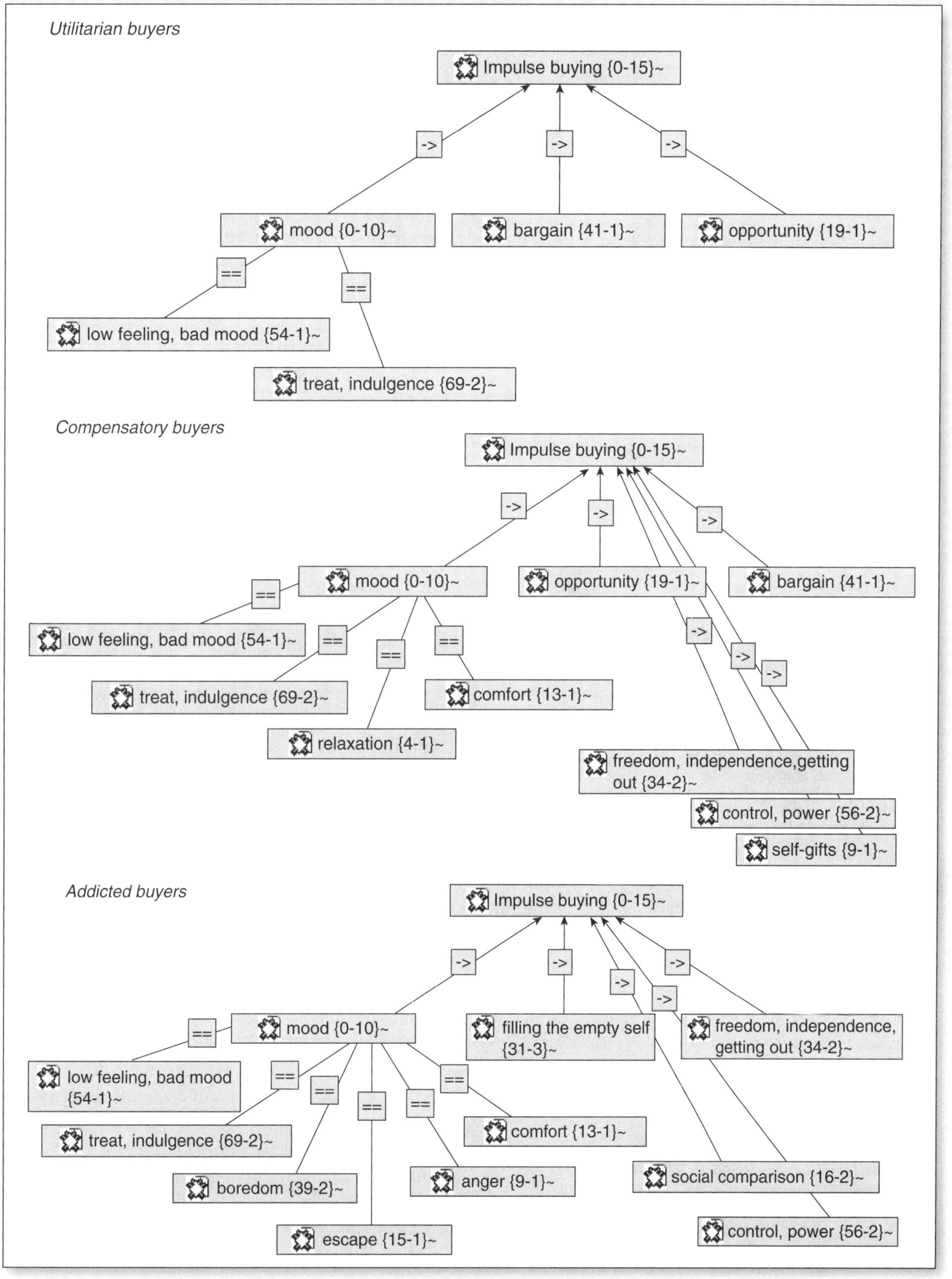

Utilitarian buyers

Compensatory buyers

Addicted buyers

Source: Friese (1999). Used with permission.

Note: >, reason for; ==, is associated with

perceived led to, or were associated with, episodes of impulse buying. Because Friese displays similar maps for less addicted buyers, the reader is presented with a quick comparative summary of how these people experienced and explained their behavior.

The use of generalist QDA software for social research is now very well established. In the previous edition of this book, the chapter written by Seale (2002) reported a survey of published studies that had used such software, finding basic coding and retrieval studies to be common but advanced features, such as concept mapping or theory building capacities, to be rare. In our impression, this situation remains, particularly for multimedia analysis, although updating such a survey of the literature now would be difficult, as the use of QDA software is now so routine that it often does not merit mention in the abstracts or methods sections of articles. Instead, we offer here an account of two somewhat specialized strands within the computer-assisted analysis of qualitative data that, in our view, will grow in the future: (1) the use for social research purposes of software developed for corpus linguistics and (2) the use of software designed for video analysis. Where possible, we will illustrate these with interview data.

Both of these areas of software development have been made feasible by other technological advances, the most important of which has been the exponential increase in the processing and storage speeds of personal computers. This means that software can become more complex and data files can become larger. Huge amounts of text and very large video files can now be processed with relative ease. Coupled with this is the reduction in the cost and size of good audio- and video-recording equipment, the advancement of graphics cards and data digitizing, and the ready availability of large quantities of text via the Internet and in the various data archives and depositories that have developed in conjunction with the Internet. Together, these developments mean that computer-assisted analysis can now support new forms of analysis on a scale that 20, or even 10, years ago would have been impossible.

◆ Adapting Corpus Linguistic Software

An interest in computerized analysis of language predates the development of generalist QDA software. Linguists and literature specialists have long used computers to generate concordances and other string-search software to analyze literary style or language-in-use through quantitative content analysis. Early use of this by social researchers is worth noting here. Bernard and Ryan (1994) identify "schema analysis" as a productive merge of the linguistic and sociological traditions and illustrate this by referring to anthropological studies of storytelling in Indian and Inuit cultures, reported by Colby (1966; Colby, Kennedy, & Milanesi, 1991), who developed a computer program (called SAGE) to analyze both the overall structural features and the linguistic content of stories. Initially, in work derived from interviews, he compared the words used by Zuni informants (a crop-growing group) with those used by Navajo (a sheep-herding group). Crop growers are concerned with weather conditions above all, sheep herders with finding good grazing land and protection from stormy weather. Words concerning different forms of moisture (snow, rain, clouds) were accordingly found more often in Zuni stories than in Navajo stories, where storms, wind, and cold featured more frequently. Because traveling was more a feature of Navajo lifestyle, home was depicted as a place of rest after a journey, and arrival home was often the end of the story; for Zuni, home was where things happened, and events there occurred at the start of stories. Colby then became interested in identifying common structures in folktales, using a computer to analyze the linguistic content of particular points in tales in order to reveal the underlying cultural themes.

WordSmith Tools is an example of a popular program used by corpus linguists. Within this subdiscipline, it is often used to compare a particular text with a language "corpus," which is a multimillion word collection of language examples, often chosen to represent typical usage of a language across a variety of genres (e.g., written, spoken, speeches, conversations, published writing, e-mails, and letters). Examples of reference corpora designed to be representative of national English usage are the British National Corpus (www.natcorp.ox.ac.uk) and the Corpus of Contemporary American English (www.americancorpus.org). If a word, a group of words, or a part of speech occurs more frequently in the text being analyzed in comparison with the reference corpus, this is often an indicator of some interesting aspect of the style or content of the text being analyzed, so that this is then a signal for further qualitative investigation of these features.

In adapting this software for social research purposes, Clive Seale and his colleagues developed a method dubbed "comparative keyword analysis"—which, instead of comparing a text with a corpus, compares one text with another. This can be appreciated by considering the material analyzed in the first project in which this method was used (Seale, Charteris-Black, & Ziebland, 2006). This involved the analysis of 97 qualitative interviews with people who had experienced breast and prostate cancer, collected some years earlier by the Health Experiences Research Group (www.healthtalkonline.org), and another archive of postings to Internet-based discussion and support groups visited by people with these illnesses, their family members, and others. The interviews contained 727,100 words of text, and the web forums contained 2,145,337 words posted by 1,534 people. Later work (e.g., Seale, Charteris-Black, MacFarlane, & McPherson, 2010) has involved analysis of various subsamples of an archive of 1,035 interviews collected by this group. This volume of material is very large by the standards of conventional qualitative research, meaning that our collection had the potential to overcome a common criticism made of qualitative research: that the emphasis on analytic depth is only possible where small and possibly unrepresentative samples are analyzed. Yet reading and coding all of this material using generalist QDA software would have taken many months, so a different method was needed.

In a sense, keyword analysis is like an aerial view of a landscape, whose undulations and patterns of vegetation growth reflect the outline of ancient buildings, only possible to be seen from above. The method helped us identify sections within the large body of texts we had assembled that would repay more detailed analysis, of a sort more recognizable by qualitative researchers. For example, in Seale et al. (2010), where the language and content of research interviews were compared with the language and content of postings to web forums, we added 43 interviews with people talking about sexual health issues to the breast and prostate cancer interview files. Postings to a web forum concerning sexual health were also added to the cancer web collection. Our purpose was to see how the web postings and interviews compared.

The method proceeds by using the software first to create a list of all of the words occurring in a body of text (e.g., all interviews on sexual health) and then producing a list of words appearing in another text with which to compare it (e.g., all postings to the sexual health website). Comparison is then made of the two word lists so that words that are more frequently used in one text than in the other are shown. These are "keywords." Thus, the word *penis* occurs 4,048 times in the e-mail queries concerning sexual health (0.44% of all of the words in all of the e-mail queries) but only 7 times in all of the transcripts of qualitative interviews about sexual health. *Penis* is placed fifth in the list of words that show the strongest difference between these bodies of texts ("corpora"), ranked according to a log-likelihood test. We therefore call *penis* a "positive keyword" in the e-mail subcorpus when it is compared with the interview subcorpus.

The software can be set to do this for two- or three-word clusters too. Figure 29.2a shows this for some of the key three-word clusters that characterize interview talk by females concerning sexual health, in comparison with postings by females to the website. The phrase "I didn't want to," which occurs 68 times in the interviews but never in the web postings, has been selected, and Figure 29.2b shows an extract from a concordance showing the words on either side of this cluster. It gives some sense of the meanings associated with these words. Figure 29.2c then does the same thing for web forum contributors compared with interviewees. "Should I do" occurs 983 times in the web forum but never in the interviews, reflecting that this was a website where people wrote in asking for advice from a "Dr. Anne," the agony aunt. The concordance extract (Figure 29.2d) gives some idea of how this can be used to explore what topics people were asking about.

In this work, which was supported by both displays of keyword lists and quotations from the texts that illustrated the use of these keywords, we concluded that interviewees produced retrospective accounts, their content guided by the interviewers' questions, which sometimes elicited rich biographical and contextual details. Internet exchanges, on the other hand, concerned participants' current experiences and contained detailed accounts of disease processes, medical procedures, bodily processes, and, in the case of sexual health, sexual practices. Conclusions were drawn about the relative usefulness of each source for inquiring into personal experience.

In this kind of analysis, deciding which positive keywords, or keyword clusters, to report, or to

Figure 29.2 Three-Word Cluster Keyword Comparisons and Concordances Using WordSmith Tools

a. Clusters more frequently used by female interviewees than by female contributors to Web forum

N	Key word	Freq.	%	. Freq.	RC. %	eyness	P
26	A LOT MORE	110	0.04	9		183.12	0.0000000000
27	BUT YOU KNOW	84	0.03	0		182.89	0.0000000000
28	AND THAT WAS	82	0.03	0		178.53	0.0000000000
29	I DON'T REALLY	113	0.04	15		165.86	0.0000000000
30	YOU KNOW IT'S	76	0.02	0		165.47	0.0000000000
31	TO TALK ABOUT	92	0.03	6		160.09	0.0000000000
32	TALK ABOUT IT	96	0.03	9		154.98	0.0000000000
33	SO IT WAS	70	0.02	0		152.41	0.0000000000
34	LOT OF PEOPLE	90	0.03	7		151.42	0.0000000000
35	DIDN'T WANT TO	68	0.02	0		148.05	0.0000000000
36	I DIDN'T HAVE	68	0.02	0		148.05	0.0000000000
37	I DIDN'T REALLY	68	0.02	0		148.05	0.0000000000

b. Concordance of "I didn't want to" in interviews with female respondents

N	Concordance
9	had gone with my best friend and so I didn't want to sleep with my next
10	I first got my proper second boyfriend I didn't want to sleep with him at all
11	Yeah, my second boyfriend I didn't want to have sex with because I
12	I mean I did kind of feel like I kind of didn't want to take too long with the
13	and I obviously wasn't because I didn't want to have sex so I found that
14	make it work again' but I decided that I didn't want to go back, I wanted to go
15	could I be put back on that and they didn't want to give it to me basically
16	my head wasn't in it but I didn't, I was. I didn't want to let him go and I was too
17	with him but if I couldn't be with then I didn't want to be with anyone else for
18	bin because it was like right, because I didn't want to be with anyone else,
19	it and felt pressured to do it 'cos they didn't want to lose their boyfriend and
20	know, the same experience that they didn't want to do it and felt pressured to

c. Clusters more frequently used by female contributors to Web forum than by female interviewees

N	Key word	Freq.	%	. Freq.	RC. %	eyness	P
1	SHOULD I DO	983	0.16	0		807.65	0.0000000000
2	I HAVE A	1,126	0.18	15		798.10	0.0000000000
3	WHAT SHOULD I	908	0.15	0		745.99	0.0000000000
4	I AM #	806	0.13	0		662.15	0.0000000000
5	DEAR DR ANN	556	0.09	0		456.69	0.0000000000
6	SHALL I DO	540	0.09	0		443.54	0.0000000000
7	CAN I DO	506	0.08	0		415.61	0.0000000000
8	CAN YOU GET	503	0.08	0		413.14	0.0000000000
9	HOW CAN I	501	0.08	0		411.50	0.0000000000
10	AND I AM	563	0.09	7		402.16	0.0000000000
11	I DONT KNOW	489	0.08	0		401.64	0.0000000000
12	I HAVE BEEN	629	0.10	16		401.59	0.0000000000

d. Concordance of "should I do?" by female contributors to Web forum

N	Concordance
176	now pregnant I stay in care and what should I do I'm still at school too please
177	and i dont want to give up. What should i do? Ok I need some help. . . . I
178	i do i have really bad period pains what should i do how long do you have to sex
179	sex i have really bad period pains what should i do i have really bad period pains
180	I did while giving a presentation. What should I do? Dear Dr. Ann, I have low
181	asked me to have sex with her. what should i do My teacher invited me round
182	my friends dad sleeps with her. whar should i do what is gay porn cause i like
183	of what they might do to me. . . what should i do????? What is the hole

Source: Used with permission from Mike Scott, creator of WordSmith Tools (Version 5.0).

analyze further, is not done on purely statistical grounds. Some positive keywords are highly significant statistically but are of trivial importance for the research questions being pursued. Choosing the keywords that best bring out the characteristics of a particular text is, then, a qualitative judgment informed by examining the meanings that these words have in the texts concerned and relating this to the purpose of the analysis. Comparative keyword analysis is therefore a conjoint qualitative and quantitative analytic method (Seale & Charteris-Black, 2010).

◆ *Using Software to Analyze Video Data*

The history of video analysis software differs slightly from that of more generalist programs. Early film work was firmly rooted in anthropology, documenting behaviors and rituals as descriptive records (see, e.g., Bateson & Mead, 1942; Flaherty, 1922). In the 1920s, Kurt Lewin, a psychologist, was one of the first to adopt a more analytical approach, and psychologists have continued to heavily influence video analysis work since (Knoblauch, Schnettler, & Raab, 2006). Kurt Lewin used film to explore types of behaviors as discrete sequences of events. For example, in a study of children's emotional expressions, he filmed moments of conflict (Lewin, 1935). Later, in 1952, an anthropologist named Ray Birdwhistell used film to explore aspects of what we now term *body language*. He coined the term *kinesics* to describe this nonverbal language. Significantly for

later software development, Birdwhistell (1952) drew heavily on descriptive linguistics to code nonverbal language. For example, he categorized more than 50 of the smallest individual units of movement (such as a head nod) and called these kinemes, just as the smallest unit of spoken words is called a phoneme. He also developed a code for analyzing the way these kinemes were used in social interactions. Since then, a large number of coding schemes have been drawn up for visual analysis, although the sheer volume of possible event types that may be coded means that researchers continue to develop new schemes ad hoc to suit their particular requirements.

Charles Goodwin (1980) was one of the first to apply conversation analysis (CA) to video rather than just audio data, examining the sequencing of verbal elements of communication with nonverbal elements such as gaze. Also in the 1980s, Christian Heath began video-analytic work on the clinical encounter and other social interactions from a conversation-analytic perspective (see, e.g., Heath, 1992; Heath & Hindmarsh, 2002). The use of CA with interview data is itself quite rare, however (see Roulston, 2006, for a review), and CA of this type of interaction using video analysis software is rarer still. Figure 29.3 shows, though, how specialized video analysis software (the ELAN program, developed at the Max Planck Institute for Psycholinguistics) can be used to examine simultaneously different levels of interaction between two individuals. While watching the video in the upper-left corner, the analyst can look at the waveform of the audio, the speech transcribed (W-Spch and W-Words), the overall bodily position

Figure 29.3 ELAN Software Showing Levels of Analysis

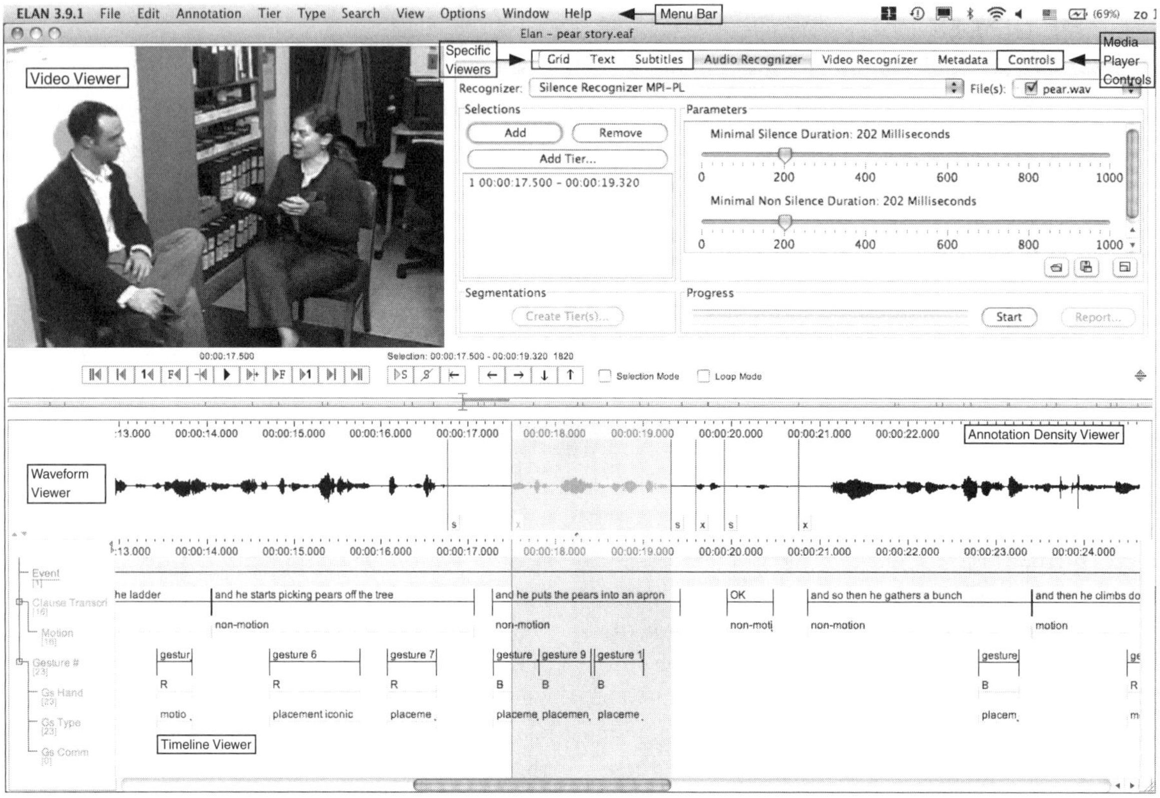

Source: Brugman and Russel (2004). Image provided by Han Sloetjes (Max Planck Institute for Psycholinguistics, Nijmegen, The Netherlands). For more information on ELAN, see http://www.lat-mpi.eu/tools/elan/.

(W-POS), and other aspects of the interaction, such as gaze and hand gestures, as these scroll past in real time.

FEATURES OF QDA VIDEO SOFTWARE

As Figure 29.3 shows, a few minutes of video can provide a huge mass of data. Video is multisensual, containing various types of audio and visual information, and these confer multiple layers of meaning. As well as the increasing incorporation of video analysis facilities within generalist QDA software, specialized programs have been developed to enable the analyst to work on and display these different levels of meaning simultaneously and to stay close to the data through the use of multiple transcripts that may be displayed together on screen. This feature has been exploited by researchers analyzing only written transcripts as well as by those analyzing video data more directly. Separate but linked transcripts may be made of body language and verbal language, or verbal communication may be represented by various conventions, each with its own transcript. The different layers of meaning may be considered diachronically (things unfold as the video plays out, which may affect subsequent events) and synchronically (e.g., a grimace and a hand gesture may occur at the same time). QDA video programs facilitate both types of analysis through the use of timelines, to which the transcripts may be linked in various ways. Most of these programs are particularly suited to diachronic analysis. DRS (Digital Replay System), a free program, differs from other QDA video software tools in a number of ways, including the way it can link different types of data synchronically according to the temporal relationship between events. ELAN (Figure 29.3) has similar functionality. Tiers—ELAN's name for transcripts—may be aligned not just in relation to the unfolding action in the main video file but also in relation to each other; they can then be ordered and reordered to make more salient particular relationships within the data.

As with text-based programs, the basic function of video analysis software is to code and retrieve. Both hierarchical and nonhierarchical relationships between codes may be represented, but the ease with which each is managed varies with the program. Some programs allow for loose connections between uncoded bits of multimodal data, using hypertext links. An example is the generalist program ATLAS.ti, which was developed by a psychologist in collaboration with linguists for bottom-up grounded theory analysis and which has recently incorporated video-analytic capabilities. A similar effect may be achieved in more structured programs by using very broad codes for collections of data, such as "beginning," "middle," and "end." The aim in these cases is to navigate around the data in a systematic fashion but without imposing structure on it too early.

Other programs, such as Transana and MaxQDA, developed initially for linguistic, conversation, and discourse analysis, prioritize top-down hierarchies— that is, videos or sections of these are stored using keywords that immediately impose some sort of coding framework on the data.

SOME EXAMPLES

Nathan, Eilam, and Kim (2007) undertook a multilayered analysis of pupils learning about pie charts in a middle school mathematics classroom, exploiting some of the capabilities of Transana. They used a specialized video analysis program to look at features such as speech, gestures, drawing, and object use, at the global level (considering the whole class), at the meso level (between participants), and at the micro level (individual students' actions and utterances). This level of complexity would have been difficult to achieve without the use of the software.

Their first step was to get a broad picture of the data by making a rough transcript and by using the waveform feature in Transana to document pauses (zero-amplitude waveform) and active parts of the recording. Transana, reflecting its roots in CA and discourse analysis, handles pause and micropause measurements with ease, but any of the QDA programs capable of video analysis can time these far more accurately than was ever possible with a watch. Next, Nathan and colleagues divided the transcript into "stanzas" of interaction, with a new stanza each time a substantively new idea or problem was introduced by participants. Stanzas were marked by time

codes, which are active in Transana—that is, they act like hypertext links to the relevant parts of the videos. Next, these researchers added to the transcripts information on gestures and on "representations"— that is, the specific use of drawings, objects, and gestures to explain pie charts.

Up to this point, all the coding was broad and top-down, to facilitate navigation around the data. Further coding involved using a more bottom-up approach, with thematic coding of both particular representations and evaluations of the representations by others in the classroom. This process was aided by the use of collections of video clips illustrating a particular type of interaction that could be analyzed for themes in the same way as a collection of text extracts. Nathan et al. (2007) next used what they called a discourse analysis approach to examine the speech events within stanzas and the times when there was agreement or disagreement (which they called the level of intersubjectivity). By this stage, they had determined that the following types of interaction were significant in their data: initiating a new topic, demonstrating it using representations, and evaluating the demonstration. They also found differences depending on whether the student or teacher had initiated a stanza and directed the way it proceeded, the types of representations that pupils used to solve the mathematical problem, and the interpretive frames that students used during representations (e.g., whether they considered a pie chart in terms of a physical pie that is eaten or as an abstract, two-dimensional concept).

Next, the researchers used particular features of Transana to consider the dynamics of what went on; that is, they mapped out the different events that they had previously determined (initiation, demonstration, evaluation, and presence [IS+] or absence [IS–] of intersubjectivity) as they occurred along the timeline. This revealed the way these events combined into simultaneous groups and also sequences through time. The maps therefore provided an alternative to the more immediate synchronic linking feature of DRS and ELAN and also provided diachronic information. It was clear from the maps that the triad of initiation–demonstration–evaluation (IDE) predominated and cycled throughout the teaching session. Intersubjectivity events tended to mark the beginning of a new IDE sequence. The maps not only served to summarize data for interpretation but also suggested more avenues for exploration; further detailed analysis of video and transcripts showed how agreement

(IS+) and disagreement (IS–) were not mutually exclusive events but that some level of disagreement could be necessary for substantive agreement to be worked out.

The researchers then stepped back to a more global analysis of the data. They constructed a map to measure the quality of representations in the entire session, which revealed that the quality of representations improved over time during the session. Their conclusion was that intersubjectivity was important in perpetuating discourse and developing understanding and that intersubjectivity was developed through the use of representations.

A number of researchers have analyzed combinations of videos of naturally occurring events with interviews with the participants and with other modes of data. Most QDA video analysis software enables different types of data to be treated in the same way, but some programs are better at handling this than others. For example, ATLAS.ti treats each type of data as a separate object, and so it can use stand-alone videos or audio, or text or images. Transana, however, has to have both a video or audio recording and a linked transcript in order to work and so cannot be used for materials that do not have accompanying sound or video (unless a dummy video is uploaded).

The different sources of data may be simultaneously displayed within different windows, which can also be hidden as required. This means that transcripts can be made directly from video within the program, although programs can also upload transcripts from other sources. Some allow several videos to be synchronized and displayed at the same time. This enables ready comparison of different scenes and events. It also means that shots of the same scene from several angles may be shown together, increasing the amount of information the analyst can use for a single scene. Some software allows windows to be "detached" and moved around the screen, arranged as the analyst wishes independently of other windows, and enlarged or made smaller. This allows windows to be juxtaposed in the most helpful ways for the analyst. In this way, Kivelä and Mylläri (2008) initially used ELAN to analyze juxtaposed videos of school pupils working in the school's computer lab, videos of associated lessons, screen capture animations from the pupils' workstations, and interviews with pupils who used the screen capture animations as prompts.

It can be seen from Figure 29.3 that ELAN displays transcripts horizontally along the timeline. This means that ELAN transcription is visually directly aligned with the video timeline, which makes it an excellent tool for multimodal analysis of various simultaneous lines of action. Other programs use the more conventional list format for transcripts, as in Figure 29.4, which shows how Transana displays data. This makes rapid comparisons less easy but is more suited to forms of analysis (e.g., CA) that require the precise syllables of overlapping talk or action to be shown.

◆ Conclusion

Our review has focused on some rather less used elements of QDA software, keyword and video analysis, and some specialized software designed to support these, because the field has moved on considerably since the first edition of this book. Then—and it was only about 10 years ago that Clive Seale (2002) was writing that chapter—QDA software, though increasingly known about and used by researchers, had not attained the same status as statistical software had done for people doing quantitative social research. In other words, it was not regarded by all as an essential tool for social scientists, to be built into the undergraduate—or at least postgraduate—research methods curriculum. There were few generic textbooks on QDA software, and the manuals that came with particular programs had to substitute for them.

Now, however, most social scientists who have come into the field in the past 10 years or so will know about and be able to use one of the generalist QDA software programs, such as NVIVO or ATLAS.ti. Textbooks, websites, and training courses have proliferated to reflect and support this. One of the themes of the earlier version of this chapter was that the actual practice of social researchers using these programs rarely went beyond a very basic level. Now, use of more advanced elements of these programs is increasingly integrated into a more sophisticated practice of qualitative research.

Because of the widespread knowledge of generalist QDA software and its basic operations, we have in this chapter paid particular attention to modes of analysis, and the software to support these, that are rarer and arguably more "advanced"—or at least are attempting to be innovative. QDA software developments in the past 10 years have enabled a substantial amount of research into the visual, material, and spoken aspects of language, communication, and interaction, including computer-mediated versions of these. Each program has its limitations and also its specializations, which depend partly on its roots and

Figure 29.4 Transana, Showing the List Format Style of Transcript

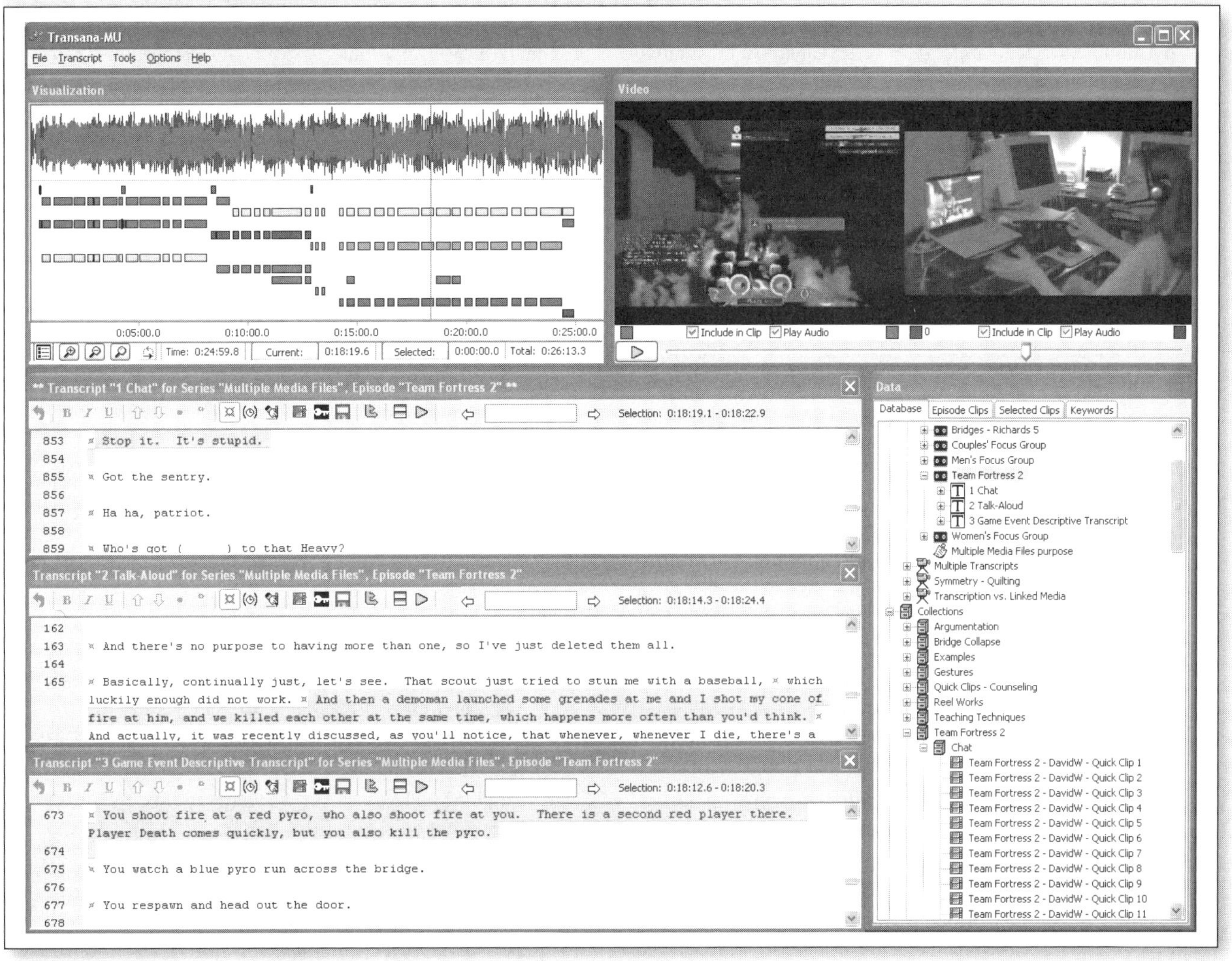

Source: Screenshot of Transana software used with permission from David Woods. For more information on Transana, see http://www.transana.org/.

on which types of media it has chosen to support and which to focus on. We hope that this chapter will have guided you through these in a reasonably clear fashion and that, in some respects, it may point to the future of qualitative research practice.

◆ *Useful Web Resources*

CAQDAS (Computer-Assisted Qualitative Data Analysis) networking project: http://caqdas.soc.surrey.ac.uk/
ATLAS.ti: www.atlasti.de
DRS: http://web.mac.com/andy.crabtree/NCeSS_Digital_Records_Node/DReSS.html
ELAN: www.let.kun.nl/sign-lang/echo/ELAN/ELAN_intro.html
ETHNOGRAPH: www.QualisResearch.com

MaxQDA: www.maxqda.com
NVIVO: www.qsr.com.au
Transana: www.transana.org/index.htm
WordSmith Tools: www.lexically.net/wordsmith/

◆ *References*

Baker, P. (2006). *Using corpora in discourse analysis*. London, England: Continuum.
Bateson, G., & Mead, M. (1942). *Balinese character: A photographic analysis*. New York, NY: New York Academy of Sciences.
Becker, H. S. (1970). Problems of inference and proof in participant observation. In H. S. Becker (Ed.), *Sociological work: Method and substance* (pp. 25–38). Chicago, IL: Aldine Press.

Becker, H. S., Geer, B., Hughes, E. C., & Strauss, A. (1961). *Boys in white*. Chicago, IL: University of Chicago Press.

Bernard, H. R., & Ryan, G. (1994). Text analysis: Qualitative and quantitative methods. In H. R. Bernard (Ed.), *Handbook of methods in cultural anthropology* (pp. 595–646). Thousand Oaks, CA: Sage.

Birdwhistell, R. L. (1952). *Introduction to kinesics: An annotated system for the analysis of body motion and gesture*. Louisville, KY: University of Louisville.

Brugman, H., & Russel, A. (2004, May). Annotating multimedia/multi-modal resources with ELAN. Poster presented at the Fourth International Conference on Language Resources and Evaluation, Lisbon, Portugal. Retrieved from http://www.lat-mpi.eu/papers/papers-2004/Brugman-ELAN.pdf

Colby, B. N. (1966). The analysis of culture content and the patterning of narrative concern in texts. *American Anthropologist, 68*, 374–388.

Colby, B. N., Kennedy, S., & Milanesi, L. (1991). Content analysis, cultural grammars and computers. *Qualitative Sociology, 14*, 373–384.

Fielding, N. G., & Lee, R. M. (1998). *Computer analysis and qualitative research*. London, England: Sage.

Flaherty, R. J. (1922). How I filmed *Nanook of the North. World's Work, October*, 632–640. Retrieved from www.cinemaweb.com/silentfilm/bookshelf/23_rf1_2.htm

Friese, S. (1999). *Self concept and identity in a consumer society: Aspects of symbolic product meaning*. Marburg, Germany: Tectum.

Gibson, W., Callery, P., Campbell, M., Hall, A., & Richards, D. (2005). The digital revolution in qualitative research: Working with digital audio data through Atlas.Ti. *Sociological Research Online, 10*, 1. Retrieved from www.socresonline.org.uk/10/1/gibson.htm

Glaser, B. G., & Strauss, A. L. (1967). *The discovery of grounded theory: Strategies for qualitative research*. Chicago, IL: Aldine Press.

Goodwin, C. (1980). Restarts, pauses, and the achievement of mutual gaze at turn-beginning. *Sociological Inquiry, 50*(3/4), 272–302.

Heath, C. (1992). The delivery and reception of diagnosis in the general-practice consultation. In P. Drew & J. Heritage (Eds.), *Talk at work: Interaction in institutional settings* (pp. 235–267). Cambridge, England: Cambridge University Press.

Heath, C., & Hindmarsh, J. (2002). Analysing interaction: Video, ethnography and situated conduct. In T. May (Ed.), *Qualitative research in action* (pp. 99–122). London, England: Sage.

Kivelä, M., & Mylläri, J. (2008, September). *Making sense of content creation in the physical and virtual in primary school*. Helsinki, Finland: University of Helsinki, Department of Education and Department of Applied Sciences of Education (InnoEdu-project). Retrieved from http://www.dream.dk/files/pdf/08Kivela.pdf

Knoblauch, H., Schnettler, B., & Raab, J. (2006). Video-analysis: Methodological aspects of interpretive audiovisual analysis in social research. In H. Knoblauch, B. Schnettler, J. Raab, & H.-G. Soeffner (Eds.), *Video-analysis methodology and methods: Qualitative audiovisual data analysis in sociology* (pp. 9–28). Frankfurt-am-Main, Germany: Peter Mann.

Lazarsfeld, P. F., & Rosenberg, M. (1955). *The language of social research: A reader in the methodology of social research*. Glencoe, IL: Free Press.

Lewin, K. (1935). A dynamic theory of personality. In *Survey of the experimental investigations* (chap. 7, pp. 239–273). New York, NY: McGraw-Hill. Retrieved from http://gestalttheory.net/archive/lewin1935.html

McEnery, A., Xiao, R., & Tono, Y. (2006). *Corpus-based language studies: An advanced resource book*. London, England: Routledge.

Nathan, M. J., Eilam, B., & Kim, S. (2007). To disagree, we must also agree: How intersubjectivity structures and perpetuates discourse in a mathematics classroom. *Journal of the Learning Sciences, 16*(4), 525–565.

Roulston, K. (2006). Close encounters of the "CA" kind: A review of literature analysing talk in research interviews. *Qualitative Research, 6*(4), 515–534.

Seale, C. (1995a). Dying alone. *Sociology of Health and Illness, 17*(3), 376–392.

Seale, C. (1995b). Heroic death. *Sociology, 29*(4), 597–613.

Seale, C. (1996). Living alone towards the end of life. *Ageing and Society, 16*, 75–91.

Seale, C. (2002). Computer-assisted analysis of qualitative interview data. In J. F. Gubrium & J. A. Holstein (Eds.), *Handbook of interview research* (pp. 651–670). Thousand Oaks, CA: Sage.

Seale, C., & Charteris-Black, J. (2010). Keyword analysis: A new tool for qualitative research. In I. L. Bourgeault, R. DeVries, & R. Dingwall (Eds.), *Handbook of qualitative health research*. Thousand Oaks, CA: Sage.

Seale, C., Charteris-Black, J., MacFarlane, A., & McPherson, A. (2010). Interviews and Internet forums: A comparison of two sources of data for qualitative research. *Qualitative Health Research, 20*, 595–606.

Seale, C., Charteris-Black, J., & Ziebland, S. (2006). Gender, cancer experience and Internet use: A comparative keyword analysis of interviews and online cancer support groups. *Social Science and Medicine, 62*(10), 2577–2590.

Shepherd, E., & Seale, C. (2010). Eating disorders in the media: The changing nature of newspaper reports. *European Eating Disorders Review, 18*(6), 486–495.

Whyte, W. F. (1981). *Street corner society: The social structure of an Italian slum* (3rd ed.). Chicago, IL: University of Chicago Press. (Original work published 1943)

Part VI

ETHICS OF
THE INTERVIEW

INFORMED CONSENT

◆ Marco Marzano

I n many respects, the history of informed consent began with the Nazi extermination camps and the dreadful violence perpetrated on their inmates and, above all, the reduction of their bodies to "objects" in the hands of experimenters devoid of humanity. That such horrors should never happen again was the unanimous conviction of public opinion worldwide after World War II. It was for this reason that the Nuremberg Code was formulated in 1947 and the Helsinki Declaration was signed by the World Medical Association in 1964 (Dingwall, 2006; Hoeyer, Dahlager, & Lynöe, 2005).

Only in subsequent decades did the idea arise that these declarations of principle could be translated into a single instrument—namely informed consent—for doctors and health care practitioners (Beauchamp & Childress, 2001). Because, as Arthur Kleinman (1997) writes, Westerners tend to be monotheist outside religious contexts as well, the enterprise of informed consent rapidly became the new moral deity: the fetish, some would say, of a secularized and individualized society. It expressed the distrust widely aroused by an expert system as esoteric and complex as medicine (Giddens, 1990) and perhaps also the crisis of trust that traverses contemporary social systems.

Put very simply, the notion of informed consent is grounded primarily on the principle of individual autonomy and secondarily on that of beneficence (Oeye, Bjelland, & Skorpen, 2007). It states the obligation to furnish the potential participants in a research study or experiment with detailed information (preferably in written form) on the purpose, duration, and methods of the research. Moreover, the risks and benefits deriving from participation in the study and the treatments must be honestly described. And guarantees must be given as to absolute confidentiality and the respondent's right to withdraw his or her consent at any time (Marshall, 2003). The correct application of the principle of informed consent is enforced by the myriad "ethical committees" charged with its enforcement.

Successful ideas travel far (Czarniawska & Joerges, 1995); "greater than the tread of mighty armies is an idea whose time has come," said Victor Hugo (quoted by Czarniawska & Joerges, 1995). The informed consent regulatory system has thus rapidly become a "universal fashion" through an isomorphic process that has reached the four corners of the world (Dingwall, 2006). From biomedicine, it has quickly spread into social research, where it has progressively increased the number of domains falling under its control (Katz, 2007). It has done so with all the unintentional consequences that inevitably accompany "translation processes" of this kind (Czarniawska & Joerges, 1995). "The translation model" has been introduced in the sociological analysis of social and organizational change by the French sociologist Bruno Latour. Latour contrasts the traditional "diffusion" model with the translation model. He wrote that "watching ideas travel, we observe a process of translation, not one of reception, rejection, resistance or acception."

In this chapter, I review some of the stages of this journey. I begin with the effects of the migration of the idea of informed consent into interview research, and into social research in general. I then measure its efficacy in the place where it first arose, namely, biomedicine. I conclude with an examination of the alternative conceptions of protecting research participants.

◆ Informed Consent in Social Research

For some decades, the idea of informed consent has migrated steadily into the territory of social research at universities and in many empirical "fields" (especially, and obviously, health care). Although this large-scale transmigration is most evident in the English-speaking countries, it now extends worldwide, and it assumes the features of an outright invasion, or an institutional and cultural hegemony. This invasion has received legitimacy from the discovery of the presumed dangers that derive from social studies, a claim bolstered by the obligatory references to the well-known studies of Humphreys (1975), Zimbardo and White (1972), and especially Milgram (1974). Van den Hoonaard (2001) refers to this growing hypersensitivity to the potential dangers of research as a "moral panic": that is, a campaign skillfully orchestrated by powerful interest groups inside and outside universities and based on exaggeration of the risks and damage to society caused by social research as a whole.

Whatever the case may be, this invasion is a social phenomenon that has compelled change in research methods and in relationships with participants. It has imposed new standards and cultural sensitivities.

But it has also provoked resistance, or at least profound malcontent, in some academic circles. This is especially true for those who use qualitative methods. There are, however, a few defenders of informed consent in social research (Bosk & De Vries, 2004; Fluehr-Lobban, 1994; Hedgecoe, 2008). These scholars argue that the differences between biomedicine and the social sciences should be substantially scaled down, given that even social research can inflict damage (obviously more moral or psychological than physical) on research subjects. The resistance raised by social researchers against informed consent and ethical committees, the defenders allege, reveals the persistence in this community of a paternalistic mentality similar to that prevalent among doctors until a few decades ago. For example, Hedgecoe (2008), based on his first-hand observations of research ethics committees (RECs), concludes that their members do not harbor a priori prejudices against qualitative research. When they rejected a project, they were sincerely sorry to do so, and they hoped in general that they might be able to foster the development of social research, not to hinder it. The defenders of informed consent hope that social research will sooner or later be able to reconcile itself to a more formalized culture of ethical control, which in their view is both necessary and inevitable (Bosk & De Vries, 2004; Hoeyer et al., 2005).

Nonetheless, the voices in favor of the migration of ethical standards from the medical to the social sciences seem the exception in the sea of protests from its opponents, who even fear for the very future of the social sciences under the new ethical regime. For example, Peter and Patricia Adler (2002) have spoken of an "Orwellian atmosphere," Haggerty (2004) of a dangerous "ethics creep," and Katz (2007) of a return to censorship and denial of legality. Others have claimed that the main problem for qualitative researchers used to be obtaining access to the field and gaining participants' trust (i.e., rapport); today, the chief obstacles have become the informed consent form and uncertainty about the decisions of ethical committees. In many countries, if researchers cannot provide RECs with a "convincing narrative" (Whittaker, 2005) that exhibits good moral intentions and a package of solutions for every possible problem that may arise in the course of the study, the research is not authorized and thus may not be initiated or continued.

The *cahier de doleances* (the list of grievances) is a long and complex one. In what follows, I shall restrict my treatment to the arguments most relevant to interview research (especially qualitative), with some inevitable digressions into the adjoining field of ethnography.

◆ Informed Consent and Cultural Differences

I begin by pointing out that informed consent safeguards certain values, primarily those of autonomy and privacy. But these values are by no means universal, in that they are not considered truly important in many (probably most) countries in the world. This is the case, for example, in China (Chan, 2004; Cong, 2004; Fan & Li, 2004) and Japan (Ohara, 2000; Tuschida, 1998), where the most important decisions concerning health care are not taken by patients but rather by their families in agreement with the doctors. But it is not necessary to go to Asia to find situations that do not fit Anglo-American norms.

In a European country such as Italy, for example, the law on the transparency of medical information is de facto a dead letter (Marzano, 2004, 2007). In fact, the majority of patients afflicted by serious pathologies are unaware of their prognoses. This is despite the fact that, in deference to the international fashion, informed consent has been formally required in Italy for years. Yet it is still a mere formality, a vacuous bureaucratic simulacrum, the effect of a *translation process* (Czarniawska & Joerges, 1995) that has come about in theory and then been nullified by extremely resilient cultural mechanisms. This has also happened in Hong Kong (Chan, 2004), where the British legislation, still fully in effect on paper, has in practice been modified, if not altogether warped, by the values of familism widespread in that society. This trend also holds in many parts of Africa, where the conduct of an interview requires prior negotiation with the leaders of the community (Chilisa, 2009; Ntseane, 2009).

One is obliged to admit that in these social realities, informed consent exists only on paper. It does not apply to the work of doctors; even less does it apply to that of social researchers, who must find other ways to conduct fieldwork ethically respectful of people's dignity (Marzano, 2007; Riessman, 2005). Instead, in some of these countries (and certainly in Italy), there is a real risk that the formal introduction of informed consent will foster what I would call a "facade of ethics," which serves to

"support" the claim that all ethical issues have been definitively resolved simply by the introduction of a printed form.

Problems arise for social scientists conducting research in foreign countries if it is decided in their home countries (usually by ethical committees) that indigenous norms should be ignored and that researchers should comply with their home country's overkill ethical guidelines. This, in essence, absolutizes informed consent and obliges researchers to obtain, for instance, written consent from people who may be illiterate (Czymoniewicz-Klippel, Brijnath, & Crockett, 2010) or who normally view a nod of the head as sufficient indication of agreement to participate. In these cases, a request for written consent before an interview may even cause offence and introduce an element of suspicion into the researcher–participant relationship (Tilley & Gormley, 2007): It becomes a marker of cultural distance and not a gesture of respect. In many cultural settings, signing a form is not an innocuous and routine act, for it evokes painful memories of colonial abuses or governmental injustices (Barata, Gucciardi, Ahmad, & Stewart, 2006; Corbie-Smith, Thomas, Williams, & Moody-Ayers, 1999; Riessman, 2005) or it reveals other unexpected meanings (Czymoniewicz-Klippel et al., 2010). Similar problems arise when studying ethnic minority groups (Barata et al., 2006) whose first language is different from that of the researchers and who are unable to understand complex passages or the terminology employed in consent forms.

◆ Flexibility of Methods, Rigidity of Norms: The Informed Consent in Qualitative Research

Cultural differences are not the only obstacles to the universal application of informed consent. To these are added, in the case of qualitative research, reasons of a strictly methodological kind. Requiring participants to sign an informed consent form at the beginning of a qualitative research project is very often premature and somewhat foolish (Adler & Adler, 2002; Murphy & Dingwall, 2007; Parker, 2007; Van den Hoonaard, 2001). Anselm Strauss (quoted in Van de Hoonaard, 2002) states that

because the analysis of these [research] data begins (in our style of research) with the very first, second, or third interview or after the first day or two of fieldwork. . . . It follows also that the next interviews and observations become informed by analytic questions and hypotheses about categories and their relationships. This guidance becomes increasingly explicit as the analysis of new data continue. (p. 13)

Unlike medical research, which is based on a deductive logic whereby the research protocols and design are rigorously established beforehand, qualitative research follows an inductive logic: The research design, the cognitive questions, and significant issues emerge only as the work proceeds. And this is precisely because the purpose of research of this kind is to understand the meanings that people ascribe to what they do or to the symbols and other cultural forms prevalent in their social environment (Katz, 2006). If all these elements were known to the researcher from the outset, there would be no need to undertake the fieldwork.

For this reason, a qualitative research project tends to be initially characterized by a certain vagueness and ambiguity. For example, if one were to conduct a series of in-depth interviews, it is very likely that the first interviews will be different from later ones. As the researcher becomes more embedded in the field, she or he learns to adapt the initial questions to the emerging topics and focal concerns (this process is akin to what Glaser and Strauss, 1967, call "grounded theory" analysis). One may therefore legitimately wonder what it is that the participants authorize when they sign the informed consent form before an interview (Howard & DeMets, 1981). To fulfill the requirements of ethical committees, semifictional details of a project can certainly be outlined at the beginning of the research, but adhering to such a design will pervert the meaning of the research. It signifies false knowledge about social phenomena that in reality are observed over time and using flexible methods, as envisaged by all the textbooks and as recommended by all the best-known researchers in the field.

In particular, open-ended interviews (like many other forms of qualitative research) involve a level of unpredictability reflected in everyday encounters in general (Miller & Boulton, 2007). What happens, for instance, if during the conversation between researcher and interviewee, there emerge (due to the unpredictability inherent in human relationships) topics and issues not envisaged in the initial plan,

and therefore not included in the text of the informed consent form and not approved by the ethical committee (Koro-Ljungberg, Gemignani, Winton Brodeur, & Kmiek, 2007)? What should the researcher do in such cases? Should she or he remind the interviewee—thereby jeopardizing the success of the interview and the discovery of new research hypotheses—that the topic is not relevant to the interview plan? Or should the researcher let the flow of thoughts elicited from the interviewee wander to topics more important for him or her? And what is to be done if, as in the case of Dingwall (Murphy & Dingwall, 2007; but see also Katz, 2006), the researcher is invited by the participants to a party where she or he gathers information that will be useful for subsequent interpretative work? Must relations of friendship also be prohibited because they were not envisaged in the informed consent form from the outset?

Moreover, the inflexible application of the informed consent procedure seriously jeopardizes one of the researcher's most valuable resources in his or her relationships with participants: trust (Librett & Perrone, 2010). It is not difficult to imagine what might happen when presentation of the informed consent form (often a lengthy document of five single-spaced pages, with special provision for different types of respondents, such as patients, relatives, non-relative family members, children, etc.) is the *first gesture* made by the researcher toward a person hitherto unknown to him or her (Gordon, 2003; Haggerty, 2004; Van den Hoonaard, 2001). Even someone well disposed toward the interviewer and willing to talk to him or her would immediately become suspicious (Plattner, 2003). Cherryl Mattingly (2005) recounts how, when presenting an informed consent form, she had to apologetically specify, "Oh well, I know how it sounds but, uh, well, it's necessary for you to sign up before I can actually interview you or anything" (p. 455). In effect, Mattingly tries to distance herself from the informed consent protocol by telling her participants that the language of the form was not her own and that she was indeed sensitive, sympathetic, and trustworthy. In reality, the gesture of submitting the consent form as the first action toward a potential interviewee amounts to suggesting that she or he should not believe in appearances, should be wary, and should not grant this person with the notebook or recorder the trust that would otherwise naturally develop (Bhattacharya, 2007). For, and this is the implicit meaning of the action, the person asking for an interview is not what she or he seems but a potentially dangerous and biased "snoop" or "busybody" whose true intentions are fortunately revealed by the wisdom of the research ethics committee. This procedure, Miller and Boulton (2007) point out, makes potential interviewees say "no" simply because they believe that they have nothing to say and the researcher cannot prove the contrary.

Moreover, when the recommendation that the interviewer constantly remind the participants of the nature and purposes of the inquiry, and that they are talking to a researcher and not to a friend or an ordinary human being, becomes an obligatory prescription applied regardless of the context, it not only undermines the relationship with respondents but ironically could produce its own undesirable, and even unethical, effects. Lawton (2001) provides an example. She has argued, when reconstructing her experience of conducting ethnographic research in a hospice, that constantly reminding terminally ill patients about the rules of informed consent and the purposes of the research may cause them further suffering, besides that inevitably produced by their situation. Oeye et al. (2007) report an episode when an exasperated participant reacted to yet another statement of the goals of the research by eloquently saying, "You know, I am not stupid. I understand the purpose of your study."

Similarly, the obsession with prior control over the ethical consequences of the research overlooks the rather elementary fact that, especially in qualitative research, numerous problems may derive from the publication of the results (Librett & Perrone, 2010). Consider, to cite only the most striking case, Marianne Boelen's (1992) revelations on the damaging consequences for many "ex–corner boys" of the publication and success of *Street Corner Society* (Whyte, 1955). In this case, informed consent, even if rigorously obtained, does not serve any purpose. Of much greater importance is the researcher's own sense of moral responsibility. This point was well illustrated by Van Maanen (1983) when he decided to denounce in his articles the brutal methods used by the police but at the same time protect the individual police officers whom he had accompanied on patrol by not testifying against them in court and not surrendering his field notes to the judge. Another example is the moral responsibility shown by

Whittaker (2005) when he refrained from reporting that many of the fathers of disabled children whom he had interviewed had said that they sometimes wished for the death of their children.

The truth is that in some cases what is considered a "good" practice for protecting research participants from a formal research ethics perspective produces a "bad" outcome for the participants. Consider, for example, what happens in numerous studies regarding the protection of respondents' identities (Haggerty, 2004; Tilley & Gormley, 2007). Anonymity is not always desired by participants, and not necessarily because in the "interview society" (Gubrium & Holstein, 2002; Silverman, 1997), they want to appear in books with their own true identity (Grinyer, 2002; Wiles, Crow, Heath, & Vikki, 2008; Wiles, Heath, Crow, & Charles, 2005). The following examples illustrate this point.

In 1997, Cherryl Mattingly (2005) met Nekia, a girl aged 4½ years, and her mother Shanelle. Some weeks previously, the girl had been diagnosed with a brain tumor. The two women—the researcher and Nekia's mother—almost immediately became friends. Shanelle asked Cherryl to videotape the most important family events and also to accompany her to appointments with the school psychologist and the speech therapist. After Nekia's death, Shanelle said that she would be very happy if the real name of her daughter appeared in Mattingly's writings. It would be a way to honor her memory, to keep her image and achievements alive. But to avoid censure by ethical committees, Mattingly decided to use the true names of the people in the story only when she spoke somewhere distant from where they lived. Something similar happened to me during my study of the experience of dying from cancer in Italy. In the book that resulted from that work (Marzano, 2004), I used pseudonyms to conceal the identities of the participants. There were some exceptions, however. The most important one was Carlo and his wife, Lina, a couple whom I met in the oncological ward to which Carlo had been admitted for advanced-stage lymphoma. They were a wonderful couple, intelligent, ironic, shrewd, wise, and courageous. They were both well-known "characters" in the ward, always ready to converse with others, to help other patients in difficulties, and sometimes to serve as mediators between them and health care personnel. The interviews that they granted me helped enormously in answering many of my questions.

When I learned of Carlo's death, I telephoned Lina, who invited me to lunch and introduced me to her entire family, her daughters and grandchildren. When we had finished lunch, she took me into what had been Carlo's study and handed me, not without a tremor, a sheet of paper on which he had written an extraordinary "decalogue" for coping with the disease: 10 recommendations on how to make suffering and death more bearable. Not only have I published that decalogue (Marzano, 2004), I have also decided not to conceal the identity of its author—to the immense satisfaction of Lina, who even today expresses her gratitude to me. My action, I hope, honors Carlo's memory and pays tribute to a fine man whom I had the good fortune to know.

◆ The Role of Ethical Committees

There is at least one further issue to discuss regarding the application of informed consent in interview research. It concerns the role of ethical committees (which have proliferated enormously in recent decades; Katz, 2006). Given different names in different countries (IRBs [institutional review boards] in the United States, RECs in the United Kingdom, Tri-Councils in Canada, *Comitati Etici* in Italy), they have the institutional task, among others, of supervising informed consent and the manner in which it is obtained. Ethical committees have provoked innumerable complaints from social researchers (Adler & Adler, 2002; Coomber, 2002; Herdman, 2000; Lincoln & Tierney, 2004). They are accused (especially hospital ethical committees, which consist largely of clinicians) (a) of privileging an inductive logic and discriminating against qualitative research (Librett & Perrone, 2010; Timmermans, 1995); (b) of being obsessed with the imaginary damage (Plattner, 2003) caused by social research; (c) of being less interested in the substance of ethical issues than in defense of the institutions that they represent; (d) of not using transparent criteria and rejecting any appeals against their decisions (Haggerty, 2004); (e) of representing the worst form of the "fetishization of rules" (Haggerty, 2004); and (f) of protecting the interests of the weakest members of society only in the abstract and on paper, in a standardized and distant manner. The action of many ethical committees is driven by the conviction that the mere infringement of a formal rule is a breach of ethics, although nobody is harmed,

or even, as Whittaker has argued (2005), by the suspicion that *all* social research is to some extent unethical insofar as it is a potential source of stress for participants and that it presumably yields scant benefits for society and even fewer for the participants. In the best of cases, it is dismissed as irrelevant; in the worst, it is condemned as harmful. In particular, ethical committees have made it extremely difficult to conduct research on certain social groups deemed vulnerable and at risk. This amounts to a form of de facto exclusion of certain groups from the world of research. The coercive authority of ethical committees stands in inverse ratio to their moral force.

◆ Where Informed Consent Is Lacking

Overall, the migration of the idea of informed consent into social research has certainly complicated the work of the social researcher. It has done so more than in other professions, especially journalism (Dingwall, 2006; Haggerty, 2004; Murphy & Dingwall, 2007). Journalists can work with greater freedom and without the constraints that, as we have seen, apply to social research. For this reason, and especially in the case of investigative journalism, they are often able to obtain substantially better results. But they do so without the rigor of social research and without its bond of trust with disadvantaged people. This can be illustrated by a story recounted by Gotlib Conn (2008), a Canadian anthropologist who began research on intersexuality in 2001 but then encountered innumerable difficulties. One day, at the clinic where Gottlib Conn was laboriously trying to complete his work, a journalist from a local magazine arrived to interview Dr. Marvin, the head researcher. The physician was so helpful to the woman that he showed her a video recording of an examination conducted on one of his young patients, naturally without requesting the consent of either the patient or the ethical committee. The content of the recording appeared 6 months later as the magazine's cover story.

Under a pseudonym—writes Gottlib Conn—the opening passage of the piece described most intimately the contents of the videotape in which a nine-year-old boy strutted provocatively in a feminine blonde wig and a pair of high-heeled shoes. Technically, this is a violation of the confidentiality and informed consent of the patient that the ethics policy is supposed to act to protect; unfortunately for this patient, this is a policy to which journalists are not accountable and Dr Marvin is well aware of this fact. (p. 511)

Gotlib Conn reaches the following bitter conclusion:

This is to say that in an anthropological account of this site the knowledge gained through field-work will most directly benefit the researcher (me) and the discipline (anthropology), advancing knowledge in this particular area, and hopefully reciprocating intellectually through its insights to the informants who have shared their work. In the journalistic account the benefits are more tangible and direct for the institution and its employees; as my informant unabashedly declares: "It's good for business!" (p. 511)

Such observations have led many scholars to conclude that as the idea of informed consent has migrated outside the territory of medicine and health care, it has created more problems than it has solved, proving to be a largely inadequate means by which to reduce risks and increase the ethicality of research. This is the first conclusion to be drawn. I am convinced, however, that if we are to gain full understanding of the consequences of the hegemony of informed consent in interview research, we must go a step further and determine how it is actually produced. In other words, we must conduct a microsociological analysis of informed consent. To this end, we must investigate the social region in which it was born, that of biomedicine; because it is there that the majority of empirical studies have been carried out.

◆ Informed Consent in Medical Settings

The studies on which such exploration can draw are not particularly numerous, but they all demonstrate that informed consent is in many respects a legal fiction, even in the world of medical sciences. And they also show that those who decide to consent (by signing a form) to either experimental medical research or normal clinical treatment do not do so for the motives attributed to them by the advocates of this form of regulation in the bioethical literature.

For example, as Corrigan (2003) has reported, sometimes patients do not fully understand the contents of the request for informed consent and its many loopholes. For example, they might believe that they are receiving treatment while in fact they are being administered a placebo. Or they may overreact to certain symbols, regardless of their particular scientific meaning. For example, if a consent form contains expressions such as "experiment" or "experimental" instead of "research," "clinical investigation," or "medical study," participation rates may decline significantly (Advisory Committee on Human Radiation Experiments, 1995; Slevin et al., 1995). More than being scrupulously informed, many patients simply want to be *treated*, and if possible *cured*, by their doctors—to the point that, in some cases (Taylor, 1988), they are angered by the doctor neutrally presenting them with different therapeutic options, for this strikes them as a stratagem to shirk the responsibilities of a healer (Corrigan, 2003). Consider this illuminating exchange reported by Taylor (1988): "Experimenter: we don't really know which surgery is best. . . . Patient: Doctor, I am asking YOU what you think is best for me. . . . For God's sake you are a doctor." Olufowote (2011) described in detail the complexity of doctor–patient communication on the "informed consent to treatment" and how doctors systematically try to manipulate the language of informed consent and to control patients' decisions on treatments.

The members of an Austrian ethical committee observed and then interviewed by Felt, Bister, Strassnig, and Wagner (2009) considered the patient's autonomy as of decidedly secondary importance. Their overriding concern was that informed consent should protect the hospital against possible legal reprisals (see also Boisaubin, 2004). But it is perhaps even more surprising that the *patients* interviewed by Felt and colleagues (2009) saw informed consent in the same way as the doctors did: It was a mere administrative formality with which the hospital *rightly* protected itself against the more "awkward" patients. In general, the tissue donor patients interviewed by Felt and colleagues (2009) declared, when asked after the interview when they had signed the informed consent form, that they had not bothered to read its 10 and more pages. Moreover, their main preoccupation was their health, and they had no intention of refusing a request made by someone able to give them crucial help at a difficult time in their lives. For some of them, their consent was part of a trade-off with the public health service. It was a sort of gift made to the state (and, indirectly, to the national community and the sick of tomorrow) in exchange for everything that had been done for them and, in general, for all the sick (see also Hoeyer & Lynöe, 2006). For others, the consent was instead a homage gladly paid to science and its progress, from which humanity as a whole would benefit, which would bring a future better than the present and which would also justify possible failures in the meantime (Dixon-Woods & Tarrant, 2009; Hoeyer & Lynöe, 2006). No mention was made of the interests of the pharmaceutical companies or of the human costs necessary to achieve such scientific progress. After all, the doctors and experimenters interviewed by Felt et al. (2009) were convinced that their professional ethics more than sufficed to guarantee the well-being of patients. And when they asked patients for their consent to experimentation, they certainly did not do so "neutrally" because they wanted the sampled group to accept the proposal at all costs. For this reason, they chose to provide the recruits with more positive and encouraging information.

A touching story of the application of informed consent in medical research is recounted by Rose Weitz (1999). In some respects, it is reminiscent of the celebrated Terry Schiavo (the American woman whose right to die was contested in court) affair. Fittingly, the story is set in the United States, the birthplace of informed consent. Weitz's narrative centers on the ordeals of her brother-in-law Brian (a fictional name), who was injured in a serious industrial accident and admitted to hospital in a critical condition. In the few instants of lucidity that preceded Brian's definitive loss of consciousness, the doctors asked him if he wanted to continue living and face the risks of painful treatment with little chance of success. Brian, close to death, presumably in shock and about to lapse into a coma, answered in the affirmative. The doctors interpreted this feeble signal as authorization to proceed with clearly futile treatment unsuited to saving Brian's life and bordering on therapeutic obstinacy. And they did so contrary to the opinion of his wife, who told them that Brian had repeatedly insisted that he would not want to survive under such circumstances. But although the wife had the legal right to decide for her husband, the doctors belittled her, withheld information

from her, and assumed decision-making authority. They preferred to communicate with Brian's father, an influential businessman, who was in favor of any treatment decided by the doctors and, in general, of letting the doctors make the most important decisions. The hospital's ethical committee proved entirely remiss by failing to intervene. Brian died a few days later, gainsaying the optimism of the physicians and after useless and prolonged agony. The story confirms the findings of numerous other studies of intensive care wards (see, e.g., Anspach, 1993) that underline the difference between the rhetoric and reality of informed consent and "the continuing power and clinical autonomy of doctors in the USA" (Weitz, 1999, p. 224).

Therefore, the guidelines on protecting medical research participants and patients through informed consent amount to "empty ethics" (Corrigan, 2003), a "false panacea" that yields none of the results promised. This is not only because doctors do not believe in them (an attitude similar to that of social researchers) or because some ethical committees are more concerned with protecting the interests of hospitals than those of patients. It is also, and above all, because the willingness of people to participate is decisively influenced by (a) comprehension of scientific research and medicine, (b) the desire to please (Bevan, Chee, McGhee, & McInness, 1993) and not to contradict physicians in any way that risks the "good patient" status (Dixon-Woods et al., 2006), (c) the disorientation and anxiety caused by suffering, and (d) uncertainty about the range of therapeutic alternatives. The decision to consent is not, as the "information paradigm" (Felt et al., 2009) would suggest, due to a rational choice by social actors wanting to act autonomously and to obtain as much information as possible for that purpose. All in all, far from being a solitary action, the granting of informed consent is the product of a *relationship* (Hoeyer & Lynöe, 2006), of a social interaction that is very often clearly asymmetrical and has regulatory effects; it is a power relation based above all on implicit gestures (Strong, 1979) and on a prior cultural habitus (Bourdieu, 1984; Dixon-Woods et al., 2006; Dixon-Woods & Tarrant, 2009).

Hoeyer and Lynöe (2006) cite in this regard the example of nurses already holding the syringe when they ask patients for permission to take, besides the amount of blood necessary for the medical examination, a sample of blood for research purposes.

The contractual pretence has the sole effect of "deresponsibilizing" doctors and shifting the burden of choice onto patients. Signing the consent form may even increase the patient's passivity (Dixon-Woods et al., 2006). It may be that these mechanisms are stronger where (e.g., in Austria, Sweden, or Italy) the health care system is entirely run by the state; but it is likely that the situation is quite common in the United States and the United Kingdom as well (see Boisaubin, 2004; Corrigan, 2003; Weitz, 1999).

At this point of our discussion, we have the many necessary elements with which to arrive at a more balanced vision of informed consent as an ethical guideline. We may conclude that the efficacy of informed consent in ensuring full, responsible, and rational assent and in protecting patients against harm is relatively low. This is even true in the domain where informed consent procedures first arose, namely medicine, where the risks of causing extreme damage are the highest.

When a patient is proposed a certain treatment or is asked to participate in an experiment and to sign the relevant consent form, the situation is not as imagined by bioethicists: that is, two rational actors, one of whom makes an offer, while the other decides, after a calculation, whether or not to accept. For also involved in that conversation, even if they are invisible, are scientific medicine, with its immense reputation; the economic and political interests of hospitals and pharmaceutical companies; the doctor's scientific career; the patient's anxiety and emotions; the patient's need to trust and rely on those caring for him or her; and the differences in education and social class between the two parties.

The encounter between an interviewer and a potential interviewee exhibits the same complexity in the context of social science research. But there are also some very significant differences. Not only does the interviewer not possess all the symbolic and power resources available to the doctor, but she or he often has to contend with ethical committees that do not understand (or do not agree with) epistemological approaches and research methodologies. The presentation of a bureaucratic form jeopardizes the trust relationship between researchers and participants that could otherwise develop naturally. Within the sort of contractual relationship that the consent form entails, the researcher is rarely able to offer something (money or other things) in exchange for an interview.

And the researcher is often forced, at least in structured organizational contexts, to rely on gatekeepers who are almost never "neutral" and with whom she or he is wrongly associated by the subjects.

The overall result is a marked curtailment of the possibility of conducting research freely, an outcome probably viewed with favor only by those universities, hospitals, or other institutions threatened by the freedom of research and its potential for challenging the status quo. Perhaps the time has come to turn around and move in the opposite direction. Namely, it may be that the journey begun with the migration of informed consent from medicine to social research can best be completed in the opposite direction, by importing into the field of health care some of the most innovative perspectives developed in the field of social research.

◆ Beyond Informed Consent

The mistrust of informed consent by social researchers has certainly not coincided with a neglect of ethical issues. On the contrary, there has been much discussion on these matters in recent decades, thanks mainly to feminism (Brabeck & Brabeck, 2009; Tronto, 1993), postmodernism (Denzin & Lincoln, 2005), critical social science (Cannella & Lincoln, 2011), emancipatory research (Swartz, 2011), and the work of Michel Foucault (Infinito, 2005). These and other currents of thought have given rise to many alternatives to the abstract and individualist viewpoint of informed consent. One such paradigm, discussed below, is the "ethics of care" (Christian, 2000; Miller & Boulton, 2007; Noddings, 2003; O'Connell Davidson, 2008), or "relational ethics" (Ellis, 2007).

For a researcher, adopting a relational approach means showing a concern for the well-being of the people studied that extends well beyond simple respect for their decision-making autonomy or the transparency of the research objectives and methods. That is to say, it extends well beyond informed consent. Respecting an ethics of care means involving the participants in the write-up of the research work or asking for their approval of the final text, caring about their general welfare, supporting their causes, being interested in their empowerment, and considering the potential benefits to them of participation in the research.

Adopting a relational approach means being concerned about what happens when a person is interviewed, when the researcher is in direct contact with participants, but also about what happens *afterward*, about the consequences of what has been written for the people studied. An ethics of care is manifest in the courage to "return" to the field some years later to discover the often painful effects of research undertaken at a time of careless ethical indifference. Such courage was shown by Carolyn Ellis (1995) when she went back to the fishing village that she had described in her first book and faced the anger of people who had considered her a friend and were resentful of how the book described them. It was also shown by Nancy Scheper-Hughes (2000) in returning to the small Irish town made famous by her book but in which hostility toward her reached such a pitch that she was forced to make an adventurous nighttime escape to safety. And there is the distress suffered by Julia O'Connell Davidson (2008) when, on resuming an issue long crucial to the feminist debate, she discussed the consequences of a person being "objectified" by a research product, of becoming a "character" in a book, especially when this person, as in the case of the former prostitute Desiree, had changed her life and rejected her former identity. Is the consent once given to be interviewed and observed valid forever? The liberal logic of informed consent asserts that it is: The original procedure of gaining consent has been respected, so that the "yes" can be considered perpetual. In an ethics of care, matters are more complicated because it requires that the researcher must never lose interest in the subjects of his or her research. Identification with the subjects and a commitment to protecting their well-being at all costs is an ongoing responsibility that transcends contractual obligations. Indeed, such dedication may go as far as the researcher being prepared to lose his or her freedom in order to protect the people studied (Brajuha & Hallowell, 1986; Van Maanen, 1983). I would argue that in essence the ethics of care is about accepting that the researcher's "moral biography" is not distinct from that of the subject and that fieldwork can and must be an occasion for moral and existential growth, a shared stage for the "moral careers" of both the researcher and the observed, a chance for being human along with others.

Espousing an ethics of care therefore necessarily entails reversing the anthropology—the conception of human and social relationships—on which the notion of informed consent is founded, at least in its current bureaucratic and standardized version. Adopting a relational perspective on the ethical plane is equivalent to abandoning the Durkheimian conception of society as a moralizing force, a factory of moral laws able to control and, if need be, repress the menacing immorality due to the egoism intrinsic to human beings. Durkheim (1972) argued that "man is a moral being only because he lives in society" (p. 101) and that "morality, in all its forms, is never met with except in society" (p. 102). "By putting himself under the wing of society, the individual makes him/herself also, to a certain extent, dependent upon it. But this is a liberating dependence; there is no contradiction in this" (p. 115).

From this point of view, immoral behavior is the consequence of imperfection, or deviation from the norm, of a defect in the processes of certification, of a selfish and presocial instinct that has unexpectedly escaped the control of the moralizing Leviathan. Society, Bauman (1989, 2008) maintains when expounding Durkheim's thought, has the right to impose its own moral codes and to aspire to absolute and uncontested hegemony, to total moral monopoly. Resisting societal demands leads directly to immorality.

This is the logic underlying informed consent and that assigns to ethical committees the role of vigilant guardians of society's interests. And this is the logic that is overturned by the ethics of care, which is rooted in the idea of *responsibility* so tenaciously defended by the philosopher Emanuel Lévinas: "We are responsible for everything and to everybody and me more than all the others." The Other exists in so far as I am responsible for it. This is a care-based mode of social action that excludes calculation, instrumentality, fear, interest, and even rationality. It is the sight of the face of the Other that enjoins me to serve it, doing so with a spontaneous action that does not derive from a constraint but instead becomes the basis of subjectivity, of an asymmetrical relationship in which my duties toward the Other prevail—duties that existed before the birth of society, which is liable to contaminate them.

It seems to me that, at least at this historical juncture, the ethics of care represents the principal alternative to the practice of informed consent. It entails constant education in the themes of respect and solidarity with others, constant reflexive attention to conduct in the field, to evaluation of the consequences of our actions—all of which is in line with the loyalty (if not the sympathy verging on complicity) that qualitative researchers have very often shown toward the people they studied (Adler & Adler, 1987; Becker, 1967; Whyte, 1955). In reality, such a view even circulates in the field of medicine as an antidote to the simplifying and hypocritical standardization of informed consent, fostering the empowerment of patients (Gubrium & Holstein, 2002; Mishler, 1986) and the growth of a narrative and listening medicine (Charon, 2006).

The rise of the ethics of care is certainly a positive development. I do not, however, believe that it would be correct to consider it the only alternative to the perspective of informed consent. For there is another approach that risks disappearing entirely in this age of legalistic obsession—that of conflict methodology (Lehmann & Young, 1974; see also Katz, 2007). In this framework, the researcher studies social groups and institutions that she or he dislikes and intends to criticize freely and amply, but not before gathering rigorous empirical documentation about them—that is, not before studying them in detail. In some cases, the researcher may resort to various forms of reticence, and often also to deceit. I would point out, however, that in these cases, unlike in that of covert research essentially motivated by the desire for scientific knowledge (among the many examples, see Festinger, Riecken, & Schacter, 1956; Humphreys, 1975), there is an ethical justification, even if it is often only an implicit one. It consists in the moral right/duty to criticize the existing social and political order, and to consider social justice as being the priority rather than the subjective rights of the people studied.

The results obtained by means of this approach have been striking in the history of social research. Providing an exhaustive list would be impossible here. I merely suggest considering what we would know about the psychological, organizational, and political mechanisms of psychiatric hospitals without the works of Rosenham (1973) and, especially, Goffman (1961). Both were the result of covert research, without a hint of informed consent.

Today, at least in the countries in which legislation on informed consent is most inflexible, it would be impossible to conduct research of this kind. Admittedly, the social world is not inhabited solely by vulnerable people in need of protection

and respect. The powerful (above all, powerful institutions) are often much better able than anyone to defend themselves against the "intrusions" of researchers into their daily lives. For them, informed consent has been a blessing because it has afforded them better protection (as if they needed it!) against researchers obliged to declare their possible critical intentions in advance (Herdman, 2000; Katz, 2007). Being required before an interview to present a form that exhaustively explains that the purpose of the research is to criticize the institution to which the interviewee belongs is not exactly an advantage for the interviewer (Herdman, 2000). From this point of view, working in a country where universities do not supervise research may be an advantage (Marzano, 2007).

Finally, I think that there are zones of ambiguity that not even the obsession with truth and sincerity in social interactions (and therefore also in interviews) can resolve. Social life is replete with ethical dilemmas, with complicated choices between values of often equal importance. These are extremely difficult issues that interrogate the consciences of us all, which no magic formula can resolve once and for all.

◆ References

Adler, P. A., & Adler, P. (1987). *Membership roles in field research.* Newbury Park, CA: Sage.

Adler, P. A., & Adler, P. (2002). Do university lawyers and the police define research values? In W. C. Van den Hoonaard (Ed.), *Walking the tightrope: Ethical issue for qualitative researchers* (pp. 34–42). Toronto, Ontario, Canada: University of Toronto Press.

Advisory Committee on Human Radiation Experiments. (1995). *Advisory Committee on Human Radiation Experiments: Final report.* Washington, DC: Author.

Anspach, R. R. (1993). *Deciding who lives: Fateful choices in the intensive-care nursery.* Berkeley: University of California Press.

Barata, P., Gucciardi, E., Ahmad, F., & Stewart, D. E. (2006). Cross-cultural perspectives on research participation and informed consent. *Social Science and Medicine, 62*(2), 479–490.

Bauman, Z. (1989). *Modernity and the Holocaust.* Ithaca, NY: Cornell University Press.

Bauman, Z. (2008). *Does ethics have a chance in a world of consumers?* Cambridge, MA: Harvard University Press.

Beauchamp, T., & Childress, J. (2001). *Principles of biomedical ethics.* Oxford, UK: Oxford University Press.

Becker, H. (1967). Whose side are we on? *Social Problems, 14*(3), 239–247.

Bevan, E. G., Chee, L. C., McGhee, S. M., & McInness, G. T. (1993). Patients' attitudes to participation in clinical trials. *British Journal of Clinical Pharmacology, 35,* 204–207.

Bhattacharya, K. (2007). Consenting to the consent form: What are the fixed and fluid understanding between the researcher and the researched? *Qualitative Inquiry, 13*(8), 1095–1115.

Boelen, M. (1992). Street corner society: Cornerville revisited. *Journal of Contemporary Ethnography, 21*(1), 11–51.

Boisaubin, E. V. (2004). Observations of physician, patient and family perceptions of informed consent in Houston, Texas. *Journal of Medicine and Philosophy, 29*(2), 225–236.

Bosk, C. L., & De Vries, R. G. (2004). Bureaucracies of mass deception: Institutional review boards and the ethics of ethnographic research. *The ANNALS of the American Academy of Political and Social Science, 595*(1), 249–263.

Bourdieu, P. (1984). *Distinction: A social critique of the judgement of taste.* Cambridge, MA: Harvard University Press.

Brabeck, M. B., & Brabeck, K. M. (2009). Feminist perspectives on research ethics. In D. M. Mertens & P. Ginsberg (Eds.), *Handbook of social research ethics* (pp. 39–53). London, England: Sage.

Brajuha, M., & Hallowell, L. (1986). Legal intrusion and the politics of fieldwork: The impact of the Brajuha case. *Journal of Contemporary Ethnography, 14*(4), 454–478.

Cannella, G. S., & Lincoln, Y. S. (2011). Ethics, research regulation and critical social sciences. In N. K. Denzin & Y. S. Lincoln (Eds.), *The SAGE handbook of qualitative research* (4th ed., pp. 81–89). Thousand Oaks, CA: Sage.

Chan, H. M. (2004). Informed consent Hong Kong style: An instance of moderate familism. *Journal of Medicine and Philosophy, 29*(2), 195–206.

Charon, R. (2006). *Narrative medicine: Honoring the story of illness.* Oxford, UK: Oxford University Press.

Chilisa, B. (2009). Indigenous African-centered ethics. In D. M. Mertens & P. E. Ginsberg (Eds.), *Handbook of social research ethics* (pp. 407–425). London, England: Sage.

Christian, C. G. (2000). Ethics and politics in qualitative research. In N. K. Denzin & Y. S. Lincoln (Eds.), *Handbook of qualitative research* (2nd ed., pp. 133–155). Thousand Oaks, CA: Sage.

Cong, Y. (2004). Doctor–family patient relationship: The Chinese paradigm of informed consent. *Journal of Medicine and Philosophy, 29*(2), 149–178.

Coomber, R. (2002). Signing your life away? Why Research Ethics Committees (REC) shouldn't always require written confirmation that participants in research have been informed of the aims of a study and their rights: The case of criminal populations. *Sociological Research Online, 7*(1).

Corbie-Smith, G., Thomas, S. B., Williams, M. V., & Moody-Ayers, S. (1999). Attitude and beliefs of African Americans toward participation in medical research. *Journal of General Internal Medicine, 14*(9), 537–546.

Corrigan, O. (2003). Empty ethics: The problem with informed consent. *Sociology of Health and Illness, 25*(3), 768–792.

Czarniawska, B., & Joerges, B. (1995). Winds of organizational change: How ideas translate in objects and actions. In S. B. Bacharach, P. Gagliardi, & B. Mundell (Eds.), *Studies of organizations in Europe* (pp. 171–209). Greenwich, CT: Jai Press.

Czymoniewicz-Klippel, M. T., Brijnath, B., & Crockett, B. (2010). Ethics and the promotion of inclusiveness within qualitative research: Case examples from Asia and the Pacific. *Qualitative Inquiry, 16*(5), 332–341.

Denzin, N. K., & Lincoln, Y. S. (2005). *The SAGE handbook of qualitative research* (3rd ed.). Thousand Oaks, CA: Sage.

Dingwall, R. (2006). Confronting the anti-democrats: The unethical nature of ethical regulation in social sciences. *Medical Sociology Online, 1,* 51–58.

Dixon-Woods, M., & Tarrant, C. (2009). Why do people cooperate with medical research? Findings from three studies. *Social Science and Medicine, 68*(12), 2215–2222.

Dixon-Woods, M., Williams, S. J., Jackson, C. J., Akkad, A., Kenyon, S., & Habiba, M. (2006). Why do women consent to surgery, even when they do not want to? An interactionist and Bourdieusian analysis. *Social Science and Medicine, 62,* 2742–2753.

Durkheim, E. (1972). *Selected writings.* Cambridge, England: Cambridge University Press.

Ellis, C. (1995). Emotional and ethical quagmires in returning to the field. *Journal of Contemporary Ethnography, 24*(1), 68–98.

Ellis, C. (2007). Telling secrets, revealing lives: Relational ethics in research with intimate others. *Qualitative Inquiry, 13*(1), 3–29.

Fan, R., & Li, B. (2004). Truth-telling in medicine: The Confucian view. *Journal of Medicine and Philosophy, 29*(2), 179–193.

Felt, U., Bister, M. D., Strassnig, M., & Wagner, U. (2009). Refusing the information paradigm: Informed consent, medical research, and patient participation. *Health, 13*(1), 87–106.

Festinger, L., Riecken, H. V., & Schacter, S. (1956). *When prophecy fails: A social and psychological study of a modern group that predicted the destruction of the world.* Minneapolis: University of Minnesota Press.

Fluehr-Lobban, C. (1994). Informed consent in anthropological research: We are not exempt. *Human Organization, 53*(1), 1–10.

Giddens, A. (1990). *The consequences of modernity.* Cambridge, MA: Polity Press.

Glaser, B. G., & Strauss, A. L. (1967). *The discovery of grounded theory.* Chicago, IL: Aldine Press.

Goffman, E. (1961). *Asylum.* Garden City, NY: Doubleday/Anchor.

Gordon, E. J. (2003). Trial and tribulations of navigating IRBs: Anthropological and biomedical perspectives of "risk" in conducting human research subjects. *Anthropological Quarterly, 76*(2), 299–320.

Gotlib Conn, L. (2008). Ethics policy as audit in Canadian clinical settings: Exiling the ethnographic method. *Qualitative Research, 8*(4), 499–514.

Grinyer, A. (2002). The anonymity of research participants: Assumptions, ethics and practicalities. *Social Research Update, 36.*

Gubrium, J. F., & Holstein, J. A. (2002). From the individual interview to interview society. In J. F. Gubrium & J. A. Holstein (Eds.), *Handbook of interview research* (pp. 3–32). Thousand Oaks, CA: Sage.

Haggerty, K. D. (2004). Ethics creep: Governing social science research in the name of ethics. *Qualitative Sociology, 27*(4), 391–420.

Hedgecoe, A. (2008). Research ethics review and the sociological research relationship. *Sociology, 42*(5), 873–886.

Herdman, E. (2000). Pearls, pith and provocation: Reflections on "making somebody angry." *Qualitative Health Research, 10*(5), 689–702.

Hoeyer, K., Dahlager, L., & Lynöe, N. (2005). Conflicting notions of research ethics: The mutually challenging traditions of social scientist and medical researchers. *Social Science and Medicine, 61*(8), 1741–1749.

Hoeyer, K., & Lynöe, N. (2006). Motivating donors to genetic research? Anthropological reasons to rethink the role of informed consent. *Medicine, Health Care and Philosophy, 9*(1), 13–23.

Howard, J. M., & DeMets, D. (1981). How informed is informed consent? The BHAT experience. *Controlled Clinical Trials, 2*(4), 287–303.

Humphreys, L. (1975). *Tearoom trade: Impersonal sex in public places.* Chicago, IL: Aldine Press.

Infinito, J. (2005). Ethical self-formation: A look at the later Foucault. *Educational Theory, 53*(2), 155–171.

Katz, J. (2006). Ethical escape routes for underground ethnographers. *American Ethnologist, 33*(4), 499–506.

Katz, J. (2007). Toward a natural history of ethical censorship. *Law & Society Review, 41*(4), 797–810.

Kleinman, A. (1997). *Writing at the margin: Discourse between anthropology and medicine.* Berkeley: University of California Press.

Koro-Ljungberg, M., Gemignani, M., Winton Brodeur, C., & Kmiek, C. (2007). The technologies of normalization and self: Thinking about IRBs and extrinsic research ethics with Foucault. *Qualitative Inquiry, 13*(8), 1075–1094.

Lawton, J. (2001). Gaining and maintaining informed consent: Ethical concerns raised in a study of dying patients. *Qualitative Health Research, 11*, 69–73.

Lehmann, T., & Young, T. R. (1974). From conflict theory to conflict methodology: An emerging paradigm for sociology. *Sociological Inquiry, 44*(1), 15–28.

Librett, M., & Perrone, D. (2010). Apples and oranges: Ethnography and the IRB. *Qualitative Research, 10*, 729–747.

Lincoln, Y. S., & Tierney, W. G. (2004). Qualitative research and institutional review boards. *Qualitative Inquiry, 10*(2), 219–234.

Marshall, P. A. (2003). Human subjects protections, institutional review boards, and cultural anthropological research. *Anthropological Quarterly, 76*(2), 269–285.

Marzano, M. (2004). *Scene finali: Morire di cancro in Italia* [Final scenes: Dying of cancer in Italy]. Bologna, Italy: il Mulino.

Marzano, M. (2007). Informed consent, deception and research freedom in qualitative research. *Qualitative Inquiry, 13*(3), 417–436.

Mattingly, C. (2005). Toward a vulnerable ethics of research practice. *Health, 9*(4), 453–471.

Milgram, S. (1974). *Obedience to authority.* New York, NY: Harper & Row.

Miller, T., & Boulton, M. (2007). Changing constructions of informed consent: Qualitative research and complex social worlds. *Social Science and Medicine, 65*(11), 2199–2211.

Mishler, E. G. (1986). *Research interviewing: Context and narrative.* Cambridge, MA: Harvard University Press.

Murphy, E., & Dingwall, R. (2007). Informed consent, anticipatory regulation and ethnographic practice. *Social Science and Medicine, 65*(11), 2223–2234.

Noddings, N. (2003). *Caring: A feminine approach to ethics and moral education.* Berkeley: University of California Press.

Ntseane, P. G. (2009). The ethics of the researcher-subject relationship: Experiences from the field. In D. M. Mertens & P. E. Ginsberg (Eds.), *Handbook of social research ethics* (pp. 295–307). London, England: Sage.

O'Connell Davidson, J. (2008). If no means no, does yes mean yes? Consenting to research intimacies. *History of the Human Sciences, 21*(49), 49–67.

Oeye, C., Bjelland, A. K., & Skorpen, A. (2007). Doing participant observation in a psychiatric hospital: Research ethics resumed. *Social Science and Medicine, 65*(11), 2296–2306.

Ohara, S. (2000). We-consciousness and terminal patients: Some biomedical reflections on Japanese civil religion. In G. K. Becker (Ed.), *The moral status of persons: Perspective on bioethics* (pp. 119–127). Atlanta, GA: Rodopi.

Olufowote, J. O. (2011). A dialectical perspective on informed consent to treatment: An examination of radiologists' dilemmas and negotiations. *Qualitative Health Research, 21*(6), 839–852.

Parker, M. (2007). Ethnography/ethics. *Social Science and Medicine, 65*(11), 2248–2259.

Plattner, S. (2003). Human subjects protection and cultural anthropology. *Anthropological Quarterly, 76*(2), 287–297.

Riessman, C. K. (2005). Exporting ethics: A narrative about research in South India. *Health, 9*(4), 473–490.

Rosenham, D. L. (1973). On being sane in insane places. *Science, 179*(4070), 250–258.

Scheper-Hughes, N. (2000). Ire in Ireland. *Ethnography, 1*(1), 117–140.

Silverman, D. (1997). *Qualitative research: Theory, method and practice*. London, England: Sage.

Slevin, M., Mossman, J., Bowling, A., Leonard, R., Steward, W., Harper, P., McIllmurray, M., Thatcher, N. (1995). Volunteers or victims: Patients' views of randomised cancer trials. *British Journal of Cancer, 71*, 1270–1274.

Strong, P. M. (1979). *The ceremonial order of the clinic: Parents, doctors and medical bureaucracies*. London, England: Routledge & Kegan Paul.

Swartz, S. (2011). "Going deep" and "giving back": Strategies for exceeding ethical expectations when researching amongst vulnerable youth. *Qualitative Research, 11*(1), 47–68.

Taylor, K. M. (1988). Telling bad news: Physicians and the disclosure of undesirable information. *Sociology of Health and Illness, 10*(2), 109–132.

Tilley, S. A., & Gormley, L. (2007). Canadian university ethics review: Cultural complications translating principles into practice. *Qualitative Inquiry, 13*(3), 368–387.

Timmermans, S. (1995). Cui bono? Institutional review board ethics and ethnographic research. *Studies in Symbolic Interaction, 19*, 153–173.

Tronto, J. C. (1993). *Moral boundaries: A political argument for an ethic of care*. London, England: Routledge.

Tuschida, T. (1998). A differing perspective on advance directives. In H.-M. Sass, R. M. Veatch, & R. Kimura (Eds.), *Advance directives and surrogate decision making in health care* (pp. 209–221). Baltimore, MD: Johns Hopkins University Press.

Van den Hoonaard, W. C. (2001). Is research-ethics review a moral panic? *Canadian Review of Sociology and Anthropology, 38*(1), 19–36.

Van den Hoonaard, W. C. (2002). *Walking the tightrope: Ethical issues for qualitative researchers*. Toronto, Ontario, Canada: University of Toronto Press.

Van Maanen, J. (1983). The moral fix: On the ethics of fieldwork. In R. M. Emerson (Ed.), *Contemporary field research* (pp. 269–287). Prospect Heights, IL: Waveland Press.

Weitz, R. (1999). Watching Brian die: The rhetoric and reality of informed consent. *Health, 3*(2), 209–227.

Whittaker, E. (2005). Adjudicating entitlements: The emerging discourses of research ethics boards. *Health, 9*(4), 513–535.

Whyte, W. F. (1955). *Street corner society: The social structure of an Italian slum*. Chicago, IL: University of Chicago Press.

Wiles, R., Crow, G., Heath, S., & Vikki, C. (2008). The management of confidentiality and anonymity in social research. *International Journal of Social Research Methodology, 11*(5), 417–428.

Wiles, R., Heath, S., Crow, G., & Charles, V. (2005). *Informed consent in social research: A literature review*. Southampton, England: ESRC National Centre for Research Methods.

Zimbardo, P. G., & White, G. (1972). *The Stanford prison experiment*. Stanford, CA: Stanford University Press.

31

PROTECTING CONFIDENTIALITY

◆ Karen Kaiser

Confidentiality refers to "agreements with persons about what may be done with their data" (Sieber, 1992, p. 52). In practice, confidentiality typically means ensuring that no one other than the researcher knows who participated in a study. Given that interview studies often contain rich descriptions of study participants, confidentiality breaches via deductive disclosure are of particular concern to interview researchers. Deductive disclosure, also known as internal confidentiality (Tolich, 2004), occurs when the traits and experiences of individuals or groups make them identifiable in research reports (Sieber, 1992). For example, if a researcher studying teachers named the school district where the research occurred, someone with knowledge of the school district could identify individual teachers based on traits such as age, gender, and number of years with the school district (Sieber, 1992).

As such, researchers face a conflict between conveying detailed, accurate accounts of the social world and protecting the identities of the individuals who participated in their research.

◆ Confidentiality of Individuals

Several researchers have published accounts of the challenges of trying to protect the identities of individual study participants. Often, these researchers struggled to assess the negative consequences respondents would face if confidentiality were compromised. Baez (2002) interviewed minority faculty members at a predominantly white university about promotion and tenure experiences. Given the few minority faculty members on campus, descriptions of specific experiences of discrimination within the university could lead to

Author's Note: This work was supported by the National Science Foundation under Grant No. 0425398 and by the National Cancer Institute, R25TCA57699-14.

identification of the minority faculty members by their colleagues. Baez's interviews produced powerful descriptions of experiences of isolation, racism, betrayal, and sexism. For example, one respondent described a colleague who stole her ideas and published them as his own. Baez was concerned that publishing these accounts would cause his study participants to be identified by their colleagues, which could lead to retaliation, stigma, or other negative career consequences.

Kaiser (2009) describes her struggles with the possibility of deductive disclosure in her study of breast cancer survivors. Her deductive disclosure concerns centered on the unique experiences of one respondent named Rachel (a pseudonym). Rachel revealed that she did not attend a cancer support group because she did not feel that she would fit in:

Well, I might as well just say it right up front, I'm a lesbian and most of the women I see at treatment, you know, they're married. They've got family, husbands, and I just didn't feel like I would fit in. I had enough stress on me, I didn't need to be trying to explain to people why I live the way I live. So that's why I didn't do that. Many times I wish I had somebody to talk to that really understood. . . . Knowing you're kind of different, anyhow, it's kind of hard to participate in those kinds of things. (p. 1633)

Rachel's comments presented Kaiser with an ethical dilemma. Although the study did not aim to address the experiences of sexual minority women, Rachel's perspective could be shared with local health care providers and could lead to improved support services. Rachel was likely one of the very few lesbian cancer patients seen in the local hospital. Thus, physicians and staff would easily identify Rachel from her comments. Although Rachel's disclosure was a powerful moment in the interview, only later did Kaiser recognize the confidentiality dilemma the data presented. To resolve the dilemma, Kaiser attempted to assess the risks to Rachel if others linked her to the comments. Rachel might feel shame or embarrassment if the staff and doctors knew of her comments. Rachel might also face discrimination if others learned that she was a lesbian. However, Rachel might also benefit if she were identified since her comments could motivate the doctors and staff to provide her with additional support. Ultimately, Kaiser decided that regardless of the risks or benefits

to Rachel, sharing her information would breach the confidentiality agreement set forth during the interview. Thus, she chose not to publish Rachel's comments with the other study results. Importantly, Kaiser (like Baez) made this decision on her own, without additional input from Rachel. If Kaiser had established a way to discuss the use of sensitive data with respondents, she could have sought Rachel's views on whether or not the data could be used. These two examples illustrate researchers' dilemmas with respect to protecting the confidentiality of individuals. In particular, each researcher struggled to weigh the potential risks to the individuals, which included loss of privacy, career damage, strained relationships, and shame. Moreover, regardless of the potential risks or benefits to the respondents, using their data would compromise the confidentiality promise given to participants in these studies (usually in the form of a signed informed consent agreement). Weiss (1994), a leading scholar in the area of research ethics, is unequivocal on the issue of confidentiality: "Nothing reported from the study, in print or in lecture, should permit identification of respondents" (p. 131). Weiss, however, also acknowledges our responsibility to make the most "useful report possible" and "to make [our respondents'] lessons known" (p. 131). Essentially, social science researchers are required to simultaneously (a) protect their individual respondents' confidentiality, (b) share their stories with a larger audience, and (c) create rigorous scientific manuscripts worthy of publication in scholarly journals. As seen in the next section, this balancing act is no less challenging when the unit of analysis is a larger social entity (e.g., groups or communities).

◆ Confidentiality of Groups

Research conducted within specific groups or communities poses confidentiality risks of its own. Social groups are often identifiable to outsiders because of their unique geographic, cultural, religious, occupational, or other characteristics. Additionally, members of the group often recognize themselves and others in research reports. As research participants, these socially identifiable communities face "collective risks," both from the outside world and from within the community (Committee on Native American Child Health [CONACH] & Committee on Community Health Services [COCHS], 2004). External risks are those harms inflicted by outsiders. For example, groups represented in research may become the targets of racism and discrimination based on their ethnic, religious, or other characteristics. External risks may affect the economic, social, legal, and political well-being of the community (CONACH & COCHS). For example, studies that detail problems within a community, such as drug use, can result in stigmatization of the community or can lead businesses to avoid the community.

The potential negative consequences of confidentiality breaches also take the form of intracommunity risks. Intracommunity risks involve the disruption of relationships, and they "may not be considered when IRBs [institutional review boards] review research involving human subjects, in part because intracommunity risks are highly localized and often not evident to those outside the community" (CONACH & COCHS, 2004, p. 149). Carolyn Ellis's research for her book *Fisher Folk* (1986) illustrates the collective risks socially identifiable communities face. Ellis's data came from a small, remote community on the marshlands of the Chesapeake Bay. Despite the use of pseudonyms in her book, the community members were able to identify themselves and their neighbors in the often unflattering content of the book (Allen, 1997). Relationships in the community were strained because of what Ellis had written. The book further stigmatized the community, which was already seen in a negative light by some. As a result, the members of the community felt betrayed and humiliated by Ellis and less trusting of outsiders (Allen, 1997; Ellis, 1995).

These examples illustrate the types of potential negative consequences when the confidentiality of a community or of individuals is compromised. As shown by the examples from Baez (2002) and Kaiser (2009), researchers often struggle in solitude, with little systematic guidance or training, to assess the risks to their respondents and decide how to handle data that might compromise confidentiality. In the remainder of this chapter, I offer a set of concrete suggestions to help interviewers manage common confidentiality dilemmas encountered in the course of social science research.

◆ Confidentiality Management

Despite emphasizing the importance of confidentiality (Grinyer, 2002), the literature on research design and the ethical codes of professional associations offer virtually no specific, practical guidance

on preventing deductive disclosure in qualitative research (Giordano, O'Reilly, Taylor, & Dogra, 2007; Kaiser, 2009; Wiles, Crow, Heath, & Charles, 2008). Thus, it is not surprising that researchers struggle with confidentiality and feel uncertain about how to maintain confidentiality (Wiles et al., 2008). There are, however, certain steps that interview researchers can take to manage confidentiality concerns. Confidentiality management occurs in three stages: (1) preinterview, (2) during the interview, and (3) postinterview.

STAGE 1: STUDY PLANNING AND APPROVAL

Prior to beginning a study, researchers must address confidentiality in applications to their institution's internal review board (IRB). Although review boards vary in their procedures (Singer & Levine, 2003), researchers are expected to protect the identities of their study participants at every stage of the research. The ultimate goal is complete confidentiality. Baez (2002) refers to the emphasis on confidentiality as the "convention of confidentiality." Confidentiality is primarily upheld as a means to protect research participants from harm. The emphasis on protection from harm is consistent with *The Belmont Report*'s guideline to ensure "beneficence" in research; in other words, researchers must not harm their study participants. The convention of confidentiality is also upheld to protect the privacy of all persons, build trust and rapport with study participants, and maintain ethical standards and the integrity of the research process (Baez).

As part of IRB approval, an informed consent form is drafted. Consent forms contain assurances of confidentiality to be read by study participants. For example, Kaiser's (2009) consent form for her study of breast cancer survivors stated that the reports resulting from the study would not contain any information that could be used to identify them. "Individual responses may be described in research reports, however all possible precautions will be taken to disguise individuals' identities so that readers of the report will be unable to link you to the study" (p. 1633). Sieber (1992) provides the following example of confidentiality statements in a consent form: "All identifying characteristics, such as occupation, city, and ethnic background, will be changed" (p. 52). Confidentiality promises within informed consent documents function not only to inform respondents of their rights but also to build respondents' trust in the researcher (Crow, Wiles, Heath, & Charles, 2006); however, some have argued that the informed consent process damages rapport by casting the interview in a cold, legalistic tone (see Marzano's "Informed Consent," this volume).

Prior to beginning interviews, researchers should also consider whether community assent is necessary. Most IRB standards are tailored to individual rights. When studying entire communities, however, collective assent may be appropriate and beneficial. There is little guidance on how to obtain community consent. Community assent can take a variety of forms, including formal approval from community leaders or informal approval from community members present at informational meetings. Research in Native American communities provides some examples of obtaining community assent. For example, some universities (e.g., University of Washington) and offices of the Indian Health Service require documentation of tribal support prior to working with Native American communities (CONACH & COCHS, 2004). Although community support does not supersede individual rights to informed consent, community involvement prior to and throughout the project facilitates study recruitment and the identification of potential risks. Community input can also point to important areas of study that might otherwise be overlooked. Kaiser (2009) suggests that researchers can lessen confidentiality concerns by considering the audience and purpose of their study prior to beginning data collection. Every project has a number of potential audiences. For example, data from a study of high school teachers' views of classroom discipline could be shared with students, parents, staff, the school board, administrators, state or city policymakers, other academics, and the general public. Dissemination can occur in a variety of formats, including presentations, drafts read by colleagues, journal articles, radio commentaries, newspaper or magazine articles, and books. Likewise, within each format, researchers will encounter different audiences with different expectations. For example, the expectations of journal reviewers and readers will vary across journals (Marvasti, 2010). Having a clear and specific plan for disseminating data makes it easier to assure respondents that their contributions will be kept confidential. Likewise, knowing how data will be used helps the researcher to discuss potential threats to confidentiality with respondents. Because many respondents participate in research out of a desire to help others, discussing the use of their data can help them better grasp the outcomes of their participation (Beck, 2005; Carter, Jordens, McGrath, & Little, 2008; Dyregrov, 2004; Hynson, Aroni, Bauld, & Sawyer, 2006).

However, as Kaiser (2009) notes, anticipating one's audience can be challenging. First, given the inductive, emergent nature of interview research, it may not be possible to anticipate the best outlets for data until we have worked with the data (James & Platzer, 1999). As Parry and Mauthner (2004) note, "The reflexive nature of qualitative research, its use of unexpected ideas that arise through data collection and its focus upon respondents' meanings and interpretations renders the commitment to informing respondents of the exact path of the research unrealistic" (p. 146; see also Merrell & Williams, 1994). Nonetheless, Kaiser (2009) argues that most outlets for research can be anticipated. Discussing whom we intend to share data with might influence what respondents say or how they behave (Crow et al., 2006; Morse, 2008). This problem, however, can be avoided by discussing the specifics of audience *after* data collection.

Serious consideration of audience not only addresses confidentiality issues but enhances study design as a whole and leads to more focused analyses and writing. Weighing potential audiences also forces researchers to consider their priorities. What are your goals? Are you striving to further scientific knowledge? Do you hope to make an impact on policy? Do you want to give back in some way to the community or organization that assisted you with recruiting participants? Answering these questions will lead researchers to the best audiences for their work. Moreover, awareness of one's audience leads to considerations of the style, tone, and format that best suit a targeted audience (Marvasti, 2010; Strauss & Corbin, 1998).

STAGE 2: THE INTERVIEW

Typically, confidentiality is addressed at the start of the interview when the researcher obtains informed consent; however, confidentiality issues also arise during the interview. For example, respondents may make statements about their confidentiality concerns. In Baez's (2002) interviews with minority faculty members, one female respondent repeatedly asked for her comments to be kept in "total confidence." In contrast, another respondent indicated that she wanted to openly share her experiences with others at the university. As Baez notes, while both respondents opened up to him about their experiences of racism and sexism, the respondent who requested "total confidence" marked some of her statements as extremely confidential and not to be shared. In contrast, in the second instance, the respondent seems to have invited him to disclose her information, even if it would identify her.

Respondents also express confidentiality concerns through emotion. The tone and emotional expressions of the respondent convey to the researcher that he or she is being given access to private, sensitive information not to be shared with others. For example, Kaiser (2009) noticed that Rachel was tentative and self-conscious when discussing her sexuality. Rachel's disclosure of her sexuality and her comments about the support group are an example of an "ethically important moment" (Guillemin & Gillam, 2004). As researchers, we receive little training on how to notice and interpret emotional cues from respondents. Ellis (1995) wishes that she would have paid greater attention to the emotional responses of her study participants during data collection. She vowed to consider respondents' emotions in the future by viewing her writing through their eyes and by imagining how she would feel if the descriptions she wrote were applied to her. Being cognizant of respondents' emotional cues builds gratitude toward study participants for sharing personal information. Awareness of respondents' emotions also builds a sense of duty to protect their information and/or a desire to make the respondents' "lessons known."

Although most interview researchers have encountered an ethically important moment or heard a respondent comment about confidentiality during the interview, interviews typically lack a procedure for discussing such moments. Two procedures can be added to the end of the interview to deal with confidentiality issues that arise during the interview. First, the interviewer can ask the respondent for permission to contact her in the future to discuss questions about her data. By introducing the possibility of recontact, researchers will find it much easier to seek respondents' input on how to use sensitive information. Second, the interviewer can use an end-of-interview document to obtain the respondent's specific wishes for data use and confidentiality. An example of an end-of-interview confidentiality form

is shown in Figure 31.1. Unlike informed consent documentation, this form considers confidentiality in light of the data shared in the interview. The form lets respondents pinpoint data they want kept strictly confidential. As such, the document gives respondents greater control of their data. Notably, this represents a shift in power (Giordano et al., 2007) that may be uncomfortable for some researchers and for some respondents. Researchers should respect a respondent's wish to defer to the researcher regarding data use. Researchers who experience discomfort in giving respondents greater control over data use may want to examine these feelings and their root causes; such examination offers an opportunity to explore loyalties, connections to others, and moral boundaries (Marzano, 2007). Giving greater control to respondents may be most difficult when researchers' primary goals are to advance their careers or contribute to scientific knowledge, rather than to better the lives of their participants (Ellis, 2007). Blind commitment to career and scientific goals can lead to "writing right" (i.e., presenting facts that contribute to theory and knowledge) but "doing wrong" by consequently hurting those who have participated in the research (Becker, 1964; Ellis, 1995, 2007; Richardson, 1992).

With this form, respondents can request or give permission to be identified in study reports. Under the convention of confidentiality, it is assumed that all respondents want confidentiality. However, even respondents typically considered to be "vulnerable" may want to be identified in our reports. In one study of parents of young adults with cancer, 75% of the parents chose to have their real names used in publications resulting from the study of the data (Grinyer, 2004). Prior research has also shown that while researchers interpret displays of painful emotion by respondents as indicating a need for confidentiality, respondents may actually want their data published as a way to feel empowered or help others (Beck, 2005; Carter et al., 2008; Dyregrov, 2004; Hynson et al., 2006; James & Platzer, 1999; Wiles, Charles, Crow, & Heath, 2006).

Additional research is needed to determine how best to use a postinterview form in different studies and with a variety of populations. There are caveats to using the form. For example, if respondents wish to be identified in research, researchers must advise them that the final reports may not be what they envision and ultimately their data may not appear in published reports. Moreover, additional formal

Figure 31.1 Postinterview Confidentiality Form

Study Title

Study #

Post-interview confidentiality form

It is our goal and responsibility to use the information that you have shared responsibly. Now that you have completed the interview, we would like to give you the opportunity to provide us with additional feedback on how you prefer to have your data handled. Please check one of the following statements:

____You may share the information just as I provided it. No details need to be changed and you may use my real name when using my data in publications or presentations.

____You may share the information just as I provided it; however, please do not use my real name. I realize that others might identify me based on the data, even though my name will not be used.

____You may share the information I provided; however, please do not use my real name and please change details that might make me identifiable to others. In particular, it is my wish that the following specific pieces of my data not be shared without first altering the data so as to make me unidentifiable (describe this data in the space below):

_____

_____

_____

____You may contact me if you have any questions about sharing my data with others. The best way to reach me is (provide phone number or email):

_____

Respondent's signature   Date

Investigator's signature   Date

Source: Kaiser (2009).

documents may overwhelm respondents or make them feel alienated from the researcher (Crow et al., 2006). A postinterview form may work best in longitudinal research, where respondents may feel more comfortable with the researcher (Carter et al., 2008). In short, researchers must determine if a postinterview confidentiality form is appropriate for their study topic and population. Finally, researchers should be prepared to work with IRBs to gain approval of postinterview forms. Researchers can facilitate approval by noting that such forms safeguard confidentiality by providing additional documentation of respondents' preferences for the use of the most sensitive data.

STAGE 3: DATA CLEANING, ANALYSIS, AND DISSEMINATION

Once interviews are completed, confidentiality is addressed during data cleaning, analysis, and preparation of results for publications and presentations. Under the convention of confidentiality, all identifiers are removed from the data. Although changing the names of people and specific places can be done rather easily by using the "Find and Replace" function available in most text-based software, changing the characteristics of individuals that are central to the science of the project (e.g., respondents' race and gender in a study of racism and sexism) and changing the details of their experiences is more difficult. For example, neither Kaiser (2009) nor Baez (2002) felt comfortable changing the details of their respondents' stories. Baez notes that altering his data could lessen accuracy by replacing "fact" with "fiction." Moreover, he felt that altering his respondents' stories of discrimination would also conceal oppressive power arrangements. Instead of altering the substance of stories, Kaiser and Baez chose to exclude them from publications and presentations that posed the risk of deductive disclosure. An end-of-interview form can help address such dilemmas and prevent rich, important data from being unused, unless that is the wish of the respondent.

Confidentiality can also be addressed by presenting data and preliminary reports back to the community, a process referred to as member checks (Maxwell, 1996). Member checks allow the community to respond to how they are portrayed in the research, including whether they are comfortable with the degree of confidentiality present in study reports. Soliciting feedback from respondents about our interpretation and presentation of data challenges the traditional power dynamics in the interview setting. The growing body of community-based participatory research (CBPR) provides some guidance on how to give greater voice and power to participants:

Rather than following a top-down, expert-driven model in which the researcher is distinctively empowered to determine research questions, methods and results, a CBPR design has the advantage of working directly with communities to ascertain their views on how the project should proceed. (Boyer, Mohatt, Pasker, Drew, & McGlone, 2007, p. 20)

One way to ensure that the community is supportive of how it is portrayed in the research is to send "progress updates" back to the community (Boyer et al., 2007). Looking back on the negative events that followed the publication of *Fisher Folk*, Ellis (1995) acknowledged that many problems and conflicts could have been prevented if she had shared her data with the respondents, informed them of her plans to publish the data, and made them aware of how they would be portrayed in the final research.

Sharing one's research with respondents is not without its challenges. Participants might not understand the research objectives, or they might be disinterested in them. Participants may object to how we

use their data or represent them in our publications (Corden & Sainsbury, 2006; Ellis, 1995; Lawton, 2001). Nonetheless, sharing our conclusions with respondents can also enhance the validity of our research by allowing respondents to comment on the accuracy of our data and interpretations (Maxwell, 1996) and, importantly, lead to the publication of data that would have been impossible to print without the input from the respondents.

◆ Conclusion

Interview research provides unique insights into the lives of individuals and the complex dynamics of communities. However, researchers may find it difficult to convey detailed, accurate accounts of the social world while protecting the identities of the individuals who live in that particular social world. Researchers should be aware of the risks that confidentiality breaches pose for individuals and communities. Other researchers' accounts of their struggles to use interview data while maintaining confidentiality highlight the need for steps to manage confidentiality at every stage of a project. By carefully addressing confidentiality during research planning, within the interview, and during data cleaning, analysis, and dissemination, researchers can protect respondent confidentiality and make our respondents' lessons known.

◆ References

Allen, C. (1997). Spies like us: When sociologists deceive their subjects. *Lingua Franca*, 7(9), 31–38.

Baez, B. (2002). Confidentiality in qualitative research: Reflections on secrets, power and agency. *Qualitative Research*, 2, 35–58.

Beck, C. T. (2005). Benefits of participating in Internet interviews: Women helping women. *Qualitative Health Research*, 15, 411–422.

Becker, H. (1964). Problems in the publication of field studies. In A. Vidich, J. Bensman, & M. Stein (Eds.), *Reflections on community studies* (pp. 267–284). New York, NY: Wiley.

Boyer, B. B., Mohatt, G. V., Pasker, R. L., Drew, E. M., & McGlone, K. K. (2007). Sharing results from complex disease genetics studies: A community based participatory research approach. *International Journal of Circumpolar Health, 66*, 19–30.

Carter, S. M., Jordens, C. F. C., McGrath, C., & Little, M. (2008). You have to make something of all that rubbish, do you? An empirical investigation of the social process of qualitative research. *Qualitative Health Research, 18*, 1264–1276.

Committee on Native American Child Health & Committee on Community Health Services. (2004). Ethical considerations in research with socially identifiable populations. *Pediatrics, 113*, 148–151.

Corden, A., & Sainsbury, R. (2006). Exploring "quality": Research participants' perspectives on verbatim quotations. *International Journal of Social Research Methodology, 9*, 97–110.

Crow, G., Wiles, R., Heath, S., & Charles, V. (2006). Research ethics and data quality: The implications of informed consent. *International Journal of Social Research Methodology, 9*, 83–95.

Dyregrov, K. (2004). Bereaved parents' experience of research participation. *Social Science & Medicine, 58*, 391–400.

Ellis, C. (1986). *Fisher folk: Two communities on Chesapeake Bay*. Lexington: University of Kentucky Press.

Ellis, C. (1995). Emotional and ethical quagmires in returning to the field. *Journal of Contemporary Ethnography, 24*, 68–98.

Ellis, C. (2007). Telling secrets, revealing lives. *Qualitative Inquiry, 13*, 3–29.

Giordano, J., O'Reilly, M., Taylor, H., & Dogra, N. (2007). Confidentiality and autonomy: The challenge(s) of offering research participants a choice of disclosing their identity. *Qualitative Health Research, 17*, 264–275.

Grinyer, A. (2002). *The anonymity of research participants: Assumptions, ethics and practicalities* (Social Research Update, No. 36). Retrieved from http://sru.soc.surrey.ac.uk/SRU36.html

Grinyer, A. (2004). The narrative correspondence method: What a follow-up study can tell us about the longer term effect on participants in emotionally demanding research. *Qualitative Health Research, 14*, 1326–1341.

Guillemin, M., & Gillam, L. (2004). Ethics, reflexivity, and "ethically important moments" in research. *Qualitative Inquiry, 10*, 261–280.

Hynson, J. L., Aroni, R., Bauld, C., & Sawyer, S. M. (2006). Research with bereaved parents: A question of how not why. *Palliative Medicine, 20*, 805–811.

James, T., & Platzer, H. (1999). Ethical considerations in qualitative research with vulnerable groups: Exploring lesbians' and gay men's experiences of health care— A personal perspective. *Nursing Ethics, 6*, 73–81.

Kaiser, K. (2009). Protecting respondent confidentiality in qualitative research. *Qualitative Health Research, 19*, 1632–1641.

Lawton, J. (2001). Gaining and maintaining consent: Ethical concerns raised in a study of dying patients. *Qualitative Health Research, 11*, 693–705.

Marvasti, A. (2010). The three faces of writing qualitative research: Practice, genre and audience. In D. Silverman (Ed.), *Qualitative research* (pp. 383–396). London, England: Sage.

Marzano, M. (2007). Informed consent, deception, and research freedom in qualitative research. *Qualitative Inquiry, 13*, 417–436.

Maxwell, J. A. (1996). *Qualitative research design: An interpretive approach*. Thousand Oaks, CA: Sage.

Merrell, J., & Williams, A. (1994). Participant observation and informed consent: Relationships and tactical decision-making in nursing research. *Nursing Ethics, 1*, 163–172.

Morse, J. M. (2008). Does informed consent interfere with induction? *Qualitative Health Research, 18*, 439–440.

Parry, O., & Mauthner, N. S. (2004). Whose data are they anyway? Practical, legal and ethical issues in archiving qualitative research data. *Sociology, 38*, 139–152.

Richardson, L. (1992). Trash on the corner: Ethics and technology. *Journal of Contemporary Ethnography, 21*, 103–119.

Sieber, J. E. (1992). *Planning ethically responsible research: A guide for students and internal review boards* (Vol. 31). Newbury Park, CA: Sage.

Singer, E., & Levine, F. (2003). Protection of human subjects of research: Recent developments and future prospects for the social sciences. *Public Opinion Quarterly, 67*, 148–164.

Strauss, A., & Corbin, J. (1998). *Basics of qualitative research: Techniques and procedures for developing grounded theory*. Thousand Oaks, CA: Sage.

Tolich, M. (2004). Internal confidentiality: When confidentiality assurances fail relational informants. *Qualitative Sociology, 27*, 101–106.

U.S. Department of Health and Human Services. (2005). *Code of federal regulations, Title 45, Part 46: Protection of human subjects*. Washington, DC: Author. Retrieved from http://www.hhs.gov/ohrp/humansubjects/guidance/45cfr46.htm

Weiss, R. S. (1994). *Learning from strangers: The art and method of qualitative interview studies*. New York, NY: Free Press.

Wiles, R., Charles, V., Crow, G., & Heath, S. (2006). Researching researchers: Lessons for research ethics. *Qualitative Research, 6*, 283–299.

Wiles, R., Crow, G., Heath, S., & Charles, V. (2008). The management of confidentiality and anonymity in social research. *International Journal of Social Research Methodology, 1*, 417–428.

32

PROTECTING PARTICIPANTS' CONFIDENTIALITY USING A SITUATED RESEARCH ETHICS APPROACH

◆ Kristin Heggen and Marilys Guillemin

Ann was one of a number of people who eagerly responded to Stefan's call for research participants. The project was on everyday life experiences of parents whose child had been diagnosed as severely obese. Stefan was the lead researcher on this project examining how parents of children who were diagnosed as severely obese understood their child's obesity and managed the condition. In recruiting participants, Stefan was acutely aware of the sensitive nature of obesity in children; he was careful to inform potential participants of the risks involved for themselves, their child, and the rest of the family. His project had been granted ethics approval, and he was very familiar with the ethical guidelines for interview research. Stefan was careful to assure potential participants that their privacy would be protected and that any identifying information would be left out of the research report; participants' names would be replaced with pseudonyms in all ensuing publications.

Ann was keen to participate in this research project and enthusiastically chose to be interviewed in her home. During the research interview, Ann talked about her family, including her two children, who she said were all "big boned." As a child, Ann had always been "large," and in her family, they strongly believed that this was just genetic. Ann felt that as a child she had been discriminated against by her teachers, who dismissed her in the belief that because she was large she was also less intelligent, and by her schoolmates, who left her out of sporting activities or social occasions. Although he was of normal weight now, Stefan had been severely obese himself as a child and empathized with Ann. As an adult, Ann had been turned down many times for jobs despite her excellent qualifications and experience; she was convinced that her body size was the main reason. Ann firmly believed that she and her family had a healthy lifestyle, had regular exercise, and ate "reasonably well." Ann deeply resented that her weight and her children's weight were made to be a problem by her doctor, her children's school, and society at large. Ann was adamant that the problem was not with her and her children but with society's refusal to accept that people are just different and that difference should be celebrated rather than demonized. Stefan was taken aback by the force of Ann's convictions; this was the first time that a participant had expressed such strong views to him. He was touched personally and was reminded about his past, as well as being excited about the interesting data being generated from Ann's participation.

At the close of the interview, just as Stefan was leaving, Ann stopped him and stated that she wanted her real name to be used in the research and any publications that arose from it. Ann claimed that she had felt silenced during most of her life and now wanted her voice to be heard. Ann saw her participation in this research as an opportunity to make her views heard and to allow the perspectives of those who had been socially stigmatized to be known.

Stefan was uncertain as to how to respond to Ann's request. He appealed to the necessity for him to abide by his university's ethics committee and their guidelines. Stefan suggested that they both consider the matter further and promised to phone Ann back.

Stefan returned to his department and discussed Ann's request with his colleagues. Many of them thought that it was not reasonable and that she did not fully understand the consequences and potential harm for herself and her children. They would have to reconsider their research design as the data analysis and the writing of papers would have to be done differently if some participants wanted to be recognized by name and others did not. Another major concern was the institution's reputation; they could imagine the severe consequences if the institution became known as a place where research participants' privacy was not guaranteed. Although Stefan was still not comfortable about this point of view, he complied with it and agreed that it was the researcher's responsibility to decide if participants' real names were to be used or not.

As promised, Stefan rang up Ann to tell her of his decision. Ann was silent, then hung up the phone.

◆ Introduction

For Stefan, protecting his participants' confidentiality was something he took for granted. Stefan understood protecting privacy and confidentiality as an obligation he must abide by and for his participants, a right to be fulfilled. It was not until he was forced to question this that he began to challenge this taken-for-granted notion.

Underlying human research are a number of key ethical principles, most notably respect for human beings and research integrity, beneficence, and justice. Although there is some debate about the universality of these principles, their importance in governing human research guidelines is widely agreed on. Of importance to this chapter are the principles of beneficence and respect, from which arise the guidelines around informed consent. To address these important principles, a number of strategies have been developed that serve to protect participants' confidentiality. Strategies such as asking for informed consent, the use of pseudonyms rather than participants' actual names, and removing identifying features from research reports are all widely acknowledged practices in research. Although these strategies may be commonly used and widely accepted, we suggest that they are not as straightforward as they may first appear, as illustrated in Ann and Stefan's story. Focusing on the practice of research ethics enables us to examine what is ethically at stake here and for whom.

We work from the premise that protecting participants' confidentiality is vitally important in research. The challenge is to consider what this means not just from a position of abstract principles but from a position of situated practice. Our argument has three moves. First, we argue that although the principles of respect and beneficence are fundamental, they are not necessarily helpful when considering how to act at the level of practice. Our second move is to consider the notion of "situated research ethics," which highlights the importance of the local and specific and the idea of ethics as relational and contextual. The notion of situated research ethics helps bring our focus from abstract principles to local practices. However, for researchers such as Stefan, what can we offer to assist them in negotiating local ethical relations in the conduct of research? This is our third move. We suggest that the features of "ethical mindfulness" are useful in assisting researchers to negotiate ethical issues with participants, including how best to protect their confidentiality.

We focus here on interview research, specifically individual interviews. Interview research poses particular challenges. The topics explored using interview research often deal with participants' personal life experiences and place private utterances in a public sphere. As opposed to quantitative methodologies, where personal characteristics can be concealed by numbers and averages, interview researchers are often working with subjective and perhaps intimate aspects of people's lives. Interviews often involve (although they are not limited to) face-to-face interactions between two people who may have never met before or may have met only briefly. The content of interview research may involve sensitive topics that may have not been previously voiced by participants. Even if the topic of research is not obviously sensitive in nature, the establishment of rapport between researcher and participant and the context of the interview setting can lead to disclosure of sensitive matters. There is often a heightened intensity in interviews where sensitive issues may be disclosed. Participants may benefit from discussing their own experiences and developing their own understanding during the interview process. Characteristically, when actually conducting research interviews, there is often little time for reflection on the part of the researcher (in contrast to research methods such as participant observation, where the researcher has the opportunity to reflect and return to the research field on another day). When ethical issues do arise in interview research, there is often

no time for considered deliberation, only a need for quick decisions on how to proceed. In sum, interview research is complex, both methodologically and ethically. Researchers are often faced with having to make ethical decisions with little time or opportunity to reflect. It is therefore imperative to pay serious attention to how best to protect participants' confidentiality in the context of interview research. Ethical questions in interview research may not necessarily be dramatic or highly visible; rather, they may be "ethically important moments" (Guillemin & Gillam, 2004). The fact that they are less visible does not, however, mean that they are less important; on the contrary, less visibility calls for a strong and reflective awareness (Brinkmann, 2010). It is here that we believe that situated perspectives and ethically mindful research practice can be useful.

In developing our argument, we first examine the ethical principles that inform the notion of research participants' confidentiality. From the position of principles, we then develop what we mean by "situated research ethics" in the interview context. Paying attention to the local practices and context leads us to a discussion of ethical mindfulness. We examine how to negotiate situated ethics using the concept of ethical mindfulness, particularly focusing on the researcher–participant relationship. We conclude with a discussion of both the benefits and the challenges of this approach.

◆ Principles of Protecting Participants' Confidentiality

The ethical principles of respect, beneficence, and justice provide a foundation for human research ethics guidelines and frameworks internationally. Following the abuses in medical research during World War II, the Nuremberg trials took place, from which the Nuremberg Code was established. This code specified the need for voluntary participation and obtaining informed consent from research participants. Following the Nuremberg Code came the Declaration of Helsinki in 1964 and the release of the Belmont Report in 1979 by the U.S. National Commission for the Protection of Human Subjects of Biomedical and Behavioral Research (U.S. Office for Human Research Protections [OHRP], 2005). From this came the development of codes of human research ethics internationally to guide the conduct of research. Examples of these guidelines include the OHRP (2005) guidelines, Australia's *National Statement on Ethical Conduct in Human Research* (commonly referred to as the *National Statement*) (National Health and Medical Research Council [NHMRC], 2007), and Norway's *Guidelines for the Research Ethics in the Social Sciences and the Humanities* and *Guidelines for Research Ethics in Science and Technology* (National Committee for Research Ethics in Science and Technology, 2008; National Committee for Research Ethics in the Social Sciences and the Humanities, 2006). These codes of ethics are significant in setting the ethical framework for the conduct of human research.

Central to these guidelines is the ethical principle of respect for persons, which involves recognition of the value of human autonomy and respecting the privacy and confidentiality of participants (Israel & Hay, 2006). The conduct of ethical research requires ensuring that the benefits of research outweigh the risks (NHMRC, 2007). Assessing potential risks to participants includes consideration of not just physical harm but also economic, psychological, legal, and social harm, such as that brought about by breaching confidentiality. Breach of confidential information may involve disclosure of personal information about the participant or sensitive information disclosed during the course of the research that may put the participant at risk. Although in most cases every attempt is made to protect participants' confidentiality, there are circumstances, such as in criminological and sociolegal research, where disclosing information given in confidence by research participants may be justifiable (Israel, 2004; Parker, 2005).

The principle of respect informs the practice of informed consent, which functions to ensure that potential research participants are provided with sufficient information to make a voluntary and informed decision whether to participate or not. It is difficult to fully guarantee confidentiality in human research. However, the practice of informed consent seeks to ensure that participants are fully informed of all known risks and given information about how these risks will be curtailed.

The primary reason why we strive to guard participants' confidentiality is to protect them from potential harm. This is the dominant view, and considerable efforts are made to offer this protection to participants. However, this dominant view is being challenged (Whittaker, 2005). As the case of Ann and Stefan demonstrates, this view can be contested by the very participants we are aiming to protect. It could be seen as disempowering to Ann not to allow her name to be made public. This calls into question the dominance of the principle of respect, when weighing up whether Stefan's attempt to protect Ann's privacy is protective or paternalistic (Patton, 2002).

Although the primary intent of the *principle of respect* and confidentiality is to protect the participant, this has been extended to the protection of institutions. For many researchers and research institutions, ensuring that participants' confidentiality is protected has more to do with protecting organizations from potential harm and, increasingly, from liability. Breaches of participants' confidentiality can result in serious harm, leading to loss of reputation, trust, and integrity for researchers and research institutions alike (Hatcher & Aragon, 2000; O'Neill, 2004; Pascal, 2006).

Clearly, ethical principles are paramount in terms of research ethics, broadly, and protecting confidentiality, more specifically. But as we have shown, these principles are not clear-cut. It is often at the level of practice that the contestations become visible, and it is not always clear how these contestations should be resolved. In addition, as researchers in the field, how do we respond when faced with requests such as Ann's to use her real name in research publications or indeed the myriad other ethical challenges that confront researchers in the field? We suggest that ethical principles at the abstract level cease to be helpful when we are faced with often unexpected ethical problems in practice. There is therefore a need for other ways of addressing confidentiality in practice, and we thus turn to the notion of "situated research ethics."

◆ Situated Research Ethics

Interview research is premised on interpersonal relations and active interaction between a researcher and one or more participants in the qualitative research context (Holstein & Gubrium, 2003; Tanggaard & Brinkmann, 2010). Topics dealt with in interview research are often closely connected with participants' real-world dilemmas, experiences, perceptions, thoughts, emotions, and values as experienced in a variety of life situations. This is well illustrated by Stefan's project examining the everyday experiences of parents with obese children. Interview research (with the exception of very structured interview designs) is often characterized as flexible and open. Interaction with research participants in an interview setting often requires the researcher to be flexible and able to adapt to the specific context. Consequently, we suggest that addressing confidentiality needs to be marked by the same openness and flexibility. As illustrated in Ann and Stefan's story, dealing with ethical issues in practice is fraught with often unexpected dilemmas and divergent interests. Addressing these ethical issues is not a straightforward application of abstract rules and principles. We argue the need for a situated research ethics reflecting the characteristics of interview research (and qualitative research more generally).

The term *situated ethics* has recently been adopted by a number of authors in the research context (Calvey, 2009; Danaher & Danaher, 2008; Piper & Simons, 2005; Simons & Usher, 2000). According to Simons and Usher (2000), situated ethics places the focus on the local and the specific rather than at the level of universal principles. This is not to suggest that principles are not helpful but rather that they are mediated by the local and the particular. In arguing for situated research ethics, we are arguing for a more dynamic concept of confidentiality. This is in contrast to a notion of protecting confidentiality as a one-off assurance when signing a consent form.

In using the term *situated research ethics*, we highlight two key points. First, interview research is *situated*; it is local and specific, occurring in a particular time and place, involving researchers and participants who have their own histories, concerns, and interests. As we go on to discuss, this is important in helping us address research ethics that is situated in local practice. The second point is that situated research ethics draws attention to the specificities of the different stages of interview research as well as the contextual factors influencing the research. We need to consider confidentiality as an ongoing process during the conduct of interview research. Confidentiality needs to be addressed in different ways depending on the stage of the research project. A situated perspective directs attention to the integration of ethics in the different stages of research

practice; we go on to illustrate this using confidentiality in interview research as the focus.

◆ Research Ethics as Situated

Our first point is that situated research ethics emphasizes the situatedness of interview research, the individuals involved, and the specificities of their interaction. To illustrate this, we return to Stefan and Ann, and their understanding of confidentiality. Thinking about Stefan and Ann as a particular researcher and a particular research participant, respectively, rather than as researchers and participants in a general sense will help highlight what we mean here. We know that Stefan is well versed in the procedural requirements of the human research ethics committee and research guidelines; however, this would be the case for most experienced researchers. What is particular about Stefan is that he had been severely obese as a child, and it is likely that his personal experience influenced his motivation for developing and undertaking this research. Stefan's personal experience also enabled him to empathize with Ann's experiences of her own childhood. Ann comes to the interview eager to participate. She is keen to share her life experiences and, in particular, is keen to have her views on obesity voiced. Having felt that she had been silenced and discriminated against, Ann sees the interview as an opportunity to have her views heard. In addition, Ann wants to be named. In this interview, confidentiality is not an abstract concept operationalized in a standard consent form; it is not a straightforward arrangement between the researcher and the participant. Because of their particular histories and interests, confidentiality in this interview becomes contested as Ann challenges Stefan and the dominant power relations where the researcher usually decides how participants are identified.

A situated research ethics perspective highlights that interview research occurs at a particular time. Ann and Stefan share a history of childhood obesity and are at a point in their lives where they can look back and reflect on their experiences. It could be expected that Ann and Stefan may share similar views. However, at the point in time when the research takes place, childhood obesity is a controversial issue imbued with considerable stigma. Although both Ann and Stefan had been severely obese as children, Stefan has now reduced his weight; for him, obesity is a problem that can be overcome, proven by his own efforts. Ann, on the other hand, is still obese, as are her children. She continues to live the discrimination and stigma associated with obesity, both for herself and for her children. For Ann, obesity is a societal problem, and she is determined to speak out, and this interview research provides her an opportunity to do so. For Ann and Stefan at this point in time, weighing up the benefits and risks of disclosing Ann's identity results in different decisions. The decision may be quite different at another point in time, reinforcing the notion of confidentiality as a dynamic concept in this kind of research.

In addition to time, a situated research ethics perspective highlights the importance of place in interview research. Ann chose to do the interview in her own home. It is possible that the outcome would have been different if the interview had been conducted in Stefan's university department or a neutral location. It is probable that Ann felt more empowered in her own surroundings and more ready to request that she be identified in the research publications. Again, this reminds us of the situatedness of confidentiality and the role of place in the way confidentiality is understood and practiced by those involved.

◆ Confidentiality in the Different Stages of Interview Research

We have proposed that confidentiality be understood as a dynamic concept rather than as a one-off consideration when informed consent is gained. It therefore follows that confidentiality may take different hues and needs to be addressed differently for different stages of interview research. We illustrate this by examining the place of confidentiality in the various stages of interview research from design to dissemination.

RESEARCH DESIGN

When designing interview research, we generally start with a research proposal. Approval must then be obtained from appropriate human research ethics committees. This approval process requires the researcher to consider potential harm to participants and to ensure that the benefits of the research will outweigh the risks, including the question of confidentiality. All aspects of the project, from the main research question to the report of findings, are subject to careful consideration. Reflection about confidentiality includes consideration of the sampling process. If the sample is small with easily identifiable informants (e.g., patients with a rare condition), it will be difficult to provide guarantees of confidentiality. This has to be discussed openly with participants and may necessitate a plan for discussing the presentation of findings with participants to ensure that they are comfortable with the way they are represented and identified. The methods of recruiting participants need serious consideration. This is particularly the case with methods where mailing lists are used or snowball methods are employed, where maintaining confidentiality may be an issue.

A reflexive approach is necessary in the design stage, encouraging researchers to reflect on their own assumptions and motivations in undertaking the research. In Stefan's case, he needs to be clear about the impact of his past experience as an obese child on his research. Is he going to be secretive about his past when recruiting participants or use his experience strategically to encourage participants to take part? These questions are relevant when considering confidentiality. Confidentiality needs to be considered from the very beginning of the research project as a dynamic and challenging aspect that affects the researcher, participants, and their ensuing interactions.

DATA COLLECTION

The data collection stage of interview research usually involves face-to-face contact between the researcher and the participant. It is the interaction between them that is the vehicle driving data generation, as well as questions of confidentiality. The researcher is dependent on building confidence and developing a trusting relationship with the participant. The purpose of establishing rapport between researcher and participant is to generate rich data while at the same time ensuring that respect is maintained between the researcher and the participant (Guillemin & Heggen, 2009). There is a considerable literature devoted to how best to negotiate the relationship with the participant, establishing rapport while resisting the temptation to push boundaries in order to get rich data at the cost of the participant's integrity (Dickson-Swift, James, Kippen, & Liamputtong, 2007; Duncombe & Jessop, 2002; Kvale & Brinkmann, 2009).

Considerations of confidentiality are important in the way these interactions develop. For Stefan, it is possible that his self-disclosure may encourage participants to reciprocate and reveal more of their own inner thoughts and feelings, creating potential confidentiality issues as the focus of the interview shifts from "research" to "therapy." From an ethical standpoint, researchers often work to maintain a particular interpretive frame in the course of the interview. For example, for some researchers, a rule of thumb to keep in mind is that the researcher–participant relationship is not a therapeutic one, where the participant is necessarily seeking help from the researcher. Instead, the research encounter is viewed as a relationship where the researcher, together with input from the participant, contributes to the production of knowledge. The point is that the data collection phase of interviewing becomes another occasion where respondents and researchers negotiate "situated ethics" and the moral boundaries of their relationship.

DATA ANALYSIS

In interview research, there is no discrete stage of data analysis. Consideration of how data will be analyzed occurs from the early design stage, together with consideration of the sample, recruitment, data collection, and dissemination. Strategies for data analysis have an impact on confidentiality. Whether the data are categorized in abstract terms or analyzed as individual life narratives will have consequences for participant confidentiality. Furthermore, in interview research, there is no single approach to data analysis. However, the aim in most methods of data analysis used in interview research is to generate patterns from the data, moving progressively toward increasing levels of abstraction from the raw data. How we think about participants in this process is of interest here. For some researchers, it is helpful during data analysis to visualize the person and the setting where the interview took place. Visualizing the participant's face, voice, body, and mannerisms and the intensity of the interaction can stimulate the analysis. It is interesting to consider how this process of personalizing participants relates to aspects of confidentiality.

For most interview researchers, it is impossible to "forget" the identity of the participants once the interview is completed. Despite the promise to use pseudonyms and remove any identifying material, it is often not possible to remove the details of the participants from the researcher's mind. The researcher's obligation to mask participants' identity and protect their privacy is challenged by the participants being present in the researcher's mind while he or she is analyzing the data. The closeness to the participant has to be balanced with the distancing of the analytical abstraction process. This abstraction might lead to participants believing that they have been falsely interpreted and may threaten the trust relationship between the researcher and the participant. The opposite is also a possibility; the researcher's fear of losing the participant's confidence might lead to suppression of certain data, with critical consequences for the production of research knowledge. In the context of data analysis, "situated ethics" focuses on the work of constructing a particular vision of the respondent. Under the guidelines of confidentially, in a sense, the researcher has to erase the actual face of the respondent from his or her memory, at least partially, and instead construct one that is reminiscent of the original but only in terms of features that are relevant for the analysis at hand.

The process of translating spoken words into written text is in itself an ethical question and demands reflection about confidentiality (Brinkmann, 2010). The use of a person outside the research team to transcribe interviews is common practice. However, there is often little consideration given to confidentiality when an external transcriber is introduced into the process; how confidentiality is protected in these circumstances requires serious attention. Whether a transcribed text is faithful to the participants' oral statements can pose issues of confidentiality. It may be tempting to reword participants' statements to present them in the most respectful way, but this may inadvertently misrepresent them. This aspect of confidentiality can be complicated and clearly links with other research ethical principles such as respect.

PUBLICATION AND DISSEMINATION

The last stage of the research project is dissemination of knowledge, and this is where confidentiality as an ethical issue is often most apparent. At this stage, data provided by participants are presented publicly. If the participants have been promised confidentiality, it is of great importance that this promise be kept. A key question is how to protect participants' privacy and anonymity without compromising the integrity of the findings. It is often in detailed description that the significance of the research comes to the fore. However, in providing such details, there is a risk that participants may recognize themselves or others, particularly with small samples or unusual research contexts. Clearly, this has the potential to cause harm to participants, their communities (Ellis, 1986, 2007; Etherington, 2007), and associated organizations (Irvine, 2003).

A situated research perspective emphasizes the importance of contextual factors influencing the production of knowledge, including the researcher's position in the research institution. Going back to Stefan, his concerns are influenced by his relationship to his colleagues and his department and possibly his concerns for fulfilling his obligations to his funding agency and having a future research career. Allowing Ann to be named in his publications is not only a question to be negotiated between Ann and Stefan; it is also a matter of how and where Stefan is situated as a researcher in an institutional context.

Our reflections indicate that there are no simple answers to questions of confidentiality in interview research. A situated research ethics perspective opens up a more dynamic and flexible concept of confidentiality. This approach highlights that confidentiality is embedded in the interactions between researcher and participant and in the context of the research. This perspective allows a more open exploration of interview research as situated and contextual and, additionally, enables an examination of confidentiality as an ongoing process affecting the different stages of interview research. Although we suggest that a situated research ethics perspective offers us a different lens with which to view confidentiality, it still operates at a conceptual level. In the next section, we offer a more practical approach, ethical mindfulness in research, which facilitates reflection-in-action.

◆ Ethical Mindfulness in Research Practice

Ethical mindfulness is a term used by Guillemin and Gillam (2006) in their discussion of everyday ethics in health care. This term refers to a group of predispositions, a set of ongoing concerns or characteristics rather than any single skill or trait. Although Guillemin and Gillam (2006) use the term to address ethically important moments in health care practice, we suggest that it also has application in the context of ethics practice in research. In a sense, "ethical mindfulness" amounts to actively attending to, and framing, the interview process in terms of its ethical implications for the researcher and the participant. Guillemin and Gillam (2006) identify five features of ethical mindfulness, which we have applied to research ethics.

ETHICALLY IMPORTANT MOMENTS

The first feature of ethical mindfulness is to acknowledge the role of ethically important moments in the everyday practice of research. Ethically important moments refer to the small moments that may be overlooked as unimportant. For example, in an interview setting, changes in tone of voice, hesitations, a sudden change of topic, and nervous shuffling may all be signs that a participant is feeling uncomfortable. Although this may not always be the case, being ethically mindful alerts the researcher that there may be something ethically significant going on. In Ann's case, it may be about paying attention to her enthusiasm to take part in the research and her eagerness to be interviewed before the interview even commences; during the interview, it may be Ann's expressions of feeling discriminated against and feeling that her voice had not been heard. Rather than passing these off as insignificant, being ethically mindful suggests that they should be noted and given serious consideration, as much as the more overt ethical obligations of providing participants with information sheets and seeking informed consent.

ATTENDING TO DISCOMFORT

The second feature of ethical mindfulness is to acknowledge the *ethical* importance of discomfort or uneasiness during or following the interview. It has been our experience when conducting interviews to leave the interview feeling that something was not quite right. This feeling of discomfort may not be recalled until some time afterward, perhaps during the transcription or analytic stage or even later when the researcher is writing the report and hesitating over particular phrasing. This may be a feeling of doubt or unease that may be initially difficult to articulate. Being ethically mindful alerts us to these feelings of discomfort as being potentially ethically significant. Again, it is possible that they may not turn out to be ethically important, but the point here is to acknowledge this doubt or unease and not dismiss it. Ellis (2007, p. 21) urges us to listen to the cues of discomfort as being of potential ethical significance. In the case of Stefan, he had felt increasingly uncomfortable at Ann's vehemence in describing her experiences of stigmatization and being ostracized. When Ann asked that her real name be used, Stefan was unprepared. In discussing Ann's request with his colleagues, Stefan considered the possible harms to the university and his own reputation as a researcher. He decided to "play it safe" and not allow Ann's request. However, Stefan still felt that he had disappointed Ann and was uncomfortable with the decision.

ARTICULATING WHAT IS ETHICALLY AT STAKE

Third, to be ethically mindful requires articulation of what is ethically at stake. It is important to both understand and identify what is of ethical importance. It is not enough to acknowledge that something is not right. To address it requires it to be identified and articulated. The language of ethical principles is very useful here as it provides a frame for understanding, communicating, and working with what we have acknowledged to be ethically troubling. In addition, codes of research ethics and ethics guidelines serve as useful operational devices for the fundamental principles of research ethics, respect, justice, and beneficence. Furthermore, articulating what is ethically at stake may require other conceptual and linguistic tools; for example, power relations are often integrally woven into ethical problems, and the tools from disciplines such as sociology may be useful. Together, these provide important resources to identify what is ethically at stake and to enable it to be communicated. This is important if we are to move beyond feeling uneasy to being able to identify and address the ethical issue in question. For Stefan, being ethically mindful would have meant not just having an understanding of the ethical principles of respect and beneficence but

being able to communicate these to Ann in a way that enabled her to be fully informed of the consequences of her request. Before the interview began, Stefan could have explained to Ann the potential harm to herself and her children of revealing her identity. The nature and length of time required for research publication and dissemination would mean that these consequences may not be played out until years later, when Ann's own circumstances and beliefs may have changed and her children's situation could have been different. There was also respect for her children's privacy to consider. On the other hand, these would need to be weighed against the benefit to Ann of having her voice heard after having felt silenced for so long. Articulating what is ethically at stake and engaging in dialogue with Ann would enable an informed decision to be negotiated between Ann and Stefan, instead of the unsatisfactory ending that ensued.

REFLEXIVITY

The fourth characteristic of ethical mindfulness is being reflexive. Reflexivity is a concept that is well-known in qualitative research, where researchers are urged to seriously consider their role and its impact on the research process (Finlay, 1998; Koch & Harrington, 1998; Mason, 1996). It is also useful to consider reflexivity in relation to research ethics (Etherington, 2007; Guillemin & Gillam, 2004; McGraw, Zvonkovic, & Walker, 2000). Being ethically mindful also means being ethically rigorous, and being reflexive enables ethical rigor. This applies to all stages of the research process, from design to dissemination. Reflexivity in Stefan's case would mean his giving due consideration to his motivation for choosing this research project and how his own childhood experiences of obesity influenced his choice of research and his approach to designing the project. In his response to Ann, being reflexive would encourage Stefan to reflect on his unease at Ann's strong beliefs that the problem was not a personal problem but rather a societal one. In discouraging Ann from self-identifying, who is Stefan actually trying to protect—Ann and her children, his own reputation as a researcher, or the reputation of his institution? Just as reflexivity is useful in ensuring methodological rigor and the validity of the knowledge produced, being reflexive and ethically mindful ensures *ethical* rigor.

COURAGE

The last feature of ethical mindfulness is courage. Although this may initially seem an oddity, on further reflection, courage is highly relevant in a research setting. Courage is required for critically questioning your own research practices and beliefs. Courage is required for changing established patterns of behavior and challenging your colleagues about their practices and, indeed, for exposing yourself to scrutiny. Challenging your own research integrity, together with accepting that you may be wrong, requires courage. The primary aim of research ethics is to protect participants; however, it requires courage on the part of the researcher to decide to act in a way that is ethically preferable but that may potentially cause emotional harm to participants. In the case of Stefan, it could be seen that he lacked courage when he responded to Ann in a way that asserted the established practice of protecting participants' privacy and confidentiality, since he had already obtained Ann's consent and agreement to the use of a pseudonym. A more courageous stance may have been to support Ann's request and accept that silencing her as a research participant was not respecting her wishes. Stefan could have discussed other possibilities with Ann to enable her to have her voice heard, for example, by independently writing and publishing her narrative while still respecting her confidentiality in the context of the research project.

As a whole, the concept of ethical mindfulness offers a way of addressing situated research ethics. Ethical principles and ethics guidelines are mediated through ethical mindfulness while still keeping the focus on the local and the particular. This is not about research ethics in the abstract but about local practices and ensuring that different research practices are ethically mindful.

◆ Conclusion

Protecting participants' confidentiality is vitally important in interview research. However, participants' right to privacy may be accompanied by other ethical problems. An important question concerning confidentiality is this: What information should be available to whom and in what form? In addressing this question, research ethics guidelines offer strategies and serve as a context for reflection on ethical decisions throughout the interview research. For Stefan, confidentiality is a major concern; his project is reviewed and approved by an institutional review board. Stefan is knowledgeable about the research ethics guidelines and is prepared to abide by them. However, the guidelines are not necessarily black and white. Stefan needs to reflect on when and how to apply the guidelines. There are always situational factors that determine the relevance and use of guidelines. This is one premise for introducing situated research ethics. Another is the fact that interview research usually has an open and flexible design, requiring the researcher to make it adaptable to specific contexts. Addressing confidentiality has, consequently, to be marked by the same openness and flexibility. We see confidentiality more as a problem area or what Kvale and Brinkmann (2009) refer to as "areas of uncertainty." We are arguing for a dynamic concept of confidentiality that is open to the uncertainties, challenges, and ambivalences arising during the research process.

In arguing for situated research ethics, we highlight two key points with special relevance for confidentiality. First, we see the interview as situated and local, occurring in a particular time and place, involving researchers and participants with specific interests. This is illustrated by Ann's personal experience of being marginalized, which influences her wish to have her name made public in Stefan's research reports. Second, ethical issues about confidentiality are embedded in all stages of interview research. We suggest that confidentiality be regarded as an ongoing process during the conduct of interview research and not just confined to seeking a signature on a consent form at the commencement of the interview. Confidentiality needs to be addressed in different ways depending on the stage of the research. Knowledge about the confidentiality issues that typically arise in the different stages can assist the researcher in making considered choices during all stages of research. To stimulate the researcher's sensitivity and awareness of ethical issues in practice, we suggest that the features of "ethical mindfulness" are useful. Being ethically mindful is being practically wise in research; it involves being able to appraise and act in response to ethical situations that arise in the doing of research. In interview research, the researcher is the instrument of the research, and data are constructed through the interaction between the researcher and the participant. Consequently, the capacity and role of the researcher is a critical factor. Therefore, addressing how researchers can learn to become ethically skilled and mindful and adopt a situated perspective on confidentiality deserves serious attention.

Learning ethical principles and being familiar with the codes of research conduct is not sufficient to become an ethical researcher. The goal is ethically mindful researchers whose research practices are oriented and sensitized to a situated ethics perspective. This begs the question of how these ethical capabilities can be developed. In this last section, we will draw the contours of a learning strategy to enable ethical craftsmanship.

A situated approach not only requires learning to be ethically mindful but also includes practical wisdom to see and ascertain that there might be something ethically significant going on. It is a perspective intimately connected with a conception of ethical knowledge as contextualized rather than abstract. Arguing the importance of a situated research ethics implies a conception of knowledge more like what Aristotle called "phronesis," or practical wisdom or judgment to deal with the particularities of ethical cases (Jonsen & Toulmin, 1988). Phronesis is the skill of clear perception and judgment; it is a craftsmanship requiring skills and personal insight acquired through training, extensive practice, and observing and reflecting together with those who are more experienced.

Kvale and Brinkmann (2009) conceive of qualitative interviewing and research ethical behavior as a craft rather than a method; they present an approach to learning ethical research behavior through mastering the art of "thick description" (pp. 76–79). Learning to "thicken" events is helpful in enabling researchers to be ethically reflective and interact respectfully toward research participants. Our presentation and reflections on Stefan's experiences serve to illustrate the way Kvale and Brinkmann would conceive of learning ethically skilled craftsmanship.

Although Kvale and Brinkmann's (2009) idea serves to support our approach, we have taken this notion further through the introduction of ethical mindfulness. There are no simple right or wrong answers to questions about confidentiality. There are always situational factors that need to be identified, articulated, and reflected on. Using Ann and Stefan's story, we have illustrated the idea of learning ethical craftsmanship where events are described in context

and located spatially and temporally. The features of ethical mindfulness are helpful for making visible the ethical complexities of an event and present a framework for reflection, which can then guide action.

We have presented some potentially useful guides for ethical practice in interview research. These conceptual tools clearly apply to more than just notions of confidentiality. As we have suggested, there is usually more than one ethical issue at stake in any given research situation. Moreover, this applies to more than just interview research and is equally applicable to other research methods involving human participants. The challenge with these conceptual tools is to actually apply them in practice. We have made the point that interview research is complex and potentially ethically laden. This means that solutions to ethical problems cannot be standardized; it is not a case of "one size fits all." However, using a situated research ethics perspective allows a more dynamic and complex notion of confidentiality, enabling research that is ethically rich and rigorous.

◆ References

Brinkmann, S. (2010). Etik i en kvalitativ verden [Ethics in the context of doing qualitative research]. In S. Brinkmann & L. Tanggaard (Eds.), *Kvalitative metoder* [Qualitative methods] (pp. 429–446). Copenhagen, Denmark: Hans Reitzels Forlag.

Calvey, D. (2009). The art and politics of covert research. Doing "situated ethics" in the field. *Sociology, 42,* 905–918.

Danaher, M., & Danaher, P. A. (2008). Situated ethics in investigating non-government organisations and showgrounds: Issues in researching Japanese environmental politics and Australian traveller education. *International Journal of Pedagogies and Learning, 4,* 58–70.

Dickson-Swift, V., James, E., Kippen, S., & Liamputtong, P. (2007). Doing sensitive research: What challenges do qualitative researchers face? *Qualitative Research, 73,* 327–353.

Duncombe, J., & Jessop, J. (2002). "Doing rapport" and the ethics of "faking friendship." In M. Mauthner, M. Birch, & T. Miller (Eds.), *Ethics in qualitative research* (pp. 107–122). London, England: Sage.

Ellis, C. (1986). *Fisher folk: Two communities in Chesapeake Bay.* Lexington: University Press of Kentucky.

Ellis, C. (2007). Telling secrets, revealing lies: Relational ethics in research with intimate others. *Qualitative Inquiry, 13,* 3–29.

Etherington, K. (2007). Ethical research in reflexive relationships. *Qualitative Inquiry, 13,* 599–616.

Finlay, L. (1998). Reflexivity: An essential component for all research? *British Journal of Occupational Therapy, 61,* 453–456.

Guillemin, M., & Gillam, L. (2004). Ethics, reflexivity and "ethically important moments" in research. *Qualitative Inquiry, 10,* 261–280.

Guillemin, M., & Gillam, L. (2006). *Telling moments: Everyday ethics in health care.* Melbourne, Victoria, Australia: IP Communications.

Guillemin, M., & Heggen, K. (2009). Rapport and respect: Negotiating ethical relations between researcher and participant. *Medicine, Healthcare and Philosophy, 12,* 291–299.

Hatcher, T., & Aragon, S. R. (2000). Rationale for and development of a standard on ethics and integrity for international HRD research and practice. *Human Resource Development International, 3*(2), 207–219.

Holstein, J. A., & Gubrium, J. F. (2003). Active interviewing. In J. F. Gubrium & J. A. Holstein (Eds.), *Postmodern interviewing* (pp. 67–81). London, England: Sage.

Irvine, H. (2003). Trust me! A personal account of confidentiality issues in an organisational research project. *Accounting Forum, 27,* 111.

Israel, M. (2004). Strictly confidential? Integrity and the disclosure of criminological and socio-legal research. *British Journal of Criminology, 44,* 715–740.

Israel, M., & Hay, I. (2006). *Research ethics for social scientists.* London, England: Sage.

Jonsen, A., & Toulmin, S. (1988). *The abuse of casuistry: A history of moral reasoning.* Berkeley: University of California Press.

Koch, T., & Harrington, A. (1998). Reconceptualizing rigour: The case for reflexivity. *Journal of Advanced Nursing, 28,* 882–890.

Kvale, S., & Brinkmann, S. (2009). *InterViews: Learning the craft of qualitative research interviewing.* London, England: Sage.

Mason, J. (1996). *Qualitative researching.* London, England: Sage.

McGraw, L., Zvonkovic, A., & Walker, A. (2000). Studying postmodern families: A feminist analysis of ethical tensions in work and family research. *Journal of Marriage and the Family, 62,* 68–77.

National Committee for Research Ethics in Science and Technology. (2008). *Guidelines for research ethics in science and technology.* Oslo, Norway: Norwegian Ministry of Education, Research and Church Affairs.

National Committee for Research Ethics in the Social Sciences and the Humanities. (2006). *Guidelines for the research ethics in the social sciences and the humanities.* Oslo, Norway: Norwegian Ministry of Education, Research and Church Affairs.

National Health and Medical Research Council, Australian Research Council, and Australian Vice-Chancellor's Committee. (2007). *National statement on ethical conduct in human research.* Canberra, ACT, Australia: Australian Government Publishing Service.

O'Neill, O. (2004). Accountability, trust and informed consent in medical practice and research. *Clinical Medicine, 4,* 269–276.

Parker, I. (2005). *Qualitative psychology: Introducing radical research.* Maidenhead, England: Open University Press.

Pascal, C. B. (2006). Issues on research integrity: A perspective. *Experimental Biology and Medicine, 231,* 1262–1263.

Patton, M. (2002). *Qualitative research and evaluation methods.* Thousand Oaks, CA: Sage.

Piper, H., & Simons, H. (2005). Ethical responsibility in social research. In B. Somekh & C. Lewin (Eds.), *Research methods in the social sciences* (pp. 56–63). London, England: Sage.

Simons, H., & Usher, R. (2000). Introduction: Ethics in the practice of research. In H. Simons & R. Usher (Eds.), *Situated ethics in educational research* (pp. 1–11). London, England: Routledge Falmer.

Tanggaard, L., & Brinkmann, S. (2010). Interviewet: Samtalen som forskningsmetode [The interview: Conversation as an interview method]. In S. Brinkmann & L. Tanggaard (Eds.), *Kvalitative metoder* [Qualitative methods] (pp. 29–54). Copenhagen, Denmark: Hans Reitzels Forlag.

U.S. Office for Human Research Protections. (2005). *Code of federal regulations, Title 45, Public Welfare, Part 46: Protection of human subjects.* Washington, DC: U.S. Department of Health and Human Services. Retrieved from http://www.hhs.gov/ohrp/humansubjects/guidance/45cfr46.html

Whittaker, E. (2005). Adjudicating entitlements: The emerging discourses of research ethics boards. *Health: An Interdisciplinary Journal for the Social Study of Health, Illness & Medicine, 9,* 513–535.

33

ASSESSING THE RISK OF BEING INTERVIEWED

◆ Anne Ryen

Concerns with ethics and protecting research participants from harm ironically represent risks of their own. Namely, to the extent that the pursuit of knowledge is the main goal of interview research, such efforts can hinder our understanding of more politically charged matters such as social justice. To better understand the inadvertent consequences of formalized research ethics (i.e., "ethicism" as embodied by the institutional review board [IRB] protocol), I consider the object of protecting research participants' privacy in the context of the professional–private divide in interview research as achieved through linguistic practices by orienting to how members make social life into a recognizable reality. This stands against the view that language is simply a passive medium used for transferring external meaning, a view that is often adopted by ethical regulators in their approach to privacy and risks. Challenging an "ethicist" approach to interview research, I will use data extracts to show how privacy and other "risks" are both negotiated in the micropolitical context of the interview itself and mediated by broader historical and cultural discourses. I argue that IRBs' contractual management of "harm," combined with a limited understanding of the nature of qualitative research, retards our scientific obligation as interview researchers to explore the many dimensions and qualities of social reality.

This chapter consists of two main, closely related sections. The first is a review of the new research ethics regime situated within the present transformation of universities. Despite variations, there is a rather unanimous agreement among qualitative researchers that the new ethics regime

Author's Note: Thanks to the Norwegian Programme for Development, Research and Education (NUFU) for financing the research program Governance, Gender and Scientific Quality (GGSQ), a collaboration of Mzumbe University, Tanzania, and University of Agder, Norway.

in different ways both complicates social science research and introduces new risks or threats. The second section illustrates how this in different ways interferes with qualitative interviewing and constructionist approaches to explore reality-constituting practices. The risk of hampering knowledge production is inextricably interwoven with disregarding the intersection of research ethics, epistemology, and methods. This has made some critics argue that institutional research ethics creeps (Haggerty, 2004) into many things other than research ethics.

◆ "Knowledge Factories" and the New Audit Culture

Yesteryear politicians concerned with higher education and universities have demanded that research be relevant and evidence based and feed immediate solutions to practical problems (Denzin, 2009b; Hammersley, 2009). Some critics argue that this process transforms universities into a neoliberal marketplace for academic capitalism. They become knowledge factories or production sites of a more material kind. This links up with Hammersley (2008, p. 4), who is concerned with the now more prominent place for the investment model of funding research, where investors expect a return that is responsive to external demands. In this model, research is no longer seen as a good thing in itself, and it follows from this that the researcher has a more marginal position in the say over what and how to research. Higher education has become a new global commercial growth industry (Kjeldstadli, 2010). Others have been more concerned with the bureaucratization that followed, with the expansion of university administrative compared with scientific staff to handle the systematic procedures for registering and measuring scientific members' activities and, more important, for regulating their research activities to ensure that they comply with the prescribed criteria. This is what Shore and Wright (1999) refer to as the "audit culture" and describe as "a product of a neo-governmentality, a function of which is a disciplinary mechanism that reforms and reduces institutional procedures, such as ethics reviews, into models of accountability, coercion and governance" (cited in Gotlib Conn, 2008, p. 500; Kushner, 2006). Thus, it is essential that we grasp the new ethical regime not as an independent occurrence but as part of a wider

transformation of universities that did not leave research communities unaffected. This transformation also has implications for qualitative inquiry in general and for trust in qualitative researchers' moral standard in particular (see the debate between Denzin, 2009b, and Fielding, 2010, on threats and gold standards).

THE NEW RESEARCH ETHICS REGIME

IRBs' main job is to protect research participants involved in federally funded studies (and their equivalent in other countries) from harm and unreasonable risks. This regulation requires that plans for any social research project be subject to approval by an ethics committee with authority to demand clarification and/or modification, to disapprove, or to potentially stop ongoing studies. If your application is disapproved, you cannot appeal (Economic and Social Research Council, 2005; Hammersley, 2008; Tinker & Coomber, 2004). More specifically, the panels demand that the researcher at the very outset write a rather detailed protocol accounting for all matters of relevance to the IRB, including showing the documents for recruiting interviewees, consent forms, and instruments to be used. They want to know if interviewees are ethically recruited and ethically treated, if questionnaires are phrased so that interviewees will understand them, and if questions, payments, compensations, and incentives are appropriate to participants (Speiglman & Spear, 2009, pp. 124–125).

The focus on universal principles has made social scientists warn against their hegemonic normative definition. As Rhonda Shaw (2010) puts it,

> Ethics typically refers to rules, maxim and principles that inform moral conduct and guide how we ought to act. In this view . . . moral agency and moral judgment are achieved by exercise of universal cognitive faculties that guide actions in a given situation. (p. 444)

It follows from this conceptualization of ethics that protecting research participants can be "outsourced" to an external control and monitoring system that presumably embodies such impeccable "universal cognitive faculties." This implies that the lone social scientist can no longer be trusted to independently assess his or her own ethical conduct. It also demonstrates "the basic assumptions inherent in universalist models such as that ethical issues can be sorted out by the start of a project and the either-or assumptions as with informed consent and harm" (Ryen, 2011, p. 422), just like bureaucratic work that can be finished before leaving the office.

The institutionalization of the new regime was implemented despite warnings from critics. According to Speiglman and Spear (2009), "the regulatory net was thrown wide" (p. 126), and they cite Israel and Hay (2006), who claim that "not surprisingly, an adversarial culture has emerged between researchers and regulators" (cited in Speiglman & Spear, 2009, p. 127). The opposition has also led to a number of reactions and initiatives, such as the first (2004) and fourth (2008) U.S. Qualitative Inquiry Congresses, which both put ethics on their agenda (International Center for Qualitative Inquiry, 2005, 2008). It is undeniably a paradox that a regime based on a biomedical model, with its heavy emphasis on factual evidence, is itself based on assumptions and anecdotal horror stories not fully supported by systematic evidence. As noted earlier, the empirical basis is missing (Atkinson, 2009). Classic incidences such as Stanley Milgram's (1963) obedience experiments or Laud Humphreys's *Tearoom Trade* (1975), from qualitative studies in the past decades (see Ryen, 2004, 2011, for more examples), do not qualify as empirical evidence to justify a systematic surveillance apparatus of qualitative researchers. According to John Johnson and David Altheide (2002), "ethics has . . . collapsed into discourses of institutional control" (p. 61) and deals with issues other than research ethics.

Jacqui Gabb (2010, p. 466) and others claim that the potential risk to participants in social science research is not comparable with that in biomedical sciences research and clinical trials. She cites Dingwall (2008), who suggests that "at most there is a potential for causing minor and reversible emotional distress or some measure of reputational damage" (Gabb, 2010, p. 466). This is reiterated by Hammersley (2009, p. 217), I. Shaw (2008), and Speiglman and Spear (2009, p. 126), who refer to social science as a "low-risk category" (Gotlib Conn, 2008, p. 504; see also Van den Hoonaard, 2001). That is, they become gatekeepers to the kind of research that gets approved and is favored by university administrations for reasons that may have little to do with ethics per se.

Malcolm M. Feeley (2007, cited in Speiglman & Spear, 2009, p. 129) claims that the boards have taken on the form and function of censorship boards, serving the universities rather than the researchers. This is in line with Patricia Adler and Peter Adler (2002), who claim that the former deception studies prompted the boards to privilege "the protection of the institutions sponsoring research (universities) from lawsuits over the informal loyalty between researchers and subjects" (p. 517; see also Christians, 2000). In the context of such observations that Speiglman and Spear (2009, p. 127) arrive at, the conclusion is that rather than promoting ethics, the primary function of IRBs seems to be institutional risk management.

Veered Amit (2000), for example, looks at the terms of censorship in terms of a mismatch between IRB demands and academic freedom. This is a serious threat to the very enterprise of social science research nurtured by the neoliberal turn, which especially undermines the methodological foundation of constructionist interview research. In addition, the procedures are expensive and time-consuming and cause delays and also much agony to interviewees. As Clifford G. Christians (2005) puts it, "This constricted environment no longer addresses adequately the complicated issues we face in studying the social world" (p. 148). I will look further into this argument later.

If social science interviewers can no longer be trusted to protect their interviewees, a brief comparison with another group of interviewers exempt from the IRB procedure will show that distrust toward social scientists is not rooted in any fact that they necessarily pose the greatest harm to their respondents or that they are inherently less ethical than other professional interviewers.

WHOSE INTERVIEWEES?

With the qualitative interview as the new technology of the self (Gubrium & Holstein, 2002, p. 6), the interview has also become the preferred method in journalism, an occupation driven by harsh market competition. This opens up a brief but interesting comparison of qualitative interviewers and journalists, who both ask questions and rely on field relations of some kind. The U.S. federal regulations' definition of research exempts certain interviews (e.g., oral history and journalistic interviews) and thus restricts the "vulnerability regime" to social science interviews only (see Bourne-Day & Lee-Treweek, 2008, p. 35). A few reports will illustrate this inconsistency (see Denzin, 2008, p. 116 [on emic vs. nomothetic studies], Footnote 16 [on journalist inquiries exempted from review]), though my point is rather to show the comparable low risk of research interviewees.

Responding to the Central Intelligence Agency's claim that stories from women in Afghanistan could make Europeans more positive toward the North Atlantic Treaty Organization's operations in the country, the journalist Anders Sømme (2010) points out that journalists can put their interview subjects at risk when revealing their identities and stories in oppressive regimes. Specifically, he refers to a report on interviews with female prisoners in Maimana (Afghanistan) giving away intimate details of forced marriages and rapes where relatives have been involved and which were sometimes the very reasons for their imprisonment. This might put the same women at risk as their oppressors could read the stories published online and retaliate against the women who disclosed such information about their tribe or family.

The journalist Ahmed Fawad Ashraf wrote an article in a newspaper under the heading "Besieged by Bloodhounds" ("Beleiret av blodhunder," 2011), where he describes his family's experiences with journalists when his sister Faiza was kidnapped (she called the police from the trunk of a car, but eventually her mobile's battery died). Unfortunately, the police could not rescue her in time and only managed to find her dead body in the snow 3 days later. Based on former experiences with young Pakistani girls reporting their family for forcing them into marriage, some journalists indicated that Faiza's family might have been involved. One of the two kidnappers, who actually had been observed when forcing her into the car at a bus stop, had long been fascinated by her, though she consistently had turned him down. Her brother, himself a journalist, raises two relevant issues. The first is ethical principles versus moral practice, and the second is sympathy or empathy with interviewees. It is a problem when editors protect their journalists by referring to principles rather than to the concrete choices journalists make when reporting a case. It is also a problem that sympathy becomes instrumental, as in cases when it is combined with angling for information, described as the "death knock" method. In this case, newspaper journalists responded by raising a critical debate on the squeeze between market pressure and moral

behavior (e.g., "Beleiret av blodhunder," 2011; "Da Faiza forsvant," 2011; "Death Knock," 2011; "Skjuler seg bak sjefen," 2011).

The African correspondent Aidan Hartley illustrates the impact of the wider context well in his book *The Zanzibar Chest* (2004), where he tells a story about traveling in a Sudanese village with a British TV cameraman after the crops had failed. Because of "donor fatigue," he says, "it had become harder to shock people in Europe and America," and he continues,

> Our guides ordered the kids to parade in front of us and display their swollen bellies and thin limbs. "I'm sorry," said the cameraman. "They're not thin enough." . . . The journalist had to get the thin ones. If he didn't, he would not be doing his job. He had been sent to find thin ones. He returned to the Africans and enunciated in a voice both load and slow. "NOT. THIN. ENOUGH!" (p. 221).

It is interesting to note that in this example written consent was never an issue.

Lesley Gotlib Conn (2008, p. 511) refers to this inconsistency when she compares journalists and social scientists based on her experiences as a qualitative interviewer and ethnographer. In the middle of her fieldwork, she came across a local freelance writer who arrived at her main field site to interview one of her informants for a popular local magazine. The journalist posed a series of critical questions, and the interview was later published as a cover story. "Before I could utter the words 'informed consent,'" she says, the journalist also showed a video of a young patient during a confidential clinical assessment. The contrasts are striking when she simultaneously compares this with the procedural exercise her local research ethics panel made her acquiesce to (involving the same informant). Hammersley (2009, p. 222, Footnote 15) reports that when the anthropologist Nancy Scheper-Hughes had problems with ethical regulation for her "undercover ethnography" of illegal trafficking of human organs, she successfully arranged to be treated as if she were a member of the school of journalism in her university (see Scheper-Hughes, 2004, pp. 44–45).

It is well-known that journalism faces problems in dealing with ethical regulations (Dash, 2007), but incidences from journalistic interviews such as the ones above interestingly do not give rise to any calls for external control (they have their own ethical codes[1]) irrespective of any harm they might cause informed as well as uninformed interviewees.

These stories are good for reflections on the "petty tyranny" that Malcolm Feeley (2007, p. 765, cited in Speiglman & Spear, 2009, p. 129) argues researchers now are subjected to by university ethics committees, which are rather totalitarian versions of the IRBs. Two interrelated issues are of particular interest in this debate. The first refers to the dilemma that the new ethical regime reflects a lack of understanding of qualitative inquiry, with grave consequences for qualitative interviewing. Second, the new regulations may themselves impede ethical research (Haimes, 2002; Hammersley, 2009; Ryen, 2011). There is a close link between the two.

It will be useful to look into the more nuanced aspect of the discord. First, the rather univocal protest against the regime gets more disintegrated when we introduce epistemology. Second, to operate, a regime needs supporters. A brief look into the supporters' and the critics' camps introduces nuances that account for some of the complexity of the research ethics dispute.

◆ Ethicism: Among Ethical Regulators and Ethical Enthusiasts

The demands and pervasiveness of the ethical regulatory regime have prompted a massive response from social scientists, such as that reflected in *The Handbook of Social Research Ethics* (Mertens & Ginsberg, 2009),[2] as well as textbook chapters, journal articles, or special journal issues (for a number of references to categories and topics, see Ryen, 2008b). These are important not only in documenting ethical dilemmas but also to voice resistance to the new regime. A few also cast a critical eye on the critics and the enthusiasts.

In his well-known article "Against the Ethicists: On the Evils of Ethical Regulation," Martyn Hammersley (2009) accurately sums up the general criticism that

given that there is such a lack of consensus within the research community, how can ethics committees claim the expertise required to legislate on what is and is not acceptable? There is insufficient

common ground to do this with any legitimate authority. (p. 214)

He also introduces concepts whereby he differentiates between the two sides in the current debate.

His concept of "ethicism" refers to an old Greek criticism of the Stoics' dogmatic claims to knowledge. Good and bad are complex phenomena because "rather, what is good or bad depends upon people and circumstances" (Hammersley, 2009, p. 211). This becomes an argument against recent forms of ethicism, in which he identifies two, somewhat overlapping groups, (1) ethical enthusiasts and (2) ethical regulators supporting the new regulatory system. The first group refers to "people who give conventionally defined ethical issues too much priority, and/or interpret them in overly simple ways" (Hammersley, 2009, p. 211). This group "treats ethicality as the pre-eminent requirement, demanding that researchers exemplify ethical ideals. In other words, they are required to meet the *highest* ethical standards (on some interpretation)" (Hammersley, 2009, p. 213). He illustrates this with the old argument that informants should control interview data and researchers should return them to the informants to be corrected and altered.

The regulator group wrongly assumes that decisions are guided by principles rather than decision making as situated. They also ignore that there may be disagreement about the recommended solution to a dilemma and that ethics cannot be separated from other decisions being made through a research process, including methodological ones. Hammersley (2009) warns against ethical enthusiasm or moralism encompassing a belief "that we cannot be 'too ethical'" (p. 219). He also argues that this

moralism involves exaggerating the importance of abstract ethical principles as against the goal of producing good quality research findings, and as against what is required in order to make reasonable judgments about what can and should be done in particular contexts. (Hammersley, 2009, p. 219)

When ethics committees intervene, "they threaten the future of social research as a worthwhile enterprise" (Hammersley, 2009, p. 221).

---

[1]See, for example, The Norwegian Press Association's *Code of Ethics of the Norwegian Press* (2011) and *Rights and Duties of the Editor* (2011). See also the newspaper articles "Beleiret av blodhunder" (2011), "Death Knock" (2011), and "Skjuler seg bak sjefen" (2011).

[2]This discussion was adapted from the introductory section in Ryen (2008b, p. 449).

Social scientists agree with his general conclusion, but less so with the linkages to the controversy over epistemology or the dispute over "an intellectual crisis." Importantly, the influence of postmodernism is more moderate in Europe than in the United States. On this ground, we may refer to the more general difference in epistemology across the ocean as "the Atlantic divide." This warns us against assuming that social scientists easily fit the same box.

◆ Contemporary Controversies

Despite fervent contributions, there is a somewhat blurred line of demarcation between some ethical enthusiasts and ethical regulators, reflecting an overall lack of consensus on the very basic question "What is research all about?" The controversy over ethicism in qualitative inquiry runs deeper than research ethics. It also reflects the dispute between proponents of knowledge production and advocates of social justice. There is nothing peculiar about this dispute; it simply reflects that research ethics, epistemology, and methodology are closely interconnected (Ryen, 2004, 2008b).

APOCALYPSE AND CRISES

In his controversial book *Questioning Qualitative Inquiry*, Hammersley (2008) states, "My starting point is that qualitative research is currently facing a crisis" (p. 1). His worry is that what he refers to as an intellectual crisis will nurture the material crisis, with funds drying up, and that the direction toward the social engineering model "is a particular problem for much qualitative work" (p. 6), but "the problems are deeper than this external threat"[3] (p. 1). This last remark refers to the *Handbook of Qualitative Research* and what he refers to as (U.S.) "avant-garde

qualitative inquiry" with a "love, care and hope" approach very deviant from the scientific ideal (p. 134; also propounded in Denzin, 2009c, conceptualizing research in terms of social justice). Hammersley's criticism triggered a rather tense dialogue with, or rather rebuttal from, Denzin.

In his one-act play "Apocalypse Now: Overcoming Resistances to Qualitative Inquiry," Denzin (2009a) makes Hammersley his main target, who gives voice to the fictional first remark in Act 1: "We need a functional, scientific approach to social science" (p. 333; cited from Hammersley, 2008, p. 3).[4] In his book, Hammersley (2008) had cited from Woody Allen's "If the impressionists had been dentists" to illustrate the intellectual crisis.[5] This provocative comment about the "artistic" interpretation of qualitative inquiry (p. 7) reflects his argument that research and art are separate activities. More precisely, he does not rule out artistic and literary forms but argues that "their use should be subordinated to the distinct purpose of research" (p. 143). However, both discussants criticize the IRBs.

Denzin had made Paul Atkinson and Sara Delamont appear as silent voices in his play. They wrote their response as a counternarrative[6] in which they, in line with their prior warning (Atkinson & Delamont, 2006), conclude that "there's really no justification for any talk of apocalypse or of crisis" (Atkinson & Delamont, 2010, p. 14). After all, they say, European social scientists are preoccupied with "the real stuff of research" (Atkinson & Delamont, 2010, p. 15; Euroqual, 2006–2010), and "these debates are all taking place in another reality . . . , when there's a much more interesting world *out there*" (Atkinson & Delamont, 2010, p. 15).

This internal epistemological controversy among qualitative researchers provides a context for a closer examination of the intersection of research ethics and epistemology in interview research, as discussed below.

---

[3]The external pressure to demonstrate practical value.

[4]Among the other voiced actors, we find Herbert Blumer, Dorothy Smith, Jan Morse, Patti and Peter Adler, Art Bochner, Carolyn Ellis, and Yvonne Lincoln, apart from Norman K. Denzin himself and some others.

[5]In Van Gogh's imaginary letter to his brother Theo, he complains about Mrs. Sol Schwimmer, who is suing him claiming that his artistic bridge does not fit her mouth and makes it impossible for her to chew. "I find it beautiful. . . . What do I care whether she can chew or not," Van Gogh comments (Hammersley, 2008, p. 2).

[6]Atkinson and Delamont (2010) appeared as silent characters in Denzin's play, hence their counternarrative "Can the Silent Speak? A Dialogue for Two Unvoiced Actors" (p. 11). They refer to the experiences from the European Science Foundation's *Euroqual* program, where steering committee members organized international qualitative method workshops in a number of European countries. These showed the diversity of different national research traditions in qualitative inquiry.

THE AUDIT PARADOX AND OTHER PARADOXES

The auditing model interferes with both interview practice and our efforts to produce new knowledge, and we see the resonance of this model across the Western research communities. In her comments, Jacqui Gabb (2010) refers to Furedi and Bristow (2008), who quite rightly complain about the "institutional cultures of risk assessment and wider cultural moves towards a 'risk averse' society" (p. 466). This takes us to the more specific implications for nonpositivist social science and interview research practice.

In their review of the history and the role of (the more aggressive) U.S. IRBs, Speiglman and Spear (2009) argue that the extensive mandatory documentations that the review panels ask for illustrate the administrative and bureaucratic burden imposed on social scientists "and, in turn, on IRB members" (p. 125). In an output-based production system, this practical side takes time away from doing research. It is the same burden that has prompted researchers to share their auto-experiences with the system, such as Monica Leisley (2008), who invites readers into the many quandaries she faced in her qualitative project in the United States on domestic violence (see also I. Shaw, 2008), and Lesley Gotlib Conn (2008), with the Canadian equivalent, the research ethics boards, in her anthropological fieldwork practice in a clinical setting. These are telling stories. They share close resemblances with the Economic and Social Research Council's Framework for Research Ethics in the United Kingdom (with some changes from their 2005 framework). We should not downplay this burden because experiences tell us that bureaucracy is hard to resist. Bureaucratic measures become organizational investments, with their own defenders.

Other risks associated with the new practice are misallocations of resources (Speiglman & Spear, 2009, p. 127), toward more panel-friendly topics and away from methods and groups that could provide us with important knowledge but with small chance of getting approval from ethics committees (Hammersley, 2009, p. 219). Case studies (Gabb, 2010, p. 468), covert observation, and innovative methods work as examples (Hammersley, 2009), all rather deviant from the biomedical tradition. To see certain groups as particularly problematic rests on an assumption of conflicting field relations. This rules out "situational co-memberships" (Erickson &

Shultz, 1982) or feminist advocacy of participating and equalizing research relations (Bourne-Day & Lee-Treweek, 2008, p. 55; Finch, 1984, on interviewing female asylum seekers). This has made qualitative inquirers such as Denzin (1997) and Murphy and Dingwall (2007) criticize the biomedical image of the standard vulnerable research subject. This image singles out not only whole categories as systematic, lacking power, and unable to advocate for themselves, such as the mentally ill, older persons (Bourne-Day & Lee-Treweek, 2008, p. 35), and children, but even a whole discipline, social science. In other words, "the contemporary governance of research ethics may itself actively participate in constituting qualitative research as a vulnerable field" (Ryen, 2011, p. 432).

Therefore,

what we have here is the audit paradox: auditing processes do not capture the phenomena they claim to be auditing, but only the capacity of people to play the role of being audited. The strategic skills needed to fill in a form do not necessarily overlap with those needed for ethical reflections. (Power, 1997, cited in Hammersley, 2009, p. 216)

When critics refer to the panels' either-or approach to research ethics in qualitative research (Ryen, 2011), ethical enthusiasts claim that these are ethical and methodological reflections researchers will follow irrespective of the new regulations. The problem is that ethical enthusiasts ignore the contextual reflexivity and the emergent processes of much qualitative empirical research (Murphy & Dingwall, 2007) and thereby ignore the complexity of research ethics. This distorted view of qualitative research in turn provides ethical regulators their legitimate authority to intervene in social science. Of course, as Christians (2005) and Pritchard (2002) argue, the problem is augmented by the fact that since IRB panels are dominated by medical and behavioral scientists, most panel members do not understand interpretive, qualitative proposals to begin with. Hammersley (2009) points to another sinister aspect:

The inner dynamic of the regulatory process—the attempt to carry out an impossible task—is likely to multiply the level and depth of surveillance, for example the extent and frequency of reporting. In other words, ethical regulation will feed on its own failure. (p. 218)

That is, the ethical regime becomes a self-perpetuating and endless system of surveillance. Hammersley (2009) concludes that

> the consequences . . . are likely to worsen the quality of research, and probably also the quality of the ethical reflection involved in it. Doing research is difficult enough at the best of times, and if the obstacles are increased then it will become even harder to do well. (p. 219)

Let us now look into interview practice. In particular, in the following section, I will show how ethnographic interviewing mediates the processes of perception and interpretation in long-lasting relations. I argue that the ability of ethnographers to negotiate these relationships with their research participants restores trust in the ethnographic interviewer as a competent and moral research practitioner.

◆ Research Ethics, Constitutive Practice, and Context

Despite the new ethics regime, "constructionism has become an intellectual movement whose empirical insights are widely recognized" (Gubrium & Holstein, 2008, p. 3). For constructionists, the interview is itself "a site of, and occasion for, producing knowledge itself" (Holstein & Gubrium, 2003, p. 3) rather than a medium for representing "true" experiences (Karo-Ljungberg, 2008, p. 431). According to Holstein and Gubrium (2004), constructionism allows us to explore how participants actively and collaboratively constitute social situations as private or public, risky or harmful, by focusing on their sequential talk-in-interaction. They also argue that we need to bring in the wider cultural and sociohistorical context to our analyses because the two "are always reflexively at play" (p. 303) and insist that we

> look at how context actually manifests its presence— how it works—in lived experience. In our view, should qualitative analysts call upon context to explain social action, they must consider social context as it is relevant to the experience of the social participants under consideration. (p. 299)

This makes context into an interpretive resource where we need to look for linkages between context and social action and how participants actually do bring context into their interaction or to "work . . . across social settings to make visible how alternative forms of meaning-making are accomplished" (p. 304) to see patterns where "distinct contexts come into play in particular contexts" (p. 305).

By sharing ethnographic experiences with our informants, we slowly come to see how participants collaboratively, in one way or another, make more distant aspects such as gender, age, ethnicity, or the regional sociopolitical history relevant in local situations. In time, such shared experiences also make us notice the very situations they are brought into. This invites us to reflect on the fine nuances across situations and displays talk and even silence as social actions. By rejecting these situation-specific approaches to knowledge production, ethical regulators have come to resemble the religious leaders who once rejected those whose knowledge challenged the dogma of the church.[7]

The following empirical section draws on my ethnographic study on Asian businesses in East Africa where the combination of ethnography, interviews, and meetings in transnational spaces (Stake & Rizvi, 2008, p. 525) across a number of years show how the research process, and research ethics by extension, is mediated through a process of perception and interpretation. Breakdowns in communication, potential violations of privacy, sexual flirtation, and ethnicity represent classic IRB worries, so let us take a closer look at how these unfolded in the actual practice of my ethnographic research.

"RUPTURES OF COMMUNICATION": ERUPTIONS IN THE FIELD

Rapport is a desired virtue as well as a source of constant worry because it invites dilemmas when one gets close to others in the research field (Ryen, 2004, 2011; Sabar, 2008; Taylor, 2010). Still, it is crucial for access to data that may lead us to local knowledge, which is a prerequisite for handling situationally emergent risks.

In the context of research ethics, some ethnographers worry about intrusions (asking too much),

---

[7]Just as with Galileo and the controversy over heliocentrism, and Socrates some centuries before Galileo.

some about leaving the field unexplored (asking too little), some about the dos and don'ts of caring, as with the feminist "ethic of care model" (Gilligan, 1983; Nodding, 1984; Porter, 1999); and finally there are those with reservations about the cathartic effect and the benefits of the raised self-consciousness created through close relations (Murphy & Dingwall, 2001, p. 340). What these various positions have in common is a tendency, or a willingness, to see ethics as something that is ultimately situated in time, place, and practice. Indeed, in the context of ethnographic research, so-called ethical dilemmas become a recurring and integral component of the research process. For example, Paul Rabinow, in his classic *Reflections on Fieldwork in Morocco* (1977), challenges the old insider–outsider view by seeing his informant as a mediator somewhere in between an insider–outsider, with no final "there." In particular, he suggests that the informant actively constructs the field rather than just telling it "as it is." In his words, the anthropologist is

> an outsider who is by definition external to his usual life-world. . . . This externality, however, is a moving ratio. It is external both for the anthropologist (it is not his own life-world) and for the informants, who gradually learn to inform. . . . It is intersubjective, between subjects. (pp. 153–154)

Rabinow argues that breakdowns or "interruptions and eruptions" (p. 154) are in fact essential in fieldwork. "Ruptures of communication" become core aspects or turning points because they start new cycles from which a new depth can develop in the communication and more can be taken for granted and shared. As Rabinow puts it, "The subjects involved do not share a common set of assumptions, experiences and traditions. . . . It is the dialectic between these poles, ever repeated, never quite the same, which constitutes fieldwork" (p. 155). I do not argue against kindness but in favor of courage to allow for a multiplicity of emotions. Conflicts or tensions are important to "the moving ratio" we search; they demand that analysts explore ruptures, the situations they are brought into, and how participants make them relevant. It is this that makes conflicts interesting data that invite us into spaces otherwise difficult to access.

As most ethnographers, I too get multiple versions of stories. A positivist would worry about the mismatch between what is told and the "truth," whereas a constructivist would explore the competing narratives as viable realities in their own right. Sometimes asking to clarify provokes my informant (yes, I do ask when it comes to certain numbers such as salaries, budgets, or shares of ownership because I do find constitutive processes leading to alternative versions interesting rather than "true"). By his "I have given you the answer to that before" or "You have asked me that twice," he rejects my delicate initiatives, but "being provoked" is also emergent and invites us to see how the more distant context is made relevant in particular contexts. Extract 33.1 (Ryen, 2008c, p. 85, Extract 1) is taken from an interview on fringe benefits that Mahid's (M) company offers its employees. Paula, one of his employees, had been very particular in telling me that she was the one who had organized the company house downtown, where some of his female employees had moved in. Later, he told me that it was he who did it (A = Anne):

Extract 33.1

1. A: and she was here in September.
2. M: yeah. When she left, it happened after that.
3. A: She said she did it. Why does she say she did it, you say you did it?
4. M: Ok, she did it, all right? Are you happy? (Uganda, 2004)

Prior to this interview, I had talked to Paula, who was next in command and who had told me about how she had got hold of this company house where she lived. Mahid had also told me about the house, but their versions did not match. The extract shows the start of what slowly escalated into a typical eruption. Mahid heard my question in Line 3, where I make the discrepancy between their versions explicit, as a provocation that prompted his recipient-designed, rather ironic and rejecting response in Line 4. Working it up from the sequential talk, both participants constitute their communication into a disagreement of some kind, though at the time I was unaware of any external reasons why exploring this issue would be such a delicate task.

When I later also asked about the total monthly value of employee benefits, there was a mismatch when the sum was compared with the total of the separate benefits. My estimation showed that this employee was given favorable treatment and exposed Mahid's miscalculations. My interest was not so much with the compensation level, since Paula held a high position, as with the boss and owner underestimating the value. This eventually left me with a feeling of intruding into unclear territory. My observations also showed that she had access to benefits that Mahid claimed she did not have, such as enjoying the company car for private use after work hours. He got very upset when I contradicted him. It is hard to tell if I got too close to the gray areas of economics or other kinds.

However, other "Goffmanian observations" indicated that Paula found my presence complicated and unclear despite my explanations about the study, and she constantly expanded her territorial space, in which my informant was included. Whenever she saw Mahid and me working, she would come over and sit down, and however awkwardly, she would first walk over to his side of the table to stroke his arm even if it were the opposite side of her own seat. After all, she had negotiated a rather close relationship with her boss, facilitated by mundane practices such as meeting over a cigarette for breaks (they were the only smokers), and I noticed that my informant would bring her an ashtray (counter to rank) before they would sit down, talking in low voices, an acknowledgment of her favored position (he would often shout at a low-rank personnel).

This does tell us that they enacted their relationship as smooth and that my presence intervened into their rhythm. They later coordinated their response to me by declaring his version the official one (positivists' favorite). This shows interviews as more than simple information gathering. As Carolyn Baker (2002) puts it, "No questions are neutral in respect to the way it characterizes the person being interviewed" (p. 785); this assertion can be applied, for example, to how I came to describe Mahid, the boss, through my interview questions and my assumptions about what he should have known regarding the allocation of employee benefits. As a whole, Baker suggests that identity and related work are products of both the questioning as well as the answering. In other words, both accounts and actions are induced through the social interaction rather than being simply "out there" (Atkinson & Coffee, 2002, p. 811).

I have accompanied Mahid across numerous meetings with people of different ages, sexes, and ethnicities. Some experiences have been very pleasant, others rather tense; and at times, Mahid has treated me in a rather hostile manner during and after such meetings,

which in time I came to see as methodologically interesting, as when we visited Nargas, a young Asian woman who was leaving the region the next morning. She already had two male visitors, and I noticed that she refrained from offering me a drink from the table next to where I was standing, and so did Mahid. Not until Nargas and Mahid had left the room did one of the two visitors pour me a drink. Her housemaid, a grown-up, local woman, came over to me when we left and apologized for the treatment. Mahid never talked to me during the visit, and when alone with him again in the car, I awaited his accusation, a phenomenon that interestingly used to follow such incidents involving deviations from events where one person has an obligation to another, as in the case of a host (Mahid) and his companion (I).

Sacks claims that we are very much aware of the moral implication of utterances (Silverman, 1998, p. 9) and that events are used to inform us about what is appropriate for us to do next. Sacks also argues that "we can be held responsible not only for our descriptions, but also for the *inferences* that can be drawn from them, that is, as to what kind of person who could say such a thing about themselves or others" (p. 16). I did not have to wait long before I heard him mutter, "What kind of woman are you who is drinking whisky!"—which I as an ethnographer came to see as a most interesting comment. Well aware of the gendered expectations, I never touched the whisky, but his description did not deal with such facts. Rather, I heard his whisky argument as recognizing that he would be held responsible for the inferences drawn from disregarding my presence at Nargas's house. Telling me that men like him do not go with whisky-drinking women like me thus becomes a moral account and a product of gender at play in our local talk-in-interaction. Ruptures such as these invite us to explore how participants make context into an interpretive resource and make us see how they accomplish alternative forms of meaning making, as in private or public. This is knowledge production in action, and it teaches us of the nuances in accomplishing local social events as, for example, public or private, which is vital to moral research practice.

First, this shows that characteristics such as "researcher" or "interviewer" are dynamically and interactionally constructed, negotiated, and renegotiated in the field. Second, it also shows the emergent and situational controversies in the field, where universal guidance by some kind of standard procedures separate from the interaction itself will not work. Rather, working across contexts allows us to explore such frictions and eruptions rather than worry about trappings (for references to such claims, see Taylor, 2010, p. 17). It also enables us to notice when situations escalate into less harmless situations and, in a glimpse of a second, prepares us to handle such actions in, it is hoped, morally acceptable ways. Third, they show the situationally embedded nature of research ethics.

FIELD RELATIONS: PRIVATE AND PUBLIC

In "the interview society" (Atkinson & Silverman, 1997), probing the lives of others through a question-and-answer format has become ubiquitous; "interviewing of all kinds mediates contemporary life" (Gubrium & Holstein, 2002, p. 9); it is an omnipresent activity. However, in modern societies, we also value privacy (Bourne-Day & Lee-Treweek, 2008, p. 56), or "the right to be left alone" (Whittaker, 1999, cited in Bourne-Day & Lee-Treweek, 2008, p. 57). Privacy is complex, as shown by Hookway (2008) when he argues that blogs are public, not private, despite a lack of consensus among social scientists (p. 105); by Mellick and Fleming (2010) when they discuss disclosure in autobiographical research; by Carolyn Ellis (2009), who writes of the "complex decisions requiring integrating our moral positions with society's call for scholarship" (p. 3); or by Mukherjee (2008, p. 84) when he discusses Allen's (1999) different types of privacy.

In their chapter "Access, a Zone of Comprehension, and Intrusion," Robert Stake and Brinda Jegatheesan (2008, p. 1) are worried that researchers may get too close or violate personal privacy in their quest for knowledge.

When we reduce interpersonal distance comprehension can be counted on to go up. . . . But at some point, with some people, with some topics and in some situations, we get too close. We intrude. We slip into that person's privacy. . . . The points that bound these zones are not points at all. They are shadings, passages. . . . [W]e need to rely on ourselves to back out. (pp. 7–8)

They are correct when they say that general ethical principles cannot guide practice and no map can help us identify "shadings." Such maps do not exist. Stake and Jegatheesan also direct our attention to the contextual, the personal, and the situational nature of privacy. As they put it, "Privacy is not defined only by the content of the disclosure, but also in terms of audiences and circumstances involved" (p. 2), and "cultures differ" (p. 3) on what they consider private and public.

By using Harvey Sacks's membership categorization device, which consists of "a collection of categories (. . . male, female = gender) and some rules about how to apply these categories," also referred to as "rules of application" (Silverman, 2006, p. 183), we can look into the dynamic nature of "private talk" in the context of ethnographic field relations. Whereas Extract 33.1, in the previous section, showed classic interview talk, the following extracts show how participants intersect interview talk with other regular talk and thereby accomplish an array of paired relations beyond that of interviewer–interviewee. This is what good rapport is all about (Ryen, 2008c).

Once in a while when Mahid (a fictional name I assign to most of my informants) was exhausted and burned out, he would ask me, "What will you do if I die?" Extract 33.2 shows our communication after his question (Ryen, 2009, p. 234, Extract 6):

Extract 33.2

1. A: I will not even know when you're gone . . .
2. M: Someone will contact you after 1–3 months and let you know.
3.   What will you do?
4. A: I go to your grave, sit down with my tape recorder and play it over again. We'll have some looong,
5.   good talks, and maybe a few conflicts, but we'll sort them out.
6. M: Laughing (Mobile communication, December 19, 2004)

In my first response (Line 1), I reject Mahid's question, or rather, I hear it as a "fragile story," in Sacks's words (Silverman, 1998, p. 92), but he is not easily distracted. He insists that I relate to his question (Lines 2 and 3), and I do, but by a short narrative with bits and pieces from our joint stock of experiences. I hear his laughter in Line 6 as accepting my narrative. Usually, one cannot legitimately reject a personal statement about bad health, but Mahid had asked me this question on several occasions to a point that this time I came to hear it as deprived of any substance. In a second, other experiences came to my mind, as when he told me that he had cancer but could not properly respond to my question on what kind of cancer he suffered from (he simply said, "It is all over"). Or the fact that his eyes were still working despite his previous claims that he would go blind "within a year." First, this excerpt shows that relations are actively constituted, that experiences across contexts feed into how we come to hear whatever we hear, and that time and settings constitute the processes in which we get informed and receive knowledge. In Mahid's case, eventually I came to identify and differentiate among the nuances in his utterances about his bad health. As situations and contexts change, they call for different responses, as shown in Extract 33.3 (Ryen, 2009, p. 233, Extract 3):

Extract 33.3

1. M: I was so depressed this morning. You were not here when I needed you the most.

2. A: I am so sorry.

3. M: I tried calling you again and again, and I must have sent you 6 sms.[8]

Here, in the middle of an even tougher period, Mahid's mood has changed (Line 1) from what it was in Extract 33.2. I come to hear his utterance here as quite different from that in the previous extract. Importantly, I do not hear his statement ("I tried calling you again and again, and I must have sent you 6 sms") as referring to an external, concrete, or "true" reality but as a brief narrative craving for contact (he may or may not have called me or sent me a text message as there were no missed calls or new text messages in my mobile). Initially, I was bewildered when he claimed that he had tried to contact me without success and even numbered his attempts. Not until more experiences unfolded did I come to hear his responses as narratives in unfolding power relations.

Relationships (between friends or researchers) are not unproblematic or without risks. In this case, we see participants negotiating over hierarchical relations and over caring obligations, a classic and complex gendered territory loaded with power. However, our relationship eventually allowed us to put privacy and power on the agenda, by which we reinforced our paired relationship as friend–friend, away from that of patient–councilor. On the other hand, there are stories Mahid has tried to tell me, but I have tried not to listen to them. Mahid had found it arrogant

and provocative that I could freely compartmentalize his life into relevant and irrelevant, a pattern of interaction that once made him verbally abusive to me. I later learned to listen also to stories not relating to my study, often crossing the passages Stake and Jegatheesan (2008) warn us against.

As challenging as these encounters were for me to navigate in real time and place, I find it remarkable that ethics panels far away from my research site (both geographically and culturally) think that they would know in advance how to handle such complex field relations better than the social scientist.

WHOSE RISKS? FLIRTATIONS

Gender is a classic topic closely associated with both care and power. When we introduce emotions, risk assumptions are more than lurking in the background.

As suggested throughout this chapter, field relations are dynamic, and lighthearted flirtation is one out of a wide arsenal of communicative devices to foster good relations. In Extract 33.4, Rajesh (R) and I are leaving my car to go inside to prepare dinner (Ryen, 2008a, p. 154, Extract 12):

Extract 33.4

1. A: would you accept me if I came to your office asking?

2. R: why not? (a bit aggressive). Would I accept you (warm)?

3. A: as an interviewer

4. R: no, you know, I don't, if you came to my office and said you wanted to interview me, I'd say Why? (aggressive)

5. Don't you know enough of me? (warm) (both laughing)

6. R: do you want to stand outside and do, if you want to do the talking outside?

7. A: eh, I think we should go inside. I need to make the dough for the rolls.

8. R: oh ok.

This flirt illustrates how emotion work works to make relations smooth. This is an activity traditionally associated with the risk of going private and one where positivists would accentuate the problem, allowing it to get out of hand and escalate.

---

[8]This is an abbreviation in my language for text messages. When Mahid communicates with me, he alternates between "sms" and "txt-msg."

Constructionists, however, would analyze the flirt to get the nuanced details of these processes. I insist that such knowledge also works to protect the (female) interviewer, because you learn to recognize the occasions and devices put into play to signal that a situation is escalating or getting out of control. In Extract 33.4, I am asking about interviewing in East Africa (Line 1), which initiates Rajesh's flirting response in Line 2. I compliment him in Line 3 with slow (not seen) precision. He follows up in a playful way (very professional in Line 4), turning sweet and emotional in Line 5. His abruption in Line 6 hardly makes sense unless we know the wider context.

The communication takes place while we are leaving my car with the bags from the local shopping mall when Rajesh is visiting my family. Interestingly, in Line 6 he violates the prior invitation to flirt as I hear it. I can see that he finds the weather chilly and rather elegantly invites us to go inside. I agree in Line 7 by referring to the dough, a rather unromantic entity. Within seconds, we transcend from a flirting relation into a mundane, practical one. The myth is busted. Flirt is collaboratively accomplished and socially enacted. This makes us see the performative qualities of talk as social actions, as opposed to the classic, rather narrow, truth-seeking version. In the car, Rajesh told me that I had deprived him of his masculinity by making him my passenger, and standing outside with shopping bags in the chilly autumn is different from romance in the bar or by the pool. This makes flirt a highly elastic, emergent activity that participants in different ways accomplish or not. We need to recognize flirt as a shared experience, how participants do flirting as well as elegantly end it and how the external contexts are being put into play in the local interpretive, ongoing work. This challenges the IRB's concerns regarding "vulnerability" of research participants and the researchers themselves by showing how we come to see, to negotiate, and to protect ourselves in muddy waters. Let us take this one step further into the intersection of sex and color.

THE COLLECTIVE OF PRIVATE MEMORIES: THE ETHNOSEXUAL FRONTIER IN THE BAR

Doing being man–woman, though often negotiated in dual, rather private communication, may be firmly based in discourses of color and gender. Extract 33.5 presents an evening bar site extract (in Ryen, 2008c, p. 95, Extract 9):

Extract 33.5

1. M: What do you want to drink?
2. A: (3.0)
3. M: can you get your bloody head to work (aggressive)
4. A: A Safari and a Sprite, thanks.
   (I turn away, but can hear him talking nicely to the African bar man. Mahid is coming over.)
5. A: What did I hear you say? (with resentment)
6. M: What do you mean? (polite)
7. A: If I ever again hear you address me that way, I will simply leave! Not even once will I hear that
8. again! (very determined)
9. M: I don't understand (1.0) what are you talking about (mild, I hear an apology)

We are the first customers and alone with the young African barman. Mahid walks over to the desk; they are chatting. He calls over to me (Line 1), and before I have given my order (3 seconds), I hear what I see as an aggressive description of me by his "can you get your bloody head to work" (Line 3). When he is back, I sanction his rude remark (Line 5) and make sure he gets my point (Lines 7 and 8). He seems puzzled (Lines 6 and 9). This extract also vividly displays the impact of audiences.

The performance takes place at a masculine Kenyan scene, the bar area, and I saw the performance as embedded in the legacy of the old British complex colonial, racial, and gendered rank system, mediating the contextual meaning of my whiteness. In this area, Mahid runs two parallel communications, one with the black barman and one with me, here a representative of the old regime. A closer look shows that Mahid with his rude remark in Line 3 does not primarily address me as I hear it (supported by his Lines 6 and 9). Rather, he is bonding with the black man over a colonizer (in East Africa I am primarily white and Western). That would make his comment a performance for his black audience (Line 3; the 3 seconds is an acceptable delay in this cultural context), which accounts for his puzzlement when he is back at our table. His responses in Lines 6 and 9 then become markers of transitions from one audience to another. Other observations also indicate that old colonial encounters are brought into local situations in certain constellations. This makes the intersectionality of gender and ethnicity into interpretive resources participants in different ways bring into play. The incident also reminds us that talk is action and that both memory and experience are social actions and a result of cultural categories that shape what is thinkable and tellable, as Atkinson and Coffee (2002, p. 810) describe it, and doable. This makes memory not a private issue but a collective cultural phenomenon.

Interestingly, Asian women have told me they have heard their ethnic men put down white women in the presence of other ethnic companions, but as always, context and audiences matter. One evening, Mahid and I accepted an invitation to join in a cookout with some other Asian businessmen (no other women) in one of their factory buildings. Listening to our sequential talk-in-interaction, I noticed the finely grained nuances that marked a transition to a more privately oriented focus by a question relating to my body. As I saw it, this called for my indirect effort to renegotiate the meeting into a relaxed dinner event. Mahid later told me that the men had hoped for an orgy but he had signaled to them that I would never allow it. Analysts do not simply replicate an informant's version, which here allocates him or her a place in the center as a mediator between "them" and "the prey," both provider and protector. Our interest, however, is in exploring the participants' methods in situ for accomplishing this occurrence and my trust in Mahid to follow him to such risky territory (I do trust him).

These incidents rightly add to the wide stock of our shared experiences based on Mahid's generosity in accepting my presence, which allows for ethnographic, cultural, and sociohistorical sensibilities. For this purpose, it is essential that we also allow eruptions and conflicts to emerge without allowing undue risk assessments to interfere with the knowledge production. This is no mechanical process that justifies a simplified either-or perception of research ethics and harm in research practice.

◆ Conclusions: Trust and Distrust as Epistemological Outcomes

Trust is too important to be left to regulators totally external to our social science models and methods. Based on Rabinow (1977), who reminded us of the problematic of the insider–outsider dichotomy, there is no argument for insisting on the researcher as the divine manager or even arbiter of truth. However, there are very good reasons to claim that the researcher should be at least as good as the regulators, as we know them by now, in finding morally acceptable solutions to particular dilemmas emerging in his or her study. This would also relieve us of the bureaucratic burden accompanying the present research ethics regime and the unhealthy power relations that come with it. What we do know and can document is that loyalty toward IRB panels means blocking off access to explore the local meaning-making processes at play in historical and cultural contexts. This illustrates the risk that the new audit regime poses to qualitative interviewing as a knowledge-producing method. It is experiences such as these that support Hammersley's (2009) argument that the new regime probably will worsen the quality of much research. Elizabeth Murphy and Robert Dingwall (2001, p. 340) are more specific in their criticism of the mechanical application of ethics codes. They worry that the ritualistic application, instead of protecting participants, may increase the risk of harm "by blunting the ethnographers' sensitivities to the method-specific issues which do arise" (p. 340). This is what the interview extracts and data tried to illustrate. It is worthwhile giving a chance to interview researchers' combination of contextual knowledge and restricted opportunity for doing excessive damage.

We will still need panels of some kind, but with philosophers and social scientists who would use their knowledge of the intersection of philosophy, epistemology, and methods to make such panels into what they should be—arenas for research ethics and risk assessments of different kinds and arenas to handle slips and violations.

It is a paradox of great concern that universities, which supposedly value intellectual freedom and independence, would institutionalize a research ethics regime where the ethical regulators authorize themselves to impose their own judgments about intellectual matters on the social science research community as a whole. Apart from arguing against those with power, social scientists also need to do what they are best qualified to do, which is to systematically uncover how participants in powerful positions themselves use their power to manipulate those without it. We have analytic tools, methods, and theories available to explore situations, processes, contexts, and eventually the policies of ethics review boards. Material is plentiful. But if we take seriously the claim that research ethics now at least partly deals with things other than research ethics, we also need to analyze how the wider contextual transformations are inextricably linked with the new regime, so "if we are to gain further analytic purchase on the role of context, we need to be constantly aware of the locally unarticulated contextual alternatives that can come into play at other times and places" and that could "direct us in specific ways to the contextual alternatives that, from the top down, might inform particular sites of social interaction" (Holstein & Gubrium, 2004, p. 304); that is to say, we need to present intelligible alternatives to the status quo.

It is imperative to counteract any assault on research as a sphere of critical thinking. Still, the ultimate consequence of ethicist arguments, however subtle, is qualitative interview research as a place for the *in*ability to think. Institutional research ethics thus indeed has come to deal with "the real stuff of research."

◆ References

Adler, P. A., & Adler, P. (2002). The reluctant respondent. In J. F. Gubrium & J. A. Holstein (Eds.), *Handbook of interview research: Context and method* (pp. 515–536). Thousand Oaks, CA: Sage.

Allen, A. L. (1999). Coercing privacy. *Mary and William Law Review, 40,* 723–757.

Amit, V. (2000). The university as panopticon: Moral claims and attack on academic freedom. In M. Strathern (Ed.), *Audit cultures: Anthropological studies in accountability, ethics and the academy* (pp. 212–235). London, England: Routledge.

Atkinson, P. (2009). Ethics and ethnography. *Academy of the Social Sciences, 4*(1), 17–30.

Atkinson, P., & Coffee, A. (2002). Revisiting the relationship between participant observation and interviewing. In J. F. Gubrium & J. A. Holstein (Eds.), *Handbook of interview research* (pp. 801–814). Thousand Oaks, CA: Sage.

Atkinson, P., & Delamont, S. (2006). In the roiling smoke: Qualitative inquiry and contested fields. *International Journal of Qualitative Studies in Education, 19*(6), 747–755.

Atkinson, P., & Delamont, S. (2010). Can the silenced speak? A dialogue for two unvoiced actors. *International Review of Qualitative Research, 3*(1), 11–15.

Atkinson, P., & Silverman, D. (1997). Kundera's immortality: The interview society and the invention of the self. *Qualitative Inquiry, 3,* 304–325.

Baker, C. D. (2002). Ethnomethodological analyses of interviews. In J. F. Gubrium & J. A. Holstein (Eds.), *Handbook of interview research* (pp. 777–795). Thousand Oaks, CA: Sage.

Beleiret av blodhunder [Besieged by bloodhounds]. (2011, February 22). *Klassekampen,* pp. 18–19.

Bourne-Day, J., & Lee-Treweek, G. (2008). Interconnected lives: Examining privacy as a shared concern for the researched and researchers. In B. Jegatheesan (Ed.), *Access: A zone of comprehension and intrusion* (Advances in Program Evaluation, Vol. 12, pp. 29–61). Bingley, England: JAI Press, Emerald.

Christians, C. (2000). Ethics and politics in qualitative research. In N. K. Denzin & Y. S. Lincoln (Eds.), *Handbook of qualitative research* (2nd ed., pp. 133–155). Thousand Oaks, CA: Sage.

Christians, C. (2005). Ethics and politics in qualitative research. In N. K. Denzin & Y. S. Lincoln (Eds.), *Handbook of qualitative research* (3rd ed., pp. 133–164). Thousand Oaks, CA: Sage.

Code of ethics of the Norwegian press. (2011). Retrieved from http://ethicnet.uta.fi/norway/code_of_ethics_of_the_norwegian_press

Da Faiza forsvant [When Faiza disappeared]. (2011, February 25–March 3). *Klassekampen,* pp. 14–15.

Dash, L. (2007). Journalism and institutional review boards. *Qualitative Inquiry, 13*(6), 871–874.

Death knock. (2011, February 23). *Klassekampen,* p. 2.

Denzin, N. K. (1997). *Interpretive ethnography: Ethnographic practices for the 21st century.* Thousand Oaks, CA: Sage.

Denzin, N. K. (2008). IRBs and the turn to indigenous research ethics. In B. Jegatheesan (Ed.), *Access: A zone of comprehension and intrusion* (pp. 97–123). Bingley, England: JAI Press, Emerald.

Denzin, N. K. (2009a). Apocalypse now: Overcoming resistances to qualitative inquiry. *International Review of Qualitative Research, 3*(1), 333–343.

Denzin, N. K. (2009b). The elephant in the living room: Or extended the conversation about the politics of evidence. *Qualitative Research, 9*(2), 139–160.

Denzin, N. K. (2009c). *Qualitative inquiry under fire: Towards a new paradigm debate.* Walnut Creek, CA: Left Coast Press.

Economic and Social Research Council. (2005). *Research ethics framework.* Retrieved from http://www.esrc.ac.uk/_images/Framework_for_Research_Ethics_tcm8-4586.pdf

Ellis, C. (2009). Telling tales on neighbours: Ethics in two voices. *International Review of Qualitative Research, 2*(1), 3–28.

Erickson, F., & Shultz, J. (1982). *The counselor as gatekeeper: Social interaction in interviews.* New York, NY: Academic Press.

Euroqual. (2006–2010). *Qualitative research in the social sciences in Europe* (An ESF program). Retrieved from http://www.esf.org/index.php?eID=tx_nawsecuredl&u=0&file=fileadmin/be_user/research_areas/social_sciences/RNPs/Euroqual.pdf&t=1287488844&hash=bbeb55fbc51e0dbe164fbc0f24036e12

Fielding, N. (2010). Elephants, gold standards and applied qualitative research. *Qualitative Research, 10*(1), 123–127.

Finch, J. (1984). It's great to have someone to talk to: The ethics and politics of interviewing women. In C. Bell & H. Roberts (Eds.), *Social researching: Politics, problems, practice* (pp. 70–88). London, England: Routledge & Kegan Paul.

Furedi, F., & Bristow, J. (2008). *Licenced to hug*. London, England: Civitas.

Gabb, J. (2010). Home truths: Ethical issues in family research. *Qualitative Research, 10*(4), 461–478.

Gilligan, C. (1983). *In a different voice: Psychological theory and women's development*. Cambridge, MA: Harvard University Press.

Gotlib Conn, L. (2008). Ethics policy as audit in Canadian clinical settings: Exiling the ethnographic method. *Qualitative Research, 8*(4), 499–514.

Gubrium, J. F., & Holstein, J. A. (2002). From the individual society to the interview society. In J. F. Gubrium & J. A. Holstein (Eds.), *Handbook of interview research* (pp. 3–32). Thousand Oaks, CA: Sage.

Gubrium, J. F., & Holstein, J. A. (2008). The constructionist mosaic. In J. A. Holstein & J. F. Gubrium (Eds.), *Handbook of constructionist research* (pp. 3–10). New York, NY: Guilford Press.

Haggerty, K. (2004). Ethics creep: Governing social science research in the name of ethics. *Qualitative Sociology, 24*(4), 391–414.

Haimes, E. (2002). What can the social sciences contribute to the study of ethics? Theoretical, empirical and substantive considerations. *Bioethics, 16*(2), 89–113.

Hammersley, M. (2008). *Questioning qualitative inquiry*. Los Angeles, CA: Sage.

Hammersley, M. (2009). Against the ethicists: On the evils of ethical regulation. *International Journal of Social Research Methodology, 12*(3), 211–225.

Hartley, A. (2004). *The Zanzibar chest*. London, England: Harper Perennial.

Holstein, J. A., & Gubrium, J. F. (2003). Inside interviewing: New lenses, new concerns. In J. A. Holstein & J. F. Gubrium (Eds.), *Inside interviewing: New lenses, new concerns* (pp. 3–30). Thousand Oaks, CA: Sage.

Holstein, J. A., & Gubrium, J. F. (2004). Context: Working it up, down and across. In C. Seale, G. Gobo, J. F. Gubrium, & D. Silverman (Eds.), *Qualitative research practice* (pp. 297–311). London, England: Sage.

Hookway, N. (2008). Entering the blogsphere: Some strategies for using blogs in social research. *Qualitative Research, 8*(1), 91–113.

Humphreys, L. (1975). *Tearoom trade* (Enlarged ed.). Chicago, IL: Aldine.

International Center for Qualitative Inquiry. (2005). *QI 2005: The first international congress of qualitative inquiry*. Retrieved from http://www.iiqi.org/C4QI/httpdocs/qi2005/index.html

International Center for Qualitative Inquiry. (2008). *QI 2008: The fourth international congress of qualitative inquiry*. Retrieved from http://www.icqi.org/qi2008/

Johnson, J. M., & Altheide, D. (2002). Reflections on professional ethics. In W. C. Van den Hoonaard (Ed.), *Walking the tightrope: Good intentions and awkward outcomes* (pp. 59–69). Toronto, Ontario, Canada: University of Toronto Press.

Karo-Ljungberg, M. (2008). A social constructionist framing of the research interview. In J. A. Holstein & J. F. Gubrium (Eds.), *Handbook of constructionist research* (pp. 429–444). New York, NY: Guilford Press.

Kjeldstadli, K. (2010). *Akademisk kapitalisme*. Oslo, Norway: Res publica.

Kushner, S. (2006, February). A lament for the ESRC [Newsletter of the British Educational Research Association]. *Research Intelligence, 94*, 9–11.

Leisley, M. (2008). Qualitative inquiry and the IRBs: Protection at all costs? *Qualitative Social Work, 7*(4), 415–426.

Mellick, M., & Fleming, S. (2010). Personal narrative and the ethics of disclosure: A case study from elite sports. *Qualitative Research, 10*(3), 299–314.

Mertens, D. M., & Ginsberg, P. (Eds.). (2009). *Handbook of social research ethics*. Newbury Park, CA: Sage.

Milgram, S. (1963). Behavioral study of obedience. *Journal of Abnormal and Social Psychology, 67*, 371–378.

Mukherjee, D. (2008). Privacy and the intrusion in ethnographic health research. In B. Jegatheesan (Ed.), *Access: A zone of comprehension and intrusion* (pp. 83–96). Bingley, England: JAI Press, Emerald.

Murphy, E., & Dingwall, R. (2001). The ethics of ethnography. In P. Atkinson, A. Coffee, S. Delamont, J. Lofland, & L. Lofland (Eds.), *Handbook of ethnography* (pp. 339–351). Los Angeles, CA: Sage.

Murphy, E., & Dingwall, R. (2007). Informed consent, anticipatory regulation and ethnographic practice. *Social Science and Medicine, 65*(11), 2223–2234.

Nodding, N. (1984). *Caring: A feminine approach to ethics and moral education*. Berkeley: University of California Press.

Porter, E. (1999). *Feminist perspectives on ethics*. Harlow, England: Pearson Education.

Pritchard, I. A. (2002). Travellers and trolls: Practitioner research and institutional review boards. *Educational Researcher, 31*(3), 3–13.

Rabinow, P. (1977). *Reflections on fieldwork in Morocco.* Berkeley: University of California Press.

Rights and duties of the editor. (2011). Retrieved from http://www.nj.no/Rights+and+duties+of+the+editor.b7C_wJzU1Y.ips

Ryen, A. (2004). Ethical issues. In C. Seale, G. Gobo, J. F. Gubrium, & D. Silverman (Eds.), *Qualitative research practice* (pp. 158–174). London, England: Sage.

Ryen, A. (2008a). Crossing borders? Doing gendered ethnographies of third-world organisations. In B. Jegatheesan (Ed.), *Access: A zone of comprehension and intrusion* (Advances in Program Evaluation, Vol. 12, pp. 141–164). Bingley, England: JAI Press, Emerald.

Ryen, A. (2008b). Trust in cross-cultural research: The puzzle of epistemology, research ethics and context. *Qualitative Social Work, 7*(4), 448–465.

Ryen, A. (2008c). Wading the field with my key informant: Exploring field relations. *Qualitative Sociology Review, 4*(3), 84–104. Retrieved from http://www.qualitativesociologyreview.org/ENG/Volume11/QSR_4_3.pdf

Ryen, A. (2009). Ethnography: Constitutive practice and research ethics. In D. Mertens & P. Ginsberg (Eds.), *Handbook of research ethics for the social sciences* (pp. 229–258). Thousand Oaks, CA: Sage.

Ryen, A. (2011). Ethics and qualitative research. In D. Silverman (Ed.), *Qualitative research: Issues of theory, method and practice* (pp. 416–438). London, England: Sage.

Sabar. (2008). Informed consent: An instrumental or deceptive principle in qualitative educational research. In B. Jegatheesan (Ed.), *Access: A zone of comprehension and intrusion* (pp. 63–82). Bingley, England: JAI Press, Emerald.

Scheper-Hughes, N. (2004). Parts unknown: Undercover ethnography of the organs-trafficking underworld. *Ethnography, 5*(1), 29–73.

Shaw, I. (2008). Ethics and the practice of qualitative research. *Qualitative Social Work, 7*(4), 400–414.

Shaw, R. (2010). Deliberating and doing ethics in body gifting practices. *Current Sociology, 58*(3), 443–462.

Silverman, D. (1998). *Harvey Sacks: Social sciences and conversational analysis.* Cambridge, England: Polity Press.

Silverman, D. (2006). *Interpreting qualitative data.* London, England: Sage.

Skjuler seg bak sjefen [Hides behind the boss]. (2011, February 24). *Klassekampen*, pp. 24–25.

Sømme, A. (2010). Kvinner vi kan gråte for. *Samtiden, 3,* 4–17.

Speiglman, R., & Spear, P. (2009). The role of institutional review board ethics: Now you see them, now you don't. In D. M. Mertens & P. E. Ginsberg (Eds.), *The handbook of social research ethics* (pp. 121–134). Los Angeles, CA: Sage.

Stake, R., & Jegatheesan, B. (2008). Access, a zone of comprehension, and intrusion. In B. Jegatheesan (Ed.), *Access: A zone of comprehension and intrusion* (pp. 1–13). Bingley, England: JAI Press, Emerald.

Stake, R., & Rizvi, F. (2008). Research ethics in transnational spaces. In D. M. Mertens & P. Ginsberg (Eds.), *Handbook of social science research in ethics* (pp. 521–536). Thousand Oaks, CA: Sage.

Taylor, J. (2010). The intimate insider: Negotiating the ethics of friendship when doing insider research. *Qualitative Research, 11*(1), 3–22.

Tinker, A., & Coomber, V. (2004). *University research ethics committees: Their role, remit and conduct.* London, England: Nuffield Foundation/Kings College.

Van den Hoonaard, W. C. (2001). Is research-ethics review a moral panic? *The Canadian Review of Sociology and Anthropology, 38*(1), 19–36.

Whittaker, R. (1999). *The end of privacy.* New York, NY: New Press.

34

TOWARD CONCILIATION

*Institutional Review Board Practices and
Qualitative Interview Research*

◆ Michelle Miller-Day

Meet the Foster family. Susan Foster is a college professor, her husband Lee is in pharmaceutical sales, and their son Jordan is a junior in high school but has stopped caring about school altogether. He believes that a traditional high school experience will not matter for his career goal of becoming an artist and is thinking about dropping out. Jordan spends much of his time in his art studio drawing and painting. Susan worries constantly about what she sees as Jordan's aimlessness, and she makes comments to him about school every chance she can. The more frequently she asks Lee to intervene (which is often), the more Lee ignores the situation, saying, "He'll come around." Jordan feels caught in a vicious circle. Painting helps relax him, but then his mom gets upset that he is not studying, which makes him withdraw to the studio. Although some may see Jordan as the problem in

this family, someone taking an *interactional view* of the family system likely sees more complexity. What roles do Jordan, Susan, and Lee each play in perpetuating this ongoing disquiet? From an interactional perspective, one tries to understand the functioning of the system and *understand the reality the system has created for itself* without making judgments about who are the good guys and bad guys.

Now meet some select members of a *Midwestern_ university_somewhere_in_the_flatlands_of_the_ United States*. Norm is a qualitative sociologist who has been conducting ethnographic field research for more than 20 years, conducting conversational unstructured interviews with community members as his primary tool for collecting information. Bob, Carol, Ted, and Alice are all members of the university in the flatlands' institutional review board (IRB). Bob, Carol, and Ted represent faculty from a variety of disciplines including biology, psychology, and architecture, and Alice is a community member. Now that we have met these characters, I hope to illustrate—through a fictional scenario involving Bob, Carol, Ted, Alice, and Norm—how an interactional perspective might be useful for understanding and addressing some of the IRB challenges faced by qualitative scholars hoping to conduct in-depth qualitative interviews.

◆ A Fictional (but Oh Too Common) Scenario

Last month, Norm submitted a research application to the university's IRB soliciting approval for his proposed research. This research involves conducting semistructured and unstructured interviews with migrant workers and local farmers. The migrant workers are employed to pick soybeans, and the interviews are intended to gather information about the skin cancer prevention efforts of these migrant workers and their employers. While Norm can guess what some of the barriers might be for migrant workers to prevent skin cancer, his hunches are just that—hunches. There is very little research literature available on this topic specifically addressing migrant populations and a pressing need to address this gap in the literature. Hence, Norm's goal is to ground his inquiry in the daily experiences of the migrant workers themselves to discover more about how any barriers are experienced in situ.

The members of any institution's IRB are generally charged with, among many things, minimizing harms and risks to human participants who might participate in this study, maximizing benefits to them, and making sure that the research procedures respect their human dignity, privacy, and autonomy. Therefore, when Bob, Carol, Ted, and Alice received Norm's application, they conscientiously examined the application for any potential risks to human participants. After the initial review, Carol considered migrant workers to be a vulnerable population; therefore, she would not approve verbal consent procedures. Instead, she wrote in her review statement that Norm "needs to provide a more formal consent procedure, including a written consent form and an interpreter

on-site for workers who do not speak English very well." Bob had different concerns. Bob would not approve the interview procedures because they were "too vague," and he wrote in his statement that "[Norm] should develop a clear protocol for each interview and include his interview schedule, including the exact questions he intends to ask the employees and employers." Finally, Alice was worried that employers might dock the worker's pay for the time it took to talk with the researcher. In her review, she wrote that the researcher "should require the employer to sign a waiver for each employee, agreeing not to sanction them for their participation in the interviews." After reading these comments, Norm believes that they are not reasonable and is ready to throw in the towel. When talking with his colleagues, he contends that this is important research, but the restrictions imposed by the IRB are making it impossible to actually conduct the study. He recognizes that members of the IRB take their responsibilities of protection seriously, but he believes that they do not understand the nature of conducting qualitative inquiry and that this lack of understanding is obstructing his ability to conduct his research in a meaningful way.[1]

From an interactional perspective, we can see that the *somewhere_in_the_flatlands* academic institution is not that different from the Foster family. Both are interdependent systems, guided by rules, where the actions of one part of the system affect and are affected by the actions of another (Federman, Hanna, & Rodriquiz, 2003). There are rules that hold these systems together, but there are also incompatible goals that threaten to pull the parts of the interdependent system in opposing directions. The funny thing about most systems is that they are infamously resistant to change (Beer & Nohria, 2000; Lewin, 1947) and their respective parts often collude in the maintenance of the status quo (Piderit, 2000).

When asked to write a chapter on IRBs and qualitative inquiry, I was excited to add my voice to the many other writings that exist on this topic (see, e.g., Koenig, Back, & Crawley, 2003; Lincoln & Tierney, 2004; Morse, Niehaus, Varnhagen, & McIntosh, 2008; Ramcharan & Cutcliffe, 2001) and offer an interactional view of this sometimes uneasy alliance in the pursuit of discovery and knowledge. My view is contextualized in my own past training

---

[1]This illustration represents an actual case. All phrases in quotation marks reflect excerpts from IRB feedback, but all names have been changed.

and experience as a qualitative researcher, family communication scholar, and previous IRB member. However, it is from this vantage point that I see a need for the scientific community to reframe the dissonance that often occurs in interactions between qualitative researchers and IRBs.

Toward that end, in this chapter, I first provide an overview of the interactional perspective and illustrate how this approach can assist us in reframing IRB/qualitative researcher relations; then I offer a discussion of some of the tensions that exist at the intersection of IRB mandate and qualitative research practice and some of the consequences of those tensions; and, finally, I cautiously propose strategies for a possible accord.

◆ An Interactional View of Qualitative Inquiry and IRB Review

Although it is beyond the scope of this chapter to provide a comprehensive discussion of the interactional view as others have done (see, e.g., Watzlawick & Weakland, 1977), there are two axioms of this perspective I would like to specifically discuss: (1) Communication = Content + Relationship and (2) all communication between interactants is either symmetrical or complementary (Watzlawick & Weakland). These axioms are useful for understanding the complexity inherent in the interactions of qualitative researchers and their IRBs.

"Communication = Content + Relationship" is shorthand for the idea that every verbal and nonverbal message (whether it is in a written IRB application, written response, or face-to-face interaction) contains a content and relationship dimension (Watzlawick, Beavin, & Jackson, 1967; Watzlawick & Weakland, 1977). Content refers to *what* is said, and relationship refers to *how* it is said and to be understood in the context of the relationship. How something is said provides information about how the information should be interpreted. For example, the prescriptive language used in the IRB feedback above, such as "needs to," "should," and "require," implies directives that must be obeyed and a paternalistic relationship between board members and researchers. These kinds of directives move past implication to reification when considering the power disparity between IRB members and individual researchers.

The interactional view pays particular attention to questions of power, control, and status (Griffin, 2010). According to this view, interchanges between interactants can be symmetrical or complementary. Symmetrical interchange refers to interactions based on equal power, and complementary interchange refers to interactions based on accepted differences of power. In the case of the IRB–investigator interface, by virtue of organizational structures and the function of the IRB, interactions—whether in writing or in person—can be almost universally characterized as complementary. Educational institutions recognize the legitimate authority of the IRB to protect human subjects and charge these boards with the authority to approve or not approve any research application that does not offer what they deem to be the necessary protections. Hence, the individual researcher begins any interaction with the IRB from a point of less legitimate power and certainly less decision-making power.

By requiring compliance and offering prescriptions and proscriptions, IRBs often establish a pattern of "one-up communication," where their comments to researchers assert control over or dominate the communication exchange. These messages order, contradict, fail to support, and sometimes outright disrespect the researcher's description of what is required for any particular investigation. Researchers are expected, in turn, to reply with "one-down communication," where any response is intended to yield control of the exchange through agreement or compliance with IRB directives. In the previous case, if Norm "throws in the towel" and does not comply with the requested revisions, then he, in effect, cedes control and power in the interaction, conveying a "one-down" message. In an educational environment where dialogue and symmetrical interchange are typically appreciated, this is an untenable situation. This is especially true when the IRB at a given institution does not possess expertise in qualitative research methods—as many do not. Within this working system, individual researchers often feel that they have no recourse and that the legitimate power of the IRB supersedes the expert power of the individual researcher to fully consider what practices are both ethical and necessary.

Additionally, a qualitative researcher may be placed in a double bind when he or she believes that the requested revisions would compromise the quality of the investigation. For Norm, the IRB message

"Do good and ethical research . . . but only with these changes" seemed to place him in a no-win situation. Either he would need to make the revisions and proceed, believing that his study was dangerously compromised, or he would neither revise nor conduct the study. Speaking as a faculty member who sat on my institution's review board for 2 years, I am bothered by this uneasy relationship. I personally know of no faculty member who sits on an IRB who would advocate for this kind of double bind. Yet, as I mentioned earlier, most systems are highly resistant to change, and this situation continues to occur in many institutions.

From where I type, I do not view this as an issue about good guys or bad guys. It is about trying to understand the reality that the IRB system has created for itself. Pursuant to this, there is a need for academics to understand the tensions inherent in this system, engage in dialogue about these tensions and the untenable relationships they promote, and consider strategies for a possible accord. A system can often be transformed only when members receive outside help to reframe their metacommunication. The next section offers a discussion of some different tension points specific to IRB mandates and qualitative interview research in particular.

◆ *Some Tensions Between IRB and Qualitative Interview Research*

According to Professor William Rand Kenan,

> IRB supervision of our research violates the First Amendment and its strictures against prior restraint. We believe that the First Amendment guarantees that the press in all of its manifestations [e.g., publication] is free from governmental interference. The IRB is a governmental intrusion on freedom of disseminating information. Review by an IRB is a prior restraint on press and academic freedom, because it requires individuals to seek the government's approval before initiating a project. . . . A better formula for demoralizing graduate students and faculty members could not be imagined. A better formula for stultifying research is beyond contemplation. That formula is today in place, thanks to the IRB. (American Association of University Professors [AAUP], 2002, para. 57)

In 2001, the AAUP Committee on Academic Freedom and Tenure was charged with developing a report on the regulation of research by IRBs, and among the AAUP committee's conclusions was that some IRBs "too often mistakenly apply standards of clinical and biomedical research to social science research, to the detriment of the latter" (pp. 55–56). Federal regulation of research on human subjects was a response to public and legislative concerns about lack of oversight of biomedical research (e.g., the study of syphilis in Tuskegee, Alabama). However, as practiced currently in most institutions, research with human participants must obtain IRB approval whether or not it imposes a serious risk of harm to its participants. Kenan's words above aptly state the fears and frustrations of many researchers, especially those who pursue qualitative inquiry. Although it is likely not their intention, IRBs often impede the conduct of interview studies.

While there are many tensions that can be identified between the artistic practice of conducting qualitative interviews and navigating the IRB system, I will focus on what I see as three salient tensions that manifest in the IRB/qualitative investigator interface: (1) competing research models, (2) paternalistic monitoring, and (3) inconsistency across institutions.

◆ *Competing Research Models*

According to Koenig et al. (2003), IRBs often judge qualitative studies using yardsticks developed for clinical trials, suggesting procedures that are often burdensome, counterproductive, and ineffective. Echoing this, in 2006, the AAUP expanded their earlier report and argued that IRBs have "unchecked power" that disadvantages inquiry, especially by researchers not employing biomedical models of research. In neither the 2002 nor the 2006 report did the AAUP advocate that IRBs provide oversight to *only* biomedical research; in fact, social science research does have the potential to cause serious psychological harm, and not all biomedical research imposes a serious risk of harm on its subjects. The AAUP organization did, however, advocate for IRBs to educate themselves on the risks, benefits, and procedures associated with certain methods, so as to better provide guidance and determine if research using those tools should possibly be exempt from review. I see the value in this suggestion and assert that there are two very important ways in which qualitative interviewing as a method contrasts with other, perhaps more positivist, tools for collecting empirical materials (data). Those points of contrast include the emergent nature of qualitative interviewing and consent as a process and not a one-time achievement.

THE EMERGENT NATURE OF QUALITATIVE INTERVIEWING

When conducting qualitative interviews, especially in naturalistic settings, there is a need for *planned flexibility*. While each researcher is guided by specific questions, these do not dictate the exact direction of a study. In fact, qualitative inquiry often takes unexpected directions leading to some of the most valuable scientific contributions (Agar, 1982; Atkinson, 1990; Bogdan & Taylor, 1976; Goffman, 1961; Kübler-Ross, 1973; Malinowski, 1950; Merton, 1968). With emergent methodological research designs such as qualitative interviewing, it is difficult to establish the balance of risks and benefits, particularly in comparison with quantitative studies where the range of questions and research procedures is known beforehand. Researchers may not know the total number of participants they will involve, how many interviews will be conducted per person, precisely what questions will be asked, or how long interviews will last. In sum, they cannot provide the exact level of detail an IRB application requires. Moreover, decision making about ethics is more of a process than an a priori plan when a researcher navigates both expected and unexpected moral dilemmas at each stage of the research process (Ramcharan & Cutcliffe, 2001). For researchers conducting qualitative interviews, planned flexibility is needed for unplanned events. I encourage researchers to develop an outline of "expected" participants, interviews, interview questions, and ethical situations given the research plan, but with the proviso that decisions will be made during the research process as needed, based on a stipulated set of ethical guidelines. As Fine and Deegan (1996) articulated, "Unplanned does not suggest that anything is possible, only that a range of things are."

It is the socially interactive nature of qualitative interviewing that often causes turbulence in the investigator–IRB interface. In this research frame, qualitative interviews are not understood as research *on human subjects* but rather as inquisitive social interaction *with other human beings*. This view of participants as active agents in their interaction with researchers stands in direct contrast with IRB protocols that often frame the interviewer–respondent interactions in terms of fixed federal guidelines (i.e., legal mandates) situating researchers as acting *on* subjects. For most of us, an interview is viewed as an interaction that is a co-constructed event, a dialogue with mutual participation. Interlocutors know that we are asking them questions in a conversational setting.

> They can thus choose how to respond. They can—and do—refuse to answer specific questions; give misleading, incomplete, inaccurate, or false information; and refuse to participate in the interview. Unlike subjects of experiments or clinical trials, they retain a great deal of personal autonomy as well as control over the research itself. (AAUP, 2002, para. 36)

Yet, just as for the Foster family introduced at the beginning of this chapter, for many IRB members and qualitative researchers, competing models of viewing the world create dissonance and tension among the interacting parties. There is a large corpus of published (see, e.g., AAUP, 2006; Lincoln & Tierney, 2004; Morse et al., 2008) and unpublished complaints about IRB/qualitative researcher interactions. Many complaints focus on the burden placed on researchers to submit increasing amounts of detailed information about their projects, in round after round of revisions, essentially stonewalling projects.

CONSENT AS AN ONGOING PROCESS AND NOT AS A SINGULAR ACHIEVEMENT

In the situation where one is conducting a singular prearranged interview, consent typically follows the biomedical research model. That is, informed consent must be obtained from the participant in the form of written documentation prior to the procedure. Under these conditions, consent is the precondition for research but not part of the research. In contrast, much qualitative interviewing takes place informally, over time, and in natural settings. In these cases, informed consent is an ongoing interaction between the researcher and participants in their community, and consent is subject to the cultural rules and understandings of that community. Consent is not obtained before one does the research but is part of the constant activities of conducting the research, involving a process of establishing trust, building rapport, and negotiating consent.

Since much qualitative interview work is relationship centered, scholars such as Hewitt (2007) argue for an ethics-of-care perspective, which prizes the relationship with and personhood of the participant. In promoting this perspective in an IRB application, a researcher would argue that negotiating consent is a relational event and that scientific rigor should be balanced with moral concerns. Sensitivity to the perceived wishes of participants is integral to the interview process, with an emphasis on empathetic awareness. The wishes of the participant, however, might come into conflict with IRB mandates such as anonymity. In some research, such as community-based participatory research or action research, the participants/coresearchers desire to be acknowledged for their contribution. In cases such as this, the needs of the participants would override concerns about participant anonymity. Instead of decisions being directed by IRB mandates, decisions are made as necessary in a way that facilitates egalitarian relationships, reciprocity, and a sense of mutuality (Hewitt, 2007).

The ethics-of-care approach may be functional in the field, but attempting to represent this approach in an IRB application is a challenge. This is another way in which competing models of research provide obstacles for positive interactions between the IRB system and qualitative researchers. Often, in an effort to fit their model into the existing IRB model, researchers will undergo endless revisions of the application to make their approach seem more conventional (Lincoln & Tierney, 2004). The different beliefs and vocabulary used by qualitative researchers and many IRB members sometimes breeds suspicion among all—including participants. One example, presented in Hewitt (2007), described an IRB that required inclusion of a frightening "Experimental Subjects Bill of Rights" in the consent form document for an interview study of decision making. The interviews were unstructured and conversational, so the participants were confused and suspicious of the document. They asked the researchers, "Why am

I being warned about risks such as physical harms and dangers?" Another situation depicted in this article described an IRB that required written—rather than verbal—consent based solely on the justification that their policy was *never* to waive written consent. Yet what about illiterate participants or participants who are suspicious of legalistic, bureaucratic jargon? For Norm, in his proposed research with migrant workers, he did not believe that a respectful, trusting relationship could be forged or honest conversation elicited if he was required to thrust a written consent form into the hands of these workers. He believed that requiring written consent in a primarily verbal community would be perceived as government intrusion into an arrangement they would otherwise enter freely. Moreover, he felt strongly that if an employer were asked to sign a waiver for each employee, agreeing not to sanction them for their participation in the interviews, this would have the adverse result of arousing suspicion! Norm also speculated that introducing such a waiver could perhaps trigger the idea of sanctions among employers who had never previously considered this idea.

At the center of much of the discord between qualitative scholars and IRBs is the chilling effect that occurs as the result of interaction between constituents—that is, researchers suppressing or limiting their work due to fear of penalization by the IRB. From an interactional perspective, IRBs' paternalistic approach to monitoring low-risk research has served to create relational turbulence among qualitative researchers and IRBs nationwide.

◆ Paternalism of IRBs

Feeling unempowered in IRB negotiations, having very little voice in the process, and perceiving real sanctions if not compliant "with higher education's version of a police state,"[2] many scholars view IRBs as obstructionist. I often hear comments from faculty indicating that they avoid the IRB at all costs because of the paternalistic nature of the interactions, with one professor indicating that he limits his work to unimportant topics to ensure exemption from review. Lincoln and Tierney (2004) stated that some IRBs

---

[2]This quote was excerpted from an account shared by a faculty member at a research institution in the northeastern United States.

are clear that their main concern is protection of the institution from damage, and he argues that this is a fundamental (and unfortunate) shift from the original purpose of ascertaining risk to human subjects and ensuring that informed consent was adequate to prepare human subjects for associated risks. IRBs at most institutions currently have extensive oversight responsibilities, including approval of research, ongoing monitoring of research progress, and receiving complaints—with virtually no policing of their own decisions.

Many IRBs, however, seem to extend beyond what might be considered reasonable oversight. The AAUP (2006) reported that a Caucasian doctoral student seeking to study career expectations in relation to ethnicity was told by the IRB that African American doctoral students could not be interviewed because it might be traumatic for them to be interviewed by a Caucasian student. They also reported that IRBs have objected to research protocols on the grounds that the participants might find it distressing even to be asked questions . . . period. The report further stated, "We regard that as an unpardonable piece of paternalism, especially when participants are autonomous adults who are free to end their participation at any time, or to refuse to participate at all" (para. 26). From the interactional perspective, I believe that paternalistic messages and monitoring of low-risk interview research has led to a demand–withdraw interaction style at institutions, where IRBs persist in demanding and researchers are withdrawing.

Although some researchers may feel powerless and withdraw because of the demands of IRBs, they are still members of an overall "system" that functions to sustain these negative interactions. Perhaps it might be prudent to consider that IRBs' persistent demands might be partly a result of lack of knowledge. Qualitative researchers would be well served to educate members of their institutions' IRBs on not just the risks of qualitative interviews but also the benefits. Review committees sometimes express concern that the interview process may be stressful to some participants. This is not generally the case, even though a participant may become upset during an interview on a sensitive topic. Generally, the experience of a qualitative interview can be a validating and therapeutic experience and stimulate self-reflection, appraisal, and/or catharsis (May, 1991; Peplau, 1988). Participants often express

appreciation that "someone has *at last listened* to their stories" (Morse & Field, 1995, p. 93). In fact, an interview might be the first opportunity interviewees have had to tell their own personal accounts, allowing them to make sense out of their experiences (Cutcliffe, 2002; Cutcliffe & Ramcharan, 2002).

In addition to a lack of awareness of different research models, IRBs at each institution have their own internal dynamics and ways of determining risks and benefits for a given proposed study. With as many as 5,000 IRBs of various sorts in operation around the country, achieving consistency in the field of human subject protection across institutions is not feasible (Coleman, 2004). Therefore, efforts to educate and change IRB processes and procedures relevant to qualitative interview research will typically need to be made at the local level. To *understand the reality the research review system has created for IRB–investigator relations*, it is imperative to examine some of the consequences of these tensions.

◆ Consequences of the Tensions

There is certainly the potential for significant and consequential risks in conducting interview research involving human participants. Yet while most scholars are aware of and consider the risks for participants, few consider the risks for the institution and researcher. The violation of participant rights or causing participants harm could result in funding support being withdrawn from a university—not just for a single transgressive project—and the host institution could lose all federal funding. Additionally, research in all departments of the university could potentially be halted during the period of investigating the abuses. For example, Johns Hopkins University and Duke University had their federal funding frozen briefly because of not properly protecting participants in biomedical research. There are real and significant risks involved when institutions are not compliant with federal guidelines. However, overzealous pursuit of human subjects' protection by IRBs, at the cost of reasonable assessment of risk, has resulted in a number of harms to researchers themselves. These harms can move beyond uncompleted studies to include loss of funding and careers. IRB review often undermines individual and institutional reputations, and "this costs students opportunities for jobs, faculty members opportunities for tenure and promotion, and academic programs opportunities to raise necessary funding to maintain their positions" (AAUP, 2002, para. 50).

The interactional perspective argues that to understand how to alter a system, members of the system must be reflexive about how each part of the system contributes to maintaining the status quo. I argue that we, as researchers, should be as reflexive about our interactions with IRBs as of our interactions with interviewees. If factors such as inequalities of power and knowledge affect the research relationship, it seems likely that these also affect the investigator–IRB relationship. Competing research models and paternalism in the research review system have, unfortunately, contributed significantly to the current status quo, where many researchers feel overburdened and experience the chilling effect of IRB sanctions.

Increasingly, academics from around the United States report a variety of complaints about the stonewalling tactics of IRBs that result in researcher burden. This is not limited to qualitative research, but competing research models may entail an inherent increased burden for the qualitative researcher to elaborate, clarify, and educate members of IRB committees about the research. This increased burden requires qualitative researchers to submit increasing amounts of detailed information about their projects. An IRB at my institution recently required a qualitative researcher to provide detailed interview scripts for her telephone interview designed to investigate expatriate experiences, despite the unstructured conversational nature of the interview. They asked that she "promise not to probe for more detail or clarification." Certainly, the committee was within its scope of responsibility to ask for the kinds of questions that were planned for the interview, but to issue a directive to probe for neither information nor detail or clarification is counterproductive and not feasible when conducting qualitative studies. Another researcher was required to complete seven revisions and resubmissions of his IRB application before receiving approval, but his frustration was not so much about the number of revisions as the fact that after the third revision, additional revisions were required to change the information back to what was *originally* proposed! By the time he received approval for his

school-based study, he had a 2-week window to complete his interviews with more than 100 youth. For another research team doing school-based research, the entire research project was shut down for more than 4 months because a consent form was returned by a parent 1 week after the annual IRB approval stamp had expired. This parent had held onto the consent form until after the deadline and returned it only then. The student was interviewed, but only after the project had been approved to continue for another year. Still, once the 1-week discrepancy was discovered, the project was shut down while an IRB official audited all of the project files and the interview data. Then, the offending interview had to be discarded—even though the interview was conducted using the same protocol and procedures approved to continue for another year. In an educational environment where dialogue and collaboration are typically encouraged and appreciated, stonewalling tactics such as these are incongruous.

The resulting overburden and perceptions of stonewalling often have a chilling effect on researchers. A *chilling effect* is a situation where speech is suppressed or limited for fear of penalization at the hands of an individual or group (Cloven & Roloff, 1993). When I hear about doctoral students changing their dissertation topics because they want as little contact with the IRB as possible, this concerns me. Intellectual curiosity, the backbone of university training, is actively discouraged by some IRBs. What some students perceive is that, despite guidance by a committee of individuals with expertise in a subject and research methods, student research must be approved by a remote group of people with no training in the method and who seem to have no faith in the student committee's ability to monitor that research. Many researchers do not want to make the effort to repair the uneasy qualitative investigator/IRB relationship because they are concerned about retaliation. They fear that their efforts might put future research approval at risk or provoke scrutiny of current research. The chilling effect that has occurred on many campuses is often accompanied by the demand–withdraw pattern of interaction, where the criticisms and demands of one party are met with avoidance, withdrawal, or defensiveness by the other, which in turn elicits more demands (Caughlin, 2002). In relationship research, there is a strong association between the demand–withdraw communication pattern and relational dissatisfaction (Caughlin, 2002). Moreover, a demand–withdraw pattern in interactional systems is associated with dissatisfaction apart from the correlation between negativity and dissatisfaction (Caughlin & Huston, 2002). I contend that viewing the qualitative investigator/IRB relationship as an interaction system within the larger context of the university culture might be fruitful for understanding and addressing the current tensions and problems experienced by both qualitative researchers and IRBs in the academy. As stated at the beginning of the chapter, when applying the interactional perspective, one tries to understand the functioning of the system and *understand the reality that the system has created for itself* without making judgments about who are the good guys and bad guys.

◆ Strategies for Possible Accord

The tensions described in the previous section in no way represent all of the tensions present in the qualitative investigator/IRB interface, but those tensions reveal some of the problematic consequences that may arise in this interdependent system. The system appears to be in need of reform in order to responsibly meet the needs of both universities and researchers. Yet the *power dynamics* that exist in this interactional system seem to determine what is defined as a problem. The findings from myriad studies in organizational communication indicate that those with the most power tend to decide whether an issue is a problem or not and what solutions may be needed (see, e.g., King & Anderson, 1995). Moreover, in healthy systems, those with power are sensitive to the needs of all members, acknowledge legitimate problems, and seek appropriate solutions (King & Anderson, 1995). In some systems, however, power is used to suppress dealing with important problems that affect the less powerful members of the system. This is part of a more general pattern of dominance, which I argue is present in the current IRB research protection system on university campuses. I believe that unless a focused strategy is adopted and concrete steps taken, very little will change in the IRB/qualitative researcher interactional system. Therefore, I offer the following strategies for a possible accord. First, I argue

that the problem needs to be defined from an interactional perspective, and then I pose both first- and second-order change strategies.

◆ Defining the Problem

Protections for human participants at most universities are carried out by local IRBs, which approve and monitor research involving human participants. These boards and the investigators who seek to conduct research with human participants communicate via word (e.g., written and verbal reviews) and deed (halting research activities). This communication takes place in existing sociocultural frameworks that guide how people relate to each other. I argue that power and communication are issues at the heart of some of the problems in the qualitative investigator/IRB relationship. Within this working relational system, the IRB possesses legitimate institutional power that supersedes the expert power of the individual researcher, leading to exchanges where researchers are expected to reply to IRB directives with "one-down communication"—yielding control of the exchange—by complying with these directives, revising, revising, and then revising again, even when those changes are not in the best interest of the research endeavor. Qualitative researchers tend to feel that they do not have a voice in the process, even though they have the expert power in the interaction.

According to the interactional perspective, one cannot *not* communicate. Both verbal and nonverbal messages conveyed by individuals and institutional entities in an interaction are consequential. As in the case of the Foster family at the beginning of the chapter, if one member of the system is withdrawing, avoiding other members, or complying only under duress from other members, this must be acknowledged. For the relationship to remain healthy, these communication cues must be addressed. As the tensions rise in the IRB/qualitative researcher system, conflicts between institutional mandates and academic freedoms are inevitable. Instead of throwing in the towel, as Norm wished to do in our earlier story, I suggest that qualitative researchers work together and move toward negotiating and defining a more palatable working relationship with IRBs. To do this, it is important to make both first- and second-order changes to the IRB system as it is currently functioning in U.S. institutions of higher education.

◆ First-Order Change

Watzlawick, Weakland, and Fisch (1974) differentiated between first- and second-order changes. First-order change entails changing individuals in a setting to attempt to fix a problem, whereas second-order change entails attending to systems and structures involved with the problem to enhance the person–environment fit (Watzlawick, Weakland, & Fisch). Second-order change is often the focus of change in larger systems such as institutions or communities.

An interactional approach posits that solid relationships forge successful communication. To strengthen the IRB/qualitative researcher relationship and improve communication, I suggest that all members of this system consider how each one *punctuates* interactions with another. Punctuation concerns how a person marks the beginning of an interaction and becomes a problem when each person sees himself or herself as only reacting to, rather than provoking, a cyclical conflict. Hence, researchers as well as review board members need to reflect on how they are each contributing to the problems in this relationship. For many academics, the dysfunction in the IRB–researcher relationship is characterized by the uneasy—sometimes adversarial—nature of the relationship regardless of the content of the communication exchanges. Perhaps it is time to reframe the relational interactions in this system? Reframing is the process of altering punctuation and looking at things in a new light. For example, just like Norm in our opening story, qualitative interview researchers often feel frustrated when completing IRB applications requiring written consent when verbal consent may be more practical or necessary. Researchers complain that IRB members do not understand the notion of consent as an ongoing and relationally negotiated phenomenon. IRB members, conversely, imply by their comments that the researcher is willfully not being compliant with the rules and cannot be trusted to make ethical judgments in the field. One possible reframing might be to view ethics more as a process and not as a one-time accomplishment.

ETHICS-AS-PROCESS

A growing number of researchers (see Booth, 1998; Cutcliffe & Ramcharan, 2002; Frank, 2004; Ramos, 1989) argue for an alternative approach to ethical decision making in qualitative research.

Ramcharan and Cutcliffe (2001) have termed this an *ethics-as-process* approach. Perhaps researchers might incorporate reflexivity into IRB applications more explicitly, critically examining their own a priori assumptions and actions by being self-conscious and self-aware and conveying an accurate picture of how the research "might" play out in the field and their role in decision making during the process. This reflexivity can serve to elucidate for IRB reviewers that, in practice, researchers must be morally sensitive, be able to identify ethical problems, and respond with moral reasoning to decide on the proper action when expected and unexpected moral dilemmas occur (Aita & Richer, 2005). Given the emergent nature of the design of most qualitative interview studies, it might not always be possible for ethics committees to balance the benefit-to-risk ratio in advance. However, the ethics-as-process approach would enable ongoing monitoring of risks-to-benefits as new potential ethical concerns are balanced against emerging benefits (Ramcharan & Cutcliffe, 2001).

By preemptively addressing the possibilities that might arise in the field and how the research might monitor the risks-to-benefits ratio, IRB members can be more fully informed about the process, trusting the researcher to make ethically sound judgments and reducing the perception of noncompliance with established (biomedical model) rules. Additionally, viewing ethics-as-process allows the qualitative researcher to tell his or her story more completely, demonstrating unique needs (e.g., for verbal rather than written consent), and educate—rather than rationalize—about the potential harm of certain protections (e.g., insisting on the supervisor's active written consent for each migrant worker interviewee) versus the benefits of establishing and maintaining rapport and trusting relationships without paternalistic interference. Reframing ethics-as-process provides both the researcher and the IRB reviewer with the flexibility to make judgments as needed—not just as prescribed by rules designed for biomedical research.

PLANNED FLEXIBILITY

Going into the field with an open mind and not an empty head (Fetterman, 1998) is one of my favorite guiding principles for qualitative research. This implies that there should be some kind of a plan, idea, or motivation for the inquiry and that the research should be guided by it. It is important to the qualitative interview process, however, to understand that while one may be *guided by* the research questions and by the sensitizing constructs of a phenomenon, these *do not dictate* the nature of the study. Qualitative researchers can acknowledge a plan for going into their interviews, but this need not be inflexible. It is up to the researcher to educate IRB members that there must be flexibility within any given research plan. Providing an outline of the guiding research questions, a listing of the interview topics (e.g., the kinds of questions one might ask in the domain of education), and strategies for addressing unanticipated issues (e.g., if the interviewee introduces the topic of his or her abuse as a child) should suffice to afford the IRB with enough information to gauge if human participants will be treated in an ethical manner, protecting them from harm, maximizing their benefits, and ensuring reasonable levels of fairness (see the National Commission for the Protection of Human Subjects of Biomedical and Behavioral Research, *Belmont Report,* 1979). The specific details about the myriad directions an interview might take are neither necessary nor warranted given the charge of most IRBs to ensure that mechanisms are in place to protect human participants. In fact, allowing for flexibility in the interview schedule or protocol might actually enhance the ethical nature of the interviewing. Koenig et al. (2003) argue that this kind of flexibility enhances the ethical nature of research because an interviewer paces his or her questioning to the subject's level of knowledge, mood, and energy level and is thus less likely to cause distress. There is a need to reframe the directive to provide comprehensive and predictive interview schedules (e.g., exact questions, the exact number of interviews, and the duration of said interviews) to include, instead, a flexible research plan. Planned flexibility would honor the IRB need to reduce uncertainty as well as the spontaneous, emergent nature of qualitative inquiry.

◆ Second-Order Change

In addition to the need for individual researchers and IRB members to introduce change in their own behaviors in their home institutions, I believe there is also a need for second-order organizational change. Organizational change has been an object of academic interest since Kurt Lewin (1947) developed his theories of organizations, groups, and change processes

(Piderit, 2000). This body of research provides a compelling amount of evidence that organizational systems such as universities are resistant to change. Grover, Jeong, Kettinger, and Teng (1995) developed a hierarchical list of 64 derived problems that affected change efforts at the institutional level. The top three problems discovered, in order of importance, were that (1) the need to manage change was not recognized, (2) top management had a short-term view and was looking for a quick fix, and (3) rigid hierarchical structures in the organization posed barriers. It is my hope that the years of dissatisfaction with the status quo, recent reports by the AAUP (2002, 2006), and increasing unrest about the "overreach" of IRB monitoring practices (Morse et al., 2008) have encouraged academic institutions to recognize that there is a problem with the current system. However, to date, I believe that many institutions have been shortsighted about the relational problems that exist and have implemented some quick-fix measures (e.g., opportunities for researchers to verbally present their cases to IRBs when a stalemate occurs); however, these are often situational efforts, with no lasting effect on current institutional practices. I argue that it is the third problem identified by Grover et al. (1995)—rigid structures that pose barriers—where institutions must focus if they are to make any lasting changes and improve the IRB/qualitative researcher relationship. Two potential strategies for reducing rigidity and minimizing barriers are to address IRB paternalism and to increase IRB–researcher partnerships. These are interconnected objectives and will be addressed here together.

ADDRESSING IRB PATERNALISM AND INCREASING PARTNERSHIP

Paternalism refers to an attitude or policy of an authority that manages the affairs of others in the manner of a father, especially in usurping individual responsibility and the liberty of choice (*Collins English Dictionary*, 2009; Sartorius, 1983). Advocates of paternalistic policies claim that an overarching moral system overrides personal freedom in some circumstances. An assumption of IRB paternalism is that IRB boards know better than researchers (some of whom have been conducting research for years) and better than human participants who may wish to enter into research relationships without government interference. As discussed earlier in the chapter, participants are autonomous adults who are free to end their participation at any time and may elect to not participate at all. I believe that IRB paternalism only serves to undermine IRB/qualitative researcher interactions, especially when none of the members of the IRB have expertise in qualitative methodologies. Hence, to reduce paternalism, it may be wise to increase true partnerships between IRBs and qualitative researchers on campuses across the United States. True partnerships would involve qualitative researchers in IRB activities. If IRBs are composed of a representative group of academics, then certainly qualitative inquiry should have representation. This requires qualitative methodologists agreeing to serve in this capacity. By participating in review processes, a qualitative researcher can help educate other board members who may not be aware of ethics-as-process, the emergent nature of qualitative inquiry, and the theoretical formulations of qualitative research.

In addition to actively soliciting qualitative researchers' participation in IRB activities, IRBs must seek to educate themselves about qualitative inquiry by inviting discussion and dialogue rather than continue to issue mandates and requirements. This change would necessitate a reframing of the IRB–researcher interface as a "relationship" that honors the contributions of both parties and leaves room for both symmetrical and complementary exchanges. This new way of conceptualizing this interface would emphasize the *discussion of* research proposals to increase understanding and clarity and promote idea development. This runs counter to the existing model in most institutions, which focuses on defending one's proposal, providing justifications, and—in the end—submitting to the will of the IRB. This reframing of the relationship would require qualitative researchers to respectfully challenge and educate members of IRBs rather than withdraw from their demands. It would also require IRBs to be receptive to continuing educational efforts.

◆ Summary

Without doubt, there are a number of tensions that exist in IRB–investigator relations in institutions across the United States, and national groups such as the AAUP (2006) are calling for regulatory reform (Slater, 2002). This chapter viewed the IRB/qualitative researcher relationship from an interactional perspective, discussed some tensions and the consequences of those tensions, and offered some

strategies for a possible accord. It is my belief that researchers such as Norm should resist the urge to withdraw from research discussions with IRBs and, instead, challenge the chilling effect IRBs have on academic freedom and creative thought by joining with other qualitative scholars to educate IRB members, participate in IRB activities, and work toward developing partnerships with IRBs. With the current power disparities and institutional mandates, this is likely a challenging road to travel. But, as indicated throughout this chapter, researchers and IRBs constitute an interdependent system, guided by rules, where the actions of each part of the system affect and are affected by the actions of another part. We must ask ourselves how we (as qualitative researchers) are colluding in the maintenance of the status quo in our relationship with IRBs and how we can reframe this relationship to encourage its transformation.

◆ References

Agar, M. H. (1982). Toward an ethnographic language. *American Anthropologist, 84,* 779–795.

Aita, M., & Richer, M. C. (2005). Essentials of research for healthcare professionals. *Nursing Health Science, 7,* 119–125.

American Association of University Professors. (2002). *For the record: Should all disciplines be subject to the common rule? Human subjects of social science research.* Paper presented at the meeting of the U.S. Department of Health and Human Services' National Human Research Protections Advisory Committee. Washington, DC: Author. Retrieved from http://www.aaup.org/AAUP/pubsres/academe/2002/MJ/For+the+Record/FTR2.htm

American Association of University Professors. (2006). *Research on human subjects: Academic freedom and the institutional review board.* Washington, DC: Author. Retrieved from http://www.aaup.org/AAUP/comm/rep/A/humansubs.htm

Atkinson, P. (1990). *The ethnographic imagination.* London, England: Routledge.

Beer, M., & Nohria, N. (2000). Cracking the code of change. *Harvard Business Review, 78*(3), 133–141.

Bogdan, R., & Taylor, S. (1976). The judged, not the judges: An insiders' view of mental retardation. *American Psychologist, 31,* 47–52.

Booth, W. (1998). Doing research with lonely people. *British Journal of Learning Disabilities, 26,* 132–134.

Caughlin, J. P. (2002). The demand/withdraw pattern of communication as a predictor of marital satisfaction over time: Unresolved issues and future directions. *Human Communication Research, 28,* 49–85.

Caughlin, J. P., & Huston, T. L. (2002). A contextual analysis of the association between demand/withdraw and marital satisfaction. *Personal Relationships, 9,* 95–119.

Cloven, D. H., & Roloff, M. E. (1993). The chilling effect of aggressive potential on the expression of complaints in intimate relationships. *Communication Monographs, 60,* 199–219.

Coleman, H. (2004). Rationalizing risk assessment in human subject research. *Arizona Law Review, 46*(1), 5–7.

Collins English dictionary: Complete and unabridged (10th ed.). (2009). Paternalism. New York, NY: HarperCollins.

Cutcliffe, J. R. (2002). Ethics committees, vulnerable groups and paternalism: The case for considering the benefits of participating in qualitative research interviews. In J. Dooher & R. Byrt (Eds.), *Empowerment and participation: Power, influence and control in health care* (pp. 204–219). London, England: Quay Books.

Cutcliffe, J. R., & Ramcharan, P. (2002). Leveling the playing field? Exploring the merits of the ethics-as-process approach for judging qualitative research proposals. *Qualitative Health Research, 12*(7), 1000–1010.

Federman, P. D., Hanna, L. E., & Rodriquiz, L. L. (Eds.). (2003). *Responsible research: A systems approach to protecting research participants.* Washington, DC: The National Academies Press.

Fetterman, D. M. (1998). *Ethnography: Step by step.* Thousand Oaks, CA: Sage.

Fine, G. A., & Deegan, J. (1996). Three principles of serendipity: Insight, chance, and discovery in qualitative research. *Qualitative Studies in Education, 9*(4), 434–447.

Frank, A. W. (2004). Ethics as process and practice. *Internal Medicine Journal, 34*(6), 355–357.

Goffman, E. (1961). *Asylums.* New York, NY: Anchor Books.

Griffin, E. (2010). *A first look at communication theory.* New York, NY: McGraw Hill.

Grover, V., Jeong, S. R., Kettinger, W. J., & Teng, J. T. (1995). The implementation of business process reengineering. *Journal of Management Information Systems, 12*(1), 109–144.

Hewitt, J. (2007). Ethical components of researcher–researched relationships in qualitative interviewing. *Qualitative Health Research, 17*(8), 1149–1159.

King, N., & Anderson, N. R. (1995). *Innovation and change in organizations.* London, England: Routledge.

Koenig, B. A., Back, A. L., & Crawley, L. M. (2003). Qualitative methods in end-of-life research: Recommendations to enhance the protection of human subjects. *Journal of Pain and Symptom Management, 25,* S43–S52.

Kübler-Ross, E. (1973). *On death and dying.* London, England: Routledge.

Lewin, K. (1947). Frontiers in group dynamics. In D. Cartwright (Ed.), *Resolving social conflicts and field theory in social science* (pp. 301–336). Washington, DC: American Psychological Association.

Lincoln, Y. S., & Tierney, W. G. (2004). Qualitative research and institutional review boards. *Qualitative Inquiry, 10,* 219–234.

Malinowski, B. (1950). *Argonauts of the Western Pacific.* New York, NY: Dutton.

May, K. A. (1991). Interviewing techniques in qualitative research: Concerns and challenges. In J. M. Morse (Ed.), *Qualitative nursing research: A contemporary dialogue* (pp. 187–201). Newbury Park, CA: Sage.

Merton, R. K. (1968). *Social theory and social structure.* New York, NY: Free Press.

Morse, J. M., & Field, P. A. (1995). *Qualitative research methods for healthcare professionals* (2nd ed.). London, England: Sage.

Morse, J. M., Niehaus, L., Varnhagen, S., & McIntosh, M. (2008). Qualitative researchers' conceptualizations of the risks inherent in qualitative interviews. In N. Denzin & M. D. Giardina (Eds.), *Qualitative inquiry and the politics of evidence* (pp. 195–218). Walnut Creek, CA: Left Coast Press.

National Commission for the Protection of Human Subjects of Biomedical and Behavioral Research. (1979). *The Belmont report: Ethical principles and guidelines for the protection of human subjects of research.* Washington, DC: Government Printing Office.

Peplau, H. (1988). *Interpersonal relations in nursing* (2nd ed.). London, England: Macmillan.

Piderit, S. K. (2000). Rethinking resistance and recognizing ambivalence: A multidimensional view of attitudes toward an organizational change. *Academy of Management Review, 25*(4), 783–794.

Ramcharan, P., & Cutcliffe, J. R. (2001). Judging the ethics of qualitative research: The "ethics as process" model. *Health and Social Care, 9*(6), 358–367.

Ramos, M. C. (1989). Some ethical implications of qualitative research. *Research in Nursing and Health, 12,* 57–63.

Sartorius, R. (1983). *Paternalism.* Minneapolis: University of Minnesota Press.

Slater, E. E. (2002). IRB reform. *New England Journal of Medicine, 346,* 1402–1404.

Watzlawick, P., Beavin, J., & Jackson, D. (1967). *Pragmatics of human communication.* New York, NY: W. W. Norton.

Watzlawick, P., & Weakland, J. H. (Eds.). (1977). *The interactional view.* Palo Alto, CA: W. W. Norton.

Watzlawick, P., Weakland, J., & Fisch, R. (1974). *Change: Principles of problem formation and problem resolution.* New York, NY: W. W. Norton.

Part VII

CRITICAL REFLECTIONS

35

STORIES ABOUT GETTING STORIES

Interactional Dimensions in Folk and Personal Narrative Research

◆ Kirin Narayan and Kenneth M. George

There is a thirst among the Paxtun women for autobiography. There is also a correct way to "seek the person out" with questions. One day, when my daughter's nanny had observed me eliciting a life story from someone, she later tried to correct me on the grounds that I did not know how to interrogate properly. "You foreigners don't know how to search [latawel] one another," she reproached me. "When we Pakistanis ask a person's story, we don't let a single detail go by. We dig in all the corners, high and low. We seek the person out. That's how we do things. We are storytellers

and story seekers. We know how to draw out a person's heart."

Grima (1991, pp. 81–82)

As this outspoken Paxtun woman from Northwest Pakistan reminds us, asking people for and about stories is a widespread practice, even though the ways of asking and the kinds of stories told may vary. Indeed, most of us are already old experts at coaxing, inviting, or outright demanding stories in our everyday lives. From a child's wheedling, "Tell me," to a friend's bright-eyed prod, "And then what happened?" we regularly make and receive such requests.

Authors' Note: The authors extend their great thanks to Lila Abu-Lughod and Maria Lepowsky for their helpful critiques of an earlier version of this chapter and to the editors of the first and second editions of this *Handbook* for their insightful comments.

Pursuing stories within an interview context, though, we bring a set of disciplinary goals and analytic reflections to storytelling transactions. The delights of a well-told tale may continue to sweep us along, but as interviewers we usually elicit and evaluate stories with particular professional agendas. Like Grima's Paxtun critic, the people we seek to interview sometimes already have their own ideas about how one should go about getting stories from others. Storytelling practices—how to tell stories, when and to whom to tell them, how to classify and interpret them, and the broader social, cultural, and political purposes to which stories are put—vary across communities. As stories move about in a range of interpersonal and institutional settings, the presence of a researcher eagerly seeking narrative materials may provide yet another occasion for retellings. In addition to scholars, there are also other specialists with their own purposes and methods for eliciting stories—therapists, shamans, lawyers, doctors, talk show hosts, priests, immigration officers, police, journalists, human rights workers, and so on. This interactive process of extracting and yielding stories plays an ongoing role in the shaping of social life.

Our task in this chapter is to describe the dynamics of interviewing for two sorts of stories: (1) personal narratives and (2) folk narratives. The distinction between them may seem commonsensical at first: personal narratives as person-centered, experiential, and idiosyncratic folk narratives as collective, traditional, and shared. We will, however, argue that such a distinction becomes blurred under closer view and that scholarly insights developed for one category can also illuminate the other. Second, we explore the interactive dynamics of eliciting stories in interviews, emphasizing the need to be aware of the social life of stories that extend beyond the interview. Third, we argue for the importance of supplementing interviews *for* stories with interviews *about* stories, to comprehend the interpretive frames that surround storytelling transactions. Finally, we point out the usefulness of critically examining interview transcripts in evolving practice.

Many excellent publications are already available with insights and guidelines for ethnographic or folkloristic interviewing more generally (Atkinson, 1998; Briggs, 1986; Holstein & Gubrium, 1995; Ives, 1995; Jackson, 1987; Langness & Frank, 1981; Spradley, 1979). Rather than rehash insights from these other works, we direct interested readers to

them. Here, we will draw on a selection of memorable examples of prior interviews for stories, working from the larger ethnographic record and also from our own fieldwork experiences.

◆ Personal and Folk Narratives

For the better part of the 20th century, most anthropologists, folklorists, and literary specialists assumed that personal narratives are uniquely individual, shaped more by the vagaries of experience than by the conventions of collective tradition. From this vantage, experience appears to dictate the content and form of personal narrative, and so the teller is of central importance. In contrast, folk narratives have been seen as highly conventional, widely shared cultural representations, mediated by the narrative community at large. As Franz Boas (1916) asserted, folk narratives, like myths, "present in a way an autobiography of the tribe" (p. 393). Yet, time and again, the people with whom anthropologists work have not made the same distinction between "personal" and "folk" in terms of the significance of stories to individuals' lives.

Personal stories are also shaped through the use of culturally recognized—and sometimes transculturally negotiated—narrative and linguistic conventions that are themselves differentially put to use by people positioned by gender, age, or class. As life story research in anthropology has shown, such stories are closely tied to cultural conceptions of personhood (Langness & Frank, 1981). So, for example, when Renato Rosaldo (1976) asked his Ilongot "brother" Tukbaw to speak about his own life, he found that Tukbaw chose to build stories around the wise words and advice of his father rather than provide introspective vignettes about feelings or events. Or when Benedicte Grima went to northwest Pakistan in the hope of researching Paxtun women's romance narratives, she soon learned that the stories the women themselves most liked to tell involved tragic tales of personal suffering, the more tragic the better. A woman who hadn't suffered was assumed not to have a life story. As a 30-year-old unmarried schoolteacher told Grima, "I have no story to tell. I have been through no hardships" (Grima, 1991, p. 84). Similarly, in northwest India, Kirin Narayan was startled when Vidhya Sharma, an educated Kangra village woman, claimed that she had no life story.

"Look, it's only when something different has happened that a woman has a story to tell," Vidhya said. "If everything just goes on the way it's supposed to, all you can think of is that you ate, drank, slept, served your husband and brought up your children. What's the story in that?" (Narayan, 2004, p. 227). Building on cultural conceptions, individuals may also elaborate their own tastes and convictions about others as appropriate subjects for life story research. Ruth Behar, for example, found that Esperanza, the Mexican peddler whose life story she recorded, followed a narrative structure that moved from suffering to rage to redemption and appeared to expect other women to follow this too. When Behar proposed to ask other women for their life stories, Esperanza objected to her choice of a respected schoolteacher, declaring, "But she, what has she suffered? I never heard that her husband beat her or that she suffered from rages" (Behar, 1993, p. 12).

While the genre that anthropologists have developed to write about people's lives is labeled "life history," we prefer the term *life story*, or even *life stories*, to draw attention to the fragmentary and constructed nature of personal narratives (cf. Peacock & Holland, 1993). Sometimes, asking someone for a "life story" may appear altogether too overwhelming or foreign a request. Asking about particular eras or incidents may do more to stimulate retellings (see also Abu-Lughod, 1993, p. 46). Whether entire life stories or passing anecdotes, personal narratives emerge to serve culturally story-worthy situations and purposes. By looking at the subjects that people choose to dwell on in narrating their lives, we are in a position to see what most matters to them, from their point of view. Describing the hunting stories that Ilongot men of the Philippines love to tell, Rosaldo (1986) observes, "Narrative can provide a particularly rich source of knowledge about the significance people find in their workaday lives. Such narratives often reveal more about what can make life worth living than about how it is routinely lived" (p. 98).

In addition to being implicitly encoded in cultural practice, conventions for talking about lives can also be actively inculcated by institutional demands of various kinds—including the many approaches toward narrative inquiry circulating in scholarly circles (Chase, 2005). Viewing orally told stories among many kinds of "autobiographical acts," Smith and Watson (2001) point to the role of "coaxers,

coaches and coercers" in eliciting personal narratives (pp. 50–52; see also Gubrium & Holstein, 2001; Holstein & Gubrium, 2000). For example, as Kenneth George (1978) learned in his fieldwork with Pastor John Sherfey, the religious doctrines and practices of evangelical Protestant congregations in the United States lead adherents to routinely "testify" to their spiritual salvation through stories about their personal conversion experience (cf. Harding, 1987, 2001; Titon, 1988; Titon & George, 1977, 1978). Or as Carole Cain (1991) has argued, Alcoholics Anonymous (AA) teaches newcomers how to tell a confessional story in which they are not just drinkers but alcoholics who have hit rock bottom and need help. Through pamphlets, the examples of others' storytelling, and feedback from fellow participants at AA meetings, people joining the group learn how to shape personal experience along the lines of this key story form. Markets, too, require life stories, especially in establishing literary or artistic reputations or in setting artistic value (cf. Bourdieu, 1993). And we would further add that governmentality always involves shaping citizenship and personal identity around the narrative demands of the nation-state.

Even as personal narratives are shaped by salient storytelling conventions, folk narratives circulating within and across communities are personalized through retellings. If we shift attention from traditional stories to the storytellers, it becomes clear that storytellers put their own creative and aesthetic stamp on folk narratives, personalizing them through retellings to fit particular occasions (Azadovskii, 1974; Degh, 1969). As Swamiji, a Hindu holy man who delighted in making moral and spiritual points through stories, once reflected to Narayan, people told stories according to their own feelings and the feelings of their audience. As Swamiji said,

> When you tell a story, you should look at the situation and tell it. Then it turns out well. If you just tell any story any time, it's not really good. You must consider the time and shape the story so it's right. All stories are told for some purpose. (Narayan, 1989, p. 37)

Occasionally, storytellers may make explicit links between their folk narratives and their lives. So, for example, Urmilaji, a woman in the Himalayan foothills, once compared the hard times she had experienced to the wanderings of an exiled king and queen in one of the folktales she had told Narayan. In making this explicit connection, Urmilaji was shedding light not just on her own life but on the traditional tale too. When Urmilaji's family priest retold the same story, forefronting the beleaguered king and downplaying the travails of his loyal wife, it became clear that both tellers were recasting the tale according to their own gendered experiences (Narayan, 1997, pp. 121–124; cf. Taggart, 1990).

Reading life histories, one can occasionally witness the subject straining against an anthropologist's conceptions of appropriate "personal" content in an interview. So, for example, when the energetic !Kung woman Nisa suggested to Margery Shostak, "Let's continue our talk about long ago. Let's also talk about the stories that the old people know" (Shostak, 1983, p. 40), it is possible that Nisa was trying to include some of her repertoire of traditional tales within the frame of her life stories. Collecting oral histories, Julie Cruikshank (1990, 1998, 2005) found that the Yukon women elders whose life stories she was recording insisted that their myths were *a part* of their lives and interspersed retellings of myth with oral histories in ways that directly inspired Cruikshank's scholarship. Similarly, Michael Young (1983) admits in the prologue to *Magicians of Manumanua: Living Myth in Kalauna* that his book emerged from an attempt to make sense of the ritual expert Iyahalina's puzzling response to a request for his life history:

> Instead of telling me tales from his childhood, recounting the circumstances of his marriage, or enumerating his mature achievements, he narrated a sequence of myths and legends that described the activities of his ancestors. He concluded with a passionate peroration on the ritual duties they had bequeathed him, the central task of which was to "sit still" in order to anchor the community in prosperity. (pp. 3–4)

As Young learned, Iyahalina and other hereditary guardians of myths on Goodenough Island identified with the heroes of their myths and drew on mythic themes to construct their own autobiographical narratives. At the same time, possession of these myths was a means of asserting status. In a related vein, Lepowsky (1993, p. 126) found that in Vanatinai, New Guinea, women could also own authoritative versions of myths, a fact that she links to women's stature within this more gender-egalitarian society.

Rather than suppress the disjunction between the kinds of stories we might seek and the stories that we obtain in an interview, interviewers can fruitfully explore this gap between analytic categories and the locally conceived genres that index social power. As the examples just cited show, reflecting on that "gap" can be a source of scholarly insight and creativity (cf. Bauman & Briggs, 1992; Ben-Amos, 1969/1976; Briggs, 1986).

Even when we receive the sorts of stories we are looking for, the underlying narrative ideology might differ, as both Susan Harding (1987, 2001) and Kenneth George (1978) discovered in their respective studies of evangelical Protestant speech in the American South. For the pastors who spoke with Harding and George, the conversations were not "interviews" so much as "testimonies" to the power of God and Christ in their personal lives and in the world more generally. These pastors were also explicit about using the interview testimonies to persuade the interviewers to confess their sins and seek forgiveness and salvation through God in Christ. In this way, the pastors were able to put Harding and George's respective scholarly endeavors to work for their own greater spiritual purpose.

Thus, narratives are not just vehicles for cultural representation; they are also potent tools in social interaction, a form of cultural work. By "cultural work," we mean the ways narrators and audiences use narrative resources for political and social ends. While stories of different kinds certainly contain representations of cultural values, concerns, and patterns, we cannot forget that stories—like all genres of speech—are also practices intended to get things done: to entertain, edify, shock, terrorize, intimidate, heal, comfort, confess, persuade, divulge, and more. Narrative form, then, does not only conjure up other worlds, whether imagined or remembered, but it is also a way to use words for social and political purposes in the immediacies of this world.

◆ Getting Stories

A researcher should always be alert to the ways stories are narrated as part of ongoing social life and to the commentaries, debates, revisions, and retellings they evoke. Yet researchers are not always so lucky as to be in the right place at the right time to participate in the many varied moments when people tell or comment on stories that circulate in everyday life. When researchers do have a chance to listen in, their very presence cannot help but shape different aspects of the storytelling occasion; even "conversationally shared stories" (see also Prasad, 2007) can be subtly transformed by the presence of a recording device. Furthermore, a single narrative performance is usually not enough to gain insight into the larger ongoing life of stories and storytelling encounters. Interviews, then, are a useful supplement to the ethnographer's taking part in social life in an engaged, observant way.

Because all storytelling events are situationally unique, narratives heard or exchanged in interviews should not be carelessly confused with or substituted for narratives that take place outside the interview context. All stories emerging from an interview will bear the mark of an interviewer's presence and goals and the hierarchical dynamics of the interview situation. Yet we should not dismiss interview narratives as artificial or contrived. Rather, like so many other social encounters, interviews are culturally negotiated events worthy of analysis (see Briggs, 1986). Since the interview can be an invitation to narrate, it is a wonderful opportunity to grasp—or to at least begin to think about—the complexity of stories exchanged elsewhere in a community.

The word *interview* has roots in Old French and at one time meant something like "to see one another." While we cannot ignore the social hierarchies of inquiry, we want to underscore how "seeing one another" in interviews requires close attentiveness and an openness to the surprises of dialogue and exchange. How an interview runs its course depends very much on all the participants involved. It is important for the interviewer to be flexible and ready to follow the unexpected paths that emerge in the course of talking together with interviewees. In fact, in our experience, interviews often end up having less to do with structured questions or answers than with the animated exchange of stories. A willingness to reveal one's own stories can also add depth to an interview, inspiring the person one is interviewing to open up.

The ethnographic interview is a bid on the part of a researcher to get a subject to converse openly about a set of issues of concern to the researcher. The political conditions surrounding the consent and participation of interviewees in ethnographic interviews—and in the negotiated elicitation of stories—have been anticipated in human subject protocols designed to hold in check the potentially coercive impulses of social scientific and humanistic inquiry. Setting up an interview becomes an invitation to narrate, albeit one that can be refused, subverted, or turned back on the interviewer.

Seeking stories through interview soon reveals a range of storytelling styles. Some people are energetic raconteurs who will use the interview as a welcome occasion to spin stories. Stories may pour toward the researcher in such dizzying numbers that all he or she needs to do is show engagement with nods or murmurs. In the presence of such practiced storytellers, an interviewer may have to struggle to redirect the stories toward subjects suited to his or her specific interests. Sometimes, the interviewer may need to clarify details. But mostly, when a storyteller takes charge, an interviewer's work is to listen with attentive care so as to formulate necessary questions when the retelling is over.

In other cases, an interviewer has to work harder. It may take a while to formulate the right questions that inspire the telling of stories. Questions that can be answered by a simple "yes" or "no" are particular hazards that give an interviewer a sense of getting nowhere at all. Sometimes, a person is more willing to tell stories outside the formal context of an interview, without recording devices or notebooks at hand. Occasionally, a person being interviewed is willing to tell stories about some things but not others. Here, for example, is a moment from Narayan's (KN) fieldwork in the Northwest Himalayan foothills, when Suman Kumari (SK), a woman who had been animatedly telling stories about her grandmother's and mother's difficult lives, seemed to lose narrative direction when it came to recounting her own life trajectory.

KN: And after that?

SK: After that what can I say? What can I say, Bahenji? (*she turns to her half sister, who along with the mother, is listening in*). After that—that's all: sons and all that, and daughters-in-law.

KN: (*seeing that SK is still speaking from the perspective of her mother, tries to turn the interview to SKs own life*) And your earliest memories were of this place? What was your childhood like?

SK: (*looking at her sister again*) What should I tell her about my childhood, Bahenji?

Sister: That you went to school in your childhood—that's just fine.

[*Both sisters laugh.*]

SK: What happened is that we went to school, we ate food. Sometimes there would be mangoes on the trees and we'd eat a lot. In the house, she (*indicating her mother*) would say, "Go to sleep." But as soon as she was asleep, then all three of us would run out!

In a cursory way, Suman Kumari gestured toward memories of school, food, mangos, and naps, yet her own life clearly did not have as much interest to her as tales of her female ancestors. Though Narayan tried to refuel the narrative with questions, these reminiscences soon sputtered to a halt.

Asking people to specify can sometimes be helpful. For example, if someone says, "Life was hard," asking for the ways that life was hard, or if there are any particular moments that stand out as being especially hard, can result in the unpacking of stories. However, the more an interviewer works at extracting a story, the less sure one can be whether this is a story already present in a person's repertoire or whether it has been created only by the interview. This is one of the reasons why including the questions that a researcher asks in the final published work can be crucial to showing how the materials emerged as part of a dialogical process (Dwyer, 1982; Mintz, 1960/1974).

In addition, it's useful to reflect on the structural relations between the interviewer and interviewee, and an interviewee's own reasons for sharing stories. For example, preparing to be interviewed by Barbara Myerhoff in Venice Beach, California, the elderly retired tailor Shmuel Goldman wrote out memories in Yiddish from his childhood in the Jewish quarter of a Polish town; he read these to her in English and elaborated with oral stories. Later, he mused,

> For myself, growing old would be altogether a different thing if that little town was there still. . . . But when I come back from these stories and remember the way they lived is gone forever, wiped out like you would erase a line of writing, then it means another thing altogether for me to accept leaving this life. If my life goes now, it

means nothing. But if my life goes, with my memories, and all that is lost, that is something else to bear. (Myerhoff, 1978, p. 74)

Shmuel sent Myerhoff home with what he called "all this package of stories"; a day later, he died in his sleep. Shmuel's words remind us that sometimes interviews are of value to not just scholars. Transmitting memories to an eager audience, ensuring the survival of stories beyond a limited lifetime, an interviewee may also have a stake in the process.

The elicitation of stories in interviews may be subject to wider constraints around narrative practice. Examples abound in many Native American communities, where storytelling is often intimately linked to seasons, especially winter. To tell or elicit stories at other times can be complicated. So, for example, if a storyteller among the Anishanaabe (Ojibwa) wishes to tell myths outside the winter months, he or she can put on a white weasel pelt, as though simulating snow. Exploring indigenous sacred traditions in the highlands of South Sulawesi, Indonesia, George (1996) had to adjust his interview work to fit with taboos that regulated the time and place for narrative activity: During the long months that stretched from the time of preparing rice fields to the time of harvest, community-wide prohibitions against storytelling and singing were in place, and so he could neither gather nor discuss narrative materials. Once the postharvest ritual season of about 2 months began, he was at liberty to record and discuss traditional songs and stories. Even then, certain taboos remained in effect. For example, *sumengo*—a genre of ritual song associated with headhunting narratives—could only be performed and discussed for 1 week of the year in any given community. As a result, George had to adjust his research, moving from community to community as sets of taboos came into effect in one yet were relaxed in another.

The kinds of stories appropriate to tell may vary not just with calendrical cycles but also with social location. Gender and age are particularly important factors to consider. For example, adult males in many of Southeast Asia's upland communities especially favor personal stories about going on journeys (see, e.g., George, 1996; Rosaldo, 1976; Steedly, 1993; Tsing, 1993). Interestingly, many of the mythic and historical narratives in these regions feature male "culture heroes" whose journeys lead to the foundation of the communities in question.

Thus, men's contemporary tales of personal journeys resonate well with the foundational narratives of any specific locale. Women in these same communities have less to say about personal journeys but comparatively more when it comes to talking about trance experience (George, 1993; Steedly, 1993; Tsing, 1993). While both men and women in these communities go on journeys and go into trance, in an important sense it is more relevantly male to make a story of personal travel and more relevantly female to talk about trance experience. The very familiarity and pervasiveness of this pattern makes it all the more striking when, for example, a woman recounts the dangers of a journey she has made. Her move into a typically "male" narrative terrain, then, is an exceptionally revealing and socially salient example of gender play and transgression.

Storytelling forms are not static. Like other genres, different kinds of stories evolve within the play of power in ongoing social life and in dialogue with other genres (Bauman & Briggs, 1992). This means that there may be shifts in the kinds of stories that are appropriate for different social groups to tell. In his long-term research among the Kwaio of the Solomon Islands, Roger Keesing (1985) at first found men ready to talk about their lives, while women "were fragmented and brief, distancing themselves from serious autobiography with reciprocal jests" (p. 29). On return visits, he found that men's efforts to codify cultural rules and conventions, or *kastom*, as a form of postcolonial resistance to outside influences had also inspired women to think of culture as an objectifiable "thing" and to lay claim to their own accounts of *kastom* in which women's importance was given its due. When Kwaio women finally spoke out, they were doing so in counterpoint to the men who had previously been working with Keesing (1985) to codify *kastom*; also, senior women recounted their lives "*as moral texts, as exemplifications of the trials, responsibilities, virtues and tragedies of A Woman's Life*" (p. 33). Speaking out, for Kwaio women, was a bid to power. While acknowledging the wider historical shifts that made women perceive their life stories as valuable texts to transact, Keesing also mentions the importance of what he terms "the politics of the elicitation situation" (p. 37)—that is, the particular interpersonal circumstances of the interview. That he was joined by a female fieldworker during the time when he was able to finally record women's stories was

also a key factor in coaxing Kwaio women, who had previously been silent about their lives, into animated speaking subjects.

For folklorists, there is an implicit understanding that any retelling is a *version* rather than *the* story. There is no urtext, no abstract cultural schema, no basically basic story or structure behind these narrations; there is instead an ongoing history of narratives and retellings that is recalled and put to use in the present (George, 1996, p. 14; cf. McGann, 1991; Smith, 1981). To track the wider life of stories and their constituent parts beyond particular iterations, folklorists have developed tools such as tale-type indexes and motif indexes. At the same time, attention to performance has shown how stories emerge within the parameters of particular contexts rather than as perfect forms that float above social life. Such attention to the surfacing of versions in performance can be applied to life histories. So, for example, Laurel Kendall was able to record multiple versions of the stories that Yongsu's mother, a Korean shaman, dramatically retold to Kendall, neighbors, and clients to make varied points about gender, the power of gods, the dangers of lapses in ritual, and so on (Kendall, 1988). George (1978; Titon & George, 1978) did much the same thing in his study of conversion narratives. He recorded Pastor John Sherfey retelling the story of his conversion nine times—three times in the context of interviews (which Sherfey regarded as testimonies) and six times in the context of preaching and chanting of improvised sermons. The differences between the versions reflected Sherfey's pragmatic rhetorical strategies for each situation, from conversations with relative strangers to sermons before a familiar audience of weekly churchgoers and to the sinners attending a tent revival.

We also would suggest that moving beyond one life story to compare several related life stories may bring narrative forms and their transgressions into clearer focus. This method of juxtaposing life stories was pioneered by Oscar Lewis (1961) in his work with a poor Mexican family, where each family member recounted his or her own stories, revealing multifaceted, cross-cutting, and even diverging perspectives on the same episodes. This method has also been used in other life histories (see Mintz 1960/1974; Viramma & Racine, 1997) to reveal how positioned perspectives and gendered conventions pervade the shaping of life stories.

To summarize, then, we would like to emphasize the value of eliciting several versions of folktales and life stories—from the same person through time, and from different people—so that one can see how the uniqueness of a particular telling emerges within larger patterns. Collecting multiple versions of folk narratives and life stories and talking to different storytellers is vital to understanding how narrative traditions are creatively reworked by particular tellers for particular social ends. Also, situating the performance of different versions within social interactions reveals the role of storytelling in the exercise of power, authority, and identity.

◆ Interviews About Stories

Getting a story during an interview still leaves unfinished the intellectual work of making sense of the story. Engaging interviewees in the interpretive process carries great rewards not only for comprehending the meanings, motives, and contexts within and around stories but also for better understanding how interviewees themselves assess the project of interviewing.

For folklore scholarship, Alan Dundes (1966) termed the move beyond eliciting texts to also comprehending indigenous meanings "oral literary criticism." Affirming the theoretical and methodological value of this method, Narayan (1995) also argued for eliciting generalized commentaries on a genre of folklore to supplement talk about particular texts. So if people might find it too revealing to explain *why* they tell a particular story, one can elicit valuable insights by asking about why people more generally tell stories and what kinds of meanings certain sorts of stories might carry.

Narayan (1997) sought to put this method to work through a collaboration with "Urmilaji" (Urmila Devi Sood), the wise woman we met earlier. After hearing Urmilaji's tales, Narayan transcribed them, thought about them, and came back to talk more—about texts in particular and what meanings they held and about storytelling in general. Sometimes her questions mystified Urmilaji, and at other times, Urmilaji expounded implicit meanings in the tales, self-evident to most Kangra people but perplexing to Narayan: for example, that characters so often, at the end of stories, dropped dead from shame because exposure had compromised their honor. Speaking with Urmilaji about her stories, Narayan also came to understand how stories can be associated with particular prior tellers, keeping their wisdom and influence alive. Urmilaji, for example, loved many of these tales because they had been gifts, lovingly imparted, by her father and aunt-in-law.

Talking to people about stories is a chance to learn how the stories work interpersonally and psychologically. Keith Basso has explored how, among the Western Apache, historical tales bearing moral points are associated with various sites in the landscape. A place called "Trail Goes Down Between Two Hills," for example, is associated with a story about lascivious Old Man Owl and how he was tricked by two beautiful girls; telling this story might comment on how someone's behavior involves uncurbed appetites and so is laughable and offensive (Basso, 1996, pp. 113–120). By telling a story instead of speaking directly, a critique is implied rather than directly stated. The moral points carried within stories become embodied within the geographical landscape, reminding people of occasions when places have been pointed out to them. As Nick Thompson, a spirited elderly Apache, explained to Basso (1996), stories "go to work on your mind and make you think about your life" (p. 58). Using the metaphor of hunting for the aiming of stories at an appropriate quarry, Thompson went on to describe how, when people acted inappropriately, someone would go hunting for them.

> So someone stalks you and tells a story about what happened long ago. It doesn't matter if other people are around—you're going to know that he's aiming that story at you. All of a sudden it *hits* you! It's like an arrow, they say. Sometimes it just bounces off—it's too soft and you don't think about anything. But when it's strong it goes in deep and starts working on your mind right away. No one says anything to you, only that story is all, but now you know that people have been watching you and talking about you. They don't like how you've been acting. So you have to think about your life. (pp. 58–59)

The messages, then, are reinforced by place: "You're going to see the place where it happened, maybe every day if it's nearby. . . . If you don't see it, you're going to hear its name and see it in your mind" (Basso, 1996, p. 59). Even when the original storytellers die, places continue to stalk the person, reminding him or her how to live right. In this conception of storytelling, then, a good story pierces deep and transforms a person from inside even while its effects are continually reinforced by the outer landscape.

In some societies, much of the power of stories lies in internalizing and embodying them—a "living myth," as Young (1983) memorably puts it. Thus, inviting someone to stand aside to extract explicit meaning, without a cultural frame of reference, may indeed be annoying. As Elsie Mather, a Yup'ik teacher, forcefully wrote to Phyllis Morrow (1995) when the question of explication came up in the course of their collaboration in documenting Yup'ik oral traditions,

Why do people want to reduce traditional stories to information, to some function? Isn't it enough that we hear and read them? They cause us to wonder about things, and sometimes they touch us briefly along the way, or we connect the information or idea into something we are doing at the moment. This is what the old people say a lot. They tell us to listen even when we don't understand, that later on we will make some meaning or that something that we had listened to before will touch us in some way. Understanding and knowing occur over one's lifetime. . . .

Why would I want to spoil the repetition and telling of stories with questions? Why would I want to know what they mean? (p. 33)

Like Nick Thompson, Morrow reminds us how stories live in ongoing reverberations through lived practices, not just in analytic reflection. Asking people for meaning isolated from particular contexts of retelling or remembering may appear to fix meaning in inappropriate ways. As Margaret Mills (1991) found in her research in Afghanistan, storytellers may actually thrive on the ambiguity of storytelling and the intertextual relations between stories, as it allows them to make sly commentaries on the sociopolitical world beyond the stories.

The analytic stance that breaks up stories may be perceived as dangerous for other reasons too. In a dramatic example of the dangers of researching stories without being cognizant of their social role or power, Barre Toelken has traced different moments of "enlightenment" in his long-term research on

Navajo Coyote tales. With growing understanding of these Coyote tales, he was told that these were not just entertainment for winter months but were also used in Navajo healing ceremonies. When Toelken discussed the use of these tales with an elderly Navajo singer one night, the singer asked, "Are you ready to lose someone in your family?" Baffled, Toelken asked him to explain. This was the cost of taking up witchcraft, the singer told him. Toelken had been unaware that because of the sorts of questions he asked, he was thought to have an interest in witchcraft, with potentially malevolent repercussions for everyone around him. As Toelken (1996) writes,

For just as the tales themselves in their narration are normally used to create a harmonious world in which to live, and just as elliptical references to the tales can be used within rituals to clarify and enhance the healing processes, so the tales can be dismembered and used outside the proper ritual arena by witches to promote disharmony and to thwart the healing processes. In discussing parts and motifs separately, by dealing with them as interesting ideas which might lead me to discoveries of my own, I had been doing something like taking all the powerful medicines to be found in all the doctors' offices in the land and dumping them by the bucketload out of a low-flying chopper over downtown Los Angeles. (p. 11)

Asking for help with interpretations, then, is like walking a razor's edge: By asking, one runs the danger of making severe cultural faux pas, like Toelken, while by not asking, one risks attributing one's own interpretative frames to subjects. The same dangers hold for both folk narrative and personal narrative, though with personal narrative people may be even more sensitive to interpretations made without consulting them.

A powerful example of the conflict that can arise when informants do not share the interpretations with their interviewers is described in an essay by Katherine Borland (1991). Borland interviewed her grandmother Beatrice Hanson about events that had taken place in 1944, when Beatrice attended a horse race and bet against the wishes of her father. Borland then wrote a student essay in which she interpreted her grandmother's actions as enacting a female struggle for autonomy and, thus, as being feminist. Yet her grandmother, after reading the essay, wrote a

14-page letter in which she pointedly objected to her feminist granddaughter's interpretation:

> So your interpretation of the story as a female struggle for autonomy within a hostile male environment is entirely YOUR interpretation. You've read into the story what you wished to—what pleases YOU. That it was never—by any wildest stretch of the imagination—the concern of the originator of the story makes such an interpretation a definite and complete distortion, and in this respect I question its authenticity. The story is no longer MY story at all. The skeleton remains, but it has become your story. Right? How far is it permissible to go in the name of folklore [or scholarship generally] and still be honest in respect to the original narrative? (Borland, 1991)

This disagreement resulted in a dialogue where both grandmother and granddaughter explained the assumptions they were working from and the different associations they brought to the term *feminist*. In the process of this conflict and the ensuing discussion, each woman stretched to understand the other's position, and each was educated in the process.

Indeed, feminist work on life stories has been at the forefront of exploring issues of possible reciprocity amid the hierarchical imbalances of interviews and their outcomes (cf. Gluck & Patai, 1991; Personal Narratives Group, 1989). The sociologist Ann Oakley (1981), for example, long ago advocated replacing a distanced interviewing technique that seeks to deflect questions aimed at the interviewer with "a different role, that could be termed 'no intimacy without reciprocity,'" especially for in-depth interviewing through time. She writes, "This involves being sensitive not only to those questions that are asked (by either party) but to those that are not asked. The interviewee's definition of the interview is important" (p. 49). Elaine Lawless (1991) has worked out a system of "reciprocal ethnography" when eliciting the life stories of Pentecostal women ministers: Even as she sought to interpret their personal narratives, she allowed the women ministers to critique and reflect on her ethnographic practices. Such openness to the perspectives of the people interviewed can radically reframe the scholarly project, enhancing accountability to the contradictions and inequalities of the real world.

◆ The Lives of Interviews: Further Reflections

Before bringing this chapter to a close, we want to remind readers that interviews take place in the daily flow of life. Although some issues and methodologies may call for structured, formal interviews that take interview subjects momentarily away from their everyday circumstances, most of what we learn as ethnographers takes place in the intersubjective flow of what Renato Rosaldo (1989) calls "observant participation." This includes interviews that, in our experience, unfold as brief informal exchanges embedded in long conversations, the routines of daily life, and the deepening bonds of collaborative friendships.

Kenneth George began working with the Indonesian painter Abdul Djalil Pirous in 1994 to study the rise of Islamic art and culture in that country. In their first months together, they would sit down for "interview" evenings—usually with Pirous's wife or children listening in—to record the artist's stories of his life and career up to that time. These storytelling sessions became a bond between them, such that Pirous invited George to help him with his 2002 retrospective show at Jakarta's National Gallery and to write his biography for the event. Working shoulder to shoulder with the artist gave George many occasions to ask about Pirous's signature Qur'anic paintings, paintings that the artist calls his "spiritual notes" (*catatan spiritual*). For example, George recounts a conversation as he helped Pirous move a particular Qur'anic painting he had just completed for a client:

> As we eased the ungainly painting off the work table, around a cabinet, and into another room, I asked how he came up with the verse for the painting. The client, Pirous began to explain, had come to him the year before saying, "Pirous, you are like a father to me. I want a painting with a lesson in it. I will hang it somewhere in my house where it will keep me company when I am old." So Pirous had the burden of selecting a passage from the *Qur'an* that would speak to the client. We leaned the canvas against a pillar, and then my friend took out an Indonesian edition of the *Qur'an* to read to me the verses featured in the painting. They were from QS 17, *Bani Isra'il*,

verses 35–7. . . . The passages were an admonition to the client. "It is a reminder to seek knowledge (*berilmu*), do good deeds (*beramal*), and to be humble (*merunduk*)," [said Pirous], "If he doesn't like it and doesn't want it, that's okay, so what? I will keep it, I like it a lot."

We stepped back and, standing side by side, looked over the painting some more. "So, do you think he'll like it?" I asked after a few moments. Pirous turned to me, shrugging. "You know, you grasp a painting as a whole," he replied, "In a single moment you either like it or you don't. It doesn't need time. But for the verse here, you need time for that, for reflection. That's why I say there is aesthetic pleasure and ethical fulfillment in my paintings." (George, 2010, pp. 99–100)

In a sense, George's long-standing friendship with the artist is an ongoing "interview" or "conversation" through which he learns not just about Qur'anic verse but about ways in which stories help turn paintings into meaningful and companionable objects.

In that same project, George also compared his interview materials about Pirous's first exploration of Qur'anic art in 1971 with published interviews the artist had granted to art historians, journalists, and others scholars. Scouring through newspapers, exhibit brochures, and clippings, George did not come across a public account of Pirous's "conversion" to Islamic aesthetics published before 1985. By the early 1990s, it is a polished and well-rehearsed story. This suggests that it took over a decade for the story to take settled form as part of the artist's broader life story and career history. Although the story earns a place in George's research, it is also fundamental to the art market's need for publicity and painterly reputations.

Narayan's interest in the ways folk narrative and personal narrative interweave led her toward family stories. For years, she has written down or taped key versions of family stories from her Indian relatives: informal interviews that serve as an affirmation of shared identity and that she has drawn on both for scholarly essay (Narayan, 2007a) and by implicitly embedding insights on interactional dynamics within a book-length family memoir (Narayan, 2007b).

We have found that a lot can be learned not just from looking at the work of others but also from looking back at one's own interview practices, whether this involves listening again to tapes or

studying transcripts. Most immediately, such a review can help a researcher frame questions about stories already recorded and so more self-consciously engage interviewees in an unfolding interpretive process. More generally, encountering one's own shortcomings can be very instructive for future practice. For example, interviewers may find moments when they have asked questions that elicit "yes" or "no" answers instead of stories, moments when they have interrupted, moments when they have radically misunderstood what someone was trying to say and taken an interview off on a new tangent, and so on. Bruce Jackson (1987) possibly summarizes what many of us feel on transcribing our own tapes when he says, "The most important thing I learned was that I talked too much" (p. 81). Revisiting interviews across time, themes that one might have previously ignored might emerge; Narayan (2009), for example, found on listening again to tapes and looking through notes many years after she had written about a Hindu guru's storytelling as a form of religious teaching that all along he had also been giving her recipes and instructions for cooking.

The mortifying process of looking back at interviews leads one to forgive oneself, to make the best of what has been done, and to look ahead to the next interview or publication. In querying one's own interview practices, it is useful to recall the poet Rilke's (1984) stricture to "Live the questions" (p. 34) rather than expect fixed and certain answers.

◆ Conclusions

The interest in "getting stories" has an institutional backdrop and a place within broader fields of everyday inquiry. As we stated in opening, it is not just scholars who want to obtain stories but the police, medical and psychiatric diagnosticians, journalists, refugee agencies, shamans, social workers, state and corporate bureaucracies, courts, and human rights organizations too. Interview narratives have been put to use not just by anthropologists or folklorists but also by colonizers seeking to comprehend "the native mind," nationalists wanting to mobilize support around an imagined "spirit of the people," and those promoting regional and state articulations of identity.

The distinction between "personal" and "folk" narrative, we have argued, is often blurred in practice, and so cross-fertilizing methodologies and theories usually associated with one body of stories or the other may be a source of creative insight. We have emphasized the need to follow other people's own conceptions of stories: as speech genres and as interpersonal, politically charged transactions with a life outside an interview context. Paying attention to the kinds of people who are storytellers, the kinds of stories appropriate to tell with social location, transformations in the kinds of stories told, and the shifting multiplicity of versions enhances appreciation for the specificity of stories that emerge within interviews.

In addition to gathering stories in interviews, we have underscored the value of talking about stories with both the storytellers and listeners. Being sensitive to indigenous conceptions of the meaning and psychological impact of stories can bring our own interpretive biases to light, to be transformed in constructive dialogues. Sometimes, cultural sensitivity may require holding back on analytic questions that carve up stories into constituent elements, cutting them away from the ongoing flow of lived experience.

Finally, we have argued for the ongoing fruits of critically examining interview tapes or transcripts, thus learning to ask and to listen with greater skill. Often, being a good interviewer for stories involves not just asking the right questions but sympathetically listening and holding questions back so that the person being interviewed can shape stories in his or her own way. Equally, being a good interviewer may involve responding to questions from an interviewee and so entering into a reciprocal exchange.

Telling and listening to stories is at the heart of social and cultural life. Much of what we understand as personhood, identity, intimacy, secrecy, experience, belief, history, and common sense turns on the exchange of stories between people. In receiving stories from people, we are often receiving gifts of self. It is incumbent on us to handle these gifts with respect as we pass them onward in our scholarly productions.

◆ References

Abu-Lughod, L. (1993). *Writing women's worlds: Bedouin stories*. Berkeley: University of California Press.

Atkinson, R. (1998). *The life story interview* (Sage University Papers Series on Qualitative Research Methods, Vol. 44). Thousand Oaks, CA: Sage.

Azadovskii, M. (1974). *A Siberian tale teller* (J. Dow, Trans.). Austin: University of Texas Press.

Basso, K. (1996). *Wisdom sits in places: Landscape and language among the Western Apache*. Albuquerque: University of New Mexico Press.

Bauman, R., & Briggs, C. L. (1992). Genre, intertextuality and social power. *Journal of Linguistic Anthropology, 2,* 131–172.

Behar, R. (1993). *Translated woman*. Boston, MA: Beacon Press.

Ben-Amos, D. (1976). Analytical categories and ethnic genres. In D. Ben-Amos (Ed.), *Folklore genres* (pp. 215–242). Austin: University of Texas Press. (Original work published 1969)

Boas, F. (1916). *Tsimshian mythology* (31st Annual Report of the Bureau of American Ethnology). Washington, DC: Smithsonian Institution.

Borland, K. (1991). "That's not what I said": Interpretive conflict in oral narrative research. In S. B. Gluck & D. Patai (Eds.), *Women's words: The feminist practice of oral history* (pp. 63–76). New York, NY: Routledge.

Bourdieu, P. (1993). *The field of cultural production: Essays on art and literature*. New York, NY: Columbia University Press.

Briggs, C. (1986). *Learning how to ask: A sociolinguistic appraisal of the role of the interview in social science research*. Cambridge, UK: Cambridge University Press.

Cain, C. (1991). Personal stories, identity acquisition and self-understanding in alcoholics anonymous. *Ethos, 19,* 210–253.

Chase, S. E. (2005). Narrative inquiry: Multiple lenses, approaches, voices. In N. K. Denzin & Y. S. Lincoln (Eds.), *The SAGE handbook of qualitative research* (3rd ed., pp. 652–679). Thousand Oaks, CA: Sage.

Cruikshank, J. (with Sidney, A., Smith, K., & Ned, A.). (1990). *Life lived like a story: Life stories of three Yukon native elders*. Lincoln: University of Nebraska Press.

Cruikshank, J. (1998). *The social life of stories: Narrative and knowledge in the Yukon Territory*. Vancouver, British Columbia, Canada: UBC Press.

Cruikshank, J. (2005). *Do glaciers listen? Local knowledge, colonial encounters, and social imagination*. Seattle: University of Washington Press.

Degh, L. (1969). *Folktales and society: Story telling in a Hungarian peasant community* (E. M. Schossberger, Trans.). Bloomington: Indiana University Press.

Dundes, A. (1966). Metafolklore and oral literary criticism. *The Monist, 60,* 505–516.

Dwyer, K. (1982). *Moroccan dialogues: Anthropology in question*. Baltimore, MD: Johns Hopkins University Press.

George, K. M. (1978). *"I still got it": The conversion narrative of John C. Sherfey* (Master's thesis). University of North Carolina, Chapel Hill.

George, K. M. (1993). Music-making, ritual, and gender in a Southeast Asian hill society. *Ethnomusicology, 37*(1), 1–27.

George, K. M. (1996). *Showing signs of violence: The cultural politics of a twentieth-century headhunting ritual*. Berkeley: University of California Press.

George, K. M. (2010). *Picturing Islam: Art and ethics in a Muslim lifeworld*. Malden, MA: Wiley-Blackwell.

Gluck, S. B., & Patai, D. (Eds.). (1991). *Women's words: The feminist practice of oral history*. New York, NY: Routledge.

Grima, B. (1991). Suffering in women's performance of *Paxto*. In A. Appadurai, F. J. Korom, & M. Mills (Eds.), *Gender, genre and power in South Asian expressive traditions* (pp. 78–101). Philadelphia: University of Pennsylvania Press.

Gubrium, J. F., & Holstein, J. A. (Eds.). (2001). *Institutional selves: Troubled identities in a postmodern world*. New York, NY: Oxford University Press.

Harding, S. (1987). Convicted by the Holy Spirit: The rhetoric of fundamental Baptist conversion. *American Ethnologist, 14*(1), 167–181.

Harding, S. (2001). *The book of Jerry Falwell: Fundamentalist language and politics*. Princeton, NJ: Princeton University Press.

Holstein, J. A., & Gubrium, J. F. (1995). *The active interview* (Sage University Papers Series on Qualitative Research Methods, Vol. 37). Thousand Oaks, CA: Sage.

Holstein, J. A., & Gubrium, J. F. (2000). *The self we live by: Narrative identity in a postmodern world*. New York, NY: Oxford University Press.

Ives, E. D. (1995). *The tape recorded interview: A manual for fieldworkers in folklore and oral history* (2nd ed.). Knoxville: University of Tennessee Press.

Jackson, B. (1987). *Fieldwork*. Urbana: University of Illinois Press.

Keesing, R. (1985). Kwaio women speak. *American Anthropologist, 87*, 27–39.

Kendall, L. (1988). *The life and hard times of a Korean shaman: Of tales and the telling of tales*. Honolulu: University of Hawaii Press.

Langness, L. L., & Frank, G. (1981). *Lives: An anthropological approach to biography*. Novato, CA: Chandler & Sharp.

Lawless, E. (1991). Women's life stories and reciprocal ethnography as feminist and emergent. *Journal of Folklore Research, 29*, 35–60.

Lepowsky, M. (1993). *Fruit of the motherland: Gender in an egalitarian society*. New York, NY: Columbia University Press.

Lewis, O. (1961). *The children of Sánchez: Autobiography of a Mexican family*. New York, NY: Random House.

McGann, J. J. (1991). *The textual condition*. Princeton, NJ: Princeton University Press.

Mills, M. (1991). *Rhetorics and politics in Afghan traditional storytelling*. Philadelphia: University of Pennsylvania Press.

Mintz, S. (1974). *Worker in the cane*. New York, NY: W. W. Norton. (Original work published 1960)

Morrow, P. (1995). On shaky ground. In P. Morrow & W. Schneider (Eds.), *When our words return: Writing, hearing and remembering oral traditions of Alaska and the Yukon* (pp. 27–51). Logan: Utah State University Press.

Myerhoff, B. (1978). *Number our days*. New York, NY: Simon & Schuster.

Narayan, K. (1989). *Storytellers, saints and scoundrels: Folk narrative in Hindu religious teaching*. Philadelphia: University of Pennsylvania Press.

Narayan, K. (1995). The practice of oral literary criticism: Women's songs in Kangra, India. *Journal of American Folklore, 108*, 243–264.

Narayan, K. (with Sood, U. D.). (1997). *Mondays on the dark night of the moon: Himalayan foothill folktales*. New York, NY: Oxford University Press.

Narayan, K. (2004). "Honor is honor after all": Silence and speech in the life stories of women in Kangra, northwest India. In D. Arnold & S. Blackburn (Eds.), *Telling lives in India: Biography, autobiography and life history* (pp. 227–251). Bloomington: Indiana University Press.

Narayan, K. (2007a). Legends and family folklore. *Indian Folklife, 25*, 4–7.

Narayan, K. (2007b). *My family and other saints*. Chicago, IL: University of Chicago Press.

Narayan, K. (2009). Breaking the crust: Reevaluating ethnography across time. *Etnofoor: Special Issue on Writing Culture, 21*(1), 61–78.

Oakley, A. (1981). Interviewing women: A contradiction in terms. In H. Roberts (Ed.), *Doing feminist research* (pp. 30–61). London, England: Routledge & Kegan Paul.

Peacock, J. L., & Holland, D. C. (1993). The narrated self: Life stories in process. *Ethos, 21*, 367–383.

Personal Narratives Group. (Eds.). (1989). *Interpreting women's lives: Feminist theory and personal narratives*. Bloomington: Indiana University Press.

Prasad, L. (2007). *Poetics of conduct: Oral narrative and moral being in a South Indian town*. New York, NY: Columbia University Press.

Rilke, R. M. (1984). *Letters to a young poet* (S. Mitchell, Trans.). New York, NY: Random House.

Rosaldo, R. (1976). The story of Tukbaw: "They listen as he orates." In F. Reynolds & D. Capps (Eds.), *The biographical process* (pp. 121–151). The Hague, The Netherlands: Mouton.

Rosaldo, R. (1986). Ilongot hunting as story and experience. In V. W. Turner & E. M. Bruner (Eds.), *The anthropology of experience* (pp. 97–138). Urbana: University of Illinois Press.

Rosaldo, R. (1989). *Culture and truth: The remaking of social analysis*. Boston, MA: Beacon Press.

Shostak, M. (1983). *Nisa: The life and words of a !Kung woman*. New York, NY: Vintage Books.

Smith, B. H. (1981). Narrative versions, narrative theories. In W. J. T. Mitchell (Ed.), *On narrative* (pp. 209–232). Chicago, IL: University of Chicago Press.

Smith, S., & Watson, J. (Eds.). (2001). *Reading autobiography: A guide of interpreting life narratives*. Minneapolis: University of Minnesota Press.

Spradley, J. P. (1979). *The ethnographic interview*. New York, NY: Holt, Rinehart & Winston.

Steedly, M. M. (1993). *Hanging without a rope: Narrative experience in colonial and postcolonial Karoland*. Princeton, NJ: Princeton University Press.

Taggart, J. M. (1990). *Enchanted maidens: Gender relations in Spanish folktales of courtship and marriage*. Princeton, NJ: Princeton University Press.

Titon, J. T. (1988). *Powerhouse for God: Speech, chant, and song in an Appalachian Baptist Church*. Austin: University of Texas Press.

Titon, J. T., & George, K. M. (1977). Dressed in the armor of god. *Alcheringa: Ethnopoetics, 3*(2), 10–31.

Titon, J. T., & George, K. M. (1978). Testimonies. *Alcheringa: Ethnopoetics, 4*(1), 69–83.

Toelken, B. (1996). From entertainment to realization in Navajo fieldwork. In B. Jackson & E. D. Ives (Eds.), *The word observed: Reflections on the fieldwork process* (pp. 1–17). Bloomington: Indiana University Press.

Tsing, A. (1993). *In the realm of the diamond queen: Marginality in an out-of-the-way place*. Princeton, NJ: Princeton University Press.

Viramma, J. R., & Racine, J. L. (1997). *Viramma: Life of an untouchable*. London, England: Verso Books.

Young, M. (1983). *Magicians of Manumanua: Living myth in Kalauna*. Berkeley: University of California Press.

36

INTERVIEW AS EMBODIED COMMUNICATION

◆ Laura L. Ellingson

No body, no voice; no voice, no body.
That's what I know in my bones.

Mairs (1997, p. 305)

We begin with the body. Although some researchers remain unconscious of it, embodiment is an integral part of the interview process—from preparation, throughout the interview, to data analysis and choices about representation of findings. For example, we select participants for an interview often based on physical characteristics (e.g., race, gender, age) and/or bodily experiences (e.g., living with multiple sclerosis, birthing a baby). In the face-to-face interview, bodies encounter each other as warm, tangible, messy, material manifestations of our selves; bodies do not wait quietly outside the room while our "real" self is interviewed by the disembodied, questioning mind of another. When we analyze interview data, we engage in reflections on how the researcher's embodied experiences are similar to and different from those of our respondents and how that affects meaning making. Even representation is an embodied act. We write or type (or draw, paint, or photograph) and discover new meanings even as we engage in the act of moving fingers across the page or equipment. Interview researchers must reject the mind/body split and embrace our participants and ourselves as whole persons who *are* bodies, not who *have* bodies. The body is not a subsidiary of the self but is intricately woven throughout all facets of the self—not deterministically but powerfully.

This chapter explores interview research as an embodied communicative process. Research across the social sciences, education, health sciences, and human services continues to probe important topics and produce valuable findings that have an impact directly on the quality of people's lives. We have the capacity to do tremendous good in the world. I contend that an awareness of and active engagement with issues of embodiment enhance our capacity as researchers to design and produce high-quality research and to share our findings widely with practitioners, professional organizations, community members, and scholars across a wide array of disciplines.

This chapter is organized to first explore how the legacy of the mind/body split pervades the social-scientific research enterprise, including, of course, studies based on interview data, followed by the role of embodiment in preparation for and conducting interviews and then during data analysis and representation. Finally, I offer specific suggestions for consciously embodying our research processes and products. I note that my attention throughout this chapter focuses primarily on the dynamics of face-to-face interviewing. However, most of the theory, application, and strategies articulated here have relevance to any type of interviewing, including phone interviewing and Internet interviewing.

Before continuing, I also want to take a moment to position myself as the embodied author of this chapter. I write from the position of a midcareer feminist, qualitative researcher with joint academic appointments (and graduate degrees) in the fields of Communication Studies and Women's & Gender Studies. My two primary areas of study include interdisciplinary teamwork in clinics and communication within extended and chosen family networks, particularly as it relates to aunts' relationships with nieces and nephews. Thus, my body/self has spent a lot of time with (the bodies of) health care workers, patients, and members of extended and chosen families. Feminist theory and methods and a focus on gendered discourse shape my research processes, including the ways in which I prepare for, co-construct, analyze, and represent interview research. Moreover, I am a female body who benefits from white, heterosexual, and middle-class privileges (among others) as they intersect with the marginalization of people with disabilities. I am a cancer survivor with my right leg amputated above the knee, and I rely on a computerized leg prosthesis for daily mobility. My troublesome body demands continual attention and makes it impossible to ignore the ways in which embodiment necessarily affects my research processes, relationships with participants, and perspectives on knowledge construction (Ellingson, 1998, 2005, 2006). Yet my body is not unique in its relevance; *all* researchers' bodies play important roles in producing interview research.

This chapter illuminates some possibilities for engaging our embodiment to deepen our understanding of the topics we research, the interview processes in which we engage, and the intersections thereof.

◆ The Mind/Body Split and the Erasure of Bodies in Research

The privileging of the mind over the body is deeply engrained in Western cultures and hence within conventional research methodologies. The mind/body separation posits "a clear division between mind, equated with self, experienced as proactive and unthreatening, and body, experienced as potentially troublesome" (Marshall, 1999, p. 71). Rationality dictates that the (higher) mind-self should seek to control its body-property, preferably to the point of rendering it absent or at least irrelevant. Furthermore, Western cultures traditionally associate "male" or "masculine" with the mind and knowledge production and "female" or "feminine" with the body and the subjectivity of emotion (e.g., du Pre, 2009). Such a mind/body split renders bodily knowledge oxymoronic; indeed, "it is as if 'facts' come out of our heads, and 'fictions' out of our bodies" (Simmonds, 1999, p. 52).

An alternative feminist epistemological perspective bridges and blurs the boundary between the mind and body: "We do not *have* bodies, we *are* our bodies" (Trinh, 1999, p. 258). We encounter the world through our bodies and engage in some forms of preconceptual learning through our interactions with others by using our senses—this is literally "sense making" (Barnacle, 2009).

> As animals we have bodies connected to the natural world, such that our consciousness and rationality are tied to our bodily orientations and interactions in and with our environment. Our embodiment is central to who we are, to what meaning is, and to our ability to draw rational inferences and to be creative. (Johnson, 1987, p. xxxviii)

In this epistemology, "instead of the body being positioned as a bar to knowledge, knowledge is produced through the body and embodied ways of being in the world" (Price & Shildrick, 1999, p. 19). Drawing on Merleau-Ponty's work, Barnacle (2009) suggests that we are "body-subjects" whose embodied senses provides the basis for us to learn cultural rules and norms, which we internalize, forming the basis for formal learning: "Not only are formal and embodied knowing integrated but the former is dependent upon the latter" (p. 30). Thus, "any adequate account of meaning and rationality must give a central place to embodied and imaginative structures of understanding by which we grasp our world" (Johnson, 1987, p. xiii).

Furthermore, beliefs about the relationship between the mind and body point to a fundamental tension surrounding what one means when one speaks of "the body." On the one hand, philosophers and scholars construct a notion of the body as a material entity whose potential meanings are constituted and circumscribed by culture(s) through particular discursive systems that privilege certain sets of norms and values (e.g., those of biomedicine, global capitalism, the U.S. prison industrial complex, or religious doctrines) (Gergen, 1994). On the other hand, bodies can also be understood as containing our essential qualities (e.g., emotions, gut instincts, physical characteristics) and material being. That is, cultural meanings certainly vary and have dramatic impact on how we come to interpret bodies, but we cannot completely disassociate such meanings from the concrete, physical reality of the body as a lived entity (e.g., Marshall, 1999).

Moreover, "*the* body" becomes an impossibility when researchers seriously consider embodiment within knowledge production. Instead, bod*ies* must be taken seriously as multiple, diverse, and situated. Bodies are never neutral but rather are "maps of the relation between power and identity" (Rose, 1999, p. 361) that cannot be separated from the politics of knowledge production (e.g., Davis, 1990). The singular body privileges those bodies on whom the status quo confers the most privilege—white, male, heterosexual, affluent, Western, able-bodied—by generalizing the experiences of the elite as normative and also as the ideal against which nonwhite, female, LGBTQ (lesbian, gay, bisexual, transgender, and queer), poor, Third World, and disabled bodies will inevitably be found wanting (Minow, 1990). Unequal power distribution becomes evident when we consider bodies in interviews, and "we are forced to take account of the ways in which our own bodies and the bodies of our participants are inscribed with power" (Del Busso, 2007, p. 313).

And yet we tend to conduct and represent research as though knowledge were produced without unruly bodies involved. The performance of "disembodied researcher" has been repeated for so long that it functions as a set of naturalized norms that privilege a masculinist rationality as the only legitimate form of knowledge, accorded only to those with sufficient social privilege to deny their feminine unruliness. Leaving (our own and others') bodies unmarked in our reports and other representations is the privilege of the powerful. Research accounts largely reflect social science norms that frame the researcher's personality, body, and other sources of subjectivity as irrelevant. Disembodied prose appears to come from nowhere, implying a disembodied author (Haraway, 1988). Researchers have used the power of academic discourse to define their bodies as essentially irrelevant to the production of knowledge (Denzin, 1997). Hence, when researchers' bodies remain unmarked in our accounts, they reinscribe the power of scholars to speak without reflexive consideration of their positionality. Of course, marginalized body markers cannot be denied by less powerful researcher-bodies who do not have the privilege of disowning their unruly physicality; scholars with queer, disabled, nonwhite, and otherwise marked bodies encounter resistance to their claims of disembodied prose and the privilege of objectivity (e.g., Brown & Boardman, 2010; Sharma, Reimer-Kirkham, & Cochrane, 2009; Simmonds, 1999). Likewise, often we render our participants' embodied experiences marginal to our research findings or else unproblematically offer their bodies up as evidence by failing to problematize them at all, thus essentializing bodily markers such as race, gender, or sexual orientation as constitutive of meanings about members of a marginalized group.

At the same time, we must not simply invert the hierarchy to privilege the body to the exclusion of the mind, thus reinforcing the dichotomy between emotional/imaginative and rational logics.

> In seeking to re-engage body-mind relations it is important not to lose sight of why the body was considered a problem in the first place, particularly if we are to avoid merely reversing established hierarchies. . . . [We need] a way of re-thinking body-mind relations that complicates rather than erases demarcation between the two. (Barnacle, 2009, p. 28)

Cartesian and Kantian reasoning reinforces dichotomies that "have made it extremely difficult to find a place in our views of human meaning and rationality for structures of imagination" that would help us think more holistically about the limits of emotional responses and the misuses of rational logics (Johnson, 1987, p. xxix).

◆ Embodiment as a Focus of Inquiry

Feminist and other critical attention to the role of embodiment in research processes has led to and paralleled interest in the varieties of embodiment as a topic of inquiry throughout the social sciences, medical and health fields, social services, and education. That is, researchers explore through interviews (and other methods) people's lived experiences of their bodies and the meanings they engender for themselves and (with) others, in terms of individual and group identity and within specific contexts. Ironically, most of the studies have followed traditional research report–writing conventions, generating texts that are embodied only to the extent that the representative quotes offered as evidence of patterns reference the body (unless it is an autoethnographic exploration of embodiment). That is, rarely is the body represented using evocative, narrative genres or other media (e.g., photographs) that would enhance an embodied representation of an exploration of embodiment. Topics explored include embodiment of whiteness and hegemonic masculinity through alcohol consumption among college-age males (Peralta, 2007); embodiment during childbirth as it reflects, resists, and negotiates between biomedical and natural birth discourses (Walsh, 2010); the paradoxical experience of embodiment by women with physical disabilities as both invisible and yet rendered highly visible (as different) (Zitzelsberger, 2005); the embodiment of prosthetic limbs among "successful" prosthetic users (i.e., those for whom using a prosthesis is part of their daily way of being in the world) (Murray, 2004); the gendered, sexualized, and ethnic embodiment of Latin musicians performing salsa music in a dance club (Román-Velázquez, 1999; for a fascinating, broader explanation of the physical and sensory embodiment of music, see Evans, 2010); older women's embodiment, especially as it relates to socioeconomic class (Dumas, Laberge, & Straka, 2005); beliefs about embodiment and brain stem death among family members making decisions to donate organs of their loved one (Haddow, 2005); the gendered embodiment of male-to-female transsexuals as they engage in "bodywork" to retrain, redecorate, and reshape their bodies (Schrock, Reid, & Boyd, 2005); the intersection of racial and cultural identities with gendered embodiment among "gender-liminal" (third sex, transgender, and transsexual) people belonging to cultures indigenous to the South Pacific (Roen, 2001); and the gendered nature of marking on bodies through tattoos, piercings, and "self-injury" or "self-cutting" (Inckle, 2007).

Embodiment is thus both a topic of inquiry and a means of framing inquiry. I now turn to embodied practices for interviewing.

◆ Embodiment in the Interview

Interaction creates meaning (Blumer, 1954). The nature of embodied cognition extends to the phenomenology of human interpersonal communication: "Intersubjective interaction is the cognition and affectively charged experience of self and other. Our bodily structure and sensorimotor skills ground our ability to make sense of the other, and vice versa" (Colombetti & Thompson, 2008, p. 57).

> The play of understanding between self and other arises out of an ongoing creative tension between what is familiar and what is unfamiliar, between self and other, between the known and the fresh textures of the unknown, between the existing framework of understanding that one brings, and the new and context-specific "reality that surpasses" such a brought framework (Gadamer, 1989, p. 109) and between general understandings from the past and the different understandings that come by being present to the otherness of "that" as it lives. (Todres, 2008, p. 1570)

Nonverbal signals such as tone of voice, rate of speech, and eye contact are rooted in the body; interviewer and interviewee adjust their communication in the moment in response to those cues. Indeed, research shows that 90% of meaning is nonverbal and that when verbal and nonverbal signals contradict, people almost always believe the nonverbal (i.e., embodied signals) (Adler & Towne, 2005).

Holstein and Gubrium (1995) suggested that researchers consider interviews to be *active*: that is, activities in which two participants generate meanings within the encounter, through verbal and nonverbal communication, less a data collection than a co-construction. In this way, the active interviewer can be understood to "virtually activat[e] narrative production" (Holstein & Gubrium, 1995, p. 123) by the interviewee with questions, signals, and so on. This includes the body as two active parties—both with agency—that interact in a site of knowledge construction, not only of information transmission, as is traditionally framed, with respondents as "vessels" from whom researchers obtain answers (see also Holstein & Gubrium, 2003). An exemplar of a researcher who indicates awareness of the encounter in which meaning is actively generated may be found in Pollock's (1999) interview study of women's birth narratives as she describes one of her participants' embodied affect:

> In whispered, halting tones—checking repeatedly to make sure no one overheard our arrangements— she asked to meet at my house rather than at her own or at some more public place. In her choice of setting and in the distance she maintained once there, Margaret seemed literally to be guarding her stories from intrusion. . . . Margaret sat on the living room chair, at a long arm's reach from the muffins and tea on the coffee table, at once trembling with anxiety and anger and practically daring me to cross the two or three feet between us. I remember especially how she left: she slid past me, out the door. . . . Margaret walked down the front path and away, her chin cocked—in embarrassment? indignation? pride?—taking her story with her. (p. 28)

Later, she describes a key moment in the interview: "She inched forward in her seat, leaning toward me—her face so bright now she seemed to have caught a spotlight—and began nervously, then fervently, to tell a third story" (Pollock, 1999, p. 28).

Del Busso (2007) pointed out that bodies communicate, sometimes in ways we do not intend as researchers, as our bodily signifiers—such as bodily grooming and clothing—are interpreted by our participants: "I felt that my body had spoken directly or indirectly to the women who took part in the research in ways that were incompatible with my feminist identity" (p. 311); her participant did not think she "looked" like a feminist because she was "too feminine" in appearance.

A full exploration of mediated interviewing via phone (see Shuy, 2002) or the Internet (see Mann & Stewart, 2002) is beyond the purview of this chapter. However, it is vital to understand that while interviews may appear to be disembodied by technology, researcher and participant bodies do not disappear or become irrelevant; they remain present and implicated in complex ways. First, bodily signals are inferred: emotions signified with signs such as emoticons, all caps, and punctuation via Internet or facial expressions assumed to align with the tone of voice on a phone call. Second, research suggests that people are assumed to conform to some linguistic stereotypes that are inferred, such as masculine and feminine styles of voice or written language (Colley & Todd, 2002) and racial structures reproduced online (Lovink, 2005). Finally, very strong and not necessarily accurate impressions of bodies are produced from different combinations of computer-mediated communication cues (Jacobson, 1999; Tanis & Postmes, 2003). In addition, as examined further in the section on representation, typing on a computer for e-mail or online chatting is a physical act, one that invokes mental processes that relate to and differ from those that arise from oral storytelling.

In the next section, I will explore the ways in which embodiment plays a critical role in analyses of interview data.

◆ Embodiment in Data Analysis

TRANSCRIPTION

Researchers typically audiotape and then transcribe in-person interviews. Far from a neutral act of transferring words from a tape to a page as traditionally framed, transcription is an act of translation between two vastly different media. Stripped of most nonverbal interaction cues and with no descriptions of the participants or setting, standard transcriptions of research interviews focus on accurately representing spoken language, placing rhetorical emphasis on the verbal content while ignoring the differences between oral and written speech. Mishler (1991) argued that moving from oral to written speech involves not accurate dictation but translation; just as moving ideas from one language to another may make it impossible to express many ideas literally, writing down oral speech renders it a different entity altogether. People do not process oral speech the same way we read it; we encounter and make sense of language in vastly different ways depending on which organs of the body take in the cues. Thus, Mishler critiques accuracy as a naive standard for evaluating transcription; retaining the *actual* dialogue in written form does not convey the *truth* of what happened in the (oral) moment. The rhetorical choices inherent in transcription typically erase bodies completely, leaving only words and sometimes series of cryptic marks that reflect conversation-analytic codes intelligible only to those trained in the techniques and not at all equivalent to the nonverbal cues for which they stand.

Indeed, Mishler argues that transcription is part of data analysis, since the decisions we make about how to represent the interactions on the page already frame our desired findings by structuring the discourse on the page in ways that reinforce the assumptions we bring to the research and our anticipated findings. Analysis of words with no attention to bodies leaves out essential aspects of the story: "Methods of reflexivity and analysis that focus solely on participants' verbal accounts cannot fully grasp the conditions through which the resulting knowledge is produced" (Del Busso, 2007, p. 313). Yet bodies lurk in the background of the disembodied transcripts. Transcript excerpts of participants' speech beg an infinite number of questions about, among other things, the setting in which the interaction took place, the appearance of the people and their positions vis-à-vis one another in the room, and the tone of the discussion. Such accounts obviously present only a very partial representation of "what happened," and of course these disembodied accounts do not favor all participants equally.

WORKING DATA WITH THE BODY

Interviewing involves embodied practices performed by actors occupying specific standpoints within cultures. The researcher's body—where it is positioned, what it looks like, what social groups or classifications it is perceived as belonging to, what experiences it has had, what its daily routines are—matters deeply in knowledge formation. Rather than apologizing for subjectivity or simply stating one's

"biases," qualitative researchers can endeavor to remain conscious of the ways in which data analysis implicates the body as the site of knowledge production. In the same way that the interaction within the interview occurred between (active) bodies, data analysis occurs by one or more embodied researchers encountering data that also reflect embodied actors and their meanings. Speaking of teaching and learning the skills of critical thinking, Barnacle (2009) argued that our "gut feelings" are not merely metaphorical but crucial sensations intricately involved in sense making:

> Being critical, therefore, becomes an aspect of how one lives one's life, and this is not reducible to a specific skill set that can be deployed or withheld at will. A gut, engaged "moodfully" with the world, to borrow from Heidegger, offers a better model for describing such a phenomenon than a conception of mind dominated by a calculating brain. (pp. 31–32)

Thus, if we consider data analysis as one manifestation of critical thinking, it follows that we must employ our guts as consciously as possible and consider those of our participants as we seek to sort through and discern patterns, construct coherent categories and typologies, and otherwise (re)assemble data into new forms. Attending to embodiment requires "a reflexivity that takes into account much more than an acknowledgement of the ways in which we 'affect' the data collected and how our own subject positions are implicated in the analyses produced" and instead requires attention to the data as encompassing meanings tied to a specific interaction in which specific bodies met each other (Burns, 2003, p. 230). We need to pay attention to gut knowing as we analyze data, and engage in embodied sense making/reasoning.

Knowledge grounded in bodily sensations encompasses uncertainty, ambiguity, and messiness in everyday life; it is inherently and unapologetically subjective, celebrating—rather than glossing over—the complexities of knowledge production. At the same time, researchers best remember that the gut is hardly infallible: "Sensibilities can orient thought in ways not necessarily beneficial and can also limit or truncate one's openness to inquiry" (Barnacle, 2009, p. 32). Moreover, our understanding of emotions and the accompanying physical sensations is subject to cultural "feeling rules" into which we are socialized and that we generally invoke without conscious reflection (Hochschild, 1983). Thus, our gut feelings and other bodily sensations arise as we reread and analyze our data—tears, muscle tension, headaches, feeling energetic, smiling, trembling—and give us clues to meanings embedded in our data (themselves a construction of our and our participants' bodies). Such clues are complex and require careful reflection and interpretation.

Miller-Day's (2004) study of relationships among adult daughters, mothers, and grandmothers illustrates not only the added richness of embodied details but also the vital context for meaning that such details render (more) intelligible for readers. Researchers must attend to "how the interviewer's own embodied subjectivity interacts with that of the respondent in the mutual construction of meanings/bodies" (Burns, 2003, p. 232) to consider the complexities of the meaning making. Describing one of a series of interviews, Miller-Day (2004) expresses awareness of the bodily connection between herself, her participant, and her sense-making processes:

Once, on a cool spring day, Kelly [participant] and I were walking together in downtown Elkwood, heading for a local pub for a late lunch. The sun was bright, but the chill in the air was palpable, so I pulled my sweater closer to my body, and Kelly placed her arm about me to provide additional warmth. As we walked into the pub I felt comforted by her presence and part of my comfort, I assume, was due to the fact that Kelly was the same age as my older sister. I suspect that some aspect of my sense-memory was stimulated by this "sisterly" hug. (p. 52)

Since this is a study of familial relationships, these details are particularly helpful in considering the position from which Miller-Day and her participants made meaning together.

◆ Embodiment in Representation

Conventional reports omit embodiment. Qualitative research reports typically were written following strictly social-scientific or medical conventions, in which the author's agency is obscured via passive voice (e.g., "The data were collected"). Currently, they more commonly employ a sanitized "I," who reports having taken actions without describing any

details of the body through which the actions were taken or the embodied being of the participants with whom the researcher acted. In addition, qualitative researchers may now own up to relevant aspects of their identity in brief statements in methods sections or footnotes of journal articles; for example, I note my identity as a cancer survivor in grounded theory analyses of clinical communication because the participants responded to my impaired body with questions and judgments that certainly affected our interactions (e.g., Ellingson, 2003). More commonly, such epistemological and methodological issues are the focus of fascinating essays that are published separately from the authoritative research accounts in spaces devoted to the development of qualitative methodology (e.g., *Qualitative Inquiry*, the "Piths, Pearls, and Provocations" section of *Qualitative Health Research*). Despite the narrative turn that has made qualitative research more credible to the social science, education, and health communities and expanded the options for writing conventions (e.g., Denzin & Lincoln, 2000), research articles, reports, and essays continue to omit details of their authors' embodied being as they relate to research processes and findings. Autoethnographic accounts and some narrative and postmodern ethnography redress these omissions (e.g., Minge, 2007; Ronai, 1992, 1995); however, the vast majority of such accounts find publication in outlets devoted to qualitative and interpretive research, segregated from research reflecting scientific norms and practices that obscure themselves as neutral standards for knowledge promoted in mainstream disciplinary journals (Ellingson, 2009).

Disembodied writing is intertwined not just with academic writing conventions but with language itself. Our bodies cannot be understood apart from our languaging of them. While bodies do of course have material being, that materiality cannot be transparently understood. Instead, the lenses of culture and language variously filter all interpretations. Words do not spring forth from nowhere; we draw language from cultural reference points to construct categories, descriptions, and labels (Wittgenstein, 1953). Hence, meanings of our bodies and those of our research participants are constructed in particular sociohistorical contexts that entail constraints of language resources, including absence of language for some experiences, feelings, and understandings. "When we try to name our bodily experiences, we are always involved in a dialogue" (Marshall, 1999, p. 71).

We make sense through our bodies and then reach for language to express ideas. "In the passage from the heard, seen, smelled, tasted, and touched to the told and the written, language has taken place" (Trinh, 1999, p. 263). Once language has taken place, meaning is created, assigned, and even imposed on the body, and we need to acknowledge that our languaging of experience and ideas can be thought of neither as somehow reporting pure bodily experience nor as purely disembodied knowledge. Likewise, audiences always jointly construct meanings with researcher/ authors when they read research reports in other, equally specific sociohistorical contexts. Language conventions also make it difficult to resist the mind/ body spilt that frames the body as the property of the self (Trinh, 1999).

Moreover, writing is done with fingers and arms and eyes: It is an embodied act, not mental conjuring:

> I encourage you to think of writing itself as an embodied practice: Come to [your topic] not with your mind and ideas, but with your whole body—your heart and gut and arms. . . . What people don't realize is that writing is physical. It doesn't have to do with thought alone. It has to do with sight, smell, taste, feeling, with everything being alive and activated. . . . You are physically engaged with the pen [or keyboard], and your hand, connected to your arm, is pouring out the record of your senses. (Goldberg, 1986, pp. 37, 50)

When we resist the Cartesian mind/body split and embrace writing about our interview research as something we enact with our whole bodies, not just our heads, we more easily recall sensuous details and construct more visceral prose and richer accounts in other media as well (e.g., Ellingson, 2011; Hayward & Harter, 2010; Quinlan, 2010; Quinlan & Harter, 2010).

In the remainder of this chapter, I turn my attention to how the body can be more consciously incorporated into research practice.

◆ Embodying Our Work: Best Practices for Interview Research

In this section, I offer strategies for engaging embodiment throughout the processes of face-to-face interview

research: preparation for the interview, the actual interview, data analysis, and choices about representation.

PREPARATION FOR THE INTERVIEW

First, I encourage researchers to learn more about embodiment by consulting the many references cited in this chapter (for beginners, I particularly recommend Burns, 2003). Designing a qualitative study involves both intensive preparation of a schedule of questions that address varying aspects of your research topic and openness to working with whatever words, actions, and signals participants offer in the moment. Effective improvisation, Janesick (2011) argues, is possible only when researchers undergo extensive preparation so that their immediate responses in the midst of an interview (or fieldwork, etc.) remain grounded in and guided by what they have learned deeply and internalized—ethical standards (e.g., do no harm), epistemological stances (e.g., social constructionism), political commitments (e.g., feminism), methodological concepts (e.g., rapport), and extant research literature. Reading about, reflecting on, and collegial discussion concerning embodiment will improve researchers' skills for all phases of interview research.

In a related vein, before conducting the first of a series of research interviews, researchers may benefit from reflecting on how their embodied selves relate to the topic and participants. For example, "stretching exercises" (Janesick, 2011); questions for ethical reflection such as those posed by Fine, Weis, Weseen, and Wong (2000); and/or "wondering" questions (Ellingson, 2009) could all be used to help researchers record their own perceptions and reasoning about embodiment. Ideally, one will return to these questions and reconsider them periodically throughout the processes of data collection, analysis, and representation, as an ongoing dialogue that may yield theoretical, pragmatic, or other insights.

Another strategy is to practice awareness of the problems of essentializing participants' body/selves in research design. Research questions for interview studies typically target people based on traits and/or bodily experiences, for example, young, black, single fathers (Coles, 2001) or elderly Iranian immigrants (Hegland, 2009). Practice awareness of what you are doing when you sort bodies into categories and then treat those categories of difference as though they are inherent to the body/selves of participants rather than socially constructed. Cultural categories such as gender, age, race, class, sexuality, and disability provide a useful starting point for exploring the impact of people's bodies on the research opportunities and challenges and for questioning taken-for-granted stereotypes, categories, and labels. Strategic essentialism involves acting as though the identity category were real, even though it cannot be fixed or definitively established (Spivak, 1987). But then we may destabilize the very categories we invoked to select participants by inquiring in the interview as to the meaning of these categories for participants. Such identifiers or specific experiences are meaningful; just remember that none of them are essential to who a person is; categories of difference form, crumble, and reform as political winds shift (Minow, 1990).

Researchers also may interrogate the ways in which recruitment was embodied. For example, the willingness of strangers to comply with a request for an interview or the ease with which one obtained access to a private corporation to conduct research interviews with employees may relate (in part) to potential participants' perceptions of the researcher as similar to them and therefore easier to understand and less threatening. Belonging to a different racial group from that of potential participants or being much older or younger than they are may spark feelings of unease that may make it more challenging to recruit participants. On the other hand, demographic differences also may be capitalized on—I once used the similarity of my age to the likely age of grandchildren of senior (over 70 years of age) oncology patients as a basis to begin conversations with seniors (Ellingson, 2005). In addition, women not wanting to go alone to interview male research participants in their homes could lead to sex and gender influences on interview data, and so on. Such factors will influence directly the methods used and the data compiled. Instead of dismissing these as peripheral concerns, they could be brought into a discussion of how research practices reflect, reinscribe, and/or subvert social power structures that shaped and are shaped by our bodies and their signifiers.

Finally, as researchers, we should consider our own performances of self through a "personal front" (Goffman, 1959), including clothing, grooming, and artifacts or objects. This is not to say that we are not entitled to dress or groom ourselves in ways that make us comfortable or that we should perform an "inauthentic" self. However, participants do read our bodies and respond in both typical and unexpected ways. Therefore, we should think carefully about how best to adapt ourselves to the circumstances of the interview, dressing in business attire to interview a CEO, for instance, but a casual outfit for interviewing child care workers (see also Annika Lillrank's chapter, "Managing the Interviewer Self," this volume).

DURING THE INTERVIEW: EMBODIMENT AS A TOOL FOR ENGAGEMENT

Think with your body. Pay attention to how your body responds to your surroundings and to your participants' emotions, body language and gestures, and proximity. Draw on all your senses. Rather than simply noting what the room looked like, describe the overchilled office building air or the scent of crayons that clings to preschool children or the squishy feel of the shag carpet lining a participant's living room. If you share a meal with a participant, savor the spicy sauce or the deep chocolate dessert with smell, taste, and touch, being present and attentive to bodily sensations as you eat.

Question the body/self understandings of participants, pressing for specific sensations, details, and movements. One strategy for understanding how to question embodiment is using "experience-based, body-anchored" interviewing techniques (Stelter, 2010).

> Experience-based, body-anchored qualitative interviewing can be defined as a specific way of conducting an interview, where the pivotal point is the participant's experiential, embodied involvement in the issues of the research interview. . . . [Researchers] can use this interview approach to deepen their understanding of how bodily reactions and body anchored experiences are related to thoughts, emotions, and actions. (Stelter, 2010, p. 859)

Ask questions that focus on embodied feelings and sensations as situations or events are recalled and brought to the present moment. Ideally, in this context, both participant and interviewer should seek to be as nonjudgmental as possible, both making a conscious effort not to impose hierarchies of value on aspects of the experience described in the interview (Stelter, 2010, pp. 863–864).

Similarly, use sensuous language when making notes during the interview. When documenting the experience of the interview, notes could be embodied using a language that is sensuous and textured: "It is the lived body that connects language to the world of experience. Such sense-making is not just logical and populated by bits of information, but is full of textures," senses, and bodily sensations (Todres, 2008, p. 1570). The richer and more descriptive the account of the interview, the more context is available for interpreting the transcripts later.

Finally, interviewers should be open to personal change as a consequence of encountering the embodied selves of participants.

When researchers recognize the encounter as an embodied communication . . . embodiment can become a *tool* as well as a text. In this encounter, the researchers, venturing into new intellectual (and often emotional) terrains, are willing to let themselves be touched and changed. (Bresler, 2006, p. 32)

Tools work on the researcher as well as the researched: "The 'flesh' of mindful embodiment yields a texture belonging as much to the other as self" (Latta & Buck, 2008, p. 322). If we are willing—and often even when we are not—we experience profound changes in our sense of who we are and how we live in the world as our sense making alters in response to every interview encounter.

EMBODIED STRATEGIES FOR DATA ANALYSIS

Data analysis may be enriched with consideration of embodiment woven throughout the process of discerning patterns or uncovering and constructing meanings (e.g., grounded theory, cultural studies critique). I will discuss issues of embodied representation in the next section; however, I should point out that decisions about analytic frameworks and techniques overlap with those about representation, since some genres, media, and audiences pair more readily with some modes of analysis than do others. So while my focus in each of these sections differs, the two may be considered even more closely intertwined than

are all of the issues about research processes discussed in this chapter.

For most qualitative researchers, the beginnings of analysis coincide with data collection, as we make notes to ourselves about emergent topics and themes, our impressions of participants' affect during interviews, and connections to existing research (e.g., Lindlof & Taylor, 2011), and as I argued earlier, transcription of interviews also involves analytic choices (Mishler, 1991). During the in-depth analysis of transcripts and notes, researchers may engage in what is generally known as reflexivity, a fairly standard component of qualitative methods across the continuum of such methods, except those near the scientific/positivist end (i.e., as far from the artistic/interpretive pole as possible) (Ellingson, 2009). Reflexivity includes many variations, and important epistemological, ontological, and methodological debates persist concerning what it means to be reflexive about researchers' involvement in meaning making (e.g., Alvesson & Skoldberg, 2000; Downe, 2007; Ezzy, 2010; Finlay, 2002; Hall & Callery, 2001; Macbeth, 2001; Madison, 2005; Pillow, 2003; Stronach, Garratt, Pearce, & Piper, 2007), all of which address embodiment to a greater or lesser extent. For interview research, I hold three particular aspects of reflexivity critical to engaging embodiment as a meaningful component of data analysis.

First, continually return attention to the *mutual* embodiment of both researcher(s) and participants in the interview data under analysis. To "limi[t] the exploration of embodiment to the other" places researchers in a "position of power that can be exploitive" of participants (Sharma et al., 2009, pp. 1647–1648; see also Edvardsson & Street, 2007). Mutuality does not erase the differences of power between participants and researchers; instead, it serves as a way to ground verbal texts in the complex realities of the intersubjective process from which they arose—that is, a conversation between (material) bodies.

Second, harness the materiality of data analysis processes. That is, pay attention to the ways in which analysis involves physical creation and manipulation of textual objects and the ways of seeing and understanding promoted by these processes (Konopásek, 2008). Konopásek (2008) explains that "analytical work is in an important sense a material praxis (and vice versa)" (para. 30). Using computer programs that assist with qualitative data analysis, "we can *create, see* and *manipulate* various objects. These objects can be of different sizes and shapes; they can be hidden, moved, split, colourised, grouped and regrouped, forgotten and rediscovered on unexpected occasions" (para. 20). Likewise, those who have used and/or continue to use printed paper copies, colored pens and pencils, scissors, paper clips, and so on for data coding and manipulation create new objects (groupings of quotes and notes) within a "textual laboratory—which has the power to shrink time and space distances between observable phenomena so that everything important is present and under control" (para. 22). The grouping, networking, coding, and commenting on of quotes enables researchers to visualize connections among ideas, deeply affecting our continual construction of meaning.

Third, consider the degree to which emergent themes or other developing findings implicate specific bodily states, practices, definitions, and experiences. Cast a discerning eye over the preliminary collection of quotes (or other evidence), and consider how participants describe their own bodily appearance, bodily sensations (e.g., pleasure as well as discomfort or pain), and experiences of bodily breakdown or failure. Also note participants' descriptions of others' responses to their bodies (e.g., how a boyfriend described her hips, how a coach criticized his calf muscles) and their thoughts and feelings about those past responses. Consider how participants' discussions of abstract principles (e.g., respect, authority) are grounded in gestures, facial expressions, or other embodied signals. Charmaz (2006) admonishes researchers to "never leave their data" (i.e., to continually refer back to data) when constructing typologies of themes because of the risk of developing themes not sufficiently grounded in participants' talk and based too much in researcher's thoughts. In the same way, I admonish researchers conducting analysis to never leave the body when constructing themes—to continually reflect on how themes reflect bodies and the interaction of bodies even as they encapsulate more abstract patterns of meaning.

EMBODIED REPRESENTATIONAL STRATEGIES

One way to position the body as producing knowledge is to write autoethnographically about

the research process (Ellis, 1997). Ellis and Bochner (2000) described autoethnography as revealing the connections of the

personal to the cultural. . . . [Autoethnographers focus] outward on social and cultural aspects of their personal experience; then, they look inward, exposing a vulnerable self that is moved by and may move through, refract, and resist cultural interpretations. (p. 739)

Autoethnography blurs the lines between the sciences and humanities (e.g., Ellingson, 1998; Ellis & Bochner, 2000) and problematizes the differentiation between researcher and researched (DeVault, 1990; Mies, 1983; Reinharz, 1992). For example, narrative and autoethnographic methods acknowledge the dialogic construction of patients' constructions of the meaning of their illness with researchers' embodied experiences (Frank, 1995). Rather than simply being the narrator or reporter of findings, the researcher serves as the main character of a story that parallels the academic narrative contained in the research report (see also Sara Crawley's chapter, "Autoethnography as Feminist Self-Interview," this volume). In layered accounts, researchers alternate sections of an article written using social science conventions (i.e., citation of relevant research and theory, presentation of a research question, explanation of methods) with brief narratives that show rather than tell about aspects of the research (Ronai, 1995); alternatively, such narratives can be placed at the beginning or end of the conventional analysis (e.g., Ellis, 1993). Autoethnographic narratives (potentially) offer embodied details, celebrate the author's position, problematize the production of knowledge, and reveal the profane in the sacred processes of interview research.

Of course, many venues do not welcome autoethnographic accounts, and not all researchers are comfortable with such forms of representation, even as supplements to other, more social-scientific analyses of the same data. It is vital to maintain a wide range of accepted genres for disseminating qualitative research. Thus, I also explore ways in which researchers' bodies can be represented in conventionally written interview research reports.

First, as other qualitative methodologists have suggested, researchers could pay more careful attention to all of their senses as they conduct interviews and include relevant details in the "thick description" of their findings (Geertz, 1973). In interview research, we want to describe our participants' meanings using concrete details about their experiences, thoughts, and feelings. Yet those descriptions of individuals in specific moments must resonate with the larger themes of the research; that is, each particular example must illustrate a broader category while retaining its ability to embody some specific aspect of an individual's life. Thus, interviewers should record as much detail as possible during interviews and then select with great care which details to include in their reports and other representations.

Second, be conscious of the direct and indirect ways in which we show up in our work. Use the first person to own your actions: *I* collected the data, *I* conducted analyses, *I* sought institutional review board approval, and so on. First-person voice usually provides the most concise way of describing research processes, findings, and implications. In addition to being present as an authorial "I," let readers know who you are in your project. Describing your standpoints can be done in the introduction or methods section or in a footnote if the outlet does not approve or if such an explanation might distract from an essay or story's aesthetic goals.

Another way to bring the body into analytic writing is to wrestle with the semantics of the body, including framing the body *as* the self rather than adhering to the Cartesian model, in which the body is the lowly property of the (higher) mind-self (i.e., I moved my body). The difficulty lies in writing intelligibly while also reflecting the embodied nature of knowledge in our body-selves. Trinh (1991), for example, discussed the "subjectivity of a non-I/plural I" (p. 192) as a strategy to counter hegemonic Western conceptualizations of the self. Along similar lines, Irigaray (1980) invoked you/I, I/you, and you/me in her discussion of the need for plurality of identity rather than reaffirmation of dichotomies (e.g., male/female, culture/nature). When I construct a research report or other representation, I struggle with language, almost inevitably linguistically possessing "my" body instead of equating or connecting body and self. The only example of blurring the mind and body I have been successful in gaining editorial approval for is in the autoethnographic reflection chapter of my ethnography of a geriatric oncology (i.e., cancer) team: "The sharp sound of pagers rips open a scab I hadn't known still lingered on my psyche, and I gasp as the blood/memory flows" (Ellingson, 2005, p. 95). This move was easier to accomplish because it was in

the context of narrative writing; such a strategy would be far more disruptive to the reader if it were placed in a more structured qualitative analysis. I encourage researchers to (gently) push the boundaries of writing conventions by trying out unusual phrasing of the body/self when doing so would enhance meaning and illuminate an embodied account of your interview research (see the discussion of "guerilla scholarship" in Ellingson, 2009, pp. 134–136).

◆ Conclusion

I opened this chapter with a quotation from Nancy Mairs, a poet and essayist who lives with multiple sclerosis. Her remarkable essay about writing, voice, and embodiment, "Carnal Acts," echoes many of the themes of embodiment that I have discussed in the context of interviewing practices. Mairs (1997) boldly asserts the need to speak our bodily truths, particularly those that have been silenced and shamed through systems of sexism, racism, classism, homophobia, ableism, and other powerful discourses that continue to inscribe indelible bodily difference on some while privileging others by positioning their bodies as irrelevant to knowledge construction. In a world of complex intersections of identities and experience, interviewing is a potentially powerful method for examining meanings in ways that acknowledge our embodied being in the world. This chapter has offered a number of practical suggestions for focusing on embodiment while preparing for, collecting, analyzing, and representing interviews. Reflecting on the role of interviewers' and interviewees' bodies at every stage of the interview process circumvents the temptation to simplify findings either by ignoring the realities of bodily differences or conversely by essentializing bodies as inherently constituting certain meanings. Conscious embodiment undoes traditional mind/body dichotomies by joining the material with the socially constructed and enabling us to co-construct research findings that are both richly nuanced and grounded in the material realities of our contemporary global world.

◆ References

Adler, R. B., & Towne, N. (2005). *Looking out, looking in: Interpersonal communication* (11th ed.). Fort Worth, TX: Harcourt Brace.

Alvesson, M., & Skoldberg, K. (2000). *Reflexive methodology*. Thousand Oaks, CA: Sage.

Barnacle, R. (2009). Gut instinct: The body and learning. *Educational Philosophy and Theory, 41*, 22–33.

Blumer, H. (1954). *Symbolic interactionism: Perspective and method*. Englewood Cliffs, NJ: Prentice Hall.

Bresler, L. (2006). Embodied narrative inquiry: A methodology of connection. *Research Studies in Music Education, 27*, 21–43.

Brown, L., & Boardman, F. K. (2010). Accessing the field: Disability and the research process. *Social Science and Medicine, 72*(1), 23–30. doi:10.1016/j.socscimed.2010.09.050

Burns, M. (2003). Interviewing: Embodied communication. *Feminism & Psychology, 13*, 229–236.

Charmaz, K. (2006). *Constructing grounded theory: A practical guide through qualitative analysis*. Thousand Oaks, CA: Sage.

Coles, R. C. (2001). The parenting roles and goals of single black full-time fathers. *Western Journal of Black Studies, 25*, 101–116.

Colley, A., & Todd, Z. (2002). Gender-linked differences in the style and content of e-mails to friends. *Journal of Language and Social Psychology, 21*, 380–392.

Colombetti, G., & Thompson, E. (2008). The feeling body: Toward an enactive approach to emotion. In W. F. Overton, U. Müller, & J. L. Newman (Eds.), *Developmental perspectives on embodiment and consciousness* (pp. 45–68). New York, NY: Lawrence Erlbaum.

Davis, A. (1990). *Women, culture, and politics*. New York, NY: Vintage Books.

Del Busso, L. (2007). Embodying feminist politics in the research interview: Material bodies and reflexivity. *Feminism & Psychology, 17*, 309–315.

Denzin, N. K. (1997). *Interpretive ethnography: Ethnographic practices for the 21st century*. Thousand Oaks, CA: Sage.

Denzin, N. K., & Lincoln, Y. S. (2000). Introduction: The discipline and practice of qualitative research. In N. K. Denzin & Y. S. Lincoln (Eds.), *Handbook of qualitative research* (2nd ed., pp. 1–28). Thousand Oaks, CA: Sage.

DeVault, M. L. (1990). Talking and listening from women's standpoint: Feminist strategies for interviewing and analysis. *Social Problems, 37*, 96–116.

Downe, P. J. (2007). Strategic stories and reflexive interruptions: Narratives of a "safe home" amidst cross-border sex work. *Qualitative Inquiry, 13*, 554–572.

Dumas, A., Laberge, S., & Straka, S. M. (2005). Older women's relations to bodily appearance: The embodiment of social and biological conditions of existence. *Ageing & Society, 25*, 883–902.

du Pre, A. (2009). *Communicating about health: Current issues and perspectives* (3rd ed.). New York, NY: Oxford University Press.

Edvardsson, D., & Street, A. (2007). Sense or no-sense: The nurse as embodied ethnographer. *International Journal of Nursing Practice, 13*, 24–32.

Ellingson, L. L. (1998). "Then you know how I feel": Empathy, identification, and reflexivity in fieldwork. *Qualitative Inquiry, 4*, 492–514.

Ellingson, L. L. (2003). Interdisciplinary health care teamwork in the clinic backstage. *Journal of Applied Communication Research, 31*, 93–117.

Ellingson, L. L. (2005). *Communicating in the clinic: Negotiating frontstage and backstage teamwork*. Cresskill, NJ: Hampton Press.

Ellingson, L. L. (2006). Embodied knowledge: Writing researchers' bodies into qualitative health research. *Qualitative Health Research, 16*, 298–310.

Ellingson, L. L. (2009). *Engaging crystallization in qualitative research: An introduction*. Thousand Oaks, CA: Sage.

Ellingson, L. L. (2011). The poetics of professionalism among dialysis technicians. *Health Communication, 26*(1), 1–12.

Ellis, C. (1993). "There are survivors": Telling a story of sudden death. *The Sociological Quarterly, 34*, 711–730.

Ellis, C. (2004). *The ethnographic I: A methodological novel about autoethnography*. Walnut Creek, CA: AltaMira Press.

Ellis, C., & Bochner, A. P. (2000). Autoethnography, personal narrative, reflexivity: Researcher as subject. In N. K. Denzin & Y. S. Lincoln (Eds.), *Handbook of qualitative research* (2nd ed., pp. 733–768). Thousand Oaks, CA: Sage.

Evans, H. M. (2010). The art of medicine: Music, medicine, and embodiment. *The Lancet, 375*, 886–887.

Ezzy, D. (2010). Qualitative interviewing as an embodied emotional performance. *Qualitative Inquiry, 16*, 163–170.

Fine, M., Weis, L., Weseen, S., & Wong, L. (2000). For whom? Qualitative research, representation, and social responsibilities. In N. K. Denzin & Y. S. Lincoln (Eds.), *Handbook of qualitative research* (2nd ed., pp. 107–132). Thousand Oaks, CA: Sage.

Finlay, L. (2002). "Outing" the researcher: The provenance, process, and practice of reflexivity. *Qualitative Health Research, 12*, 531–545.

Frank, A. W. (1995). *The wounded storyteller: Body, illness, and ethics*. Chicago, IL: University of Chicago Press.

Geertz, C. (1973). *The interpretation of cultures*. New York, NY: Basic Books.

Gergen, K. J. (1994). *Realities and relationships: Soundings in social construction*. Cambridge, MA: Harvard University Press.

Goffman, E. (1959). *The presentation of self in everyday life*. Garden City, NY: Doubleday.

Goldberg, N. (1986). *Writing down the bones: Freeing the writer within*. Boston, MA: Shambhala.

Haddow, G. (2005). The phenomenology of death, embodiment and organ transplantation. *Sociology of Health & Illness, 92–113.*

Hall, W. A., & Callery, P. (2001). Enhancing the rigor of grounded theory: Incorporating reflexivity and relationality. *Qualitative Health Research, 11,* 257–272.

Haraway, D. (1988). Situated knowledges: The science question in feminism and the privilege of partial perspective. *Feminist Studies, 14,* 575–599.

Hayward, C. (Director), & Harter, L. M. (Producer). (2010). *The art of the possible* [Motion picture]. Athens: University of Ohio.

Hegland, M. E. (2009). Losing, using, and crafting spaces for aging: Muslim Iranian American seniors in California's Santa Clara Valley. In J. Sokolovsky (Ed.), *The cultural context of aging: World wide perspectives* (pp. 302–324). Westport, CT: Greenwood.

Hochschild, A. R. (1983). *The managed heart: Commercialization of human feeling.* Berkeley: University of California Press.

Holstein, J. A., & Gubrium, J. F. (1995). *The active interview.* Thousand Oaks, CA: Sage.

Holstein, J. A., & Gubrium, J. F. (2003). Active interviewing. In J. F. Gubrium & J. A. Holstein (Eds.), *Postmodern interviewing* (pp. 67–80). Thousand Oaks, CA: Sage.

Inckle, K. (2007). *Writing on the body? Thinking through gendered embodiment and marked flesh.* Newcastle, England: Cambridge Scholars.

Irigaray, L. (1980). When our lips speak together (C. Burke, Trans.). *Signs: Journal of Women in Culture and Society, 6,* 69–79.

Jacobson, D. (1999). Impression formation in cyberspace: Online expectations and offline experiences in text-based virtual communities. *Journal of Computer-Mediated Communication, 5.* Retrieved from http://jcmc.indiana.edu/vol5/issue1/jacobson.html

Janesick, V. J. (2011). *Stretching exercises for qualitative researchers* (3rd ed.). Thousand Oaks, CA: Sage.

Johnson, M. (1987). *The body in the mind: The bodily basis of meaning, imagination, and reasoning.* Chicago, IL: University of Chicago Press.

Konopásek, Z. (2008). Making thinking visible with Atlas.ti: Computer assisted qualitative analysis as textual practices. *Forum Qualitative Sozialforschung/Forum: Qualitative Social Research, 9*(2), Art. 12. Retrieved from http://www.qualitative-research.net/index.php/fqs/article/view/420/911

Latta, M. M., & Buck, G. (2008). Enfleshing embodiment: "Falling into trust" with the body's role in teaching and learning. *Educational Philosophy and Theory, 40,* 315–329.

Lindlof, T. R., & Taylor, B. C. (2011). *Qualitative communication research methods* (3rd ed.). Thousand Oaks, CA: Sage.

Lovink, G. (2005). Talking race and cyberspace: An interview with Lisa Nakamura. *Frontiers, 26,* 60–65.

Macbeth, D. (2001). On "reflexivity" in qualitative research: Two readings and a third. *Qualitative Inquiry, 7,* 35–68.

Madison, D. S. (2005). *Critical ethnography: Method, ethics, and performance.* Thousand Oaks, CA: Sage.

Mairs, N. (1997). Carnal acts. In K. Conboy, N. Medina, & S. Stanbury (Eds.), *Writing on the body: Female embodiment and feminist theory* (pp. 296–305). New York, NY: Columbia University Press.

Mann, C., & Stewart, F. (2002). *Internet interviewing.* In J. F. Gubrium & J. A. Holstein (Eds.), *Handbook of interview research: Context and method* (pp. 603–628). Thousand Oaks, CA: Sage.

Marshall, H. (1999). Our bodies, ourselves: Why we should add old fashioned empirical phenomenology to the new theories of the body. In J. Price & M. Shildrick (Eds.), *Feminist theory and the body: A reader* (pp. 64–75). New York, NY: Routledge.

Mies, M. (1983). Towards a methodology for feminist research. In G. Bowles & R. D. Klein (Eds.), *Theories of women's studies* (pp. 117–138). London, England: Routledge.

Miller-Day, M. A. (2004). *Communication among grandmothers, mothers, and adult daughters: A qualitative study of maternal relationships.* Mahwah, NJ: Lawrence Erlbaum.

Minge, J. M. (2007). The stained body: A fusion of embodied art on rape and love. *Journal of Contemporary Ethnography, 36,* 252–280.

Minow, M. (1990). *Making all the difference: Inclusion, exclusion and the American law.* Ithaca, NY: Cornell University Press.

Mishler, E. G. (1991). Representing discourse: The rhetoric of transcription. *Journal of Narrative and Life History, 1,* 255–280.

Murray, C. D. (2004). An interpretative phenomenological analysis of the embodiment of artificial limbs. *Disability and Rehabilitation, 26,* 963–973.

Peralta, R. L. (2007). College alcohol use and the embodiment of hegemonic masculinity among European American men. *Sex Roles, 56,* 741–756.

Pillow, W. (2003). Confession, catharsis, or cure? Rethinking the uses of reflexivity as methodological power in qualitative research. *International Journal of Qualitative Studies in Education, 16,* 175–196.

Pollock, D. (1999). *Telling bodies, performing birth.* New York, NY: Columbia University Press.

Price, J., & Shildrick, M. (Eds.). (1999). *Feminist theory and the body: A reader.* New York, NY: Routledge.

Quinlan, M. M. (2010). Fostering connections among diverse individuals through multi-sensorial storytelling. *Health Communication, 25,* 91–93.

Quinlan, M. M., & Harter, L. M. (2010). Meaning in motion: The embodied poetics and politics of Dancing Wheels. *Text and Performance Quarterly, 30*, 374–395.

Reinharz, S. (1992). *Feminist methods in social research.* New York, NY: Oxford University Press.

Roen, K. (2001). Transgender theory and embodiment: The risk of racial marginalisation. *Journal of Gender Studies, 10*, 253–263.

Román-Velázquez, P. (1999). The embodiment of salsa: Musicians, instruments and the performance of a Latin style and identity. *Popular Music, 18*, 115–131.

Ronai, C. R. (1992). Managing aging in young adulthood: The "aging" table dancer. *Journal of Aging Studies, 6*, 307–317.

Ronai, C. R. (1995). Multiple reflections of childhood sex abuse: An argument for a layered account. *Journal of Contemporary Ethnography, 23*, 395–426.

Rose, G. (1999). Women and everyday spaces. In J. Price & M. Shildrick (Eds.), *Feminist theory and the body: A reader* (pp. 359–370). New York, NY: Routledge.

Schrock, D., Reid, L., & Boyd, E. M. (2005). Transsexuals' embodiment of womanhood. *Gender & Society, 19*, 317–335.

Sharma, S., Reimer-Kirkham, S., & Cochrane, M. (2009). Practicing the awareness of embodiment in qualitative health research: Methodological reflections. *Qualitative Health Research, 19*, 1642–1650.

Shuy, R. W. (2002). *In-person versus telephone interviewing.* In J. F. Gubrium & J. A. Holstein (Eds.), *Handbook of interview research: Context and method* (pp. 537–556). Thousand Oaks, CA: Sage.

Simmonds, F. N. (1999). My body, myself: How does a black woman do sociology? In J. Price & M. Shildrick (Eds.), *Feminist theory and the body: A reader* (pp. 50–63). New York, NY: Routledge.

Spivak, G. (1987). *In other worlds: Essays in cultural politics.* New York, NY: Routledge.

Stelter, R. (2010). Experience-based, body-anchored qualitative research interviewing. *Qualitative Health Research, 20*, 859–867.

Stronach, I., Garratt, D., Pearce, C., & Piper, H. (2007). Reflexivity, the picturing of selves, the forging of method. *Qualitative Inquiry, 13*, 179–203.

Tanis, M., & Postmes, T. (2003). Social cues and impression formation in CMC. *Journal of Communication, 53*, 676–693.

Todres, L. (2008). Being with that: The relevance of embodied understanding for practice. *Qualitative Health Research, 18*, 1566–1573.

Trinh, T. M. (1991). *When the moon waxes red: Representation, gender and cultural politics.* New York, NY: Routledge.

Trinh, T. M. (1999). Write your body: The body in theory. In J. Price & M. Shildrick (Eds.), *Feminist theory and the body: A reader* (pp. 258–266). New York, NY: Routledge.

Walsh, D. J. (2010). Childbirth embodiment: Problematic aspects of current understandings. *Sociology of Health & Illness, 32*, 486–501.

Wittgenstein, L. (1953). *Philosophical investigations.* Malden, MA: Blackwell.

Zitzelsberger, H. (2005). (In)visibility: Accounts of embodiment of women with physical disabilities and differences. *Disability & Society, 20*, 389–403.

37

THE (EXTRA)ORDINARY PRACTICES OF QUALITATIVE INTERVIEWING

◆ Tim Rapley

By failing to consider the effects of the interview situation on responses, we circumvent the vital process of examining our own contribution to the generation of the data. Focusing on what the natives say and do thus keeps us from having to ask tough questions with regard to the effects of our actions on the data, and on the people we are studying.

Charles Briggs (1986, p. 124)

All trajectories of research on interviews have highlighted the work of the interviewer in encounters with interviewees. Within the positivist and neopositivist traditions, the interviewer should, ideally, closely moderate and monitor his or her potential impact. In this space, interviewer neutrality is not only good but also necessary practice. In the more romantic, feminist, constructionist, and postmodern traditions, the interviewer is viewed as an active participant who collaborates with interviewees to share and generate knowledge. Of the works that focused explicitly on the relatively fine-grained analysis of interactional practices in qualitative interviews, those by Baker (1983, 1984), Baruch (1981), Briggs (1986), Mishler (1986), and Watson and Weinburg (1982) were central in beginning to document how the work of the interviewer comes off in real time. Since then, we have seen a slow but steady growth in work that focuses on various aspects of interaction in interviews (see Roulston, 2006, for a review). This chapter outlines some of the trajectories of that work and asks what, if anything, we can learn from research on interaction in interviews.

◆ Social Studies of Interaction in Interviews

INTERVIEWERS' WORK IN INTERVIEWS

The interviewer is an essential part of the trajectory of the talk. This seems like quite a mundane observation, but scholarly work is often silent about this, where a discussion of the work of the interviewer is generally left to the methodology, discussion, or limitation sections of a paper. The classic way to show this in action is to contrast different formats of presenting interview talk.

First, let us view a section of transcript as it routinely appears in scholarly publications. Extract 37.1a is taken from research I conducted into the diagnostic pathways of children with arthritis. In this case, the mother of a child with arthritis, to whom I (Tim) have given the pseudonym Gill, has been describing how she has been going back and forth to health professionals and that no one has been able to offer a diagnosis.

Extract 37.1a

Gill: I was petrified because I didn't know what it was and then, you can tell when it's like, on the big body scan they says "Oh her kidney doesn't look right," but he didn't tell us nothing else. That was it.

In this case, we are only given access to the mother's talk. Clearly, we can get a sense of her concern and fear, in part further compounded by her lack of information. Let us review this talk, but placed in its local context, with some of the talk that led up to it (see Extract 37.1b).

Extract 37.1b

Gill: and she had x-rays, she had scans, she was taken to the BlueHospital for a scan like a full-body scan where they put the like the dye stuff to stick to her bones?

Tim: Ah yeah.

Gill: Ah ha, erm she had kidney scans because one of her kidneys looked bigger than the other kidney erm and then

Tim: I mean how scared were you when all of this was going on?

Gill: I was petrified because I didn't know what it was and then, you can tell when it's like, on the big body scan they says "Oh her kidney doesn't look right," but he didn't tell us nothing else. That was it.

We can now see how Gill's description of her state of mind as "petrified" and her subsequent unpacking of why she felt like this—only being told that her child's kidney doesn't look right—was incited by the interviewer's question. Prior to the question, she was offering quite a pragmatic unpacking of the various processes that they went through. The question explicitly asks her to talk in a language of emotions ("How scared were you?") to describe her emotional reaction. In this case, we can see that the interviewers' questions affect the trajectory of the talk, its form, and its content. As Watson and Weinburg (1982) noted, in all interviews, interviewers are central in directing the overall trajectory of the talk: They initiate the topic; they follow up specific issues.

Let us view the same extract, but with another layer of verbal interactional detail, viewing it through the lens of a Jeffersonian transcription notation (see Extract 37.1c).

Extract 37.1c

1	Gill:	erm and she had x-rays, she had sca:ns (.)
2		she- (.) she was taken to the BlueHospital for
3		a scan=>like a full body scan<=where
4		they put the:: (0.5) like the dye stuff? to
5		stick to h[er bones,]
6	Tim:	[Ahhhh,] yeah? okay. [>yeah, yeah,] yeah<
7	Gill:	[Ah ha]
8		errrm she had kidney scans=because one
9		of her kidneys looked bigger than the
10		other kidney. (0.5) errrm (0.8) and then (.)
11	Tim:	>I mean how scared were you< when all of

12		this was going [o n]?
13	Gill:	[I was] petrified
14		(0.5)
15	Tim	[(Okay.)]
16	Gill:	[e r m] (0.5) because I didn't know what it
17		was=and=then (.) you cou- you can tell when
18		(0.4) it's like (0.8) the- on the big body scan
19		they says "Oh her kidney doesn't look
20		right" but he didn't tell us nothing else.
21	Tim:	°mm hm°=
22	Gill:	=That was it. erm (.) so we ((continues))

From this vantage point—and this is only showing some aspects of the verbal work, and the nonverbal is lost—we can begin to see some of the interactional dynamics, some of the *work* that both participants are engaged in. In terms of the interviewer, the action of asking the question (Lines 11–12) is one part of the broader trajectory of actions.

This whole sequence of talk was initiated about 3 minutes beforehand, when I asked Gill to describe when someone had actually told her that arthritis was causing her child's problem. During this stretch of talk, at various points, I asked specific questions to follow up a specific aspect of her unfolding narrative.

Returning to Extract 37.1c, at Lines 4–5, Gill tentatively attempts to describe a specific diagnostic test in quite everyday terms, seeking some kind of confirmation, and Tim works to show that he understands what she is getting at (Line 6: "[Ahhhh,] yeah? okay"), although he does not offer the technical term to further demonstrate his understanding. Gill, while overlapping with Tim's talk, then shows that she sees his response as enough to carry on (Line 7: " Ah   ha   "), and Tim confirms this (Line 6: "yeah?"). Later in the talk, at Line 21, Tim also demonstrates that he is following what she is saying ("mm hm"), and this comes off just as this aspect of her talk about the scan comes to a close. We can also see how, just after Gill describes herself as being "petrified" (Line 13), a gap in the talk emerges (Line 14). Tim could have come in with another follow-up question, but both speakers start to talk at the same point. Tim merely acknowledges her answer, saying what I can only hear on the tape as "okay" (Line 15)—implicitly marking what Gill said was a "good enough answer to the question, please

carry on." She then goes on to explain aspects of why she was petrified (Line 16: "because . . . ").

So, even in this small extract, we can begin to see some of the work that interviewers undertake in interviews. Centrally, they do some very "mundane work": They ask questions about specific topics; they ask follow-up questions, following up specific aspects of talk and remaining silent about others; and they, in time with the interviewees' talk, offer responses such as "yeah," "okay," and "mm hm." And this mundane work has some quite clear effects. It directs, incites, and encourages interviewees to talk on specific topics. And the interactional turn asks people to consider that work when reviewing, analyzing, and presenting their transcripts. In this sense, to borrow a phrase from social studies of science, it argues for a more *symmetrical* approach to the analysis of interviews.

IDENTITY WORK IN INTERVIEWS

This work has also focused more explicitly on the identity work in interviews, exploring how interviewees (and to a lesser extent interviewers) work to produce themselves as specific types of people in relation to the topics of talk. The talk in Extract 37.2 is taken from an interview with a drug peer educator that I have transcribed following Jeffersonian transcription notation. It is the first moment in the interview when the identity "drug peer educator" and, importantly, the topic, "drugs," are made explicitly relevant. Note that the interviewer's (IR) question is an open question; it is up to the interviewee, Dan, to offer the details as to why he put himself forward.

Extract 37.2

1	IR:	°°<(all right). (.) <u>o</u>kay.°°>=> .h< so can you tell me	
2		why why did you put yourself forward at that stage,	
3	Dan:	erm<u>:</u>, phh Well,=it is the sort of thing erm:. (0.4) I like to do	←1
4		and I do= I enjoy you know (.) <u>learn</u>ing things I didn't	←1a
5		know before and=then you know teaching it its	←1b
6		°>things that I do you know° I teach a lot of other things	
7		as well as drama< and so forth so um .hh quite used to doing	
8		°it°.=and I come from <u>a</u> medical family so er:, (0.3)	←1c
9		[>you know drugs and so forth< we do	
10	IR:	[mm:.	
11	Dan:	it we discuss quite a lo<u>t</u> °and er°	
12	IR:	=yeah.	
13	Dan:	°and it is something it doe- did interest me really°	
14	IR:	okay=was there any other particular interest in the	
15		fact that it was drugs >I mean< is that something	
16		that is <u>mean</u>ingful to <u>you</u>: pa[rticularly or not=	

After Dan's initial gloss of his motivation, that this is the "sort of thing" he *likes to* do (Arrow 1), he works to unpack the gloss. He first states, "I enjoy you know (.) <u>learn</u>ing things I didn't know before" (Lines 4–5). Dan produces himself as someone who, in general, irrespective of the topic—note the utterance "things" (Line 4)—actively enjoys learning. He produces himself as a "seeker of new knowledge," which is a praiseworthy activity. Dan then marks that he also enjoys teaching what he's learned" (Arrow 1b), another praiseworthy activity. Then, at Arrow 1c, he does some lovely identity work; he implicitly marks why the topic of the peer education, drugs, is relevant to him: He "come[s] from a *medical* family" (Arrow 1c), and they discuss "drugs *and so forth*" (Line 9), so drugs is marked as just one of the things they discuss together.

So Dan works to mark his motivation for becoming a "drug peer educator." He moves initially from distancing himself from having any specific interest in the role (it's just the sort of thing he does), to motivations produced as generally available reasons specifically connected to the job (he likes learning/teaching), to motivations produced as more biographical in origin (he comes from a medical family). All these reasons

have predicates centered on the type of person who has such motivations. He works to mark himself as a specific type of person, whose motivation for becoming a drug peer educator is not a product of him being a drug user or having contact with other drug users.

By marking himself as someone who is interested in learning and teaching irrespective of the topic, the fact that he will be gaining knowledge about drugs is produced as being of only minor importance. He then works to produce himself as someone who is potentially hearable as a "non–drug user," as he marks that any interest in drugs that has entered his life has only entered through legitimate and ordinary ways, through both a medical and a familial context. He does not connect an interest in drugs to any other part of his life, be it friends, school, or strangers or a desire to help drug users. So Dan works to negate that he is a seeker of drug knowledge because he does, intends to, or is thinking about using drugs. All this work comes off as an answer to IR's open and nonleading question.[1]

The talk under analysis begins to demonstrate how interviewees actively work to manage identities. In this case, Dan works to produce himself as "morally adequate" (see also Baker, 1984, 1997; Baruch, 1981).

---

[1]For analysis of this style of "neutral and facilitative" interviewing, see Rapley (2001, 2004).

One of the fundamental ways to document your moral adequacy is to demonstrate how you, or the topics you are speaking about, are "ordinary" (see Lawrence, 1996; Sacks, 1984). In other contexts, such identity work may be more explicitly tied to issues of expertise and knowledge (see Bryman & Cassell, 2006; Roulston, 2001) or specific rights and responsibilities (see Baruch, 1981). Centrally, this work argues that before we make assertions about what people are saying, how they behave, or what they believe in, we can (and maybe should) examine how both interviewers and interviewees work to locally manage their identities and how such work is central to the trajectory of talk.

MUTUALITY AND DIFFERENCE WORK IN INTERVIEWS

A quite broad, focused view of issues of mutuality and difference is found in Enosh and Buchbinder's (2005) work on narrative styles in domestic violence research. They highlight four narrative formats that emerged in their interviews. The styles of "self-observation" and "negotiation" emerge at moments when interviewees have accepted and worked with the interviewers' position—that violence existed in their domestic relationship—that was articulated through their questions. So in "narrative as negotiation," the interviewee might accept that violence had occurred but would work to redefine the meanings and context of the violence. The styles of "struggle" and "deflection" marked stretches of talk when the interviewees actively disagreed with, minimized, or dismissed the interviewers' line of questioning and version of the situation. Irrespective of the topic, the dynamics they outline are an essential part of all interviews.[2] Interviewers and interviewees have to *constantly work* to define and agree on the emergent and unfolding trajectory, focus, and meanings of the talk.

With the exception of those advocating more adversarial styles of interviewing (see Brinkmann, 2007; Dinkins, 2005), interviewers routinely work hard to maintain a mutual definition of the situation and avoid overt or extended tension. Clearly, questions, although

essential to the action, are not the only resources that interviewers work with to enact mutuality. Those apparently mundane moments of talk, such as "yeah," "uh huh," "mm," "right," "okay," and so on, also shape trajectories of interview talk and sense making (see, e.g., Rapley, 2001). And clearly, face-to-face interviews come off in a multimodal world of bodies and material culture; we interact in and through artifacts, gaze, gestures, touch, and so on. Researchers interested in interaction in interviews have begun to explore specific aspects of the phenomena that emerge in interviews, including complaints (Roulston, 2000; Roulston, Baker, & Liljestrom, 2001), laughter (Grønnerød, 2004), and self-disclosure (Abell, Locke, Condor, Gibson, & Stevenson, 2006). This work begins to throw light on how mutuality unfolds.

In reviewing my own archive of interviews, I've observed that doing self-disclosure talk—in the form of a biographical account—is a routine feature of some of the questions I ask or responses I give to an account.[3] Extract 37.3 is again taken from research I conducted into the diagnostic pathways of children with arthritis. We had been discussing the information-searching practices that Mel (the mother of a child with arthritis) had been undertaking.

At this moment, despite starting something hearable as a question or formulation of prior talk (Line 2), it is abandoned. Instead, the interviewer offers an account of his own mother's relationship with sources of medical information (Lines 3–7). This self-disclosure talk works to incite Mel to produce a nice, vivid account, which goes beyond the talk shown in Extract 37.2 and covers illness information work and familial dynamics.

It also does some specific interactional work. Much earlier in the interview, Mel had described looking up her child's symptoms and becoming extremely concerned about the range of illnesses her child could have. About a minute before this extract she had also noted that she only visits a single website now. In this way, the interviewer's self-disclosure works to both document that he had been closely following the prior talk as well as produce the position of being "cautious" about searching for medical information as being understandable and "ordinary,"

---

[2]See also Gubrium and Holstein's (2009) discussion of narrative editing and narrative composition.

[3]I've also observed how I do what could be referred to as "research disclosure," by disclosing either in specific or in general terms what other research participants have said in prior interviews. This seems to emerge in two distinct contexts, one interactional—especially around asking potentially delicate questions or hearing potentially delicate answers—and the other more structural, where the interview is close to coming to an end, especially when interviewees ask questions centered on whether this encounter was "useful" for me.

Extract 37.3

1	Mel:	Anything to help ((Smiley voice))
2	Tim:	Okay so >so so so< you did this searching, which=I
3		mean yeah=I mean (0.4) it jus- yeah (.) my mum
4		always refused, to have a medical book in the
5		house=because it was-because=she knew what
6		it would do to her (.) because it would
7		just scare her, [.hhh (.) as if]
8	Mel:	[My mother has] a one
9		this thic[k and she does my] head in
10	Tim:	[yeah=yeah (.) yep] yep yep=
11	Mel:	=because I don't tell her half of it
12	Tim:	yep, yep yep [yep yep yep]
13	Mel:	[because erm] (.) we have an I- erm
14		information pack on her new medication= ((continues))

especially for people in the category "mum." Notice also the work that Tim does to mark his understanding of Mel's talk (Lines 10 and 12), saying something like "I hear what you are saying, and I've experienced it as well."

With direct reference to methodological discussions of rapport and power inequalities, Abell et al. (2006) closely analyzed moments when researchers did self-disclosure in interviews with young people. As in Extract 37.3 above, they found that disclosing a personal narrative can work to produce quite elaborated follow-up talk from the interviewee. However, they also show that what they call "doing similarity" can close down a trajectory of talk when interviewees orientate to the disclosure as demonstrating some evidence of difference between the speakers; in their research, this difference was situated in the context of age and ethnicity. Interestingly, interviewees can also orientate to the disclosure as demonstrating that they are less knowledgeable and so less entitled to speak on the topic than the interviewer. In these cases, again, interviewees offer minimal responses or shift topics.

In a related area, Soilevuo Grønnerød (2004) has explored how laughter emerges in the interviews she conducted with men involved in amateur rock bands. She nicely highlights the diverse moments when laughter emerges and the potential interactional work it can do. Laughter can mark interviewees' (or interviewers') talk as ironic, thus softening the impact of something hearable as potentially contentious, or highlight some aspect of contradiction in their talk. Also, laughter can

unfold between interviewer and interviewee; in some contexts, this can work to enact mutuality and encourage talk. Lack of mutual laughter can also mark potential distance or difference. As she notes, her analysis of laughter "revealed the subtle conflicts and tensions . . . [and] demonstrated the instability of interactive positions and categorisations" (p. 46).

◆ So What?

Although there is some work on the dynamics of accounting practices, in real terms we still know very little about the interactional work of qualitative interviews beyond the very basics. However, the existing empirical literature and the discussion articles that engage with it do offer some potential directions, ranging from quite practical, therapeutic issues to more radical, epistemological ones.

SO WHAT: REPRESENTATIONAL DIRECTIONS

When you read articles reporting quotes from interviews, you often lose the interactional nature of those encounters as things such as interviewers' questions, pauses, response tokens (words such as "uh huh," "yeah," etc.), tone, and laughter are rarely given. And just as the interviewers' work is central to the trajectory of talk, their talk should also be part of the *representation* of data.

However, the work of the interviewer is not the only action sometimes lost in our transcription practices. The overall interactional texture is often rendered as rather flat. As Potter and Hepburn (2005) describe it, by drawing on conventional textual punctuation and ordered, grammatically complete sentences, transcripts can read like the scripts of a play. A clean transcript, devoid of the intimacies of talk—the hesitations, the reworkings, the emotion, the stress, the perturbations, and so on—can create distance from the lived work of the speakers, from the lived reality of its production.[4]

Clearly, as Briggs (2007) suggests, following Bruno Latour, transcripts are very useful devices; they are "immutable mobiles," in that they allow focused and directed exchanges between researchers in a research team or between the author and reader. If we directly worked with and from the recordings, if they were the central part of day-to-day analytic work and the rhetoric of our demonstrations, we would probably transform our relationship to interview "data."

Our current routine practice is to get the audio (or video) recording of the interview transcribed, to whatever level of detail, often by other researchers, support staff, or an outside agency. We then relisten to the recording against the transcript, adjusting specific words, tidying it, or adding whatever additional features we feel might be relevant. The transcript is then worked on—divided, labeled, reordered, and sections connected to other sections—talked about, and written on. The interaction, or rather the recording of the interaction, is lost, hidden from the analytic action, and rarely returned to. In this way, our current routines configure a specific order of analytic reasoning and action.

However, we already have at hand a suite of technologically mediated options to unite analysis, talk, and text. The field of audio and video interaction–orientated work has already developed potential practical solutions, where transcripts of talk are tied directly to the recordings; so on finding that moment in a transcript that we think is key, interesting, or just puzzling, we could easily hear that as a moment of talk. Ideally, and with the appropriate ethical reviews

and informed consent, such a practice could be extended to more public presentations, be it data sessions, conferences, or publication.

To date, the "verbatim" transcript reigns supreme. Given that this is the case, you still have to make a choice as to the degree of "tight" or "loose" coherence with the original recording that you are working from. The tighter the coherence, the more technical your transcript will have to become. Above, I've used Jeffersonian transcription, the industry standard for those doing conversation-analytic work. It relies on a quite specific series of notation devices to render various aspects of the interactional texture and can appear as an overly technical and complex way of textually reproducing talk. Clearly, it is not for everyone, as few have the analytic interest, time, technical expertise, or budget to undertake such work. However, Poland (2002) has developed a useful list of things that he feels should be included in interview transcripts: features such as pauses, laughing, and other features of talk such as sighing or coughing, interruptions and overlapping talk, garbled talk, emphasis and held sounds, reported speech, mimicking, and paraphrasing of others' or self-thoughts.

So issues of representation have implications for two areas of practice. They relate not only to the more public transcripts we make available to others in research reports and articles but also to our working, analytic transcripts that we use on a day-to-day basis to think with. Whatever be the level of analytic detail you prefer to work with, having as a baseline the sort of detail that Poland (2002) argues for is very useful in making you and your audience think and explore (however briefly) how the "data" emerged in and through interaction. How you choose to represent your data publicly will ultimately depend on the types of analytic claims you want to make. With the transcripts I used above, I explicitly chose the form of representation that would make some analytic points in the context of this chapter;[5] it is not something I would want or expect to offer to all audiences.

Above all, if we are to learn something from the work on interactions in interviews, it is that we should include the work of interviewers, to demonstrate their often central role in inciting the trajectory

---

[4]I'm not trying to suggest an overly naive view, in that the audio or video recording of an interview somehow stands for the interaction. Clearly, recordings artificially frame the event; we have a lot of work before and after a recording, as well as a lot of lived, situated, emotional, embodied work, that recording devices can never render available.

[5]And the transcripts given above are somewhat cleaner and tidied up from my analytic or working transcripts! The ones I made initially, when I was repeatedly listening to small sections of the recording, have other features, including attempts to notate the intonation to a finer degree and comments about tone and emphasis.

of the talk. Also, I feel that, whenever possible, we should make a habit of returning to our recordings (alongside our field notes and embodied rememberings) when reflecting on and arguing from specific moments of our transcripts.

SO WHAT: THERAPEUTIC DIRECTIONS

When we as social scientists study the "other," we routinely feed back our findings in the hope that they will engage with them and create new styles of thought and action. Part of the history of ethnomethodological and conversation-analytic work has been centered on redescribing anew the seen but unnoticed, taken-for-granted aspects of routine practice, providing people with resources to reflect on their practical action and reasoning. So findings from social studies of interviewee–interviewer interaction can also be used by people to reflect on and help them make sense of their own interviewing practice.

Such a stance can be particularly helpful to novice researchers. As I have briefly outlined elsewhere (Rapley, 2004), the how-to interview literature means that novices are surrounded by a range of directives and instructions about how to conduct interviews, ranging from the appropriate lexical design of questions to moments of bodily comportment. This is most clear in the literature that seeks to produce a neutralistic interviewer, where researchers are asked to closely monitor talk and gesture, to maintain a veil of neutrality and interestedness. However, the literature surrounding more engaged and active forms of interviewing also describes an array of empathetic technologies of the self. As Roulston (2010) argues, we could be actively encouraging researchers to transcribe their own interview recordings and ask them to focus on how they interact, as opposed to solely focusing on the topical content of interviewees' talk. I feel that it is potentially helpful and illuminating for novices, in the sense that it provides them with both a space and, it is hoped, some analytic distance, to actively reflect on their role in the emergent trajectory of talk as well as review their interactional routines and habits.

Making your interactional practice "strange" can, at times, be quite disconcerting, and you can easily become overly critical. You can realize how easily you fall short of the abstract ideals of interviewing practice that you have gained through teaching and texts. However, such a reading should, ideally, be undertaken with some practical knowledge of the interaction-in-interviews literature, in part so that you can come to terms with the fact that what you do echoes the mundane practices of others, that others enact such abstract ideals in an as ad hoc way as you do. As Roulston (2010) outlines it, some of the assumptions about good question design do not always make sense in situated interaction. For example, she shows examples of how closed questions, rather than being "bad" somehow, are at times useful devices we draw on to establish our understanding.

Relatedly, (re)engaging with specific interviews, especially those we feel went "badly," can be intellectually rewarding. As Tanggaard (2007) outlines, moments of "objection," where interviewees momentarily question or refuse the assumptions embedded in interviewers' talk, can be a therapeutic intervention for researchers, in that they may learn to question or reflect on their own practice. Reflecting on such "failed" interviews can also invoke a quite substantive analytic insight (Callon & Rabeharisoa, 2004) as well as redirect the overall approach toward your research topic (Nairn, Munro, & Smith, 2005). It might also help you question the idea of what a "good" or "great" interview is. Does the sense of "good" emerge from the here-and-now interaction, that you got on well, that you thought the interviewee was a really interesting person, that you presented yourself as a good person? Does it emerge from broader analytic issues, from the interviewee being highly quotable, offering you a great "sound bite" for an analytic point you are thinking through? Or is it tied to the interviewee making you think anew, that something he or she uttered has thrown a new area or idea into relief?

Reviewing transcripts, or ideally the recordings of them, can affect the day-to-day conduct of our interviewing and the broader analytic trajectories of our interview research. Reading *for* interaction can intimately shape our assumptions and our specific research questions; it can also help us highlight the silences, in terms of what was left unsaid by just that interviewee or what is left unexplored through our questions.

SO WHAT: INTERACTIONAL DIRECTIONS

As the archive of work on interaction in interviews is beginning to show—albeit very lightly and from a distance—no single trajectory, no single set of norms, ideals, or position that you take up as an interviewer will automatically produce something that gives you "better data." All the interactional work—whether doing neutrality or mutuality, whether engaged, confessional, supportive, or adversarial—*takes work and does work*. It has effects. None of these effects in the trajectory of talk can be assumed, can be established a priori; with each interview, they are worked out in the here and now. In this way, we cannot assume that a specific interviewing style or format will produce a specific effect and so produce "better" data. However, this raises the following question: Why follow a specific style, format, or tradition of interviewing? Clearly, our choices routinely emerge from our training, our intellectual habitus, and our disciplinary grounding. However, we need to critically reflect on these often diffuse legacies. For me, the only reason to prefer a specific style over another stems more from a desire to produce or enact a specific ideology, theory, or politics with just that interviewee.

If you seek to follow the theoretical tradition of work, where the interviewer is supposed to create "bias"—and this should be minimized through close self-inspection of question wording, probes, and others' responses and bodily gestures—fine. Following quite a strict code, and closely monitoring you actions, may make you feel better as you are enacting a theoretical ideal. However, you still cannot somehow automatically extract and silence the work of the interviewer; the interviewer is active, and interviewees' talk is emergent and unfolds in and through just this dynamic context.

If you feel, for personal and/or theoretical reasons, that mutuality is essential, you can engage in acts of mutual self-disclosure or draw on other forms of talk or gesture that you feel enact intimacy. However, offering a self-report does not necessarily mean that people will offer up analytically rich second stories. As Abell et al. (2006) show, such work can create and sustain difference as much as generate connection and similarity. Talk or gestures that demonstrate some form of intimate, empathetic listening do not necessarily create reciprocity. Personally, I'm only interested in making people feel at ease out of an ethico-moral sense. They have given me their time, and so I should respect them for that. I do not like being seen or orientated to as overly distant or neutralistic, in part as I act as a proxy for a range of actors, including my university, the funder, and, in my research area, specific departments of hospitals that interviewees use. However, I don't assume that "doing intimacy and understanding" will have a specific effect on the analytic quality or possibilities of the talk.

In this way, my fundamental task in interviews is to attempt to explore, with just this participant, his or her practical experience and knowledge about a specific topic or range of issues. I've come to this participant because he or she offers a point of access to a specific issue; this participant can, potentially, throw some light on a research question or idea that I or the broader research team I'm part of are trying to explore. I cannot know, a priori, what specific interactional dynamics are going to emerge. I cannot know a priori what specific trajectory of questions is going to help the participant explore, with me, the issues that the research is centered on. Such things are emergent; they are a product of the here-and-now interaction. With this is mind, I'm generally quite relaxed about the form of my talk. Clearly, I'm interested in trying to coordinate the talk, to coordinate the "essential tension" (Mazeland & Have, 1996), to actively manage the here-and-now trajectories of ideas, thoughts, and comments with those of the broader research, with the ideas, thoughts, and comments that have emerged from the initial research idea, past and current reading, conversations, interviews, and analysis.

Interactionally speaking, my job is to try to incite the participant to speak and to explore in some detail. What's fascinating is the way we—as interviewers—sometimes have to work to practically show the interviewee the sort of talk we are expecting and are interested in. In rare cases, you offer up an initial question, and then, some 10, 20, or 30 minutes later, the interviewee comes up for breath. Until that point, all you've been doing is nodding, offering token responses or other utterances that do some version of appreciation. However, more often you have to implicitly (and sometimes explicitly) show the interviewee the kind of style, format, and trajectory of talk you're interested in. This work emerges prior to the meeting, through information sheets and recruitment conversations, as well as in those introductory, meet-and-greet phases where you are (again) unpacking the project and the reason for the interview for the interviewee.

Although we have no extensive archive of empirical work on this, just reviewing your transcripts can show you the range of interactional resources that we rely on. Clearly, topically initiating questions do some work to define, in some broad sense, the possibilities of response. We then rely on various devices to encourage the participant to offer more. As interviewers, we do such work through silence—by not responding with a new question at points when the talk is hearable as coming to a close; with utterances, specific intonational contours such as "yeah," "oh yeah," "uh huh," which can work to say, "I'm following you, please continue"; as well as with follow-up questions, where we ask the interviewees to focus on and unpack a specific aspect of their prior talk or self-reports, where you offer your own or other experiences. In this way, these and other verbal and gestural resources can work to encourage the interviewee to learn how to be the sort of interviewee we want him or her to be. And we see this overtly expressed when interviewees offer a question directed at the form of their own talk, what van Enk (2009), following Goffman, calls parenthetical remarks, with utterances such as "Is this what you're interested in hearing about?" or "Does that answer your question?"

In this way, I prefer a more "conversational" style of interviewing. The interview is clearly not a "naturally occurring" conversation, but it comes off in and through coordinating, in the here and now, quite unspectacular and mundane conversational resources (Hester & Francis, 1994; Rapley, 2004). So, for example, I'm not too concerned if my question is too leading or, following Holstein and Gubrium (1995, 1997), "active," in that it asks the participants to talk in a specific, focused way, say to talk in a language of "emotions" or a specific identity, such as a "concerned mother." I'm not concerned because I will have this in mind when I analyze the data; I don't assume that the trajectory of interviewees' talk is somehow devoid of the work of the interviewer. Also, I don't assume that a question or topic is automatically and inherently delicate or sensitive; as delicacy is emergent, it unfolds and can become quite palpable. This is not to say that anything goes or that you should boldly ask potentially difficult or uncomfortable (for you or the participant) questions.[6] And clearly, we also live in a world where our broad topics and specific questions, our very conduct, are subject to the gaze of institutional review boards or research ethics committees, as well as an array of disciplinary, organizational, and laical ethico-moral expectations.

Remember to let the interviewees speak; you've come to see them in order to explore their situated knowledge about a specific topic. However, you also need to use this space to create and challenge your

emergent knowledge. Centrally, each methodological position comes off in the here and now—it has to be enacted—and has local, here-and-now interactional effects. Those ideals can only exist in the here and now, and we (re)produce them. We hope that we will not (re)produce them uncritically and will reflect on their impact on the unfolding trajectory of the talk. In this way, our analysis needs to focus on both actors, to focus on how specific topics emerge, and *to make sense of our data in just this context.* You can also begin to ask, "How does this refer to the just then, to the just prior, or to the overall trajectory of talk as well as the broader trajectory of the series of interviews you are working with and the overarching focus of the research?"

SO WHAT: RADICAL AND PRAGMATIC ANALYTICAL DIRECTIONS

A focus on how interview talk emerges in and through the here-and-now emergent interaction potentially leads to quite a critical view of the possibilities of analytic knowledge emerging from interviews. Hammersley (2003) offers an overview (and subsequent critique) of the three directions of what he describes as the "radical criticism" that such a position is based on, and I'm going to focus on each one in turn.

1. Given that we have no access to what goes on inside people's heads, we cannot assume that what people say in interviews is what people think.

If we view (interview) talk as a social action, that in and through language we produce a specific version of the self, interviews cannot offer us some kind of privileged access to a more "authentic," "private," or "inner" voice (Atkinson & Silverman, 1997). As Potter and Hepburn (2005) note,

Interviewees are typically recruited as members of a social category of some kind. There may well be an expectation that they have a stake in that category. Yet this is often combined with questions that treat the participant as a broadly neutral informant on their own practices. (p. 295)

---

[6] I often reflect afterward and think I should (or should not) have pushed an interviewee more on this or that topic. I find that with some people, at some moments, I get a sense that they don't want to unpack or discuss a specific topic. Sometimes I pursue the issues, and at other times I don't. This can emerge elsewhere in the interview, and then you follow it up, or you can work to position the question as emerging from your role as a researcher, doing your job, by orientating to the interview schedule as the source of the question.

Once we reject a simple correlation between talk and essential meaning, we should then focus on how interviewees (and interviewers) construct or perform identities and subjectivities. For example, Holstein and Gubrium's (1995) concepts of active interviewing draw on this epistemic position, that we actively encourage interviewees to speak as specific types of persons. As they note, "Treating subject positions and their associated voices seriously, we might find that an ostensibly single interview could actually be, in practice, an interview with several subjects, whose particular identities may only be partially clear" (Gubrium & Holstein, 2002, p. 23). So those informed by more emancipatory and postmodern impulses seek to highlight and explore the multiple and fragmentary performances of the self (Denzin, 2002; Fontana, 2002).

2. Given that we only have access to people's accounts of events, we can only view what people say in interviews as one possible version.

If we understand interviews as giving access to versions, that they are providing one possible version, we need to be aware that these versions are not somehow created in a social, historical, or cultural vacuum. As Silverman (1993) notes, "In studying accounts, we are studying displays of cultural particulars as well as displays of members' artful practices in assembling those accounts" (p. 781).

In this way, interviews offer us some access to "some of the discourses, identities, narratives, repertoires, rhetorics *that are available to people* to talk about a . . . specific topic" (Rapley, 2001, p. 318). So, for example, as Baker's (1983, 1984, 1997, 2000, 2002) work has repeatedly shown, interviewees (and interviewers) draw on, work with, negotiate, and (re)produce social orders. She outlines the practico-moral reasoning, the social and cultural norms, that interviewers and interviewees assemble in and through interview talk.

3. Given that what people say is produced in and through interaction with an interviewer, we cannot assume that what they say in interviews has any relation to what they would say or do in other (noninterview) contexts.

If we understand interviews as unique situated interactions, where the talk is co-constructed in and through the ongoing collaborative work of the interviewer and interviewee, we have no real sense of how the talk relates to talk or actions beyond the interview space. As Dingwall (1997) notes,

"The interview is an artefact, a joint accomplishment of interviewer and respondent. As such, its relationship to any 'real' experience is not merely unknown but in some senses unknowable" (p. 56).

The interaction-in-interviews work, described in part above (see also Roulston, 2006), takes this quite seriously, viewing the interview as a naturally occurring interaction, a space in which to explore the interactional norms, routines, and practices through which we locally produce such a research instrument.

All three of these positions emerge from various directions of the constructionist tradition and linguistic turn, where talk in interviews is viewed as a topic rather than as a transparent resource that gives some form of unmediated access to the world beyond. If you feel, for good theoretical reasons, that language is somehow transparent, that what interviewees say in an interview can be treated relatively uncritically, albeit with a suitable dose of caution in relation to either questions of bias (hence, interviewers adequately followed the strictures of neutral but facilitative questions) or questions of creating deep connection (hence, interviewers adequately followed the strictures of intimacy), then you don't really need to worry. Otherwise, at the very least, you need to focus on *how* the talk is produced, prior to or alongside focusing on *what* is actually said or *why* it is said in that way (Gubrium & Holstein, 2002). More radically, you could, whenever possible, prioritize observation over interviewing or combine both.

Given their preference for working with (recordings of) naturalistic materials, Silverman (e.g., 1993, 2007) and Potter (e.g., 2002, 2004; see also Potter & Hepburn, 2005) have both been central to a more general sustained critique of the dominant role of interviews in social science research. For them, the researcher as an interviewer creates too much "noise" and so pollutes our understanding of the phenomena that are at the center of the research. It is almost too complex to manage, filter, or put to one side the noise that interviewers bring to their analysis. Not only does such noise emerge from the way we as social scientists ask interviewees to act as lay social observers and reporters, to work with our social science agendas, so that these are spaces layered with identity work, but also, as Silverman (personal communication) describes it, "People do so much more than they can ever put into words." I have a lot of sympathy for this position, in part because of the way we do not (and simply cannot) reflect or make available the quite amazingly artful, subtle, and intricate ways in which we do social life.[7] For these authors, interviews should always be, at the very least, the second choice. They should only be undertaken and analyzed when you cannot gain access to the phenomena by any other means.

Such a position, highlighting the problems of relying *exclusively* on interviews, also emerges in a less radical form in the work of ethnographers like Hammersley (2003) and Strong (1980), where direct observation is understood as a good source of support. In this context, the noise of interviews creates doubt, not a radical doubt but a cautious uncertainty around an uncritical overreliance on the interview. As Hammersley (2003) notes, the questions about whether talk in interviews relates to actions elsewhere echoes older methodological accounts about the potential problems of interviews,

> about likely errors and biases in interviewees' reports of past events or behaviour, about the dangers of reactivity, about problems involved in drawing valid inferences from what people say in interviews to conclusions about stable attitudes or perspectives that shape their behaviour in other contexts. (p. 123)

However, as Briggs (1986) pointed out, such a classical discussion of interviewer bias assumed that this is something that we can remove or reduce with better technique or analysis. As I've tried to outline repeatedly above, there is no time out; we cannot, in some ways, work to exclude the interactional nature of data collection—in fact, we rely on this: We rely on the creative and emergent nature of the interaction; otherwise, we might choose to undertake structured interviews.

◆ Social Studies of Interview Studies

It is interesting to reflect on how the trajectory of your research briefly aligns with an interviewee's world (see C. A. B. Warren's chapter "Interviewing as Social Interaction," this volume). For interviewees, the interview can be a fleeting encounter, a brief, potentially storyable event, in which they "helped out someone doing some research." For us, these interactions are vital, and the recordings of the event, in terms of audio files, videotapes, field notes, and transcripts, alongside our embodied recollections and

reactions, become objects that we then focus large numbers of hours on. Clearly, research interviews can and do have strong resonances on interviewees' lives (and others in their lives) and can remain strong in people's memories. And clearly, discussing some topics can raise distinct issues for both interviewees and interviewers. However, those resonances are routinely of a different order and play out in radically different contexts. For us, as researchers, the resonances are never just "personal" or "emotional" per se; they are also deeply analytic.

Briggs (2007), in his argument for an anthropology of interviewing, criticized some of the work on interaction in interviews:

> Our framework suggests that the conversation analysts' frequent insistence that interviews are "mundane talk" is a product of limiting the analysis to the interview alone (e.g. Rapley, 2004). Although mundane interactional practices are certainly at play, the shaping of interviews by preceding events and texts (research proposals, formulation of questions, etc.) and their orientation towards recontextualization in quite different settings (such as scholarly publications or policy decisions) suggests that this "mundane" quality is a powerful illusion. (p. 562)

Following Briggs (2007), I would suggest a need to shift from a focus on the mundane interactional work *in* interviews to a broader focus on the situated, pragmatic work *of* interview research projects.

When we discuss the work in interviews, we routinely position them as moments of talk or events, somehow isolated from the broader trajectory of our research projects. However, when we analyze them, we rarely focus, analytically, on just this interview. We relate just that issue not only with the question we asked just then, or with prior sequences of talk, but also with a much broader and layered trajectory of work. In the process of "analysis"—whatever that is, as I'm not actually sure when analysis begins or starts—we are directed and inspired by a range of issues. So as I read a specific transcript, we have a complex configuration of actions. We work to relate just that emerging idea or stretch of talk to the prior and following on-tape and off-tape talk, to the recruitment conversations, to other conversations, to emerging issues from a prior interview or a reading that we wish to explore, alongside the research protocol, objectives and aims, and so on.

---

[7]However, as the narrative turn highlights, stories are an artful, subtle, and intricate way of doing (a specific aspect of) social life.

In this way, we rarely treat interviews as one-off encounters. Instead, they are engaged with within a broader trajectory of analytic work. That includes the work of reading, thinking, noting, marking, labeling and coding, discussing, and writing (to name but a few). What is central is that, with the possible exception of the first interview, we always analyze an interview in relation to the prior interviews we have already conducted on this issue. And for me, this is reflected not only in my "desk work" but also in the interview interactions. For me, the questions I ask in an interview and the areas I choose to follow up are not somehow isolated from my prior desk and field-work but rather are informed by them. In this way, interviews are not only moments when I and the participants engage in something like analysis but moments in which I and the informant are also engaging with aspects of those prior interviews, of the prior reading, of the emerging analytic ideas, alongside broader trajectories of social experiences, norms, ideas, and values.

Following Briggs's (2007) intervention, when we review and explore the interview as a center of coordination, as a moment when different trajectories and social worlds weave together, we begin to see a deeply complex space—a space of cultural, interactional, political, and theoretical work. In this sense, interviews, or rather the broader trajectory of interview research in which interviews occur, are truly extraordinary. Viewed in this way, they are extraordinary both as an interactional practice and in the sense of all the layers of work—all the trajectories of mundane, situated, practical action and reasoning—that they combine and demonstrate. As Briggs (2007) notes, "Post-interview procedures strip away the indexical traces of diverse knowledge-making practices in order to make the material seem to embody a particular social scientific cartography" (p. 576). What is fascinating is how, through our analytic practice, we routinely manage to hold them in check, to silence, ignore, or smooth over this work. It is clearly time to recover the (extra)ordinary practical action and reasoning of interview research.

◆ References

Abell, J., Locke, A., Condor, S., Gibson, S., & Stevenson, C. (2006). Trying similarity, doing difference: The role of interviewer self-disclosure in interview talk with young people. *Qualitative Research, 6*(2), 221–244.

Atkinson, P., & Silverman, D. (1997). Kundera's immortality: The interview society and the invention of the self. *Qualitative Inquiry, 3*(3), 304–325.

Baker, C. D. (1983). A "second look" at interviews with adolescents. *Journal of Youth and Adolescence, 12*(6), 501–519.

Baker, C. D. (1984). The search for adultness: Membership work in adolescent-adult talk. *Human Studies, 7,* 301–323.

Baker, C. D. (1997). Membership categorization and interview accounts. In D. Silverman (Ed.), *Qualitative research: Theory, method and practice* (pp. 162–176). London, England: Sage.

Baker, C. D. (2000). Locating culture in action: Membership categorization in texts and talk. In A. Lee & C. Poynton (Eds.), *Culture and text: Discourse and methodology in social research and cultural studies* (pp. 99–113). Sydney, New South Wales, Australia: Allen & Unwin.

Baker, C. D. (2002). Ethnomethodological analyses of interviews. In J. F. Gubrium & J. A. Holstein (Eds.), *Handbook of interview research: Context and method* (pp. 777–796). Thousand Oaks, CA: Sage.

Baruch, G. (1981). Moral tales: Parents' stories of encounters with the health profession. *Sociology of Health & Illness, 3*(3), 275–296.

Briggs, C. (1986). *Learning how to ask: A sociolinguistic appraisal of the role of the interview in social science research*. Cambridge, England: Cambridge University Press.

Briggs, C. (2007). Anthropology, interviewing, and communicability in contemporary society. *Current Anthropology, 48*(4), 551–580.

Brinkmann, S. (2007). Could interviews be epistemic? An alternative to qualitative opinion polling. *Qualitative Inquiry, 13,* 1116–1138.

Bryman, A., & Cassell, C. (2006). The researcher interview: A reflexive perspective. *Qualitative Research in Organizations and Management: An International Journal, 1*(1), 41–55.

Callon, M., & Rabeharisoa, V. (2004). Gino's lesson on humanity: Genetics, mutual entanglements and the sociologist's role. *Economy and Society, 33*(1), 1–27.

Denzin, N. (2002). The cinematic society and the reflexive interview. In J. F. Gubrium & J. A. Holstein (Eds.), *Handbook of interview research: Context and method* (pp. 833–848). Thousand Oaks, CA: Sage.

Dingwall, R. (1997). Accounts, interviews and observations. In G. Miller & R. Dingwall (Eds.), *Context and method in qualitative research* (pp. 51–65). London, England: Sage.

Dinkins, S. C. (2005). Shared inquiry: Socratic-hermeneutic interviewing and interpreting. In P. Ironside & N. Diekelmann (Eds.), *Interpretive studies in health-care and the human sciences* (pp. 111–147). Madison: University of Wisconsin Press.

Enosh, G., & Buchbinder, E. (2005). The interactive construction of narrative styles in sensitive interviews: The case of domestic violence research. *Qualitative Inquiry, 11,* 588–617.

Fontana, A. (2002). Postmodern trends in interviewing. In J. F. Gubrium & J. A. Holstein (Eds.), *Handbook of interview research: Context and method* (161–180). Thousand Oaks, CA: Sage.

Grønnerød, J. S. (2004). On the meanings and uses of laughter in research interviews: Relationships between interviewed men and a woman interviewer. *Young, 12*(1), 31–49.

Gubrium, J. F., & Holstein, J. A. (2002). From the individual interview to the interview society. In J. F. Gubrium & J. A. Holstein (Eds.), *Handbook of interview research: Context and method* (pp. 3–32). Thousand Oaks, CA: Sage.

Gubrium, J. F., & Holstein, J. A. (2009). *Analyzing narrative reality*. Thousand Oaks, CA: Sage.

Hammersley, M. (2003). Recent radical criticism of interview studies: Any implications for the sociology of education. *British Journal of Sociology of Education, 24*(1), 119–126.

Hester, S., & Francis, D. (1994). Doing data: The local organization of a sociological interview. *British Journal of Sociology, 45,* 675–695.

Holstein, J. A., & Gubrium, J. F. (1995). *The active interview*. Thousand Oaks, CA: Sage.

Holstein, J. A., & Gubrium, J. F. (1997). Active interview. In D. Silverman (Ed.), *Qualitative research: Theory, method and practice* (pp. 140–161). London, England: Sage.

Lawrence, S. G. (1996). Normalizing stigmatized practices: Achieving co-membership by "doing being ordinary." *Research on Language and Social Interaction, 29*(3), 181–218.

Mazeland, H., & Have, P. ten. (1996). Essential tensions in (semi-)open research interviews. In I. Maso & F. Wester (Eds.), *The deliberate dialogue: Qualitative perspectives on the interview* (pp. 87–113). Brussels, Belgium: VUB University Press.

Mishler, E. G. (1986). *Research interviewing: Context and narrative*. Cambridge, MA: Harvard University Press.

Nairn, K., Munro, J., & Smith, A. B. (2005). A counter-narrative of a "failed" interview. *Qualitative Research, 5*(2), 221–244.

Poland, B. D. (2002). Transcription quality. In J. F. Gubrium & J. A. Holstein (Eds.), *Handbook of interview research:*

Context and method (pp. 629–650). Thousand Oaks, CA: Sage.

Potter, J. (2002). Two kinds of natural. *Discourse Studies, 4,* 539–542.

Potter, J. (2004). Discourse analysis. In M. Hardy & A. Bryman (Eds.), *Handbook of data analysis*. London, England: Sage.

Potter, J., & Hepburn, A. (2005). Qualitative interviews in psychology: Problems and possibilities. *Qualitative Research in Psychology, 2,* 281–307.

Rapley, T. (2001). The art(fulness) of open-ended interviewing: Some considerations on analysing interviews. *Qualitative Research, 1*(3), 303–323.

Rapley, T. (2004). Interviews. In C. Seale, G. Gobo, J. F. Gubrium, & D. Silverman (Eds.), *Qualitative research practice* (pp. 15–33). London, England: Sage.

Roulston, K. (2000). The management of "safe" and "unsafe" complaint sequences in research interviews. *Text, 20*(3), 1–39.

Roulston, K. (2001). Data analysis and "theorizing as ideology." *Qualitative Research, 1,* 279–302.

Roulston, K. (2006). Close encounters of the "CA" kind: A review of literature analyzing talk in research interviews. *Qualitative Research, 6,* 515–534.

Roulston, K. (2010). Considering quality in qualitative interviewing. *Qualitative Research, 10,* 199–228.

Roulston, K., Baker, C. D., & Liljestrom, A. (2001). Analyzing the researcher's work in generating data: The case of complaints. *Qualitative Inquiry, 7*(6), 745–772.

Sacks, H. (1984). On doing "being ordinary." In J. M. Atkinson & J. Heritage (Eds.), *Structures of social action* (pp. 413–429). Cambridge, England: Cambridge University Press

Silverman, D. (1993). *Interpreting qualitative data: Methods for analysing talk, text and interaction*. London, England: Sage.

Silverman, D. (2007). *A very short, fairly interesting, and reasonably cheap book about qualitative research*. London, England: Sage.

Strong, P. M. (1980). Doctors and dirty work: The case of the alcoholic. *Sociology of Health & Illness, 2,* 24–47.

Tanggaard, L. (2007). The research interview as discourses crossing swords. *Qualitative Inquiry, 13,* 160–176.

van Enk, A. A. J. (2009). The shaping effects of the conversational interview: An examination using Bakhtin's theory of genre. *Qualitative Inquiry, 15,* 1265–1286.

Watson, D. R., & Weinberg, T. S. (1982). Interviews and the interactional construction of accounts of homosexual identity. *Social Analysis, 11,* 56–78.

38

EIGHT CHALLENGES FOR INTERVIEW RESEARCHERS

◆ Jonathan Potter and Alexa Hepburn

There is little need to provide further evidence here of the ubiquity of the open-ended research interview across the range of contemporary social sciences. Chapters in this volume and its predecessor (Gubrium & Holstein, 2002) make this point very effectively, as does a survey of the content of contemporary qualitative methods handbooks such as Denzin and Lincoln (2005) and Willig and Stainton-Rogers (2008). In some cases, the term *interview* is not even mentioned, as this method of eliciting material from participants has become hardwired into the commonplaces of social science. A diligent reader need only read through the content of the past full year of mainstream journals in sociology, social psychology, geography, and anthropology to see that where qualitative research is conducted, it is overwhelmingly done using some forms of interviews. Cutting things up another way, the open-ended interview is the preeminent data generation technique in methodological traditions as disparate as ethnography, phenomenology (in its different forms), psychoanalysis, narrative psychology, grounded theory, and (much) discourse analysis.

Our aim in this chapter is to make the case that interviewing has been too easy, too obvious, too little studied, and too open to providing a convenient launching pad for poor research. We will argue that interview research will be made better if it faces up to a series of eight challenges that arise in the design, conduct, analysis, and reporting of qualitative interviews. Some research studies already face up to some of these challenges; few studies face up to all of them. We will make our case strongly and bluntly with the aim of provoking debate where not enough has taken place. These challenges are overlapping, but we have separated them in the way we have for clarity. It is important to emphasize that our aim is not to criticize interviews but to make them better.

There are two contexts for this chapter for us. First, the past 20 years have seen an extraordinary development of our understanding of what might be called the central motor of interviews, the question-and-answer pair. Profound work in the tradition of conversation analysis (Schegloff, 2007) has been done on the organization of questions and answers in institutional settings such as television news interviews (e.g., Clayman & Heritage, 2002), courtrooms (e.g., Atkinson & Drew, 1979), police interrogations (e.g., Stokoe & Edwards, 2008), help lines (e.g., Hepburn & Potter, 2010), and medical examinations (e.g., Boyd & Heritage, 2006), as well as in mundane settings such as everyday phone calls and family mealtimes (Heritage & Raymond, in press; Stivers & Hayashi, 2010). Such work has started to unpack some of the basic design features of questions, such as how they embody preferences, manage neutralism, build presuppositions, and work to constrain the actions of the recipient in different ways (Clayman & Heritage, 2002; Raymond, 2003). Researchers are starting to turn the analytic searchlight from this tradition onto the operation of social science methods (Antaki & Rapley, 1996; Houtkoop-Steenstra, 2000; Maynard, Houtkoop-Steenstra, Schaeffer, & van der Zouwen, 2002; Puchta & Potter, 1999). In this chapter, we will draw on this tradition and shine a bit of its light on the qualitative research interview.

The second context is a more biographical one. Both of us started our research careers doing research with open-ended interviews. Both of us have published widely using interview research (e.g., Hepburn, 2000; Wetherell & Potter, 1992) and on the nature and role of interviews (Potter & Hepburn, 2005b; Potter & Mulkay, 1985; Potter & Wetherell, 1995); yet both of us became increasingly dissatisfied with what was possible, particularly as we have become more sophisticated in the analysis of interaction. In a way, this chapter is an attempt to make sense of that dissatisfaction and provide a more positive set of suggestions for interview research. The current chapter develops two earlier discussions of the status of research on open-ended interviews and highlights the general implications beyond the field of psychology (Potter & Hepburn, 2005a, 2005b, 2007).

We have arranged the eight challenges into two groups. Four of them can be addressed by attending to the reporting of the interview in the research study. These challenges can be met by

1. improving the transparency of the interview setup,

2. more fully displaying the active role of the interviewer,

3. using representational forms that show the interactional production of interviews, and

4. tying analytic observations to specific interview elements.

The aim will be to provide a set of suggestions for how any interview study can be reported, so as to support more comprehensive evaluation by readers. Currently, interview studies often provide only the most limited possibilities for auditing by other researchers. These four suggestions will extend those possibilities.

The second set of challenges arises in the analysis of the interview. They require interview researchers to pay more attention to

5. how interviews are flooded with social science categories, assumptions, and research agendas;

6. the varying footing of interviewer and interviewee;

7. the orientations to stake and interest on the part of the interviewer and interviewee; and

8. the way cognitive, individualist assumptions about human actors are presupposed.

These analytic issues are potentially highly consequential for how the talk of the interviewee is understood in relation to the claims of any research study. These are by no means the only analytic challenges, but all are potentially relevant for any researcher who wishes to make adequately grounded claims on the basis of an interview study.

After describing these challenges, we will make two broader sets of suggestions. First, work on questions and interaction should feed back into the design, conduct, and analysis of interviews as well as into the training of interviewers and the strategic exploitation of interviewer conduct. In particular, open-ended interviews should be viewed as a range of rather different conversational occasions, and the research should be designed to build a particular kind of occasion as suitable for the specifics of the research. Second, we believe that there needs to be more consideration of whether research aims could be furthered more effectively by using other forms of data generation, including working with records of natural interaction.

◆ Reporting

1. MAKE THE INTERVIEW SETUP EXPLICIT

One thing that is striking about much contemporary interview research is how little is said about how participants were recruited. The concern here is not with sampling; it is with the sort of potentially highly consequential interaction that goes on when interviewees are introduced to the study. In particular, there are two elements of the interview setup that are likely to be important.

The first is the issue of the category that participants have been explicitly recruited under. For example, were they recruited as "adolescent recreational drug users," "young adult unemployed," or "active waste recyclers"? Researchers typically recruit participants grouped into such categories, which are themselves key parts of the research arguments that are being pursued. Such recruitment is itself an active part of the research process, not unlike the social identity salience manipulations in social identity theory research studies (Turner, Hogg, Oakes, Reicher, & Wetherell, 1987), and it may figure in the introduction to the research that the participant is given, the ethics procedures, the administrative arrangements, and so on.

Note that this issue is separate from the issue of sampling. It is not a matter of the category embedded in the abstract research design; it is a matter of the processes through which particular individuals are actually recruited and told about their recruitment and role in the research. It is during these processes that particular category memberships can in various ways be made central to the research. Thus, a study might be concerned with the beliefs of "depressed students" about the causes of their problems. When such students are recruited, the category "depressed student," and potentially a range of related categories, is likely to be made central, formulated, and reworked. Indeed, recruitment itself often has some of the characteristics of an interview.

During recruitment, a particular understanding of how each participant is relevant to the research may be delivered to them; and such an understanding is, at least potentially, highly consequential for their conduct during the interview.

The second issue that becomes live in the interview setup is the understanding of the task that participants are given. This involves issues such as what the interview will be *about* (healthy and unhealthy eating, say), what the research will be used *for* (influencing government health policy), and what *tasks* the interviewees will be performing in the interview (e.g., explaining how their eating preferences have changed as they grew up).

In many ways, it is not surprising that these matters are rarely included in research studies. Full records are often not kept, and when asked for full transcripts and sound files, researchers typically cite tensions between generating ethical consent and collecting full records. Adequate consent procedures may depend on prior description of the interview topics and the rationale for recruitment. Nevertheless, given how potentially consequential for the research outcomes such category membership ascriptions and topic and task formulations are, it is important to attempt to capture these features of recruitment. One possibility is including textual materials relating to recruitment and attempting a descriptive overview of the early interaction between participant and researcher. Crucially, when the actual interview takes place, the recording should be started as early as possible, so that the researcher's formulation of the nature of the interview and its goals is captured and made available for scrutiny.

This issue has received almost no attention in previous discussions of methodology. Our aim is to signal both its neglect and its importance and to start to indicate some ways in which the situation can be improved.

2. DISPLAY THE ACTIVE ROLE OF THE INTERVIEWER

Contemporary interview studies regularly emphasize that what goes on in interviews is interactional. Yet this is rarely followed through in the research practice. We will try to illustrate this point without picking on individual studies; it would be invidious to pick any one paper out of the thousands published every year.

But we have no doubt that readers will find what we are illustrating here instantly recognizable. Anyone still not sure should sit down with the past few years of any mainstream social science journal from sociology, human geography, nursing, or qualitative psychology and count the number of extracts that include both interviewers and interviewees in relation to the number that simply include the latter. Expect a ratio of 1 to 10 or more! We will use an example from our own materials so that readers can refer to the audio record if they wish to and to spare the blushes of others.

The quotation in Extract 38.1 comes from a corpus of interviews conducted by Alexa Hepburn as part of a project looking at the different ways bullying appears in school settings (published papers using this corpus include Hepburn, 1997a, 1997b; Hepburn & Brown, 2001). The extract has been rendered in the style typical of contemporary qualitative research.

Extract 38.1

I think all teachers are stressed. Because they're stressed they may react inappropriately in certain situations, because they are near the edge themselves. If you're tired and stressed you're not always in the best situation to make good judgements. The children I think at least are slightly more aware of this than they used to be in the past.

Let us make some observations about the form as presented here.

First, note what is absent. The interviewer's question has not been reproduced. The extract comes only from the talk of the interviewee, the teacher. And we are not told if this is an entire turn of talk that is responsive to a question or if it is a fragment from a longer turn. This has the effect of framing the talk as an abstract pronouncement on the nature of teachers and the effects of stress; it is not framed as a specific answer to a specific question put by a specific interviewer.

Second, note that the extract uses a conventional orthographic representation of talk. It is rendered as a form of play script; it has been turned into mostly grammatical sentences and uses conventional punctuation marks. Some of what is missing can be clarified by simply extending the extract using the same orthographic form of representation. Material absent from Extract 38.1 is rendered in bold in Extract 38.2 to show the kind of contextual and interviewer talk that is commonly omitted.

Extract 38.2

Interviewer:	**So do you feel then that the constraints on teachers' time and the resources that are available to you actually err constrain your ability to do your job well to deal effectively with kids**
Teacher:	**yes** I think all teachers are stressed err because they're stressed they may react **um** inappropriately in certain situations because they are near the edge themselves **(Int: yes yes) erm** if you're tired and stressed you're not always in the best situation to make good judgements **(Int: oh yeah yeah)** the children I think at least are slightly more aware of this than they used to be in the past **(Int: mm mm) but yes I would say it can affect it**

With the introduction of the interviewer's question and various contributions during the teacher's turn of talk, we get more of a sense of what is going on here as an interaction. Crucially, we can start to see how the form of the answer may be occasioned by the form of the question. Nevertheless, the talk is still rendered as a play script. This makes it hard to identify the precise actions going on here—it is left to the reader to animate the talk as it must have sounded. One crucial thing we are missing here is information about the delivery of the talk—the prosody, the delay and overlap, the emphasis and volume, the tempo and various features of voice quality—everything that turns it back into normal human interaction.

It might be observed at this point that interview data analysis and representation are always partial and incomplete (Andrews, 2008). The key question is what kinds of information may be consequential for understanding what is going on in the interview. Information about what color of socks each party is wearing is unlikely to be relevant to how the interview unfolds. However, information about whether the interviewer receipted an interviewee turn with "oh," whether interviewee intonation is closing or questioning at some point, or where the parties are speaking in overlap is much more likely to be consequential. If we are going to take seriously the idea that the interview is an interactional occasion, surely this kind of information should be available in some form. It is ironic that as we claim to be social scientists, rather than students of literature, we have been wiping out the embodied and voiced nature of talk.

3. REPRESENT TALK IN A WAY THAT CAPTURES ACTION

For nearly half a century, interaction analysts, and particularly conversation analysts, have found that if they are to understand the actions that are being done in talk, they need to pay close attention to actual talk. This means listening closely to recordings, watching the video, if one exists, and combining this with a representation of talk that captures what is interactionally relevant. It is common in interview studies to get the recordings done

by a transcription service (usually untrained speed typists); and then the recordings are boxed away, and the researcher works with these impoverished transcripts.

It is important to consider what is missed by doing this. The transcription conventions for representing talk as delivered were developed by the late Gail Jefferson (2004; for a broader discussion, see Hepburn & Bolden, in press; a brief summary is given in the appendix to this chapter, Table 38.1). Extract 38.3a shows the same research interview exchange now represented using Jeffersonian transcription.

Extract 38.3a

```
01   Int:   So d'you feel then that the constrai:nts on teachers'
02          ti::me and the resources that are available to you
03          actually .hh (0.2) c- er constrain your ability to
04          do your job ↑well to deal effectively with- (0.2)
05          °with kids: an° (0.2) [((inaudible))]
06   Tch:                         [ U : : m : ] (0.9)
07          ((swallows)) Ye:s, (0.7) I think all teachers are
08          stressed
09          (0.2)
10   Int:   Mm:.
11   Tch:   Er because they're stressed (.) they may react (0.5)
12          u::m inappropriately,
13   Int:   Mhm,
14          (0.2)
15   Tch:   in certain situatio[ns,]
16   Int:                      [M]hm.
17          (0.4)
18   Tch:   Because they (.) are near (.) the edge themse:[lves, ]
19   Int:                                                 [Yeah.]
20          (0.4)
21   Int:   °Yeah.
22   Tch:   Er::m (0.9) if you're ti:red, (.) an stressed, (.) erm
23          you're not always in the best: situation to make
24          good judge[ments. ]
25   Int:             [↑Oh ye]ah. °yeah. [°Mm.]
26   Tch:                               [Er:  ]m (0.4) the CHILdren
27          I think at least are slightly more aware of this
28          [than they used to] be in [the pa:]st.
29   Int:   [ M m : : : .      ]       [M m: :.]
```

(Continued)

Extract 38.3a (Continued)

30	Int:	Mm:.
31		(0.2)
32	Tch:	Er::m:=
33	Int:	=Mm.
34		(0.9)
35	Int:	°Mm.
36		(1.5)
37	Tch:	BUT (huh)YEs I would sayhh (0.2) er it can affect it. (The audio record of this extract is available online—search for Loughborough Discourse and Rhetoric Group)

This is a brief extract. Yet it shows up a wide range of hearable, and therefore potentially interactionally consequential, features of the talk compared with the play script version. Note the overlaps, closing intonation, latching of turns to one another, rising and falling intonation, raised volume, stretched vowel sounds, and different kinds of breaths and laugh particles. In contemporary social science articles, there is a pervasive failure to capture features of delivery such as these.

The fuller transcript allows the identification of a number of potentially consequential interviewer actions. For example, note the "acknowledgment tokens" (Clayman & Heritage, 2002; Jefferson, 1985) on Lines 10, 13, and 16. Such tokens have a range of jobs, including displaying attentiveness and passing the opportunity to take a turn. Note also the news receipt and agreeing second assessment (Heritage, 2002; Pomerantz, 1984) on Line 25. As we will see, such objects are particularly interesting in research interviews. Our general argument is that such elements are universally treated as relevant *by the parties to the interaction* (Hepburn & Bolden, in press) and so will be consequential for the conduct of the interview and how it is understood. They, therefore, ought to be represented in a way that makes them available to readers.

4. TIE ANALYTIC OBSERVATIONS TO SPECIFIC FEATURES OF INTERVIEWS

In a recent critical piece about the qualitative analysis of interviews, and particularly the uses of discourse analysis, Antaki, Billig, Edwards, and Potter (2007) argue that researchers pervasively underanalyze their materials. They highlight six different forms of underanalysis. These include underanalysis through summary, underanalysis by taking sides, underanalysis through overquotation or through isolated quotation, the identification of discourses from mental constructs (and vice versa), overgeneralizing claims, and ad hoc feature spotting. Our aim here is not to repeat this argument, which is fully documented with examples of interview analysis in the original piece. Instead, our focus will be on the issue of how links between specific analytic claims and specific sections or elements of interviews are made plain to the reader.

One of the consequences of conventional orthographic representation is that it often makes it unclear what specific elements of the interviewee's talk are being referred to. In part, this is because this form of transcript collapses together groups of different conversational elements. More technically speaking, the interviewee's answer (and the interviewer's question) can be built from a number of different practices that are not easy to separate because of the representational form used. For example, Extract 38.1 allows for a highly restricted consideration of the way different aspects of the interviewee's answer are built and what elements of the interviewer's talk they are responsive to. Even the simple procedure of putting the interviewer's and the interviewee's talk on separate lines allows for a much clearer understanding of what is going on. The additional, and equally simple, procedure of adding line numbers allows for much more precision in referring to segments of talk. It is common in contemporary interview studies to find large blocks of text combined with analytic observations that are hard to clearly link to specific elements in the talk of the interviewee.

Challenges in Reporting Interviews

In proposing these ways of improving the quality of representational practice with interview research, we are mindful that there are difficult tensions between practices that support the thorough academic auditing of research claims and practices that simplify the process of interview research. We are asking the question rather than offering a template. Transcription, in particular, both is time-consuming to conduct and requires training and effort (Hepburn & Bolden, in press). Where transcription has been addressed by interview researchers, it has often been with an argument for "Jefferson Lite"—transcription that captures words and some of the grosser elements of stress and intonation but leaves pauses untimed and does not attempt to capture more subtle elements such as closing and continuing intonation, latching, and so on. Poland (2002) offers a relatively sophisticated version of this position.

There is an argument that attention to what seem to be merely micro aspects of talk will detract from broader themes or ideological organization. However, an alternative argument is that broader themes and organizations are in practice understood through working with the concrete specifics across a number of examples of talk; therefore, analysis will benefit from an engagement with a form of transcript that goes beyond the reconstructed, simplified, and distorted version of interaction that comes from many transcription services. A further argument for attending to the specifics is that this is what participants do, pervasively and thoroughly, in the course of their own interaction. The full Jeffersonian transcript drags into the open the jointly constructed, socially engaged nature of what is going on in interviews, including the close dependence of what the interviewee says on the interviewer's question design and delivery in all its specifics.

Even if the interview researcher is happy to work with a reduced form of representation, there is still the issue of how the research is to be adequately evaluated by others. Insofar as the evaluation of the research is a communal endeavor for journal referees and readers, there is a strong argument that the researchers should provide a form of transcription that will offer readers a much fuller understanding of what is going on and, moreover, an understanding less likely to have already embedded their own theoretical assumptions within it. Over the years, we have refereed many articles using interviews in different social science areas. There are often important cases where the interviewee's talk is constrained by the actions of the interviewer, and yes, this is obscured by the form of representation. Our feeling is that some moves in this direction are overdue and need to be encouraged by journal editors.

Jeffersonian transcription is a slow process—done well it involves a recording to transcription time ratio of at least 1 to 20 hours. However, the aim would not necessarily be to do a full transcript of the complete interview corpus; rather, the full transcript would be reserved for the instances of some analytically identified theme. For example, in conversation-analytic studies working with large corpuses of institutional talk, it is common to work with collections of fully transcribed extracts that relate to particular questions.

It may be that some of what we are suggesting can be provided by making audio or video records available via the web. These could be comprehensive, illustrative, or just provide the recording of the extracts that are reproduced in the papers. Ethics procedures would need to be adjusted accordingly. The provision of audio and video materials would help address a further problem with the representation of interview material, which is that the transcript may be faulty. Sometimes, the transcribed form is such that it "sounds" impossible to a trained ear, or the formulations offered seem pragmatically odd. On those occasions when such doubts have led us to ask if we can check the recording ourselves, we have been told that ethics preclude this or the recordings are unavailable. While this may be true, it does not promote a social research practice that is publically accountable and transparent.

We do not underestimate the extra effort involved in moving in this direction. However, we have made strong arguments for the value of that effort. It is up to others to show that it is unnecessary and these arguments are wrong. A defense of the current practice will need to do more than say that the researcher is not interested in interaction, as Morgan (2010) has argued; researchers defending the status quo will need to show that the close dependence of both the form and the content of the "answer" on the design and delivery of the "question" is not of general consequence.

Analysis

The first part of this chapter has focused on the issues that arise in the representation of interviews in research publications. In the second part, we will focus on some challenges that face researchers when they are analyzing interviews. Again, these are challenges that are brought into focus by a familiarity with interaction research. These highlight features of research interviews that are pervasive and yet hard to successfully manage analytically. Although we are describing them as challenges, we do not mean that they are typically seen in this way by interview analysts; indeed, for the most part they are overlooked. The point is that they are consequential for understanding how the interview should be interpreted. We will work through them in turn.

5. FLOODING

Research interviews are flooded with social science agendas of different kinds. The notion of a "social science agenda" is meant to capture the loose set of concerns and orientations that are central to the researcher who is conducting social research. Researchers have spent years developing particular views of social organizations and structures, the nature and competence of human subjects, and so on. They often work with a "factors and variables" picture of how different elements of sociality affect one another. Such pictures are often taken for granted to the point of invisibility. Agendas of this kind are expressed in various ways, including the research recruitment briefings, the kinds of questions asked and how they position recipients, the categories they use, and the way questions are organized into narratives that build particular researcher concerns.

It is the apparent invisibility of such agendas that makes their influence on the actions of research participants hard to identify. Sometimes, clearly technical or quasi-technical terms such as *internalized homophobia* (Giorgi & Giorgi, 2003) mark the way the participant is being recruited into a particular social science tradition. However, the relevant social science agenda is often developed much less explicitly.

Let us look more closely at the initial question from Extract 38.3a (see Extract 38.3b).

Extract 38.3b

01	Int:	So d'you <u>fee</u>l then that the constrai:nts on teachers'
02		ti::me and the re<u>sou</u>rces that are a<u>vai</u>lable to you
03		<u>actual</u>ly .hh (0.2) c- er constr<u>ai</u>n your ability to
04		<u>do</u> your job ↑well to deal effectively with- (0.2)
05		°with kids: an° (0.2) [[((inaudible))]]

This question has the feel of something put together on the spot. The delay, hitches, and an "er" on Lines 3 to 5 give a sense of the interviewer building the question locally rather than rehearsing something preformed. The trailing off to quiet on 5 and then the overlapped inaudible element contribute to this sense. Nevertheless, this is a highly recognizable and recurrent form of social research question. Indeed, Puchta and Potter (2004) suggest that the display of informality here is part of what constitutes it as a standard question from an open-ended interview (as opposed to a systematic survey question). These features help in the production of informality and manage potentially problematic epistemic asymmetries between interviewer and interviewee.

When we drill down further into what is going on here, however, things are a bit more complex. This informality is combined with a question form that is highly constraining. A polar question, or yes/no interrogative, advances a candidate proposition and sets the terms from within which participants' responses are to be interpreted (Heritage & Raymond, in press).

Let us consider this candidate proposition a bit more closely. It does not draw on terms from one of the obvious social science dictionaries ("internalized homophobia"). Nevertheless, it is built with references to abstract objects ("teachers' time"—Line 2) and processes ("constraints"—Lines 1 and 3). Moreover, the category is the generic "teachers" rather than a reference to specific teachers at a particular school.

The point here is not that such questions are poorly designed or use illegitimate constructions but rather that such types of question can subtly coach the participant in a relevant social science agenda. This is not in itself a bad thing; the challenge is how to work with it in a way that avoids circularity.

Although interview questions are an obvious place to look for the development of a social science agenda, it can also be seen in other kinds of interviewer contribution to the interaction. The exchange in Extract 38.3c comes a little later in Extract 38.3a.

Extract 38.3c

18	Tch:	Because <u>they</u> (.) are near (.) the edge them<u>se</u>:[lves,]
19	Int:	[<u>Yeah.</u>]
20		(0.4)
21	Int:	°Yeah.
22	Tch:	Er::m (0.9) if you're <u>ti</u>:red, (.) an <u>stressed</u>, (.) erm
23		you're <u>not</u> always in the best: situation to make
24		good <u>judge</u>[ments.]
25	Int:	[↑Oh <u>ye</u>]ah. °yeah. [°Mm.]

The point we want to highlight here is the difference between the interviewer's contributions on Lines 19, 21, and 25. While the interviewee's turn on Line 18 receives only an acknowledgment token (Jefferson, 1985)—a conversational object that specifically holds off doing a number of potential actions—her contribution on Lines 22 through 24 is responded to with an "oh-prefaced" agreement (Heritage, 2002). These interviewer responses are markedly different in what they display about the status of the propositions advanced. We will say more about that later in relation to footing. For the moment, just note the way such interviewer turns are a vehicle for the broader social science agenda. They potentially lead the interviewee down a desired path.

Crucially, the challenge is to avoid the interview taking the form of a circular rediscovery of preexisting social science ideas and assumptions. How can the analysis cut down the possibility that it is chasing its own tail, offering back a refined or filtered form of the ideas and intuitions that went into the building of the original schedule and briefing of participants?

6. FOOTING

One of the key observations made by Erving Goffman (1981) was that when people speak to one another, they do so from a range of different positions, or "footings." Interaction has a "participation framework," where a speaker may be the origin of ideas, for example, or may represent the ideas of another speaker (compare a national president and his or her speechwriters) and recipients may be directly addressed, say, or be in a position to overhear the conversation.

Interview talk can be considered in this way, focusing in particular on the different bases on which participants are speaking. Interviewees are typically recruited as members of particular categories (lesbian parents, teachers, multiple sclerosis sufferers, etc.). But when they are speaking, they can be speaking as an individual with her or his own unique beliefs and preferences; as a category member, where the answers are intended to reflect the category as a whole; or, more likely, as some complicated mix of the two. There are subtle but important differences between the two. Moreover, if they are speaking as a category member, what precisely is the relevant category?

We will illustrate the analytic significance of footing with examples from Extract 38.3a. Consider first the question design and its use of categories (see Extract 38.3d).

Extract 38.3d

01	Int:	So d'you <u>feel</u> then that the constrai:nts on teachers'
02		ti::me and the res<u>ources</u> that are a<u>vail</u>able to you
03		<u>actu</u>ally .hh (0.2) c- er constr<u>ain</u> your ability to
04		<u>do</u> your job ↑well to deal effectively with- (0.2)
05		°with kids: an° (0.2) [((inaudible))]
06	Tch:	[U : : m :] (0.9)
07		((swallows)) <u>Ye</u>:s, (0.7) I think <u>a</u>ll teachers are
08		<u>stressed</u>_
09		(0.2)
10	Int:	<u>Mm</u>:.

The interviewee has been recruited as a category member (a teacher), and she is addressed in a way that invokes her category membership ("teachers' time," "your job"). Yet she is addressed in direct personal terms ("you"—Line 1) in a way that separates out her stance on the category that she is, here, relevantly, a member of. As we noted above, in virtue of its yes/no interrogative form, the question restricts the response options. Anything other than a yes/no response will be type-nonconforming (Raymond, 2003) and therefore liable to inspection by the questioner for what it is doing in departing from the terms of the question. Thus, the respondent could build an answer that separates her from the category—most teachers say X, but I find Y—but this would involve unpacking the terms of the question. Instead, she offers (after an extended um and delay, which may be occasioned by the trail-off in the question but more likely relates to the potentially challenging nature of the question) a standard response with the type-conforming "yes" and the expansion "I think all teachers are stressed." The general point is that participants can answer questions in a "personal" or "institutional" capacity, and without careful analytic attention to this,

researchers risk making misleading inferences from their material. Here, the challenging nature of the question makes answering in a more generalized way a more useful resource.

The footing of interviewers is also complicated. For example, are they treated by the interviewee as the addressed recipient? Or is their participant status as a conduit or reporter? Take television news interviews. Here, both interviewer and interviewee treat the overhearing audience as the relevant recipient of the talk. One interactional feature that displays this is the absence of "oh" receipts. There is no interactional need for news anchors to mark a "change of state." Indeed, they may be asking questions to which they already know the answer or in which they have no personal interest. The issue, then, is not the news interviewer's change of knowledge state but how informed the audience is (Clayman & Heritage, 2002; Heritage & Greatbatch, 1991).

Again, we can consider the issue of footing as it is played out practically in the conduct of the interviewer and the interviewee. Interviewer turns can display different footing positions. Compare the simple acknowledgment token "mm." in Line 10 of Extract 38.3d with the turns on Lines 25 and 29 in Extract 38.3e.

Extract 38.3e

22	Tch:	Er::m (0.9) if you're ti:red, (.) an stressed, (.) erm
23		you're not always in the best: situation to make
24		good judge[ments.]
25	Int:	[↑Oh ye]ah. °yeah. [°Mm.]
26	Tch:	[Er:]m (0.4) the CHILdren
27		I think at least are slightly more aware of this
28		[than they used to] be in [the pa:]st.
29	Int:	[M m : : : .] [M m : :.]
30	Int:	Mm:.

In these turns, the interviewer is displaying full recipiency, with oh-prefaced agreement on Line 25 and stretched acknowledgment tokens on Line 29. By indexing existing relevant knowledge and views in this way, the interviewer builds herself or himself as a fully active participant (Heritage, 2002) rather than a neutral, disinterested recorder of what is said by the interviewee.

This form of engagement can be part of a process where the interview productively becomes "an interventionist and confrontative arena" (Potter & Wetherell, 1987, p. 164). However, note that what

we have here is not something consistent through the whole extract, let alone the whole interview. The different interviewer footing appears selectively in different positions in relation to different interviewee turns. Footing itself is a somewhat limited notion (see the debate in Leudar & Antaki, 1996; Potter, 1996), and there is a range of further possibilities for how footing can be displayed in interviewee talk (Ensink, 2003; Lee & Roth, 2004). Our point is that these are subtle, complex, and yet potentially consequential matters that up to now have been barely considered by analysts of interviews.

7. STAKE AND INTEREST

A central feature of interaction is that people orient to issues of potential stake and interest (Edwards & Potter, 1992). They may respond to what other people say as a product of interests and manage the potential interestedness of their own talk. This can play out in complex ways in open-ended interviews.

Consider the interviewee. She or he will typically have been recruited as a member of a social category; and she or he is likely to be treated as having a stake in that category. At the same time, interviewees are typically treated as being broadly neutral informants of their own practices. This combination of being more or less neutral and having a stake in a category is an analytic commonplace of more discourse-focused work on interviews (e.g., Edley, 2001),

although that does not make the analysis easy to do. And such issues are more or less ignored in most qualitative interview analyses.

Now take the interviewer. Much qualitative research is conducted on doctoral programs, and here it is overwhelmingly the case that the interviewer and the researcher are the same person. Moreover, it is not just common but expected for those researchers to care deeply about the topic they are studying. So there is a profound issue of how this potentially live stake is managed. It is interesting to compare this with market research settings, where there is often an explicit focus on the potential interestedness of the interviewer or moderator. Extract 38.3f shows the kind of construction that is recurrent at the start of market research focus groups.

Extract 38.3f

```
01   Mod:   As I say I <↑don't make> the adver↓tising,
02          (0.5) I don't sell cars.=I don't work for
03          ei:ther company that doe:s:. .hhh s:o: er::
04          ↑whilst (0.3) >this research has clearly
05          been commissioned< by: (.) er a >company
06          that does< both. An >you'll see (as we go
07          through) who 'tis.<
08          (.)
09   Mod:   ↑I don't have a vested interest.
10          (0.2)
11   Mod:   °Right, >so I don't really mind what you< say:. (Puchta & Potter, 2004)
```

When the moderator introduces herself to the group like this, she emphasizes her independence from the firm that has commissioned the focus group and how she was not involved in producing the advertising for its products (something that participants might expect). Note the very explicit denial of having an interest (Line 9) and the assertion of the implication of this for the conduct of the participants (Line 11). Note that the converse implication here is that the moderator otherwise might have had an interest in what is being discussed and might mind it being criticized!

In academic qualitative social science work with interviews, this kind of asserted separation between the interests of the researcher and the topic is much less common. The researcher is unlikely to be able to plausibly and honestly assert his or her disinterest. Researchers do on occasion introduce the issue

of their own stake in the topic at hand—although this is probably more common offstage during the interview setup. An important area of future metastudy will be the way such avowals of concern (or relevant membership) play out in the trajectory of the interview.

As with footing, issues of stake and interest vary through the trajectory of the interview. They appear in different places and in different ways. We have already noted an example. Consider Extract 38.3e again.

Note again here the interviewer's displays of investment in the topic in Lines 25 and 29. The teacher is being interviewed about the potentially delicate topic of punishment of children (and how some of the schoolchildren interviewed have suggested the phenomenon of teacher bullying). The teacher is building an account for "inappropriate"

Extract 38.3e

22	Tch:	Er::m (0.9) if you're <u>ti</u>:red, (.) an <u>stre</u>ssed, (.) erm
23		you're <u>not</u> always in the best: situation to make
24		good <u>judge</u>[ments.]
25	Int:	[↑Oh <u>ye</u>]ah. °yeah. [°Mm.]
26	Tch:	[Er:]m (0.4) the CHILdren
27		I think at least are slightly more a<u>ware</u> of this
28		[than they used to] be in [the pa:]st.
29	Int:	[M m : : : .] [M m: :.]
30	Int:	Mm:.

actions, prompted by a question that indexes certain constraints on "dealing effectively with kids." By employing an "oh-prefaced" agreement, the interviewer treats its contents as "already known," thereby more strongly aligning with this account and encouraging the teacher to be less guarded.

Agreements (and disagreements, of course) can display broader alignments and interest in topics (see Koole, 2003). For the moment, we will just note again that if we take this seriously, it makes the process of interview analysis considerably more complicated than is often presented. And it highlights the powerful role of interviewer activities. Our point is not that such activities should be driven out of interviews. Agreements show attentive listening and engagement (often glossed as "rapport" in methods texts). However, they do more than this, and their specific placement deserves analytic attention.

Our general point is that the interactional organization of interviews is complex and consequential, yet it is rarely explicitly addressed. To take it into account during analysis is a major challenge (for a research example that highlights the subtlety of the challenge, see Edwards, 2003). However, to fail to take it into account risks interview conclusions that are based more on researchers' prior expectations than on analysis of actual interview conduct.

8. COGNITIVISM AND INDIVIDUALISM

One of the pervasive but almost unnoticed by-products of interview research is the reproduction of a kind of cognitive individualism. The point is not that such a perspective is necessarily wrong; it is that there is no way of testing it when it is reproduced in this way. It is a vision of human life presupposed rather than discovered in most interview research. There is something particularly ironic about this given that many researchers who draw on qualitative interviews espouse a critical, nonindividualist perspective on social life. We will focus on two ways in which cognitive individualism is reproduced: (1) the privileging of conceptual meditation over action and (2) the treatment of cognitive language as referential.

Privileging Conceptual Rumination

Qualitative interviews recruit participants to report on events, actions, social processes, and various kinds of cognitive objects (attitudes, beliefs, etc.). This kind of explicit conceptual meditation is treated as providing a way into participants' minds or social organizations. Participants orient to this in their answers, offering up their reflexive thoughts as skilled participant theorists. Note the syllogistic pattern in Extract 38.3g, and the way causal relationships are adduced.

Extract 38.3g

06	Tch:	[U : : m :] (0.9)
07		((swallows)) <u>Ye</u>:s, (0.7) I think <u>a</u>ll teachers are
08		<u>stressed</u>
09		(0.2)
10	Int:	<u>Mm</u>:.

11	Tch:	Er be<u>ca</u>use they're stressed (.) they <u>ma</u>y react (0.5)
12		u::m inap<u>prop</u>riately,
13	Int:	Mhm,
14		(0.2)
15	Tch:	in <u>ce</u>rtain situatio[ns,]

The teacher here is being asked as a teacher not to be a teacher but to reflexively formulate aspects of the lives of teachers and to provide causal observations.

Looked at in one way, this is a restatement of the basic rationale for doing interviews in the first place. People are asked about what they do and what they think, and they helpfully tell you about these things. However, looked at another way, what is going on here is that people are being treated as being in a special epistemic position with respect to their own conduct—not just actions and events but also causal and developmental relationships, intrapsychic processes, and so on. The interview depends on a range of ambitious cognitive judgments and feats of memory and analysis.

Cognitive Language

The contemplative picture of interview talk goes hand in hand with the kinds of referential understanding of specifically cognitive language that were criticized by Wittgenstein, whose critiques were refined in different ways by discursive psychology (Edwards, 1997) and conversation analysis (Sacks, 1992). Recent studies have started to consider the role of cognitive language in social research settings. Myers (2004) and Puchta and Potter (2002, 2004; Potter & Puchta, 2007) looked at the role of what focus group researchers call POBA terminology (perceptions, opinions, beliefs, and attitudes). For example, Puchta and Potter (2004) note that questions constructed in POBA terms make it harder for participants to produce "don't know" and slow responses (people are treated as having immediate and privileged access to their own opinions and attitudes). And they also show how the interactional organization of social research can be used to generate POBAs as objects within individuals (Puchta & Potter, 2002).

Consider the interviewer's question that starts our illustrative extract:

| 01 | Int: | So d'you ↑feel then that the constrai:nts |
| 02 | | on teachers' ti:me and the resources >that are |

Note the interviewer's use of the POBA term *feel* at the start of this topic's initial question. Asking for a "feeling" softens the epistemic demands of the question while heightening the interactional demands. Your "feeling" may not be subject to the same scrutiny as a factual claim; however, you are expected to know and be able to report on your own feelings.

Similar sorts of issues arise with the interviewee's use of psychological or cognitive terminology. To take one example, the interviewee uses the term *stressed* on three occasions in this sequence (Lines 8, 11, and 22). Whatever referential role this term has, careful analysis will be needed to consider what it is being used to do in this sequence. For example, Hepburn and Brown (2001), in an analysis of these interviews, highlight some of the practical uses of stress talk in managing accountability and linking individual actions with broader institutional roles and relationships.

Our point is that to fully understand what is going on in qualitative interviews, researchers will need to be attentive to the practical role of cognitive and psychological language in the talk of both interviewer and interviewee. Conversely, we will need to be cautious when treating such talk as a way of referring to inner psychological objects of some kind.

◆ The Conduct and Analysis of Interviews

Recent interaction work in the tradition of ethnomethodology, conversation analysis, and discursive psychology has revolutionized our understanding of questions as social actions. This has two kinds of implication for the way qualitative open-ended interviews have been used in social research.

First, it throws up a series of challenges. Once we recognize the subtlety and complexity of interaction in social research interviews, we are faced with the importance of representing that interaction in ways that allow fuller inspection. Not recording the potentially consequential work of the recruitment and setup makes it harder to appreciate the basis on which the interviewee is talking. The representation of the actual interaction in the interview needs to allow the reader to appreciate the active role of the interviewer and, most crucial, the way the interview questions are built. The pervasive failure to reproduce the interviewer's questions is simply not acceptable now that we know the impact of different question designs and the way questions can embody different social science agendas. The second set of challenges is to do with the way the interview is analyzed and how far that analysis is able to take seriously the way social science agendas are hardwired into the interview, the way footing and stake and interest are managed, and the tendency of the very interview setup to analyze everything in terms of individual cognitive objects.

Second, it throws up a set of opportunities. This literature can feed into the training of interviewers and the way interview schedules are developed. Work on news interviewers shows the way a range of subtle and challenging question forms can be effectively deployed. Social researchers have the opportunity to learn from this sophistication and improve their own practices. There is the potential for more control over the unfolding conduct of the interview than has currently been claimed in how-to methods books, with the possibility of managing issues of argument and displays of stake and interest

to generate particular kinds of challenges and to provide a particular context to answering. The irony is that qualitative interviews are massively overused but their potential has been massively restricted.

This kind of research also allows us to move on to a subtler position on issues of bias, neutrality, and leading questions. The way questions "prefer" particular kinds of answers is now better understood (Clayman & Heritage, 2002). Once we have the resources to identify such preferences analytically, we can move beyond bias as a problem toward considering how questions with different kinds of pressures can be used to open up issues for the interviewee. Despite the sophistication that is now possible, more systematic work on the social institution of the research interview is long overdue. Very few studies carefully describe the institution of interviewing and the different practices that make up that institution. This contrasts with the massive reliance of modern social research on the qualitative interview.

We started with the observation that interviews have often been used on the basis that they are the obvious way of doing any qualitative social research, with few alternatives. Part of this increased sophistication in the conduct and analysis of interviews puts us in a position where we can make a more informed judgment on the choice of research approach. And the recognition of this choice starts to put the onus on researchers who are using interviews to fully justify that choice.

◆ *Appendix*

Table 38.1 Basic Transcription Conventions

[ ]	Square brackets mark the start and end of overlapping speech.
↓ ↑	Vertical arrows precede marked pitch movement, over and above normal rhythms of speech.
Under<u>lin</u>ing	Underlining signals vocal emphasis.
CAPITALS	Capitals mark speech that is obviously louder than surrounding speech.
°practical°	"Degree" signs enclose obviously quieter speech.
(0.4)	Numbers in round brackets measure pauses in seconds (in this case, four tenths of a second).
she wa::nted	Colons show elongation of the prior sound: the more colons, the more elongation.
bu-u-	Hyphens mark a cutoff from the preceding sound.
solid.= =We had	"Equals" signs mark the immediate "latching" of successive talk, whether of one or more speakers, with no interval.
hhh	Aspiration (out-breaths): the more the longer.
.hhh	Inspiration (in-breaths): the more the longer.

Yeh,	The comma marks continuation, signaling that the speaker has not finished; intonationally it is a fall–rise or weak rising intonation.
y'know?	Question marks signal stronger, "questioning" intonation, irrespective of grammar.
Yeh.	Periods (full stops) mark falling, stopping intonation ("final contour"), irrespective of grammar.

Note: See Hepburn and Bolden (in press) for further details.

◆ References

Andrews, M. (2008). Never the last word: Revisiting data. In M. Andrews, C. Squire, & M. Tamboukou (Eds.), *Doing narrative research* (pp. 86–101). London, England: Sage.

Antaki, C., Billig, M., Edwards, D., & Potter, J. (2007). Discourse analysis means doing analysis: A critique of six analytic shortcomings. In J. Potter (Ed.), *Discourse and psychology: Theory and method* (Vol. 1, pp. 331–347). London, England: Sage.

Antaki, C., & Rapley, M. (1996). "Quality of life" talk: The liberal paradox of psychological testing. *Discourse and Society, 7*, 293–316.

Atkinson, J. M., & Drew, P. (1979). *Order in court: The organisation of verbal interaction in judicial settings.* London, England: Macmillan.

Boyd, E. A., & Heritage, J. (2006). Taking the patient's medical history: Questioning during comprehensive history-taking. In J. Heritage & D. Maynard (Eds.), *Communication in medical care: Interactions between primary care physicians and patients* (pp. 151–184). Cambridge, England: Cambridge University Press.

Clayman, S., & Heritage, J. C. (2002). *The news interview: Journalists and public figures on the air.* Cambridge, MA: Cambridge University Press.

Denzin, N. K., & Lincoln, Y. S. (Eds.). (2005). *Handbook of qualitative research* (3rd ed.). London, England: Sage.

Edley, N. (2001). Analysing masculinity: Interpretative repertoires, ideological dilemmas and subject positions. In M. Wetherell, S. Taylor, & S. J. Yates (Eds.), *Discourse as data: A guide to analysis* (pp. 198–228). London, England: Sage.

Edwards, D. (1997). *Discourse and cognition.* London, England: Sage.

Edwards, D. (2003). Analysing racial discourse: The discursive psychology of mind-world relationships. In H. van den Berg, M. Wetherell, & H. Houtkoop-Steenstra (Eds.), *Analysing race talk: Multidisciplinary approaches to the interview* (pp. 31–48). Cambridge, England: Cambridge University Press.

Edwards, D., & Potter, J. (1992). *Discursive psychology.* London, England: Sage.

Ensink, T. (2003). The frame analysis of research interviews: Social categorization and footing in interview discourse. In H. van den Berg, M. Wetherell, & H. Houtkoop-Steenstra (Eds.), *Analyzing race talk: Multidisciplinary approaches to the interview* (pp. 156–177). Cambridge, England: Cambridge University Press.

Giorgi, A. P., & Giorgi, B. M. (2003). The descriptive phenomenological method. In P. M. Camic, J. E. Rhodes, & L. Yardley (Eds.), *Qualitative research in psychology: Expanding perspectives in methodology and design* (pp. 243–274). Washington, DC: American Psychological Association.

Goffman, E. (1981). *Forms of talk.* Oxford, England: Basil Blackwell.

Gubrium, J. F., & Holstein, J. A. (Eds.). (2002). *Handbook of interview research: Context and method.* London, England: Sage.

Hepburn, A. (1997a). Discursive strategies in bullying talk. *Education and Society, 15*, 13–31.

Hepburn, A. (1997b). Teachers and secondary school bullying: A postmodern discourse analysis. *Discourse and Society, 8*, 27–48.

Hepburn, A. (2000). Power lines: Derrida, discursive psychology and the management of accusations of teacher bullying. *British Journal of Social Psychology, 39*, 605–628.

Hepburn, A., & Bolden, G. (in press). Transcription for conversation analysis. In J. Sidnell & T. Stivers (Eds.), *Blackwell handbook of conversation analysis.* Oxford, England: Blackwell.

Hepburn, A., & Brown, S. J. (2001). Teacher stress and the management of accountability. *Human Relations, 54*(6), 531–555.

Hepburn, A., & Potter, J. (2010). Recipients designed: Tag questions and gender. In S. Speer & E. Stokoe (Eds.), *Conversation analysis and gender* (pp. 137–154). Cambridge, England: Cambridge University Press.

Heritage, J. (2002). The limits of questioning: Negative interrogatives and hostile question content. *Journal of Pragmatics, 34*, 1427–1446.

Heritage, J. C., & Greatbatch, D. (1991). On the institutional character of institutional talk: The case of news interviews. In D. Boden & D. H. Zimmerman (Eds.), *Talk and social structure: Studies in ethnomethodology and conversation analysis* (pp. 93–137). Cambridge, MA: Polity Press.

Heritage, J. C., & Raymond, G. (in press). Navigating epistemic landscapes: Acquiescence, agency and resistance in responses to polar questions. In J.-P. de Ruiter (Ed.), *Questions*. Cambridge, England: Cambridge University Press.

Houtkoop-Steenstra, H. (2000). *Interaction and the standardized survey interview: The living questionnaire.* Cambridge, England: Cambridge University Press.

Jefferson, G. (1985). Notes on a systematic deployment of the acknowledgement tokens "Yeah" and "Mmhm." *Papers in Linguistics, 17,* 197–216.

Jefferson, G. (2004). Glossary of transcript symbols with an introduction. In G. H. Lerner (Ed.), *Conversation analysis: Studies from the first generation* (pp. 13–31). Amsterdam, The Netherlands: John Benjamins.

Koole, T. (2003). Affiliation and detachment in interviewer answer receipts. In H. van den Berg, M. Wetherell, & H. Houtkoop-Steenstra (Eds.), *Analyzing race talk: Multidisciplinary approaches to the interview* (pp. 178–199). Cambridge, England: Cambridge University Press.

Lee, Y.-J., & Roth, W.-M. (2004, January). Making a scientist: Discursive "doing" of identity and self-presentation during research interviews. *Forum: Qualitative Social Research, 5*(1), Art. 12. Retrieved from http://www.qualitative-research.net/fqs-texte/1-04/1-04leeroth-e.htm

Leudar, I., & Antaki, C. (1996). Discourse participation, reported speech and research practices in social psychology. *Theory & Psychology, 6,* 5–29.

Maynard, D. W., Houtkoop-Steenstra, H., Schaeffer, N. C., & van der Zouwen, J. (Eds.). (2002). *Standardization and tacit knowledge: Interaction and practice in the survey interview.* New York, NY: Wiley.

Morgan, D. L. (2010). Reconsidering the role of interaction in analysing and reporting focus groups. *Qualitative Health Research, 20,* 718–722.

Myers, G. (2004). *Matters of opinion: Talking about public ideas.* Cambridge, England: Cambridge University Press.

Poland, B. D. (2002). Transcription quality. In J. F. Gubrium & J. A. Holstein (Eds.), *Handbook of interview research: Context and method* (pp. 629–649). London, England: Sage.

Pomerantz, A. M. (1984). Agreeing and disagreeing with assessments: Some features of preferred/dispreferred turn shapes. In J. M. Atkinson & J. Heritage (Eds.), *Structures of social action: Studies in conversation analysis* (pp. 57–101). Cambridge, England: Cambridge University Press.

Potter, J. (1996). Right and wrong footing. *Theory and Psychology, 6,* 31–39.

Potter, J., & Hepburn, A. (2005a). Action, interaction and interviews: Some responses to Hollway, Mischler and Smith. *Qualitative Research in Psychology, 2,* 319–325.

Potter, J., & Hepburn, A. (2005b). Qualitative interviews in psychology: Problems and possibilities. *Qualitative Research in Psychology, 2,* 281–307.

Potter, J., & Hepburn, A. (2007). Life is out there: A comment on Griffin. *Discourse Studies, 9,* 277–283.

Potter, J., & Mulkay, M. (1985). Scientists' interview talk: Interviews as a technique for revealing participants' interpretative practices. In M. Brenner, J. Brown, & D. Canter (Eds.), *The research interview: Uses and approaches* (pp. 247–271). London, England: Academic Press.

Potter, J., & Puchta, C. (2007). Mind, mousse and moderation. In A. Hepburn & S. Wiggins (Eds.), *Discursive research in practice* (pp. 104–123). Cambridge, England: Cambridge University Press.

Potter, J., & Wetherell, M. (1987). *Discourse and social psychology: Beyond attitudes and behaviour.* London, England: Sage.

Potter, J., & Wetherell, M. (1995). Discourse analysis. In J. Smith, R. Harré, & L. van Langenhove (Eds.), *Rethinking methods in psychology* (pp. 80–92). London, England: Sage.

Puchta, C., & Potter, J. (1999). Asking elaborate questions: Focus groups and the management of spontaneity. *Journal of Sociolinguistics, 3,* 314–335.

Puchta, C., & Potter, J. (2002). Manufacturing individual opinions: Market research focus groups and the discursive psychology of attitudes. *British Journal of Social Psychology, 41,* 345–363.

Puchta, C., & Potter, J. (2004). *Focus group practice.* London, England: Sage.

Raymond, G. (2003). Grammar and social organisation: Yes/no interrogatives and the structure of responding. *American Sociological Review, 68,* 939–967.

Sacks, H. (1992). *Lectures on conversation* (Vols. 1 & 2; G. Jefferson, Ed.). Oxford, England: Basil Blackwell.

Schegloff, E. A. (2007). *Sequence organization in interaction: A primer in conversation analysis* (Vol. 1). Cambridge, England: Cambridge University Press.

Stivers, T., & Hayashi, M. (2010). Transformative answers: One way to resist a question's constraints. *Language in Society, 39,* 1–25.

Stokoe, E., & Edwards, D. (2008). Did you have permission to smash your neighbour's door? Silly questions and their answers in police–suspect interrogations. *Discourse Studies, 10*(1), 89–111.

Turner, J. C., Hogg, M. A., Oakes, P. J., Reicher, S. D., & Wetherell, M. S. (1987). *Rediscovering the social group: A self categorization theory.* Oxford, England: Blackwell.

Wetherell, M., & Potter, J. (1992). *Mapping the language of racism: Discourse and the legitimation of exploitation.* London, England: Columbia University Press.

Willig, C., & Stainton-Rogers, W. (Eds.). (2008). *The SAGE handbook of qualitative research in psychology.* London, England: Sage.

AUTHOR INDEX

Abell, J., 545, 546, 549
Abramson, P. R., 79
Abu-Lughod, L., 118, 151, 208, 513
Acker, J., 151
Ackerman, T. F., 341
Adams, J., 53
Adams, T. E., 149
Adhikari, R. P., 103, 104
Adler, P. A., 32, 56, 108, 155, 209, 210, 212,
    222, 223, 307, 308, 338, 340, 444, 445, 448,
    453, 479
Adler, R. B., 528
Adorno, T. W., 16, 17
Agar, M., 342
Agar, M. H., 499
Ahmad, F., 354, 445
Aita, M., 504
Akita, K., 263
Akkad, A., 450, 451
Alasuutari, P., 28, 403, 404
Alise, M. A., 360
Allan, G., 245
Allen, A. L., 487
Allen, B., 118
Allen, K., 245
Allen, M. W., 245
Allen, P. C., 459
Allen-Kelsey, G. J., 354
Allport, G., 116
Altheide, D. L., 39, 105, 110, 479
Althusser, L., 233
Alvesson, M., 281, 534
Alwin, D. F., 91
Amit, V., 479
Anderson, B. A., 79
Anderson, D., 245, 248
Anderson, K., 52

Anderson, L., 147, 148, 150, 153, 155, 262, 319
Anderson, N. R., 503
André-Bechely, L. N., 381, 386, 388
Andrews, M., 281, 282, 283, 289, 292, 369, 558
Ani, M., 257
Anspach, R. R., 450
Antaki, C., 404, 405, 410, 556, 560, 564
Antonow, K., 170
Antunes, L., 361
Aquilino, W. S., 88
Aragon, S. R., 468
Arendell, T., 281, 285
Arksey, H., 244
Armstrong, D. J., 245
Aroni, R., 460, 461
Ashworth, P., 325
Astedt-Kurki, P., 248
Atkinson, J. M., 556
Atkinson, P., 31, 36, 39, 46, 125, 179, 208, 257, 307,
    319, 349, 368, 479, 482, 486, 490, 499, 550
Atkinson, R., 17, 101, 115, 119, 120, 121, 512
Ault, A., 309
Azadovskii, M., 513

Babbie, E. R., 51, 209
Back, A. L., 496, 498, 505
Back, K. W., 23
Baez, B., 457, 459, 460, 463
Bakardjieva, M., 178, 185
Baker, C. D., 70, 404, 405, 486, 541, 544, 545, 551
Baker, P., 427
Baker, R. P., 88
Bakera, J., 213
Baldwin, A. K., 88
Baldwin, S., 341
Bales, K., 11
Balfe, M., 336

SUBJECT INDEX

Elder function, 117
Electroconvulsive therapy (ECT), 135, 139
Electronic interviewing, 52–53
Embodied communication process, 525–526
  active interviews, meaning making and, 529
  autoethnography and, 151–153, 155, 535–536
  best practices, embodied interview research, 532–536
  body, meaning of, 527
  body-mind relations, re-engagement of, 527–528
  body-subjects, embodied senses and, 527
  data analysis and, 529–531, 534–535
  disembodied researcher, performance of, 527
  during interviews, embodied engagement and, 533–534
  embodied knowledge and, 530–531
  embodiment, research processes and, 528
  feminist perspective, blurred mind/body boundary and, 526–527
  interviews, embodiment in, 528–529
  medicated interviewing and, 529
  mind/body split, absence of body in research and, 526–528
  preparation for interviews and, 532–533
  representation, embodiment in, 531–532, 535–536
  social locations, embodiment of, 145
  transcription process and, 529–530
Emotional labor, 285–286
  autoethnographic turn and, 288
  challenges of, 287
  defended subjects, interaction of, 291–292
  examples of, 286–287
  interviews, joint construction of, 289–290
  managing interviewer self, doing justice and, 288–289
  managing interviewer self example and, 290–291
  managing interviewer self, illness narratives and, 289
  reflexive interviewer, managing emotional intensity and, 327–328
  sensitive topics and, 286
  See also Interviewer self
Empowerment, 35, 36, 271, 272, 416
Error, 18–19
  active interviews, meaning making and, 529
  coverage error, 78
  interviewer effects and, 78
  measurement error, 78
  nonresponse error, 78, 84
  sampling error, 77–78
  total error perspective and, 77–78
Essentialist perspective on culture, 256–257
  anti-essentialism, critiques of, 257–258
  essentialism, critiques of, 257
  See also Culture work
Ethical mindfulness, 472
  courage and, 474
  discomfort/unease, attention to, 472–473
  ethically important elements, articulation of, 473
  ethically important moments and, 472
  reflexivity and, 473
  See also Ethics; Situated research ethics approach
Ethic of care model, 451–453, 485, 500

Ethics:
  autoethnography and, 155
  beneficence and, 110, 443, 459, 466, 467
  codes of human research ethics and, 467–468
  communities, protection of, 110
  consent, negotiation of, 326
  deprivatization of lived experience and, 110
  ethical reflexivity, 318, 325–328
  human rights, 111
  in-depth interviewing and, 108–111
  Internet interviewing and, 183–187
  netiquette and, 186
  principals of, 110
  privacy concerns, 110, 187
  public/private spaces and, 185–186
  relational interviews and, 124
  release forms and, 124
  research subjects, protection of, 109–110
  respect for all, 110, 466, 467
  respondent construction and, 308–310
  social justice and, 110, 111
  truth telling, 110
  zones of ambiguity and, 453
  See also Confidentiality; Ethical mindfulness; Informed consent; Risks in interview research; Situated research ethics approach
ETHNOGRAPH software, 53, 427, 429
Ethnography, 14, 515
  analytic ethnography, 110
  autoethnography, 55–56
  cultural criticism and, 153
  essentialism and, 257
  new ethnography, 122
  online ethnography, 178
  reciprocal ethnography, 520
  respondent as member/informant and, 307–308
  standpoint epistemologies and, 110
  See also Autoethnography; Folk narrative research; Institutional ethnography; Life story interview; Personal narrative research
Ethnomethodological perspectives, 22, 49, 50–51
  ethnographic interviewing, sensuous turn in, 54
  methods of interaction and, 129
  place-as-ethnographic knowledge and, 54–55
ETHNO software, 53
Evocative autoethnography, 147–148
Excel software, 428, 430

Fabrication, 140
Face-to-face interviews, 8, 14, 77, 78
  computer-assisted personal interviewing and, 87–88
  interaction design and, 85
  participation, incentives for, 84–85
  random sampling and, 83
  supervision of, 92–93
  See also Social/interpersonal interaction
Facebook, 188
Falsification incidence, 93

survey interviewing and, 78
truth, unfolding of, 137
vessels of topics, interview transcripts and, 140–141
See also Culture work; Focus group interviews; Folk
    narrative research; Personal narrative research
Sociopolitical perspective, 14
Software. *See* Qualitative data analysis (QDA) software
Split-panel/split-ballot tests, 83
Stage plays, 56
Standardized interviewing, 86–87
    benefits of standardization, 89
    conversational elements, suppression of, 89
    effectiveness evaluation of, 88–90
    in-depth interviewing and, 107
    interviewer behavior, flexibility in, 89–90
    nonstandardized interviewer behavior and, 88–89
    questions, wording/interpretation of, 89
    rapport issue and, 89
    See also Survey interviewing
Standpoint epistemologies, 110, 145–146
Statistical Package for the Social Sciences (SPSS), 427,
    428, 430
Statistical software. *See* Qualitative data analysis (QDA)
    software
Stigma, 333–334
    co-construction/management of, 335, 337
    combative qualitative interviews and, 340–341
    continuum of, 335–336, 336 (figure)
    contractual nature of research and, 339
    definitions of, 334
    discreditable, interviewing of, 337–338
    discredited, stigmas of, 336–337
    experience of stigmatization and, 337
    logic of unity, silenced participants and, 340
    normal/stigmatized persons, interactions between, 337
    paid research participants and, 341–342
    power dynamics, interview encounter and, 335, 338–342
    research interviews and, 334–336
    social processes and, 334
    unnatural nature of research interviews and, 339–340
Stimulus-response model, 22–23
StoryCorps project, 61
Storytelling, 115, 511–512
    analytic stance and, 519–520
    constituencies/communities of action and, 368
    culture, intergenerational transmission of, 115
    eliciting stories and, 514–518
    forms of stories and, 517
    internalized/embodied stories, 519
    interviews about stories and, 518–520
    narrative linkages and, 250
    relational activity of, 368
    storytelling transactions and, 512
    styles of, 515
    universal pattern in, 115
    See also Folk narrative research; Interview subjectivity;
        Life story interview; Narrative practice; Personal
        narrative research; Postmodern interviewing trends
Structured interview method, 13, 14, 194
Subjectivity. *See* Interview subjectivity; Q methodology (QM)

Subject positions. *See* Culture work
Supervision, 13, 36, 65, 78, 92–93, 287, 317
Surveillance, 29, 178
Survey interviewing, 11–12, 15, 22, 23, 77–78
    behavior coding and, 82, 83
    cognitive processing perspective and, 91
    computer-assisted interviewing and, 87–88
    conversational interviews, social basis of, 90–92
    converter interviewers and, 85–86
    coverage error and, 78
    fact-to-face vs. telephone surveys and, 78, 86
    falsification incidence and, 93
    field pretesting questions and, 82–83
    fieldwork phase and, 78
    Internet-based surveys, 31, 77
    interviewer demographic characteristics and, 78–79
    interviewer effects and, 78
    interviewer recruitment/selection and, 78–80
    interviewer training and, 80–81
    interviewer/respondent interaction and, 78
    interviewing process, 86–92
    interviewing ratings and, 82–83
    measurement error and, 78
    motivation for participation and, 84–85, 87, 91
    nonresponse error and, 78, 84
    planning phase of, 78
    pretesting questions, cognitive interviewing and, 81–82
    questionnaire drafts, peer review of, 83
    random sampling and, 83
    rational choice perspective and, 91
    relevance, principle of, 91
    resistance to cooperation, survey design/interaction
        variables and, 84–85
    respondent debriefings and, 82
    respondent as reporter and, 305–306
    respondent selection/participation and, 83–86
    respondent training and, 86–87
    response analysis and, 83
    sampling error and, 77–78
    sampling process and, 83–84
    satisficing respondent behavior and, 91–92
    split-panel/split-ballot tests and, 83
    standardization, evaluative studies of, 88–90
    standardized interviewing and, 86–90
    steps in, 78, 79 (figure)
    supervision/quality control and, 92–93
    survey questions, design/evaluation of, 81–83, 86
    tasks in, 80
    think-aloud interviews and, 81, 82
    total error perspective and, 77–78
Synchronous interviews, 179–180
Synthesized interviews, 196, 196 (figure)

Teenage Cancer Trust (TCT), 226–227
Telephone interviewing, 24, 77, 78
    disembodied interviews and, 529
    interaction design and, 85
    interviewer vocalizations, compliance
        rates and, 85
    participation, incentives for, 84–85

ABOUT THE EDITORS

Jaber F. Gubrium is Professor and Chair of Sociology at the University of Missouri. He has an extensive record of research on identity in everyday life and the social organization of care in human service institutions. His publications include numerous books and articles on aging, family, the life course, medicalization, and representational practice in a therapeutic context.

James A. Holstein is Professor of Sociology in the Department of Social and Cultural Sciences at Marquette University. His research and writing have addressed social problems, deviance and social control, mental health and illness, family, and the self, all approached from an ethnomethodologically informed, constructionist perspective.

Collaborating for more than 25 years, Gubrium and Holstein have authored and edited dozens of books, many of them dealing with qualitative research methods and interviewing, including *Varieties of Narrative Analysis*, *Analyzing Narrative Reality*, *The New Language of Qualitative Method*, *The Active Interview*, *Handbook of Constructionist Research*, *Handbook of Interview Research* (first edition), *The Self We Live By*, *Constructing the Life Course*, and *What Is Family?*

Amir B. Marvasti is Associate Professor of Sociology at Pennsylvania State University, Altoona. His research focuses on the social construction of deviant identities. He is the author of *Being Homeless: Textual and Narrative Constructions* (Lexington Books, 2003), *Qualitative Research in Sociology* (Sage, 2003), *Middle Eastern Lives in America* (with Karyn McKinney; Rowman & Littlefield, 2004), and *Doing Qualitative Research: A Comprehensive Guide* (with David Silverman; Sage, 2008). His articles have been published in *Journal of Contemporary Ethnography*, *Qualitative Inquiry*, *Symbolic Interaction*, and *Critical Sociology*.

Karyn D. McKinney is Associate Professor of Sociology and Women's Studies at Pennsylvania State University, Altoona. Her research has focused on the role of race and racism in identity construction. Her publications include *Being White: Stories of Race and Racism* (Routledge, 2005), *Middle Eastern Lives in America* (with Amir Marvasti; Rowman & Littlefield, 2004), and *The Many Costs of Racism* (with Joe Feagin; Rowman & Littlefield, 2003). In addition, she has published articles in journals such as *Race and Society*, *Social Identities*, and *Critical Sociology*.

ABOUT THE CONTRIBUTORS

Robert Atkinson is Professor of Human Development, Multicultural Studies, and Religious Studies, director of the Life Story Center, and senior research fellow at the Osher Lifelong Learning Institute (OLLI) National Resource Center at the University of Southern Maine (USM), where he has been since 1987. He is the author, coauthor, or editor of seven books, including *Latino Voices in New England* (SUNY Press, 2009); his memoir, *Remembering 1969: Searching for the Eternal in Changing Times* (2008); *The Beat of My Drum: An Autobiography* (assisting Babatunde Olatunji, 2005); *The Life Story Interview* (Sage, 1998; translated into Italian, 2002, and Romanian, 2006); and *The Gift of Stories: Practical and Spiritual Applications of Autobiography, Life Stories, and Personal Mythmaking* (1995; translated into Japanese, 2005). He was a faculty member on the Semester at Sea program of the University of Virginia, sailing around the world in 100 days and visiting 10 countries, in the fall of 2002. From 2002 to 2004, he served as the first Diversity Scholar for the College of Education and Human Development at USM. His website for the Life Story Center, on the home page of the OLLI National Resource Center, features a searchable archive of 300 life stories and an interactive life storytelling protocol.

Ben K. Beitin is an associate professor of marriage and family therapy at Seton Hall University. His research has focused on couple relationships and coping and expanded into an interest in the wonders and complexities of interviewing partners and family members together in qualitative research. He has published several chapters and articles related to interviewing couples and families, social justice, diversity, and the interactions between family systems and societies. He has been recently studying health and relationships in immigrant couples.

Linda Liska Belgrave is an associate professor of sociology at the University of Miami. Her scholarly interests are primarily in the substantive areas of medical sociology, social psychology, and social justice (broadly defined). She uses a variety of qualitative methods, including in-depth interviews, focus group interviews, participant observation, and variations on autoethnography, to pursue topics such as elders' experiences and definitions of well-being, the daily lives of African American caregivers of family members with Alzheimer's disease, and, most recently, political controversy in the classroom from the perspectives of both faculty and students. She currently serves as chair for a National Institutes of Health Special Emphasis Panel/Scientific Review Group on Health Literacy.

Christian L. Bolden is an assistant professor in criminology at Indiana University, Pennsylvania. His current research interests include reconciling interpretations of gang behaviors and processes with the viewpoints of actual gang members, examining the social network dynamics of populations labeled as deviant, assessing territory and crime hot spots through GIS crime mapping, and studying homicide trends. His recent work can be found in the *Journal of Gang Research* and *Deviant Behavior.*

Michael Ian Borer is an associate professor of sociology at the University of Nevada, Las Vegas. He is the author of *Faithful to Fenway: Believing in Boston, Baseball, and America's Most Beloved Ballpark* (NYU Press, 2008) and editor of *Varieties of Urban Experience: The American City and the Practice of Culture* (2006). He has published articles in *City and Community*, *Journal of Popular Culture*, and *Symbolic Interaction*, among others. He is currently coauthoring a textbook on the connections between the cultures and communities in cities, suburbs, and towns and is conducting ethnographic research on people watching and the sacred landscape of Las Vegas. He is the 2011–2012 vice president of the Society for the Study of Symbolic Interaction.

Hugh Busher is a senior lecturer in education, University of Leicester, UK. Using mainly qualitative and visual methods, he is currently researching students' and teachers' perspectives on education and teaches courses on research methods, on leadership of inclusive schooling and learning communities. Among his more recent publications are *Understanding Educational Leadership: People, Power and Culture* and, with Nalita James, *Online Interviewing.*

Shannon K. Carter is an assistant professor of sociology at the University of Central Florida. Her primary research interest is gender and reproduction, with an emphasis on narratives of the body. Her work is published in journals such as *Sociology of Health & Illness*, *Gender Issues*, *National Women's Studies Association Journal*, and *Journal of Family Issues*. Her current research focuses on public discourses of breast-feeding and race differences in women's institutional breast-feeding experiences.

Kathy Charmaz is a professor of sociology and the director of the Faculty Writing Program at Sonoma State University, California, a program that supports faculty members' scholarly writing. Her research interests include the experience of illness and disability, the social psychology of time, and ethics in qualitative research. She has written, coauthored, or coedited nine books, including *Constructing Grounded*

Theory: A Practical Guide Through Qualitative Analysis, which received a Critics' Choice award from the American Educational Studies Association and has been translated into Chinese, Japanese, Polish, and Portuguese. Her recent multiauthored books are *Five Ways of Doing Qualitative Analysis: Phenomenological Psychology, Grounded Theory, Discourse Analysis, Narrative Research, and Intuitive Inquiry* and *Developing Grounded Theory: The Second Generation.* She recently received the Goldstein award for scholarship from Sonoma State University and has also received the George Herbert Mead award for Lifetime Achievement and the Feminist Mentors Award from the Society for the Study of Symbolic Interaction. Throughout her career, she has conducted professional development workshops and classes on grounded theory methods, intensive interviewing, and writing for publication.

Kay E. Cook is a senior research fellow in the Centre for Applied Social Research at RMIT University, Melbourne, Australia. She is a sociologist who uses qualitative methods, particularly critical approaches, to explore how social policies affect the lives of marginalized groups. This work has an explicitly political focus and has contributed to several government inquiries and reforms, including the recent Australian Law Reform Commission inquiry into family violence and family law. Her recent nationally funded grants have examined the health and social consequences of Australia's welfare-to-work reforms and the impact of erratic child support payments on the social inclusion of low-income children.

Sara L. Crawley is an associate professor of sociology at the University of South Florida and regularly teaches in the Department of Women's and Gender Studies. Trained in both qualitative sociology and women's studies, Crawley focuses on the interdisciplinary space compelled by feminist and queer theories, especially on and about topics of the body and bodily experience, and regularly employs autoethnography as method. Crawley's book *Gendering Bodies* (coauthored with Lara J. Foley and Constance L. Shehan) adds interpretive sociology to gender and sexualities theories to explain how gender gets written on and produced by bodies. Having published autoethnographic work in *Feminism and Psychology, Feminist Teacher, Journal of Lesbian Studies, Journal* of *Contemporary Ethnography*, and *Cultural Studies ↔ Critical Methodologies*, Crawley recently was invited to hold workshops on feminist theory, queer theory, and interpretive methods in Ukraine for scholars from post-Soviet countries; some of Crawley's works have recently been translated into Russian.

Marjorie L. DeVault is professor of sociology in the Maxwell School of Citizenship and Public Affairs at Syracuse University. Her research focuses on gender and work, including unpaid household and family work, and she has written extensively on qualitative and feminist research methodologies, especially institutional ethnography. She is the author of *Feeding the Family: The Social Organization of Caring as Gendered Work* and *Liberating Method: Feminism and Social Research* and editor of *People at Work: Life, Power, and Social Inclusion in the New Economy*.

Ingunn T. Ellingsen is a qualified social worker and a research associate professor in the Faculty of Social Sciences at the University of Stavanger, Norway. Her doctoral thesis was based on her research on family perceptions in child welfare settings. In this research, she used Q methodology as the main data collection instrument.

Laura L. Ellingson is an associate professor of Communication Studies and Women's & Gender Studies at Santa Clara University. She teaches courses in qualitative methods, feminist methods, health communication, communication and gender, and gender, health, and sexuality. Her research focuses on gender in extended families, feminist and qualitative methodologies, embodiment, and interdisciplinary teamwork in health care organizations. She is the author of *Communicating in the Clinic: Negotiating Frontstage and Backstage Teamwork* (2005, Hampton) and *Engaging Crystallization in Qualitative Research* (2009, Sage) and coauthor with Patty Sotirin of *Aunting: Cultural Practices That Sustain Family and Community Life* (2010, Baylor University Press). She is the senior editor for Qualitative, Interpretive, and Rhetorical Methods and senior editor of the Defining Moments section of the journal *Health Communication*. She has served as president of the Organization for the Study of Communication, Language, and Gender and as chair of the Ethnography Division of the National Communication Association. Currently, she is investigating representations of aunts in contemporary North American popular culture and the personal, professional, and

health care experiences of long-term cancer survivors living with the "late effects" of treatment.

Christopher A. Faircloth is an associate professor and chair of the Department of Sociology at Xavier University, Louisiana. His primary research interests are the "chronic illness experience," health disparities, sociology of the body, interpretive sociology, and qualitative research methods. He has edited or coedited two volumes, *Aging Bodies* (AltaMira Press) and *Medicalized Masculinities* (Temple University Press), with Dana Rosenfeld. In addition, he has published numerous articles in journals such as *Sociology of Health and Illness*, *Qualitative Health Research*, *Ageing and Society*, and *Journal of Aging Studies*. He is currently researching the effects that the treatment of leukemia and lymphoma have on perceptions of body and self among cancer patients. He served as the 2010–2011 vice president for the Society for the Study of Symbolic Interactionism and is on the editorial board of *Symbolic Interaction*.

Linda Finlay is an integrative-existential psychotherapist and freelance academic consultant. In addition to her psychotherapy practice, she teaches psychology and writes for the Open University, United Kingdom. She also offers training and mentorship on how to do qualitative research. Her particular interests include working with trauma and researching the lived experience of disability using phenomenological approaches that embrace hermeneutic, reflexive, and relational forms. She has published widely, including *Reflexivity: A Practical Guide for Researchers in Health and Social Science*, a volume coedited with Brendan Gough; *Qualitative Research for Allied Health Professionals*, a volume coedited with Claire Ballinger; *Relational Centred Research for Psychotherapists*, a book coauthored with Ken Evans; and, most recently, *Phenomenology for Therapists* (2011, Wiley).

Lara J. Foley is Chair and Associate Professor of Sociology at the University of Tulsa. She is also codirector of the University of Tulsa Institute for Trauma, Abuse and Neglect. Her research focuses on gender and occupational identity, especially in medical and legal fields. She is the coauthor of *Gendering Bodies* (2008, with Sara L. Crawley and Constance L. Shehan) as well as numerous articles.

Andrea Fontana is Professor Emeritus of Sociology at the University of Nevada, Las Vegas. He has published articles on aging, leisure, theory, and postmodernism. He is the author of the *Last Frontier: The Social Meaning of Growing Old*, coauthor of *Social Problems, Sociologies of Everyday Life*, and coeditor of *The Existential Self in Society* and *Postmodernism and Social Inquiry*. He is a former president of the Society for the Study of Symbolic Interaction and a former editor of the journal *Symbolic Interaction*. Among his last published essays are a deconstruction of the work of the painter Hieronymus Bosch; a performance/play about Farinelli, the castrato; an ethnographic narrative about land speed records at the Bonneville Salt Flats; and a performance based on *Six Feet Under*. He recently published *The Interview: From Formal to Postmodern* and *Death in America*.

Kenneth M. George has been Professor of Anthropology at the University of Wisconsin–Madison since 1999, having served previously at Harvard University and the University of Oregon. He is a specialist on Southeast Asia and a past editor of the *Journal of Asian Studies* (2005–2008). His ethnographic research in Indonesia has focused on the cultural politics of minority ancestral religions (1982–1992) and, more recently (1994–2008), on a long-term collaboration with the painter A. D. Pirous, exploring the aesthetic, ethical, and political ambitions shaping Islamic art and art publics in that country. His books include *Showing Signs of Violence: The Cultural Politics of a Twentieth-Century Headhunting Ritual*, awarded the 1998 Harry J. Benda Prize for best book on Southeast Asia by the Association for Asian Studies; *Picturing Islam: Art and Ethics in a Muslim Lifeworld*; and *Spirited Politics: Religion and Public Life in Contemporary Southeast Asia* (coedited with Andrew C. Willford). Ken has been the recipient of major postdoctoral fieldwork fellowships from the Social Science Research Council, the Wenner-Gren Foundation for Anthropological Research, and the Aga Khan Trust for Culture. His fellowships for writing and study include awards from the National Endowment of the Humanities, the John Simon Guggenheim Foundation, and the Institute for Advanced Study. His early work on personal narrative in evangelical oratory appeared in the pages of *Alcheringa: Ethnopoetics*.

Anne Grinyer is a medical sociologist and senior lecturer in the Division of Health Research at Lancaster University. Her research over the past 10 years has focused on the life stage effects of cancer in teenagers and young adults and covers four main phases.

The first phase focused on the impact a cancer diagnosis at this age has on family dynamics, particularly in terms of the life stage of the teenagers and young adults. The second phase was based on interviews with young adults with cancer to understand the life stage issues from their perspective. The third phase examined long-term survivorship and the ongoing impact of life stage at diagnosis. The fourth phase addressed palliative and end-of-life care for the age group and the challenge of providing age-appropriate care. Each phase of the research has resulted in a number of publications, including books based on the qualitative data collected from participants. The books are *Cancer in Young Adults: Through Parents' Eyes* (Open University Press, 2002), *Young People Living With Cancer: Implications for Policy and Practice* (Open University Press, 2007), *Life After Cancer in Adolescence and Young Adulthood: Late Effects and Long Term Survivorship* (Routledge, 2009), and *Palliative and End of Life Care for Children and Young People: Hospital, Hospice and Home* (Wiley, in press). She also has an interest in the ethics of health research and in research design and has published a number of articles on this topic.

Marilys Guillemin is an associate professor and the director of the Centre for Health and Society, School of Population Health, University of Melbourne, Australia. She teaches postgraduate subjects in qualitative research design and research methods, and health ethics. She has published widely in the areas of sociology of health, illness and technology, innovative research methodologies, research practice, narrative ethics, and ethical practice in research and in health care. She has completed a number of key research projects that include the management of menopause within specialized clinic settings; middle-aged women and heart disease, particularly focusing on women's understanding of risk and prevention of heart disease; deafness and genetic testing; and examination of how ethics committee members and health researchers understand research ethics and how they address ethical issues in practice. She is the author (with Lynn Gillam) of *Telling Moments: Everyday Ethics in Health Care* (2006). Her current research focuses on the role of trust in human research from the perspectives of researchers and research participants.

Kristin Heggen is Professor of Health Sciences and Deputy Dean of Studies at The Faculty of Medicine,

University of Oslo, Norway. Her scholarly work concentrates on professional education, focusing on the interdependence of liberal education and professional training. She has been involved in numerous studies of the power dynamics in health care, including care for the elderly, supervision of care, acute psychiatry, and acute hospital care. She is recognized for her expertise in qualitative methodologies, and she is an experienced user of unstructured observation in complex care settings and of interviews with participants who are patients, care persons, and health professionals. Her publications reflect an ongoing interest in research ethics practice. She teaches courses for master's degree and PhD students on general research design, qualitative methodology, and research ethics. A strong collaboration with Dr. Marilys Guillemin from The University of Melbourne, Australia, has led to an innovative narrative approach in the ethics education of novice researchers.

Alexa Hepburn is Reader in Conversation Analysis in the Social Sciences Department at Loughborough University. Her broad interests include theoretical and analytical innovations in psychology and understanding the rights and competencies of young people. Recent studies focus on the notation and analysis of laughing and crying, advice resistance, tag questions, aspects of self-repair, and threats in adult–child interaction, and the empirical grounding of these issues in a variety of data, for example, child protection help line phone calls and videos of family mealtimes. She is the author of *An Introduction to Critical Social Psychology* and coeditor (with Sally Wiggins) of *Discursive Research in Practice*. She is currently coauthoring *Transcribing for Social Research* (with Galina Bolden).

Hanna Herzog is a professor of sociology at Tel Aviv University and heads the interdisciplinary program on Women and Gender Studies. She is codirector, with Professor Naomi Chazan, of the Center for Advancement of Women in the Public Sphere at the Van Leer Jerusalem Institute in Israel. Herzog specializes in political sociology, political communication, sociology of knowledge, generation as a sociological phenomenon, and sociology of gender. She has written many articles and several books on the politics of ethnic and racial relations, women in politics and politics of women, Palestinian women citizens of Israel, Jewish women in the Holocaust, and gender, religion, and politics. Her works, based on qualitative research methods, analyze the reciprocal relations

between the excluded and the excluders and the role of weakened groups in social structuring. As a feminist researcher, she emphasizes everyday activities and experiences as a part of social construction and social change.

Nalita James is lecturer in employment studies in the Centre for Labour Market Studies at the University of Leicester, England. She has used both online and offline qualitative research methods to research teachers' identities and learning, and is currently researching students' education to work transitions. She also teaches courses on, and writes about, qualitative research methods. Her recent research work has explored the use of the Internet in qualitative research. With Hugh Busher, she has presented and published widely on topics related to Internet interviewing. She is coauthor of *Online Interviewing* (2009) and continues to research and write about the methodological capacities of the Internet.

John M. Johnson is Professor of Justice Studies at Arizona State University, where he has taught for 40 years. He has used qualitative methods to study religious crusades, prisons, child abuse, sexual abuse, organizations, politics, violence against women, justice, human rights, and the death penalty. He is a former winner of the George Herbert Mead Award for outstanding career contributions to symbolic interaction and the Mentor Excellence Award, both from the Society for the Study of Symbolic Interaction. He has won many racquetball tournaments in his age division.

Karen Kaiser is a research assistant professor in the Department of Medical Social Sciences in the Feinberg School of Medicine at Northwestern University, Chicago. She utilizes qualitative and mixed methods to examine individual, interpersonal, organizational, social, and policy influences on health behaviors and health outcomes. Most recently, she has examined the experiences of women with breast cancer, racial and ethnic disparities in breast cancer, and patient experiences of cancer-related symptoms and side effects.

Annika Lillrank is senior lecturer of social work at the Swedish School of Social Science, University of Helsinki, Finland, and an associate professor of social work and health care at Jyväskylä University, Finland. Her scholarly work focuses on narrative methods in the study of health experience, and she has an extensive research record involving the study of parents' experiences of encounters with the health services in association with severe illness in their children and of pain sufferers in interaction with health care. Currently, she is working on a qualitative research project focusing on professional practices in maternity health care, seen from the point of view of pregnant immigrant women and their families.

Marco Marzano is a professor of sociology at the University of Bergamo, Italy. He has been a visiting scholar at many American and European universities. He cofounded and coedits *Etnografia e Ricerca Qualitativa*, the first Italian journal entirely devoted to qualitative research. His major interests include qualitative methodology, research ethics, death and dying, illness narratives, religion, and Catholicism. He has published several books, book chapters, and articles, mostly in Italian.

Liza McCoy is an associate professor of sociology at the University of Calgary in Alberta, Canada. Her research focuses on the social organization of knowledge and everyday practice in the areas of health, immigration, employment, and visual representation.

Michelle Miller-Day is an associate professor of communication arts and sciences, and bioethics and medical humanities at the Pennsylvania State University. She is the founding director of the Penn State Qualitative Research Interest Group, an interdisciplinary community of researchers involved in and supporting qualitative inquiry at Penn State University. Her research addresses human communication and health, including areas such as substance use prevention, suicide, and families and mental health. Her community-embedded research has involved numerous creative projects to translate research findings into social change. For the past 20 years, she has served as the principal qualitative methodologist for a National Institute on Drug Abuse line of research. This work has developed one of the most successful evidence-based substance use prevention programs in the United States and reaches youth in 43 countries worldwide.

David L. Morgan is a professor of sociology at Portland State University. He is a sociological social psychologist who specializes in focus groups and mixed methods. In addition to further developments in focus groups, his current scholarship is devoted to developing two-person interviews as a new format for qualitative interviewing.

Janice M. Morse is a professor and Presidential Endowed Chair at the University of Utah College of Nursing and Professor Emerita, University of Alberta, Canada. She was the founding director of the International Institute for Qualitative Methodology (IIQM, 1997–2007), University of Alberta and the founding editor of the *International Journal of Qualitative Methods*; since 1991, she has served as the founding editor for *Qualitative Health Research*. She is the recipient of the Episteme Award (Sigma Theta Tau) and honorary doctorates from the University of Newcastle, Australia, and Athabasca University, Canada. She was an inaugural inductee to the Researcher Hall of Fame (2010) and received the Lifetime Achievement Award, International Center for Qualitative Inquiry, 2011. She is the author of 420 articles and 19 books on qualitative research methods, suffering, comforting, and patient falls. Her most recent book (with Linda Niehaus) is *Mixed Method Design: Principles and Procedures* (2009).

Kirin Narayan is Professor of Anthropology at the University of Wisconsin–Madison. She is the author of *Storytellers, Saints and Scoundrels: Folk Narrative in Hindu Religious Teaching* (Pennsylvania, 1989), awarded the 1990 Victor Turner Prize for Ethnographic Writing from the American Anthropological Association and cowinner of the 1990 Elsie Clews Parsons Prize for Folklore from the American Folklore Society; *Love, Stars and All That* (Pocket Books, 1994), a novel; *Mondays on the Dark Night of the Moon: Himalayan Foothill Folktales* (Oxford, 1997), an ethnography composed around folktales retold by Urmila Devi Sood; *My Family and Other Saints* (Chicago, 2007), a family memoir; and *Alive in the Writing: Crafting Ethnography in the Company of Chekhov* (Chicago, 2012), a manual that offers ways to generate writing through examples and exercises.

Pirjo Nikander is a professor at the Institute for Advanced Social Research, University of Tampere, Finland, and adjunct professor at the University of Helsinki, Finland. She has studied institutional interaction, decision making in meetings, age in interaction, ageism, and moral discourse. Her publications include *Age in Action: Membership Work and Stage of Life Categories in Talk* (2002) and numerous chapters and articles on discourse analysis, age and ageism, membership categorization analysis, and transcription and translation. She has also coedited books on women and ageing, and the analysis of interviews.

Jennifer Platt is Emeritus Professor of Sociology at the University of Sussex, England. Her research interests are aspects of the logic and sociology of research methods, and the history of sociology. Her main publications include "Cases of Cases . . . of Cases?" in *What Is a Case?* (edited by H. S. Becker & C. Ragin); "Research Methods and the Second Chicago School" in *A Second Chicago School?* (edited by Gary A. Fine); *A History of Sociological Research Methods in America, 1920–1960*; *The British Sociological Association: A Sociological History*; and "Sociology" in *The History of the Social Sciences Since 1945* (edited by Roger E. Backhouse and Philippe Fontaine). She has been concerned to extend the history of sociology beyond its traditional study of the thought of prominent theorists and so has also written on intellectual migration, the position of women in British sociology, and topics in the social system of sociology, such as editorial boards and presidential addresses. She is currently Vice President for Publications of the International Sociological Association and was for many years an officer of its Research Committee on the History of Sociology. In the past, she has been president of the British Sociological Association and editor of its journal *Sociology*; recently, she chaired the American Sociological Association's Section on the History of Sociology.

Jonathan Potter is Professor of Discourse Analysis and Dean of the School of Social, Political and Geographical Sciences at Loughborough University. He has worked on fundamental issues to do with the nature of human action and social science method. His most recent books include *Representing Reality*, which attempts to provide a systematic overview, integration, and critique of constructionist research in social psychology, postmodernism, rhetoric, and ethnomethodology, and *Conversation and Cognition* (with Hedwig te Molder), in which different researchers consider the implications of studies of interaction for understanding cognition. He is one of the founders of discursive psychology.

Tim Rapley is a staff scientist at the Institute of Health & Society at Newcastle University, England. His current research interests are in empirical studies of medical work, knowledge, and practice, and social studies of research. He is the author of *Doing Conversation, Discourse and Document Analysis* (Sage, 2007), and recently, he wrote a chapter he is quite proud of, "Some Pragmatics of Data Analysis," for the third edition of David Silverman's (2010) edited collection *Qualitative Research: Theory, Method & Practice*.

Catherine Kohler Riessman is a medical sociologist and Emerita Professor at Boston University. She is currently a research professor in the Sociology Department at Boston College. Her most recent book is *Narrative Methods for the Human Sciences* (Sage, 2008). Throughout her long career, she has studied and compared the narratives women and men develop to account for biographical disruptions, including divorce, infertility, and chronic illness in midlife. She has been the author of many journal articles and book chapters in recent years, and her early books include *Divorce Talk* (1990) and *Narrative Analysis* (1993). She has been awarded Leverhulme, British Academy, and Fulbright fellowships and has served as a visiting professor at the University of London, Victoria University in Melbourne, and the University of Western Sydney in Australia.

Carol Rivas undertakes research and teaching at Barts and the London School of Medicine and Dentistry, Queen Mary, University of London. She was previously based at St. Mary's Hospital, London. Before that she was a medical journalist, and she has undertaken commercial projects writing health communications and clinician training materials and developing telemedicine and multimedia educational resources. She currently lectures in medical sociology and teaches qualitative research methods to undergraduates and postgraduates. Her main research interests are in ethnicity and culture, communication, and cognition. She has undertaken several studies on access to health care and its improvement, involving various approaches to data collection and analysis. She is particularly interested in encouraging other researchers to take up computer-assisted methods of video analysis. Her current projects are a video-based exploration of communication in medical consultations and development of an associated web-based multimedia educational and research resource.

Kathryn Roulston is an associate professor in the Qualitative Research Program in the Department of

Lifelong Education, Administration, and Policy at the University of Georgia, where she teaches qualitative research methodology. Her research interests include qualitative research methods, qualitative interviewing, analyses of talk-in-interaction, topics in music education, and the preparation of qualitative researchers. She is the author of *Reflective Interviewing: A Guide to Theory and Practice* (2010) and has published articles and chapters on qualitative interviewing and analysis of interview data.

Timothy Rowlands received his PhD in 2009 from the faculty of Justice and Social Inquiry, School of Social Transformation, Arizona State University. His dissertation will be published in November 2011 on Video Game Worlds. Since his graduation, he has worked as research manager of a three-university longitudinal study of early infant and child care.

Anne Ryen is Associate Professor of Sociology and Vice Dean of the Faculty of Economics and Social Sciences at University of Agder, Norway. She is a former president of the European Sociological Association (ESA) Research Network on Qualitative Methods and present member of the ESA Executive Committee. Her research has focused on fringe benefits in private companies, cross-cultural research, and research ethics and the qualitative interview, and her publications include *Verneverdig. Barnevern, forskning og metode* (*Child Care, Research, and Ethics,* with Pål Repstad, 2001), *Det kvalitative intervjuet: fra vitenskapsteori til feltarbeid* (*The Qualitative Interview: From Theory of Science to Fieldwork,* 2002), and *Hvordan kan frynsegoder bli belønning?* (*How Can Fringe Benefits Become Remuneration?* with Knud Knudsen, 2005). In addition to writing articles and chapters in handbooks, she has been guest editor of journals such as *Journal of Qualitative Social Work* (2008), *Qualitative Sociology Review* (with Krzysztof Konecki, 2009), and *International Journal of Social Research Methodology: Theory and Practice* (with Giampietro Gobo, 2011).

Clive Seale is a professor of medical sociology in Barts and the London School of Medicine and Dentistry, Queen Mary, University of London. He is the editor of the journal *Sociology of Health and Illness* and author or editor of numerous books, including *Constructing Death: The Sociology of Dying and Bereavement* (Cambridge University Press, 1998) and *The Quality of Qualitative Research* (Sage, 1999). His edited methods textbook *Researching Society and*

Culture will be published in its third edition by Sage in 2012. He is interested in computer-assisted methods of text analysis using software developed for the discipline of corpus linguistics and carries out research using this and a variety of other methods. Currently, he is working with audio- and videotaped data to understand the communication issues involved in multilingual consultations in primary care in East London, where he now works.

David Shemmings is a professor of social work at the University of Kent, England, and a visiting professor of child protection research at Royal Holloway, University of London, England. He is currently the director of the Assessment of Disorganised Attachment and Maltreatment Project, which focuses on the detection and assessment of child abuse as well as how best to help families. Prior to moving to Kent, he was a professor of social work research at Middlesex University, England. He qualified in 1974 and worked with traumatized children for 5 years. He has spent the past 15 years undertaking research into attachment theory in close relationships. He has used Q methodology in the study of later life filial attachment and has presented papers in a number of international settings.

Royce A. Singleton Jr. is Professor Emeritus of Sociology at the College of the Holy Cross, where he taught for 32 years until his retirement in 2009. A quantitative researcher, he has conducted numerous surveys on a broad range of topics. His most recently published work, based on a series of campus surveys, addresses issues of student alcohol consumption and voluntarism. He is the coauthor, with Bruce Straits, of *Approaches to Social Research* (2010). He currently serves on the editorial board of *Sociological Perspectives*.

Bruce C. Straits is Professor Emeritus of Sociology at the University of California, Santa Barbara. His research areas include social demography, cigarette smoking and cessation, the social psychology of research settings, the influence of personal networks on individuals' attitudes and behavior, and research methodology. He is the coauthor, with Royce Singleton, of *Social Research: Approaches and Fundamentals* (Oxford University Press, 2011).

John B. Talmage is a professor of sociology at the University of Mobile. He has done research on homelessness and aging and has been involved in applied research. In addition to his academic career, he has been a business executive, a counsellor, and University Chaplain.

Carol Thomas is a professor of sociology at Lancaster University in the United Kingdom and is based in the School of Health and Medicine. She is currently director of the *Centre for Disability Research* at Lancaster University. She is best known for her publications in disability studies—including her books *Female Forms: Experiencing and Understanding Disability* (Open University Press, 1997) and *Sociologies of Disability and Illness: Contested Ideas in Disability Studies and Medical Sociology* (Palgrave Macmillan, 2007). She has also researched and published widely on the experiences of "patients" and "carers" of living with cancer and has recently completed a project funded by the Economic and Social Research Council (ESRC) on illness narratives in cancer contexts (ESRC project: RES-000-22-2031). Publications on narrative analysis have followed, notably in debate context in Volume 32, Issue 4 of *Sociology of Health and Illness*.

Jinjun Wang is a professor in the School of Foreign Languages at Yunnan University, People's Republic of China. She was a visiting scholar at the University of Sunderland, England, in 2005. Her academic interests include systemic functional linguistics, discourse analysis, sociolinguistics, and pragmatics. So far, she has published three books and nearly forty articles and has cotranslated three English–Chinese dictionaries. She has obtained seven research grants at the nation, province, and university levels. Now she is a vice director of the Foreign Languages and Literatures Research Institute of Yunnan University and acts as a directing member of the China Association of Functional Linguistics and the China Association of Comparative Studies of Chinese and English.

Carol A. B. Warren, Professor Emerita, taught at the University of Southern California for 17 years and the University of Kansas for 13, retiring in 2003. Her research interests over the years have included qualitative methods (ethnographic, historical, and interviewing), law and society, social control, gender, and the history of medicine and psychiatry. Her most recent books are *Doing Qualitative Research*, with Xavia Karner (2010) and *Pushbutton Psychiatry: A Cultural History of Electroshock in America*, with Timothy Kneeland (2008). Recent articles include "The Eyes Have It" (*Ethnography*, 2011), "Pride, Shame and Stigma in Private Spaces" (*Ethnography*, 2010), and "Interviewing Elderly Residents in Assisted Living," with Kristine N. Williams (*Qualitative Sociology*, 2008).

Ying Yan has research interests that include systemic functional linguistics and discourse analysis. She has explored metadiscourse in English movie reviews for her master's thesis. In 2009, she was chosen to study at the Yuan Ze University in Taiwan. Within a year's stay at the university, her excellence in academic research and university activities was appreciated by her teachers and colleagues.

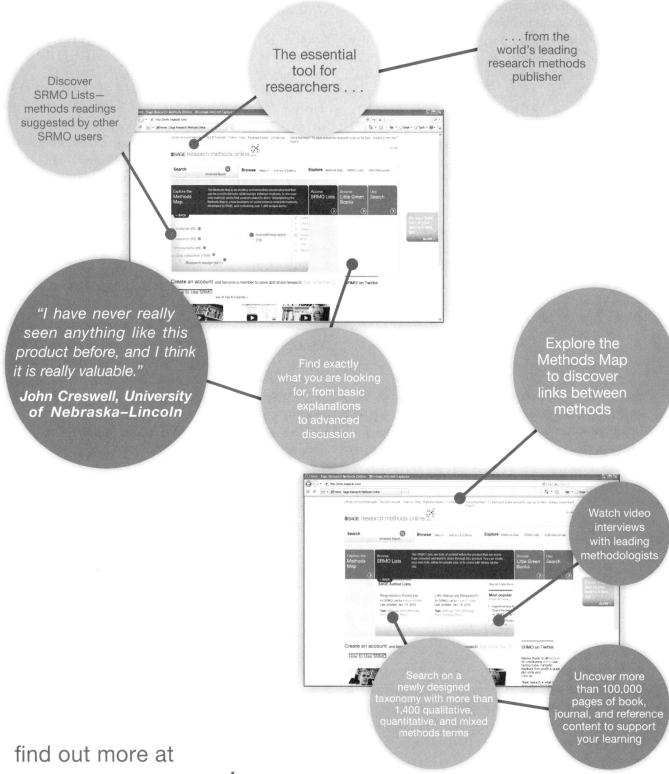